IF FOUND, please notify and arrange return to owner. This text is important for the owner's federal income tax and other accounting classes or continuing professional education.

Name of Accounting
Student or Practitioner: _Tammy Franasco_

Address: _____

City, State, Zip: _____

Telephone: (_____) _____

Additional copies of *Federal Tax Objective Questions and Explanations* are available for $16.95 direct from

> Gleim Publications, Inc.
> P.O. Box 12848
> University Station
> Gainesville, Florida 32604
> (800) 87-GLEIM
> (904) 375-0772

Other similar available study manuals:

Auditing & EDP Objective Questions and Explanations ($16.95)
Business Law/Legal Studies Objective Questions and Explanations ($16.95)
Financial Accounting Objective Questions and Explanations ($16.95)
Managerial Accounting Objective Questions and Explanations ($16.95)

Also available are:

CIA Examination Review, Volume I -- Outlines and Study Guides, 4th Ed. ($23.95)
CIA Examination Review, Volume II -- Problems and Solutions, 4th Ed. ($23.95)
CIA 1992 Updating Edition ($15.95)
Save $8.85! Order all three ($55.00)

CMA Examination Review, Volume I -- Outlines and Study Guides, 5th Ed. ($24.95)
CMA Examination Review, Volume II -- Problems and Solutions, 5th Ed. ($24.95)

Order forms for these and all of our other publications are provided at the back of this book.

All mail orders must be prepaid. Shipping charges will be added to telephone orders, and to library and company orders which may be on account. Add applicable sales tax to shipments within Florida. All payments must be in U.S. funds and payable on a U.S. bank. Please write or call for prices and availability of all foreign country shipments. Book(s) will usually be shipped the day after your order is received. Allow 10 days for delivery in the United States. Please contact us if you do not receive your shipment within 2 weeks.

Gleim Publications, Inc. guarantees the immediate refund of all resalable texts returned within 30 days. Shipping and handling charges are nonrefundable.

REVIEWERS AND CONTRIBUTORS

Maria M. Bolanos, B.A., University of Florida, is our production manager. She coordinated and supervised the production staff and reviewed the final manuscript.

Holger D. Gleim, LL.M., CPA, co-authored the first four editions.

Grady M. Irwin, J.D., provided editorial assistance throughout the five editions.

Sandra S. Kramer, Associate Professor of Accounting at the University of Florida, co-authored the first four editions and reviewed and edited Chapter 17 in this edition.

John F. Rebstock, CIA, is a graduate of the Fisher School of Accounting at the University of Florida. He has passed the CPA exam, and is a CMA candidate. Mr. Rebstock reviewed the entire text and prepared the page layout.

The following provided assistance in the First, Second, Third, and Fourth Editions through reviewing, editing, and/or writing first drafts to many answers:

    Michael Ake, M.Acc. (Taxation), works for a national accounting firm.
    Laura Alderman, M.Acc. (Taxation), works for a national accounting firm.
    Kim Allen, M.Acc. (Taxation), works for a national accounting firm.
    Thomas Christmann, LL.M. (Taxation), is a senior partner in a Gainesville, Florida law firm.
    Linda Garrett, LL.M., M.Acc. (Taxation), teaches at the University of Central Florida.
    Russ Gillis, CPA, is a J.D. candidate at the University of Florida.
    Michael L. Goodson, M.Acc. (Taxation), works for a national accounting firm.
    Windy Kemp, B.S.Ac. (Auditing), works for a national accounting firm.
    Michael McLamb, M.Acc. (Taxation), works for a national accounting firm.
    Joan Millett, CPA, is a J.D. candidate at the University of Florida Law School.
    Anne Morley, M.Acc. (Taxation), works for a national accounting firm.
    Douglas Munson, J.D., CPA, works for a national accounting firm.
    Raquel Ortega, M.Acc. (Taxation), works for a national accounting firm.
    Douglas Phillips, M.Acc. (Taxation), works for a national accounting firm.
    Drew Rogers, M.Acc. (Taxation), works for a national accounting firm.
    Mary Ann Vorce, M.Acc. (Auditing), works for a national accounting firm.

The following Fisher School of Accounting Master's graduates and candidates provided editorial assistance and drafts for many answers in this Fifth Edition:

Michael Fell	Sam Khoury
Kurt Frahn	Andy Mason
Russ Gillis	Michelle Mihalik

A PERSONAL THANKS

    This manual would not have been possible without the extraordinary efforts and dedication of Ann Finnicum, Janice Martin, Cathy Smith, and Connie Steen, who typed the entire manuscript and all revisions, as well as prepared the camera-ready pages.

    The authors also appreciate the proofreading and editing assistance of Laura David, Greg Mullins, Paul Phillips, Rhonda Ray, Cathy Smith, and Aimee Westerson, and the reviewing and production assistance of Gillian Hillis.

    Finally, we appreciate the encouragement, support, and tolerance of our families throughout this project.

Fifth Edition
FEDERAL TAX
Objective Questions and Explanations

by

Irvin N. Gleim, Ph.D., CPA, CIA, CMA

John L. Kramer, Ph.D.

ABOUT THE AUTHORS

Irvin N. Gleim is Professor Emeritus in the Fisher School of Accounting at the University of Florida and is a member of the American Accounting Association, American Business Law Association, American Institute of Certified Public Accountants, Association of Government Accountants, Florida Institute of Certified Public Accountants, Institute of Internal Auditors, Institute of Certified Management Accountants, and the National Association of Accountants. He has had articles published in the *Journal of Accountancy*, *The Accounting Review*, and *The American Business Law Journal* and is author/coauthor of numerous accounting and aviation books and CPE courses. He has enjoyed over 20 years as accounting professor at Pittsburg State University, Illinois State University, and the University of Florida.

John L. Kramer is the Arthur Andersen Professor of Accounting at the Fisher School of Accounting at the University of Florida. For the past 12 years he has directed the graduate program in taxation. In addition, he has served as Director of the Fisher School of Accounting and Interim Dean of the College of Business Administration. He is co-editor of a three-volume undergraduate taxation series published by Prentice Hall and a co-author of a graduate corporate taxation text also published by Prentice Hall. He is a past president of the American Taxation Association and former Editor of the *Journal of the American Taxation Association*. Professor Kramer teaches for a number of national public accounting firms. He has had over 50 articles published in a variety of professional and academic journals including *The Journal of Taxation*, *The Tax Adviser*, *The Accounting Review*, and *The Journal of the American Taxation Association*.

Gleim Publications, Inc.
P.O. Box 12848
University Station
Gainesville, Florida 32604
(800) 87-GLEIM
(904) 375-0772

Library of Congress Catalog Card No. 91-70567
ISBN 0-917537-44-0

Copyright © 1991 by Gleim Publications, Inc.
Third Printing: May 1992

ALL RIGHTS RESERVED. No part of this material may be reproduced in any form whatsoever without express written permission from Gleim Publications, Inc.

ACKNOWLEDGMENTS

Material from Uniform Certified Public Accountant Examination questions and unofficial answers, Copyright © 1972, 1973, 1974, 1975, 1976, 1977, 1978, 1979, 1980, 1981, 1982, 1983, 1984, 1985, 1986, 1987, 1988, 1989, and 1990 by the American Institute of Certified Public Accountants, Inc., is reprinted and/or adapted with permission.

The authors also appreciate and thank the Institute of Management Accounting of the National Association of Accountants for permission to use problem materials from past CMA examinations, Copyright © 1977, 1978, 1979, 1980, 1981, 1982, 1983, 1984, 1985, 1986, 1987, 1988, 1989, and 1990 by the National Association of Accountants.

The authors also appreciate and thank the Internal Revenue Service for its cooperation. Questions have been used from the 1977, 1978, 1979, 1980, 1981, 1982, 1983, 1984, 1985, 1986, 1987, 1988, 1989, and 1990 Special Enrollment Examinations.

This publication is designed to provide accurate and authoritative information with regard to the subject matter covered. It is sold with the understanding that the publisher is not engaged in rendering legal, accounting, or other professional service.

If legal advice or other expert assistance is required, the services of a competent professional person should be sought.

(From a declaration of principles jointly adopted by a Committee of the American Bar Association and a Committee of Publishers.)

PREFACE FOR TAX STUDENTS

The purpose of this study manual is to help you understand federal taxation concepts and their application. In turn, these skills will enable you to perform better on your undergraduate examinations, as well as look ahead to (and prepare for) professional certification examinations, including the IRS Special Enrollment Exam.

One of the major benefits of this study manual is comprehensive coverage of federal taxation topics. Accordingly, when you use this study manual to help prepare for federal taxation courses and examinations, you are assured of covering virtually all topics that could reasonably be expected to be studied in typical college or university tax courses.

The question-and-answer format is designed and presented to facilitate effective study. Students should be careful not to misuse this text by referring to the answers before independently answering each question.

In addition to being a student study guide, this book is designed to be a basic review text for the Special Enrollment Examination. Given that you have had exposure to the typical university tax courses or equivalent, this study manual should be sufficient to prepare for successful completion of the Special Enrollment Exam.

While many of the questions in this study manual are from past CMA and CPA examinations, this study manual should not be relied upon to prepare for these professional examinations. You should use review manuals specifically developed for each examination. *CMA Examination Review* and *CPA Examination Review* (and also *CIA Examination Review*) are up to date and comprehensively cover all material necessary for successful completion of each examination.

Most of the questions taken from the CMA, CPA, and Enrollment exams have been modified to update them. All questions and answers have been updated to be in accord with the tax laws in effect March 1991. Thus, the Revenue Reconciliation Act of 1990 is covered. In addition, we have tried to be as complete as possible about including judicial decisions and government promulgations issued through March 1991. Note, however, that certain questions test the old law still in effect from earlier transactions. Additional changes have been made to questions to clarify them and/or to emphasize a point of law or its application.

Although the last major tax law change is the Revenue Reconciliation Act of 1990, the individual and corporate estimated tax rules have been modified in 1991 and 1992 by P.L. 102-164 (the Emergency Unemployment Compensation Act of 1991) and 102-244. A number of deduction, tax credit, and tax preference exemptions have had their lives extended by P.L. 102-227 (the Tax Extension Act of 1991). References to these changes have been added to modules in Chapters 5, 8, 10, 12, 18, and 19 where appropriate. Updating has not been done for the 1992 changes occurring as a result of the mandated annual inflation adjustments that are made to the individual tax rate brackets, standard deduction, personal and dependency exemptions, etc.

Thank you for your interest in this study manual. We deeply appreciate the many letters, suggestions, and questions received from accounting students and educators during the past years, as well as CIA, CMA, and CPA candidates. Please send us your suggestions, comments, and corrections. The last page in this study manual has been designed to help you note corrections and suggestions throughout your study process.

Please read the first three chapters carefully. They are very short but nonetheless very important.

Good Luck on Your Exams,

Irvin N. Gleim
John L. Kramer

May 1992

PREFACE FOR ACCOUNTING AND TAX PRACTITIONERS

The first purpose of this study manual is to permit you to assess your technical proficiency concerning tax laws, regulations, and procedures. The second purpose is to facilitate your review and update of most federal taxation topics with our compendium of approximately 2,522 objective questions. The third purpose is to provide CPE credit for your self-assessment and review/update study effort.

This approach to CPE is both interactive and intense. You should be continuously challenged to answer each question correctly. When you answer a question incorrectly or have difficulty, you should pursue a complete understanding by reading the answer explanation and consulting other reference sources as necessary.

Most of the questions in *Federal Tax Objective Questions and Explanations* were taken from various professional examinations, but many have been revised and adapted to provide broader and up-to-date coverage of the tax laws. In addition, hundreds of publisher questions cover material not directly tested on certification examinations.

Finally, we ask for any supplemental comments, reactions, suggestions, etc., that you may have as you complete our CPE program. The last page of this study book has been designed to help you note corrections and suggestions throughout your study process. Please attach it to your Course Evaluation (handwritten notes are fine).

The first three chapters of *Federal Tax Objective Questions and Explanations* are directed primarily to accounting students and enrolled agent candidates. Those practitioners interested in multiple certification, however, may find the discussion of the CPA, CIA, and CMA certification programs in Chapter Three to be useful. If, as you work through this study book and take the open-book CPE final exams, you find you need to refer to a current textbook, Chapter One contains a list of current titles. You should be sure to carefully read the introductory chapter in the accompanying CPE book, as well as the opening page for each course.

Thank you for your interest, and we look forward to hearing from you.

Best Wishes in Your CPE Endeavors,

Irvin N. Gleim
John L. Kramer

March 1991

TABLE OF CONTENTS

	Page
PREFACE for Tax Students	v
PREFACE for Accounting and Tax Practitioners	vi
1. How to Use This Book	1
2. Multiple-Choice Question Answering Technique	15
3. The IRS Special Enrollment Examination and Other Professional Accounting Examinations	17

INDIVIDUAL

4. Gross Income	41
5. Exclusions from Gross Income	73
6. Business Expenses and Losses	95
7. Limitations on Losses	133
8. Other Deductions for Adjusted Gross Income	147
9. Deductions from AGI	167
10. Individual Tax Computations	219
11. Credits	253

PROPERTY

12. Basis	285
13. Depreciation, Amortization, and Depletion	311
14. Capital Gains and Losses	333
15. Sale of Business Property	359
16. Nontaxable Property Transactions	381

OTHER ENTITIES

17. Partnerships	401
18. Corporate Formations and Operations	459
19. Advanced Corporate Topics	533
20. Income Taxation of Estates and Trusts	581

OTHER TOPICS

21. Accounting Methods	603
22. Employment Taxes and Withholding	643
23. Wealth Transfer Taxes	663
24. Preparer Rules and Practice Before the IRS	695
25. Federal Tax Process and Procedure	721
INDEX	763

CONTRIBUTING PROFESSORS

We are especially grateful to the following professors who submitted questions for this and previous editions. Their participation has made *Federal Tax Objective Questions and Explanations* truly a community project. We welcome further submissions of questions either for the Sixth Edition of *Federal Tax Objective Questions and Explanations* or for future editions of our other Objective Question and Explanation books.

Bradley, David B.	Lyndon State College
Bunn, Radie	Southwest Missouri State University
Burns, Joseph G.	North Carolina A&T State University
Byrd, Sandra	Southwest Missouri State University
Craig, C.K.	Illinois State University
Dugopolski, Christiana	University of Missouri at St. Louis
Fenton, Jr., Edmund D.	Eastern Kentucky University
Fernandez, Ramon	University of St. Thomas
Grams, Edsel	University of Wisconsin at Eau Claire
Greenberg, Ira S.	University of North Carolina at Greensboro
Hite, Peggy A.	Indiana University - Bloomington
Karl III, Peter A.	State University of New York at Utica/Rome
Markou, P.J.	North Adams State University
McLean, John P.	University of Scranton
McMullen, Kyle G.	Marshall University
Premont, Marion F.	Siena College
Rosson, Gerald W.	Lynchburg College
Ruble, John M.	Bradley University
Skender, C.J.	North Carolina State University
Suttles, Donald R.	Catawba College
Trebby, James P.	Marquette University
Wallace, William	University of Mississippi
Waters, Gary L.	University of Texas - Austin
Whiteman, Michael J.	University of Massachusetts
Yates, Mary	Central Missouri State University

CHAPTER ONE
HOW TO USE THIS BOOK

> *Our Use of Modules* 2
> *Sources of Objective Questions* 2
> *Identification of the Source of Each Question* 3
> *Order of Questions in Each Module* 3
> *Uniqueness of Objective Questions* 4
> *Answer Explanations Alongside the Questions* 4
> *Using Objective Questions to Study* 5
> *Citations to Authoritative Tax Sources* 6
> *Tax Forms on the Special Enrollment Examination* 6
> *Preparing for Essay Questions and Computational Problems* 6
> *Cross-References to Federal Tax Textbooks* 7

This chapter explains how and why this study manual was written. More importantly, it directs you on how to use it efficiently and effectively.

The format and content of this study manual are innovative in the federal tax text market. The first purpose is to provide accounting students with a well-organized, comprehensive compendium of objective questions covering all topics and issues that could reasonably be expected to be studied in a typical federal tax course. The second purpose is to provide accounting professionals with a comprehensive presentation of objective questions for diagnostic use and for review of taxation topics.

This study manual consists solely of objective questions and answer explanations, with the exception of the first three chapters:

1. How to Use This Book

2. Multiple-Choice Question Answering Technique

3. The IRS Special Enrollment Examination and Other Professional Accounting Examinations

The chapter titles and organization of Chapters 4 through 25 are based on current federal tax books listed below and on page 2.

Commerce Clearing House, Inc., *Federal Taxation: Advanced Topics*, 1991 Edition, Commerce Clearing House, Inc.

Commerce Clearing House, Inc., *Federal Taxation: Basic Principles*, 1991 Edition, Commerce Clearing House, Inc.

Commerce Clearing House, Inc., *1991 Federal Tax Course*, 1990 Edition, Commerce Clearing House, Inc.

Everett, Boley, Duncan, and Jamison, *HBJ Federal Tax Course*, 1991 Edition, Harcourt Brace Jovanovich, Inc.

Hoffman and Raabe, *Corporations, Partnerships, Estates and Trusts*, 1991 Edition, West Publishing Co.

Hoffman and Willis, *Federal Taxation: Comprehensive Volume*, 1991 Edition, West Publishing Co.

Hoffman, Willis, and Smith, *Individual Income Taxes*, 1991 Edition, West Publishing Co.

Kramer and Phillips, *Prentice Hall's Federal Taxation 1991: Comprehensive Volume,* Prentice Hall, Inc., 1990.

Kramer and Phillips, *Prentice Hall's Federal Taxation 1991: Corporations, Partnerships, Estates and Trusts*, Prentice Hall, Inc., 1990.

Phillips and Kramer, *Prentice Hall's Federal Taxation 1991: Individuals*, Prentice Hall, Inc., 1990.

Pratt, Burns, and Kulsrud, *Corporate, Partnership, Estate and Gift Taxation*, 1991 Edition, Richard D. Irwin, Inc., 1990.

Pratt, Burns, and Kulsrud, *Federal Taxation*, 1991 Edition, Richard D. Irwin, Inc., 1990.

Pratt, Burns, and Kulsrud, *Individual Taxation*, 1991 Edition, Richard D. Irwin, Inc., 1990.

Prentice Hall, Inc., *1991 Federal Tax Course*, Prentice Hall, Inc.

Raby, Tidwell, and White, *Introduction to Federal Taxation*, 1991 Edition, Prentice Hall, Inc.

Sommerfeld and Jones, *Federal Taxes and Management Decisions*, 1991-1992 Edition, Richard D. Irwin, Inc., 1990.

Sommerfeld, Madeo, and Milliron, *An Introduction to Taxation*, 1991 Edition, Harcourt Brace Jovanovich, Inc.

Some textbooks may have been inadvertently omitted from the above list, for which we apologize. The last section in this chapter (beginning on page 7) contains the tables of contents of the above books with cross-references to modules in this book.

OUR USE OF MODULES

Each chapter is divided into subtopics (i.e., groups of questions) to assist your study program. We call these subtopics modules. Choosing modules and arranging questions for federal taxation was difficult. We wanted the number of questions to be large enough for comprehensive coverage without presenting an insurmountable task. We defined each module to be narrow enough to cover a single topic, but broad enough so the questions are not redundant.

The true-false questions, where they are used, appear at the end of each module. While true-false questions are not ideal for examination use (since they result in an expected score of 50%, given no knowledge), they are a useful study vehicle. Also, they are heavily used on the Special Enrollment Exam.

SOURCES OF OBJECTIVE QUESTIONS

The Special Enrollment Exam is the primary source of questions included in this study manual. Questions from past CMA and CPA examinations are also included. The contents of these exams are discussed further in Chapter 3.

In addition, your authors (coded in this text as *Publisher*) have prepared questions based upon the content of the federal tax textbooks listed on pages 1 and 2. These *Publisher* questions were developed where questions on important points were either not available from the other sources or were not suitable. Similarly included are questions submitted by professors from around the country.

Chapter 1: How to Use This Book

The source for each question appears in the first line of its answer explanation, in the column to the right of the question. Summary of objective question sources:

CMA	Certified Management Accountant Examination
CPA	Uniform Certified Public Accountant Examination
Publisher	Your authors
SPE	Special Enrollment Examination
Professor Name	Professor who submitted the question

IDENTIFICATION OF THE SOURCE OF EACH QUESTION

After each source code (except Publisher and professor's name), codes for the following information are given:

Month and year	(e.g., 1289)
Exam part	(see below)
Question number	(see below)

All SPE questions are coded with the year, the month of September or October, and Roman numerals for exam parts. Arabic numerals signify the parts of the CMA exam, e.g., 1, 2, 3, 4, 5. The parts of the CPA exam covered in this book are coded as follows:

L	Business Law
P	Practice I
Q	Practice II

Examples:

(CMA 690 3-17)	CMA exam, June 1990, Part 3, question 17
(CPA 1190 Q-31)	CPA exam, November 1990, Practice II section, question 31
(SPE 990 II-48)	Special Enrollment Exam, September 1990, Part II, question 48
(Publisher)	Prepared by your authors
(E.D. Fenton)	Prepared by Professor E.D. Fenton

Most questions were modified to update them to current tax law, i.e., to cover 1991 based on changes made by the various laws enacted in 1990, principally the Revenue Reconciliation Act of 1990 and the various judicial decisions and government promulgations issued on or before March 1, 1991. Many questions and/or answer selections have also been modified for clarity or for overall consistency of format and style.

ORDER OF QUESTIONS IN EACH MODULE

Within most modules, the multiple-choice questions precede the true-false questions. Each group of questions is in a sequence from general to specific, elementary to advanced, etc., to provide an effective learning sequence. Duplicate questions are kept to a minimum. Some repetitive SPE true-false questions are presented to emphasize the repetitive testing areas of the Special Enrollment Examination.

UNIQUENESS OF OBJECTIVE QUESTIONS

The major advantage of objective questions is the ability to cover (i.e., to study or to test) a large number of topics with relatively little time and effort when compared to essay questions and computational problems.

A multiple-choice question is actually a group of four statements of which all but one are incorrect given the facts of the question. The advantage of multiple-choice questions over true-false questions is that they require more analysis and result in a lower score for those with little or no knowledge. Random guessing on questions with four answer choices results in an expected grade of 25%. The same approach on a true-false test question results in an expected grade of 50%.

Students and practitioners both like multiple-choice questions. Students find them relatively easy to answer because they present alternative answers from which only one needs to be selected. Professors like objective questions because they are easy to grade and because much more material can be tested in the same period of time.

ANSWER EXPLANATIONS ALONGSIDE THE QUESTIONS

Our efficient format presents questions and answer explanations side by side. The answer explanations appear to the right of each question. The example below is question 87 from Part I of the September 1989 SPE.

In 1991, Mr. A, a sole proprietor, made interest payments of $800 on his personal credit cards, $650 on his business truck loan, $3,000 to the bank for a loan origination fee (charge for services) for his Veterans Administration mortgage, and $8,000 on his home mortgage. What is the total allowable interest deduction on Schedule A, Form 1040?
 	
   a. $12,450.
   b. $11,800.
   c. $9,520.
   d. $8,000.
	The correct answer is (d). *(SPE 989 I-87)*
	REQUIRED: The allowable interest deduction on Schedule A for 1991.
	DISCUSSION: After 1990 personal interest is no longer allowed as an itemized deduction. Therefore, the $800 of credit card interest is not deductible. The $650 interest on the business truck loan would probably be deducted as business interest on Schedule C; it would not be a deduction on Schedule A. Points paid on a Veterans Administration loan are not deductible as interest. Note also, that points charged as compensation for services are not deductible as interest. Therefore, none of the $3,000 loan origination fees (points) would be deductible as interest. The $8,000 of home mortgage interest would be deductible in full. Mr. A's interest deduction on Schedule A for 1991 would be $8,000.

The format in this study manual is designed to facilitate your study of the objective questions, their answers, and the answer explanations. The intent is to save you the **time and effort** of turning pages back and forth from questions to answers.

Be careful, however. You must exercise restraint against misusing this format by consulting the answers **before** you have answered the questions. Misuse of the readily available answers will give you a false sense of security and result in your performing poorly on examinations. The best way to use this study manual is to cover the answer explanations with a sheet of paper as you read and answer each question. As a crucial part of the learning process, you must honestly commit yourself to an answer before looking at the answer explanation. Whether you are right or wrong, your memory of the concept tested will be **reinforced** by this process.

USING OBJECTIVE QUESTIONS TO STUDY

Testing experts increasingly favor multiple-choice questions as a valid means of testing various levels of knowledge. For example, 60% of each part of the CPA examination now consists of objective questions. The AICPA now proposes using 85% objective questions beginning in 1994. Using objective questions to study for these professional certification examinations and undergraduate examinations is an important tool in obtaining a passing grade.

The following suggestions can be used as a guideline for your study purposes in conjunction with any of the Gleim Series of Objective Question and Explanation books (see our order form at the back of this book).

1. Locate the chapter and module that contains questions on the topic you are currently studying. The end of Chapter 1 has cross-references to the tables of contents of most textbooks.

2. Work through a series of questions, one or more modules at a time.
    a. Cover up the answers and explanations with your hand or with a piece of paper as you work the questions (see 3. below).
    b. Circle the answer you think is correct.
    c. Check your answer.

3. **Do not consult the answer or answer explanations on the right side of each page until after you have chosen and written down an answer.**
    a. It is crucial that you cover up the answer explanations and intellectually commit yourself to an answer. This approach will help you understand the concept much better, even if you answered the question incorrectly.

4. **Study** the explanations to each question you answered incorrectly. In addition to learning and understanding the concept tested, analyze **why** you missed the question. Did you misread the question? Misread the requirement? Make a computational error? Not know the concept tested? Identify your weaknesses in answering multiple-choice questions and take corrective action (before you take a test).
    a. Studying the important concepts that we provide in **our answer explanations** will help you understand the principles to the point that you can answer that question (or any other like it) successfully.

5. Prepare a summary analysis of your work on each module (topic). It will show your weaknesses (areas needing more study) and also your strengths (areas of improvement). You can improve your performance on objective questions both by increasing your percentage of correct answers and by decreasing the time spent per question. Here are sample column headings for the summary analysis:

Date	Module	Time to Complete	Number of Questions	Minutes Per Question	Number Correct	Percent Correct

The Gleim Series of Objective Question and Explanation books really works! You can pretest yourself before class to see if you are strong or weak in the assigned area. You can retest after class to see if you really understand the material. The questions in these books cover all topics in your related courses, so you will rarely encounter questions on your exams for which you are not well prepared. Furthermore, each book covers the material generally taught in two or three courses, so your cost per course is minimal.

CITATIONS TO AUTHORITATIVE TAX SOURCES

Almost all answer explanations contain a citation to the source of the law, regulation, or procedure on which the answer is based. These citations are abbreviated as follows:

Sec.	Section of the Internal Revenue Code
Reg.	Treasury regulation
Prop. Reg.	Proposed Treasury regulation
Temp. Reg.	Temporary Treasury Regulation
Rev. Rul.	Revenue ruling issued by the IRS
Rev. Proc.	Revenue procedure issued by the IRS
CFR	Code of Federal Regulations
Soliman	Judicial decision with citation given

See the first module in Chapter 25, Federal Tax Process and Procedure, for explanations of the authoritative value of these sources of tax law, regulation, and procedure. Treasury Department Circular No. 230, cited in Chapter 24, is a publication containing the part of federal regulations dealing with the practice before the IRS of enrolled agents, attorneys, CPAs, and others.

References to prior major tax acts are abbreviated; e.g., "1988 TAMRA" is used for the Technical and Miscellaneous Revenue Act, "1986 TRA" for Tax Reform Act of 1986, and "1984 TRA" for Tax Reform Act of 1984.

TAX FORMS ON THE SPECIAL ENROLLMENT EXAMINATION

Tax forms are often presented to use for computation on the Special Enrollment Examinations. They are not included in this book because they are not needed to complete the solutions to the questions. Tax students and exam candidates should be able to undertake the required computations without the forms. Furthermore, referring to the forms during the exam may confuse SPE candidates once they understand the theory, especially if they are not familiar with the forms.

PREPARING FOR ESSAY QUESTIONS AND COMPUTATIONAL PROBLEMS

The Special Enrollment Examination, which is all multiple-choice and true-false, needs no essay question preparation.

In studying for the other certification exams, however, do not overemphasize studying objective questions at the expense of underemphasizing essay questions and computational problems. Remember, 40% of each part of the CPA exam and well over 50% of each part of the CMA exam consist of essay questions and/or computational problems. Thus, a complete study program must include working essay questions and computational problems as well as objective questions under exam conditions.

When working federal tax essay questions and/or computational problems, survey the question/problem and set a time budget, e.g., 10, 15, or 20 minutes. Then, complete the question or problem in the budgeted time. Question answering techniques are discussed and illustrated in Chapter 3 of *CIA Examination Review*, *CMA Examination Review*, and *CPA Examination Review*.

CROSS-REFERENCES TO FEDERAL TAX TEXTBOOKS

The next 8 pages contain the tables of contents from current federal tax textbooks with cross-references to the corresponding modules in this study manual. The texts are presented in the order listed on pages 1 and 2 of this chapter. As you study a particular chapter in your federal tax textbook, you can easily determine which module(s) to study in this manual. You should review all questions in each module.

Commerce Clearing House, Inc., *Federal Taxation: Advanced Topics*, **1991 Edition, Commerce Clearing House, Inc.**

Chapter   1 - Introduction to Federal Taxation
Chapter   2 - Tax Research and Planning - 25.1, 25.2
Chapter   3 - Business Taxation--An Overview - 6.1-6.5, 11.8-11.15, 13.1-13.8, 21.1, 21.2
Chapter   4 - Taxation of Corporations--Basic Concepts - 18.1-18.16, 19.6, 19.7
Chapter   5 - Corporate Nonliquidating Distributions - 18.17, 18.18, 19.1, 19.2
Chapter   6 - Corporate Distributions in Complete Liquidations - 19.3, 19.4
Chapter   7 - Corporate Reorganizations - 19.5
Chapter   8 - Accumulated Earnings and Personal Holding Company Taxes - 19.8, 19.9
Chapter   9 - Partnerships--Formation and Operation - 17.1-17.9, 17.13, 17.14
Chapter 10 - Partnerships--Distributions, Sales and Exchanges - 17.10-17.12
Chapter 11 - S Corporations - 19.10-19.16
Chapter 12 - Federal Estate Tax - 23.7-23.11
Chapter 13 - Federal Gift Tax, Generation-Skipping Transfer Tax, and Valuation - 10.5, 12.2, 12.3, 23.1-23.6, 23.12-23.14
Chapter 14 - Income Taxation of Trusts and Estates - 4.10, 20.1-20.6
Chapter 15 - Deferred Compensation and Retirement Plans
Chapter 16 - Tax Accounting - 21.1-21.8
Chapter 17 - Tax Administration, Procedure, and Practice - 25.3-25.10

Commerce Clearing House, Inc., *Federal Taxation: Basic Principles*, **1991 Edition, Commerce Clearing House, Inc.**

Chapter   1 - Introduction to Federal Taxation
Chapter   2 - Understanding the Tax Law - 25.1-25.6
Chapter   3 - Individual Taxation--An Overview - 10.1-10.5
Chapter   4 - Gross Income - 4.1-4.9, 5.1, 5.7, 21.1
Chapter   5 - Gross Income--Exclusions - 5.1-5.7, 16.4
Chapter   6 - Deductions: General Concepts and Trade or Business Deductions - 6.1-6.9, 7.1-7.3, 8.1-8.4, 13.1-13.8
Chapter   7 - Deductions: Business/Investment Losses and Passive Activity Losses - 7.1-7.3
Chapter   8 - Deductions: Itemized Deductions - 9.1-9.7
Chapter   9 - Tax Credits, Prepayments, and Special Methods - 10.6, 11.1-11.15
Chapter 10 - Property Transactions: Determination of Basis and Gains and Losses - 12.1-12.8
Chapter 11 - Property Transactions: Nonrecognition of Gains and Losses - 16.1-16.4
Chapter 12 - Property Transactions: Treatment of Capital and Section 1231 Assets - 14.1-14.8, 15.1-15.6
Chapter 13 - Accounting Periods and Methods - 21.1-21.8
Chapter 14 - Deferred Compensation and Retirement Plans
Chapter 15 - Tax Planning for Individuals
Chapter 16 - Partnerships, Corporations, and S Corporations - 17.1-17.14, 18.1-18.18, 19.1-19.4, 19.8-19.16
Chapter 17 - Estate and Gift Tax - 23.1-23.14
Chapter 18 - Income Taxation of Trusts and Estates - 4.10, 20.1-20.6

Commerce Clearing House, Inc., *1991 Federal Tax Course,* **1990 Edition, Commerce Clearing House, Inc.**

Part I: Overview
    1 - The Federal Revenue System - 25.1
Part II: Individual Taxpayers
    2 - Taxation of Individuals - 10.1-10.7
Part III: Determining Taxable Income
    3 - Tax Accounting - 21.1-21.3, 21.6-21.8
    4 - Gross Income - 4.1-4.10, 5.1, 5.7
    5 - Exclusion from Gross Income - 5.1-5.7, 16.4
    6 - Trade or Business Expenses - 6.1-6.9, 8.1-8.3
    7 - Depreciation and Depletion - 13.1-13.7
    8 - Nonbusiness Deductions - 8.1-8.4, 9.1-9.7
    9 - Realization and Recognition of Gain or Loss - 12.1-12.8, 4.8, 16.1-16.4
    10 - Character of Gain or Loss - 14.1-14.8, 15.1-15.6
    11 - Bad Debts and Losses - 6.2, 6.9, 7.1-7.3, 9.5
Part IV: Determining Tax Liability
    12 - Tax Computations - 10.1-10.8
    13 - Tax Credits - 11.1-11.15
    14 - Procedure and Administration - 10.9, 21.9, 24.6, 25.3-25.10
Part V: Corporations and Other Entities
    15 - Decedents -- Estates -- Trusts - 20.1-20.6
    16 - Corporations - 18.1-18.16, 19.6, 19.7
    17 - Corporate Distributions - 18.17, 18.18, 19.1-19.5, 19.8
    18 - S Corporations - 19.10-19.16
    19 - Partnerships - 17.1-17.14
Part VI: Special Topics
    20 - Federal Tax Research - 25.1, 25.2
    21 - Special Accounting Methods - 21.3-21.6
    22 - Net Operating Losses - 7.1, 18.10
    23 - Specially Taxed Corporations - 19.9
    24 - Taxation of Securities - 12.8, 14.2
    25 - Retirement Plans
    26 - Gift Tax - 23.1-23.6
    27 - Estate Tax - 23.7-23.11

Everett, Boley, Duncan, and Jamison, *HBJ Federal Tax Course,* **1991 Edition, Harcourt Brace Jovanovich, Inc.**

Chapter 1 - An Introduction
Chapter 2 - Sources and Uses of Tax Law - 25.1-25.10
Chapter 3 - Calculating an Individual's Income Tax - 10.1-10.5
Chapter 4 - Gross Income - 4.1, 4.9, 21.1, 21.2, 21.8
Chapter 5 - Inclusions and Exclusions - 4.1-4.10, 5.1-5.7
Chapter 6 - Business Income - 21.1-21.8
Chapter 7 - General Requirements for a Deduction and Employment-Related Deductions - 6.1, 6.3, 6.6, 8.1, 9.6, 9.7
Chapter 8 - Business Deductions - 6.1-6.9, 7.1
Chapter 9 - Personal Deductions for Individual Taxpayers - 9.1-9.7
Chapter 10 - Sales of Investment Properties - 12.1-12.8, 14.1-14.8
Chapter 11 - Sales of Business Properties - 15.1-15.6
Chapter 12 - Nontaxable Exchanges - 16.1-16.4
Chapter 13 - Investment Properties: Income, Deduction and Tax-Shelter Opportunities and Limitations - 7.2, 7.3, 8.2, 8.3
Chapter 14 - Tax Credits - 11.1-11.15
Chapter 15 - The Tax Computation - 10.6-10.7, 22.4
Chapter 16 - Corporations and Other Entities - 17.1-17.14, 18.1-18.18, 19.1, 19.10-19.16, 20.1-20.3

Chapter 1: How to Use This Book

Hoffman and Raabe, *Corporations, Partnerships, Estates and Trusts*, 1991 Edition, West Publishing Co.

Chapter 1 - Understanding and Working with the Federal Tax Law - 25.1, 25.2
Chapter 2 - Corporations: Introduction, Operating Rules, and Related Corps. - 18.1, 18.2, 18.6-18.16
Chapter 3 - Corporations: Organization, Capital Structure, and Dividend Distribution - 14.6, 18.3-18.5, 19.6, 19.7
Chapter 4 - Corporations: Redemptions and Liquidations - 18.17, 18.18, 19.1, 19.2
Chapter 5 - Alternative Minimum Tax and Certain Penalty Taxes Imposed on Corporations - 18.14, 18.15
Chapter 6 - Corporations: Reorganizations - 19.5
Chapter 7 - Partnerships: Formation, Operation, and Distributions - 17.1-17.10, 17.14
Chapter 8 - Partnerships: Transfer of Interests; Distributions; Family and Limited Partnerships - 17.11-17.13
Chapter 9 - S Corporations - 19.10-19.16
Chapter 10 - Comparative Forms of Doing Business; Exempt Entities
Chapter 11 - Taxation of International Transactions - 5.7, 11.7
Chapter 12 - Multistate Corporate Taxation
Chapter 13 - Tax Administration and Practice - 24.1-24.6, 25.3-25.10
Chapter 14 - The Federal Gift and Estate Taxes - 23.1-23.14
Chapter 15 - Family Tax Planning
Chapter 16 - Income Taxation of Trusts and Estates - 20.1-20.6

Hoffman and Willis, *Federal Taxation: Comprehensive Volume*, 1991 Edition, West Publishing Co.

Chapter 1 - An Introduction to Taxation and Understanding the Federal Tax Law - 25.1, 25.2
Chapter 2 - Tax Determination: Personal and Dependency Exemptions; An Overview of Property Transactions - 10.1-10.5, 12.1, 12.8, 14.1-14.4, 14.7
Chapter 3 - Gross Income: Concepts and Inclusions - 4.1-4.9, 5.7, 21.1-21.3, 21.8
Chapter 4 - Gross Income: Exclusions - 5.1-5.7
Chapter 5 - Deductions and Losses: In General - 6.1, 6.3, 6.6, 21.1-21.3
Chapter 6 - Passive Activity Losses - 7.3
Chapter 7 - Deductions and Losses: Certain Business Expenses and Losses - 6.2, 6.9, 7.1, 9.5, 14.5, 14.6
Chapter 8 - Depreciation, Cost Recovery, Amortization, and Depletion - 13.1-13.8
Chapter 9 - Deductions: Employee Expenses - 6.3, 6.6, 8.1, 9.6, 9.7, 22.2
Chapter 10 - Deductions and Losses: Certain Itemized Deductions - 9.1-9.7
Chapter 11 - Tax Credits - 11.1-11.15
Chapter 12 - Property Transactions: Determination of Gain or Loss, Basis Considerations, and Nontaxable Exchanges - 12.1-12.8, 16.1-16.4
Chapter 13 - Property Transactions: Capital Gains and Losses, Section 1231, and Recapture Provisions - 12.8, 14.1-14.8, 15.1-15.8
Chapter 14 - Alternative Minimum Tax - 10.6
Chapter 15 - Accounting Periods and Methods - 21.1-21.8
Chapter 16 - Corporations: Operating Rules, Organization, and Capital Structure - 18.1-18.16
Chapter 17 - Corporations: Distributions Not in Complete Liquidation - 18.17, 18.18, 19.1, 19.2
Chapter 18 - Corporations: Distributions in Complete Liquidation and an Overview of Reorganizations - 19.3-19.5
Chapter 19 - Corporate Accumulations - 19.8, 19.9
Chapter 20 - S Corporations - 19.10-19.16
Chapter 21 - Partnerships - 17.1-17.14
Chapter 22 - Tax-Exempt Entities
Chapter 23 - Taxation of International Transactions - 5.7, 11.7
Chapter 24 - Tax Administration and Practice - 25.3-25.10
Chapter 25 - The Federal Gift and Estate Taxes - 23.1-23.14
Chapter 26 - Income Taxation of Trusts and Estates - 20.1-20.6
Chapter 27 - Working with the Tax Law - 25.1, 25.2

Hoffman, Willis, and Smith, *Individual Income Taxes,* 1991 Edition, West Publishing Co.

Chapter   1 - An Introduction to Taxation and Understanding the Federal Tax Law - 25.3-25.7
Chapter   2 - Working with the Tax Law - 25.1, 25.2
Chapter   3 - Tax Determination; Personal and Dependency Exemptions; an Overview of Property Transactions - 10.1-10.5, 12.1, 12.8, 14.1-14.4, 14.7
Chapter   4 - Gross Income: Concepts and Inclusions - 4.1-4.9, 5.7, 21.1-21.3, 21.8
Chapter   5 - Gross Income: Exclusions - 5.1-5.7
Chapter   6 - Deductions and Losses: In General - 6.1, 6.3, 6.6, 21.1-21.3
Chapter   7 - Passive Activity Losses - 7.3
Chapter   8 - Deductions and Losses: Certain Business Expenses and Losses - 6.2, 6.9, 7.1, 9.5, 14.5, 14.6
Chapter   9 - Depreciation, Cost Recovery, Amortization, and Depletion - 13.1-13.8
Chapter 10 - Deductions: Employee Expenses - 6.3, 6.6, 8.1, 9.6, 9.7, 22.2
Chapter 11 - Deductions and Losses: Certain Itemized Deductions - 9.1-9.7
Chapter 12 - Alternative Minimum Tax - 10.6, 22.1-22.7
Chapter 13 - Tax Credits and Payment Procedures - 11.1-11.15
Chapter 14 - Property Transactions: Determination of Gain or Loss and Basis Considerations - 12.1-12.8
Chapter 15 - Property Transactions: Nontaxable Exchanges - 16.1-16.4, 18.3, 18.4
Chapter 16 - Property Transactions: Capital Gains and Losses - 12.8, 14.1-14.5, 14.7, 14.8
Chapter 17 - Property Transactions: Section 1231 and Recapture Provisions - 15.1-15.6
Chapter 18 - Accounting Periods and Methods - 21.1-21.9
Chapter 19 - Deferred Compensation
Chapter 20 - Corporations and Partnerships - 17.1-17.10, 18.1-18.18, 19.1-19.4, 19.10-19.16

Kramer and Phillips, *Prentice Hall's Federal Taxation 1991: Comprehensive Volume,* Prentice Hall, Inc., 1990.

Chapter   1 - An Introduction to Taxation - 25.1, 25.2
Chapter   2 - Determination of Tax - 10.1-10.5
Chapter   3 - Gross Income--Inclusions - 4.1-4.10
Chapter   4 - Gross Income--Exclusions - 5.1-5.8
Chapter   5 - Property Transactions--Capital Gains and Losses - 12.1-12.8, 14.1-14.4
Chapter   6 - Deductions and Losses - 6.1, 6.3-6.8, 8.1-8.3, 14.7, 14.8, 21.1, 21.2
Chapter   7 - Itemized Deductions - 9.1-9.7
Chapter   8 - Losses and Bad Debts - 6.2, 6.9, 7.1, 7.3, 9.5
Chapter   9 - Employee Expenses - 6.3, 6.6, 8.1, 9.6, 9.7
Chapter 10 - Depreciation, Cost Recovery, Depletion, Amortization, and Inventory Costs - 13.1-13.8, 21.6
Chapter 11 - Accounting Periods and Methods - 21.1-21.8
Chapter 12 - Property Transactions--Nontaxable Exchanges - 16.1-16.4
Chapter 13 - Property Transactions--Section 1231 and Recapture - 15.1-15.6
Chapter 14 - Special Tax Computation Methods, Payment of Tax, and Tax Credits - 10.6, 10.7, 11.1-11.15
Chapter 15 - Formation of the Corporation - 18.1-18.5
Chapter 16 - The Corporate Income Tax - 18.6-18.16, 19.6, 19.7
Chapter 17 - Corporate Nonliquidating Distributions - 18.17, 18.18, 19.1, 19.2
Chapter 18 - Corporate Liquidating Distributions - 19.2-19.4
Chapter 19 - Corporate Acquisitions and Reorganizations - 19.5
Chapter 20 - Partnership Formation and Operation - 17.1-17.9, 17.13, 17.14
Chapter 21 - Special Partnership Issues - 17.10-17.12
Chapter 22 - S Corporations - 19.10-19.16
Chapter 23 - The Gift Tax - 23.1-23.6
Chapter 24 - The Estate Tax - 23.7-23.14
Chapter 25 - Income Taxation of Trusts and Estates - 20.1-20.6
Chapter 26 - U.S. Taxation of Foreign-Related Transactions - 5.7, 11.7
Chapter 27 - Administrative Procedures - 10.7, 18.16, 25.3-25.10

Kramer and Phillips, *Prentice Hall's Federal Taxation 1991: Corporations, Partnerships, Estates and Trusts,* **Prentice Hall, Inc., 1990.**

Chapter   1 - Tax Research - 25.1
Chapter   2 - Formation of the Corporation - 18.1-18.5
Chapter   3 - The Corporate Income Tax - 18.6-18.16, 19.6, 19.7
Chapter   4 - Other Corporate Tax Levies - 18.14, 19.8, 19.9
Chapter   5 - Corporate Nonliquidating Distributions - 18.17, 18.18, 19.1, 19.2
Chapter   6 - Corporate Liquidating Distributions - 19.2-19.4
Chapter   7 - Corporate Acquisitions and Reorganizations - 19.5
Chapter   8 - Consolidated Tax Returns - 19.6
Chapter   9 - Partnership Formation and Operation - 17.1-17.9, 17.13, 17.14
Chapter 10 - Special Partnership Issues - 17.10-17.12
Chapter 11 - S Corporations - 19.10-19.16
Chapter 12 - The Gift Tax - 23.1-23.6
Chapter 13 - The Estate Tax - 23.7-23.14
Chapter 14 - Income Taxation of Trusts and Estates - 20.1-20.6
Chapter 15 - U.S. Taxation of Foreign-Related Transactions - 10.7
Chapter 16 - Administrative Procedures - 10.7, 18.16, 24.1-24.6, 25.3-25.10

Phillips and Kramer, *Prentice Hall's Federal Taxation 1991: Individuals,* **Prentice Hall, Inc., 1990.**

Chapter   1 - An Introduction to Taxation - 25.1, 25.2
Chapter   2 - Determination of Tax - 10.1-10.5
Chapter   3 - Gross Income -- Inclusions - 4.1-4.10, 5.1, 5.3, 5.7
Chapter   4 - Gross Income -- Exclusions - 5.2-5.7
Chapter   5 - Property Transactions -- Capital Gains and Losses - 12.1-12.8, 14.1-14.4
Chapter   6 - Deductions and Losses - 6.1, 6.3-6.8, 8.1-8.3, 14.7, 14.8, 21.1, 21.2
Chapter   7 - Itemized Deductions - 9.1-9.7
Chapter   8 - Losses and Bad Debts - 6.2, 6.9, 7.1-7.3, 9.5
Chapter   9 - Employee Expenses and Deferred Compensation - 6.3, 6.6, 8.1, 9.6, 9.7
Chapter 10 - Depreciation, Cost Recovery, Depletion, Amortization, and Inventory Costs - 13.1-13.8, 21.6
Chapter 11 - Accounting Periods and Methods - 21.1-21.8
Chapter 12 - Property Transactions -- Nontaxable Exchanges - 16.1-16.4
Chapter 13 - Property Transactions -- Section 1231 and Recapture - 15.1-15.6
Chapter 14 - Special Tax Computation Methods, Payment of Tax, and Tax Credits - 10.6, 10.7, 11.1-11.15
Chapter 15 - Partnerships and S Corporations - 17.1-17.14, 19.10-19.16
Chapter 16 - Corporations - 18.1-18.18, 19.1
Chapter 17 - Tax Considerations for Investors - 7.2, 7.3, 8.2, 8.3

Pratt, Burns, and Kulsrud, *Corporate, Partnership, Estate and Gift Taxation,* **1991 Edition, Richard D. Irwin, Inc., 1990.**

Chapter   1 - Income Taxation of Corporations - 18.1, 18.2, 18.6-18.16
Chapter   2 - Corporate Formation and Capital Structure - 14.6, 18.3-18.5
Chapter   3 - Corporate Distributions: Cash, Property, and Stock Dividends - 18.17, 18.18, 19.1, 19.2
Chapter   4 - Corporate Distributions: Stock Redemptions, Partial Liquidations, and Corporate Divisions - 19.1-19.5
Chapter   5 - Complete Liquidations - 19.3, 19.4
Chapter   6 - Penalty Taxes on Corporate Accumulations - 19.8, 19.9
Chapter   7 - Corporate Reorganizations - 19.5
Chapter   8 - Consolidated Tax Returns - 19.6, 19.7
Chapter   9 - International Taxation - 5.7, 11.7
Chapter 10 - Taxation of Partnerships and Partners - 17.1-17.9
Chapter 11 - Special Partnerships, Asset Distributions, and Dispositions of Partnership Interests - 17.10-17.14
Chapter 12 - S Corporations - 19.10-19.16
Chapter 13 - Estate and Gift Taxation - 23.1-23.14
Chapter 14 - Income Taxation of Estates and Trusts - 20.1-20.6
Chapter 15 - Family Tax Planning - 4.9, 10.5, 14.8, 17.13, 20.4
Chapter 16 - Sources and Applications of Federal Tax Law - 25.1, 25.2
Chapter 17 - Tax Practice and Procedure - 10.3, 24.1-24.12, 25.3-25.10

Pratt, Burns, and Kulsrud, *Federal Taxation*, 1991 Edition, Richard D. Irwin, Inc., 1990.

Chapter 1 - An Overview of Federal Taxation
Chapter 2 - Sources and Applications of Federal Tax Law - 25.1, 25.2
Chapter 3 - Taxable Entities, Tax Formula, Introduction to Property Transactions - 10.4, 18.13
Chapter 4 - Personal and Dependency Exemptions; Filing Status; Determination of Tax for an Individual; Filing Requirements - 10.1-10.5, 10.7
Chapter 5 - Gross Income - 4.1, 4.9, 21.1-21.3, 21.8
Chapter 6 - Gross Income: Inclusions and Exclusions - 4.1-4.10, 5.1-5.8
Chapter 7 - Overview of Deductions and Losses - 6.1, 6.3, 6.6, 21.1-21.3
Chapter 8 - Certain Business Deductions and Losses - 6.2, 6.9, 7.1, 9.5, 14.5, 14.6
Chapter 9 - Employee Business Expenses - 6.3, 6.4, 6.6, 8.1, 9.6, 9.7
Chapter 10 - Capital Recovery: Depreciation, Amortization, and Depletion - 13.1-13.8
Chapter 11 - Deductions for Investment Expenses and Certain Personal Items - 7.3, 8.2, 19.1-19.4
Chapter 12 - The Alternative Minimum Tax and Tax Credits - 10.6, 11.1-11.15
Chapter 13 - Property Transactions: Basis Determination, Recognition of Gain or Loss - 12.1-12.8
Chapter 14 - Nontaxable Exchanges - 16.1-16.4
Chapter 15 - Property Transactions: Character of Gain or Loss Recognized; Capital Assets and Trade or Business Property - 12.1-12.8, 14.1-14.5, 14.7, 14.8, 15.1-15.3
Chapter 16 - Special Tax Accounting Problems - 21.4-21.7
Chapter 17 - Employee Compensation and Retirement Plans - 4.2, 5.2
Chapter 18 - Corporations: Formation and Operation - 14.6, 18.3-18.13
Chapter 19 - Corporate Distributions, Redemptions, and Liquidations - 18.18, 19.1-19.5
Chapter 20 - Taxation of Corporate Accumulations - 19.8-19.9
Chapter 21 - Taxation of Partnerships and Partners - 17.1-17.5, 17.13
Chapter 22 - S Corporations - 19.10-19.16
Chapter 23 - The Federal Transfer Taxes - 23.1-23.14
Chapter 24 - Income Taxation of Estates and Trusts - 20.1-20.6
Chapter 25 - Family Tax Planning
Chapter 26 - Aspects of International Taxation - 5.7, 11.7

Pratt, Burns, and Kulsrud, *Individual Taxation*, 1991 Edition, Richard D. Irwin, Inc., 1990.

Chapter 1 - An Overview of Federal Taxation - 10.3, 25.6
Chapter 2 - Sources and Applications of Federal Tax Law - 25.1, 25.2
Chapter 3 - Taxable Entitles, Tax Formula, Introduction to Property Transactions - 10.4, 18.13
Chapter 4 - Personal and Dependency Exemptions; Filing Status; Determination of Tax for an Individual; Filing Requirements - 10.1-10.5, 10.7
Chapter 5 - Gross Income - 4.1, 4.9, 21.1-21.3, 21.8
Chapter 6 - Gross Income: Inclusions and Exclusions - 4.1-4.8, 5.1-5.8
Chapter 7 - Overview of Deductions and Losses - 6.1, 6.5, 6.6, 8.3
Chapter 8 - Certain Business Deductions and Losses - 6.2-6.9, 7.1-7.3, 8.1, 8.2, 9.6, 9.7, 14.5, 14.6
Chapter 9 - Employee Business Expenses - 6.3, 6.6, 8.1, 9.6, 9.7
Chapter 10 - Capital Recovery: Depreciation, Amortization, and Depletion - 6.8, 13.1-13.8
Chapter 11 - Deductions for Investment Expenses and Certain Personal Items - 7.3, 8.2, 19.1-19.4
Chapter 12 - The Alternative Minimum Tax and Tax Credits - 10.6, 11.1-11.15
Chapter 13 - Property Transactions: Basis Determination, Recognition of Gain or Loss - 4.1, 12.1-12.7, 14.2, 14.8
Chapter 14 - Nontaxable Exchanges - 16.1-16.4
Chapter 15 - Property Transactions: Character of Gain or Loss Recognized; Capital Assets and Trade or Business Property - 12.8, 14.1-14.7, 15.1-15.6
Chapter 16 - Special Tax Accounting Problems - 21.4-21.7
Chapter 17 - Employee Compensation and Retirement Plans - 4.2, 5.2
Chapter 18 - Taxation of Business Forms and Their Owners - 17.1-17.8, 18.1-18.18, 19.10-19.16

Prentice Hall, Inc., *1991 Federal Tax Course***, Prentice Hall, Inc.**

    Chapter 1 - An Introduction to Federal Taxes
Figuring the Individual Income Tax
    Chapter 2 - Individuals - Returns, Filing Status, Personal Exemptions and Rates - 10.1-10.5
Gross Income - Property Transactions - Gain or Loss
    Chapter 3 - Gross Income - Exclusions - 4.1, 4.7, 5.1, 5.3, 5.4, 5.7
    Chapter 4 - Gross Income - Inclusions - 4.1-4.9, 5.1, 5.2, 5.5
    Chapter 5 - Property Transactions: Gain or Loss, Basis, Recognition - 12.1-12.8, 16.1, 16.2, 18.3
    Chapter 6 - Property Transactions: Gain or Loss, Involuntary Conversion, Sale of Residence - 16.3, 16.4
    Chapter 7 - Property Transactions: Capital Gains and Losses of Individuals - 12.8, 14.1-14.8, 15.1-15.6
Business and Personal Deductions
    Chapter 8 - Deductions - Business Expenses - 6.1, 6.3-6.7, 8.1-8.3, 9.6, 9.7
    Chapter 9 - Deductions - Personal Expenses - 9.1-9.4
    Chapter 10 - Deductions - Depreciation - 13.1-13.7
    Chapter 11 - Deductions - Depletion, Mining and Farmers' Expenses - 6.8, 13.8
    Chapter 12 - Deductions - Losses - 6.9, 7.1-7.3, 9.5, 14.6-14.8
    Chapter 13 - Deductions - Bad Debts - 6.2, 14.5
Tax Computation - Retirement Plans - Inventories - Accounting
    Chapter 14 - Special Tax Computations - Tax Credits - Estimated Tax - 10.6, 11.1-11.15
    Chapter 15 - Retirement Plans
    Chapter 16 - Inventory - 21.6
    Chapter 17 - Accounting - 21.1-21.3, 21.7, 21.8
    Chapter 18 - Installment and Deferred Payment Sales - 21.4, 21.5
Handling Taxes of Partnerships
    Chapter 19 - Organizing and Operating a Partnership - 17.1-17.8
    Chapter 20 - Partnerships: Distributions, Transfers, and Terminations - 17.9-17.14
Figuring Corporation Tax - Special Corporation Problems
    Chapter 21 - Corporations - Tax Rates, Income, Deductions, Gains and Losses - 18.1-18.18, 19.6, 19.8
    Chapter 22 - S Corporations - 19.10-19.16
    Chapter 23 - Corporations - Reorganizations - Stock Redemptions - 19.1-19.5
    Chapter 24 - Corporations - Personal Holding Companies, Etc. - Exempt Organizations - 19.9
Taxation of Estates and Trusts
    Chapter 25 - Estates and Trusts - 20.1-20.5
Estate and Gift Taxes - Foreign Income Taxpayers - Payroll Taxes
    Chapter 26 - Estate and Gift Taxes - 23.1-23.14
    Chapter 27 - Foreign Income, Foreign Taxpayers - 10.7
    Chapter 28 - Payroll Taxes - 22.1-22.5
Filing Returns - Paying Taxes - Getting Refunds
    Chapter 29 - Returns and Payment of Tax - 10.3, 10.7, 18.15, 18.16, 22.7
    Chapter 30 - Assessment, Collection, Refunds - 25.3-25.10

Raby, Tidwell, and White, *Introduction to Federal Taxation***, 1991 Edition, Prentice Hall, Inc. (see page 14)**

Sommerfeld and Jones, *Federal Taxes and Management Decisions***, 1991-1992 Edition, Richard D. Irwin, Inc., 1990.**

Chapter 1 - An Introduction
Chapter 2 - The Income Concept: General Rules and Common Misconceptions
Chapter 3 - Taxable Entities
Chapter 4 - Tax Aspects of Selecting a Business Form - 17.1-17.8, 18.1-18.18, 19.10-19.16
Chapter 5 - Accounting Method Options - 21.1-21.8
Chapter 6 - The Alternative Minimum Tax - 10.6, 21.1-21.8
Chapter 7 - Capital Gains and Losses - 12.8, 14.1-14.8, 15.1-15.8
Chapter 8 - Special Limitation on Passive-Activity Losses - 7.3
Chapter 9 - Compensation Considerations
Chapter 10 - Tax Factors in the Acquisition, Use, and Disposition of Fixed Assets - 11.10-11.15, 13.1-13.8, 15.2, 15.3
Chapter 11 - The Nontaxable Transactions - 16.1-16.4, 18.3, 18.4
Chapter 12 - Corporate Acquisitions, Mergers, Divisions, and Liquidations - 18.1-18.18, 19.1-19.5, 19.8-19.16
Chapter 13 - Common Tax Traps
Chapter 14 - Family Tax Planning - 14.8, 17.13, 20.4, 23.1-23.14
Chapter 15 - The Taxing Process

Raby, Tidwell, and White, *Introduction to Federal Taxation*, 1991 Edition, Prentice Hall, Inc.

Part One - The Nonbusiness Taxpayer
    Chapter   1 - Taxes and Choices
    Chapter   2 - Income - 4.1-4.10, 5.1-5.7
    Chapter   3 - Deductions from Income - 8.1-8.4, 9.1-9.7
    Chapter   4 - Tax Calculation - 10.1-10.7, 11.1-11.15
    Chapter   5 - Taxable Property Transactions - 12.1-12.8, 14.1-14.8, 15.1-15.6
    Chapter   6 - Nontaxable Property Transactions - 16.1-16.4
Part Two - The Taxpayer in Business
    Chapter   7 - The Business Individual 6.1-6.9, 7.1-7.3, 8.1, 8.2, 11.7-11.9, 21.1
    Chapter   8 - Tax Accounting for Business - 6.2, 21.1-21.8
    Chapter   9 - Asset Acquisition, Use, and Disposition - 11.10-11.15, 13.1-13.8, 15.2, 15.3
    Chapter 10 - Partnerships and Partners - 17.1-17.13
    Chapter 11 - The S Corporation - 19.10-19.16
    Chapter 12 - Corporations: A First Look - 18.1-18.18, 19.8
    Chapter 13 - Advanced Corporate Tax Topics - 19.1-19.5, 19.9
Part Three - Other Opportunities
    Chapter 14 - Fiduciaries - 20.1-20.6
    Chapter 15 - Family Tax Planning, Including Estate Tax and Gift Tax - 14.8, 17.13, 20.4, 23.1-23.14
    Chapter 16 - Alternative Minimum Tax - 10.6, 18.14
    Chapter 17 - Tax Shelters - 7.2, 7.3
    Chapter 18 - Employee Benefit Plans and Retirement Income
    Chapter 19 - Tax Practice and Procedure - 24.1-24.6, 25.3-25.10
    Chapter 20 - Tax Research - 25.1, 25.2
    Chapter 21 - Analyzing Tax-Planning Opportunities

Sommerfeld, Madeo, and Milliron, *An Introduction to Taxation*, 1991 Edition, Harcourt Brace Jovanovich, Inc.

Part One - An Overview of Taxation
    Chapter   1 - Taxation as a Policy Tool
    Chapter   2 - The Evolutionary Nature of U.S. Taxation
    Chapter   3 - Legal Processes and Responsibilities - 25.1-25.10
Part Two - Basic Concepts
    Chapter   4 - Income: General Concepts - 4.1-4.10, 5.1-5.8
    Chapter   5 - Deductions: General Concepts - 6.1-6.8
    Chapter   6 - Losses: General Concepts
    Chapter   7 - Tax Accounting (Including the AMT) - 4.9, 10.5, 10.6, 21.1-21.3, 21.7, 21.8
    Chapter   8 - Taxable Entities and Tax Rates - 17.1-17.14, 18.1-18.14, 19.7, 19.10-19.16, 20.1-20.6
    Chapter   9 - Tax Basis - 12.1-12.8
Part Three - The Individual Taxpayer
    Chapter 10 - The Individual Tax Computation - 10.1-10.5, 10.7, 11.1-11.7
    Chapter 11 - Itemized Deductions - 9.1-9.5
    Chapter 12 - Miscellaneous Itemized Deductions - 9.6, 9.7
    Chapter 13 - Incentives for Savings: Pension Plans
Part Four - Business Income and Deductions
    Chapter 14 - Business Income and Credits - 6.1-6.9, 7.1, 11.8-11.15, 18.2, 21.1-21.3, 21.8
    Chapter 15 - Depreciation and Cost Recovery - 13.1-13.8
Part Five - Property Transactions
    Chapter 16 - Capital Gains and Losses - 14.1-14.7
    Chapter 17 - Nontaxable Exchanges - 16.4, 18.3, 18.4, 18.17, 18.18
Part Six - Perspective
    Chapter 18 - Tax Practice, Planning, and Education

CHAPTER TWO
MULTIPLE-CHOICE QUESTION ANSWERING TECHNIQUE

You need a personalized control system (**technique**) for answering multiple-choice questions, essay questions, and computational problems. The objective is to obtain complete, correct, and well-presented answers. Because this study manual is limited to multiple-choice questions, this chapter is limited to discussion of a multiple-choice question answering technique. Developing answers to computational problems and essay questions is discussed and illustrated in *CIA Examination Review*, *CMA Examination Review*, and *CPA Examination Review*.

The following series of steps is suggested for answering multiple-choice questions. The important point is that you need to devote attention to and develop **the technique that works for you**. Personalize and practice **your** multiple-choice question answering technique on questions in this study manual. Modify the following suggested steps to suit your individual skills and ability. For example, you will need to cover the readily available answer explanations at the right of each question. There will be none of these on your exam! Begin now, and develop **your** control system.

1. **Budget your time.**

    We make this point with emphasis. Just as you would fill up your gas tank prior to reaching empty, so too would you finish your exam before time expires.

    a. Calculate the time allowed for each multiple-choice question after you have allocated exam time to the other overall questions on the exam; e.g., if one overall question consists of 20 individual multiple-choice questions and is allocated 40 minutes on your exam, you should spend a little under 2 minutes per individual multiple-choice question (always budget extra time for transferring answers to answer sheets, if provided, interruptions, etc.).

    b. Before beginning a series of multiple-choice questions, write the starting time on the exam near the first multiple-choice question.

    c. As you work through the individual multiple-choice questions, check your time; e.g., assuming the above time allocation of 40 minutes for 20 questions, if you have worked five multiple-choice questions in 9 minutes, you are fine, but if you spent 11 minutes on five questions, you need to speed up.

2. **Answer the questions in chronological order.**

    a. Do **not** agonize over any one question. Stay within your time budget.

    b. Mark any unanswered questions with a big "?" and return to them later if time allows.

3. **For each question**

    a. **Cover up the answer choices** with your hand or a piece of scratch paper. Do not allow the answer choices to affect your reading of the question.

    1) For example, if four answer choices are presented, three of them are incorrect. They are called **distractors** for a very good reason.

b. **Read the question** stem carefully (the part of the question that precedes the answer choices) to determine the precise requirement.

1) You may wish to underline or circle key language or data used in the stem.

2) Focusing on what is required enables you to ignore extraneous information and to proceed directly to determining the correct answer.

a) Be especially careful to note when the requirement is an **exception**; e.g., "All of the following are taxable interest income **except**:"

c. **Determine the correct answer** before looking at the answer choices.

1) By adhering to the steps above, you know what is required and which are the relevant facts.

d. **Read the answer choices** with close attention.

1) Even if answer (a) appears to be the correct choice, do **not** skip the remaining answer choices. Answer (b), (c), or (d) may even be better.

2) Treat each choice as a true-false question. Consider marking a "T" or "F" next to each answer choice as you analyze it.

e. **Select the best answer.** Circle the most likely or "best" answer choice on the test paper. If you are uncertain, you must decide whether to guess.

1) Most examinations do not penalize guessing because the score is determined by the number of correct responses. In this situation, you should answer every question.

2) When a subtraction from the total of correct answers **is** made for incorrectly answered questions (and no subtraction for unanswered questions), guessing is penalized. Therefore you must decide whether the payoff outweighs the risk of guessing.

4. After you have answered all the questions, **transfer your answers to the answer sheet** (if one exists).

a. Do this after completing all multiple-choice questions.

b. Make sure you are within your time budget so that you will be able to perform this vital step in an unhurried manner.

c. Do not wait to transfer answers until the very end of the exam session when you may run out of time.

d. Double check that you have transferred the answers correctly, e.g., recheck every fifth or tenth answer from your test paper to your answer sheet.

CHAPTER THREE
THE IRS SPECIAL ENROLLMENT EXAMINATION AND OTHER PROFESSIONAL ACCOUNTING EXAMINATIONS

IRS Special Enrollment Examination (SPE)	*17*
Enrollment to Practice Before the IRS--Form 23	*18*
Overview of the Special Enrollment Examination	*18*
Qualifications for the Examination	*19*
Dates of the Examination	*19*
How to Apply for the Special Enrollment Examination--Form 2587	*19*
Examination Sites	*20*
Grading Examinations and Notifying Candidates	*21*
Types of Questions Appearing on the SPE	*21*
IRS Study Material Listing	*21*
Enrollment Examination Pass Statistics	*22*
Self-Analysis of Your Knowledge	*22*
Preparing for Exam Success	*23*
Arrival at the Exam Site	*24*
Calculators	*25*
Special Enrollment Exam Answer Sheets	*25*
Time Budgeting	*28*
Chapters in This Book Cross-Referenced to the SPE	*29*
Overview of Accounting Certification Programs	*29*
Rationale for Accounting Certification Programs	*31*
Examination Content for CIA, CMA, and CPA Exams	*31*
Individual State CPA Requirements	*35*
Exam Schedules and Future Dates	*36*
How to Apply for the Certification Examinations	*38*

The purpose of this chapter is to explain the IRS Special Enrollment Examination (which is abbreviated SPE in this book) and to introduce you to the CIA, CMA, and CPA examinations. You should be conversant with all of these designations. Attorneys and CPAs are automatically eligible to practice before the IRS. If you are not a CPA or an attorney, you may wish to sit for the IRS Special Enrollment Examination.

IRS SPECIAL ENROLLMENT EXAMINATION (SPE)

The IRS has developed a 2-day examination to assure the technical competence and ethical appreciation of persons (other than attorneys and certified public accountants) who practice before the Internal Revenue Service. Practice before the Internal Revenue Service includes all matters connected with presentations to the Service relating to a client's rights, privileges, and liabilities under laws or regulations administered by the Service. Such presentations include

1. The preparation and filing of documents;
2. All communications with the Service; and
3. The representation of a client at conferences, hearings, and meetings.

Preparing a tax return, appearing as a witness for the taxpayer, and furnishing information at the request of the Service are not considered practice before the Service.

ENROLLMENT TO PRACTICE BEFORE THE IRS -- FORM 23

Within 1 year from the date of the letter notifying a successful candidate that (s)he passed the Special Enrollment Examination, eligible persons who wish to be enrolled to practice before the Service must complete and submit a 4-page application, Form 23, in duplicate, with a $25 application fee, in accordance with instructions on the form. Form 23 is sent to candidates who successfully complete the exam. Each application is investigated to determine whether statements made are correct and whether facts or circumstances exist which reflect unfavorably on the candidate. This procedure takes from 2 to 4 months. All questions on the application must be completely answered. An incomplete application will take longer to process.

If the investigation raises a question about an applicant's eligibility for enrollment, that applicant will be informed, permitted to submit additional information, and given an opportunity to be heard. Each applicant whose investigation is satisfactory will be enrolled to practice before the Internal Revenue Service, and an enrollment card will be issued.

IRS enrolled agents must meet certain continuing professional education (CPE) requirements every 3 years. The current enrollment cycle ends January 31, 1993, during which each enrolled agent must earn 72 hours of CPE credit. This is prorated to 2 hours per month for new enrolled agents. A minimum of 16 hours is required each year.

OVERVIEW OF THE SPECIAL ENROLLMENT EXAMINATION

The 11-hour written examination covers federal taxation and tax accounting and the use of tax return forms for individuals, partnerships, corporations, trusts, estates, and gifts. It also covers ethical considerations and procedural requirements in Circular 230, and Conference and Practice Requirements, 26 C.F.R. 601.501 (both of these pamphlets are available from the IRS at no charge).

The exam consists of four parts, which take 2 days to complete. Parts I and II (3 hours each) are given on the morning and afternoon of the first day. Parts III (3 hours) and IV (2 hours) are given on the morning and afternoon of the second day. The questions on the examination are directed toward the tasks that enrolled agents must perform to complete and file forms and tax returns, and to represent taxpayers before the Internal Revenue Service. The examination includes true-false and multiple-choice questions and covers the following tax topics:

Part I - Individuals

Part II - Sole Proprietorships and Partnerships

Part III - Corporations (including S corporations), Fiduciaries, and Estate and Gift Taxes

Part IV - Ethics, Recordkeeping Procedures, Appeal Procedures, Exempt Organizations, Retirement Plans, Practitioner Penalty Provisions, Research Materials, and Collection Procedures

Note we do not cover two SPE topics: exempt organizations and deferred compensation. Together they usually constitute less than 5% of the examination, i.e., several questions on each. IRS Publications 557, *Tax-Exempt Status for Your Organization*, and 590, *Individual Retirement Arrangements (IRAs)*, cover this material.

The questions are assigned various weights according to their importance and degree of difficulty.

Kind of Question	No. of Points
True-False	1
Noncomputational multiple-choice	2
Computational multiple-choice *(do not appear on Part IV)*	3

A passing grade is determined for each of the four parts. You are required to take all four parts when taking the examination for the first time. If you pass one, two, or three parts, you will be given credit for the part(s) you passed, but you must pass all remaining parts on next year's exam. In other words, you must pass all four parts within a successive 2-year period or retake the examination in its entirety.

QUALIFICATIONS FOR THE EXAMINATION

Although no particular experience or educational requirements are specified, examination candidates should be able to answer income tax accounting questions on the intermediate college course level.

DATES OF THE EXAMINATION

The enrollment examination is generally given on a Thursday and Friday in September or October. The exact dates, determined in January of each year, are scheduled to avoid religious holidays. In 1992, the exam is scheduled for September 24 and 25.

HOW TO APPLY FOR THE SPECIAL ENROLLMENT EXAMINATION -- FORM 2587

The application form is revised every year to reflect the scheduled examination date. Forms are available the week of June 1 each year. Obtain the application form (Form 2587) by calling your IRS district office and requesting the Special Enrollment Exam application booklet (Publication 1470). It will include such items as

1. Form 2587 - The application form (the 1989 form is reproduced on page 20; the 1992 form will be identical except for a question asking for permission to release your name and address to companies offering SPE study assistance)
2. Form 4190A - Special Enrollment Examination Study Material Request and Mailing Label
3. Special Enrollment Examination Background Material for Applicants
4. Rules for Tax Return Preparers
5. The prior year's exam with answers
6. Information pamphlet on the exam

Applicants must complete Form 2587 in its entirety and submit it with the examination fee as explained in the instructions included in the application materials. The application must be mailed to the IRS (use the address below) by July 31 (or the specific date given in the instructions). However, to avoid problems created by a last-minute rush, the application should be mailed at the earliest possible date.

Internal Revenue Service
P.O. Box 845854
Dallas, TX 75284-5854

No extensions for filing will be granted, and incomplete applications will be returned.

The examination fee for applicants taking all four parts of the examination in 1991 was $50. For applicants taking fewer than four parts, the examination fee was $40. See the current Form 2587 for 1992 fees. The fee is nonrefundable, but a credit may be granted toward the next year's examination fee under some circumstances, e.g., illness or death in the family, as explained in the instructions for Form 2587.

Form 2587 for the 1989 enrollment examination is reproduced below for your information. The form for subsequent years should be similar. IRS publication 1470 is a complete package on the enrollment examination that becomes available each June.

SEE SEPARATE INSTRUCTIONS

Department of the Treasury Internal Revenue Service **Form 2587** (Rev. April 1988)	**Application for Special Enrollment Examination** MAIL BY DUE DATE — NO EXTENSIONS GRANTED	1. Candidate No.	OMB No. 1545-0949 Expires 1-31-89

In accordance with section 10.4(a), Treasury Department Circular No. 230, I apply for permission to take the Special Enrollment Examination. (Mail both parts of this form by the due date with your fee to the address shown in the separate instructions. Please type, or print firmly with ballpoint.

2. Signature of applicant	Date	3. Daytime telephone no. (Include area code)	4. Social Security Number

5. Parts to be taken: ☐ Part I ☐ Part II ☐ Part III ☐ Part IV ☐ All Parts

6. Name and address (Street, City, State, ZIP code) (Type or print clearly with ballpoint within marked area)

BEFORE YOU MAIL THIS FORM, PLEASE MAKE SURE YOU HAVE: SIGNED AND DATED IT; CHECKED THE BOXES SHOWING THE PARTS OF THE EXAM YOU WANT TO TAKE; AND INCLUDED YOUR EXAMINATION FEE (CHECK OR MONEY ORDER MADE PAYABLE TO INTERNAL REVENUE SERVICE).

7. Preferred examination site (City and State)

8. Location Code (See instructions)

Part 1 - National Office Copy

EXAMINATION SITES

The examination is offered in each city an Internal Revenue district headquarters office is located and in foreign countries upon application. The District Director may designate other locations within the district if requested by enough candidates. In item 7 of Form 2587, the candidate may indicate a preference for an examination site. A list of sites is provided in the application booklet.

GRADING EXAMINATIONS AND NOTIFYING CANDIDATES

After the examination is over, the completed examination papers are sent to the Office of the Director of Practice in Washington, D.C., for grading. The answer sheets are computer graded. A passing score between 60% and 70% is established on each part of the examination. Thus, the grading is curved to accommodate the difficulty of the examination. The pass rate on each part of the exam is usually about 50%. Also see the sideheading, Enrollment Examination Pass Statistics on page 22.

Occasionally, a question is faulty, e.g., contains typographical errors, two or more correct answers, no correct answer, etc. All candidates are given credit for these questions. These problems usually come to the attention of the IRS as the answer patterns for each question are analyzed. For example, a question that most candidates answered incorrectly needs a close review.

Candidates will receive formal notification of their test results in late December.

TYPES OF QUESTIONS APPEARING ON THE SPE

The table below shows the distribution of true-false and multiple-choice questions per part on previous Special Enrollment Exams.

	Part I	Part II	Part III	Part IV
1987	30 TF 60 MC 90	29 TF 61 MC 90	41 TF 49 MC 90	55 TF 20 MC 75
1988	41 TF 49 MC 90	35 TF 53 MC 88	46 TF 44 MC 90	59 TF 21 MC 80
1989	30 TF 65 MC 95	30 TF 60 MC 90	35 TF 55 MC 90	62 TF 18 MC 80
1990	30 TF 65 MC 95	30 TF 60 MC 90	32 TF 56 MC 88	54 TF 36 MC 90
1991	25 TF 65 MC 90	25 TF 65 MC 90	30 TF 60 MC 90	59 TF 31 MC 90

IRS STUDY MATERIAL LISTING

In the past, each year's exam usually covered the tax law in effect the previous December 31. For example, the 1991 exam covered the tax law in effect December 31, 1990. This delay allows 9 to 10 months for preparation of the examination.

The IRS publishes a list of study materials in Publication 1470, which is the pamphlet describing the examination. The listing is composed of standard IRS publications. For example, the listing for the 1991 exam is presented below.

Publication 1	*Your Rights as a Taxpayer*
Publication 17	*Your Federal Income Tax*
Publication 216	*Conference and Practice Requirements*
Publication 334	*Tax guide for Small Business*
Publication 541	*Tax Information on Partnerships*
Publication 542	*Tax Information on Corporations*
Publication 553	*Highlights of 1988 Tax Changes*
Publication 560	*Self-Employed Retirement Plans*
Publication 586A	*The Collection Process (Income Tax Accounts)*
Publication 589	*Tax Information on S Corporations*
Publication 590	*Individual Retirement Arrangements*
Publication 594	*The Collection Process (Employment Tax Accounts)*

ENROLLMENT EXAMINATION PASS STATISTICS

The following table indicates that for those who sit for all four parts, about 25% pass all four parts. About 45% complete one, two, or three parts, and about 30% fail all four parts. For candidates attempting to pass remaining parts, about 55% are successful. Remember, if you do not pass all four parts on your first sitting, you must pass the remaining parts the next year or you lose credit for the parts previously passed.

Year	Total Applicants	No Shows	Candidates Taking Examination	Passed (%)	Partial (%)	Failed (%)	Passed (%)	Failed (%)	Total Who Passed Exam (%)
1986	8,079	1,859	6,220	1,019 (23)	1,926 (43)	1,522 (34)	897 (51)	856 (49)	1,916 (31)
1987	7,781	1,965	5,816	1,047 (24)	2,143 (48)	1,228 (28)	802 (57)	596 (43)	1,849 (32)
1988	7,989	2,150	5,839	1,113 (26)	1,797 (43)	1,310 (31)	927 (57)	692 (43)	2,040 (35)
1989	7,975	2,191	5,784	1,132 (25)	2,258 (51)	1,048 (24)	749 (56)	597 (44)	1,881 (33)
1990	7,720	2,018	5,702	977 (23)	1,691 (41)	1,488 (36)	727 (47)	819 (53)	1,704 (30)

(Candidates Who Took All Parts; Retook Part of Exam)

SELF-ANALYSIS OF YOUR KNOWLEDGE

Once you have made the commitment to take the examination, apply to sit for the exam and make sure your application form is sent in well before the July 31 deadline (for 1991). Verify the deadline for subsequent years.

Next, you should assess your ability by answering all of the questions appearing on the previous year's exam. You will receive last year's exam, complete with answers (but not explanations of the answers) in your application packet. Taking this test is an 11-hour task that is broken up into four sessions (three sessions of 3 hours each plus 2 hours for Part IV).

After completing each of the four parts of the exam, grade yourself to determine how you have done. If you have 60% to 70% correct, you are doing fine. Recall that the passing grade is generally in that range (60% to 70%).

If you have a substantially higher score on this practice test, you are doing even better. As you review further, e.g., answering questions in this study manual, you will probably find yourself well prepared. Accordingly, you will be able to tailor your review program.

On the other hand, if you answer less than 60% of the sample test questions correctly, you should determine whether you need to study additional textual material prior to attempting the questions in this book. The further your score falls below 60%, the more we recommend a subject-matter study program prior to using the questions in this book as a review.

Also, as you review your sample test, you should analyze each question you answered incorrectly to ascertain why you missed the question. Reasons include

1. Lack of knowledge
2. Misunderstanding the requirements
3. Misreading the fact situation
4. Misreading the alternative answers
5. Failure to apply an efficient question answering technique to individual questions
6. Failure to apply an examination strategy, e.g., time budgeting
7. Computational errors, including sloppiness

The results of this self-analysis have important ramifications for your study program; e.g., your problem may be in taking tests rather than in your knowledge of federal taxation topics.

PREPARING FOR EXAM SUCCESS

A. **The Preparation Process**--In order to be successful on examinations, you need to undertake the following steps:

1. **Understand the exam, including coverage, content, format, administration, and grading.** Virtually all certification programs, admission tests, and other established exams have information books such as Publication 1470 developed by those responsible for the examination. Review manuals and test prep books such as *Federal Tax Objective Questions and Explanations* usually exist to help you become conversant with the exam. The better you understand the examination process from beginning to end, the better you will perform.

2. **Learn and understand the subject matter tested.** Obtain content specification outlines for established exams. Outline recommended reference books. Confirm coverage by looking at past examinations (if available) and/or review manuals.

3. **Practice answering recent exam questions to perfect your exam answering techniques.** Improve your objective question answering technique by studying the explicit detailed steps you undertake when answering objective questions (see Chapter 2). In addition to practicing your exam answering techniques, answering recent exam questions helps you understand the standards to which you will be held.

4. **Plan and practice exam execution.** Anticipate the exam environment and prepare yourself with a plan including: When will you arrive? How dressed? With which exam supplies? How many questions and what format? Order of answering questions? Time to spend on each question?

    a. Expect the unexpected and adjust! Remember that your sole objective when taking an examination is to maximize your score. Most examinations are curved and you must out-perform your peers.

5. Most importantly, develop and assure success with a controlled preparation program followed by confident execution during the examination.

B. **Control**--You have to be in control to be successful during the exam preparation and execution. Perhaps more importantly, control can also contribute greatly to your personal and other professional goals.

What is Control? Control is a process whereby you

1. Develop expectations, standards, budgets, plans.
2. Undertake activity, production, study, learning.
3. Measure the activity, production, output, knowledge.
4. Compare actual activity with expected, budgeted.
5. Modify the activity, behavior, or production to better achieve the expected or desired outcome.
6. Revise expectations, standards in light of actual experience.
7. Continue the process.

The objective is to improve performance as well as be confident that the best possible performance is being generated. Most accountants study this process in relation to standard costs, i.e., establish cost standards and compute cost variances.

Every day you rely on control systems implicitly. For example, when you comb, brush, and/or fix your hair, you utilize a control system. You have expectations as to what you want your hair to look like and how long it will take. Implicitly you monitor your progress and make adjustments as appropriate, e.g., brush it a different way, speed up, etc.

The point is that either you have and enforce standards or you do not, or you are somewhere in between. In all of your endeavors, you do or do not exercise control, implicitly or explicitly. Unless you are a natural artist at something, most endeavors will improve with explicit control. This is particularly true with certification examinations, and also applies to other tests.

1. Practice your question answering techniques (and develop control) as you answer practice questions during your study program.
2. Develop an explicit control system over your study programs.
3. Think about using more explicit control systems over any and all of your endeavors.

ARRIVAL AT THE EXAM SITE

Your application form (Form 2587, reproduced on page 20) has two parts, i.e., it is in duplicate. You will receive a letter (examination credential) from the District Coordinator to gain admittance to the exam room. The exam proctor will have Part 2 to compare to your letter of admittance. Plan to get to the exam site at least 1 hour prior to the exam if you have not been there before to avoid parking problems or other delays.

If the candidate gives prompt notice of accident, illness, or other emergency (reasonable cause) that prevents his/her taking the examination, credit toward the application fee for next year's examination will be approved by endorsement of the district SPE coordinator on the back of the candidate's examination credential. In such cases, the district SPE coordinator will return the credential to the applicant with the endorsement and advise him/her to submit the endorsed examination credential in lieu of an application fee with next year's application form.

A candidate arriving late for any part of the examination may, at the discretion of the SPE coordinator, be allowed to take that part provided the candidate has a reasonable excuse such as car failure, unusual traffic problems, family emergency, etc. Additionally, the candidate must sign and date a statement that (s)he did not discuss the examination with anyone prior to arrival and that (s)he must complete that part within the original allotted time frame. For instance, if the time frame was 9:00 to 12:00, the candidate cannot go beyond 12:00.

A candidate who fails to sit (without a reasonable excuse) for any required part(s), may not receive credit for any additional required part(s) passed, and should be so advised. The Director of Practice will determine if credit will be allowed. To receive credit for any part(s) passed, the candidate must have a reasonable excuse and send a letter containing a full statement of facts and circumstances to

> Internal Revenue Service
> Office of the Director of Practice
> HR:DP
> 1111 Constitution Avenue, N.W.
> Washington, D.C. 20224

The exam booklet cover provides complete instructions on examination procedure. The instructions that appear on Parts I, II, and III of the 1989 SPE are reproduced on the next page. They are similar to the instructions on previous examinations and are expected to remain much the same during the next few years. It is **imperative** that you read the instructions carefully before beginning each part of the exam.

Since the examination is designed to provide complete instructions to the candidate, the proctor should not have to provide any information pertaining to questions. There is a possibility, however, that flaws will appear due to printing errors that were not discovered during review and editing. The proctor will make any interpretations necessary to remedy the situation.

CALCULATORS

Electronic calculators have not been permitted on past Special Enrollment Examinations, but this policy may be changed. Contact your regional IRS office for more information. Assuming that calculators are not permitted on the exam, you should study without a calculator, especially when answering and studying the questions in this book.

SPECIAL ENROLLMENT EXAM ANSWER SHEETS

A separate machine-gradable answer sheet will be provided for each part of the examination. A sample answer sheet from the 1990 exam appears on page 27. Your exam proctor will tell you the IRS region and district numbers that you must fill in on the answer sheet. Your candidate number will be on your copy of Form 2587. Fill in all of these required numbers carefully.

Transfer all of your answers from your exam booklet to the answer sheet at one time as explained under the next sideheading. Use the number 2 pencil provided by the test proctor. Mark each answer carefully so you completely blacken the corresponding circle, but do not mark outside the circle. If you wish to change an answer, erase carefully and thoroughly (without erasing other pencil marks).

Special Enrollment Examination

Part I

Individuals

Instructions:

The time allotted for this part of the examination is 3 hours. No additional time will be granted.

On your answer sheet in the spaces provided you should enter the following:

1. Sign your name (First, M.I., Last).
2. IRS Regional office number.
3. IRS District office number.
4. Date of this examination.
5. Print your name (Last, F.I., M.I.) in the boxes provided. Immediately below the boxes darken the circle corresponding to each letter you have printed, as in the Sample Name Grid. Darken only one circle in each column below a box in which you have printed a letter. Make no marks in the columns below boxes you have left blank.
6. Enter your candidate number and immediately below, darken the circle corresponding to each number you have entered.

Important:

The answer sheet should not be folded, spindled, stapled, punctured or paper clipped since it will be machine graded.

Read the examination questions carefully. All references are to the Internal Revenue Code as amended through December 31, 1988. Unless otherwise stated all questions relate to the calendar year 1988.

You will be given a No. 2 pencil by the monitor. Darken completely only one circle under the corresponding letter on the answer sheet. In making corrections, erase errors completely. You will be allowed to keep your examination question books after completion of the examination. Scratch paper will be provided, but you may make necessary computations in the question books. Raise your hand to attract the monitor's attention when you need extra supplies or for permission to leave the room.

When you finish the examination, your answer sheet must be turned in to the monitor before leaving the room. The examination will be graded in Washington, D.C., by the Office of Director of Practice, Internal Revenue Service. You will receive formal notification of your examination results on or about December 31, 1989.

General Grading Information:

The questions in this examination have been assigned values of 1 to 3 points. All true or false questions have a value of 1 point each; the multiple choice questions in Section B have a value of 2 points each; and the multiple choice questions in Section C have value of 3 points each.

The examination is graded on the basis of correct answers. If more than one circle is darkened in answering a question, the answer will be considered incorrect.

The Service will include the answers with your formal notification of examination results. Several commercial tax services also publish the examination with their suggested answers. Therefore, you may want to mark your answers in your examination question book and retain it for purposes of your own future comparison.

Chapter 3: The IRS Special Enrollment Examination and Other Professional Accounting Examinations

TIME BUDGETING

You have 180 minutes (3 hours) for each part of the exam (except 120 minutes on Part IV). Each part will have about 90 multiple-choice and true-false questions, i.e., about 2 minutes per question. Part IV consisted of 54 true-false and 36 multiple-choice questions in 1990; expect about the same number of questions in 1991 and 1992.

1. Answer the questions in order, i.e., be systematic.
2. Apply your question answering technique to each question, as explained in Chapter 2 of this study guide.
3. Mark your answer on your exam book. You are permitted to write on your exam book (and take it with you when you leave).
    a. Do not waste time going back and forth to your answer sheet between each question.
4. If you are unsure about the answer to a question, put a big "?" next to the question in the margin of the exam book to remind yourself to review it later.
5. If you temporarily skip a question, put a big "X" next to the question in the margin of the exam book to remind yourself to answer it later.
6. Approximately every 30 minutes, write down your time beside the question you are working on.
    a. Are you working multiple-choice questions at the rate of one every 2 minutes and true-false questions at the rate of one every 1 to 1½ minutes?
        1) Remember to pace yourself throughout the exam, not just during the last 30 or 60 minutes.
    b. Practice this pacing and time management as you answer questions in this study manual in preparation for the examination.
7. After your first "pass" through the exam, transfer all of your answers to your answer sheet.
    a. Mark the correct answer carefully by darkening the entire circle. Make no marks outside the desired circle.
    b. Be careful not to get the answers out of order or they will probably all be incorrect; e.g., every 5 or 10 answers, check to make sure the answer numbers on your answer sheet agree with your question numbers to assure that you do not skip or miss an answer.
    c. WATCH YOUR TIME. Transfer all of your answers before you go back to rework the "?" and "X" questions. You do not want the exam stopped and your answer sheet picked up before your answers are transferred from your exam booklet to your answer sheet.
8. Go back and rework "?" and "X" items.
    a. Budget your remaining time among these items.
    b. Carefully check (and change, if appropriate) each answer on the answer sheet (or you may forget or run out of time to go back).
9. Review your other questions as time permits.

CHAPTERS IN THIS BOOK CROSS-REFERENCED TO THE SPE

For each of the four parts of the Special Enrollment Exam, the applicable chapters in this book are cross-referenced on the table on pages 39 and 40. Additionally, space has been provided for you to write in the dates on which

1. You complete the questions in each chapter.
2. You reassess your proficiency on topics in each chapter.
3. You complete your final review of topics in each chapter.

The intent is to help you organize your study program. Paper clip these pages for easy access.

Note that only certain modules of some chapters apply to particular parts of the exam. These are indicated by the listing of modules to be studied under the chapter title. For example, only the Bad Debt Expense and Business Use of Home modules in Chapter 6 are tested on Part I of the Special Enrollment Examination. The X's indicate that you are not to study the entire chapter (only the modules listed). The asterisk (*) used in the table denotes light coverage on the SPE.

In some chapters, you may notice an occasional question or two from another part of the exam, but these are not significant enough to worry about.

Note that this book contains CPA, CMA, Professor, and Publisher (author-developed) questions in addition to SPE questions. Virtually all questions in this book relate to material tested on the IRS Special Enrollment Exam. Thus, all questions should be studied diligently. Sometimes, a question on a particular topic from one of these other sources may be included in this book rather than a current IRS question because the former may be better from an educational point of view.

OVERVIEW OF ACCOUNTING CERTIFICATION PROGRAMS

The CPA (Certified Public Accountant) exam is the grandfather of all of the professional accounting examinations. It had its origin in the 1896 public accounting legislation of New York. In 1916 the American Institute of CPAs (AICPA) began to prepare and grade a uniform CPA exam. It is currently used to measure the technical competence of those applying to be licensed as CPAs in all 50 states, Guam, Puerto Rico, the Virgin Islands, and the District of Columbia. Over 140,000 candidates sit for the two CPA exams each year.

The CIA (Certified Internal Auditor) and CMA (Certified Management Accountant) examinations are newcomers when compared to the CPA exam. The CMA exam was first administered in 1972, and the first CIA exam was in 1974. Why were these certification programs begun? Generally, the requirements of the CPA designation instituted by the boards of accountancy, especially the necessity for public accounting experience, led to development of the CIA and CMA programs.

CIA, CMA, CPA EXAMINATION SUMMARY

	CIA	CMA	CPA
Sponsoring Organization	Institute of Internal Auditors 249 Maitland Avenue P.O. Box 1119 Altamonte Springs, FL 32701 (407) 830-7600 (800) CIA-DESK	National Association of Accountants 10 Paragon Drive Montvale, NJ 07645-1959 (201) 573-6300 (800) 562-4262	American Institute of Certified Public Accountants 1211 Ave. of the Americas New York, NY 10036 (212) 575-6495
Passing Score	75%	70%	75%
Average Pass Rate by Exam Part	45%	45%	30%
Year Examination Was First Administered	1974	1972	1916
Major Exam Sections and Length	I. Theory and Practice of Internal Auditing (3½ hours) II. Theory and Practice of Internal Auditing (3½ hours) III. Management, Quantitative Methods, and Information Systems (3½ hours) IV. Accounting, Finance, and Economics (3½ hours)	1. Economics, Finance, and Management (4 hours) 2. Financial Accounting and Reporting (4 hours) 3. Management Reporting, Analysis, and Behavioral Issues (4 hours) 4. Decision Analysis and Information Systems (4 hours)	1. Auditing (3½ hours) 2. Business Law (3½ hours) 3. Accounting Theory (3½ hours) 4. Accounting Practice (9 hours)
Length of Exam	14 hours	16 hours[1]	19½ hours[2]
Candidates Sitting for Exam:			
1974	654	633	72,052*
1975	719	723	80,433*
1976	1,099	1,037	86,464*
1977	1,227	2,046*	93,148*
1978	2,091	2,355*	104,791*
1979	2,250	2,734*	113,629*
1980	2,653	3,301*	120,937*
1981	3,137	3,790*	128,793*
1982	4,989*	4,538*	138,677*
1983	4,070*	4,578*	142,564*
1984	3,610*	4,934*	137,918*
1985	3,574*	4,734*	139,454*
1986	3,534*	4,711*	139,647*
1987	3,408*	4,557*	136,997*
1988	3,531*	4,595*	139,117*
1989	3,892*	4,879*	142,114*
1990	4,363*	4,839*	143,572*

[1] Reflects change from 5-part to 4-part exam in December 1990.
[2] To change to 2-day, 15½ hours in May 1994.

* Total number of candidates sitting for two examinations; many are repeaters.

Other professional accounting-related designations include: CBA (Chartered Bank Auditor), CDP (Certificate in Data Processing), CFA (Chartered Financial Analyst), CISA (Certified Information Systems Auditor), Enrolled Agent (one enrolled to practice before the IRS).

Copyright © 1991 Gleim Publications, Inc.

Certification is important to professional accountants because it provides

1. Participation in a recognized professional group.
2. An improved professional training program arising out of the certification program.
3. Recognition among peers for attaining the professional designation.
4. An extra credential for the employment market/career ladder.
5. The personal satisfaction of attaining a recognized degree of competency.

These reasons hold particularly true in the accounting field due to the wide recognition given to the CPA designation. Accountants and accounting students are frequently asked if they are CPAs when people learn they are accountants. Thus, there is considerable pressure for accountants to become certified.

A new development is multiple certification, which is important for the same reasons as initial certification. Accounting students and recent graduates should look ahead and obtain multiple certification. The CIA, CMA, and CPA Examination Summary on page 30 provides an overview of the three accounting examinations.

RATIONALE FOR ACCOUNTING CERTIFICATION PROGRAMS

The primary purpose of the CIA, CMA, and CPA examinations is to measure the technical competence of candidates. This includes technical knowledge, ability to apply such knowledge with good judgment, and comprehension of professional responsibility. Additionally, the nature of these examinations (low pass rate, broad and rigorous coverage, etc.) has several important effects.

1. Candidates are forced to learn all of the material that should have been presented and learned in a good accounting educational program.
2. Relatedly, candidates must integrate the topics and concepts which are presented in individual courses in accounting educational programs.
3. The content of each examination provides direction to accounting educational programs; i.e., what is tested on the examinations will be taught to students.

EXAMINATION CONTENT FOR CIA, CMA, AND CPA EXAMS

The content of each of these examinations is specified by their governing boards by means of lists of topics to be tested. In all three review manuals -- *CIA Examination Review*, *CMA Examination Review*, and *CPA Examination Review*[1] -- the material tested is subdivided into subtopics or modules. A module is a more manageable study unit than the overall parts of each exam. The listings of topics on pages 32 through 34 provide an overview of the content of the three examinations.

---

[1] Published by John Wiley & Sons, Inc.

> **CIA EXAMINATION REVIEW***
>
> **Parts I and II:** **THEORY AND PRACTICE OF INTERNAL AUDITING**
> - Nature of Internal Auditing
> - Administration of the Internal Audit Department
> - Administration of the Internal Audit Assignment
> - Internal Control
> - Audit Evidence
> - EDP Auditing
> - Statistical Sampling
> - Audit Communications
> - Ethics
> - Fraud
>
> **Part III:** **MANAGEMENT, QUANTITATIVE METHODS, AND INFORMATION SYSTEMS**
> - Management Behavior
>   - Nature and Theories of Management
>   - Planning
>   - Organization Theory
>   - The Directing Process
>   - The Controlling Process
> - Quantitative Methods
> - Management Information Systems
> - Current Related Topics
>
> **Part IV:** **ACCOUNTING, FINANCE, AND ECONOMICS**
> - Management Accounting
> - Financial Accounting
> - Finance
> - Economics (Micro and Macro)
>
> *These are the modules in the Fourth Edition of *CIA Examination Review* by Irvin N. Gleim

1. The CIA exam lasts 14 hours (four 3½-hour parts).

2. The first two parts of the CIA exam focus on the theory and practice of internal auditing. The body of knowledge of internal auditing consists of

   a. The typical undergraduate auditing class (as represented by auditing texts, e.g., Arens and Loebbecke, Taylor and Glezen, etc.).

   b. Internal auditing textbooks, e.g., Sawyer and Sumners, *The Practice of Modern Internal Auditing,* and Atkisson, Brink, and Witt, *Modern Internal Auditing*.

   c. Various IIA (Institute of Internal Auditors) pronouncements, e.g., IIA Code of Ethics, Standards for the Professional Practice of Internal Auditing, and Statement of Responsibilities of Internal Auditing.

3. The remaining 50% of the exam (7 hours) covers seven topics with a minimum of 120 multiple-choice questions in addition to a variety of other objective questions.

   a. Since management cannot personally observe the functioning of all officers, employees, and specialized functions (finance, marketing, operations, etc.), each has its own special point of view. Only internal auditing is in a position to take a total company point of view.

   b. Thus, Parts III and IV of the CIA exam assure that internal auditors are conversant with topics, methodologies, and techniques ranging from individual and organizational behavior to economics, both macro and micro.

4. Parts I and II each consists of 50 multiple-choice questions that constitute 50% of the grade. Part III includes at least 50 multiple-choice questions and a variety of other objective questions. Part IV has 70 multiple-choice questions only.

Chapter 3: The IRS Special Enrollment Examination and Other Professional Accounting Examinations   33

CMA EXAMINATION REVIEW*

Part 1: ECONOMICS, FINANCE, AND MANAGEMENT
- Microeconomics
- Macroeconomics
- International Economics
- Institutional Environment of Business
- Working Capital Finance
- Capital Structure Finance
- Organization Theory
- Motivation and the Directing Process
- Planning and Budgeting
- Communication
- Ethics and the Management Accountant

Part 2: FINANCIAL ACCOUNTING AND REPORTING
- Financial Accounting: Development of Theory and Practice
- Financial Statement Presentation
- Special Financial Reporting Problems
- SEC Reporting Requirements
- Ratio and Accounts Analysis
- Internal Control
- External Auditing
- Income Taxes

Part 3: MANAGEMENT REPORTING, ANALYSIS, AND BEHAVIORAL ISSUES
- Process and Job Order Costing
- Direct (Variable) Costing
- The Controlling Process
- Budgeting and Responsibility Accounting
- Standard Costs and Variance Analysis

Part 4: DECISION ANALYSIS AND INFORMATION SYSTEMS
- Incremental Costing
- Cost-Volume-Profit Analysis
- Capital Budgeting
- Decision Making Under Uncertainty
- Inventory Models
- Quantitative Methods
- Information Systems
- Internal and Operational Auditing

*These are the modules in the Fourth Edition of *CMA Examination Review* by Irvin N. Gleim

---

1. The ICMA decided in January 1990 to convert the CMA exam from a 5-part, 2½-day, 17½-hour exam to a 4-part, 2-day, 16-hour exam beginning December 1990.

2. Each of the four parts of the CMA exam is 4 hours long.

3. The CMA exam provides expanded and more rigorous coverage of CIA Parts III and IV.

4. The CMA examination has broader coverage than the CPA examination in several areas. For example,

    a. The management information systems area of EDP is tested more extensively on the CMA exam.

    b. SEC Financial Reporting Releases and Cost Accounting Standards Board pronouncements are covered on the CMA exam but not on the CPA exam.

    c. Topics like economics, finance, and management on Part 1 of the CMA exam are covered lightly, if at all, on the CPA exam.

    d. The CMA examination tests internal auditing to a far greater degree than does the CPA exam.

    e. The CMA exam tests business ethics, but not business law.

5. About 30% of each part of the CMA exam consists of multiple-choice questions.

6. CMA questions are generally more analysis oriented than CPA questions. On the CPA exam, the typical requirement is the solution of an accounting problem, e.g., consolidated worksheet, funds statement, etc. The CMA exam generally has an additional requirement to analyze the impact of the data in the accounting presentation or to explain how the accounting data are used.

> **CPA EXAMINATION REVIEW***
>
> **ACCOUNTING THEORY**
>   General Concepts, Principles, Terminology, and
>   Other Professional Standards
>   Measurement, Valuation, Realization, and
>   Presentation of Assets
>   Valuation, Recognition, and Presentation of
>   Liabilities
>   Ownership Structure, Presentation, and Valuation of
>   Equity Accounts
>   Measurement and Presentation of Income and
>   Expense Items
>   Other Financial Topics
>   Cost Accumulation, Planning, and Control
>   Not-for-Profit and Governmental Accounting
>
> **BUSINESS LAW**
>   The CPA and the Law
>   Business Organizations
>   Contracts
>   Debtor-Creditor Relationships
>   Government Regulation of Business
>   Uniform Commercial Code
>   Property
>
> **ACCOUNTING PRACTICE**
>   Presentation of Financial Statements or Worksheets
>   Measurement, Valuation, Realization, and
>   Presentation of Assets
>   Valuation, Recognition, and Presentation of
>   Liabilities
>   Ownership Structure, Presentation, and Valuation of
>   Equity Accounts
>   Measurement and Presentation of Income and
>   Expense Items
>   Other Financial Topics
>   Cost Accumulation, Planning, and Control
>   Not-for-Profit and Governmental Accounting
>   Federal Taxation - Individuals, Estates, and Trusts
>   Federal Taxation - Corporations, Partnerships, and
>   Exempt Organizations
>
> **AUDITING**
>   Professional Responsibilities
>   Internal Control
>   Evidence and Procedures
>   Reporting
>   Other Reporting Considerations
>
> *From the AICPA Content Specification Outlines.

1. The schedule for the CPA exam is

Accounting Practice, Part I	Wednesday	1:30 - 6:00	4½ hours
Auditing	Thursday	8:30 - 12:00	3½ hours
Accounting Practice, Part II	Thursday	1:30 - 6:00	4½ hours
Business Law	Friday	8:30 - 12:00	3½ hours
Accounting Theory	Friday	1:30 - 5:00	3½ hours

   Only one grade is given for the Practice section since it is treated as one part, even though it is 9 hours long. Practice and Theory cover the same general topics, except that Federal Income Taxation is tested only in Practice.

2. In addition to multiple-choice questions, the Practice section of the CPA exam consists of typical accounting problems. The other sections contain multiple-choice questions and essay questions rather than computational problems.

3. Currently, 60% of each section of the CPA exam consists of multiple-choice questions, largely due to advice from testing experts indicating that the testing quality of multiple-choice questions can be defended statistically. The AICPA is planning to increase objective question coverage to 85% beginning in May 1994 in conjunction with a reorganization of the CPA exam into a 4-part, 2-day examination.

INDIVIDUAL STATE CPA REQUIREMENTS

Even though there is a Uniform CPA Examination, there is no national CPA certificate. Candidates must comply with the requirements of a specific state to receive a CPA certificate. The following comments and the table of individual state requirements on page 37 are general and subject to revision, exceptions, interpretations, etc.

1. **Residency.** Most jurisdictions have a residency requirement of some form, e.g., legal residency, employment, or a business office in the state. About one-half of the jurisdictions require U.S. citizenship or intent to apply for U.S. citizenship.

2. **Education.** Generally, a college degree or equivalent is required, although many states allow candidates to take the exam in their last quarter or semester. Some jurisdictions administer an exam or accept experience in lieu of education. An AICPA policy adopted in October 1990 recommends to state authorities that they require CPA candidates to complete educational requirements before applying to sit for the examination.

3. **Experience Requirements.** Most state boards have experience requirements, with many exceptions, substitutes, etc., prior to issuing a permit or license to practice public accounting. A popular example, is the substitution of postgraduate study for a portion or all of the experience requirements. Many states allow some form of experience other than public accounting.

4. **Application Dates.** Candidates are precluded from sitting for the exam if they fail to apply within the stated registration period.

5. **Conditional Requirements.** Conditional status is granted to candidates who pass some, but not all, sections. Conditional candidates are only required to take the remaining sections of the exam. States generally limit the length of conditional status. If candidates do not successfully complete the remaining sections within the time limit, they must retake all four sections, i.e., start over.

6. **Exam Fee.** The fees listed on the accompanying table are for first-time candidates. The fee for reexamination candidates is usually less than for first-time candidates. Conditional candidates' fees are usually based on the sections remaining.

7. **Ethics Exam.** The majority of states require a special examination or course in professional ethics, which may be offered through either the AICPA or the individual state board.

8. **CPA Certificate.** Some jurisdictions will grant the CPA Certificate upon successful completion of the education requirements and the Uniform CPA Examination. In the majority, however, a separate permit or license to practice public accounting is issued after specific experience requirements have been met.

9. **Continuing Education Requirements.** (Not listed on the accompanying table.) There is a substantial movement toward requiring CPAs to undertake continuing professional education. The requirements are generally specified as a number of hours per year(s), e.g., 40 hours per year, or 80 hours in 2 years, with a specified minimum per year.

10. Contact your state board to confirm the data appearing on page 37 or for an interpretation of your specific situation. The information provided changes continually and may be subject to interpretation.

The following is an explanation of the requirements listed on the table presented on the opposite page.

Residency: If required, R indicates Residency, E is Employment, and O is Office. A "1" means U.S. citizenship is required.

Education beyond high school (in years) required to take exam/apply for certificate: B = bachelors; A = emphasis in accounting; + = hours in excess of bachelors.

Experience (in public accounting) required to practice: Years correspond to education levels just to left. Varying education requirements and varying experience requirements are separated by slashes. For example, California permits persons to take the CPA exam with either 2 years of college or a bachelors degree with an accounting major, and then requires 3 years or 2 years experience, respectively, before a CPA certificate is issued.

Application deadlines: New candidates, followed by repeat candidates.

Condition requirement: Number of parts to pass, or P for practice, followed by minimum grade requirement (if any) on other parts to achieve conditional status.

Exam fee: For all four parts, usually less if one has established conditional status.

Ethics test: If required, E indicates separate ethics test. Asterisk means required at time of certification, not at time of examination.

Certificate separate from license to practice: Indicated by an "X."

EXAM SCHEDULES AND FUTURE DATES

The CPA exam schedule is presented on page 34. The exam is generally given during the first week of May and November. Future CPA exam dates are

1991	1992
May 8, 9, 10	May 6, 7, 8
November 6, 7, 8	November 4, 5, 6

The CIA exam is given the Thursday and Friday following the CPA examination. Parts I and II are given Thursday morning and afternoon, respectively. Parts III and IV are on Friday morning and afternoon, respectively. Morning exams are from 8:30 to 12:00, and afternoon exams are from 1:30 to 5:00. Future CIA exam dates are

1991	1992
May 9, 10	May 14, 15
November 14, 15	November 12, 13

The CMA exam is offered in the second week of June and December. Parts 1 and 2 are given Thursday morning and afternoon, respectively. Parts 3 and 4 are given on Friday morning and afternoon, respectively. Future CMA exam dates are

1991	1992
June 13, 14	June 11, 12
December 12, 13	December 10, 11

Note that all three exams can be taken within a 6-week period, which is ideal owing to the great amount of overlap of the material tested. The formats of the three exams are very similar, which also contributes to the synergy of preparing for and taking all three exams together.

CPA REQUIREMENTS BY STATE

NOTE: The information below continually changes. Contact your State Board for complete up-to-date requirements.

STATE BOARD • Address	Telephone #	Residency	Education	Experience	Application Deadline First Time	Application Deadline Re-Exam	Condition Requirements	Exam Fee	Ethics	Separate Certif.
AK P.O. Box D • Juneau, AK • 99811	(907) 465-2580	R	2/B/BA	4/3/2	60 days	60 days	2 or P	$100	E	
AL 12 Com. Row • 529 S. Perry St. • Montgomery, AL • 36104-3503	(205) 834-7651	1	B	2	2/28; 8/31	3/31; 9/30	2 or P	$175	E*	⟩
AR 1515 W. 7th Street, Suite 320 • Little Rock, AR • 72201-3934	(501) 682-1520	R/E	BA/+	2/1	60 days	30 days	2 or P, 50	$150	--	⟩
AZ 3110 N. 19th Avenue • Suite 140 • Phoenix, AZ • 85015	(602) 255-3648	R	BA/+	2/1	2/28; 8/31	2/28; 8/31	2 or P	$175	E*	
CA 2135 Butano Drive • Suite 112 • Sacramento, CA • 95825	(916) 920-7121	--	2/BA	3/2	3/1; 9/1	3/1; 9/1	2 or P	$185	E*	
CO 1560 Broadway, Suite 1370 • Denver, CO • 80202	(303) 866-2869	--	BA/+	1/0	3/1; 9/1	3/1; 9/1	2 or P	Varies	E*	
CT 30 Trinity Street • Hartford, CT • 06106	(203) 566-7835	R/E	BA/+	3/2	60 days	60 days	2 or P, 50	$230	E	
DC P. O. Box 37200 • Washington, DC • 20013-7200	(202) 727-7468	--	BA	2	90 days	60 days	2 or P, 50	$120	--	⟩
DE P.O. Box 1401 • Dover, DE • 19903	(302) 736-4522	--	2/BA/+	4/2/1	3/1; 9/1	3/1; 9/1	2 or P, 50	$150	E*	
FL 4001 NW 43rd St. • Suite 16 • Gainesville, FL • 32606-4599	(904) 336-2165	--	BA+	0	2/1; 8/1	3/1; 9/1	2 or P, 50	$175	E	
GA 166 Pryor Street, S.W. • Atlanta, GA • 30303	(404) 656-3941	--	BA	2	2/1; 8/1	3/1; 9/1	2, 40	$150	--	
GU P.O. Box P • Agana, GU • 96910	(671) 646-6987	R1/E/O	BA/+	2/1	60 days	60 days	2 or P, 50	$ 35	--	
HI P.O. Box 3469 • Honolulu, HI • 96801-3469	(808) 548-7471	--	BA+	2	3/1; 9/1	3/1; 9/1	2 or P, 50	$225	E	
IA 1918 S.E. Hulsizer Avenue • Ankeny, IA • 50021	(515) 281-4126	R/E/O	0/BA/+	3/2/1	2/28; 8/31	2/28; 8/31	2 or P, 50	$150	--	X
ID 500 S. Tenth Street • Suite 104 • Boise, ID • 83720	(208) 334-2490	R	BA	1	3/1; 9/1	3/1; 9/1	2 or P, 50	$100	E	
IL 10 Admin. Bldg • 506 S. Wright St. • Urbana, IL • 61801-3260	(217) 785-0800	--	4A	1	3/1; 9/1	3/1; 9/1	2 or P, 50	$180	--	X
IN 1021 State Office Building • Indianapolis, IN • 46204-2246	(317) 232-3898	R	BA/+	3/2	3/1; 9/1	3/1; 9/1	2, 50	$135	E	
KS 900 S.W. Jackson Street • Topeka, KS • 66612-1220	(913) 296-2162	R/E/O	B/BA/+	4/2/½	3/15; 9/15	3/15; 9/15	2, 50	$125	E*	X
KY 332 W. Broadway • Suite 310 • Louisville, KY • 40202-2115	(502) 588-3037	R/E/O	BA/+	2/1	3/1; 9/1	3/1; 9/1	2 or P, 50	$125	E*	
LA 1515 WTC • 2 Canal Street • New Orleans, LA • 70130	(504) 566-1244	R	BA/+	2/1	3/1; 9/1	3/1; 9/1	2 or P, 50	$125	--	⟩
MA 100 Cambridge St. • Room 1514 • Boston, MA • 02202	(617) 727-1753	--	B/+	3/2	3/15; 9/15	3/15; 9/15	2 or P, 50	$200	--	
MD 501 St. Paul Place • Room 902 • Baltimore, MD • 21202-2272	(301) 333-6322	--	BA	0	60 days	60 days	2 or P, 50	$ 80	E	
ME State House Station 35 • Augusta, ME • 04333	(207) 582-8723	R/E	B/+	2/1	4/1; 10/1	4/1; 10/1	2 or P	$120	--	X
MI P.O. Box 30018 • Lansing, MI • 48909-7518	(517) 373-0682	R/E/O	BA/+	2/1	60 days	60 days	2 or P, 50	$120	--	
MN 133 E. 7th St., 3rd Floor • St. Paul, MN • 55101	(612) 296-7937	R/E/O	0/2/B/BA/+	6/5/3/2/1	60 days	60 days	2, 50	$115	E	X
MO P.O. Box 613 • Jefferson City, MO • 65102-0613	(314) 751-0012	R/E/O	BA	2	3/1; 9/1	3/1; 9/1	2 or P, 50	$150	E*	X
MS 961 Highway 80 E., Suite A • Clinton, MS • 39056-5246	(601) 924-8457	R	B/BA	2/1	3/15; 9/15	3/15; 9/15	2 or P, 45	$107	--	X
MT 1424 9th Avenue • Helena, MT • 59620-0407	(406) 444-3739	--	B/BA	2/1	3/15; 9/15	3/15; 9/15	2 or P, 50	$100	E*	X
NC P.O. Box 12827 • Raleigh, NC • 27605-2827	(919) 733-4222	R1	2/BA/+	4/2/1	2/28; 8/31	2/28; 8/31	2 or P	$150	--	
ND Box 8104 • University Station • Grand Forks, ND • 58202	(701) 777-3869	R	0/BA	4/0	3/15; 9/15	3/15; 9/15	2 or P	$125	E	
NE P.O. Box 94725 • Lincoln, NE • 68509-4725	(402) 471-3595	R/E/O	B	2	3/31; 9/30	3/31; 9/30	2 or P, 50	$120	E*	X
NH 57 Regional Drive • Concord, NH • 03301-8506	(603) 271-3286	R/E/O	4/+	2/1	3/15; 9/15	3/15; 9/15	2 or P, 50	$200	--	
NJ 1100 Raymond Blvd • Room 507-A • Newark, NJ • 07102-5205	(201) 648-3240	--	BA	2	3/1; 9/1	3/1; 9/1	2 or P, 50	$100	--	
NM 4125 Carlisle Boulevard, N.E. • Albuquerque, NM • 87107	(505) 841-9108	R/O	B/BA	3/1	3/1; 9/1	3/1; 9/1	2	$125	E	X
NV One E. Liberty Street • Suite 311 • Reno, NV • 89501-2110	(702) 786-0231	--	BA	2	3/1; 9/1	3/1; 9/1	2 or P, 35	$100	E*	
NY Cultural Ed. Center • Room 9A47 • Albany, NY • 12230-0001	(518) 474-3836	--	0/BA/+	15/2/1	90 days	60 days	2 or P	$220	--	
OH 77 S. High St., 18th Fl. • Ste 222 • Columbus, OH • 43266-0301	(614) 466-4135	--	BA/+	2/1	3/1; 9/1	4/1; 10/1	1, 40	$155	E	
OK 4545 Lincoln Blvd., Ste 165 • Ok. City, OK • 73105-3413	(405) 521-2397	R	0/BA	3/0	60 days	60 days	2 or P	$100	--	
OR Comm. Bldg 1st Fl • 158 12th St. N.E. • Salem, OR • 97310-0001	(503) 378-4181	--	0/BA/+	2/2/1	3/1; 9/1	3/1; 9/1	2 or P, 50	$150	E*	
PA P.O. Box 2649 • Harrisburg, PA • 17105-2649	(717) 783-1404	--	BA/+	2/1	2/15; 8/15	3/1; 9/1	1, 20	$103.75	--	
PR Box 3271 • San Juan, PR • 00904-3271	(809) 722-2122	R1/E/O	0/B/BA	6/4/0	60 days	60 days	2	$ 50	--	
RI 233 Richmond St., Ste 236 • Providence, RI • 02903-4236	(401) 277-3185	R/E	BA/+	2/1	3/15; 9/15	3/15; 9/15	2 or P	$170	E	
SC 800 Dutch Square Blvd • Ste 260 • Columbia, SC • 29210	(803) 737-9266	R	BA	2	3/15; 9/15	3/15; 9/15	2 or P, 40	$140	E*	
SD 301 E. 14th St., Ste. 200 • Sioux Falls, SD • 57104	(605) 339-6746	--	2A/BA/+	2/2/1	60 days	60 days	2 or P, 50	$175	E	⟩
TN 500 J. Robertson Pkwy, 2nd Fl • Nashville, TN • 37243-1141	(615) 741-2550	R/E	BA/+	2/1	3/1; 9/1	3/1; 9/1	2 or P, 50	$150	E	⟩
TX 1033 LaPosada • Suite 340 • Austin, TX • 78752-3892	(512) 451-0241	1	B/BA/+	4/2/2	2/28; 8/31	2/28; 8/31	2 or P	$100	E*	
UT 160 E 300 S • Box 45802 • Salt Lake City, UT • 84145-0802	(801) 530-6628	--	BA/BA+	3/1	60 days	60 days	2 or P, 50	$165	E	⟩
VA 3600 West Broad Street • Richmond, VA • 23230-4915	(804) 367-8505	--	4A/BA/+	2/2/1	60 days	60 days	2 or P, 50	$100	E	⟩
VI 1-B King St. • Christiansted, St. Croix • VI • 00820-4933	(809) 773-0096	R/E/O	0/B/BA	6/3/2	3/15; 9/15	3/15; 9/15	2	$100	--	
VT 26 Terrace Street • Montpelier, VT • 05602-2198	(802) 828-2363	E/O	0/1A	2/2	4/1; 10/1	4/1; 10/1	2 or P, 50	$150	E	
WA P.O. Box 9131 • Olympia, WA • 98504-2321	(206) 753-2585	--	0/BA	1/1	3/1; 9/1	3/1; 9/1	2 or P, 50	$125	E*	⟩
WI P.O. Box 8935 • Madison, WI • 53708-8935	(608) 266-3020	--	BA	3	3/1; 9/1	3/1; 9/1	2, 50	$102.50	E	
WV 201 L&S Bldg • 812 Quarrier St. • Charleston, WV • 25301-2617	(304) 348-3557	R/O	BA	2	2/15; 8/15	2/15; 8/15	1	$125	E	
WY Barrett Building • Third Floor • Cheyenne, WY • 82002-0001	(307) 777-7551	R/E/O	BA	2	3/15; 9/15	3/15; 9/15	2 or P	$175	E	⟩

HOW TO APPLY FOR THE CERTIFICATION EXAMINATIONS

Sit for all three examinations as soon as you can. Both the CIA and CMA exams can be taken by students in their senior year and offer a 50% reduction in fees to full-time students. In many states, you may also take the CPA exam in your last quarter or semester. If you are graduating in June, you may take the CPA exam the first week of May, the CIA exam the second week of May, and the CMA exam the second week of June. Your preparation program for all three exams is quite synergistic and not appreciably more work than preparing for just the CPA exam.

The CPA designation is controlled by the individual boards of accountancy in the 50 states, Guam, Puerto Rico, the Virgin Islands, and the District of Columbia. Fortunately, all boards of accountancy use the Uniform Certified Public Accountant Examination, which is prepared and graded by the examinations division of the American Institute of Certified Public Accountants (AICPA). For information on taking the examination, write to the board of accountancy for your state; the addresses are provided in the table on page 37.

> The American Institute of CPAs
> 1211 Avenue of the Americas
> New York, NY 10036
> (212) 575-6945

The CIA certification program is sponsored by the Institute of Internal Auditors, which was organized to develop the professional status of internal auditing.

> The Institute of Internal Auditors
> 249 Maitland Avenue
> P.O. Box 1119
> Altamonte Springs, FL 32701-4201
> (407) 830-7600

The National Association of Accountants (NAA) was conceived as an educational organization to develop the individual management accountant professionally and to provide business management with the most advanced techniques and procedures. The Institute of Certified Management Accountants (ICMA) was formed in 1972 by the NAA to offer and administer the CMA examination.

> Institute of Certified Management Accountants
> 10 Paragon Drive
> Montvale, NJ 07645-1759
> (201) 573-6300

Chapter 3: The IRS Special Enrollment Examination and Other Professional Accounting Examinations   39

The following table is discussed on page 29.

	Date Questions Completed	Self-Assessment	Date of Final Review
PART I: INDIVIDUALS			
Chapter 4 - Gross Income			
Chapter 5 - Exclusions from Gross Income			
Chapter 6 - Business Expenses • *Bad Debt Expense* • *Business Use of Home*	XXX	XXX	XXX
Chapter 7 - Limitations on Losses			
Chapter 8 - Other Deductions for AGI			
Chapter 9 - Deductions from AGI			
Chapter 10 - Individual Tax Computations			
Chapter 11 - Credits • *Refundable Credits* • *Nonrefundable Personal Credits* • *Foreign Tax Credit** • *Investment Credit**	XXX	XXX	XXX
Chapter 12 - Basis			
Chapter 13 - Depreciation, Amortization, and Depletion			
Chapter 14 - Capital Gains and Losses			
Chapter 16 - Nontaxable Property Transactions			
Chapter 21 - Accounting Methods			
Chapter 23 - Employment Taxes and Withholding*			
PART II: SOLE PROPRIETORSHIPS AND PARTNERSHIPS			
Chapter 4 - Gross Income			
Chapter 6 - Business Expenses			
Chapter 7 - Limitations on Losses			
Chapter 10 - Individual Tax Computations • *Minimum Tax*	XXX	XXX	XXX
Chapter 11 - Credits • *All General Business Credits*	XXX	XXX	XXX
Chapter 12 - Basis			
Chapter 13 - Depreciation, Amortization, and Depletion			
Chapter 14 - Capital Gains and Losses			
Chapter 15 - Sale of Business Property			
Chapter 16 - Nontaxable Property Transactions			
Chapter 17 - Partnerships			
Chapter 21 - Accounting Methods			
Chapter 22 - Employment Taxes			

X = study only the module(s) listed.
* = light coverage on the SPE.

(continued on next page)

	Date Questions Completed	Self-Assessment	Date of Final Review
PART III: CORPORATIONS (including S Corporations), FIDUCIARIES, AND ESTATE AND GIFT TAX			
Chapter 4 - Gross Income • Income on Final Returns	xxx	xxx	xxx
Chapter 11 - Credits • Investment Credit*	xxx	xxx	xxx
Chapter 14 - Capital Gains and Losses • Section 1244 Stock	xxx	xxx	xxx
Chapter 18 - Corporate Formations and Operations			
Chapter 19 - Advanced Corporate Topics			
Chapter 20 - Income Taxation of Estates and Trusts			
Chapter 21 - Accounting Methods			
Chapter 22 - Withholding			
Chapter 23 - Wealth Transfer Taxes			
PART IV: ETHICS, RECORDKEEPING PROCEDURES, APPEAL PROCEDURES, EXEMPT ORGANIZATIONS, RETIREMENT PLANS, PRACTITIONER PENALTY PROVISIONS, AND RESEARCH MATERIALS			
Chapter 10 - Individual Tax Computations • Estimated Tax Payments • Claims for Refunds	xxx	xxx	xxx
Chapter 21 - Accounting Methods • Recordkeeping Requirements	xxx	xxx	xxx
Chapter 24 - Preparer Rules & Practice Before IRS			
Chapter 25 - Federal Tax Process and Procedure			

CHAPTER FOUR
GROSS INCOME

4.1	Identification of Items Included	(24 questions)	41
4.2	Income from Employment	(10 questions)	48
4.3	Income from Self-Employment	(11 questions)	51
4.4	Interest Income	(11 questions)	53
4.5	Income from Stocks and Bonds	(18 questions)	56
4.6	Rental Income	(7 questions)	61
4.7	Income from Annuities	(7 questions)	63
4.8	Income from a Divorce	(8 questions)	65
4.9	Assignment of Income	(8 questions)	68
4.10	Income on Final Returns	(6 questions)	71

4.1 Identification of Items Included

1. Which of the following payments received by a member of a U.S. military service is not taxable?

a. Reenlistment bonus.
b. Family separation allowances because of overseas assignments.
c. Armed services academy pay.
d. Reserve training pay.

The correct answer is (b). *(SPE 987 I-48)*
REQUIRED: The item of income that is not taxable.
DISCUSSION: Gross income means all income from whatever source derived unless specifically excluded by a provision in the Internal Revenue Code (Sec. 61). Some forms of compensation to armed forces personnel are excluded. Most are "fringe benefit" type items. In addition to subsistence, uniform, and quarters allowances, family separation allowances as a result of overseas duty are specifically excluded.
Answers (a), (c), and (d) are incorrect because military pay is included in gross income. Bonuses to enlist or reenlist are included, as well as pay received while in an academy, in training, or at school.

2. Which of the following does not have to be included in gross income?

a. Unemployment compensation.
b. Damages from personal injury suit involving back injuries.
c. Prize from church raffle.
d. Free tour from travel agency for organizing a group of tourists.

The correct answer is (b). *(Publisher)*
REQUIRED: The item which does not have to be included in gross income.
DISCUSSION: Gross income means all income from whatever source derived unless specifically excluded (Sec. 61). This is an intentionally broad and all-encompassing definition. However, Sec. 104(a)(2) excludes damages awarded for personal injuries involving physical injury or physical sickness.
Answer (a) is incorrect because unemployment compensation is included in gross income under Sec. 85. Answer (c) is incorrect because a prize received in a raffle (whether from a church or any other organization) is included in gross income under Sec. 74. Answer (d) is incorrect because the fair market value of a free tour is the receipt of an economic benefit which is included in gross income as compensation since no provision excludes it.

Module 4.1: Identification of Items Included

3. Which of the following is not subject to federal income tax?

   a. Interest on U.S. Treasury bills, notes, and bonds issued by an agency of the United States.

   b. Interest on federal income tax refund.

   c. Interest on New York State bonds.

   d. Discount income in installment payments received on notes bought at a discount.

The correct answer is (c). *(SPE 1081 I-49)*
REQUIRED: The item of income which is not subject to federal income tax.
DISCUSSION: Gross income is defined under Sec. 61 as all income from whatever source derived which is not specifically excluded. Sec. 103 specifically excludes from gross income interest on most obligations of a state or any political subdivision thereof.
Answers (a) and (b) are incorrect because the exclusion under Sec. 103 does not apply to obligations of the federal government. Answer (d) is incorrect because discount income (the excess of the face amount of a debt over the purchase price) is a form of interest income included in gross income by Secs. 61 and 1272.

4. Which of the following should not be included in Mr. W's gross income for 1991?

   a. $200 in dental work Mr. W received in exchange for repairs made by Mr. W to his dentist's residence.

   b. $5,000 in executor fees received from the estate of Mr. W's brother.

   c. Life insurance proceeds of $10,000 received as a beneficiary as a result of the death of Mr. W's brother who owned the policy.

   d. A new car worth $7,000 given to Mr. W by his employer for his valuable services.

The correct answer is (c). *(SPE 1080 I-47)*
REQUIRED: The item which is excluded from gross income.
DISCUSSION: Although life insurance proceeds would fall within the broad definition of gross income, Sec. 101(a) specifically excludes from gross income amounts received under a life insurance contract if such amounts are paid by reason of death of the insured.
Answers (a) and (d) are incorrect because if services are paid for with property, the fair market value of the property received in payment must be included in income as compensation [Reg. 1.61-2(d)]. Answer (b) is incorrect because compensation for services, including executor fees, is included in gross income.

5. Generally, which of the following should be included in gross income?

   a. Life insurance proceeds.

   b. Child support payments.

   c. Cash rebate from a dealer when a car is purchased.

   d. Moving expense reimbursements from your employer.

The correct answer is (d). *(SPE 984 I-57)*
REQUIRED: The item that must be included in gross income.
DISCUSSION: Sec. 82 specifically provides that gross income includes amounts received as reimbursement of moving expenses that are attributable to employment. A corresponding itemized deduction (from adjusted gross income) may be allowed for part or all of the moving expenses.
Answer (a) is incorrect because life insurance proceeds are specifically excluded under Sec. 101(a). Answer (b) is incorrect because Sec. 71(c) excludes payments for the support of children. Answer (c) is incorrect because a rebate on a new automobile is merely a reduction of the purchase price of the automobile, not income.

6. John Budd is single with no dependents. During 1991, John received wages of $11,000 and state unemployment compensation benefits of $2,000. He had no other source of income. The amount of state unemployment compensation benefits that should be included in John's 1991 gross income is

   a. $2,000.

   b. $1,000.

   c. $500.

   d. $0.

The correct answer is (a). *(CPA 588 Q-1)*
REQUIRED: The amount of unemployment compensation to be included in gross income.
DISCUSSION: There is no exclusion for unemployment compensation benefits (prior to 1987, all or part could be excluded). Since there is no exclusion, all of the unemployment compensation benefits of $2,000 must be included in John's gross income [Sec. 85(a)].

Module 4.1: Identification of Items Included

7. Which of the following is not considered actual receipt or "constructive receipt" of income in 1990?

a. Taxpayer A was informed his check for services rendered was available on December 15, 1990, but he waited until January 15, 1991 to pick up the check.

b. A payment on a sale of real property was placed in escrow on December 15, 1990, but not received by Taxpayer A until January 10, 1991 when the transaction was closed.

c. Earned income of Taxpayer A was received by his agent on December 29, 1990, but not received by A until January 5, 1991.

d. Taxpayer B received a check on December 30, 1990 for services rendered, but was unable to make a deposit until January 4, 1991.

The correct answer is (b). *(SPE 1079 II-60)*
REQUIRED: The occurrence which is not considered "constructive receipt" of income.
DISCUSSION: Income, although not actually in a taxpayer's possession, is constructively received in the taxable year during which it is credited to his/her account, set apart for him/her, or otherwise made available so that (s)he may draw upon it at any time, or so that (s)he could have drawn upon it during the taxable year if notice of intention to withdraw had been given (Reg. 1.451-2). However, income is not constructively received if the taxpayer's control of its receipt is subject to substantial limitations or restrictions. Since the taxpayer's control of the receipt of the funds in the escrow account is substantially limited until the transaction has closed, the taxpayer has not constructively received the income until the closing of the transaction in 1991.
Answer (a) is incorrect because the check (and therefore the funds) for services rendered was made available to the taxpayer during 1990. Answer (c) is incorrect because the receipt of the income by the taxpayer's agent makes it available to the taxpayer and therefore is constructively received. Answer (d) is incorrect because the receipt of a check is the receipt of the income, regardless of the ability to cash or deposit it.

8. Colin Rosson is a free-lance writer who reports income on the cash basis. Some of his 1991 transactions follow:

Cash fees received for articles, etc.	$55,000
Color TV won in resort promotion (had to attend promotion to win)	300
Loss on sale of business furniture	(100)
Appreciation on investment property	1,000

What is Colin's gross income?

a. $55,000.
b. $55,900.
c. $55,300.
d. $55,200.

The correct answer is (c). *(G.W. Rosson)*
REQUIRED: The taxpayer's gross income from the listed transactions.
DISCUSSION: Under Sec. 61, gross income includes income from whatever source derived. The cash fees are compensation for services. The TV won in the promotion is a prize included in gross income under Sec. 74. These two items total $55,300.
Appreciation on property is not included in gross income until there is a sale or exchange or some other event causing the taxpayer to realize or receive the economic benefit. Losses (if deductible) are deducted from gross income; i.e., they do not affect the computation of gross income.

9. In 1991, Emil Gow won $5,000 in a state lottery and spent $400 for the purchase of lottery tickets. Emil elected the standard deduction on his 1991 income tax return. The amount of lottery winnings that should be included in Emil's 1991 taxable income is

a. $0.
b. $2,000.
c. $4,600.
d. $5,000.

The correct answer is (d). *(CPA 588 Q-2)*
REQUIRED: The amount of state lottery winnings included in gross income.
DISCUSSION: Under Sec. 61, gambling winnings (whether legal or illegal) are included in gross income. Therefore, Emil must include the full $5,000 in gross income. Gambling losses, i.e., amounts spent on nonwinning tickets, may be deductible, but only as an itemized deduction after the total gambling winnings are included in gross income.

Module 4.1: Identification of Items Included

10. Based on the following, how much should Mr. B include in income in his federal income tax return?

Punitive damages awarded by jury	$10,000
Kickbacks received on sale of goods (not treated as a reduction elsewhere)	5,000
Money borrowed from a bank	8,000
Increase in the value of an asset	1,000

a. $10,000.
b. $15,000.
c. $16,000.
d. $23,000.

The correct answer is (b). *(SPE 1082 II-52)*
REQUIRED: The amount of the items listed which must be included in gross income.
DISCUSSION: Punitive damages are included in gross income under the broad concept of Sec. 61 which includes all income from whatever source derived unless specifically excluded. Punitive damages are unlike damages for personal injury or property damage which are considered a return of capital. Sec. 104(a) excludes punitive damages from gross income only in situations involving physical injury or physical sickness. Kickbacks on the sale of goods are also included in gross income (even if illegal) since they are not specifically excluded from gross income (and often represent payment for services). Mr. B should include $15,000 in gross income ($10,000 punitive damages + $5,000 kickbacks).

Money borrowed from a bank is not included in gross income because there is a legal obligation to return it. The increase in the value of an asset is not included in income because there has been no event causing the taxpayer to realize or receive the economic benefit.

11. During 1990, Larcenous paid $500 of estimated state income tax payments which she also deducted for federal income tax purposes. Early in 1991, Larcenous received a refund of $300 of these state tax payments. Larcenous immediately placed an illegal bet at 5-to-1 odds and won an additional $1,500. Later in the year, Larcenous was short of money and robbed a tavern of $4,000. How much should Larcenous include in her income for 1991?

a. $0.
b. $1,500.
c. $1,800.
d. $5,800.

The correct answer is (d). *(Publisher)*
REQUIRED: The amount that the recipient of a state tax refund and illegally obtained money must include in gross income.
DISCUSSION: All of the amounts received, which total $5,800, must be included in gross income. The state tax refund is included in income since it was previously deducted when paid. Under Sec. 111 (known as the "tax benefit rule"), recovery of previously paid taxes is excluded from gross income only if the prior deduction did not reduce the taxpayer's federal income tax. Income from betting, whether legal or illegal, must be included in gross income. Likewise, the $4,000 of proceeds from the robbery must also be included in gross income. Larcenous took the money with an expectation of an unrestricted right to it ("claim of right" doctrine).

12. During 1991, Henry Thompson, a single taxpayer, received a $2,000 income tax refund from the IRS and a $1,500 tax refund from New York State for his 1990 tax filings. Henry did not itemize his deductions on his tax returns. How much income must Henry include in his 1991 tax return as a result of these refunds?

a. $3,500.
b. $2,000.
c. $1,500.
d. $0.

The correct answer is (d). *(M. Premont)*
REQUIRED: The amount of tax refunds that must be included in gross income.
DISCUSSION: Under Sec. 111, recovery of previously deducted taxes is excluded from gross income only if the prior deduction did not reduce the taxpayer's federal income tax. Since federal income taxes are not deductible, the refund of them is not included in income. Because the state taxes did not reduce federal income taxes (since Henry did not itemize), their refund is not included in income.

Module 4.1: Identification of Items Included

13. Roger Burrows, age 19, is a full-time student at Marshall College and a candidate for a bachelor's degree. His tuition and fees were $4,000 per year. During 1991 he received the following payments:

State scholarship for 10 months	$3,600
Loan from college financial aid office	1,500
Cash support from parents	3,000
Cash dividends on qualified investments	700
Cash prize awarded in contest	500
	$9,300

What is Burrows' gross income for 1991?

- a. $1,100.
- b. $1,200.
- c. $4,800.
- d. $9,300.

The correct answer is (b). *(CPA 581 P-60)*
REQUIRED: The taxpayer's gross income for 1991.
DISCUSSION: Gross income includes all income from whatever source derived unless specifically excluded. Sec. 117 excludes, to the extent of actual tuition and fees, amounts received as a scholarship from a government or other qualified organization. Therefore, the $3,600 state scholarship is excluded from gross income. The $1,500 loan is not considered income as long as there is a bona fide obligation to repay it. The cash support from the parents of $3,000 is a gift which is excluded from gross income under Sec. 102(a). The $700 of dividends should be included in gross income in full. The cash prize of $500 is specifically included by Sec. 74. The taxpayer's total gross income is $1,200 ($700 dividends + $500 prize).

14. Morbid was always interested in making a "fast buck." When Morbid's father was very ill and unlikely to live very much longer, Morbid purchased an existing life insurance policy on Father's life from a brother who acquired the policy several years ago and was not aware of the serious illness. Morbid paid $10,000 for the policy and received $20,000 in proceeds shortly thereafter when Father died. Under Father's will, all his property was bequeathed to Morbid's mother, except that the income earned from the property during the administration of the estate was bequeathed to Morbid. The estate had $15,000 of income which was distributed to Morbid in the same year as the insurance proceeds. How much must Morbid include in his income for the year?

- a. $0.
- b. $10,000.
- c. $15,000.
- d. $25,000.

The correct answer is (d). *(Publisher)*
REQUIRED: The amount of gross income from the life insurance proceeds and the inheritance of income.
DISCUSSION: Although life insurance proceeds payable by reason of death are generally excluded under Sec. 101(a), when a life insurance policy has been assigned for valuable consideration, the amount excluded by the assignee may not exceed the amount paid for the policy. Therefore, $10,000 from the life insurance policy ($20,000 proceeds − $10,000 purchase price) must be included in Morbid's gross income.
Property received by gift or inheritance is generally excluded from gross income under Sec. 102(a). However, the income from such property is not excluded, and Sec. 102(b) requires a gift or inheritance of income from property to be included in gross income. See Chapter 20, "Income Taxation of Estates and Trusts," for more detail. Morbid must include $25,000 in gross income ($10,000 life insurance proceeds + $15,000 inheritance of income).

15. Wheeler purchased two parcels of real property for $10,000 each in 1989 and held the property for investment. These properties appreciated in value and were reassessed for property tax purposes at $15,000 each in 1990. In 1991, Wheeler sold one parcel for $20,000 to Dealer and exchanged the other parcel for a lot on an island which was worth $22,000 on which he planned to build his vacation home. Which of the following is a correct statement of the amount and time when Wheeler recognized income from the property transactions?

- a. $10,000 in 1991 only.
- b. $22,000 in 1991 only.
- c. $10,000 in 1990 and $12,000 in 1991.
- d. $10,000 in 1990 and $5,000 in 1991.

The correct answer is (b). *(Publisher)*
REQUIRED: The amount and time of recognition of income from transactions in property.
DISCUSSION: Income is realized when there is a transaction, event, or occurrence which is sufficient to give rise to an economic benefit. It does not include mere appreciation in value. For property, there generally must be a sale or exchange for there to be realization. Therefore, Wheeler realized income in 1991 when the properties were sold and exchanged. The gain realized that must be recognized is determined under Sec. 1001 as the sum of money received, plus the fair market value of other property received, less the adjusted basis in the property given up. $10,000 was realized on the first property ($20,000 cash − $10,000 basis). $12,000 was realized on the second property ($22,000 fair market value received − $10,000 basis), for a total of $22,000.

16. Shifty borrowed $10,000 from Easy. When Easy tried to collect the debt, she discovered that Shifty had moved to another state. Easy tracked Shifty down and demanded payment. Knowing it would cost Easy a substantial amount of time and money to collect the debt, Shifty offered to pay $5,000 on the condition that Easy cancel the remainder of the debt. Easy agreed to accept the $5,000 and cancel the remaining $5,000 of the debt. Which of the following statements is correct?

   a. Shifty has $5,000 of income when Easy cancels the debt.
   b. Easy has $5,000 of income upon collection of half of the debt.
   c. Shifty had $10,000 of income upon obtaining the loan.
   d. Neither Shifty nor Easy has any income from this transaction.

The correct answer is (a). *(Publisher)*
REQUIRED: The correct statement of income recognized from a loan and settlement of the debt at a lesser amount.
DISCUSSION: Under Sec. 61(a)(12), gross income includes income from the discharge of indebtedness. When Easy canceled the remainder of the debt, Shifty was relieved of an obligation and must recognize $5,000 of income.
Answer (b) is incorrect because the receipt of payment on a debt is merely the return of capital, not income. Answer (c) is incorrect because the receipt of a loan is not income since there is an obligation to repay it. Answer (d) is incorrect because Shifty must recognize $5,000 of income from the cancellation of indebtedness.

17. Optimistic borrowed $20,000 to buy a machine for his printing business. Shortly thereafter, the economy went into a deep recession and Optimistic was not able to repay the debt although he was not insolvent. In 1991 the creditor reduced the debt by $10,000 so Optimistic could afford to pay it. As a result of this reduction of debt,

   a. The purchase price of the machine is adjusted to reduce Optimistic's basis in the machine.
   b. Optimistic has $10,000 of income.
   c. The debt is qualified business indebtedness and the basis of the machine must be reduced.
   d. Any tax effect from the reduction of the debt is deferred until final payment by Optimistic.

The correct answer is (b). *(Publisher)*
REQUIRED: The tax effect of a reduction of a debt from the purchase of business property.
DISCUSSION: The cancellation of indebtedness is included in gross income under Sec. 61(a)(12). Under Sec. 108, the discharge of indebtedness is excluded from gross income only if the debtor is insolvent, in reorganization bankruptcy, or a farmer. Since Optimistic is none of these, the $10,000 reduction of debt is included in Optimistic's income.
Answer (a) is incorrect because a reduction of purchase-money debt is treated as a purchase price adjustment only if the creditor is the seller of the property. Answer (c) is incorrect because the reduction of basis for qualified business indebtedness is not available after 1986. Answer (d) is incorrect because the discharge of indebtedness causes immediate recognition of income by a solvent taxpayer who is not a farmer.

18. Photo Gray worked as an employee in a camera store and made $15,000 each year. Photo also had a one-third interest in a calendar-year partnership. The partnership had $9,000 of taxable income for the year, none of which was distributed to the partners. Photo was also one of two beneficiaries of a trust set up by her rich uncle. The trust earned $4,000 of income and it was all distributed to Photo during the year. Photo's gross income for the year is

   a. $22,000.
   b. $15,000.
   c. $20,000.
   d. $18,000.

The correct answer is (a). *(Publisher)*
REQUIRED: An employee's gross income from salary, a partnership, and a trust.
DISCUSSION: An employee's salary is fully included in gross income under Sec. 61(a)(1). A partner's share of partnership income is included in the partner's gross income, whether distributed or not, under Sec. 702(a). The beneficiary of a trust is also required to include the total amount distributed from the trust to the extent of the trust's income. It does not matter that there was another beneficiary since all the income was distributed to Photo. Therefore, Photo must include $22,000 in gross income ($15,000 salary + $3,000 share of partnership income + $4,000 trust income). See Chapters 17 and 20 for more detail on partnership and trust income, respectively.

Module 4.1: Identification of Items Included

19. Dr. Y, a cash-basis taxpayer, received a check for $250 after banking hours on December 31, 1990 from a patient. Since Dr. Y could not deposit the check in his business checking account until January 3, 1991, the fee of $250 is not included in his income for 1990.

The correct answer is (F). *(SPE 1080 II-7)*
DISCUSSION: A check is the equivalent of cash; therefore, both a cash-basis and an accrual-basis taxpayer must report income received in the form of a check in the year in which the check is received. The ability to cash or deposit the check is not relevant unless the check is known to be worthless.

20. Medical expenses recovered after being claimed as a deduction in the previous year must be included in your income in the year of recovery to the extent that the deductions decreased the income taxes paid in the year they were deducted.

The correct answer is (T). *(SPE 1077 I-1)*
DISCUSSION: If a taxpayer obtains a deduction for an item in one year which reduces taxes and later recovers all or a portion of the prior deduction, the recovery is included in gross income in the year it is received [Sec. 111 and Reg. 1.213-1(g)]. Note that to the extent the expense did not reduce federal income taxes in the earlier year, the recovery is excluded from income.

21. In 1991, Mary recovered a bad debt she had claimed as a deduction on her 1990 return. Mary must include the amount as income in 1991 to the extent it reduced her taxes in 1990.

The correct answer is (T). *(SPE 990 II-10)*
DISCUSSION: The recovery of an amount previously deducted as a bad debt is generally included in gross income under Sec. 61. To the extent that the previous deduction for a bad debt did not reduce taxes, the recovery is excluded from gross income under Sec. 111. This means that the recovery payment must be included in income to the extent that the prior deduction decreased taxes.

22. A scholarship received by a student that represents compensation for his past, present, or future services is includable in gross income.

The correct answer is (T). *(SPE 1077 I-99)*
DISCUSSION: Although Sec. 117 excludes from gross income amounts received as qualified scholarships to be used for tuition and related expenses, this exclusion does not apply to any amount received which represents compensation for past, present, or future services [Sec. 117(c)].

23. Compensation for damages to your character or for personal injury or illness is taxable.

The correct answer is (F). *(SPE 1077 I-135)*
DISCUSSION: Compensation for damages to your character or for personal injury or illness is paid to replace the personal capital destroyed. Sec. 104(a)(2) specifically excludes such compensation from income. The exclusion does not apply to any punitive damages awarded in a case not involving physical injury or sickness.

24. You must include in income, at the time received, the fair market value of property or services you receive in bartering.

The correct answer is (T). *(SPE 984 II-5)*
DISCUSSION: Bartering involves the sale or exchange of property or services (but not for cash). Reg. 1.61-2(d)(1) provides that, if services are paid for with property, the fair market value of the property must be included in income as compensation. If services are paid for by exchanging other services, the fair market value of such other services must be included in income as compensation. If property or services are received in exchange for other property, the taxpayer must compute gain or loss as if the property had been sold.

4.2 Income from Employment

25. All of the following income items are includable in an employee's gross income except

    a. Severance pay for cancellation of employment.

    b. Vacation allowance.

    c. Payments from employer while sick or injured.

    d. Medical insurance premium paid by employer for employee and spouse.

The correct answer is (d). *(Publisher)*
REQUIRED: The item that is not includable in an employee's gross income.
DISCUSSION: Gross income includes all income from whatever source derived unless specifically excluded. Sec. 106 excludes contributions by an employer to accident or health plans for employees. Reg. 1.106-1 extends the exclusion to contributions for the employee's spouse or dependents.
Answers (a), (b), and (c) are incorrect because no provision excludes these amounts from gross income.

26. For 1991, Dan's employer paid the following:

Premium on $30,000 of nondiscriminatory group-term life insurance of which Dan's wife was the sole beneficiary	$400
Premiums on $30,000 nondiscriminatory ordinary life insurance of which Dan's wife was the sole beneficiary	800
Rental of car used by Dan for commuting to and from work	1,500

In addition, the union to which Dan belonged went on strike and Dan received $1,000 of strike benefits from the union. What amount must Dan include in gross income for 1991?

    a. $1,200.

    b. $1,500.

    c. $3,300.

    d. $3,700.

The correct answer is (c). *(SPE 990 I-58)*
REQUIRED: The amount of fringe benefits and union strike benefits includable in gross income for 1991.
DISCUSSION: Fringe benefits received from an employer must be included in the employee's gross income unless specifically excluded. Sec. 79 specifically excludes premiums paid by an employer for up to $50,000 of nondiscriminatory group-term life insurance for each employee. However, the $800 of premiums on the ordinary life insurance must be included in Dan's income. The cost of commuting to and from work is considered a personal expense, so the car rental must be included in gross income. Strike benefits are also included in gross income.

Ordinary life insurance premiums	$ 800
Car rental	1,500
Strike benefits	1,000
Gross income	$3,300

27. Corporation X made the following payments to or on behalf of Mr. B, a cash-basis taxpayer:

Note received in lieu of bonus (fair market value $3,000, no payments in current year)	$5,000
Advance commissions for services to be performed in the future	600
Ham received at Christmas party	20
Sick pay due to illness paid directly by Corporation X	1,000
Group-term life insurance premium paid by Corporation X on nondiscriminatory insurance coverage of $50,000	100

What amount should Mr. B report as income?

    a. $4,600.

    b. $4,620.

    c. $4,720.

    d. $6,720.

The correct answer is (a). *(SPE 1082 I-72)*
REQUIRED: The amount received from an employer that an employee must include in gross income.
DISCUSSION: Sec. 61(a)(1) specifically provides that compensation for services is to be included in gross income. Due to the relationship between an employee and an employer, almost everything received by the employee from the employer is included in gross income as compensation. As a cash-basis taxpayer, Mr. B must include the fair market value of the note in gross income in the current year. When the note is subsequently paid, an additional $2,000 will be included ($5,000 − $3,000). The advance commissions of $600 are also included in gross income regardless of when the services are to be performed. Sick pay is included in gross income as part of the employee's compensation for not working when sick. These three amounts total $4,600 and should be reported by Mr. B as income.

The ham worth $20 is not included in gross income under Sec. 132(a)(4) which excludes de minimis fringe benefits. Under Sec. 79, the cost of up to $50,000 of nondiscriminatory group-term life insurance paid by an employer on behalf of employees is not included in the employees' gross incomes.

28. Bill Walden received a $2,100 grant from his employer and, as required by his employer, used all of the money for tuition and fees to take three graduate-school courses during the period September 1 to December 31, 1991. Walden is not a candidate for a degree and has never received a scholarship or fellowship grant before. He had previously met the minimum educational requirements for his employment position; however, due to new requirements established by his employer, these courses were necessary for him to retain his job. In computing his 1991 taxable income, Walden should include

a. Gross income of $2,100 and an education expense deduction of $2,100.
b. Gross income of $2,100 and no education expense deduction.
c. No gross income and no education expense deduction.
d. Gross income of $0 and an education expense of $2,100.

The correct answer is (a). *(CPA 574 Q-18)*
REQUIRED: The proper treatment of an educational grant from an employer used for courses to retain a job.
DISCUSSION: The grant was received from an employer by reason of employment and therefore is included in income as compensation for services. It does not qualify for exclusion under Sec. 117 as a scholarship or fellowship. The facts do not provide enough information for an exclusion under Sec. 127 as a qualified educational assistance program (which basically requires a written plan which is not discriminatory). However, the amounts actually expended are deductible as an education expense to meet an employer's requirements to retain a job since he had already met the minimum education requirements to obtain the job (Reg. 1.162-5).

29. During the current year, Hal Leff sustained a serious injury in the course of his employment. As a result of this injury, Hal received the following payments during the year:

Workers' compensation	$2,400
Reimbursement from his employer's accident and health plan for medical expenses paid by Hal and not deducted by him	1,800
Damages for personal injuries	8,000

The amount to be included in Hal's gross income for the current year should be

a. $12,200.
b. $8,000.
c. $1,800.
d. $0.

The correct answer is (d). *(CPA 586 Q-49)*
REQUIRED: The amount of gross income from the payments received as a result of the injury.
DISCUSSION: Sec. 104 excludes from gross income compensation for personal injuries and sickness whether received as workers' compensation benefits, accident or health insurance benefits, or as damages received by suit or agreement. Therefore, none of the payments should be included by Hal in gross income.
Note that the Sec. 104 exclusion does not apply to any punitive damages received by suit or agreement in connection with a case not involving physical injury or physical sickness.

30. Roberta Warner and Sally Rogers formed the Acme Corporation on October 1, 1991. On the same date Warner paid $75,000 cash to Acme for 750 shares of its common stock. Simultaneously, Rogers received 100 shares of Acme's common stock for services rendered. How much should Rogers include as taxable income for 1991, and what will be the basis of her stock?

	Taxable Income	Basis of Stock
a.	$0	$0
b.	$0	$10,000
c.	$10,000	$0
d.	$10,000	$10,000

The correct answer is (d). *(CPA 1181 P-46)*
REQUIRED: The amount of taxable income and the basis of stock received in exchange for services rendered.
DISCUSSION: Sec. 83 provides that if property is received in exchange for the performance of services, the excess of the fair market value of such property over the amount paid for such property is included in gross income. Since Rogers did not pay anything for the stock, the fair market value of the stock ($10,000) is included in her gross income as payment (revenue) for her services. The basis of property is its "tax cost basis," the amount paid for the property ($0) increased by the amount which was included in income ($10,000) [Reg. 1.61-2(d)(2)]. Therefore, Rogers' basis in the stock is her tax cost of $10,000.

31. For 1991, the records of Reverend Lamb, an ordained minister of a qualifying religious organization, reflected the following:

Salary	$10,000
Offerings for marriages, baptisms, funerals, etc., performed by Lamb but given directly to the organization	800
Offerings for marriages, baptisms, funerals, etc., performed by Lamb and given directly to him	550
Lamb's other outside earnings donated by him to the organization	750
Rental value of home provided to Lamb as part of his pay	1,750

What is the amount of income that Lamb should include in his gross income for 1991?

a. $11,300.
b. $12,100.
c. $12,300.
d. $13,050.

The correct answer is (a). *(SPE 990 I-60)*
REQUIRED: The amount that an ordained minister must include in gross income.
DISCUSSION: Under Sec. 61, salaries and fees for personal services are always included in gross income. Lamb should include his salary, the offerings given directly to him for marriages, baptisms, funerals, etc., and the other outside earnings donated by him to the organization in his gross income for a total of $11,300. Reg. 1.107-1 excludes from gross income the rental value of a home, including utilities, furnished to a minister as a part of his/her compensation. Lamb should also exclude the offerings made directly to the organization from his gross income. Lamb must include:

Salary	$10,000
Fees for marriages	550
Other outside earnings	750
Total	$11,300

32. In 1990, Alex Burg, a cash-basis taxpayer, earned an annual salary of $80,000 at Ace Corp., but elected to take only $50,000. Ace, which was financially able to pay Burg's full salary, credited the unpaid balance of $30,000 to Burg's account on the corporate books in 1990, and actually paid this $30,000 to Burg on April 30, 1991. How much of the salary is taxable to Burg in 1990?

a. $50,000.
b. $60,000.
c. $65,000.
d. $80,000.

The correct answer is (d). *(CPA 1184 Q-37)*
REQUIRED: The amount of salary from an employer that an employee must include in gross income when received over 2 years.
DISCUSSION: Sec. 61(a)(1) specifically provides that compensation for services is to be included in gross income. Here, Burg must report the full $80,000 in 1990 because it was his and not the employer's choice to receive only a portion of it in 1990. The $30,000 that was not actually received until 1991 is considered to have been constructively received in 1990. Under the general rule of Sec. 451(a) and Reg. 1.451-1(a), a taxpayer using the cash method of accounting includes an item in gross income when it is actually or constructively received.

33. On January 1, 1990, Corporation Y, a cash-basis taxpayer, entered into a contract to pay Mr. A, a cash-basis taxpayer, for his services to be rendered in 1990. Mr. A is to receive 200 shares of Y's common stock, 100 shares on July 1, 1990 and 100 shares on February 1, 1991. The fair market value of the stock on the relevant dates is

January 1, 1990	$50 per share
July 1, 1990	$75 per share
February 1, 1991	$40 per share

Mr. A must report $8,000 as compensation from Corporation Y in 1990.

The correct answer is (F). *(SPE 1078 III-11)*
DISCUSSION: If property is received in connection with the performance of services, the fair market value of such property (at the time of inclusion in income) is included in the taxpayer's gross income under Sec. 83. Since Mr. A is a cash-basis taxpayer, the compensation is included in gross income when actually or constructively received (as long as it is not subject to a substantial risk of forfeiture under Sec. 83). Mr. A must include the FMV of the shares received in 1990 in his 1990 gross income at the July 1 value (100 shares x $75 = $7,500). In 1991, he must include the FMV of the shares received in 1991 at the February 1 value (100 shares x $40 = $4,000).

34. Highly compensated persons must include in their income excess reimbursements from a self-insured medical reimbursement plan that discriminates in favor of highly compensated persons. These excess reimbursements must be included in income in the taxpayer's tax year in which the plan year ends, regardless of when they are received.

The correct answer is (T). *(SPE 1081 I-24)*
DISCUSSION: The Sec. 105 exclusion for medical expense reimbursements from an employer does not apply to discriminatory amounts paid to a highly compensated individual under a self-insured medical reimbursement plan which discriminates in favor of highly compensated persons. These excess reimbursements are included in the taxpayer's income in his/her tax year in which the plan year ends. (See Module 5.2 for more detail.)

4.3 Income from Self-Employment

35. Mr. A works as an employee for Never Peel Painting Company. While on vacation in 1991, Mr. A painted the residence of his dentist in exchange for dental services having a fair market value of $1,500. His dentist provided all of the paint and supplies. For income tax purposes, Mr. A has

a. No income or expense.

b. $1,500 in wages and $1,500 in medical expenses.

c. $1,500 in self-employment income and $0 in medical expense.

d. $1,500 in self-employment income and $1,500 in medical expense.

The correct answer is (d). *(SPE 987 I-53)*
REQUIRED: The income and expense due to an exchange of services.
DISCUSSION: Reg. 1.61-2(d)(1) provides that, if services are paid for with other services, the fair market value of such other services must be included in income as compensation. Since Mr. A provided services and received dental services with a fair market value of $1,500, he must include that amount in his income.
At the same time, Mr. A is treated as having paid $1,500 for the dental services. Dental services are medical expenses generally deductible subject to certain limits.

36. Gross income from self-employment includes all but which of the following?

a. Damage awards for lost profits.

b. Book royalties.

c. Income from general partnerships.

d. Improvements on rental property left by a lessee.

The correct answer is (d). *(Publisher)*
REQUIRED: The item which is not gross income from self-employment.
DISCUSSION: Income from self-employment is included in gross income under Sec. 61(a)(1) and (2). Improvements on rental property left by a lessee at the termination of the lease are not included in gross income under Sec. 109. They would be included only if made in lieu of rent. Even if such amounts were included in gross income, they would not be self-employment income.
Answer (a) is included in self-employment income since the damage awards replace profits which would have been earned and included in income. Answer (b) is included in self-employment income because the recipient of book royalties is generally an independent contractor. Answer (c) is included in self-employment income because general partners are considered self-employed.

37. During 1991, Mrs. R, a cash-basis lawyer, had the following transactions:

Cash fees for legal services	$100,000
Gain on sale of personal auto	300
Her business building's appreciation in value	20,000
Fair market value of stock received for services	10,000
Interest on personal loan to her son	10,000

What is Mrs. R's gross income in respect to her business?

a. $100,000.

b. $110,000.

c. $120,300.

d. $130,000.

The correct answer is (b). *(SPE 1078 II-63)*
REQUIRED: The taxpayer's gross income from her business, i.e., self-employment income.
DISCUSSION: The gain on the sale of a personal automobile and the interest on a personal loan are not income from the taxpayer's business, although they are items of gross income. The appreciation on the taxpayer's building is not included in gross income since there has been no event causing the realization of the income, e.g., a sale or exchange. Mrs. R's only self-employment income consists of $100,000 of cash fees and the $10,000 value of stock received (Sec. 83), which total $110,000.

Module 4.3: Income from Self-Employment

38. Dr. Chester is a cash-basis taxpayer. His office visit charges are usually paid on the date of visit or within 1 month. However, services rendered outside the office are billed weekly, and are usually paid within 2 months as patients collect from insurance companies. Information relating to 1991 is as follows:

Cash received at the time of office visits	$ 35,000
Collections on accounts receivable	130,000
Accounts receivable, January 1	16,000
Accounts receivable, December 31	20,000

Dr. Chester's gross income from his medical practice for 1991 is

a. $165,000.
b. $169,000.
c. $181,000.
d. $185,000.

The correct answer is (a). *(CPA 583 P-41)*
REQUIRED: The amount of gross income from the medical practice of a cash-basis taxpayer.
DISCUSSION: Since Dr. Chester is a cash-basis taxpayer, income is recognized at the time cash is actually or constructively received, whichever is earlier. Dr. Chester's 1991 income consists of the $35,000 received at the time of office visits plus the $130,000 collected on accounts receivable, for a total of $165,000.
Since Dr. Chester is not an accrual-basis taxpayer, the amount of accounts receivable at the beginning and end of the year do not affect his gross income.

39. Carl Slater was the sole proprietor of a high-volume drug store which he owned for 25 years before he sold it to Statewide Drug Stores, Inc. in 1991. Besides the $800,000 selling price for the store's tangible assets and goodwill, Slater received a lump sum of $60,000 in 1991 for his agreement not to operate a competing enterprise within 10 miles of the store's location, for a period of 6 years. How will the $60,000 be taxed to Slater?

a. As $60,000 ordinary income in 1991.
b. As ordinary income of $10,000 a year for 6 years.
c. As part of the gain on the sale of the store.
d. It is excluded since it was not for the performance of services.

The correct answer is (a). *(CPA 1181 Q-44)*
REQUIRED: The tax treatment of an amount received for a covenant not to compete.
DISCUSSION: The taxpayer received the $60,000 as compensation for agreeing not to enter into an income producing activity. Since this payment replaces what would otherwise be ordinary income, the $60,000 is treated as ordinary income in the year received under Sec. 61. Income received in advance is included in gross income when received.

40. M, an accrual-method taxpayer using the calendar year, had the following transactions during 1990:

Recovery of an account receivable written off in a prior year but which did not reduce his taxes	$ 5,000
Sales to a customer who is directed to transmit the payment to M's brother	3,500
Amounts received in settlement of a breach of contract suit	22,500
Goods shipped on consignment December 15, 1990 and sold by M's agent on January 10, 1991	13,000

What amount must M include in gross income in 1990?

a. $8,500.
b. $26,000.
c. $27,500.
d. $31,000.

The correct answer is (b). *(SPE 1081 II-73)*
REQUIRED: The amount the taxpayer must include in gross income in 1990.
DISCUSSION: Since the taxpayer's tax was not reduced in the year the account receivable was written off, no income is recognized upon the recovery of the receivable (Sec. 111). The taxpayer must include in his/her gross income the $3,500 from the sale to the customer since income cannot be avoided by assigning the right to collection of the income to another. The amounts received in the settlement of the breach of contract suit represent lost income, so the $22,500 must be included in gross income. Title to goods shipped on consignment remains with the seller until the goods are sold by the consignee. Since the goods were not sold until 1991, the $13,000 is not included in the taxpayer's 1990 gross income. Therefore, the taxpayer must include $26,000 ($3,500 sale to customer + $22,500 settlement) in gross income.

41. For 1990, Mr. F, in his first year of operating a business, sustained a net operating loss of $2,000. Uncollectible accounts receivable in the amount of $5,000 were deducted in arriving at the loss. During 1991, $4,000 of the amount deducted as bad debts in 1990 was recovered. F's 1990 loss was completely absorbed in 1991. What is the amount of the recovery that F must include in his gross income for 1991?

    a. $5,000.
    b. $4,000.
    c. $3,000.
    d. $1,000.

The correct answer is (b). *(SPE 988 II-60)*
REQUIRED: The amount included in income upon the recovery of a bad debt previously deducted.
DISCUSSION: Under the general concept of Sec. 61, recovery of a bad debt must be included in income the same as any other receipt. Only if the prior deduction of the bad debt did not reduce taxes would the recovery not be included in income under Sec. 111. Since the bad debt deduction reduced taxes (was completely absorbed per the language of the question), the entire $4,000 must be included in gross income for 1991.

42. An honorary director of a corporation, who served as an active director for many years but who is no longer required to perform services, does not have to include the fees from the corporation in self-employment income.

The correct answer is (F). *(SPE 986 II-32)*
DISCUSSION: The fees paid to the now inactive director are paid because of his/her prior service, not as a gratuitous gift. Compensation for prior services is gross income under Sec. 61.

43. In 1991, Mr. L, a cash-basis attorney, provided services for Corporation M. In return he received 1% of M's common stock that had a fair market value of $4,000. Mr. L must report this $4,000 as income on his 1991 tax return.

The correct answer is (T). *(SPE 1083 III-11)*
DISCUSSION: Compensation for services is gross income under Sec. 61. If services are paid for with property, the fair market value of the property taken in payment must be included in gross income as compensation (Sec. 83).

44. For compensation from his employer, Mr. White received a note in December 1990 that had a fair market value of $3,000. Payment of the note plus $75 interest is received in May 1991. Mr. White should report the entire $3,075 in gross income in 1991.

The correct answer is (F). *(SPE 1077 I-115)*
DISCUSSION: If services are paid for in property, the fair market value of the property taken in payment must be included in income as compensation (Sec. 83). Therefore, the taxpayer must include the fair market value of the note of $3,000 in his gross income in 1990. When the note is paid in 1991, the taxpayer must include only the $75 of interest in his gross income.

45. Abe set up the accounting system for John's construction business. They agree that John will furnish material and build a shed in Abe's yard in exchange for the service. Abe usually charges $500 for this type of service and that seems fair to John. Abe must include $500 in his gross income for this transaction.

The correct answer is (T). *(SPE 990 I-12)*
DISCUSSION: Bartering involves the sale or exchange of property or services (but not for cash). Reg. 1.61-2(d)(1) provides that, if services are paid for with property or by exchanging other services, the fair market value of such property or services must be included in gross income as compensation.

4.4 Interest Income

46. All of the following are taxable interest income except:

    a. Interest on a federal tax refund.
    b. Interest on an IRA before withdrawal.
    c. Interest on GI insurance dividends.
    d. Interest on U.S. Treasury bills.

The correct answer is (b). *(SPE 987 I-49)*
REQUIRED: The type of interest income which is excluded from gross income.
DISCUSSION: Interest income is included in gross income under Sec. 61 unless specifically excluded in another section. Sec. 408 provides in most cases that individual retirement accounts (IRAs) are taxed to the owner only on distribution.
Answers (a), (c), and (d) are incorrect because there is no exclusion for interest on U.S. government obligations derived from tax refunds, GI insurance, or Treasury bills.

Module 4.4: Interest Income

47. During 1991, Clark received the following interest income:

On Veterans Administration insurance dividends left on deposit with the V.A.	$20
On state income tax refund	30

What amount should Clark include for interest income in his 1991 return?

a. $50.
b. $30.
c. $20.
d. $0.

The correct answer is (b). *(CPA 1188 Q-4)*
REQUIRED: The amount of interest income the taxpayer should include on his 1991 tax return.
DISCUSSION: Interest income is included in gross income under Sec. 61 unless specifically excluded in another section. Although Sec. 103 provides an exclusion for interest on certain obligations of states and municipalities, it does not apply to interest on state income tax refunds. Therefore, the interest on the state income tax refund is included in Clark's gross income. The interest on Veterans Administration insurance dividends left on deposit with the Veterans Administration is excluded from gross income (Rev. Rul. 91-14). Therefore, Clark should include all the interest ($30) in gross on his 1991 tax return.

48. In 1991 Uriah Stone received the following interest payments:

Interest of $400 on refund of federal income tax for 1989.
Interest of $300 on award for personal injuries sustained in an automobile accident during 1988.
Interest of $1,500 on municipal bonds.
Interest of $1,000 on United States savings bonds (Series HH).

What amount, if any, should Stone report as interest income on his 1991 tax return?

a. $0.
b. $700.
c. $1,700.
d. $3,200.

The correct answer is (c). *(CPA 580 P-48)*
REQUIRED: The amount the taxpayer should include as interest income on his 1991 tax return.
DISCUSSION: Unless otherwise excluded in another section, Sec. 61 includes interest in gross income. Sec. 103 excludes from gross income interest on most obligations of states or political subdivisions of a state (e.g., municipal bonds). This exclusion does not apply to the obligations of the United States. Therefore, the taxpayer's interest income includes the $400 of interest on the refund of federal income taxes, and the $1,000 of interest on the United States Series HH savings bonds which is paid by check semiannually. Although an award for personal injuries is tax-exempt under Sec. 104, the interest income earned on the award is not tax-exempt. A total of $1,700 ($400 + $1,000 + $300) is included in gross income.

49. From the items listed below, determine the interest income includable on Mr. F's tax return for 1991:

Received on deposits in a federal savings and loan association	$320
Received on share accounts in a credit union	125
Received on money market certificates at fixed intervals of 1 year or less	50
Toaster received for opening an account in a mutual savings bank	16
Increase in the value of prepaid premiums applied to the payment of premiums due on a life insurance policy	95

a. $445.
b. $465.
c. $511.
d. $606.

The correct answer is (d). *(SPE 1081 I-67)*
REQUIRED: The amount of interest income includable in the taxpayer's tax return for 1991.
DISCUSSION: Sec. 61 includes interest in gross income, whether received in cash or property, unless specifically excluded in another section. None of the items listed is excluded from income. A toaster received to open an account is equivalent to interest since it is paid to induce a deposit; i.e., a payment for the use of money by the bank. The increase in value of prepaid premiums is due to interest on the prepayments. It is taxable even though not directly received, since Mr. F has the benefit of it. Therefore, all of the items listed are includable interest income and total $606.

50. Ms. B received the following interest:

Luggage for purchasing a 4-year certificate of deposit (fair market value)	$ 50
Interest on passbook savings account	15
Interest on certificate of deposit	200
Dividends on share account in credit union	150
Interest on State of Mississippi bonds issued to finance state highway construction	300

What is the amount of interest income to be included in income?

a. $265.
b. $365.
c. $415.
d. $715.

The correct answer is (c). *(SPE 1082 I-73)*
REQUIRED: The amount of interest income to be included in gross income.
DISCUSSION: Under Sec. 61, gross income includes interest, whether received in cash or property, unless specifically excluded by another section. Interest is a payment for the use of money. Luggage for purchasing a certificate of deposit is a payment to obtain the use of the taxpayer's money, so it is interest and must be included in gross income. The interest on the passbook savings account and certificate of deposit are items of interest income. Dividends on a share account in a credit union are the equivalent of interest and must be included in gross income as such. The total of these amounts is $415, which must be included in Ms. B's gross income.
Sec. 103 excludes interest on most state and local governmental obligations. The interest on the state bonds to finance highway construction is excluded from gross income.

51. In 1991, Ms. Smith withdrew her funds from a time-savings account before maturity and was charged a penalty of $2,000 for early withdrawal. The interest earned on the account in 1991 was $1,600. Ms. Smith had no other interest income. How should Ms. Smith report this transaction on her 1991 individual income tax return?

a. Report $1,600 interest income; $2,000 penalty is not deductible.
b. Report $1,600 interest income; deduct penalty of $2,000 as an adjustment to income to arrive at adjusted gross income.
c. Report $1,600 interest income; deduct penalty of $2,000 as an itemized deduction.
d. Report $1,600 interest income; deduct penalty of $1,600 as an adjustment to income to arrive at adjusted gross income.

The correct answer is (b). *(SPE 990 I-37)*
REQUIRED: The correct way to report interest earned on a time savings account and the penalty for its early withdrawal.
DISCUSSION: Interest income earned must be reported in full. The $1,600 of interest must be included in gross income. The $2,000 interest penalty is a deduction for adjusted gross income under Sec. 62(a)(9).
Answers (a) and (c) are incorrect because the full amount of the interest earned must be reported, and the penalty is deductible as an above-the-line deduction. Answer (d) is incorrect because the full amount of the penalty is deductible, i.e., the deduction is not limited to the interest income.

52. Mrs. Green, a widow whose husband died on April 5, 1991, chose to receive the proceeds of her husband's $200,000 life insurance policy in twenty yearly installments of $15,000 each. The payments are based on a guaranteed interest rate. How much of each payment is interest income to be included in Mrs. Green's adjusted gross income each year?

a. $3,000.
b. $4,000.
c. $5,000.
d. $10,000.

The correct answer is (c). *(SPE 989 I-62)*
REQUIRED: The amount of interest includable in gross income from a life insurance policy paid in installments.
DISCUSSION: The amount of each payment in excess of the death benefit prorated over the period of payment is interest income. Mrs. Green will receive $15,000 each year. Of this amount, $10,000 ($200,000 ÷ 20 years) is death benefits and $5,000 ($15,000 − $10,000) is interest. This interest is fully included in gross income.

53. All of the following are considered interest to be included in income:

(1) Dividends on share accounts in a mutual savings bank.
(2) Fair market value of gift received for opening an account with a savings institution.
(3) Interest received on obligations of a state.
(4) Interest charged at an illegal rate. State law does not require application of amount to principal.

The correct answer is (F). *(SPE 1085 I-18)*
DISCUSSION: Sec. 103 excludes from gross income interest on most obligations of states or any political subdivision of a state, so (3) would not be included in income. Dividends on share accounts in a mutual savings bank are considered interest, and gifts received for opening an account are also considered equivalent to interest since they are made to induce a deposit. Illegal income must also be included in gross income, and interest in excess of the legal rate is still interest.

54. On December 31, 1990, Mr. B's bank credited his savings account with interest earned from October 1, 1990 through December 31, 1990. The bank posted this interest to Mr. B's passbook on January 15, 1991 when he made a withdrawal. Mr. B, a calendar-year, cash-method taxpayer, must report this interest on his 1990 income tax return.

The correct answer is (T). *(SPE 1082 I-9)*
DISCUSSION: A depositor in a bank is required to report interest income under the doctrine of "constructive receipt" when his/her account is credited with the interest by the bank. That is when the depositor is entitled to the interest. When the interest is posted to the depositor's passbook or when a withdrawal is made is irrelevant. Since the interest was credited to Mr. B in 1990, he is required to report it in 1990.

55. U.S. Treasury bills are issued at a discount. The difference between the issue price and the face value at maturity is taxable interest income to the holder reported when the bill is paid at maturity.

The correct answer is (T). *(SPE 984 I-10)*
DISCUSSION: Sec. 454(b) provides that, for a U.S. obligation issued on a discount basis and payable without interest at a fixed maturity date not exceeding 1 year from the date of issue, the amount of discount shall not be considered to accrue until the obligation is paid at maturity, sold, or otherwise disposed of. U.S. Treasury bills generally are issued with a maturity date 1 year or less from the issue date.

56. In 1991, Mr. Black received a condemnation award from the state of Texas for land to be used as a state park. With the award, Mr. Black received interest of $4,000. The interest received on a condemnation award of a state is tax exempt interest.

The correct answer is (F). *(SPE 1077 I-30)*
DISCUSSION: Although Sec. 103 excludes from gross income interest received on obligations of a state, interest on such an obligation is not excluded if the obligation is not issued in registered form [Sec. 103(b)(3)]. Since the interest on the condemnation award is not interest on a state obligation issued in registered form, the interest is not excluded under Sec. 103.

4.5 Income from Stocks and Bonds

See Chapter 5 for certain dividend and interest exclusions and Chapter 18 for distributions to shareholders.

57. Al and Iris Oran, who are married, received $10,000 in 1991 as dividends from taxable domestic corporations. In the Orans' 1991 joint return, the amount of these dividends subject to tax is

a. $10,000.
b. $9,900.
c. $9,800.
d. $8,500.

The correct answer is (a). *(CPA 588 Q-5)*
REQUIRED: The amount of cash dividends from domestic corporations subject to tax.
DISCUSSION: Sec. 61(a)(7) lists dividends as being included in gross income. They are included in their entirety unless there is a specific exclusion. There is no exclusion for dividends received by an individual from a taxable domestic corporation (provided the dividends are paid out of earnings and profits which is the assumed case unless other information is provided in a question). Therefore, the entire $10,000 of dividends are included in their gross income.

58. Mr. Z owned 200 shares of Corporation K common stock. During 1991, Mr. Z received distributions from Corporation K of $600 in cash dividends, 100 additional shares of K's common stock, and rights to purchase 100 more shares. The distributions were not disproportionate and the shareholders were not given an option to receive cash instead of the stock and stock rights. The fair market value of the total stock and the total stock rights were $200 and $100, respectively. What is the amount of income from these distributions that is includable in Mr. Z's income for 1991?

a. $600.
b. $700.
c. $900.
d. $1,000.

The correct answer is (a). *(SPE 988 I-58)*
REQUIRED: The amount of income a shareholder must report from dividends of cash, stock, and rights to purchase the stock.
DISCUSSION: The $600 in cash dividends are included in taxable income under the general rule of Sec. 61(a)(7). Cash dividends from taxable domestic corporations are included in income provided they are paid out of earnings and profits (which is assumed unless information is given otherwise in the question). However, under Sec. 305(a), gross income generally does not include a stock dividend. Rights to purchase stock are also treated as a stock dividend for this purpose. There are exceptions under Sec. 305(b), but the usual stock dividend paid on common stock falls within the general rule and is not included in the shareholder's income. Therefore, Mr. Z does not have to include any gross income from the stock dividend or distribution of stock rights.
Mr. Z's total taxable income from these distributions is the $600 of cash dividends. Note that under Sec. 307(a), Mr. Z will be required to allocate some of the basis of his original shares of common stock to the stock and stock rights received as distributions.

59. Ms. X received notice from her mutual fund that it has realized a long-term capital gain in 1991 on her behalf in the amount of $2,500. It also advised her that it has paid a tax of $500 on this gain. The mutual fund indicated that it will not distribute the net amount. All of the following statements are correct except

a. X must report a long-term capital gain of $2,500.
b. X is allowed a $500 credit for the tax since it is considered paid by X.
c. X is allowed to increase her basis in the stock by $1,650.
d. X does not report a long-term capital gain because nothing was paid to her.

The correct answer is (d). *(SPE 986 I-50)*
REQUIRED: The false statement concerning an undistributed long-term capital gain in a mutual fund.
DISCUSSION: A mutual fund is a regulated investment company, the taxation of which is determined by Sec. 852. Shareholders are taxed on dividends paid by the mutual fund. If part or all of the dividend is designated as a capital gain dividend, it must be treated as such by the shareholders. Undistributed capital gains must also be included in income by shareholders, but they are allowed a credit for their proportionate share of any tax on the capital gain paid by the mutual fund.
Answer (a) is true because X must include the undistributed capital gain in income. Answer (b) is true because X is allowed a credit for her share of the tax paid by the mutual fund on the capital gain. Answer (c) is true because X does increase her basis by 66% of the undistributed capital gain she includes in income [Sec. 853(b)(3)(D)].

60. Mr. J sold a corporate bond to Mr. K on March 31, 1991. The bond, which matures in 1993, has a face value of $1,000 and an annual interest rate of 10%. Interest is payable on June 30 and December 31 of each year. How much interest should Mr. K include in income for 1991?

a. $0.
b. $50.
c. $75.
d. $100.

The correct answer is (c). *(SPE 984 I-68)*
REQUIRED: The interest income from a corporate bond purchased between interest dates.
DISCUSSION: When corporate bonds are purchased between interest dates, the taxpayer theoretically pays an amount equal to the accrued interest on the bond for the right to receive the entire interest payment. When the interest payment is received, the amount paid for the right to receive that interest is deducted as a return of capital. In this manner, the seller is taxed on the interest accrued before the sale, and the purchaser is taxed on the interest accrued after the sale. Mr. K should include $75 (.10 x $1,000 x 9/12) interest in income.

Module 4.5: Income from Stocks and Bonds

61. On June 2, 1982 (before the 1982 TRA change in original issue discount rules), Ms. J, a calendar-year taxpayer, purchased XYZ Corporation's 10-year, 10% bonds at original issue for $12,000. The bonds had a stated redemption price of $15,000. What amount of the original issue discount must Ms. J report as interest income on her 1991 tax return?

- a. $0.
- b. $25.
- c. $175.
- d. $300.

The correct answer is (d). *(SPE 1080 II-69)*
REQUIRED: The amount of the original issue discount the taxpayer must report as interest income on her 1991 tax return.
DISCUSSION: Sec. 1272(b) requires the holder of corporate bonds issued at a discount before July 2, 1982 to include in gross income the ratable monthly portion of the original issue discount multiplied by the number of complete months the holder held the bond during the taxable year. The original issue discount is equal to the difference between the issue price and the stated redemption price at maturity ($15,000 − $12,000 = $3,000). The bond will be outstanding for 10 years, or 120 months, so the ratable monthly portion of the original discount is $25 ($3,000 ÷ 120 months). The taxpayer held the bond for 12 months of the taxable year, so she must include $300 as interest income ($25 x 12 months) on her 1991 tax return.
Note that original issue discount on bonds issued after July 1, 1982 is included in income on a daily basis using the "yield" method (rather than straight-line amortization) under Sec. 1272(a).

62. The income tax rules for reporting original issue discount (OID) on publicly offered instruments apply to which one of the following?

- a. U.S. Savings Bonds (long-term).
- b. Zero-coupon bonds (long-term).
- c. Tax-exempt obligations that are not stripped bonds or coupons (long-term).
- d. Short-term obligations (fixed maturity date of 1 year or less from date of issue).

The correct answer is (b). *(SPE 989 I-41)*
REQUIRED: The instrument to which the income tax rules for reporting original issue discount (OID) apply.
DISCUSSION: Zero coupon bonds bear no stated rate of interest and are issued at a discount. As the stated redemption price at maturity exceeds the issue price, the provisions of Sec. 1272(a) with regard to original issue discount are applicable.
Answers (a), (c), and (d) are incorrect because Sec. 1272(a)(2) provides an exception for tax exempt obligations, U.S. Savings Bonds and short-term obligations with a fixed maturity date of 1 year or less from the date of issue. None of these items would be subject to the income tax rules for reporting original issue discount.

63. On January 1, 1991, Joe Green purchased XYZ Corporation's 10-year, 10% bonds at original issue for $12,000. The bonds had a stated redemption price of $15,000. How much original issue discount must Green include in gross income in 1991 assuming a current market yield for bonds of similar quality of 14%?

- a. $120.
- b. $180.
- c. $300.
- d. $420.

The correct answer is (b). *(Publisher)*
REQUIRED: The amount of original issue discount includable in gross income in 1991.
DISCUSSION: For original issue discount bonds issued after July 1, 1982, Sec. 1272(a) requires the inclusion in gross income of an amount equal to the sum of the daily portions of the original issue discount for each day during the taxable year the instrument was held. The daily portions are determined under Sec. 1272(a)(3) as the ratable portion of the excess of the product of the bond's yield to maturity and its adjusted issue price over the interest payable for the bond year. The adjusted issue price is the original issue price adjusted for the original issue discount previously taken into income (which is zero in 1991).

Yield times adjusted issue price (14% x $12,000)	$1,680
Less: interest payable (10% x $15,000)	(1,500)
Ratable portion (entire year)	$ 180

Module 4.5: Income from Stocks and Bonds 59

64. On January 1, 1987, Ira Ostire, who is not a dealer, purchased ten $1,000, 5% bonds of the state of California for $10,400 (maturity date of January 1, 2006). Interest is payable January 1 and July 1 each year. On December 31, 1990, he sold four of the bonds at a total price of $4,386 exclusive of interest. In computing Mr. Ostire's 1990 taxable income, the receipt of interest on the bonds and the sale of the bonds will increase his gross income by

a. $603.
b. $258.
c. $90.
d. $0.

The correct answer is (b). *(CPA 573 Q-6)*
REQUIRED: The amount by which the receipt of interest on the bonds and the sale of the bonds will increase the taxpayer's adjusted gross income.
DISCUSSION: The bonds are obligations of a state, the interest of which is generally tax-exempt under Sec. 103. Therefore, the interest received on the bonds will not increase adjusted gross income. The gain on the sale of the bonds is long-term capital gain since the bonds were not issued at a discount (they were issued at a premium). The bond premium (at $40 per bond) must be amortized to determine the basis of the bonds under Sec. 1016(a)(5); however, the amortization is not deductible under Sec. 171 because they are tax-exempt bonds. The amortization for the four bonds is $32 ($160 premium divided by 20-year life of bonds, times 4-year holding period). Therefore, the basis of the bonds is $4,128 ($4,160 − $32). The effect on gross income is as follows:

Sales price	$4,386
Less: Adjusted basis	(4,128)
Gain included in gross income	$ 258

65. Mr. D, a cash-method taxpayer, died and left his beneficiary a $1,000 Series EE bond. D bought the bond for $500 and had not chosen to report the increase in value each year. At D's death, the bond had a $750 redemption value. The executor did not elect to include any interest earned in the decedent's final income tax return. D's beneficiary, a cash-method taxpayer, did not elect to report the increase in value of the bond each year. The beneficiary cashed the bond and received $800. What amount must the beneficiary include in interest income in the year she cashed the bond?

a. $1,000.
b. $750.
c. $300.
d. $250.

The correct answer is (c). *(SPE 987 III-88)*
REQUIRED: The interest income when a Series EE bond is redeemed.
DISCUSSION: Series EE bonds are issued at a discount and redeemable for fixed amounts which increase at stated intervals. Sec. 454(a) allows a cash-basis taxpayer to elect to either include in gross income the annual increment in redemption value or defer recognition of any interest income until the bond is actually redeemed. Since none of the owners of the bond, Mr. D, the executor, and D's beneficiary, elected to include the annual increments and redemption value in income, the entire redemption amount in excess of the original purchase is interest. Since Mr. D purchased the bond for $500 and D's beneficiary cashed the bond for $800, the interest income is $300.
Note that the basis of the bond was not increased to its redemption value at D's death as normally occurs with property held by a decedent, because the increase in value is due to interest that was already earned but not paid. The appreciation income that is earned, but not yet taxed, does not receive a step-up in basis at death because it is income in respect of a decedent (see Module 20.6 for more detail).

66. Mr. P invested in Park Place Corporation, a real estate investment trust (REIT). Park Place declared a dividend on October 1, 1990, and made it payable to its shareholders of record on October 17, 1990. Park Place actually paid the dividend on January 5, 1991. Mr. P received $1,500. How should P report this dividend for federal income tax purposes?

a. $1,500 in taxable income for 1990.
b. $1,500 in taxable income for 1991.
c. $1,125 in taxable income for 1990, $375 in taxable income for 1991.
d. $1,000 in taxable income for 1990, $500 in taxable income for 1991.

The correct answer is (a). *(SPE 989 I-43)*
REQUIRED: The correct reporting of a dividend from a REIT declared and made payable October 17, 1990 and paid January 5, 1991.
DISCUSSION: Dividends declared by a REIT in October, November, or December and made payable to shareholders of record in these months are deemed to have been paid by the REIT and received by its shareholder on December 31 of the same year, provided that the dividends are actually paid in January of the following year [Sec. 857(b)(8)].
Answers (b), (c), and (d) are incorrect because all are improper reporting treatments.

67. Marnie purchased a Series HH bond on November 15, 1990, for $2,100. $200 of the purchase price represented accrued interest. She received $210 in interest income on the bond on December 2, 1990. What is the proper treatment of the $210 interest income for federal income tax purposes?

a. $200 return of capital, the $10 can be currently included as interest income or deferred until the bond is cashed.

b. Marnie can elect to include the $210 as interest income in 1990 or defer the reporting until she cashes the bond.

c. $210 taxable as interest income.

d. Report the total payment as taxable interest, then report $200 as an adjustment on Schedule B.

The correct answer is (d). *(SPE 990 I-36)*
REQUIRED: The proper treatment of interest income from a Series HH bond purchased between interest dates.
DISCUSSION: When a bond is sold between interest dates the interest accrued up to the sale date is added to the selling price of the bond - in this case $200. Marnie would report the full interest payment of $210 on Schedule B as taxable interest in the year received along with a corresponding adjustment of $200 representing the amount already paid to (and taxable to) the seller. In this way the bond holder will include in income only the interest attributable to the portion of the year during which the bond was held.
Answer (a) is incorrect because none of the payment represents a return of capital. Answer (b) is incorrect because Series HH bonds are issued at face value and interest must be reported in the year received. Answer (c) is incorrect because $200 of the interest payment has already been remitted to the seller by way of an increased purchase price and is taxable to the seller.

68. Dacey Corporation issued a stock option in 1989 to Crown, an employee, to purchase 100 shares of Dacey stock at $10 per share. Dacey stock was not traded on an exchange, but it was estimated that its stock was worth $9 per share. The stock options were considered not to have a readily ascertainable value. In 1991, Crown exercised the stock options when it was determined that the stock was worth $18 per share based on several offers by competitors to buy out the company. How much and when must Crown report income from the receipt and exercise of the stock options?

a. No income or loss.

b. $100 loss in 1989.

c. $800 in 1991.

d. $900 in 1991.

The correct answer is (c). *(Publisher)*
REQUIRED: An employee's income from a nonqualified and nonstatutory stock option which does not have a readily ascertainable value.
DISCUSSION: The rules for taxation of nonqualified and nonstatutory stock options are contained in Reg. 1.83-7. When a stock option does not have a readily ascertainable value, the employee is not taxed until the option is exercised. At that time, the amount of income is measured by the difference between the stock's fair market value and the amount paid for the stock under the option. It is considered ordinary income. Therefore, Crown must report $800 of ordinary income in 1991 [100 shares x ($18 – $10) = $800].
Note that if the option is subject to restrictions, no income will be recognized until the restrictions lapse (Sec. 83).

69. Mr. T, a cash-basis taxpayer, may either defer reporting the interest on Series EE bonds until he cashes the bonds or he may choose to report the increase in redemption value as interest each year.

The correct answer is (T). *(SPE 1080 I-10)*
DISCUSSION: Series EE bonds are savings bonds issued at a discount and are redeemable for fixed amounts which increase at stated intervals. The income from these bonds is received when the bonds are redeemed and is equal to the difference between the purchase price and the amount received on redemption. No interest payments are actually made while the bond is held. Sec. 454(a) allows a cash-basis taxpayer to elect to either include in gross income the annual increment in redemption value or defer recognition of any interest income until the bond is redeemed.

70. A cash-basis taxpayer must report interest received on series HH United States Savings Bonds, issued at face value, as income in the year received.

The correct answer is (T). *(SPE 988 I-6)*
DISCUSSION: Interest on United States bonds is taxable. The interest must be reported in the year received. Only for U.S. Savings Bonds issued at a discount and redeemable for fixed amounts increasing at stated intervals is the interest not reported currently. It is reported when the bond is redeemed because that is when the interest is received (although an election is available to report the interest as the bond increases in redemption value).

71. When bonds are sold between interest dates, a portion of the sales price is accrued interest. The seller does not report the interest income. The purchaser will report the total interest income and deduct the accrued interest payment as a return of capital.

The correct answer is (F). *(SPE 1085 I-19)*
DISCUSSION: The purchaser has theoretically paid an amount equal to the accrued interest on the bond for the right to receive the entire interest payment. The seller reports this amount as interest income. When the purchaser receives the interest payment, the amount paid for the right to receive that interest is deducted as a return of capital. In this manner, the seller is taxed on the interest accrued before the sale, and the purchaser is taxed on the interest accrued after the sale.

72. Original issue discount (OID) is the difference between the larger principal amount (stated redemption price at maturity) of a long-term debt instrument, such as a bond, note, or other obligation, and the smaller issue price.

The correct answer is (T). *(SPE 986 I-19)*
DISCUSSION: Original issue discount (OID) is equal to the difference between the issue price and the stated redemption price at maturity. OID exists only if the discount exceeds 1/4 of 1% of the stated redemption price times the number of years to maturity [Sec. 1273(a)(3)].

73. Zero-coupon bonds are generally long-term debt instruments that pay no interest prior to maturity and are presumed to be issued at a discount. The discount is generally includable in income.

The correct answer is (T). *(SPE 990 I-5)*
DISCUSSION: The difference between the stated redemption price at maturity and the issue price of a zero-coupon bond is considered to be original issue discount. Under Sec. 1272(a) the original issue discount on bonds issued after July 1, 1982 must be included in income and is computed on a daily basis using the "yield" method.

74. On March 5, 1991, Mr. B purchased a corporate bond for $8,200. The bond, which was issued January 1, 1990, has a face value of $10,000, no stated interest, and will mature December 31, 1992. Mr. B's gross income for 1991 should include a portion of the original issue discount on the corporate bond.

The correct answer is (T). *(SPE 1085 II-7)*
DISCUSSION: Under Sec. 1272(a), the original issue discount on bonds issued after July 1, 1982 must be included in income, computed on a daily basis using the "yield" method.

4.6 Rental Income

75. Paul Bristol, a cash-basis taxpayer, owns an apartment building. The following information was available for 1991

- An analysis of the 1991 bank deposit slips showed recurring monthly rents received totaling $50,000 for the year.
- On March 1, 1991, the tenant in apartment 2B paid Bristol $2,000 to cancel the lease expiring on December 31, 1991.
- The lease of the tenant in apartment 3A expired on December 31, 1991 and the tenant left improvements valued at $1,000. The improvements were not in lieu of any required rent.

In computing net rental income for 1991, Bristol should report gross rents of

   a. $50,000.
   b. $51,000.
   c. $52,000.
   d. $53,000.

The correct answer is (c). *(CPA 583 P-42)*
REQUIRED: The amount of gross rents given monthly rents, leasehold improvements, and a cancellation payment.
DISCUSSION: Gross rents include the $50,000 of recurring rents plus the $2,000 lease cancellation payment. The cancellation payment is in lieu of rent so it must be included in income the same as rent.
The $1,000 of leasehold improvements are excluded from income since they were not in lieu of rent (Sec. 109).

Module 4.6: Rental Income

76. Gewald enters into an agreement to lease a house to Dorschuk. Although the fair rental value of the house is $5,000 per year, Dorschuk is required to pay only $3,000 per year in return for building a patio, a sundeck, and a hot tub which will be left on the premises at the end of the lease. The lease is to last for 2 years. Dorschuk finishes all the improvements in the first year of the lease. How much and when must Gewald recognize rental income from this transaction?

   a. $3,000 in the first year and $3,000 in the second year.
   b. $5,000 in the first year and $5,000 in the second year.
   c. $7,000 in the first year and $3,000 in the second year.
   d. $3,000 in the first year and $7,000 in the second year.

The correct answer is (c). *(Publisher)*
REQUIRED: The amount and timing of rental income when the lessee makes improvements in lieu of rent.
DISCUSSION: Sec. 61(a)(5) includes rents in gross income whether received in cash, property, or as services. Improvements made by a lessee on the lessor's property are generally excluded from income under Sec. 109 unless they are made in lieu of rent. In this case, the improvements made by Dorschuk are made in lieu of $2,000 of rent in the first year of the lease and $2,000 of rent in the second year of the lease. Improvements in lieu of rent are included in the lessor's income when the improvements are completed or placed on the property (the same as if cash rent had been received at that time). Since Dorschuk paid $3,000 in cash in the first year and completed the improvements in the first year, Gewald must recognize $7,000 of rental income in the first year. Gewald must also recognize $3,000 of rental income in the second year when it is received.

77. Mr. Wolf, a cash basis taxpayer, owns an apartment building. His records reflect the following information for 1991.

Tenant G paid cost of floor repairs that were Mr. Wolf's responsibility	$ 950
Security deposits to be returned to tenants upon expiration of their leases in 1994	1,350
Advance rents received in December for the first 6 months of 1992	3,000

What is the amount of gross rental income Mr. Wolf should include on his 1991 Schedule E?

   a. $2,300.
   b. $3,950.
   c. $4,350.
   d. $5,300.

The correct answer is (b). *(SPE 990 I-66)*
REQUIRED: A landlord's rental income from various types of payments.
DISCUSSION: Both cash and accrual basis taxpayers must include amounts in gross income upon actual or constructive receipt if the taxpayer has an unrestricted claim to such amounts under Reg. 1.61-8(b). Since Mr. Wolfe has an unrestricted claim to the $3,000 of rent paid in advance, it would be included in his rental income. The security deposits of $1,350 would not be included in rental income since they were not intended as advance rental payments. (Mr. Wolfe does not have an unrestricted claim since they must be returned unless there are damages or rent is not paid.) The expenses of $950 paid by a tenant are also gross income unless intended as a gift. Therefore Mr. Wolfe's gross rental income is $3,950.

78. Mr. G rents an apartment to Mr. B. If Mr. B pays any of G's expenses, G must include the payments in his rental income. G may deduct the expenses paid by B if they are otherwise deductible.

The correct answer is (T). *(SPE 984 I-14)*
DISCUSSION: As a general rule, if a lessee pays any of the expenses of his/her lessor, such payments are additional rental income to the lessor [Reg. 1.61-8(c)]. Since the expenses are in effect treated as if paid by the lessee to the lessor, and then paid by the lessor to a third party, the lessor may deduct them.

79. An amount called a security deposit which is to be used as a final payment of rent should not be included in rental income in the year received, but should be included in income in the year the lease expires.

The correct answer is (F). *(SPE 1080 I-11)*
DISCUSSION: Advance rental payments are included in gross income in the year of receipt regardless of the period covered or the method of accounting employed by the taxpayer [Reg. 1.61-8(b)]. Therefore, if a security deposit is intended as an advance rent payment, it must be included in income in the year received.

80. In 1991 Mrs. G received $5,000 in advance payments under a 50-month lease agreement. The $5,000 represented the entire amount due under the lease. There were no restrictions on the use or enjoyment of the payments. Mrs. G must include the $5,000 as income in 1991.

The correct answer is (T). *(SPE 1078 I-9)*
DISCUSSION: Rent is included in gross income under Sec. 61. Furthermore, gross income includes advance rentals, which must be included in income for the year of receipt regardless of the period covered or the method of accounting employed by the taxpayer [Reg. 1.61-8(b)]. Therefore, in 1991 Mrs. G must include the $5,000 of advance rent in income.

81. Mr. and Mrs. Peach, whose principal residence is in a resort town, went out of town for 3 weeks. While they were gone they rented out their residence for $2,000. Mr. and Mrs. Peach are not required to include the $2,000 in their gross income.

The correct answer is (F). *(SPE 990 I-9)*
DISCUSSION: Rent is included in gross income under Sec. 61. Sec. 280A(g) provides that, if a dwelling unit is used as a residence and rented out for less than 15 days per year, then (1) none of the rental income is included in gross income, and (2) no deduction for the rental use will be allowed. As Mr. and Mrs. Peach rented their residence for 3 weeks, the provisions of Sec. 280A(g) do not apply and the entire $2,000 will be included in gross income.

4.7 Income from Annuities

82. Mary Wilson, a calendar-year taxpayer, purchased an annuity contract for $3,800 that would pay her $110 a month beginning on January 1, 1991. Her expected return under the contract is $11,000. How much of this annuity is excludable from gross income for the 1991 calendar year?

   a. $0.
   b. $456.
   c. $864.
   d. $1,320.

The correct answer is (b). *(J. McLean)*
REQUIRED: The amount of an annuity the taxpayer may exclude from gross income in the current year.
DISCUSSION: Sec. 72(b) allows the taxpayer to exclude from income the proportion of each payment from an annuity contract that the investment in the contract bears to the expected return under the contract. In the current year the taxpayer will receive $1,320 ($110 x 12 months) from the annuity contract. Of this amount, the taxpayer may exclude 34.55% (the $3,800 investment in the contract divided by the $11,000 expected return). The exclusion is $456 ($1,320 x 34.55%).

83. Mr. Kitten purchased an annuity contract for $50,000 from the XYZ Company on March 31, 1991. He is to receive $1,000 per month starting April 1, 1991 and continuing for life. He has a life expectancy of 10 years as of March 31, 1991. Mr. Kitten's reportable annuity income for 1991 is

   a. $3,750.
   b. $5,000.
   c. $5,250.
   d. $12,000.

The correct answer is (c). *(SPE 1077 II-35)*
REQUIRED: The taxpayer's income in the first year of a life annuity.
DISCUSSION: Amounts received as an annuity are included in gross income under Secs. 61 and 72. However, Sec. 72(b) permits the taxpayer to exclude from income as a return of capital the proportion of each payment that the investment in the contract bears to the expected return under the contract. The expected return is the annual amount to be paid to the taxpayer multiplied by the number of years of life expectancy. Kitten's expected return in the annuity contract is $1,000 per month times 120 months (10 years), or $120,000. The investment in the contract is $50,000; therefore, the taxpayer may exclude 41 2/3% ($50,000 ÷ $120,000) of the payments received as a return of capital.

Amount received	$9,000
Exclusion (41 2/3% x $9,000)	(3,750)
Annuity income	$5,250

84. Dick Jones retired on May 31, 1986 and receives a monthly pension benefit of $800 payable for life. The first pension check was received on June 15, 1986. During his years of employment, Dick contributed $27,200 to the cost of his company's pension plan. How much of the pension amounts received may Dick exclude from taxable income in 1991?

   a. $0.
   b. $2,400.
   c. $3,200.
   d. $4,800.

The correct answer is (a). *(Publisher)*
REQUIRED: The amount of pension payments the employee may exclude from taxable income for 1991.
DISCUSSION: If an employee can fully recover his/her contribution to a pension plan within 3 years of the date of the receipt of the first payment, and this first payment is prior to July 2, 1986, then all amounts received from the pension are excluded from gross income until an amount equal to the employee's contribution has been excluded [Sec. 72(d)]. Dick will receive $800 per month from the pension and therefore will recover his contribution of $27,200 with his 34th payment, i.e., the March 1989 payment. No additional amounts can be excluded after the March 1989 check is received. Dick can exclude none of the $9,600 received in 1991.

85. Tina T. retired on December 31, 1990. Her employer-sponsored pension is $500 a month starting on January 31, 1991. Her pension cost was $8,000 and her expected return after the contract is $80,000. The amount of the pension to be included as income on Tina's 1991 tax return is

   a. $0.
   b. $600.
   c. $5,400.
   d. $6,000.

The correct answer is (c). *(Publisher)*
REQUIRED: The amount of pension first received by an employee after July 1, 1986 to be included in gross income in the first year of receipt.
DISCUSSION: Since this annuity began after July 1, 1986, the prior law rule allowing an employee to exclude all the annuity until recovery of his/her investment (when it would occur within 3 years) does not apply. Instead, this annuity is treated as any other annuity and an exclusion ratio is computed ($8,000 investment ÷ $80,000 expected return = 10%). Tina will receive $6,000 ($500 x 12 months) in 1991. She can exclude 10% of this, so $5,400 (90% of $6,000) must be included in gross income.

86. Tony D. retired on June 30, 1991 when his life expectancy was 10 years. Tony received $500 a month from a life annuity beginning July 31. During his working years Tony paid in a total of $20,000 as his contribution to the retirement plan. If Tony lives more than 10 years, how much of his retirement pay is includable in income in 2002?

   a. $0.
   b. $3,600.
   c. $4,000.
   d. $6,000.

The correct answer is (d). *(Publisher)*
REQUIRED: The amount of the annuity includable in income after recovery of the investment.
DISCUSSION: For annuities which began before 1987, the exclusion ratio is used for all payments even if the actual return is greater than the expected or estimated return. For annuities which begin after 1986, the total exclusion is limited to the investment. Tony's investment of $20,000 was fully recovered in 2001 (the end of his life expectancy on which the exclusion ratio was based). Therefore, all of the annuity is included in gross income in 2002.
Relatedly, if a person dies before recovering his/her investment in an annuity, the unrecovered portion is allowed as a deduction on his/her last tax return. But if a refund is to be paid to beneficiaries of the deceased annuitant, those beneficiaries are entitled to the deduction.

Module 4.8: Income from a Divorce

87. Peter has made contributions to an IRA for a number of years including both deductible and nondeductible contributions. He retires in 1991 and decides to withdraw the balance of the IRA as an annuity. Which of the following statements is correct about the taxability of the distribution?

 a. Peter is taxed on the entire amount he receives.
 b. Peter can exclude the portion of each annuity payment received in 1991 equal to his investment (nondeductible IRA contributions) in the contract divided by the annuity's expected return.
 c. Peter can exclude the portion of each annuity payment received in 1991 equal to his total contributions to the IRA divided by the annuity's expected return.
 d. Peter is not taxed on any amount he receives.

The correct answer is (b). *(Publisher)*
REQUIRED: The amount the taxpayer must include in his income as a result of receiving an annuity from his IRA.
DISCUSSION: The IRA distribution received after 1986 is taxed under the rules of Sec. 72 [as modified by Sec. 408(d)(2)]. If the benefits payable by an IRA are in the form of an annuity, then the recipient can exclude the amount of the payments received times the ratio that his investment in the contract (his nondeductible contributions to the IRA) bears to the annuity's expected return.
 Answer (a) is incorrect because the distribution is taxed as an annuity and Peter has an investment in the annuity from his nondeductible contributions. Answer (c) is incorrect because only nondeductible contributions provide Peter with an investment in the annuity. Answer (d) is incorrect because IRA distributions generally are taxable except when there is an investment in the annuity.

88. During July 1991, Mrs. R withdrew $5,000 from her IRA. At the end of 1991, the fair market value of her account, including earnings, was $17,500. Through 1991, her deductible contributions totaled $8,000 and her nondeductible contributions totaled $4,050. She did not have any tax-free withdrawals in earlier years. How much of the $5,000 distribution must Mrs. R include in her income for 1991?

 a. $0.
 b. $900.
 c. $4,100.
 d. $5,000.

The correct answer is (c). *(SPE 989 IV-75)*
REQUIRED: The amount the taxpayer must include in her income as a result of receiving a nonannuity distribution from her IRA.
DISCUSSION: If an IRA distribution is not in the form of an annuity, Sec. 408(d)(1) provides that it will be taxed under Sec. 72(e). The excluded portion of Mrs. R's payments equal the amount distributed in the year times the ratio that Mrs. R's investment in the contract (her nondeductible contributions to the IRA) bears to the sum of the value of the IRA at the end of the year plus the amounts distributed from the IRA during the year. The excludable portion of the 1991 payments equals $4,050 ÷ ($17,500 1991 year-end value + $5,000 1991 distributions) = 0.18. Mrs. R's exclusion equals $900 (0.18 x $5,000), therefore, her gross income inclusion is $4,100 ($5,000 − $900).

4.8 Income from a Divorce

89. Gertrude and Boomer were divorced in 1984 before July 18 (the effective date of the 1984 TRA). Boomer made the following payments to Gertrude in 1991 in accordance with the provisions of their decree:

Payments for children's welfare	$ 5,000
Indefinite periodic payments	12,000

How much must Gertrude include in her income as alimony in 1991?

 a. $0.
 b. $5,000.
 c. $12,000.
 d. $17,000.

The correct answer is (c). *(Publisher)*
REQUIRED: The amount the taxpayer must include in her income as alimony in 1991, if divorced in 1984.
DISCUSSION: Alimony payments are taxable to the recipient and deductible by the payor if such payments are periodic payments made pursuant to a decree of divorce or separate maintenance, pursuant to a written separation agreement, or pursuant to a decree for support executed prior to 1985. The payments also must be in discharge of a legal obligation arising from the marital or family relationship (old Sec. 71). Old Sec. 71(b) specifically provided that payments to support minor children are not alimony if the terms of such payments are fixed in the decree, instrument, or agreement. The $12,000 indefinite periodic payments are included in the taxpayer's income as alimony.

Module 4.8: Income from a Divorce

90. Richard and Alice Kelley lived apart during 1991 and did not file a joint tax return for the year. Under the terms of the written separation agreement they signed on July 1, 1991, Richard was required to pay Alice $1,500 per month of which $600 was designated as child support. He made six such payments in 1991. Additionally, Richard paid Alice $1,200 per month for the first six months of 1991, no portion of which was designated as child support. Assuming that Alice has no other income, her return for 1991 should show gross income of

- a. $0.
- b. $5,400.
- c. $9,000.
- d. $12,600.

The correct answer is (b). *(CPA 581 P-42)*
REQUIRED: The taxpayer's gross income arising from periodic payments from her spouse.
DISCUSSION: Sec. 71(b)(2) requires the recipient of cash payments made pursuant to a written separation agreement (entered into after 1984) to include these payments in gross income if they do not live together and if the payments are not required after the death of the recipient spouse. If the agreement specifies that a fixed portion is for support of a minor child, then that portion is excluded from gross income [Sec. 71(c)]. Since $600 was specifically designated as child support, only $900 ($1,500 minus $600) of each monthly payment is included in Alice's gross income for a total of $5,400 ($900 x 6 months). The $1,200 per month paid for the first six months is not included in Alice's gross income since these payments were made before the written separation agreement [Sec. 71(b)].

Questions 91 and 92 are based on the following data. Ana and Gus were granted a divorce in 1991. They had no children. In accordance with the decree, which specified that payments would cease at Ana's death, Gus made the following payments to Ana in 1991:

Lump-sum alimony settlement which the divorce decree specifies is not income to Ana or deductible by Gus	$25,000
Indefinite periodic payments	2,100

---

91. How much should Ana include in her 1991 taxable income as alimony?

- a. $0.
- b. $2,100.
- c. $25,000.
- d. $27,100.

The correct answer is (b). *(CPA 585 Q-21)*
REQUIRED: The amount includable in taxable income as alimony for 1991.
DISCUSSION: Payments to former spouses under a divorce decree entered after 1984 are treated as alimony if made in cash and if the divorce decree does not designate the payments as not included in gross income [Sec. 71(b)]. Since the divorce decree specifies that the lump-sum cash settlement is not income to Ana, it is not alimony. If the divorce decree had not specified this, the lump-sum payment would be alimony and treated as an excess alimony payment under Sec. 71(f). See Question 95.

92. Gus does not itemize his deductions. How much can Gus deduct as alimony in his 1991 return?

- a. $0.
- b. $2,100.
- c. $25,000.
- d. $27,100.

The correct answer is (b). *(CPA 585 Q-22)*
REQUIRED: The amount the payor may deduct as alimony.
DISCUSSION: Sec. 215 allows an above-the-line deduction for alimony paid in the amount which is includable in the gross income of the recipient under Sec. 71. Since it is an above-the-line deduction, it does not matter that Gus does not itemize.

Module 4.8: Income from a Divorce

93. Ed and Ann Ross were divorced in January 1991. In accordance with the divorce decree, Ed transferred the title in their home to Ann in 1991. The home, which had a fair market value of $150,000, was subject to a $50,000 mortgage that had 20 more years to run. Monthly mortgage payments amount to $1,000. Under the terms of settlement, Ed is obligated to make the mortgage payments on the home for the full remaining 20-year term of the indebtedness, regardless of how long Ann lives. Ed made 12 mortgage payments in 1991. What amount is taxable as alimony in Ann's 1991 return?

  a. $0.
  b. $12,000.
  c. $100,000.
  d. $112,000.

The correct answer is (a). *(CPA 1190 Q-25)*
REQUIRED: The amount taxable as alimony in Ann's gross income.
DISCUSSION: The monthly payments to Ann would normally be alimony to the extent of $1,000 a month. However, since they are required even if Ann dies, they are not alimony. In addition, receipt of the home does not qualify as alimony since it is not cash.

94. Stan and Anne were divorced in January 1991. The requirements of the divorce decree and Anne's performance follow:

Transfer the title in their resort condo to Stan. At the time of the transfer the condo had a basis to Anne of $75,000, a fair market value of $95,000, and was subject to a mortgage of $65,000.
Anne is to make the mortgage payments for 17 years regardless of how long Stan lives. Anne paid $8,000 in 1991.
Anne is to pay Stan $1,000 per month, beginning in February, for 10 years or until Stan dies. Of this amount, $300 is designated as child support. Anne made five payments of $900 each in 1991 (February - June).

What is the amount of alimony from this settlement that is includable in Stan's gross income for 1991?

  a. $3,000.
  b. $3,500.
  c. $11,000.
  d. $38,500.

The correct answer is (a). *(SPE 990 I-83)*
REQUIRED: The amount included in Stan's gross income in 1991 as alimony.
DISCUSSION: Sec. 71(a) provides that gross income includes amounts received as alimony or separate maintenance payments. Alimony is a payment in cash if such payment is received by a spouse under a divorce decree entered after 1984, but subject to certain requirements. Stan's receipt of title to the resort condo does not qualify as alimony since the payment was not in cash. The mortgage payments could be considered alimony even though paid to a third party since they are for the benefit of the payor's ex-spouse. Since they are required even if Stan dies, they are not alimony.

The monthly payments to Stan would normally be alimony to the extent of $700 per month (the amount in excess of that specified for child support). However, Anne did not pay the full amount of any of the payments in 1991. Sec. 71(c)(3) provides that, if any payment is less than the amount specified in the instrument, the payment should first be considered child support, and any excess will be alimony. Stan received alimony of $600 for each of the five payments, a total of $3,000 of alimony in 1991.

95. Jim and Ann were divorced in 1989 and the following alimony payments were made by Jim to Ann under their divorce decree:

$45,000 in 1989
$30,000 in 1990
$10,000 in 1991

How much must Jim include in gross income in 1991?

a. $0.
b. $5,000.
c. $17,500.
d. $25,000.

The correct answer is (c). *(Publisher)*
REQUIRED: The excess alimony payments included in the payor's gross income in the third year.
DISCUSSION: To prevent the front loading of alimony payments for early tax deductions, excess alimony payments from the first and second years are included in the payor's income in the third year (and are deductible by the recipient in the third year).

Excess alimony in the second year is alimony paid in the second year minus the sum of the statutory amount of $15,000 plus alimony paid in the third year. For Jim this is $5,000 [$30,000 − ($15,000 + $10,000)].

Excess alimony in the first year is alimony paid in the first year minus the sum of (1) $15,000 plus (2) the average of (a) alimony paid in the second year less excess alimony in the second year plus (b) alimony paid in the third year. For Jim, this is calculated as follows:

1st year alimony paid		$ 45,000
Less statutory amount		(15,000)
Less average of:		
2nd year alimony paid	$30,000	
Less 2nd year excess alimony	(5,000)	
3rd year alimony paid	10,000	
	$35,000	
Divided by 2	÷ 2	(17,500)
1st Year Excess Alimony		$ 12,500

The total excess alimony in the amount of $17,500 ($5,000 + $12,500) is included in Jim's income in 1991.

96. A provision agreed to by both parties in a divorce instrument, that payments otherwise qualifying as alimony will not be so treated for tax purposes, will be recognized and followed for federal income tax purposes.

The correct answer is (T). *(SPE 987 I-18)*
DISCUSSION: Payments to former spouses under a divorce decree entered after 1984 are treated as alimony if made in cash and if the divorce decree does not designate the payments as not included in gross income [Sec. 71(b)]. If the divorce instrument (decree) specifies that payments will not be treated as alimony (included in the recipients gross income), this provision will be recognized and followed for federal income tax purposes.

4.9 Assignment of Income

97. Big Bucks owns corporate bonds with detachable interest coupons. Interest of $1,000 is payable each January 1 and July 1. On December 31, 1990, Big Bucks gave his son the coupons for the interest payments due on January 1 and July 1, 1991. When the interest is received by Son in 1991, how is it taxed?

a. $1,000 to Big Bucks and $1,000 to Son.
b. $2,000 to Son.
c. $2,000 to Big Bucks.
d. None, since $2,000 was taxed to Big Bucks in 1990.

The correct answer is (c). *(Publisher)*
REQUIRED: The taxation of interest from coupons transferred by gift.
DISCUSSION: Income earned from property is taxed to the person who owns the property. Interest coupons only represent the income and are not the property which earns the income. The corporate bonds are considered to be the property which earns the interest. Therefore, Big Bucks was merely assigning income when he gave the coupons to his son. The entire $2,000 is taxed to Big Bucks when it is received by Son since he still owns the bonds.

This is known as the fruit and the tree doctrine. The fruit (income) cannot be separated from the tree (property).

Module 4.9: Assignment of Income

98. Use the same facts as in the previous question, except that Big Bucks transfers the bonds and the coupons on December 31, 1990. How is the income taxed?

    a. $1,000 to Big Bucks and $1,000 to Son.

    b. $2,000 to Son.

    c. $2,000 to Big Bucks.

    d. $1,000 to Big Bucks and $2,000 to Son.

99. Janice purchased $10,000 in Series HH bonds with her own money and had them issued in her and her son's name as co-owners. During 1991, Janice and her son received $600 in interest on the bonds. Janice allowed her son Mark to keep the full $600 of interest income. For 1991, how should the interest be reported for federal income tax purposes?

    a. Neither Janice or Mark have to report interest income.

    b. $300 by Janice and $300 by Mark.

    c. $600 by Janice.

    d. $600 by Mark.

100. On January 1, 1991, Mr. J invested in two Series HH bonds. Bond No. 1 was issued in his and his son's name as co-owners. Bond No. 2 was issued in J's son's name with Mr. J named as the sole beneficiary. In 1991, Bonds No. 1 and No. 2 paid interest of $900 and $1,000, respectively. What amount of interest income should be reported by Mr. J and his son for 1991?

	Mr. J	Mr. J's Son
a.	$450	$1,450
b.	$950	$950
c.	$1,450	$450
d.	$1,900	$0

The correct answer is (a). *(Publisher)*
REQUIRED: The taxation of interest from bonds when the bonds and coupons are transferred by gift.
DISCUSSION: Income earned from property is taxed to the person who owns the property. Bonds are the property on which the interest is earned. Interest accrued prior to the transfer is taxed to Big Bucks when it is received by Son and interest accrued after the transfer is taxed to Son. Big Bucks and Son will each be taxed on $1,000 in 1991.

The correct answer is (b). *(SPE 989 I-39)*
REQUIRED: The correct reporting of interest income received by the co-owners of series HH bonds.
DISCUSSION: Income earned from property is taxed to the person who owns the property. When Janice purchased the bonds with her own money and named herself and her son as co-owners, she made a gift of one-half of the bonds to her son. One-half of the interest ($300) is taxable to each co-owner.
Author's Note: Alternatively, if one assumes that a completed gift of one-half of the bond is not made until Janice does more than make Mark a co-owner, then all $600 is reported by Janice.

The correct answer is (c). *(SPE 986 I-47)*
REQUIRED: The amount of interest income to be reported by owners of bonds.
DISCUSSION: Income earned from property is taxed to the person who owns the property. When Mr. J purchased Bond No. 1, he made a gift of one-half of the bond to his son. Therefore, each taxpayer should include one-half of the interest from Bond No. 1 in his income. Although Mr. J put Bond No. 2 in the name of his son, he did not really make a complete transfer since he is the beneficiary. Therefore, all the interest from Bond No. 2 will be included in Mr. J's income.
Mr. J's interest income is thus $1,450 ($450 from Bond No. 1 and $1,000 from Bond No. 2). The son's interest income is $450 from Bond No. 1.
Author's note: Again, if one assumes that a completed gift of one-half of Bond No. 1 is not made until Mr. J. does more than make his son a co-owner, then all $1,900 is reported by Mr. J.

101. Carter obtained a new job in Washington, D.C. in which she was to receive a substantially larger salary than before. Carter decided to give one-half of this salary to her spouse and they executed a legal document under which Carter's spouse was required to receive one-half of her salary. This document was given to Carter's employer with directions to issue two checks each pay period, one to Carter and one to Carter's spouse. Carter's salary for the year 1991 is $100,000. What are the tax consequences of this transaction?

  a. Carter must include $50,000 in gross income and Carter's spouse must include $50,000 in gross income.
  b. Carter must include $100,000 in gross income.
  c. Carter has made a taxable gift of $50,000.
  d. The person actually receiving the checks must include them in his/her gross income.

The correct answer is (b). *(Publisher)*
REQUIRED: The tax effect of an assignment of an employee's salary to his/her spouse.
DISCUSSION: The person who earns income is taxed on it. Although the money or property received as income can be legally assigned, the person who earned the income still must report it as his/her gross income. The amount that the assignee then receives may be a gift. Since Carter earned the $100,000 of salary, Carter must include all of it in gross income.

Answer (a) is incorrect because Carter's spouse need not include any amount in gross income. Answer (c) is incorrect because there is a deduction for gifts to a spouse in computing taxable gifts under Sec. 2523. If Carter assigned part of her salary to another person, a taxable gift might be made. Answer (d) is incorrect because the person who earns the salary must include it in income, not the person who receives the checks.

Note that in states with community property law (AZ, CA, ID, LA, NV, NM, TX, WA, WI), each spouse is usually considered to earn one-half of each other's earnings. This is valid for income tax purposes also.

102. Tycoon owned an office building subject to a lease on which the rent for the year was paid at year-end in December. Tycoon legally assigned the lease to her daughter on July 1, 1991. In December 1991, Daughter received $12,000 of rent under the lease. How is this rental income taxed?

  a. $12,000 to Daughter.
  b. $12,000 to Tycoon.
  c. $6,000 to Tycoon and $6,000 to Daughter.
  d. $12,000 to Tycoon and $12,000 to Daughter.

The correct answer is (b). *(Publisher)*
REQUIRED: The amount and person taxed on rental income when a lease is transferred by gift.
DISCUSSION: Income earned on property is taxed to the person who owns the property. A lease merely represents the right to income from property. The building is the property on which rental income is earned. Therefore, the assignment of a lease is merely the assignment of income. Tycoon will be taxed on the entire amount of rent received by Daughter under the lease. Daughter has no income because she is merely the recipient of an assignment of income.

103. Use the same facts as in the previous question, except that Tycoon transfers her entire interest in the office building on July 1, 1991. How is the income taxed?

  a. $12,000 to Daughter.
  b. $12,000 to Tycoon.
  c. $6,000 to Daughter and $6,000 to Tycoon.
  d. $6,000 to Tycoon and $12,000 to Daughter.

The correct answer is (c). *(Publisher)*
REQUIRED: The person and amount taxed on rental income when the entire property is transferred by gift.
DISCUSSION: Income earned on property is taxed to the person who owns the property. Since Tycoon owned the building for the first half of the year, she will be taxed on one-half of the rental earned on the building. Since Daughter owned the building for the second half of the year, she will be taxed on the other one-half of the income earned from the building. In this case, only $6,000 of income was assigned (the amount attributable to the period of time during which Tycoon owned the building). Remember, the fruit (income) follows the tree (property).

Module 4.10: Income on Final Returns

104. During 1987, Mr. P furnished the money to buy Series EE U.S. Savings Bonds issued in his name and his brother's name (as co-owners). No election was made to report the interest earned in income each year. During 1991, P's brother cashed the bonds and kept all of the proceeds for his personal use. Mr. P's brother must include the interest earned on the bonds in his gross income for 1991.

The correct answer is (F). *(SPE 988 I-7)*
DISCUSSION: The IRS takes the position that when one person purchases Series EE U.S. Savings Bonds solely with his/her own money and names another person as co-owner, the interest is taxable to the person who furnished the money even if the other co-owner redeems the bond and keeps all of the proceeds. Therefore, in the question, all of the interest would be taxed to Mr. P since he furnished the money to buy the bond (Rev. Rul. 54-143).

If it can be proven that a gift was made equal to one-half the value of the bond when the bond is issued in both names, then one-half interest should be taxable to each co-owner. This might be proven by a written and signed declaration of gift, filing a gift tax return, etc.

4.10 Income on Final Returns

105. All of the following items of income are reported on a cash basis decedent's final income tax return except

a. Paycheck received 1 day before death, cashed 1 week after death.

b. Cash dividend declared before death and received 2 days after death.

c. Distributive share of partnership income for the partnership's tax year ending within or with the decedent's last tax year.

d. Earnings on certificate of deposit credited to decedent's account before death.

The correct answer is (b). *(SPE 990 III-51)*
REQUIRED: The income item not reported on a cash basis decedent's final income tax return.
DISCUSSION: For a cash basis taxpayer, only those amounts actually or constructively received prior to death are included in the final return. A cash dividend declared before death and received after death would not be actually or constructively received before death and would not be reported on the decedent's final tax return.

Answers (a) and (d) are incorrect because both the paycheck and the interest earnings to the date of death would be considered constructively received and would be reported as income on the final return. Answer (c) is incorrect because under Sec. 706(a), a partner would include his/her distributive share of partnership income if the partnership's taxable year ends within the partner's taxable year.

106. Mr. K, a calendar-year, cash-basis taxpayer, died on September 30, 1991. From the following transactions, determine the amount of gross income that would not be includable in Mr. K's final income tax return.

Salary received January 1 until his death	$ 8,000
Commission earned that was not received in 1991	10,000
Rental income due 9/30/92, collected 10/15/91	3,350
Passbook savings account interest income credited to K from 1/1/91 to 9/30/91	930
Passbook savings account interest credited to K for the period 10/1/91 to 12/31/91	200

a. $8,000.
b. $8,930.
c. $13,550.
d. $22,280.

The correct answer is (c). *(SPE 1082 III-83)*
REQUIRED: The amount of gross income that is not included on the decedent's final return.
DISCUSSION: As a cash-basis taxpayer, Mr. K recognized income only when actually or constructively received. Therefore, only those amounts actually or constructively received prior to his death are included in his final return. The items which are not included in his final return are the commission paid after death, the rental income collected after death, and the passbook savings interest accruing after death.

Commission	$10,000
Rental income	3,350
Interest after 9/30/91	200
Income not in final return	$13,550

107. All of the following statements are correct regarding the final return of a decedent except

    a. On the final return of a deceased taxpayer, all income is reported on the accrual method.

    b. A net operating loss from business operations sustained by a decedent during his/her last tax year is deductible only on the decedent's final income tax return.

    c. If medical expenses incurred in the year of death are paid by the estate during the 1-year period beginning with the day after death, the executor may elect to treat all or part of the medical expenses as paid by the decedent and deduct them on the final return if deductions are itemized.

    d. Any credit that applied to the decedent before death may be claimed on the final income tax return.

The correct answer is (a). *(SPE 1085 I-50)*
REQUIRED: The item that is false regarding the final return of a decedent.
DISCUSSION: On the final return of a deceased taxpayer, all income is reported using the same accounting method the taxpayer used before death. For most taxpayers, this is the cash method. If the accrual method is used, income accruable to the date of death is included, but not income accruable only because of death [Sec. 451(b)].
Answers (b), (c), and (d) are incorrect because each is a true statement.

108. Mr. D, a single, calendar-year, cash-method taxpayer, died on October 1, 1991. Mr. D owned and operated an auto repair shop until his death. Income and expenses with respect to this business for 1991 are as follows:

Fees billed but unpaid at 10/1/91	$ 500
Checks from customers not yet cashed	100
Fees deposited since 1/1/91	1,000
Supplies purchased but unpaid at 10/1/91	200
Supplies purchased and paid for at 10/1/91	400

Mr. D's final return, Form 1040, should reflect $1,000 in gross receipts and $400 in expenses.

The correct answer is (F). *(SPE 1078 III-46)*
DISCUSSION: Since the decedent is a cash-method taxpayer, income is recognized if actually or constructively received prior to death and expenses are deducted if actually paid prior to death. Checks from the customers on hand but uncashed constitute income received by the taxpayer prior to his death because they are the equivalent of cash. These must be included in gross income along with the fees deposited, giving Mr. D gross income of $1,100. Only the supplies purchased and actually paid for prior to the decedent's death are recognized as expenses, i.e., $400.

109. Mr. F, a cash-basis farmer, died on June 30, 1991. Before his death he sold and delivered corn worth $10,000; however, payment was not received until July 1, 1991. The $10,000 should be included in Mr. F's final income tax return.

The correct answer is (F). *(SPE 1079 I-2)*
DISCUSSION: Since the decedent is a cash-basis taxpayer, income is recognized only if actually or constructively received prior to his death. Since he did not actually or constructively receive the payment for the corn prior to his death, the $10,000 should not be included in his final income tax return.

110. Mr. W, a cash basis accountant, rendered services in the amount of $5,000 during May 1991. Mr. W died on June 1, 1991 and the $5,000 payment was received on June 15, 1991. The $5,000 should be included in Mr. W's final return.

The correct answer is (F). *(SPE 989 III-24)*
DISCUSSION: Since the decedent is a cash-basis taxpayer, income is recognized only if actually or constructively received prior to death. As Mr. W did not actually or constructively receive payment for the services prior to his death, the $5,000 should not be included in his final income tax return.

CHAPTER FIVE
EXCLUSIONS FROM GROSS INCOME

5.1 Dividends and Interest	(6 questions)	73
5.2 Compensation for Injuries or Sickness	(6 questions)	75
5.3 Employee Benefits	(26 questions)	77
5.4 Social Security Benefits	(5 questions)	86
5.5 Payments Made at Death	(7 questions)	87
5.6 Scholarships and Fellowships	(5 questions)	89
5.7 Foreign Income Exclusions	(6 questions)	91
5.8 Gifts and Prizes	(6 questions)	93

5.1 Dividends and Interest

See Chapter 18 for stock dividends and other distributions to shareholders.

1. Henry Adams, an unmarried taxpayer, received the following amounts during 1991

Interest on savings accounts	$1,000
Interest on municipal bonds used for road construction	500
Dividends on General Steel common stock	750
Dividends on life insurance policies	200

Adams should report taxable income, after exclusions, if any, from dividends and interest for 1991 in the total amount of

a. $1,650.
b. $1,750.
c. $1,850.
d. $2,150.

The correct answer is (b). *(CPA 581 P-45)*
REQUIRED: The amount of taxable dividend and interest income after exclusions.
DISCUSSION: The interest on the savings account is included in gross income. The interest on municipal bonds is generally excluded by Sec. 103. The dividends on life insurance policies are generally considered a return of premiums or capital and are not included in gross income (provided the cumulative dividends do not exceed the cumulative premiums paid). There is no exclusion for the dividends from U.S. corporations unless such dividends are a return of capital to the taxpayer (see Chapter 18). Therefore, Adams should report income of $1,750 ($1,000 interest + $750 of General Steel dividends).

2. Gary and Gladys invest in bonds. In 1991, they received the following interest

California general revenue bonds	$ 800
New York City sanitation fund bonds	1,000
Seattle School District bonds	400
AT&T 20-year bonds	600

The bonds are neither private activity bonds nor arbitrage bonds. How much interest income may Gary and Gladys exclude from gross income on their joint return?

a. $0.
b. $800.
c. $1,800.
d. $2,200.

The correct answer is (d). *(Publisher)*
REQUIRED: The amount of interest income from bonds excludable from gross income.
DISCUSSION: Under Sec. 103, gross income does not include interest on obligations of a state or any political subdivision thereof. The use of the proceeds of the bonds does not ordinarily change the taxation of the interest (although special rules apply in the case of private activity bonds and arbitrage bonds).
Therefore, Gary and Gladys may exclude the interest from all the municipal bonds (as listed below) but must include the $600 of interest from the AT&T bonds in gross income.

California general revenue bonds	$ 800
New York City sanitation fund bonds	1,000
Seattle School District bonds	400
Total excluded interest	$2,200

Module 5.1: Dividends and Interest

3. Which of the following distributions is nontaxable?
   a. Mutual fund distribution from its net realized long-term capital gains in the amount of $1,000. You have an adjusted basis of $10,000 in the mutual fund.
   b. Return of capital distribution from a utility company in the amount of $2,000. You have a zero basis in this stock.
   c. Dividend on insurance policy in the amount of $1,000. As of the date of this dividend, your net premiums exceed the total dividends by $3,500.
   d. Your share of an ordinary dividend received by an S corporation in the amount of $25,000.

The correct answer is (c). *(SPE 986 I-49)*
REQUIRED: The distribution that is nontaxable.
DISCUSSION: Dividends on insurance policies are treated under Sec. 72(e). They are excluded from gross income when the cumulative dividends do not exceed the cumulative premiums (provided the cash value does not exceed the net investment, which it normally does not).
Answer (a) is incorrect because mutual fund (regulated investment company) distributions of capital gains are included in the shareholders' incomes (Sec. 852). Answer (b) is incorrect because a return of capital distribution is taxable as a gain when it exceeds basis. Answer (d) is incorrect because a dividend received by an S corporation is taxable to the shareholder whether or not it is distributed.

4. Which of the following bonds can be a tax-exempt bond if issued in 1991 so that the interest therefrom may be excluded from gross income?
   a. A $1 million bond issued by a municipality with 50% of the proceeds to be used by a private developer to create an industrial neighborhood of offices and warehouses, and the developer will use sales and rents to repay 50% of the bond issue.
   b. A $1 million bond issued by a city with 50% of the proceeds to be invested in higher yielding corporate bonds.
   c. A $1 million bond issued by a state with all the proceeds to be used to finance student loans.
   d. A $1 million bond issued by a city with all the proceeds to be used to help finance a sports stadium owned by a nongovernment company.

The correct answer is (c). *(Publisher)*
REQUIRED: The bond issued in 1991 which may qualify as tax-exempt.
DISCUSSION: Under Sec. 103, interest on a state or local government bond is tax-exempt if the bond is not a private activity bond (unless it meets certain qualifications), is not an arbitrage bond, and if it is properly registered. If the proceeds are used to finance student loans, it might be a private activity bond if the loans are provided through private banks. But even if it is a private activity bond, it is tax exempt because the proceeds are used for student loans.
Answers (a) and (d) are incorrect because each describes a private activity bond (more than 10% of the proceeds are for a nongovernmental trade or business and to be repaid by the same) to be used for nonqualified industrial development purposes. Answer (b) is incorrect because it describes an arbitrage bond, i.e., where funds acquired through low-interest bonds are reinvested in higher yielding bonds.

5. Which of the following is a requirement for the exclusion of interest from U.S. savings bonds issued at a discount?
   a. The bonds must be issued after 1989.
   b. The entire amount of the bonds must be used for higher education expenses.
   c. The bonds must be redeemed by the child(ren) attending school.
   d. The taxpayer redeeming them must have adjusted gross income of $50,000 or more.

The correct answer is (a). *(Publisher)*
REQUIRED: The statement which is a correct requirement in order to exclude interest from a U.S. savings bond.
DISCUSSION: A new Sec. 135 provides an exclusion for interest on U.S. savings bonds issued at a discount (Series EE bonds) to the extent spent on higher education for the year. One of the requirements, in order to exclude such interest, is that the bonds be issued after 1989.
Answer (b) is incorrect because the total amount of the bonds need not be used for higher education expenses. If the total redemption amount (principle and interest) exceeds the education expenses for the year, a proportional part of the interest is excluded. Answer (c) is incorrect because the bonds must be redeemed by the person to whom they are issued. Furthermore, the bonds must be issued to an individual age 24 or more and may not be transferred or the interest is no longer eligible. Answer (d) is incorrect because the exclusion is phased out as modified adjusted gross income exceeds $40,000 or $60,000 (adjusted after 1990 for inflation) if filing a joint return.

6. Mr. T elected to participate in the dividend reinvestment plan of Power & Light, a public utility. Under the plan, he chose to use the dividends paid to him by the utility to purchase additional shares in Power & Light at the current market price in place of receiving cash. In 1991, Mr. T received 20 shares of common stock from Power & Light instead of a $2,000 cash dividend. Mr. T may exclude the $2,000 from his gross income in 1991.

The correct answer is (F). *(SPE 990 I-6)*
DISCUSSION: Prior to 1986, in a public utility dividend reinvestment plan, shareholders could elect to receive stock of the utility rather than cash or other property and exclude it from gross income. However, the exclusion is no longer available after 1985; therefore, Mr. T must include the dividend in gross income.

5.2 Compensation for Injuries or Sickness

7. Which of the following is not excluded from gross income of the recipient taxpayer?

   a. Workers' compensation benefits.
   b. Payments in lieu of wages (while not able to work due to an injury) from an insurance policy paid for by the taxpayer.
   c. Payments in lieu of wages (while not able to work due to an injury) from an insurance policy paid for by the taxpayer's employer.
   d. Lump-sum payment from an insurance policy for loss of a hand in an automobile accident.

The correct answer is (c). *(Publisher)*
REQUIRED: The item included in the gross income of the recipient taxpayer.
DISCUSSION: Sec. 104 generally excludes amounts received through accident or health insurance for personal injuries or sickness. However, Sec. 105 provides that amounts received by an employee through accident or health insurance paid for by the employer are included in the employee's gross income unless the amounts are for medical care or loss of a body part. Therefore, the payments in lieu of wages from an insurance policy paid for by the taxpayer's employer must be included in the employee's gross income.
Answer (a) is incorrect because Sec. 104(a) specifically exempts workers' compensation benefits for personal injuries or sickness. Answer (b) is incorrect because Sec. 104(a) specifically exempts amounts received through accident or health insurance for personal injuries or sickness provided the insurance policy is not paid for by the employer. Answer (d) is incorrect because Sec. 104(a) specifically exempts amounts received through accident or health insurance for personal injuries, and Sec. 105(c) exempts payments for loss of a body part even if the insurance is paid for by the employer.

8. In 1990, John incurred $2,000 of medical expenses but was able to deduct $500 of them because of deduction limitations. In 1991, John received a reimbursement from his insurance company (he pays his own premiums) of $1,600 of his 1990 medical expenses. How much of the insurance reimbursement can John exclude?

   a. $0.
   b. $1,100.
   c. $1,500.
   d. $1,600.

The correct answer is (b). *(Publisher)*
REQUIRED: The amount of an insurance reimbursement for medical expenses that can be excluded when part of the expenses were previously deducted.
DISCUSSION: Sec. 104(a) specifically excludes amounts received through accident or health insurance for personal injuries or sickness, but not to the extent that the medical expenses were deducted in a prior year. Since John deducted $500 of the medical expenses in 1990, only $1,100 of the insurance reimbursement ($1,600 − $500) is excluded in 1991. John must include the other $500 of the reimbursement in gross income.

9. Mrs. R is covered under her employer's medical insurance policy. The annual premium for Mrs. R's coverage is $2,000, of which Mrs. R's employer pays 75%. Mrs. R pays the rest. In 1991, Mrs. R received reimbursement of $200 from the insurance company in excess of her actual medical expenses. What amount must Mrs. R include in her gross income?

  a. $0.
  b. $50.
  c. $150.
  d. $200.

The correct answer is (c). *(SPE 984 I-80)*
REQUIRED: The amount of health insurance reimbursement to be included in gross income.
DISCUSSION: Sec. 105(a) provides that amounts received by an employee through accident and health insurance shall be included in gross income to the extent such amounts (1) are attributable to contributions by the employer that were not includable in the gross income of the employee, or (2) are paid by the employer. Sec. 105(b) excludes amounts that would normally be included in gross income under Sec. 105(a) if such amounts are paid to reimburse the taxpayer for expenses incurred for medical care. Since Mrs. R received reimbursement of $200 in excess of her medical expenses, Sec. 105(a) requires that 75% of this amount ($150) be included in her income.

10. Ivan Turner, a truck driver, was injured in an accident in the course of his employment in 1991. As a result of injuries sustained, he received the following payments in 1991:

Damages for back injuries	$5,000
Workers' compensation	500
Reimbursement from his employer's accident and health plan for medical expenses paid by Turner in 1991. (The employer's contribution to the plan was $475 in 1991.)	750

The amount to be included in Turner's 1991 gross income should be

  a. $5,000.
  b. $750.
  c. $475.
  d. $0.

The correct answer is (d). *(CPA 574 Q-24)*
REQUIRED: The amount included in gross income arising from payments received from a job-related accident.
DISCUSSION: Sec. 104(a) specifically excludes from gross income amounts received under workers' compensation acts as compensation for personal injuries or sickness and the amount of any damages received (whether by suit or agreement) on account of personal injuries or sickness. Therefore, the damages for personal injuries and workers' compensation Turner received would not be included in gross income. Sec. 105(b) excludes payments received from an employer as medical expense reimbursements except to the extent such amounts relate to medical expenses which were deducted by the taxpayer in a prior year. Therefore, Turner's 1991 gross income should include none of the payments listed.

11. Donald, an accountant, was falsely accused of fraud by a local newspaper. He sued the newspaper for libel claiming damages both to his personal reputation in the community and to his business. In 1991 the jury awarded Donald the following:

$10,000 for his personal reputation
$70,000 for his business loss
$70,000 as punitive damages (to punish the newspaper)

How much can Donald exclude from gross income?

  a. $0.
  b. $10,000.
  c. $30,000.
  d. $80,000.

The correct answer is (b). *(Publisher)*
REQUIRED: The amount of a recovery from a libel lawsuit that may be excluded from gross income.
DISCUSSION: Sec. 104(a)(2) excludes from gross income "the amount of any damages received (whether by suit or agreement and whether as lump sums or periodic payments) on account of personal injuries or sickness." The Revenue Reconciliation Act of 1989 amended Sec. 104(a) by making punitive damages received by suit or agreement in connection with a case not involving physical injury or physical sickness no longer excludable from gross income under Sec. 104(a). If the $10,000 awarded to Donald as damages to his personal reputation is considered to be a personal injury under Sec. 104(a)(2), then the exclusion will apply in spite of his having no physical injury or physical sickness. The $70,000 of punitive damages are not generally excludable under Sec. 104(a) since they do not arise out of physical injury or physical sickness. A transitional rule applies to suits filed on or before July 10, 1989 or agreements entered into, court decrees issued, or mediation awards in effect on July 10, 1989. The $70,000 for business loss is taxable to Donald as a substitute for compensation he would have otherwise earned.

12. Disability payments received from a health or accident plan whose premiums were paid entirely by the employee are taxable if they total more than 50% of the individual's adjusted gross income.

The correct answer is (F). *(Publisher)*
DISCUSSION: Disability payments are generally to replace income lost when an employee is injured or sick. Sec. 104(a) specifically excludes amounts received through accident or health insurance for personal injuries or sickness. It does not matter whether they are reimbursement for medical expenses or for lost income. The entire amount is excluded regardless of the individual's adjusted gross income.

5.3 Employee Benefits

Author's Note: The Tax Extension Act of 1991 (P.L. 100-227) extended the following income exclusion provisions for 6 months:

Code Sec.	Income Exclusion Provision
120	Employer-provided group legal services
127	Employer-provided educational assistance benefits

For tax years beginning in 1992, the exclusion is generally available only for amounts paid or provided by the employer before July 1, 1992.

13. Mr. Hawk, a factory assembly line worker, received the following benefits from his employer during 1991:

Medical insurance plan policy	$250
Christmas bonus	125
Reimbursement for college physics course under a nondiscriminatory written plan	450
$40,000 nondiscriminatory group-term life insurance policy	475
Membership in a local health club	550

How much is includable in Mr. Hawk's income?

a. $675.
b. $925.
c. $1,050.
d. $1,125.

The correct answer is (a). *(Publisher)*
REQUIRED: The amount of fringe benefits includable in gross income.
DISCUSSION: Benefits received from an employer are compensation for services and included in gross income under Sec. 61 unless provided otherwise. Sec. 106 excludes from gross income contributions to accident or health plans (a medical insurance plan) made by an employer on behalf of the employee. Sec. 79 provides for the inclusion in gross income of the cost of group-term life insurance paid by the employer, but only to the extent that such cost exceeds the cost of $50,000 of such insurance provided the plan is not discriminatory. The cost of Mr. Hawk's group-term life insurance would not be included in gross income.
  Sec. 127, which provides an exclusion of payments made to reimburse an employee for educational expenses, was amended by the 1990 tax act to apply to tax year 1991. Therefore, the reimbursement for the physics course would be excluded from income. As there is no provision excluding Christmas bonuses or memberships in off-premises health clubs, $675 ($125 bonus + $550 membership) is includable in gross income.

14. Which of the following will be included in the gross income of a highly compensated employee if provided to such employees on a discriminatory basis?

a. No-additional-cost service.
b. Working condition fringe.
c. De minimis fringe.
d. Free parking.

The correct answer is (a). *(Publisher)*
REQUIRED: The fringe benefit included in income if provided on a discriminatory basis.
DISCUSSION: Each of the listed fringe benefits is excluded under Sec. 132. However, no-additional-cost services and employee discounts are excludable by an officer, owner, or highly compensated employee only if they are also available at substantially the same terms to the other employees [Sec. 132(h)(1)]. The other fringe benefits may be provided by an employer on a discriminatory basis (except for eating facilities).

Module 5.3: Employee Benefits

15. Eagle Airlines operates solely as an air carrier. It allows all its employees to fly at no charge on any of its flights provided that paying customers are not displaced. Eagle has a reciprocal agreement with Diversified, Inc. (which is in both the airline and hotel businesses) under which the employees of one company may use the facilities of the other without charge provided that paying customers are not displaced. Which of the following benefits may an Eagle employee exclude from gross income?

  a. A flight on an Eagle airplane only.
  b. A flight on an Eagle airplane or a Diversified airplane.
  c. A flight on either company's airplane and use of Diversified's hotels.
  d. None. Services provided by an employer are income.

The correct answer is (b). *(Publisher)*
REQUIRED: The no-additional-cost service that may be excluded from gross income.
DISCUSSION: Sec. 132(a)(1) excludes from gross income no-additional-cost services provided by an employer to an employee. The service must be one normally sold to customers in the ordinary course of business and in the same line of business in which the employee works. Also, the employer must not incur substantial additional costs. Employees may also exclude the same type of services provided by another related employer if the employers have a reciprocal agreement. Since an Eagle employee works in the airline business, (s)he may exclude a flight provided by Eagle or Diversified.
Answer (a) is incorrect because an airline employee may exclude a flight on either company's airplane, since the companies have a reciprocal agreement. Answer (c) is incorrect because an Eagle employee does not work in the hotel business, so (s)he cannot exclude use of one of Diversified's hotels. Answer (d) is incorrect because Sec. 132 permits the exclusion of this kind of fringe benefit.

16. Midwest Department Stores allows all its employees to purchase goods worth up to $1,000 in retail value each year at a 50% discount. Mark, an employee of Midwest, took full advantage of this policy 1 year and received a $500 discount. Midwest's gross profit percentage on sales to customers is 45%. The normal industry discount was only 30%. How much must Mark include in gross income?

  a. $0.
  b. $50.
  c. $200.
  d. $500.

The correct answer is (b). *(Publisher)*
REQUIRED: The amount of an employee discount that must be included in gross income.
DISCUSSION: Sec. 132(a)(2) provides an exclusion from gross income for qualified discounts provided by an employer to an employee. The amount of the discount must not exceed the employer's gross profit percentage based on the price normally sold to customers.
Since Midwest's gross profit percentage is normally 45%, any discount in excess of 45% must be included in the employee's gross income. Here the excess discount is 5% (50% − 45%). Accordingly, Mark must include $50 in his gross income (5% x $1,000).

17. Mary is a CPA who works for a public accounting firm. How much of the following fringe benefits are excluded from her gross income if paid for or provided by her employer?

Membership in CPA association	$ 75
Subscription to a banking association journal (she has several bank clients)	40
Parking at her office	250
Personal photocopying on office machine	10
Coffee and doughnuts	20

  a. $135.
  b. $290.
  c. $385.
  d. $395.

The correct answer is (d). *(Publisher)*
REQUIRED: The amount of fringe benefits excludable by an employee from gross income.
DISCUSSION: Sec. 132 provides an exclusion from gross income of an employee for working condition fringe benefits and de minimis fringe benefits provided by an employer. A CPA's membership in a CPA association and a subscription to a banking association journal for someone who has bank clients are considered working condition fringe benefits. Parking is specifically listed as a fringe benefit under Sec. 132(h)(4). Personal use of a photocopy machine and free coffee and doughnuts are examples of de minimis fringe benefits. Hence, all of the fringe benefits listed are excludable from Mary's gross income. These benefits total $395.

Module 5.3: Employee Benefits

18. For 1991, all of the following fringe benefits may be excluded from gross income except

a. Qualified employee discounts.

b. On-premises athletic facilities.

c. Payments under a plan for educational assistance for graduate level courses and advanced degrees.

d. Employer-provided transportation, such as a van pool, used for commuting purposes.

The correct answer is (d). *(SPE 989 I-38)*
REQUIRED: The type of fringe benefits which may not be excluded from income for 1991.
DISCUSSION: Code Sec. 124, which formerly provided an exclusion for qualified transportation provided by an employer, such as an employer-provided van pool, has been repealed for tax years after 1985, and the amount of such a fringe benefit must be included in income.
Answer (a) is incorrect because Sec. 132 provides an exclusion from gross income for qualified discounts provided by an employer to an employee. Answer (b) is incorrect because Sec. 132(h)(5) provides an exclusion for the value of on-premises athletic facilities. Answer (c) is incorrect because the Revenue Reconciliation Act of 1990 amended Sec. 127, which provides an exclusion for educational assistance programs, to include payments made under such a plan for graduate level courses and advanced degrees. The 1990 tax act also extended the provision to apply to taxable years beginning before December 31, 1991.

19. Mr. T has been a night watchman at Y Company for 10 years. During 1991, he received the following payments from Y Company

Salary	$15,000
Hospitalization insurance premiums	3,600
Required lodging on Y's premises for Y's convenience as a condition to T's employment	2,400
Reward for preventing a break-in	1,000
Christmas ham (value)	15

What amount is includable in Mr. T's gross income for 1991?

a. $17,400.

b. $16,015.

c. $16,000.

d. $15,000.

The correct answer is (c). *(SPE 1080 I-66)*
REQUIRED: The amount includable in Mr. T's gross income.
DISCUSSION: The hospitalization insurance premiums paid by Mr. T's employer are excluded from gross income under Sec. 106. Since Mr. T was required to live on Y's premises both for Y's convenience and as a condition for his employment, the cost of such lodging is excluded from gross income under Sec. 119. The Christmas ham is excluded from gross income under Sec. 132 as a de minimis fringe. Therefore, Mr. T's salary of $15,000 and the reward of $1,000 are the only items included in gross income as compensation for services rendered (Sec. 61).

20. Ernest Sosa files a joint return with his wife. Sosa's employer pays 100% of the cost of all employees' group-term life insurance under a qualified plan. What is the maximum amount of coverage that may be provided tax-free by his employer under this plan?

a. $5,000.

b. $10,000.

c. $50,000.

d. $100,000.

The correct answer is (c). *(CPA 1183 Q-40)*
REQUIRED: The maximum amount of group-term life insurance that may be provided by an employer tax-free to an employee.
DISCUSSION: Sec. 79 excludes the cost of up to $50,000 of group-term life insurance provided by an employer to an employee. The plan must be nondiscriminatory, and this one probably is since all employees are covered. The cost of group-term life insurance in excess of $50,000 of coverage is included in an employee's gross income.

Module 5.3: Employee Benefits

21. From the items listed below, determine the amount of income to be included in Mr. E's tax return for 1991

Medical insurance premium paid by employer under a plan	$375
Nondiscriminatory group permanent life insurance premiums paid by employer	225
The excess of fair market value over the purchase price paid for property acquired from employer (not a qualified discount)	400
Amount of interview expense allowance received from employer in excess of actual expenses	250

a. $475.
b. $650.
c. $875.
d. $1,250.

The correct answer is (c). *(SPE 1081 I-66)*
REQUIRED: The amount of income includable in Mr. E's tax return.
DISCUSSION: Mr. E would include in gross income the premiums paid by his employer for group permanent life insurance ($225) since Sec. 79 excludes such premiums only if paid for group-term life insurance (up to $50,000). The excess of fair market value over the purchase price for property acquired from the employer ($400) is additional compensation for services rendered. The excess reimbursement for interview expenses ($250) is also income. (If Mr. E made an adequate accounting to his employer for his interview expenses, he may report the excess reimbursement as miscellaneous income and would not have to include the full amount of reimbursement in gross income with a corresponding deduction for the actual expenses [Reg. 1.162-17(b)(2)].) These three amounts total $875.

The medical insurance premiums paid by the employer are excluded from gross income under Sec. 106.

22. Employee Y, who is 55 years old, is provided with $120,000 of nondiscriminatory group-term life insurance by his employer. Based on the IRS uniform premium cost table, the total annual cost of a policy of this type is $9.00 per $1,000 of coverage. Y's required contribution to the cost of the policy is $2.00 per $1,000 of coverage per year. Y was covered for the full 12 months of 1991. How much of the cost must Y include in his income for 1991?

a. $0.
b. $390.
c. $630.
d. $840.

The correct answer is (b). *(SPE 987 I-67)*
REQUIRED: The amount of premium for group-term life insurance that is included in the employee's gross income.
DISCUSSION: Under Sec. 79, the cost of qualified group-term life insurance paid by an employer is included in the employee's gross income to the extent that such cost exceeds the cost of $50,000 of such insurance. The includable cost is determined on the basis of uniform premiums prescribed by regulations, rather than actual cost. Therefore, we do not need to know what the actual premiums were in order to compute the answer.

The includable cost is the total cost (based on uniform premiums prescribed by regulations minus the employee's contribution) of the employer less the amount otherwise excluded. The total cost of the employer is $7 per $1,000 of insurance per year because Y is paying $2. The excludable cost is $9 per $1,000 for the first $50,000 of insurance. Computation is below.

Employer's cost of policy ($7 x 120)	$840
Less excludable portion ($9 x 50)	(450)
Amount included in Y's income	$390

23. The Rosco Corporation has a medical reimbursement plan under which employees are reimbursed for their medical expenses directly by the corporation. In order for the amount received by a highly compensated employee in 1991 to be entirely excluded from income, which of the following is correct?

　a. A self-insured plan may not discriminate but an insured plan may.

　b. The plan must be insured.

　c. All employees must be covered by the plan.

　d. Both diagnostic medical procedures and those to treat, cure, or test a known illness must be provided in a nondiscriminatory manner.

The correct answer is (a). *(Publisher)*

REQUIRED: The correct statement regarding the exclusion of medical reimbursements from the income of a highly compensated employee in 1991.

DISCUSSION: Sec. 105(b) excludes from an employee's gross income amounts which are paid, directly or indirectly, to the employee as reimbursements for expenses incurred by the employee, spouse, and dependents for medical care. Sec. 105(h) provides that a self-insured medical expense reimbursement plan may not discriminate in favor of highly compensated employees. If the plan is discriminatory, the discriminatory portion of the reimbursements will be included in the income of the highly compensated employees. The nondiscriminatory provisions of Sec. 105 apply only to self-insured plans, however, and an insured medical reimbursement plan may discriminate in favor of highly compensated employees. Therefore, an amount received by a highly compensated employee under an insured plan would be excluded from income under Sec. 105 regardless of whether the plan was nondiscriminatory or not.

Answer (b) is incorrect because a medical reimbursement plan may be insured or self-insured and still come within the provisions of Sec. 105. Answer (c) is incorrect because an insured plan may cover any employees, even in a discriminatory manner, and even a self-insured plan can exclude certain employees from coverage (i.e., part-time, seasonal, and employees under age 25). Answer (d) is incorrect because the nondiscriminatory provisions of Sec. 105 apply only to self-insured medical reimbursement plans.

24. Which of the following will not be a characteristic (not considering cost-of-living adjustments) of a highly compensated individual for self-insured medical expense reimbursement plans in 1991?

　a. Owns more 10% in value of the employer's stock.

　b. Receives compensation in excess of $75,000.

　c. One of the five highest paid officers.

　d. Among the highest paid 25% of all employees (excluding all employees who are not plan participants).

The correct answer is (b). *(Publisher)*

REQUIRED: The characteristic which will not identify a highly compensated individual in 1991.

DISCUSSION: A highly compensated individual is a term used to identify certain employees to determine if employee benefits are discriminatory. For purposes of self-insured medical expense reimbursement plans, Sec. 105(h)(5) defines a highly compensated employee as one of the five highest paid officers, a shareholder who owns more than 10% of the value of an employer's stock, or one who is among the highest paid 25% of all employees (excluding nonparticipants). Answer (b) is not a characteristic of a highly compensated employee for self-insured medical reimbursement plans.

Answers (a), (c), and (d) are incorrect because they define an individual as highly compensated for purposes of Sec. 105.

25. If an employer provides a health plan for its employees, in which of the following situations will a highly compensated individual be required to include part or all of the amount in gross income in 1991?

a. Premiums for medical insurance of a highly compensated employee if continuation coverage is not provided for all covered employees.

b. Payment by an insurance company of medical expense reimbursements to a highly compensated employee if continuation coverage is not provided for all covered employees.

c. Self-insured medical expense reimbursements to a highly compensated employee if the plan is discriminatory.

d. Premiums for medical insurance of a highly compensated employee if the plan is discriminatory.

The correct answer is (c). *(Publisher)*
REQUIRED: When a highly compensated employee may not exclude an employer-provided health benefit.
DISCUSSION: Sec. 105(h) provides that if a medical expense reimbursement plan for employees is discriminatory, the highly compensated employees must include the excess benefit in gross income. This applies only to self-insured medical expense reimbursement plans and not to insured plans.

Answers (a) and (b) are incorrect because the absence of continuation coverage no longer affects includability of group health plan benefits in employee's income. Instead, new Sec. 4980B now provides an excise tax for group health plans that do not provide continuation coverage. However, if the employer has fewer than 20 employees on a typical business day during the prior year, no continuation of coverage is required. Answer (d) is incorrect because premiums paid for medical insurance of a highly compensated employee are still excluded under Sec. 106 even if the plan is discriminatory. It is the benefits that may be included in gross income of a highly compensated employee if the plan is discriminatory.

26. Which of the following is true with respect to nondiscrimination requirements of group-term life insurance plans for employees in 1991?

a. If the plan is discriminatory, none of the employees may exclude the benefit from gross income.

b. If the plan is discriminatory, key employees must include the cost of the group-term life insurance provided to them in their gross income.

c. A plan is nondiscriminatory if the benefits available under the plan do not discriminate in favor of participants who are key employees.

d. The amount of life insurance provided employees under the plan may not bear a uniform relationship to the total compensation of such employees.

The correct answer is (b). *(Publisher)*
REQUIRED: The correct statement concerning the nondiscrimination requirements of group-term life insurance plans for employees in 1991.
DISCUSSION: Sec. 79(a) provides an exclusion of the cost of up to $50,000 in group-term life insurance from an employee's gross income when the cost of the insurance is paid by the employer. However, Sec. 79(d) provides that if the group-term life insurance plan discriminates in favor of key employees [as defined in Sec. 416(i)(1)] then the key employees must include the greater of the actual cost of their group-term life insurance coverage or the cost of their group-term life insurance coverage determined in tables provided in the Treasury Regulations in gross income.

Answer (a) is incorrect because only key employees must include the benefit in gross income when a plan is discriminatory. Other employees still receive the exclusion. Answer (c) is incorrect because a plan is nondiscriminatory only if the eligibility to participate in the plan and the type and amount of benefits available are provided for on a nondiscriminatory basis. Answer (d) is incorrect because Sec. 79(d)(5) specifically provides that a plan will not be considered discriminatory merely because the amount of life insurance provided employees under the plan bears a uniform relationship to the total compensation of such employees.

Module 5.3: Employee Benefits

27. Which of the following qualifications is not necessary in an employer's self-insured accident and health plan to prevent the plan from being considered discriminatory?

    a. All benefits provided for participants who are highly compensated individuals must be provided for all other participants.

    b. The plan may not discriminate in favor of highly compensated individuals as to eligibility to participate.

    c. All employees having completed 3 years of service must be participants in the plan.

    d. The plan must not discriminate in favor of highly compensated individuals as to benefits provided under the plan.

The correct answer is (c). *(Publisher)*
REQUIRED: The qualification not needed to prevent an employer's accident and health plan from being considered discriminatory.
DISCUSSION: Sec. 105(h) provides the requirements a plan must meet in order to be considered nondiscriminatory. In determining whether eligibility to participate in the plan is discriminatory, certain employees, such as part-time or seasonal employees or employees who have not attained the age of 25, are excluded from consideration. Therefore, answer (c) is not a necessary qualification for a plan to be considered nondiscriminatory.
Answers (a), (b), and (d) are incorrect because they are all requirements of nondiscriminatory plans as outlined in Sec. 105(h).

28. Ginger Corporation provides a nondiscriminatory plan under which its employees are able to choose their fringe benefits up to $2,000 in value per year from the following:

    Cash
    Medical reimbursements
    Premiums on major medical insurance
    Premiums on up to $50,000 of group-term life insurance

If in 1991 an employee chooses medical insurance premiums worth $950, medical reimbursements of $300, group-term life insurance premiums of $50, and cash of $700, how much may the employee exclude from gross income?

    a. $0.
    b. $300.
    c. $1,250.
    d. $1,300.

The correct answer is (d). *(Publisher)*
REQUIRED: The amount of benefits from a cafeteria plan that an employee may exclude from gross income.
DISCUSSION: The cafeteria plan is one in which the employees may choose among their fringe benefits. Under Sec. 125, the use of a cafeteria plan does not cause the benefits to be included in the gross income of the participants, provided the plan does not discriminate in favor of highly compensated or key employees. However, the only benefits allowed under the cafeteria plan are cash and qualified benefits (not allowed are scholarships and fellowship grants or tuition reductions under Sec. 117, educational assistance under Sec. 127, or fringe benefits under Sec. 132). Since only cash and qualified benefits are allowed, Ginger's cafeteria plan qualifies. The taxation of the benefits depends on which are chosen. Medical reimbursements by an employer are excluded from gross income under Sec. 105(b) and major medical insurance premiums paid by an employer are excluded under Sec. 106. Premiums on up to $50,000 of qualified group-term life insurance are excluded by Sec. 79. There is no exclusion for cash payments to an employee. Therefore, the employee who chooses medical insurance premiums worth $950, medical reimbursements of $300, and group-term life insurance premiums of $50 may exclude this $1,300 from gross income.

29. During 1991, Employee A received tangible personal property as a safety achievement award from her employer. The award was not a qualified plan award. The property cost the employer $500 and had a fair market value of $600. How much must A include in her 1991 gross income?

    a. $0.
    b. $200.
    c. $500.
    d. $600.

The correct answer is (b). *(SPE 981 I-51)*
REQUIRED: The amount an employee must include in income from a safety achievement award.
DISCUSSION: Sec. 74(c) allows an employee to exclude from gross income the value of an employee achievement award to the extent the employer may deduct it under Sec. 274(j). An employee achievement award is an item of tangible personal property provided by an employer for length of service achievement or for safety achievement. Sec. 274(j) allows a deduction of up to $400 per award (or up to $1,600 under a qualified plan) provided the average awards do not exceed $400. Since the award was not a qualified plan award, the limitation is $400. Any excess value received by an employee must be included in gross income. Therefore, A must include $200 ($600 value − $400 excludable) in gross income.

Module 5.3: Employee Benefits

30. Elmer has been a faithful employee of the Bold Dairy Co. for 25 years. In recognition of Elmer's length of service, Bold Dairy held a banquet and presented Elmer with a gold watch and a brass cow, with a cost and value of $500. The award was not a qualified plan award. Elmer's meal at the banquet was valued at $30. Bold Dairy was able to expense the banquet in full and $400 of the gifts. Later in the year, Elmer received a cash Christmas gift of $50 (as did other employees) and Bold Dairy was able to expense $25. How much income must Elmer report?

a. $0.
b. $150.
c. $475.
d. $550.

The correct answer is (b). *(Publisher)*
REQUIRED: The amount an employee must include in income from gifts and awards from the employer.
DISCUSSION: An employee may exclude from gross income the value of an employee achievement award to the extent the employer may deduct it under Sec. 274(j). Elmer must include the excess of the $500 award over the $400 employer deduction, or $100 [Sec. 74(c)]. The value of the meal is excluded as a de minimis fringe benefit under Sec. 132. The entire $50 Christmas gift must be included in Elmer's income under Sec. 102(c), which disallows an exclusion for gifts by an employer to an employee. The cash gift is not de minimis because it is in cash and easily accounted for.

31. Zippy worked at the Maxwell Hotel as a desk clerk. Since there was no one to replace him during the dinner hour, the Maxwell Hotel provided Zippy's meal out of the dining room free of charge. Zippy was allowed to go and eat elsewhere but was encouraged to eat at the hotel and mind the desk. The cost of the meals to the Maxwell Hotel was $450 and the fair market value of the meals was $800. How much must Zippy include in gross income?

a. $0.
b. $350.
c. $450.
d. $800.

The correct answer is (a). *(Publisher)*
REQUIRED: The amount that an employee must include in gross income for meals furnished by an employer.
DISCUSSION: Sec. 119 provides an exclusion for meals furnished on the business premises of the employer if they are furnished to the employee for the convenience of the employer. The convenience of the employer is served by keeping Zippy at the desk during dinner. In the case of meals, the fact that the employee may accept or decline such meals is not taken into account. Therefore, Zippy may exclude the entire amount of the meals from his gross income. Note that the relevant amount Zippy would have to include in gross income if the meals did not meet the requirements of Sec. 119 is the fair market value of the meals.

32. Hansel and Gretel were employed as managers of a motel. Part of their job requirements was to live on the premises so that they would be available to watch the desk and take care of any guest's problems. They were provided with living quarters and groceries free of charge. The living quarters were worth $3,000 per year and the groceries were worth $2,500 per year. How much must Hansel and Gretel include in gross income?

a. $0.
b. $2,500.
c. $3,000.
d. $5,500.

The correct answer is (b). *(Publisher)*
REQUIRED: The amount that an employee must include in gross income from an employer who provides living quarters and groceries.
DISCUSSION: Sec. 119 provides an exclusion for meals and lodging furnished on the business premises of the employer if they are furnished for the convenience of the employer. Having motel managers remain on the premises to register and take care of guests is for the convenience of the employer. For lodging (but not meals) the employee must be required to accept the lodging as a condition of employment. Since these requirements are met for Hansel and Gretel, they may exclude the entire value of their living quarters. However, while the value of meals may be excluded, there is no exclusion for groceries. Therefore, Hansel and Gretel must include the value of groceries ($2,500) in their gross income.

33. Dependent care assistance paid by an employer to an employee must be included in the employee's income.

The correct answer is (F). *(Publisher)*
DISCUSSION: Under a qualified program, up to $5,000 of dependent care assistance may be excluded (Sec. 129) on a joint return.

34. The exclusions for employer-provided educational assistance benefits and for group legal services plan benefits are not available after 1991.

The correct answer is (F). *(Publisher)*
DISCUSSION: The Tax Extension Act of 1991 extended the educational assistance benefits paid to employees under a qualified plan through June 30, 1992. A similar extension was provided for group legal service benefits. The educational assistance exclusion is Sec. 127 and the group legal services exclusion is Sec. 120.

35. An educational assistance program is a separate written plan of an employer to provide excludable educational assistance to employees. The exclusion does not apply to payments for graduate-level courses leading to a law, medical or similar advanced academic or professional degree.

The correct answer is (F). *(SPE 990 I-27)*
DISCUSSION: Sec. 127 provides an exclusion from an employee's gross income of amounts paid by the employer for educational assistance. The payments must be made pursuant to an educational assistance program as defined in that section. Sec. 127 was amended by the Revenue Reconciliation Act of 1990 so as to allow payments for graduate-level courses leading to a law, medical or similar advanced academic or professional degree to be excluded from an employee's gross income.

36. Mr. J, a highly compensated employee, has group-term life insurance coverage of $100,000 paid for by his employer in 1991. The plan discriminates in favor of key employees. J must include the actual cost of the entire $100,000 of coverage in his income.

The correct answer is (T). *(SPE 986 I-10)*
DISCUSSION: Under Sec. 79, the cost of up to $50,000 of group-term life insurance in a nondiscriminatory plan may be excluded from each employee's income. If the plan discriminates in favor of key employees, the key employees are not eligible for the exclusion and must include in gross income the greater of the actual premiums paid or the amount calculated from the Uniform Premiums Table provided at Reg. 1.79-3T. The term key employee is defined in Sec. 416(i)(1) as being certain highly-compensated owners and officers.

37. During 1991, Mrs. S worked for a university which has a qualified tuition reduction program. Her son, an undergraduate, whom she is entitled to claim as a dependent, received a tuition reduction of $5,500 in 1991. He does not have to include the $5,500 in his income for federal income tax purposes.

The correct answer is (T). *(SPE 989 I-21)*
DISCUSSION: The amount of any qualified tuition reduction provided for an employee, the employee's spouse, or dependent child is excluded from gross income under Sec. 117(d). The tuition reduction may be used only toward undergraduate education unless it is for an employee who is a graduate student engaged in teaching or research activities for his/her employer.

38. If an employer-provided cafeteria benefit plan gives an employee an option of receiving the benefits in cash, all benefits provided under the plan are taxable to the employee.

The correct answer is (F). *(Publisher)*
DISCUSSION: A cafeteria benefit plan is one in which the employees may choose among their fringe benefits. However, the only benefits allowed under the cafeteria plan are cash and qualified benefits. An option to receive all benefits in cash does not disqualify the cafeteria plan.

5.4 Social Security Benefits

39. The "base amount" for married taxpayers filing a joint return that determines whether Social Security benefits are to be taxed is

a. $18,000.
b. $25,000.
c. $30,000.
d. $32,000.

The correct answer is (d). *(R. Bunn)*
REQUIRED: The income on a joint return above which Social Security benefits are taxed.
DISCUSSION: Under Sec. 86, part of Social Security benefits are taxed when the sum of "modified" adjusted gross income plus one-half of the Social Security benefits exceeds a base amount. This base amount is $32,000 for a joint return and $25,000 for a single return.

40. Mr. & Mrs. Birch are both over 65 years of age and are filing a joint return. Their income for 1991 consisted of the following:

Taxable interest	$ 6,000
Taxable dividends	8,000
Social Security payments (Mr. & Mrs. Birch combined)	15,000
Tax-exempt interest	4,000
Taxable pension	15,000

They did not have any adjustments to income. What amount of Mr. & Mrs. Birch's Social Security benefits is taxable?

a. $0.
b. $4,250.
c. $7,500.
d. $7,750.

The correct answer is (b). *(SPE 989 I-67)*
REQUIRED: The amount of Social Security benefits included in gross income for 1991.
DISCUSSION: Under Sec. 86, if the sum of the "modified" adjusted gross income plus one-half of Social Security benefits exceeds $32,000 on a joint return, part of the Social Security benefits will be included in gross income. Modified adjusted gross income equals adjusted gross income plus tax-exempt interest [Sec. 86(b)(2)]. The includable portion of Social Security benefits is the lesser of one-half of the Social Security benefits or one-half of the excess as noted above. Mr. and Mrs. Birch would include $4,250 since it is less than one-half of the Social Security benefits ($15,000 x .50 = $7,500).

Modified AGI ($6,000 + $8,000 + $4,000 + $15,000)	$33,000
One-half Social Security benefits	7,500
Less $32,000 base amount	(32,000)
	$ 8,500
50% of excess or	$ 4,250
50% of Social Security (50% x $15,000)	$ 7,500

41. Ms. Green is single and over 65 years old. She received the following income in 1991:

Interest from certificates of deposit	$ 3,000
Tax-exempt interest	6,000
Taxable dividends	5,000
Taxable pension	20,000
Wages from consulting work	9,000
Social Security	14,000

She did not have any adjustments to income. What is the taxable amount of Ms. Green's Social Security?

a. $7,000.
b. $9,000.
c. $9,500.
d. $12,500.

The correct answer is (a). *(SPE 990 I-70)*
REQUIRED: The amount of Social Security benefits to be included in gross income for 1991.
DISCUSSION: If the sum of a single individual's modified adjusted gross income plus 50% of the Social Security benefits exceeds $25,000, part of the Social Security benefits is included in gross income. The includable portion is the lesser of 50% of Social Security benefits or 50% of the excess in the previous sentence. Modified adjusted gross income equals adjusted gross income plus tax-exempt interest [Sec. 86(b)(2)]. Therefore, Ms. Green's modified adjusted gross income is $43,000 ($20,000 pension + $3,000 taxable interest + $6,000 tax-exempt interest + $5,000 dividends + $9,000 consulting wages). The taxable portion of Social Security is $7,000 because it is less than 50% of the excess of modified AGI over $25,000 ($12,500 computed below).

Modified AGI	$43,000
One-half Social Security	7,000
Less $25,000 base amount	(25,000)
	$25,000
50% of excess or	$12,500
50% of Social Security (50% x $14,000)	$ 7,000

Module 5.5: Payments Made at Death

42. After Hughes died, his daughter Jane was entitled to receive Social Security benefits for education. During the year, she received $2,800 for tuition. However, she also earned $27,000 from part-time work. How much of the Social Security benefits must Jane include in her income?

a. $0.
b. $1,400.
c. $1,700.
d. $2,800.

The correct answer is (b). *(Publisher)*
REQUIRED: The Social Security educational benefits includable by a surviving child.
DISCUSSION: Social Security educational benefits provided to survivors are excluded from gross income to the extent not required to be included under Sec. 86. If the sum of a single individual's modified adjusted gross income plus 50% of the Social Security benefits exceeds $25,000, part of the Social Security benefits are included in gross income. The includable portion is the lesser of 50% of Social Security benefits or 50% of the excess in the previous sentence. Jane's includable portion is $1,400 (50% x $2,800 Social Security benefits) because it is less than the computation below.

Modified AGI	$27,000
One-half Social Security	1,400
Less $25,000 base amount	(25,000)
	$ 3,400
50% of excess or	$ 1,700
50% of Social Security benefits	$ 1,400

43. During 1991, Mr. A, who is 67 years old, received Social Security benefits of $12,000. This amount was reported to him at year end on a Form SSA-1099. Because he received a Form SSA-1099, Mr. A must include this amount as income on his 1991 income tax return.

The correct answer is (F). *(SPE 988 I-9)*
DISCUSSION: Social Security benefits are not taxed unless the sum of one-half of the Social Security benefits plus modified adjusted gross income exceeds a base amount. This base amount is $32,000 for a joint return and $25,000 for a single return. Receiving a Form SSA-1099 does not require Social Security benefits to be included in gross income.

5.5 Payments Made at Death

44. On September 18, 1991, Dennis was killed in an automobile accident. In October 1991, his widow received a lump sum death benefit from his employer in the amount of $15,000. Dennis had no right to the $15,000 prior to death. For 1991, what amount should his widow include in adjusted gross income, assuming a joint tax return was filed?

a. $0.
b. $10,000.
c. $14,000.
d. $15,000.

The correct answer is (b). *(CPA 1179 Q-40)*
REQUIRED: The amount of a lump sum death benefit which must be included in adjusted gross income.
DISCUSSION: Gross income does not include amounts (limited to $5,000) received by the beneficiaries or the estate of an employee if such amounts are paid by or on behalf of an employer and are paid by reason of the death of the employee [Sec. 101(b)]. Furthermore, the deceased employee must not have had a nonforfeitable right to receive such amounts. Dennis's widow should exclude $5,000 of death benefits under this section and therefore would include $10,000 in adjusted gross income.

45. Frank Clarke, an employee, was covered under a noncontributory pension plan. Frank died on April 15, 1991 at age 64 and, pursuant to the plan, his widow received monthly pension payments of $500 beginning May 1, 1991. Mrs. Clarke also received an employee death payment of $10,000 in May 1991. How much should she exclude from her gross income for 1991?

a. $5,000.
b. $9,000.
c. $10,000.
d. $14,000.

The correct answer is (a). *(CPA 581 P-46)*
REQUIRED: The amount of monthly pension payments and/or the amount of a lump sum death benefit which is excluded from gross income.
DISCUSSION: Sec. 101(b) provides for the exclusion of up to $5,000 in death benefits received by the beneficiaries or estate of an employee if such payments are made by or on behalf of the employer and are paid by reason of the death of the employee. Since Mrs. Clarke received $10,000 from her husband's employer by reason of his death, she should exclude up to $5,000 of these death benefits. No part of the pension payments may be excluded unless Frank made contributions to the pension plan.

Module 5.5: Payments Made at Death

46. Howard, an employee of Ogden Corporation, died on June 30, 1991. During July, Ogden made employee death payments of $10,000 to his widow and $10,000 to his 15-year-old son. What amounts should be included in gross income by the widow and son in their respective tax returns for 1991?

	Widow	Son
a.	$0	$0
b.	$5,000	$5,000
c.	$5,000	$10,000
d.	$7,500	$7,500

The correct answer is (d). *(CPA 582 P-47)*
REQUIRED: The death benefits a widow and son should each include in gross income.
DISCUSSION: Sec. 101(b) provides for the exclusion of up to $5,000 of death benefits received by the beneficiaries of an employee if such payments are made by or on behalf of an employer and are paid by reason of the death of the employee. This $5,000 exclusion must be apportioned among the beneficiaries on the basis of each beneficiary's percentage of the total death benefits received [Reg. 1.101-2(c)(1)]. The widow and son each received $10,000 out of the total $20,000 of death benefits. Each is entitled to 50% of the $5,000 exclusion. The widow and son must each include $7,500 in gross income ($10,000 − $2,500).

47. Mrs. D, a widow since 1985, elected to receive the proceeds of her deceased husband's $100,000 life insurance policy in 10 yearly installments of $12,000 instead of a lump sum payment. The payments are based on a guaranteed interest rate. What amount of interest should Mrs. D include in her income each year?

a. $0.
b. $500.
c. $1,000.
d. $2,000.

The correct answer is (c). *(SPE 1085 I-68)*
REQUIRED: A surviving spouse's annual gross income from a life insurance policy received in installments if the spouse died on or before October 22, 1986.
DISCUSSION: The proceeds of a life insurance policy, if paid by reason of the death of the insured, are excluded from gross income under Sec. 101(a). Mrs. D will receive $10,000 ($100,000 ÷ 10 years) of the insurance proceeds per year and she may exclude this amount each year from gross income. Sec. 101(d) permits a surviving spouse to exclude the first $1,000 of interest collected on the proceeds of an insurance policy paid in installments if the spouse died on or before October 22, 1986. In addition to the $10,000 exclusion, Mrs. D may also exclude $1,000 of interest each year. Therefore, she must include $1,000 ($12,000 − $10,000 − $1,000) each year.

48. Mrs. Dee's husband died in 1991. She chose to receive the proceeds of her husband's $100,000 life insurance policy over a 10-year period. The monthly installments are $1,200 each. What is the amount of the annual payments that represents taxable income to Mrs. Dee?

a. $0.
b. $2,000.
c. $4,400.
d. $14,400.

The correct answer is (c). *(SPE 990 I-61)*
REQUIRED: A surviving spouse's annual gross income from a life insurance policy received in installments if the spouse died after October 22, 1986.
DISCUSSION: Mrs. Dee will receive $10,000 ($100,000 ÷ 10 years) of the insurance proceeds per year and may exclude this amount each year from gross income. The remaining $4,400 [($1,200 x 12) − $10,000] received each year is interest. The 1986 TRA repealed the Sec. 101(d) exclusion of $1,000 of interest on installment payments of life insurance for surviving spouses when the deceased died after October 22, 1986. Since Mrs. Dee's husband died in 1991, she must include the entire $4,400 of interest in her gross income each year.

Module 5.6: Scholarships and Fellowships

49. Al, a cash-basis taxpayer, died on September 30, 1991. From January 1 until his death he received a salary of $15,000. In addition, he earned commissions of $6,500 which were not received, although a check for $2,000 had been available since September 15, 1991. On December 15, 1991, Al's widow, Paula, received a $6,000 death benefit from his employer in consideration of his past services rendered. Assuming a joint return is properly filed, gross income for Paula and the decedent for 1991 should be

  a. $27,500.
  b. $23,000.
  c. $18,000.
  d. $16,000.

The correct answer is (c). *(CPA 574 Q-26)*
REQUIRED: The gross income Paula and the decedent should report on a joint tax return.
DISCUSSION: An individual's tax year ends on the date of his/her death [Reg. 1.443-1(a)(2)]. Under Sec. 6013, a joint return may be filed including the decedent's short year and the surviving spouse's entire year. The joint return will include all the income a decedent received before his/her death and all the income the surviving spouse received for the entire year. The commissions not received by Al will be taxed to his estate (and excluded from his final return) except for the $2,000 which had been available under the doctrine of constructive receipt (Reg. 1.451-1). Paula will be entitled to exclude $5,000 of the death benefit under Sec. 101(b). Therefore, the joint return should include

Salary	$15,000
Commissions	2,000
Death benefit ($6,000 – $5,000)	1,000
Gross income	$18,000

50. When Sylvester was 16 years old, his uncle died and left him $100,000. After Sylvester received the $100,000, interest income of $10,000 was earned before the end of the year. Sylvester's uncle also left $1,000,000 to a charity but Sylvester was to receive the income from the money for a period of 5 years. It produced $80,000 worth of income before year-end. How much must Sylvester include in his gross income for the year?

  a. $0.
  b. $80,000.
  c. $90,000.
  d. $110,000.

The correct answer is (c). *(Publisher)*
REQUIRED: The amount of income a beneficiary of a bequest of property and a bequest of income must include in gross income.
DISCUSSION: Under Sec. 102(a), income does not include the value of property acquired by gift, bequest, or inheritance. Therefore, the bequest of $100,000 to Sylvester is excluded from gross income. Sec. 102(b) provides, however, that both income from a bequest or inheritance of property and from a bequest or inheritance of income are included in gross income. Therefore, the $10,000 of interest income earned on the bequest is included in Sylvester's gross income, as well as the $80,000 income received from the bequest made to charity. Sylvester must include a total of $90,000 in gross income for the year.

5.6 Scholarships and Fellowships

51. For which of the following items may a scholarship or grant not be paid if the recipient is to exclude the scholarship or grant from gross income?

  a. Tuition.
  b. Books and supplies.
  c. Equipment required for courses.
  d. Services provided to the grantor.

The correct answer is (d). *(Publisher)*
REQUIRED: The item for which a reimbursement will be included in the recipient's income.
DISCUSSION: Sec. 117 provides an exclusion from gross income for amounts received as a scholarship or as a fellowship grant by a degree candidate. Any amount which represents payment for services required as a condition to receive the scholarship or grant is not excluded from gross income even if the services are required of all candidates for a particular degree as a condition of receiving the degree.
Answers (a), (b), and (c) are items for which a reimbursement in the form of a scholarship or fellowship grant for a degree candidate will be excluded from gross income, provided these items are incident to such scholarship or fellowship grant and the amounts are so expended by the recipient.

Module 5.6: Scholarships and Fellowships

52. Mr. R is a candidate for a master's degree at State University. During 1991 he was granted a fellowship that provided

$8,000 for tuition
$1,500 for books and supplies
$9,500 for room
$8,000 for board

What is the amount Mr. R may exclude from gross income for 1991?

a. $12,500.
b. $11,500.
c. $9,500.
d. $8,000.

The correct answer is (c). *(SPE 987 I-73)*
REQUIRED: The amount of a scholarship a candidate for a degree may exclude.
DISCUSSION: Sec. 117 provides an exclusion from gross income for amounts received as a scholarship or fellowship grant by a degree candidate. But only amounts actually used for tuition, fees, books, supplies, and equipment required for instruction qualify for this exclusion. Room and board does not qualify.

Tuition	$8,000
Books and supplies	1,500
Total amount excluded	$9,500

53. In 1987 Lee was beginning his undergraduate education. In January 1987 Lee was awarded a scholarship of $500 per month from a tax-exempt educational foundation to continue as long as Lee was a full-time student until he received his degree. Lee remained a full-time student and graduated at the end of August 1991. Lee received the scholarship each month from January 1991 through August 1991. How much must Lee include in gross income from the scholarship in 1991?

a. $0.
b. $1,600.
c. $2,400.
d. $4,000.

The correct answer is (a). *(Publisher)*
REQUIRED: The amount of income the recipient of a scholarship who is a candidate for a degree must include in gross income.
DISCUSSION: A candidate for a degree may exclude the amount received as a scholarship at an educational organization. There is no limit on the time for which the scholarship may be received. Only amounts actually used for tuition, fees, books, supplies, and equipment required for instruction qualifies for this exclusion. Therefore, Lee need not include any amount in gross income from the scholarship in 1991 provided the monies are spent for the requisite items.

54. In February 1991, Jane received a $7,000 scholarship for the 1991 spring semester at State University where she is a candidate for a degree. The scholarship was for the following:

Room and board	$2,000
Payment for being a teaching assistant	2,500
Tuition	2,000
Books and supplies	500

The services Jane provided as a teaching assistant are a condition of receiving the grant and are required of all candidates for the degree. Assuming all other conditions are met, what amount must Jane include in her 1991 taxable income?

a. $2,000.
b. $2,500.
c. $4,000.
d. $4,500.

The correct answer is (d). *(SPE 989 I-66)*
REQUIRED: The amount to be included in taxable income from a scholarship.
DISCUSSION: Sec. 117 excludes from gross income the amount received as a scholarship or grant by a candidate for a degree. The term scholarship includes only the amount used for tuition, fees, books, supplies and equipment and does not include the value of services and accommodations such as room and board. Therefore, the $2,000 for room and board must be included in Jane's gross income. Also, the exclusion under Sec. 117 does not apply if past, present, or future services are a condition of the scholarship. As Jane is required to be a teaching assistant, the $2,500 payment for being a teaching assistant must be included in Jane's gross income. Jane must include a total of $4,500 ($2,000 + $2,500) in gross income for 1991.

55. Mr. P received a fellowship grant from the State of Virginia in December 1990 for a special research project on education. During 1991, he received $700 per month for the period June 1 to December 31. P is not a candidate for a degree. What amount of the fellowship may P exclude from gross income?

   a. $0.
   b. $2,100.
   c. $3,500.
   d. $4,900.

The correct answer is (a). *(SPE 984 I-56)*
REQUIRED: The amount of a fellowship granted to a nondegree candidate that may be excluded from gross income.
DISCUSSION: Sec. 117 excludes from gross income scholarships and fellowship grants provided that the payments are not made for services of the recipient, that the grants are not made primarily for the benefit of the grantor, and the recipient is a candidate for a degree. Since Mr. P is not a candidate for a degree, none of the fellowship may be excluded.

5.7 Foreign Income Exclusions

56. In January 1990, Bush, a vice-president of Dearborn National Bank (DNB), was transferred to France to work in a French subsidiary of DNB. Bush has qualified as a bona fide foreign resident of France since his arrival in the country. During 1991, Bush was paid a salary of $65,000 and had interest income of $24,000 from U.S. savings accounts. Bush's U.S. gross income for the year is

   a. $0.
   b. $24,000.
   c. $65,000.
   d. $89,000.

The correct answer is (b). *(Publisher)*
REQUIRED: The gross income of a U.S. citizen who has earned income from a foreign country and is a bona fide foreign resident.
DISCUSSION: Under Sec. 911, a qualified individual may elect to exclude from gross income any foreign earned income for the taxable year up to a maximum of $70,000. A qualified individual includes someone whose tax home is in a foreign country, is a citizen of the United States, and is a bona fide resident of the foreign country for an uninterrupted period which includes an entire taxable year or is present in foreign countries for at least 330 days of a consecutive 12-month period. Earned income means wages, salaries, professional fees, and other amounts received as compensation for personal services actually rendered. Since Bush is a qualified individual, foreign earned income of $65,000 can be excluded from gross income. Therefore, gross income for the year is the $24,000 of interest income from the U.S. savings accounts.

57. During all of 1989, 1990, and 1991, Una Dostres, a U.S. employee of Math Corporation, lived in Spain and worked in a Spanish subsidiary of Math. In 1991, Una received a $75,000 salary plus a housing allowance from her employer for her actual qualifying housing costs of $11,200. Assume the 1991 federal salary at grade GS-14 is $50,342. Una's gross income to be reported on her U.S. tax return is

   a. $0.
   b. $5,000.
   c. $13,055.
   d. $16,200.

The correct answer is (c). *(Publisher)*
REQUIRED: The U.S. gross income of an individual who works in a foreign country and receives a housing allowance.
DISCUSSION: Under Sec. 911, a qualified individual may separately elect to exclude foreign earned income and a housing allowance. A qualified individual includes someone who is a citizen or resident alien of the U.S. who is either a bona fide resident of a foreign country for an entire tax year or is present in foreign countries for at least 330 days of a consecutive 12-month period. Una meets this second test, if not also the first.

The foreign earned income exclusion is limited to $70,000 so Una must include $5,000 of her $75,000 salary. The housing allowance exclusion is limited to the qualifying housing costs ($11,200) less 16% of the current pay rate for a U.S. government employee of step 1 of grade GS-14 (assumed to be $50,342 in 1991). 16% of $50,342 is $8,055, so Una's exclusion is limited to $3,145 ($11,200 − $8,055). Therefore, she must include $13,055 ($8,055 of her housing allowance + $5,000 of earned income) for 1991.

Module 5.7: Foreign Income Exclusions

58. Mr. H is a foreign student studying for a degree in the United States. There is no income tax treaty between his country and the United States. During the nine months of the school year, Mr. H is employed part-time by a corporation incorporated in his home country doing business in the U.S. During summer vacation Mr. H returns home where he is employed by the same company. Which of the following statements is correct regarding U.S. taxes?

a. All income is taxable on a U.S. tax return.

b. All income is excludable and filing is not required.

c. Only income earned for services in the U.S. is taxable.

d. All income is taxable on a U.S. tax return and credit is allowed for foreign taxes paid for the income taxes paid on his summer income.

The correct answer is (c). *(SPE 1085 I-65)*
REQUIRED: The U.S. taxation of compensation earned both in the U.S. and abroad by a foreign student in the U.S.
DISCUSSION: Under Sec. 871, income from U.S. sources which is effectively connected with a U.S. trade or business must be included in a nonresident alien's U.S. gross income. The performance of personal services in the U.S. constitutes a trade or business in the U.S. (Sec. 864). Therefore, the income earned by Mr. H while employed part-time in the U.S. is taxable.

Answers (a) and (d) are incorrect because a nonresident alien has no U.S. income when the personal services income is earned outside the U.S. and is not connected with the conduct of a U.S. trade or business. Answer (b) is incorrect because the income earned in the U.S. is taxable.

59. Jean Blanc, a citizen and resident of Canada, is a professional hockey player with a U.S. hockey club. Under Jean's contract, he received $68,500 for 165 days of play during 1991. Of the 165 days, 132 days were spent performing services in the United States and 33 playing hockey in Canada. What is the amount to be included in Jean's gross income on his 1991 Form 1040NR?

a. $0.

b. $34,250.

c. $54,800.

d. $68,500.

The correct answer is (c). *(SPE 988 I-90)*
REQUIRED: The U.S. gross income of a nonresident alien who performs services in the U.S. for part of the year.
DISCUSSION: A nonresident alien must include in U.S. gross income that income from U.S. sources which is effectively connected with the conduct of a trade or business in the U.S. (Sec. 871). Under Sec. 864, the performance of personal services in the U.S. constitutes a trade or business in the U.S. If income is derived therefrom, it is considered to be from a U.S. source. According to the IRS and the courts, services of a professional hockey player are allocable to U.S. and non-U.S. time periods during the pre-season training camp, the regular season, and post-season playoffs, but not the off-season. Therefore, Jean must include the portion of his income which is attributable to the performance of personal services in the U.S., i.e., 80% (132 ÷ 165 days). Eighty percent of $68,500 is $54,800, which must be reported as U.S. income.

60. An executive is assigned to work in his company's Paris, France office for an 18-month period from April 1, 1990 through September 30, 1991. He retained his United States residence and returned home each month for 4 days. A portion of the income earned in Paris may be excluded from gross income.

The correct answer is (F). *(SPE 1077 I-107)*
DISCUSSION: Under Sec. 911, a U.S. citizen or resident alien may exclude earned foreign income (up to certain limits) if his/her tax home is in a foreign country, and (s)he either is a bona fide resident of a foreign country for an uninterrupted period including an entire tax year or is present in a foreign country for at least 330 days during 12 consecutive months.

The executive apparently does not meet the bona fide foreign resident test because the retention of the U.S. residence and the frequent visits to the U.S. indicate a lack of assimilation into French life. (Visits to the U.S. do not, per se, preclude establishing bona fide foreign residence.) In addition, the executive was not a resident of France for an entire tax year. The executive also fails the 330 day test, since his French residence has not lasted for 330 days during 12 consecutive months (365 days − 48 days = 317 days).

Module 5.8: Gifts and Prizes

61. Vesco, a U.S. citizen working abroad, qualifies for the foreign earned income exclusion in 1991. Vesco has a $72,000 salary plus $7,000 in interest earned in U.S. banks. The tax due on the interest income is calculated using the highest individual tax rate.

The correct answer is (F). *(Publisher)*
DISCUSSION: The rate at which an individual is taxed is dependent on the amount of his/her taxable income. The amount of taxable income is reduced by any exclusions from gross income. Sec. 911 provides an exclusion of up to $70,000 for foreign earned income. An individual with only $9,000 of gross income would not be in the highest tax bracket.

5.8 Gifts and Prizes

62. Rupert wanted to give his son and daughter a gift of $10,000. However, the son was not trustworthy enough to receive such a large sum of money at one time. Therefore, Rupert decided to keep the son's $10,000 invested for him and only give the son the income each year. In 1991, this income amounted to $1,200 which Rupert transferred to the son. Rupert's daughter received her $10,000 outright in 1991. How much income must the son and daughter report respectively in 1991 as a result of the gift?

	Son	Daughter
a.	$0	$0
b.	$1,200	$0
c.	$1,200	$10,000
d.	$10,000	$10,000

The correct answer is (a). *(Publisher)*
REQUIRED: The amount of gross income recognized by the recipients of a gift.
DISCUSSION: Sec. 102(a) excludes the value of property acquired by gift from gross income. However, Sec. 102(b) provides that income from property acquired by gift or a gift of income from property is not excluded from gross income. The $10,000 received by the daughter is a gift under Sec. 102(a) and is excluded from her gross income. The $1,200 received by the son is also a gift of property which is excluded from his gross income. It is not income from a gift of property or a gift of income because the $10,000 was never given or legally set aside for the son. Rupert simply made a gift of $1,200 in 1991 which happened to be determined by the amount of income earned on $10,000. Rupert must include the $1,200 in his income and the son includes no amount in his income.

63. Silly became a contestant on a daytime television game show. Silly was lucky and won a fur coat with a retail price of $3,000 and a television with a fair market value of $400. Silly lived in Florida, so (s)he sold the fur coat the next day, but was only able to receive $2,500 for it. One month later, the television broke and Silly discovered there was no warranty on it. How much must Silly include in gross income for the year?

a. $0.
b. $2,500.
c. $2,900.
d. $3,400.

The correct answer is (c). *(Publisher)*
REQUIRED: The amount that the recipient of prizes must include in gross income.
DISCUSSION: Amounts received as prizes or awards are generally included in the recipient's gross income (Sec. 74). The fair market value of the fur coat was $2,500 (the amount Silly could receive for it) since most products are no longer worth their retail price once taken out of the store. The fair market value of the television was $400 regardless of events occurring after receipt, such as its breaking. Therefore, Silly must include $2,900 in gross income from the prizes.

Module 5.8: Gifts and Prizes

64. Brain invented a new product but did not know who would be willing to market it. Brain asked her friend Rooster for some help. Rooster recommended someone who would be likely to market the product. The product turned out to be a success and Brain was so happy that she went to Rooster and said, "I want to make you a gift since you were so good to me." Brain gave Rooster $5,000. Which of the following statements is correct?

a. Rooster must include the $5,000 in gross income.
b. Rooster may exclude the $5,000 as a gift.
c. Rooster may exclude the $5,000 as a prize.
d. Rooster must pay the gift tax on the $5,000.

The correct answer is (a). *(Publisher)*
REQUIRED: The correct statement concerning a gratuitous transfer of money for help received in producing income.
DISCUSSION: Sec. 102(a) excludes from gross income the value of property acquired by gift. Under the Duberstein case, 363 U.S. 278 (1960), a gift must be made from "detached and disinterested generosity." In this situation, Brain did not make the "gift" out of detached and disinterested generosity; rather the "gift" was made in return for the information Rooster gave. Therefore, Rooster must include the $5,000 in his gross income.
Answer (b) is incorrect because the $5,000 is not considered a gift under the Duberstein case. Answer (c) is incorrect because the $5,000 is not a prize, and prizes are included in gross income as a general rule anyway. Answer (d) is incorrect because there is no gift on which to pay gift tax. Even if the $5,000 were a gift, the donor would be liable for the gift tax.

65. J. Ripper spent several years studying the human body. Finally, her research provided a new method for making surgical incisions that left no scars. Much to Ripper's astonishment, she was awarded a Nobel Prize that year. Ripper was awarded $50,000 outright (which was paid directly to a recognized charity designated by Ripper) and another $75,000 on the condition that she continue her research. How much must Ripper include in gross income for the year?

a. $0.
b. $50,000.
c. $75,000.
d. $125,000.

The correct answer is (c). *(Publisher)*
REQUIRED: The amount that the recipient of a scientific prize must include in gross income.
DISCUSSION: Sec. 74(b) excludes from gross income prizes and awards made primarily in recognition of charitable, scientific, educational, etc. achievement if the recipient was selected without any action on his/her part, is not required to render substantial future services as a condition of receiving the prize or award, and the payor transfers it to a governmental unit or a charity designated by the award recipient. Ripper received a Nobel Prize in recognition of scientific achievement, she did not take any action to enter the proceeding, and she assigned $50,000 of it to charity. However, $75,000 of the prize was awarded on the condition that substantial future services be rendered. Therefore, only $50,000 is excluded and Ripper must include the $75,000 in gross income.

66. In 1991 Joan accepted and received a $10,000 award for outstanding civic achievement. Joan was selected without any action on her part, and no future services are expected of her as a condition of receiving the award. What amount should Joan include in her 1991 gross income in connection with this award?

a. $0.
b. $4,000.
c. $5,000.
d. $10,000.

The correct answer is (d). *(CPA 1185 Q-9)*
REQUIRED: The amount of a civic achievement award the recipient must include in gross income.
DISCUSSION: Prizes and awards made primarily in recognition of charitable, scientific, educational, etc., achievement are excluded from gross income only if the recipient was selected without any action on his/her part, is not required to render substantial future services as a condition of receiving the prize or award, and assigns it to charity. Thus, Joan cannot exclude any amount of the $10,000 award from gross income once she receives it.

67. George Generous operates as a sole proprietorship and employs Ned Needy. Knowing that Ned's son Tiny Tim needed an operation, George made a gift to Ned of $1,000 in 1991 purely out of the goodness of his heart. The $1,000 is excluded from Ned's gross income.

The correct answer is (F). *(Publisher)*
DISCUSSION: Sec. 102(a) normally excludes gifts from the gross income of the recipient. However, the 1986 TRA added Sec. 102(c), which provides that gifts by an employer to an employee are not excluded from the employee's gross income.

CHAPTER SIX
BUSINESS EXPENSES AND LOSSES

6.1 Ordinary and Necessary Expenses	(46 questions)	95
6.2 Bad Debt Expense	(11 questions)	106
6.3 Business Travel and Entertainment	(28 questions)	110
6.4 Business Gifts	(8 questions)	118
6.5 Employee Compensation	(13 questions)	120
6.6 Business Use of Home	(8 questions)	123
6.7 Rental Expense	(7 questions)	126
6.8 Farm Expense	(9 questions)	128
6.9 Casualty and Theft Loss	(10 questions)	130

6.1 Ordinary and Necessary Expenses

1. State X imposes a tax based upon the amount of fixed assets a business owns. An individual proprietor would deduct this tax on which schedule?

a. Schedule A.
b. Schedule C.
c. Schedule E.
d. Schedule SE.

The correct answer is (b). *(SPE 1077 I-174)*
REQUIRED: The schedule on which an individual proprietor should deduct a state tax imposed upon the business's fixed assets.
DISCUSSION: A tax imposed on business assets is an expense of that business and is deductible under Sec. 162. As an ordinary and necessary expense of the business, it is reported on Schedule C which is used to report the income and expenses of a sole proprietorship, the net income (or loss) of which is carried onto page 1 of Form 1040.
Answer (a) is incorrect because Schedule A is used to compute itemized deductions. Answer (c) is incorrect because Schedule E is used to report supplemental income such as rents and royalties, and income from partnerships, estates and trusts. Answer (d) is incorrect because Schedule SE is used for computation of the Social Security self-employment tax.

2. Hamlet hires the Rosencrantz and Guildenstern rock opera ensemble to perform indefinitely at his night spot, The Sweet Prince. They perform nightly and are paid by the hour. Hamlet withholds the players' share of FICA taxes from their wages and pays both this and the employer's share to the government. Both Hamlet and the players claim income tax deductions for the FICA taxes. Which of the following is a true statement?

a. Hamlet should not deduct FICA taxes as a business expense.
b. The players properly claimed their share of FICA taxes as an income tax deduction.
c. Hamlet may deduct his share of FICA taxes but the players may not.
d. Hamlet should not withhold FICA taxes from the players' wages.

The correct answer is (c). *(Publisher)*
REQUIRED: The correct statement concerning the deduction of FICA taxes.
DISCUSSION: Sec. 164(a) lists the taxes which may be deducted by any person. FICA taxes are not listed as deductible. However, Sec. 164(a) does provide that taxes not described, but which are paid or accrued in carrying on a trade or business, may also be deducted. Since Hamlet is carrying on a trade or business, he may deduct the employer's share of the FICA taxes. The players (employees) are not allowed to deduct FICA taxes.
Answers (a) and (b) are incorrect because the employer is allowed to deduct FICA taxes while the employees are not. Answer (d) is incorrect because an employer is required to withhold the employees' share of FICA taxes from their wages and pay them to the government. Failure to do so can cause the employer to be liable for the full amount of the taxes.

Module 6.1: Ordinary and Necessary Expenses

3. George Michael, a sole proprietor, may deduct various taxes imposed by federal, state, local, and foreign governments, if he incurs them in the ordinary course of his business. All of the following are deductible on Schedule C, Form 1040, except

a. Real estate taxes on real property used in his business.

b. State and local income taxes on net income.

c. Personal property taxes on personal property used in his business.

d. Gasoline taxes included in the cost of fuel used in his business.

The correct answer is (b). *(SPE 984 II-55)*
REQUIRED: The tax that is not deductible on Schedule C, Form 1040.
DISCUSSION: State income taxes are imposed on an individual after income from all taxable sources is aggregated. State income taxes are a personal expense (deductible under Sec. 164) and not an expense of the source of income, e.g., a sole proprietorship. They are deducted from adjusted gross income and are reported as an itemized deduction on Schedule A.
Answers (a), (c), and (d) are incorrect because each is an expense of the business and deductible on Schedule C, Form 1040.

4. Jim Domuch, a calendar-year taxpayer, operates a novelty shop as a sole proprietor. During 1991 he incurred the following expenses in his business. Which is not deductible in 1991?

a. Property tax paid on business premises.

b. Sales taxes on the purchase of $50,000 of equipment used in the business.

c. Sales taxes on the purchase of supplies used in the business.

d. Business license tax imposed by the city.

The correct answer is (b). *(Publisher)*
REQUIRED: The tax that is not deductible by a business in 1991.
DISCUSSION: Sec. 164(a) lists the taxes that may be deducted by any person. Sales taxes are not listed as deductible for tax years beginning after 1986. Sec. 164(a) also provides that taxes not listed but paid or accrued in a trade or business may be deducted, except that any tax not listed that is paid or accrued to purchase property is to be treated as part of the cost of the property. Therefore, the sales tax on the equipment must be capitalized and only deducted as depreciation over the recovery period of the asset.
Answer (a) is incorrect because property taxes are listed in Sec. 164 as a deductible tax. Answer (c) is incorrect because, although the sales taxes on the purchase of supplies must be treated as part of the cost of supplies, this entire cost is deductible as an ordinary and necessary expense. Answer (d) is incorrect because the occupational license tax is an ordinary and necessary business expense.

5. Which of the following insurance premiums paid for policies related to a business is deductible as a business expense?

a. Owner's share of premiums on a split dollar life insurance plan.

b. Employee fidelity or performance bonds.

c. Self-insurance reserve funds.

d. Insurance against loss of employer's earnings due to sickness or disability.

The correct answer is (b). *(SPE 986 11-44)*
REQUIRED: The insurance premium that is deductible as a business expense.
DISCUSSION: Sec. 162(a) allows a deduction for all ordinary and necessary expenses paid or incurred during the taxable year in carrying on any trade or business. An expense is ordinary if it is customary in the kind of business conducted by the taxpayer and is not capital in nature. An expense is necessary if it is appropriate and helpful. Insurance to cover losses from employee malfeasance or nonperformance qualifies as such an expense.
Answer (a) is incorrect because the policy-owner's share of life insurance premiums is a personal (not business) expenditure. Answer (c) is incorrect because self-insurance reserve funds are not deductible until paid out and only then if for a deductible loss. Answer (d) is incorrect because insurance on the loss of the employer's earnings is not a deductible expense. Only if it were for the reimbursement of overhead expenses would such premiums be deductible.

Module 6.1: Ordinary and Necessary Expenses

6. All of the following insurance premiums are ordinarily deductible as a business expense except:

   a. Workers' compensation on behalf of partners in a business partnership.
   b. Life insurance on the life of an employee with the employee's wife as the beneficiary.
   c. Group health insurance that does not contain continuation coverage to employees.
   d. Malpractice insurance covering a professional's personal liability for negligence resulting in injury to business clients.

The correct answer is (a). *(SPE 990 II-39)*
REQUIRED: The insurance premium not ordinarily deductible as a business expense.
DISCUSSION: Workers' compensation insurance premiums paid on behalf of employees are deductible as a business expense. However, for this purpose, partners are not considered employees of the partnership (they are considered self-employed owners) and the insurance premiums on their behalf are not deductible.

Answer (b) is incorrect because life insurance premiums paid on the life of an employee are deductible as long as the employer is not the beneficiary. These life insurance premiums are effectively compensation to the employee unless excluded as part of a group term life insurance plan. Answer (c) is incorrect because for tax years beginning after 1988, there is an excise tax under Sec. 4980B if an employer has group health insurance not containing continuation coverage for employees. For 1986 through 1988, the premiums were not deductible. Answer (d) is incorrect because malpractice insurance is deductible as an ordinary business expense.

7. Mr. C operates a business as a calendar-year, cash-basis proprietorship. During the year, C purchased the following insurance policies:

Description of Policy	Total Cost	Date Paid
One-year policy that pays C for lost earnings owing to sickness or disability effective January 1, 1991	$ 600	1/5/91
One-year life insurance policy on a key employee of which C is beneficiary effective January 1, 1991	360	1/5/91
One-year life insurance policy on his own life taken out on June 30, 1991, required by bank for C to obtain a business loan	240	6/30/91
Two-year fire and theft policy effective December 1, 1991	2,400	1/6/92

What is C's deductible insurance expense for 1991?

   a. $0.
   b. $700.
   c. $1,180.
   d. $3,480.

The correct answer is (a). *(SPE 1083 II-73)*
REQUIRED: The taxpayer's ordinary and necessary business insurance deduction.
DISCUSSION: Sec. 162(a) allows a deduction for all ordinary and necessary expenses paid or incurred during the taxable year in carrying on any trade or business. Insurance premiums paid for carrying on a trade or business are deductible. The 1-year policy that pays C for lost earnings is personal, thus the premiums are not deductible as a trade or business expense. The premiums paid for the 1-year life insurance policy on the key employee are not deductible since C is the beneficiary [Sec. 264(a)]. The premiums on the 1-year life insurance policy on C's own life are also not deductible because the policy is personal even though required by the bank for C to obtain a business loan. The premiums paid on the 2-year fire and theft policy will be deductible, but since C is a cash-basis taxpayer, the premiums are not deductible until paid. Furthermore, the premiums will have to be apportioned over the 2-year period of the policy but cannot be deducted before they are paid.

8. Which of the following is not a test in determining whether an employee's pay is deductible?

   a. Ordinary and necessary.
   b. Reasonable.
   c. Services rendered.
   d. Control of individual.

The correct answer is (d). *(SPE 988 II-37)*
REQUIRED: The item not used to determine if an employee's pay is deductible.
DISCUSSION: Sec. 162(a)(1) allows a deduction for a reasonable allowance of salaries or other compensation for personal services actually rendered. There is no requirement that the employer have legal control over the individual. A concept of controlling the individual goes to whether the person is an employee or independent contractor.

Answer (a) is incorrect because all trade or business expenses must be ordinary and necessary. Answers (b) and (c) are incorrect because Sec. 162(a)(1) specifically requires the amount to be reasonable and the services to be actually rendered in order to deduct compensation.

9. The Gotham Goliaths ball club of the World Baseball League insures the life of its star center-fielder, Mickey Mays, for $1 million. The annual premium is $10,000 and the Goliaths club named itself as beneficiary. The club also pays an annual premium of $5,000 for insurance to recover overhead expenses in the event of a strike by the ballgirls who retrieve foul balls and thrown bats. It also has property insurance covering the club's chewing tobacco for which the annual premium is $1,000. What amount may the Gotham Goliaths deduct for its annual insurance premiums?

   a. $0.
   b. $1,000.
   c. $6,000.
   d. $16,000.

The correct answer is (c). *(Publisher)*
REQUIRED: The amount of premiums that a business may deduct for various insurance.
DISCUSSION: Sec. 162(a) allows a deduction for ordinary and necessary expenses paid or incurred in carrying on a trade or business. Insurance to recover overhead expenses is deductible. Property insurance is also deductible for any property owned by the business. Sec. 264(a) provides, however, that no deduction is allowed for premiums on a life insurance policy covering the life of an employee if the taxpayer is directly or indirectly a beneficiary. These are generally known as "key man" insurance policies. Since the Gotham Goliaths club is the beneficiary, the $10,000 premium is not deductible. Therefore, the total deduction for insurance premiums is $6,000 ($5,000 for overhead insurance and $1,000 for property insurance).

10. Carbozo was an officer of a corporation in the business of selling hospital supplies. Due to stiff competition, the corporation went bankrupt. Carbozo contracted with the Hoover Corporation to purchase hospital supplies for it on commission. In order to reestablish relations with suppliers of hospital supplies that Carbozo had known in his previous capacity, and to solidify his credit standing, Carbozo decided to pay certain debts of the former corporation that went bankrupt. Which of the following statements is correct concerning these payments?

   a. The payments are not deductible because they are not necessary.
   b. The payments are not deductible because they are not ordinary.
   c. The payments are deductible as ordinary and necessary business expenses.
   d. The payments are not deductible because they were not Carbozo's debts.

The correct answer is (b). *(Publisher)*
REQUIRED: The correct statement concerning a deduction for payment of another's debts.
DISCUSSION: Sec. 162(a) allows a deduction for the ordinary and necessary expenses paid or incurred in carrying on a trade or business. Courts have held that ordinary does not mean habitual or normal in terms of frequency, rather that it is the common and accepted means of dealing with the situation. Courts have also held that the payment of debts of others without legal obligation or a definite business requirement is not considered ordinary and is not deductible.
Answer (a) is incorrect because necessary has generally been defined as useful and helpful, which the payments made by Carbozo were. Answer (c) is incorrect because the payments are not deductible since they are not ordinary. Answer (d) is incorrect because the mere fact that Carbozo was not liable did not make the debts nondeductible. If the payments had been required by the suppliers in order for Carbozo to continue in business, they may have been considered ordinary even though they were not his legal obligations.

11. AMJ Enterprises is a small book publisher. It incurred the following as its miscellaneous expenses:

Bank service charges	$ 70
Office supplies	100
Advertising	600
Fees to attorneys and CPAs	2,400
Interest for the entire period of a 5-year loan taken out on January 1	2,500

How much of the above may AMJ Enterprises deduct for the current year?

   a. $770.
   b. $3,570.
   c. $3,670.
   d. $5,670.

The correct answer is (c). *(Publisher)*
REQUIRED: The amount that a business can deduct for the miscellaneous expenses listed.
DISCUSSION: Professional fees are deductible under Sec. 162, the same as compensation to an employee, provided they are reasonable in amount. Advertising and bank service charges are deductible as general expenses. Office supplies are also deductible under Reg. 1.162-3. Sec. 461(g) requires prepaid interest to be capitalized and allocated to the periods to which it relates. Since the interest was prepaid for 5 years, only one-fifth of the interest may be deducted in the current year.

Bank service charges	$ 70
Office supplies	100
Advertising	600
Professional fees	2,400
Interest (1/5 x $2,500)	500
Deductible business expenses	$3,670

12. Frank Fronton decided to become a professional jai alai player. In January, Fronton joined a jai alai club where he could train to become a jai alai player. After training for the first 7 months of the year, Fronton received a contract and began to play professionally; however, he continued to use the club for ongoing training and practice. Fronton paid $12,000 for the use of the club during the year ($1,000 per month). He purchased equipment in January costing $1,500. Replacement equipment after receiving the contract cost $500, and transportation to out-of-town games cost $800 for the remainder of the year. How much can Fronton deduct as business expenses?

a. $800.
b. $6,300.
c. $7,800.
d. $12,800.

The correct answer is (b). *(Publisher)*
REQUIRED: The amount that a person entering a new business may deduct as business expenses.
DISCUSSION: The playing of professional jai alai would be considered a trade or business; however, the preparation for entering that business is not conducting that trade or business.
Therefore, the $1,000 monthly club dues for the first 7 months are not deductible, whereas the dues for the last 5 months are deductible. The $1,500 initially spent for equipment is also not deductible since it is a preoperating cost. Replacement equipment is deductible assuming it does not have a life substantially longer than the current year. Transportation expenses are also deductible provided there is adequate documentation.

Training club dues ($1,000 x 5 months)	$5,000
Replacement equipment	500
Transportation	800
Total business deductions	$6,300

13. Mr. M, a cash-basis sole proprietor, secured two business loans from two different banks. The following information pertains to the loans. Assume all costs have been paid by M.

	Loan 1	Loan 2
Date of Loan	1/1/89	1/1/91
Term	10 years	10 years
Loan origination fee	$1,000	$2,000
Mortgage commission	250	500
Abstract fees	150	300
Recording fees	100	200
Interest for 1991	5,000	7,000

On December 31, 1991, Mr. M paid off Loan 1 and had to pay a prepayment penalty of $1,500. What deductions can Mr. M take in 1991 with respect to these loans?

	Interest Expense	Other Costs
a.	$14,500	$500
b.	$14,000	$2,500
c.	$13,500	$3,000
d.	$12,000	$4,500

The correct answer is (a). *(SPE 1083 II-72)*
REQUIRED: The amount and character of deductions for miscellaneous loan costs.
DISCUSSION: Interest is deductible under Sec. 163 as well as other payments made in lieu of interest. The prepayment penalty is in lieu of interest. The loan origination fees are also in lieu of interest since they are unreasonably large to be actual fees for processing a loan. As prepaid interest, the loan origination fees must be amortized over the period of each loan, but the balance of unpaid origination fees on Loan 1 is deductible in 1991 when the loan was paid off.
All other expenditures are costs of obtaining a loan and are deductible over the period of each loan as Sec. 162 business expenses. The balance on Loan 1 is deductible in 1991 when the loan was paid off.

Stated interest on both loans	$12,000
Prepayment penalty on Loan 1	1,500
Loan 1 origination fee ($1,000 – $200 amortized in 1989 and 1990)	800
Loan 2 origination fees ($2,000 ÷ 10 years)	200
Total 1991 interest	$14,500
Loan 1 fees ($500 – $100 amortized in 1989 and 1990)	$ 400
Loan 2 fees ($1,000 ÷ 10 years)	100
Other deductible costs	$ 500

Module 6.1: Ordinary and Necessary Expenses

14. Mr. B paid the following amounts in 1991 in connection with his business property:

New motor for a truck which extended its useful life by 3 years	$ 600
Replacement parts to maintain machinery in efficient operating condition	3,000
Labor to maintain the above equipment	1,800
Cost of replacing gravel driveway with heavy duty concrete	12,000
Cost of repainting factory building	1,400

What is Mr. B's allowable deduction for repairs and maintenance expense on his 1991 Schedule C, Form 1040?

a. $2,400.
b. $6,200.
c. $6,800.
d. $18,800.

The correct answer is (b). *(SPE 1080 II-56)*
REQUIRED: The taxpayer's allowable deduction for repairs and maintenance expense.
DISCUSSION: Repairs and maintenance that do not materially add to the value of property or prolong its life may be deducted. All other expenditures should be capitalized and depreciated (Reg. 1.162-4). The expenditures made for a new truck motor with a useful life of 3 years and the cost of replacing the driveway should be capitalized. The $3,000 cost of replacement parts and the $1,800 in labor costs to maintain the equipment in operating condition are deductible. The $1,400 cost of repainting the factory building is also deductible as a repair and maintenance item. These total $6,200 for repair and maintenance expenses which are deductible in the current year.

15. The Saturn Titans of the Planetary Football League have a team spaceship. The spaceship developed a leak between the power source and living area causing dangerous fumes to occasionally enter. This was fixed at a cost of $100,000. The power source also needed an overhaul which was done at a cost of $500,000. As a result of the overhaul, the useful life of the spaceship was not changed but it can now make the trip to the players' home in the United States on Earth in half the former time and at a substantial fuel savings. How should these expenditures be treated?

a. The repair of the leak should be deducted while the overhaul should be capitalized.
b. The overhaul should be deducted and the repair of the leak should be capitalized.
c. Both the repair of the leak and the overhaul should be deducted.
d. Both the repair of the leak and the overhaul should be capitalized.

The correct answer is (a). *(Publisher)*
REQUIRED: The proper treatment of expenditures for repair and maintenance of business property.
DISCUSSION: Repairs and maintenance, which do not materially add to the value of property or prolong its life, may be deducted. All other repair and improvement expenditures should be capitalized and depreciated (Reg. 1.162-4). Expenditures to repair damage and put the property back in the same condition as it was before the damage are generally deductible as repairs, provided that they do not materially add to the value of the property or prolong its life. This would be true in the case of fixing the leak. However, the cost of a major overhaul which changes the operation of a vehicle, such as increasing its speed and saving fuel costs, would be considered to add materially to the value of the property. Therefore, the overhaul of the powerplant in the spaceship may not be deducted. It must be capitalized and depreciated.

16. Mr. R is a self-employed over-the-road trucker who uses the cash method of accounting. Which one of the following expenses paid during 1991 would be deductible on Mr. R's 1991 Schedule C?

a. Penalty for late delivery of cargo paid to Corporation V.
b. Fine for speeding in business truck paid to city A.
c. Overweight fine paid to State B.
d. Contribution to Bull Moose Political party in an attempt to receive a trucking contract.

The correct answer is (a). *(SPE 987 II-47)*
REQUIRED: The item which is a deductible business expense.
DISCUSSION: Although fines and penalties paid to a government are generally not deductible, the payment of a penalty for nonperformance of a contract is generally deductible. This penalty usually represents damages which one contracting party was willing to incur in order to avoid performing under the contract. This is a business decision and the damages are deductible under Sec. 162(a).
Answers (b) and (c) are incorrect because each is a fine or penalty paid to a government or governmental agency and is specifically not deductible under Sec. 162(f).
Answer (d) is incorrect because political contributions are not deductible as business expenses.

17. During 1991, Mr. C was forced to permanently abandon business property in a foreign country. The property consisted of the following items:

	Fair Market Value	Cost	Adjusted Basis
Truck	$5,000	$7,000	$3,000
Furniture	2,000	3,000	1,000
Building	45,000	50,000	40,000

Mr. C's abandonment loss for 1991 is:

a. $0.
b. $44,000.
c. $52,000.
d. $60,000.

The correct answer is (b). *(SPE 1081 II-50)*
REQUIRED: The taxpayer's deductible loss arising from the forced abandonment of business property in a foreign country.
DISCUSSION: Sec. 165 allows a deduction for an uncompensated loss sustained during the year which is incurred in a trade or business. A loss from abandonment of assets is deductible in the year the assets are actually abandoned with no claim for reimbursement (Reg. 1.165-2 and Reg. 1.167(a)-8). The amount of the loss is the adjusted basis of the property provided in Sec. 1011 for determining the loss from the sale or other disposition of property. The taxpayer's adjusted basis in the property was $3,000 for the truck, $1,000 for the furniture, and $40,000 for the building. The total loss is $44,000.

18. Toys-or-Bust, a toy manufacturer, had the following items recorded on its books for the year ending December 31, 1991:

Direct labor	$15,000
Inventory on hand (12/31/91)	3,500
Inventory on hand (12/31/90)	4,000
Legal fees	500
Purchase of office equipment	8,000
Purchase of manufacturing materials	50,000
Rent expense - auto	1,000
Shipping expense - freight out	600
Supplies - office	400
Supplies - manufacturing	2,500

What is the cost of goods sold for Toys-or-Bust?

a. $67,000.
b. $68,000.
c. $76,000.
d. $78,500.

The correct answer is (b). *(SPE 1085 II-63)*
REQUIRED: The taxpayer's cost of goods sold for 1991.
DISCUSSION: Cost of goods sold is computed by starting with the beginning inventory, adding the cost of materials purchased during the year and the cost of production, and subtracting the ending inventory. Under Code Sec. 263A, manufacturers are required to use the full absorption method of costing which means that both direct and indirect production costs must be included. Freight charges are always added to the cost of the goods purchased.

Legal fees, auto rental, costs to ship to the purchaser, and office supplies are selling expenses, not costs of inventory. Office equipment costs are capitalized.

Beginning inventory		$ 4,000
Plus materials and labor:		
Direct labor	$15,000	
Manufacturing materials	50,000	
Manufacturing supplies	2,500	67,500
Goods available for sale		$71,500
Less ending inventory		(3,500)
Cost of goods sold		$68,000

19. Which of the following expenditures incurred in the operation of a business is not required to be capitalized?

a. Cost of replacing an old shingle roof with a new tile roof.
b. Cost of changing from one heating system to another.
c. Cost of replacing an old truck used for business delivery.
d. Cost of replacing small tools.

The correct answer is (d). *(SPE 1080 II-55)*
REQUIRED: The expenditure which should not be capitalized.
DISCUSSION: Small tools used in a business normally do not have to be capitalized under the theory that either they do not have a useful life substantially beyond the taxable year or that their cost is so small so as not to materially distort income. Items costing a small amount may normally be expensed as long as a consistent policy is followed.

Answers (a), (b), and (c) are incorrect because each is an expenditure for property having a useful life substantially beyond the taxable year [Reg. 1.263(a)-2].

Module 6.1: Ordinary and Necessary Expenses

20. All of the following expenses incurred in the course of operating a business are deductible business expenses except:

a. Cost of sending communications to members of Congress.

b. Public service advertising that keeps the name of the business before the public.

c. Advertising in a concert program the local church is sponsoring.

d. Advertising in a convention program of a political party. The proceeds from the publication of the program are for the local use of the political party.

The correct answer is (d). *(SPE 990 II-41)*
REQUIRED: The expense not deductible as a business expense.
DISCUSSION: Sec. 162(e)(2)(A) provides that contributions to a political party or candidate are not deductible as business expenses. The proceeds from the convention program are for the use of a political party. Therefore, the expenses incurred to advertise in that program are not deductible.
Answer (a) is incorrect because lobbying expenses are deductible under Sec. 162. Answers (b) and (c) are incorrect because advertising expenses are also deductible under Sec. 162.

21. Mr. E, a sole proprietor, made the following payments in 1991. Which payment is not a capital expenditure?

a. Freight paid on new equipment purchased.

b. Rewiring of building to install a new computer.

c. A payment made to eliminate competition for 5 years.

d. Moving machinery from one location to another.

The correct answer is (d). *(SPE 1080 II-51)*
REQUIRED: The payment that is not a capital expenditure.
DISCUSSION: Capital expenditures include those which add to the value or prolong the life of property, or adapt the property to a new or different use. Moving machinery to a new location does not increase the value of the machinery, prolong its life, or adapt it to a new or different use. Therefore, the cost of moving the machinery is not a capital expenditure (it is deductible under Sec. 162).
Answer (a) is incorrect because freight paid on new equipment purchased is a cost of acquisition, which is a capital expenditure. Answer (b) is incorrect because the cost of rewiring a building to install a new computer adapts the building to a new or different use, which is a capital expenditure. Answer (c) is incorrect because a payment made to eliminate competition increases the value of the business, and is a capital expenditure.

22. All of the following expenses paid or incurred in the course of operating a business are deductible as business expenses except:

a. Lobbying expenses.

b. Political contributions.

c. Penalty for nonperformance of a contract.

d. Reimbursements to job applicants in connection with interviews.

The correct answer is (b). *(SPE 989 II-44)*
REQUIRED: The expense not deductible as a business expense.
DISCUSSION: Contributions to a political party or candidate are not deductible as business expenses under Sec. 162(e)(2)(A).
Answers (a), (c), and (d) are incorrect because lobbying expenses, penalties for nonperformance of a contract, and reimbursements to job applicants in connection with interviews are all deductible business expenses under Sec. 162.

23. On September 1, 1991, Mr. Z, a cash basis, calendar year, self-employed mechanic, borrowed $10,000 at 10% for 5 years to purchase equipment with a useful life of 10 years. Z paid the lender a loan origination fee of $3,000 on the loan date. This fee was solely for the use of the money. How much of the $3,000 fee may Z deduct on his Schedule C for 1991?

a. $100.

b. $200.

c. $630.

d. $3,000.

The correct answer is (b). *(SPE 989 II-43)*
REQUIRED: The current year deduction for points paid to obtain a loan.
DISCUSSION: Loan origination fees or points are effectively interest paid in advance. Prepaid interest is not deductible in advance except for the ordinary points paid on a home mortgage. The points must be amortized over the period of the loan. The loan is for a 5-year period, so the points should be amortized over 60 months (5 years x 12 months). Since there are 4 months left in 1991 after the loan is taken out, $200 ($3,000 ÷ 60 months x 4 months) is deductible as interest expense in 1991.

24. Real estate assessments by a municipal government against business property for construction of public parking facilities benefiting the business are not deductible by the business as a tax expense.

The correct answer is (T). *(SPE 987 II-20)*
DISCUSSION: Real property taxes do not include assessments for local benefit, e.g., streets, sidewalks, curbing, and other like improvements, since such assessments tend to increase the value of the property (Reg. 1.164-4). The cost of such assessments is added to the adjusted basis of the taxpayer's property. According to the IRS and the courts the public parking facilities are a similar improvement.

25. Whitney is a self-employed cash-basis carpenter. On July 1, 1991 she purchased a new piece of equipment that is 5-year MACRS property, for use in her business. The state sales tax on the equipment was imposed on Whitney. She can deduct the state sales tax as a business expense on her Schedule C for 1991.

The correct answer is (F). *(SPE 987 II-21)*
DISCUSSION: Sec. 164 requires state and local general sales taxes related to the purchase of property to be included as a cost of the property.

26. Trust Me Company, a sole proprietorship, paid Mr. J, an employee of Trust Me, $35,000 in 1991 to compensate him for injuries sustained while at work. The company was reimbursed for $15,000 by its insurance carrier. Trust Me can deduct $20,000 on its 1991 income tax return as an ordinary and necessary business expense.

The correct answer is (T). *(SPE 990 II-6)*
DISCUSSION: Under Sec. 162(a), a business may deduct, as an ordinary and necessary business expense, reasonable amounts paid for sickness, injury, or disability benefits. In this case, Trust Me Company paid Mr. J $35,000 to compensate him for injuries sustained while at work. Trust Me was reimbursed for $15,000 by its insurance company; thus, the $20,000 of unreimbursed expenditures is deductible.

27. Mr. C, owner of a sole proprietorship, purchased an insurance policy that will pay for business overhead expenses in the event he is disabled for a long time. The premiums on this policy are deductible as an insurance expense.

The correct answer is (T). *(SPE 1083 II-20)*
DISCUSSION: The premiums on an insurance policy that will pay for business overhead expenses in the event the sole proprietor is disabled for a long time are an ordinary and necessary business expense. The premiums paid are deductible under Sec. 162(a).

28. Mr. N cannot get business insurance coverage for certain business risks; therefore, he periodically contributes to a reserve he set up for self-insurance. Mr. N may deduct these periodic payments as an expense.

The correct answer is (F). *(SPE 1082 II-23)*
DISCUSSION: Sec. 162 allows a deduction for ordinary and necessary trade or business expenses only if they were paid or incurred during the taxable year. Since no expense is paid or incurred when a reserve is set aside for self-insurance, no deduction is allowed.

29. An employer may deduct premiums paid on an ordinary life insurance policy covering the life of an officer-employee if the employer is the direct beneficiary.

The correct answer is (F). *(SPE 986 II-11)*
DISCUSSION: Sec. 264 disallows a deduction for premiums paid on any life insurance policy covering the life of any person financially interested in the trade or business carried on by the taxpayer, when the taxpayer is directly or indirectly a beneficiary under such policy.

30. Beginning in 1991, if you are self-employed, you can no longer deduct as a business expense, up to 25% of the amount you pay for medical insurance for yourself and your family, as an adjustment to income on your individual income tax return.

The correct answer is (F). *(SPE 990 I-20)*
DISCUSSION: Sec. 162l permits a deduction of up to 25% of amounts paid for health insurance by a self-employed person for themselves, their spouse, and dependents. The provision is applicable for tax years beginning after 1986 and before 1992. Therefore, the statement is false.

31. Brian borrowed $10,000 from his local bank in order to fund the cost of a business venture. The bank required Brian to take out a life insurance policy on his own life as security for the loan. Premiums paid on this policy are deductible as a business expense since they are related to a business venture.

The correct answer is (F). *(SPE 1085 II-12)*
DISCUSSION: If the taxpayer died, the insurance proceeds would be used to pay the loan. Therefore, the taxpayer is indirectly a beneficiary. Sec. 264 disallows a deduction for life insurance premiums when the insured is directly or indirectly a beneficiary.

32. In 1991, Mr. H established a self-insured medical reimbursement plan that covers medical expenses for all eligible employees. The plan has eligibility requirements that favor highly compensated individuals of the company. Mr. H may not deduct payments under the plan.

The correct answer is (F). *(SPE 1081 II-7)*
DISCUSSION: The cost of a medical reimbursement plan is deductible under Sec. 162(a) regardless of whether the plan discriminates in favor of highly compensated employees. Under Sec. 105(h), however, such highly compensated employees who receive payments under this plan may not be able to exclude all the payments from gross income.

33. Lisa Johnson started a dry cleaning business in June 1991. In April 1991, prior to beginning business operations, she incurred costs totaling $1,500 for the purpose of securing prospective suppliers and customers. The $1,500 is a capital expenditure that cannot be deducted as an expense or amortized.

The correct answer is (F). *(SPE 984 II-4)*
DISCUSSION: The cost of securing suppliers and customers before going into business is a start-up expense which must be capitalized. It is not a business expense because the business has not yet begun. Such costs may be amortized over a period of not less than 60 months (Sec. 195).

34. In 1991, Mr. X incurred $12,000 in qualified expenses to make a public transportation vehicle used in his business more accessible to handicapped people. Mr. X may deduct the expenses in 1991.

The correct answer is (T). *(SPE 1081 II-17)*
DISCUSSION: Sec. 190 allows a taxpayer to elect to deduct up to $15,000 of qualified expenditures which remove architectural and transportation barriers to the handicapped and the elderly. Sec. 44 permits a disabled access credit to be claimed in 1991 for qualified expenditures incurred by an eligible small business to remove architectural and transportation barriers to the handicapped and elderly. The available credit is 50% of eligible expenditures in excess of $250 but not in excess of $10,250. Any amounts for which a credit is claimed cannot be deducted under Sec. 190 [Sec. 44(d)(7)]. Since the Sec. 190 limit of $15,000 exceeds the Sec. 44 limit of $10,000, some of the expenditures will be deducted under Sec. 190 even though the credit election is made for the $10,000 limit.

35. Since the seller gets capital gain treatment on the sale of goodwill, the buyer must amortize the value of purchased goodwill over not less than 60 months.

The correct answer is (F). *(SPE 1077 I-77)*
DISCUSSION: Goodwill is normally not amortizable since its life is usually indeterminate and often extends for an unlimited period [Reg. 1.167(a)-3]. The seller of a business gets capital gain treatment on the sale of goodwill, but that is irrelevant to amortization.

36. Mr. C considers it necessary to his business to pay kickbacks to the purchasing agents of his customers. The employers of the purchasing agents are unaware of these payments. The kickbacks are in violation of the law in the state in which Mr. C resides and the law is generally enforced. Mr. C may deduct the kickbacks as a business expense.

The correct answer is (F). *(SPE 988 II-12)*
DISCUSSION: Illegal bribes and kickbacks are specifically disallowed as deductions under Sec. 162(c)(2), provided the law is generally enforced.

Module 6.1: Ordinary and Necessary Expenses

37. Mr. X, an insurance broker, pays kickbacks to car dealers who refer insurance companies to him. There is a state law against such payments but the law is never enforced. There is no federal law against such payments. Mr. X can deduct the kickback payments.

The correct answer is (T). *(SPE 984 II-19)*
DISCUSSION: Illegal bribes and kickbacks are specifically disallowed as deductions under Sec. 162(c)(2), provided the law is generally enforced. When such a state law is not generally enforced, the kickbacks are deductible.

38. Mr. K, a long-haul trucker, incurred fines in 1991 for violation of state maximum highway weight laws. These fines are deductible because they are both ordinary and necessary in the operation of the business.

The correct answer is (F). *(SPE 1079 II-26)*
DISCUSSION: No deduction is allowed for any fine or similar penalty paid to a government for the violation of any law [Sec. 162(f)]. Although such fines may be ordinary and necessary in the trucking business, a deduction would be in violation of public policy and is therefore specifically disallowed.

39. Interest and penalties paid on an individual income tax deficiency are deductible as a business expense if the deficiency was related to income from a business.

The correct answer is (F). *(SPE 1082 II-22)*
DISCUSSION: After 1986 personal interest is only deductible in part (not at all after 1990). Interest paid on an individual's income tax deficiency is personal interest, even if the income was from a business. To the extent personal interest is deductible, it is deductible as an itemized deduction rather than as a business expense. Penalties paid are not deductible [Sec. 162(f)].

40. In 1991 Mr. Z purchased an apartment building. As part of a major restoration plan to make the apartments suitable for tenants, he painted all of the rooms. Mr. Z can deduct the cost of the paint as a repair expense in 1991.

The correct answer is (F). *(SPE 984 II-12)*
DISCUSSION: Since the painting was done as part of a major restoration, the cost of the paint should be capitalized as an amount paid for permanent improvements or betterments made to increase the value of the apartment building [Sec. 263(a)(1)].

41. If part of the purchase price of a business is clearly for a covenant not to compete, and the covenant is for a fixed number of years, the amount paid for it is deductible as a business expense proportionately over the life of the covenant.

The correct answer is (T). *(SPE 984 II-7)*
DISCUSSION: If an intangible asset has a known useful life which may be estimated with reasonable accuracy, the asset may be subject to amortization [Reg. 1.167(a)-3]. A covenant not to compete may be amortized over the life of the covenant, provided its purchase price is separately stated in the purchase agreement.

42. During 1991 DN Corporation constructed a building for use in its business. DN borrowed $200,000 during the production period that was used to pay construction costs. The wages paid to employees to construct the building and the entire amount of interest paid on the production period loan can be deducted as a current operating expense.

The correct answer is (F). *(SPE 990 II-4)*
DISCUSSION: The Uniform Capitalization Rules of Sec. 263A apply to real or tangible personal property produced by the taxpayer for use in a business [Sec. 263A(b)(1)]. Sec. 263A requires all direct costs and a proper share of indirect costs allocable to property produced by the taxpayer to be capitalized. Wages paid to employees for constructing a new building would be direct costs allocable to that building and have to be capitalized [Sec. 263A(a)(2)]. Sec. 263A(f) requires interest paid or incurred during the production period on real property produced by the taxpayer to be capitalized. These costs are depreciated as part of the cost of the building.

43. Mr. X purchased a vacant lot he plans to use later as a parking lot for his business. While the lot remains vacant and unimproved, Mr. X must capitalize the annual taxes and mortgage interest that are otherwise currently deductible.

The correct answer is (F). *(SPE 1082 II-3)*
DISCUSSION: Interest and taxes paid on vacant land that is held for investment, or merely waiting to be improved, are deductible.

44. During 1980 Mr. H bought a building for use in his business. He demolished the building in 1991 at a cost of $5,000, because repairs were abnormally high, and he had an opportunity to rent the land at an acceptable fee. Mr. H can deduct the $5,000 as an ordinary expense, and he can claim the undepreciated basis of the building as a loss.

The correct answer is (F). *(SPE 986 II-18)*
DISCUSSION: All costs of demolishing structures, and any losses sustained, must be allocated to the land (Sec. 280B). Therefore, the $5,000 cost to demolish the building must be capitalized. Neither this $5,000 nor the undepreciated basis of the building demolished is deductible.

45. Scott Kyzar is a self-employed, cash-basis restaurant owner. During 1991 he paid off the mortgage on his restaurant building, and he had to pay the lending bank a penalty for early payment. Scott may deduct the penalty as interest on his Schedule C for 1991.

The correct answer is (T). *(SPE 987 II-19)*
DISCUSSION: When a person pays off a mortgage early, and is required to pay the lender a penalty for doing so, the penalty is deductible in the year the interest is paid.

46. On July 1, 1991, Mr. K, a calendar-year, cash-basis sole proprietor, paid $3,000 in commitment fees to his bank to have business funds made readily available to him over a period of 3 years as needed. Mr. K did not borrow any of these funds in 1991. Mr. K may deduct $500 of these fees as interest on his Schedule C for 1991.

The correct answer is (F). *(SPE 988 II-9)*
DISCUSSION: Loan commitment fees are a cost of obtaining a loan. They are deductible over the period of the loan. If the loan is never taken out, a loss is deductible for the loan commitment fees in the year the right to borrow the funds expires. Therefore, Mr. K cannot deduct any loan commitment fees in 1991, since he did not take out a loan, and the right to borrow the funds has not yet expired.

6.2 Bad Debt Expense

47. Gary, an accrual basis taxpayer, operates a retail jewelry business as a sole proprietor. Before 1987, Gary used the reserve method for determining his bad debt deduction. The balance in Gary's bad debt reserve account on December 31, 1986 was $4,000. During 1990 Gary recovered two bad debts. One was for $3,000 from 1988 and the other was for $1,000 from 1989. What is the total amount of recovered bad debts and the recovery of bad debt reserve account that Gary must include in his income for 1990?

   a. $0.
   b. $1,000.
   c. $4,000.
   d. $5,000.

The correct answer is (d). *(SPE 989 II-67)*
REQUIRED: The total amount of recovered bad debts and the recovery of bad debt reserve to be included in income for 1990.
DISCUSSION: For tax years beginning after 1986, the reserve method of deducting bad debts is no longer allowed and Gary must use the specific write-off method. Gary would include in income, over 4 years, his bad debt reserve balance existing at December 31, 1986. Beginning in 1987 $1,000 ($4,000 ÷ 4 years) would be included in income each year for the next 4 years. In 1990, Gary would recover the remaining $1,000 balance in the reserve account. In addition, the recoveries of the two previously written-off bad debts should be included in income in the year it is collected under the tax benefit rule. Thus, $5,000 ($1,000 recovery of reserve account + $4,000 recoveries of previously written-off bad debts) should be included in income for 1990.

Module 6.2: Bad Debt Expense

48. Landon, a sole proprietor, made the following loans in 1991. Two loans were closely related to his business operation, and the other two were personal.

To	Amount	Type	Unrecoverable Debt Written Off Landon's Books in 1991
A	$2,000	Nonbusiness	$1,000
B	$1,000	Nonbusiness	$1,000
C	$3,000	Business	$1,000
D	$5,000	Business	$2,000

What is the total maximum tax deduction Landon can take for business and nonbusiness worthless debt in 1991?

a. $2,000.
b. $3,000.
c. $4,000.
d. $5,000.

The correct answer is (c). *(SPE 1081 II-52)*
REQUIRED: The maximum deduction available for the business and nonbusiness bad debts.
DISCUSSION: A partially worthless nonbusiness debt is not deductible (Reg. 1.166-5), and a wholly worthless nonbusiness debt is treated as a loss from the sale or exchange of a capital asset held for 1 year or less, i.e., a short-term capital loss [Sec. 166(d)]. Notice that the Sec. 1211 limit of $3,000 for a capital loss deduction is not reached in this problem. Partially worthless business debts may be deducted under Sec. 166(a) to the extent they are specifically written off. Landon's bad debt deduction is

A	$	0
B		1,000
C		1,000
D		2,000
Deduction		$4,000

49. CW Enterprises is in financial difficulties. It manufactures seagull-shaped sports cars for the jet set. The board of directors is highly paid and all members loaned funds to the company, hoping to retain their positions (they own no stock in the company). They instituted a policy requiring the assembly line workers to lend 5% of their wages, or face discharge. The officers have all made voluntary loans to the company. In addition, the majority shareholder made a substantial loan. If CW defaults on all these loans, who is not entitled to a business bad debt deduction?

a. The assembly line workers.
b. The officers.
c. The board of directors.
d. The majority shareholder.

The correct answer is (d). *(Publisher)*
REQUIRED: Those who are not entitled to a bad debt deduction for loans to a company.
DISCUSSION: A loss from a business debt is an ordinary loss, while a loss from a nonbusiness debt is treated as a short-term capital loss (Sec. 166). A nonbusiness bad debt is a debt other than one incurred or acquired in connection with the trade or business of the taxpayer. An investment is not considered a trade or business, and a shareholder who makes a loan to a corporation to protect his/her investment is not considered to have made a business loan. Therefore, the majority shareholder's bad debt will be deductible as a short-term capital loss.
Answers (a), (b), and (c) are incorrect because employment has been held to constitute an employee's trade or business, and loans made to protect an employee's job are considered business loans. Therefore, such loans will be considered a business bad debt if not paid.

50. Which of the following may be deducted as a business bad debt by Mr. B, an accrual-basis taxpayer?

a. Worthless loan to son for college tuition - $500.
b. Worthless trade receivable - $1,000.
c. Partially worthless note from a friend - $1,500.
d. Worthless corporate security - $2,000.

The correct answer is (b). *(SPE 1078 I-55)*
REQUIRED: The item deductible as a business bad debt by an accrual-basis taxpayer.
DISCUSSION: An accrual-basis taxpayer includes trade receivables in gross income, and a worthless trade receivable is deductible as a business bad debt under Sec. 166(a).
Answer (a) is incorrect because a worthless loan to the taxpayer's son for college tuition may not be a bona fide debt, and is not a business debt in any event. Answer (c) is incorrect because a loan to a friend is not a business debt. Answer (d) is incorrect because a worthless corporate security is not considered a bad debt [Sec. 166(e)]; it is treated as a loss under Sec. 165(g).

Module 6.2: Bad Debt Expense

51. On January 1, 1991, Ms. C loaned $10,000 to her son to pay tuition expenses for college. Her son repaid $2,000 on July 1, 1991, and Ms. C forgave the balance upon her son's agreement to enter her business. What is the amount and character of the loss that Ms. C may deduct on her individual income tax return?

a. $0.
b. $4,000 short-term capital loss.
c. $4,000 long-term capital loss.
d. $8,000 nonbusiness bad debt.

The correct answer is (a). *(SPE 990 I-95)*
REQUIRED: The amount deductible for a forgiven debt owed by a related party.
DISCUSSION: A bad debt deduction may be taken only for a bona fide debt arising from a valid debtor-creditor relationship based upon a valid and enforceable obligation to pay a fixed or determinable sum of money [Reg. 1.166-1(c)]. The taxpayer either made a gift to her son of the balance of the debt owed, or released the debt in consideration of her son's agreement to enter the business. Therefore, no bad debt exists, and no deduction is available.

52. Mr. X, a dentist and calendar year taxpayer, has consistently reported income and expenses from his business on the cash basis. All cash and checks he receives are deposited and included in income. X's records for 1991 reflect the following information:

Uncollectible receivables	$2,000
Patients' uncollectible returned checks	500
Recovery of an uncollectible receivable from 1990	1,000
Business related loan to a supplier that became totally worthless	3,000

Mr. X has chosen not to use the nonaccrual-experience method of reporting bad debts. What is the amount of X's bad debt expense for 1991?

a. $2,500.
b. $3,500.
c. $4,500.
d. $5,500.

The correct answer is (b). *(SPE 989 II-66)*
REQUIRED: The amount of bad debt expense for 1991.
DISCUSSION: Mr. X has consistently reported income and expenses on the cash basis, and cash and checks received are deposited and included in income. Therefore the $2,000 in accounts receivable have not been included income, and accordingly, no deduction will arise from their uncollectibility. The recovery of an uncollectible receivable from 1990 of $1,000 will be included in income, and will not be netted against bad debt expense. Bad debt expense for 1991 will be $3,500: the $500 in returned checks has been included in income, so a bad debt deduction is proper, and the $3,000 business bad debt would also be deductible.

53. Mr. Jones, who operates a small tools supply company, guaranteed payment of a $10,000 note for Black Hardware store, one of Mr. Jones's largest clients. Black Hardware later filed for bankruptcy and defaulted on the loan. Mr. Jones made full payment to satisfy the note. Mr. Jones's payment should be considered:

a. A business bad debt.
b. A nonbusiness bad debt.
c. A gift.
d. An investment.

The correct answer is (a). *(SPE 988 II-42)*
REQUIRED: The characterization of a loss on a guarantee of a customer's debt.
DISCUSSION: A business bad debt is deductible in full as an ordinary loss under Sec. 166. A loss on a guarantee of a debt is treated the same as a primary debt in determining whether it is business or nonbusiness. To be a business bad debt, it must be closely related to one's trade or business. However, guaranteeing the debt of a primary customer does not necessarily make it a business debt. If making the guarantee was required to retain the customer, the payment on the guarantee would be a business bad debt.

This question does not specify that the guarantee was required to retain the customer. But the Special Enrollment Exam seems to assume that guaranteeing the debt of a primary customer is closely related to one's trade or business. On that basis it would be a business bad debt.

54. All of the following statements regarding the nonaccrual-experience method of accounting for bad debts are true except:

   a. Under this method you do not have to accrue income that you do not expect to collect.
   b. This method cannot be used if interest or penalties are required to be paid for late payments.
   c. This method can only be used for amounts to be received that are earned by performing services.
   d. This method can be used for amounts to be received that are earned from any source.

The correct answer is (d). *(SPE 989 II-39)*
REQUIRED: The incorrect statement regarding the nonaccrual-experience method of accounting for bad debts.
DISCUSSION: An accrual method of accounting taxpayer meeting certain qualifications may use the nonaccrual-experience method of accounting for bad debts [Sec. 448(d)(5)]. The nonaccrual-experience method may be used only for amounts to be received for the performance of services which would otherwise be included in income. This method may not be used for amounts to be received from activities other than the performance of services. Amounts arising from lending money, selling goods, or acquiring receivables from other parties would not be eligible for treatment under the nonaccrual-experience method.
Answers (a), (b), and (c) are incorrect because all are true statements regarding the nonaccrual-experience method of accounting for bad debts.

55. Under the specific charge off method of computing bad debts, partially worthless bad debts may be deducted for tax purposes even though no charge off is taken on the books.

The correct answer is (F). *(SPE 990 II-9)*
DISCUSSION: Partially worthless bad debts are deductible under Sec. 166(a)(2). When satisfied that a debt is recoverable only in part, the amount not in excess of the part charged off within the taxable year is allowed as a deduction.

56. Mr. N lent his good friend, Mr. W, $5,000 with the understanding it would be paid back. W repaid $1,000 of the loan but came upon hard times and could not pay the remaining $4,000. Mr. N forgave the debt. N has a deductible bad debt.

The correct answer is (F). *(SPE 989 I-29)*
DISCUSSION: A bad debt deduction may be taken only for a bona fide debt arising from a valid debtor-creditor relationship based upon a valid and enforceable obligation to pay a fixed or determinable sum of money. Since Mr. N forgave the debt, no bad debt exists, and no deduction is available.

57. Mr. E is an accrual-basis taxpayer. In 1990, E charged off $1,000 from K's outstanding account that totaled $5,000. E received property worth $3,000 from K as final payment in 1991. This property had an adjusted basis of $2,000 to K. The remaining amount owed was determined to be worthless in 1991. E can deduct only $1,000 as a bad debt loss in 1991.

The correct answer is (T). *(SPE 1083 I-4)*
DISCUSSION: Worthless debts are deductible only to the extent of the adjusted basis of the debt [Sec. 166(b)]. Since Mr. E is on the accrual basis, he apparently included $5,000 in income without receiving payment, so he has a $5,000 basis in the debt. He recovered $1,000 in 1990, and $3,000 in 1991, leaving a balance of $1,000. E can deduct this $1,000 as a bad debt loss in 1991, since the remaining amount owed was determined to be worthless in 1991.

6.3 Business Travel and Entertainment

58. Mr. Pine, a self-employed engineer in Boston, traveled to Chicago in 1991 in order to attend a course on new engineering techniques. He spent 2 weeks attending the course, and remained in Chicago for an additional 6 weeks on personal matters. The air flight cost $200, hotel $600, meals $300, and the tuition for the course $500. How much of these expenses may Mr. Pine deduct on his return?

a. $500.
b. $710.
c. $725.
d. $910.

The correct answer is (b). *(SPE 1077 III-1)*
REQUIRED: The deductible amount of travel expenses incurred for both business and personal activities.
DISCUSSION: A deduction for adjusted gross income is allowed for travel expenses while away from home in connection with a trade or business [Sec. 162(a)]. However, transportation is deductible only if the trip is primarily related to the taxpayer's trade or business (Reg. 1.162-2). If more days are spent for personal purposes than for business purposes, none of the transportation is deductible. Since Mr. Pine spent 6 out of his 8 weeks in Chicago on personal matters, the cost of the flight to Chicago is not deductible. Meals and lodging must always be allocated between personal and business. Under Sec. 274(n), business meals are deductible at only 80% of their cost. The expenses for 2 weeks out of 8 weeks are deductible. Educational expenses are deductible if the education maintains or improves skills required in the taxpayer's business (Reg. 1.162-5).

Hotel (2/8 x $600)	$150
Meals (2/8 x $300 x 80%)	60
Tuition	500
Total deduction	$710

59. Phil Collins is actively engaged in the oil business and owns numerous oil leases in the Southwest. During 1991 he made several trips to inspect oil wells on the leases and to consult about future oil wells to be drilled on these sites. As a result of these overnight trips, he paid the following:

Plane fares	$4,000
Hotels	1,000
Meals	800
Entertaining lessees	500

Of the $6,300 in expenses incurred, he can claim as deductible expenses

a. $6,300.
b. $6,040.
c. $5,300.
d. $5,000.

The correct answer is (b). *(CPA 579 Q-39)*
REQUIRED: The amount of expenses incurred on overnight trips that are deductible.
DISCUSSION: A deduction is allowed for travel expenses while away from home in the pursuit of a trade or business [Sec. 162(a)]. Meals are deductible under Sec. 162 provided they are currently related to the active conduct of a trade or business, the expense is not lavish or extravagant under the circumstances, and the taxpayer (or an employee) is present during the meals. Entertainment expenses must be directly related to or associated with business to be deductible. Under Sec. 274(n), both meal and entertainment expenses are limited to 80% of their cost. Also, all these expenditures must be substantiated under Sec. 274(d). Assuming that Collins' expenses meet the above requirements, his total deduction is as follows:

Plane fares	$4,000
Hotels	1,000
Meals ($800 x 80%)	640
Entertainment ($500 x 80%)	400
Total deduction	$6,040

Module 6.3: *Business Travel and Entertainment*

60. Willy, a self-employed laboratory consultant, flew to Buffalo in 1991 where he stayed 3 days (2 days were on business). Airfare was $300. Meals were $20 and lodging was $20 per day. From Buffalo, Willy flew to Toronto, Canada, where he spent 2 weeks on business and 1 week with relatives. Airfare to Toronto and back home was $600. In Toronto, food was $100 and lodging was $200 per week. What is Willy's deductible travel expense for the trip?

   a. $680.
   b. $1,332.
   c. $1,532.
   d. $1,920.

The correct answer is (b). *(Publisher)*
REQUIRED: The travel expense deduction for both domestic and foreign travel.
DISCUSSION: Under Reg. 1.162-2(b), on a trip made primarily for business the entire amount for transportation may be deducted, but the food and lodging must be allocated between business and personal time. However, under Sec. 274(c) and Reg. 1.274-4, travel outside the United States must be allocated between business and personal (including the transportation) if the travel is in excess of 1 week when more than 25% of the time is for nonbusiness activity.

The airfare on the trip to Buffalo is entirely deductible, while food and lodging are only deductible for 2 days. On the trip to Toronto, the airfare must be apportioned (2/3 business) as well as the food and lodging. Under Sec. 274(n), meals are deductible at only 80% of their cost. Assuming Willy's meals met the requirements for business meals, his business deduction is

Buffalo:	
Airfare	$ 300
Lodging (2 days x $20)	40
Meals (2 days x $20 x 80%)	32
Toronto:	
Airfare (2/3 x $600)	400
Lodging (2 weeks x $200)	400
Meals (2 weeks x $100 x 80%)	160
Total travel expense deduction	$1,332

61. Willy, a self-employed laboratory consultant specializing in white mice, attended a convention in Paris in 1991 concerning the care and feeding of white mice. The convention was held in Paris since most of the white mice specialists in the world are located in France. Willy's expenses were $1,600 for airfare, $400 for food, and $400 for lodging. Willy spent 5 days at the convention and 3 days visiting friends. How much can he deduct for the trip?

   a. $0.
   b. $1,450.
   c. $2,100.
   d. $2,400.

The correct answer is (b). *(Publisher)*
REQUIRED: The amount that a taxpayer can deduct for travel to a convention outside of North America.
DISCUSSION: Sec. 274(h) provides that no deduction is allowed for travel expenses to attend a convention held outside North America unless the meeting is directly related to the active conduct of his/her trade or business, and it is as reasonable for the meeting to be held outside North America as within. Willy's convention in France will satisfy these tests.

However, this trip is still subject to the rules under Sec. 274(c), which require all foreign travel for more than 1 week to be allocated between business and personal time when more than 25% of the time is spent on nonbusiness affairs. Therefore, Willy may deduct only 5/8 of the transportation, food, and lodging expenses. Meals are limited to 80% of total cost. His deduction is as follows:

Airfare (5/8 x $1,600)	$1,000
Lodging (5/8 x $400)	250
Meals (5/8 x $400 x 80%)	200
Total travel expense deduction	$1,450

Module 6.3: Business Travel and Entertainment

62. Partiers Unlimited sent one of its employees to attend an association meeting on behalf of the company in 1991. It is customary, and good for business, for spouses to attend these meetings and participate in the social activities in the evenings. The employee took her spouse along for this purpose. Airfare for the employee was $200, food was $100, and lodging was $200. Airfare for the spouse was $200, food was $100, and lodging was $150. Partiers reimbursed its employee for these amounts, but included $450 on the employee's W-2 as compensation at the end of the year. How much, and in what manner should Partiers deduct for these expenses?

   a. $500 as travel expense.
   b. $950 as travel expense.
   c. $480 as travel expense and $450 as compensation.
   d. $660 as travel expense and $250 as compensation.

The correct answer is (c). *(Publisher)*
REQUIRED: The amount and method of deducting travel expenses for an employee and spouse.
DISCUSSION: An employer may deduct reimbursements to an employee for business travel under Sec. 162(a) subject to the restrictions in Sec. 274. However, the expenses of an employee's spouse on a trip are not deductible, unless the spouse actually renders substantial services on behalf of the employer. It is not sufficient that the spouse is along for customary social activities. Therefore, the expenses relating to the spouse in this question are not deductible.

Under Sec. 274(e), if an employer treats the nondeductible travel expenses as compensation to the employee, they may be fully deducted as compensation. Treating them as compensation requires withholding income tax, including the amounts on the employee's W-2, and deducting them in the employer's tax return as compensation. When the employee is reimbursed for the cost of meals and entertainment, the 80% limitation applies to the party making the reimbursement. Therefore, Partiers may deduct the following:

Spouse's expenses as compensation	$450
Employee's expenses as travel	
Airfare	$200
Meals ($100 x 80%)	80
Lodging	200
Deductible amount	$480

63. Bob, a calendar year, cash basis taxpayer, owns an insurance agency. Bob has four people selling insurance for him. The salesmen incur ordinary and necessary meals and entertainment expenses for which Bob reimburses them monthly. During 1991, Bob reimbursed his agents $10,000 for meals and $26,000 for entertainment. How much of the reimbursement can Bob deduct on his 1991 federal income tax return?

   a. $28,800.
   b. $30,800.
   c. $34,000.
   d. $36,000.

The correct answer is (a). *(SPE 989 II-62)*
REQUIRED: The amount an employer may deduct for meal and entertainment expenses.
DISCUSSION: Under Sec. 162(a), an employer may deduct reimbursements to an employee subject to the restrictions of Sec. 274. There is an 80% limitation for meals and entertainment when the employer does not treat the expenses as compensation, thus Bob's deduction for 1991 meal and entertainment expenses is $28,800 [($10,000 + $26,000) x 80%].

64. Happy Lucky drove her car a total of 18,000 miles during 1991. Of this, 12,000 miles was related to business for JR Enterprises. Happy paid $1,950 for gas, $600 for repairs, and $400 for tires during the year. Happy accounted to JR for these actual expenses and received a reimbursement for the business portion. How much may JR deduct as travel and transportation expense?

   a. $0.
   b. $1,967.
   c. $2,700.
   d. $3,705.

The correct answer is (b). *(Publisher)*
REQUIRED: The amount an employer may deduct for reimbursed automobile expenses paid to an employee.
DISCUSSION: Under Sec. 162(a), an employer may deduct reimbursements paid to an employee for use of his/her personal car, subject to the substantiation rules of Sec. 274. Although an employee is allowed to report to an employer either the actual expenses or a standard mileage rate for the business miles driven, the employer is only allowed to deduct what is actually reimbursed to the employee. JR reimbursed Happy $1,967 (2/3 x $2,950). This represented an allocation of Happy's total automobile expenses, based on the number of business miles driven as compared to the total miles driven. JR may only deduct $1,967.

Module 6.3: Business Travel and Entertainment 113

65. In January 1991, Mr. D, who is self-employed, purchased a new automobile which he uses 100% for business. During 1991 he drove the car 14,000 miles. Mr. D also owns another automobile which he uses occasionally for business but is primarily used for personal purposes. During 1991 he drove the second car 2,000 business miles. The second car is not fully depreciated. What is the amount of Mr. D's automobile expense deduction using the standard mileage rate?

   a. $3,840.
   b. $4,010.
   c. $4,160.
   d. $4,400.

The correct answer is (d). *(SPE 988 I-65)*
REQUIRED: The allowable automobile expense deduction using the standard mileage rate.
DISCUSSION: Automobile expenses pertaining to a trade or business are deductible under Sec. 162 as ordinary and necessary business expenses. The taxpayer may either deduct the portion of actual operating cost of the automobile attributed to business use, or compute the deduction based on standard mileage rate. In 1991, the standard mileage rate is $.275 per mile for all miles driven. Mr. D's deduction for 1991 is $4,400 (16,000 miles x $.275).

66. Mr. D purchased an automobile for use in his business in 1987. For the years 1987 through 1990 he used the maximum standard mileage rate to figure his car expense deduction. What would Mr. D's car expense deduction be in 1991, using the standard mileage rate, if the auto was driven 20,000 miles for business use, and the business mileage from prior years is 50,000 miles?

   a. $3,700.
   b. $4,150.
   c. $4,800.
   d. $5,500.

The correct answer is (d). *(SPE 1085 II-67)*
REQUIRED: The allowable automobile expense deduction for 1991 using the standard mileage rate.
DISCUSSION: Automobile expenses pertaining to a trade or business are deductible under Sec. 162 as ordinary and necessary business expenses. The taxpayer may either deduct the portion of actual operating cost of the automobile attributed to business use, or compute the deduction based on the standard mileage rate. In 1991, the standard mileage rate is $.275 per mile for all miles of business use.
The deduction for 1991 is $5,500 (20,000 miles x $.275).

67. Which of the following is a correct statement with respect to the business use of automobiles and other property placed in service after December 31, 1985?

   a. The maximum purchase price of an automobile is $12,800.
   b. Both transportation and entertainment property must be used over 50% for business to claim the investment tax credit.
   c. Automobiles must be used over 50% for business to deduct depreciation at an accelerated rate.
   d. Depreciation on automobiles and entertainment property is limited to $3,200 per year for each item.

The correct answer is (c). *(Publisher)*
REQUIRED: The correct statement with respect to the business use of automobiles and other property placed in service after December 31, 1985.
DISCUSSION: Sec. 280F(b)(2) provides that if the business use of an automobile does not exceed 50%, the alternative depreciation system under Sec. 168(g) must be used (i.e., straight-line method).
Answer (a) is incorrect because there is no maximum purchase price for an automobile, although the limitations on depreciation are equivalent to depreciation on a $12,800 asset. Answer (b) is incorrect because the investment tax credit was generally repealed for tangible personal property (other than special energy property) placed in service after December 31, 1985. Answer (d) is incorrect because recovery deductions (depreciation and Sec. 179 expense) are limited to the following amounts:

$2,660	for first taxable year
4,200	for second taxable year
2,550	for third taxable year
1,475	for each succeeding taxable year in the recovery period.

68. After 1986, all of the following statements relating to entertainment facilities are true except:

a. The part of the dues or fees applicable to the use of a club for quiet business meals and beverages to discuss business is considered associated entertainment expense.

b. A membership or initiation fee you pay only once to join a club is a capital expense if the useful life of the membership extends beyond the first year.

c. In figuring whether a club is used more than 50% for business, you do not count the days the club is not used.

d. If part of the expenses of a facility were deductible as entertainment expenses, the sale or other disposition of the facility must be treated as a disposition of two pieces of property.

The correct answer is (a). *(SPE 989 II-41)*
REQUIRED: The false statement about entertainment expenditures.
DISCUSSION: Under Reg. 1.274-2(c)(6), all club dues shall be considered "directly related" to the active conduct of the taxpayer's trade or business if it is established that the club dues were allocable to business meals. Thus, statement (a) is false since it says such portion of club dues are an "associated with" entertainment expense.
Answers (b), (c), and (d) are incorrect because each is a correct statement about entertainment expenditures.

69. Mr. Giglia's 1991 dues to Country Club F were $3,500. Mr. and Mrs. Giglia used the country club a total of 160 days in 1991. Mr. Giglia's records reflect that 70 days were used for business; 30 days were used by Mr. Giglia's wife when entertaining wives of prospective customers; and 60 days were personal or family use. What is Mr. Giglia's entertainment deduction for 1991?

a. $0.
b. $1,530.
c. $1,750.
d. $2,188.

The correct answer is (a). *(SPE 1079 II-57)*
REQUIRED: The amount of country club dues that may be deducted.
DISCUSSION: Sec. 274 disallows a deduction for expenditures made with respect to a facility used in connection with entertainment or recreation (e.g., a country club), unless the facility is used primarily for business purposes (over 50%). Since the taxpayer used the facility for business purposes less than 50% of the time (70 days out of a total of 160 days), a deduction for the country club dues is disallowed. Mrs. Giglia's entertaining wives of prospective customers is not considered business use. Any expenses incurred at the club for meals, golf, etc., which qualify as business entertainment may be deducted at 80% of their cost.

70. Mr. C, a self-employed insurance salesman, maintains a country club membership. He establishes by appropriate documentation the following for 1991:

20% of the use of the club is directly related to his insurance sales.
An additional 35% of the use of the club is associated with his insurance sales.
Club dues are $100 per month for all of 1991.
Other expenses incurred at the club for meals, golf, and other events were $1,800, of which $1,200 is bona fide business entertainment.

What is the total amount in club dues and other entertainment expenditures that Mr. C can deduct on his Schedule C, Form 1040, for 1991?

a. $960.
b. $1,152.
c. $1,488.
d. $1,584.

The correct answer is (b). *(SPE 1080 II-76)*
REQUIRED: The total amount of club dues and entertainment expenses deductible on Schedule C.
DISCUSSION: Schedule C is used to report the profit or loss from the business of a sole proprietor. Sec. 274 disallows a deduction for expenditures made with respect to a facility used in connection with entertainment or recreation (e.g., a country club) unless the facility is used primarily for business; i.e., over 50% of the use must be for business purposes. When applying the primary use test, business use includes that associated with and directly related to business. Once the primary use test is satisfied, only the portion of expenses directly related to business qualifies for the deduction.
Mr. C met the primary use test, since 55% of the use of the club was for business purposes (20% directly related + 35% associated). Nevertheless, only that portion of the dues directly related to business is deductible and limited to 80% of cost, i.e., $192 (80% x $100 x 12 months x 20%). The bona fide business entertainment is also deductible as long as it is properly documented, i.e., $960 ($1,200 x 80%). His total deduction is $1,152 ($192 club dues + $960 entertainment).

Module 6.3: Business Travel and Entertainment

71. Mr. Norman, who is self-employed, belongs to a country club to which he pays dues of $1,500 per year. During 1991, he used it for business meals 20% of the time, directly related entertainment 25% of the time, and 15% for associated entertainment. What is the amount of the dues Mr. Norman can deduct as a business expense for 1991?

a. $0.
b. $240.
c. $540.
d. $720.

The correct answer is (c). *(SPE 989 I-84)*
REQUIRED: The taxpayer's allowable deduction for country club dues.
DISCUSSION: Sec. 274 disallows a deduction for expenditures made with respect to a facility used in connection with entertainment or recreation (e.g., a country club) unless the facility is used primarily (i.e., over 50%) for business purposes. Mr. Norman used the club for business purposes 60% of the time (20% for business meals, 25% for directly related entertainment, 15% for associated entertainment), so he has met the primary use test.
Once the test is met, only that portion of the dues directly related to business is deductible, which includes directly related entertainment and business meals. Business meals are considered directly related to business [Reg. 1.274-2(c)] provided the meals are currently related to the active conduct of a trade or business, are not lavish or extravagant, and the taxpayer is present during such meals.
Therefore, Mr. Norman may deduct 45% of the club dues (20% for business meals + 25% for directly related entertainment), up to the 80% of costs limitation. The deduction is $540 ($1,500 x 45% x 80%).

72. Which of the following is not required to substantiate a business entertainment expense deduction?

a. Social Security number of the person entertained.
b. Date the entertainment took place.
c. Type of entertainment, name of person entertained, and name and address or location where it took place.
d. Reason for the entertainment or nature of business derived or expected to be derived.

The correct answer is (a). *(SPE 1080 II-59)*
REQUIRED: The information not required to substantiate a business entertainment expense deduction.
DISCUSSION: Sec. 274(d) disallows a deduction for business entertainment expenses unless the taxpayer substantiates the expenditure by adequate records or corroborating evidence showing the amount, time, place, business purpose, and the business relationship to the taxpayer of each person entertained. The Social Security number of the person entertained is not required to substantiate a business entertainment expense.
Answers (b), (c), and (d) are incorrect because the business entertainment expense is not deductible unless each one is substantiated.

73. Which one of the following statements concerning the recordkeeping requirements for travel and entertainment is correct?

a. Social Security numbers of business guests must be recorded to support entertainment expenses.
b. If the business purpose of a meal is not recorded, other evidence may be used to substantiate the business purpose.
c. Receipts must be kept for all transportation expenditures over $25.
d. A canceled check, by itself, is adequate evidence to support an entertainment expense.

The correct answer is (b). *(SPE 990 IV-64)*
REQUIRED: The true statement of recordkeeping requirements for travel and entertainment expenses.
DISCUSSION: Sec. 274(d) requires the taxpayer to substantiate by adequate records or by sufficient corroborating evidence any deduction for travel and entertainment.
Answer (a) is incorrect because the Social Security numbers of business guests are not required. Answer (c) is incorrect because receipts for transportation expenditures are not required even if over $25. Answer (d) is incorrect because a canceled check alone is not proper documentary evidence for recordkeeping requirements.

74. Documentary evidence is required to prove all lodging expenses while traveling away from home and for any other expense, except transportation costs if evidence is not readily available, exceeding a total of $25.

The correct answer is (T). *(SPE 987 IV-1)*
DISCUSSION: Sec. 274(d) requires the taxpayer to substantiate by adequate records or corroborating evidence all expenditures made for travel or entertainment. In addition, documentary evidence, such as a receipt, is required for all lodging while traveling away from home, even if the amount is less than $25. Documentary evidence is required of all other travel and entertainment expenditures (except transportation) if the expense is greater than $25.

75. A membership or initiation fee, paid only once to join a country club for business use, is a capital expenditure which is not currently deductible if the useful life of the membership extends beyond the year of acquisition.

The correct answer is (T). *(SPE 1080 II-19)*
DISCUSSION: If an expenditure is for an asset having a useful life that extends substantially beyond the close of the taxable year, then the cost of the asset must be capitalized (Sec. 263). The expenditure may be amortized or depreciated over its useful life if the life may be estimated with reasonable accuracy.

76. Standing alone, canceled checks payable to hotels and restaurants constitute adequate substantiation for travel and entertainment expenses.

The correct answer is (F). *(SPE 1079 I-13)*
DISCUSSION: The taxpayer must maintain an account book, diary, statement of expenses or similar record and documentary evidence which, in combination, are sufficient to establish the amount, time, place, business purpose, and the business relationship to the taxpayer of each person entertained (Reg. 1.274-5). A canceled check may provide documentary evidence in place of a receipt, but is not adequate substantiation by itself.

77. The dues paid to a country club for 1991 are not deductible unless the club is used more than 183 days during the year for business purposes.

The correct answer is (F). *(SPE 1077 I-7)*
DISCUSSION: Country club dues are deductible only if the club is used primarily for business purposes with the requirement of over 50% of the actual use of the facility being for business purposes. The primary use test considers only the days the facility was used, and business use includes entertainment that is either associated with or directly related to business. If the primary use test is satisfied, only that portion of the dues directly related to business entertainment qualifies for the deduction.

78. For an entertainment expense to meet the directly related test, a taxpayer must show that:

    1. (S)he had more than a general expectation of getting income or some other specific business benefit at some future time,
    2. (S)he did engage in business with the person being entertained during the entertainment period, and
    3. (S)he had a clear business purpose, and business income or other benefit actually resulted from each entertainment expense.

The correct answer is (F). *(SPE 1083 II-17)*
DISCUSSION: The requirements for an expense to be considered directly related are set out in Reg. 1.274-2(c)(3). Under this Section, it is not required that business income or other benefit result from each entertainment expense. The taxpayer need only show (s)he had more than a general expectation of deriving income or some other specific business benefit.

79. Mr. Austin, owner of an advertising firm, paid $300 for entertainment in a hospitality room at a business convention. Mr. Austin used the convention to display and discuss his products with potential clients. The entertainment is not directly related entertainment.

The correct answer is (F). *(SPE 990 II-11)*
DISCUSSION: Sec. 274 allows a deduction for 80% of the costs of entertainment expenses if the entertainment is directly related to or associated with business. Directly related entertainment includes expenditures in a clear business setting and directly in furtherance of the taxpayer's trade or business. A hospitality room to display and discuss products is an example given in Reg. 1.274-2(c)(4).

80. One of the requirements that must be met for meal and entertainment expenses to meet the directly related test is that the taxpayer must show that business income or business benefit actually resulted from each meal or entertainment expense.

The correct answer is (F). *(SPE 989 II-6)*
DISCUSSION: The requirements for meal and entertainment expenses to meet the directly related test are set out in Reg. 1.274-(2)(c)(3). No deduction shall be allowed for any expenditure for entertainment unless the taxpayer establishes the expenditure was directly related to the active trade or business. This means the taxpayer had more than a general expectation of deriving income or some other business benefit. It is not required that business income or other benefit result from each entertainment expense.

81. Mr. G, a businessman, entertains his customer, Mr. C, by taking him to a cocktail party at the country club and afterwards to the theater. No business discussions took place during the party or at the theater. However, Mr. G and Mr. C had spent several hours earlier in the evening discussing new product lines. Mr. G may deduct as an entertainment expense 80% of the cost of entertaining Mr. C.

The correct answer is (T). *(SPE 984 II-16)*
DISCUSSION: The cost of entertaining Mr. C is considered an associated with business expense because it occurs directly after a substantial business discussion. Expenses associated with business entertainment must serve a clear business purpose such as to obtain new business or continue existing business. The expenditures qualify for deduction at the rate of 80% of the cost if they directly precede or follow a bona fide business discussion [Reg. 1.274-2(d)(3)(ii)].

82. In 1991, Ms. Painter, an attorney, rented a skybox for only one football game at the local sports stadium. Ms. Painter invited and entertained 10 of her best clients. Business discussions took place both before and during the game. 80% of the cost for renting the skybox would be an allowable entertainment expense.

The correct answer is (T). *(SPE 987 II-17)*
DISCUSSION: The cost of tickets and entertaining clients and business customers at sporting events is an entertainment expense. The deduction for entertainment expenses is limited to 80% of the otherwise allowed expense [Sec. 274(n)]. Although Sec. 274(l)(2) contains other limitations on the deduction of skybox rental, that provision only applies when a skybox is leased for more than one event. Since Ms. Painter rented the skybox for only one football game, the additional limitations do not apply and 80% of the cost is deductible as an entertainment expense.

83. Instead of deducting the actual cost of meals and incidental expenses while you are away from home on business, you may deduct expenses based on an allowance of $26 per day for meals and incidental expenses ($34 for high-cost areas) for each day of your stay.

The correct answer is (T). *(SPE 986 II-15)*
DISCUSSION: Instead of deducting the actual cost of meals and incidental expenses while traveling away from home on business, a taxpayer may deduct meals and incidental expenses per diem rate. This allowance is $26 per day in most areas and $34 per day in designated high-cost areas (Rev. Proc. 90-60). The final deduction is then 80% of this amount.

84. In June 1991, Mr. O, a real estate broker, went to Paris, France to attend a convention on "Art as an Investment." Mr. O spent $2,000 on travel expenses on his trip. Mr. O would be able to deduct the cost of the trip on his Schedule C for 1991.

The correct answer is (F). *(SPE 987 II-15)*
DISCUSSION: A convention on investing in art is not an ordinary and necessary expense of carrying on a real estate trade or business. It would only be deductible as an expense related to the production of income. These types of investment seminars and conventions are no longer deductible under Sec. 274(h)(7).

85. Randy Donain lives with his family in Oberlin, Ohio, but for the last 3 years has worked in Cleveland where he resides in a hotel and eats in restaurants Monday through Friday. On weekends he returns to his Oberlin home. Randy's tax home is in Oberlin and he can deduct his expenses for travel, meals, and lodging in Cleveland.

The correct answer is (F). *(SPE 986 I-23)*
DISCUSSION: A person's tax home is his/her main place of business regardless of the location of the family home. Therefore, Randy's tax home is Cleveland. Since his trips to Oberlin are for personal reasons, they are not deductible.

6.4 Business Gifts

86. During 1991 Ashley Corporation charged the following payments to miscellaneous expense:

Travel expense of $300 for the company president to offer voluntary testimony at the state capital against proposed legislation regarded as unfavorable to its business.
Christmas gifts to 20 customers at $75 each.
Contribution of $600 to local political candidate.

The maximum deduction that Ashley can claim for these payments is

- a. $800.
- b. $1,400.
- c. $1,800.
- d. $2,400.

The correct answer is (a). *(CPA 580 Q-39)*
REQUIRED: The maximum deduction available for the listed payments.
DISCUSSION: The travel expenses of $300 to provide testimony with regard to legislation are deductible as an ordinary and necessary business expense under Sec. 162(e). Christmas gifts to customers are also deductible as ordinary and necessary business expenses. Sec. 274(b) limits the deduction for business gifts to $25 per donee in a single year. Accordingly, the taxpayer may only deduct $500 ($25 x 20 customers) for the Christmas gifts. No deduction is allowed for political contributions. The maximum deduction Ashley can claim is $800 ($300 in travel expenses + $500 in business gifts).

87. Gulp Oil Company gives miniature souvenir oil rigs with its name imprinted on them to its suppliers and customers. Each costs the company $2 and is worth $5. Sometimes it gives large quantities of these oil rigs to major wholesalers to be given out to retail customers. Gulp Oil also furnishes display racks to dealers that can be used for both Gulp products and other products. These display racks cost the company $40 and are worth $50. In 1991, 20,000 oil rigs and 500 display racks were given away. How much can Gulp Oil deduct for these gifts?

- a. $52,500.
- b. $60,000.
- c. $112,500.
- d. $125,000.

The correct answer is (b). *(Publisher)*
REQUIRED: The amount a taxpayer may deduct for business gifts of small items and display racks.
DISCUSSION: Gifts can constitute a business deduction under Sec. 162(a). They are limited by Sec. 274(b) to $25 per recipient per year. There are exceptions for items that do not cost the taxpayer in excess of $4, and on which the name of the taxpayer is clearly imprinted, and for signs and display racks to be used on the recipient's business premises. These may be given without limit as long as they meet the ordinary and necessary test under Sec. 162(a). Since the miniature oil rigs did not cost more than $4, there is no limit on the deduction for giving them away. Similarly, the display racks are not limited to $25 per recipient. Consequently, the cost of these items may be deducted in full. The total deduction is $60,000 ($2 per oil rig x 20,000) + ($40 per display rack x 500).

88. Mr. Brown is a self-employed lawyer, his wife a self-employed dentist, and they file calendar year joint returns. During 1991, Mr. Brown gave five of his clients gifts costing $50 each. In addition, he gave one of his part-time employees, Kathleen, a gift costing $75. During 1991, Mrs. Brown gave four of her clients gifts costing $60 each. None of Mrs. Brown's clients were Mr. Brown's clients and vice versa. However, Mrs. Brown also employed Kathleen as a part-time employee and gave her a gift costing $55. What is the amount of the Browns' deductible business gift expense in 1991?

- a. $250.
- b. $275.
- c. $355.
- d. $620.

The correct answer is (c). *(SPE 989 II-68)*
REQUIRED: The deduction allowed for the business gifts listed.
DISCUSSION: Sec. 274(b) limits the deduction for gifts to $25 per recipient per year. The Sec. 274(b) limit only applies to items excludable from gross income under Sec. 102. Gifts to employees are not excludable by the employees under Sec. 102 [Sec. 102(c)]. Therefore, the entire $130 paid to the Browns' employee Kathleen should be deductible. Thus, the total deduction allowable is $355 (Mr. Brown's 5 gifts x $25) + (Mrs. Brown's 4 gifts x $25) + (Kathleen's $130).

Module 6.4: Business Gifts

89. If Mihalick Company gives gift certificates of $30 each to its employees for Christmas in 1991, only $25 per employee is deductible by Mihalick.

The correct answer is (F). *(Publisher)*
DISCUSSION: Sec. 274(b) limits the deduction for gifts to $25 per recipient per year. However, this section only applies to items excludable under Sec. 102. After 1986, "gifts" to employees are not excludable under Sec. 102. Therefore, the entire $30 per employee is deductible as compensation and must be included in income by each employee.

90. If a partnership gives business gifts, the partnership and the partners are treated as one taxpayer for figuring the $25 per recipient limitation.

The correct answer is (F). *(SPE 1082 II-11)*
DISCUSSION: The deduction for business gifts is generally limited to $25 per recipient under Sec. 274(b). In the case of a partnership, the $25 limitation applies first at the partnership level and then to each partner. This is not the same as treating both the partnership and partners as one taxpayer.

91. To take a deduction for business gifts, you must prove all the following elements: cost, date of gift, description of gift, reason for giving gift, and business relationship of person receiving gift.

The correct answer is (T). *(SPE 1081 I-18)*
DISCUSSION: Sec. 274(d) disallows a deduction for any business gift unless the taxpayer substantiates by adequate records the amount (cost) of the gift, the date and description of the gift, the business purpose of the gift, and the business relationship to the taxpayer of the person receiving the gift.

92. If you provide tickets to a theater performance or sporting event for a business customer, and do not go with the customer to the performance or event, you may treat the tickets either as a gift or as entertainment, whichever is to your advantage.

The correct answer is (T). *(SPE 986 II-16)*
DISCUSSION: Sec. 274 does not specify that the taxpayer providing the entertainment for a business customer must be present at the entertainment event (as is required in the case of meals). However, the taxpayer must establish that the entertainment was directly related to, or associated with, the active conduct of the taxpayer's trade or business. The taxpayer has the option of treating the entertainment tickets as a gift, but under Sec. 274(b), the limit for deduction is $25 per person per year. If the taxpayer treats the tickets as entertainment, then the deduction is limited to 80% of the cost of the tickets.

93. If a husband and wife both give business gifts, both are treated as one taxpayer, even if they have separate businesses or are separately employed, and even if each has an independent connection with the recipient.

The correct answer is (T). *(SPE 1083 II-19)*
DISCUSSION: Sec. 274(b) disallows a business expense deduction for gifts to any individual in excess of $25 per year. For purposes of this limitation, a husband and wife are treated as one taxpayer regardless of their business relationship or type of return filed.

6.5 Employee Compensation

94. Oscar Cinema Studios rewards its retiring officers with miniature gold statuettes if at least 10 years of service have been completed. Each statuette costs Oscar $400 and is worth $600. Rank-and-file employees receive plastic replicas of the studio's back lot, costing $50 apiece, when they retire and have completed 30 years of devoted service. These plastic replicas are each worth $70. In 1991, Oscar gave two retiring officers each a miniature statuette during a meaningful presentation. How much can Oscar deduct for these gifts?

a. $50.
b. $100.
c. $800.
d. $1,200.

The correct answer is (c). *(Publisher)*
REQUIRED: The amount that an employer may deduct for gifts to employees by reason of length of service.
DISCUSSION: Sec. 274(j) limits the deduction for employee achievement awards. These are items of tangible personal property awarded to an employee by reason of length of service or safety achievement, and the award is given as part of a meaningful presentation and under circumstances that do not create a significant likelihood that the payment is disguised compensation. The deduction limit is $400, or $1,600 if it is a qualified plan award (which requires a permanent written plan or program that does not discriminate in favor of highly compensated employees).
In this case the plan does discriminate in favor of officers, so the deduction is limited to $400 per recipient. Since each statuette costs Oscar $400, the amount is deductible in its entirety. The total deduction is $800.

95. Flora Corporation made the following awards of tangible personal property to employees during 1991 under a written, qualified, nondiscriminatory plan:

Name	Reason for Award	Value Received
Mike	20 years' employment	$250
Kurt	20 years' employment	250
Steve	35 years' employment	450
Casey	40 years' employment	550
George	2 year safety award	200

No other safety awards were awarded during 1991. The amount Flora can deduct related to these awards is

a. $400.
b. $1,300.
c. $1,500.
d. $1,700.

The correct answer is (d). *(Publisher)*
REQUIRED: The amount an employer can deduct for awards to employees under a qualified plan.
DISCUSSION: Sec. 274(j) limits the deduction for employment achievement awards (tangible personal property awarded to an employee by reason of length of service or safety achievement) to $400 per employee per year, or $1,600 per employee per year if it is a qualified plan award. A qualified plan award is an item awarded as part of a permanent, written plan or program that does not discriminate in favor of highly compensated employees. An item may not be treated as a qualified plan award if the average cost of all items awarded exceeds $400. Under Sec. 274(j)(4), further limitations on employee awards are provided whereby length of service awards must not be awarded until after the recipient has worked over 5 years, and the recipient has not received any such award during the applicable year or any of the 4 prior years. Safety achievement awards are also not deductible if, during the taxable year, such awards have previously been awarded to more than 10% of the other employees or to a manager, clerical employee, or other professional employee. Here, since all the requirements of a qualified plan award are met, the full amount of each award, or a total of $1,700, is deductible.

96. Mr. Z, the sole proprietor of Z's Wholesale, transferred an automobile used in his business to Mr. Y, an employee of Z's Wholesale, for business related services rendered during 1991. Z's adjusted basis in the automobile was $6,000 and the fair market value was $8,000 at the time of the transfer. Z had purchased the automobile 2 years ago for $11,000. During 1991, Z paid $80,000 in employee salaries, not including the automobile given to Mr. Y. Z is a cash basis taxpayer. What is his total salary and wage deduction for 1991?

a. $48,000.
b. $80,000.
c. $86,000.
d. $88,000.

The correct answer is (d). *(SPE 990 II-64)*
REQUIRED: The amount of the employer's deduction for property paid to an employee.
DISCUSSION: Sec. 162(a)(1) allows a deduction for reasonable compensation for personal services actually rendered. Sec. 83(a) allows the deduction to an employer equal to the fair market value of property given to the employee when the property is transferable or is not subject to a substantial risk of forfeiture. Therefore, Mr. Z's salary and wage deduction is $88,000 ($80,000 + $8,000 FMV of car).

Module 6.5: Employee Compensation

97. Bunker is an officer of Westerfeld Enterprises. Bunker is provided a car for business use and is reimbursed for travel and entertainment. Bunker also uses the car to commute home. Bunker has not been very careful in documenting his travel and entertainment; therefore, the requirements of Sec. 274(d) are not met. How should Westerfeld Enterprises treat the payments to Bunker in order to obtain the maximum tax advantage?

   a. Include the commuting use of the car and nondocumented travel and entertainment in Bunker's W-2 and withhold on it.
   b. Include the commuting use of the car and nondocumented travel in Bunker's W-2 and not withhold on it.
   c. Include the commuting use of the car in Bunker's W-2 but deduct the rest as travel and entertainment.
   d. Deduct everything as car expense and travel and entertainment since this is what the expenditures were for.

The correct answer is (a). *(Publisher)*
REQUIRED: An employer's most advantageous treatment of an employee's personal use of a company car and nondocumented travel and entertainment.
DISCUSSION: The employee's personal use of an employer's property is additional compensation to the employee. Commuting to and from work is a personal expense that should be deducted by the employer as additional compensation. Nondocumented travel and entertainment is not deductible by the employer unless treated as additional compensation to the employee under Sec. 274(e)(2). All such forms of compensation are subject to withholding.
Answer (b) is incorrect because failure to withhold could result in the employer's being liable for the employee's share of withholding and a 100% penalty. Answer (c) is incorrect because the nondocumented travel and entertainment is not deductible under Sec. 274 (except as compensation). Negligent deduction of such items could result in additional taxes, interest, and a 20% penalty. Answer (d) is incorrect because these items must be reported as additional compensation to the employee in order to be deductible by the employer.

98. Mickie Mays, centerfielder for the Gotham Goliaths, Inc. baseball team is also the majority shareholder. He performs no services other than playing as centerfielder for the team. His salary is twice that of the next highest paid player in the league, even though his performance is below average for a centerfielder. What is the most likely treatment of his salary upon audit of the Gotham Goliaths by the IRS?

   a. It is not deductible at all.
   b. It is deductible in full.
   c. It is deductible up to the amount of the next highest paid player.
   d. It is deductible to the amount of the reasonable value of Mays' services.

The correct answer is (d). *(Publisher)*
REQUIRED: The correct treatment of a salary paid to a shareholder-employee.
DISCUSSION: Sec. 162(a)(1) permits a deduction for a reasonable allowance for salaries or other compensation for personal services actually rendered. In determining what is reasonable, it is important to compare what other businesses would pay for similar services under similar circumstances (Reg. 1.162-7). Since Mays is below average in performance, he should receive the fair value of his services and not twice that of the next highest paid player in the league.
Answer (a) is incorrect because the salary is deductible to the extent that it is a reasonable allowance for services. Answer (b) is incorrect because the salary is probably not deductible in full due to the shareholder relationship, and due to the extraordinary amount of the salary. Answer (c) is incorrect because there is no reason to measure Mays' salary by that of the next highest paid player in the league if Mays is not one of the best players.

99. During 1991, Mr. Y, a cash basis sole proprietor, paid the following:

Base wages to his 4 employees	$100,000
Year-end bonuses paid to 2 employees for establishing new sales records	20,000
Christmas gifts to his 4 employees in appreciation for past services ($50 per gift)	200

What is the total amount Mr. Y can deduct on his 1991 income tax return?

   a. $100,000.
   b. $120,000.
   c. $120,100.
   d. $120,200.

The correct answer is (d). *(SPE 990 II-65)*
REQUIRED: The deductible amount for salary payments, bonuses, and gifts.
DISCUSSION: Sec. 162(a)(1) permits a deduction for a reasonable allowance for salaries or other personal services actually rendered, including bonuses. In addition, Sec. 274(b) limits the deduction for gifts up to $25 per recipient per year. However, this section only applies to gifts excludable under Sec. 102. Sec. 102(c) explicitly disallows an exclusion from income for employee gifts. Thus, the entire $200 of employee gifts are deductible. Generally, such amounts are taxable to the employee as compensation, although they may be tax-exempt as a <u>de minimis</u> fringe benefit or a qualified employee achievement award. Mr. Y may deduct $120,200 on his 1991 return ($100,000 base wages + $20,000 bonuses + $200 gifts to employees).

100. Willy Mantle is the rightfielder for the Gotham Goliaths, Inc., a major league baseball team. He is not a shareholder nor is he related to any shareholder. Nevertheless, he is the highest paid rightfielder in the league by a substantial margin. His performance is outstanding, and many other clubs would like to sign him. How should this compensation be treated?

  a. The deduction should be limited to what other rightfielders are paid.
  b. The deduction should be limited to the IRS determination of fair market value of the services.
  c. The deduction should be allowed in full.
  d. The compensation should be treated as a dividend to the extent that the salary is excessive.

The correct answer is (c). *(Publisher)*
REQUIRED: The correct treatment of a very large salary to a nonshareholder employee.
DISCUSSION: Compensation is deductible under Sec. 162(a)(1) as long as it is a reasonable allowance for personal services actually rendered. The determination of what is a reasonable salary is a major issue in closely held corporations, or when a shareholder-employee is in control of a corporation, but is rarely an issue for a nonshareholder employee. Furthermore, the fact that Mantle is an outstanding rightfielder and in demand by other clubs will justify an unusually large salary. Accordingly, the salary should be deductible in full.

Answer (a) is incorrect because a salary may be reasonable based on the employee's outstanding performance even if in excess of what is normally paid to employees in similar positions. Answer (b) is incorrect because the IRS has no justification to substitute its opinion of the value of an employee's services if the employer has acted in an arm's length manner. Answer (d) is incorrect because excessive or unreasonable salaries will be treated as a dividend only to shareholders.

101. All of the following payments made to employees would be currently deductible as business expenses except:

  a. Wages paid to employees for constructing a new building to be used in the business.
  b. Vacation pay paid to an employee when the employee chooses not to take a vacation.
  c. Reasonable salary paid to a corporate officer owning a controlling interest for services she rendered.
  d. Lump-sum payment made to the beneficiary of a deceased employee that is reasonable in relation to the employee's past services.

The correct answer is (a). *(SPE 989 II-35)*
REQUIRED: The payment to an employee not currently deductible.
DISCUSSION: Normally, Sec. 162(a)(1) allows a deduction for a reasonable allowance for salaries or other compensation for personal services actually rendered. However, Sec. 263A requires all direct costs and a proper share of indirect costs allocable to property produced by the taxpayer to be capitalized. Wages paid to employees for constructing a new building would be direct costs allocable to that building. Those costs are capitalized and depreciated as part of the cost of the building rather than currently deductible.

Answers (b), (c), and (d) are incorrect because each is a currently deductible compensation expense provided they are not an indirect cost of producing property.

102. Mr. Bryan, a calendar-year taxpayer, employs his mother and uses the accrual method of accounting. On December 31, 1991, he accrued $10,000 of his mother's salary. She uses the calendar year and the cash method of accounting. The $10,000 accrued salary was paid on March 31, 1992. Mr. Bryan can deduct the accrued salary on his 1991 tax return.

The correct answer is (F). *(SPE 1082 II-21)*
DISCUSSION: Sec. 267(a)(2) provides that payments otherwise deductible (e.g., salary) made to a related person are not deductible until includable in the income of the recipient. The effect is to prevent an accrual-basis taxpayer from deducting payments made to a related cash-basis taxpayer until the payments are made. Related persons include members of a family, so Mr. Bryan cannot deduct the salary to his mother until 1992.

103. On February 16, 1992, Mr. E paid his employees a $10,000 bonus. Mr. E is an accrual-basis taxpayer on a calendar year, and the employees are not related to him. The amount and date of payment was fixed by agreement dated December 31, 1991. Mr. E is entitled to take the bonus deduction on his 1991 income tax return.

The correct answer is (T). *(SPE 1079 II-15)*
DISCUSSION: Sec. 162(a) allows a deduction for ordinary and necessary business expenses paid or incurred during the taxable year, including a reasonable allowance for salaries or other compensation. Since the amount and date of payment were fixed by an agreement dated prior to the end of the taxable year, all the events had occurred to determine the fact and the amount of the liability. Therefore, it is deductible in 1991 (Reg. 1.461-1).

Module 6.6: Business Use of Home   123

104. To be deductible for an accrual-method taxpayer, compensation must be ordinary, necessary and reasonable. Payment must be for services rendered and the expense must have been paid or incurred during the tax year.

The correct answer is (T). *(SPE 1080 II-12)*
DISCUSSION: Sec. 162(a) allows a deduction for all ordinary and necessary business expenses paid or incurred during the taxable year, including a reasonable allowance for salaries or other compensation for personal services actually rendered.

105. Group life insurance premiums paid by the employer covering the lives of employees who designate their own beneficiaries are not deductible.

The correct answer is (F). *(SPE 988 II-5)*
DISCUSSION: Life insurance premiums paid by the employer on the lives of employees is deductible as compensation to the employees provided the employees designate their own beneficiaries. It is when the employer is the beneficiary that the premiums are not deductible [Sec. 264(a)].

106. If an employee is required to include the fair market value of a noncash fringe benefit in their gross income, the employer can deduct that amount as compensation for services.

The correct answer is (F). *(SPE 987 II-12)*
DISCUSSION: It is the position of the IRS (and the Special Enrollment Exam) that only the cost of noncash fringe benefits (such as meals) provided to employees may be deducted. However, note that under Sec. 83(a), an employee includes property received for services in income at the fair market value of the property. Under Sec. 83(h), the employer is entitled to an equivalent deduction. However, if the employer did take a deduction for the fair market value of the property provided to an employee, the employer would also have to recognize income for the excess of the fair market value over its cost, so the net effect is that the employer winds up with a deduction equal to the cost.

6.6 Business Use of Home

107. Mr. K uses 10% of his home regularly and exclusively for business purposes. Mr. K's net income from his business operation (before taking into account expenses of his home) is $550. In 1991 he had the following total expenses on his home

Taxes	$1,500
Interest	3,000
Insurance	400
Utilities	600
Depreciation	1,200

How much can Mr. K deduct for his home office as an expense of his CPA practice?

a. $100.
b. $450.
c. $550.
d. $670.

The correct answer is (c). *(SPE 1081 I-81)*
REQUIRED: The taxpayer's allowable deduction for the business use of his home.
DISCUSSION: Sec. 280A disallows a business expense deduction for an office located in the taxpayer's residence unless the office is used exclusively and on a regular basis as the taxpayer's principal place of business or as a place of business to meet with patients, clients, or customers. In addition, the allowable business expense deduction may not exceed the excess of the net income from the business activity (not taking into account expenses of the home) over the deductions allowable whether or not the home was used for business purposes, e.g., interest and taxes.

Net income		$550
Less expenses allowable whether or not home is used for business:		
Taxes	$1,500	
Interest	3,000	
	$4,500 x 10%	(450)
Mr. K's allowable deductions		$100

The total allowable deductions are $550 ($450 taxes and interest + $100 insurance and utilities). No deduction is available for any of the depreciation since the insurance and utilities allocable to the office exactly equal the amount of other deductions that can be deducted [Prop. Reg. Sec. 1.280A-2(i)(7)].

Module 6.6: Business Use of Home

108. Kilgore is a flight instructor who assists in the writing of aviation books. She uses a room in her apartment as an office. It is also used to store personal effects and as an occasional second bedroom. It takes up 25% of the space of the apartment and is used 50% of the time as an office. Kilgore's rent is $400 per month and utilities are $50 per month. How much may Kilgore deduct for this office?

a. $0.
b. $675.
c. $1,350.
d. $2,700.

The correct answer is (a). *(Publisher)*
REQUIRED: The amount that a self-employed person may deduct for an office in the home.
DISCUSSION: Under Sec. 280A, no deduction is allowable with respect to a dwelling unit used during the year as a residence. There is an exception for regular and exclusive use of a portion of the dwelling unit as a principal place of business of the taxpayer. In this case Kilgore did not use the bedroom exclusively as an office; therefore, no deduction is allowable.

If Kilgore had used the bedroom exclusively as an office, a ratable portion of the rent and utilities would be deductible since it was her principal place of business.

109. During 1991, Mrs. A operated a business from her personal residence. She used 20% of her residence exclusively for business purposes. The income and expenses attributable to the business portion of her residence were as follows:

Gross income	$4,000
Supplies expense	2,000
20% of interest on residence	600
20% of taxes on residence	800
20% of maintenance, insurance, utilities on residence	400
Allowable depreciation on residence	1,200

Mrs. A's 1991 return should reflect:

a. A net loss from business of $1,000.
b. No gain or loss from business and a $1,000 expense carryover to 1992.
c. A net profit from business of $600, and a $1,000 expense carryover to 1992.
d. No gain or loss from business, and no carryover to 1992.

The correct answer is (b). *(SPE 987 I-81)*
REQUIRED: The taxpayer's allowable business expense deduction for an in-home office.
DISCUSSION: Since Mrs. A uses 20% of her residence exclusively for business purposes, she may deduct 20% of the expenses of her residence plus any expenses directly applicable to the business. The deduction is limited to the excess of the net income derived from her business activity (not taking into account expenses of the home) over the deductions allowable whether or not the home was used for business purposes, e.g., interest and taxes. This limit is $600 as computed below. Since the other home expenses are $1,600 ($400 maintenance, insurance, utilities + $1,200 depreciation), she will have a $1,000 ($1,600 – $600) expense carryover to 1992 with no gain or loss from the business in 1991.

Gross income	$4,000
Less	
Supplies	(2,000)
20% of interest	(600)
20% of taxes	(800)
Limit on other deductions	$ 600

Module 6.6: Business Use of Home

110. Mr. G, a plumber, owns his own building which he uses exclusively in his business. On January 1, 1990, Mr. G purchased a residence and began using the entire basement as an office and workshop for his business. The size of Mr. G's residence is 2,000 square feet including the basement, which has an area of 800 square feet. During 1991, Mr. G's net income attributable to the business use of his home (before taking into account expenses of the home) was $10,000. In addition, Mr. G incurred the following costs with respect to his residence:

Mortgage interest	$15,000
Real estate taxes	2,500
Utilities	2,000
Insurance and maintenance expenses	2,500

Assuming $1,500 of depreciation on the basement portion each year, what is Mr. G's depreciation deduction with respect to his residence?

   a. $1,500.
   b. $1,456.
   c. $1,364.
   d. $1,200.

The correct answer is (d). *(SPE 986 I-76)*
REQUIRED: The depreciation that may be deducted for an office in a taxpayer's home.
DISCUSSION: Under Sec. 280A, a deduction for the business use of a dwelling unit also used as a residence is allowed only if a portion of the unit is used exclusively on a regular basis as the principal place of business, or as a place of business to meet with patients or customers, or if it is a separate structure that is used in connection with the taxpayer's trade or business.

The expenses of the residence must be apportioned based on the area used exclusively for business. Mr. G's business portion is 40% (800 ÷ 2,000 feet). However, the business deduction is limited to net income from the business activity (not taking into account expenses of the home) less the expenses deductible regardless of the business activity, e.g., interest and taxes. Under Prop. Reg. 1.280A-2(i)(5), expenses deductible only as a result of business use that are not adjustments to basis are deducted first, and then those business deductions affecting basis (e.g., depreciation).

Net income	$10,000
Mortgage interest (40% x $15,000)	(6,000)
Taxes (40% x $2,500)	(1,000)
Utilities (40% x $2,000)	(800)
Insurance & maintenance (40% x $2,500)	(1,000)
Limitation on depreciation	$ 1,200

111. A taxpayer who is entitled to a deduction for the use of a portion of his home in his work can base the deduction on the cost to rent equivalent commercial space.

The correct answer is (F). *(SPE 1077 I-81)*
DISCUSSION: If the taxpayer is allowed a deduction for the business use of a portion of his/her home, the taxpayer must allocate the total expenses of operating the home between business and personal use. Accordingly, actual allocated expenses are deductible, not the cost of equivalent commercial space.

112. Michelle Lee operates a babysitting service out of her home four days a week. The state in which she resides has licensed her as a day care center. No part of her home is used exclusively for her business. Michelle Lee is not entitled to claim any depreciation deductions attributable to the business use of her home.

The correct answer is (F). *(SPE 1083 I-35)*
DISCUSSION: Under Sec. 280A, a deduction for the business use of a dwelling unit also used as a residence is allowed only if a portion of the unit is used exclusively on a regular basis as the principal place of business, as a place of business to meet with patients or customers, or it is a separate structure and is used in connection with the taxpayer's trade or business. Sec. 280A(c)(4) provides an exception to this general rule for any portion of a dwelling unit used in the trade or business of providing day care for children.

113. An employee who rents a portion of his home to his employer in 1991 (for the employee to work in) may deduct all expenses allocable to the office space.

The correct answer is (F). *(Publisher)*
DISCUSSION: No deduction is available (except for otherwise allowable interest and taxes) for the business use of a home by an employee when it is rented by the employer [Sec. 280A(c)(6)].

6.7 Rental Expense

114. If a residence is completely converted to business use and not used at all as a dwelling, any carryover "office in home" deductions may be deducted in full regardless of net income.

The correct answer is (F). *(Publisher)*
DISCUSSION: When home office deductions exceed the net income from a business, this excess is carried over to future years. However, these carryover deductions are limited to net income from the business whether or not the dwelling unit is used as a residence during each such succeeding taxable year [Sec. 280A(c)].

115. In October 1991, Nanette, a calendar-year taxpayer, leased a building for 5 years, beginning November 1, 1991 and ending October 31, 1996. Under the terms of the lease, her rent is $24,000 per year. She paid the first year's rent on November 1, 1991. What amount can Nanette deduct as rent expense on her 1991 income tax return?

 a. $2,000.
 b. $4,000.
 c. $12,000.
 d. $24,000.

The correct answer is (b). *(SPE 988 II-58)*
REQUIRED: The amount of rent deduction when rent has been prepaid.
DISCUSSION: Prepaid rent may not be deducted by either a cash-basis or accrual-basis taxpayer. To do so would violate the requirement that the taxpayer's method of accounting must clearly reflect income [Sec. 446(b)]. Furthermore, an expenditure that creates an asset having a useful life extending substantially beyond the close of the taxable year is not deductible [Reg. 1.461-1(a)]. Only the $4,000 of rental expense allocable to the current year ($24,000 x 2/12 months) is deductible in 1991.

116. On January 2, 1991, Melanie paid $9,000 to acquire a lease on a new building for a term of 20 years. At her request, the lease also included two renewal options of 5 years each. Of the above cost, $6,000 was for the original lease and $1,500 for each of the two renewal options. Melanie is a cash-basis taxpayer. What is her allowable deduction for 1991?

 a. $0.
 b. $300.
 c. $450.
 d. $9,000.

The correct answer is (b). *(SPE 1078 II-65)*
REQUIRED: The allowable deduction in the year of acquisition for the cost of acquiring a long-term lease.
DISCUSSION: A cash-basis taxpayer normally deducts expenses in the year paid. However, the lease is an asset with a useful life that extends substantially beyond the close of the taxable year, so the cost of it must be capitalized and amortized over the life of the lease [Reg. 1.461-1(a)]. Since less than 75% of the cost of acquiring the entire lease is attributable to the basic or initial term of the lease ($6,000 ÷ $9,000 = 67%), the term of the lease is treated as including all periods for which the lease may be renewed (Sec. 178). The taxpayer's allowable deduction in the current year is $300 ($9,000 ÷ 30-year useful life).

117. Harvey Haberdasher leased a building for his clothing store. Harvey has a 5-year lease with an option to renew it for another 5 years. He constructed a storeroom in 1991 at the rear of the building which cost $10,000. Over what period may Harvey depreciate the storeroom?

 a. 5 years.
 b. 10 years.
 c. 27.5 years.
 d. 31.5 years.

The correct answer is (d). *(Publisher)*
REQUIRED: The depreciable life a lessee may use for improvements constructed on the premises.
DISCUSSION: Under prior law, leasehold improvements made by a lessee were deductible over the shorter of the property's ACRS recovery period or the portion of the lease term remaining on the date the property was acquired. After 1986, the lessee recovers capital costs under the general depreciation rules in every case. After 1987 real property, other than residential rental property, is depreciated over 31.5 years.

Module 6.7: Rental Expense

118. An agreement may be considered a conditional sales contract rather than a lease if any of the following are true except

    a. You pay rent that is much more than current fair rental value for the property.

    b. At the end of the lease you obtain title to the property by paying its fair market value.

    c. The agreement applies part of each "rent" payment toward an equity interest that you will receive.

    d. The lease designates some part of the "rent" payments as interest.

The correct answer is (b). *(SPE 1085 II-41)*
REQUIRED: The factor that would not cause an agreement to be considered a conditional sales contract rather than a lease.
DISCUSSION: By having to pay the fair market value of the property, and not just a nominal payment at the end of the lease, the agreement would not be considered a conditional sales contract, since the actual sale would not take place until the lease is over. Any rental payments throughout the life of the lease would be deductible as rent, and not capitalized as payments toward ownership of the property.
Answer (a) is incorrect because the average person would not pay well above the current fair rental value for property unless such person expected an additional interest in the property. Answer (c) is incorrect because, under such agreement, the lessee gets an increasing interest in the property with each payment. Answer (d) is incorrect because such a situation would be treated as if the lessee is actually financing the property with the lessor.

119. Mr. B leased a sprinkler system for his warehouse. The system had an estimated useful life of 40 years and a cost to the lessor of $20,000. Under the agreement, Mr. B will rent the system for 5 years at a yearly rate of $5,000 for a total rent of $25,000. Mr. B must insure the system for an amount at least equal to the total rentals and will bear the risk of any loss. The lessor's liability for any defect is limited to $1,000. The lease may be renewed for another 5-year period at $200 a year. The lease payments may be deducted by Mr. B as rent expense.

The correct answer is (F). *(SPE 984 II-10)*
DISCUSSION: Although the transaction takes the form of a rental, it is in substance a financed sale, since the taxpayer is required to provide insurance and maintenance for the system and bear the risk of loss. The lessor has almost no liability for the system. Furthermore, the renewal period of the lease is for a nominal amount, indicating that the system has already been paid for. In essence, Mr. B has made a capital expenditure for which Sec. 263 disallows a deduction. Instead, he must capitalize and amortize or depreciate the asset over its useful life.

120. A lease that provides for 85% of the periodic payments to be applied to the purchase price upon exercise of a purchase option by the lessee will normally constitute a conditional sale, and the purchase price (net of interest) should be capitalized.

The correct answer is (T). *(SPE 1078 II-10)*
DISCUSSION: A transaction in the form of a lease but in substance a purchase is treated as a purchase so that the rent is not deductible and the purchase price must be capitalized and depreciated. When a substantial portion of the payments can be applied to acquire title, the transaction is considered to be a purchase.

121. Mr. T, a lessee of part of an office building from an unrelated lessor, made permanent improvements in 1991 which had a recovery period longer than the remaining term of the lease. Mr. T may amortize the cost of the improvement over the remaining term of the lease.

The correct answer is (F). *(SPE 1082 II-14)*
DISCUSSION: Improvements made or erected on leased property after 1986 are amortized under the general depreciation rules in every case. Therefore, the remaining term of the lease is not a factor in computing the amortization (depreciation). The recovery class or class life of the improvements determines the recovery period.

6.8 Farm Expense

122. On May 4, 1991, Taxpayer A expected a yield of 50,000 bushels of corn from his farm. The December futures price at that time was $2.05 a bushel. To protect himself against a loss, he sold 10 December futures contracts of 5,000 bushels each. The price did not drop, but rose to $2.25 a bushel. He sold his 50,000 bushels of raised corn for $2.25 a bushel. He also purchased his futures obligations of corn at $2.25 a bushel to close out the futures transactions. He paid a broker's commission of $500 for the in and out futures transactions. What is his loss on these futures transactions?

a. $10,225.
b. $10,500.
c. $11,250.
d. $102,500.

The correct answer is (b). *(SPE 1079 II-82)*
REQUIRED: The taxpayer's loss incurred on the sale and purchase of futures contracts.
DISCUSSION: Taxpayer A has engaged in a short sale generally regulated under Sec. 1233. A short sale occurs when securities (e.g., commodity futures) are sold now to be delivered in the future. The price of the commodity used to cover (deliver) the prior short sale determines the gain or loss as compared to the selling price in the short sale. Taxpayer A incurred a loss of $10,500 [(50,000 bushels x $.20 price increase) + $500 commission]. This was a hedging transaction which farmers engage in to protect against price drops in the commodity. Because the hedge was made to protect ordinary income from farming, the loss is also ordinary.

123. In 1991 Taxpayer A had gross income from Farms X and Y of $20,000 ($10,000 from each). During 1991 A spent $12,000 on Farm X on deductible soil and water conservation expenditures under a plan approved by his state's Soil Conservation Service of the Department of Agriculture. How much of the soil and water conservation expenditures can Taxpayer A deduct for 1991?

a. $2,500.
b. $5,000.
c. $10,000.
d. $12,000.

The correct answer is (b). *(SPE 1079 II-51)*
REQUIRED: The deductible amount of soil and water conservation expenditures.
DISCUSSION: Sec. 175 allows a taxpayer engaged in the business of farming to treat expenditures for the purpose of soil or water conservation on land used for farming as deductible expenses rather than capital expenditures, provided the expenditures are approved by the Soil Conservation Service of the Department of Agriculture for the area in which the land is located. The deduction for any year is limited to 25% of the gross income derived from farming during the year. The gross income includes that from all the taxpayer's farming, not just from the land on which the soil and water conservation expenditures were made. Taxpayer A may deduct $5,000 ($20,000 x 25%) of the soil and water conservation expenditures. The remaining $7,000 may be carried over and deducted in succeeding taxable years subject to the 25% limit each year.

124. In 1991 Frankie had gross income from farming of $60,000 and taxable income from farming of $25,000. Frankie spent $6,500 on land clearing expenses during 1991. How much of the land clearing expenses can Frankie deduct in 1991?

a. $0.
b. $3,250.
c. $5,000.
d. $6,500.

The correct answer is (a). *(SPE 1081 II-56)*
REQUIRED: The amount of land clearing expenses deductible in the current year.
DISCUSSION: A taxpayer engaged in the business of farming may no longer elect to treat expenditures to clear land for the purpose of making such land suitable for farming as deductible expenses rather than capital expenditures because Sec. 182 has been repealed. Land clearing expenses incurred after 1986 must be capitalized.

125. Alma Knack is a calendar-year, cash-basis farmer who grows corn and raises hogs on a large farm in Iowa. On December 26, 1991 Alma purchased a 6-month supply of feed for the hogs costing $4,000. At the same time, she also purchased a new hybrid variety of seed costing $1,000 for the spring planting period. Her other farm expenses for the year were $9,000. Of the feed and seed purchased on December 26, Alma may deduct

a. Only $1,000 in 1991.
b. Only $4,000 in 1991.
c. Only $4,500 in 1991.
d. All $5,000 in 1991.

The correct answer is (c). *(Publisher)*
REQUIRED: When a farmer can deduct prepaid feed and seed.
DISCUSSION: Under Reg. 1.162-12, farmers are allowed to deduct prepaid feed and seed that will not be used until subsequent years. However, this must be a consistent method of accounting from year to year, and after 1986 the deduction for prepaid expenses may not exceed 50% of other farming expenses. Therefore, Alma can deduct only $4,500 (50% x $9,000) in 1991.
Note that a farming syndicate (any business enterprise, other than a regular corporation, an interest in which is a security subject to regulation by the SEC) may not deduct prepaid feed and seed; these are only deductible when actually used or consumed (Sec. 464). These and other restrictions on deductions by farming syndicates are designed to curb their use as tax shelters.

126. Mr. Cryzer, a calendar-year taxpayer who itemizes his deductions, raises cows in his spare time and on weekends. In 1991, he sold 25 cows for a total of $7,000 and incurred the following expenses directly related to raising those cows:

Medicine and veterinarian bills	$ 2,000
Taxes	1,000
Feed	5,000
Depreciation	1,000

What is Mr. Cryzer's net profit or loss to be included in his individual income tax return assuming that the activity is not engaged in for profit?

a. ($2,000) loss.
b. ($1,000) loss.
c. $0.
d. $1,000 profit.

The correct answer is (c). *(SPE 990 II-72)*
REQUIRED: The profit or loss of a taxpayer who raises cows as a hobby.
DISCUSSION: A farmer or cattleman deducts expenses under Sec. 162 for a trade or business, or under Sec. 212 for the production or collection of income. However, if the activity is merely a hobby and not engaged in for profit, Sec. 183 limits the deductions to the gross income from the activity. Mr. Cryzer's gross income from raising cows was $7,000 and his expenses were $9,000. He may deduct $7,000, so he has no profit or loss.
In order to determine whether an activity is a hobby or engaged in for profit, the presumption of Sec. 183(d) may be used: if a profit is made for three or more of five consecutive taxable years, the activity will be presumed to have been engaged in for profit.

127. A farmer, trading in commodity future contracts within the range of his production, can deduct a $5,000 loss on such contracts on Schedule F as an ordinary business expense.

The correct answer is (T). *(SPE 1077 I-149)*
DISCUSSION: A farmer who trades in commodity futures within the range of his/her production (both amount and type of commodity) is considered to be engaged in hedging to protect against loss in the event of a decline in the price of the commodity farmed. As such, the hedging is deemed a part of the farming operation, and any gain or loss is considered ordinary.

128. If you rent a farm for farming, the rental expense that represents the fair rental value of the farm residence is not deductible.

The correct answer is (T). *(SPE 1085 II-27)*
DISCUSSION: The rental value of the farm residence is a personal expense which is not deductible. Only that portion of the rental expense attributable to the land and buildings actually used for farming is deductible.

129. Morgan Donegan, a cash-basis farmer, sold cattle that he had raised for $8,000. His feed, veterinarian fees, and other costs of raising the cattle totaled $4,000. His gross income from this sale is $4,000.

The correct answer is (F). *(SPE 986 II-24)*
DISCUSSION: Gross income from the sale of cattle is the amount received, or $8,000. Furthermore, a farmer's expenses of raising the cattle are generally deducted, not capitalized.

130. Michael Wright purchased several brood mares in 1985, expecting to breed them and sell their offspring. His Schedule C reflected the following:

1985	$ 5,000	loss
1986	9,900	loss
1987	3,500	loss
1988	10,800	profit
1989	4,250	loss
1990	2,700	loss
1991	17,250	profit

Wright's activity is presumed to be for profit.

The correct answer is (T). *(SPE 1081 I-15)*
DISCUSSION: Sec. 183 applies to activities that are not engaged in for profit and allows a deduction only to the extent of gross income. There is a presumption that an activity is engaged in for profit if it shows a profit in at least 3 of any 5 consecutive years (2 out of 7 years if breeding horses). Since the taxpayer's activity showed a profit in 1988 and 1991 that is substantially the same amount as the losses, the horse breeding activity is presumed to be for profit.

6.9 Casualty and Theft Loss

131. Mr. Smith constructed a building at a cost of $80,000 on land that he leases. He uses half of the building for business purposes and lives in the other half. In 1991 a flood damaged the entire building. Mr. Smith's records reflect the following information.

Cost of building	$80,000
Depreciation properly deducted	4,800
Fair market value of building immediately before the flood	76,000
Fair market value of building immediately after the flood	64,000
Insurance reimbursement received during 1991	8,000
Mr. Smith's adjusted gross income for 1991	50,000

What is the amount of Mr. Smith's business and personal casualty losses after any limitations?

a. $0 business; $0 personal.
b. $2,000 business; $0 personal.
c. $2,000 business; $1,800 personal.
d. $900 business; $2,000 personal.

The correct answer is (b). *(SPE 990 II-79)*
REQUIRED: The deductible loss resulting from a flood of an insured building.
DISCUSSION: Sec. 165 allows a deduction for a loss sustained during the taxable year and not compensated for by insurance. Since Mr. Smith uses the building for business purposes 50% of the time, his business casualty loss would be calculated as follows:

Fair market value before flood	$76,000 x 50% =	$38,000
Fair market value after flood	$64,000 x 50% =	(32,000)
Loss due to flood		$ 6,000
Insurance reimbursement	$8,000 x 50% =	(4,000)
Business casualty loss		$ 2,000

This amount was determined under Sec. 165 rules which state the loss for partial destruction of business property is the lesser of the taxpayer's adjusted basis in the property or the difference between the fair market value of the property immediately before and after the casualty.

Since Mr. Smith's 50% personal use of the building is subject to the $100 floor for each casualty item, and the total casualty does not exceed 10% of adjusted gross income of the individual, no personal deduction can be claimed [the 10% of AGI limitation of $5,000 (10% x $50,000 = $5,000) is greater than the $1,900 personal casualty loss].

132. Dawson's office was flooded in 1991 when an upriver dam broke. The office furniture had been purchased in 1990 at a total cost of $6,000, and Dawson had claimed $1,500 in depreciation before the flood. The fair market value of the furniture before the flood was $5,000 and after the flood was $1,000. Dawson was reimbursed $2,000 by insurance. Dawson's casualty loss was

a. $2,000.
b. $2,500.
c. $3,000.
d. $4,000.

The correct answer is (a). *(Publisher)*
REQUIRED: The deductible casualty loss resulting from the partial destruction of office furniture.
DISCUSSION: Sec. 165 allows a deduction for a loss sustained during the taxable year and not compensated for by insurance. The amount of the loss for partial destruction of business property is the lesser of the taxpayer's adjusted basis in the property or the difference between the fair market value of the property immediately before and immediately after the casualty. Dawson's adjusted basis in the property was $4,500 (original cost of $6,000 − $1,500 in depreciation), while the reduction in the fair market value of the property due to the flood was $4,000. Therefore, Dawson's deductible loss is $2,000 (the $4,000 reduction in the property's fair market value − the $2,000 insurance reimbursement).

Module 6.9: Casualty and Theft Loss

133. A machine that Mrs. Cunningham used in her business was partially destroyed by a fire. The machine had an adjusted basis of $25,000 and a fair market value of $50,000 just before the fire. The fair market value was $20,000 after the fire and before any repairs were made. Ms. Cunningham's insurance company immediately reimbursed her $35,000. What is her gain or loss from the casualty?

a. $15,000 gain.
b. $10,000 gain.
c. ($15,000) loss.
d. ($30,000) loss.

The correct answer is (b). *(SPE 986 II-73)*
REQUIRED: The gain or loss from a casualty when an insurance reimbursement is received.
DISCUSSION: Sec. 165 allows a deduction for a loss sustained during the taxable year and not compensated for by insurance. The amount of the loss for partial destruction of business property is the lesser of the taxpayer's adjusted basis in the property or the difference between the fair market value of the property immediately before and immediately after the casualty. Ms. Cunningham's adjusted basis in the property was $25,000 while the reduction in the fair market value was $30,000 ($50,000 − $20,000). Therefore, Ms. Cunningham's loss before her insurance recovery was $25,000. Since her insurance recovery was $35,000, she had no deductible loss, but instead a $10,000 gain ($35,000 − $25,000).

134. Ernest Kopp started a security guard business. Kopp rented an office and furnished it with used furniture and a typewriter from his home. He also converted one of the family cars to business use. On the second day of operations, the company car was stolen while Kopp was installing a security system. On the third day, the office was burglarized and the typewriter stolen. Kopp's basis in the typewriter was $200 and its fair market value when put in the office was $300. The car had cost Kopp $1,500 but it was worth only $1,000 when converted to business use. What is Kopp's casualty deduction?

a. $1,000.
b. $1,100.
c. $1,200.
d. $1,800.

The correct answer is (c). *(Publisher)*
REQUIRED: The casualty loss deduction for property converted from personal to business use.
DISCUSSION: Under Regs. 1.165-9(c) and 1.165-7(b), the amount of a loss by theft is the lesser of the fair market value of the property or its adjusted basis. However, the adjusted basis for property converted from personal to business use is the lesser of its cost basis or its fair market value on the date of conversion. For the typewriter, the lesser amount is its $200 basis. For the car, the lesser amount is its $1,000 fair market value. Kopp may deduct the total of $1,200 ($200 for the typewriter and $1,000 for the car). The deduction is not subject to the $100 and 10% of adjusted gross income limitations since the property was used in a trade or business.

135. In April 1991, Mr. Beach, an accrual basis taxpayer, had a $25,000 theft loss from inventory items held for sale to customers in the ordinary course of his business. In August 1991 he received a $25,000 reimbursement from his insurance company to cover the loss. Which of the following is a correct method of reporting the loss and reimbursement on Beach's income tax return?

a. Include the $25,000 in ordinary income; the loss is accounted for in the cost of goods sold.
b. Do not report the loss as a separate item; do not include the $25,000 in ordinary income.
c. Include the $25,000 in ordinary income; decrease the cost of goods sold by the $100 casualty loss rule.
d. Apply the 10% adjusted gross income rule to the loss; the amount of the deductible loss would be the amount of the reimbursement to be included in ordinary income.

The correct answer is (a). *(SPE 990 II-46)*
REQUIRED: The correct method of reporting a loss of inventory and an insurance reimbursement.
DISCUSSION: If opening and closing inventories are properly reported, a theft or casualty loss to inventory will automatically be claimed through the increase in cost of goods sold. In such event, an insurance reimbursement must be included in ordinary income. Alternatively, the loss can be shown separately and reduced by the insurance reimbursement. But then either opening inventory or purchases must be adjusted downward so that the loss is also not automatically claimed through cost of goods.
Answer (b) is incorrect because if the loss is not reported as a separate item (which means it is automatically claimed through cost of goods sold), then the $25,000 must be included in ordinary income. Answer (c) is incorrect because the $100 casualty loss rule does not apply to inventory, it only applies to personal losses. Answer (d) is incorrect because the 10% of adjusted gross income rule does not apply to business losses, it only applies to personal losses. Also, the deductible loss is not determined by the amount of reimbursement to be included in income.

136. Lynn Newburger owned an office building that she used in her trade or business. A hurricane damaged the building and shrubbery. The building had a fair market value before the hurricane of $100,000 and an adjusted basis of $60,000. After the hurricane, the building had a fair market value of $55,000. The shrubbery had a fair market value of $3,000 before the hurricane and an adjusted basis of $1,000. After the hurricane, the shrubbery had a fair market value of $1,000. Lynn's casualty loss deduction is:

a. $46,000.
b. $47,000.
c. $61,000.
d. $62,000.

The correct answer is (a). *(Publisher)*
REQUIRED: The loss deduction when a building and shrubbery are partially destroyed in one casualty.
DISCUSSION: Under Reg. 1.165-7(b), the amount of a casualty loss deduction is the lesser of the decrease in fair market value or the amount of the adjusted basis of the property destroyed. When there is a casualty loss of real property and improvements not used in a trade or business, the casualty loss is computed on the property as a whole, not each individual part. However, when a loss is incurred in a trade or business, the loss must be computed on each separate item.
Lynn's loss on the building is the decrease in fair market value of $45,000. The loss on the shrubbery is its adjusted basis of $1,000. The total casualty loss deduction is $46,000.

137. When property damaged or destroyed by a casualty is owned partly for personal use and partly for business use, the casualty loss deduction must be figured as if there were two separate casualties.

The correct answer is (T). *(SPE 1082 II-33)*
DISCUSSION: Both business and personal casualty losses are deductible under Sec. 165. Unlike business casualties, the deduction for personal casualties has a $100 floor for each casualty, and the total personal casualties for the year must exceed 10% of adjusted gross income of the individual. Consequently, a casualty on property used partly for personal use and partly for business use must be computed as if there were two casualties.

138. An uninsured casualty or theft loss of inventory may be reflected in cost of goods sold.

The correct answer is (T). *(SPE 1083 II-29)*
DISCUSSION: The normal casualty or theft loss rules do not apply to inventories [Reg. 1.165-7(a)(4)]. If opening and closing inventories are properly reported, the casualty or theft loss attributable to inventory will automatically be reported through cost of goods sold.

139. Christy embezzled $10,000 from Saidy in 1990. However, the theft was not discovered until 1991. The insurance recovery in 1991 was $9,500. Saidy can deduct a $400 casualty loss for 1990.

The correct answer is (F). *(SPE 1079 I-19)*
DISCUSSION: A loss arising from theft is treated as sustained during the taxable year in which the taxpayer discovers the loss [Sec. 165(e)]. Since the taxpayer discovered the loss in 1991, it would be deductible in that year. Assuming Saidy's loss was incurred in her trade or business, she may claim a casualty loss of $500. The $100 casualty floor does not apply to business thefts.

140. In 1991, Gus Grizzum, who operates an auto parts store, incurred a $25,000 inventory loss due to fire and submitted an insurance claim for $20,000, his maximum coverage. The insurance reimbursement was not received by the end of the year. Gus could deduct the entire $25,000 loss in 1991 and include the insurance proceeds in income in the year received.

The correct answer is (F). *(SPE 987 II-27)*
DISCUSSION: The normal casualty or theft loss rules do not apply to inventories [Reg. 1.165-7(a)(4)]. If opening and closing inventories are properly reported, the casualty or theft loss to inventory will automatically be reported through cost of goods sold. Because there is the prospect of a $20,000 recovery, either the opening inventory or cost of goods sold must be adjusted downward so that the entire $25,000 loss is not claimed through cost of goods sold until the reimbursement is received or the claim is denied and the loss is deducted.

CHAPTER SEVEN
LIMITATIONS ON LOSSES

```
7.1  Net Operating Loss .............................. (13 questions)  133
7.2  At-Risk Rules ................................... (11 questions)  137
7.3  Passive Activities .............................. (16 questions)  141
```

These loss limitations are presented here because, to the extent allowed, the losses reduce income in computing adjusted gross income. For example, an allowable loss from either a direct investment or from a limited partnership is deductible for adjusted gross income. Also, these loss limitations generally apply across the board to varied types of transactions. For other limitations on losses from specific transactions, see

Module 6.6	Business Use of Home
Module 6.9	Casualty and Theft Loss (Business)
Module 9.5	Casualty and Theft Losses (Personal)
Module 14.7	Capital Loss Limitations and Carryovers
Module 14.8	Sales to Related Parties (Capital Assets)
Module 15.5	Sales to Related Parties (Depreciable Property)
Module 17.6	Partnership Losses
Module 18.10	C Corporation Net Operating Losses
Module 19.12	S Corporation Losses

7.1 Net Operating Loss

1. In computing an individual's net operating loss, which of the following is not considered business income or deduction(s)?

a. Wages.
b. Personal casualty loss.
c. Gain on sale of investment property.
d. Gain on sale of business property.

The correct answer is (c). *(SPE 1081 II-59)*

REQUIRED: The item not considered business income or deductions in computing an individual's net operating loss.

DISCUSSION: Business and nonbusiness income and deductions need to be distinguished because nonbusiness deductions are deductible in computing a net operating loss only to the extent of nonbusiness income [Sec. 172(d)]. Nonbusiness deductions and income are those that are not attributable to, or derived from, a taxpayer's trade or business. Also, capital losses are only deductible to the extent of capital gains. A gain on the sale of investment property is a capital gain and not business income.

Answer (a) is incorrect because employment is considered a trade or business; therefore, wages are business income. Answer (b) is incorrect because a personal casualty loss is treated as a business deduction [Reg. 1.172-3(a)(3)]. Answer (d) is incorrect because a gain on the sale of business property is considered business income.

2. In computing an individual's net operating loss, all of the following are considered business income or deductions except

a. Contributions made by a self-employed person to a personal retirement plan.
b. Moving expenses paid in connection with beginning work at a new principal place of employment.
c. State income taxes on net income from business profits.
d. Loss from the rental of property for the year.

The correct answer is (a). *(SPE 1078 II-51)*
REQUIRED: The item not considered business income or deduction in computing an individual's net operating loss.
DISCUSSION: Contributions made by a self-employed person (or an employee) to a retirement plan are not treated as attributable to the trade or business of the taxpayer [Sec. 172(d)(4)]. Therefore, they are treated as a nonbusiness deduction.
Answer (b) is incorrect because employment is considered a trade or business. Therefore, employee moving expenses are business expenses. Answer (c) is incorrect because state income taxes on net income from business profits are attributable to the taxpayer's trade or business. Answer (d) is incorrect because the loss from a rental property is a business loss for purposes of Sec. 172 (Rev. Rul. 70-40).

3. Which one of the following is deductible in computing a net operating loss for an individual taxpayer?

a. Nonbusiness deductions in excess of nonbusiness income.
b. Loss on disposition of rental property.
c. NOL carryovers from other years.
d. Business capital losses in excess of business capital gains.

The correct answer is (b). *(SPE 990 II-44)*
REQUIRED: The item deductible in computing a net operating loss for an individual taxpayer.
DISCUSSION: A loss on the disposition of rental property is allowed in computing net operating loss under Sec. 172.
Answers (a), (c), and (d) are incorrect because each is nondeductible in computing NOL under Sec. 172(d). These and other items must be added back to the individual taxpayer's loss as modifications in computing NOL.

4. Which of the following is not a modification required to calculate an individual net operating loss?

a. Add back a net operating loss deduction from any other year used in computing taxable income.
b. Add back excess nonbusiness capital losses over nonbusiness capital gains.
c. Add back personal exemptions and exemptions for dependents.
d. Add back all itemized deductions.

The correct answer is (d). *(SPE 1077 I-152)*
REQUIRED: The item which is not a modification required to calculate an individual NOL.
DISCUSSION: In computing a net operating loss, nonbusiness deductions are allowable to the extent of nonbusiness income. Itemized deductions or the standard deduction are nonbusiness deductions. However, all itemized deductions or the standard deduction need not be added back, only those in excess of nonbusiness income.
Answers (a), (b), and (c) are incorrect because each is a modification required to calculate an individual's net operating loss under Sec. 172(d).

Module 7.1: Net Operating Loss

5. What is the amount of the net operating loss for 1991 based on the following information?

Total income:
- Interest on savings — $425
- Net long-term capital gain on sale of business property — 2,000

Total deductions:
- Net loss from business (sales of $87,000 less expenses of $92,000) — $5,000
- Net nonbusiness short-term capital loss on sale of stock — 1,000
- Personal exemption — 2,150
- Standard deduction — 3,400

a. $0.
b. $1,475.
c. $2,575.
d. $3,000.

The correct answer is (d). *(SPE 989 II-71)*
REQUIRED: The taxpayer's net operating loss for 1991.
DISCUSSION: A net operating loss is defined as the excess of allowable deductions (as modified) over gross income [Sec. 172(c)]. An NOL generally includes only items which represent business income or loss. Personal casualty losses and wage or salary income are included as business items. Nonbusiness income in excess of nonbusiness deductions must be included. Interest and dividends are not business income.

Net loss from business	$(5,000)
Capital gain on business property	2,000
Net operating loss	$(3,000)

The nonbusiness capital loss cannot be offset against the business-related capital gain. The nonbusiness deductions (the standard deduction) exceed the nonbusiness income (interest) and both items are excluded from the NOL calculation. No deduction is allowed for the personal exemption in arriving at the NOL.

6. What is the amount of Ms. Joseph's net operating loss for 1991, based on the following information?

Income:
- Salary from part-time employment — $9,000
- Interest income from savings — 1,000
- Net long-term capital gain from sale of investment property — 1,000

Deductions:
- Net loss from business (sales of $100,000 less expenses of $120,000) — $20,000
- Personal exemption — 2,150
- Standard deduction — 3,400
- 1990 net operating loss carryover — 2,000

a. $14,000.
b. $12,900.
c. $11,000.
d. $10,000.

The correct answer is (c). *(SPE 990 II-73)*
REQUIRED: The taxpayer's net operating loss for 1991.
DISCUSSION: A net operating loss is defined as the excess of allowable deductions (as modified) over gross income [Sec. 172(c)]. An NOL generally includes only items which represent business income or loss. Personal casualty losses and wage or salary income are included as business items. Nonbusiness deductions in excess of nonbusiness income must be excluded. Interest is not business income. Interest and capital gains from the sale of the investment property are an offset to nonbusiness deductions (the standard deduction). Since nonbusiness deductions ($3,400 standard deduction) exceed nonbusiness income ($1,000 + $1,000), they have no effect on the NOL.

Net loss from business	$(20,000)
Salary	9,000
Net operating loss	$(11,000)

No deduction is allowed for the personal exemption or 1990 NOL carryover in arriving at the 1991 NOL.

Module 7.1: Net Operating Loss

7. Nancy, who is single, started her business in 1991 and had a $40,000 net operating loss for the year. Her 1988 income tax return reflects the following:

Salary	$50,000
Deduction for capital loss	(1,000)
Adjusted gross income	49,000
Charitable contributions	30,000
Limited to 50% of adjusted gross income	24,500
Medical expense [$4,675 − $3,675 (7.5% of AGI)]	1,000
Personal exemption	1,950

Assuming the $40,000 net operating loss is carried back to 1988, what is Nancy's net operating loss to be carried back to 1989?

  a. $15,925.
  b. $18,450.
  c. $20,400.
  d. $21,400.

The correct answer is (a). *(SPE 990 II-74)*
REQUIRED: The amount of the taxpayer's 1991 net operating loss to be carried back to 1989.
DISCUSSION: The entire amount of the net operating loss (NOL) for any taxable year is carried first to the earliest of the taxable years to which it may be carried. The NOL is used to reduce the income (as modified) to zero in such earliest year, and to the extent not so used, it is carried to succeeding years. The modifications to the income of the carryback year are those used in computing NOL, except the deduction for a net operating loss is not disallowed, and nonbusiness deductions are not limited to nonbusiness income. When recomputing Nancy's 1988 taxable income, the deductions for the capital loss and personal exemption are not allowed. The limitations on the charitable contributions and the medical expenses must be recomputed in light of the modified adjusted gross income [Reg. 1.172-5(a)(2)(ii)].

AGI		$50,000
Charitable contributions		(25,000)
Medical expenses	$4,675	
Less: 7.5% of AGI	3,750	(925)
Modified income for 1988		$24,075
1991 NOL		(40,000)
1991 NOL carryback to 1989		$15,925

8. Mr. Trim sustained a net operating loss (NOL) for 1991. If Trim does not elect to forgo the carryback period, to what years may he carry the NOL?

  a. Back 3 years; forward 7.
  b. Back 5 years; forward 15.
  c. Back 3 years; forward 5.
  d. Back 3 years; forward 15.

The correct answer is (d). *(SPE 990 II-43)*
REQUIRED: The years to which a net operating loss may be carried.
DISCUSSION: A net operating loss may be carried back to each of the 3 taxable years preceding the taxable year of such loss (oldest first), and may be carried forward to each of the 15 taxable years following the taxable year of the loss. Alternatively, the taxpayer may elect to forgo the carryback entirely, and only carry the net operating loss forward.

9. Morgan, a single taxpayer, was employed for the first 6 months of 1991 and earned $15,000 in wages. On July 1, 1991, he started a business and sustained a loss of $20,000. Interest income for 1991 was $300. Morgan has a net operating loss for 1991 which he elects to carry back to 1988. His adjusted gross income for 1988 consisted of wages of $11,750 and a capital loss of $1,000. The standard deduction amount for 1988 was $3,000 and the personal exemption amount was $1,950. What is Morgan's 1988 taxable income after the carryback of the net operating loss?

  a. $2,750.
  b. $1,800.
  c. $800.
  d. $0.

The correct answer is (c). *(SPE 1080 II-77)*
REQUIRED: The taxpayer's taxable income for 1988 after the carryback of the 1991 NOL.
DISCUSSION: First, the net operating loss (NOL) for 1991 must be computed.

Gross income:		
Salary	$15,000	
Interest	300	$15,300
Modified deductions:		
Business loss	$(20,000)	
Standard deduction limited to nonbusiness income	(300)	(20,300)
1991 NOL		$(5,000)

The 1988 taxable income is then computed with the NOL carryback. Remember, taxable income is adjusted gross income reduced by itemized deductions or the standard deduction and the personal exemption.

Wages	$11,750
Capital loss	(1,000)
1991 NOL carryback	(5,000)
Standard deduction	(3,000)
Personal exemption	(1,950)
1988 taxable income	$ 800

Module 7.2: At-Risk Rules 137

10. In figuring the current year's net operating loss (NOL), an individual can include any NOL carryovers from the prior 15 years.

The correct answer is (F). *(SPE 990 II-15)*
DISCUSSION: When computing an NOL, the allowable deductions are modified under Sec. 172(d). These modifications disallow deductions for NOLs from other years and for personal exemptions.

11. Mr. Folgers has been granted an automatic extension for filing his 1991 calendar-year return. On August 30, 1992, Mr. Folgers filed his 1991 return reflecting a net operating loss. On his return, Mr. Folgers made an election to forgo the carryback period. Mr. Folgers is ineligible to make the election to forgo the carryback period.

The correct answer is (T). *(SPE 1081 II-19)*
DISCUSSION: A net operating loss (NOL) may be carried back 3 years and forward 15 years. A taxpayer may elect to relinquish the entire carryback period if the election is made by the due date (including extensions of time) for filing the taxpayer's return for the year of the NOL [Sec. 172(b)(3)(C)]. The automatic extension gave an additional 4 months to file the return, thus making it due on 8/15/92 (ignoring Saturdays, Sundays, and holidays). Since Mr. Folgers failed to file the return and make the election prior to the due date, he is ineligible to make the election to forgo the carryback period.

12. In figuring the amount of a net operating loss that can be absorbed in a carryback or carryover year, all capital losses incurred in the year to which the net operating loss is carried must be eliminated.

The correct answer is (F). *(SPE 987 II-24)*
DISCUSSION: When carrying an NOL back to an earlier year, modifications to income of the carryback year are those used in computing an NOL except the deduction for a net operating loss is not disallowed and nonbusiness deductions are not limited to nonbusiness income. Capital losses can still be used to offset capital gains or deducted up to the individual limitation.

13. If two or more net operating losses are carried back to a tax year, they must be deducted in the order they were incurred.

The correct answer is (T). *(SPE 989 II-12)*
DISCUSSION: A net operating loss (NOL) may be carried back to each of the 3 taxable years preceding the taxable year of such loss (oldest first). If you suffer an NOL in both 1990 and 1991, the 1990 loss must be carried back, and completely offset the income from 1987, 1988, or 1989 before the 1991 loss may be carried back to 1988 and 1989.

7.2 At-Risk Rules

14. The at-risk rules

a. Limit a taxpayer's deductible losses from investment activities.
b. Limit the type of deductions in income-producing activities.
c. Apply to business and income-producing activities on a combined basis.
d. Apply at the entity level for partnerships and S corporations.

The correct answer is (a). *(Publisher)*
REQUIRED: The correct statement concerning the at-risk rules.
DISCUSSION: The at-risk rules are contained in Sec. 465 and limit a taxpayer's deductible losses from each business and income-producing activity to the amount for which the taxpayer is at risk with respect to that activity. Although originally designed to limit deductible losses from tax shelters, the at-risk rules apply across the board to most activities.
Answer (b) is incorrect because it is the losses from each activity that are limited, not the type of deductions.
Answer (c) is incorrect because the at-risk rules apply to each business and income-producing activity separately.
Answer (d) is incorrect because the at-risk rules apply at the partner or shareholder level for "pass-through" entities such as partnerships and S corporations.

15. The at-risk rules do not apply to

   a. A corporation owned more than 50% during the last half of the year by five or fewer individuals.
   b. The holding of real property placed in service in 1988.
   c. A closely held corporation for which 50% or more of its gross receipts are from equipment leasing.
   d. Exploring for oil and gas resources.

The correct answer is (c). *(Publisher)*
REQUIRED: The activity to which the at-risk rules do not apply.
DISCUSSION: The at-risk rules apply to most business and income-producing activities. However, there is an exception for a closely held corporation actively engaged in equipment leasing. A closely held corporation for this purpose is defined as one owned more than 50% during the last half of the year by five or fewer individuals. At least 50% of the gross receipts must be from equipment leasing for the corporation to be considered "actively engaged" in equipment leasing.
Answer (a) is incorrect because this is the definition of a closely held corporation to which the at-risk rules apply. The at-risk rules do not apply to other C corporations.
Answer (b) is incorrect because the holding of real property is generally subject to the at-risk rules after 1986. Answer (d) is incorrect because exploring for oil and gas resources is an activity specifically included in the at-risk rules by Sec. 465(c)(1)(D).

16. All of the following statements relating to net operating losses and the at-risk limits are true except

   a. In applying at-risk limits to individuals, each item of leased Sec. 1245 equipment, farm, or oil and gas property is treated as a separate activity.
   b. If the amounts that you borrow for use in the activity are secured by property not used in the activity, the amount considered at-risk is limited to the net fair market value (the fair market value on the date the property is pledged less any prior or superior claims to which it is subject) of your interest in the property.
   c. If you have a loss in excess of your at-risk investment, the loss disallowed will not be allowed in subsequent years unless you increase your at-risk investment.
   d. You are considered at-risk for the amount of money you borrow to contribute to an activity, other than activities involving the holding of real property, if the lender's recourse is only to your interest in the activity.

The correct answer is (d). *(SPE 986 II-47)*
REQUIRED: The false statement concerning at-risk limitations on losses.
DISCUSSION: Sec. 465 generally limits losses from an activity for each year to the amount the taxpayer has at-risk in the activity at year-end. A taxpayer is generally considered at-risk for money and the adjusted basis of property contributed to the activity and amounts borrowed for use in the activity. But amounts borrowed for use in the activity are not included as at-risk if the lender has no recourse against the borrower personally, except for certain qualified financing with respect to real property.
Answers (a), (b), and (c) are all correct statements with respect to the at-risk rules.

17. Mr. Condor began producing picture films in January 1991. During 1991, he made the following contributions to his business

Cash	$10,000
Equipment (adjusted basis to Condor)	15,000
(fair market value)	30,000
Loan from First Bank which he personally promised to repay	20,000
Loan from Second Bank for which he is not personally liable, but secured by a mortgage on his home	10,000
Loan from Third Bank for which he is not personally liable, but secured by equipment used in his business	25,000

Under the at-risk rules, Mr. Condor is considered to be at risk in the amount of:

a. $45,000.
b. $55,000.
c. $60,000.
d. $80,000.

The correct answer is (b). *(SPE 990 I-68)*
REQUIRED: The amount for which a taxpayer is considered at risk.
DISCUSSION: A taxpayer is considered at risk for cash contributions to the activity, the adjusted basis of other property contributed to the activity, and amounts borrowed for use in the activity, if the taxpayer is personally liable on the debt or has pledged property not used in the at-risk activity as security for the debt. A taxpayer is generally not considered at risk for nonrecourse debt secured by property used in the activity. Mr. Condor is considered at risk for the following:

Cash	$10,000
Basis of property	15,000
Loan from First Bank	20,000
Loan from Second Bank	10,000
Total amount at risk	$55,000

18. In February 1991, Kathy purchased a small apartment building for $200,000. She used $25,000 of her own money and $25,000 that she borrowed from her father to make the down payment. She signed a note to pay the remainder of the purchase price to the seller. Both the loan from her father and the debt to the seller were nonrecourse, secured only by the apartment building. The terms of both debts were commercially reasonable and on substantially the same terms as loans involving unrelated persons. Kathy's at-risk limitation on losses is:

a. $25,000.
b. $50,000.
c. $175,000.
d. $200,000.

The correct answer is (b). *(SPE 989 I-60)*
REQUIRED: The amount an individual is considered at risk for holding real property when there are nonrecourse loans.
DISCUSSION: The at-risk rules of Sec. 465 apply to the holding of real property in general after 1986. However, qualified nonrecourse financing may be treated as an amount at risk for the holding of real property. Qualified nonrecourse financing means an amount borrowed by the taxpayer with respect to the holding of real property, that is not convertible debt, for which no one is personally liable, and borrowed from a qualified person.

A qualified person is someone actively and regularly engaged in the business of lending money. It does not include persons from whom the taxpayer acquired the property or who are related to the taxpayer. However, a related person will qualify if the terms of the loan are commercially reasonable, and on substantially the same terms as loans involving unrelated persons.

Therefore, Kathy is at risk with respect to $25,000 of her own money and the $25,000 borrowed from her father, because the terms of the nonrecourse debt are commercially reasonable and on substantially the same terms as loans involving unrelated persons. The debt owed to the seller of the property does not qualify as at risk.

19. Jill Perry invested $10,000 for a 5% interest in a limited partnership on January 1, 1990. There is one general partner with a 50% interest. In 1990, the partnership purchased an office building to rent and incurred a nonrecourse debt of $100,000 to a bank paying interest only for 5 years. The debt has no conversion feature. The partnership incurred a loss of $150,000 in 1990 and a loss of $200,000 in 1991. How much can Jill deduct each year ignoring any passive loss rules?

	1990	1991
a.	$7,500	$2,500
b.	$7,500	$7,500
c.	$7,500	$10,000
d.	$10,000	$10,000

The correct answer is (b). *(Publisher)*
REQUIRED: The at-risk limitation on losses deductible by a limited partner.
DISCUSSION: A limited partner in a partnership is considered to have at risk the amount of cash and adjusted basis of property contributed to the partnership (or used to purchase the partnership interest), and also a share of any qualified nonrecourse financing on real estate. The existence of a general partner does not affect the fact that Jill will receive a 5% allocation of the nonrecourse debt, provided that no partner has any personal liability on this particular debt. Therefore, Jill's at-risk amount is $15,000 ($10,000 invested + $5,000 share of nonrecourse debt).
Her share of loss in 1990 is $7,500 ($150,000 loss x 5% interest), which may be deducted in full. Her share of loss in 1991 is $10,000 ($200,000 loss x 5% interest), but the limitation on the 1991 deduction is $7,500 ($15,000 at risk − $7,500 deducted in 1990). Note that there may be further limitations on the deduction of a loss based on the passive loss rules.

20. In 1990, Angie purchased a general partnership interest in Partnership X. Angie was at risk for $20,000. In 1990, Angie's share of losses was $25,000 and in 1991 the partnership broke even. Which of the following is correct with respect to the at-risk rules?

a. Angie can deduct $5,000 in 1991 if she increases her amount at risk by $5,000.

b. Angie can deduct only $2,500 in 1991 even if she increases her amount at risk by $5,000.

c. Angie cannot deduct any amount in 1991, even if the partnership incurs nonrecourse debt on tangible personal property, and Angie's share is $10,000.

d. Angie can deduct $5,000 only when her share of the partnership income is at least $5,000.

The correct answer is (a). *(Publisher)*
REQUIRED: The carryover of unused loss limited by the at-risk rules.
DISCUSSION: Any loss from an activity not allowed for a taxable year due to the limitations of Sec. 465 may be treated as a deduction in succeeding taxable years. In the next taxable year, the at-risk rules will be applied again to the carryover amount. If an individual's at-risk amount increases, the unused loss from a prior year may be deducted to the extent of the increased at-risk amount. Therefore, if Angie's amount at risk is increased by $5,000 in 1991, she can deduct the $5,000 not deductible in 1990.
Answer (b) is incorrect because the carryover of unused loss is deductible in full to the extent that the at-risk amount is increased. Answer (c) is incorrect because the at-risk basis will increase if nonrecourse debt is "qualified." A nonrecourse debt is "qualified" only if the debt is incurred with respect to an activity holding real property. Answer (d) is incorrect because Angie can increase her at-risk amount by contributions to the partnership, earnings of the partnership, or purchases of additional interest in the partnership, as well as by increasing her share of debt in the partnership.

21. A person who receives a fee with respect to a taxpayer's investment in real property may be a qualified person to borrow money from with respect to the at-risk rules in 1991.

The correct answer is (F). *(Publisher)*
DISCUSSION: Persons from whom the taxpayer acquired the property, who received a fee with respect to the taxpayer's investment, or who are related to either of the foregoing, usually do not qualify with respect to the at-risk rules.

22. The activity of holding real property does not include the provision of any incidental services.

The correct answer is (F). *(Publisher)*
DISCUSSION: The activity of holding real property includes the holding of personal property and the provision of services incidental to making the real property available as living accommodations.

23. Doug invested in a limited partnership in 1985. In 1991 the partnership purchased an apartment building for rent. The at-risk rules do not apply to Doug's share of any losses from operation of the apartment building.

The correct answer is (F). *(Publisher)*
DISCUSSION: Sec. 465 applies to the holding of real property placed in service after December 31, 1986. Therefore, a partner of a partnership which invests in property in 1991, and incurs losses, will be subject to the at-risk rules.

24. Partnership C acquired an office building in 1985 to rent. It incurs substantial tax losses on this office building each year. Sally acquired a partnership interest in Partnership C in 1991. The at-risk rules do not apply to Sally's share of the loss.

The correct answer is (F). *(Publisher)*
DISCUSSION: The at-risk rules applying to real property are effective for losses attributable to an interest in a partnership (or S corporation or other pass-through entity) that is acquired after December 31, 1986. Since Sally acquired her partnership interest in 1991, she is subject to the at-risk rules for losses from the real property, even if other partners may not be subject to the at-risk rules.

7.3 Passive Activities

25. Which of the following is a correct statement concerning losses from passive activities?

    a. Losses from each passive activity are not deductible, regardless of income earned in other passive activities.
    b. The losses may offset passive income such as interest and dividends, but not business income or earned income.
    c. The rules apply to losses but not credits.
    d. Losses from one passive activity may offset income from another passive activity.

The correct answer is (d). *(Publisher)*
REQUIRED: The correct statement concerning losses from passive activities.
DISCUSSION: In general, losses from passive activities may not offset other income such as salary, interest, dividends, or active business income (Sec. 469). However, deductions from one passive activity may offset income from the same passive activity, and losses from one passive activity may generally offset income from another passive activity.
Answer (a) is incorrect because losses from a passive activity are deductible to the extent of income from other passive activities. Answer (b) is incorrect because losses from passive activities may not offset income such as interest and dividends, which are considered portfolio income. Answer (c) is incorrect because the passive loss rules apply to credits as well as losses.

26. If an individual taxpayer's passive losses and credits relating to rental real estate activities cannot be used in the current year, then they may be carried

    a. Back 3 years, but they cannot be carried forward.
    b. Forward up to a maximum period of 15 years, but they cannot be carried back.
    c. Back 3 years or forward up to 15 years, at the taxpayer's election.
    d. Forward indefinitely or until the property is disposed of in a taxable transaction.

The correct answer is (d). *(CPA 1188 Q-5)*
REQUIRED: The correct statement concerning the carryover or carryback of unused passive losses and credits.
DISCUSSION: Disallowed passive activity losses (and credits) are carried forward and used to offset passive activity income (and taxes) in later years. This applies to passive losses and credits from rental real estate activities or from any other passive activity. The carryover is accomplished by treating the disallowed loss from each activity as a deduction for the activity in the following year. In this manner, the carryforward is indefinite. If the entire interest in a passive activity is disposed of in a taxable transaction in a later year, the passive loss may be used at that time.
Answers (a), (b), and (c) are incorrect because the carryforward is indefinite and there is no carryback of disallowed passive losses or credits.

27. Which of the following is not an example of a passive activity for tax years beginning after 1986?

   a. The rental of apartments with no provision of unusual services.
   b. A limited partner's interest in a limited partnership.
   c. The farming of land when the taxpayer owning the land has hired others to manage operations.
   d. A working interest in oil and gas property, when the taxpayer-owner has unlimited liability, and does not materially participate in the activity.

The correct answer is (d). *(Publisher)*
REQUIRED: The activity not considered a passive activity.
DISCUSSION: Passive activities generally include any activity involving the conduct of a trade or business or the production of income and in which the taxpayer does not materially participate (Sec. 469). However, Sec. 469(c)(3) excludes from the passive activity definition any working interest in oil or gas property in which the form of ownership does not limit liability. This is true whether or not the taxpayer-owner materially participates in the activity.
Answer (a) is incorrect because most rental activities are treated as passive activities. Answer (b) is incorrect because a limited partnership interest is treated as an activity in which the taxpayer does not materially participate. However, the IRS has provided temporary regulations which provide some exceptions to this rule. Answer (c) is incorrect because a farming operation which others are hired to manage is an example of a passive activity.

28. Which of the following is treated as income from a passive activity with respect to loss limitations of Sec. 469?

   a. Interest on bank accounts.
   b. An individual's fees for managing a passive activity.
   c. Annuity income from an insurance contract.
   d. Rental income from an office building in which the owner materially participates but nothing more than usual services are provided to the tenants.

The correct answer is (d). *(Publisher)*
REQUIRED: The income treated as passive income.
DISCUSSION: In general, a passive activity is any activity that involves the conduct of a trade or business or the production of income and in which the taxpayer does not materially participate [Sec. 469(c)(1)]. A rental activity is treated as a passive activity, whether or not the taxpayer materially participates. But if the rental period is short, and significant personal services are provided along with the rentals, the activity may not be considered a rental activity and therefore may be subject to the material participation test.
Answers (a) and (c) are incorrect because interest on bank accounts and annuity income from an insurance contract are treated as portfolio income. Portfolio income is excluded from the definition of passive activity income. Answer (b) is incorrect because income received by an individual in the performance of personal services with respect to a passive activity is not treated as income from a passive activity.

29. The passive loss rules of Sec. 469 do not apply to

   a. Personal service corporations.
   b. Widely held corporations.
   c. Closely held corporations.
   d. Trusts.

The correct answer is (b). *(Publisher)*
REQUIRED: The types of entity to which the passive loss rules do not apply.
DISCUSSION: Under Sec. 469(a)(2), the passive loss rules apply to individuals, estates, trusts, closely held corporations, and personal service corporations. A corporation is considered closely held if, at any time during the last half of the year, 50% or more of the value of its stock is held by five or fewer individuals. The passive loss rules do not apply to widely held corporations, which would be any other C corporation.
Answers (a), (c), and (d) are incorrect because the passive loss rules apply to each of them.

30. With regard to the passive loss rules involving rental real estate activities, which one of the following statements is correct?

   a. The term "passive activity" includes any rental activity without regard to whether or not the taxpayer materially participates in the activity.
   b. Gross investment income from interest and dividends not derived in the ordinary course of a trade or business is treated as passive activity income that can be offset by passive rental activity losses when the "active participation" requirement is not met.
   c. Passive rental activity losses may be deducted only against passive income, but passive rental activity credits may be used against tax attributable to nonpassive activities.
   d. The passive activity rules do not apply to taxpayers whose adjusted gross income is $300,000 or less.

The correct answer is (a). *(CPA 589 Q-54)*
REQUIRED: The correct statement involving rental real estate activities.
DISCUSSION: Passive activities generally include any activity involving the conduct of a trade or business or the production of income in which the taxpayer does not materially participate (Sec. 469). However, a passive activity includes any rental activity, whether or not the taxpayer participates in the activity [Sec. 469(c)(2)].
Answer (b) is incorrect because gross investment income from interest and dividends not derived in the ordinary course of business is not treated as income from passive activities [Sec. 469(e)]. Answer (c) is incorrect because passive rental activity credits may not be used against tax attributable to nonpassive activities. Answer (d) is incorrect because the passive activity rules apply to taxpayers without regard to their adjusted gross income. Special rental real estate loss rules apply to taxpayers who actively participate in the activity and whose adjusted gross income is below $150,000 [Sec. 469(i)].

31. Mrs. King is a general partner with a 20% interest in a partnership that leases equipment on a long-term basis. She is not regularly involved in the partnership business. During 1991, the partnership has a $200,000 loss which includes a $250,000 loss from operations and $50,000 of interest income on funds the partnership plans to use to buy more equipment. What is Mrs. King's passive loss for 1991?

   a. $0.
   b. $30,000.
   c. $40,000.
   d. $50,000.

The correct answer is (d). *(Publisher)*
REQUIRED: A partner's passive loss when the passive activity has portfolio income.
DISCUSSION: A passive activity includes a rental activity where the average rental period is not short-term. However, portfolio income of an activity (e.g., interest, dividend, royalty, or annuity income earned on funds set aside for the future use of the activity) is not treated as passive income from the activity. Therefore, it is the $250,000 loss from operations which is a loss from a passive activity. Mrs. King's passive loss is $50,000 (20% interest x $250,000).

32. All of the outstanding stock of Bryant Corporation is owned equally by three individuals. Bryant is not a personal service corporation. During 1991, Bryant had net operating (active) income of $250,000, a loss on the rental of an office building (acquired in 1989) of $300,000, and portfolio income of $150,000. How much of Bryant's income may be offset by the rental loss?

   a. $250,000 operating income and $50,000 portfolio income.
   b. $250,000 operating income and $0 portfolio income.
   c. $0 operating income and $150,000 portfolio income.
   d. No income may be offset.

The correct answer is (b). *(Publisher)*
REQUIRED: The amount of active business income and portfolio income that may be offset by passive losses for a closely held corporation.
DISCUSSION: Bryant Corporation is a closely held corporation because more than 50% of the value of its stock is held by five or fewer individuals during the last half of the year. In the case of closely held corporations that are not personal service corporations, Sec. 469(e)(2) permits passive losses to offset net active income, but does not permit them to offset portfolio income. Therefore, Bryant's passive loss (a rental activity is treated as a passive activity) may offset the $250,000 of active operating income. It may not offset any of the portfolio income.

Module 7.3: Passive Activities

33. Don Wolf became a general partner in Gata Associates on January 1, 1991, with a 5% interest in Gata's profits, losses, and capital. Gata is a distributor of auto parts. Wolf does not materially participate in the partnership business. For the year ended December 31, 1991, Gata had an operating loss of $100,000. In addition, Gata earned interest of $20,000 on a temporary investment while awaiting delivery of equipment that is presently on order. The principal will be used to pay for this equipment. Wolf's passive loss for 1991 is

   a. $0.
   b. $4,000.
   c. $5,000.
   d. $6,000.

The correct answer is (c). *(CPA 1190 Q-27)*
REQUIRED: The amount treated as a passive loss for 1991.
DISCUSSION: In general, losses arising from one passive activity may be used to offset income from other passive activities, but may not be used to offset active or portfolio income. Wolf's $5,000 operating loss (5% x $100,000) may not be used to offset his $1,000 portfolio income (i.e., interest and dividends are portfolio income) (5% x $20,000). Therefore, his passive loss for 1991 is his $5,000 operating loss.

34. A taxpayer who actively participates in rental real estate activities in 1991 may offset some losses and credits from the activity against nonpassive income (salary, self-employment earnings, etc.) provided that adjusted gross income is under $150,000 and the taxpayer has a minimum percentage interest in the real estate investment of

   a. 75%.
   b. 50%.
   c. 33 1/3%.
   d. 10%.

The correct answer is (d). *(P. Karl III)*
REQUIRED: The minimum investment a taxpayer must have in 1991 to claim additional losses from active participation in rental real estate activities.
DISCUSSION: After 1986, Sec. 469 limits losses from passive activities. Passive activities are generally deemed to include any rental activity. However, in the case of rental real estate activities in which an individual actively participates, up to $25,000 in losses and credits (in a deduction-equivalent sense) from such activities are allowed each year to offset nonpassive income. An individual is not treated as actively participating in a rental real estate activity unless his/her (and spouse's) interest is at least 10% of all interests in the activity.

35. In 1991, the Aloha Gardens apartment complex had rental losses of $40,000. Which of the following is true?

   a. Steve and his wife Barbara each have a 5% interest in the property and manage the apartments. They had nonpassive income of $30,000 for the year. They may offset their share of the rental loss against their nonpassive income.
   b. T Trust has a 40% interest in the property. The trustee is active in managing the apartments. The trust may offset its portion of the rental loss against other income earned during the year.
   c. John's estate has a 20% interest in the property. John was actively involved in managing the complex from 1983 until his death in 1986. His estate may offset its portion of the rental loss against any nonpassive income.
   d. Kathy has an interest as a limited partner in the property. Her nonpassive income for the year is $50,000. She may offset her portion of the rental loss against her nonpassive income up to $25,000.

The correct answer is (a). *(Publisher)*
REQUIRED: The correct statement concerning the deduction of rental losses by various property owners.
DISCUSSION: In the case of rental real estate activities in which an individual actively participates, up to $25,000 of losses from such activities are allowed each year against nonpassive income. Active participation requires only participation such as making management decisions on lease terms, tenant approvals, repair versus replacement decisions, etc., even if an agent handles day-to-day matters. An individual is not treated as actively participating in a rental real estate activity if the individual's and spouse's interests are less than 10% of all interests in the activity. Since Steve and his wife together own 10% of the property and manage the apartments, they qualify for allowing up to $25,000 of rental real estate losses against nonpassive income. Their share of the losses is $4,000 (10% x $40,000).
Answer (b) is incorrect because trusts do not qualify for this $25,000 allowance of passive losses against nonpassive income. Answer (c) is incorrect because an estate is considered to actively participate in an activity for only 2 years following the death of a taxpayer who actively participated in the year of death. Answer (d) is incorrect because an interest as a limited partner is usually not treated as an activity in which the taxpayer actively participates.

Module 7.3: Passive Activities

36. Miss Jones owns several rental properties which she acquired in January 1990, and actively participates in all activities connected with the rentals. She received a salary of $42,300 from her advertising job. Her net rental loss for 1991 was $60,000. What is the amount of rental loss that Miss Jones can deduct in 1991?

a. $0.
b. $25,000.
c. $42,300.
d. $60,000.

37. Maria, a single taxpayer, had losses totaling $30,000 from a rental real estate activity in which she actively participated. Maria also had $15,000 of income from another rental real estate activity in which she actively participated. She acquired both investments in 1991. If Maria has no other passive income and adjusted gross income before passive losses of $70,000, how much loss from rental activities can she use to offset her portfolio and active income?

a. $0.
b. $15,000.
c. $25,000.
d. $30,000.

38. Dr. J has adjusted gross income (AGI) for 1991 of $130,000 before the deduction for a $2,000 contribution to his IRA, and before any potential deduction for $40,000 of losses from rental real estate activities in which he actively participates. How much of the rental losses may he deduct if the rental real estate activities were acquired in 1989?

a. $0.
b. $10,000.
c. $11,000.
d. $25,000.

The correct answer is (b). *(SPE 989 I-46)*
REQUIRED: The amount of rental loss which may be deducted in 1991.
DISCUSSION: In the case of rental real estate activities in which an individual actively participates, up to $25,000 of losses from such activities are allowed each year against nonpassive income. Since Miss Jones had an adjusted gross income of less than $100,000, no phase-out calculation is necessary, and the full $25,000 of losses may be deducted against her $42,300 of nonpassive (earned) income.

The correct answer is (b). *(SPE 990 I-67)*
REQUIRED: The amount of passive losses from rental real estate activities an individual may use to offset other income.
DISCUSSION: The $25,000 allowance of losses from rental real estate activities in which an individual actively participates is applied by first netting the income and losses from all rental real estate activities in which the taxpayer actively participates. If there is a net loss for the year from such activities, net passive income (if any) is then applied against it to determine the amount eligible for the $25,000 allowance. Maria's net loss from active participation activities is $15,000 ($15,000 income – $30,000 losses). This is the amount that Maria may use to offset portfolio income and active income. Note that no phase-out of the $25,000 allowance is necessary since Maria's adjusted gross income before passive losses is less than $100,000.

The correct answer is (b). *(Publisher)*
REQUIRED: The amount a taxpayer may deduct for losses from active participation in rental real estate activities when adjusted gross income is in excess of $100,000.
DISCUSSION: The $25,000 allowance of losses from active participation in rental real estate activities against nonpassive income is reduced by 50% of the amount by which adjusted gross income (determined without regard to Social Security, IRA contributions, and passive losses) exceeds $100,000. Dr. J's adjusted gross income exceeds $100,000 by $30,000. Therefore, the $25,000 allowance is reduced by $15,000 (50% x $30,000). This leaves $10,000 of losses that can be deducted.

39. Sandra purchased a limited partnership interest in 1989. She had nondeductible passive losses of $30,000 in 1989 and $20,000 in 1990 from the partnership. If she sells her partnership interest in 1991 for a $10,000 gain, has $15,000 of income from the partnership up to the sale, and $100,000 of nonpassive income, how much can she deduct in 1991?

   a. $10,000.
   b. $15,000.
   c. $25,000.
   d. $50,000.

The correct answer is (d). *(Publisher)*
REQUIRED: The amount of previously nondeductible losses that may be deducted when a passive activity is sold.
DISCUSSION: The cumulative total of disallowed losses from an activity are allowed in full when the taxpayer disposes of his/her entire interest in a passive activity in a taxable transaction. The losses are allowed against income in the following order: (1) income or gain from the passive activity for the year, (2) net income or gain for the year from all passive activities, (3) any other income or gain. Sandra may first use the $50,000 of losses to offset both the partnership income of $15,000 and the gain of $10,000 from sale of the partnership interest. She may then use the remaining $25,000 to offset her nonpassive income. Her total deduction for the losses is $50,000 in 1991.

40. Taxpayer A had $5,000 of passive losses in 1990 from pre-October 22, 1986 investments in which he does not materially participate and $30,000 of passive losses from rental real estate acquired in 1985 in which he actively participates. He also had $100,000 of nonpassive income. How much of the losses can A deduct in 1990?

   a. $25,000.
   b. $26,000.
   c. $34,000.
   d. $35,000.

The correct answer is (b). *(Publisher)*
REQUIRED: The amount of losses from passive activities acquired prior to October 22, 1986 which may be deducted in 1990.
DISCUSSION: Interests in passive activities acquired by the taxpayer on or before October 22, 1986 are eligible for the passive loss phase-in rules. Under the phase-in rules, 90% of passive losses from preenactment interests will be disallowed in 1990 (and 100% thereafter). The phase-in percentage applies to the passive loss remaining after allowing up to $25,000 of losses from rental real estate activities in which the taxpayer materially participates.
   All of Taxpayer A's losses are from passive activities. $25,000 of the passive losses from rental real estate in which he actively participates is deductible in full regardless of when the interest in passive activities was acquired. The remaining $5,000 from the rental activity and the $5,000 of other passive losses are subject to the phase-in rules. 90% of this $10,000 will be disallowed or 10% will be allowed. Therefore, Taxpayer A can deduct $26,000 ($25,000 + $1,000).

CHAPTER EIGHT
OTHER DEDUCTIONS FOR
ADJUSTED GROSS INCOME

 8.1 Trade and Business Expenses of Employees .... (6 questions) 147
 8.2 Rental Property Expenses .... (11 questions) 150
 8.3 Expenses Related to the Production of Income .... (8 questions) 154
 8.4 Alimony .... (12 questions) 157
 8.5 Contributions to IRAs .... (17 questions) 161
 8.6 Contributions to Keogh Plans .... (7 questions) 165

For other deductions for adjusted gross income (above-the-line), see

       Chapter 6 - Business Expenses and Losses
       Chapter 7 - Limitations on Losses
       Chapter 13 - Depreciation, Amortization, and Depletion
       Chapter 14 - Capital Gains and Losses

8.1 Trade and Business Expenses of Employees

1. During 1991, Mike Daniel, who is single, had the following income and expenses:

Salary	$50,000
Interest income	2,300
Travel expenses for employer	800
Contribution to IRA	2,000

Mike accounted to his employer for the travel expenses, which were then reimbursed by his employer. Mike Daniel is not an active participant in an employer provided pension plan. What is Mike's adjusted gross income?

   a. $49,500.
   b. $49,660.
   c. $50,300.
   d. $51,500.

The correct answer is (c). *(Publisher)*
REQUIRED: An employee's adjusted gross income when there are reimbursed travel expenses and a contribution to an IRA.
DISCUSSION: Adjusted gross income is defined in Sec. 62 as gross income minus specified deductions, including reimbursed employee expenses and contributions to an IRA. The employee must account to the employer for the expenses and not receive a reimbursement in excess of the expenses accounted for. Since the travel expenses were accounted for, the reimbursement need not be included in gross income, and the expenses are not deducted. Since Mike is not an active participant in an employer provided pension plan, he can deduct the $2,000 amount of the IRA contribution. Mike's adjusted gross income is $50,300 ($50,000 salary + $2,300 interest − $2,000 IRA contribution).
   Note that if the travel expenses were not accounted for, they would be included in gross income, and would only be deductible as an itemized deduction subject to an 80% limit on meals and entertainment. If any meals or entertainment are included in Mike's $800, it would be the employer, not Mike, for whom the 80% limitation would apply, since the expenses were reimbursed.

Module 8.1: Trade and Business Expenses of Employees

2. Justin Peter earned a salary of $30,000 during 1991. During the year, he was required by his employer to take several overnight business trips, and he received an expense allowance of $1,500 for travel and lodging. In the course of these trips, he incurred the following expenses which were either adjustments to income or deductions from adjusted gross income.

Travel	$1,100
Lodging	500
Entertainment of customers	400

What is Justin's adjusted gross income if he does not account to his employer for the expenses?

a. $29,500.
b. $29,900.
c. $30,000.
d. $31,500.

The correct answer is (d). *(CPA 1180 Q-31)*
REQUIRED: The taxpayer's adjusted gross income.
DISCUSSION: An employee's business expenses do not need to be included in and deducted from gross income in arriving at AGI if the employee accounts to his/her employer for the expenses and the expenses equal the reimbursement. All other business expenses incurred by employees (except those incurred by a qualified performing artist) are deducted from adjusted gross income [Sec. 63(b)]. Justin's gross income was $31,500 ($30,000 salary + $1,500 expense allowance). When the employee receives an allowance and does not account to the employer for the expenses, the expense allowance is included in gross income and the expenses are deducted as an itemized deduction.

Therefore, Justin's adjusted gross income is $31,500, and his travel, lodging, and entertainment expenses are deductible from adjusted gross income.

3. Ron Mohollic received a salary of $60,000 from his employer in 1991. As a salesman, Ron was expected to incur various travel, transportation, meal, and entertainment expenses. His employer required an accounting of all these expenses and reimbursed Ron, provided they met the employer's requirements. In 1991, Ron incurred $3,000 of transportation and lodging expenses, and $2,000 of meal and entertainment expenses. He properly accounted to his employer and received a $5,000 reimbursement. How much of the reimbursement must Ron include in gross income, and how much of the expenses can he deduct from gross income?

	Include in GI	Deduct for AGI
a.	$0	$0
b.	$5,000	$3,000
c.	$5,000	$4,600
d.	$5,000	$5,000

The correct answer is (a). *(Publisher)*
REQUIRED: The amount of an employee's business expense reimbursement included in income and the deduction for AGI.
DISCUSSION: Under Sec. 61, an expense reimbursement from an employer is included in gross income, and under Sec. 62(a)(2), reimbursed business expenses of employees for which the employee accounts to the employer (and is not eligible for any reimbursement in excess of the expenses accounted for) are deductible for adjusted gross income. But if the employee accounts to his/her employer for the expenses, the reimbursement does not have to be included in gross income and the employee does not deduct the expenses, provided the reimbursement does not exceed the expenses and the expenses do not exceed the reimbursement [Reg. 1.162-17(b)].

Since Ron accounted to his employer and the reimbursement was equal to the expenses, he does not include the reimbursement in income and he does not deduct the expenses.

Module 8.1: Trade and Business Expenses of Employees

4. Jon is employed by a consulting firm and is required to account to his employer for travel expenses. During 1991 he paid the following business expenses and accounted to his employer for all of them.

Travel expenses incurred while away from home overnight	$3,000
Executive search consultant fees paid in securing a new job in the same profession	1,200
Professional society dues	500
Transportation expenses	750

During 1991 Jon received travel expense reimbursements totaling $2,500 from his employer. How much should Jon deduct as employee business expenses in arriving at his adjusted gross income for 1991?

a. $0.
b. $500.
c. $2,500.
d. $3,750.

The correct answer is (c). *(SPE 990 I-59)*
REQUIRED: The amount the taxpayer may deduct in arriving at adjusted gross income.
DISCUSSION: Each of the expenses listed is deductible as a trade or business expense under Sec. 162. In the case of an employee, trade and business expenses are deducted from gross income in arriving at adjusted gross income only if they are reimbursed expenses for which the employee accounts to the employer or are incurred by a qualified performing artist [Sec. 62(a)(2)]. If the employee accounts to his/her employer for the expenses, the reimbursement is not included in gross income as long as the expenses equal the reimbursement. If the expenses exceed the reimbursement, the reimbursement is reported as income and expenses up to the reimbursement amount are deductible from gross income. Excess expenses are deductible from adjusted gross income, subject to the 2% floor.

Therefore, Jon must include the $2,500 reimbursement in gross income and should deduct $2,500 of the travel expenses for AGI. The additional $500 of travel expenses and all the other expenses are deductible from adjusted gross income (subject to limitations covered in Chapter 9 including a deduction of only 80% of any meal expenses included in the $500 of unreimbursed travel expenses).

5. Michelle is a Broadway actress. During 1991, she earned $15,000 from performing in three separately produced plays. She incurred expenses of $2,000 for make-up, costumes, and other expenses attributable to her services as an actress. Assuming she had no other income or expenses, what is her adjusted gross income for 1991?

a. $15,000.
b. $14,500.
c. $14,000.
d. $13,000.

The correct answer is (d). *(Publisher)*
REQUIRED: The adjusted gross income of a performing artist.
DISCUSSION: An exception to the requirement that an employee's business expenses must be reimbursed to be deductible for adjusted gross income is the expenses of a qualified performing artist. Sec. 62(a)(2)(B) allows the deduction for AGI of expenses incurred after 1986 relating to the performance of services in the performing arts as an employee if the taxpayer:

1. Performs services in the performing arts as an employee for two or more employers during the taxable year,
2. Has expenses relating to the performance of such services which exceed 10% of the taxpayer's gross income attributable to the performance of such services, and
3. Has adjusted gross income (determined without regard to this deduction) of $16,000 or less [Sec. 62(b)].

Since Michelle meets the above three requirements, she may deduct her expenses of $2,000 in full to arrive at her adjusted gross income of $13,000 ($15,000 – $2,000).

6. Brian is a violinist and toured the United States with two different orchestras during 1991. He incurred expenses of $3,000 related to his services as a violinist, and had adjusted gross income of $25,000. Brian may deduct the $3,000 of expenses to arrive at adjusted gross income of $22,000.

The correct answer is (F). *(Publisher)*
DISCUSSION: Sec. 62(a)(2)(B) allows expenses incurred after 1986 by a qualified performing artist in connection with his/her services in the performing arts as an employee to be deducted from gross income to arrive at adjusted gross income. However, Brian is not considered a qualified performing artist under Sec. 62(b) because his adjusted gross income of $25,000 exceeds the $16,000 maximum.

8.2 Rental Property Expenses

7. During 1991, Mr. C had the following expenditures relating to his rental property

Local assessment for repair of sidewalk	$ 200
Property tax on rental house #1	900
Mr. C's portion of property tax paid on rental house #2 sold in 1991	350
Local assessment for connection to newly constructed sewage system	1,200

What is the amount of the above expenditures that must be capitalized?

- a. $0.
- b. $550.
- c. $1,200.
- d. $1,400.

The correct answer is (c). *(SPE 988 II-65)*
REQUIRED: The amount of property assessments and taxes which must be capitalized.
DISCUSSION: Property taxes on rental property are deductible under Sec. 164, the same as for any other property. When property is sold during the year, the seller's portion of the property tax is deductible. Assessments tending to increase the value of property are not deductible as taxes [Sec. 164(c)]. However, if the assessment is allocable to maintenance as in the case of the assessment for sidewalk repairs, then it is deductible as a maintenance or repair expenditure. The same concept applies as with the decision to capitalize or deduct any other repair expenses. The fact that it is an assessment from a local government does not affect the determination. Only the assessment for connection to a newly constructed sewage system needs to be capitalized. This payment increases the value of the property, and accordingly must be capitalized.

8. Carla Meehan, a cash-basis taxpayer, owns the Ritz Regency Apartments, which contain 10 identical units. Carla and her husband, Charles, live in Apartment 13 and rent out the remaining apartments. Income and expenses for 1991 were reported by David Richter, their accountant, as follows:

Gross rental income	$37,800
Depreciation of building	$12,500
Maintenance and repairs	3,750
Utilities	4,250
Interest and taxes	500
Total expenses	$21,000

What amount of net rental income should be reported by Carla and Charles for 1991?

- a. $16,800.
- b. $17,300.
- c. $18,900.
- d. $37,800.

The correct answer is (c). *(M.F. Premont)*
REQUIRED: The amount the taxpayers should report as net rental income.
DISCUSSION: Sec. 212 allows a deduction for all ordinary and necessary expenses paid or incurred during the taxable year for the production of income. The costs of maintenance, repairs, and utilities are deductible expenses incurred for the production of income under Sec. 212. Sec. 167 and Sec. 168 allow a deduction for depreciation on property held for the production of income. Secs. 163 and 164 allow deductions for interest and taxes, respectively. The total amount of these expenses is $21,000 ($12,500 + $3,750 + $4,250 + $500). However, one-tenth of these expenses were personal and may not be deducted as rental expenses (Sec. 262). The net rental income is

Gross rental income	$37,800
Less expenses ($21,000 x 90%)	(18,900)
Net rental income	$18,900

Note that the $50 of interest and taxes related to the Meehans' apartment is deductible as an itemized deduction (from AGI).

9. Mr. Smith, a cash-basis, calendar-year taxpayer, owns a duplex. He lives in one unit and rents the other unit to an unrelated individual. The two units are approximately equal in size. On July 1, 1991, Mr. Smith paid the property insurance on the duplex for the 3-year period July 1, 1991 through June 30, 1994. The total premium was $360. For 1991, Mr. Smith's rental expense for this insurance policy is

- a. $30.
- b. $60.
- c. $120.
- d. $360.

The correct answer is (a). *(SPE 987 I-72)*
REQUIRED: The portion of insurance the taxpayer may deduct as rental expense.
DISCUSSION: Insurance premiums paid on rental property are deductible as rental expenses. However, Sec. 262 disallows a deduction for personal expenses unless otherwise provided in another section. Mr. Smith must allocate the insurance expense between the personal unit and the rented unit. Since the units are approximately equal in size, one-half of the total premium should be allocated to the rental unit ($180). However, only the portion of the premium applying to the current year is deductible in 1991. The insurance premium is for 3 years or 36 months. The rental portion comes to $5 per month ($180 ÷ 36 months). Since there are 6 months left in 1991, Mr. Smith's rental expense for the insurance policy is $30 ($5 per month x 6 months).

Module 8.2: Rental Property Expenses

10. Mr. C owns a duplex. He lives in one unit and rents the other unit to an unrelated individual. The two units are equal in size. On July 1, 1991, Mr. C paid the real estate taxes on the duplex for the year in the amount of $1,190. How would Mr. C report the real estate taxes paid on his income tax return for 1991?

 a. Schedule-C $595, Schedule-E $595

 b. Schedule-A $595, Schedule-E $595

 c. Schedule-A $595, Schedule-C $595

 d. Schedule-A $1,190

The correct answer is (b). *(SPE 988 I-45)*
REQUIRED: The proper reporting of real property taxes.
DISCUSSION: Sec. 164 allows a deduction for real property taxes. All the taxes are deductible; however, the personal portion (for the unit Mr. C lives in) is deductible on Schedule A, as an itemized deduction and the portion allocable to the rental unit is deductible on Schedule E, used to report rental income and rental expenses.

11. Mr. and Mrs. Snyder own a house at the beach which was rented to unrelated parties for 8 weeks during 1991. Mrs. Snyder and the children used the house 18 days for their vacation during the year. After properly dividing the expenses between rental and personal use, it was determined that a loss was incurred as follows:

Gross rental income		$ 4,000
Less: Allocated interest and taxes	$3,500	
Other allocated expenses	1,000	(4,500)
Net rental loss		$ (500)

What is the correct treatment of the rental income and expenses on Mr. and Mrs. Snyder's joint income tax return for 1991?

 a. A $500 loss should be shown on Schedule E of Form 1040.

 b. The interest and taxes should be deducted on Schedule A of Form 1040 as itemized deductions.

 c. Since the house was used more than 14 days personally by the Snyders, rental expenses (other than interest and taxes) are limited to the gross rental income in excess of deductions for interest and taxes allocated to rental use.

 d. Mr. and Mrs. Snyder should include none of the income or expenses from the beach house in their 1991 income tax return.

The correct answer is (c). *(SPE 1080 I-58)*
REQUIRED: The correct treatment of the rental income and expenses related to a vacation home.
DISCUSSION: When a dwelling unit is used by the taxpayer as a residence, Sec. 280A disallows a deduction for expenses in excess of the gross income derived from the rents received reduced by the deductions allowable (e.g., taxes and interest), whether or not the unit was used for rental purposes. A taxpayer is deemed to use a dwelling unit as a residence if (s)he uses it for personal purposes for a number of days which exceeds the greater of 14 days or 10% of the number of days during the year for which the unit is rented at fair rental value [Sec. 280A(d)]. These rules only apply if the vacation home is rented for 15 days or more. If the rental is for fewer than 15 days, no rental expenses are deductible (and no rent is includable in gross income) per Sec. 280A(g).

Answer (a) is incorrect because a rental loss is not allowed when the taxpayer personally uses the dwelling unit more than 14 days during the year or 10% of the number of days rented, whichever is greater. Answer (b) is incorrect because only the interest and taxes not allocated to the rental portion should be deducted as itemized deductions. Answer (d) is incorrect because all income and all deductible expenses must be reported when a dwelling unit is rented for more than 14 days during the year.

Module 8.2: Rental Property Expenses

12. Taxpayer W rented the apartment in the basement of his personal residence to an unrelated married couple for the entire year of 1991. The apartment consists of 1,000 square feet which represents 25% of the total space in the residence. W's total expenses in 1991 are as follows:

Interest	$2,500
Taxes	900
Utilities (all paid by W)	1,200
Repairs (to apartment plumbing)	150
Insurance (covers period January 1, 1991 through December 31, 1993)	600
Fair market value of Mr. W's time applied to maintenance	200
Depreciation of residence	1,000

What is the amount of rental expenses that may be deducted on Mr. W's Schedule E (assuming no passive loss limitations)?

- a. $1,600.
- b. $1,700.
- c. $1,800.
- d. $2,350.

The correct answer is (a). *(SPE 1080 I-77)*
REQUIRED: The amount of rental expenses the taxpayer may deduct on Schedule E.
DISCUSSION: Since 25% of the residential space was used for rental purposes, the taxpayer should allocate 25% of each expense relating to the entire residence to the rental activity. In this case the repairs only apply to the apartment, so they are 100% deductible. Sec. 212 allows a deduction for ordinary and necessary expenses paid or incurred during the taxable year for the production of income. The cost of utilities, repairs, and insurance allocable to the rental activity are deductible under this section. Sec. 164 allows a deduction for real estate taxes, and Sec. 163 allows a deduction for interest. Secs. 167 and 168 allow a deduction for depreciation of property held for the production of income. Only the insurance relating to the current year is deductible (1/3 x $600 = $200). The value of the owner's time is not deductible.

Interest (25% x $2,500)	$ 625
Taxes (25% x $900)	225
Utilities (25% x $1,200)	300
Repairs	150
Insurance (25% x $200)	50
Depreciation (25% x $1,000)	250
Rental expenses	$1,600

The interest and taxes on the personal residence portion of the residence are deductible on Schedule A.

13. Mrs. R owns a beach cottage which she rented out for 3 months, lived in for 1 month, and tried unsuccessfully to rent for the rest of the year. Mrs. R received rental income of $5,600. Her total expenses for the cottage were as follows:

Interest	$3,000
Taxes	1,800
Utilities	1,500
Maintenance	900
Depreciation	2,400

What is Mrs. R's net rental income or loss to be reported on her income tax return for 1991?

- a. $4,000 loss.
- b. $800 income.
- c. $0.
- d. (b) or (c).

The correct answer is (d). *(SPE 986 I-69)*
REQUIRED: The net rental income or loss to be reported for 1991.
DISCUSSION: When a dwelling unit is used by the taxpayer as a residence, Sec. 280A disallows a deduction for expenses exceeding the gross income derived from rents reduced by deductions allowable (e.g., taxes and interest), whether or not the unit was used for rental purposes. Under Prop. Reg. 1.280A-3(d)(3), the order of deductions is: (1) the allocable portion of expenses deductible regardless of rental activity, (2) deductions not affecting basis, and (3) those that do affect basis.

The allocation of all deductions between rental and personal use is based on the total days actually used per the IRS (i.e., 3/4 of each of R's expenses is deductible as a rental expense, limited to income). However, the case of Bolton, 51 AFTR 2d 83-305 (CA-9, 1982) allocates the interest and taxes based on the total days of the year (i.e., 3/12 of each is deductible as rental expense). The remaining interest and taxes are deductible as an itemized deduction.

	IRS	Bolton
Gross rent	$5,600	$5,600
Interest	(2,250)	(750)
Taxes	(1,350)	(450)
Allowable other deductions	$2,000	$4,400
Utilities and maintenance	(1,800)	(1,800)
Depreciation	(200)	(1,800)
Income	$ 0	$ 800

Under Bolton the remaining interest and taxes would be deductible on Schedule A.

Module 8.2: Rental Property Expenses

14. On January 31, 1991, Mr. Fund, a cash basis taxpayer, purchased a commercial building in Acorn City. As part of the transaction, he agreed to pay the 1990 property tax of $6,000 due on February 1, 1991. The city converted the area around the building into a pedestrian mall and financed the construction with 10-year bonds. The full cost was assessed against the affected properties. Mr. Fund's portion of the assessment was $1,100 ($1,000 for principal and $100 for interest on the bonds). On December 31, 1991, he paid property taxes of $7,600, including the assessment. What is the amount of Mr. Fund's real estate tax deduction on this property for 1991?

   a. $5,948.
   b. $6,039.
   c. $6,600.
   d. $12,600.

The correct answer is (b). *(SPE 990 II-71)*
REQUIRED: The real estate tax deduction for 1991.
DISCUSSION: Sec. 164 allows a deduction for state and local real property taxes. That section also allows a deduction for real property taxes incurred in carrying on a trade or business or an activity described in Sec. 212 (relating to expenses for production of income). Special assessments for improvements to the land are not deductible but are added to the basis of the land. The interest expense on the bonds is deductible under Sec. 163.

The total real estate tax expense for 1991 is $6,600 ($7,600 − $1,000 special assessment). Real estate taxes must be apportioned between the buyer and seller based on the number of days the property was held by each in the year of sale. Mr. Fund owned the property for 334 days in 1991 (February 1 to December 31). His real estate tax deduction on the property for 1991 is $6,039 (334/365 days × $6,600). The real estate taxes for 1990 that were paid by Mr. Fund in 1991 are not deductible by Mr. Fund since he did not incur the expense. Instead, he must capitalize the $6,000 amount as part of the building's cost.

15. Mr. X owns a cabin that he used for 20 days during 1991. X rented the cabin for 220 days at a fair rental during the year. X's rental income was $6,000 and his expenses, less a portion for personal use, totaled $6,900. X's deductible rental expenses are not limited to his rental income of $6,000.

The correct answer is (T). *(SPE 1083 I-17)*
DISCUSSION: Sec. 280A restricts the deductions with respect to a dwelling unit used by the taxpayer as a residence. A taxpayer is deemed to use a dwelling unit as a residence if (s)he uses it for personal purposes for a number of days that exceeds the greater of 14 days or 10% of the number of days during the year for which the unit is rented at a fair rental. Since Mr. X rented the cabin for 220 days, he was allowed to use it for personal purposes for 22 days without treating it as a residence. Thus, Mr. X's deductible rental expenses are not limited to his rental income.

16. Mr. Z owns a beach cottage which he and his family use during the last 3 weeks in May. He offers the cottage for rent from June 1 through August 31. He was able to rent the property for only the first 2 weeks in July. On Schedule E he is allowed no deductions attributable to the rental and does not include any rental income in gross income.

The correct answer is (T). *(SPE 989 I-11)*
DISCUSSION: Sec. 280A restricts the deductions with respect to a dwelling unit which is used by the taxpayer as a residence. Sec. 280A(g) provides, however, that if a residence is actually rented for fewer than 15 days during the year, no deductions are allowable for the rental use and no rental income is included in gross income. Since Mr. Z's summer home was rented for fewer than 15 days, no expenses are deductible (and no rent is included in gross income).

17. Mrs. W rented a portion of her personal residence to Ms. E, a college student. In allocating the expenses between the rented portion and the personal portion of the residence she used, it is not necessary for Mrs. W to allocate taxes and mortgage interest.

The correct answer is (F). *(SPE 1080 I-12)*
DISCUSSION: A taxpayer who rents a portion of a personal residence must allocate all expenses, including taxes and interest, between the rented and personal portions of the residence, because Sec. 62(a)(4) requires expenses attributable to rented property to be deducted for adjusted gross income. The remainder of the interest and taxes is deductible from adjusted gross income under Sec. 63.

8.3 Expenses Related to the Production of Income

Author's Note: The Tax Extension Act of 1991 (P.L. 100-227) extended the deduction for health insurance costs of self-employed individuals under Sec. 162(1). For tax years beginning in 1992, the deduction is available only for amounts paid before July 1, 1992 for insurance coverage for periods before July 1, 1992.

18. Rickey Spillane earned royalties from writing books on a part-time basis. He did all his writing at home in his kitchen. His expenses included

Paper, pencils, supplies	$ 80
Typing services	700
Rent on apartment (apportioned)	600

Rickey also had to make several trips to the publisher's offices under his royalty contract. Air fare, 80% of the meals, and lodging for these trips cost $900. How much can Rickey deduct for adjusted gross income?

a. $0.
b. $780.
c. $1,680.
d. $2,280.

The correct answer is (c). *(Publisher)*
REQUIRED: The amount of royalty expenses that can be deducted for adjusted gross income.
DISCUSSION: Expenses incurred in the production of income are deductible under Sec. 212 even if they are not trade or business expenses. However, these expenses may be deductible for adjusted gross income or from adjusted gross income. Royalty expenses are deductible for adjusted gross income under Sec. 62(a)(4).
Rickey can deduct the cost of the paper, pencils, supplies, typing services, and trips to the publisher's office since these are all incurred to produce the royalty income. The total of these expenses is $1,680 (assuming the hobby loss rules do not apply). The rent on the kitchen portion of the apartment is not deductible at all since Sec. 280A requires exclusive use of part of a dwelling for business purposes for the rent allocable thereto to be deductible.

19. Dick Mixon was a retired politician who decided to write about his life in politics. In his first year (1987), Dick received prepublication royalties. He worked sporadically, and it took 6 years to complete the first draft. In the meantime, he submitted articles to gossip magazines under a pen name. Dick's expenses and income were as follows:

	Income	Expenses
1987	$16,000	$2,000
1988	50	3,500
1989	200	4,000
1990	600	4,200
1991	900	4,000

How much can Dick deduct as royalty expense in 1991?

a. $0.
b. $50.
c. $900.
d. $4,000.

The correct answer is (c). *(Publisher)*
REQUIRED: The business deduction when only 1 year has been profitable.
DISCUSSION: The expenses of an author are deductible under Sec. 162(a) as trade or business expenses or under Sec. 212 as expenses for the production of income. In either case, they are deductible for adjusted gross income under Sec. 62(a)(4). If an activity is not engaged in for profit, however, Sec. 183 limits deductions to those which are allowed regardless of whether the activity is engaged in for profit (e.g., taxes and interest), plus the excess of gross income over the deductions which are allowed regardless of whether the activity is engaged in for profit. An activity is presumed to be engaged in for profit if the gross income from the activity exceeds the deductions attributable to the activity for 3 or more of 5 consecutive taxable years which end with the current taxable year.
Since Mixon only earned a profit in one of the 5 years, he does not satisfy the safe harbor presumption that his activity was engaged in for profit found in Sec. 183(d). His deductions will be limited to the amount of income earned from the activity ($900 in 1991) unless he can substantiate his profit motive based on the facts and circumstances.

20. The portion of expenses which exceeds income from an activity is not deductible if that activity is classified as a hobby. A taxpayer may, however, establish the presumption that an activity (one not related to horses) is a bona fide business engaged in for profit if

a. The activity shows a profit at least 50% of the time.
b. The activity is profitable at least 2 out of 5 consecutive years.
c. The activity is profitable at least 2 out of 7 consecutive years.
d. The activity is profitable at least 3 out of 5 consecutive years.

The correct answer is (d). *(SPE 990 II-42)*
REQUIRED: The statutory profit requirement at which an activity (not related to horses) is presumed engaged in for profit.
DISCUSSION: The presumption test under Sec. 183(d) is 3 out of 5 years of profitability for most businesses. This test is used if there is a question as to whether an activity is actually a hobby or a business which has been engaged in for profit. If a profit is shown in at least 3 out of the last 5 consecutive years which end with the current taxable year, the burden of proving the activity is a hobby is shifted to the IRS. For activities associated with horses, the requirement is 2 out of 7 years.

21. For the year 1991 Frances Quinn had a time savings account with the Benevolent Savings Bank. The following entries appeared in her passbook for 1991

March 30, interest credited	$150
June 29, interest credited	160
July 25, penalty forfeiture because of a premature withdrawal	125
September 28, interest credited	80
December 28, interest credited	85

The above information should be reported by Ms. Quinn on her 1991 tax return as

a. Interest income of $350.

b. Interest income of $475.

c. Interest income of $475 and an itemized deduction for interest expense of $125.

d. Interest income of $475 and a deduction of $125 in arriving at adjusted gross income.

The correct answer is (d). *(CPA 580 P-49)*
REQUIRED: The method of reporting interest income and premature withdrawal penalties.
DISCUSSION: Interest income is included in gross income [Sec. 61(a)(4)] as of the date it is credited to the account and is available for withdrawal. During the taxable year, Ms. Quinn received $475 in interest income ($150 on March 30, $160 on June 29, $80 on September 28, and $85 on December 28). This income must be reported in full and may not be netted with the withdrawal penalty.
Sec. 165(c)(2) allows an individual to deduct losses incurred during the taxable year on any transaction entered into for profit. The $125 forfeiture penalty is a loss incurred on a transaction entered into for profit and is deductible. The loss is deducted from gross income in arriving at adjusted gross income [Sec. 62(a)(9)].

22. Which of the following is deductible to arrive at adjusted gross income in 1991?

a. Unreimbursed dues to AICPA by an employee of an accounting firm.

b. Unreimbursed union dues by an employee of a company.

c. 25% of the medical insurance expense of a self-employed individual.

d. One-half of a net short-term capital gain in excess of a net long-term capital loss.

The correct answer is (c). *(CPA 575 Q-30)*
REQUIRED: The item which is deductible from gross income in arriving at adjusted gross income.
DISCUSSION: Sec. 162(l) allows a self-employed individual to deduct 25% of the insurance for family medical expenses as business expenses. Trade and business expenses of an individual other than as an employee are deductible for adjusted gross income [Sec. 62(a)(1)]. This is not available if the taxpayer is eligible for coverage by an employer of the taxpayer or spouse.
Answers (a) and (b) are incorrect because business deductions of employees are deductible for adjusted gross income only if they are accounted for to the employer and reimbursed by the employer, or they are certain expenses of performing artists. The unreimbursed dues may be deducted under Sec. 63 from adjusted gross income as an itemized deduction subject to the 2% of adjusted gross income floor. Answer (d) is incorrect because there is no capital gain deduction.

23. Barney, who is self-employed, spent $7,000 for medical insurance for himself and his family. Barney's wife is not employed. Barney's records for 1991 reflect the following

Profit on Schedule C, Form 1040	$2,000
Contribution to Keogh plan	500
Alimony paid to former wife	6,000

What is the amount of Barney's self-employed health insurance deduction for 1991?

a. $1,478.
b. $1,500.
c. $1,750.
d. $2,000.

The correct answer is (a). *(SPE 989 I-86)*
REQUIRED: The amount deductible for self-employed health insurance in 1991.
DISCUSSION: Self-employed persons may deduct up to 25% of the amount paid for medical insurance covering the self-employed individual and his family from gross income as a business expense. The deduction is limited to the earnings of the business for which the insurance plan was established. The balance of the medical insurance premiums not deducted as a business expense would be treated as medical expenses and subject to the 7.5% of AGI limitation. Code Sec. 162(l)(6) authorizes this deduction for amounts paid before July 1, 1992. Barney's self-employed health insurance deduction is computed below.

Amount paid for medical insurance in 1991	$7,000
Deduction percentage	x 25%
Tentative deduction	$1,750

The deduction is limited to the lesser of $1,750 or earned income {less net earnings from self-employment times one-half of the self-employment tax rate and contribution to Keogh [Secs. 162(l)(2) and 401(c)(2)(A)]}.

Schedule C profit	$2,000
Less: Self-employment taxes ($2,000 x .1530 x ½)	(153)
Keogh contribution [($2,000 − $153) x 0.20]	(369)
Earned income limitation	$1,478

Barney's deduction for 1991 is $1,478.

24. Mr. D works full-time as a systems analyst for a consulting firm. In addition, he sells plants which he raises himself in a greenhouse attached to his residence. During the past 5 years the results from raising and selling the plants have been as follows:

Year	Net Profit (Loss)
1987	$(2,000)
1988	(1,200)
1989	1,000
1990	2,500
1991	(500)

Lacking evidence to the contrary, this activity is presumed to be an activity carried on for profit and the $500 loss in 1991 can be taken on D's 1991 tax return.

The correct answer is (F). *(SPE 986 II-1)*
DISCUSSION: If an activity is not engaged in for profit, Sec. 183 limits deductions to those allowed regardless of whether the activity is engaged in for profit (e.g., taxes and interest), plus the excess of gross income over the deductions which are allowed regardless of whether the activity is engaged in for profit. An activity is presumed to be engaged in for profit if the gross income from the activity exceeds the deductions attributable to the activity for 3 or more of 5 consecutive taxable years which end with the current taxable year [Sec. 183(d)]. Mr. D's activity was profitable for only 2 of 5 consecutive years.

25. Most expenses incurred for the production of income (Sec. 212) are deductible for adjusted gross income.

The correct answer is (F). *(Publisher)*
DISCUSSION: Sec. 212 allows a deduction for ordinary and necessary expenses paid or incurred for the production or collection of income, and for the management, conservation, or maintenance of property held for the production of income. Only those expenses attributable to rents and royalties are deductible for adjusted gross income [Sec. 62(a)(4)]. The other expenses incurred for the production of income which are deductible must be deducted from (not for) adjusted gross income under Sec. 63.

8.4 Alimony

26. Which one of the following types of allowable deductions can be claimed as a deduction in arriving at an individual's 1991 adjusted gross income?

a. Unreimbursed business expenses of an outside salesman-employee.
b. Personal casualty losses.
c. Charitable contributions.
d. Alimony payments.

The correct answer is (d). *(CPA 1188 Q-10)*
REQUIRED: The deduction allowable above the line for arriving at adjusted gross income.
DISCUSSION: Sec. 215 allows the deduction by the payor of amounts includable as alimony in the recipient's gross income. This is a deduction for adjusted gross income (above the line).
Answer (a) is incorrect because business expenses of an employee (whether an outside salesman or not) are deductible as a miscellaneous itemized deduction, unless the expenses are reimbursed and the employee accounts to the employer for the expenses. Answer (b) is incorrect because personal casualty losses are an itemized deduction (from adjusted gross income). Answer (c) is incorrect because charitable contributions are also an itemized deduction.

27. Which of the following is deductible as alimony under separation agreements or court decrees entered into before 1985?

a. A periodic payment required under the terms of the divorce decree.
b. A periodic payment that does not arise out of the marital or family relationship.
c. Payment made before the decree of divorce.
d. Lump-sum cash required by a decree of divorce.

The correct answer is (a). *(SPE 1077 I-163)*
REQUIRED: The payment that is deductible as alimony under agreements and decrees entered into before 1985.
DISCUSSION: Sec. 215 allows a deduction by the payor of amounts includable as alimony in the recipient's gross income under Sec. 71. To be considered alimony under Sec. 71 (for court decrees and separation agreements entered into before 1985), the payments must be periodic; made under a decree of divorce or separate maintenance, a written separation agreement, or a decree for support; and due to the marital or family relationship.
Answer (b) is incorrect because the periodic payment must arise out of the marital or family relationship. Answer (c) is incorrect because the payment must be required by a court decree or written separation agreement to be deductible. Answer (d) is incorrect because the payment must be periodic (i.e., over more than 10 years or contingent).

28. Mr. and Mrs. Wright were legally divorced in 1984. The court decree of divorce was entered into on April 20, 1984. Mr. Wright is required to pay Mrs. Wright $3,000 a month from May 1, 1984 through May 1, 1992. The payments are not subject to contingencies. Mr. Wright also made a voluntary payment of $1,000 to Mrs. Wright on April 1, 1991. Assuming Mr. Wright made all of the payments required by the divorce decree, what is the amount of alimony deductible on his 1991 return?

a. $0.
b. $1,000.
c. $36,000.
d. $37,000.

The correct answer is (a). *(SPE 984 I-76)*
REQUIRED: The amount of alimony deductible under a 1984 decree of divorce.
DISCUSSION: Sec. 215 allows the payor a deduction for payments that are required to be included in the recipient's gross income as alimony under Sec. 71. For payments under court decrees or separation agreements entered into before 1985, Sec. 71 requires the payments to be periodic, which means they must last for more than 10 years unless they are subject to a contingency. Therefore, the $3,000 per month is not deductible. The voluntary payment of $1,000 on April 1 is considered a gift and not deductible.
For divorce or separation instruments executed after 1984, the Tax Reform Acts of 1984 and 1986 have amended Sec. 71 and the requirements for alimony and separate maintenance payments.

Module 8.4: Alimony

29. Which of the following is not a requirement to be met for a payment received by a spouse or former spouse under a divorce or separation instrument to be considered alimony?

a. The payments must be paid directly to the spouse or former spouse and not to a third party.
b. The payments must be in cash, including checks or money orders.
c. The spouses cannot file a joint return.
d. There must be no liability to make any payment, in cash or property, after the death of the recipient spouse.

The correct answer is (a). *(SPE 989 I-51)*
REQUIRED: The requirement which must be met for a payment to be considered alimony.
DISCUSSION: Sec. 71 states that the term "alimony or separate maintenance payment" means any payment in cash if (1) such payment is received by (or on behalf of) a spouse under a divorce or separation instrument, (2) the instrument does not designate the payment as not includable in gross income, (3) the payor spouse and the payee spouse are not members of the same household at the time the payment is made, and (4) there is no liability to make such payment after the death of the payee spouse. Assuming these requirements are satisfied, a payment of cash by a payor spouse to a third party under the terms of the divorce or separation agreement will qualify as a payment received "on behalf of" the payee spouse and will be considered alimony [Prop. Reg. 1.71-1T(b)].

30. Your divorce decree, which became final in 1990, requires that you pay $400 a month, of which $250 is specified as child support. During 1991 you pay only $4,000, although in no month did you pay less than $250. What amount may you deduct and must your former spouse report as alimony?

a. $1,000.
b. $1,800.
c. $2,500.
d. $3,000.

The correct answer is (a). *(SPE 1077 II-1)*
REQUIRED: The amount the payor may deduct and the recipient must report as alimony.
DISCUSSION: Any part of a payment which the terms of the decree specify as a sum payable for the support of minor children is not includable in the recipient's gross income and is not deductible by the payor [Sec. 71(c)]. If any payment is less than the amount specified in the decree, it will first be considered child support, until all the child support obligation is paid. The decree specified that $250 per month ($3,000) was for child support. The remaining $1,000 is includable in the recipient's gross income and deductible by the payor as alimony.

31. Rick and Stacy were divorced in February 1991. Requirements of the divorce decree and Stacy's performance follow:

Transfer title to their residence to Rick. Stacy's basis was $95,000, the fair market value was $105,000, and the residence was subject to a mortgage of $90,000.
Make the mortgage payments of $1,000 per month (beginning in March) for the remaining 20 years or until Rick dies, if sooner.
Pay Rick $500 per month (beginning in March) for 6 years or until Rick dies, if sooner. Of this amount, $200 is designated as child support.

Stacy's 1991 alimony deduction for 1991 is

a. $3,000.
b. $13,000.
c. $15,000.
d. $18,000.

The correct answer is (b). *(Publisher)*
REQUIRED: The deduction for alimony paid under a 1991 decree of divorce.
DISCUSSION: Sec. 215 allows a deduction for alimony or separate maintenance payments as defined under Sec. 71. Sec. 71(b) defines alimony as any payment in cash if (1) it is received under a divorce or separation agreement, (2) the agreement does not designate the payment as not includable in gross income, (3) the payee and payor are not members of the same household at the time the payment is made, and (4) there is no liability to make such payment for any period after the death of the payee spouse.
The transfer of title to the residence is not considered alimony since it is not a payment in cash. The mortgage payments are considered alimony. Even though they are made to a third party, they are for the benefit of Rick. The $500 monthly payment includes $200 of child support that is not includable as alimony [Sec. 71(c)]. Stacy's 1991 alimony deduction is $13,000 [10 months x ($1,000 + $300)].

Module 8.4: Alimony

32. On January 2, 1990 Ms. S divorced her spouse. The divorce decree calls for her to pay her former spouse $500 a month as alimony starting in January. In June 1990 her former spouse remarried. S was not aware of this and continued to make payments until February 1991. Under state law, S's legal obligation to make the payments ended when her former spouse remarried. What are the correct amounts that must be reported on Ms. S's and her former spouse's tax returns for 1990?

	Ms. S Alimony Deduction	Former Spouse Alimony Income	Other Income
a.	$3,000	$3,000	$0
b.	$3,000	$3,000	$3,000
c.	$3,000	$6,000	$0
d.	$6,000	$3,000	$3,000
e.	$6,000	$6,000	$0

The correct answer is (a). *(SPE 1083 I-76)*
REQUIRED: The amount of alimony income and deduction under a 1990 divorce decree.
DISCUSSION: A deduction for alimony is allowed under Sec. 215. Alimony is required to be included in the recipient's income under Sec. 71(a). In order to be considered alimony, payments must be made under a decree of divorce or separate maintenance, a written instrument incident to such a decree, or a written separation agreement. The payments made after Ms. S's legal obligation ended are not alimony. They are treated as gifts, and are not included in the recipient's income nor deductible by the payor.
The alimony at $500 per month for 6 months (January through June) equals $3,000.

33. Mr. K paid $500 a month for 3 months to his estranged wife while they were negotiating a written separation agreement. Mr. K filed a separate return for 1991. An agreement reached June 1, 1991 required Mr. K to pay $300 a month as alimony. Mr. K made payments of $2,100 for the period June 1, 1991 to December 31, 1991. What is Mr. K's correct alimony deduction for 1991?

a. $900.
b. $2,100.
c. $3,000.
d. $3,600.

The correct answer is (b). *(SPE 1081 I-52)*
REQUIRED: The taxpayer's alimony deduction for 1991.
DISCUSSION: Sec. 215 allows a deduction by the payor of amounts includable in the recipient's gross income as alimony under Sec. 71. Sec. 71 requires inclusion in the recipient's gross income of cash payments made under a divorce or separation agreement entered into after 1984. The taxpayer may deduct only the $2,100 of payments made under the written separation agreement. The payments made prior to June 1 are neither deductible by Mr. K nor includable in his wife's income.

34. Mr. D is required, under his 1989 divorce decree, to make cash alimony payments to his former spouse of $30,000 in each of the calendar years 1989 through 1993. The payments are to stop if she remarries. D made cash payments totaling $30,000 in 1989. In 1990, his payments totaled only $14,000 because his former wife remarried. Under the recapture rule limiting front-loaded payments, what is the amount of alimony payments D will have to recapture in 1991?

a. $0.
b. $8,000.
c. $15,000.
d. $16,000.

The correct answer is (a). *(SPE 989 I-85)*
REQUIRED: The amount of alimony payments that must be recaptured in 1991.
DISCUSSION: Sec. 71(f) requires a spouse who makes "excess" alimony payments in the first or second post-separation year to recapture part of those payments in the third post-separation year. Sec. 71(f) supplies a formula for determining the amount of the payments that are considered "excess" and the amount of these payments that must be recaptured by the payor. Sec. 71(f)(5)(A) provides an exception to the general recapture rule. Under that exception, if either spouse dies before the close of the third post-separation year, or if the payee spouse remarries before the close of the third post-separation year, the payor spouse is relieved of the recapture requirement. Because Mr. D's former spouse remarried before the close of the third post-separation year, he does not have to recapture any of the alimony payments made in the previous years.

Module 8.4: Alimony

35. Mr. A was divorced in 1988. Under the court decree he is to pay his former wife $100,000 in installments of $15,000 a year for 5 years and $5,000 a year for the following 5 years. The payments are not subject to any contingencies. Mr. A may deduct the $15,000 he paid in 1991 as alimony.

The correct answer is (T). *(SPE 1085 I-27)*
DISCUSSION: Divorce decrees executed after 1986 are subject to a 3-year recapture rule. "Excess alimony" is recaptured commencing with the third post-separation taxable year. Recapture occurs by having the payor-spouse include such amounts in gross income and the payee-spouse deducting such amounts. Excess alimony is the sum of the excess payments made in the first and second post-separation taxable years according to formulas found in Secs. 71(f)(3) and (4). To be recaptured the alimony payment must be at least $15,000. Since the payments are constant for the first 5 years and do not exceed $15,000 in the example, we do not have any excess alimony, and even if excess alimony existed it would not affect the payor's deduction.

36. Payment of a former wife's medical expenses is deductible as alimony. A divorce decree requires that the husband pay the wife's future medical expenses in addition to qualifying alimony.

The correct answer is (T). *(SPE 1082 I-21)*
DISCUSSION: Only those payments which are included in the recipient's income as alimony under Sec. 71 are deductible by the payor under Sec. 215. For a divorce decree entered prior to 1985, payments from the ex-spouse are included in the recipient's income if they are periodic payments in discharge of a legal obligation which arose under the marital or family relationship, and which are imposed under the decree of divorce. If the divorce decree requires the husband to pay the wife's future medical expenses, they are periodic since they are contingent, and they are deductible as alimony. For divorce decrees entered after 1984, the payments would have to be made in cash, and there could be no liability to make payments after the former wife's death. If these requirements are met, the medical payments would be deductible as alimony for divorce decrees after 1984.

37. Paul and Joan divorced in 1991. They have two children, ages 5 and 10. The divorce decree requires Joan to pay $300 a month to Paul and does not specify the use of the money. According to the decree, the payments will stop after the children reach 18. Joan may deduct the payments as alimony.

The correct answer is (F). *(SPE 990 I-19)*
DISCUSSION: Sec. 71(c) requires that, if a payment to a former spouse will be reduced when a child attains a certain age, that payment shall be treated as an amount payable for the support of the child. Child support payments are not deductible as alimony.

8.5 Contributions to IRAs

38. P was eligible for, and set up as his only retirement plan, an individual retirement arrangement for 1990 on January 27, 1991. On February 15, 1991, P contributed $1,700 to his account. Mr. P's income for 1990 consisted of the following

Wages	$9,000
Interest income	3,000
Dividend income	2,000

What is P's deduction for 1990?

a. $0.
b. $1,350.
c. $1,700.
d. $2,100.

The correct answer is (c). *(SPE 1081 IV-86)*
REQUIRED: The taxpayer's deduction for his contribution to an IRA.
DISCUSSION: The maximum amount of a contribution to an IRA that a taxpayer may deduct is the lesser of $2,000 or an amount equal to the compensation which is includable in the individual's gross income for the taxable year [Sec. 219(b)]. In 1990, P had wages of $9,000; thus, his maximum deduction is limited to $2,000. Since P only made a contribution of $1,700, he may deduct only $1,700. The deduction is for adjusted gross income [Sec. 62(a)(7)].
A contribution can be made after year-end if it is made on account of the prior year and no later than the due date of the tax return (without extensions) for such prior year.

39. All of the following types of income are considered earned compensation in determining whether an Individual Retirement Account can be set up and contributions made except

a. Self-employment income.
b. Partnership income of an active partner providing services to the partnership.
c. Alimony.
d. Rental income from a property in which the taxpayer has active participation.

The correct answer is (d). *(SPE 990 IV-73)*
REQUIRED: The item not treated as compensation with respect to contributions to an IRA.
DISCUSSION: Sec. 219(f) defines compensation as earned income. Rental income is not generally considered earned income, rather it is treated as a passive form of income.
Answers (a), (b), and (c) are incorrect because each is a common example of earned income.

40. Ms. Seburn had the following during 1991

Taxable alimony received	$ 4,000
Wages	12,000
Net loss from self-employment	(10,000)
Interest income	3,000

For purposes of an IRA, Ms. Seburn had "compensation" for 1991 of

a. $2,000.
b. $6,000.
c. $16,000.
d. $19,000.

The correct answer is (c). *(SPE 987 IV-77)*
REQUIRED: The total amount of compensation for an IRA of an individual.
DISCUSSION: Sec. 219(f) defines compensation as earned income. Wages is the most common example of earned income. Taxable alimony is included as compensation for this purpose. There is no provision for reducing earned income by net losses from self-employment. Interest income is not earned income. Therefore, Ms. Seburn had compensation for IRA purposes of

Taxable alimony	$ 4,000
Wages	12,000
Total compensation	$16,000

41. Glenn and Lisa are married. They both work and both have IRAs. Neither is an active participant in an employer plan. For 1991, Glenn earned $1,800 and Lisa earned $28,000. Their maximum allowable IRA contribution and deduction on a joint return is

a. $4,000.
b. $3,800.
c. $2,250.
d. $2,000.

The correct answer is (b). *(SPE 986 IV-72)*
REQUIRED: The maximum deduction a husband and wife may claim on their joint tax return for contributions to separate IRAs.
DISCUSSION: The maximum amount that any taxpayer may claim as a deduction for a contribution to an IRA is limited by Sec. 219 to the lesser of $2,000 or an amount equal to the compensation includable in the taxpayer's gross income for the year. This limitation applies separately to each spouse who has compensation and makes a contribution to a separate IRA. Lisa's limit is $2,000 and Glenn's limit is $1,800 (his compensation since it is less than $2,000). Their total deduction is $3,800 ($2,000 + $1,800).

42. Mr. Knox wants to make contributions to an IRA (spousal IRA), for his wife. For Mr. Knox to be eligible to make such contributions, all of the following requirements must be met except

a. They must file a joint return for the tax year.
b. He must have compensation that must be included in his income for the tax year.
c. They must be married at the end of the tax year.
d. His wife must have no taxable compensation for the tax year.

The correct answer is (d). *(SPE 990 IV-70)*
REQUIRED: The item that is not a requirement for making contributions to an individual retirement account for a spouse.
DISCUSSION: Sec. 219(c) provides rules for deducting contributions to a spousal IRA. If one spouse is eligible to make deductible IRA contributions, that spouse may contribute up to $2,250 if a joint return is filed. The additional $250 spousal IRA deduction is available if the other spouse has no compensation for the year, or if an election is made to treat the other spouse as having no compensation for the year. Therefore, it is not a requirement that the wife have no compensation for the tax year.

43. Sol and Julia Crane are married and filed a joint return for 1990. Sol earned a salary of $80,000 in 1990 from his job at Troy Corp., where he is covered by his employer's pension plan. In addition, Sol and Julia earned interest of $3,000 in 1990 on their joint savings account. Julia is not employed and the couple had no other income. On January 15, 1991, Sol contributed $2,000 to an IRA for himself, and $250 to an IRA for his spouse. The allowable IRA deduction in the Cranes' 1990 joint return is

a. $0.
b. $250.
c. $2,000.
d. $2,250.

The correct answer is (a). *(CPA 1188 Q-11)*
REQUIRED: The allowable deduction for a contribution to an IRA when the employee is covered by another plan.
DISCUSSION: Contributions may be made to an IRA and deducted even if an employee is covered by an employer's plan. However, the deduction for contributions to an IRA when the taxpayer or spouse is an active participant in an employer's retirement plan is phased out. The deduction is eliminated if the adjusted gross income is $50,000 or more for a joint return. Thus, the Cranes are not eligible for the deduction.
However, the Cranes are allowed to make a contribution to an IRA but the contributions are nondeductible. The earnings will accumulate tax free, and only the earnings will be taxable at distribution.

44. Larry and Marge Strong are married and living together. They have decided to file separate federal income tax returns for 1991. Larry is an active participant in his employer's pension plan. Marge is not an active participant in any plan. Each contributed $2,000 to their 1991 Individual Retirement Account (IRA). Larry's modified adjusted gross income is $50,000 and Marge's is $6,000. Marge's compensation from her employer is $4,000. The deductible portion of Marge's compensation to her IRA is

a. $0.
b. $800.
c. $1,200.
d. $2,000.

The correct answer is (b). *(SPE 990 IV-69)*
REQUIRED: The deductible portion of contributions made to an IRA by an individual whose spouse is covered by an employer's pension plan.
DISCUSSION: Sec. 219(g) limits the deduction for contributions made to an IRA by an individual, or the spouse of an individual, who is an active participant in an employer's pension plan. The limitation is based on filing status and modified adjusted gross income. Modified adjusted gross income is adjusted gross income computed without regard to the IRA deduction, the foreign earned income exclusion, the foreign housing exclusion or deduction, or the exclusion of Series EE bond interest.
In the case of a married individual who lives with his/her spouse during the taxable year and who files a separate return, the deduction is reduced if modified AGI is between zero and $10,000, and eliminated if modified AGI is $10,000 or more. The allowable deduction is computed by first subtracting the individual's modified AGI from $10,000 and multiplying the result by 20%. The amount obtained is then compared to the individual's IRA contributions (limited to $2,000) and compensation received in the tax year. The smallest of the three amounts is the allowable deduction. Marge's deduction is limited to $800 [($10,000 − $6,000 modified AGI) x 20%, compared to her IRA contribution ($2,000) and compensation ($4,000)]

Module 8.5: Contributions to IRAs 163

45. Mr. and Mrs. Smith are both employed and file joint federal income tax returns. Mr. Smith is covered by his employer's retirement plan. For 1991, Mr. Smith's salary was $35,000 and Mrs. Smith's $10,000. They both have IRAs and their combined modified adjusted gross income was $45,000. Mr. Smith contributed $2,000 to his IRA and Mrs. Smith $1,500 to her IRA. What is the maximum IRA deduction each is entitled to for 1991?

	Mr. Smith	Mrs. Smith
a.	$2,000	$1,500
b.	$1,000	$1,000
c.	$0	$1,500
d.	$0	$0

The correct answer is (b). *(SPE 989 IV-73)*
REQUIRED: The maximum deduction a husband and wife may claim on their joint tax return for contributions to separate IRAs when one spouse is covered by an employer's retirement plan.
DISCUSSION: Sec. 219(g) limits the deduction for contributions made to separate IRAs by individuals filing a joint tax return when one or both are covered by an employer's retirement plan. The allowable deduction is based on the spouses' combined modified adjusted gross income, which is adjusted gross income computed without regard to the IRA deduction, the foreign earned income exclusion, the foreign housing exclusion or deduction, or the exclusion of Series EE bond interest. For married individuals who file a joint tax return, the allowable deduction is phased out if their combined modified AGI is between $40,000 and $50,000, and eliminated if their combined modified AGI equals or exceeds $50,000.

The allowable deduction is computed by first subtracting combined modified AGI from $50,000 and multiplying the result by 20%. Each spouse then compares the amount obtained to his/her IRA contribution and his/her compensation received in the tax year. The allowable deduction for each spouse is the smallest of the three amounts. For Mr. and Mrs. Smith, their individual limits are the smaller of: 20% of $50,000 minus combined modified AGI [.20 x ($50,000 − $45,000) = $1,000], their IRA contribution ($2,000 for Mr. Smith and $1,000 for Mrs. Smith) and compensation ($35,000 for Mr. Smith and $10,000 for Mrs. Smith). Each can thus contribute $1,000.

46. On April 15, 1991, Mr. Y filed Form 4868, Application for Automatic Extension of Time to File, extending the due date for filing his 1990 federal tax return to August 15, 1991. By what date must he make his IRA payment to qualify for the deduction on his 1990 return?

a. December 31, 1990.
b. April 15, 1991.
c. June 30, 1991.
d. August 15, 1991.

The correct answer is (b). *(SPE 1085 IV-72)*
REQUIRED: The due date for an IRA payment made after the close of the tax year in order for it to be deductible in the prior year.
DISCUSSION: A contribution can be made to an IRA after year-end and apply to the prior year if it is made on account of the prior year and no later than the due date of the tax return (without extensions) for such prior year. Mr. Y's 1990 tax return is due April 15 (without extension), so this is the last date on which he may make a deductible contribution to his IRA for 1990.

47. Your IRA is a trust or custodial account created by a written document and must meet all of the following requirements except

a. The amount in your account must be fully vested at all times.
b. You can be your own trustee.
c. Your account must be set up in the United States.
d. You must start receiving distributions from your account by April 1 of the year following the year in which you reach age 70½.

The correct answer is (b). *(SPE 989 IV-74)*
REQUIRED: The item that is not a requirement for setting up an individual retirement account.
DISCUSSION: Under Secs. 219(d) and 408, an IRA account must be fully vested at all times, it must be set up in the United States, and you must begin receiving distributions from the account by April 1 of the year following the year in which you reach age 70½. An IRA account must be set up in the hands of a third party; therefore, you cannot be your own trustee.

48. Jean is single and not an active participant in her employer's pension plan. She received taxable compensation of $1,200 in 1990 and $1,600 in 1991. Her modified adjusted gross income was $24,000 in both years. In 1990, she contributed $1,400 to her IRA, but deducted only $1,200 on her income tax return. In 1991, she again contributed $1,400, but deducted $1,600 on her income tax return. Which of the following statements is correct?

    a. Jean properly handled her IRA contributions and deductions.

    b. Jean must pay 6% excise tax on the excess contribution in 1990 and for each year after that until she withdraws the excess.

    c. When Jean withdraws the excess contribution she will be assessed a 10% tax for early withdrawal.

    d. Jean should only claim $1,400 as an IRA deduction in 1991.

The correct answer is (a). *(SPE 990 IV-71)*
REQUIRED: The taxpayer's deduction for her contribution to an IRA.
DISCUSSION: Under Sec. 219(b), the deduction for contributions to an IRA is limited to the lesser of the compensation that must be included in gross income, or $2,000. In 1990, Jean's allowable deduction was limited to $1,200, which was the amount of her taxable compensation.
In 1991, Jean's taxable compensation was $1,600 and her IRA contributions totaled $1,400. Under Sec. 219(f)(6), Jean may treat the $200 unused contributions from 1990 as having been made in 1991. Therefore, her allowable deduction for IRA contributions in 1991 is $1,600. The allowable deduction in 1991 will still be limited to the lesser of taxable compensation or $2,000.

49. A deduction is allowable for a contribution of property to an individual retirement plan.

The correct answer is (F). *(SPE 1077 I-110)*
DISCUSSION: A deduction is provided for in Sec. 219(a) for a qualified retirement contribution. Sec. 219(e)(1) defines a qualified retirement contribution as cash paid by the individual or on his/her behalf to an IRA. Thus, deductions are not allowable for a contribution of property to an IRA.

50. Ms. D died on July 5, 1991. Her son, who is 25 years of age and had compensation of $25,000 in 1991, inherited her IRA. Ms. D's son may treat the IRA as one established on his behalf and deduct payments that he made to the inherited IRA in 1991.

The correct answer is (F). *(SPE 1085 IV-44)*
DISCUSSION: A person may deduct contributions made to an inherited IRA only if the IRA was inherited from a spouse. Contributions made to an IRA inherited from someone who died after December 31, 1983, and who was not a spouse, are not deductible.

51. If excess contributions are made to an IRA, an excise tax of 10% will be charged on the excess amounts that remain in the IRA for the year of the excess contribution and for each year thereafter unless corrected.

The correct answer is (F). *(SPE 989 IV-46)*
DISCUSSION: Under Sec. 4973, a nondeductible 6% penalty tax is imposed on excess contributions to an IRA. A 10% penalty tax is assessed on premature distributions from an IRA.

52. If you make contributions to your simplified employee pension IRA (SEP-IRA), you can deduct them the same as contributions to a regular IRA, up to the amount of your deduction limit or 100% of your taxable compensation for the year, whichever is less.

The correct answer is (T). *(SPE 989 IV-48)*
DISCUSSION: For purposes of computing contributions and deductions, simplified employee pension IRAs (SEP-IRAs) are treated in the same manner as regular IRAs. You can deduct up to $2,000 or 100% of your taxable compensation for the year, whichever is less.

53. Mr. Green was 70 years old on February 20, 1990. He must take a minimum distribution from his Individual Retirement Account based on the joint life expectancy of himself and his wife, who is his beneficiary. He will be assessed a 50% excise tax on the required minimum amount unless he takes a distribution by no later than April 1, 1991.

The correct answer is (T). *(SPE 990 IV-33)*
DISCUSSION: Retirement payments must begin no later than April 1st following the calendar year in which the individual reaches age 70½. Under Sec. 4974, if the amount distributed during the taxable year is less than the minimum required distribution for such taxable year, a tax will be imposed equal to 50% of the amount by which the minimum required distribution exceeds the actual amount distributed during the taxable year.

Module 8.6: Contributions to Keogh Plans

54. Employees may no longer make deductible voluntary contributions to their employer's retirement plan.

The correct answer is (T). *(SPE 987 IV-44)*
DISCUSSION: In order to obtain a deduction for a contribution to an IRA, the IRA must be an individual retirement account, individual retirement annuity, or individual retirement bonds. Prior to 1987, as an alternative, contributions could be made to an employer's retirement plan and deducted as a contribution to an IRA. This deduction is no longer available, although a voluntary (nondeductible) contribution may still be made to an employer's retirement plan.

8.6 Contributions to Keogh Plans

55. Mr. Barnes, a self-employed individual, has a qualified defined contribution plan. For 1991, Barnes' earned income from his business before payment to his plan was $20,000, and his adjusted gross income was $30,000. What is the maximum deduction allowed B for 1991?

a. $3,694.
b. $4,000.
c. $5,000.
d. $20,000.

The correct answer is (a). *(SPE 984 IV-82)*
REQUIRED: The maximum amount that a self-employed person may deduct as a contribution to a defined contribution plan.
DISCUSSION: The deduction for contributions on behalf of a self-employed individual is the same as for corporate contributions to an employee plan. Under Sec. 415(c), the contribution limit is 25% of the earned income derived by the self-employed individual from the trade or business, or $30,000, whichever is less. However, Sec. 401(c) requires the earned income to be reduced by the amount of the deductible contribution. This is a circular computation and the contribution percentage is modified for convenience to 20%. Starting in 1990, one-half of the self-employment tax rate times the net earnings from self-employment will also reduce the earned income amount that is calculated under Sec. 401(c).

The maximum deduction allowed is calculated as follows:

Earned income as given	$20,000
Less: self-employment tax adjustment ($20,000 x .1530 x ½)	(1,530)
Contribution base	$18,470
Times: 20%	x 0.20
Allowable deduction	$ 3,694

56. Kirk Bennett, a cash-basis taxpayer, is a self-employed accountant. During 1991 he established a qualified defined contribution retirement plan of which he will be the only beneficiary. In examining his records for 1991, the following information is available:

Earned income from self-employment	$40,000
Interest income	6,000
Dividend income	4,000
Net long-term capital gains	10,000
Adjusted gross income	$60,000

What is the maximum amount that Kirk can deduct as a contribution to his qualified retirement plan for 1991?

a. $7,388.
b. $7,500.
c. $8,000.
d. $10,000.

The correct answer is (a). *(CPA 578 Q-31)*
REQUIRED: The maximum amount that can be deducted as a contribution to the self-employed individual's qualified retirement plan for 1991.
DISCUSSION: Under Sec. 415(c), the maximum amount that can be deducted for a contribution on behalf of a self-employed individual is the lesser of $30,000 or 25% of the self-employed individual's earned income. Kirk's only income which qualifies as earned income is $40,000. However, Sec. 401(c) requires the earned income to be reduced by the amount of the deductible contribution. This is a circular computation and the contribution percentage is modified for convenience to 20%. Starting in 1990, one-half of the self-employment tax rate times the net earnings from self-employment will also reduce the earned income amount calculated under Sec. 401(c).

The maximum deduction allowed is calculated as follows:

Earned income	$40,000
Less: self-employment tax adjustment ($40,000 x .1530 x ½)	(3,060)
	$36,940
Times: 20%	x 0.20
Allowable deduction	$ 7,388

57. Only self-employed persons may deduct contributions to a qualified Keogh plan.

The correct answer is (T). *(SPE 1085 IV-34)*
DISCUSSION: A Keogh plan is for the self-employed, and only self-employed persons may deduct contributions to a Keogh plan. The contributions for employees of a self-employed person (proprietor or a partner in a partnership) are deductible by the self-employed person as a business expense.

58. If you are an owner-employee, payments may be deducted to a Keogh plan only if you have net earnings from self-employment.

The correct answer is (T). *(SPE 1085 IV-37)*
DISCUSSION: The deduction for contributions to a Keogh plan are limited to 25% of the earned income derived by the self-employed individual from the trade or business. If an owner-employee does not have net earnings from self-employment, the deduction limitation is zero.

59. Contributions to defined contribution plans for self-employed persons in excess of the limits for a year may not be carried forward to later years.

The correct answer is (F). *(SPE 1081 IV-45)*
DISCUSSION: If the contributions to a defined contribution plan for a self-employed person are in excess of the limit for that tax year, any excess will be deductible in each succeeding taxable year under Sec. 404(a)(1)(D), up to the limit in any one year. However, after 1986 there is a 10% tax on the excess portion of the contribution (Sec. 4972).

60. If your contributions to a Keogh plan are less than the deductible limit, you can carry the unused amount over to a later year.

The correct answer is (F). *(SPE 988 IV-45)*
DISCUSSION: Each year the annual limit on deductions to a Keogh plan start again. If in a prior year deductions are made in an amount less than the limitation, the unused limitation may not be carried forward to another year.

61. XYZ, a cash-basis partnership, provides a retirement plan for all its employees. On March 21, 1991, the partnership made a payment to the plan administrator, with the designation that it was for 1990. The partnership return for 1990 was filed on April 15, 1991 and this payment was included in the retirement plan deduction. This payment was properly included in the 1990 return.

The correct answer is (T). *(SPE 1082 IV-42)*
DISCUSSION: A contribution to a retirement plan is deemed to have been made on the last day of the preceding year, if the payment is made on account of such year, and is made no later than the time for filing the return for such year, including extensions of time to file [Sec. 404(a)(6)]. The partnership return for 1990 was not due until April 15, 1991, at which time it was filed. Since the contribution was made no later than the time for the filing of the tax return and was designated for 1990, it was properly deducted in the tax return for 1990.

CHAPTER NINE
DEDUCTIONS FROM AGI

9.1 Medical Expenses	(19 questions)	167
9.2 Taxes	(17 questions)	173
9.3 Interest Expense	(23 questions)	177
9.4 Charitable Contributions	(28 questions)	184
9.5 Casualty and Theft Losses	(23 questions)	193
9.6 First-Tier Miscellaneous Itemized Deductions	(15 questions)	199
9.7 Second-Tier Miscellaneous Itemized Deductions	(45 questions)	204
9.8 Limitation on Itemized Deductions for High-Income Taxpayers	(5 questions)	217

9.1 Medical Expenses

1. Which one of the following expenses does not qualify as a deductible medical expense?

 a. Cost of braille books over cost of regular books.
 b. Special school for a deaf child to learn lip reading.
 c. Cost of keeping a mentally retarded person in a relative's home.
 d. Cost and care of guide dogs used by a blind person in his business.

The correct answer is (c). *(SPE 1081 I-55)*
REQUIRED: The expense that does not qualify as a deductible medical expense.
DISCUSSION: Sec. 213 allows a deduction for expenses paid for medical care of the taxpayer, spouse, and dependents to the extent such expenses exceed 7.5% of adjusted gross income. The term medical care includes amounts paid for the diagnosis, cure, mitigation, treatment, or prevention of a disease or physical handicap, or for the purpose of affecting any structure or function of the body [Sec. 213(d)]. The cost of keeping a mentally retarded person in a relative's home is an expenditure for the support of the person and does not fall within the definition of medical care. The cost of institutional care could be deductible as a medical expense.
Answers (a), (b), and (d) are incorrect because each is an expenditure for the mitigation of a disease or physical handicap. Therefore, each is a deductible medical expense.

2. Which one of the following expenditures qualifies as a deductible medical expense for tax purposes?

 a. Vitamins for general health not prescribed by a physician.
 b. Health club dues.
 c. Transportation to physician's office for required medical care.
 d. Mandatory employment taxes for basic coverage under Medicare A.

The correct answer is (c). *(CPA 1190 Q-33)*
REQUIRED: The expenditure that qualifies as a deductible medical expense for tax purposes.
DISCUSSION: Sec. 213(d) defines medical care as including transportation for needed medical care.
Answers (a) and (b) are incorrect because each is incurred for the purpose of improving the taxpayer's general health and not for the purpose of curing any specific ailment or disease. Answer (d) is incorrect because Medicare A premiums are not deductible unless voluntarily paid by a taxpayer otherwise ineligible for coverage (Rev. Rul. 79-175). The amounts withheld from wages (or paid on self-employment income) under Medicare A are considered to be paid as taxes.

3. Which of the following qualify as deductible medical expenses?

1. Payments to physician
2. Payments for a cosmetic face-lifting operation
3. Medical portion of your auto insurance premium (although not separately stated)
4. Payments for acupuncture service
5. Domestic help

    a. 1, 3, and 5.

    b. 1.

    c. 1, 2, and 4.

    d. 1 and 4.

The correct answer is (d). *(SPE 1078 I-51)*
REQUIRED: The expenditure(s) qualifying as deductible medical expenses.
DISCUSSION: Payments to a physician and payments for acupuncture service are both expenditures made for the diagnosis, cure, mitigation, treatment, or prevention of disease, or for the purpose of affecting any structure or function of the body. Accordingly, they fall within the definition of medical care under Sec. 213 and are deductible expenses.
    Answers (a), (b), and (c) are incorrect because expenditure 2 is no longer a deductible expense under Sec. 213 for tax years beginning after December 31, 1990, unless the procedure was necessary to "ameliorate a deformity arising from, or directly related to, a congenital abnormality, a personal injury resulting from an accident or trauma, or disfiguring disease." Expenditures 3 and 5 are also not deductible medical expenses. Although insurance covering medical care is a deductible medical expense, if the insurance contract covers losses other than medical care and the charge for the medical insurance is not separately stated, no portion of the premium may be deducted as a medical expense. Domestic help does not fall within the definition of medical care under Sec. 213(e) and is not deductible.

4. Premiums paid for insurance policies that provide for the payment or reimbursement of the following expenses are all deductible as medical expenses except premiums for

    a. Replacement of contact lenses.

    b. Membership in an association furnishing cooperative or "free-choice" medical service.

    c. Prescription drugs.

    d. A guaranteed amount for each week the taxpayer is hospitalized for sickness or injury.

The correct answer is (d). *(SPE 984 I-60)*
REQUIRED: The expenditure for insurance that is not deductible as a medical care expense.
DISCUSSION: Sec. 213(d) provides that the term "medical care" includes amounts paid for insurance covering medical care. A policy that will pay a guaranteed amount for each week the taxpayer is hospitalized for sickness or injury does not meet the definition of medical care since the amount it pays is unrelated to the medical expense.
    Answers (a), (b), and (c) are incorrect because each meets the definition of medical care expenses.

5. Scott is an 8-year-old with a rare lung problem. His doctor wants him to be examined by a specialist at the Mayo Clinic. Scott and his mother travel to Rochester, Minnesota. Scott is not sick enough to be admitted to the hospital, so he stays in a nearby hotel from which he can go to the hospital daily for the specialist to monitor his reaction to a new drug. Scott and his mother have separate rooms so that Scott can rest properly. They remain for 10 nights and the rooms each cost $60 per night. How much is allowable as a medical expense?

    a. $500.

    b. $600.

    c. $1,000.

    d. $1,200.

The correct answer is (c). *(Publisher)*
REQUIRED: The amount paid for lodging away from home that is deductible as a medical expense.
DISCUSSION: Sec. 213(d)(2) provides special rules for amounts paid for lodging away from home related to medical care. The amounts paid for lodging will be considered paid for medical care if the medical care is provided by a physician in a licensed hospital and if there is no significant element of personal pleasure, recreation, or vacation in the travel away from home. The amount for lodging is limited to $50 for each night for each individual (including a parent with his/her child). Therefore, Scott and his mother are limited to $100 per night for 10 nights, or $1,000.

Module 9.1: Medical Expenses

6. During 1991, Mr. E spent $10,000 to construct an entrance ramp and to widen doorways in his personal residence to make the home accessible to his wife, who is confined to a wheelchair. The $10,000 expenditure increased the value of the residence by $2,000. How much of the $10,000 is a deductible medical expense for 1991?

   a. $0.
   b. $2,000.
   c. $8,000.
   d. $10,000.

The correct answer is (c). *(SPE 987 I-56)*
REQUIRED: The amount of home improvements deductible as a medical expense.
DISCUSSION: Capital expenditures are generally not deductible as medical expenses [Reg. 1.213-1(e)(1)(iii)]. However, a capital expenditure related to the care of a sick person is deductible. The IRS's position is that home-related capital expenditures incurred by a physically handicapped individual are deductible only to the extent the expenditures exceed any increase in the value of the property. Therefore, Mr. E may only deduct $8,000 ($10,000 – $2,000 increase in value).

The Committee Reports to the 1986 TRA indicated an intent to allow a deduction for the full cost of such expenditures, but such a provision was not actually included in the law. Nevertheless, the IRS did publish a list of certain capital expenses that it feels do not ordinarily increase the value of a residence. Two of the items on this list are constructing ramps and widening doorways. But since the facts of the question indicate a definite increase in value, only the excess is deductible.

7. Mr. E, a single taxpayer, had an adjusted gross income of $10,000 for 1991. In addition, he paid the following expenses:

Surgeon's fee (outpatient)	$600
Psychiatrist's fee	700
Hospital bill as follows:	
Medical services	300
Meals in hospital	200
Hospital room charge	500
Transportation to/from doctor's office and hospital	50
Contact lenses	200
Prescription drugs	80
Vitamins for general health	60
Weight-loss program	300
Chiropractor's fee	400

Mr. E also paid $900 for medical insurance premiums and received reimbursement of $850 from the insurance company on claims for the above expenses. Compute Mr. E's 1991 medical deduction for Schedule A.

   a. $2,180.
   b. $2,330.
   c. $2,580.
   d. $3,080.

The correct answer is (b). *(SPE 1083 I-79)*
REQUIRED: The medical expense deduction for 1991 on Schedule A.
DISCUSSION: Sec. 213 allows a deduction for medical care expenses to the extent that they exceed 7.5% of adjusted gross income. Medicine and drugs are limited to prescription drugs and insulin. Vitamins and the weight-loss program are not deductible because they are for the purpose of improving the taxpayer's general health and not for a specific ailment. The total amount of expenses paid during the year must be reduced by the amount of insurance reimbursements received.

Surgeon's fee	$ 600
Psychiatrist's fee	700
Hospital bills ($300 + $200 + $500)	1,000
Transportation	50
Contact lenses	200
Prescription drugs	80
Chiropractor's fee	400
Medical insurance premium	900
	$3,930
Less insurance reimbursement	(850)
	$3,080
Less 7.5% of AGI	(750)
Medical expense deduction	$2,330

169

Module 9.1: Medical Expenses

8. Tom Tucker had a $10,000 salary this year but he also had numerous medical expenses as listed below:

Doctor bills	$1,000
Health insurance	500
Car transportation	100

For 1991, what amount of the deductions is to be included with Tom's other itemized deductions if he was reimbursed $200 for the expenses?

a. $400.
b. $650.
c. $900.
d. $1,400.

The correct answer is (b). *(P. Hite)*
REQUIRED: The taxpayer's allowable medical expense deduction.
DISCUSSION: Sec. 213 permits the taxpayer to deduct medical expenses only to the extent they exceed 7.5% of adjusted gross income. Amounts paid for health insurance are treated as other medical expenses. Transportation to obtain medical care is also deductible. Reimbursements for medical expenses reduce the amount deductible. Tom's medical expense deduction is

Doctor bills	$1,000
Health insurance	500
Car transportation	100
Total expenses	$1,600
Less: Reimbursements	(200)
7.5% of AGI	(750)
Allowable medical expense deduction	$ 650

9. Jim and Nancy Walton had adjusted gross income of $25,000 in 1991. During the year they paid the following medical-related expenses:

Over-the-counter medicines	$100
Prescription drugs	300
Doctor fees	825
Health club membership (recommended by the family doctor for general health care)	400
Medical care insurance	280

How much may the Waltons use as medical expenses in calculating itemized deductions for 1991?

a. $1,380.
b. $980.
c. $30.
d. $0.

The correct answer is (d). *(CPA 581 P-48)*
REQUIRED: The taxpayers' allowable medical expense deduction for 1991.
DISCUSSION: The cost of the health club membership is not included in the computation of the medical expense deduction since the cost is incurred for the purpose of improving the taxpayers' general health, not for curing a specific ailment or disease [Reg. 1.213-1(e)]. Only prescription drugs and insulin are deductible, so the over-the-counter medicines are not included.

Medical care insurance	$ 280
Doctor fees	825
Prescription drugs	300
Total expenses	$1,405
Less 7.5% of AGI	(1,875)
Allowable medical expense deduction	$ 0

10. Al Daly's adjusted gross income for the year ended December 31, 1991 was $20,000. He was not covered by any medical insurance plan. During 1991 he paid $500 to a physician for treatment of a heart condition. He also owed the physician $900 for an operation performed in December 1991, which he paid in January 1992. In addition, Daly incurred a $1,700 hospital bill in 1991 which he charged to his bank credit card in December 1991 and paid to the bank in January 1992. Daly's total allowable medical deduction for 1991 is

a. $0.
b. $700.
c. $1,200.
d. $2,200.

The correct answer is (b). *(CPA 1183 Q-22)*
REQUIRED: The allowable medical expense deduction for 1991.
DISCUSSION: The taxpayer may only deduct medical expenses that were paid during the year. The taxpayer may not deduct as a medical expense the balance owed for an operation performed during the year, but it will be deductible in 1992 when paid. The taxpayer may deduct the medical expense charged on a bank credit card, even though the bank was not paid until the following year. Daly's total allowable medical expense deduction is

Payment to physician	$ 500
Hospital bill	1,700
Total expenses	$2,200
Less 7.5% AGI	(1,500)
Allowable medical expense deduction	$ 700

Module 9.1: Medical Expenses 171

11. Gail and Jeff Payne are married and filed a joint return for 1991. In 1991 they paid the following doctors' bills for

Gail's mother, who received over half of her support from Gail and Jeff, but who does not live in the Payne household, and who earned $2,000 in 1991 for baby-sitting.	$700
Their unmarried 26-year-old son, who earned $4,000 in 1991, but was fully supported by his parents. He is not a full-time student.	500

Disregarding the adjusted gross income percentage test, how much of these doctors' bills may be included on the Paynes' joint return in 1991 as qualifying medical expenses?

a. $0.
b. $500.
c. $700.
d. $1,200.

The correct answer is (d). *(CPA 586 Q-56)*
REQUIRED: The total amount of qualifying medical expenses.
DISCUSSION: Sec. 213(a) allows a deduction for expenses paid for medical care of the taxpayer, spouse, or a dependent. Dependent is defined in Sec. 152 to include the mother of the taxpayer and the son of the taxpayer if each received over half of his/her support from the taxpayer. Gail's mother and son are thus considered dependents for purpose of the medical deduction, regardless of their gross income or filing status (these other factors do affect the availability of the dependency exemption). Therefore, all the medical expenses incurred by Gail and Jeff ($1,200) for their son and Gail's mother are considered qualifying medical expenses.

12. During 1991, A charged $5,000 on his credit card for the medical expenses of his son whom he could claim as a dependent. In the same year he also paid $1,000 in medical expenses for his wife who died in 1990. What is the amount of A's 1991 deductible medical expenses before the limitation?

a. $0.
b. $1,000.
c. $5,000.
d. $6,000.

The correct answer is (d). *(SPE 988 I-44)*
REQUIRED: The deductible amount of medical expenses paid for a spouse who died in the prior year and also a son.
DISCUSSION: Sec. 213(a) allows a deduction for expenses paid for medical care of the taxpayer, spouse, or a dependent. Therefore, the $5,000 of medical expense paid for the son is deductible. The fact that it was charged on a credit card does not affect the deduction. Medical expenses are deductible in the year in which they are paid. Therefore, the $1,000 of medical expenses paid for the wife who died in the prior year are deductible in 1991. A's total deductible expenses before the limitation are $6,000 ($5,000 + $1,000).

13. Kathy and Rob have been legally divorced since 1989. Their son, Tommy, lived with Kathy for all of 1991. Kathy and Rob provide 100% of Tommy's support. Kathy, as the custodial parent, was allowed to claim Tommy as a dependent on her 1991 federal income tax return. Rob paid for $1,000 of Tommy's medical expenses. Rob cannot include the $1,000 as a medical expense on his 1991 federal income tax return because he was not allowed the exemption for Tommy.

The correct answer is (F). *(SPE 989 I-15)*
DISCUSSION: Sec. 213(d)(5) provides that any child of divorced or separated parents shall be treated as a dependent of both parents for purposes of the medical expense deduction.

14. The cost and maintenance of a guide dog for a blind person is a qualified medical expense.

The correct answer is (T). *(SPE 1077 I-47)*
DISCUSSION: Sec. 213(d) includes in the definition of medical expense amounts paid for the mitigation of disease or handicap. The cost and maintenance of a guide dog for a blind person is an expenditure made for the mitigation of the taxpayer's handicap.

Module 9.1: Medical Expenses

15. To alleviate an obesity problem, a doctor puts his patient on a special diet. The total cost of the patient's food for the special diet is a deductible medical expense.

The correct answer is (F). *(SPE 1077 I-60)*
DISCUSSION: The normal cost of a taxpayer's food is not deductible as a medical expense since it is necessary for the taxpayer's general health [Reg. 1.213-1(e)]. If the taxpayer's doctor prescribes a special diet to alleviate an obesity problem, however, any additional food costs the taxpayer incurs due to the special diet may be deductible as a medical expense.

16. Cosmetic surgery is no longer a deductible medical expense under Sec. 213 for tax years beginning after 1990.

The correct answer is (T). *(Publisher)*
DISCUSSION: The Revenue Reconciliation Act of 1990 amended Sec. 213(d) so that medical care does not include cosmetic surgery or other similar procedures, unless the surgery or procedure is necessary to ameliorate a deformity arising from, or directly related to, a congenital abnormality, a personal injury resulting from an accident or trauma, or disfiguring disease. The amendment defines cosmetic surgery as "any procedure which is directed at improving the patient's appearance and does not meaningfully promote the proper function of the body or prevent or treat illness or disease."

17. During 1991 Mr. R paid medical expenses for his wife, who died during 1990. He remarried and is filing a joint return for 1991 with his second wife. Mr. R may not include the medical expenses on the joint return with his second wife.

The correct answer is (F). *(SPE 1081 I-23)*
DISCUSSION: Medical expenses are deductible in the year in which they are paid. Since Mr. R incurred the expenditures for the medical care of his first wife in 1990, he may deduct the expenditures in the year they are paid [Reg. 1.213-1(a)], even on a joint return filed with his second wife.

18. For 1991 Mr. Q had adjusted gross income of $10,000. His itemized deductions included qualifying medical expenses of $1,000. A reimbursement of 1990 medical expenses in the amount of $400 was received in 1991. If Mr. Q itemizes in 1991, he must reduce his medical expenses by the $400 received.

The correct answer is (F). *(SPE 1083 I-27)*
DISCUSSION: Reg. 1.213-1(g)(1) provides that, when a reimbursement for medical expenses is received in a taxable year subsequent to a year in which the expense was deducted, the reimbursement must be included in gross income in the year received.

19. In 1990 Mrs. D installed an elevator in her house on the advice of her doctor because of a persistent heart condition. The elevator cost $10,000 and the fair market value of Mrs. D's house increased $5,000 due to the elevator being installed. In 1991 Mrs. D paid $1,000 for repairs to the elevator. The $1,000 is deductible by Mrs. D as a medical expense for 1991.

The correct answer is (T). *(SPE 988 I-12)*
DISCUSSION: Home-related capital expenditures incurred by a physically handicapped individual are deductible. An example is an elevator needed for someone with a heart condition. Once a capital expense qualifies as a medical expense, amounts paid for the operation and upkeep also qualify as a medical expense. This is true even if the original capital expenditure was not entirely deductible (because it may have increased the fair market value of the residence). Therefore, the entire $1,000 for repairs to the elevator is deductible as a medical expense.

9.2 Taxes

20. Mr. Adams derives his entire income from the operation of his grocery store business. On which schedule should he deduct the state income taxes imposed on this income?

   a. Schedule A.
   b. Schedule C.
   c. Schedule D.
   d. Schedule E.

The correct answer is (a). *(SPE 1078 I-52)*
REQUIRED: The schedule on which a taxpayer should deduct state income taxes.
DISCUSSION: Sec. 164 allows a deduction for state income taxes. Since this is not a deduction allowable in arriving at adjusted gross income as defined in Sec. 62, it is an itemized deduction as defined in Sec. 63(d). Itemized deductions are reported on Schedule A.
Answer (b) is incorrect because Schedule C is used to report income and expenses from a business. The income taxes are not a business expense because the income from a sole proprietorship is reported by the individual and the income taxes are a personal expense. Answer (c) is incorrect because Schedule D is used to report capital gains and losses. Answer (d) is incorrect because Schedule E is used to report supplemental income from rents and royalties, partnerships, and estates and trusts.

21. All of the following taxes are deductible on Schedule A (Form 1040) except

   a. State or local inheritance tax.
   b. State income tax.
   c. State real estate tax on a personal residence.
   d. Occupational tax charged at a flat rate by a locality for the privilege of working there.

The correct answer is (a). *(SPE 987 I-57)*
REQUIRED: The tax not deductible on Schedule A of Form 1040.
DISCUSSION: No deduction is allowed for state or local inheritance taxes. On the federal estate tax return a credit may be allowed, but for income tax purposes no deduction is available.
Answer (b) is incorrect because Sec. 164(a) specifically lists state income taxes as a deduction. Answer (c) is incorrect because Sec 164(a) also specifically lists state and local (and foreign) real property taxes as a deduction. Answer (d) is incorrect because Sec. 164(a) provides a deduction for taxes paid or accrued in carrying on a trade or business or activity related to the production of income. An occupational tax paid by an employee would be deductible on Schedule A (subject to the 2% floor on miscellaneous itemized deductions). A similar tax paid by a self-employed individual is deductible on Schedule C.

22. Which of the following taxes may be deducted on Form 1040, Schedule A, for 1991?

   a. Homeowners' association charges.
   b. Assessments for sewer lines.
   c. State income taxes on municipal bond interest.
   d. State and local taxes on gasoline.

The correct answer is (c). *(SPE 1081 I-56)*
REQUIRED: The tax that may be deducted on Form 1040, Schedule A.
DISCUSSION: Sec. 164(a) allows a deduction for state income taxes (even if the income is exempt from federal tax). Since this is not allowed as a deduction in arriving at adjusted gross income as defined in Sec. 62, it is an itemized deduction as defined in Sec. 63(d) and is reported on Schedule A.
Answer (a) is incorrect because homeowners' association charges are not a tax; they are a type of private dues for services provided. Answer (b) is incorrect because an assessment for sewer lines is a payment for a special benefit tending to increase the value of the property and is not deductible under Sec. 164. Answer (d) is incorrect because gasoline taxes are not deductible except as a business expense.

23. George Burke, a salaried taxpayer, paid the following taxes which were not incurred in connection with a trade or business during 1991:

Federal income tax (withheld by employer)	$1,500
State income tax (withheld by employer)	1,000
FICA tax (withheld by employer)	700
State sales taxes	900
Federal auto gasoline taxes	200
Federal excise tax on telephone bills	50

What taxes are allowable deductions from Burke's adjusted gross income for 1991?

- a. $2,850.
- b. $2,550.
- c. $1,900.
- d. $1,000.

The correct answer is (d). *(CPA 579 Q-33)*
REQUIRED: The taxes that are allowable deductions from adjusted gross income.
DISCUSSION: Sec. 164(a) lists the taxes that are deductible from adjusted gross income. These include the state income tax of $1,000.

Sec. 164 does not allow a deduction for federal income taxes in any case. FICA tax, federal gasoline taxes, and federal excise taxes are only deductible if incurred as trade or business expenses or for the production of income. After 1986, sales taxes are not deductible unless incurred in a trade or business or for the production of income. If the sales taxes were incurred in connection with the acquisition of property (as is usually the case), they must be capitalized.

---

24. During 1991 Jack and Mary Bronson paid the following taxes:

Taxes on residence (for period January 1 to September 30, 1991)	$2,700
State motor vehicle tax on value of the car	360

The Bronsons sold their house on June 30, 1991 under an agreement in which the real estate taxes were not prorated between the buyer and sellers. What amount should the Bronsons deduct as taxes in calculating itemized deductions for 1991?

- a. $1,800.
- b. $2,160.
- c. $2,700.
- d. $3,060.

The correct answer is (b). *(CPA 582 P-52)*
REQUIRED: The amount the taxpayers can deduct as taxes in calculating itemized deductions.
DISCUSSION: Sec. 164(a) allows a deduction for state, local, and foreign real property taxes, and for state and local personal property taxes. Real estate taxes must be apportioned between the buyer and seller on the basis of the number of days the property was held by each in the year of sale, regardless of an agreement not to prorate them [Sec. 164(d)]. The taxpayers held the property for 6 months of the 9-month period the taxes covered. The amount of the taxes apportioned to the Bronsons is $1,800 ($2,700 x 6/9). The state motor vehicle tax on the value of the car is a tax on the value of personal property, so the $360 may also be deducted. The taxpayers may deduct a total of $2,160 as taxes in calculating their itemized deductions.

---

25. During 1991, Paul and Mary Davis, cash basis taxpayers, paid the following taxes:

State income tax	$ 300
Estimated federal income tax	250
Estimated state income tax	1,500
Sales tax on 1991 auto used 60% for business	1,400
State gift tax	1,000
Property tax, including $50 for trash pick-up	2,600
Property tax on their vacation home in Canada	1,000

What amount can Mary and Paul claim as an itemized deduction on their 1991 federal income tax return?

- a. $4,350.
- b. $5,350.
- c. $6,350.
- d. $6,400.

The correct answer is (b). *(SPE 990 I-84)*
REQUIRED: The amount of taxes paid that can be claimed as an itemized deduction in 1991.
DISCUSSION: Sec. 164(a) allows a deduction for state, local, and foreign real property taxes. This would include $1,000 tax on the vacation home and $2,550 of other property taxes ($2,600 – $50 trash pick-up fee). A deduction is also allowed for state income taxes. This would include the $300 of state income taxes withheld and the $1,500 of estimated state income taxes paid. Sec. 164 does not allow a deduction for federal income taxes in any case and sales taxes are deductible only if incurred as a trade or business expense or for the production of income. The business portion of the sales tax paid on the automobile would be deducted as a business expense on the taxpayer's Schedule C through the claiming of a depreciation deduction, not as an itemized deduction on Schedule A. Sec. 164 does not allow a deduction for gift taxes. The $50 fee paid for trash pick-up would not be allowed as an itemized deduction.

State income tax	$ 300
Estimated state income tax	1,500
Property tax ($2,600 – $50 trash pick-up)	2,550
Property tax-vacation home	1,000
	$5,350

26. In 1991, Smith paid $6,000 to the tax collector of Big City for realty taxes on a two-family house owned by Smith's mother. Of this amount, $2,800 covered back taxes for 1990, and $3,200 covered 1991 taxes. Smith resides on the second floor of the house, and his mother resides on the first floor. In Smith's itemized deductions on his 1991 return, what amount was Smith entitled to claim for realty taxes?

   a. $6,000.
   b. $3,200.
   c. $3,000.
   d. $0.

The correct answer is (d). *(CPA 1190 Q-32)*
REQUIRED: The amount of deductible property taxes paid by a person who does not own the property but resides in half of the property.
DISCUSSION: Taxes may only be deducted by the person on whom they are legally levied. Since Smith does not own the house, none of the taxes paid by Smith can be deducted by Smith. Smith's mother is entitled to the deduction only if she pays the taxes.

27. Ms. L, a cash-basis taxpayer, lives in a county where the real estate tax year runs from July 1 to June 30. The tax bills are due in two installments-- July 1 and January 1. Ms. L purchased her first house on September 1, 1991. As part of her purchase price, she reimbursed the sellers $700 for her share of the 1991 real estate taxes. At the date of purchase she also paid her mortgage company $450, which was credited to her tax escrow account. From her monthly mortgage payments in 1991, a total of $600 was credited to her tax escrow account. On January 4, 1992 the bank paid the escrow balance to the county tax office. L's real estate tax deduction for 1991 is

   a. $450.
   b. $700.
   c. $1,150.
   d. $1,750.

The correct answer is (b). *(SPE 1083 I-64)*
REQUIRED: The real estate tax deduction for 1991.
DISCUSSION: Sec. 164(d) provides for the apportionment of taxes on real property between sellers and purchasers. Ms. L paid her share of the real estate taxes in 1991 ($700). The amounts credited to her account by the mortgage company and held in escrow are not deductible as taxes until the tax is actually paid. The $1,050 ($450 + $600) held by the mortgage company in escrow will be deductible by Ms. L in 1992, the year paid.

28. Mr. & Mrs. Smith's real property tax year is the calendar year. Real estate taxes for the previous year are assessed in their state on January 2 and become due on May 1 and October 1. The tax becomes a lien on May 1. The Smiths bought a home on July 1, 1991. The 1990 real estate taxes on the home due in 1991 were $1,000. The Smiths agreed to pay the $1,000 after the sale. They paid $500 in late taxes on August 1, and $500 on October 1. How should the Smiths treat the tax payments for federal income tax purposes for 1991?

   a. The entire $1,000 is deductible.
   b. They may deduct only the $500 payment made on October 1.
   c. They may not deduct any amount but must add the $1,000 to the cost of their home.
   d. They may deduct only the $500 payment made on August 1 as a settlement fee or closing cost.

The correct answer is (c). *(SPE 989 I-52)*
REQUIRED: The correct tax treatment of the payment of back taxes by the purchasers of real property.
DISCUSSION: Real property taxes are generally deductible only by the person against whom the tax is imposed. Sec. 164(d) requires real estate taxes to be apportioned between the buyer and seller based on the number of days in the real property tax year that the property was held by each. If the buyer pays the seller's taxes, they are capitalized as an additional cost of the property. The Smiths paid $1,000 in 1990 real estate taxes after they purchased the property in 1991. They have, in effect, paid taxes owed by the seller and will not be able to deduct any of the amount and instead must add the $1,000 to the basis of the property.
Answers (a), (b), and (c) are incorrect because taxes may only be deducted by the person upon whom they are levied. All $1,000 of the taxes in question were levied on the prior owner of the property and no part of the amount is deductible by the Smiths.

29. Fred Harvey, a cash-basis taxpayer, elected to itemize his deductions on his 1990 income tax return. Harvey plans to itemize again in 1991 and the following information relating to his state income taxes is available:

Taxes withheld in 1991	$2,500
Refund received in 1991 of 1990 tax	500
Assessment paid in 1991 of 1989 tax	700

The above information should be reported by Harvey in his 1991 tax return as

a. State and local income taxes of $2,500.
b. State and local income taxes of $2,700.
c. State and local income taxes of $3,200.
d. State and local income taxes of $3,200 and income from state and local income tax refund of $500.

The correct answer is (d). *(CPA 581 P-56)*
REQUIRED: The correct tax treatment of state income tax withholdings, refund, and assessment.
DISCUSSION: State and local income taxes are deductible under Sec. 164. A cash-basis taxpayer is entitled to deduct state income taxes withheld by his/her employer in the year such amounts are withheld. Assessments of state income taxes are deductible in the year of payment by a cash-basis taxpayer even if the payments relate to prior years. A refund of a prior year's tax payment must be included in the taxpayer's gross income in the year received if the taxpayer deducted the taxes in an earlier year.
In 1991, Harvey should deduct the taxes withheld of $2,500 and the assessment paid of $700. He should include the $500 refund he received in gross income.

30. Mr. Jones filed an amended federal income tax return during 1991 for an earlier tax year. This amended return resulted in an additional tax payment of $400, a penalty of $100, and an interest payment of $40. How much of these payments will be deductible on the 1991 tax return?

a. $440.
b. $40.
c. $8.
d. $0.

The correct answer is (d). *(G.L. Waters)*
REQUIRED: The amount of payments made with an amended return that is deductible.
DISCUSSION: Federal income taxes and penalties imposed by the IRS are never deductible, and the deduction for personal interest under Sec. 163 has been phased out over the years 1987 through 1990. There is no deduction for personal interest for tax years after 1990. None of the payments made by Jones are deductible in 1991.

31. In certain circumstances it is possible to have two taxpayers deduct the same state tax. Which of the following is such an example?

a. A retailer separates the state sales tax collected from his revenues. Both he and the consumer may deduct the tax on their federal returns.
b. A retailer separates the state sales tax on gasoline sold from his revenues. The consumer claims a state tax on gasoline on his federal return.
c. A retailer includes the state tax on gasoline in his revenues, and claims a deduction for the tax. The consumer claims the tax as a proper business expense.
d. A retailer includes the state tax on gasoline in his revenues, and claims a deduction for the tax. The consumer claims the tax as a personal deduction on his federal return.

The correct answer is (c). *(D. Suttles)*
REQUIRED: When the same state taxes may be deducted by two taxpayers.
DISCUSSION: When a retailer includes state gasoline taxes in his gross revenues, he may deduct the amount as a tax on his return. The consumer who claims the gasoline purchase as business expense may show the tax portion separately as a tax. Note, however, that including the tax in gross revenue is not a proper method of accounting by the retailer.
Answers (a) and (b) are incorrect because the retailer may not deduct the tax if he has not included it in his total revenues. Answer (d) is incorrect because the consumer may not claim the state tax on gasoline as a personal deduction.

Module 9.3: Interest Expense 177

32. On January 31, 1991, John and Mary Green paid property tax of $3,000 on their home to cover the period January 1 to September 30, 1991. John and Mary sold their home on June 30, 1991 under an agreement in which the real estate taxes were not prorated between buyer and seller. Since the Greens paid the tax, they will be able to claim $3,000 as an itemized deduction on their 1991 return.

The correct answer is (F). *(SPE 990 I-22)*
DISCUSSION: Real property taxes are generally deductible only by the person against whom the tax is imposed. Sec. 164(d) requires real estate taxes to be apportioned between the buyer and seller based on the number of days in the real property tax year that the property was held by each. Reg. 1.164-6(a) provides that this proration is required whether or not the seller and the purchaser actually apportion the tax. Therefore, the Greens may deduct only $2,000 ($3,000 x 6/9) of the property taxes.

33. In 1990, Mrs. R, an accrual-method taxpayer, was assessed real property taxes. During that year, she filed a formal protest with Z County in accordance with local law. Mrs. R paid the contested liability in 1991 and is entitled to a deduction in the year of payment.

The correct answer is (T). *(SPE 1079 II-27)*
DISCUSSION: When a liability is honestly disputed, an accrual method taxpayer may not deduct the amount until the dispute is settled or adjudicated under general accrual principles. But Sec. 461(f) allows the deduction when the amount is paid, even if an honest dispute continues after the payment.

34. Beginning in 1991, state and local income taxes may no longer be deducted as an itemized deduction on Schedule A.

The correct answer is (F). *(SPE 987 I-19)*
DISCUSSION: State and local income taxes are deductible per Sec. 164(a)(1). Furthermore, they are deducted as an itemized deduction on Schedule A. State and local sales taxes, however, may not be deducted after 1986 unless incurred in a trade or business or for the production of income. Generally, sales taxes must be capitalized as a cost of the acquisition of property.

35. State and local income taxes for a sole proprietor are only deductible on Schedule A, Form 1040, even if the only source of income is from a business.

The correct answer is (T). *(SPE 986 I-26)*
DISCUSSION: State and local income taxes are deducted from adjusted gross income and are reported on Schedule A regardless of whether the source of the income is from a business.

36. If state law imposes the sales tax on the seller or retailer and allows the seller or retailer to state it separately or pass it on to the consumer, the consumer may deduct the sales tax paid in purchasing a capital item in 1991 as a business expense.

The correct answer is (F). *(SPE 1085 II-14)*
DISCUSSION: After 1986, sales taxes are not deductible unless incurred in a trade or business or for the production of income. If the sales taxes were incurred in connection with the acquisition of property (as is usually the case), the sales taxes must be capitalized.

9.3 Interest Expense

37. Bill Bullar incurs a substantial amount of personal or consumer interest each year on charge cards, auto loans, and other personal loans. What percentage of this interest can he deduct in 1989, 1990, and 1991?

	1989	1990	1991
a.	80%	85%	90%
b.	20%	10%	0%
c.	20%	10%	5%
d.	40%	20%	10%

The correct answer is (b). *(Publisher)*
REQUIRED: The percentage of personal interest deductible in 1989, 1990, and 1991.
DISCUSSION: Personal interest [defined in Sec. 163(h)(2)] is not deductible after 1990. Until then, only a portion is deductible.

Year	Deductible	Not Deductible
1989	20%	80%
1990	10%	90%
1991 and thereafter	0%	100%

38. Which of the following types of interest is not subject to the interest deduction limitation under the Tax Reform Act of 1986 (100% disallowance beginning in 1991 with a phase-in over the interim period):

a. Student loan interest.

b. Interest owed to the IRS stemming from an audit on a 1987 income tax return.

c. Interest on a judgment.

d. All of the above are subject to the interest deduction limitation.

The correct answer is (d). *(P. Karl III)*
REQUIRED: The type of interest still fully deductible after 1986.
DISCUSSION: After 1986 the deduction for personal or consumer interest is phased out over a five-year period. Choices (a), (b), and (c) are all personal interest [Sec. 163(h)(2)].

The major exception is the interest on a debt secured by a principal or second residence of a taxpayer (called "qualified residence interest"). This interest is generally deductible subject to some limitations on the total amount of debt which will qualify. Investment interest, interest incurred in a trade or business, and interest incurred in a passive activity are covered by other rules.

39. Which of the following is treated as personal interest of Individual A after 1986?

a. Interest incurred on refinancing A's home if the funds are used for a vacation.

b. Interest incurred to purchase bonds as an investment.

c. Interest incurred by a limited partnership in which A is a limited partner.

d. Interest incurred on an ordinary bank loan if the funds are used to provide medical care for a dependent of A.

The correct answer is (d). *(Publisher)*
REQUIRED: The interest expense treated as personal interest after 1986.
DISCUSSION: Personal interest (not deductible after 1990 and only partially deductible during tax years 1987 through 1990) is defined in Sec. 163(h)(2) as any interest other than qualified residence interest, investment interest, interest taken into account in computing income or loss from a passive activity, interest in connection with a business, and interest during certain extensions of time to pay the estate tax. Interest on an ordinary bank loan incurred for medical care is personal interest.

Answer (a) is incorrect because interest on debt secured by one's residence may be qualified residence interest regardless of the use of the funds. Answer (b) is incorrect because this is investment interest. Answer (c) is incorrect because a limited partnership is generally a passive activity and the interest is deductible subject to the passive activity loss limitations rules (see Chapter 7).

40. In 1991, Mr. A, a sole proprietor, made interest payments of $800 on his personal credit cards, $650 on his business truck loan, $3,000 to the bank for a loan origination fee (charge for services) for his Veterans Administration mortgage, and $8,000 on his home mortgage. What is the total allowable interest deduction on Schedule A, Form 1040?

a. $12,450.

b. $11,800.

c. $9,520.

d. $8,000.

The correct answer is (d). *(SPE 989 I-87)*
REQUIRED: The allowable interest deduction on Schedule A for 1991.
DISCUSSION: After 1990 personal interest is no longer allowed as an itemized deduction. Therefore, the $800 of credit card interest is not deductible. The $650 interest on the business truck loan would probably be deducted as business interest on Schedule C; it would not be a deduction on Schedule A. Points paid on a Veterans Administration loan are not deductible as interest. Note also, that points charged as compensation for services are not deductible as interest. Therefore, none of the $3,000 loan origination fees (points) would be deductible as interest. The $8,000 of home mortgage interest would be deductible in full. Mr. A's interest deduction on Schedule A for 1991 would be $8,000.

41. Jo Jackson, married and who files a joint return, purchased her principal residence for $500,000 in 1989 and the balance of her original mortgage is $400,000 in July 1991. Assume the fair market value of the home is $550,000 in July 1991. Which of the following is a correct statement of deductibility of interest on additional debt secured by the home?

a. Interest on a second mortgage (home equity loan) of $120,000 incurred in July 1991 is deductible in full as qualified residence interest.

b. Interest on a second mortgage (proceeds used to make a financial investment) of $85,000 incurred in July 1991 is deductible in full as qualified residence interest.

c. Interest on a second mortgage (home equity loan) of $200,000 incurred in July 1991 is limited to $150,000, the difference between the FMV and the acquisition indebtedness on the home.

d. Interest on a second mortgage of $700,000 incurred in July 1991 is fully deductible if the proceeds are used to remodel and add on to the house.

The correct answer is (b). *(Publisher)*
REQUIRED: The correct statement concerning the deduction for qualified residence interest.
DISCUSSION: Qualified residence interest is deductible in full, subject to limitations, and is defined in Sec. 163(h)(3). Effective for tax years beginning after December 31, 1987, the general rule classifies qualified residence interest as interest on two categories of debt secured by a taxpayer's principal or second residence. Acquisition indebtedness is debt used to purchase, build, or substantially improve the residence. The limit on acquisition indebtedness is $1,000,000. Home equity indebtedness is any debt secured by the residence other than acquisition indebtedness. Home equity indebtedness is limited to the lesser of $100,000 or the excess FMV of the residence over any acquisition indebtedness ($150,000).
Since Jo's $85,000 home equity debt is less than both the difference between the FMV and acquisition indebtedness of the residence, and the $100,000 home equity indebtedness limitation, the interest paid on the second mortgage is fully deductible. Note that the interest on the $85,000 of debt is deductible as qualified residence interest even if it is also investment interest.
Answers (a) and (c) are incorrect because home equity debt is limited to $100,000. Answer (d) is incorrect because total acquisition indebtedness is limited to $1,000,000.

42. Which of the following payments may be deducted in full in 1991 as interest expense on Form 1040, Schedule A?

1. Mortgage prepayment penalty
2. Interest relating to tax-exempt interest income
3. Installment plan interest for clothes purchases
4. Mortgage interest
5. Credit investigation fees

a. 1, 3, and 5.
b. 1 and 4.
c. 2, 4, and 5.
d. 3 and 4.

The correct answer is (b). *(SPE 1082 I-61)*
REQUIRED: The payments that may be deducted as interest expense.
DISCUSSION: Sec. 163 allows a deduction for certain interest paid or accrued within the taxable year on indebtedness. Interest is compensation for the use or forbearance of money. Personal interest is not deductible after 1990, but mortgage interest is generally deductible, provided that it is "qualified residence interest" as defined in Sec. 163(h)(3). Mortgage prepayment penalties have also been held to be compensation for the use of money and are deductible as interest.
Answers (a) and (c) are incorrect because credit investigation fees are not paid as compensation for the use or forbearance of money; they are paid for services to obtain a loan. Answer (c) is also incorrect because no deduction is permitted for interest on debt incurred to purchase or carry tax-exempt bonds (Sec. 265). Answers (a) and (d) are incorrect because after 1990, installment plan interest is not deductible as personal interest.

43. The amount of investment interest deductible in 1991 is limited to

a. Net investment income.
b. Net investment income plus $10,000.
c. Net investment income plus 10% of the excess, limited to $1,000.
d. Net investment income plus $4,000.

The correct answer is (a). *(Publisher)*
REQUIRED: The amount of investment interest deductible in 1991.
DISCUSSION: After 1986, Sec. 163(d) limited the deduction for investment interest to the net investment income for the year plus the following amount:

Year	Additional Amount Deductible
1989	20% of excess, limited to $2,000
1990	10% of excess, limited to $1,000
After 1990	-0-

44. Investment interest generally includes

  a. Interest expense for rental activity in which the taxpayer materially participates.
  b. Interest expense for an investment in property subject to a net lease.
  c. Interest expense to acquire a limited partnership interest.
  d. Interest expense to acquire stocks and bonds.

The correct answer is (d). *(Publisher)*
REQUIRED: The type of interest expense that constitutes investment interest.
DISCUSSION: Investment interest includes interest paid or accrued on indebtedness incurred or continued to purchase or carry property held for investment, and interest expense for a business activity in which the taxpayer does not materially participate, if that activity is not treated as a passive activity under Sec. 469 [Sec. 163(d)]. Interest to acquire stocks and bonds meets the first part of this definition as interest on indebtedness incurred to purchase property held for investment.

Answers (a) and (b) are incorrect because investment property does not include any interest in a passive activity under Sec. 469 and passive activity includes most rental activities. Answer (c) is incorrect because a limited partnership interest is also treated as a passive activity in most instances, so it is not investment property under Sec. 163(d).

45. The Tax Reform Act of 1986 placed several limitations on the deductions for interest paid. Which of the following types of interest payments, not allowed because of one of the limitations, may be carried over to the next year?

  a. Interest on a personal car loan.
  b. Interest on credit cards.
  c. Interest on a personal residence mortgage.
  d. Interest on money borrowed to buy stocks.

The correct answer is (d). *(SPE 987 I-60)*
REQUIRED: The type of disallowed interest deduction that may be carried over to a subsequent year.
DISCUSSION: The deduction for interest on investment indebtedness is limited by Sec. 163(d) to the amount of net investment income for taxable years after 1990. Any disallowed investment interest may be carried over and treated as investment interest paid or accrued in the succeeding taxable year [Sec. 163(d)(2)].

Answers (a) and (b) are incorrect because both are types of personal interest and any disallowed deduction is lost forever. Answer (c) is incorrect because any qualified residence interest in excess of the amount deductible is treated as nondeductible personal interest.

46. Mr. and Mrs. L are calendar-year, cash-basis taxpayers. They have their own business which they operate as a sole proprietorship. In addition, they own several investments including a 4-year-old rental property in whose operations they do not materially participate. In 1991, the rental property produced a net loss of $40,000 including interest expense of $90,000. In addition, Mr. and Mrs. L paid the following amounts of interest expense:

Interest on home mortgage	$ 4,500
Interest on business loan	35,500
Interest on loan to purchase 10,000 shares of ABC Corporation stock	45,000
	$85,000

Mr. and Mrs. L had no dividend or interest income in 1991. If they file a joint return, what is the total amount deductible as investment interest on their 1040 for 1991?

  a. $0.
  b. $2,000.
  c. $9,000.
  d. $37,500.

The correct answer is (a). *(SPE 1083 I-81)*
REQUIRED: The total investment interest deductible for 1991.
DISCUSSION: The deduction for interest on investment indebtedness is limited by Sec. 163(d) to the amount of net investment income in 1991. Net investment income is the excess of investment income over investment expenses. Gross income and any net gains on property held for investment are considered investment income to the extent such amounts are not derived from the conduct of a trade or business. Investment income does not include any income derived from a passive activity as defined in Sec. 469(c). Rental of real property is generally considered a passive activity. Investment expenses are those associated with the investment income.

Mr. and Mrs. L's ordinary interest is $40,000 ($4,500 home mortgage (qualified residence interest) + $35,500 business loan). Their investment interest is only the $45,000 on the loan to purchase stock. The $90,000 interest on the rental property is not considered investment interest under Sec. 163(d)(3)(B) because it is interest taken into account under Sec. 469 in computing income or loss on a passive activity. Since Mr. and Mrs. L have no net investment income, their investment interest deduction is $0 in 1991.

Module 9.3: Interest Expense

47. For the year ended December 31, 1991, David Roth, a married taxpayer filing a joint return, reported the following:

Investment income from dividends and interest	$24,000
Long-term capital gains on stock held for investment	25,000
Investment expenses	4,000
Interest expense on funds borrowed in 1991 to purchase investment property	70,000

What amount can Roth deduct in 1991 as investment interest expense?

a. $22,000.
b. $45,000.
c. $47,000.
d. $70,000.

The correct answer is (b). *(CPA 1180 Q-30)*
REQUIRED: The amount of investment interest the taxpayer may deduct in 1991.
DISCUSSION: Sec. 163(d) limits the deduction on investment interest to the amount of net investment income in 1991. Investment income includes gross income from property held for investment and any net gain attributable to the disposition of property held for investment, to the extent that such amounts are not derived from the conduct of a trade or business.

Roth had investment income of $49,000 ($24,000 + $25,000) and investment expenses of $4,000, or net investment income of $45,000. His investment interest deduction is limited to $45,000.

The $25,000 of disallowed investment interest ($70,000 − $45,000 deductible in 1991) may be carried over and treated as investment interest paid or accrued in the succeeding taxable year [Sec. 163(d)(2)].

48. Mr. B, a cash-basis taxpayer, signed a note for $1,200 on June 1, 1991 to buy his wife a fur coat. Interest was stated at 12% (which exceeds the federal rate) and Mr. B received $1,056 from the bank. Repayment is to be $100 a month starting on July 1, 1991. Mr. B also paid $18 of interest on his department store credit card. How much interest can Mr. B deduct in 1991?

a. $0.
b. $18.
c. $32.
d. $72.

The correct answer is (a). *(SPE 1080 I-80)*
REQUIRED: The amount of interest the taxpayer may deduct in 1991.
DISCUSSION: For tax years after 1990 no deduction is allowed for personal interest. The interest on the note used to buy the fur coat and the credit card interest are personal interest and Mr. B will have no interest deduction in 1991 arising from these items.

49. Charles Wolfe purchased the following long-term investments at par during 1991:

$20,000 general obligation bonds of Burlington County (wholly tax-exempt)
$10,000 debentures of Arrow Corporation

Wolfe financed these purchases by obtaining a $30,000 loan from Union National Bank. For 1991 Wolfe made the following interest payments:

Union National Bank	$3,600
Qualified residence interest on home mortgage	3,000
Interest on credit card charges	500

Wolfe's net investment income for the year was $10,000. What amount can Wolfe utilize as interest expense in calculating itemized deductions for 1991?

a. $4,200.
b. $4,250.
c. $4,700.
d. $7,100.

The correct answer is (a). *(CPA 582 P-51)*
REQUIRED: The amount of interest expense allowed in computing itemized deductions.
DISCUSSION: Sec. 163 allows a deduction for certain interest paid or accrued during the year on indebtednesses. Investment interest is deductible up to the taxpayer's net investment income for the year in 1991. Personal or consumer interest is disallowed beginning after 1990. Qualified residence interest is deductible under Sec. 163(h)(3). Sec. 265 disallows a deduction for interest on debt incurred to purchase or carry tax-exempt securities. Since Wolfe used two-thirds of the loan from Union National Bank to purchase tax-exempt securities, two-thirds of the interest on this loan is disallowed as a deduction. Wolfe may deduct

Union National Bank (1/3 × $3,600)	$1,200
Interest on home mortgage	3,000
Interest deduction	$4,200

Module 9.3: Interest Expense

50. All of the following statements regarding deductible interest expense are true except:

a. The day you mail a check for the payment of interest is the date the interest is paid.
b. "Points" paid by a seller are deductible as interest.
c. A mortgage prepayment penalty is deductible as interest.
d. "Points" paid by the borrower for the use of money are deductible as interest either ratably as the loan is repaid or in the year of payment.

The correct answer is (b). *(SPE 987 I-59)*
REQUIRED: The false statement concerning deductible interest expense.
DISCUSSION: Points are generally a fee paid for processing, placing, or finding a loan. Points are deductible as interest if considered compensation to a lender for the use of the money. However, points paid by a seller are not deductible as interest because the debt on which they are paid is not the debt of the seller. Instead, they are treated as a reduction of the selling price.
Answers (a), (c), and (d) are incorrect because each is a true statement concerning the deduction of interest expense.

51. Phil and Joan Crawley made the following payments during 1991:

Interest on bank loan (loan proceeds used to purchase U.S. Series HH savings bonds)	$4,000
Interest on installment charge accounts	500
Interest on home mortgage for period April 1 to December 31, 1991	2,700
Points paid to obtain conventional mortgage loan on April 1, 1991	900

The Crawleys had net investment income of $3,000 for the year. What is the maximum amount that the Crawleys can deduct as interest expense in calculating itemized deductions for 1991?

a. $3,600.
b. $6,600.
c. $7,600.
d. $7,650.

The correct answer is (b). *(CPA 581 P-41)*
REQUIRED: The maximum amount the taxpayers can deduct as interest expense.
DISCUSSION: Sec. 163 allows a deduction for certain interest paid or accrued during the taxable year on indebtedness. The interest on U.S. savings bonds is taxable, so Sec. 265 does not deny the interest deduction on the loan to purchase them. Since Sec. 163(d) limits investment interest to net investment income in 1991, the Crawleys may deduct only $3,000 of investment interest. The interest on the installment charge accounts is personal interest, none of which is deductible in 1991. The home mortgage interest is deductible assuming it is qualified residence interest as defined in Sec. 163(h)(3). Sec. 461(g) allows the deduction for points on a conventional mortgage loan even though the points represent prepaid interest. The Crawleys' maximum interest deduction is

Interest on bank loan	$3,000
Interest on home mortgage	2,700
Points	900
Interest deduction	$6,600

52. During 1991 William Clark was assessed a deficiency on his 1990 federal income tax return. As a result of this assessment he was required to pay $1,120 determined as follows:

Additional tax	$900
Late filing penalty	60
Negligence penalty	90
Interest	70

What portion of the $1,120 qualifies as itemized deductions for 1991?

a. $0.
b. $14.
c. $70.
d. $914.

The correct answer is (a). *(CPA 1180 Q-39)*
REQUIRED: The portion of the payment to the IRS which qualifies as an itemized deduction.
DISCUSSION: Federal income taxes and penalties are not deductible in any year. The $70 of interest paid on the amounts owed to the IRS is considered personal interest and is not deductible under Sec. 163, for tax years after 1990. Therefore, none of the amounts is deductible in 1991.

Module 9.3: Interest Expense 183

53. Mr. X, a farmer, borrowed $50,000 from the local bank. The loan was secured by a first mortgage on his farm where he resides. Proceeds from the loan were used to construct an addition to an equipment shed and to pay fertilizer costs for the following spring. How will Mr. X handle the interest paid on his mortgage?

   a. Deduct all interest on Schedule A.
   b. Deduct all interest on Schedule F.
   c. Prorate interest between farm property and residential property and deduct on Schedules A and F accordingly.
   d. Deduct all interest on either Schedule A or F as he chooses.

The correct answer is (b). *(SPE 1085 I-57)*
REQUIRED: The method of deducting farm interest.
DISCUSSION: Interest on a farm is generally deductible on Schedule F. Since the proceeds of this mortgage were used for farming operations, it is entirely deductible on Schedule F.
If the mortgage had been incurred to purchase the farm, then the interest would have to be prorated between farm property (deducted on Schedule F) and residential property (deducted on Schedule A).

54. During 1991, Ms. Nancy used corporate stock that she held for investment as collateral to borrow funds. The funds were used to purchase property for use in her business. Which of the following statements concerning the interest expense paid or incurred by Ms. Nancy is true?

   a. The expense is limited by the personal interest limitation.
   b. The expense is fully deductible in the year paid or incurred.
   c. The expense is limited by the investment interest limitation.
   d. The expense must be capitalized.

The correct answer is (b). *(SPE 989 II-42)*
REQUIRED: The correct statement regarding interest expense on a loan used to purchase business property when the loan was secured by investment property.
DISCUSSION: Interest expense incurred in a trade or business is deductible from gross income. It is the use to which borrowed funds are put, not the security behind the obligation, which is the determining factor in deciding whether interest is a business or nonbusiness expense deduction. Ms. Nancy used the borrowed funds to purchase property for use in her business, so the interest expense is deductible as a business expense without regard to the nature of the collateral.
Answer (a) is incorrect because the interest is not personal interest. Answer (c) is incorrect because the interest is business interest, not investment interest, in spite of the fact that the obligation was secured by investment property. Answer (d) is incorrect because the provisions of Sec. 263A do not apply to interest expense which is incurred on a loan used to buy property for use in a trade or business.

55. Mr. O is in the business of constructing houses. Owing to poor market conditions in his area, he offers zero interest financing to his prospective customers. Mr. and Mrs. B purchased one of Mr. O's houses for $40,000 and, as offered, financed their purchase with a noninterest-bearing 10-year mortgage to Mr. O for the purchase price. Since Mr. and Mrs. B's mortgage payments reduce principal only, they are not entitled to deduct any interest expense even if they itemize their deductions on Schedule A.

The correct answer is (F). *(SPE 1083 I-28)*
DISCUSSION: Sec. 483 imputes interest to deferred payments for the sale or exchange of property when there is unstated interest. Unstated interest is the excess of the sum of the payments over the sum of the present values of the payments using a discount rate equal to the appropriate federal rate. Imputed interest is determined in accordance with the original issue discount rules.

56. On August 18, 1991 Mr. Q's original home mortgage had a balance of $30,000. On that date he took out a $20,000 second mortgage. $5,000 was used for paving his driveway and $15,000 was used to buy a new car. After the improvement, Mr. Q's residence has an adjusted basis of $45,000 and a fair market value of $60,000. All of the interest paid by Mr. Q on his first and second mortgages is fully deductible.

The correct answer is (T). *(SPE 988 I-13)*
DISCUSSION: Mr. Q's first mortgage is acquisition indebtedness which has fully deductible interest. Of the second mortgage, $5,000 is acquisition indebtedness because it was used to improve the residence. The remaining $15,000 is home equity indebtedness which is limited to the lesser of the home's FMV over the acquisition indebtedness ($60,000 − $35,000) or $100,000. The home equity portion of the debt meets these limits and interest on this loan is also fully deductible.

57. On August 1, 1991, Ms. M, a cash-basis taxpayer, borrowed $2,000 from her bank, payable in 90 days at 15% annual interest. On October 31, 1991, Ms. M made the payment with a new note from her bank for $2,075 due January 31, 1992. The $75 is deductible as interest expense by Ms. M.

The correct answer is (F). *(SPE 986 I-27)*
DISCUSSION: A cash-basis taxpayer cannot deduct interest until paid. Paying interest with another debt instrument is only substitution of a debt. Only when the debt is paid with cash or other property will the interest be deductible.

58. On August 1, 1991, Mr. G borrowed $10,000 in order to meet margin requirements on his investment in the commodities market. On August 5, 1991 Mr. G bought five contracts of May 1992 corn and sold five contracts of June 1992 corn. On December 24, 1991, Mr. G sold the May 1992 contracts realizing a loss of $20,000 and bought five contracts of July 1992 corn. Interest on the loan amounted to $800 which Mr. G paid in 1991. Mr. G may deduct the $800 as interest expense on his 1991 tax return.

The correct answer is (F). *(SPE 1085 I-29)*
DISCUSSION: Under Sec. 263(g), interest on indebtedness incurred or continued to purchase or carry personal property which is part of a straddle is not deductible in general to the extent that interest and other carrying charges exceed ordinary income derived from the straddle property. The interest must be capitalized. Mr. G's corn contracts constitute a straddle because he has offsetting positions, i.e., he has contracts to buy and sell at the same time [Sec. 1092(c)].

59. Commitment fees that you incur to have business funds made readily available to you over a period of time, but not for actual use of the funds, are not deductible as interest payments. However, these fees are costs of getting your loan, and you can deduct a part of the fees in each tax year during the period of the loan.

The correct answer is (T). *(SPE 990 II-13)*
DISCUSSION: Commitment fees do not represent interest incurred so they are not deductible under Sec. 163. The expense is, however, deductible as a business expense under Sec. 162. Loan commitment fees in this case are capitalized and deducted ratably over the term of the loan since the outlay relates not to the tax year in which the loan is obtained but to the entire term of the loan.

9.4 Charitable Contributions

60. All of the following are qualified organizations for charitable contribution purposes except

  a. Civic league.
  b. War veterans' organization.
  c. Nonprofit volunteer fire company.
  d. Medical research organization.

The correct answer is (a). *(SPE 1085 I-58)*
REQUIRED: The organization that is not a qualified charitable organization.
DISCUSSION: A contribution is deductible only if made to a state or possession of the U.S. or any subdivisions thereof; a corporation, trust, community chest, fund, or foundation that is situated in the United States and is organized and operated exclusively for religious, charitable, scientific, literary, or educational purposes or for the prevention of cruelty to children or animals; a veterans' organization; a fraternal organization operating under the lodge system; or a cemetery company [Sec. 170(c)]. A civic league does not fall within these categories of qualified organizations.
Answer (b) is incorrect because a veterans' organization is listed as a qualified organization. Answer (c) is incorrect because a fire company is operated for charitable purposes. Answer (d) is incorrect because a medical research organization is operated for scientific and educational purposes.

Module 9.4: Charitable Contributions

61. Donations to all of the following organizations are deductible as charitable contributions except a

 a. Charitable community chest.

 b. Local chamber of commerce.

 c. Nonprofit hospital.

 d. Charitable fund of a domestic fraternal society operating under the lodge system.

The correct answer is (b). *(SPE 988 I-46)*
REQUIRED: The organization that is not a qualified charitable organization.
DISCUSSION: A contribution is deductible only if made to an organization described in Sec. 170(c). The organizations listed include a state or possession of the United States or any subdivisions thereof; a corporation, trust, community chest, fund, or foundation that is situated in the United States and is organized and operated exclusively for religious, charitable, scientific, literary, or educational purposes, or for the prevention of cruelty to children or animals; a veterans' organization; a fraternal organization operating under the lodge system; or a cemetery company. The Chamber of Commerce does not fall within these categories.
Answers (a), (c), and (d) are incorrect because each meets the criteria of a qualified organization described in Sec. 170(c).

62. During 1991, Mr. K, who is single and 45 years of age, made cash contributions of $500 to his church. Mr. K is taking the standard deduction on his 1991 return. What is the amount of Mr. K's deduction for charitable contributions?

 a. $500.

 b. $300.

 c. $75.

 d. $0.

The correct answer is (d). *(SPE 987 I-61)*
REQUIRED: The deduction for charitable contributions when the standard deduction is taken.
DISCUSSION: Charitable contributions are allowed in Sec. 170 as itemized deductions (below the line to arrive at taxable income). Itemized deductions are an election in lieu of taking the standard deduction. Since Mr. K claimed the standard deduction, he is not entitled to any additional deduction for a charitable contribution.

63. On December 20, 1991, Mr. and Mrs. Garrison purchased four tickets for a New Year's Eve party at their church, a qualified charitable organization. Each ticket cost $75 and had a fair market value of $50. The Garrisons gave two of the tickets to a needy family in the community. Mr. Garrison tended bar at the party from 8 PM to 4 AM and was paid $40. The usual charge for such services is $80. Immediately before midnight, Mr. Garrison pledged $200 to the building fund and delivered a check for that amount on January 2, 1992. Of the amounts described above, the total amount which the Garrisons can include as a charitable contribution deduction for 1991 on a joint return is

 a. $340.

 b. $140.

 c. $100.

 d. $50.

The correct answer is (c). *(CPA 574 Q-21)*
REQUIRED: The total amount the taxpayers can include as a charitable contribution deduction for 1991 on a joint return.
DISCUSSION: The taxpayers may deduct as a charitable contribution the excess of what they gave over the probable fair market value of what they received, or $100. The taxpayers gave $300 (4 tickets x $75 per ticket) to a qualified charitable organization in return for property with a fair market value of $200 (4 tickets with a fair market value of $50 each).
The donation of the two tickets to the needy family was not a donation to a qualified organization and therefore was not deductible. No deduction is allowable for a contribution of services [Reg. 1.170A-1(g)], so the taxpayer may not deduct the value of his time. The pledge of $200 is not deductible until actually paid, i.e., in 1992.

Module 9.4: Charitable Contributions

64. Mr. Q's records for 1991 contain the following information:

Donated stock having a fair market value of $1,000 to a qualified charitable organization. He acquired the stock 5 months previously at a cost of $800.

Paid $3,000 to a church school as a requirement for the enrollment of his daughter.

Paid $200 for annual homeowner's association dues.

Drove 300 miles in his personal auto that were directly related to services he performed for his church (actual costs were not available).

Paid $40 in parking fees and tolls in connection with the 300 miles.

What is Mr. Q's charitable contribution deduction for 1991?

  a. $876.
  b. $1,076.
  c. $4,036.
  d. $4,076.

The correct answer is (a). *(SPE 989 I-88)*
REQUIRED: The portion of the contributions deductible in 1991.
DISCUSSION: The amount of a charitable contribution of property is the fair market value of the property reduced by the amount of gain which would not have been long-term capital gain if the property had been sold by the taxpayer at its fair market value [Sec. 170(e)(1)(A)]. Accordingly, Q will be allowed a deduction of $800 ($1,000 − $200) on the contribution of the stock. The 300 miles driven in the personal auto directly related to services performed for the church and would, therefore, constitute a deductible contribution. The amount of the contribution would be $36 (300 x $.12) [Sec. 170(i)]. The $40 in parking fees and tolls associated with the travel would also qualify as a charitable contribution.

Contribution of stock ($1,000 − $200)	$800
Mileage (300 x $.12)	36
Parking fees and tolls	40
Total	$876

The tuition payments of $3,000 are required for the daughter's enrollment and do not qualify as a charitable contribution. Neither are the homeowner's association dues considered a charitable contribution under Sec. 170.

65. During 1991 Vincent Tally gave to the municipal art museum title to his private collection of rare books that was appraised and valued at $60,000. However, he reserved the right to the collection's use and possession during his lifetime. For 1991 he reported an adjusted gross income of $100,000. Assuming that this was his only contribution during the year, and that there were no carryovers from prior years, what amount can he deduct as contributions for 1991?

  a. $0.
  b. $30,000.
  c. $50,000.
  d. $60,000.

The correct answer is (a). *(CPA 1179 Q-37)*
REQUIRED: The current deduction for a contribution when the donor reserves the right to use the property during his/her lifetime.
DISCUSSION: Payment of a charitable contribution which consists of a future interest in tangible personal property is treated as made only when all intervening interests and rights to the actual possession and enjoyment of the property have expired or are held by persons other than the taxpayer or those related to the taxpayer [Sec. 170(a)(3) and (f)(3)]. Therefore, the contribution of the rare books will be treated as made only when Tally's intervening lifetime right to use and possess the books has terminated, i.e., at his death.

66. Under a written agreement between Mrs. Norma Lowe and an approved religious exempt organization, a 10-year-old girl from Vietnam came to live in Mrs. Lowe's home on August 1, 1991 in order to be able to start school in the U.S. on September 3, 1991. Mrs. Lowe actually spent $500 for food, clothing, and school supplies for the student during 1991, without receiving any compensation or reimbursement of costs. What portion of the $500 may Mrs. Lowe deduct on her 1991 income tax return as a charitable contribution?

  a. $0.
  b. $200.
  c. $250.
  d. $500.

The correct answer is (b). *(CPA 1181 Q-45)*
REQUIRED: The portion of the expenditures for the student's maintenance the taxpayer may deduct as a charitable contribution for 1991.
DISCUSSION: Amounts paid by a taxpayer to maintain an individual other than a dependent as a member of his/her household under a written agreement between the taxpayer and a qualified organization to provide educational opportunity for pupils or students in private homes are deductible up to $50 per month [Sec. 170(g)]. The student must attend full-time in the 12th or any lower grade of a qualified educational organization located in the United States. The deduction is only available for the months the child is a full-time student, which is 4 months in this case: September - December. Mrs. Lowe's expenditures qualify under this provision as a charitable contribution deduction of $200 ($50 x 4 months in 1991).

Module 9.4: Charitable Contributions

67. Mr. U is actively involved in church activities in his community. During 1991, he incurred the following church-related expenses:

Cash contributed to the church	$2,000
Round-trip mileage to attend church services (400 miles x .12)	48
Round-trip mileage to do church volunteer work (500 miles x .12)	60
Fair market value of used clothing given to church mission	500
Raffle tickets purchased from the church	200
Value of time and services contributed to the church	400

Mr. U's adjusted gross income is $25,000 and he itemizes his deductions on his tax return. What is his charitable contribution deduction?

a. $2,500.
b. $2,560.
c. $2,760.
d. $3,160.

The correct answer is (b). *(SPE 990 I-85)*
REQUIRED: The amount of the charitable contribution deduction for 1991.
DISCUSSION: The cash contribution of $2,000 to the church will be fully deductible. The $60 at the standard mileage rate for church-related volunteer work will also be deductible [Sec. 170(i)]. The clothing donated is capital gain property and the donation would be $500.

Cash	$2,000
Mileage for volunteer work	60
Value of used clothing	500
Total	$2,560

The mileage to and from church does not constitute a charitable contribution for Mr. U. The purchase price of raffle tickets, also, is not a deductible charitable contribution. The value of a service rendered to a charitable organization is not deductible as a contribution, either. Mr. U may not deduct, then, the $48 in mileage to attend church services, the cost of the raffle tickets or the $400 in services contributed to the church.

68. On December 15, 1991, Donald Calder made a contribution of $500 to a qualified charitable organization by charging the contribution on his bank credit card. Calder paid the $500 on January 20, 1992 upon receipt of the bill from the bank. In addition, Calder issued and delivered a promissory note for $1,000 to another qualified charitable organization on November 1, 1991 which he paid upon maturity 6 months later. If Calder itemizes his deductions, what portion of these contributions is deductible in 1991?

a. $0.
b. $500.
c. $1,000.
d. $1,500.

The correct answer is (b). *(CPA 1182 P-52)*
REQUIRED: The amount of contributions which is deductible in 1991.
DISCUSSION: Charitable contributions are deductible under Sec. 170 in the year in which payment is made. A promissory note is not payment of a charitable contribution until the note is paid, since it is merely a promise made by the donor to the charitable organization. However, a contribution made by bank credit card is considered payment in the year charged even though the credit card obligation may not be paid until the following year. This is because the charitable organization is entitled to the funds and the donor is obligated to a third party (the bank). As a result, $500 of the contributions are deductible in 1991 for the credit card charge, but none for the promissory note until it is paid.

69. An individual may deduct contributions to most charities up to 50% of adjusted gross income. However, some contributions have other limits. These limits are

a. 40% and 30%.
b. 30% and 10%.
c. 30% and 20%.
d. 40% and 20%.

The correct answer is (c). *(SPE 1082 I-62)*
REQUIRED: The percentage limitations for charitable contributions other than the 50% limitation.
DISCUSSION: The annual limit for the deduction of an individual's contributions to most charities is 50% of adjusted gross income for the year [Sec. 170(b)(1)(A)]. Another limitation is 30% of adjusted gross income for contributions to charities to which the 50% limitation does not apply [Sec. 170(b)(1)(B)], and also for contributions of long-term capital gain property which is included at full fair market value and not reduced by any of its appreciation [Sec. 170(b)(1)(C)]. The third limitation is 20% of the taxpayer's adjusted gross income for long-term capital gain property given to charities to which the 50% limitation does not apply (e.g., private nonoperating foundations) [Sec. 170(b)(1)(D)].

Module 9.4: Charitable Contributions

70. The following information is available for Rufus Hirsch and his wife Mavis who file a joint return for 1991:

	Rufus	Mavis
Adjusted gross income	$20,000	$5,000
Cash contributions to recognized charities	600	3,000
Cash contributions to political parties	1,000	100

What is the maximum amount of the above that they can deduct in calculating itemized deductions for 1991?

a. $3,100.
b. $3,600.
c. $4,100.
d. $4,700.

The correct answer is (b). *(CPA 578 Q-27)*
REQUIRED: The maximum amount the taxpayers can deduct in calculating itemized deductions.
DISCUSSION: By filing a joint income tax return, the Hirsches' charitable deduction limitation is $12,500 (50% x combined adjusted gross income of $25,000). Political parties are not qualified organizations under Sec. 170. Therefore, the taxpayers' charitable contribution to qualified organizations is $3,600 ($600 by Rufus and $3,000 by Mavis). The taxpayers may deduct the full $3,600, since this amount is within their charitable contribution deduction limitation.

71. Mr. Q is single and has adjusted gross income of $7,250 in 1991. He made the following contributions in December 1991:

Appraisal fee on donated property	$ 250
Nonprofit hospital - cash	400
War veterans' organization - land held as inventory - fair market value	4,000
basis	2,200
Domestic fraternal society (to be used exclusively for a qualified charitable purpose) - cash	850
Value of land used for church picnic	300

What is his allowable contribution deduction?

a. $2,575.
b. $3,625.
c. $3,700.
d. $4,000.

The correct answer is (a). *(SPE 1081 I-78)*
REQUIRED: The taxpayer's allowable charitable contribution deduction.
DISCUSSION: An appraisal fee paid on donated property is not an amount paid to a qualified organization and therefore is not deductible as a charitable contribution. It is deductible as a miscellaneous itemized deduction. The value of the use of the taxpayer's land is also not deductible [Sec. 170(f)(1)]. The deduction for the $2,200 contribution to the war veterans' organization and the $850 contribution to the domestic fraternal society are limited to 30% of the taxpayer's adjusted gross income [Sec. 170(b)(1)(B)], since these are charitable organizations to which the 50% limit does not apply. The taxpayer may also deduct the $400 contribution to the nonprofit hospital (a 50% charity).

War veterans' organization	$2,200	
Fraternal society	850	
Limited to 30% of AGI ($7,250)	$3,050	$2,175
Nonprofit hospital		400
Allowable contribution deduction (limited to 50% of $7,250 = $3,625)		$2,575

72. Mr. E donated stock which he had held for 5 months to his church. The stock had a fair market value of $1,000 at the time of the gift, but had only cost Mr. E $800. What amount can he deduct as a charitable contribution?

a. $200.
b. $600.
c. $800.
d. $1,000.

The correct answer is (c). *(SPE 1080 I-57)*
REQUIRED: The amount the taxpayer may deduct as a charitable contribution.
DISCUSSION: The amount of a charitable contribution of property is the fair market value of the property reduced by the amount of gain which would not have been long-term capital gain if the property contributed had been sold by the taxpayer at its fair market value [Sec. 170(e)(1)]. The fair market value of the stock at the time of the contribution was $1,000, and the amount of the gain which would not have been a long-term capital gain was $200 ($1,000 FMV − $800 basis). Accordingly, the amount E can deduct as a charitable contribution is $800 ($1,000 − $200).

73. For 1991, Ms. S had adjusted gross income of $20,000. She contributed $12,000 to a church and $3,000 to a private nonoperating foundation which is subject to the 30% limitation. What is the amount of B's charitable contribution for 1991 and the amount to be carried over?

	Deduction for 1991	Carryover
a.	$10,000	$0
b.	$10,000	$2,000
c.	$10,000	$5,000
d.	$15,000	$0

The correct answer is (c). *(SPE 989 I-89)*
REQUIRED: The charitable contribution deduction for the current year and the amount to be carried over to the following year.
DISCUSSION: All $15,000 ($12,000 + $3,000) of contributions made by Ms. S are deductible contributions. However, the deduction allowed in any tax year is limited to a percentage of the taxpayer's "contribution base" (AGI computed without regard to NOL carrybacks). The percentage is determined by the type of property contributed and the type of organization to which the property is contributed [Sec. 170(b)(1)]. The $12,000 in contributions to a church would be subject to a 50% limitation while the other $3,000 in contributions is subject to a 30% limitation.

Contribution to church	$ 12,000
Contribution to nonoperating foundation subject to $6,000 ($20,000 x 30%) limitation	3,000
Total contributions	$ 15,000
Less deduction for current year subject to $10,000 ($20,000 x 50%) limitation	(10,000)
Carryforward to 1992	$ 5,000

Note that the carryforward to 1992 would consist of the following amounts and can be carried forward up to 5 years.

Contribution subject to 50% limitation	$ 2,000
Contribution subject to 30% limitation	3,000
Total carryforward	$ 5,000

74. Malcolm owned real property which he held for investment for several years. The property had a fair market value of $20,000 and a basis of $10,000. In 1991 Malcolm contributed this property to a hospital qualifying for a charitable contribution. If Malcolm's adjusted gross income in 1991 is $30,000, he may deduct

a. $20,000 in 1991.

b. $15,000 in 1991 with no carryover.

c. $9,000 in 1991 with no carryover.

d. $10,000 in 1991 with no carryover or $9,000 in 1991 with an $11,000 carryover.

The correct answer is (d). *(Publisher)*
REQUIRED: The charitable contribution deduction for long-term capital gain real property.
DISCUSSION: The amount of a charitable contribution of the real property is the fair market value of the real property. Under Sec. 170(b)(1)(C), the deduction is limited to 30% of adjusted gross income because the contribution was not reduced by the long-term capital gain portion. 30% of $30,000 adjusted gross income is a contribution limitation of $9,000 in 1991. A 5-year carryover of the remaining $11,000 is allowed.

However, Sec. 170(b)(1)(C) also allows a taxpayer to reduce the contribution by the long-term capital gain portion and be subject to the 50% rather than the 30% limit. If Malcolm so elects, he reduces the amount of the contribution from $20,000 to $10,000. The entire amount would be deductible under the 50% limit, but there would be no carryover.

Module 9.4: Charitable Contributions

75. Stuart Green had adjusted gross income during the year of $200,000 and made contributions to qualified charities as follows:

	Basis	FMV
Cash	$10,000	$10,000
Inventory	6,000	8,000
IBM stock	8,000	5,000

Green's charitable contribution deduction is

a. $21,000.
b. $23,000.
c. $24,000.
d. $26,000.

The correct answer is (a). *(I.S. Greenberg)*
REQUIRED: The charitable contribution deduction for the property contributed.
DISCUSSION: The taxpayer is allowed a deduction for the full amount of the cash contributed ($10,000). Inventory contributed to a charitable organization is considered ordinary income property. If such property is contributed, Sec. 170(e)(1)(A) limits the deduction to its fair market value less the amount of ordinary income that would have been reported if the property had been sold (in most instances, the deduction is limited to the cost basis of the property). The deduction for inventory is thus limited to $6,000. The IBM stock is valued at its fair market value ($5,000) because there would be no long-term capital gain if sold at its FMV. Green's total deduction is $21,000 ($10,000 cash + $6,000 inventory + $5,000 IBM stock).
Note that Green will not be able to deduct the loss on the stock (FMV less than basis). Thus, such assets may not make a good choice for a charitable contribution.

76. Ruth Lewis has adjusted gross income of $100,000 for 1991 and itemizes her deductions. On September 1, 1991, she made a contribution to a private nonoperating foundation (not a 50% charity) of stock held for investment for 2 years that cost $25,000 and had a fair market value of $70,000. The foundation sold the stock for $70,000 on the same date. Assume that Lewis made no other contributions during 1991. How much should Lewis claim as a charitable contribution deduction for 1991?

a. $50,000.
b. $30,000.
c. $25,000.
d. $20,000.

The correct answer is (d). *(CPA 583 P-52)*
REQUIRED: The amount of charitable contribution deduction for stock contributed to a private nonoperating foundation.
DISCUSSION: Generally, contributions to private operating foundations are limited to 30% of the taxpayer's adjusted gross income. But contributions of long-term capital gain property to private nonoperating foundations are limited to 20% of the taxpayer's adjusted gross income [Sec. 170(b)(1)(D)]. Lewis's charitable contribution deduction should be limited to $20,000 (20% x $100,000).
For deduction purposes, the contribution is equal to $25,000 ($70,000 fair market value − $45,000 long-term capital gain) because it is being made to a private nonoperating foundation [Sec. 170(e)(1)(B)]. $20,000 can be deducted in 1991. The remaining $5,000 can be carried forward for up to 5 years.

77. All of the following statements relating to a contribution of $500 or more of charitable deduction property (property other than money or publicly traded securities) are true except:

a. An organization that received such property in July 1990 and sells it in December 1991 must file a special return Form 8282, Donee Information Return, within 90 days after the disposition.

b. An organization selling such property must provide the donor with a copy of Form 8282, Donee Information Return, or be subject to a penalty.

c. The donor of such property is required to get a qualified appraisal if the claimed value of the property exceeds $1,000.

d. The organization receiving such property is not a qualified appraiser for the purpose of making a qualified appraisal.

The correct answer is (c). *(SPE 987 IV-78)*
REQUIRED: The false statement concerning a noncash charitable contribution.
DISCUSSION: A donor of noncash charitable contributions is not required to obtain a qualified appraisal unless the value of the property exceeds $5,000. If the value of the property exceeds $500 but is not over $5,000, then the person making the contribution must retain a description of the property including its fair market value and how the fair market value was computed.
Answer (a), (b), and (d) are incorrect because each is a true statement.

Module 9.4: Charitable Contributions

78. In 1990, T contributed $8,000 cash and also some appreciated intangible capital gain property, which T had held for 2 years, to the University of Illinois. The appreciated capital gain property had a basis to T of $3,000 and a FMV of $5,000. In 1991 T contributed $1,000 cash to the University. For 1990 and 1991, T had AGI of $20,000 and $8,000, respectively. T itemized his deductions in both years. What is T's charitable deduction carryforward, if any, to 1992?

   a. $0.
   b. $600.
   c. $2,400.
   d. $3,400.

The correct answer is (b). *(J.G. Burns)*
REQUIRED: The charitable contribution carryforward to 1992.
DISCUSSION: All contributions were made to a 50% charitable organization. Under Sec. 170(b)(1)(C), intangible long-term capital gain property is subject to a 30% limitation that also applies to carryforwards. (Note that the taxpayer can elect the 50% limitation with a contribution amount of the fair market value minus the long-term capital gain.)

Calculation for 1990

Cash	$ 8,000
Capital gain property subject to $6,000 ($20,000 x .30) limitation	5,000
	$13,000
Deduction subject to $10,000 ($20,000 x .50) limitation	(10,000)
Carryforward subject to 30% limit	$ 3,000

Calculation for 1991

Cash	$ 1,000
$3,000 carryforward with $2,400 ($8,000 x .30) limitation	2,400
Deduction, subject to $4,000 ($8,000 x .50) limitation	$ 3,400

The $2,400 limitation results in a carryforward to 1992 of

Carryover from 1990	$ 3,000
1991 deduction of 1990 carryforward	(2,400)
Carryforward to 1992 still subject to a 30% limitation	$ 600

79. The Veterans of Foreign Wars of the United States is a qualified charitable organization.

The correct answer is (T). *(SPE 1077 I-116)*
DISCUSSION: A post or organization of war veterans organized in the United States and no part of the net earnings of which inures to the benefit of any private shareholder or individual is a qualified organization [Sec. 170(c)(3)].

80. A donation made to the "Boy Scouts of Mexico" is a deductible charitable contribution.

The correct answer is (F). *(SPE 1077 I-9)*
DISCUSSION: Since the donation is not made to an organization created or organized in the United States or any of its possessions, the donation is not to a qualified organization under Sec. 170(c)(2) and is not deductible. Limited contributions to foreign charities are deductible under U.S. tax treaties. Mexico, however, is not one of the eligible countries.

81. An appraisal fee, paid to determine the fair market value of property donated to a charitable organization, is deductible as a charitable contribution and is subject to the limitations thereon.

The correct answer is (F). *(SPE 987 I-21)*
DISCUSSION: The appraisal fee incurred in determining the fair market value of property given to a qualified organization is not an amount paid to such organization or an expenditure incident to rendering services to the organization, so it is not deductible as a charitable contribution (Rev. Rul. 67-461). However, it is deductible as a miscellaneous itemized deduction subject to a 2% of AGI limitation.

82. Mr. C contributed $100 to the presidential campaign in 1991. Mr. C can deduct the $100.

The correct answer is (F). *(SPE 1081 I-30)*
DISCUSSION: Sec. 170(c)(2)(D) specifically provides that an organization is not qualified if it participates in any political campaign on behalf of any candidate for public office.

83. An individual donates land that he has held for 2 years to his town. The fair market value of this land may qualify as a charitable contribution.

The correct answer is (T). *(SPE 1077 I-84)*
DISCUSSION: The charitable contribution of property is valued at fair market value, although the annual deduction for long-term capital gain property is limited to 30% of the taxpayer's contribution base (adjusted gross income computed without regard to a net operating loss carryback) [Sec. 170(b)(1)(C)].

84. In 1991, Mr. F, a farmer, contributed a mower that he used on his farm to a church. The fair market value of the mower is $400. Mr. F purchased it in 1988 for $600 and has claimed $300 depreciation. The amount of Mr. F's contribution deduction is $100.

The correct answer is (F). *(SPE 1081 I-27)*
DISCUSSION: The amount of any charitable contribution of property must be reduced by the amount of gain which would not have been long-term capital gain if the property had been sold [Sec. 170(e)]. If the taxpayer had sold the mower for its fair market value of $400, he would have realized a gain of $100 ($400 realized − $300 basis). This $100 gain would have been characterized as ordinary income under the recapture provisions of Sec. 1245. Thus, the $400 FMV of the mower is reduced by the $100 of gain which would not be long-term capital gain if Mr. F sold the property, giving him a charitable contribution deduction of $300.

85. Farmer A donated a hog that he had raised and was holding for sale to his church for its annual picnic on July 3, 1991. Farmer A can deduct the fair market value of the hog as a charitable contribution on his 1991 return.

The correct answer is (F). *(SPE 987 I-22)*
DISCUSSION: Inventory contributed to a charitable organization is considered ordinary income property. Sec. 170(e) limits the deduction to its fair market value less the amount of ordinary income that would have been reported if the property had been sold (in most instances, the deduction is limited to the cost basis of the property). A farmer who raises animals generally has no cost basis in them because the cost of raising animals is deducted currently. Therefore, Farmer A would have no basis in the hog and would not be able to claim any deduction for the charitable contribution.

86. Mrs. S donated two pints of her blood to the Red Cross. The fair market value per pint on the dates the blood was given was $25 and $30. The $55 is deductible by Mrs. S as a noncash contribution.

The correct answer is (F). *(SPE 986 I-29)*
DISCUSSION: A person has no basis in one's own blood. If sold, the gain would not be long-term capital gain according to the IRS. Therefore, the contribution is reduced by the entire gain, i.e., its value, under Sec. 170(e)(1)(A).

87. Child care expenses that are incurred while you perform services for a qualified charitable organization are not deductible.

The correct answer is (T). *(SPE 990 I-23)*
DISCUSSION: Expenses incurred by taxpayers in caring for their children while performing gratuitous services for charitable organizations are nondeductible personal expenses under Sec. 262 and, therefore, not deductible as charitable contributions (Treasury Information Release 1267).

9.5 Casualty and Theft Losses

See Chapter 6 for Casualty and Theft Losses incurred in a business.

88. Which of the following are casualty losses for tax purposes?

1. Damage to fur coat by moths
2. Water damage to rugs caused by bursting water heater
3. Damage to old water heater that burst
4. Damage to residence by earthquake
5. Citrus trees killed by a freeze

   a. 1, 3, and 5.
   b. 2, 3, and 4.
   c. 2, 4, and 5.
   d. 2, 3, 4, and 5.

The correct answer is (c). *(SPE 1077 I-185)*
REQUIRED: The losses that are casualty losses for tax purposes.
DISCUSSION: A casualty is defined as the complete or partial destruction of property resulting from some sudden, unexpected, or unusual cause. Water damage to rugs caused by a bursting water heater, damage to a residence by earthquake, and freeze damage to citrus trees are all losses resulting from sudden and unexpected events. Each is a casualty loss for tax purposes.
  Answers (a), (b), and (d) are incorrect because items 1 and 3 are not sudden events. Damage to a fur coat by moths and damage to an old water heater that burst are losses from events that occur slowly over time. Hence, they are not casualty losses for tax purposes.

89. Which of the following events is a casualty loss that is deductible?

   a. Damage to a house from wood rotting.
   b. Decline in value of a home due to mudslides which damaged only neighboring homes.
   c. Damage to a building from a fire which was intentionally set by an enemy of the taxpayer.
   d. Loss of a seawall from the waves continually striking it.

The correct answer is (c). *(Publisher)*
REQUIRED: The event that is a casualty for tax deduction purposes.
DISCUSSION: A casualty is defined as the complete or partial destruction of property from a sudden, unexpected, or unusual cause. A fire is a sudden and unexpected event causing damage to a building. It does not matter that the fire was intentionally set as long as it was not intentionally set by the taxpayer incurring the loss.
  Answer (a) is incorrect because damage from rotting wood is not considered a loss from a sudden event. Answer (b) is incorrect because it has been held that physical damage to the taxpayer's property must occur to sustain a casualty loss. Answer (d) is incorrect because the loss of or damage to a seawall from the continual pounding by waves is not from a sudden or unexpected event.

90. Mr. A lives in an area that had been hit by a flood in 1991. Mr. A's house was not damaged. An appraisal of A's property indicates the following:

Cost	$50,000
Improvements	5,000
Fair market value, December 31, 1991	45,000

In addition, A spent $3,500 for a drainage system around his house because of potential flooding. Without considering any limitations, what is the amount of A's deductible casualty loss for 1991?

   a. $0.
   b. $3,500.
   c. $10,000.
   d. $13,500.

The correct answer is (a). *(SPE 988 I-72)*
REQUIRED: The deductible casualty loss for reduced value in a residence from neighborhood flooding.
DISCUSSION: A casualty is defined as the complete or partial destruction of property from a sudden, unexpected, or unusual cause. Although a flood is a sudden cause, it has been held that physical damage to the taxpayer's property must occur to sustain a casualty loss. Since the value of Mr. A's property decreased only because there was a flood in the surrounding area and not because the house was actually flooded itself, no casualty loss is available. The amount spent to add a drainage system around the house is a capital improvement which increases the cost basis in his residence.

91. All of the following events ordinarily qualify as casualty losses except

a. Flood damage.
b. Sonic boom damage.
c. Vandalism damage.
d. Termite damage.

The correct answer is (d). *(SPE 987 II-53)*
REQUIRED: The event that is not a casualty event.
DISCUSSION: A casualty is defined as the complete or partial destruction of property from a sudden, unexpected, or unusual cause. Termite damage is not a sudden event and does not qualify as a casualty.
Answers (a), (b), and (c) are incorrect because each is a sudden event which will qualify as a casualty.

92. Several years ago, Mr. B purchased an antique vase for his personal use at a flea market sale for $500. This vase was stolen on July 1, 1991, when its fair market value was $1,000. Mr. B had insurance on the vase, but only for $300 with no deductible amount. B had no other casualty losses. What is the amount of B's allowable casualty loss for 1991, disregarding the limitation based on adjusted gross income?

a. $100.
b. $200.
c. $500.
d. $600.

The correct answer is (a). *(SPE 989 I-91)*
REQUIRED: The amount of the casualty loss deduction for 1991 without regard to the adjusted gross income limitation.
DISCUSSION: Disregarding the adjusted gross income limitation, Mr. B's casualty loss deduction would be $100 computed as follows:

Adjusted basis in vase	$ 500
Less insurance reimbursement	(300)
Loss sustained	$ 200
Less floor amount for casualty losses	(100)
Casualty loss deduction	$ 100

Note that casualty losses are generally limited to the amount that each loss exceeds $100. After the $100 floor limitation is applied to each loss, all losses are aggregated and are deductible to the extent that they exceed 10% of the taxpayer's adjusted gross income [Sec. 165(h)(2)].

93. Kultchurd went to a museum wearing a very expensive ring. She was jostled several times in crowds and upon leaving the museum, she realized the ring was missing. Kultchurd had bought the ring several years earlier for $5,000 and its fair market value before it was lost was $9,000. What is Kultchurd's theft loss deduction?

a. $0.
b. $4,900.
c. $5,000.
d. $8,900.

The correct answer is (a). *(Publisher)*
REQUIRED: The theft loss deduction for lost property.
DISCUSSION: Theft includes larceny, embezzlement, and robbery [Reg. 1.165-8(d)]. It does not include misplacing property or other loss by inadvertence. Without some proof or specific indication that a theft actually occurred, there can be no deduction for a theft loss.

94. Which of the conditions below is not required for a taxpayer to claim a casualty loss deduction if his/her personal residence is demolished or relocated after a disaster?

a. The residence is damaged as a result of the disaster.
b. The residence is located in an area designated to warrant assistance under the Disaster Relief Act of 1974.
c. The residence has been rendered unsafe for use as a residence owing to the disaster.
d. Within 120 days of the disaster relief determination, the state or local government orders the residence demolished or relocated.

The correct answer is (a). *(S. Byrd)*
REQUIRED: The condition that is not a requirement for a casualty loss deduction if a personal residence is demolished or relocated after a disaster.
DISCUSSION: Sec. 165(k) allows a casualty loss deduction to taxpayers whose personal residences are demolished or relocated as a result of a disaster. The requirements for the casualty loss treatment are that the residence be located in an area designated to warrant assistance under the Disaster Relief Act of 1974, the residence has been rendered unsafe for use as a residence owing to the disaster, and the taxpayer is ordered by the state or local government, not later than 120 days after the federal determination, to demolish or relocate the residence.
However, there is not a requirement that the residence actually be damaged.

Module 9.5: Casualty and Theft Losses

95. The following information pertains to Cole's personal residence, which sustained casualty fire damage in 1991:

Adjusted basis	$150,000
Fair market value immediately before the fire	200,000
Fair market value immediately after the fire	180,000
Fire damage repairs paid for by Cole in 1991	10,000

The house was uninsured. Before consideration of any "floor" or other limitation on tax deductibility, the amount of this 1991 casualty loss was

a. $30,000.
b. $20,000.
c. $10,000.
d. $0.

The correct answer is (b). *(CPA 1188 Q-15)*
REQUIRED: The casualty loss (before any limitations) when a residence is damaged by fire.
DISCUSSION: The amount of a casualty loss under Sec. 165 is the lesser of the decrease in the fair market value of the property resulting from the casualty or the taxpayer's adjusted basis in the property. The decrease in the fair market value of Cole's residence is $20,000 ($200,000 − $180,000). This is less than the adjusted basis, so the casualty loss is $20,000.
The repairs paid by Cole are not an additional loss. Instead, they are an effort by Cole to replace the loss which has already occurred.

96. Keith wrecked his speedboat on Lake George during the summer of 1991. Damage to the boat was estimated at $30,000. Original cost was $25,000. The boat was partially insured and Keith received an insurance reimbursement of $15,000. Keith's adjusted gross income is $50,000 and he had no other losses during the year. What amount can Keith deduct on his 1991 tax return?

a. $4,900.
b. $5,000.
c. $9,900.
d. $14,900.

The correct answer is (a). *(M.F. Premont)*
REQUIRED: The amount of a casualty loss to be deducted on the 1991 tax return.
DISCUSSION: Personal losses are allowed only to the extent that total losses exceed 10% of adjusted gross income and to the extent that each loss exceeds $100. The amount of the casualty loss is the lesser of the asset's basis ($25,000) or the decrease in fair market value ($30,000). Hence, the loss is limited to $25,000, reduced by the insurance reimbursement of $15,000, the $100 limitation, and 10% of AGI.

Loss	$25,000
Less: Insurance	(15,000)
$100 per casualty	(100)
10% of AGI	(5,000)
Deductible casualty loss	$ 4,900

97. In October 1991 John Dill's wife was involved in an accident while driving the family automobile. Damage to the automobile was estimated at $300. Though fully insured, Dill was fearful that his automobile insurance rates would rise as a result of the accident. He did not notify his insurance company and had the automobile repaired at his own expense. What amount can he deduct as a casualty loss on his income tax return for 1991 if his adjusted gross income is $1,000?

a. $0.
b. $100.
c. $200.
d. $300.

The correct answer is (a). *(CPA 1180 Q-36)*
REQUIRED: The amount the taxpayer may deduct as a casualty loss when an insurance claim is not made.
DISCUSSION: A deduction for a personal casualty loss is allowed by Sec. 165(c). However, any loss is deductible only to the extent it is not compensated for by insurance or otherwise. Since Dill's automobile was fully insured, the loss he sustained resulted from his choice not to collect the insurance proceeds rather than from a casualty. Sec. 165(h)(4)(E) requires an insurance claim to be timely filed if the loss is covered by insurance.

98. In 1985 Mr. P bought a residential lot for $8,000 and built a house on it at a cost of $52,000. He added an inground swimming pool costing $15,000 in 1987. The house was destroyed by fire in 1991 and he received a $45,000 insurance settlement. The fair market value of the property was determined to be $115,000 immediately before the fire, and $25,000 immediately after. Mr. P's adjusted gross income for 1991 was $65,000. What is the amount of his nonbusiness casualty loss deduction?

a. $8,500.
b. $15,400.
c. $23,400.
d. $38,400.

The correct answer is (c). *(SPE 987 I-79)*
REQUIRED: The casualty loss deduction when a residence is destroyed by fire leaving land and a swimming pool intact.
DISCUSSION: The amount of a casualty loss under Sec. 165 is the lesser of the decrease in the fair market value of the property resulting from a casualty or the adjusted basis. In the case of a residence (not used for business purposes), no allocation is required among the land and improvements [Reg. 1.165-7(b)(2)]. Therefore, Mr. P's basis of the residence for purposes of determining the casualty loss is $75,000 ($8,000 + $52,000 + $15,000). Since this is less than the decrease in fair market value of $90,000 ($115,000 − $25,000), the casualty loss is $75,000.

The casualty loss must be reduced by the insurance proceeds and a deduction is only allowed to the extent the loss exceeds $100 and to the extent it also exceeds 10% of the taxpayer's adjusted gross income. Mr. P's casualty loss is $23,400 as computed below:

Loss	$75,000
Less: Insurance	(45,000)
$100 per occurrence	(100)
10% of AGI	(6,500)
Deductible casualty loss	$23,400

99. Mr. F constructed a building at a cost of $40,000 on land that he leases. He uses half of the building for business purposes and lives in the other half. In 1991, a flood damaged the entire building. The fair market value of the building was $38,000 immediately before the flood and $32,000 immediately after. Mr. F had deducted $2,400 in depreciation on the business portion of the building. Mr. F's insurance company reimbursed him $4,000 for the damage. Mr. F's adjusted gross income for 1991 was $25,000. What is the amount of Mr. F's deductible business casualty loss and personal casualty loss?

a. $1,000 personal; $0 business.
b. $0 personal; $1,000 business.
c. $900 personal; $1,000 business.
d. $1,000 personal; $1,000 business.

The correct answer is (b). *(SPE 986 II-72)*
REQUIRED: The taxpayer's deductible personal and business casualty losses for 1991.
DISCUSSION: Personal casualty losses of an individual are deductible to the extent that the loss from each casualty exceeds $100. The amount of either a personal or business casualty loss is the lesser of the decrease in fair market value or the adjusted basis of the property, less any insurance reimbursement. If there are no personal casualty gains, the aggregate of all casualty losses for the year are deductible only to the extent they exceed 10% of adjusted gross income [Sec. 165(h)(2)].

Personal

Lesser of adjusted basis ($20,000) or decrease in FMV ($3,000)	$3,000
Less: Insurance reimbursement	(2,000)
$100 per occurrence	(100)
10% of AGI	(2,500)
Deductible casualty loss	No deduction

Business

Lesser of adjusted basis ($20,000 − $2,400 = $17,600) or decrease in fair market value ($19,000 − $16,000 = $3,000)	$3,000
Less insurance reimbursement	(2,000)
Deductible casualty loss	$1,000

Module 9.5: Casualty and Theft Losses

100. Determine the deductible casualty loss for Mr. J for 1991. Mr. J's adjusted gross income is $40,000.

Asset	J's Adj. Basis	FMV Before	FMV After	Ins. Reimbursement
T	$ 300	$ 2,000	$ 500	$ 50
O	14,000	10,000	4,000	1,000
P	600	3,000	2,775	125

Each asset was damaged in a separate casualty during 1991. All casualty losses were nonbusiness personal property losses and none occurred in a federally declared disaster area.

a. $13,725.
b. $9,725.
c. $2,550.
d. $1,050.

The correct answer is (d). *(SPE 984 I-83)*
REQUIRED: The deductible casualty loss for 1991.
DISCUSSION: Each loss must be calculated separately, and the $100 limitation applies to each loss [Sec. 165(h)].

	Asset		
	T	O	P
Loss amount (lesser of decrease in FMV or adjusted basis)	$ 300	$6,000	$ 225
Less:			
Insurance	(50)	(1,000)	(125)
$100 floor	(100)	(100)	(100)
Casualty loss	$ 150	$4,900	$ 0

The total casualty loss of $5,050 ($150 + $4,900 + $0) is deductible to the extent it exceeds $4,000 (10% x $40,000 adjusted gross income). Accordingly, J's deduction for 1991 is $1,050.

101. In 1991, Mr. Gear completely demolished his personal automobile in a car accident. Damage to the auto was estimated at $30,000. Gear purchased the car in 1989 for $28,000. Gear received an insurance reimbursement of $25,000. Gear's adjusted gross income for 1991 was $25,000 and he incurred no other losses during the year. What amount can he deduct as a casualty loss on his 1991 income tax return?

a. $400.
b. $500.
c. $2,900.
d. $3,000.

The correct answer is (a). *(SPE 990 I-88)*
REQUIRED: The amount of the taxpayer's deduction for a casualty loss.
DISCUSSION: A deduction is allowed for personal casualty losses only to the extent the loss from each casualty exceeds $100 and the aggregate of all such losses during the tax year exceeds 10% of the taxpayer's adjusted gross income [Sec. 165(h)]. The amount of a casualty loss is the lesser of the decrease in fair market value as a result of the casualty or the adjusted basis of the property. Gear's casualty loss was $28,000 (adjusted basis in the car) as this is less than the $30,000 decrease in the fair market value of the car.

Loss on car	$28,000
Less: Insurance	(25,000)
$100 per occurrence	(100)
10% AGI	(2,500)
Deductible casualty loss	$ 400

102. Kate Harris had adjusted gross income in 1991 of $60,000. The following information pertains to her beach house which was destroyed by a hurricane.

Cost basis	$ 90,000
Value before hurricane	100,000
Value after hurricane	5,000
Insurance recovery	85,000

Her city apartment was also broken into and a necklace with a cost of $3,000 and a value of $5,000 was stolen. She recovered $5,000 from the insurance company. What is her casualty loss deduction for 1991?

a. $0.
b. $2,000.
c. $3,900.
d. $4,900.

The correct answer is (b). *(Publisher)*
REQUIRED: The total casualty loss deduction for 1991.
DISCUSSION: Sec. 165(h) allows a casualty deduction for nonbusiness casualty losses to the extent that each uninsured loss exceeds $100 and the aggregate of all such losses during the year exceeds 10% of AGI. The amount of a loss is the lesser of the decrease in the fair market value of the property resulting from the casualty or the property's adjusted basis. If any insurance reimbursements result in casualty gains, the gains are netted against casualty losses before computing the casualty loss deduction. In any case, a deduction for casualty losses is allowed to the extent of casualty gain, without regard to the 10% test.

	Beach House	Jewelry
Lesser of decrease in FMV or adjusted basis	$ 90,000	$ 3,000
Less insurance recovery	(85,000)	(5,000)
$100 floor on losses	(100)	---
Casualty loss (gain)	$ 4,900	$(2,000)

The net casualty loss is zero because the casualty loss of $4,900 less the casualty gain of $2,000 does not exceed 10% of AGI, or $6,000. The casualty loss for 1991 is therefore limited to the casualty gain of $2,000.

Module 9.5: Casualty and Theft Losses

103. While driving home from work, Mr. B's car unavoidably skidded on ice and struck the car in front of him, causing extensive damage to both cars. B may not deduct a casualty loss since the accident was solely his fault.

The correct answer is (F). *(SPE 1083 I-30)*
DISCUSSION: A casualty is defined as the complete or partial destruction of property resulting from some sudden, unexpected, or unusual cause. An auto accident meets this definition if it was not caused by the taxpayer's willful act or willful negligence. The damage to B's car is deductible as a casualty loss [Reg. Sec. 1.165-7(a)(3)(i)].

104. For purposes of determining a casualty loss, the amount offered for a vehicle as a trade-in on a new vehicle is the acceptable measure of fair market value.

The correct answer is (F). *(SPE 1077 I-143)*
DISCUSSION: Under Reg. 1.165-7(a)(2), fair market value must generally be ascertained by appraisal. The loss can also be determined by the cost of repairs if they are necessary, not excessive, and do not increase the value of the property. Trade-in offers are often inflated to generate business.

105. Mr. T's boat was damaged by a storm in 1990. Due to some financial difficulty he put off having the boat repaired until 1991. Mr. T may claim the casualty loss on the boat in 1991.

The correct answer is (F). *(SPE 1082 I-26)*
DISCUSSION: A deduction for a casualty loss is allowed only for the taxable year in which loss is sustained unless there exists a claim for reimbursement with a reasonable prospect for recovery, but about which there is some uncertainty. In such a case, the loss is deducted when it can be ascertained with reasonable certainty whether such reimbursement will be received [Reg. 1.165-1(d)]. Mr. T must deduct the casualty loss in 1990.

106. An election exists whereby a loss in a federally declared disaster area can be deducted on the tax return for the year immediately preceding the year in which the disaster occurred.

The correct answer is (T). *(SPE 990 I-25)*
DISCUSSION: Sec. 165(i) provides that a taxpayer who has suffered a disaster loss which is allowable as a deduction under Sec. 165(a) may, if the disaster is in an area that warrants assistance from the federal government under the Disaster Relief and Emergency Assistance Act, elect to deduct such loss for the taxable year immediately preceding the taxable year in which the disaster occurred.

107. In July 1991, Mr. P, a calendar-year taxpayer, incurred a casualty loss as a result of an event declared to be a federal disaster. He can claim the loss on his 1990 return if he amends the 1990 return within 3 years of its filing date or due date, whichever is later.

The correct answer is (F). *(SPE 987 I-23)*
DISCUSSION: Under Sec. 165(i), a loss attributable to a disaster occurring in an area declared by the federal government to be a disaster area may be deducted in the year prior to the disaster if the taxpayer so elects. In order to make this election, a statement indicating the election must be filed with the IRS by the later of the due date (without extensions) of the tax return for the year when the loss occurred or the due date (with extensions) of the prior year return. Mr. P would generally have to file the election by April 15, 1992.

108. The amount of a nonbusiness casualty loss must be reduced by the expected insurance recovery even though the insurance proceeds are not received until a later year.

The correct answer is (T). *(SPE 987 I-24)*
DISCUSSION: A casualty loss must be reduced by any insurance recovery which is expected to be received even if the proceeds are not received until a later year. If the reimbursement actually received is less than expected, the difference is claimed as a loss in such later year. If the reimbursement actually received is more than expected, the difference is included in income at such later year.

109. If a nonbusiness casualty loss occurs on property covered by insurance, but a claim is not filed, the total loss may be claimed as a casualty loss subject to the 10% limit and $100 reduction.

The correct answer is (F). *(SPE 989 I-17)*
DISCUSSION: Sec. 165(h)(4) provides that a taxpayer must file a timely insurance claim on a casualty loss covered by insurance in order to be able to deduct the loss. In such a case, the deductible casualty loss would be limited to the amount of the loss which was not covered by the insurance.

110. An individual may elect to deduct as a casualty loss a loss of deposits in an insolvent or bankrupt financial institution. The loss is the difference between your deposit and the amount you can expect to receive from the bankrupt institution.

The correct answer is (T). *(SPE 990 I-24)*
DISCUSSION: Sec. 165(l) provides that a taxpayer incurring a loss on deposits in a bankrupt or insolvent financial institution may choose to treat the loss as an ordinary loss or casualty loss rather than as a nonbusiness bad debt. This treatment is allowed provided that the taxpayer is not at least a 1% owner or officer of the financial institution or related to that owner or officer. The loss would be subject to the $100 floor and 10% of AGI limitations.

9.6 First-Tier Miscellaneous Itemized Deductions

111. Which of the following expenses is not deductible in full as an itemized deduction?

a. Moving expenses.
b. Reimbursed business expenses of an employee which are not substantiated to the employer.
c. Expenses of a handicapped individual to be able to work.
d. Gambling losses to the extent of gambling winnings.

The correct answer is (b). *(Publisher)*
REQUIRED: The itemized deduction not allowed in full.
DISCUSSION: Some miscellaneous itemized deductions are allowed in full and some miscellaneous itemized deductions are only deductible to the extent that they exceed 2% of adjusted gross income. Therefore, we call those deductible in full first-tier miscellaneous itemized deductions and those subject to the 2% of adjusted gross income floor, second-tier miscellaneous itemized deductions. After 1988, employee business expenses must be substantiated to the employer and reimbursed to be deductible for adjusted gross income. Otherwise, they are deductible as second-tier miscellaneous itemized deductions.
Answers (a), (c), and (d) are incorrect because each of these is a first-tier miscellaneous itemized deduction.

112. Which one of the following statements is correct with regard to an individual taxpayer who has elected to amortize the premium on a bond that yields taxable interest?

a. The amortization is treated as an itemized deduction.
b. The amortization is not treated as a reduction of taxable income.
c. The bond's basis is reduced by the amortization.
d. The bond's basis is increased by the amortization.

The correct answer is (c). *(CPA 1190 Q-34)*
REQUIRED: The correct statement regarding bond premiums amortized on a bond yielding taxable interest income.
DISCUSSION: Sec. 171 permits an election to be made to amortize the premium on a bond yielding taxable interest income. Sec. 1016(a)(5) requires the basis of the bond to be reduced by the amount of premium that is amortized.
Answers (a) and (b) are incorrect because, for bonds issued after 1987, the bond premium amortized is an offset against the interest income from the bond. Answer (d) is incorrect because the basis of the bond is reduced.

113. Marc Clay was unemployed for the entire year of 1990. In January 1991, Clay obtained full-time employment 40 miles away from the city where he had resided during the 10 years preceding 1991. Clay kept his new job for the entire year 1991. In January 1991, Clay paid direct moving expenses of $300 in relocating to his new city of residence, but he received no reimbursement for these expenses. In his 1991 income tax return, Clay's direct moving expenses are

a. Not deductible.
b. Fully deductible only if Clay itemizes his deductions.
c. Fully deductible from gross income in arriving at adjusted gross income.
d. Deductible subject to a 2% threshold if Clay itemizes his deductions.

The correct answer is (b). *(CPA 1190 Q-31)*
REQUIRED: The proper tax treatment of unreimbursed moving expenses.
DISCUSSION: Sec. 217 provides that an employee may deduct as an itemized deduction the reasonable expenses of moving himself and his family from one location to another, provided that the move is related to the commencement of work in a new location. To be eligible for the deduction the new place of work must be at least 35 miles farther from the taxpayer's old residence than his old residence was from his old place of work. Also, the taxpayer must be employed full-time for at least 39 weeks during the 12-month period following the move. As Clay has met the commencement-of-work test, the distance test and the length of employment test, and has received no reimbursement, he may deduct the moving expenses as a first-tier itemized deduction not subject to the 2% of adjusted gross income threshold provided that deductions are itemized.
Answer (a) is incorrect because the expenses are deductible as explained above. Answer (c) is incorrect because unreimbursed moving expenses are not deductions for gross income. Answer (d) is incorrect because moving expenses are first-tier itemized deductions not subject to the 2% of adjusted gross income threshold.

114. Which of the following expenses associated with selling or moving from your old residence does not qualify as a deductible moving expense?

a. Settling your lease at the old location.
b. Attorney fee.
c. Real estate commission.
d. Improvements to enhance salability of old residence.

The correct answer is (d). *(SPE 1079 I-55)*
REQUIRED: The expense associated with selling or moving from a residence that does not qualify as a deductible moving expense.
DISCUSSION: The definition of moving expenses under Sec. 217(b) includes the reasonable expenses constituting qualified residence sale, purchase, or lease expenses. These are reasonable amounts paid or incurred for expenses incidental to the sale or exchange of a former residence, the purchase of a new residence, the settlement of an unexpired lease, or the acquisition of a lease [Sec. 217(b)(2)]. Improvements to enhance the salability of an old residence do not qualify as moving expenses.
Answers (a), (b), and (c) are incorrect because each represents a qualified moving expense.

115. Which of the following is a nondeductible moving expense?

a. Cost of lodging and 80% of meals while in transit.
b. Loss on sale of your personal residence.
c. Attorney fees to sell personal residence.
d. Real estate commissions to sell personal residence.

The correct answer is (b). *(SPE 1081 I-51)*
REQUIRED: The item that is a nondeductible moving expense.
DISCUSSION: Although qualified real estate expenses are included in the definition of moving expenses in Sec. 217(b), loss on the sale of a personal use asset is not deductible.
Answer (a) is incorrect because the reasonable expense of traveling, including meals and lodging, from the former residence to the new residence is a moving expense under Sec. 217(b)(1)(B). However, the 80% limitation on the deduction for meals applies [Sec. 274(n)(2)(D)]. Answers (c) and (d) are incorrect because qualified residence sales, purchase, or lease expenses include reasonable expenses incidental to the sale or exchange of the former residence [Sec. 217(b)(2)(A)].

Module 9.6: First-Tier Miscellaneous Itemized Deductions

116. All of the following will qualify as a moving expense for computing the allowable moving expense deduction except:

a. Cost of transporting members of the taxpayer's family to the new home.

b. Amount of security deposit placed on an apartment at the new location.

c. Cost of breaking a lease on an apartment at the old location.

d. Cost of moving personal and household articles to the new residence.

The correct answer is (b). *(SPE 990 I-48)*
REQUIRED: The item not qualifying as a deductible moving expense.
DISCUSSION: The definition of moving expenses under Sec. 217(b) includes qualified residence sale, purchase or lease expenses. These are defined under Sec. 217(b)(2), but do not include security deposits. Reg. 1.217-2(b)(7)(iv) specifically provides that no deduction is permitted for payment or prepayments of rent or for payments representing the cost of a security or other similar deposit.
Answers (a) and (d) are incorrect because each is specifically included as a moving expense in Sec. 217(b)(1). Answer (c) is incorrect because the cost of breaking a lease on the former apartment residence is a qualified moving expense under Sec. 217(b)(2).

117. Mr. P and his nonworking spouse made a move that qualifies for the moving expense deduction. They paid the following expenses in 1991 after Mr. P got his new job:

Transportation of household goods	$ 8,000
Pre-move travel for househunting	900
Travel from old residence to new	400
Temporary living expenses for 20 consecutive days in new location	1,900
Real estate commission on sale of old residence	4,800

What is their 1991 moving expenses deduction?

a. $3,000.
b. $11,000.
c. $11,400.
d. $13,400.

The correct answer is (c). *(SPE 984 I-75)*
REQUIRED: The taxpayers' allowable moving expense deduction.
DISCUSSION: Sec. 217(a) allows a deduction for moving expenses paid or incurred in connection with the commencement of work by the taxpayer at a new place of work. The expenses of actually moving the taxpayer, family, and household goods are deductible without limit. Expenses of househunting and temporary quarters for up to 30 days are limited to $1,500. Expenses to sell the old residence are limited to $3,000 less the deduction for househunting and temporary quarters.

Expenses of the actual move:		
Household goods		$ 8,000
Family		400
Househunting	$ 900	
Temporary living expense	1,900	
Limited to $1,500	$2,800	1,500
Real estate commission ($4,800, limited to $3,000 − $1,500)		1,500
Moving expense deduction		$11,400

118. All of the following statements regarding moving expenses are true except:

a. If you are an employee, you must work full-time, for the same employer, for at least 39 weeks during the first 12 months after arrival in the new job area.

b. If you are self-employed, you must work full-time for at least 39 weeks during the first 12 months and for a total of at least 78 weeks during the first 24 months after arrival in the new job area.

c. You do not have to meet the time test to deduct your moving expenses if you moved to the United States because you retired.

d. If you are married and file a joint return and both you and your spouse work full-time, either of you may satisfy the full-time work test.

The correct answer is (a). *(SPE 989 I-53)*
REQUIRED: The incorrect statement regarding moving expenses.
DISCUSSION: In order to deduct moving expenses, an employee must work full-time for at least 39 weeks during the first 12 months after arrival in the new job area; however, the work need not be for the same employer.
Answers (b), (c), and (d) are incorrect because each is a true statement regarding moving expenses.

Module 9.6: First-Tier Miscellaneous Itemized Deductions

119. Mr. Flynn, a single individual, was transferred by his employer to another city in 1991. He incurred the following expenses which were not reimbursed by his employer:

Travel to new location	
Transportation (400 miles @ .09)	$ 36
Lodging	250
Meals	120
Moving household goods	3,000
Temporary living expenses (15 days)	
Hotel room	1,400
Meals	400
Premove househunting trip	
Transportation	250
Lodging	350
Meals	200
Improvements to old home	2,000

Mr. Flynn's adjusted gross income for 1991 was $30,000. Assuming the time and distance tests are met, what is the amount of Flynn's deductible moving expense?

    a. $4,882.
    b. $4,906.
    c. $5,902.
    d. $6,382.

The correct answer is (a). *(SPE 989 I-92)*
REQUIRED: The taxpayer's moving expense deduction.
DISCUSSION: Sec. 217(a) allows the deduction for moving expenses paid or incurred in connection with the commencement of work by a taxpayer at a new place of work. The expenses of actually moving a taxpayer and household goods are deductible without limit. However, only 80% of the meals are deductible. Instead of actual expenses, a mileage rate of $.09 per mile can be used for driving one's own automobile. Expenses of househunting and temporary quarters for up to 30 days are limited to $1,500. Improvements to the old home are not deductible as moving expenses. The cost of the improvements would be capitalized and added to the basis of the old home.

Expenses of actual move:		
Moving household goods		$3,000
Transportation		36
Lodging		250
Meals ($120 x 80%)		96
		$3,382
Househunting:		
Transportation	$ 250	
Lodging	350	
Meals ($200 x 80%)	160	
Temporary living:		
Hotel	1,400	
Meals ($400 x 80%)	320	
(Limited to $1,500)	$2,480	1,500
Moving expense deduction		$4,882

---

120. Ms. C, a single taxpayer, accepted a new job which required a move from Chicago, Illinois to Miami, Florida in 1991. She incurred and paid the following moving expenses:

Real estate commission on sale of residence	$2,000
Cost of moving household and personal goods	2,200
Travel expenses to new residence	550
Cost of decorating new apartment residence	1,200
Temporary (15 days) living expenses at new location	750
Loss of membership in the country club at old residence	1,000

Ms. C was reimbursed $2,500 by her employer who did not include this amount in the wages reported on her W-2 form for 1991. Assume the distance and time requirements were properly met. What is Ms. C's allowable moving expense deduction for 1991?

    a. $2,700.
    b. $3,000.
    c. $4,200.
    d. $5,500.

The correct answer is (d). *(SPE 1080 I-74)*
REQUIRED: The taxpayer's allowable moving expense deduction for 1991.
DISCUSSION: A reimbursement for moving expenses must be included in gross income under Sec. 82. The deduction for the moving expenses is provided in Sec. 217 when a taxpayer commences employment at a new place of work which is at least 35 miles farther from the old residence than was the old place of work. If the moving expense reimbursement is incorrectly omitted from gross income (as in this case since the taxpayer would report only what was on her W-2), Reg. 1.217-2(j)(2) provides that the moving expense is not deductible to the extent the reimbursement is not included in gross income.

The expenses to sell the old residence include the real estate commission. The cost of decorating the new residence and the loss of membership in the country club are not deductible. Ms. C's moving expense deduction is

Moving household goods	$2,200
Travel to new residence	550
Temporary living expenses (lesser of $750 actual or limit of $1,500)	750
Expenses to sell old residence (lesser of $2,000 actual or limit of $3,000 – $750 temporary living expense)	2,000
	$5,500

No adjustment should be made in the deductible expense because the employer omitted $2,500 from the W-2 form. Under Sec. 82, this amount is included in gross income regardless of its treatment on the W-2 form.

Module 9.6: First-Tier Miscellaneous Itemized Deductions

121. Mr. B, a single taxpayer, moved to a new city in 1990 to start a new job and properly deducted moving expenses on his 1990 income tax return. In 1991, the expenses became nondeductible because Mr. B failed to meet the full-time work test when he voluntarily quit the job. Which of the following is the proper action to take?

   a. Mr. B can secure an extension for the 39-week test.
   b. Mr. B must include the expenses in gross income on his return in the year he returns to work.
   c. Mr. B must either amend his 1990 return or report the amount previously deducted as income on his 1991 return.
   d. Mr. B must amend his 1990 return, but can reduce the gain on the sale of his residence by the amount of the moving expenses.

The correct answer is (c). *(SPE 1080 I-53)*
REQUIRED: The proper action when a taxpayer becomes ineligible after deducting moving expenses.
DISCUSSION: To be eligible for a moving expense deduction, an employee must be employed on a full-time basis at the new location for 39 weeks in the 12-month period following the move [Sec. 217(c)(2)]. Reg. 1.217-2(d)(3) provides that a taxpayer, who deducts moving expenses and then is no longer able to satisfy the minimum period of employment condition, may either include the amount previously deducted in the current year's gross income, or file an amended return for the year in which the deduction was taken and not claim the deduction.
  Answer (a) is incorrect because the 39-week test may not be extended. Answer (b) is incorrect because if the prior tax return is not amended, the expenses must be included in gross income in the current year. Answer (d) is incorrect because the prior year's tax return need not be amended; and moving expenses may not reduce the gain on the sale of a residence unless they are selling expenses.

122. Mr. K moved to a new home to be nearer to his new job location, which is 40 miles farther from his former home than his old job location was. Mr. K meets the distance test for purposes of deducting moving expenses.

The correct answer is (T). *(SPE 984 I-17)*
DISCUSSION: Sec. 217(c) provides that a deduction is only allowed for moving expenses if the taxpayer's new principal place of work is at least 35 miles farther from the old residence than was the former principal place of work. In the event there was no former principal place of work, the new principal place of work must be at least 35 miles from the old residence.

123. Pre-move househunting expenses are deductible moving expenses up to certain dollar limits if they are incurred after the job is secured in the new area and the primary purpose of the visit is to look for a new place to live.

The correct answer is (T). *(SPE 1082 I-13)*
DISCUSSION: Sec. 217(b)(1)(C) provides that moving expenses include the cost of traveling, after obtaining employment, to and from the former residence to the general location of the new place of work, provided the principal purpose is to search for a new residence. Reg. 1.217-2(b)(5) also includes the cost of transportation, meals, and lodging while at the general location of the new place of work to search for a new residence. Deductions for househunting expenses and temporary living expenses may not exceed a total of $1,500.

124. Rich and Lisa moved in May, 1991, because Lisa was starting a new job in June, 1991. The following distances relate to the move:

Miles from former home to former job - 10
Miles from new home to former job - 47
Miles from new home to new job - 7
Miles from former home to new job - 41

Rich and Lisa have met the distance test for deducting their moving expenses.

The correct answer is (F). *(SPE 989 I-19)*
DISCUSSION: Sec. 217 allows a deduction only if the taxpayer's new principal place of work is at least 35 miles farther from the old residence than was the former principal place of work.

Former home to new job	41 miles
Less former home to former job	(10 miles)
Difference	31 miles

Rich and Lisa have failed to meet the distance test for deducting moving expenses as the new principal place of work is only 31 miles farther from the old residence than was the former principal place of work.

125. Fred lived in Michigan and attended a local university. Upon graduation, he secured a job in Houston, Texas. This will be Fred's first full-time job. Fred's moving expenses are not deductible.

The correct answer is (F). *(SPE 1083 I-23)*
DISCUSSION: Sec. 217(c) requires the taxpayer's new principal place of work to be at least 35 miles farther from his/her former residence than the former principal place of work was. However, if the taxpayer had no former principal place of work, the new place of work must be at least 35 miles from his/her former residence. There are no other requirements concerning a former place of work.

9.7 Second-Tier Miscellaneous Itemized Deductions

126. Which of the following is a correct statement concerning changes made to miscellaneous itemized deductions by the Tax Reform Act of 1986?

a. Most miscellaneous itemized deductions are allowed only to the extent they exceed 2% of adjusted gross income.

b. Most miscellaneous itemized deductions are limited to 2% of adjusted gross income.

c. Reimbursed employee business expenses are deductible as miscellaneous itemized deductions, but unreimbursed employee business expenses are not deductible.

d. Many of the miscellaneous itemized deductions allowed under prior law are no longer deductible at all.

The correct answer is (a). *(Publisher)*
REQUIRED: The changes made to miscellaneous itemized deductions by the 1986 TRA.
DISCUSSION: After 1986, some miscellaneous itemized deductions are available in full and some are allowed only to the extent that they exceed 2% of adjusted gross income. The first group we call first-tier miscellaneous itemized deductions and the second group (subject to the 2% floor) we call second-tier miscellaneous itemized deductions.
Answer (b) is incorrect because most miscellaneous itemized deductions are second-tier and are allowed only to the extent in total they exceed 2% of adjusted gross income. Answer (c) is incorrect because reimbursed employee business expenses are still deductible for adjusted gross income (above the line) provided the employee substantiates the expenses to the employer. Unreimbursed employee business expenses are second-tier miscellaneous itemized deductions. Answer (d) is incorrect because most former miscellaneous itemized deductions are now second-tier miscellaneous itemized deductions.

127. All of the following items are nondeductible miscellaneous expenses except:

a. Adoption expenses for children with special needs.

b. Expenses generating tax-exempt income.

c. Governmental fines and penalties, such as parking tickets.

d. Subscriptions to professional journals and trade magazines related to your work as an employee.

The correct answer is (d). *(SPE 989 I-55)*
REQUIRED: The item which is deductible as a miscellaneous expense.
DISCUSSION: Amounts paid by an individual for work-related professional journals and trade magazines would be deductible as unreimbursed employee business expenses. Such expenses are second-tier miscellaneous itemized deductions and subject to the 2% of AGI floor.
Answer (a) is incorrect because adoption expenses are personal in nature and a deduction for personal expenditures is not allowed under Sec. 262. Answer (b) is incorrect because a deduction is not allowed under Sec. 265 for any expense allocable to the earning of tax-exempt income. Answer (c) is incorrect because penalties and fines are not deductible as such a deduction would tend to frustrate public policy [Reg. 1.212-1(p)].

Module 9.7: Second-Tier Miscellaneous Itemized Deductions

128. Which of the following types of itemized deductions is included in the category of unreimbursed expenses that is deductible only if the aggregate amount of such expenses exceeds 2% of the taxpayer's adjusted gross income?

a. Employee moving expenses.
b. Tax return preparation fees.
c. Medical expenses.
d. Interest expense.

The correct answer is (b). *(CPA 1188 Q-14)*
REQUIRED: The itemized deduction subject to the 2% of AGI floor.
DISCUSSION: Sec. 67 provides that certain itemized deductions are only allowed to the extent that the aggregate of such deductions exceeds 2% of adjusted gross income. The itemized deductions subject to this 2% floor are those other than the ones listed in Sec. 67(b). Tax return preparation fees are an itemized deduction allowed by Sec. 212 and not listed in Sec. 67(b). Therefore, it is only deductible to the extent it exceeds 2% of AGI.
Answer (a) is incorrect because employee moving expenses are deductible as a miscellaneous itemized deduction but they are a first-tier miscellaneous deduction and not subject to the 2% of AGI floor. Answers (c) and (d) are incorrect because medical expenses and interest expense are not a miscellaneous itemized deduction subject to the 2% floor, but they are itemized deductions.

129. Each of the following expenses is considered a deductible employee expense on Schedule A (Form 1040) except

a. Firefighter's uniform.
b. Union membership dues.
c. Small tools used for work.
d. Painter's work clothing and standard shoes required by the union.

The correct answer is (d). *(SPE 984 I-63)*
REQUIRED: The expenses incurred that are not deductible as itemized deductions.
DISCUSSION: A deduction is allowed under Sec. 212 for all ordinary and necessary expenses paid or incurred during the taxable year for the production or collection of income. The items in (b) and (c) are deductible under Sec. 212 as second-tier miscellaneous deductions. Protective clothing and equipment are also deductible if they are required as a condition of employment and are not adaptable to regular wear. A firefighter's uniform qualifies under this definition, but a painter's work clothing and standard shoes do not.

130. Which of the following miscellaneous deductions is not subject to the 2% of adjusted gross income limit?

a. Work clothes and uniforms.
b. Safe deposit box rental.
c. Clerical help in caring for investments.
d. Gambling losses to the extent of gambling winnings.

The correct answer is (d). *(SPE 990 I-51)*
REQUIRED: The miscellaneous deduction not subject to the 2% of AGI floor.
DISCUSSION: Gambling losses are deductible to the extent of gambling winnings (Reg. 1.165-10). They are a loss deduction for adjusted gross income if gambling is a trade or business, but in most cases they are a first-tier miscellaneous itemized deduction (not subject to the 2% of AGI floor).
Answer (a) is incorrect because special clothing and equipment are deductible as a miscellaneous deduction provided they are required as a condition of employment and not adaptable to regular wear. When deductible, they are subject to the 2% of AGI floor. Answer (b) is incorrect because safe deposit box rental is deductible under Sec. 212 provided it is used to store documents or other data for the production or collection of income, not personal effects. If deductible, it is subject to the 2% of AGI floor. Answer (c) is incorrect because clerical help in caring for investments is deductible under Sec. 212 and is subject to the 2% of AGI floor.

Module 9.7: Second-Tier Miscellaneous Itemized Deductions

131. Which of the following expenses may be claimed as an "Other Miscellaneous Deduction" on Schedule A of Form 1040?

   a. Legal expenses to collect taxable alimony.
   b. Expenses of attending stockholders' meeting.
   c. Bar exam fees.
   d. Fee paid to a broker to buy investment property such as stocks or bonds.

The correct answer is (a). *(SPE 990 I-50)*
REQUIRED: The expense which may be claimed as an "other miscellaneous deduction" on Schedule A.
DISCUSSION: Legal expenses incurred to collect taxable alimony would be allowed as an "other miscellaneous deduction" on Schedule A. Because the alimony is taxable income, legal costs incurred in the collection of the income may be deducted under Sec. 212.
  Answer (b) is incorrect because the expense of attending a stockholders' meeting is not directly related to the production or collection of income, but rather, is generally a personal expense and disallowed under Sec. 262. Answer (c) is incorrect because bar exam fees are also personal expenses and are not deductible under Sec. 262. Answer (d) is incorrect because fees paid to a broker to buy investment property such as stocks or bonds are added to the cost of such property and recovered upon its sale or other disposition.

132. All of the following expenses may be claimed on Schedule A as an expense of producing income except

   a. Investment counsel fee paid for managing your investments.
   b. Trustee's administrative fees that are billed separately and paid in connection with your individual retirement arrangement.
   c. Custodian fees and service charges to subscribers in a dividend reinvestment plan.
   d. Fee paid to a broker to buy investment property such as stocks or bonds.

The correct answer is (d). *(SPE 986 I-54)*
REQUIRED: The expense not allowable as an expense of producing income.
DISCUSSION: A fee paid to a broker to acquire stocks or bonds is a cost of acquiring the property that should be included in the basis of the stocks or bonds under Sec. 1012. A cost to acquire property which is included in the basis of the property is not deducted.
  The expenses in (a), (b), and (c) are allowable as deductions under Sec. 212 for ordinary and necessary expenses paid or incurred for the production or collection of income, or for the management, conservation, or maintenance of property held for the production of income. However, these expenses are considered second-tier miscellaneous itemized deductions, and are deductible to the extent that total second-tier miscellaneous itemized deductions exceed 2% of AGI.

133. Mr. and Mrs. White's adjusted gross income for 1991 was $100,000. During the year they incurred and paid the following:

Business publications	$ 200
Tax return preparation fee	600
Fees for will preparation	1,000
Life insurance premiums	2,000
Union dues	2,400

Assuming they can itemize, how much should the Whites claim as miscellaneous deductible expenses?

   a. $1,200.
   b. $3,200.
   c. $4,200.
   d. $6,000.

The correct answer is (a). *(SPE 990 I-89)*
REQUIRED: The amount taxpayers can claim as miscellaneous itemized deductions.
DISCUSSION: Under Sec. 262, life insurance premiums and the preparation of a will are personal expenses for which a deduction is disallowed. The business periodicals ($200), tax return preparation fee ($600), and union dues ($2,400) are deductible under Sec. 212 as "second-tier" miscellaneous itemized deductions, to the extent they exceed 2% of AGI. Total deductible items thus amount to $1,200 [$3,200 − (.02 × $100,000)].

134. For 1991, Mr. A had adjusted gross income of $26,000 which consisted of $20,000 in wages, $4,000 in dividend income from taxable domestic corporations, and $2,000 in gambling winnings. His expenses for 1991 included:

Investment counseling fee	$ 700
Attorney fee for preparing a will	200
Union dues	400
Tax return preparation fee	150
Gambling losses	2,500

What is the amount deductible by A for the above items?

a. $1,250.
b. $2,730.
c. $2,930.
d. $3,950.

The correct answer is (b). *(SPE 987 I-80)*
REQUIRED: The deductible amount of various expenses.
DISCUSSION: Under Sec. 262, the cost of preparation of a will is a personal expense for which a deduction is disallowed. Gambling losses are deductible to the extent of winnings (Reg. 1.165-10). They are first-tier deductions without further limitation. Investment counseling fees, union dues, and tax preparation fees are second-tier miscellaneous itemized deductions. However, they are only deductible to the extent they exceed 2% of adjusted gross income. The computation is shown below.

First-tier deduction		
Gambling losses (limited to winnings)		$2,000
Second-tier deductions		
Investment counseling	$ 700	
Union dues	400	
Tax preparation	150	
	$1,250	
Less 2% of AGI	(520)	730
Total deductible expenses		$2,730

135. Education expenses may be deductible as a miscellaneous itemized deduction as well as any related travel and transportation expenses. Which of the following may also be true concerning education expenses?

a. The education expense is deductible, even though it may qualify one for an additional trade or business, as long as it improves one's skills in an established trade or business.

b. The expenses related to education are deductible if the education is primarily to bring one up to the minimum level of knowledge or skills required by the employer.

c. As long as one has met the minimum knowledge or skill requirements for one's established employment, trade, or business, all additional expenses are deductible.

d. Education expenses are for the most part deductible as long as one has already met the minimum requirements for one's established employment, trade, or business, the education does not qualify one for a new trade or business, and the education is necessary to keep a present job status or pay rate.

The correct answer is (d). *(D. Suttles)*
REQUIRED: The true statement concerning education expenses.
DISCUSSION: Expenditures made by an individual for education include amounts spent on correspondence courses, travel and transportation costs, supplies and books, and tuition. They are deductible as second-tier miscellaneous itemized deductions if the education maintains or improves skills required of the individual in his/her employment or other trade or business, or if it meets the express requirements of the individual's employer or the requirements of applicable law or regulations imposed as a condition to the retention by the individual of an established employment relationship, status, or rate of compensation [Reg. 1.162-5(a)]. Note that travel itself as a form of education is not a deductible expense.
Answer (a) is incorrect because education that qualifies one for a new trade or business is not deductible. Answer (b) is incorrect because one of the requirements for education expense to be deductible is to have already met the minimum level of education or skills required of employment. It is the additional education which may be deductible. Answer (c) is incorrect because this is only one requirement and does not guarantee the deduction, e.g., if the education does qualify one for a new trade or business, it is not deductible even if one does not intend to enter the new trade or business.

Module 9.7: Second-Tier Miscellaneous Itemized Deductions

136. Mr. G, a full-time accountant with a CPA firm, incurred the following deductible education expenses in 1991 and substantiated them to his employer:

Travel and transportation	$ 400
Tuition	1,000
Books	200

G's employer reimbursed him $800 for these expenses and included the reimbursement on G's Form W-2 for 1991. What amount may G deduct for tuition and books to arrive at adjusted gross income?

- a. $0.
- b. $600.
- c. $800.
- d. $1,200.

The correct answer is (b). *(SPE 984 I-84)*
REQUIRED: The amount that may be deducted for tuition and books to arrive at adjusted gross income.
DISCUSSION: Education expenses include books, tuition, and transportation and travel. They are deductions from adjusted gross income unless the employee substantiates the expenses to the employer and is reimbursed by the employer. G received a reimbursement of $800, which should be applied to each of the expenses proportionately when it is not a reimbursement for a specific expense. The tuition and books are 3/4 ($1,200 ÷ $1,600) of the total expenses, so $600 (3/4 x $800) of the reimbursement is treated as for tuition and books. Therefore, G may deduct $600 for tuition and books to arrive at AGI.

The remaining $600 of tuition and books is deductible from AGI as a second-tier miscellaneous itemized deduction to the extent that total second-tier deductions exceed 2% of AGI.

137. Betty Brunett spent $2,000 in unreimbursed business expenses associated with her $20,000 annual salary. Included in those expenses were $1,000 of travel and $1,000 of dues and subscriptions. Because of $5,000 of interest expense on her home, she will be filing Schedule A of Form 1040. In 1991 how much of her $2,000 expenses will be deductions "for" and "from" AGI?

	For	From
a.	$0	$1,600
b.	$1,000	$1,000
c.	$0	$2,000
d.	$1,000	$600

The correct answer is (a). *(P. Hite)*
REQUIRED: The deduction for second-tier miscellaneous itemized deductions.
DISCUSSION: Unreimbursed business expenses of an employee are deductible as miscellaneous itemized deductions. They are second-tier miscellaneous itemized deductions and only allowed to the extent that in total they exceed 2% of adjusted gross income. Since Brunett's adjusted gross income was $20,000, the unreimbursed business expenses are deductible only to the extent they exceed $400 (2% x $20,000). Therefore, $1,600 of the expenses ($2,000 minus $400) are deductible from adjusted gross income. None of the expenses are deductible for adjusted gross income.

138. Mr. N, an employee of AM Corporation, paid $10,000 for use of a country club for 1991. N used the club in the following manner:

Associated entertainment	10%
Business meals	15%
Directly related entertainment	40%
Personal use	35%

What is the amount of the dues that Mr. N may deduct on his 1991 income tax return, disregarding the 2% of adjusted gross income limitation?

- a. $3,200.
- b. $4,400.
- c. $5,500.
- d. $6,500.

The correct answer is (b). *(SPE 990 I-81)*
REQUIRED: The amount of country club dues deductible as a miscellaneous itemized deduction.
DISCUSSION: Sec. 274 allows a deduction for dues and fees paid with respect to a facility used in connection with entertainment or recreation (e.g., country club) when the facility is used more than 50% for business purposes. If the 50% requirement is met, the portion of the dues and fees directly related to the business use of the club may be deducted. The deduction would also be subject to the 80% limitation for meals and entertainment. Mr. N used the club only 35% for personal use, and therefore 65% for business, and his deduction would be computed as follows:

Business meals ($10,000 x 15%)	$1,500
Directly related entertainment ($10,000 x 40%)	4,000
	$5,500
Meals and entertainment limitation	x 80%
Total deduction	$4,400

Note that the lack of a direct relationship between club expenditures and the taxpayer's business prevents Mr. N from deducting the portion of the dues allocable to "associated entertainment." No deduction is allowed for the portion of the dues allocable to personal use.

Module 9.7: Second-Tier Miscellaneous Itemized Deductions

139. Mr. B uses the standard mileage rate in calculating the expense of operating his car for business purposes. He is an employee who is not reimbursed for his transportation expenses. B purchased the car in 1988 and has driven the car 15,000 business miles each year through 1990. In 1991 B drove 20,000 business miles and his adjusted gross income is $40,000. Mr. B had no other miscellaneous deductions. B has a

- a. $4,700 adjustment to income to arrive at adjusted gross income.
- b. $4,700 miscellaneous itemized deduction.
- c. $3,875 miscellaneous itemized deduction.
- d. $4,400 miscellaneous itemized deduction.

The correct answer is (b). *(SPE 987 I-75)*
REQUIRED: The deduction for use of an automobile in business.
DISCUSSION: Unreimbursed business expenses are deductible as a miscellaneous itemized deduction to the extent they exceed 2% of adjusted gross income. The standard mileage rate in 1991 $.275 per mile for all miles driven. B's deductible amount is $5,500 (20,000 miles x $.275 per mile). However, his actual deduction is limited to the amount that exceeds 2% of adjusted gross income. His final deduction is $4,700 [$5,500 − (2% x $40,000)]. Note that all mileage is eligible for the 27.5 cent rate in 1991 and later years. Prior to the 1991 tax year, an 11 cent rate applied to business use in excess of 15,000 miles in the year, or to fully depreciated vehicles.

140. Mr. Speed drives a race car in his spare time and on weekends in 1991. His records regarding this activity reflect the following information for:

Income	$3,000
Expenses:	
Entry fees	1,000
Depreciation on car	700
Tires	200
Interest on loan for race car	800
Insurance premiums	1,000

What is the allowable deduction for depreciation assuming that this activity is not engaged in for profit and Mr. Speed can itemize his deductions?

- a. $0.
- b. $380.
- c. $480.
- d. $700.

The correct answer is (d). *(SPE 989 II-70)*
REQUIRED: The depreciation deduction for an asset used in an activity not engaged in for profit.
DISCUSSION: The activity engaged in by Mr. Speed would be considered a "hobby" as it is an activity not engaged in for profit. Expenses and losses of such an activity, known as hobby losses, are deductible only to the extent of any income produced by the hobby activity (Sec. 183; Reg. 1.183-1 through 1.183-4). Certain expenses are deductible even if they exceed hobby income, such as taxes, interest, and casualty losses. The deduction of these expenses, though, reduces the amount of hobby income against which hobby expenses may be offset. After deducting these amounts, hobby expenses are applied to hobby income in the following order: (1) operating expenses other than depreciation, and (2) depreciation and other basis adjustment items. The calculation for Mr. Speed would be:

Hobby income	$3,000
Interest on race car loan	-0-
Entry fees	(1,000)
Tires	(200)
Insurance premiums	(1,000)
Remaining hobby income (against which depreciation may be deducted)	$ 800

The full $700 depreciation deduction would be available for Mr. Speed because the $800 interest on the race car loan is personal interest and nondeductible.

141. Which of the following is not required when using the standard mileage rate to compute deductible transportation expenses?

- a. You may use only one car at a time in the business.
- b. You must own the vehicle.
- c. You may not use the vehicle for hire, such as a taxi.
- d. You must use the vehicle over 50% of the time for business.

The correct answer is (d). *(SPE 984 II-53)*
REQUIRED: The item not required when using the standard mileage rate.
DISCUSSION: The standard mileage rate is allowed under Rev. Proc. 90-59. Instead of deductions for actual costs, depreciation, etc., $.275 per mile is deductible for all miles driven in 1991. There is no required percentage of business use of the vehicle. The standard mileage rate can be used for any occasional business use of a vehicle.
Answers (a), (b), and (c) are incorrect because each is a requirement for use of the standard mileage rate.

142. Which one of the following is a deductible transportation expense?

a. Hauling tools and equipment in a vehicle while commuting to and from a regular place of work.

b. Use of a vehicle which displays material that advertises one's business while commuting to and from work.

c. Use of vehicles by Armed Forces Reservists to attend weekend meetings in the general area of their homes.

d. Use of a vehicle to report to and return home each evening from a temporary or minor assignment beyond the general area of one's regular place of work.

The correct answer is (d). *(SPE 989 I-50)*
REQUIRED: The item which is a deductible transportation expense.
DISCUSSION: An employee is permitted a deduction for transportation expenses paid in connection with services performed as an employee (Sec. 162). The use of a vehicle to report to and return home each evening from a temporary or minor assignment beyond the general area of one's regular place of work would qualify as a deductible transportation expense under Sec. 162. Rev. Proc. 90-23 has extended the transportation expense deduction to include the cost of any travel by a taxpayer having a regular place of business between home and temporary work stations, regardless of the distances. Thus, not only the costs mentioned in answer (d), but also costs related to assignments in the general area of one's regular place of business are now deductible.
Answer (a) is incorrect because a taxpayer may not deduct the costs of commuting to and from work as a transportation expense even if hauling tools and equipment (extra costs, such as renting a trailer to haul equipment could, however, be deducted). Answer (b) is incorrect because the use of the car to display advertising for your business will not change the nature of commuting from personal use to business use and personal use for commuting is not deductible. Answer (c) is incorrect because the cost of transportation to an armed forces reserve meeting in the general area of the taxpayer's home is commuting expense and is not, therefore, deductible.

143. In 1991, Mr. L, a salesperson, drove his car 36,000 miles, of which 24,000 miles pertained to business. The total operating costs and other costs were as follows:

Gas and oil	$3,250
Auto license tag	50
Insurance	380
Repairs	320
Tires	200
Parking (incurred during business use)	175
Depreciation for business use of car	2,000

What is Mr. L's greatest allowable auto expense deduction?

a. $6,240.
b. $6,415.
c. $6,600.
d. $6,775.

The correct answer is (d). *(SPE 1082 I-76)*
REQUIRED: A salesperson's maximum automobile expense deduction.
DISCUSSION: Mr. L's automobile expenses must be allocated between business use and personal use. One method is to take the business portion of the general expenses and add the direct business expenses. L's general expenses of gas and oil, license, insurance, repairs, and tires total $4,200. The business use of the automobile is two-thirds of total use (24,000 ÷ 36,000 miles), so the deductible part of these expenses is $2,800 (2/3 x $4,200). Parking and depreciation are direct business expenses which total $2,175. Operating costs total $4,975.
Alternatively, L can use the standard mileage rate authorized by the IRS which, in 1991, is $.275 per mile for all miles driven. Nonautomobile expenses may be added to this, e.g., parking of $175. The standard mileage rate of $6,600 (24,000 x $.275) plus parking equals $6,775. Since this amount is greater than actual operating costs, the standard mileage rate of $6,775 will be deducted.

144. Paul Dunyan works for a logging company. He uses the standard mileage rate of $.275 per mile for all business use of his car. During 1991, Paul incurs the following:

Mileage commuting to and from work	2,400
Mileage on inspection jobs at work	3,000
Mileage to testify for the company on new timber laws	420
Air fare to visit another company facility for a day	$350

How much can Paul Dunyan deduct as transportation expenses before the 2% of AGI limitation (round to nearest dollar)?

a. $350.
b. $821.
c. $1,291.
d. $1,747.

The correct answer is (c). *(Publisher)*
REQUIRED: The amount the employee can deduct as transportation expenses.
DISCUSSION: An employee is permitted a deduction from adjusted gross income for transportation expenses paid in connection with services performed as an employee (Sec. 162). Transportation expenses include the cost of transporting the employee from one place to another in the course of employment while not away from home in a travel status. The cost of commuting to and from work is not deductible because it is considered a personal rather than a business expense.
Dunyan's transportation expenses are $1,291 [$350 air fare + ($.275 x 3,420 miles)].

145. Which of the following items is a deductible travel expense if not substantiated to and reimbursed by the employer?

a. Mr. A pays taxi fares to and from his job and home each day.
b. Mr. B, an employee of an insurance company, incurs the cost of meals on days when he services clients 15 miles from his office.
c. Mr. C, an employee, incurred an expense for meals while returning from a 6-hour business trip.
d. Mr. D, a Pittsburgh lawyer, incurred laundry expenses while in Boston defending a client.

The correct answer is (d). *(SPE 1081 II-53)*
REQUIRED: The expenditure that is deductible as a travel expense.
DISCUSSION: A deduction is allowed for travel expenses, including amounts spent for meals and lodging, while away from home in the performance of services as an employee (Sec. 162). Travel expenses are those incurred while away from home overnight or for a period of time long enough to require a rest period. Travel expenses include transportation, meals, lodging, and expenses incident to travel, including reasonable laundry expenses and are subject to the 2% of adjusted gross income floor.
Answer (a) is incorrect because commuters' fares are not considered business expenses and are not deductible [Reg. 1.162-2(e)]. Answers (b) and (c) are incorrect because the taxpayers have not met the overnight test and thus have not incurred travel expenses (which is necessary to deduct the cost of meals).

146. Mr. N, a practicing CPA in New York, attended his profession's annual convention June 10-19, 1991 in San Francisco. His employer did not reimburse him for his expenses. Which of the following expenses incurred during the trip is not deductible?

a. Round trip air fare from New York to San Francisco - $400.
b. Lodging and 80% of the cost of meals in San Francisco - $600.
c. Laundry expenses - $75.
d. Air fare from San Francisco to Honolulu for a weekend visit with friends - $150.

The correct answer is (d). *(SPE 1080 II-57)*
REQUIRED: The expense incurred during the business trip that is not deductible.
DISCUSSION: Sec. 162(a)(2) allows a deduction for travel expenses while away from home in pursuit of a trade or business. Travel expenses include transportation, meals, lodging, and expenses incidental to travel. Only such travel expenses as are reasonable and necessary in the conduct of the taxpayer's business (employment) and directly attributable to it may be deducted [Reg. 1.162-2(a)]. The personal air fare from San Francisco to Honolulu is not deductible, but the weekend visit did not disqualify the rest of the trip to San Francisco since the overall trip was "primarily" for business.
Answers (a), (b), and (c) are incorrect because all are deductible as reasonable and necessary travel expenses incurred in the conduct of the taxpayer's business (employment).

147. Mr. Mack, a self-employed engineer, traveled to Boston for a 5-day seminar concerning engineering techniques. Mack took his wife, who performed minor entertainment services, and stayed an extra 10 days to visit family. Mr. Mack paid the following expenses.

Plane fare ($500 each)	$1,000
Hotel (single occupancy would have cost $1,500)	1,650
Meals (Mr. Mack $450; Mrs. Mack $400)	850

What is the amount of travel expenses Mr. Mack can deduct on his income tax return?

a. $0.
b. $500.
c. $620.
d. $650.

The correct answer is (c). *(SPE 990 II-68)*
REQUIRED: The amount of travel expenses to be deducted by the taxpayer.
DISCUSSION: Travel expenses are deductible if incurred in the pursuit of a trade or business activity or are related to the taxpayer's employment. If the purpose for the travel is primarily personal, no deduction is permitted except for the specific expenditures directly related to the trade or business or employment related activity. As Mr. Mack attended the seminar for 5 days and stayed for 10 additional personal days, none of the plane fare to and from Boston would be deductible. In addition, when a spouse accompanies a taxpayer on a business trip, expenses attributable to the spouse's travel are not deductible unless it can be shown that the spouse's presence on the trip served a bona fide business purpose. Reg. 1.162-2(c) requires that the spouse must perform services that are more than incidental in nature. Mack's deduction is limited to his specific expenditures incurred in attending the convention. As discussed, no portion of the plane fare nor any portion of the expense relating to Mack's spouse will be permitted as a deduction. Mack's deduction is computed as follows:

Hotel ($1,500 x 5/15)	$500
Meals ($450 x 5/15 x 80%)	120
Deductible travel expense	$620

148. During 1991, Mr. H, an employee of Corporation Z, flew to Seattle to meet with a client and incurred the following expenses that were directly related to his business.

Plane fare	$450
3 days lodging	300
Meals	100
Theater tickets with a face value of $50 each for H and his client	200

Mr. H's employer reimbursed him $450 for plane fare, $300 for lodging and $150 for meals and entertainment. The reimbursement was not included on Mr. H's W-2. What is the amount of the deduction Mr. H may claim on his 1991 return, disregarding the 2% of adjusted gross income limitation?

a. $0.
b. $40.
c. $50.
d. $80.

The correct answer is (b). *(SPE 989 I-83)*
REQUIRED: The amount of the deduction related to partially reimbursed business expenses not included on the taxpayer's W-2 form.
DISCUSSION: No deduction will be allowed for the expenses incurred by Mr. H which were reimbursed by his employer. Therefore, no deduction will be allowed relating to the plane fare ($450), the lodging ($300) and $150 of meals and entertainment. Additionally, the deduction relating to the cost of a ticket for an entertainment activity is limited to the face value of the ticket. The total deduction is computed as follows:

Meals and entertainment expense incurred:	
Meals	$ 100
Tickets (face value = $50 x 2)	100
	$ 200
Reimbursed by employer	(150)
Unreimbursed portion of meals and entertainment	$ 50
Meal and entertainment limitation	x 80%
Total deduction allowed	$ 40

149. During 1991, Joe spent $1,000 in travel expenses to attend the annual stockholders' meeting for ABC Corporation. Joe has stock in ABC for investment purposes only. How much of the travel expense can Joe deduct in 1991 if his adjusted gross income is $20,000?

a. $0.
b. $600.
c. $800.
d. $1,000.

The correct answer is (a). *(SPE 989 II-40)*
REQUIRED: The amount of the deduction for travel expenses incurred in attending shareholder meetings.
DISCUSSION: Transportation and other expenses paid to attend stockholders' meetings of companies in which the taxpayer owns stock but has no other interest are not deductible travel expenses. In general no expenses of attending conventions, seminars, or similar meetings for investment purposes may be deducted. Joe will not be permitted a deduction for travel expenses in this situation.

Module 9.7: Second-Tier Miscellaneous Itemized Deductions 213

150. For 1991, Mr. G, a construction worker, had adjusted gross income of $20,000. He incurred the following employment-related and investment-related miscellaneous expenses.

Safety shoes	$ 100
Union initiation fees	2,000
Union dues	300
Life insurance	800
Jeans & flannel shirts used for work	200
Management fees on taxable income producing investments	1,200
Legal expenses for drafting a will	100

He was not reimbursed for any of the employment-related expenses. What is the amount of his miscellaneous expense deduction after any limitations?

a. $3,200.
b. $3,400.
c. $3,600.
d. $4,800.

The correct answer is (a). *(SPE 989 I-93)*
REQUIRED: The amount of the miscellaneous expense deduction after limitations.
DISCUSSION: Dues and initiation fees paid for union membership and the cost of safety shoes are unreimbursed employee business expenses and are deductible as second-tier itemized deductions subject to the 2% of AGI limitation. Management fees on investments producing taxable income are other expenses also deductible as second-tier deductions subject to the 2% of AGI floor. The cost of life insurance, clothing suitable for normal wear (jeans and flannel shirts) and legal expenses for drafting a will are all personal expenditures and may not be included in itemized deductions (Sec. 262). Mr. G's deduction is calculated as follows:

Safety shoes	$ 100
Union initiation fees	2,000
Union dues	300
Management fees on investments	1,200
	$3,600
Less AGI limitation ($20,000 x .02)	(400)
Miscellaneous expense deduction after limitation	$3,200

151. You may deduct as miscellaneous itemized deductions fees paid to a broker, a bank, or a similar agent to collect your bond interest or dividends on stock. But you may not deduct as a miscellaneous itemized deduction a fee you paid to a broker to buy investment property, such as stocks or bonds.

The correct answer is (T). *(SPE 984 I-30)*
DISCUSSION: The fees paid to a broker to buy investment property such as stocks or bonds are added to the cost of such property and recovered upon its sale or other disposition. Note that the deductible items are second-tier miscellaneous itemized deductions, subject to the 2% of AGI limitation.

152. Mr. A uses one room in his home to read financial periodicals and reports, clip bond coupons, and perform similar investment activities. Mr. A uses this room regularly and exclusively for this purpose. These activities are not a part of Mr. A's trade or business. Mr. A can take a miscellaneous deduction on Schedule A for the use of this room.

The correct answer is (F). *(SPE 984 I-29)*
DISCUSSION: No deduction is allowed for an in-home office unless a portion of the residence is used exclusively on a regular basis as the taxpayer's principal place of business or as a place of business to meet with patients, clients, or customers (Sec. 280A).

153. For 1991, the allocated investment expenses of "publicly offered" mutual funds are not subject to the 2% of adjusted gross income limit.

The correct answer is (T). *(SPE 989 I-23)*
DISCUSSION: Sec. 67(c)(1) prevents the indirect deduction by using pass-through entities of amounts which are not allowable as a deduction because of the 2% floor on miscellaneous itemized deductions if such amounts were directly paid or incurred by an individual. An exception to this general disallowance rule is found in Sec. 67(c)(2) which permits investment expenses of "publicly offered" regulated investment companies (such as mutual funds) to be deducted by individuals without regard to the 2% floor.

154. B, a trust officer in a bank, is required by the bank to get a law degree. B registered at the local university's law school in 1991 for the regular curriculum that leads to a law degree. For 1991, B paid $7,000 for tuition, etc. which the bank reimbursed in full. The bank included the $7,000 on B's W-2. The $7,000 is deductible by B as an education expense.

The correct answer is (F). *(SPE 986 I-30)*
DISCUSSION: The education expenditures in earning a law degree are not deductible because they qualify the taxpayer for a new trade or business, that of being a lawyer. The fact that the law degree was required by B's employer to retain his employment status does not cause the expenditures to be deductible.

155. Employment agency fees in seeking employment in a new trade or business are deductible if employment is secured.

The correct answer is (F). *(SPE 1077 I-93)*
DISCUSSION: Although employment agency fees for seeking employment in the same trade or business are deductible under Sec. 212 whether or not a new job is secured, such expenses incurred in seeking employment in a new trade or business are not deductible regardless of whether employment is secured.

156. Ms. Q is a college professor with a master's degree. She takes additional courses toward a doctorate that is needed to qualify her for an appointment as president of a junior college. Ms. Q may deduct her educational expenses for the additional courses leading toward the doctorate.

The correct answer is (T). *(SPE 987 I-25)*
DISCUSSION: All teaching and related duties are considered the same general kind of work. This includes a teacher whose duties change from classroom teacher to school administrator. Since Ms. Q's education expenses to qualify as president of a junior college are not considered as qualifying her for a new trade or business, they are deductible.

157. Mr. Good holds a permanent teaching certificate in State A and was employed as a teacher by that state for several years. In August 1991, he moved to State B and was promptly hired by the state to teach school. He is required, however, to complete certain prescribed courses to get a permanent teaching certificate in State B. Mr. Good may deduct his educational expenses for the additional courses to get a permanent teaching certificate in State B.

The correct answer is (T). *(SPE 988 I-17)*
DISCUSSION: Teaching educational courses in one state is considered the same kind of work as teaching educational courses in another state. Therefore, completing courses for a teaching certificate in a new state is not considered qualifying the individual for a new trade or business. The cost of these additional courses is deductible.

158. Jody is a high school Spanish teacher. During her summer vacation in 1991, Jody traveled around Spain to improve her knowledge of the Spanish language. She took pictures to use in her classroom, visited Spanish schools, and attended movies and plays to improve her Spanish language skills. Jody may deduct the cost of the trip to Spain because it is directly related to her work.

The correct answer is (F). *(SPE 989 I-20)*
DISCUSSION: Under Sec. 274(m)(2) no deduction is generally allowed for travel as a form of education. A travel deduction, which would otherwise be allowed on the grounds that the travel itself served an educational purpose, is not permitted by Sec. 274(m).

159. Mr. W attends classes at the local university two nights a week and on Saturdays. His qualifying educational expenses are deductible. On Tuesday and Thursday nights, Mr. W goes directly from work to his night classes. On Saturday, he goes from his home to his classes. Mr. W may deduct the transportation expenses incurred in going from work to his classes and from home to classes.

The correct answer is (F). *(SPE 984 I-28)*
DISCUSSION: Education expenses include books, tuition, transportation, and travel. However, the cost of local transportation between home and school on a nonworking day is treated as a personal commuting expense and is not deductible.

160. For 1991, you may not deduct educational expenses your employer reimbursed or paid for you under a qualified education assistance program which are excluded from your income. However, amounts received under the qualified educational assistance program that are not excluded from income and qualify as educational expenses, may be deducted on Schedule A, Form 1040 as a miscellaneous deduction subject to the 2% limitation.

The correct answer is (T). *(SPE 989 I-22)*
DISCUSSION: Code Sec. 127 allows up to $5,250 a year received by an employee under an educational assistance program to be excluded from gross income, in which case no deduction for educational expenses would be allowed. Amounts received under an educational assistance program that are included in income (e.g., excess reimbursements), which are qualified educational expenses, are to be deducted as a miscellaneous deduction on Schedule A [Sec. 62(c)]. The deduction would be subject to the 2% of AGI floor. Sec. 62(c), effective beginning in 1989, requires employees to include the reimbursement in income and to itemize expenses when excess reimbursements are received. This section applies to all employee expenses.

161. A corporate officer who incurs entertainment expenses primarily for his own personal benefit can claim a deduction up to the amount of any reimbursement by the employer.

The correct answer is (F). *(SPE 1078 I-18)*
DISCUSSION: Sec. 274(a) specifically disallows a deduction for entertainment expenses unless the taxpayer establishes that the expense was directly related to the active conduct of the taxpayer's trade or business, or the expense was incurred directly preceding or following a substantial and bona fide business discussion, and that the expense was associated with the active conduct of the taxpayer's trade or business.

162. Mr. B, a commissioned car salesperson who works primarily at his employer's business location, can deduct the cost of entertaining his best customers whether or not he itemizes his deductions on Schedule A for 1991.

The correct answer is (F). *(SPE 1080 I-19)*
DISCUSSION: Entertainment expenses are deductible from adjusted gross income (subject to the provisions of Sec. 274) and can be taken only if the taxpayer itemizes his/her deductions, unless the taxpayer substantiates the expenses to the employer and they are reimbursed by the employer. In that case, the expenses are deductible for adjusted gross income.

163. To qualify an expense as directly related entertainment, you are required to show that business income or other business benefit actually resulted from each and every entertainment expenditure.

The correct answer is (F). *(SPE 1079 II-9)*
DISCUSSION: To qualify an expense as directly related to entertainment, the taxpayer must have had more than a general expectation of deriving some income or business benefit at some indefinite future time from the making of the expenditure. A taxpayer is not required to show that income or other business benefit actually resulted from every expenditure for which a deduction is claimed [Reg. 1.274-2(c)(3)].

164. If you work at two places in 1 day for two employers, you may deduct the expense of getting from one place of employment to the other.

The correct answer is (T). *(SPE 1077 I-74)*
DISCUSSION: An employee is permitted a deduction from adjusted gross income for unreimbursed transportation expenses paid in connection with services performed as an employee (Sec. 162). Transportation expenses include only the cost of transporting the employee from one place to another in the course of employment while not away from home in a travel status. The expense of getting from one job to another is deductible, while the expense of commuting to and from home or between the taxpayer's home and one or more regular places of employment or business, unless they are temporary workstations that are not the taxpayer's regular place of business, is not deductible (Rev. Proc. 90-23).

165. Mr. A, a steamfitter, has a temporary assignment beyond the general area of his tax home (place of employment). He leaves his tax home early each morning and returns home each evening. Mr. A cannot deduct the daily round-trip transportation expenses because they are commuting expenses and are nondeductible personal expenses.

The correct answer is (F). *(SPE 1081 I-17)*
DISCUSSION: Transportation expenses associated with temporary assignments beyond the general area of the tax home are an exception to the general rule that commuting expenses are nondeductible. The reason is that as long as the assignment is temporary, the employee's tax home (place of employment) has not changed, and the transportation is not between his personal home and his tax home (which is a personal commuting expense).

166. Mr. C, a construction worker who does not work beyond the general area of his employment, hauls his tools in his automobile between his residence and the job site each day. He incurs no additional costs in doing so. Mr. C can use the standard mileage rate to deduct the daily round trip between his home and the job site, providing he maintains the necessary records.

The correct answer is (F). *(SPE 1080 I-17)*
DISCUSSION: An employee who uses an automobile to transport tools to work will be allowed a deduction for transportation expenses only if additional costs are incurred, such as renting a trailer. A deduction is allowed only for the additional costs incurred to transport the tools to work. Therefore, Mr. C is not entitled to a deduction for transporting his tools.

167. Ms. X lives with her family in San Francisco, but works in Los Angeles. While in Los Angeles, Ms. X stays in a hotel and eats in restaurants during the week. She returns to San Francisco every weekend. Ms. X can deduct her expenses for travel, meals, and lodging while in Los Angeles.

The correct answer is (F). *(SPE 984 I-24)*
DISCUSSION: Travel expenses are deductible only when the employee is away from home for a temporary period. Since Ms. X permanently works in Los Angeles, this is the location of her tax home for purposes of determining travel expenses. Travel expenses to San Francisco are not deductible since Ms. X's absence from her tax home does not relate to her trade or business.

168. Mr. K, a welder living in St. Louis, takes a job on the construction crew for a large power plant in Phoenix that will take several years to complete. Mr. K maintains his residence in St. Louis and comes home occasionally to be with his family. Mr. K cannot deduct his travel expenses from his occasional visits home to be with his family because Phoenix is now his tax home.

The correct answer is (T). *(SPE 1082 I-15)*
DISCUSSION: Travel expenses are deductible only when the employee is away from home on business for a temporary period [Sec. 162(a)(2)]. The business location is considered the employee's tax home. A temporary construction job out of town for a period of up to 1 year does not necessarily change the employee's tax home. However, a job that will take several years to complete changes the taxpayer's home to the place of construction. Therefore, Mr. K cannot deduct his travel expenses for the occasional visits to his family.

169. Reimbursed employee business expenses not reported on a W-2 or 1099, are deducted as a miscellaneous itemized deduction subject to a 2% of adjusted gross income floor.

The correct answer is (F). *(SPE 989 I-14)*
DISCUSSION: If the reimbursement for employee business expense is equal to the expense incurred and an adequate accounting has been made, both the reimbursement and the expense are omitted from the employee's tax return. When reimbursed expenses are not included on a W-2 or 1099 the employee has recognized no income relating to the reimbursed expenses. Therefore, no corresponding deduction for the expense is permitted.

170. Unreimbursed employee business expenses not reported on a W-2 or 1099 are deducted as a miscellaneous itemized deduction subject to a 2% of adjusted gross income floor.

The correct answer is (T). *(SPE 990 I-18)*
DISCUSSION: Unreimbursed employee business expenses are deductible from AGI. The unreimbursed expense relating to meals and entertainment are subject to the 80% rule, and all unreimbursed employee expenses are subject to the 2% of AGI floor.

9.8 Limitation on Itemized Deductions for High-Income Taxpayers

171. Which of the following expenses is not subject to disallowance when applying the overall limitation or itemized deductions for high-income taxpayers provided for under Sec. 68?

a. Mortgage interest.
b. State income taxes.
c. Personal property taxes.
d. Medical expenses.

The correct answer is (d). *(Publisher)*
REQUIRED: The item not subject to disallowance under Sec. 68.
DISCUSSION: For tax years beginning after 1990, taxpayers with adjusted gross income in excess of a certain threshold amount are required to reduce the amount of itemized deductions allowed by the lesser of 3% of the excess of AGI over the threshold amount or 80% of allowable itemized deductions, not including certain deductions (Sec. 68). With regard to the 80% calculation, deductions for medical expenses, investment interest, casualty losses and wagering losses to the extent of wagering gains are not considered. This effectively prevents any reduction in the amount of the deduction claimed for these expenses.
Answers (a), (b), and (c) are incorrect because these items would be included in making the overall limitation calculation provided for by Sec. 68.

172. Andrea Brown is a single taxpayer. In 1991 she had adjusted gross income of $180,000 and itemized deductions of $20,000. All of the deductions arose from state income taxes and charitable contributions. Taking into account the overall limitation on itemized deductions for high-income taxpayers, what amount may Andrea deduct in determining her taxable income?

a. $20,000.
b. $17,600.
c. $16,000.
d. $4,000.

The correct answer is (b). *(Publisher)*
REQUIRED: The amount of the taxpayer's itemized deductions for 1991.
DISCUSSION: For tax years beginning after 1990, an individual with adjusted gross income in excess of a threshold amount will be required to reduce the amount of itemized deductions allowed by 3% of that excess. The total reduction may not exceed 80% of the total itemized deductions allowed, not including deductions arising from medical expenses, investment interest, casualty losses, or wagering losses to the extent of wagering gains. For 1991, the threshold amount is $100,000 ($50,000 for married persons filing a separate return). The total itemized deduction that is allowed is computed as follows:

Taxpayer's AGI	$180,000
Less threshold amount	(100,000)
Excess over threshold amount	$ 80,000
Limitation percentage	x .03
Tentative reduction	$ 2,400

The reduction will be equal to the lesser of $2,400 or 80% of total itemized deductions (not including medical expenses, investment interest, etc.).

Total itemized deductions allowed	$20,000
Times overall limitation percentage	x .80
Overall limit on reduction	$16,000

The taxpayer's reduction is $2,400 and she may claim a total of $17,600 ($20,000 − $2,400) in itemized deductions on her 1991 return.

173. Paul and Jodi are married taxpayers who file jointly. Their adjusted gross income for 1991 is $220,000. They also had the following itemized deductions:

Medical expenses (after 7.5% of AGI limitation)	$12,000
Mortgage interest	2,500
Investment interest	4,500
State income taxes	1,500
	$20,500

What amount may Paul and Jodi deduct as itemized deductions in determining taxable income?

a. $20,500.
b. $17,300.
c. $16,900.
d. $16,400.

The correct answer is (b). *(Publisher)*
REQUIRED: The amount of the taxpayers' itemized deductions allowed in 1991.
DISCUSSION: For tax years beginning after 1990, taxpayers with adjusted gross income in excess of a threshold amount will be required to reduce the amount of itemized deductions allowed by 3% of that excess. The total reduction may not exceed 80% of the total itemized deductions allowed, not including deductions arising from medical expenses, investment interest, casualty losses, or wagering losses to the extent of wagering gains. For 1991 the threshold amount is $100,000 ($50,000 for married persons filing a separate return). The total itemized deduction that is allowed is computed as follows:

Taxpayer's AGI	$220,000
Less threshold amount	(100,000)
Excess over threshold amount	$120,000
Limitation percentage	x .03
Tentative reduction	$ 3,600

The reduction for 1991 will be equal to the lesser of $3,600 or 80% of the total itemized deductions allowed. Note that for purposes of the overall 80% limitation, medical expenses, investment interest, casualty losses and wagering losses to the extent of wagering gains are not included.

Total deductions allowed ($2,500 + $1,500)	$4,000
Times: Overall limitation percentage	x .80
Overall limit on reduction	$3,200

The taxpayers' reduction then is $3,200 for 1991, and they may claim a total of $17,300 ($20,500 – $3,200) in itemized deductions for 1991.

174. For single individuals and married taxpayers filing joint returns, the threshold amount beyond which a reduction in itemized deductions will occur under Sec. 68 is $100,000 for 1991.

The correct answer is (T). *(Publisher)*
DISCUSSION: Sec. 68 provides for a reduction in the amount of itemized deductions allowed for taxpayers whose adjusted gross income exceeds a specified threshold amount. In 1991, the threshold amount for single taxpayers and married taxpayers filing jointly is $100,000. For married taxpayers filing separately the limit is $50,000 in 1991.

175. The reduction in itemized deductions for high-income taxpayers provided for in Sec. 68 is applied only after taking into account other code provisions determining the amount of a particular type of expense which may be deducted, such as the 2% of AGI floor on miscellaneous deductions.

The correct answer is (T). *(Publisher)*
DISCUSSION: The reduction in itemized deductions provided for under Sec. 68 is applied only after taking into account other code provisions limiting deductions, such as the 2% floor on miscellaneous itemized deductions. Additionally, in determining the correct treatment of state income tax refunds, the tax benefit rule will continue to apply in the same manner as it did prior to the enactment of Sec. 68.

CHAPTER TEN
INDIVIDUAL TAX COMPUTATIONS

10.1 Personal Exemptions	(25 questions)	219
10.2 Filing Status	(22 questions)	226
10.3 Filing Requirements	(20 questions)	232
10.4 Tax Calculations	(16 questions)	236
10.5 Unearned Income of a Minor Child	(7 questions)	242
10.6 Minimum Tax	(14 questions)	245
10.7 Estimated Tax Payments	(13 questions)	249

10.1 Personal Exemptions

1. Which of the following is included in determining the total support of a dependent for 1991?

   a. Fair rental value of lodging provided.
   b. Allocable portion of mortgage payment on lodging facility.
   c. Social Security benefits added to savings account.
   d. Life insurance premiums.

The correct answer is (a). *(SPE 987 I-46)*
REQUIRED: The item considered in determining the total support of a dependent.
DISCUSSION: A taxpayer must provide over one-half of the support for a person to be considered a dependent [Sec. 152(a)]. The term support includes food, shelter, clothing, medical and dental care, education, and other items contributing to the individual's maintenance and livelihood [Reg. 1.152-1(a)(2)]. Shelter or lodging is determined as the fair rental value of the room, apartment, or house in which the person lives.
  Answer (b) is incorrect because the fair rental value of lodging is used for support instead of an allocable portion of mortgage payments. Answer (c) is incorrect because amounts added to savings are not part of support. Support refers to amounts spent for an individual's maintenance and livelihood. Answer (d) is incorrect because life insurance premiums do not contribute to the maintenance and livelihood of an individual.

2. When figuring if a dependent child, who is a full-time student, meets the support test, all of the following items are taken into account in determining total support except:

   a. Food.
   b. Scholarships.
   c. Recreation.
   d. Birthday presents.

The correct answer is (b). *(SPE 990 I-34)*
REQUIRED: The item not taken into account in determining total support of a dependent child who is a full-time student.
DISCUSSION: To determine whether an individual received half of his/her support from the taxpayer, the amount of support received from the taxpayer is compared to the entire amount of support received from all sources, including support which the individual supplied. However, amounts received as a scholarship are not taken into account in determining whether the individual received more than half of his/her support from the taxpayer [Sec. 152(d)].
  Answers (a), (c), and (d) are incorrect because food, recreation, and birthday presents all constitute expenses of support.

219

Module 10.1: Personal Exemptions

3. All of the following are includable in calculating the total support of a dependent except

   a. Child care even if you are claiming the credit for the expense.
   b. Amounts veterans receive under the GI bill for tuition and allowances while in school.
   c. Medical insurance benefits, including basic and supplementary Medicare benefits received.
   d. Tax-exempt income, savings, or borrowed money used to support a person.

The correct answer is (c). *(SPE 986 I-45)*
REQUIRED: The item not taken into account in determining total support of a dependent.
DISCUSSION: A taxpayer must provide over one-half of the support for a person to be considered a dependent [Sec. 152(a)]. The term support includes food, shelter, clothing, medical and dental care, education, and other items contributing to the individual's maintenance and livelihood [Reg. 1.152-1(a)(2)]. Although medical care is an item of support, medical insurance benefits are not included. Medical insurance premiums are included.
Answers (a), (b), and (d) are incorrect because child care, education, and any funds used to support a person, whether tax exempt, borrowed, or from savings, all contribute to the maintenance and livelihood of the individual and are considered support.

4. Jim Planter, who reached age 65 on January 1, 1991, filed a joint return for 1991 with his wife Rita, age 50. Mary, their 21-year-old daughter, was a full-time student at a college until her graduation on June 2, 1991. The daughter had $6,500 of income and provided 25% of her own support during 1991. In addition, during 1991 the Planters were the sole support for Rita's niece, who had no income. How many exemptions should the Planters claim on their 1991 tax return?

   a. 2.
   b. 3.
   c. 4.
   d. 5.

The correct answer is (c). *(CPA 580 P-60)*
REQUIRED: The number of exemptions to which the taxpayers are entitled.
DISCUSSION: Sec. 151(b) provides an exemption for the taxpayer. On a joint return, there are two taxpayers and an exemption is allowed for each [Reg. 1.151-1(b)]. The Planters are entitled to an exemption for both Mary and the niece because Sec. 151(c) provides an exemption for each dependent whose gross income for the taxable year is less than the exemption amount ($2,150 in 1991), or who is a child of the taxpayer and is a full-time student (under age 24) at an educational organization during 5 months of the taxable year. No additional exemptions are allowed for being age 65 or over or for blindness. Thus, the Planters are entitled to four exemptions, one for each spouse, and one for each dependent.

5. Mr. and Mrs. P are filing a joint return for 1991. They have two children. Marie, who is 18, earned $2,400 from a part-time job. James, who is 24, and attends college as a full-time student, earned $2,400 during the summer. Mr. and Mrs. P provide over one-half of their children's support. Mr. P's mother also lives with them, but is self-supporting. How many exemptions can Mr. and Mrs. P claim on their 1991 return?

   a. 2.
   b. 3.
   c. 4.
   d. 5.

The correct answer is (b). *(SPE 988 I-32)*
REQUIRED: The number of exemptions to which the taxpayers are entitled.
DISCUSSION: Sec. 151(c) allows an exemption for each dependent whose gross income for the taxable year is less than the exemption amount ($2,150 in 1991), or who is a child of the taxpayer and has either not attained the age of 19 or is a student under age 24.
Mr. and Mrs. P are not permitted an exemption for Mrs. P's mother because she is not a dependent (she is self-supporting). They are permitted an exemption for their daughter, Marie, since she has not attained age 19. Although James is a full-time student, the taxpayers are not allowed an exemption since he has attained age 24 and has more than $2,150 of gross income. On a joint return, each spouse is entitled to an exemption. The P's are allowed three exemptions (Mr. P, Mrs. P, and Marie).

Module 10.1: Personal Exemptions

6. Mr. and Mrs. D file a joint return for 1991. Mr. D is 67 years old and Mrs. D is 52 years old. They provide 80% of the support for their son, Tom. Tom is 17 years old, single, and had wages of $4,000 in 1991. On their respective tax returns for 1991, Mr. and Mrs. D and their son, Tom, should claim which of the following number of personal exemptions?

	Mr. & Mrs. D	Tom
a.	4	1
b.	3	1
c.	3	0
d.	2	1

The correct answer is (c). *(SPE 987 I-45)*
REQUIRED: The number of exemptions allowed to the parents and child.
DISCUSSION: Sec. 151(c) allows an exemption for each dependent whose gross income for the taxable year is less than the exemption amount ($2,150 in 1991), or who is a child of the taxpayer and has not attained the age of 19. Even though Tom has gross income in excess of the exemption amount, Mr. and Mrs. D are entitled to an exemption for him since he has not attained age 19 and meets the other requirements for being a dependent. They are also each entitled to their own exemption, therefore Mr. and Mrs. D are entitled to a total of three exemptions.

Sec. 151(d)(2) states that no personal exemption may be taken on the return of an individual who can be claimed as a dependent on another taxpayer's return. Since Tom's parents are entitled to claim him as a dependent on their return, Tom is not entitled to a personal exemption himself.

7. In 1991, Sam Dunn provided more than half the support for his wife, his father's brother, and his cousin. Sam's wife was the only relative who was a member of Sam's household. None of the relatives had any income, nor did any of them file an individual or a joint return. All of these relatives are U.S. citizens. Which of these relatives should be claimed as a dependent or dependents on Sam's 1991 joint return?

a. Only his wife.
b. Only his father's brother.
c. Only his cousin.
d. His wife, his father's brother, and his cousin.

The correct answer is (b). *(CPA 1187 Q-17)*
REQUIRED: The relative(s) who could be claimed as a dependent on the taxpayer's return.
DISCUSSION: Sec. 152(a) lists those relatives who may be claimed as dependents if they receive over half of their support from the taxpayer. The taxpayer's uncle is included in this list, so Sam's father's brother may be claimed by him as a dependent.

Answers (a) and (d) are incorrect because Sam's wife is entitled to her own personal exemption and is not classified as a dependent. Answers (c) and (d) are incorrect because Sec. 152(a) does not include cousins in its list of relatives, and Sam's cousin was not a member of the household.

8. Mr. and Mrs. X, both age 50, are filing a joint return and have AGI of $75,000. Their son, who is blind, is a full-time student and is entirely supported by Mr. and Mrs. X. Mr. and Mrs. X also contributed more than half of the total support of their daughter who lived with them until her marriage in November. Their daughter and her husband had gross income for the year of $1,000 and $980 respectively, and filed a joint return to recover income tax withheld. What amount can Mr. and Mrs. X claim for exemptions for 1991?

a. $8,000.
b. $8,200.
c. $8,600.
d. $10,000.

The correct answer is (c). *(SPE 986 I-44)*
REQUIRED: The total amount the taxpayers can claim for exemptions.
DISCUSSION: An exemption is allowed under Sec. 151(c) for each dependent whose gross income for the taxable year is less than the exemption amount ($2,150 for 1991), or who is a child of the taxpayer and has either not attained the age of 19 or is a full-time student under age 24. No additional exemption is allowed for blindness or for being age 65 or over. Also, no exemption is allowed for any dependent who files a joint return with his/her spouse [Sec. 151(c)(2)], unless the joint return is filed solely to receive a refund.

Mr. and Mrs. X are thus entitled to four exemptions, one each for themselves, and one for each of their two dependent children. Their daughter qualifies since her joint return was filed solely to receive a refund. No additional exemption is allowed for their son's blindness. The amount of the personal exemption for 1991 is $2,150. The total amount of four exemptions in 1991 is $8,600 (4 x $2,150).

9. Assume the same facts as in the preceding example except that Mr. and Mrs. X instead report AGI of $200,000 for 1991. What amount can Mr. and Mrs. X claim for exemptions in 1991?

   a. $0.
   b. $4,300.
   c. $5,160.
   d. $8,600.

The correct answer is (c). *(Publisher)*
REQUIRED: The amount which the taxpayers can claim as exemptions in 1991.
DISCUSSION: For tax years beginning after 1990, if a taxpayer's adjusted gross income exceeds a specific threshold amount (based on filing status), the deduction allowed for personal and dependency exemptions is reduced by 2% for each $2,500, or fraction thereof, by which the adjusted gross income exceeds the threshold amount. The threshold amounts are:

Joint returns or surviving spouse	$150,000
Head of household	125,000
Single taxpayers	100,000
Married filing separately	75,000

The amount of Mr. and Mrs. X's four exemptions is $8,600 (4 x $2,150). The amount of the exemptions subject to phaseout is calculated as follows:

Adjusted gross income	$200,000
(Less threshold amount for joint returns)	(150,000)
Excess amount subject to 2% for each $2,500	$ 50,000

The X's exemption amount is reduced by 40%. This results from dividing the excess over the threshold amount ($50,000) by $2,500 and multiplying the result by 2% ($50,000 ÷ $2,500) x 2% = 40%. As a result, the X's $8,600 exemption is reduced by $3,440 (40% of $8,600) and the allowable exemption deduction is $5,160 ($8,600 − $3,440).

10. Mr. and Mrs. W file a joint return for 1991. During the year they provided more than 50% support for the following individuals, all U.S. citizens.

Mr. W's widowed mother, age 70, who lived with the W's and had no income.

Mrs. W's widowed father, age 64, who lived alone and whose sole source of income was Social Security of $3,600.

Mr. W's nephew, age 10, who lived with the W's all year and had no income.

Mr. W's cousin, age 30, who is single, fully disabled, had no income, and lived with the W's all year.

The W's daughter, age 25, who lived with the W's until she was married in May. She had no income but filed a joint return with her husband, who had wages of $15,000 for the year.

How many exemptions can the W's claim on their 1991 return?

   a. 7.
   b. 6.
   c. 5.
   d. 4.

The correct answer is (b). *(SPE 989 I-36)*
REQUIRED: The number of exemptions to which the taxpayer is entitled.
DISCUSSION: To qualify for the dependency exemption, the taxpayer must provide over 50% of the support of a U.S. citizen who meets certain relationship tests stated in Sec. 152(a). Each of the individuals listed qualifies under the relationship test of Sec. 152. Sec. 151(c) imposes additional limitations on the dependency exemption. These include a limit on gross income for each dependent of less than the exemption amount, unless (s)he is a child of the taxpayer and is under 19 years of age or a full-time student under 24 years of age. The dependency exemption is not allowed if a dependent has filed a joint return with his/her spouse for the taxable year.

Mr. and Mrs. W are entitled to one exemption each for themselves. They are also entitled to one exemption each for Mr. W's widowed mother, Mrs. W's widowed father, Mr. W's nephew, and Mr. W's cousin, for a total of six. Each qualifies as a dependent by passing all the dependency tests. Social Security is not included in gross income at his level of income, so Mrs. W's father does not fail the gross income test. The W's are not entitled to a dependency exemption for their daughter since she did not file a joint return with her spouse solely to secure a refund.

Module 10.1: Personal Exemptions

11. Sara Hance, who is single and lives alone in Idaho, has no income of her own and is supported in full by the following persons:

	Amount of Support	Percent of Total
Alma (an unrelated friend)	$2,400	48
Ben (Sara's brother)	2,150	43
Carl (Sara's son)	450	9
Total	$5,000	100

Under a multiple support agreement, Sara's dependency exemption can be claimed by

   a. No one.
   b. Alma.
   c. Ben.
   d. Carl.

The correct answer is (c). *(CPA 585 Q-30)*
REQUIRED: The person entitled to a dependency exemption under a multiple support agreement.
DISCUSSION: A dependent is defined in Sec. 152(a), which requires the taxpayer to provide over one-half of the support of the individual. An exception to the support test permits one of a group of taxpayers, otherwise eligible to claim the exemption and who together furnish more than one-half of the support of a dependent, to claim a dependency exemption even when no one person provides more than 50% of the support [Sec. 152(c)]. Any such individual who contributed more than 10% of the support is entitled to claim the exemption if each of the other persons in the group who contributed more than 10% signs a written consent filed with the return of the claiming taxpayer.
Ben can claim the dependency exemption because, as Sara's brother, he would otherwise be entitled under Sec. 152(a) to claim her as a dependent, and he contributed over 10% of her support. Carl cannot because he did not contribute over 10%. Alma cannot because she is not related to Sara.

12. D provides 20% of her own support. She has four children, daughters K and L and twin sons M and W, who provide the balance of her support. For 1991, K provided 40%, L 20%, M 12%, and W 8% of D's support. K and L file joint tax returns with their spouses. M files as a head of household, and W files as a single taxpayer. Taxable income in 1991, as reported on their returns, was $30,000 for K, $26,000 for L, $30,000 for M, and $34,000 for W. The four siblings come to you on April 1, 1992 and inquire about a multiple support agreement. Moreover, if one is able to claim D as a dependent, they want you to determine which individual to choose to maximize tax savings. Which of the following matches the advice you should give to K, L, M, and W?

	Must Be Party to Agreement	Should Claim Exemption
a.	K, L, M, W	W
b.	K and L or K and M	K
c.	K, L, M	M
d.	K, L, M	K

The correct answer is (c). *(J.G. Burns)*
REQUIRED: The correct application of the requirements for a multiple support agreement and an analysis of the structure of the tax rate tables.
DISCUSSION: Sec. 152(c) sets out the requirements of a multiple support agreement. All individuals who provide over 10% of D's support and are otherwise eligible to claim D as a dependent must agree that one of their number will claim D. No one individual can have provided over 50% of support. K, L, and M must be party to the agreement since each provided over 10% of D's support.
Of the three, M is subject to the highest tax rates since a head of household is subject to higher rates (28%) than a married person filing jointly (15%) when the two individuals have $30,000 of taxable income. Consequently, M will derive the greatest benefit from the exemption.
Form 2120 is used as a declaration that the persons who sign it (K and L) will not claim the individual (D) as a dependent. The taxpayer claiming the exemption (M) files it with his tax return.

13. In which of the following situations will the divorced custodial parent be entitled to the dependency exemption for the child?

   a. The noncustodial parent provides $1,500 of support for the child and the custodial parent provides $1,200.
   b. The custodial and noncustodial parent both provide $1,500 of support for the child.
   c. The custodial parent provides $1,500 of support for the child and the noncustodial parent provides $1,200.
   d. All of the above.

The correct answer is (d). *(SPE 990 I-35)*
REQUIRED: The situation(s) in which a divorced custodial parent will receive the dependency exemption for a child.
DISCUSSION: Sec. 152(e) provides that the custodial parent is allowed the exemption for a child unless (s)he releases the claim to the exemption for that year. There is no dollar requirement for support under these rules, but the child's support must come from the parents combined. If the custodial parent signs a written declaration releasing the exemption, the noncustodial parent must attach this declaration to his/her return.

Module 10.1: Personal Exemptions

14. Mr. C and Ms. D are the divorced parents of one child. Together they provide all the child's support and have custody of the child for more than half the year. Their 1984 divorce decree gives the exemption for the child to C, who is the noncustodial parent. There have been no modifications to the decree. Which of the following requirements must C also meet in order to claim the exemption?

a. He must pay at least $600 in child support during the year.
b. He must pay at least $2,150 in child support during the year.
c. He must provide over half the support for the child during the year.
d. None of the above.

The correct answer is (a). *(SPE 989 I-37)*
REQUIRED: The requirement for a noncustodial parent to claim a dependency exemption pursuant to a 1984 divorce decree.
DISCUSSION: The dependency exemption for a child of divorced taxpayers generally goes to the parent having custody of the child for the greater part of the year. This rule applies only when the child has received over half his support from divorced parents and was in the custody of one or both parents for more than half the year. Three exceptions exist to the general rule that a custodial parent is entitled to the dependency exemption, one of which is when a pre-1985 divorce decree or separation agreement between the parents grants the exemption to the noncustodial parent. In order for the noncustodial parent to claim the exemption in this situation, (s)he must provide at least $600 of support for the child during the year in question.
Answers (b) and (c) are incorrect because these are not requirements which must be met in order for a noncustodial parent to claim a dependency exemption pursuant to a pre-1985 divorce decree. Answer (d) is incorrect because the noncustodial parent must pay at least $600 toward the support of the child during the tax year as discussed above.

15. For 1991 tax returns, if you claim a dependent who is at least 1 year old by the end of a tax year, you must list the dependent's Social Security number on your Form 1040 or 1040A.

The correct answer is (T). *(SPE 987 I-3)*
DISCUSSION: Sec. 6109(e)(2) requires the taxpayer to provide on his/her return the Social Security number of any dependent 1 year of age or older for whom a personal exemption is claimed. For tax years 1989 and 1990, age 2 was the minimum for needing to provide a Social Security number.

16. Mr. and Mrs. Chung are married and are filing a joint return. Their daughter, Anne, age 20 and single, worked during the year and earned $2,600 in wages. Anne was not a full-time student during 1991. Mr. and Mrs. Chung provided over one-half of Anne's support during 1991. Mr. and Mrs. Chung may claim the dependency exemption for Anne.

The correct answer is (F). *(SPE 990 I-4)*
DISCUSSION: Sec. 151(c) allows an exemption for each dependent whose gross income for the taxable year is less than the exemption amount ($2,150 in 1991). Anne does not qualify for the exemption because she fails the gross income test. If Anne had been a full-time student or was less than 19 years old, she would have qualified as a dependent even though she failed the gross income test.

17. Miss V's friend, Miss D, who is single and a U.S. citizen, was a member of V's household during the entire year of 1991. V supported D for the entire year since D was unable to find employment and had no gross income. V may claim D as a dependent on her 1991 tax return.

The correct answer is (T). *(SPE 1083 I-5)*
DISCUSSION: Provided the other dependency requirements are met (i.e., gross income is less than his/her personal exemption amount), an individual who has his/her principal place of abode for the entire year in the home of the taxpayer and is a member of the taxpayer's household may be claimed as a dependent [Sec. 152(a)(9)].

18. Mr. B's son receives a $3,000 scholarship to X University. In the same year Mr. B provides $500 to his son as the only other support. The other dependency tests are met. Mr. B is entitled to claim his son as a dependent on his 1991 return.

The correct answer is (T). *(SPE 1079 I-1)*
DISCUSSION: To claim an exemption for a dependent, the taxpayer must provide over half of the dependent's support [Sec. 151(a)]. Amounts received as scholarships for study at an educational organization are not considered in determining whether the individual received more than half of his/her support from the taxpayer [Sec. 152(d)]. Therefore, Mr. B is considered to have supplied the only support for his son and is entitled to claim his son as a dependent.

Module 10.1: Personal Exemptions

19. Funds paid into a trust for the purpose of a child's future education are includable in determining support for dependency purposes.

The correct answer is (F). *(SPE 1078 I-5)*
DISCUSSION: Only support provided during the current taxable year is considered in determining whether an individual is a dependent [Sec. 152(a)]. Reg. 1.152-1(a)(2) specifies that only amounts received are taken into account as support. Funds put into trust for future education are not yet received, nor do they provide support during the current year.

20. Mrs. K, Mrs. N, and Mrs. S, who are sisters, together provided the total support of their mother. The amount of support given by each was Mrs. K, 45%; Mrs. N, 45%; Mrs. S, 10%. For Mrs. K to claim her mother as a dependent, all three sisters must sign a multiple support declaration (Form 2120), which must be filed with Mrs. K's return.

The correct answer is (F). *(SPE 989 I-4)*
DISCUSSION: Under Sec. 152(c)(4), only persons, other than the taxpayer, who contributed over 10% toward the support of the dependent must sign a multiple support declaration (a declaration that (s)he will not claim the individual as a dependent). Only Mrs. N is required to sign the declaration, which will be filed with Mrs. K's return.

21. Mr. T divorced his wife in December 1991. If he contributed all her support for the year, he can claim her as a dependent on his 1991 income tax return.

The correct answer is (F). *(SPE 1080 I-6)*
DISCUSSION: Even if the ex-spouse had her principal place of abode in the home of the taxpayer and was a member of the taxpayer's household during the year, if she was at any time during the taxable year the spouse of the taxpayer, she may not be considered a dependent [Sec. 152(a)(9)].

22. A and B are the divorced parents of one child and they furnish all his support. The divorce decree entered in 1988 gives the exemption for the child to B who has custody of the child. B provided $1,000 support for the child and A provided $1,100. A is entitled to the exemption for the child.

The correct answer is (F). *(SPE 1085 I-9)*
DISCUSSION: Sec. 152(e) provides that the custodial parent is allowed the exemption for a child unless (s)he makes a written declaration releasing the exemption. There are no dollar requirements for support under these rules.

23. During 1991, under the terms of a divorce, A had custody of his minor child for 8 months while his former wife B had custody the other 4 months. In each instance the custodial parent contributed 100% of the support (approximately $200 a month) while the child was in his/her custody. A gave B a signed written declaration that he would not claim the dependency exemption for the child. B can claim the exemption if she attaches this declaration to her return.

The correct answer is (T). *(SPE 986 I-5)*
DISCUSSION: Under Sec. 152(e), a noncustodial parent may claim the dependency exemption for a child if the custodial parent signs a written declaration stating that (s)he will not claim the child as a dependent. The noncustodial parent must attach this declaration to his/her return.

24. Mr. R is divorced from his wife who has custody of their child. The divorce decree entered in 1984 provides that Mr. R must pay his former wife $15 per week toward the child's support, which he did throughout the calendar year. The decree also provides that he may claim the child as his exemption. R's former wife can prove that during the year she contributed $7,500 toward the support of the child. Mr. R is entitled to claim the exemption for the child in 1991.

The correct answer is (T). *(SPE 1083 I-7)*
DISCUSSION: A noncustodial parent can claim the dependency exemption when the divorce decree was entered before 1985, if it provides for the noncustodial parent to have the exemption, and if the parent not having custody furnished at least $600 for the support of the child during the calendar year [Sec. 152(e)(4)]. Mr. R provided $780 ($15 x 52 weeks) of support and the divorce decree awarded him the exemption. Mr. R is thus entitled to the exemption in 1991.

25. Mr. and Mrs. K are filing a joint return for 1991. They provided more than half the support of their daughter and her husband who lived with them the entire year while they were full-time students at the local university. Neither their daughter nor her husband is required to file a return but they file a joint return to get a refund and no tax liability exists for either spouse on separate returns. All are U.S. citizens. Mr. and Mrs. K are entitled to claim their daughter and son-in-law as their dependents.

The correct answer is (T). *(SPE 989 I-5)*
DISCUSSION: In general, a married child may be claimed as a dependent by his or her parents only if the child does not file a joint return and would otherwise qualify as a dependent. An exception to the general rule exists, however, and a parent may claim a married child and his or her spouse as dependents in spite of their filing a joint return, provided that neither is required to file a return for the year and that the filing was solely for the purpose of obtaining a refund of tax withheld (Rev. Ruls. 54-567 and 65-34).

10.2 Filing Status

26. For federal income tax purposes, an individual is considered married for the whole year in all of the following situations except:

   a. If on the last day of the tax year the individual has not remarried after being widowed during the tax year.
   b. If on the last day of the tax year the individual is separated under an interlocutory (not final) decree of divorce.
   c. Lived with another individual over half the year as husband and wife in a state that does not recognize a common law marriage.
   d. The individuals are married with no dependents and lived apart the whole year but are not legally separated under a decree of divorce or separate maintenance.

The correct answer is (c). *(SPE 989 I-32)*
REQUIRED: The situation in which an individual would not be considered married for the entire year for tax purposes.
DISCUSSION: For federal income tax purposes, an individual is considered to have been married for the entire year if on the last day of the tax year the taxpayer is living together in a common law marriage which is recognized in the state where the taxpayer is currently living or the state where the common law marriage began. A taxpayer who lived with another individual over half the year as husband and wife in a state not recognizing common law marriage is not considered to be married for federal income tax purposes.
Answers (a), (b), and (d) are incorrect because these are all circumstances under which a taxpayer would be treated as having been married for the entire tax year.

27. John and Mary Arnold are a childless married couple who lived apart (alone in homes maintained by each) for all of 1991. On December 31, 1991, they were legally separated under a decree of separate maintenance. Which of the following is the only filing status choice available to them for 1991?

   a. Single.
   b. Head of household.
   c. Married filing separate return.
   d. Married filing joint return.

The correct answer is (a). *(CPA 583 P-58)*
REQUIRED: The filing status of married individuals living apart.
DISCUSSION: According to Sec. 7703(a)(2), an individual who is legally separated under a decree of separate maintenance is not considered married. Neither John nor Mary is eligible to file as head of household. Therefore, each must file as a single person.

28. During 1991, Robert Moore, who is 50 years old and unmarried, maintained his home in which he and his widowed father, age 75, resided. His father had $2,300 interest income from a savings account and also received $2,400 from Social Security during 1991. Robert provided 60% of his father's total support for 1991. What is Robert's filing status for 1991, and how many exemptions should he claim on his tax return?

   a. Head of household and two exemptions.
   b. Single and two exemptions.
   c. Head of household and one exemption.
   d. Single and one exemption.

The correct answer is (d). *(CPA 583 P-56)*
REQUIRED: The filing status and number of exemptions for an unmarried taxpayer who supports his father.
DISCUSSION: Robert's father has more than $2,150 of gross income in 1991, so he does not qualify as Robert's dependent [Sec. 151(c)(1)]. Only the interest income is considered when determining the amount of gross income, but it is more than $2,150. Since his father does not qualify as a dependent, Robert does not qualify for head of household filing status [Sec. 2(b)]. Robert must file as a single person with only one exemption (his personal exemption).

Module 10.2: Filing Status

29. All of the following are considered part of keeping up a home for head of household filing status except

    a. Real estate taxes.

    b. Rental value of the home you own.

    c. Rent.

    d. Food eaten in the home.

The correct answer is (b). *(SPE 990 I-32)*
REQUIRED: The item not part of keeping up a home for head of household filing status.
DISCUSSION: Reg. 1.2-2(d) provides that the cost of maintaining a household for head of household status includes the expenses incurred for the mutual benefit of the occupants. The rental value of the home is not considered part of keeping up a home since it is not an actual expense.
Answers (a), (c), and (d) are incorrect because each is an expense incurred for the mutual benefit of the occupants.

30. Which of the following is not a requirement that must be met in determining if a taxpayer is unmarried for head of household filing status purposes?

    a. You must file a separate return.

    b. You must have paid more than half the cost of keeping up your home for the tax year.

    c. Your spouse must not have lived in your home the entire tax year.

    d. Your home was, for more than half the year, the main home of your child, stepchild, or adopted child whom you or the noncustodial parent can properly claim as a dependent.

The correct answer is (c). *(SPE 989 I-35)*
REQUIRED: The item which is not a requirement in determining if a taxpayer is unmarried for head of household filing status purposes.
DISCUSSION: In determining if a taxpayer qualifies for head of household filing status, the taxpayer is considered unmarried if the following requirements are met.

1. The taxpayer filed a separate return.
2. The taxpayer paid more than half the cost of keeping up the home for the tax year.
3. The taxpayer's spouse did not live in the home during the last 6 months of the tax year.
4. The home was, for more than half the year, the main home of the taxpayer's child, stepchild, or adopted child whom the taxpayer or the noncustodial parent can properly claim as a dependent.

Therefore, answer (c) is correct, as the requirement is that the spouse may not have lived in your home during the last 6 months of the tax year, not the entire year [Sec. 7703(b)].
Answers (a), (b), and (d) are incorrect because each is a requirement for the taxpayer to be considered unmarried for the purpose of determining head of household filing status.

31. Which dependent relative does not have to live in the same household as the taxpayer claiming head of household filing status?

    a. Daughter.

    b. Mother.

    c. Uncle.

    d. Sister or brother.

The correct answer is (b). *(SPE 990 I-31)*
REQUIRED: The relative who does not have to live in the same household as the taxpayer claiming head of household filing status.
DISCUSSION: Sec. 2(b) provides head of household status for an unmarried taxpayer who maintains a household which constitutes the principal place of abode of the taxpayer's father or mother, but only if the taxpayer is entitled to a dependency deduction for the parent. The taxpayer is considered as maintaining a household only if (s)he furnishes over half of the cost of maintaining it. In the case of anyone other than the taxpayer's father or mother, such person(s) must actually occupy the taxpayer's own household for the taxpayer to be considered a head of household.

32. Mrs. Oak was divorced on January 1, 1991. She had an unmarried son living in her home for the entire 1991 year. It cost $3,000 to maintain Mrs. Oak's home for 1991, of which she contributed $2,000 and Joe Oak, ex-husband, contributed $1,000 through support payments. Joe Oak, however, provides more than one-half of the son's total support and claims him as his dependent. Which is the most advantageous filing status for which Mrs. Oak can qualify?

   a. Married filing joint return.
   b. Head of household.
   c. Married filing separately.
   d. Single.

The correct answer is (b). *(SPE 1077 I-165)*
   REQUIRED: The most advantageous filing status for which the taxpayer qualifies.
   DISCUSSION: The determination of whether an individual is married is made as of the close of the taxable year, so Mrs. Oak is unmarried. Mrs. Oak is not a surviving spouse, and the tax rates for a head of household are lower than those for a single taxpayer. To qualify for head of household rates, she must maintain (furnish over half the cost of) a household as her home which is the domicile of her unmarried child, regardless of whether she is entitled to the dependency exemption for the son [Sec. 2(b)]. Mrs. Oak meets these requirements for head of household status.
   Answers (a) and (c) are incorrect because Mrs. Oak is unmarried at year-end. Answer (d) is incorrect because head of household status is more advantageous than single.

33. Mr. W died in early 1991. Mrs. W remarried in December of 1991 and therefore was unable to file a joint return with Mr. W. What is the filing status of the decedent, Mr. W?

   a. Single.
   b. Married filing separate return.
   c. Married filing joint return.
   d. Head of household.

The correct answer is (b). *(SPE 989 I-33)*
   REQUIRED: The filing status of a decedent whose spouse remarried in the same year as the decedent's death.
   DISCUSSION: Generally, a surviving spouse may file a joint return for him- or herself and the decedent. In that case, the decedent's filing status on the final return would be married filing jointly. However, a joint return with the deceased spouse may not be filed if the surviving spouse remarried before the end of the year of the decedent's death. In this case, the filing status of the deceased spouse is that of married filing separate return [Sec. 6013(a)(2)].
   Answer (a) is incorrect because the decedent was married up until the time of his death and will not use single filing status. Answer (c) is incorrect because a joint return may not be filed for a deceased taxpayer whose spouse has remarried before the end of the year of the decedent's death. Answer (d) is incorrect because the decedent does not meet the requirements for head of household filing status.

34. Emil Gow's wife died in 1989. Emil did not remarry, and he continued to maintain a home for himself and his dependent infant child during 1990 and 1991, providing full support for himself and his child during these years. For 1989, Emil properly filed a joint return. For 1991, Emil's filing status is

   a. Single.
   b. Head of household.
   c. Qualifying widower with dependent child.
   d. Married filing joint return.

The correct answer is (c). *(CPA 1188 Q-16)*
   REQUIRED: The filing status of a widower whose wife died during the second preceding year.
   DISCUSSION: Emil qualifies as a surviving spouse whose spouse died in either of the two preceding tax years, who has not remarried, and who maintains a household which constitutes a principal place of abode of a dependent who is a child or step-child of the taxpayer [Sec. 2(a)]. A qualifying widower is another term for a surviving spouse and it is used by the IRS (and sometimes on the CPA exam).
   Answer (a) is incorrect because a surviving spouse may not use the tax rates of a single taxpayer. Answer (b) is incorrect because a surviving spouse is not a head of household [Sec. 2(b)(1)]. Answer (d) is incorrect because Emil was not married at the end of 1991.

35. Mr. A, a calendar-year taxpayer, died January 15, 1991. His widow, Mrs. A, remarried December 15, 1991. The last year for which a joint return may be filed by or for Mr. and Mrs. A is

a. 1990.
b. 1991.
c. 1992.
d. 1993.

The correct answer is (a). *(SPE 987 I-47)*
REQUIRED: The last year a joint return may be filed by a decedent whose surviving spouse remarried before year-end.
DISCUSSION: The determination of whether an individual is married is made as of the close of the taxable year, except that if his/her spouse dies during the taxable year, such determination is made as of the time of the death [Sec. 7703(a)]. Since the decedent was married at the time of his death, he is considered married for purposes of filing status. A decedent (through a personal representative) and a surviving spouse may file a joint return under Sec. 6013(a)(2) unless the surviving spouse remarries before year-end. Since Mrs. A remarried prior to the end of 1991, they may not file a joint return for 1991. The last year they could file a joint return was 1990.

36. Mrs. W's husband died in 1989. She has not remarried and has maintained a home for herself and her dependent son whose personal exemption she can claim. In the summer of 1991, the son was killed in an automobile accident. What is Mrs. W's filing status for 1991?

a. Single.
b. Married filing separate return.
c. Surviving spouse.
d. Head of household.

The correct answer is (c). *(SPE 1080 I-42)*
REQUIRED: The filing status of a widow whose dependent died during the year.
DISCUSSION: A surviving spouse is a taxpayer whose spouse died in either of the two preceding taxable years, and who maintains a household which constitutes the principal place of abode of a dependent who is a child or step-child of the taxpayer and with respect to whom the taxpayer is entitled to a dependency deduction [Sec. 2(a)]. Reg. 1.2-2(c)(1) provides that a dependent's death during the year will not prevent the taxpayer from qualifying as a surviving spouse. Mrs. W is a qualifying widow and can file as a surviving spouse.
Answer (a) is incorrect because a surviving spouse may not use the tax rates for a single individual [Sec. 1(c)] and would not want to since single rates are higher. Answer (b) is incorrect because Mrs. W was not married at year-end. Answer (d) is incorrect because a surviving spouse is not a head of household [Sec. 2(b)(1)].

37. Mrs. Doe, by herself, maintains her home in which she and her unmarried daughter resided for the entire year. Her daughter, however, does not qualify as her dependent. Mrs. Doe's husband died in 1990. What is Mrs. Doe's filing status for 1991?

a. Surviving spouse.
b. Married filing jointly.
c. Single.
d. Head of household.

The correct answer is (d). *(SPE 990 I-33)*
REQUIRED: The filing status of a widow whose child does not qualify as a dependent.
DISCUSSION: An unmarried taxpayer who is not a surviving spouse is considered a head of household if the taxpayer maintains as his/her home a household which constitutes the principal place of abode of a child or step-child of the taxpayer [Sec. 2(b)(1)]. The taxpayer need not be entitled to a dependency deduction for the child unless such child is married at the close of the taxable year. Mrs. Doe is not a surviving spouse since she is not entitled to a dependency deduction for her daughter [Sec. 2(a)(1)(B)]. Accordingly, Mrs. Doe is a head of household.
Answer (a) is incorrect because, as discussed above, surviving spouses must maintain a home for a child or step-child with respect to whom the taxpayer is entitled to a deduction under Sec. 151. Answer (b) is incorrect because Mrs. Doe was not married at year-end. Answer (c) is incorrect because a head of household may not use the tax rates for single individuals [Sec. 1(c)].

38. Ms. N, who is married, wants to file as a single person for 1991. Which of the following will prevent her from filing as a single person?

   a. Her spouse lived in her home for the final 6 months of 1991.
   b. She and her husband did not commingle funds for support purposes.
   c. She paid more than half the cost of keeping up her home for the tax year.
   d. Her home was, for more than 6 months of the year, the principal home of her son whom she can claim as a dependent.

The correct answer is (a). *(SPE 989 I-34)*
REQUIRED: The item which will prevent the taxpayer from filing as a single person.
DISCUSSION: The determination of whether an individual is married is made as of the close of the taxable year. A taxpayer's filing status is single if the taxpayer is unmarried or is separated from his or her spouse by a divorce or separate maintenance decree and does not qualify for another filing status. As Ms. N is married, the fact that her spouse lived in her home for the final 6 months of the tax year will prevent her from filing as a single person.

Answer (b) is incorrect because the fact that she and her husband did not commingle funds for support purposes will not prevent her from filing as a single person. Answers (c) and (d) are incorrect because, although these are requirements which must be met in order to file as a head of household, neither would prevent Ms. N from filing as a single taxpayer. Note, however, that, if all the requirements are met, it would be advantageous for the taxpayer to file as a head of household, because lower tax rates apply than for a taxpayer filing as a single person or a married person filing a separate return.

39. All of the following are reasons for not holding the "innocent" spouse liable for the tax (or any later assessments of tax, interest or penalty) related to a joint return except

   a. The innocent spouse did not know, and had no reason to know, that there was a substantial understatement of the tax.
   b. Taking into account the facts and circumstances, it would be inequitable to hold the innocent spouse liable.
   c. The other spouse's omitted income item resulted in a joint tax understated by more than $500.
   d. The divorce decree states that the other spouse will be responsible for any amounts due on previously filed joint returns.

The correct answer is (d). *(R. Fernandez)*
REQUIRED: When an innocent spouse may be liable for an understatement of tax on a joint return.
DISCUSSION: If a joint return is filed, husband and wife are jointly and severally (individually) liable for any tax, including any later assessments, related to the joint return. A divorced taxpayer may still be jointly and severally liable for tax, interest, and penalties due on a joint return filed before the divorce, regardless of what the divorce decree says.

Answers (a), (b), and (c) are incorrect because these three provisions must be met in order to absolve the innocent spouse from any tax liability resulting from the joint return [Sec. 6013(e)].

40. X and Y were married on December 31, 1991. This is the first marriage for both. Since they were single for the majority of the tax year, they must file single tax returns for 1991.

The correct answer is (F). *(SPE 984 I-2)*
DISCUSSION: Under Sec. 7703(a), the determination of marital status is made on the last day of the taxable year. Since X and Y were married on the last day of the taxable year, they must file as married.

41. A married couple who file separate returns may change to a joint return any time within 3 years from the original due date of the separate returns.

The correct answer is (T). *(SPE 990 I-3)*
DISCUSSION: Sec. 6013(b) provides that individuals may file a joint return after filing separate returns if they do so within 3 years from the due date, not including any extensions, of the separate returns.

42. A and B are married and timely filed a joint return for 1991. They may change to separate returns within 3 years from the due date of the joint return.

The correct answer is (F). *(SPE 988 I-2)*
DISCUSSION: Once a joint return has been filed, separate returns are not allowed after the time for filing the return has expired [Reg. 1.6013-1(a)(1)]. Therefore, A and B may not change to separate returns after the due date of the joint return.

43. Mrs. Brown's husband died on February 10, 1991. On December 30, 1991, Mrs. Brown married Mr. White. Mrs. White (previously Mrs. Brown), may elect to file a joint return with either the decedent or Mr. White.

The correct answer is (F). *(SPE 990 I-2)*
DISCUSSION: The determination of whether an individual is married is made at the end of the year [Sec. 7703(a)]. Therefore, a taxpayer who remarries is considered married to the new spouse at year-end and may file a joint return only with the new spouse [Sec. 6013(a)]. Note that in this situation the filing status of the deceased spouse would be married filing separately for his final return [Sec. 6013(a)(2)].

44. Mrs. B filed a timely joint 1990 income tax return for herself and her husband who died October 1, 1990. An executor for the decedent was appointed on April 20, 1991. The executor can revoke the joint return by filing a separate return for the decedent on or before April 15, 1992.

The correct answer is (T). *(SPE 1079 I-3)*
DISCUSSION: A joint return for a decedent must be filed by the personal representative of the estate unless one is not appointed prior to the due date for the surviving spouse's return (April 15). In that case the surviving spouse may file it. Per Sec. 6013(a)(3), if a personal representative is subsequently appointed, (s)he may revoke the joint return by filing a separate return for the decedent within 1 year after the due date of the surviving spouse's return (April 15, 1992).

45. An executor may elect to file a joint return for a decedent and the surviving spouse providing the surviving spouse has not remarried and the spouse elects to file a joint return.

The correct answer is (T). *(SPE 1078 I-4)*
DISCUSSION: A taxpayer whose spouse has died during the taxable year may file a joint return unless (s)he has remarried before year-end [Sec. 6013(a)(2)]. Both spouses must elect to file a joint return, but the executor makes this election for the decedent [Sec. 6013(a)(3)].

46. A person who qualifies as an abandoned spouse (e.g., married, but meets the tests for consideration as unmarried) automatically qualifies to file as head of household.

The correct answer is (T). *(R. Fernandez)*
DISCUSSION: To qualify as abandoned spouse, the individual must file a separate return and pay more than half the cost of keeping up a home which is his/her home and that of a son or daughter (step or adopted children included) for whom a dependency exemption is or could be claimed. The child must live in the home for more than half the taxable year and the taxpayer's spouse must not live in the home at any time during the last 6 months of the year [Sec. 7703(b)]. If these requirements are met, an abandoned spouse also qualifies as a head of household [Sec. 2(b)(1)].

47. Mary's husband died in 1989, and she has not remarried. She was entitled to file a joint return with her husband for 1989. Mary has continued to pay the entire cost of keeping up a home in which she and her dependent child have resided for the entire year. For 1991, Mary can file her federal income tax return claiming qualifying widow status.

The correct answer is (T). *(SPE 989 I-2)*
DISCUSSION: As Mary's husband died within the two preceding tax years and she has continued to maintain her home as a household which constitutes the principal place of abode of her dependent child for whom she is entitled to a personal exemption, Mary is a surviving spouse, also known as a qualifying widow or widower [Sec. 2(a)]. A qualifying widow or widower is entitled to use the same tax rates as married individuals filing joint returns.

10.3 Filing Requirements

48. Ms. T is age 20, single, and cannot be claimed as a dependent by another taxpayer. She is required to file an income tax return for 1991 if her gross income equals or exceeds what amount?

- a. $500.
- b. $2,150.
- c. $3,400.
- d. $5,550.

The correct answer is (d). *(SPE 984 I-46)*
REQUIRED: The minimum amount of gross income for which a single individual return must be filed.
DISCUSSION: Generally, a taxpayer must file a return if his/her gross income equals or exceeds the sum of the personal exemption to which (s)he is entitled plus the standard deduction amount applicable to the taxpayer [Sec. 6012(a)(1)(A)]. Sec. 151 allows a $2,150 exemption for each taxpayer in 1991. For a single taxpayer, the standard deduction is $3,400 in 1991 [Sec. 63(c)]. Ms. T must file a tax return if her gross income is at least $5,550.

49. Mr. and Mrs. X plan to file a joint return for 1991. Neither is over 65 or blind, nor do they have any dependents. What is the amount of gross income required before they must file a return.

- a. $2,150.
- b. $5,700.
- c. $9,800.
- d. $10,000.

The correct answer is (d). *(SPE 987 I-42)*
REQUIRED: The minimum amount of gross income for which a joint return must be filed when there are no dependents.
DISCUSSION: In general, a return must be filed if a taxpayer's gross income equals or exceeds the sum of the personal exemption and the standard deduction [Sec. 6012(a)(1)]. Sec. 151 allows a $2,150 exemption for each taxpayer in 1991. For a joint return, the standard deduction is $5,700 in 1991 and no additional standard deductions are allowed for taxpayers who are not over age 65 or blind. The couple must file a return if their gross income equals or exceeds $10,000 ($5,700 + $2,150 + $2,150).

50. During 1991, Student D, who is single, was claimed as a dependent by his parents. D earned $1,500 from a part-time job at a gas station. How much interest or other unearned income would D have to receive to require him to file an income tax return for 1991?

- a. $1.
- b. $550.
- c. $3,400.
- d. $5,550.

The correct answer is (a). *(SPE 1080 I-43)*
REQUIRED: The unearned income that would require filing an income tax return.
DISCUSSION: In general, an individual must file an income tax return if his/her gross income equals or exceeds the sum of the personal exemption and standard deduction [Sec. 6012(a)]. But in the case of an individual who is claimed as a dependent on another's tax return, (s)he must file if unearned income exceeds $550 or total income exceeds the standard deduction. For such a person, the standard deduction is limited to the greater of (1) $550, or (2) the individual's earned income [Sec. 63(c)(5)]. Since D was claimed as a dependent by his parents, his standard deduction is limited to his earned income of $1,500. Therefore, if D receives $1 of unearned income, his total income will exceed his standard deduction and he must file a tax return. Note that D is not entitled to a personal exemption because he was claimed as a dependent by his parents.

51. Mr. and Mrs. Jones, both over age 65, elect joint return status. They must file a return for 1991 if their combined gross income equals or exceeds

- a. $7,000.
- b. $10,000.
- c. $11,000.
- d. $11,300.

The correct answer is (d). *(Publisher)*
REQUIRED: The minimum amount of gross income for which a joint return must be filed in 1991 when taxpayers are over age 65.
DISCUSSION: In general, a return must be filed if the taxpayer's gross income equals or exceeds the sum of the personal exemption and standard deduction [Sec. 6012(a)]. Sec. 151 allows a $2,150 exemption for each taxpayer in 1991. For a joint return the basic standard deduction is $5,700 in 1991. In addition, Mr. and Mrs. Jones are allowed two additional standard deductions of $650 each for being age 65 or over [Sec. 63(f)]. The couple must file a return if their gross income equals or exceeds $11,300 ($5,700 + $650 + $650 + $2,150 + $2,150).

Module 10.3: Filing Requirements

52. Which of the following taxpayers must file a return for 1991?

a. Married taxpayers filing jointly who have income of $11,000 for the year and one child who is a dependent.

b. A single taxpayer, age 67, with interest and dividend income of $6,000.

c. A single taxpayer, claimed as a dependent by his parents, who earns $2,000 from a part-time job and has no unearned income.

d. A taxpayer who files as a head of household with two dependents and who earns $13,000.

The correct answer is (d). *(Publisher)*
REQUIRED: The taxpayer who must file a return for 1991.
DISCUSSION: Generally, a taxpayer must file a tax return if his/her gross income equals or exceeds the sum of the personal exemption and standard deduction [Sec. 6012(a)]. Sec. 151 allows a $2,150 personal exemption for each taxpayer in 1991. Standard deductions in 1991 are $5,700 for married filing jointly, $5,000 for heads of household, and $3,400 for unmarried individuals. A taxpayer who files as a head of household with two dependents must file a return if his/her gross income equals or exceeds $11,450 ($5,000 + $2,150 + $2,150 + $2,150).
Answers (a) is incorrect because gross income is less than the standard deduction plus exemptions. Answer (b) is incorrect because gross income is less than the standard deduction (basic plus additional for age 65) plus his/her exemption. Answer (c) is incorrect because (s)he has no unearned income and his/her earned income is not greater than his/her standard deduction [Sec. 63(c)(5)].

53. Silvia House, a calendar-year taxpayer, owed an additional $600 tax on her 1990 tax return which she filed on June 25, 1991. Ms. House failed to request an extension for filing her return. What are her failure to file and failure to pay penalties?

	Failure to File Penalty	Failure to Pay Penalty
a.	$100	$0
b.	$100	$9
c.	$91	$9
d.	$81	$9

The correct answer is (b). *(M. Yates)*
REQUIRED: The failure to file and failure to pay penalty when a very small amount of additional tax is due.
DISCUSSION: Sec. 6651(a) normally provides for a penalty of 5% of the tax due per month (or fraction thereof) when a return is not filed timely. In this case, House's penalty is only $90 ($600 x .05 x 3 months), reduced by the failure to pay penalty.
However, Sec. 6651(a) also provides for a failure to file minimum penalty of the lesser of $100 or 100% of the additional tax due for returns that are more than 60 days past due. When this rule applies, the failure to file penalty is not reduced by the failure to pay penalty. House's failure to file penalty is $100 and her failure to pay penalty is $9 ($600 x .005 x 3 months).

54. Sam Johnson, a calendar-year taxpayer, applied for and received an extension for filing his 1990 tax return. Mr. Johnson filed his tax return on June 2, 1991 and paid the balance due. The return reflected a tax liability of $50,000 and estimated tax payments made timely of $45,000. Based on these facts, Mr. Johnson owes

	Failure to File Penalty	Failure to Pay Penalty
a.	$0	$50
b.	$0	$25
c.	$500	$50
d.	$250	$25

The correct answer is (a). *(M. Yates)*
REQUIRED: A taxpayer's penalty when payment of tax is made at the time of filing an extended return.
DISCUSSION: Payment of tax is due by the due date for filing a tax return. The tax return is due April 15th for a calendar-year taxpayer. Since Mr. Johnson received an extension to file his tax return and filed it before the end of the extension period, there is no failure to file penalty.
The penalty for failure to pay tax is 0.5% of the amount due for each month (or fraction thereof) during which such tax remains unpaid. The maximum penalty under this provision is 25% (Sec. 6651). Mr. Johnson's failure to pay penalty is computed as follows:

Additional tax due on return	$5,000
Penalty rate per month	x .005
Penalty for 1 month	$ 25
Number of months past due	x 2
Failure to pay penalty	$ 50

The failure to pay penalty is computed only on the amount of tax due. There is no penalty for failure to pay estimated taxes because 90% of the total tax was paid as estimated payments during the year.

55. George Webster, a calendar-year taxpayer, filed his 1990 tax return on July 22, 1991. Mr. Webster did not request an extension for filing this return. The tax liability reflected on the tax return is $10,000. Mr. Webster had $9,000 withheld for federal income taxes by his employer. What are the failure to file and failure to pay penalties for this return?

	Failure to File Penalty	Failure to Pay Penalty
a.	$0	$20
b.	$200	$0
c.	$180	$20
d.	$0	$200

The correct answer is (c). *(M. Yates)*
REQUIRED: The taxpayer's penalty when a tax return is not filed timely and payment of tax is not made until the return is filed.
DISCUSSION: Mr. Webster's tax return was due on April 15th. Since he did not file for an extension of time to file his 1990 tax return, he is subject to a penalty for failure to file. Under Sec. 6651 this penalty is 5% of the tax due on the return for each month (or fraction thereof) that the return is not filed. The failure to file penalty is reduced by any failure to pay penalty. Mr. Webster is also liable for a failure to pay penalty since he did not pay the balance of his tax by the due date of his return. The failure to pay penalty is 0.5% of the unpaid tax for each month (or fraction thereof) that the tax is not paid.

Failure to pay penalty:
($1,000 x .005 x 4 months) $ 20
Failure to file penalty:
($1,000 x .05 x 4 months) $200
Less the failure to pay penalty   (20)   180
Total penalties $200

56. Mr. R, who is single and under age 65, had the following items of income and expense during 1991:

Gross receipts of sole proprietorship	$9,000
Cost of goods sold of sole proprietorship	5,000
Other expenses of sole proprietorship	1,500
Interest income (personal savings account)	2,000
Cash dividends	500

Mr. R is required to file a return for 1991.

The correct answer is (T). *(SPE 986 I-1)*
DISCUSSION: A taxpayer must file an income tax return if (s)he has gross income equal to or in excess of the standard deduction plus his/her personal exemptions [Sec. 6012(a)]. The gross income of a merchandising business is sales less cost of goods sold [Reg. 1.61-3(a)]. Therefore, Mr. R's total gross income is $6,500 ($4,000 from sole proprietorship + $2,000 interest + $500 dividends). This amount is greater than R's standard deduction of $3,400 plus his 1991 personal exemption of $2,150, so R must file a return.
A tax return is also required to report net self-employment income of $400 or more.

57. Taxpayer C's income for 1991 was $450 in wages and $250 in tips. Social Security was not collected or reported on the tips. No tax return is required to be filed because total income is less than $750.

The correct answer is (F). *(SPE 1078 I-1)*
DISCUSSION: If Social Security is not collected or reported on tips, the employee is required to pay the tax [Sec. 3102(c)(4)]. The taxpayer must file a tax return to pay the tax.

58. During the year 1991, Mr. and Mrs. P had combined gross income of $10,800. Mr. P was 66 on May 3, 1991, and Mrs. P's 65th birthday will be January 1, 1992. They are required to file an individual income tax return.

The correct answer is (F). *(SPE 1080 I-1)*
DISCUSSION: The taxpayers must file an income tax return if their gross income equals or exceeds the sum of the personal exemptions and the standard deduction [Sec. 6012(a)]. Sec. 151 allows a $2,150 exemption for each taxpayer in 1991. On a joint return, the standard deduction in 1991 is $5,700. Additional standard deductions of $650 are available if the taxpayer is blind or is age 65 or over [Sec. 63(f)]. An individual is considered 65 on the first moment of the day preceding his/her 65th birthday. Therefore, Mrs. P is considered age 65 on December 31, 1991. The taxpayers are entitled to $4,300 of exemptions and have a total standard deduction of $7,000 ($5,700 + $650 + $650). Since the taxpayers' combined gross income of $10,800 is less than $11,300 ($4,300 exemptions + $7,000 standard deduction), they are not required to file a return.

59. In 1991, a child who may be claimed as a dependent by another taxpayer, and who has earned income of $400 and unearned income of $200, must file a tax return.

The correct answer is (T). *(SPE 988 I-1)*
DISCUSSION: In the case of an individual who is claimed as a dependent on another's tax return, (s)he must file if unearned income exceeds $550 or total income exceeds the standard deduction. For such a person, the standard deduction is limited to the greater of (1) $550, or (2) the individual's earned income [Sec. 63(c)(5)]. The child who has unearned income of only $200 need only file a return if total income exceeds the standard deduction. In this case the total income of $600 does exceed the standard deduction of $550. The standard deduction is limited to $550 since this is greater than earned income.

60. Mr. K, age 66 and single, is a retired plumber. During 1991, he received $2,180 interest on savings, $490 net earnings from his neighbors for plumbing work, and $5,000 in nontaxable Social Security income. Mr. K is required to file a tax return.

The correct answer is (T). *(SPE 1085 I-1)*
DISCUSSION: In general, a taxpayer does not have to file a return if his/her gross income is less than the sum of the personal exemption and the standard deduction [Sec. 6012(a)].
But a self-employed individual must file a tax return to report net earnings from self-employment of $400 or more (Sec. 6017).

61. Mr. and Mrs. M's 1990 income consisted of the following:

Salary (Mr. M)	$33,000
Salary (Mrs. M)	18,000
Dividend income	400
Interest income	500
Unemployment compensation	1,200

Mr. and Mrs. M may use Form 1040A if they do not itemize.

The correct answer is (T). *(SPE 1082 I-3)*
DISCUSSION: Generally, Form 1040A may be filed for tax year 1990 if the taxpayers do not itemize, and if their taxable income is less than $50,000 and consists only of wages, salaries, tips, taxable scholarships and fellowships, unemployment compensation, interest, dividends, taxable Social Security and railroad retirement benefits, pensions, annuities, and IRA distributions. The taxpayers' gross income, all of which is from qualifying sources, is $53,100. They will be entitled to two personal exemptions of $2,150 each and the standard deduction of $5,700. Therefore, their taxable income will be less than $50,000 and they may file Form 1040A.

62. Mr. R is single, has no dependents, and is under 65 years of age. During 1990, his sole source of income was wages of $45,000. R does not have enough deductions to itemize. He may use Form 1040EZ for filing his 1990 income tax return.

The correct answer is (T). *(SPE 1083 I-2)*
DISCUSSION: Form 1040EZ is available for uncomplicated returns. The requirements are that the taxpayer must be single, (s)he may claim no additional exemptions for being age 65 or blind, (s)he may not itemize, taxable income must be less than $50,000, (s)he may have no dividend income, and (s)he may have only salary, wages, tip income, taxable scholarships and fellowships, and interest income of $400 or less.

63. Mr. Mercury does not have sufficient gross income to require the filing of a tax return; however, he has $100 in income tax withheld, so he should file a return in order to collect his taxes withheld.

The correct answer is (T). *(SPE 1077 I-27)*
DISCUSSION: Even if the taxpayer is not required to file, a tax return should be filed to get a refund if income tax was withheld from pay or if the taxpayer can take the earned income credit.

64. If you are a resident alien for the entire year, you must file a tax return the same as a U.S. citizen.

The correct answer is (T). *(SPE 984 I-45)*
DISCUSSION: Sec. 6012(a) provides the general rules concerning who must file a tax return for the year. Nonresident aliens are subject to different rules, but resident aliens are not.

65. An individual may obtain an automatic 4-month extension to file his/her individual income tax return and pay any balance of tax due by filing Form 4868, Application for Automatic Extension of Time to File U.S. Individual Income Tax Return.

The correct answer is (F). *(SPE 989 I-1)*
DISCUSSION: An individual who is required to file an income tax return is allowed an automatic 4-month extension of time to file the return by filing Form 4868. However, no extension of time is allowed for payment of the tax due. A taxpayer desiring an extension of time to file his/her tax return and avoid the failure to pay penalty must file Form 4868, accompanied by the payment of tax estimated to be owed for the year and not yet paid, by the normal due date of the tax return.

66. The final return of a cash basis calendar-year individual must be filed within 3½ months following the month in which (s)he died.

The correct answer is (F). *(SPE 986 I-6)*
DISCUSSION: The final return of a cash-basis calendar-year individual must be filed by April 15th of the year following the year of death. There is no requirement that the final return of a decedent be filed any earlier than (s)he would have if (s)he had not died.

67. If the Internal Revenue Service has granted a taxpayer an extension of time to file beyond the automatic 4-month extension and later justifiably renders the extension null and void, the taxpayer will have to pay the failure-to-file penalty on any tax not paid by the original due date of the return.

The correct answer is (T). *(SPE 986 I-2)*
DISCUSSION: A failure to file penalty is not imposed if the taxpayer has validly obtained an extension of time to file. But if the extension of time was not valid and is rendered null and void, the taxpayer must pay the failure-to-file penalty from the original due date of the return.

10.4 Tax Calculations

68. Which of the following is not true about adjusted gross income (AGI)?

a. It is a determining factor in the calculation of deductible medical and dental expenses.
b. It is a determining factor in the calculation of nonbusiness theft or casualty losses.
c. It may include a deduction for the unreimbursed qualifying educational expenses (tuition and books) of an employee.
d. It may include a deduction for qualifying alimony payments.

The correct answer is (c). *(R. Fernandez)*
REQUIRED: The false statement about adjusted gross income.
DISCUSSION: Unreimbursed qualifying educational expenses of an employee are itemized deductions, i.e., deductions after or from AGI. However, a taxpayer may deduct business expenses that have been substantiated to and reimbursed by an employer in arriving at AGI (Sec. 62).
Answer (a) is incorrect because AGI is used in determining the deduction for medical and dental expenses. Answer (b) is incorrect because AGI is used in calculating nonbusiness theft or casualty losses. Answer (d) is incorrect because qualifying alimony payments are deductible for AGI.

69. Scott and Trish Edwards are married and file a joint return. In 1991, Scott earned a salary of $48,000 and Trish earned $30,000. They received $600 of dividends during the year. They had unreimbursed expenses for moving household goods of $5,000 after both found new jobs across the country. What is their adjusted gross income for 1991?

a. $73,600.
b. $75,600.
c. $78,400.
d. $78,600.

The correct answer is (d). *(C.J. Skender)*
REQUIRED: The AGI for a couple with salaries, dividend income, and moving expenses.
DISCUSSION: $78,000 of salaries is included in AGI. All $600 of dividends is included in AGI because the 1986 TRA repealed the dividend exclusion for individuals. Moving expenses are a first-tier itemized deduction from AGI. Therefore, the Edwards' AGI equals $78,600.

Module 10.4: Tax Calculations

70. Donna Weber, age 24 and single, provided the following information on her 1991 income tax return:

Adjusted gross income	$30,000
Total itemized deductions	3,600
Personal exemption	2,150

Donna should report taxable income for 1991 of

a. $21,300.
b. $24,250.
c. $24,450.
d. $26,400.

The correct answer is (b). *(Publisher)*
REQUIRED: The taxpayer's taxable income for 1991.
DISCUSSION: Taxable income is defined as adjusted gross income minus the standard deduction (or total itemized deductions) and the deduction for personal exemption(s) (Sec. 63). For a single taxpayer in 1991, the basic standard deduction is $3,400. However, since Donna's itemized deductions exceed the standard deduction, she will elect to use the larger amount. Donna's taxable income is

Adjusted gross income	$30,000
Itemized deductions	(3,600)
Personal exemption	(2,150)
Taxable income	$24,250

71. Mike Law was married and filed a joint return with his wife in 1991. Neither Mike nor his wife is 65 or over or blind. Assuming he does not itemize, what is Mike's standard deduction for 1991?

a. $2,150.
b. $5,000.
c. $5,400.
d. $5,700.

The correct answer is (d). *(Publisher)*
REQUIRED: The standard deduction for a married taxpayer filing a joint return in 1991.
DISCUSSION: The standard deduction is allowed by Sec. 63 in lieu of itemizing. Additional standard deductions are allowed for those taxpayers who are age 65 or over or blind. In 1991, the basic standard deduction for those filing joint returns is $5,700.

72. Darren Cantrelle, age 21, is a full-time student and receives over half of his support from his parents. His other income is from a part-time job, from which he earned $750 in 1991. If Darren's parents claim him as a dependent for the year, what will his standard deduction be in 1991?

a. $550.
b. $750.
c. $2,150.
d. $3,400.

The correct answer is (b). *(Publisher)*
REQUIRED: The standard deduction for a taxpayer claimed as a dependent.
DISCUSSION: If an individual is eligible to be claimed as a dependent (Sec. 151) by another taxpayer for the taxable year, that individual's basic standard deduction cannot exceed the greater of (1) $550, or (2) that individual's earned income. Since Darren's parents claimed him as a dependent for 1991, his 1991 standard deduction will be limited to his earned income of $750.

73. George and Lillian Smith are married and file a joint return for 1991. They are both over age 65 and George is legally blind. They have adjusted gross income for the year of $15,000. What is the Smiths' taxable income for 1991?

a. $3,050.
b. $3,700.
c. $5,000.
d. $9,300.

The correct answer is (a). *(Publisher)*
REQUIRED: The taxpayers' taxable income for 1991.
DISCUSSION: An additional standard deduction of $650 is available if, during the taxable year, the taxpayer and/or his spouse is age 65 or over, and if the taxpayer and/or his spouse is blind. The Smiths will receive three additional standard deductions in 1991. Their taxable income for the year is

Adjusted gross income	$15,000
Basic standard deduction	(5,700)
Additional standard deductions ($650 x 3)	(1,950)
Personal exemptions ($2,150 x 2)	(4,300)
Taxable income	$ 3,050

74. Jeff Gibson, who is 26 years old and single, claimed one exemption and provided the following information for his 1991 return:

Salary	$40,000
Charitable contributions	3,100
State sales tax paid	410

Gibson's taxable income for 1991 is

a. $34,340.
b. $34,450.
c. $34,750.
d. $36,600.

The correct answer is (b). *(Publisher)*
REQUIRED: The taxpayer's taxable income for 1991.
DISCUSSION: Taxable income is defined as adjusted gross income minus (1) the standard deduction (or total itemized deductions if greater) and (2) the deduction for personal exemptions (Sec. 63). For a single taxpayer in 1991, the basic standard deduction is $3,400. Since there is no deduction for state and local sales tax, only Gibson's charitable contributions are allowable as an itemized deduction. He will therefore use the standard deduction, since it exceeds the amount of itemized deductions. The amount of the personal exemption in 1991 is $2,150. Gibson's taxable income is

Salary	$40,000
Standard deduction	(3,400)
Personal exemption	(2,150)
Taxable income	$34,450

---

75. Robert Francis, a single taxpayer, had adjusted gross income of $23,000 in 1991. Upon examining his records, he listed the following deductions for the year:

Medical expenses	$2,000
Charitable contributions	2,300
State income taxes paid	1,160
Business expenses reimbursed by employer, but not substantiated	1,500

The amount of his allowable itemized deductions for 1991 is

a. $3,735.
b. $4,775.
c. $5,235.
d. $5,460.

The correct answer is (b). *(Publisher)*
REQUIRED: The taxpayer's allowable itemized deductions for 1991.
DISCUSSION: If a taxpayer's allowable itemized deductions are greater than his standard deduction he may use these itemized deductions in computing his taxable income for the year. Qualifying medical expenses in excess of 7.5% of AGI may be deducted [Sec. 213(a)]. State and local income taxes (Sec. 164) and qualifying charitable contributions (Sec. 170) also may be deducted. Beginning in 1989, employee's business expenses must be substantiated to the employer and reimbursed to be deductible above the line. Otherwise, they are a miscellaneous itemized deduction subject to the 2% of AGI floor.

Medical expenses	$2,000	
Less: 7.5% of AGI ($23,000 x .075)	(1,725)	
Allowable medical expenses		$ 275
Charitable contributions		2,300
State income taxes paid		1,160
Business expenses	$1,500	
Less: 2% of AGI	(460)	1,040
		$4,775

---

76. For the year 1991, Frances had an adjusted gross income figure of $60,000. She is single and incurred the following expenses:

Medical expenses unreimbursed	$5,000
State income taxes	4,000
Real estate property taxes	1,000
State sales taxes	2,500
Contribution to church	6,000
Credit card interest	1,500
Home mortgage interest	7,000
Auto loan interest (personal)	500

Her allowable itemized deductions for 1991 are

a. $21,000.
b. $20,500.
c. $18,900.
d. $18,500.

The correct answer is (d). *(E. Fenton, Jr.)*
REQUIRED: The amount of itemized deductions allowable for 1991.
DISCUSSION: The medical expense deduction is limited to the portion greater than 7.5% of AGI [Sec. 213(a)], and the state sales taxes are not deductible. Consumer personal interest (credit card and auto loan interest) is not allowed as a deduction for 1991. The computations are

Medical [$5,000 − ($60,000 x .075)]	$ 500
State income taxes	4,000
Real estate property taxes	1,000
State sales tax	0
Contributions	6,000
Home mortgage interest	7,000
Allowable itemized deductions	$18,500

77. For the year 1991, Carolyn earned $40,000 and incurred the following expenses:

Moving expenses	$ 500
Credit card interest	250
Mortgage interest (qualified residence interest)	1,200
Tax return preparation fees	100
Unreimbursed employee business expenses	750

Assuming she had no other expenses, what are her total deductions for 1991?

a. $2,800.
b. $2,000.
c. $1,775.
d. $1,750.

The correct answer is (d). *(Publisher)*
REQUIRED: The amount of deductions allowable given gross income and total expenses.
DISCUSSION: All of Carolyn's expenses for 1991 are deductible from adjusted gross income (AGI) so her gross income and her AGI are the same, $40,000. Qualified residence interest is deducted in full. None of any personal interest (such as credit card interest) is deductible in 1991. Moving expenses are first-tier miscellaneous expenses and are deductible in full. Tax return preparation fees and unreimbursed employee business expenses are second-tier miscellaneous deductions and under Sec. 67 are deductible only to the extent that in total they exceed 2% of AGI.

Mortgage interest		$1,200
Moving expenses		500
Tax return preparation fees	$100	
Employee business expenses	750	
	$850	
2% of AGI ($40,000 x 2%)	(800)	
Allowable second-tier misc. itemized deductions		50
Total deductions		$1,750

78. Jerry Samson is single, age 35, and had $180,000 in adjusted gross income for 1991. All of Jerry's income is salary income. Jerry claimed one personal exemption of $2,150. Samson's taxable income for 1991 is

a. $174,450.
b. $175,826.
c. $177,850.
d. $180,000.

The correct answer is (b). *(Publisher)*
REQUIRED: The taxable income for a single taxpayer in 1991.
DISCUSSION: For tax years beginning after 1990, if a taxpayer's adjusted gross income exceeds a specific threshold amount (based on filing status), the deduction allowed for personal and dependency exemptions is reduced by 2% for each $2,500, or fraction thereof, by which the adjusted gross income exceeds the threshold amount. For a single taxpayer, the threshold amount is $100,000 in 1991. The standard deduction for a single taxpayer is $3,400 in 1991. Samson's taxable income computation is as follows:

Adjusted gross income	$180,000
Standard deduction	(3,400)
Personal exemption	(774)
Taxable income	$175,826

The personal exemption amount is calculated as follows:

($180,000 AGI − $100,000 threshold) ÷ $2,500 =
32 x 2% = 64%

Exemption for 1991	$2,150
Disallowance percentage	x .64
Disallowed exemption amount	$1,376

The deduction for Samson's personal exemption is $774 ($2,150 − $1,376).

79. John and Barbara are married, age 46 and 44, respectively, have no dependents, and file a joint return for 1991. The following information is obtained from their 1991 tax return:

John's salary	$100,000
Barbara's salary	120,000
Dividend income (jointly-owned stock)	30,000
Itemized deductions	40,000
Personal exemptions	4,300

The itemized deductions consist of: mortgage interest, $30,000; investment interest, $4,000; medical expenses (in excess of 7.5% of AGI limitation), $1,500; and charitable contributions, $4,500. John and Barbara's taxable income for 1991 is

a. $205,700.
b. $213,640.
c. $241,140.
d. $245,700.

The correct answer is (b). *(Publisher)*
REQUIRED: The amount of the taxpayer's taxable income for 1991.
DISCUSSION: For tax years beginning after 1990, the deduction allowed for personal and dependency exemptions is reduced for taxpayers whose adjusted gross income exceeds a specified threshold amount. Similarly, the amount of itemized deductions allowed is also reduced when the taxpayer's AGI exceeds a certain threshold. For married taxpayers filing jointly, the threshold amounts are $150,000 and $100,000 for personal exemptions and itemized deductions, respectively.

Note that the total reduction in itemized deductions may not exceed 80% of allowable itemized deductions, not including the deductions for medical expenses, investment interest, casualty losses, or wagering losses to the extent of wagering gains. The overall limitation did not apply in this situation.

Overall limitation on disallowed deductions:

Mortgage interest	$30,000
Charitable contributions	4,500
Total deductions	$34,500
Times: disallowance percentage	x .80
Maximum disallowed deduction	$27,600

Exemption limitation:
($250,000 AGI − $150,000 threshold) ÷ $2,500 =
40 x 2% = 80%

Exemptions for 1991 (2 x $2,150)	$ 4,300
Disallowance percentage	x .80
Disallowed exemption amount	$ 3,440
Total exemption allowed ($4,300 − $3,440)	$ 860

Itemized deduction limitation:

($250,000 AGI − $100,000 threshold) x 3% =	$ 4,500
Total itemized deductions allowed ($40,000 − $4,500) =	$ 35,500

Taxable income:

Adjusted gross income	$250,000
Exemptions allowed	(860)
Itemized deductions allowed	(35,500)
	$213,640

80. Marty and Michelle Hall, both under 65 years of age, file a joint return in 1991. Their adjusted gross income for the year is $51,000, and their itemized deductions amount to $6,600. They claim one child as a dependent. Their income tax liability for 1991 is

a. $5,100.00
b. $6,206.00
c. $7,980.50
d. $8,012.00

The correct answer is (b). *(Publisher)*
REQUIRED: The taxpayers' tax liability for 1991.
DISCUSSION: For taxpayers filing a joint return in 1991, the rates in Sec. 1(h)(2)(A) should be applied to their taxable income, defined as adjusted gross income minus the standard deduction (or total itemized deductions if greater) and the deduction for personal exemptions (Sec. 63). Each spouse on a joint return in 1991 is entitled to a $2,150 personal exemption, and a $2,150 exemption for each dependent [Secs. 151(b) and (c)]. The taxpayers' taxable income is $37,950 ($51,000 adjusted gross income − $6,600 itemized deductions − $6,450 personal exemptions). The Halls' tax liability for 1991 is

15% x $34,000	=	$5,100
28% x $3,950	=	1,106
		$6,206

Module 10.4: Tax Calculations

81. Harold and Tina Skaggs, both over age 65, file a joint return in 1991. They have adjusted gross income for the year of $60,000 and $4,100 of itemized deductions. The Skaggs' tax liability for 1991, rounded to the nearest dollar, is

a. $9,216.
b. $9,580.
c. $10,021.
d. $10,509.

The correct answer is (a). *(Publisher)*
REQUIRED: The taxpayers' tax liability for 1991.
DISCUSSION: For taxpayers filing a joint return in 1991, the rates in Sec. 1(a) should be applied to their taxable income, defined as adjusted gross income minus the standard deduction (or total itemized deductions if greater) and the deduction for personal exemptions (Sec. 63). The Skaggs will use the standard deduction since it is greater than their itemized deductions. Their standard deduction is the $5,700 basic standard deduction plus two additional standard deductions of $650 each because they are over age 65. Each spouse on a joint return is entitled to a $2,150 personal exemption in 1991. The Skaggs' taxable income is $48,700 ($60,000 adjusted gross income − $5,700 basic standard deduction − $1,300 additional standard deductions − $4,300 personal exemptions). Their tax liability for 1991 is $9,216 [(15% x $34,000) + (28% x $14,700)].

82. Judy Tower, age 34, is single. Her adjusted gross income for 1991 is $95,000. Included in this total is $5,000 of net long-term capital gains. Judy claims the standard deduction and one personal exemption. Judy's income tax liability for 1991 is

a. $23,455.
b. $23,605.
c. $25,175.
d. $25,325.

The correct answer is (a). *(Publisher)*
REQUIRED: The taxpayer's tax liability for 1991.
DISCUSSION: For tax years after 1990, income is to be taxed at three rates: 15%, 28% and 31%. The threshold amounts for each rate vary depending upon the taxpayer's filing status. Additionally, the maximum tax rate applied to net capital gains (the excess of net long-term capital gains over net short-term capital losses) is 28% for tax years beginning after 1990. Net short-term capital gains are taxed at ordinary rates. If taxable income, not including net capital gains, exceeds the amount of taxable income in the 15% bracket, the total tax liability would be equal to the sum of the regular tax on taxable income (minus net capital gain) and 28% of the net capital gain as follows:

Adjusted gross income	$95,000
Less: Net capital gain	(5,000)
Standard deduction	(3,400)
Personal exemption	(2,150)
Amount to be taxed at ordinary rates	$84,450

The tax on this amount would be determined using the 1991 tax rate schedules for single taxpayers.

First $49,300	$11,158.50
Excess $35,150 ($84,450 − $49,300) x 31%	10,896.50
Regular tax on taxable income	$22,055.00
Tax on net capital gain ($5,000 x 28%)	1,400.00
Total tax liability	$23,455.00

83. Calvin and Alice Hobbs, both under 65, file a joint return for 1991. Their adjusted gross income is $98,000. Included in this total is $30,000 of net long-term capital gains. Calvin and Alice claim the standard deduction and two personal exemptions. The Hobbs' income tax liability for 1991 is

a. $20,220.
b. $20,395.
c. $21,921.
d. $23,495.

The correct answer is (a). *(Publisher)*
REQUIRED: The taxpayer's income tax liability for 1991.
DISCUSSION: For tax years after 1990, income is to be taxed at three rates: 15%, 28% and 31%. The threshold amounts for each rate vary depending upon the taxpayer's filing status. Additionally, the maximum tax rate applied to net capital gains (the excess of net long-term capital gains over net short-term capital losses) is 28% for tax years beginning after 1990. Net short-term capital gains are taxed at ordinary rates. If taxable income, not including net capital gain, exceeds the amount of taxable income in the 15% bracket, the total tax liability would be equal to the sum of the regular tax on taxable income (minus net capital gain) and 28% of the net capital gain as follows:

Adjusted gross income	$98,000
Less: Net capital gain	(30,000)
Standard deduction	(5,700)
Personal exemption	(4,300)
Amount to be taxed at ordinary rates	$58,000

The tax on this amount would be determined using the 1991 adjusted tax rate tables for married taxpayers filing jointly.

First $34,000 x 15%	$ 5,100
Excess $24,000 ($58,000 − $34,000) x 28%	6,720
Regular tax on taxable income	$11,820
Tax on net capital gain ($30,000 x 28%)	8,400
Total tax liability	$20,220

10.5 Unearned Income of a Minor Child

84. When will a minor's income be taxed at his/her parent's rate?

a. When a child has any income and is under age 14.

b. When a child has net unearned income regardless of his/her age.

c. When a child has unearned income and is under age 14.

d. When a child has net unearned income and is under age 14 with at least one living parent.

The correct answer is (d). *(Publisher)*
REQUIRED: When a minor's parent's rates will be used to tax a minor's income.
DISCUSSION: For tax years beginning after 1986, Sec. 1(g) provides in general that unearned income of certain minor children will be taxed to the child at the top rate of the parents. For this purpose, a minor is any child under 14 years of age at the end of the tax year who has at least one living parent. The provision applies to net unearned income, which is specially defined (see Q. 86).
Answer (a) is incorrect because this provision only applies to net unearned income. Answer (b) is incorrect because this provision only applies to children under age 14. Answer (c) is incorrect because this provision only applies to net unearned income, not just unearned income.

Module 10.5: Unearned Income of a Minor Child

85. Jamie is 13 years old. She received income in 1991 from the following sources:

Babysitting for neighbor	$ 80
From a trust created and funded by her grandparents	1,000
Dividends from stocks given by her parents	200
Interest on a bank account (deposits are from last year's babysitting)	50

What is Jamie's unearned income for 1991?

a. $200.
b. $1,200.
c. $1,250.
d. $1,330.

The correct answer is (c). *(Publisher)*
REQUIRED: A minor child's unearned income given various sources.
DISCUSSION: Unearned income is simply income which is not earned. The only earned income of Jamie is the $80 from babysitting for neighbors. All the rest of the income is considered unearned income. The source of the unearned income and whether it was from assets provided by third parties or from parents does not matter. Unearned income may commonly come from a trust, a bank account, or from assets held by a custodian or guardian under the Uniform Gifts to Minors Act. Jamie's unearned income is $1,250 ($1,000 from the trust + $200 from dividends + $50 interest).

86. Marcy, age 12, earned $400 from babysitting during 1991. Her parents claim her as a dependent. She also had interest and dividends of $2,500 during the year. She did not itemize deductions. What is her net unearned income for 1991?

a. $2,900.
b. $2,000.
c. $1,950.
d. $1,400.

The correct answer is (d). *(Publisher)*
REQUIRED: The amount of a child's net unearned income.
DISCUSSION: Net unearned income is defined in Sec. 1(g)(4) as unearned income less the sum of (1) $550, plus (2) the greater of $550 or, if the child itemizes, the amount of allowable deductions directly connected with the production of the unearned income. However, unearned income may not exceed the child's taxable income. Marcy's unearned income consists of $2,500 of interest and dividends. Her net unearned income is $1,400 [$2,500 − ($550 + $550)].

Note that this is not in excess of her taxable income because her standard deduction is limited to $550 and she may not claim a personal exemption since she is a dependent of her parents.

87. Jodi, a 10-year-old and an only child, has $3,000 of unearned income in 1991 and no earned income. Her parents claim her as a dependent but do not elect to include her income in their income. Their taxable income is $100,000, on which their tax is $24,115. What is Jodi's 1991 tax (round to the nearest dollar)?

a. $367.
b. $589.
c. $671.
d. $999.

The correct answer is (c). *(Publisher)*
REQUIRED: The tax on the net unearned income of a minor child when the parents have no other minor children.
DISCUSSION: The tax imposed on a minor child's income is the greater of the tax on the child's income without regard to Sec. 1(g), or the sum of (1) tax on the child's income not including net earned income, plus (2) the "allocable parental tax." The allocable parental tax is the tax on the parent's income including the net unearned income of all minor children less the tax on the parent's income alone. Jodi's tax is the greater of A or B below. Since total tax under method B is greater, her tax is $671.

A. ($3,000 total income − $550 standard deduction) x .15 applicable rate = $367
B. The sum of
 (1) ($3,000 total income − $1,900 NUI − $550 standard deduction) x .15 applicable rate = $ 82
 Plus
 (2) Parents' tax on $101,900 $24,704
  Less parents' tax on $100,000   (24,115)
  $ 589
  Multiplied by $1,900 Jodi's NUI ÷ $1,900 total children's NUI   x 1   = 589
  $671

88. Mr. and Mrs. Martinez had joint taxable income of $50,000 in 1991 on which their tax is $9,580. Their marginal tax rate is 28% and they did not elect to include their children's income in their own income. Their children had the following unearned income: daughter Linda, 13 - $3,000; son Luis, 11 - $2,200; and son Jose, 9 - $1,500. The children had no other income. What is Luis's tax for 1991 (round to the nearest dollar)?

a. $247.
b. $308.
c. $390.
d. $952.

The correct answer is (c). *(Publisher)*
REQUIRED: The tax on the net unearned income (NUI) of a minor child whose parents have other minor children.
DISCUSSION: The tax imposed on a minor child's income is computed as in the previous question. The child's portion is the allocable parental tax times the ratio of the child's NUI over the total of all NUI of the parent's minor children.

Linda's NUI is $1,900 [$3,000 − ($550 + $550)].
Jose's NUI is $400 [$1,500 − ($550 + $550)].
Luis's NUI is $1,100 [$2,200 − ($550 + $550)].

Luis's tax is computed as the greater of A or B below. Since total tax under method B is greater, Luis's tax is $390.

A. ($2,200 total income − $550 standard
    deduction) x .15 applicable rate   = $247
B. The sum of
    (1) ($2,200 total income − $1,100
        NUI − $550 standard deduction)
        x .15 applicable rate   = $ 82
    Plus
    (2) Parents' tax on $53,400 $10,532
        Less parents' tax on $50,000   (9,580)
                                       $ 952

        Multiplied by $1,100
        Luis's NUI ÷ $3,400
        total children's NUI   x .3235   308
                                                   $390

89. Parents may elect to include in their own return income over $1,100 of their children under age 14 who have net unearned income.

The correct answer is (T). *(Publisher)*
DISCUSSION: Sec. 1(g)(7) allows the parents of a child who is subject to the "kiddie tax" to include the child's income in excess of $1,100 in the parent's own tax return. The purpose is to simplify the inconvenience of the child paying tax on his/her unearned income. Parents will also have to pay a tax equal to the lesser of $82 or 15% of the excess of the child's gross income over $550.

90. If a child's parents elect to include the child's income in the parents' return, the child will still be required to file a return in most cases.

The correct answer is (F). *(Publisher)*
DISCUSSION: Under Sec. 1(g)(7) a child is treated as having no gross income and not required to file a return if the parents elect to include the child's income in their own return. Once the parents have included in the child's income in their own return and paid the additional tax equal to the lesser of $82 or 15% of the excess of the child's gross income over $550, there is no need for a child to file a return and pay tax. But if there has been withholding on the child's income or estimated tax payments have been made for the child, the child will need to file a return to recover these amounts.

10.6 Minimum Tax

Author's Note: The Tax Extension Act of 1991 (P.L. 100-227) extended the exemption for untaxed appreciation of charitable contributions of tangible personal property from the list of tax preference items for the alternative minimum tax [Sec. 57(a)(6)]. For tax years beginning in 1992, the exclusion is generally available only for contributions made before July 1, 1992.

91. The alternative minimum tax for individuals after 1991 is

a. The excess of (1) a tentative tax of 24% of alternative minimum taxable income reduced by an exemption amount over (2) the regular tax.
b. The excess of 24% of alternative minimum taxable income over the regular tax.
c. 24% of alternative minimum taxable income reduced by an exemption amount.
d. 24% of taxable income adjusted for tax preferences.

The correct answer is (a). *(Publisher)*
REQUIRED: The definition of alternative minimum tax after 1991 for individuals.
DISCUSSION: The alternative minimum tax for tax years after 1991 is imposed by Sec. 55 for both individuals and corporations. The tax for individuals is the excess of (1) a tentative tax of 24% of alternative minimum taxable income reduced by an exemption amount over (2) the regular tax.
Answer (b) is incorrect because alternative minimum taxable income is reduced by an exemption amount before the 24% tax rate is applied. Answer (c) is incorrect because the amount computed is only added to tax to the extent it exceeds the regular tax. Answer (d) is incorrect because it takes into account neither adjustments to taxable income other than tax preferences nor the exemption amount.

92. A single individual may have to pay alternative minimum tax if taxable income for regular tax purposes, plus any adjustments and preference items exceeds:

a. $10,000.
b. $20,000.
c. $25,000.
d. $30,000.

The correct answer is (d). *(SPE 988 II-52)*
REQUIRED: The alternative minimum tax exemption for single individual taxpayers.
DISCUSSION: Sec. 55(d) provides an exemption amount for individuals for purposes of computing the alternative minimum tax. The amount of this exemption for individuals who are not married and not a surviving spouse is $30,000. As a result, a single individual will not have to pay alternative minimum tax until his/her alternative minimum taxable income exceeds $30,000.

93. Alternative minimum taxable income after 1986 is

a. Taxable income increased by tax preferences and adjusted by various other statutory modifications.
b. The sum of all tax preferences.
c. Computed the same for individuals and corporations.
d. Taxable income adjusted by tax preferences and reduced by an exemption amount.

The correct answer is (a). *(SPE 989 I-58)*
REQUIRED: The definition of alternative minimum taxable income.
DISCUSSION: Taxable income is adjusted by various statutory items to arrive at alternative minimum taxable income. There are numerous adjustments to items taken into account in taxable income as well as some additional adjustments. Tax preference items are also added to taxable income to arrive at alternative minimum taxable income.
Answer (b) is incorrect because the sum of all tax preferences is only one adjustment to taxable income to arrive at alternative minimum taxable income. Answer (c) is incorrect because many of the adjustments differ for individuals and corporations, although many are the same. Answer (d) is incorrect because the exemption amount is subtracted from alternative minimum taxable income before the tax rate is applied.

94. Scott and Cindy Muir had alternative minimum taxable income of $125,000 in 1991 and file a joint return. For purposes of computing the alternative minimum tax, their exemption is:

a. $20,000.
b. $30,000.
c. $35,000.
d. $40,000.

The correct answer is (d). *(SPE 990 I-56)*
REQUIRED: The alternative minimum tax exemption for taxpayers filing a joint return in 1991.
DISCUSSION: Sec. 55(d) provides an exemption amount for individuals for purposes of computing the alternative minimum tax. The amount of this exemption for joint returns is $40,000. Note that this amount would be phased out by reducing the exemption for 25% of the excess of alternative minimum taxable income over a certain amount ($150,000 for joint returns). As the Muirs did not exceed this threshold, no reduction in the exemption was made.

95. For property placed in service after 1986, which of the following is a correct statement of the adjustment required for alternative minimum taxable income?

a. The alternative depreciation system of Sec. 168(g) is used in its entirety.
b. The alternative depreciation system of Sec. 168(g) is used with the 150%-declining-balance method (switching to straight-line when larger) for personal property.
c. There is no adjustment for depreciation on real property.
d. It is the same as for property placed in service prior to 1987.

The correct answer is (b). *(Publisher)*
REQUIRED: The correct statement concerning the adjustment for depreciation on property placed in service after 1986.
DISCUSSION: The deduction allowed for depreciation of tangible property (personal and real) placed in service after 1986 is generally determined under the alternative depreciation system of Sec. 168(g). However, for personal property, the 150%-declining-balance method is used and switches to a straight-line method in the first year the straight-line method yields a larger deduction. For nonresidential real property and residential rental property, the straight-line method is used over a 40-year recovery period.
Answer (a) is incorrect because the 150%-declining-balance method is used for personal property. Answer (c) is incorrect because real property must generally be depreciated over 40 years instead of 27.5 years or 31.5 years, depending on which type of property it is. Answer (d) is incorrect because, for property placed in service prior to 1987, accelerated depreciation over straight-line is a tax preference item and this only applies to real property.

96. All of the following are considered adjustments for arriving at alternative minimum taxable income except:

a. Real property taxes.
b. Personal exemptions.
c. Home mortgage interest (debt used to purchase, build or substantially improve a residence).
d. Standard deduction.

The correct answer is (c). *(SPE 990 I-57)*
REQUIRED: The item which is not an adjustment for arriving at alternative minimum taxable income.
DISCUSSION: Taxable income must be adjusted to arrive at alternative minimum taxable income. The adjustments are described in Secs. 56 and 58, with tax preferences in Sec. 57. The adjustments with respect to itemized deductions of an individual are contained in Sec. 56(b)(1). No adjustment is made to taxable income for home mortgage interest in order to arrive at alternative minimum taxable income [Sec. 56(b)(1)(C)(i)].
Answers (a), (b), and (d) are incorrect because real property taxes, personal exemptions and the standard deduction are not allowed as deductions in arriving at alternative minimum taxable income under Sec. 56(b), and, therefore, must be added back as adjustments to taxable income for arriving at alternative minimum taxable income.

97. All of the following are considered tax preference items in computing alternative minimum tax in 1991 except

a. The excess of depletion deductions over adjusted basis.
b. Tax-exempt interest on private activity bonds issued after August 7, 1986.
c. Excess depreciation claimed on real property placed in service in 1985.
d. The untaxed appreciation on charitable contributions of appreciated tangible personal property.

The correct answer is (d). *(Publisher)*
REQUIRED: The item not considered a tax preference in computing alternative minimum tax in 1991.
DISCUSSION: Tax preference items are listed in Sec. 57. They increase adjusted taxable income to arrive at alternative minimum taxable income [Sec. 55(b)]. For 1991 (and the period January 1, 1992 through June 30, 1992), the untaxed appreciation on contributions of tangible personal property (other than inventory, or other ordinary income property, or short-term capital gain property) is not considered to be a tax preference item [Sec. 57(a)(6)(B)]. A carryover of excess charitable contribution deductions arising from the contribution of appreciated tangible personal property in 1991 does not generate a tax preference item in 1992 and later years (Rev. Rul. 90-111).
Answers (a), (b), and (c) are incorrect because each is a tax preference item listed in Sec. 57.

Module 10.6: Minimum Tax

98. Which of the following is a tax preference item to be considered in computing the alternative minimum tax for individuals in 1991?

a. Tax-exempt interest on any municipal bonds.
b. Excess accelerated depreciation over straight-line depreciation for real property placed in service before 1987.
c. Interest on savings accounts over $10,000.
d. Net capital gain deduction.

The correct answer is (b). *(SPE 989 I-59)*
REQUIRED: The item considered a tax preference item in 1991.
DISCUSSION: Tax preference items increase adjusted taxable income to arrive at alternative minimum taxable income [Sec. 55(b)]. Sec. 57(a)(7) lists excess depreciation as a tax preference item for real property placed in service prior to 1987. Depreciation on assets placed in service after 1986 is specially computed as an adjustment under Sec. 56(a)(1) rather than as a tax preference.
Answer (a) is incorrect because only tax exempt interest on private activity bonds issued after August 7, 1986 is a tax preference item. Answer (c) is incorrect because Sec. 57 does not list interest on savings accounts over $10,000 as a tax preference item. Answer (d) is incorrect because the Tax Reform Act of 1986 repealed the net capital gain deduction.

99. In 1991, Dr. and Mrs. McCoy had four dependent children, filed jointly, and had adjusted gross income of $70,000, and $10,000 of tax-exempt interest on private activity bonds issued in 1987. They took a depreciation deduction of $15,000 for a vacation home placed in service in 1986 (straight-line depreciation would have been $6,000). They also had deductible residence interest of $5,000, property taxes of $8,000, and medical expenses of $8,000. Their regular tax is $7,158. The McCoys' alternative minimum tax for 1991 is

a. $762.
b. $1,002.
c. $1,722.
d. $3,162.

The correct answer is (d). *(Publisher)*
REQUIRED: The taxpayers' alternative minimum tax for 1991.
DISCUSSION: A tentative tax at the rate of 24% is computed on the excess of alternative minimum taxable income over an exemption amount. The minimum tax is the excess of this tentative minimum tax over the regular tax [Sec. 55(a)]. The McCoys' alternative minimum tax for 1991 is $3,162 computed as follows:

Adjusted gross income	$70,000
Plus tax preferences:	
Tax-exempt interest	10,000
Excess ACRS depreciation over straight-line	9,000
Less itemized deductions:	
Interest	(5,000)
Medical expenses [$8,000 − (10% x $70,000 AGI)]	(1,000)
Alternative minimum taxable income	$83,000
Less exemption	(40,000)
Alternative minimum tax base	$43,000
Alternative minimum tax rate	x .24
Total tentative tax	$10,320
Less regular tax	(7,158)
Alternative minimum tax	$ 3,162

100. Ms. K is a single taxpayer. What is her alternative minimum tax for 1991 based on the following information?

Taxable income	$41,500
Regular income tax before credits	9,314
The following adjustments or preferences:	
Miscellaneous itemized deductions after taking account of the 2% floor from Schedule A	2,500
Taxes from Schedule A	3,500
Depreciation adjustment for property placed in service after 1986	1,500
Adjustment on passive activity loss on continuing investment	10,000
Appreciated property charitable deduction preference item	7,500
Depletion preference item	15,000

- a. $0.
- b. $1,250.
- c. $1,762.
- d. $3,562.

The correct answer is (c). *(SPE 988 II-90)*
REQUIRED: The taxpayer's alternative minimum tax for 1991.
DISCUSSION: Tentative tax at a rate of 24% is computed on the excess of alternative minimum taxable income over an exemption amount. The minimum tax is the excess of this tentative tax over the regular tax [Sec. 55(a)]. In computing alternative minimum taxable income, all of the items listed in the question need to be added back to taxable income. In addition, one personal exemption needs to be added back because it was deducted in computing taxable income but is not allowed in computing alternative minimum taxable income. The Revenue Reconciliation Act of 1990, effective for tax year 1991 and the first half of 1992, specifies appreciation on tangible personal property (other than inventory or other ordinary income property, or short-term capital gain property) donated as a qualifying charitable contribution shall not be considered a tax preference item. There is a $30,000 statutory exemption available for single taxpayers under the minimum tax. The computation follows:

Taxable income	$41,500
Add back:	
Personal exemption	2,150
Miscellaneous itemized deductions	2,500
Taxes	3,500
Passive activity loss adjustment	10,000
Depreciation adjustment	1,500
Plus tax preferences:	
Charitable contribution deduction	0
Depletion	15,000
Alternative minimum taxable income	$76,150
Less exemption	(30,000)
Alternative minimum tax base	$46,150
x	.24
Total tentative tax	$11,076
Less regular tax	(9,314)
Alternative minimum tax	$ 1,762

101. In 1990 Ron and Cindy had an alternative minimum tax (AMT) liability of $19,000. This is the first tax year in which they ever paid the AMT. They recompute the AMT amount using only exclusion preferences and adjustments and it results in a $8,500 AMT liability. In 1991 Ron and Cindy have a regular tax liability of $45,000. Their tentative minimum tax liability is $42,000. What is the amount of Ron and Cindy's minimum tax credit (MTC) carryover to 1991? What is the amount of the carryover that can be used in 1991?

	Carryover to 1991	Carryover Used
a.	$19,000	$3,000
b.	$19,000	$0
c.	$10,500	$3,000
d.	$8,500	$3,000

The correct answer is (c). *(Publisher)*
REQUIRED: The taxpayer's MTC carryover for 1990 and the amount used in 1991.
DISCUSSION: For the first tax year that the AMT is owed, the MTC is the portion of the AMT attributable to deferral preferences or adjustments. Deferral preferences or adjustments are: disallowed itemized deductions or standard deduction, personal exemptions, excess percentage depletion, tax-exempt interest from private activity bonds, and the appreciation portion of contributions of appreciated property (other than appreciated tangible property donated during 1991). In 1990 the exclusion preferences and adjustments result in a $10,500 MTC ($19,000 − $8,500). This credit can be carried over to 1991 and used to the extent that the regular tax liability exceeds the tentative minimum tax. This amount is $3,000 ($45,000 − $42,000).

102. The depreciation adjustment with respect to tangible personal property placed in service after December 31, 1986 for alternative minimum taxable income uses the 200%-declining-balance method, switching to the straight-line method in the year it would result in a larger deduction.

The correct answer is (F). *(Publisher)*
DISCUSSION: Sec. 56 provides for adjustments in computing alternative minimum taxable income. Among these adjustments is a depreciation adjustment for tangible personal property placed in service after December 31, 1986. In computing alternative minimum taxable income, the depreciation method used is the 150%-declining-balance (not 200%), switching to straight-line in later years when straight-line results in a greater deduction.

103. Among the adjustments which increase alternative minimum taxable income is the excess of accelerated depreciation over straight-line depreciation for property other than realty placed in service after December 31, 1986.

The correct answer is (F). *(SPE 990 I-30)*
DISCUSSION: Sec. 56 defines the adjustments in computing alternative minimum taxable income. Among these adjustments is a depreciation adjustment for tangible personal property placed in service after December 31, 1986. Depreciation is recomputed using the 150% declining-balance method, switching to straight-line depreciation in later years when it results in a greater deduction. Depreciation on realty also requires an adjustment for property placed in service after December 31, 1986. The recomputed depreciation for realty uses a 40-year recovery period (and the straight-line method) instead of a 31.5-year or 27.5-year recovery period for commercial real estate and residential rental property, respectively.

104. Net operating losses can be used to offset no more than 90% of alternative minimum taxable income.

The correct answer is (T). *(Publisher)*
DISCUSSION: The Sec. 56 adjustments in computing alternative minimum taxable income provides for an alternative net operating loss (NOL) deduction. The alternative NOL deduction is adjusted for tax preference items and other alternative minimum taxable income adjustments, and it, along with the alternative minimum tax foreign tax credit (if any), cannot offset more than 90% of alternative minimum taxable income [Sec. 59(a)(2)].

10.7 Estimated Tax Payments

Author's Note: For tax years beginning after December 31, 1991, individuals cannot use the 100%-of-prior-year's-liability safe harbor if: (1) their AGI increased by more than $40,000 when compared with the preceding tax year ($20,000 if married individuals filing separately); (2) their AGI for the current tax year exceeds $75,000 ($37,500 for married individuals filing separately); and (3) they paid estimated taxes (or paid an IRS assessment for underpayment of estimated taxes) during any of the 3 preceding tax years. Individual taxpayers can continue to use the 100%-of-prior-year's-liability safe harbor for the first quarter of the tax year and for any other quarter where their annualized AGI is estimated to be less than the $40,000/$75,000 thresholds. Special rules or exemptions apply to individuals receiving income pass-throughs from partnerships and S corporations, having gain from involuntary conversions of property, or recognizing gain from the sale of a personal residence (P.L. 102-164, 11/15/1991).

105. For estimated tax purposes, the calendar year is divided into four payment periods. Which of the following payment periods is incorrect?

a. January 1 through March 31.
b. April 1 through June 30.
c. June 1 through August 31.
d. September 1 through December 31.

The correct answer is (b). *(SPE 988 I-34)*
REQUIRED: The months which do not compose a quarter of a calendar year for estimated tax purposes.
DISCUSSION: Sec. 6654(a) provides a penalty for the underpayment of estimated taxes. In order to avoid the penalty, estimated tax payments are due quarterly. The first payment is due April 15 for the months January through March. The second payment is due June 15 for the months of April and May. The third payment is due September 15 for the months June through August. The fourth payment is due January 15 of the following year for the months September through December.

Module 10.7: Estimated Tax Payments

106. For 1992, Paul and Mary, calendar year taxpayers, received all of their gross income of $80,000 from their dairy farm. As of December 31, 1992, they had not made any estimated tax payments for 1992. Which of the following will allow them to avoid the estimated tax penalty (ignoring Saturdays, Sundays, or holidays)?

a. Make one estimated tax payment by January 15, 1993.

b. File their 1992 federal income tax return by March 15, 1993.

c. File their 1992 federal income tax return by April 15, 1993, pay all of the tax and attach a statement that they are qualified farmers.

d. File their 1992 federal income tax return by March 15, 1993, and pay all the tax due.

The correct answer is (a). *(SPE 990 II-48)*
REQUIRED: The action which will allow the taxpayers to avoid the estimated tax penalty.
DISCUSSION: Farmers or fishermen expecting to receive at least two-thirds of their gross income from farming or fishing activities, or who received at least two-thirds of their gross income for the prior tax year from farming or fishing, may pay estimated tax for the year in one installment. As Paul and Mary received all of their gross income from farming, they may wait until January 15, 1993 to make their 1992 estimated tax payment without penalty. The entire estimated tax for the year must be paid at that time. However, the January payment date may be ignored provided that the farmer or fisherman files his return for 1992 and pays the entire tax due by March 1, 1993. Farmers and fishermen who satisfy the two-thirds requirement are not subject to the post-1992 estimated tax requirements for taxpayers experiencing substantial income increases.

Note that, when a farmer or fisherman files a joint return, the gross income of the spouse must be considered in determining whether two-thirds of the gross income is from farming or fishing.

Answers (b), (c), and (d) are incorrect because, to avoid the underpayment of estimated tax penalty, the farmer or fisherman must either pay the entire estimated tax by January 15, 1993 or file the 1992 return and pay the entire tax due by March 1, 1993.

107. For 1992, all of the following situations will qualify as exceptions to the penalty for underpayment of estimated tax except

a. All of your 1992 income was from salaries, wages, and tips reported on line 7 of the Form 1040.

b. You have less than $500 tax due.

c. You had no tax liability for 1991 and your AGI increased by $15,000 from 1991.

d. You made estimated tax payments of 80% of the tax shown on your 1992 Form 1040.

The correct answer is (d). *(SPE 988 I-35)*
REQUIRED: The situation which is not an exception to the penalty for underpayment of estimated tax.
DISCUSSION: One exception to the penalty for estimated tax is if the taxpayer makes estimated payments of 90% of the tax shown on the return for the year. Paying 80% will not meet this exception. Note the payments must be made quarterly.

Answer (a) is incorrect because if all income is from salaries, wages, and tips, the employer will have withheld adequate taxes to avoid the penalty. Answer (b) is incorrect because another exception precludes the penalty if there is less than $500 tax due. Answer (c) is incorrect because another exception is to pay 100% of the tax liability for the prior year. If there was no tax liability for the prior year, no estimated tax payments are due. But, for tax years beginning after December 31, 1991, individuals cannot use the 100%-of-prior-year's-liability safe harbor in certain circumstances, e.g., if the (single) individual's AGI increased by more than $40,000 when compared with the preceding tax years.

108. Charles is a self-employed attorney and files a joint return. He reported AGI of $60,000 and taxable income of $46,800 in 1991 and paid a tax liability of $12,000 after credits. In 1992, he expects his AGI to increase about 25%. In setting up his estimated tax payments so as to avoid any penalty for underpayment of his 1992 liability, Charles should

a. Pay quarterly installments of 25% of $12,000.

b. Make only one estimated payment late in 1992 when he can more clearly estimate his 1992 income.

c. Pay at least 25% more tax each quarter than he paid in 1991.

d. Pay quarterly installments of 90% of 25% of $12,000.

The correct answer is (a). *(J.M. Ruble)*
REQUIRED: The estimated tax payments to avoid an underpayment penalty.
DISCUSSION: Sec. 6654(a) provides a penalty for the underpayment of estimated taxes. The taxpayer can avoid the imposition of the penalty for underpayment of estimated taxes by paying quarterly installments that would equal or exceed the lesser of 90% of the current year's tax liability or 100% of the prior year's tax liability since his AGI did not increase by more than $40,000. Thus, Charles could avoid the penalty by paying quarterly installments of 25% of $12,000, his prior year's tax liability.

Answer (b) is incorrect because the installments must be made on a quarterly basis. Answer (c) is incorrect because there is no provision for paying 25% more tax each quarter than paid in the previous year. Answer (d) is incorrect because the quarterly installments must equal or exceed 100% of the prior year's actual tax liability.

Module 10.7: Estimated Tax Payments

109. Taxpayer B filed a declaration of estimated tax for 1992 and paid $2,000 in four equal installments of $500. He had $6,000 withheld from his salary during 1992. The actual tax for 1992 was $12,000. B's 1992 adjusted gross income increased by $4,000 from 1991. Taxpayer B had no other credits or payments. What is his underpayment of tax for each installment?

a. $0.
b. $400.
c. $700.
d. $1,000.

The correct answer is (c). *(SPE 1080 I-90)*
REQUIRED: The amount of underpayment of estimated tax for each installment.
DISCUSSION: A penalty is provided in Sec. 6654(a) for the underpayment of estimated taxes. For tax years beginning after 1987, the amount of underpayment of each installment is the excess of the installment due if the estimated tax was 90% of that shown on the return over the amount of the installment timely paid. The estimated tax is due in four installments. Income tax withheld is considered paid equally on each installment date [Sec. 6654(g)(2)]. Therefore, the taxpayer is considered to have made estimated payments of $2,000 in each quarterly installment ($500 + 1/4 of $6,000). The amount of each installment payment should have been $2,700 (1/4 x 90% x $12,000 actual tax). B's underpayment of tax for each installment is $700 ($2,700 − $2,000).

110. Ms. W, who is single, determined that her total tax liability for 1992 would be $10,000 and that her AGI would increase by less than $40,000. W is required to make estimated tax payments if

a. Her 1991 tax liability was $12,000 and her 1992 income tax withholding will be $9,750.
b. Her 1991 tax liability was $12,000 and her 1992 income tax withholding will be $9,000.
c. Her 1991 tax liability was $5,000 and her 1992 income tax withholding will be $6,000.
d. Her 1991 tax liability was $9,000 and her 1992 income tax withholding will be $8,500.

The correct answer is (d). *(SPE 986 I-61)*
REQUIRED: When the taxpayer would be required to make estimated tax payments.
DISCUSSION: In general, individuals must make estimated tax payments or be subject to a penalty (Sec. 6654). Amounts withheld from wages are treated as estimated tax payments. For tax years beginning after 1987 the annual estimated payment that must be made is equal to the lesser of (1) 90% of the tax for the current year, or (2) 100% of the tax for the prior year. Assuming Ms. W's tax liability for 1992 is $10,000 and her 1991 tax liability was $9,000, the $8,500 withheld from her 1992 wages does not meet the required annual estimated payment.

111. G's 1992 tax liability after credits was $12,000. Tax withheld by his employer for the year totaled $8,000. G earned his taxable income evenly throughout the year and used the standard deduction. G's 1991 tax liability per his return was $10,000. Estimated tax payments for 1992 were made as follows:

Installment	Date of Payment	Amount
1st	April 15, 1992	$800
2nd	June 30, 1992	$800
3rd	September 15, 1992	$800
4th	January 15, 1993	$800

Assuming there are no circumstances justifying a waiver for the second installment period and that G's AGI increased by less than $40,000 in 1992, what is the underpayment of estimated tax for the second installment payment period?

a. $1,000.
b. $600.
c. $200.
d. $0.

The correct answer is (c). *(SPE 987 I-66)*
REQUIRED: The underpayment of estimated tax for the second quarter.
DISCUSSION: A penalty is provided in Sec. 6654(a) for the underpayment of estimated taxes. Since G's AGI increased by less than $40,000 in 1992, the penalty is avoided by paying quarterly payments that would equal or exceed the lesser of 90% of the current tax liability or 100% of the prior year's tax liability. 90% of the current year's tax liability is $10,800 (90% x $12,000). 100% of the prior year's tax liability is $10,000. Therefore, the minimum quarterly payments to avoid the penalty for underpayment of estimated taxes are $2,500 ($10,000 ÷ 4).

Tax withheld by an employer is paid equally on each installment date. Therefore, G is treated as having paid $2,000 ($8,000 ÷ 4) on each estimated tax due date. That leaves $500 of estimated payments required each quarter ($2,500 − $2,000). Since G paid $800 on the first due date of April 15, he overpaid by $300. He did not make his timely payment on June 15, so he underpaid by $200 ($2,500 − $2,000 withheld − $300 carried over from April 15).

112. Taxpayer C elected to apply his 1991 overpayment of income tax to his 1992 estimated tax. The overpayment was more than the amount due on the first installment of the estimated tax owed for 1992. Therefore, C does not have to make an estimated tax payment until June 15, 1992.

The correct answer is (T). *(SPE 1079 I-23)*
DISCUSSION: An overpayment of tax of a prior year may be applied to the current year's tax. The overpayment will be treated as an estimated payment of tax for the earliest payment due. Even if an overpayment of prior year's tax is determined after the due date of the first estimated payment (e.g., when an extension of time to file the prior tax return has been obtained) the overpayment may be applied to the first estimated payment. June 15 is the due date of the second installment of estimated tax for a calendar-year taxpayer.

113. Mrs. X files her 1992 Form 1040 on January 1, 1993 and pays the balance of the tax due. Mrs. X is not required to pay the last installment of her estimated tax due on January 15, 1993.

The correct answer is (T). *(SPE 1079 IV-52)*
DISCUSSION: At the election of the individual, the final installment of the estimated tax may be paid by filing the tax return for the tax year before January 31 following the tax year and paying in full the tax computed on the return [Sec. 6654(h)]. By filing the income tax return on January 1 and paying the balance of the tax due, the taxpayer has paid her last installment prior to the due date.

114. The penalty for underpayment of estimated tax can be waived for reasonable cause.

The correct answer is (T). *(SPE 1079 IV-53)*
DISCUSSION: A penalty is imposed on the underpayment of estimated tax under Sec. 6654(a), unless the taxpayer falls within one of the exceptions provided in Sec. 6654(e)(3)(A). A waiver is allowed if by reason of casualty, disaster, or other unusual circumstance, the imposition of a penalty would be against equity and good conscience.

115. If you know early in the year that you will realize substantial income late in that year and that the income will be subject to estimated tax, you must make your first payment of estimated tax by April 15.

The correct answer is (F). *(SPE 986 I-8)*
DISCUSSION: If substantial income is to be earned late in the year, estimated tax payments can be annualized [Sec. 6654(d)(2)]. This allows estimated tax payments to be made later in the year when income is earned later in the year.

116. Ms. B is a waitress at Mary's restaurant. Since she is a good waitress, her tips are substantial. Her regular wages are too small for her employer to withhold the taxes due on the tips. She had previously been giving her employer extra money to pay these taxes. Ms. B may pay estimated tax instead of giving her employer the extra money.

The correct answer is (T). *(SPE 1083 I-13)*
DISCUSSION: Anyone may make estimated tax payments. The penalty for underpayment of estimated tax is based on the amount of underpayment each quarter after treating amounts withheld from wages as being paid in equal parts on each due date of estimated taxes. Therefore, either withholding or timely payment of estimated taxes will avoid the penalty.
Ms. B's employer is required to withhold income tax and Social Security tax and pay the employer's Social Security tax on tips reported by the employee. Employees must report to the employer cash tips in excess of $20 in a month. If Ms. B receives substantial tips, her employer should be withholding on these tips which should obviate the need to make part or all of the estimated tax payments. Any additional amounts which must be paid in by the employee in excess of the amounts withheld can be paid through quarterly estimated tax payments rather than giving the money to her employer.

117. Mr. Johns is married and files a joint return. His gross income from farming was $60,000 while his wife's gross income from an unrelated business was $40,000. For purposes of his estimated tax, Mr. Johns meets the gross income test and qualifies as a farmer.

The correct answer is (F). *(SPE 1083 II-33)*
DISCUSSION: Sec. 6654(i) provides special rules for estimated tax payments by farmers and fishermen. There is only one estimated tax payment due each year and it is not due until January 15 following the tax year. However, to qualify, the individual's gross income from farming or fishing must be at least 66 2/3% of the total gross income. Mr. John's gross income from farming is only 60% of total gross income.

CHAPTER ELEVEN
CREDITS

	Refundable Credits		
11.1	Earned Income Credit	(12 questions)	253
11.2	Other Refundable Credits	(3 questions)	257
	Nonrefundable Personal Credits		
11.3	Child Care Credit	(16 questions)	258
11.4	Credit for the Elderly	(8 questions)	262
11.5	Interest on Home Mortgage Credit	(2 questions)	264
11.6	Limitations on Nonrefundable Personal Credits	(2 questions)	265
11.7	Foreign Tax Credit	(4 questions)	266
	General Business Credit		
11.8	Research and Experimentation Credit	(10 questions)	268
11.9	Targeted Jobs Credit	(5 questions)	270
	Investment Tax Credit (ITC)		
11.10	Business Energy Credit	(7 questions)	271
11.11	Rehabilitation Credit	(8 questions)	273
11.12	ITC Recapture	(10 questions)	275
11.13	Low-Income Rental Housing Credit	(13 questions)	278
11.14	Limitations and Carryovers of the General Business Credit	(12 questions)	280
11.15	Disabled Access Credit	(3 questions)	284

Author's Note: The Tax Extension Act of 1991 (P.L. 100-227) extended the following tax credit provisions for 6 months:

Code Sec.	Credit Provision
25	Credit for interest on certain home mortgages
28	Credit for expenses incurred in clinical testing of drugs for rare diseases or conditions
41	Credit for increasing research activities
42	Low-income housing credit
48	Business energy tax credit for solar and geothermal property
51	Targeted jobs credit.

For tax years beginning in 1992, the credit is generally available only for amounts paid before July 1, 1992.

11.1 Earned Income Credit

1. Which of the following items is considered earned income for the earned income credit in 1991?

a. Income earned abroad and excluded from taxable income.
b. Interest on savings accounts.
c. Capital gains on stock sales.
d. Rental income for which no services are performed.

The correct answer is (a). *(SPE 984 I-67)*
REQUIRED: The item of earned income for purposes of the earned income credit.
DISCUSSION: Sec. 32(c)(2) defines earned income as wages, salaries, tips, and other employee compensation, plus the amount of the taxpayer's net earnings from self-employment. This includes income earned abroad even though it is excluded from taxable income.
Answer (b) is incorrect because interest and dividends are prime examples of what is not earned income.
Answer (c) is incorrect because capital gains are also not considered earned income. Answer (d) is incorrect because rental income for which the taxpayer performs no services is not earned income.

Module 11.1: Earned Income Credit

2. All of the following statements regarding qualification for the earned income credit are correct except

a. The tax return claiming the credit must cover a full 12 months (unless a short period return is required due to the taxpayer's death).
b. The taxpayer's principal residence must be in the United States.
c. The taxpayer's filing status must be either married filing a joint return or head of household.
d. The taxpayer must have received earned income during the year.

The correct answer is (c). *(SPE 990 I-54)*
REQUIRED: The item that is not required to qualify for the earned income credit.
DISCUSSION: The earned income credit is a refundable tax credit for low-income taxpayers under Sec. 32. The credit is based on a taxpayer's earned income subject to certain limitations. An individual is eligible for the earned income credit if (s)he has a qualifying child for the tax year. A qualifying child is one who bears the necessary relationship to the taxpayer, has the same principal abode as the taxpayer for more than one-half of the tax year, and who meets the necessary age and identification requirements. A married taxpayer is eligible for the credit only if (s)he files a joint return or is treated as not married under Sec. 7703(b) (e.g., certain married individuals living apart). Thus, single taxpayers and heads of households may qualify for the earned income credit.
Answer (a) is incorrect because the earned income credit is disallowed if the taxpayer's taxable year covers a period of less than 12 months, unless the tax year is closed by reason of death. Answer (b) is incorrect because in order to be eligible for the earned income credit, a taxpayer's principal residence must be in the United States. Answer (d) is incorrect because the credit is based on earned income, so there must be some earned income during the year.

3. If a taxpayer qualifies for the earned income credit, such credit can be subtracted from

a. Gross income to arrive at adjusted gross income.
b. Adjusted gross income to arrive at taxable income after personal exemptions.
c. The tax owed, or can result in a refund, but only if the taxpayer had tax withheld from wages.
d. The tax owed, or can result in a refund, even if the taxpayer had no tax withheld from wages.

The correct answer is (d). *(CPA 586 Q-43)*
REQUIRED: The effect of the earned income credit.
DISCUSSION: The earned income credit is a refundable credit for low-income taxpayers under Sec. 32. Having taxes withheld from wages is not a requirement for using the earned income credit.
Answers (a) and (b) are incorrect because the earned income credit is subtracted from the tax owed by the taxpayer. Answer (c) is incorrect because the taxpayer need not have tax withheld from wages to use the credit.

4. If a taxpayer qualifies for the earned income credit, such credit may

a. Be carried back or forward if unused.
b. Be subtracted from adjusted gross income to arrive at taxable income.
c. Result in a refund even if the taxpayer had no tax withheld from wages.
d. Result in a refund only if the taxpayer had tax withheld from wages.

The correct answer is (c). *(CPA 589 Q-53)*
REQUIRED: The effect of the earned income credit.
DISCUSSION: The earned income credit is a refundable credit for low-income taxpayers under Sec. 32. Having taxes withheld from wages is not a requirement for using the earned income credit.
Answer (a) is incorrect because the earned income credit may not be used in a carryforward or carryback year. Answer (b) is incorrect because the earned income credit is subtracted from the tax owed by the taxpayer. Answer (d) is incorrect because having taxes withheld from wages is not a requirement.

Module 11.1: Earned Income Credit

5. In 1991, Alex Burgos paid $600 to Rita, his ex-wife, for child support. Under the terms of his 1991 divorce decree, Alex claims the exemption for his 5-year-old son, William, who lived with Rita for the entire year. Alex's only income in 1991 was from wages of $6,700, resulting in an income tax of $172. How much is Alex's earned income credit for 1991?

a. $0.
b. $172.
c. $1,119.
d. $1,159.

6. Bill and Mary Olds have combined wages of $12,000, dividends of $50, and interest of $100 in 1991. Their 6-year-old son resides with them and qualifies as their dependent. What is their earned income credit for 1991?

a. $0.
b. $107.
c. $1,085.
d. $1,192.

7. Russ Olson is a married taxpayer who files a joint return with his wife Suzie. In 1991 Russ earns wages of $17,000 and dividends of $400. Russ and Suzie have one child, Evan, 6 months old at the end of 1991, who resides with them and qualifies as their dependent. What is their earned income credit for 1991?

a. $0.
b. $458.
c. $596.
d. $1,192.

The correct answer is (a). *(CPA 1181 Q-57)*
REQUIRED: The amount of the taxpayer's earned income credit in 1991.
DISCUSSION: Sec. 32(a) allows an earned income credit for an eligible individual. An eligible individual includes one who is married and entitled to an exemption under Sec. 151 for a child, is a surviving spouse, or is a head of household [Sec. 32(c)]. Alex Burgos is neither married, a surviving spouse, nor a head of household, so he is not an eligible individual entitled to the earned income credit. In order for him to be a head of household, his son would have to live with him [Sec. 2(b)].

The correct answer is (c). *(Publisher)*
REQUIRED: The amount of the earned income credit in 1991.
DISCUSSION: Sec. 32(a) allows an eligible individual having one qualifying child a credit equal to 16.7% of the earned income for the taxable year that does not exceed $7,140 (in 1991). The amount of the credit allowable for 1991 is limited to $1,192, reduced by 11.93% of the taxpayer's adjusted gross income (or earned income if larger) above $11,250 [Sec. 32(b)].
Bill and Mary are eligible individuals because they are married and have a child. Their earned income consists of the $12,000 of wages. The dividends and interest are excluded from earned income but are included in AGI. Thus, their AGI is $12,150 ($12,000 wages + $100 interest + $50 dividends).

Credit limit ($7,140 x 16.7%)	$1,192
Less 11.93% x ($12,150 – $11,250)	(107)
Earned income credit	$1,085

The correct answer is (c). *(Publisher)*
REQUIRED: The amount of the earned income credit and supplemental young child credit for 1991.
DISCUSSION: Sec. 32(a) allows an eligible married couple filing a joint return having one qualifying child a credit equal to 16.7% of the earned income for the taxable year that does not exceed $7,140 in 1991. The amount of the credit allowable for 1991 is limited to $1,192 reduced by 11.93% of the taxpayer's adjusted gross income (or earned income if larger) above $11,250 [Sec. 32(b)].
A supplemental young child credit is added to the basic earned income credit if the taxpayers have a qualifying child who has not attained the age of 1 by the end of the calendar year in which the taxpayer's tax year ends. The supplemental credit increases the credit by 5 percentage points and increases the recapture by 3.57 percentage points.
Russ and Suzie are eligible individuals because they are married and have a child under age 1 at the end of the tax year. Their earned income consists of $17,000 in wages. Their dividends are excluded from earned income, but they are included in AGI. Thus, their AGI is $17,400 ($17,000 wages + $400 dividends).

Credit limit ($7,140 x 21.7%)	$1,549
Less 15.50% x ($17,400 – $11,250)	(953)
Earned income credit	$ 596

Module 11.1: Earned Income Credit

8. Sandy and John Smith have combined wages of $20,000 and interest of $300 in 1991. Their 4-year-old son and 6-year-old daughter reside with them and qualify as their dependents. What is their earned income credit for 1991?

a. $1,235.
b. $1,119.
c. $116.
d. $0.

The correct answer is (c). *(Publisher)*
REQUIRED: The amount of the earned income credit for 1991 when the taxpayers have two qualifying children.
DISCUSSION: Sec. 32(a) allows an earned income credit for an eligible individual. For taxpayers with two qualifying children, this credit is equal to 17.30% of the earned income for the taxable year that does not exceed $7,140 in 1991. The amount of the credit allowable for 1991 is limited to $1,235 reduced by 12.36% of the taxpayer's adjusted gross income (or earned income if larger) above $11,250 [Sec. 32(b)].

Sandy and John are eligible for the increased credit rate because they have two dependent children living with them. Their interest income is excluded from their earned income, but is included in their AGI. Thus, their AGI is $20,300 ($20,000 wages + $300 interest).

Credit limit ($7,140 x 17.30%)	$1,235
Less 12.36% x ($20,300 − $11,250)	(1,119)
Earned income credit	$ 116

9. David and Margaret Stone have combined wages of $17,000 and no other income in 1991. Their 6-year-old daughter resides with them and qualifies as their dependent. David's employer does not provide any health care insurance coverage so the Stones purchased their own coverage for $900. What is the amount of the Stones' supplemental health insurance credit? How much of their health care insurance premium can be counted as medical expenses should they elect to itemize their deductions?

	Credit	Deduction
a.	$428	$900
b.	$182	$718
c.	$182	$900
d.	$0	$900

The correct answer is (b). *(Publisher)*
REQUIRED: The amount of their health insurance credit and the amount of their medical expense deduction.
DISCUSSION: Sec. 32(a) allows a health insurance tax credit to be claimed. The tax credit is available to individuals otherwise eligible to claim the basic earned income credit. The credit is based on an individual's earned income subject to certain limitations. The individual must be married with a dependent child living within the home and a joint return must be filed, a head of household with a child living in the home for more than one-half of the year, or a surviving spouse with a dependent child. The Stones met these requirements.

The Stones' tentative health insurance credit is 6% of the taxpayer's earned income up to $7,140, or $428 (6% x $7,140). The tentative credit is reduced by 4.285% of the taxpayer's earned income in excess of $11,250, or $246 [($17,000 − $11,250) x 4.285%]. The actual credit that can be claimed is $182 ($428 − $246). Sec. 213(f) requires the medical expenses claimed for the Stones' health insurance to be reduced by the amount of the credit, so the net health insurance premium that is deductible is $718 ($900 − $182).

10. Mr. X meets all of the requirements for claiming an earned income credit except he is not entitled to claim the exemption for his child because he released his claim in writing to his child's other parent. Even though X does not meet this requirement he is still entitled to an earned income credit.

The correct answer is (T). *(SPE 989 I-27)*
DISCUSSION: A parent's releasing of his claim to the exemption for his child to another parent does not disqualify him for claiming the earned income credit. If the parent meets all the eligibility requirements in Sec. 32(c), then he may still receive the earned income credit, no matter which parent receives the exemption.

11. A taxpayer who qualifies for the earned income credit may be entitled to a refund.

The correct answer is (T). *(SPE 1077 I-75)*
DISCUSSION: The earned income credit is not limited to the amount of the taxpayer's tax liability. It is refundable even for taxpayers who have a tax liability less than the credit.

12. Unless the employee is claiming an exemption from withholding on Form W-4, an employer is required to notify an employee not having income tax withheld that (s)he may be eligible for a tax refund because of the earned income credit.

The correct answer is (T). *(SPE 987 I-40)*
DISCUSSION: Reg. 31.6051-1(h) requires an employer to furnish Notice 797 to an employee who has not had income tax withheld that (s)he may be eligible for a tax refund based on the earned income credit. This does not apply if the employee claimed an exemption from withholding. If there has been withholding, an employee may elect advance payment of the earned income credit under Sec. 3507. This is accomplished by the employer making the payments to the employee who has filed an earned income eligibility certificate.

11.2 Other Refundable Credits

13. Which of the following may not be treated as a credit against the income tax or refunded to the taxpayer if in excess of the taxpayer's income tax?

   a. Amounts withheld from an employee's wages.
   b. Amounts withheld as a tax from nonresident aliens.
   c. Amounts paid as a gasoline tax for personal automobiles.
   d. Overpayments of the income tax.

The correct answer is (c). *(Publisher)*
REQUIRED: The amount that is neither a tax credit nor refundable if in excess of the income tax.
DISCUSSION: Amounts paid as a gasoline tax for personal automobiles are personal expenditures and are therefore nondeductible. Certain taxpayers may take a credit for the taxes paid on gasoline used in special circumstances, such as off-road nonrecreational use, e.g., farming [Sec. 34(a)].
Answers (a), (b), and (d) are incorrect because each is a credit against income tax that may be refunded per Secs. 31, 1446, 1462, and 35, respectively.

14. Mr. A worked for only one employer in 1991. A's salary for 1991 was $60,000 and his employer withheld Social Security (FICA) tax on the entire amount. Mr. A may claim a credit against his income tax for the excess FICA tax withheld.

The correct answer is (F). *(SPE 984 I-44)*
DISCUSSION: In 1991, FICA tax applies to the first $53,400 of wages or self-employment income. The portion of the FICA taxes (1.45%) or self-employment tax (2.90%) applying to Medicare hospital insurance applies to the first $125,000 of wages. Excess FICA withheld when an employee works for only one employer may not be used as a credit against income taxes. A's employer should adjust the error.

15. Kenny, a sole proprietor, purchases gasoline for a forklift he uses in his business. The forklift is not a highway vehicle and is not required to be registered for highway use. Kenny may claim a credit or refund for the federal excise taxes paid on this gasoline.

The correct answer is (T). *(SPE 984 II-45)*
DISCUSSION: Sec. 34(a)(2) provides a credit equal to the amount determined under Sec. 6421 for taxes paid on gasoline used for nonhighway business purposes. Kenny's forklift qualifies for the credit since it is not a highway vehicle.

11.3 Child Care Credit

16. Which of the following statements is not a general requirement to qualify for the child and dependent care credit?

   a. You must maintain a household that includes a qualifying individual.
   b. Your expenditures must be necessary to enable you to be gainfully employed.
   c. Your payments for services must not be dependent relatives.
   d. You must be divorced or legally separated when you incur the expense.

The correct answer is (d). *(SPE 990 I-52)*
REQUIRED: The statement that is not a general requirement to qualify for the child care and dependent care credit.
DISCUSSION: Sec. 21 allows a credit for employment-related expenses for an individual who maintains a household which includes as a member one or more qualifying individuals. A qualifying individual is a dependent of the taxpayer who is under the age of 13, a dependent of the taxpayer who is physically handicapped, or a spouse of the taxpayer if (s)he is incapable of caring for him/herself. The taxpayer need not be divorced or separated when the expense is incurred.
Answer (a) is incorrect because you must maintain a household which includes the qualifying individual.
Answer (b) is incorrect because the credit is for employment-related expenses for the care of a qualifying individual.
Answer (c) is incorrect because payments for services to a dependent relative are not permitted.

17. All of the following qualify as work-related expenses for computing the child and dependent care credit except

   a. The parent-employer's portion of Social Security tax paid on wages for a person to take care of dependent children while the parents work.
   b. Payments to a nursery school for the care of dependent children while the parents work.
   c. The cost of meals for a housekeeper who provides necessary care for a dependent child while the parents work.
   d. Payments to a housekeeper who provides dependent care while the parent is off from work because of illness.

The correct answer is (d). *(SPE 986 I-57)*
REQUIRED: The child or dependent care expense that does not qualify as employment-related.
DISCUSSION: Employment-related expenses are paid for household services and for the care of a qualifying individual [Sec. 21(b)(2)]. Expenses are only classified as work-related if they are incurred to enable the taxpayer to be gainfully employed. An expense is not considered to be work-related merely because it is incurred while the taxpayer is gainfully employed [Reg. 1.44A-1(c)(1)].
Answers (a), (b), and (c) are incorrect because each is an expense incurred to enable the taxpayer to be gainfully employed.

18. Bethany is single and has adjusted gross income of $40,000. Bethany works full-time and keeps up a home for herself and her dependent father, who is not able to care for himself. She pays a housekeeper $1,100 per month to care for and provide meals to her father. What is the maximum amount of annual housekeeper expenses that Bethany can use to compute her dependent care credit?

   a. $1,320.
   b. $2,400.
   c. $2,640.
   d. $3,600.

The correct answer is (b). *(SPE 986 I-85)*
REQUIRED: The maximum amount of dependent care expenses allowable in computing the dependent care credit.
DISCUSSION: The amount of employment-related expenses incurred during any taxable year for the care of a qualifying individual may not exceed $2,400 if there is one qualifying individual, or $4,800 if there are two or more qualifying individuals, in computing the dependent care credit [Sec. 21(c)]. A qualifying individual includes any dependent of the taxpayer who is physically incapable of caring for him/herself.

Module 11.3: Child Care Credit

19. Mr. and Mrs. Donegan are filing a joint return for 1991. Mr. Donegan was employed the full year. Mrs. Donegan was a full-time student for 9 months and was not employed at anytime during the year. For the 9 months that Mrs. Donegan was a student, she paid $500 per month to a child care center to care for their 4-year-old daughter. For purposes of the child care credit, Mrs. Donegan is considered to have 1991 earned income of

 a. $1,800.
 b. $2,400.
 c. $3,600.
 d. $4,800.

The correct answer is (a). *(SPE 987 I-90)*
REQUIRED: The amount of earned income a spouse is treated as having while a full-time student.
DISCUSSION: Sec. 21(d) limits the amount of employment-related expenses to the individual's earned income or the earned income of his/her spouse (whichever is less). A full-time student at an educational institution is deemed to have earned $200 per month while a student with one qualifying individual. Since Mrs. Donegan was a full-time student for 9 months, her earned income is deemed to be $1,800 ($200 x 9 months).

20. Miss Dunn, a single parent who keeps up a home for herself and her two preschool children, paid work-related expenses of $5,200 for child care at a nursery school. Her adjusted gross income is $20,000, the sole source of which is wages. What amount can she claim as a child care credit?

 a. $1,152.
 b. $1,200.
 c. $1,248.
 d. $1,300.

The correct answer is (b). *(SPE 988 I-88)*
REQUIRED: The amount of the taxpayer's child and dependent care credit.
DISCUSSION: The child care credit is equal to the applicable percentage of employment-related expenses paid during the taxable year [Sec. 21(a)]. The applicable percentage is 30%, reduced (but not below 20%) by one percentage point for each $2,000 (or fraction thereof) by which adjusted gross income exceeds $10,000. Miss Dunn's applicable percentage is 25% {30% − [($20,000 − $10,000) ÷ $2,000]}. The amount of employment-related expenses incurred during any taxable year that may be taken into account in computing the credit may not exceed $2,400 if there is one qualifying individual and $4,800 if there are two or more qualifying individuals [Sec. 21(c)]. Miss Dunn's employment-related expenses are $5,200, which exceeds the $4,800 limit. Therefore, her child care credit is $1,200 (25% x $4,800 maximum employment-related expenses for two qualifying individuals).

21. Mr. Bently works and maintains a home for himself, his wife, and their two children. During 1991 Mr. Bently had earned income of $40,000. They file a joint return and have itemized deductions of $6,260. Mrs. Bently was a full-time student for 5 months in 1991 and had no earned income. They paid $3,000 of qualified work-related expenses while Mrs. Bently was a student. What is the amount of child and dependent care credit for 1991?

 a. $0.
 b. $400.
 c. $500.
 d. $600.

The correct answer is (b). *(SPE 1085 I-89)*
REQUIRED: The taxpayers' maximum allowable credit for child care.
DISCUSSION: Sec. 21(a) allows a credit equal to the applicable percentage of employment-related expenses. The applicable percentage is 30%, reduced (but not below 20%) by one percentage point for each $2,000 (or fraction thereof) by which adjusted gross income exceeds $10,000. The Bently's adjusted gross income exceeded $10,000 by more than $20,000, so the applicable percentage is 30% − 10% = 20%.

The taxpayers incurred $3,000 of employment-related expenses. However, Sec. 21(d) limits the amount of employment-related expenses to the individual's earned income or the earned income of his/her spouse, whichever is less. A full-time student at an educational institution is deemed to have earned $400 per month while a student with two or more qualifying individuals ($200 per month if only one qualifying individual). Mrs. Bently's deemed earned income is $2,000 ($400 per month x 5 months). Their credit for child care is $400 ($2,000 x 20%).

Module 11.3: Child Care Credit

22. Jim and Jan Cain filed a joint return for 1991 reflecting a tax liability before any credits of $3,427. Jim and Jan had earned income of $20,000 and $25,000, respectively, and reported adjusted gross income of $35,000. During 1991, for Jan to be gainfully employed, the Cains paid the following employment related expenses for their 8-year-old son.

Fine Day Care Center	$1,500
Best Home Cleaning Service	1,000

Assuming that the Cains do not claim any other credits against their tax, what is the amount of the child care credit they should report on their income tax return for 1991?

a. $300.
b. $600.
c. $720.
d. $750.

The correct answer is (a). *(SPE 990 I-90)*
REQUIRED: The amount of the child care tax credit allowed to the taxpayers.
DISCUSSION: Sec. 21(a) allows a credit equal to the applicable percentage of employment-related expenses. The applicable percentage is 30% reduced (but not below 20%) by one percentage point for each $2,000, or fraction thereof, by which the taxpayer's adjusted gross income for the taxable year exceeds $10,000. Since the taxpayers had adjusted gross income of $35,000 during the taxable year, their applicable percentage is 20%.

Housecleaning services do not qualify as eligible expenses, so the taxpayers incurred only $1,500 of qualifying employment-related expenses during the year. Sec. 21(c) limits the amount of employment-related expenses which may be taken into account in computing the credit to $2,400, but the $1,500 of actual expenses is less than this amount. Accordingly, the taxpayer's child care credit for the year is 20% of actual expenses incurred, or $300 ($1,500 x .20).

23. Jeanne incurs $2,000 of expenses to care for her 3-year-old daughter in order for Jeanne to work. Her employer reimburses Jeanne for $1,200 of these expenses under a plan so the reimbursement is exempt from tax under Sec. 129. Only $800 of Jeanne's expenses will qualify for the child care credit.

The correct answer is (T). *(Publisher)*
DISCUSSION: The child and disabled dependent care credit is equal to the applicable percentage of the employment-related expenses paid during the taxable year [Sec. 21(a)]. Only those amounts which are not reimbursed under a Sec. 129 plan qualify as child care expenses.

24. Mr. and Mrs. Anagnos are married and filed jointly. For 1991, they had adjusted gross income of $25,000 from Mrs. Anagnos's full-time employment. Mr. Anagnos was totally disabled and unable to care for himself the entire year. While she worked, Mrs. Anagnos paid an unrelated party $3,000 to care for Mr. Anagnos. Mr. and Mrs. Anagnos's tax liability before the child and disabled dependent care credit was $2,700. The applicable percentage for the credit is 22%. Mr. and Mrs. Anagnos qualify for a credit of $594.

The correct answer is (F). *(SPE 984 I-40)*
DISCUSSION: The child and disabled dependent care credit is equal to the applicable percentage of the employment-related expenses paid during the taxable year [Sec. 21(a)]. The amount of employment-related expenses incurred during any taxable year that may be taken into account in computing the credit may not exceed $2,400 if there is one qualifying individual, and $4,800 if there are two or more qualifying individuals. Mr. and Mrs. Anagnos's credit is $528 (22% x $2,400 maximum employment-related expenses).

25. To be a qualifying individual for purposes of the child care credit, a dependent under the age of 13 must be the taxpayer's child.

The correct answer is (F). *(SPE 1083 I-48)*
DISCUSSION: Included in the definition of a qualifying individual is a dependent of the taxpayer who is under the age of 13 and for whom the taxpayer is entitled to a personal exemption [Sec. 21(b)(1)]. Sec. 151(c) allows a personal exemption for each dependent of the taxpayer whose gross income for the year is less than $2,150 (for 1991), so the dependent need not be the taxpayer's child. Furthermore, a dependent or a spouse who is incapable of caring for him/herself is a qualifying individual.

Module 11.3: Child Care Credit

26. A divorced custodial parent of a 10-year-old child is not entitled to claim the child as a dependent if the noncustodial parent furnished at least $600 of the child's support for the year, and can claim the exemption for the child under a pre-1985 divorce instrument. However, the custodial parent is entitled to consider the child as a "qualifying person" for purposes of the child care credit as long as more than half of the child's support is received from one or both parents.

The correct answer is (T). *(SPE 987 I-37)*
DISCUSSION: Sec. 21(a) allows a child care credit to an individual who maintains a household that includes one or more qualifying individuals (a dependent under age 13 for whom the taxpayer is entitled to an exemption under Sec. 151(c). However, a divorced taxpayer having custody of a disabled or under-age-13 child is entitled to the child care credit even though (s)he is not entitled to an exemption under terms of a pre-1985 divorce decree [Sec. 21(e)].

27. Mrs. Neat's daughter, Nancy, is physically handicapped and unable to care for herself. She is 23 years old and her gross income for 1991 was $2,150. She could be claimed as a dependent by Mrs. Neat except for the gross-income limitation. If Mrs. Neat incurs and pays expenses for Nancy's care so that she (Mrs. Neat) can work, Mrs. Neat can claim the child and dependent care credit.

The correct answer is (T). *(SPE 989 I-24)*
DISCUSSION: A qualifying individual under Sec. 21(b) is a dependent of the taxpayer under age 13 and for whom the taxpayer is entitled to a personal dependency exemption, a dependent who is physically or mentally incapable of caring for him/herself, or the spouse of the taxpayer who is physically or mentally incapable of caring for him/herself. In order to qualify under the first test, the dependent may not have gross income in excess of $2,150 (for 1991); otherwise, the taxpayer is not entitled to a dependency exemption for the person. However, the second test only requires the qualifying person to be a dependent of the taxpayer who is physically or mentally incapable of caring for him/herself. A child is a dependent of the taxpayer provided the taxpayer provides more than 50% of the support. There is no gross income test here. Thus, Nancy meets the second test, and Mrs. Neat may claim the child and dependent care credit on her return.

28. A payment to a nursing home for the day care of your disabled and dependent father may qualify as an "employment-related" expense for the disabled dependent care credit.

The correct answer is (T). *(SPE 1077 I-88)*
DISCUSSION: The credit is allowed under Sec. 21 with respect to employment-related expenses incurred for services performed outside the household of the taxpayer, but only if the expenses are incurred for the care of a qualifying individual who is a dependent under the age of 13, or someone who spends at least 8 hours per day in the taxpayer's household [Sec. 21(b)(2)(B)]. The payment to the nursing home will qualify, as long as the father comes home for at least 8 hours per day.

29. A single individual, not otherwise employed, is considered "gainfully employed" for purposes of the child care credit if such individual is a full-time student for at least 5 calendar months during the year.

The correct answer is (F). *(SPE 1077 I-123)*
DISCUSSION: A full-time student is deemed to be gainfully employed only if (s)he is a spouse [Sec. 21(d)(2)]. A single individual is not considered gainfully employed by being a full-time student.

30. Steve Steffler, a single taxpayer, earned $10,000 in wages in 1991 as a truck driver. He maintains a home for his two dependent children, ages 10 and 12. Steve paid his mother, who is not his dependent, $2,000 to care for his children while he works. Steve may claim a child care credit on his 1991 Form 1040 income tax return.

The correct answer is (T). *(SPE 1081 I-41)*
DISCUSSION: The child care credit is allowed under Sec. 21 for employment-related expenses for the care of a qualifying individual. The term "qualifying individual" includes a dependent of the taxpayer who is under the age of 13 and for whom the taxpayer is entitled to a personal exemption [Sec. 21(b)(1)]. Although the credit is disallowed if the payments are made to related individuals, for purposes of the credit, a related individual is one for whom the taxpayer is entitled to a personal exemption, or who is a child of the taxpayer under the age of 19 [Sec. 21(e)(6)]. Therefore, Steve remains eligible to claim the credit.

31. Mr. and Mrs. J hired a housekeeper to care for their 8-year-old and 10-year-old children while they work. The housekeeper spends most of the time taking care of the children and doing the regular household work of cleaning and cooking, and spends 30 minutes a day driving Mr. and Mrs. J to and from work. The total amount ($4,800) paid to the housekeeper would qualify as work-related expenses for computing the child and dependent care credit.

The correct answer is (T). *(SPE 1085 I-43)*
DISCUSSION: Employment-related expenses which are used to calculate the credit include (1) expenses for household services and (2) expenses for the care of qualifying individuals [Sec. 21(b)(2)(A)]. Regulations define expenses for household services as amounts paid for ordinary and necessary services for the maintenance of a household, but only if the expenses are attributable in part to the care of the qualifying individual [Reg. 1.44A-1(c)(2)]. Therefore, the housekeeper's salary qualifies as employment-related expenses for the child care credit. When a portion of the expenses is for other than household purposes, a reasonable allocation must be made. But if the portion for other purposes is de minimis, no allocation is necessary, as in this case for the 30 minutes of chauffeuring [Reg. 1.44A-1(c)(6)].

11.4 Credit for the Elderly

32. All of the following statements regarding the "Credit for the Elderly and the Permanently and Totally Disabled" are true except

 a. The amount of the credit is based on age and filing status.

 b. Married persons living together must file a joint return to be eligible for the credit.

 c. A person under 65 must be retired on disability and must have been permanently and totally disabled upon retirement to be eligible for the credit.

 d. The amount of the credit which is not absorbed can be carried back 3 years or carried forward 5 years.

The correct answer is (d). *(SPE 1085 I-63)*
REQUIRED: The item that is not true with regard to the credit for the elderly and the permanently and totally disabled.
DISCUSSION: Sec. 22 provides a credit for qualified individuals based on age and filing status. Sec. 22 does not provide for any carryback or carryforward of unused credit. Any credit not used currently expires.
Answers (a), (b), and (c) are incorrect because each is a true statement regarding the credit for the elderly and the permanently and totally disabled.

33. Mr. and Mrs. Seifert, both U.S. citizens, are 67 and 64 years old, respectively. Neither is permanently and totally disabled. They filed a joint return for 1991 on which they reported adjusted gross income of $13,400. Together they received $1,200 from Social Security, all of which was nontaxable. They received no other nontaxable income. Mr. and Mrs. Seifert's tax before credits is $412. What is the amount of the credit for the elderly that Mr. and Mrs. Seifert may claim on their 1991 Form 1040?

 a. $0.
 b. $180.
 c. $255.
 d. $315.

The correct answer is (d). *(SPE 988 I-89)*
REQUIRED: The amount the taxpayers may claim as a credit for the elderly.
DISCUSSION: In the case of an individual who has attained age 65 before the close of the taxable year, Sec. 22(a) allows a credit equal to 15% of the individual's Sec. 22 amount. When only one spouse is eligible for the credit, the Sec. 22 amount is equal to an initial amount of $5,000 reduced by any amounts received as tax exempt Social Security benefits and also reduced by one-half of the excess of AGI over $10,000 (in the case of a joint return).

Initial Sec. 22 amount	$5,000
Less Social Security	(1,200)
Less AGI limitation [50% x ($13,400 − $10,000)]	(1,700)
Sec. 22 amount	$2,100
	x 15%
Seiferts' credit for the elderly	$ 315

Since the taxpayers' tax before credits exceeds the credit for the elderly, the entire credit can be claimed.

Module 11.4: Credit for the Elderly

34. Mr. K is 67 years old, single, and retired. During 1991 he received a taxable pension from his former employer in the amount of $4,000. His adjusted gross income is $10,500, and he received $500 of Social Security benefits. His tax before credits is $615. What is Mr. K's credit for the elderly?

a. $0.
b. $270.
c. $450.
d. $525.

The correct answer is (c). *(Publisher)*
REQUIRED: The amount of the taxpayer's credit for the elderly.
DISCUSSION: An individual who has attained age 65 is allowed a credit equal to 15% of the individual's Sec. 22 amount [Sec. 22(a)]. For a single individual, the initial Sec. 22 amount is $5,000, reduced by any amounts received as Social Security benefits or otherwise excluded from gross income [Sec. 22(c)(3)]. The Sec. 22 amount is also reduced by one-half of the excess of AGI over $7,500 (for a single individual).

Initial Sec. 22 amount	$5,000
Less AGI limitation [50% x ($10,500 – $7,500)]	(1,500)
Less Social Security	(500)
Sec. 22 amount	$3,000
	x 15%
K's credit for the elderly	$ 450

Since the taxpayer's tax before credits exceeds the credit for the elderly, the entire credit can be claimed.

35. Mr. and Mrs. Porpoise are both over 65 and file a joint return. During 1991, they received $5,000 from Social Security and their adjusted gross income was $13,000. How much can they claim as a credit for the elderly?

a. $0.
b. $150.
c. $450.
d. $900.

The correct answer is (b). *(SPE 990 I-91)*
REQUIRED: The amount the taxpayers may claim as a credit for the elderly.
DISCUSSION: In the case of an individual who has attained age 65 before the close of the taxable year, Sec. 22(a) allows a credit equal to 15% of the individual's Sec. 22 amount. On a joint return when both spouses are eligible for the credit, the Sec. 22 amount is equal to an initial amount of $7,500 reduced by any amounts received as Social Security benefits or otherwise excluded from gross income [Sec. 22(c)(3)]. The Sec. 22 amount is also reduced by one-half of the excess of adjusted gross income over $10,000 (in the case of a joint return), which is $1,500 [($13,000 – $10,000) x 50%] for the Porpoises.

Initial Sec. 22 amount	$ 7,500
Less Social Security	(5,000)
Less AGI limitation	$(1,500)
Sec. 22 amount	$ 1,000
	x 15%
Porpoises' tentative credit for the elderly	$ 150

The Porpoises' tax before credits will be $255 for 1991, thereby permitting the entire credit for the elderly to be claimed.

36. Mr. and Mrs. Troast are married and filing a joint return. Both are qualified individuals for purposes of credit for the elderly and the permanently and totally disabled. No Social Security benefits are received by the Troasts. They will not be eligible for the credit if their adjusted gross income is at least

a. $27,500.
b. $25,000.
c. $20,000.
d. $17,500.

The correct answer is (b). *(SPE 986 I-58)*
REQUIRED: The level of adjusted gross income at which a married couple filing a joint return will lose eligibility for the credit for the elderly.
DISCUSSION: A qualified individual is entitled to a credit of 15% of his/her Sec. 22 amount, so the level at which the credit is no longer allowed is the level at which the Sec. 22 amount becomes zero.

The Sec. 22 amount for Mr. and Mrs. Troast is the initial amount of $7,500 less one-half of the excess of AGI over $10,000. Solve for AGI by setting the initial amount equal to zero.

$$\$7,500 - 1/2(AGI - \$10,000) = \$0$$
$$1/2 AGI = \$12,500$$
$$AGI = \$25,000$$

37. Mr. Babyface was a truck driver until he retired on disability in 1985. He has a statement from his doctor that due to a back injury he will never be able to drive a truck again. He is 54 years old and now does volunteer work as a bookkeeper for a charitable organization. He sets his own hours, averaging 20 hours per week, and is not paid. Mr. Babyface is eligible for the credit for the elderly and the permanently and totally disabled.

The correct answer is (F). *(SPE 1085 I-44)*
DISCUSSION: Sec. 22 allows a credit for individuals who retire on disability and are permanently and totally disabled. Sec. 22(e)(3) defines permanently and totally disabled as being unable to engage in ANY substantial gainful activity by reason of any medically determinable physical or mental impairment.

38. Nontaxable social security payments received during the year do not affect the computation of the credit for the elderly.

The correct answer is (F). *(SPE 989 I-25)*
DISCUSSION: The initial Sec. 22 amount is reduced by nontaxable Social Security benefits received [Sec. 22(c)(3)], and therefore affects the computation of the credit for the elderly in this manner.

39. Ms. F, age 65, received a distribution from a qualified Individual Retirement Arrangement that she has contributed to because her employer did not provide a pension plan. The distribution she received qualifies for tax credit for the elderly if she meets all other requirements.

The correct answer is (T). *(SPE 1085 IV-47)*
DISCUSSION: A distribution from a qualified Individual Retirement Account such as the one described is taxable as income to the recipient. Therefore, since Ms. F meets all the other requirements, she may use the tax credit for the elderly to offset any taxes due on the IRA distribution.

11.5 Interest on Home Mortgage Credit

40. Judy purchased her first home in January 1991. She obtained a new mortgage and paid $6,000 of interest in 1991. Her state has elected to issue mortgage credit certificates in lieu of mortgage subsidy bonds. If Judy receives a mortgage credit certificate specifying a 20% credit rate, how much is her income tax credit and interest deduction?

	Credit	Deduction
a.	$1,200	$0
b.	$1,200	$4,800
c.	$1,200	$6,000
d.	$2,000	$4,000

The correct answer is (b). *(Publisher)*
REQUIRED: The taxpayer's income tax credit for home mortgage interest and the interest deduction for 1991.
DISCUSSION: Sec. 25 allows a credit to home purchasers who receive mortgage credit certificates in an amount equal to a specified percentage of the interest that the home purchaser pays or accrues during the taxable year on the mortgage on his/her principal residence. This percentage may not exceed 50% (but may not be less than 10%) of the interest on the qualifying indebtedness. If the percentage exceeds 20%, the credit is limited to $2,000. The amount of the home buyer's interest deduction in any year is reduced by the amount of the mortgage credit certificate interest for that year. Judy is entitled to a credit of $1,200 ($6,000 mortgage interest paid x 20% applicable credit rate). She may deduct the balance of the interest for the year ($4,800) as an itemized deduction.

41. The maximum credit for interest on a home mortgage is $2,000.

The correct answer is (F). *(Publisher)*
DISCUSSION: Sec. 25(a) limits the credit for interest on home mortgages to $2,000 only when the credit rate exceeds 20%. If the credit rate is less than 20%, there is no maximum credit.

11.6 Limitations on Nonrefundable Personal Credits

42. Linda and Jerry Brown have a tax liability for 1991 of $2,600 before credits. They have the following tentative credits:

Child care credit	$ 800
Interest on home mortgage credit	2,200

How much of these credits will be available for carryover to 1992 and how will any carryforward be treated?

a. $0. The credits must all be used in the year in which they arise.

b. $400. The carryforward is treated as a general nonrefundable personal credit in applying the limitation next year.

c. $400. The carryforward is treated as a child care credit. The other credits are used first in the current year.

d. $400. The carryforward is treated as an interest on home mortgage credit. It is the only one of these credits that may be carried forward.

The correct answer is (d). *(Publisher)*
REQUIRED: The amount of nonrefundable personal credits that may be carried over and used in 1992, and the treatment of the carryforward.
DISCUSSION: Sec. 26(a) limits the amount of nonrefundable personal credits such as the child care credit, the credit for the elderly, and the interest on home mortgage credit to the excess of taxpayer's regular tax liability for the year over the tentative minimum tax for the taxable year (excluding the alternative minimum tax foreign tax credit) [Sec. 26(a)]. Thus, the Browns are only allowed a credit in 1991 of $2,600.

The excess of $400 is carried forward for 3 years as an interest on home mortgage credit. There is no provision to carry forward the child care credit. Sec. 25(e)(1) provides that the carryover is the amount by which the interest on home mortgage credit exceeds the tax liability less the other nonrefundable personal credits. It is treated as an interest on home mortgage credit in the subsequent year.

43. Joe and Martha Phillips have a tax liability for 1991 of $2,800 before credits. They have the following tentative credits

Child care credit	$ 900
Interest on home mortgage credit	2,000

What is the maximum credit Joe and Martha may use in 1991?

a. $1,400.
b. $2,380.
c. $2,800.
d. $2,900.

The correct answer is (c). *(Publisher)*
REQUIRED: The maximum amount of nonrefundable personal credits for the taxpayers in 1991.
DISCUSSION: Nonrefundable credits, i.e., the child care credit, the credit for the elderly, and the interest on home mortgage credit are limited to the excess of the taxpayer's regular tax liability for the year over the tentative minimum tax for the taxable year (determined without regard to the alternative minimum tax foreign tax credit) [Sec. 26(a)]. Joe and Martha are limited to a credit of $2,800, their tax liability for 1991 assuming their tentative minimum tax liability is zero.

11.7 Foreign Tax Credit

44. For 1991, Gannon Corporation has U.S. taxable income of $500,000, which includes $100,000 from a foreign division. Gannon paid $45,000 of foreign income taxes on the income of the foreign division. Assuming Gannon's U.S. income tax for 1991 before credits is $170,000, its maximum foreign tax credit for 1991 is

a. $45,000.
b. $42,500.
c. $34,000.
d. $20,250.

The correct answer is (c). *(CMA 1289 3-23)*
REQUIRED: The foreign tax credit that can be claimed in 1991.
DISCUSSION: The foreign tax credit is allowed under Secs. 27 and 901 for foreign income taxes paid or accrued during the year and is limited by Sec. 904(a). The limitation is the proportion of the taxpayer's tentative U.S. income tax (before the foreign tax credit) which the taxpayer's foreign source taxable income bears to his/her worldwide taxable income for the year. The following calculation should be made

$$\frac{\text{Foreign Source Taxable Income}}{\text{Worldwide Taxable Income}} \times \text{U.S. Income Tax}$$

$$= \text{Foreign Tax Credit Limitation}$$

$$\frac{\$100,000}{\$500,000} \times \$170,000 = \$34,000$$

The unused credit of $11,000 ($45,000 − $34,000) may be carried back to the 2 preceding years and then forward to the following 5 taxable years [Sec. 904(c)].

45. In 1991, Kraco Corporation had worldwide taxable income of $200,000, of which $120,000 was U.S. source taxable income. Its tentative U.S. income tax was $61,250. Kraco paid foreign income taxes of $8,000 on $20,000 of nonbusiness related interest earned in Country Y. Kraco also paid $18,000 in foreign income taxes on $60,000 of foreign source business earnings. Kraco's foreign tax credit for 1991 is

a. $18,375.
b. $24,125.
c. $24,500.
d. $26,000.

The correct answer is (b). *(Publisher)*
REQUIRED: The foreign tax credit available when foreign nonbusiness interest income is earned in addition to foreign business income.
DISCUSSION: The foreign tax credit is allowed under Secs. 27 and 901 and is limited by Sec. 904(a). The limitation is the proportion of the taxpayer's tentative U.S. income tax (before the foreign tax credit) which the taxpayer's foreign taxable income bears to his/her worldwide taxable income for the year. Under Sec. 904(d), however, this limitation must be applied separately to nonbusiness interest income. For Kraco, these limits are

Nonbusiness interest income:
  $20,000 ÷ $200,000 x $61,250 = $6,125

Foreign business income:
  $60,000 ÷ $200,000 x $61,250 = $18,375

The credit for foreign taxes paid on interest income is limited to $6,125, so $1,875 of unused credit ($8,000 − $6,125) can be carried back 2 years and forward 5 years. The full $18,000 of foreign tax on other source income can be used. Total foreign tax credit is $24,125 ($6,125 + $18,000).

46. Smithco, Inc., a domestic corporation, was paid $20,000 of the total of $100,000 in dividends paid by a foreign corporation in 1991. Smithco owned 20% of the foreign corporation's stock. The foreign corporation paid $35,000 in foreign taxes and had accumulated profits of $120,000 after payment of its foreign taxes for years 1987-1991. Smithco also had $1,000 in taxes withheld by the foreign country on the dividend. Smithco has a foreign tax credit before limitation of

- a. $1,000.
- b. $5,833.
- c. $6,833.
- d. $8,000.

The correct answer is (c). *(Publisher)*
REQUIRED: The foreign tax credit (before limitation) of a U.S. corporation that received dividends from a foreign corporation subject to foreign taxes on its income.
DISCUSSION: The foreign tax credit is allowed under Secs. 27 and 901(a) for taxes paid by the corporation and those deemed to have been paid under Sec. 902. Sec. 902(a) provides that a domestic corporation owning at least 10% of the voting stock of a foreign corporation and receiving a dividend is deemed to have paid the foreign taxes which the foreign corporation paid on its profits accumulated after 1986. The dividend must be paid out of profits accumulated after 1986, and the amount of foreign taxes deemed paid is in the same proportion as that of the dividend to the profits accumulated after 1986 in excess of the post-1986 foreign taxes. The amount of taxes deemed paid by Smithco is

$$\frac{\text{Dividends } \$20,000}{\text{Post-1986 accum. profits } \$120,000} \times \$35,000 \text{ taxes}$$

$$= \$5,833 \text{ deemed paid credit}$$

Since Smithco also paid $1,000 in tax through withholding, the total foreign taxes are $6,833, the foreign tax credit before limitation. In computing its U.S. tax liability, Smithco must add the deemed taxes paid of $5,833 to its $20,000 of foreign income.

47. Which one of the following statements about the foreign operations of Nora Corporation is correct?

- a. Nora may take a credit, but not a deduction, for the income taxes paid to a foreign country.
- b. Nora may take a deduction, but not a credit, for the income taxes paid to a foreign country.
- c. Nora may elect to take either a credit or a deduction, but not both, for the income taxes paid to a foreign country.
- d. Nora may exclude both revenues and expenses of the foreign operations from its federal income tax return.

The correct answer is (c). *(CMA 686 3-24)*
REQUIRED: The correct statement about the foreign operations of a domestic corporation.
DISCUSSION: Sec. 164 allows a deduction for foreign income taxes paid or accrued during the taxable year. Alternatively, Secs. 27 and 901(a) permit both individual taxpayers and corporations to claim a foreign tax credit on income earned and subject to tax in a foreign country or U.S. possession. One may not claim both the deduction and the credit [Sec. 275(a)(4)].

Answers (a) and (b) are incorrect because a taxpayer may either deduct foreign income taxes or take a credit. Answer (d) is incorrect because worldwide income must generally be included on a federal income tax return.

11.8 Research and Experimentation Credit

48. All of the following statements regarding the research credit are correct except

a. The credit is equal to 20% of your qualified research expenses for the year over the product of (1) your "fixed base" percentage and (2) the average amount of your annual gross receipts for the 4 preceding tax years, plus 20% of your basic research payments.

b. The research credit applies only to research and development work that is incurred in your trade or business.

c. Wages paid to an individual that are used in figuring the targeted jobs credit may be included in arriving at your research credit.

d. The cost of acquiring someone else's product or process does not qualify for the credit.

The correct answer is (c). *(SPE 1085 II-55)*
REQUIRED: The item that is not correct with regard to the research and development credit.
DISCUSSION: Sec. 41(a) allows a credit against the income tax equal to 20% of the excess of the qualified research expenses for the taxable year over the base period research expenses plus 20% of your basic research payments. Qualified research expenses means the sum of the in-house research expenses and contract research expenses paid or incurred by the taxpayer during the taxable year in carrying on any trade or business [Sec. 41(b)]. Sec. 41(b)(2)(D) explicitly excludes wages taken into account in determining the targeted jobs credit from qualified research expenses.
Answers (a), (b), and (d) are incorrect because each is a true statement about the research credit.

49. Which of the following research expenditures qualify for the research and experimentation credit in 1991?

1. Research activities conducted in Brazil by a U.S. company
2. Research funded by the U.S. government
3. Research done by a state university under contract for a U.S. corporation

a. 1.
b. 2.
c. 3.
d. 1 and 3.

The correct answer is (c). *(Publisher)*
REQUIRED: The expenditure(s) that qualify for the research and experimentation credit.
DISCUSSION: Qualified research does not include research conducted outside the United States, research in the social sciences or humanities, and research to the extent funded by any grant, contract, or otherwise by another person or governmental entity [Sec. 41(d)]. However, 20% of cash expenditures by a corporation in excess of the sum of (1) a fixed research floor plus (2) an amount reflecting any decrease in nonresearch giving to qualified organizations as compared to such giving during a fixed base period qualifies for the credit [Sec. 41(e)]. Qualified organizations include institutions of higher education [Sec. 41(e)(6)].
Answers (a), (b), and (d) are incorrect because research outside the U.S. or funded by a governmental entity is not qualified.

50. Mihalco Corporation incurs $170,000 of qualified research expenses in 1991. Mihalco's ratio of total qualified research expenses over total gross receipts for the period 1984-1988 is 0.15. Gross receipts for 1987-1990 are as follows

Year	Gross Receipts
1987	$500,000
1988	550,000
1989	650,000
1990	700,000

Mihalco Corporation's income tax liability and tentative minimum tax for 1991 are $61,250 and $31,000, respectively. It did not have any other tax credits. For 1991, Mihalco's research and development credit is

a. $13,000.
b. $16,000.
c. $22,000.
d. $34,000.

The correct answer is (b). *(Publisher)*
REQUIRED: The taxpayer's research and development credit before limitations.
DISCUSSION: Sec. 41(a) allows a credit equal to 20% of the excess of the qualified research expenses for the taxable year over its base amount. The base amount is defined as the product of (1) the taxpayer's fixed-base percentage times (2) the average annual gross receipts for the 4 tax years preceding the credit year. The base amount, however, may not be less than 50% of the qualified research expenses for the credit year. The fixed base percentage is the aggregate of qualified research expenditures for tax years 1984-1988 divided by the aggregate gross receipts of the taxpayer for that period. In this case, Mihalco's research and development credit for 1991 as calculated below is $16,000.

$$\$16,000 = \left\{ .20 \times \left[\$170,000 - \left(.15 \times \frac{\$2,400,000}{4} \right) \right] \right\}$$

The full amount of the credit can be claimed since the general business credit limitation is $30,250 ($61,250 − $31,000).

Module 11.8: Research and Experimentation Credit

51. In 1991, Mr. P, in an attempt to improve his business, incurred contract research expenses of $20,000 and in-house research expenses of $110,000. The ratio of total qualified research expenses over total gross receipts for the period 1984-1988 is 0.14. Annual gross receipts for the period 1987-1990 averaged $400,000. Mr. P's income tax liability for 1991 is $70,000. He did not have any other tax credits for 1991. What amount may Mr. P claim as a research and development credit?

a. $12,300.
b. $13,400.
c. $14,800.
d. $26,000.

The correct answer is (a). *(Publisher)*
REQUIRED: The taxpayer's research and experimentation credit with contract research.
DISCUSSION: Sec. 41(a) allows a credit equal to 20% of the excess of the qualified research expenses for the taxable year over the base amount research expenses. For contract research expenses, 65% of the amount paid or incurred is included [Sec. 41(b)(3)]. The base amount research expenses is defined as the product of (1) the taxpayer's fixed base percentage times (2) the average amount of gross receipts for the 4 tax years preceding the credit year. The fixed base percentage is the aggregate of qualified research expenditures for tax years 1984-1988 divided by the aggregate gross receipts of the taxpayer for that period. The base amount research expenses may not be less than 50% of the qualified research expenses [Sec. 41(d)].

In-house research	$110,000
Contract research (65% x $20,000)	13,000
Qualified research expense	$123,000
Base amount research expenses ($56,000*, but may not be less than 50% x $123,000)	(61,500)
Eligible expenditures	$ 61,500
Times: credit rate	x 20%
Mr. P's research credit	$ 12,300

*$56,000 = (.14 x $400,000)

52. XYZ Company incurs $300,000 of research expenses in 1991 deductible under Sec. 174. These same expenses entitle XYZ to a research credit of $20,000. XYZ will only be able to deduct $280,000 of the research expenses.

The correct answer is (T). *(Publisher)*
DISCUSSION: Sec. 280C(c) requires the deduction for research expenses under Sec. 174 to be reduced by 100% of the research credit. Alternatively, if the taxpayer elected to capitalize research expenses, the amount capitalized must also be reduced by 100% of the research credit. Since XYZ's research credit is $20,000, XYZ can only deduct $280,000 ($300,000 – $20,000) of the research expenses.

53. A taxpayer may elect not to take the research credit.

The correct answer is (F). *(Publisher)*
DISCUSSION: The Sec. 41(h) election not to take the research credit was repealed for tax years beginning after December 31, 1988. A new election permits a taxpayer to avoid reducing the Sec. 174 deduction by 100% of the credit claimed by electing to reduce the credit by 50% of the credit times the maximum corporate tax rate imposed by Sec. 11(b)(1). The election is an annual election that is irrevocable and must be made no later than the filing date for the tax return (including extensions).

54. The research credit cannot be taken for any of the following

1) Research to find and evaluate gas and oil deposits
2) Research in the social sciences or humanities
3) Management efficiency surveys

The correct answer is (T). *(SPE 984 II-41)*
DISCUSSION: None of the listed work qualifies for the research credit. Sec. 41(d) defines qualified research as meaning the same as in Sec. 174, and also excludes research in the social sciences or humanities, and efficiency surveys and management studies. Sec. 174(d) excludes exploration and evaluation of oil and gas deposits.

55. Mr. A and Mr. B formed a calendar-year partnership C in November 1991. The partnership passed through the following items to A and B in 1991

Ordinary loss	$50,000
Research credit from qualifying research	11,250

Mr. A has an income tax liability of $20,000 before research credits. Mr. A may claim his proportionate share of the research credit from partnership C on his 1991 tax return.

The correct answer is (F). *(SPE 984 II-42)*
DISCUSSION: Sec. 41(g) limits a partner's use of the research credit passed through from a partnership to the tax attributable to the partner's share of taxable income from the partnership. Since the partnership has no taxable income, neither A nor B may use the research credit in 1991.

56. Research related to style, taste, cosmetic, or seasonal design factors does not qualify for the research credit.

The correct answer is (T). *(Publisher)*
DISCUSSION: Sec. 41(d)(3) states that items which do not qualify as research purposes are those which relate to style, taste, cosmetic, or seasonal design factors.

57. The tax credit for increased research and development expenditures only applies to expenses incurred before 1992.

The correct answer is (T). *(Publisher)*
DISCUSSION: The increased research activities credit has been scheduled to expire a number of times. The Revenue Reconciliation Act of 1990 has extended the credit through December 31, 1991.

11.9 Targeted Jobs Credit

58. All the following groups are targeted groups for the targeted jobs credit except

a. Trade Readjustment Act beneficiaries.
b. Economically disadvantaged youths.
c. Supplemental Security Income recipients.
d. Youths participating in a cooperative education program.

The correct answer is (a). *(SPE 984 II-62)*
REQUIRED: The group not considered a targeted group for purposes of the targeted jobs credit.
DISCUSSION: Sec. 51(d) provides a list of the groups that are considered targeted groups for purposes of the targeted jobs credit. Trade Readjustment Act beneficiaries are not included among the list of targeted groups.
Answers (b), (c), and (d) are incorrect because each is a group included as a targeted group in Sec. 51(d).

59. During 1991, Toni Painta hired an economically disadvantaged Vietnam veteran for 99 days to perform duties related to her business. Toni Painta paid the employee a total of $6,500 during 1991. What is the amount Toni Painta may claim as a jobs credit?

a. $0.
b. $2,400.
c. $2,600.
d. $3,000.

The correct answer is (b). *(SPE 988 II-87)*
REQUIRED: The amount of the targeted jobs credit.
DISCUSSION: Under Sec. 51, the amount of the targeted jobs credit is equal to 40% of the first $6,000 of wages paid to a qualified employee in his/her first year of service. Miss Painta paid the employee $6,500, so the credit is limited to $2,400 (40% x $6,000).
Note that the employee completed 90 days of service which meets one requirement of the credit [Sec. 51(i)(3)].

60. Red Baron hired two employees under a targeted jobs program and claimed the following credit in 1991

Employee X, hired 10/1/90, $3,000 salary x 40%	$1,200
Employee Y, hired 9/1/90, $4,000 salary x 40%	1,600
	$2,800

On January 10, 1991, Red Baron terminated Employee X for poor job performance. On February 15, 1991, Employee Y was laid off for lack of work in Red's business. What amount, if any, of the credit claimed in 1990 will Red Baron recapture in 1991?

a. $0.
b. $600.
c. $700.
d. $1,400.

The correct answer is (a). *(SPE 1079 II-49)*
REQUIRED: The amount of credit claimed in 1990 that the taxpayer will recapture in 1991.
DISCUSSION: The targeted jobs credit is provided in Sec. 38, and operating rules are contained in Secs. 51 and 52. The purpose of the credit is to provide incentives for employers to hire certain groups of employees who have found it hard to find employment. The credit is equal to the sum of 40% of the first $6,000 of wages paid to a qualified employee in his/her first year of service. Employees must have completed at least 90 days or 120 hours of service in order for their wages to be used in computing the credit [Sec. 51(i)(3)]. The employer is required to reduce his/her deduction for wages by the amount of the credit. There is no provision for recapture of the credit when an employee is terminated.

61. A deduction for wages paid during the year is reduced by the full amount of the targeted jobs credit, even if the total credit is not used, because of the tax liability limitation.

The correct answer is (T). *(SPE 1080 II-47)*
DISCUSSION: A deduction for wages paid during the year is reduced by the full amount of the targeted jobs credit even if the total credit is not utilized in that year [Sec. 280C(a)]. Both a deduction and a credit are not allowed for the same wages paid. Any unused portion of the credit may be carried back 3 years and carried forward 15 years.

62. The targeted jobs credit only applies to wages paid to employees who begin work prior to 1992.

The correct answer is (F). *(Publisher)*
DISCUSSION: The targeted jobs credit of Sec. 51 has been scheduled to expire a number of times. The targeted jobs credit has been extended by the Tax Extension Act of 1991 to cover wages paid to eligible employees hired before July 1, 1992.

11.10 Business Energy Credit

63. Which of the following energy properties does not qualify for the business energy credit for 1991?

a. Wind energy property.
b. Ocean thermal property.
c. Solar property.
d. Geothermal property.

The correct answer is (a). *(Publisher)*
REQUIRED: The type of energy property not qualifying for the business energy credit in 1991.
DISCUSSION: The business energy credit has been scheduled to expire a number of times. The Tax Extension Act of 1991 extended the credit through June 30, 1992, for solar, geothermal, and ocean thermal property. The credit for wind energy property expired December 31, 1985.

Module 11.10: Business Energy Credit

64. Which of the following statements on business energy credit property is not correct?

  a. The property may be used property.
  b. The property must be a depreciable or amortizable property.
  c. The property must be used in connection with a structure within the United States.
  d. The property may be structural components.

The correct answer is (a). *(SPE 1081 II-66)*
REQUIRED: The statement about business energy credit property that is not correct.
DISCUSSION: Energy property is defined in Sec. 48(a)(3). One of the requirements is that the taxpayer claiming the credit must have constructed or erected the property or acquired and have the original use of the property. This means the property must be new, not used [Sec. 48(a)(2)(B)].
Answer (b) is incorrect because energy property must be property with respect to which depreciation or amortization is allowable [Sec. 48(a)(3)(C)]. Answer (c) is incorrect because energy property must generally meet the requirements of Sec. 50(b)(1) under which the property may not be used predominantly outside the U.S. Answer (d) is incorrect because structural components of a building may qualify for the energy credit [Reg. 1.48-9(b)(1)].

65. In 1991, Pianca Corp. bought solar panels for $8,000 and depreciated them as 7-year property under the modified accelerated cost recovery system. What is Pianca's business energy credit for 1991?

  a. $480.
  b. $800.
  c. $960.
  d. $1,200.

The correct answer is (b). *(Publisher)*
REQUIRED: The business energy credit for solar panels.
DISCUSSION: Sec. 38 allows a credit against the income tax for investing in certain depreciable property. The amounts of the credit for energy property are in Sec. 48(a)(2)(A). Solar property qualifies for a 10% credit in 1991. Pianca's credit is $800 ($8,000 x 10%).

66. Solar property installed as a structural component of a building may not qualify for the business energy credit.

The correct answer is (F). *(SPE 1081 II-41)*
DISCUSSION: Energy property has included structural components of a building even though such components generally did not qualify as investment tax credit (Sec. 38) property [Reg. 1.48-9(b)(1)]. Energy property includes solar property, and solar property installed as a structural component of a building may qualify for the business energy credit.

67. The at-risk rules are applicable to the energy credit.

The correct answer is (T). *(Publisher)*
DISCUSSION: The energy credit is equal to the energy percentage times the basis of each energy property placed in service during the taxable year [Sec. 48(a)(1)]. The at-risk rules are extended to energy credit property by Sec. 49(a). The credit base of any eligible property is reduced by the nonqualified nonrecourse financing with respect to the credit base (as of the close of the taxable year the property is placed in service). This reduction limits the investment eligible for the credit to the amount at risk.

68. For energy property placed in service after 1982, the basis of the property must be reduced by 50% of the business energy credit claimed.

The correct answer is (T). *(Publisher)*
DISCUSSION: Under Sec. 50(c)(3), the basis of energy property must be reduced by 50% of the business energy credit claimed. This basis reduction will, for purposes of Sec. 1245 and Sec. 1250, be treated as depreciation, and it may, therefore, result in recapture of ordinary income upon later sale of the property.

Module 11.11: Rehabilitation Credit

69. The business energy credit remains at 15% until its expiration on June 30, 1992.

The correct answer is (F). *(Publisher)*
DISCUSSION: The business energy credit was extended until December 31, 1991 for three types of property [Sec. 48(a)(2)(A)]. However, the credit percentage varies by type of property and year as follows:

Energy Property	Amount of Credit		
	1986	1987	1988-1990
Solar	15%	12%	10%
Geothermal	15%	10%	10%
Ocean thermal	15%	15%	15%

For tax years beginning after December 31, 1990, all three energy property categories are eligible for the credit at a 10% rate.

11.11 Rehabilitation Credit

70. Expenditures that can qualify for the tax credit for rehabilitated buildings in 1991 include

1. Cost of acquiring a business building which is more than 33 years old
2. Cost of replacing all floors and plumbing in a 60-year-old office building
3. Cost of enlarging a certified historic structure used as a restaurant so that kitchen facilities can be modernized

    a. 1.
    b. 2.
    c. 3.
    d. 2 and 3.

The correct answer is (b). *(Publisher)*
REQUIRED: The item(s) qualifying for the tax credit for rehabilitated buildings.
DISCUSSION: Sec. 47(c)(2) defines qualified rehabilitation expenditures as amounts chargeable to capital for nonresidential real property, residential rental property, real property with a class life of more than 12.5 years, or improvements to any of the above-named properties and which are spent in connection with the rehabilitation of a qualified rehabilitated building. The cost of replacing floors and plumbing in a 60-year-old office building is a qualified expenditure since it will be capitalized, and the 60-year-old office building is a qualified rehabilitated building because it was placed in service before 1936 [Sec. 47(c)(1)(B)].
Answers (a), (c), and (d) are incorrect because qualified expenditures include neither the cost of acquiring a building or an interest in a building, nor the cost of enlarging a building [Sec. 47(c)(2)(B)].

71. In 1989, Sunset Corporation acquired a 60-year-old building at a cost of $320,000 and used it for 2 years. Sunset had the interior of the building rehabilitated at a cost of $200,000 in 1991 when the adjusted basis of the building was $300,000. All work was completed during 1991 when Sunset moved back into the building. The building was not a certified historic structure. The available tax credit for the rehabilitation before any limitation is

    a. $0.
    b. $30,000.
    c. $40,000.
    d. $50,000.

The correct answer is (a). *(Publisher)*
REQUIRED: The available tax credit for the rehabilitated building.
DISCUSSION: Sec. 47(c)(1) defines a qualified rehabilitated building for purposes of computing the credit as one placed in service before the rehabilitation began, and one in which 50% or more of the existing external walls are retained as external walls, 75% of existing external walls are retained as internal or external walls, and 75% of existing internal structural framework is retained. In addition, the building must have been placed in service before 1936 if it is not a certified historic structure, and substantial rehabilitation must have occurred. Rehabilitation is substantial if its cost exceeds the greater of the adjusted basis of the property or $5,000.
The basis in the building acquired by Sunset Corporation was $300,000 at the time the rehabilitation began. The cost of the rehabilitation was only $200,000, which does not meet the requirement for substantial rehabilitation. The tax credit will be $0.

Module 11.11: Rehabilitation Credit

72. Aged Corporation built an office building in 1931 at a cost of $100,000 to be used as its corporate headquarters. The building was fully depreciated, and it had a basis of $14,000 in 1991 when Aged began rehabilitating the structure. Rehabilitation expenditures of $200,000 were incurred during 1991, and Aged moved back into the building in December 1991. Aged's credit for rehabilitation expenditures is

 a. $20,000.
 b. $21,400.
 c. $32,100.
 d. $40,000.

The correct answer is (a). *(Publisher)*
REQUIRED: The taxpayer's credit for rehabilitation expenditures.
DISCUSSION: Aged Corporation rehabilitated a building that had been placed in service before 1936. Substantial rehabilitation has occurred because the cost of rehabilitation exceeded the basis of $14,000 [Sec. 47(c)(1)(C)]. Under Sec. 47(a)(2), the rehabilitation credit for a rehabilitated building other than a certified historic structure is 10%. Thus, Aged's tentative rehabilitation credit is $20,000 ($200,000 rehabilitation expenditures x 10%).

73. In 1990, C.P. Aye acquired a 45-year-old residence, which was a certified historic structure, at a cost of $75,000. In a certified rehabilitation, Aye spent $90,000 converting the house into an office for her accounting practice. Aye completed the rehabilitation in 1991. Aye's credit for rehabilitation of the building and her basis in the building after the rehabilitation are

 a. $18,000 credit and $147,000 basis.
 b. $18,000 credit and $156,000 basis.
 c. $22,500 credit and $153,750 basis.
 d. $22,500 credit and $142,500 basis.

The correct answer is (a). *(Publisher)*
REQUIRED: The credit for rehabilitation of a certified historic structure and its basis.
DISCUSSION: Rehabilitation of a certified historic structure results in a credit of 20% of the qualified expenditures [Sec. 47(a)(2)]. Aye invested $90,000 in rehabilitating the structure. Accordingly, she can claim a credit of $18,000 ($90,000 x 20%). The basis of rehabilitated certified historic structures must be adjusted by 100% of the credit claimed. Therefore, Aye's new basis in the building is equal to the original cost of $75,000, plus the amount of the rehabilitation expenditure ($90,000), less 100% of the credit ($18,000), for a total basis of $147,000 [Sec. 50(c)(1)].

74. Which of the following must be true for a building other than a certified historic structure to be considered a qualified rehabilitated building?

 a. The building must have been placed in service prior to 1936.
 b. At least 50% of existing external walls must remain in place as external walls.
 c. At least 75% of existing external walls must remain in place as internal or external walls.
 d. All of the above.

The correct answer is (d). *(Publisher)*
REQUIRED: The requirement necessary for a building other than a certified historic structure to be considered a qualified rehabilitated building.
DISCUSSION: Under Sec. 47(c)(1)(B), the requirement listed in answer (a) is necessary for a building other than a certified historic structure, to be considered a qualified rehabilitated building. The requirements listed in answers (b) and (c) are necessary for any building to be considered a qualified rehabilitated building. In addition, at least 75% of existing internal structural framework must remain in place [Sec. 47(c)(1)(A)].

75. Basis in a building placed in service before 1936 which is not a certified historic structure must be reduced by any credit for rehabilitation expenditures claimed after 1986.

The correct answer is (T). *(Publisher)*
DISCUSSION: Under Sec. 50(c), the basis in a building for which a credit for rehabilitation expenditures is claimed after 1986 must be reduced by the full amount of the credit claimed, even if the building is not a certified historic structure.

76. Accelerated depreciation can be claimed on qualified rehabilitation expenditures.

The correct answer is (F). *(Publisher)*
DISCUSSION: If a credit is claimed for qualified rehabilitation expenditures, amortization or accelerated methods of depreciation may not be used on the property [Sec. 47(c)(2)(B)(i)].

77. George leased an apartment building on April 2, 1987 for a term of 30 years. On May 1, 1991, George completed qualified rehabilitation on the apartment building costing $100,000. The lease term was not extended. George's expenses qualify for the rehabilitation credit.

The correct answer is (F). *(Publisher)*
DISCUSSION: Expenditures incurred by a lessee do not qualify for the rehabilitation credit unless the remaining lease term on the date the rehabilitation is completed is at least as long as the applicable recovery period under the general depreciation rules (27.5 years for residential rental property and 31.5 years for nonresidential real property) [Sec. 47(c)(2)(B)(vi)]. On the date George completed the rehabilitation, there were only 26 years left on the lease term and not the required 27.5.

11.12 ITC Recapture

78. The investment tax credit (or investment credit) includes all but which of the following?

  a. Reforestation credit.
  b. Energy credit.
  c. Rehabilitation credit.
  d. Low-income housing credit.

The correct answer is (d). *(Publisher)*
REQUIRED: The type of credit not considered part of the investment tax credit.
DISCUSSION: The investment tax credit is defined in Sec. 46 as being composed of the reforestation credit, the energy credit, and the rehabilitation credit. The low-income housing credit of Sec. 42 is not part of the investment tax credit.
Answer (a) is incorrect because the rehabilitation credit is part of the investment tax credit. Answer (b) is incorrect because the energy credit is part of the investment tax credit and is available through 1991. Answer (c) is incorrect because the rehabilitation credit is also part of the investment tax credit.

79. Which one of the following transactions is not a disposition of property that would cause a recapture of the investment tax credit?

  a. Property transferred by gift.
  b. Property converted by theft.
  c. Property that has been abandoned.
  d. Property transferred as security for a loan.

The correct answer is (d). *(SPE 1081 II-67)*
REQUIRED: The transaction that does not cause recapture of the investment tax credit.
DISCUSSION: Under Sec. 50(a)(1)(A), if property is disposed of or otherwise ceases to be owned by the taxpayer, the taxpayer must recapture the investment tax credit. This means his/her tax is increased for the current year by part or all of the credit previously taken. The transfer of property as security for a loan is not considered to be a disposition and would not cause any recapture.
Answers (a), (b), and (c) are incorrect because each is a disposition of property that causes the recapture of ITC.

80. Which of the following transactions is not a disposition of property that would cause a recapture of investment tax credit?

  a. Business property converted to personal use.
  b. Transfer of property by foreclosure.
  c. Property transferred by reason of death.
  d. Property destroyed by casualty.

The correct answer is (c). *(SPE 1080 II-65)*
REQUIRED: The transaction that is not a disposition that causes recapture of the investment tax credit.
DISCUSSION: Sec. 50(a)(1)(A) requires the recapture of the investment tax credit if property on which it has been taken is disposed of prematurely. Under Sec. 50(a)(4)(A), a transfer by reason of death is specifically excluded from dispositions that would result in the recapture of the investment tax credit.
Answers (a), (b), and (d) are incorrect because each is a disposition of property that causes the recapture of ITC.

81. On June 3, 1989, Universal Corporation purchased $50,000 of solar panels. The company claimed the maximum possible solar energy property credit and then the maximum depreciation, but did not use the Sec. 179 expensing election. On August 2, 1991, the equipment was sold for $38,000. Universal Corporation's energy tax credit recapture on the disposition of the solar panels amounts to

   a. $0.
   b. $3,000.
   c. $4,000.
   d. $5,000.

The correct answer is (b). *(Publisher)*
REQUIRED: The amount of energy tax credit that must be recaptured.
DISCUSSION: Since 1988, solar energy panels have been entitled to a 10% credit. Thus, in 1989, Universal Corporation received a $5,000 ($50,000 x .10) energy tax credit. Since Universal sold the property before the full credit had been earned, they must recapture part of the credit, and add it directly to their 1991 tax liability.
   Under Sec. 50(a)(1)(B), the recapture percentage is 100% if the property is disposed of within the first year of being placed in service. For each year thereafter, the recapture percentage declines by 20%. Universal held the property for 2 years, thus their recapture percentage is 60% [100% − (2 years x 20%)]. Thus, Universal's energy tax credit recapture is $3,000 (60% x $5,000).

82. Solo Corporation built an office building in 1931 to be used as its corporate headquarters. The building was rehabilitated in 1988 with rehabilitation expenditures of $300,000 being incurred. Solo occupied the building in October 1988 and claimed a $30,000 credit for its rehabilitation expenditures. Solo Corporation was acquired by Large Corporation in June 1991. The Solo Corporation corporate headquarters were sold in December, 1991 at a $150,000 profit. What is the recapture of the rehabilitation building credit in 1991?

   a. $0.
   b. $12,000.
   c. $18,000.
   d. $30,000.

The correct answer is (b). *(Publisher)*
REQUIRED: The amount of the rehabilitation credit that must be recaptured.
DISCUSSION: The credit for rehabilitation expenditures must be recaptured if the rehabilitated structure is disposed of in less than 5 years. Under Sec. 50(a)(1)(B), the recapture percentage is 100% of the credit taken if the property is disposed of within the first year after being placed in service. For each year the property is held after the first year, the recapture percentage declines by 20%.
   Solo Corporation held the property for 3 years, so they must recapture 40% [100% − (3 years x 20%)] of the original credit amount

Rehabilitation credit	$30,000
Times: Recapture percentage	40%
Recapture amount	$12,000

83. The four partners of the ABCD Partnership share the profits and losses equally. In April 1988, ABCD acquired new business assets including solar energy property in the amount of $100,000 and the partners together claimed an energy tax credit of $10,000. In July 1991, A sold his interest to Ms. E. A had properly claimed his full share of the investment credit for 1988. What is the amount A must add to his 1991 income tax liability under the energy credit recapture rules?

   a. $2,500.
   b. $2,000.
   c. $1,500.
   d. $1,000.

The correct answer is (d). *(SPE 989 II-88)*
REQUIRED: The amount of energy credit recapture.
DISCUSSION: Under Sec. 50(a)(1)(B), if the energy property in question is sold within 5 years, part of the energy tax credit taken on the property must be recaptured. The recapture percentage is 100% of the credit taken, if the property is disposed of within the first year after being placed in service. For each year thereafter, the recapture percentage declines by 20%.
   In this case, A's share of the partnership's credit is $2,500 ($10,000 credit ÷ 4 equal partners). Since A was in the partnership for only 3 years, he must recapture 40% of the credit [100% − (3 years x 20%)]. Therefore, A's recapture amount is $1,000 ($2,500 x 40%).

Module 11.12: ITC Recapture

84. In January, 1989, TexAnn Corporation, an S corporation, purchased solar heating panels for $150,000 from Ark Company. TexAnn paid $35,000 in cash and financed the remaining $115,000 on a recourse basis with Ark Company. TexAnn took an energy credit of $15,000. In January 1991, Ark and TexAnn modified their financing arrangement so that TexAnn no longer had any liability for the $75,000 of the debt which was not yet paid. How much of the investment tax credit taken in 1989 must TexAnn recapture?

   a. $0.
   b. $7,500.
   c. $9,000.
   d. $12,000.

The correct answer is (b). *(Publisher)*
REQUIRED: The amount of energy tax credit taken in 1989 that must be recaptured.
DISCUSSION: Under Sec. 49(b)(1), if a taxpayer ceases to be at risk with regard to property for which the energy tax credit was previously claimed, (s)he must recapture the amount of credit that would not have been able to be claimed if (s)he had not been at risk with respect to that amount when the property was placed in service. Ark and TexAnn modified their financing arrangement so that TexAnn was no longer liable for $75,000 of the debt. Therefore, $7,500 (10% x $75,000) must therefore be recaptured in 1991.

85. The credit for rehabilitation expenditures must be recaptured if the rehabilitated structure is disposed of in fewer than 5 years.

The correct answer is (T). *(Publisher)*
DISCUSSION: The credit for rehabilitation expenditures must be recaptured if the rehabilitated structure is disposed of in less than 5 years. Under Sec. 50(a)(1)(A), the recapture percentage is 100% of the credit taken if the property is disposed of within the first year after being placed in service. For each year the property is held after the first year, the recapture percentage declines by 20%. After the property has been held for 5 full years, the recapture percentage is zero.

86. The transfer of investment tax credit property due to the death of the property's owner is not considered to be a disposition of property that could result in the recapture of the investment tax credit.

The correct answer is (T). *(SPE 986 II-30)*
DISCUSSION: The death of a taxpayer is not a disposition for purposes of Sec. 50, and no investment tax credit should be recaptured on the decedent's final return [Sec. 50(a)(4)(A)]. In effect, investment tax credit property held by a taxpayer at death is treated as if held for the time required to avoid recapture.

87. If you have previously taken an investment credit on qualified property, and later, before the end of its useful life, traded it for other qualified property, there will be a recapture of investment credits for the original property and an investment credit available for the new property in the year of trade.

The correct answer is (T). *(SPE 1079 II-30)*
DISCUSSION: When property on which ITC has been claimed is disposed of, the taxpayer may have to recapture part of the investment tax credit depending on how long the property has been held (Sec. 50). This applies even if the taxpayer trades the original property for other property which qualifies for the credit. When traded before the property has been held for the required period of time, the taxpayer must recapture a portion of the tax credit originally claimed on the original property. A new tax credit may then be claimed for the new qualified property, if such a credit is available.

11.13 Low-Income Rental Housing Credit

88. On June 1, 1989, Herman placed in service a residential rental apartment building for low-income individuals. The qualified basis of the building is $450,000. The building is not federally subsidized. The monthly low-income housing credit percentage for June, 1989, is 9.21%. How much low-income housing credit may Herman be eligible for in 1991?

a. $4,144.
b. $20,722.
c. $40,500.
d. $41,445.

The correct answer is (d). *(Publisher)*
REQUIRED: The low-income housing credit for rental property.
DISCUSSION: For buildings placed in service after 1986, Sec. 42 provides a credit that may be claimed by owners of residential rental projects providing low-income housing, in lieu of other credits. The credit is taken over a 10-year period (the credit period) starting in the year the building or a rehabilitation of the building is placed in service. The credit amount is determined by applying a percentage to the qualified basis amount in each year. The percentage in 1987 was 9% for new buildings not federally subsidized and 4% for new buildings that are federally subsidized and also for used buildings. For buildings placed in service after 1987, the credits are adjusted monthly. But once determined, the credit remains the same for the taxpayer each year. Herman's eligible credit amount is $41,445 ($450,000 x 9.21%).

89. Which of the following statements is not a requirement that must be met in order for residential rental property to be eligible for the low-income housing credit?

a. 20% or more of the aggregate residential rental units must be occupied by individuals with incomes of 50% or less of the area median incomes.
b. 40% or more of the aggregate rental units must be occupied by individuals with incomes of 60% or less of the area median incomes.
c. The gross rent paid by families in the rent-restricted units may not exceed 30% of the qualifying income for a family of its size.
d. Qualified residential rental properties must remain as rental property and meet the minimum low-income set-aside requirements for 20 consecutive years.

The correct answer is (d). *(Publisher)*
REQUIRED: The false statement regarding eligibility for the low-income housing credit for residential rental property.
DISCUSSION: Sec. 42(g) requires that qualified residential rental property remain as rental property and meet the minimum low-income set-aside requirements for 15 consecutive years in order to be eligible for the low-income housing credit.
Answers (a) and (b) are incorrect because they are the minimum low-income set-aside requirements under Sec. 42. Note that only (a) or (b), not both, must be met. Answer (c) is incorrect because it is a rent limitation that also must be met for 15 years.

90. In 1989, Brian Baseball purchased an apartment project in which 30% of the basis qualified as low-income rental housing for individuals with incomes of 50% or less of area median incomes. His low-income credit each year is $15,000, but it would have been $10,000 if calculated ratably over 15 years instead. In 1991, only 24% of the basis of the project qualifies because vacancies have been filled by nonqualifying tenants. What is Bob's recapture of the low-income credit excluding interest?

a. $2,000.
b. $3,000.
c. $5,000.
d. $10,000.

The correct answer is (a). *(Publisher)*
REQUIRED: The amount of recapture of the low-income housing credit when fewer units are occupied by qualified tenants.
DISCUSSION: Under Sec. 42(j), recapture may occur as a result of one of the following during the 15-year compliance period: noncompliance with the minimum requirements, failure to use part of the building for low-income housing, or sale of the building (unless the original owner posts a bond and it is expected the building will continue to qualify). The amount of recapture is the accelerated portion of the credit (actual credit in excess of the amount if it had been taken over 15 years) in all prior years attributable to the portion of basis that no longer qualifies.
Low-income use of the project decreased by 20% (6% ÷ 30%). The accelerated portion of Bob's credit each year was $5,000 ($15,000 − $10,000). His recapture is for 2 years (1989 and 1990). The recapture amount is $2,000 (20% x $5,000 x 2 years) plus interest.

Module 11.13: Low-Income Rental Housing Credit

91. For qualified low-income housing buildings placed in service after 1987, the annual credit percentage for the low-income housing credit is 9% for new buildings not federally subsidized and 4% for existing buildings or new buildings that are federally subsidized.

The correct answer is (F). *(Publisher)*
DISCUSSION: The low-income rental housing credit of Sec. 42(b) is a 70% present value credit for new buildings that are not federally subsidized and a 30% present value credit for existing buildings or new buildings that are federally subsidized. For buildings placed in service in 1987 only, the 70% credit is 9% annually for 10 years and the 30% credit is 4% annually for 10 years. For years after 1987, the percentages will be determined by the IRS to reflect the 70% and 30% present values for the month the building is placed in service.

92. The low-income rental housing credit is available for rehabilitated as well as new buildings.

The correct answer is (T). *(Publisher)*
DISCUSSION: Low-income housing property costs which qualify for the credit include rehabilitation costs as well as the cost of new buildings [Sec. 42(d)(1) and (2)].

93. The eligible basis for new and existing buildings includes expenditures incurred before the close of the first tax year in the credit period.

The correct answer is (T). *(Publisher)*
DISCUSSION: The eligible basis for both new and certain existing buildings is determined as of the close of the first tax year in the credit period and is the adjusted basis of such property [Sec. 42(d)(1) and (2)]. Thus, expenditures incurred before the close of the first tax year in the credit period are includable in the eligible basis. The determination of eligible basis is made before any adjustments to basis are made for depreciation allowable in the first tax year.

94. The qualified basis used to compute the low-income rental housing credit may be based on the proportion of the floor space devoted to low-income units.

The correct answer is (T). *(Publisher)*
DISCUSSION: The qualified basis amounts are computed as the proportion of eligible basis in a qualified low-income building attributable to the low-income rental units. This proportion is the lesser of the proportion of low-income units to all residential rental units, or the proportion of floor space of the low-income units to the floor space of all residential rental units (Sec. 42(c)].

95. The eligible basis of low-income rental housing includes the cost of land.

The correct answer is (F). *(Publisher)*
DISCUSSION: Eligible basis is the adjusted basis of a new building or the adjusted basis of existing buildings attributable to the cost of acquisition and the cost of rehabilitation, if any, incurred before the close of the first taxable year of the credit. It excludes the cost of land.

96. The eligible basis of low-income rental housing is reduced by a portion of the adjusted basis attributable to non-low-income units.

The correct answer is (T). *(Publisher)*
DISCUSSION: Low-income rental housing's eligible basis is reduced by the portion of the adjusted basis attributable to non-low-income units above the average quality standard of the low-income units [Sec. 42(d)(3)].

97. A new owner may be eligible for the low-income rental housing credit.

The correct answer is (T). *(Publisher)*
DISCUSSION: A new owner of a building during its 15-year compliance period is eligible to continue to receive the credit as if the new owner were the original owner.

98. If the low-income rental housing credit has been claimed in prior years, failure to meet minimum requirements will result in recapture of only a portion of the credit.

The correct answer is (T). *(Publisher)*
DISCUSSION: The amount of recapture of the low-income housing credit is the accelerated portion of the credit in all prior years attributable to the portion of basis that no longer qualifies, plus interest [Sec. 42(j)]. The accelerated portion of credit each year is the actual amount of credit for the year in excess of what the credit would have been if the total credit had been allowed ratably over the 15-year compliance period.

99. The basis of the property is reduced by the low-income rental housing credit.

The correct answer is (F). *(Publisher)*
DISCUSSION: The basis is unaffected by the credit.

100. The low-income housing credit may be claimed by the owner of a low-income housing project only through December 31, 1991.

The correct answer is (T). *(Publisher)*
DISCUSSION: The Revenue Reconciliation Act of 1990 extended the low-income housing credit that may be claimed by the owner of a qualified low-income housing project through December 31, 1991.

11.14 Limitations and Carryovers of the General Business Credit

101. In 1991, Mr. L.E. Phant purchased geothermal energy property with a 5-year recovery period for his business from an unrelated firm. The property cost $40,000; Mr. Phant paid $10,000 down and borrowed the remaining $30,000 from First Bank where he had been a customer for years. Mr. Phant had no personal liability on the $30,000 note. The note was due in three annual installments beginning in 1992. Mr. Phant's tentative 1991 geothermal energy credit is:

  a. $0.
  b. $1,000.
  c. $2,000.
  d. $4,000.

The correct answer is (d). *(Publisher)*
REQUIRED: The tentative energy credit for geothermal property acquired with nonrecourse debt.
DISCUSSION: Under Sec. 49(a)(1)(A), the basis of property included in the qualified investment is limited to the amount for which the taxpayer is at risk with respect to such property. Since Phant has no personal liability on the $30,000, he generally would not be considered at risk for $30,000 of the property. Under an exception, however, a taxpayer is considered at risk on nonrecourse debt if (s)he is at risk with respect to at least 20% of the basis of the property, if the property was not acquired from a related person, and if the borrowed amount is from a qualified person (which includes a bank). Phant meets these requirements. Therefore, the amount borrowed is also considered at risk, and the qualified investment is $40,000. Under Sec. 48(a)(2), the geothermal energy credit is $4,000 ($40,000 x 10%) for 1991.

102. In 1991, Ms. Green purchased solar energy property with a 5-year recovery period for use in her business at a total cost of $10,000. Ms. Green paid $2,000 down and signed a note agreeing to pay the seller the remaining amount plus interest over the next four years. The seller had a lien on the solar property to secure the note, but Ms. Green had no personal liability. The tentative energy credit available to Ms. Green in 1991 is

  a. $0.
  b. $200.
  c. $800.
  d. $1,000.

The correct answer is (b). *(Publisher)*
REQUIRED: The tentative energy credit for property acquired with nonrecourse debt.
DISCUSSION: Property will qualify for the energy credit only to the extent the taxpayer is at risk with respect to it [Sec. 49(a)(1)(A)]. Since Ms. Green does not have any personal liability for $8,000 of the cost of the solar property, only the $2,000 for which she was at risk will qualify. The tentative credit in 1991 is 10% of the qualified investment of $2,000, which equals $200.

103. The maximum amount of income tax liability that can be offset by the general business credit in 1991 is limited to

a. 100% of net income tax liability.
b. 100% of first $25,000 of net income tax liability, 75% of the amount in excess of $25,000.
c. 100% of excess of net income tax liability over tentative minimum tax amount.
d. 100% of excess of net income tax liability over the greater of (1) the tentative minimum tax amount or (2) 25% of the net income tax liability in excess of $25,000.

The correct answer is (d). *(Publisher)*
REQUIRED: The general business credit limitation for 1991.
DISCUSSION: In 1991, the maximum amount of general business credit that may be used to offset an income tax liability is 100% of the taxpayer's net income tax over the greater of (1) the tentative minimum tax for the taxable year, or (2) 25% of the taxpayer's regular tax liability exceeding $25,000 [Sec. 38(c)(1)]. The term "net income tax" includes the sum of the regular tax liability and the alternative minimum tax reduced by certain allowable credits.

104. All of the following credits are applied against income tax before the general business credit can be allowed except

a. Credit for household and dependent care.
b. Foreign tax credit.
c. Earned income credit.
d. Interest on home mortgage credit.

The correct answer is (c). *(SPE 1085 II-54)*
REQUIRED: The tax credit that is not applied against income tax before the general business credit can be allowed.
DISCUSSION: Sec. 38(c)(1) defines the limitation on the general business credit, and states that the credit shall not exceed the excess of the taxpayer's net income tax over the greater of (1) the tentative minimum tax or (2) 25% of the taxpayer's net regular tax liability exceeding $25,000. Net income tax liability is defined as the sum of the regular tax liability plus the alternative minimum tax reduced by the sum of nonrefundable personal credits and the foreign tax credit. The earned income credit is a refundable personal credit and is applied after the general business credit.
Answers (a) and (d) are incorrect because they are nonrefundable personal credits subtracted from the income tax liability to get the net income tax liability. Answer (b) is incorrect because the foreign tax credit also is subtracted before the general business credit.

105. Zenda has a general business credit of $18,000 available for 1991. Her net income tax liability is $53,000. Her tentative minimum tax liability is $40,000. What is the amount of the general business tax credit that Zenda can take in 1991?

a. $0.
b. $13,000.
c. $18,000.
d. $53,000.

The correct answer is (b). *(Publisher)*
REQUIRED: The limit on the general tax credit that may be taken in 1991.
DISCUSSION: Sec. 38(c) states that the general business credit is limited to the taxpayer's net income tax over the greater of (1) the tentative minimum tax for the taxable year, or (2) 25% of the net regular tax liability exceeding $25,000. Applying this formula, Zenda's general business credit is $53,000 minus the greater of (1) $40,000 or (2) 25% x ($53,000 − $25,000) = $7,000. Forty thousand dollars is greater than $7,000, therefore Zenda's general business credit limitation is $53,000 − $40,000 = $13,000.

106. Celaine, a calendar-year taxpayer, hired two employees from a targeted group on April 1, 1991. In 1991, the employees each received $14,000 in qualified wages. Celaine has no unused jobs credit carried over into 1991. How much of the targeted jobs credit is usable in 1991 if Celaine had a regular tax liability before credits of $8,000 a tentative minimum tax liability of zero, and a research credit of $2,100?

a. $4,800.
b. $5,900.
c. $6,000.
d. $8,000.

The correct answer is (a). *(SPE 1080 II-90)*
REQUIRED: The allowable amount of targeted jobs credit.
DISCUSSION: Under Sec. 51, the targeted jobs credit is 40% of the first $6,000 of wages paid to each qualified employee during the first year of service. Therefore, Celaine's tentative jobs credit is $4,800 (2 x 40% x $6,000).
Sec. 38 combines the targeted jobs credit, the research credit, and five other credits as one general business credit. The credit allowed is limited to the taxpayer's net income tax over the greater of (1) the tentative minimum tax or (2) 25% of the taxpayer's net regular tax liability exceeding $25,000. Celaine's general business credit is thus limited to $8,000 ($8,000 − $0). Her entire $4,800 jobs credit is usable in 1991 because her total general business credit of $6,900 ($4,800 + $2,100) is less than the limit.

107. Mr. Z has a targeted jobs credit of $12,000 for 1991 and a carryover of $32,000 of eligible general business credit from other tax years. His regular tax liability, not considering these credit items, is $47,000. His tentative minimum tax liability is $6,000. What is the amount of the general business credit that Z can take for 1991?

a. $25,000.
b. $40,250.
c. $41,000.
d. $47,000.

The correct answer is (c). *(SPE 989 II-87)*
REQUIRED: The amount of general business credit allowable.
DISCUSSION: In 1991, the maximum amount of general business credit that may be used to offset the net income tax liability is 100% of the net income tax over the greater of (1) the tentative minimum tax or (2) 25% of the taxpayer's net regular tax liability exceeding $25,000. Therefore, Mr. Z may take a general business credit of $41,000.

Net income tax liability		$47,000
Minus greater of		
(1) tentative minimum tax	$6,000	($6,000)
(2) 25% (of net regular tax minus $25,000)		
25% x ($47,000 − $25,000)	$5,500	
		$41,000

108. John Rich is a sole proprietor. During 1991, he purchased business property for $90,000 that qualifies for a 10% business energy credit. He takes the maximum amount of the business energy credit but also makes the Sec. 179 election. He also has a $950 child care credit. If Mr. Rich's regular tax liability before credits is $8,000 and tentative minimum tax liability is zero, how much of the general business credit may he use this year?

a. $7,050.
b. $8,000.
c. $8,050.
d. $9,000.

The correct answer is (a). *(Publisher)*
REQUIRED: The amount of the general business credit that may be used along with the child care credit.
DISCUSSION: The Sec. 179 expense of $10,000 reduces the cost of the property for computing the energy credit [Sec. 179(d)(9)]. Rich's energy credit is thus $8,000 ($80,000 x 10%).
Sec. 38(c) limits the amount of the general business credit to the taxpayer's net income tax over the greater of (1) the tentative minimum tax or (2) 25% of the taxpayer's net regular tax liability exceeding $25,000. Rich's net regular tax liability is the gross tax liability ($8,000), reduced by any nonrefundable personal credits or foreign tax credits. The child care credit is a nonrefundable personal credit, which reduces Rich's gross tax liability to $7,050. Rich is limited to $7,050 of general business credits, which equals 100% of his net tax liability.

109. Ancient Corporation built an office building in 1931 at a cost of $100,000 which it used as its corporate headquarters. The building had a basis of $14,000 in 1991 when Ancient began rehabilitating the structure. Rehabilitation expenditures of $400,000 were incurred during 1991, and Ancient moved back into the building in December 1991. Ancient's regular tax liability before credits for 1991 was $50,000 and Ancient had a foreign tax credit of $10,000. Ancient's tentative minimum tax liability is $12,000. Ancient's credit for rehabilitation expenditures which can be claimed in 1991 is

a. $0.
b. $18,000.
c. $28,000.
d. $40,000.

The correct answer is (c). *(Publisher)*
REQUIRED: The general business credit that can be claimed when the corporation also has foreign tax credits.
DISCUSSION: Under Sec. 48(a)(2), the rehabilitation credit for a building placed in service prior to 1936 is 10%. Ancient's tentative tax credit is $40,000 ($400,000 x 10%). Under Sec. 38(c)(1), the limitation for the credit which can be claimed in 1991 is equal to the taxpayer's net income tax over the greater of (1) the tentative minimum tax or (2) 25% of the taxpayer's net regular tax liability exceeding $25,000. For purposes of this calculation, tax liability is first reduced by the foreign tax credit

Income tax liability before credits	$50,000
Less foreign tax credit	(10,000)
Net income tax liability	$40,000

Ancient's allowable credit is therefore equal to $40,000 − $12,000 = $28,000

110. Suppose ATO Corporation could not apply the full amount of its general business credit in 1991 because the maximum limitation was reached. The excess credit from 1991 would

a. Expire and could not be applied to any other years.
b. Only be carried forward 7 years.
c. Be carried back 3 years and carried forward 15 years.
d. Be carried forward 10 years if ATO elects not to carry back the credit.

The correct answer is (c). *(CMA 681 3-6)*
REQUIRED: The carryback and carryover rules for the general business credit.
DISCUSSION: Sec. 38 combines several business credits, and applies the limitations to them as a general business credit. Under Sec. 39, if the general business credit for a taxable year exceeds the maximum limit, the excess credit may be carried back to each of the 3 taxable years preceding the current year, and carried forward to each of the 15 taxable years following the current year.
Answer (a) is incorrect because the credit does not expire unless it goes unused during the carryback and carryover years. Answers (b) and (d) are incorrect because the credit must be carried back 3 years and forward 15 years without an opportunity to elect otherwise.

111. Ms. T, a calendar-year taxpayer, has $3,000 of unused general business credit for 1991 available as a carryback to 1988. Her income tax for 1988 was $2,500, general business credit for 1988 was $1,000, and unused credit carryback from 1990 was $1,000. What amount of the unused credit for 1991 can be used in 1988?

a. $250.
b. $500.
c. $1,000.
d. $2,500.

The correct answer is (b). *(SPE 1080 II-88)*
REQUIRED: The unused general business credit from 1991 that may be used in 1988.
DISCUSSION: Sec. 38 combines several business credits and applies the limitations to them as a general business credit. Sec. 39 provides that any unused general business credit is to be carried back 3 years and forward 15 years. It is carried to the oldest available year first. In each year, carryovers are used first, then current business credits, and lastly carrybacks.
In 1988, Ms. T had a tax liability of $2,500 which was offset by a $1,000 general business tax credit for that year and an unused credit carryback from 1990 of $1,000. This leaves $500 of tax liability to which the 1991 tax credit may be applied.

112. For 1991, Crystell Ball, who operates a sole proprietorship, had a regular tax liability before credits of $5,000. She had no tentative minimum tax liability. The only tax credit she had was a targeted jobs credit of $5,200. Crystell Ball will have an unused credit of $200 available for carryback or carryover.

The correct answer is (T). *(SPE 1083 II-47)*
DISCUSSION: The targeted jobs credit is included as one of the general business credits under Sec. 38. The total amount of general business credit allowed is equal to the excess of the taxpayer's net income tax over the greater of (1) the tentative minimum tax or (2) 25% of the taxpayer's net tax liability exceeding $25,000. Thus, Crystell Ball's targeted jobs credit for 1991 is $5,000 (100% of her tax liability). She will have an unused credit of $200 available for carryback to 1988 through 1990 or carryover to 1992 and later years under Sec. 39.

11.15 Disabled Access Credit

113. Which one of the following statements about the disabled access credit is false?

a. The credit is available in the current year only to businesses having gross receipts that were less than $1 million or no more than 30 full-time employees in the preceding tax year.
b. The credit equals 50% of eligible expenditures in excess of $250 and less than $10,250.
c. No deduction is allowed for any amount for which the disabled access credit is claimed.
d. The credit is a refundable credit for individuals and corporations.

The correct answer is (d). *(Publisher)*
REQUIRED: The incorrect statement regarding the disabled access credit.
DISCUSSION: Under Sec. 44(a), a credit is available to individuals and corporations that make expenditures to provide access to disabled individuals. The disabled access credit is not a refundable credit because it is part of the general business credit. Excess general business credits may be carried back 3 years or forward 15 years, but not refunded.
Answers (a), (b), and (c) are incorrect because all are correct statements about the disabled access credit.

114. Eligible expenditures for the disabled access credit include amounts spent for all but which one of the following?

a. Removing architectural barriers restricting access to a business.
b. Modification of equipment or devices for disabled individuals.
c. Making a new building accessible to the disabled.
d. Providing interpreters for hearing-impaired individuals.

The correct answer is (c). *(Publisher)*
REQUIRED: The incorrect statement regarding the disabled access credit.
DISCUSSION: Code Sec. 44(c)(2) states that the disabled access credit is available for certain kinds of expenditures incurred in order to enable small businesses to comply with the Americans with Disabilities Act. Included in eligible expenditures are these related to removing architectural barriers restricting access to a business, for modifications of equipment or devices for disabled individuals, and for providing interpreters for making aurally delivered materials available to individuals with hearing impairments.
Making a new building accessible for the disabled is not an expenditure for which the disabled access credit may be used [Sec. 44(c)(4)], thus answer (c) is the incorrect statement regarding the disabled access credit.

115. In 1991 Jones Corporation incurred $25,000 in expenditures in making its three-story office building accessible to wheelchair bound individuals. Its 1991 regular tax liability is $61,250 and its tentative minimum tax liability is $40,000. What is the amount of its disabled access credit:

a. $0.
b. $5,000.
c. $12,500.
d. $25,000.

The correct answer is (b). *(Publisher)*
REQUIRED: The amount of the disabled access credit.
DISCUSSION: The amount of the disabled access credit for any tax year is equal to 50% of the amount of the eligible access expenditures for that year that exceed $250 but do not exceed $10,250. Jones's disabled access credit is $5,000 (lesser of $25,000 actual expenditures or $10,250 limitation minus $250 floor times 50% credit rate). The disabled access credit is included as part of the general business credit, and thus, is subject to the Sec. 38(c) rules that limit the amount of the general business credit for any given year. The $5,000 credit is less than the $21,250 ($61,250 net income tax − greater of $40,000 tentative minimum tax or $9,062 that is 25% of the net regular tax liability in excess of $40,000) limitation for the general business credit.

CHAPTER TWELVE
BASIS

12.1	Purchased Property	(22 questions)	285
12.2	Property Received by Gift	(8 questions)	291
12.3	Inherited Property	(9 questions)	293
12.4	Property Received for Services	(7 questions)	296
12.5	Property Received in a Nontaxable Transaction	(16 questions)	298
12.6	Stock Dividends and Stock Rights	(8 questions)	303
12.7	Adjustments to Asset Basis	(8 questions)	305
12.8	Holding Period	(12 questions)	307

12.1 Purchased Property

1. Mr. Black purchased a house in March 1991 for $41,000. In addition, Mr. Black incurred the following expenses:

$360 for 3 years of casualty insurance
$820 for new driveway
$250 interior painting
$145 title insurance
$400 exterior painting
$405 new gutters

What is Mr. Black's basis in this house?

a. $42,225.
b. $42,370.
c. $42,630.
d. $43,020.

The correct answer is (b). *(SPE 1077 II-9)*
REQUIRED: A purchaser's basis in a house after incurring purchase costs and repair expenses.
DISCUSSION: Under Sec. 1012, the basis of property is the cost of the property. In addition, basis includes expenditures for major improvements and costs to acquire title. The costs which are not capitalized are the casualty insurance, the interior painting, and the exterior painting. Painting is usually considered ordinary maintenance. Furthermore, these costs are not deductible unless the house is rental property, i.e., unless the costs were incurred for the production of income. Basis is computed as follows:

Purchase price	$41,000
Title insurance	145
New driveway	820
New gutters	405
Basis in house	$42,370

2. The basis of property acquired by purchase includes all of the following except:

a. Amount paid in notes to the seller.
b. Freight, installation, and testing charges.
c. Unstated interest on any time-payment plan.
d. Sales tax charged on the purchase.

The correct answer is (c). *(SPE 990 I-43)*
REQUIRED: The costs that should be included in the basis of property acquired by purchase.
DISCUSSION: The basis of purchased property does not include unstated interest on time-payment plans. Interest is deductible as an expense.
Answer (a) is incorrect because the amount paid in notes to the seller is part of the cost of the property. Answer (b) is incorrect because freight, installation and testing charges are acquisition costs included as part of the cost of the property. Answer (d) is incorrect because sales tax paid in connection with the acquisition of property is treated as a cost of the property [Sec. 164(a)].

3. During 1991, Mrs. Brown paid $15,000 for the demolition of a warehouse she was using in her business. At the time of the destruction, Mrs. Brown had an adjusted basis in the warehouse of $25,000 and a basis of $12,000 in the land where the warehouse stood. How should Mrs. Brown treat the cost of demolishing the warehouse for federal income tax purposes?

a. $15,000 business expense; $25,000 recognized loss.

b. $15,000 business expense; $25,000 addition to basis of land.

c. $40,000 business expense.

d. $40,000 addition to basis of land.

The correct answer is (d). *(SPE 989 II-45)*
REQUIRED: The tax treatment for demolishing a warehouse.
DISCUSSION: All costs associated with demolishing structures (and any losses sustained) must be allocated to the land (Sec. 280B). The original cost of the warehouse is added to the basis of the land.

Cost of warehouse	$25,000
Cost of demolition	15,000
Addition to basis of land	$40,000

4. Taxpayer J purchased a business building with a fair market value of $60,000 and a business auto with a fair market value of $10,000. Both were acquired in a bargain purchase for a total cost of $49,000. What is the basis of the auto?

a. $5,000.

b. $7,000.

c. $10,000.

d. $49,000.

The correct answer is (b). *(SPE 1079 II-68)*
REQUIRED: The allocation of a lump-sum purchase price to individual assets.
DISCUSSION: The basis of property is defined in Sec. 1012 as its cost. When several assets are purchased for a lump sum, the basis of each asset is determined by allocating the total cost based on the relative fair market value of each asset. The basis of the auto is computed as the fair market value of the individual asset over the fair market value of all the assets times the total cost.

$$\frac{\$10,000}{\$70,000} \times \$49,000 = \$7,000$$

5. Mr. Y purchased a high-volume drug store on January 1, 1991, for a lump-sum price of $963,000 with no liabilities assumed. The fair market values of the assets at the time of the purchase were as follows:

Cash	$200,000
U.S. Government securities	250,000
Furniture	56,000
Building	115,000
Equipment	302,000

Mr. Y intends to operate the drug store using the same name as before the purchase. What is Mr. Y's basis for goodwill or going concern value?

a. $0.

b. $40,000.

c. $96,300.

d. $115,560.

The correct answer is (b). *(SPE 990 II-59)*
REQUIRED: The basis for goodwill on going concern value acquired as part of the purchase price of a going concern.
DISCUSSION: Under Sec. 1060, both the buyer and seller involved in a transfer of assets that amount to a trade or business must allocate the purchase price among the assets using the "residual method." The residual method requires the purchase price to first be allocated to cash, then to near cash items such as CDs and government securities, and other marketable securities, then to other tangible and intangible assets such as equipment, buildings, land, accounts receivable, and covenants not to compete. The allocation of the purchase price may not exceed the fair market value for each of these categories. Then any residual purchase price is allocated to intangible assets such as goodwill and going concern value.

In this case, Mr. Y's purchase price of $963,000 is in excess of the fair market value of all the assets listed ($923,000). Therefore, the purchase price is allocated to each asset listed based on its fair market value and the remaining $40,000 ($963,000 purchase price − $923,000 listed assets) is allocated to goodwill or going concern value.

Sec. 1060 following the Revenue Reconciliation Act of 1990 now provides that the transferor and transferee may agree in writing as to the allocation of consideration, or as to the fair market value of any assets. This agreement is binding on the transferor and transferee unless determined inappropriate by the IRS.

Module 12.1: Purchased Property

6. Kathy purchased the Blue Restaurant, an operating business, from Mr. Hungry for $180,000. The following items were included in Kathy's purchase:

Cash	$20,000
Inventory, fair market value	20,000
Equipment, fair market value	80,000
Real estate, fair market value	100,000

What is Kathy's basis in the real estate?

a. $60,000.
b. $70,000.
c. $80,000.
d. $81,818.

The correct answer is (c). *(SPE 990 II-60)*
REQUIRED: The allocation of a lump-sum purchase price to real estate.
DISCUSSION: Under Sec. 1060, both the buyer and seller involved in a transfer of assets that amount to a trade or business must allocate the purchase price among the assets using the "residual method." The residual method requires the purchase price to first be allocated to cash, then to near cash items such as CDs and government securities, and other marketable securities, then to other tangible and intangible assets such as equipment, buildings, land, accounts receivable, and covenants not to compete. The allocation of the purchase price may not exceed the fair market value for each of these categories. Then any residual purchase price is allocated to intangible assets such as goodwill and going concern value.

In this case Kathy paid $180,000 which is less than the total fair market value of the assets ($220,000). Twenty thousand is first allocated to cash. The basis of each noncash tangible and intangible asset is then determined by allocating the total cost allocable to the noncash assets based on their relative fair market values. Kathy's basis in the real estate is its fair market value ($100,000) divided by the fair market value of all noncash assets ($200,000) times the total cost of the noncash assets. The total cost of the noncash assets is $160,000 ($180,000 total cost − $20,000 cash). The allocation to the real estate is

$$\frac{\$100,000}{\$200,000} \times \$160,000 = \$80,000$$

Sec. 1060 following the Revenue Reconciliation Act of 1990 now provides that the transferor and transferee may agree in writing as to the allocation of consideration, or as to the fair market value of any assets. This agreement is binding on the transferor and transferee unless determined inappropriate by the IRS.

7. Mr. X constructed a building for use in his business. The costs that he incurred were as follows:

Land	$25,000
Wages paid to employees for construction of building	30,000
Building materials	40,000
Architect's fees	10,000
Building permit fees	3,000
Equipment rental for construction	7,000

Mr. X had an allowable targeted jobs credit of $1,000 on the wages paid to employees for construction of the building. What is Mr. X's basis in the building?

a. $60,000.
b. $89,000.
c. $114,000.
d. $115,000.

The correct answer is (b). *(SPE 987 II-65)*
REQUIRED: The costs that should be included in the basis of a constructed building.
DISCUSSION: Under Sec. 1012, the basis of property is defined as its cost. When property is constructed, the cost includes all expenditures necessary to prepare the building for its intended use. The uniform capitalization rules of Sec. 263A apply to the construction of real or tangible personal property to be used in a business. These rules require capitalization of all direct costs and an allocable portion of most indirect costs. Costs to be capitalized are those for the building materials, compensation paid to the employees constructing the building, rent for equipment used in construction, the architect's fee, and the building permit fees. These costs total $90,000. However, the wages must be reduced by the targeted jobs credit that applies to them. Therefore, Mr. X's basis in the building is $89,000 ($90,000 − $1,000 targeted jobs credit).

Module 12.1: Purchased Property

8. Mr. A constructed a factory building costing $1,500,000 for use in his business. The construction started on January 2, 1990 and was completed and placed in service on July 1, 1991. During the construction period, Mr. A incurred and paid interest and real property taxes of $10,000 attributable to the construction. Mr. A must

   a. Amortize the $10,000 over a 10-year period starting in 1990.
   b. Amortize the $10,000 over a 10-year period starting in 1991.
   c. Capitalize the $10,000 as part of the building cost.
   d. Capitalize the $10,000 as part of the land cost.

The correct answer is (c). *(SPE 987 II-48)*
REQUIRED: The correct treatment of interest and real property taxes during construction of property to be used in a business.
DISCUSSION: Prior to 1987, construction period interest and taxes was amortizable over a 10-year period. However, after 1986, no amortization is allowed and Sec. 263A requires production costs (direct and indirect) to be capitalized. Therefore, the construction period interest and taxes must be capitalized as part of the building cost.

9. Ms. F had an old truck with an adjusted basis of $2,700, which she traded in on a new one costing $12,800. The dealer allowed Ms. F $4,000 on the old truck and Ms. F paid $8,800 in cash. What is Ms. F's basis in the new truck?

   a. $6,700.
   b. $8,800.
   c. $11,500.
   d. $12,800.

The correct answer is (d). *(SPE 987 I-83)*
REQUIRED: The basis of personal use property acquired in an exchange.
DISCUSSION: The basis of property is generally its cost (Sec. 1012). In the case of a taxable exchange of property, the cost is the value of the property given up plus any additional cash paid. Ms. F's basis in the new truck is the $4,000 value of the old truck plus $8,800 cash, for a total of $12,800.
   Ms. F will also have a gain of $1,300 ($4,000 received for old truck – $2,700 basis). This exchange is taxable because the problem does not state that the truck was held for use in a trade or business or held for investment. Note that the IRS treated this as a nontaxable exchange (although these are not enough facts to support such treatment) so their answer was $11,500 ($2,700 Ms. F's basis + $8,800 cash paid). Beware on the exam.

10. Tom runs a sole proprietorship that rents out tables and chairs. He purchased new chairs in 1991. The invoice showed $2,000 for the chairs and $100 sales tax for a total due of $2,100. Which of the following statements is correct?

   a. Tom should deduct the $100 sales tax as an expense on Schedule C.
   b. Tom's depreciable basis in the chairs is $2,100.
   c. Tom should deduct $100 on Schedule A.
   d. Sales taxes are no longer deductible.

The correct answer is (b). *(SPE 990 II-40)*
REQUIRED: The correct statement regarding a purchase of personal property used in a business.
DISCUSSION: The basis of property is generally its cost (Sec. 1012). Additionally, sales taxes paid on the acquisition of depreciable personal property must also be capitalized [Sec. 164(a)]. Therefore, Tom's depreciable basis in the chairs is $2,100 ($2,000 + $100).
   Answers (a) and (c) are incorrect because the sales tax is added to the basis of the purchased property, as discussed above. Also, business expenses of a sole proprietorship are not deducted on Schedule A. Answer (d) is incorrect because, if the cost of the property is a business expense, such as the cost of supplies, any sales tax paid would be deductible as part of the business expense.

Module 12.1: Purchased Property

11. JCN Enterprises exchanged 30% of the stock of a closely held corporation which it owns for improved real property. The real property had a fair market value of $100,000 and an adjusted basis of $75,000 at the date of the exchange. The fair market value of the stock is unknown, although the shareholder's basis was $10,000 at the date of the exchange. What is JCN's basis in the real property after the exchange?

a. $10,000.
b. $75,000.
c. $100,000.
d. $110,000.

The correct answer is (c). *(Publisher)*
REQUIRED: The basis of property acquired in an exchange when the fair market value of the assets given up is not known.
DISCUSSION: The basis of property is generally its cost (Sec. 1012). In an exchange, the cost of the property acquired is the fair market value of the property given up. If the fair market value of the property given up is not known, it is assumed to be the same as the fair market value of the property received when the transaction is at arm's-length. Since the value of the stock used to buy the land is not known, the value of the stock is assumed to be the fair market value of the property purchased. Therefore, JCN Enterprises will have a basis in the land of $100,000.

JCN will also have a gain of $90,000 ($100,000 received − $10,000 basis) on the disposition of the stock. This transaction is not tax-free because the properties are not like-kind.

12. Mr. T purchased an apartment building on December 15, 1991. Mr. T's costs in connection with the purchase were as follows:

Cash paid to seller	$25,000
Secured notes to seller	55,000
Assumed an existing mortgage on the property	15,000
Sales commission paid to broker	3,000
Transfer taxes	600
Paid back taxes owed by seller	700
Paid interest on mortgage from date of purchase to end of December	100

What is the amount of Mr. T's basis in the building?

a. $80,000.
b. $95,600.
c. $99,300.
d. $99,400.

The correct answer is (c). *(SPE 989 I-68)*
REQUIRED: The basis of property acquired by taking it subject to an existing mortgage.
DISCUSSION: The basis of property is its original cost (Sec. 1012), reduced by allowable depreciation [Sec. 1016(a)(2)]. The cost of property includes debt to which the property is subject (Crane, 331 U.S. 1, 1947). Consequently, the basis of the property includes the cash paid, any notes to the seller and the liability to which the property was subject. Closing costs such as commissions paid to a broker are also included as part of the purchase cost. Taxes paid by a buyer which were not the legal responsibility of the buyer are also allocated to the purchase price (they are not deductible under Sec. 164). Mortgage interest paid is deductible (not included in cost). Mr. T's basis in the building is

Cash	$25,000
Secured notes	55,000
Mortgage	15,000
Sales commission	3,000
Transfer taxes	600
Seller's taxes	700
	$99,300

13. In 1988, Hilary Leary purchased three lots of XYZ Company common stock as follows: March 1, 100 shares at $50 per share; June 15, 100 shares at $55; October 1, 100 shares at $60. On January 15, 1991, Hilary sold 200 shares at a price of $70 per share. Under IRS regulations, which two of the following cost flow assumptions are acceptable in determining the cost basis to be used in measuring Leary's gain on the sale?

a. FIFO or LIFO.
b. Specific identification or weighted average.
c. FIFO or weighted average.
d. Specific identification or FIFO.

The correct answer is (d). *(D.B. Bradley)*
REQUIRED: The cost flow methods acceptable for determining the basis to be used in measuring a gain on the sale of stock.
DISCUSSION: Reg. 1.1012-1(c)(1) provides that, if the taxpayer can specifically identify the lots being sold, this method may be used. If they cannot be specifically identified, the taxpayer must assume that they are being sold on the first-in, first-out (FIFO) basis.

14. Mr. G bought 100 shares of Corporation H stock in 1987 for $5,000. In 1988 he bought another 100 shares for $11,000. In 1989, Mr. G gave his son 50 shares he had purchased in 1988 and purchased an additional 100 shares for $9,000. In 1991 Mr. G sold 220 shares for $22,500. Mr. G was unable to identify the specific shares sold. What was Mr. G's basis in the 220 shares that were sold?

 a. $16,800.
 b. $17,160.
 c. $17,800.
 d. $22,500.

The correct answer is (a). *(SPE 987 I-84)*
REQUIRED: The basis in shares of stock purchased in several lots when the shares cannot be specifically identified.
DISCUSSION: Reg. 1.1012-1(c)(1) provides that, if the taxpayer cannot specifically identify the lots being sold, the taxpayer must assume that the shares of stock are sold in the first in, first out (FIFO) basis. Therefore, Mr. G must assume that 100 of his shares were those purchased in 1987, 50 were of those purchased in 1988 since he had given 50 of those away which could be specifically identified to such purchase and the remaining 70 shares were part of those purchased in 1989 for $9,000. The computation is below.

100 shares	$ 5,000
50 shares (50% x $11,000)	5,500
70 shares (70% x $9,000)	6,300
Total basis	$16,800

15. Mary purchased stock for $5,000 from her brother Tom. Tom had a basis in the stock of $9,000 but could not recognize his loss on the sale. Mary's basis in the stock is

 a. $1,000.
 b. $4,000.
 c. $5,000.
 d. $9,000.

The correct answer is (c). *(Publisher)*
REQUIRED: A purchaser's basis in property acquired from a related party who could not recognize a loss.
DISCUSSION: A loss on the sale of property to a related party (including siblings) cannot be recognized (Sec. 267). Nevertheless, the purchaser's basis is his/her cost and is not affected by the nonrecognized loss. Mary's basis is $5,000. On a subsequent sale, Mary's gain will be recognized only to the extent it exceeds Tom's unrecognized loss (i.e., since Tom's unrecognized loss is $4,000; if Mary sells the stock for $10,000, her realized gain is $5,000, but she will only recognize $1,000 of it).

16. In 1991, Mr. T purchased a tract of land. In order to have city water, he had to pay the water company $5,000 to extend the water line to his property. The $5,000 cost is an addition to the basis of the land.

The correct answer is (T). *(SPE 1080 II-3)*
DISCUSSION: Expenditures chargeable to capital are adjustments to basis under Sec. 1016. Since the $5,000 cost for the extended water line would be charged to capital, it is an addition to the basis of the land.

17. Mr. B purchased a new automobile for $8,000. He received a $1,000 cash rebate from the auto manufacturer. Mr. B should report the $1,000 as taxable income.

The correct answer is (F). *(SPE 1082 I-11)*
DISCUSSION: Cash rebates received by a purchaser of property are treated as a reduction in purchase price rather than income. Therefore, Mr. B's basis in the new automobile is $7,000 ($8,000 cost − $1,000 cash rebate).

18. Mr. B bought land and a building to be used in his business. In connection with this acquisition, he paid $50,000 to the seller as the purchase price of the property, $5,000 to his attorney for reviewing the purchase contract, and $3,000 to the seller for property taxes incurred up to the date of sale. Mr. B's cost basis in the property is $58,000.

The correct answer is (T). *(SPE 1078 I-27)*
DISCUSSION: Sec. 1012 defines the basis of property as its cost. The cost Mr. B incurred in acquiring the land was the $50,000 purchase price, plus $5,000 in attorney's fees and $3,000 for prior property taxes. The property taxes are an acquisition cost and are not deductible because they were pre-purchase taxes not allocated to Mr. B [Sec. 164(a)]. Mr. B's cost basis in the property is $58,000.

19. In 1991, Mr. Y, a sole proprietor, purchased a new van to be used in his delivery business. He paid $500 in state sales taxes on the purchase. Mr. Y may elect to capitalize the $500 and include it in the basis.

The correct answer is (F). *(SPE 984 II-18)*
DISCUSSION: Sales tax was normally deducted under Sec. 164 before 1987. Sales taxes paid on the acquisition of personal property must be capitalized (it is not elective) beginning after December 31, 1986 [Sec. 164(a)].

Module 12.2: Property Received by Gift

20. P purchased a building for $40,000 cash and assumed the existing mortgage of $25,000. His basis in the property is $65,000.

The correct answer is (T). *(SPE 986 I-31)*
DISCUSSION: The basis of property is its cost (Sec. 1012). Cost includes cash paid and any debt to which the property is subject, regardless of whether the debt is recourse or nonrecourse. Including debt as part of basis was affirmed by the Crane case (331 U.S. 1, 1947).

21. The cost of renting construction equipment to build a storage facility for use in your business must be capitalized as part of the cost of the building.

The correct answer is (T). *(SPE 988 II-6)*
DISCUSSION: The uniform capitalization rules of Sec. 263A apply to the construction of real or tangible personal property to be used in a trade or business. The uniform capitalization rules require all direct costs to be capitalized as well as an allocable portion of most indirect costs. The cost of renting construction equipment must be capitalized as part of the cost of the completed building and expensed through depreciation.

22. The basis for nonbusiness property changed to business use is the greater of the adjusted basis of the property or its fair market value on the date it is converted to business use.

The correct answer is (F). *(SPE 1080 I-29)*
DISCUSSION: When nonbusiness property is converted to business use, its basis for determining loss or depreciation is the lesser of the adjusted basis of the property or its fair market value at the date of conversion [Regs. 1.165-9 and 1.167(g)]. There is no similar provision for determining gains, so the basis for gain is the adjusted basis.

12.2 Property Received by Gift

23. Mr. R received bonds as a gift from his mother. At the time of the gift the bonds had a fair market value of $5,000 and an adjusted basis to R's mother of $6,000. No gift tax was paid. Six months later R sold the bonds for $6,500. What was R's basis in the bonds for computing gain?

a. $0.
b. $5,000.
c. $6,000.
d. $6,500.

The correct answer is (c). *(SPE 989 I-70)*
REQUIRED: The donee's basis for computing gain in property received as a gift.
DISCUSSION: The basis of property acquired by gift is generally the donor's adjusted basis [Sec. 1015(a)]. Since the property had a basis in the mother's hands of $6,000, Mr. R's basis in the property is the same. No basis adjustment is required for gift taxes since none were paid on the transfer [Sec. 1015(b)]. The basis of the property for loss purposes is its fair market value on the date of the gift, or $5,000.

24. Paula gave a diamond necklace to her granddaughter, Joan. Paula had purchased the necklace in 1960 for $12,000. The fair market value of the necklace at the time of the gift was $36,000. Gift taxes of $9,000 were paid. What is Joan's adjusted basis in the necklace?

a. $12,000.
b. $18,000.
c. $21,000.
d. $36,000.

The correct answer is (b). *(SPE 990 I-75)*
REQUIRED: The donee's basis in property on which gift tax was paid.
DISCUSSION: The basis of property acquired by gift is generally the donor's adjusted basis [Sec. 1015(a)], increased by any gift tax paid applicable to appreciation [Sec. 1015(d)]. The gift tax applicable to appreciation is the appreciation divided by the fair market value times the gift tax.

Donor's adjusted basis	$12,000
Gift tax*	6,000
Donee's basis	$18,000

$$*\frac{\$36,000 - \$12,000}{\$36,000} \times \$9,000 = \$6,000$$

25. Esther gave an old truck to Lamont for use in his business. Esther's basis in the truck was $2,000 and its fair market value on the date of the gift was $500. Esther paid $90 of gift tax on the transaction. What is Lamont's basis for depreciation?

a. $500.
b. $590.
c. $2,000.
d. $2,090.

The correct answer is (a). *(Publisher)*
REQUIRED: The basis in property received as a gift when its fair market value is less than basis and it is converted to business use.
DISCUSSION: Under Sec. 1015, the basis of property received as a gift is the donor's basis prior to the gift. However, if the fair market value is less than the donor's basis, the basis for purposes of computing a loss is the fair market value on the date of the gift. This basis is increased by the amount of gift tax paid attributable to the appreciation in the value of the gift. Since there was no appreciation in the value of the gift, no part of the gift tax may be added to basis.
For purposes of depreciation, the basis of property received by gift is the basis for gain. In this case, that is $2,000. Prop. Reg. 1.168-2(j)(6) provides, however, that the basis of property which has not been used in a trade or business and which is converted to such use is the fair market value on such date if less than the adjusted basis. For purposes of depreciation, Lamont's basis in the truck is $500.

Questions 26 through 28 are based on the following information. Laura's father, Albert, gave Laura a gift of 500 shares of Liba Corporation common stock in 1991. Albert's basis for the Liba stock was $4,000. At the date of this gift, the fair market value of the Liba stock was $3,000.

---

26. If Laura sold the 500 shares of Liba stock in 1991 for $5,000, her basis is

a. $5,000.
b. $4,000.
c. $3,000.
d. $0.

The correct answer is (b). *(CPA 584 Q-26)*
REQUIRED: The basis of property acquired by gift and sold at a gain.
DISCUSSION: The basis of property acquired by gift is generally the donor's adjusted basis, plus any gift tax attributable to appreciation (Sec. 1015). This rule applies when the donee determines any gain on a sale of the property. Since no gift tax was paid attributable to appreciation, Laura's basis is the same as her father's, or $4,000.

27. If Laura sold the 500 shares of Liba stock in 1991 for $2,000, her basis is

a. $4,000.
b. $3,000.
c. $2,000.
d. $0.

The correct answer is (b). *(CPA 584 Q-27)*
REQUIRED: The basis of property acquired by gift and sold at a loss.
DISCUSSION: The basis of property acquired by gift is usually the donor's adjusted basis, increased by any gift tax applicable to appreciation (Sec. 1015). For determining loss, however, the basis may not exceed the fair market value of the property at the time of the gift. Since the donor's adjusted basis ($4,000) was greater than the fair market value ($3,000), basis is limited to $3,000.

28. If Laura sold the 500 shares of Liba stock in 1991 for $3,500, what is the reportable gain or loss in 1991?

a. $3,500 gain.
b. $500 gain.
c. $500 loss.
d. $0.

The correct answer is (d). *(CPA 584 Q-28)*
REQUIRED: The amount of gain (loss) to be reported upon the sale of property acquired by gift.
DISCUSSION: For determining gain on the sale of property acquired by gift, the basis is the donor's adjusted basis. Laura's sale results in no gain ($3,500 sales price − $4,000 basis = no gain).
For determining loss on the sale of property acquired by gift, the basis may not exceed the fair market value of the property at the date of the gift. Hence, there is no loss ($3,500 sales price − $3,000 basis = no loss).

29. During 1991 Mr. C received a gift of property having a fair market value of $25,000 at the time of the gift. The donor's adjusted basis in the property at the time of the gift was $21,000. The donor paid a gift tax of $700 on the property. Mr. C's basis in the property is $21,700.

The correct answer is (F). *(SPE 1082 I-28)*
DISCUSSION: The basis of property received by gift is the donor's adjusted basis in the gift. This basis is increased by the portion of the gift tax paid which is attributable to the appreciation in the value of the gift. The appreciation in the gift is $4,000 ($25,000 fair market value − $21,000 basis). The increase in the basis for the gift tax is $112 [$700 gift tax x ($4,000 ÷ $25,000)]. Mr. C's total basis is $21,112.

30. In 1991 Mr. T received a gift of rental property that had a fair market value of $10,000 at the time of the gift. The donor's adjusted basis in the property at the time of the gift was $12,000. Mr. T's basis for computing depreciation is $12,000.

The correct answer is (T). *(SPE 1081 I-31)*
DISCUSSION: Sec. 1015 provides that the basis of property acquired by gift is the donor's adjusted basis plus the gift tax paid applicable to the appreciation. Since there was no appreciation, there was no addition to basis for gift tax. Therefore, Mr. T's basis is $12,000. It is this basis that is used to calculate depreciation.
Note that the limitation of basis to fair market value only applies to determine loss, not to compute depreciation.

12.3 Inherited Property

31. On August 15, 1991, Harold received 100 shares of stock as an inheritance from his mother Mona, who died January 20, 1991. Mona's adjusted basis in the stock was $45,000. The stock had a fair market value of $50,000 on January 20, 1991. On July 19, 1991, its value was $65,000 and on the date Harold received it, its value was $48,000. The alternative valuation date was not selected. Harold's basis in the inherited stock is:

 a. $45,000.
 b. $48,000.
 c. $50,000.
 d. $65,000.

The correct answer is (c). *(SPE 990 I-72)*
REQUIRED: The basis of inherited property when the alternate valuation date is not elected.
DISCUSSION: The basis of property received from a decedent is generally the fair market value of the property on the date of the decedent's death [Sec. 1014(a)]. If the alternate valuation date for the estate tax return is elected by the executor, the basis of the assets is their fair market value 6 months after death. Harold's basis in the stock is the $50,000 fair market value on January 20, 1991 (the date of Mona's death).

32. Mr. Ray inherited farm land from his father who died in 1991. The farm had an adjusted basis in his father's hands of $100,000 and a fair market value on the date of death of $800,000. The estate qualified and elected the alternate valuation date fair market value of $900,000. The estate did not elect to value the property on the basis of its use as a farm. Estate tax attributable to the farm property amounted to $60,000. What is Mr. Ray's basis in the property inherited during 1991?

 a. $100,000.
 b. $800,000.
 c. $900,000.
 d. $960,000.

The correct answer is (c). *(SPE 988 I-78)*
REQUIRED: The basis of inherited property when the alternate valuation date is elected.
DISCUSSION: The basis of property received from a decedent is generally the fair market value of the property on the date of the decedent's death [Sec. 1014(a)]. If the executor elects the alternate valuation date for the estate tax return, the basis of the assets is their fair market value 6 months after death or the date of sale or distribution, if earlier. Mr. Ray's basis in the farm land is the $900,000 fair market value 6 months after his father's death. No basis adjustment is made for the estate taxes paid.

33. Mrs. N inherited property from a decedent where an estate tax return was not required to be filed. The decedent's adjusted basis in the property at the time of death was $75,000. A local real estate agent, qualified as an appraiser, placed a valuation of $100,000 on the property at the date of death. The appraised value for state inheritance tax purposes was $90,000. What is Mrs. N's basis in the property?

 a. $100,000.
 b. $90,000.
 c. $75,000.
 d. $0.

The correct answer is (b). *(SPE 989 I-48)*
REQUIRED: The basis of inherited property when a federal estate tax return is not required to be filed.
DISCUSSION: The basis of property received from a decedent is generally the fair market value of the property on the date of the decedent's death [Sec. 1014(a)]. The value of the property for basis purposes is normally the value as appraised for the federal estate tax return, but if no federal estate tax return is required to be filed, the value as appraised for state inheritance tax purposes is used [Reg. 1.1014-3(a)]. Therefore, the basis is $90,000.

34. Hoss McDonald sold his farm for $200,000. He received $50,000 cash at closing and a promissory note for $150,000 to be paid in equal installments over a 10-year period. Hoss reported the income from the sale on the installment method. After collecting the first payment on the note, Hoss died, leaving all his property to his daughter. The fair market value of the promissory note at Hoss's death was $100,000 and its basis was $45,000. $135,000 plus interest was still due and owing on the note. What is the daughter's basis in the note for the purpose of selling it or collecting on it?

 a. $135,000.
 b. $100,000.
 c. $45,000.
 d. $0.

The correct answer is (c). *(Publisher)*
REQUIRED: The basis of an installment note received from a decedent.
DISCUSSION: Normally, the basis of property received from a decedent is the fair market value of the property on the date of the decedent's death [Sec. 1014(a)]. This rule does not apply to income in respect of a decedent [Sec. 1014(c)]. Income in respect of a decedent is income which has been earned or created by a decedent, but which is not properly included in his/her final tax return. Installment income is an example of income in respect of a decedent since the sale occurred prior to death but all the income was not properly included in the decedent's final tax return. Accordingly, the daughter's basis in the installment note is the decedent's basis of $45,000.

35. In 1984 Edwin Ryan bought 100 shares of a listed stock for $5,000. In June 1991, when the stock's fair market value was $7,000, Edwin gave it to his sister, Lynn. No gift tax was paid. Lynn died in October 1991, bequeathing the stock to Edwin, when the stock's fair market value was $9,000. Lynn's executor did not elect the alternate valuation date. What is Edwin's basis for this stock after he inherits it from Lynn's estate?

 a. $0.
 b. $5,000.
 c. $7,000.
 d. $9,000.

The correct answer is (b). *(CPA 1183 Q-26)*
REQUIRED: The basis of property received from a decedent when the beneficiary had given it to the decedent within the previous year.
DISCUSSION: Sec. 1014(a) provides that a person who acquires property from a decedent is generally entitled to a basis equal to the fair market value of the property on the date of death. If, however, appreciated property is acquired by the decedent by gift within 1 year of death and passes back to the donor by reason of the decedent's death, the beneficiary's basis in the property is its adjusted basis immediately prior to the decedent's death [Sec. 1014(e)].
Since Lynn received the stock as a gift from Edwin within 1 year of her death, Edwin assumes Lynn's basis ($5,000), which was Edwin's basis when he made the gift.

Module 12.3: Inherited Property

36. Donora made a gift of a farm to her daughter with the stipulation that Donora would continue to live on and use the land for the rest of her life. Donora's basis in the farm was $40,000 and its fair market value was $160,000 at the date of the gift. When Donora died, the fair market value of the farm was $180,000. The personal representative of the estate elected to value the estate property at the alternate valuation date, six months after death. At this date, the fair market value of the farm was $200,000. What is the daughter's basis in the farm?

  a. $40,000.
  b. $160,000.
  c. $180,000.
  d. $200,000.

The correct answer is (d). *(Publisher)*
REQUIRED: A donee's basis in property received prior to the donor's death but which is included in the donor's gross estate.
DISCUSSION: Sec. 1014(a) provides that the basis of property received from a decedent is the fair market value of the property on the date of the decedent's death, or on the alternate valuation date if the alternate valuation date is elected. Although the daughter received the gift prior to Donora's death, Sec. 1014(b)(9) provides that property is considered to be acquired from a decedent if the property is required to be included in the decedent's gross estate for estate tax purposes. The farm would be included in Donora's estate under Sec. 2036 because she gave it away without full and adequate consideration and retained the right to use the property for life. Therefore, the daughter is considered to have acquired the farm from a decedent and is entitled to a basis equal to the fair market value of the farm on the alternate valuation date ($200,000).

37. In 1989 Mr. Green received a gift of rental property from Mr. Blue. Mr. Blue retained the power to transfer this property to his son in his will. At the time of the gift, Mr. Blue's adjusted basis in the property was $18,000 and its fair market value was $24,000. No gift tax was paid. In 1989 and 1990, Mr. Green deducted a total of $2,000 of depreciation. In 1991 Mr. Blue died but did not exercise his power to transfer the property. The rental property given to Mr. Green was included in the gross estate as a revocable transfer. The value of the rental property for estate tax purposes was the fair market value at Mr. Blue's death, $28,000. What is Mr. Green's basis in the property after Mr. Blue's death?

  a. $18,000.
  b. $22,000.
  c. $26,000.
  d. $28,000.

The correct answer is (c). *(SPE 1077 I-166)*
REQUIRED: The basis of property received as a revocable gift before the transferor dies.
DISCUSSION: The basis of property acquired from a decedent is the fair market value of the property at the date of the decedent's death (Sec. 1014). If the property is acquired before the death of the decedent, the basis is reduced by the depreciation deduction allowed the donee. Mr. Green's basis in the property is

Fair market value at Mr. Blue's death	$28,000
Less depreciation	(2,000)
Basis in the property	$26,000

The property was included in Mr. Blue's taxable estate under Sec. 2038 because he retained the right to revoke the transfer to Mr. Green.

38. Olympia Husky and her husband, Merlin, lived in Walla Walla, Washington. Their residence was owned by them as community property and has a basis of $60,000. Upon Olympia's death, all her property was bequeathed to Merlin. At the date of death, the fair market value of the residence was $120,000. What is Merlin's basis in the residence?

  a. $60,000.
  b. $75,000.
  c. $90,000.
  d. $120,000.

The correct answer is (d). *(Publisher)*
REQUIRED: The basis to a surviving spouse of property which was community property prior to the decedent's death.
DISCUSSION: Sec. 1014(a) provides that property acquired from a decedent shall have a basis equal to the fair market value of the property on the date of the decedent's death. Merlin will acquire a basis of $60,000 in the one-half of the property owned by Olympia and bequeathed to him. Sec. 1014(b)(6) provides that the surviving spouse's one-half share of community property is considered to have been acquired from a decedent (for the purpose of basis) if at least one-half of the entire community property interest was included in the decedent's gross estate. Under Sec. 2031, Olympia's estate would include her one-half share of community property, so Merlin will acquire a basis in his one-half equal to its fair market value on the date of Olympia's death. Merlin's basis in the entire house is $120,000.

39. Freida Farina purchased a rooming house in Waldo, Florida. In order to avoid probate, Freida took title to the rooming house with her daughter, Farrah, as joint tenants with right of survivorship. Freida paid $10,000 cash and signed a promissory note and mortgage for $40,000. Several years later, Freida died when the house was worth $80,000 and there was still a $30,000 mortgage on the property. What is Farrah's basis in the house?

   a. $50,000.
   b. $65,000.
   c. $80,000.
   d. $110,000.

The correct answer is (c). *(Publisher)*
REQUIRED: A daughter's basis after her mother's death in property which they held as joint tenants with right of survivorship.
DISCUSSION: The basis of property in the hands of a person acquiring the property from a decedent is the fair market value of the property on the date of the decedent's death [Sec. 1014(a)]. Since Farrah already had an interest as a joint tenant, it is not clear what she received from the decedent. However, Sec. 1014(b)(9) provides that property acquired from a decedent by reason of form of ownership acquires a basis equal to its fair market value on the date of the decedent's death to the extent the property is required to be included in the decedent's gross estate. Under Sec. 2040(a), property held jointly by nonspouses is included in the decedent's gross estate unless it can be proven that consideration for the property was provided by another joint tenant. Since Farrah provided no consideration for the property, the entire value will be included in Freida's gross estate. Therefore, Farrah will obtain a basis in the house equal to its fair market value of $80,000 on the date of Freida's death. The amount of the mortgage has no effect on the basis.

12.4 Property Received for Services

40. Mr. P developed a patent on a machine that could be used in his trade or business. Mr. P made no election to currently deduct any of his developmental expenses. Which of the following expenditures may not be included in the basis of Mr. P's patent?

   a. Research expenditures.
   b. Drawing fees.
   c. Governmental fees.
   d. Value of Mr. P's time.

The correct answer is (d). *(SPE 1078 II-48)*
REQUIRED: The developmental expense which may not be included in the basis of a patent.
DISCUSSION: If no election is made to either expense in the current year or defer and amortize research and experimental expenses, then these expenses are capitalized. Sec. 1012 defines the basis of property as its cost, and cost is the amount paid for the property in cash or other property. Since Mr. P did not pay for his time in cash or other property, he may not include it in the basis of the patent.
Answers (a), (b), and (c) are incorrect because each represents an expenditure paid in cash or other property to develop an asset (patent). Therefore, each may be included in the basis of the patent.

41. Mr. C performed legal services for Ms. S in exchange for a car. At the time of the exchange, the car had a fair market value of $7,000 and an adjusted basis to Ms. S of $4,000. The value of Mr. C's services was $6,000. The price of C's services was not agreed to beforehand. What is the amount Mr. C must include in his income and what is his basis in the car?

	Income	Basis
a.	$4,000	$4,000
b.	$6,000	$4,000
c.	$7,000	$4,000
d.	$7,000	$7,000

The correct answer is (d). *(SPE 989 I-47)*
REQUIRED: The amount to be included in gross income and the basis to be taken in property exchanged for services performed.
DISCUSSION: Sec. 83 provides that the receipt of property for services provided is a taxable transaction. Reg. 1.61-2(d)(1) provides that if property or services are paid for with property, the fair market value of the property must be included in gross income as compensation. Accordingly, Mr. C would include $7,000 in gross income and take an adjusted basis in the car equal to its fair market value of $7,000.

Module 12.4: Property Received for Services

42. Dr. Jekyll, a surgeon, performed an operation on Mr. Hyde. The usual cost of such service is $5,000. In lieu of cash, Hyde deeded to Jekyll a parcel of real estate with a fair market value of $8,000 encumbered by a $2,000 mortgage. What is Jekyll's basis in this property?

a. $0.
b. $5,000.
c. $6,000.
d. $8,000.

The correct answer is (d). *(Publisher)*
REQUIRED: The basis in encumbered property received for services.
DISCUSSION: Under Sec. 83(a), Jekyll is required to recognize income equal to the fair market value of property received (less any amount paid) for the performance of his services. The $2,000 mortgage is considered an amount paid so Jekyll will recognize income of $6,000 ($8,000 FMV − $2,000 liability). Jekyll then has a basis in the property equal to the amount paid ($2,000 liability) plus the amount of income he recognized on its receipt ($6,000). Jekyll's total basis in the property is $8,000. The concept of including the amount of income recognized on the receipt of property is known as "tax cost basis." This concept is not provided by statute but is applied in Reg. 1.61-2(d)(2).

43. Belle, an attorney, drew up a partnership agreement for the AB partnership when it was formed. Belle invested an additional $100 and received a 10% capital and profits interest worth $2,000 in the partnership. Belle's basis in his partnership interest is

a. $0.
b. $100.
c. $1,900.
d. $2,000.

The correct answer is (d). *(Publisher)*
REQUIRED: The basis of a partnership interest received for cash and services.
DISCUSSION: One does not receive a basis in property for one's services unless there is a taxable transaction. The taxable transaction was that Belle received property in exchange for services under Sec. 83. Belle must recognize income from services equal to the value of the property received ($2,000) less any amount paid ($100), or $1,900. Therefore, Belle has a basis in his partnership interest of $2,000 from paying $100 and recognizing income of $1,900 (a tax cost basis).

44. During 1991, Bruce, a self-employed attorney, performed legal services for Zoom Corporation. Bruce received 10 shares of Zoom's stock for his services. Which of the following statements concerning this transaction is true?

a. Bruce's basis in the stock is zero and he does not report any income until he sells the stock.
b. Bruce's basis in Zoom's stock is the amount he usually charges for his services but he does not report any income until he sells the stock.
c. Bruce should include in income the fair market value of the stock on Schedule C (Form 1040) in 1991.
d. Bruce's basis in the stock is the same as Zoom's basis and he should include this amount on Schedule C (Form 1040) in 1991.

The correct answer is (c). *(SPE 990 I-41)*
REQUIRED: The proper treatment of stock received for services performed.
DISCUSSION: Under Sec. 83(a), Bruce is required to recognize income equal to the fair market value of property received (less any amount paid) for the performance of his services. The income is reported in the year the property is received if it is not subject to a substantial risk of forfeiture and there are no restrictions on Bruce's ability to transfer it. Here, Bruce would include in 1991's income the fair market value of the 10 shares of Zoom stock he received for services performed. Schedule C (Form 1040) is used to report profit or loss from business conducted as a sole proprietor.

45. Karlyle purchased 100 shares of stock in TB Corporation (her employer) on June 1, 1987 for $1,000. The fair market value of the stock on the purchase date was $6,000. Karlyle agreed to sell the stock back to TB Corporation at $1,000 should she leave her job within 5 years. During the 5-year period Karlyle could make no other transfer of the shares. Karlyle made no election under Sec. 83(b). Her basis in the stock on June 1, 1991 is

a. $0.
b. $1,000.
c. $4,000.
d. $6,000.

The correct answer is (b). *(Publisher)*
REQUIRED: The basis of restricted stock in the taxpayer's employer corporation.
DISCUSSION: The purchase of stock from an employer below fair market value is in essence a bonus paid to the employee. In this case, the stock is restricted so Karlyle has no bonus unless she stays with the company for 5 years and the value of the stock at the end of the 5 years exceeds Karlyle's own investment. Sec. 83 provides in such a case that Karlyle does not recognize income until the restriction ends, so her basis is equal only to the $1,000 investment. When the restriction ends, Karlyle will recognize ordinary income equal to the difference between the fair market value of the stock on that date and the amount she paid for the shares in 1987. On that date her basis will increase by the amount of ordinary income recognized.

46. Mr. Birch, an appliance repairman, usually charges $10 per hour for his services. On one of his repair jobs that lasted 3 hours, a customer had no cash on hand and instead gave him 10 shares of stock valued at $50 by a major stock exchange. Mr. Birch included the $50 in income. His basis in the stock is $30.

The correct answer is (F). *(SPE 1077 I-20)*
DISCUSSION: Since Mr. Birch included the $50 market value of the stock in his income, he has a "tax cost basis" of $50 in the stock. This refers to the fact that he has already been taxed on $50 and should not be taxed on this amount again if he sells the stock. This concept is not provided by statute but is applied in Reg. 1.61-2(d)(2).

12.5 Property Received in a Nontaxable Transaction

47. Kelly Green's automobile, used exclusively for business, had an adjusted basis of $1,600 when she traded it in on a new one. The dealer allowed her $1,800 on the old automobile and she had to pay $3,200 in cash. What is Ms. Green's adjusted basis in her new auto?

a. $3,200.
b. $3,400.
c. $4,800.
d. $5,000.

The correct answer is (c). *(SPE 1077 III-4)*
REQUIRED: The basis of an automobile received in a like-kind exchange.
DISCUSSION: The basis of property received in a like-kind exchange is the adjusted basis of the property surrendered, increased by any boot given and any gain recognized, and decreased by any boot received [Sec. 1031(d)]. Boot is generally money or nonlike-kind property. Green's realized gain on the trade would not be recognized since this is a like-kind exchange under Sec. 1031, and gain is recognized only to the extent of boot received. Green's basis in the new automobile is equal to her adjusted basis in the old automobile of $1,600, increased by the $3,200 she gave in cash, for a total of $4,800.

48. Henry traded a truck with an adjusted basis of $4,000 and a fair market value of $6,000 for another truck that had a list price of $12,000. Henry also paid an additional $5,000 and was eligible for a $500 rebate that will be mailed to him in 4 weeks from date of purchase. What is Henry's basis in the new truck?

a. $12,000.
b. $10,500.
c. $9,000.
d. $8,500.

The correct answer is (d). *(SPE 990 I-71)*
REQUIRED: The basis of a truck acquired in a like-kind exchange.
DISCUSSION: The basis of property received in a like-kind exchange is equal to the adjusted basis of the property surrendered, decreased by any boot received, and increased by any gain recognized or boot given [Sec. 1031(d)]. Since no boot is received or gain recognized by Henry, his basis in the new truck is equal to his adjusted basis in the old truck of $4,000, increased by the $5,000 he paid in cash and reduced by the $500 rebated for a total of $8,500.

49. Mr. R owned a printing press with an adjusted basis of $2,000 that he used in his business. On July 17, 1991, he transferred this property to Ms. A in exchange for the following assets:

	A's Adjusted Basis	Fair Market Value
Printing press (to be used for business)	$4,000	$6,000
Truck (for personal use)	1,000	2,000
Cash	2,000	2,000

What is R's basis in the new printing press and the truck after the exchange?

	New Press	Truck
a.	$2,000	$2,000
b.	$4,000	$1,000
c.	$6,000	$2,000
d.	$6,400	$1,600

The correct answer is (a). *(SPE 1083 II-65)*
REQUIRED: The basis of two assets acquired in a like-kind exchange.
DISCUSSION: The basis of property received in a like-kind exchange is equal to the adjusted basis of the property surrendered, decreased by any boot received, and increased by any gain recognized or boot given [Sec. 1031(d)]. Since this is a like-kind exchange (one press for another) and Mr. R received boot along with the like-kind property, he will recognize gain to the extent of the lesser of the realized gain or the value of boot received. Mr. R's realized gain is $8,000 ($10,000 total FMV received – $2,000 basis). Of this amount, he recognizes only $4,000, the value of the boot received (the truck plus the cash).
The basis in the new printing press (the like-kind property) will be the basis of the property transferred ($2,000), minus the amount of boot received ($4,000), plus the amount of gain recognized ($4,000), or $2,000. The basis of the truck received will be its fair market value ($2,000).

50. A fire destroyed Mr. C's business automobile. Mr. C originally paid $8,000 for the automobile and up to the time of the fire had been allowed $5,000 in depreciation. Within 3 months the insurance company replaced the old automobile with a new one which was worth $7,000. What is the basis of the new automobile for purposes of computing depreciation?

a. $3,000.
b. $5,000.
c. $7,000.
d. $8,000.

The correct answer is (a). *(SPE 1082 I-81)*
REQUIRED: The basis of property received as a replacement for destroyed property.
DISCUSSION: If property is destroyed in an involuntary conversion, the basis of property acquired in replacement is the same as the basis of the property destroyed (decreased by any money received and increased by any gain recognized) if the replacement property (rather than cash) is received for the destroyed property [Sec. 1033(b)]. Since Mr. C did receive the new automobile from the insurance company (instead of receiving cash and buying a new automobile), Mr. C's basis in the new automobile is the same as his $3,000 basis in the old automobile ($8,000 – $5,000 depreciation).
Mr. C's holding period of the new automobile will include the holding period of the old automobile because there was a transferred basis.

51. A hurricane destroyed a bus owned by the Gator Booster Club. The bus originally cost $10,000, and $4,000 of depreciation had been allowed up to the time of the hurricane. The Gator Booster Club received $9,000 in insurance proceeds which they used to purchase a new bus by paying an additional $3,000 cash. The Gator Booster Club elected to defer gain recognition on the involuntary conversion. What is the basis of the new bus?

a. $6,000.
b. $7,000.
c. $9,000.
d. $12,000.

The correct answer is (c). *(Publisher)*
REQUIRED: The basis of property purchased with funds received from an involuntary conversion of old property.
DISCUSSION: Under Sec. 1033(b), the basis of replacement property acquired with cash received in payment for an involuntary conversion of old property is the cost of the replacement property decreased by the amount of gain not recognized. The Gator Booster Club realized a gain of $3,000 ($9,000 – $6,000 basis), but it recognized no gain under Sec. 1033(a) since the entire proceeds were reinvested in replacement property similar or related in use. The club's basis in the new bus is $9,000 ($12,000 cost – $3,000 gain not recognized).

Module 12.5: Property Received in a Nontaxable Transaction

52. Speculator has owned a tract of land for several years. She paid $100,000 for it and it is now worth $200,000. Speculator decides to form a corporation to subdivide and develop the land. Speculator transfers the land plus $10,000 cash to a newly formed corporation in exchange for all of the stock in the corporation. What is Speculator's basis in the stock?

a. $100,000.
b. $110,000.
c. $200,000.
d. $210,000.

The correct answer is (b). *(Publisher)*
REQUIRED: A shareholder's basis in stock acquired in exchange for appreciated property.
DISCUSSION: The basis in stock is generally what the shareholder pays for it (Sec. 1012). However, Sec. 358 provides that the basis of stock received by a shareholder without the recognition of gain under Sec. 351 is the same as the basis of the property exchanged. Sec. 351 provides that no gain or loss is recognized when property is transferred to a corporation solely in exchange for stock in such corporation and immediately after the exchange, such person is in control (80% or more ownership) of the corporation.
Since Speculator owns 100% of the corporation after the exchange, she will not recognize gain on the transfer of the appreciated property to the corporation. Speculator's basis in the stock is $110,000 ($100,000 transferred basis from the land + $10,000 cash).

53. Using the same facts as in the previous question, what is the corporation's basis in the land received from Speculator?

a. $90,000.
b. $100,000.
c. $190,000.
d. $200,000.

The correct answer is (b). *(Publisher)*
REQUIRED: A corporation's basis in property received in exchange for stock.
DISCUSSION: Sec. 362 provides that property received by a corporation in a Sec. 351 transaction shall have the same basis as in the hands of the transferor increased by the amount of any gain recognized on the transfer. Since Speculator recognized no gain under Sec. 351 in the previous question, the corporation will take a transferred basis from Speculator of $100,000.

54. Mr. C's building, which was used in his business, was partially destroyed in a storm. The building cost $125,000 and had an adjusted basis of $75,000. The fair market value was $85,000 before the storm and $45,000 immediately after. Mr. C received a $20,000 reimbursement from his insurance company. What is the adjusted basis of the building before any repairs are made?

a. $55,000.
b. $35,000.
c. $30,000.
d. $15,000.

The correct answer is (b). *(SPE 1085 II-78)*
REQUIRED: The basis in a building which was partially destroyed by storm and for which partial reimbursement was received by insurance.
DISCUSSION: Sec. 1016 provides that adjustments shall be made to the basis of property for receipts and losses (among other items) properly chargeable to capital. These are, in effect, recoveries of capital for which an adjustment to basis is needed so the taxpayer does not receive a double benefit. Here, there is a $40,000 decline in fair market value ($85,000 − $45,000). The $20,000 unreimbursed loss is a reduction in basis and the $20,000 receipt of insurance proceeds is also a reduction in basis. Mr. C's basis in the building before repairs is $35,000 ($75,000 − $20,000 − $20,000). If repairs are made, the basis will be increased by their cost.

55. Ms. H, age 45, sold her principal residence on September 1, 1991 for $55,000. She paid a $3,500 real estate commission on the sale. The residence was purchased in 1985 for $35,000. In 1987 a garage was added at a cost of $2,500. In 1989 she deducted $5,000 as a casualty loss due to a flood. She did not receive any insurance reimbursement. On August 15, 1991, the house was repainted at a cost of $1,500. Ms. H purchased a new residence November 15, 1991 for $48,000. What is the adjusted basis of H's new residence?

a. $31,000.
b. $32,500.
c. $44,500.
d. $48,000.

The correct answer is (a). *(SPE 1078 I-75)*
REQUIRED: The adjusted basis of a new residence after nonrecognition of the gain on the sale of the old residence.
DISCUSSION: Under Sec. 1034, the basis of a new residence is reduced by the amount of gain not recognized on the sale of the old residence. Ms. H realized a gain of $19,000 on the sale of the old residence.

Sales price	$55,000
Commission paid	(3,500)
Adjusted basis *	(32,500)
Gain realized	$19,000

* The adjusted basis of Ms. H's old house is her original cost ($35,000), plus the garage ($2,500), minus the casualty loss ($5,000).

Ms. H will recognize a gain on the sale of the old residence of $2,000 (the excess of the adjusted sales price over the cost of the new residence). The adjusted sales price was $50,000 (the amount realized of $51,500 less the fixing-up expenses of $1,500) and the cost of the new residence was $48,000; therefore, the excess was $2,000.

The unrecognized portion of Ms. H's realized gain is $17,000 ($19,000 − $2,000), and her adjusted basis in the new residence is $31,000 ($48,000 − $17,000).

56. In the previous question, assume Ms. H was 65 when the residence was sold and elected the exclusion of gain on sale of a residence available to taxpayers age 55 or older. What is the adjusted basis of her new residence?

a. $31,000.
b. $36,600.
c. $42,300.
d. $48,000.

The correct answer is (d). *(SPE 1078 I-76)*
REQUIRED: The adjusted basis of a new residence when the purchaser elects to exclude gain on the sale of the old residence.
DISCUSSION: Under Sec. 121, a taxpayer age 55 or older may exclude up to $125,000 of gain on the sale of a personal residence. This is a once in a lifetime election. Ms. H would exclude her entire $19,000 gain with this election. This is an exclusion provision (unlike the deferral under Sec. 1034), so basis in the new residence does not have to be reduced. Her basis is $48,000, the purchase price.

57. Darwin contributed land with a fair market value of $40,000 and a basis of $45,000 to the Double Dee Partnership for a 50% partnership interest. The partnership assumed a $10,000 liability on the land but had no other liabilities. Darwin's basis in his partnership interest is

a. $30,000.
b. $35,000.
c. $40,000.
d. $45,000.

The correct answer is (c). *(Publisher)*
REQUIRED: The basis of a partnership interest acquired in exchange for property which is subject to a debt.
DISCUSSION: The basis of a partnership interest acquired by a contribution of property to the partnership is equal to the adjusted basis of such property to the contributing partner at the time of contribution (Sec. 722). Under Sec. 752, an assumption of an individual partner's liabilities by the partnership is considered a distribution of money to the partner by the partnership, and this reduces the basis of the partner's interest under Sec. 733. The other partners in the Double Dee Partnership assumed $5,000 of Darwin's individual liabilities ($10,000 x 50%). His basis in the partnership interest is equal to the adjusted basis of the land contributed reduced by the liabilities assumed ($45,000 − $5,000 = $40,000).

58. On September 1, 1991, Mr. G traded in his old car which was used 50% for business and 50% for pleasure. His old car originally cost $5,000 and he had claimed $800 of depreciation in earlier years. He was given a $2,000 trade-in allowance on his old car. The sales price on the new car (also to be used 50% for business and 50% for pleasure) is $7,000. The $5,000 difference between the sales price and the trade-in allowance was paid in cash. What is Mr. G's depreciable basis of the new car?

a. $3,500.
b. $3,700.
c. $4,200.
d. $4,600.

The correct answer is (c). *(SPE 1081 I-82)*
REQUIRED: The depreciable basis of a new car used 50% for business and acquired in a like-kind exchange.
DISCUSSION: Secs. 167 and 168 define the depreciable basis of an asset as the adjusted basis used for determining gain. Only the portion of the car used for business is depreciable. The business portions of the cars also qualify as a like-kind exchange under Sec. 1031, and no gain or loss is recognized on the disposal of the old car. The basis of the newly acquired asset is the adjusted basis of the property surrendered, plus the boot given, minus gain recognized. These computations only apply to the one-half of the car used for business.

Original cost of old car	$2,500
Less depreciation	(800)
Adjusted basis of old car	$1,700
Plus boot given (1/2 of $5,000 cash)	2,500
Depreciable basis of new car	$4,200

59. Mr. A sold a truck used in his business with an adjusted basis of $2,000 for $500 to a salvage yard in 1991. He purchased a replacement truck 2 months later for $8,000. Mr. A's basis in the new truck is $9,500.

The correct answer is (F). *(SPE 1080 I-24)*
DISCUSSION: Since Mr. A sold the old truck to a salvage yard and purchased the replacement truck 2 months later, the two transactions are independent and would not qualify as a like-kind exchange under Sec. 1031. Mr. A would fully recognize the loss on the sale of the old business truck, and the basis of the new truck would be its cost of $8,000.

60. Mr. V transfers real property with a basis of $50,000 to Corporation X solely in exchange for 90% of the stock in that corporation. The basis of the stock to Mr. V is $50,000.

The correct answer is (T). *(SPE 984 III-12)*
DISCUSSION: Since this transaction qualifies under Sec. 351, the basis of the stock received by Mr. V is determined under Sec. 358. The basis of the stock received will be that of the property given up ($50,000).

61. Mrs. K transfers a building with an adjusted basis of $120,000 to Corporation Z in exchange for 90% of Z's stock plus $1,000 in cash. The basis of the building to Corporation Z is $120,000.

The correct answer is (F). *(SPE 984 III-9)*
DISCUSSION: Since this transaction qualifies under Sec. 351, the basis of the building to Corporation Z is determined under Sec. 362. The building has the same basis for Z as in the hands of Mrs. K, plus the amount of gain recognized by Mrs. K on the transfer. Under Sec. 351, any realized gain is recognized to the extent of cash received. The facts given are not sufficient to determine the amount of realized gain. Assuming that the fair market value of the building was at least $121,000, however, Mrs. K would have recognized a $1,000 gain on the transfer, and the building's basis to Corporation Z is most likely $121,000.

62. Corporation A received land valued at $80,000 from Town E as an incentive to develop an industrial park there. The basis of the land to Corporation A is $0.

The correct answer is (T). *(SPE 984 III-11)*
DISCUSSION: Under Sec. 362(c), property other than money contributed by a nonshareholder to the capital of a corporation has a basis of $0 to the corporation.

12.6 Stock Dividends and Stock Rights

63. In January 1991 Joan Hill bought one share of Orban Corp. stock for $300. On March 1, 1991, Orban distributed one share of preferred stock for each share of common stock held. This distribution was nontaxable. On March 1, 1991, Joan's one share of common stock had a fair market value of $450, while the preferred stock had a fair market value of $150. After the distribution of the preferred stock, Joan's bases for her Orban stocks are

	Common	Preferred
a.	$300	$0
b.	$225	$75
c.	$200	$100
d.	$150	$150

The correct answer is (b). *(CPA 586 Q-54)*
REQUIRED: The tax bases of common stock and preferred stock received as a nontaxable dividend.
DISCUSSION: Since the preferred stock dividend was nontaxable, the original basis of the common stock would be allocated between the common stock and the preferred stock based on the relative fair market value of each on the date of the stock dividend (Reg. 1.307-1). The market values of Joan's common and preferred stock on the date of the dividend were $450 and $150, respectively. Joan's tax basis in the common stock after the receipt of the dividend is

$$\$450 \div \$600 \times \$300 = \$225$$

Joan's tax basis in the preferred stock is

$$\$150 \div \$600 \times \$300 = \$75$$

64. Kathy owns 100 shares of preferred stock in Duck Corporation. She had purchased this stock for $5,000 in 1982. In 1991, Kathy received a stock dividend of 10 additional shares of preferred stock in Duck. On the date of distribution the preferred stock had a fair market value of $60 per share. What is Kathy's basis in the stock dividend from Duck?

a. $600.
b. $590.
c. $500.
d. $0.

The correct answer is (a). *(SPE 990 I-65)*
REQUIRED: The basis of stock received as a distribution on preferred stock.
DISCUSSION: When a tax-free distribution of stock is received by a shareholder, the basis in the new stock is determined by allocating the basis in the old stock between the new stock and the old stock. However, a distribution of preferred stock made with respect to preferred stock is included in gross income [Sec. 305(b)]. Kathy's basis in the new stock received from Duck Corporation is $600 (10 shares x $60 FMV per share). This is the amount that Kathy will have to include in gross income and for which she will receive a basis under Sec. 301(d).

65. Joe Blue owns 100 shares of common stock in the Sky Corporation previously purchased for $5,000. In 1991 Blue receives a nontaxable distribution of stock rights to purchase 40 additional shares of stock in the Sky Corporation. The fair market value of the common stock was $100 per share on the date of distribution and the fair market value of the stock rights was $2,000. What is Blue's basis in the stock rights?

a. $0.
b. $833.
c. $1,000.
d. $2,000.

The correct answer is (b). *(Publisher)*
REQUIRED: The basis of stock rights received in a distribution from a corporation.
DISCUSSION: Under Sec. 307(a), the basis of stock rights distributed tax-free to a shareholder is determined by allocating the basis of the stock between the stock rights and the stock. Since the fair market value of the rights is at least 15% of the fair market value of the underlying stock, Sec. 307(b) requires a basis allocation to take place. The allocation is based on the relative fair market values of the stock and the stock rights on the date of the distribution. Blue's basis in the stock rights is $833, as computed below.

$$\frac{\$2,000 \ FMV \ stock \ rights}{\$12,000 \ FMV \ stock + FMV \ rights} \times \$5,000 = \$833$$

Module 12.6: Stock Dividends and Stock Rights

66. Joe Blue also owned 200 shares of common stock in the Water Corporation. These were purchased several years ago for $2,000. In 1991 Blue received a nontaxable distribution of stock rights to purchase 20 additional shares of stock in the Water Corporation for $10 each. The fair market value of the common stock was $40 per share on the date of distribution and the fair market value of the stock rights was $600. What is Blue's lowest basis in the stock rights?

a. $0.
b. $70.
c. $140.
d. $600.

The correct answer is (a). *(Publisher)*
REQUIRED: A shareholder's basis in stock rights received as a distribution when the stock rights are worth less than 15% of the value of the stock.
DISCUSSION: Under Sec. 307(a), the basis of stock rights received in a nontaxable distribution is generally determined by allocating the basis of the stock between the stock rights and the stock. Sec. 307(b) provides, however, that if the fair market value of the stock rights at the time of distribution is less than 15% of the fair market value of the stock, the basis of the stock rights is zero unless the shareholder elects to determine the basis under Sec. 307(a). The stock rights in the Water Corporation had a fair market value of $600, which is less than 15% of the $8,000 fair market value of the stock, so Blue's basis in the stock rights is zero (unless he elects to allocate basis).

67. In 1977, Toni purchased 100 shares of common stock in Corporation B for $5,500. In 1988, B declared a stock dividend of one share of its common stock for each 10 shares held. In 1991, B's common stock split 2 for 1 at a time when the fair market value was $80 a share. What is Toni's basis in each of her shares of B's stock if both distributions were tax-free?

a. $25 per share.
b. $55 for 100 shares and $0 for all additional shares.
c. $50 for 110 shares and $80 for 110 shares.
d. $80 per share.

The correct answer is (a). *(SPE 990 I-73)*
REQUIRED: A shareholder's basis in stock after a stock dividend and a stock split.
DISCUSSION: A distribution of common stock as a stock dividend on common stock is generally a tax-free distribution. The same is true for a stock split. Under Sec. 307(a), the basis of the original stock is allocated between it and the distributed stock based on their relative fair market values. Here, all the stock has the same fair market value, so the basis per share is calculated as total basis divided by total number of shares. Toni's total number of shares is 220 [(100 + 10) x 2]. Her basis per share is $25 ($5,500 ÷ 220 shares).

68. On January 2, 1989, Mr. Z purchased 100 shares of common stock in Corporation D for $40 per share. Six months later he purchased 60 more shares at $50 per share. On December 1, 1991, Mr. Z received a 25% nontaxable stock dividend. The new and the old stock are identical. What is the amount of Z's basis in each share of stock?

a. 200 shares at $35 per share.
b. 200 shares at $43.75 per share.
c. 125 shares at $32 per share and 75 shares at $40 per share.
d. 125 shares at $40 per share and 75 shares at $50 per share.

The correct answer is (c). *(SPE 989 I-73)*
REQUIRED: A shareholder's basis in stock with different bases after a stock dividend.
DISCUSSION: The stock dividend made by Corporation D is a tax-free distribution under Sec. 305(a). The basis of the new stock is determined by allocating the basis of the old stock between the new stock and the old stock [Sec. 307(a)]. This allocation of basis in the stock is made based on the relative fair market values on the date of distribution for each different lot of stock, rather than by averaging them. Mr. Z owns 125 (100 + 25) shares with a basis of $4,000, or $32 per share and 75 (60 + 15) shares with a basis of $3,000, or $40 per share.

69. The basis of taxable stock dividends received by a shareholder is equal to the par value of the stock plus any income tax that resulted from the inclusion of the dividends in the shareholder's gross income.

The correct answer is (F). *(SPE 988 I-19)*
DISCUSSION: In general, the basis of property received as a taxable stock dividend from a corporation is the fair market value of the stock [Sec. 301(d)].

70. If nontaxable stock rights are allowed to expire, they have no basis.

The correct answer is (T). *(SPE 1080 I-24)*
DISCUSSION: Under Sec. 307, the basis of nontaxable rights is $0 unless the taxpayer elects or is required to allocate part of the basis of the stock. Under Reg. 1.307-1(a), allocation of basis to stock rights can occur only if the rights are sold or exercised.

12.7 Adjustments to Asset Basis

See Chapter 13 for depreciation, ACRS, cost recovery, depletion, and amortization that reduce bases of assets.

71. Morris Chevy purchased a horse farm in Ocala, Florida. $10,000 of the purchase price was properly allocated to the barn. Several months after the purchase, Morris built an addition to the barn at a cost of $2,000. In the subsequent year, Morris expended $800 to paint the barn, repair broken windows, and have the inside thoroughly cleaned. What is Morris's basis in the barn at the end of the second year, excluding depreciation?

a. $10,000.
b. $10,800.
c. $12,000.
d. $12,800.

The correct answer is (c). *(Publisher)*
REQUIRED: The basis of property on which expenditures have been made for both repairs and improvements.
DISCUSSION: Under Reg. 1.162-4, repairs are deductible while improvements that prolong the life of property or materially increase its value must be capitalized. Under Sec. 1016(a)(1), expenditures properly chargeable to capital increase the basis of property. An addition to a barn is considered an improvement, but fixing broken windows, painting, and cleaning are generally considered repairs. Morris's basis (excluding depreciation) is $12,000 ($10,000 purchase price + $2,000 improvements).

72. Susan Surety is the sole shareholder of the Surety Company. She purchased all the outstanding stock for $15,000 two years ago. The company was in financial difficulty so Susan contributed an additional $5,000 in cash and some land to the company. The land had a fair market value of $4,000 and a basis of $2,000. What is Susan's adjusted basis in the stock?

a. $15,000.
b. $20,000.
c. $22,000.
d. $24,000.

The correct answer is (c). *(Publisher)*
REQUIRED: A shareholder's basis in stock after a contribution of cash and property.
DISCUSSION: A shareholder recognizes no gain on the voluntary contribution of capital to a corporation. The contribution of capital merely increases the shareholder's basis in the corporation (Reg. 1.118-1). The shareholder's basis is increased by the basis in the property contributed, not by the fair market value. Susan will recognize no gain and her basis is

Cost of stock	$15,000
Contribution of cash	5,000
Contribution of property (basis)	2,000
Adjusted basis in stock	$22,000

73. Beth owned a large parcel of property. She had purchased it in one transaction for $80,000. In 1991, Beth was badly in need of cash, so she sold one-fourth of the land for $20,000 and sold one-half of the original land for $30,000 to another person, although it was all of approximately equal value. What is Beth's basis in the remaining land that she owns?

a. $20,000.
b. $30,000.
c. $50,000.
d. $80,000.

The correct answer is (a). *(Publisher)*
REQUIRED: Remaining basis in land after selling three-fourths of an original tract at varying prices.
DISCUSSION: When a part of a larger property is sold, the cost or basis of the entire property must be equitably apportioned among the several parts (Reg. 1.61-6). This is generally done on the basis of the relative fair market values of each part. If all the land is of approximately equal value, the basis is allocated based on the amount of land sold in each transaction. Since Beth sold three-fourths of the land and still owns one-fourth, her basis is $20,000 (1/4 x $80,000).

74. A fire in Mr. White's residence resulted in a loss of $2,200. Mr. White recovered only $1,600 from his insurance company and deducted a casualty loss of $500 ($600 unreimbursed loss, less $100 nondeductible on property used for personal purposes). By what amount must Mr. White reduce his basis before considering any reinvestment of the insurance proceeds in repairs on the house?

a. $600.
b. $1,600.
c. $2,100.
d. $2,200.

The correct answer is (c). *(SPE 1077 II-39)*
REQUIRED: The adjustment to the basis of a personal residence after a casualty loss.
DISCUSSION: Mr. White received $1,600 in insurance proceeds and recognized a casualty loss of $500. These are considered recovered costs for tax purposes and Mr. White must reduce his basis by $2,100. The remaining $100 loss for which he received no tax benefit does not reduce his basis.

75. On January 1, 1991, Mr. D owned rental property which had an adjusted basis to him of $250,000. Mr. M made the following expenditures during 1991:

Ordinary painting of the building	$ 5,000
Repair of one section of the roof (useful life not appreciably extended)	2,500
Legal fees paid to defend title	10,000
Property taxes	6,000
Assessment for local improvement of street that increased the value of the property appreciably	15,000

Not considering depreciation, what is Mr. D's basis in the property at year-end?

a. $225,000.
b. $240,000.
c. $260,000.
d. $275,000.

The correct answer is (d). *(SPE 987 II-63)*
REQUIRED: The basis of property at year-end after expenditures were made.
DISCUSSION: Under Reg. 1.162-4, repairs are deductible while improvements that prolong the life of property or materially increase its value must be capitalized. Therefore, the ordinary painting of a building and repair of a roof which does not appreciably extend the useful life are deductible and do not increase basis. Property taxes are also deductible under Sec. 164 and therefore do not increase basis. But assessments for local improvements of the street that increase the value of the property are not deductible and do increase the basis of property [Sec. 164(c)(1)]. Also, expenses paid or incurred in defending or perfecting title of property constitute a part of the cost of property and are not deductible [Reg. 1.212-1(k)]. Therefore, Mr. D's basis in the property is as follows:

Beginning basis	$250,000
Fees to defend title	10,000
Assessment for improvements	15,000
Basis at year-end	$275,000

76. In 1991 Mr. A sold an asset that originally cost $7,000. Mr. A incorrectly claimed $4,000 depreciation over a 5-year period. He should have claimed $5,000 depreciation. What was the adjusted basis when sold?

a. $2,000.
b. $3,000.
c. $5,000.
d. $7,000.

The correct answer is (a). *(SPE 1081 I-53)*
REQUIRED: The adjusted basis of an asset that was depreciated by an amount less than the amount allowable.
DISCUSSION: Under Sec. 1016, an adjustment is made to the basis of an asset for the amount of depreciation allowed in previous years, but the adjustment cannot be less than the amount allowable under Secs. 167 or 168. The amount of depreciation allowable on this asset was $5,000. Mr. A must reduce his basis by this amount. The adjusted basis of the asset when sold was $2,000 ($7,000 − $5,000).

77. Which of the following items is not a reduction to the basis of an asset?

a. Casualty loss.
b. Amount received for granting an easement on property.
c. Personal property tax.
d. Rehabilitated building credit.

The correct answer is (c). *(SPE 1082 II-51)*
REQUIRED: The item which would not cause a reduction in the basis of an asset.
DISCUSSION: Under Sec. 1016, expenditures, receipts, losses, or other items properly chargeable to capital result in an adjustment in the basis of the property. However, there is no adjustment for deductible taxes. A personal property tax is deductible and does not reduce the basis of the asset.
Answer (a) is incorrect because casualty losses do reduce the basis of an asset. Answer (b) is incorrect because the grant of an easement requires a portion of the basis to be allocated. Answer (d) is incorrect because the basis of an asset is reduced by 100% of the credit for rehabilitation of buildings [Sec. 50(c)].

78. The basis of property will be increased by adding to its capital account all of the following except:

a. Section 179 deduction.
b. Zoning costs.
c. Legal fees for defending and perfecting title.
d. Costs of extending utility service lines to the property.

The correct answer is (a). *(SPE 990 II-34)*
REQUIRED: The item which does not increase basis.
DISCUSSION: The Section 179 deduction is a depreciation deduction which allows the taxpayer to expense up to $10,000 of the acquisition cost of tangible personal business property eligible to be depreciated, which is acquired by purchase, and is to be used in a trade or business. To qualify for the deduction, the Sec. 179 election must be made in the year the asset is placed in service. This deduction decreases the basis in the asset.
Answer (b) is incorrect because zoning costs also tend to increase the value of property and are almost always treated as capital expenditures. Answer (c) is incorrect because fees to defend and perfect title are treated as a cost of the property. Answer (d) is incorrect because extending utility service lines generally increases its value and is considered a capital expenditure.

12.8 Holding Period

79. For assets acquired after 1987, the holding period for determining long-term capital gains and losses is more than

a. 6 months.
b. 9 months.
c. 12 months.
d. 15 months.

The correct answer is (c). *(CPA 586 Q-41)*
REQUIRED: The long-term holding period for capital assets acquired after 1987.
DISCUSSION: Under Sec. 1222, capital assets must be held for more than 1 year in order for the gain or loss on sale or exchange to be treated as long-term. This holding period applies to assets acquired after 1987.

Module 12.8: Holding Period

80. Exel contributed land (a capital asset) to a partnership for a 30% partnership interest on March 1, 1990. Exel had purchased the land on June 15, 1987 for $25,000, and the land had a fair market value of $50,000 in March 1990. The partnership sold the land on December 10, 1990 for $55,000. In April 1991 Exel sold his/her partnership interest. The holding period for Exel's partnership interest began

a. March 1, 1990.
b. June 15, 1987.
c. One-half began June 15, 1987 and one-half began March 1, 1990.
d. December 10, 1990.

The correct answer is (b). *(Publisher)*
REQUIRED: The holding period for a partnership interest acquired in exchange for a contributed capital asset.
DISCUSSION: If the property received in an exchange has the same basis as the property given (substituted basis), the holding period of the property given will be tacked to the period for the property received [Sec. 1223(1)]. This rule applies only if the assets are capital assets or Sec. 1231 assets. Under Sec. 722, the basis of a partnership interest is equal to the adjusted basis of property contributed to the partnership in exchange for such interest. Therefore, Exel's holding period for the partnership interest runs from the date (s)he acquired the land (capital asset) contributed to the partnership, which was June 15, 1987.
Note that the partnership's holding period in the land is also tacked under Sec. 1223(2) since the partnership has a transferred basis under Sec. 723.

81. On July 1, 1990, Dora Flora purchased a greenhouse for use in her garden. On September 1, 1990, she started a nursery business and converted the greenhouse to business use. Dora decided to incorporate the business and transferred all her business assets, including the greenhouse, to the Flora Corporation in exchange for 100% of its stock on June 1, 1991. Flora Corporation sold the greenhouse on August 1, 1991. What is Flora Corporation's holding period for the greenhouse?

a. 2 months.
b. 11 months.
c. 13 months.
d. 14 months.

The correct answer is (c). *(Publisher)*
REQUIRED: The holding period of property converted from personal to business use, and then transferred to a corporation in exchange for stock.
DISCUSSION: The holding period of property generally begins on the date of acquisition. When property has the same basis in whole or in part as it had in the hands of a prior holder, however, the holding period of the prior holder is tacked to the present owner's holding period [Sec. 1223(2)]. The transfer of business assets by Dora to the Flora Corporation qualified under Sec. 351 as a tax-free exchange and the corporation took Dora's basis in the assets. Therefore, the corporation's holding period also includes Dora's. When Dora converted the greenhouse from personal to business use, the holding period of the greenhouse was not affected. As a result, Flora Corporation's holding period ran from July 1, 1990 to August 1, 1991, or 13 months.

82. On January 1, 1991, Sanders contributed inventory with a basis of $10,000 and a fair market value of $14,000 to ASTEC Corporation and received 100 shares of ASTEC stock. All the requirements of Sec. 351 were met. Sanders had acquired the inventory on December 1, 1990 in the normal operation of business. By April 15, 1991, all the inventory was sold. Sanders' holding period for the ASTEC stock

a. Began January 1, 1991.
b. Began December 1, 1990.
c. Began April 15, 1991.
d. Is short-term because the stock was received for an ordinary income asset.

The correct answer is (a). *(Publisher)*
REQUIRED: The holding period of stock acquired in a nontaxable exchange for ordinary income property.
DISCUSSION: When a capital or Sec. 1231 asset is acquired in exchange for an ordinary income asset in a nontaxable transaction, the holding period begins on the date the capital or Sec. 1231 asset is acquired. The holding period for an ordinary income asset cannot be tacked to the holding period of a capital asset. Sanders' holding period began on the date of the exchange, January 1, 1991.

Module 12.8: Holding Period

83. In 1987 Iris King bought a diamond necklace for her own use, at a cost of $10,000. In 1991, when the fair market value was $12,000, Iris gave this necklace to her daughter, Ruth. No gift tax was due. Ruth's holding period for this gift

  a. Starts in 1991.
  b. Starts in 1987.
  c. Depends on whether the necklace is sold by Ruth at a gain or at a loss.
  d. Is irrelevant because Ruth received the necklace for no consideration of money or money's worth.

The correct answer is (b). *(CPA 1187 Q-18)*
REQUIRED: The holding period of property acquired by gift.
DISCUSSION: Under Sec. 1015, the basis of property acquired by gift is generally the same as the basis in the hands of the donor. Under Sec. 1223(2), the holding period of property which has a transferred basis (the same basis as the prior holder's) includes the holding period of the prior owner. Ruth's holding period, therefore, begins in 1987 when Iris purchased the necklace.
Answer (a) is incorrect because Ruth will tack Iris's holding period on to her own. Answer (c) is incorrect because fair market value is greater than the basis at the time of the gift so Ruth will always use Iris's basis whether she sells it at a gain or a loss. Answer (d) is incorrect because the holding period is relevant in the event that Ruth sells the necklace. The necklace is a capital asset and the holding period affects whether it is a long-term or short-term capital gain or loss.

84. Webster received 100 shares of Gator Corporation stock as a gift from Aunt Clara on August 1, 1991 when the fair market value of the stock was $4,000. Clara purchased the stock on June 1, 1990 for $5,000. On September 15, 1991, Webster sold the stock for $3,700. Webster's loss and its character are

  a. $1,300 long-term capital loss.
  b. $1,300 short-term capital loss.
  c. $300 long-term capital loss.
  d. $300 short-term capital loss.

The correct answer is (d). *(Publisher)*
REQUIRED: The amount and character of a loss incurred on the sale of stock acquired by gift.
DISCUSSION: The basis of property acquired by gift (to compute a loss) is the lower of the donor's basis or the fair market value of the property on the date of the gift (Sec. 1015). The FMV on the date of the gift was lower than Aunt Clara's basis, so Webster's basis was $4,000. Webster sold the stock for $3,700 and realized a loss of $300. Since Webster did not receive a transferred basis from Clara, the holding period was not tacked on under Sec. 1223(2). Webster's holding period ran from the date of the gift, which is less than 1 year (from August 1 to September 15, 1991), so the character of the loss is short-term (Sec. 1222).

85. On September 30, 1990, Mr. C purchased investment land. On April 15, 1991, C traded his land for some other investment land in a nontaxable exchange. On October 5, 1991, C sold the land received in the exchange for a gain. C's gain will be treated as

  a. A short-term capital gain.
  b. A long-term capital gain.
  c. Part short-term capital gain, part long-term capital gain.
  d. Part nontaxable, part long-term capital gain.

The correct answer is (b). *(SPE 984 II-58)*
REQUIRED: The character of gain on a sale of land acquired in a like-kind exchange.
DISCUSSION: If property received in an exchange has the same basis in whole or in part as that of the property given (and if the property given is a capital asset or a Sec. 1231 asset), the holding period of the property received includes the period for which the property given was held [Sec. 1223(1)]. Since the basis of the land C received is the same as the adjusted basis of the land he traded as adjusted for the factors in Sec. 1031(d), the holding period of the land traded is added to the holding period of the land acquired. Therefore, C is deemed to have held the investment land sold since September 30, 1990. C's gain will receive long-term capital gain treatment.

86. Speedo purchased a new car on May 1, 1991. Speedo died June 1, 1991. The personal representative of the estate distributed the property to Speedo's son, Rollo, on July 1, 1991. Rollo sold the car on October 31, 1991. What is Rollo's holding period for the property?

a. 4 months.
b. 5 months.
c. 12 months.
d. More than 12 months.

The correct answer is (d). *(Publisher)*
REQUIRED: A beneficiary's holding period for property acquired from a decedent and sold within 1 year of the decedent's death.
DISCUSSION: Sec. 1223(11) provides that a person who acquires property from a decedent and sells such property within 1 year after the decedent's death is considered to have held the property for more than 1 year. Rollo acquired the car from a decedent since it was distributed from Speedo's estate, and he sold it within 1 year of Speedo's death. Therefore, Rollo is considered to have held the car for more than 1 year regardless of actual holding period.

87. Rollo purchased a new car for use in his business on January 1, 1990 for $10,000. On July 1, 1991, a fire destroyed the car. The car was still worth $10,000 and $1,000 of depreciation had been claimed. The insurance company replaced the car with another car worth $10,000 on September 1, 1991. Rollo sold this replacement car on January 1, 1992. What is Rollo's holding period for the replacement car?

a. 4 months.
b. 5 months.
c. 6 months.
d. 2 years.

The correct answer is (d). *(Publisher)*
REQUIRED: The holding period of a car received in an involuntary conversion.
DISCUSSION: Under Sec. 1033(b), the basis of property replaced as a result of a casualty is the same as the basis in the destroyed property (increased by any gain recognized and decreased by any cash received). Under Sec. 1223(1), the holding period for a capital or Sec. 1231 asset acquired in an exchange includes the holding period of the property exchanged if the basis of the acquired property has the same basis in whole or in part as the property exchanged. Sec. 1223(1)(A) specifically states that an involuntary conversion shall be considered an exchange for purposes of applying the holding period rules.
Rollo's basis in the new car is the same as the basis in the old car. Under Sec. 1223(1), his holding period for the new car includes the holding period for the destroyed car, so his holding period for the new car is 2 years.

88. For purposes of determining the holding period for property, the holding period begins on the day you acquired the property and ends on the day before the sale of the property.

The correct answer is (F). *(SPE 1082 II-31)*
DISCUSSION: The general rule for the holding period of property is that the date the property was acquired is excluded and the date of disposition is included (Rev. Rul. 66-5). Also, the holding period is determined by calendar months.

89. If you receive a gift of property acquired by the donor in 1975 and your basis is determined by the donor's basis, the first day of your holding period is the date you received the gift.

The correct answer is (F). *(SPE 1077 I-14)*
DISCUSSION: The holding period begins on the same date the appropriate basis valuation arises. If the donor's basis is used (transferred basis), the holding period includes the donor's holding period [Sec. 1223(2)].

90. If you receive a nontaxable stock dividend, your holding period includes the holding period of the stock on which the dividend was distributed.

The correct answer is (T). *(Publisher)*
DISCUSSION: Under Sec. 1223(5), the holding period for stock, the basis of which is determined under Sec. 307, includes the period the taxpayer held the stock in the distributing corporation before the distribution. The basis of stock is determined under Sec. 307 when a shareholder receives a nontaxable stock dividend from the corporation.

CHAPTER THIRTEEN
DEPRECIATION, AMORTIZATION, AND DEPLETION

13.1 Depreciable Assets and Recovery Property	(10 questions)	311
13.2 Depreciable Basis	(6 questions)	313
13.3 Depreciation (Assets Acquired Before 1981)	(4 questions)	315
13.4 Election to Expense	(8 questions)	317
13.5 Depreciation (Assets Acquired 1981 - 1986)	(6 questions)	319
13.6 Depreciation (Assets Acquired after 1986)	(22 questions)	321
13.7 Amortization	(10 questions)	328
13.8 Depletion	(3 questions)	331

13.1 Depreciable Assets and Recovery Property

1. Which of the following assets are depreciable for federal income tax purposes?

1. Land
2. Personal residence
3. Rental residence
4. Inventory
5. Goodwill
6. Business automobile

   a. 3, 5, and 6.
   b. 1, 2, and 3.
   c. 1 and 4.
   d. 3 and 6.

The correct answer is (d). *(SPE 1077 I-157)*
REQUIRED: The assets that may be depreciated for income tax purposes.
DISCUSSION: Sec. 167(a) provides a depreciation deduction with respect to property used in a trade or business or held for the production of income. A rental residence and a business automobile are both used in a trade or business or for the production of income. Therefore, they are depreciable.
Answers (a), (b), and (c) are incorrect because land, a personal residence, inventory, and goodwill are not depreciable. Land is generally not subject to a decrease in value due to wear and tear, so it may not be depreciated. A personal residence may not be depreciated because it is not used in a trade or business or for the production of income. Inventory may not be depreciated because it is not used in a business; instead, it is sold. Goodwill may not be depreciated because it does not have a limited useful life [Reg. 1.167(a)-3].

2. Which of the following is not depreciable under the modified accelerated cost recovery system (MACRS)?

   a. Customer list, distinguishable from goodwill, with certain value and certain life in excess of 1 year.
   b. Low-income housing.
   c. Technical books with a 5-year useful life.
   d. Business auto driven by business owner.

The correct answer is (a). *(Publisher)*
REQUIRED: The asset that is not recovery property.
DISCUSSION: Prior to 1987, Sec. 168(c) defined recovery property as tangible property of a character subject to depreciation that is used in a trade or business or held for the production of income. The 1986 TRA revised Sec. 168 and does not use the term "recovery property" for the Modified ACRS depreciation system. Instead, Sec. 168 now applies to tangible property depreciable under Sec. 167. In effect, however, the same property is included so the term "recovery property" is still useful. A customer list is not tangible property, and therefore is not included in the definition of recovery property.
Answers (b), (c), and (d) are incorrect because each is tangible property used in a trade or business and qualifies as recovery property.

3. Intangible property may be depreciated (or amortized) if its use in the business or in producing income is definitely limited in duration. Which one of the following may not be depreciated (or amortized)?

   a. Patent.
   b. Baseball contract.
   c. Trademark.
   d. Leasehold.

The correct answer is (c). *(D.B. Bradley)*
REQUIRED: The intangible asset that may not be depreciated for income tax purposes.
DISCUSSION: Sec. 167(a) provides a depreciation deduction with respect to property used in a trade or business or held for the production of income. The deduction is not allowed if an asset lacks a determinable useful life. Since the usefulness of a trademark is considered to be of indefinite duration, it may not be depreciated or amortized.
  Answers (a), (b), and (d) are incorrect because each has a definite useful life and may be depreciated or amortized.

4. Which of the following assets qualifies for Modified ACRS treatment?

   a. Asset purchased and placed in service in 1985 as 5-year property.
   b. Real property acquired in 1991 from a related party who had acquired the property in 1986.
   c. A truck purchased in 1991 used entirely for trade or business purposes.
   d. Real property purchased in 1991 and leased back to its 1986 owner.

The correct answer is (c). *(SPE 984 II-51)*
REQUIRED: The asset(s) qualifying for Modified ACRS treatment.
DISCUSSION: To be eligible for Modified ACRS treatment, an asset must be tangible property used in a trade or business or held for the production of income and not excluded by Sec. 168(f). Sec. 168(f) excludes property acquired by the taxpayer after 1986 if the property was owned by a related person at any time during 1986, and property acquired after 1986 and leased to any person who owned the property at any time during 1986. The new rules also generally do not apply to property placed in service before 1987 (with some exceptions and transitional rules).
  Answers (a), (b), and (d) are incorrect because each is an example of property excluded by Sec. 168(f) and thus ineligible for Modified ACRS treatment.

5. Which of the following placed in service in 1991 is not a class of recovery property?

   a. 3-year property.
   b. 7-year property.
   c. 15-year property.
   d. Low-income housing.

The correct answer is (d). *(Publisher)*
REQUIRED: The item that is not a class of recovery property.
DISCUSSION: Sec. 168(e) defines the classes of recovery property as 3-year, 5-year, 7-year, 10-year, 15-year, 20-year, residential rental, and nonresidential real property. Low-income housing does not have a separate class and is generally residential real property depreciable using the straight-line method over 27.5 years.
  Answers (a), (b), and (c) are incorrect because each is a class of recovery property under Sec. 168(e).

6. Which of the following characteristics helps in assigning recovery property to a particular class?

   a. Business use.
   b. Tangible or intangible.
   c. Asset Depreciation Range midpoint.
   d. Listed property or not.

The correct answer is (c). *(Publisher)*
REQUIRED: The characteristic that is helpful in classifying recovery property.
DISCUSSION: The assignment of recovery property to classes is determined on the basis of the property's Asset Depreciation Range (ADR) midpoint. Each recovery class has a midpoint range into which the property must fall.
  Answer (a) is incorrect because only property used in a trade or business or held for the production of income is depreciable. Whether used in a business or held for production of income does not affect its classification. Answer (b) is incorrect because only tangible property is treated as recovery property (intangible property must be depreciated under Sec. 167), but it does not affect the assignment to a particular class. Answer (d) is incorrect because whether the property is classified as listed property or not under Sec. 280F(d)(4) has no effect on the recovery class to which a property is assigned.

Module 13.2: Depreciable Basis

7. Recovery property is tangible property of a character that is subject to the allowance for depreciation. It is used in a trade or business or held for the production of income and must have been placed in service after 1980.

The correct answer is (T). *(SPE 984 II-13)*
DISCUSSION: In general, recovery property is tangible property of a character subject to the allowance for depreciation and used in a trade or business or held for the production of income [Secs. 168(a) and 167(a)]. The property must have been placed in service after 1980.

8. In 1991, Marty purchased assets to be used in his business. One of the assets purchased was a copyright. The copyright is considered to be recovery property subject to the allowance for depreciation under Modified ACRS.

The correct answer is (F). *(SPE 1083 II-13)*
DISCUSSION: Recovery property is tangible property of a character subject to the allowance for depreciation. Since a copyright is not tangible property, it is not subject to the allowance for depreciation under the Modified ACRS rules. However, it is generally depreciable (or amortizable) under Sec. 167.

9. Ms. Bird moved to a new residence in September 1991. In October 1991, she began renting out her former residence that she had purchased in 1980. Ms. Bird is required to compute depreciation on the rental property under the ACRS method of depreciation.

The correct answer is (F). *(SPE 990 I-10)*
DISCUSSION: Although Ms. Bird converted the property to business use after 1980, she owned the property in 1980. Sec. 168(f) excludes real property from ACRS or MACRS treatment if owned by the taxpayer in 1980.

10. Mr. Parker's lease agreement for equipment used in his business is intended to be a conditional sales contract rather than a lease. Mr. Parker should capitalize the lease payments and depreciate them over the recovery period for the asset.

The correct answer is (T). *(SPE 1081 II-8)*
DISCUSSION: Since the equipment will be used in Mr. Parker's business and is intended to be a conditional sale, the asset should be capitalized. The capitalized lease payments should be depreciated over the asset's recovery period.

13.2 Depreciable Basis

Also see Chapter 12, Basis, for additional questions.

11. Dorothy purchased a car in 1991 to be used three-fourths of the time in her business and one-fourth of the time for personal purposes. The car cost $8,000 and is 5-year recovery property. No Sec. 179 expense deduction is taken. The basis for ACRS depreciation is

   a. $1,600.
   b. $2,000.
   c. $6,000.
   d. $8,000.

The correct answer is (c). *(Publisher)*
REQUIRED: The depreciable basis of an asset used for business and personal purposes.
DISCUSSION: The basis of property for depreciation is determined under the general basis rules. Under Sec. 1012, the basis for an asset is generally its cost. The cost of the car is $8,000, which must be allocated between business and personal use. Since she uses the car three-fourths for business, the basis for depreciation is $6,000 (75% x $8,000). Since no Sec. 179 expense deduction was taken, there are no other reductions to basis.

12. The Hockenbury Heavenly Hoist Corp. purchased a new truck in 1985 for use in the business. The truck was 5-year recovery property, cost $20,000, and was eligible for an investment tax credit. No Sec. 179 deduction was taken and no election was made to reduce the investment tax credit which was taken. What is the depreciable basis for ACRS?

   a. $20,000.
   b. $19,400.
   c. $19,000.
   d. $18,000.

The correct answer is (c). *(M.F. Premont)*
REQUIRED: The depreciable basis for ACRS of a business asset after claiming an investment tax credit.
DISCUSSION: Since Hockenbury elected to take the full investment tax credit, the original cost of the asset must be reduced by one-half of the amount of the investment tax credit claimed in pre-1986 tax years [Sec. 48(q) prior to amendment]. The investment tax credit was 10% of the qualified investment, which for 5-year property is 100% of the cost. The investment tax credit is 10% x (100% x $20,000), which equals $2,000. Therefore, the depreciable basis is $19,000 ($20,000 − ½ of $2,000). Note: The investment tax credit generally is not available after 1985.

Module 13.2: Depreciable Basis

13. For figuring depreciation on assets acquired after 1985, the basis of investment credit property must be reduced by what percentage of the amount of the regular investment credit taken?

  a. 10%.
  b. 35%.
  c. 50%.
  d. 100%.

14. Mr. Anderson, a sole proprietor, purchased $12,000 worth of office equipment and furniture in 1991 for use in his business. He elected to take the maximum Sec. 179 deduction. What is Mr. Anderson's basis for the Modified ACRS computation?

  a. $12,000.
  b. $7,000.
  c. $2,000.
  d. $0.

15. Mrs. Howser converted her personal residence (originally acquired in 1981) to rental property in 1991. At the time of the change in use, the property had an adjusted basis of $45,000, of which $5,000 was for the land and $40,000 for improvements. The fair market value at the time of the change was $50,000, of which $11,000 was for land and $39,000 for improvements. What is Mrs. Howser's basis for determining depreciation?

  a. $39,000.
  b. $40,000.
  c. $45,000.
  d. $50,000.

16. In 1970, Billy Idoll built his home for $50,000 on a lot that cost $8,000. Before he converted the property to rental use in 1991, he had added $10,000 of permanent improvements and claimed a $3,000 deduction for a casualty loss to the house. Mr. Idoll also paid $20,000 in real estate taxes from 1970 to 1990. On the date of use change, Idoll's property had a fair market value of $72,000, of which $9,000 was for the land and $63,000 for the house. What is Mr. Idoll's basis in the house for depreciation purposes?

  a. $50,000.
  b. $57,000.
  c. $63,000.
  d. $77,000.

The correct answer is (d). *(Publisher)*
REQUIRED: The percentage of the investment credit that reduces the basis of property for computing depreciation.
DISCUSSION: Generally, the investment tax credit is repealed for property placed in service after December 31, 1985. Some taxpayers will still be able to claim the credit after 1985 due to transitional rules. However, the basis of the property must be reduced by 100% of the investment credit taken after 1985 [Sec. 49(d) prior to amendment].

The correct answer is (c). *(SPE 984 I-77)*
REQUIRED: The depreciable basis for Modified ACRS after taking the full Sec. 179 deduction in 1991.
DISCUSSION: The original cost of an asset must be reduced for any Sec. 179 expense. Since Mr. Anderson took the Sec. 179 expense deduction ($10,000 in 1991), he must reduce the cost of his property. Mr. Anderson's depreciable basis is

Original cost	$12,000
Less Sec. 179 deduction	(10,000)
Depreciable basis	$ 2,000

The correct answer is (a). *(SPE 1081 I-83)*
REQUIRED: The depreciable basis of a personal residence converted to rental property.
DISCUSSION: If personal use assets are converted to business or income-producing use, the basis for ACRS and Modified ACRS depreciation is the lower of the adjusted basis or the fair market value when converted [Prop. Reg. 1.168-2(j)(6)]. Only the basis of the house is considered because the land is not depreciable.

Since the fair market value of the house on the date of conversion ($39,000) is less than the adjusted basis ($40,000), the depreciable basis of Mrs. Howser's rental property is $39,000.

The anti-churning rules of Sec. 168(f)(5) do not apply to residential rental property or nonresidential real property [Sec. 168(f)(5)(B)(i)]. Therefore, even though the property was acquired in a pre-MACRS tax year, the MACRS depreciation rules will be used to depreciate the property.

The correct answer is (b). *(SPE 987 I-85)*
REQUIRED: The depreciable basis of a personal residence converted to rental property.
DISCUSSION: Reg. 1.167(g)-1 and Prop. Reg. 1.168-2(j)(6) state that if personal use assets are converted to business or income-producing use, the basis for depreciation is the lower of the adjusted basis or the fair market value when the property is converted. The adjusted basis of the property is its cost under Sec. 1012, plus adjustments under Sec. 1016 for capital expenditures and losses. Since the basis of the house is $57,000 (computed below) and the fair market value is $63,000, Idoll's basis for depreciation is $57,000.

Cost	$50,000
Add improvements	10,000
Less casualty loss	(3,000)
Depreciable basis	$57,000

13.3 Depreciation (Assets Acquired Before 1981)

17. Mr. Lion purchased a new factory building for $300,000 on January 1, 1980. The land was valued at $60,000. The building has an estimated useful life of 50 years. Compute the depreciation for 1991 using the 150%-declining-balance method.

a. $4,996.
b. $5,150.
c. $5,309.
d. $7,200.

The correct answer is (b). *(SPE 1077 III-32)*
REQUIRED: The 1991 depreciation using the 150%-declining-balance method.
DISCUSSION: Under Reg. 1.167(b)-2, declining-balance depreciation is computed by applying a uniform rate to the unrecovered basis of the property. The constant rate of depreciation (applied to the unrecovered basis each year) is 3% (150% x 1/50). The original basis of the building was $240,000 ($300,000 – $60,000). The depreciation amounts are as follows:

Cost		$240,000
Less 1980 depreciation	($240,000 x .03)	(7,200)
Less 1981 depreciation	($232,800 x .03)	(6,984)
Less 1982 depreciation	($225,816 x .03)	(6,774)
Less 1983 depreciation	($219,042 x .03)	(6,571)
Less 1984 depreciation	($212,471 x .03)	(6,374)
Less 1985 depreciation	($206,097 x .03)	(6,183)
Less 1986 depreciation	($199,914 x .03)	(5,997)
Less 1987 depreciation	($193,917 x .03)	(5,817)
Less 1988 depreciation	($188,099 x .03)	(5,643)
Less 1989 depreciation	($182,456 x .03)	(5,474)
Less 1990 depreciation	($176,982 x .03)	(5,309)
Basis at beginning of 1991		$171,674
x uniform rate		x .03
1991 depreciation amount		$ 5,150

18. On June 30, 1980, Sandy Beech, single and a sole proprietor, purchased a new machine for $40,000 to be used in her business. The machine was estimated to have a useful life of 12 years with a salvage value of $3,000. Beech used the straight-line method of depreciation and elected to record additional first-year depreciation in 1980. What is her depreciation expense in 1991?

a. $2,917.
b. $3,083.
c. $3,167.
d. $3,333.

The correct answer is (c). *(CPA 1179 Q-39)*
REQUIRED: The maximum depreciation expense under the straight-line method for 1991.
DISCUSSION: Prior to 1981, Sec. 179 allowed an election of additional first-year depreciation in the year of acquisition of new or used, tangible, depreciable, personal property with a useful life of 6 or more years. The deduction was 20% of the cost of the first $10,000 of qualifying property in any 1 year ($20,000 on a joint return). Beech's additional first-year depreciation was $2,000 (20% x $10,000).

The basis for straight-line depreciation is reduced by both additional first-year depreciation and salvage value. Sec. 167(f) allows the salvage value of personal property with a useful life of 3 years or more to be reduced by 10% of the basis of such property.

Cost	$40,000
Less salvage [$3,000 – (10% x $40,000)]	0
Less additional first-year depreciation	(2,000)
Depreciable basis	$38,000
Divided by estimated useful life	÷ 12
Annual straight-line depreciation	$ 3,167

Module 13.3: Depreciation (Assets Acquired Before 1981)

19. Hutton Corporation purchased new factory equipment that was installed and put in service on December 31, 1980 at a total cost of $112,000. The equipment will be depreciated over 12 years using the sum-of-the-years'-digits method, with no salvage value. Hutton elected to take the additional first-year depreciation deduction. What is the maximum amount that Hutton can deduct as depreciation on its tax return for the year ended December 31, 1991?

a. $1,410.
b. $2,821.
c. $4,230.
d. $9,167.

The correct answer is (b). *(CPA 1180 P-56)*
REQUIRED: The depreciation expense for 1991 using the sum-of-the-years'-digits method and additional first-year depreciation.
DISCUSSION: Prior to 1981, Sec. 179 allowed additional first-year depreciation up to 20% of the cost of the first $10,000 of qualifying property in any one year. Hutton's additional first-year depreciation is $2,000 (20% x $10,000), which reduces the basis of the property in computing ordinary depreciation.
Reg. 1.167(b)-3(a) states that annual depreciation under the sum-of-the-years'-digits method is computed by applying changing fractions to the cost of the property reduced by estimated salvage value. The fraction is the remaining life at the beginning of the year divided by the sum-of-the-years'-digits of the estimated life of the asset.

Cost	$112,000
Less additional first-year depreciation	(2,000)
Depreciable base	$110,000
SYD fraction*	2/78
1991 depreciation	$ 2,821

*Remaining life at beginning of year/SYD,
where: SYD = $n(n + 1)/2$, and
n = estimated useful life.

20. Mr. Pig purchased a new machine on January 1, 1980. The machine cost $20,000, has a useful life of 12 years, and has a salvage value at the end of 12 years of $2,000. If Mr. Pig did not elect additional first-year depreciation and no election was made to switch to straight-line depreciation at any time, what is his depreciation for 1991 under the 200%-declining-balance method?

a. $0.
b. $538.
c. $1,667.
d. $2,691.

The correct answer is (d). *(SPE 1077 III-20)*
REQUIRED: The 1991 depreciation using the 200%-declining-balance method.
DISCUSSION: The constant rate of depreciation (applied to the unrecovered basis each year) is 16.67% (200% x 1/12 years). 1991 is the twelfth year, so the remaining basis is depreciated in 1991. The problem of decreased depreciation in later years and a large last year depreciation amount is why an election to switch to straight-line is available when it will exceed declining balance so the later years can be depreciated at an even amount.

Cost		$20,000
Less 1980 depreciation	($20,000 x 16.67%)	(3,334)
Less 1981 depreciation	($16,666 x 16.67%)	(2,778)
Less 1982 depreciation	($13,888 x 16.67%)	(2,315)
Less 1983 depreciation	($11,573 x 16.67%)	(1,929)
Less 1984 depreciation	($9,644 x 16.67%)	(1,608)
Less 1985 depreciation	($8,036 x 16.67%)	(1,340)
Less 1986 depreciation	($6,696 x 16.67%)	(1,116)
Less 1987 depreciation	($5,580 x 16.67%)	(930)
Less 1988 depreciation	($4,650 x 16.67%)	(775)
Less 1989 depreciation	($3,875 x 16.67%)	(646)
Less 1990 depreciation	($3,229 x 16.67%)	(538)
Basis at beginning of 1991		$ 2,691

13.4 Election to Expense

21. Taxpayers can elect to treat all or part of the cost of qualifying property as a currently deductible expense rather than as a capital expenditure. The maximum annual amount of this capital expensing deduction for 1991 is

a. $5,000.
b. $7,500.
c. $10,000.
d. 10% of the total cost of qualified property placed into service.

The correct answer is (c). *(CMA 685 3-1)*
REQUIRED: The maximum amount deductible under Sec. 179 for 1991.
DISCUSSION: Sec. 179 allows a taxpayer to treat all or part of the cost of Sec. 179 property as an expense which is deducted, not charged to the capital account. Sec. 179 property is defined as any tangible property subject to depreciation, which is Sec. 1245 property, and acquired by purchase for use in a trade or business. Property acquired for investment will not qualify.
The maximum cost each year for 1991 that may be taken into account under Sec. 179 and deducted is $10,000.

22. All of the following statements regarding the Sec. 179 deduction are true except:

a. The amount that is not deductible due to the taxable income limitation can be carried forward.
b. The amount expensed cannot exceed the taxable income derived from any trade or business during the tax year.
c. The maximum deductible amount is reduced if property placed in service during the tax year exceeds $200,000.
d. The maximum cost that is deductible for a tax year is $5,000.

The correct answer is (d). *(SPE 990 II-37)*
REQUIRED: The false statement concerning Sec. 179 expense.
DISCUSSION: There are several limitations on the deduction allowed by Sec. 179. One limitation is taxable income and to the extent that causes an amount to be nondeductible, such amount may be carried forward to be deducted in future years. This carryover is subject to all the limitations as if it was an expense of the current year. The maximum cost that is deductible for a tax year is $10,000 (before 1987 it was $5,000). This amount is reduced if the Sec. 179 property placed in service during the year exceeds $200,000.
Answers (a), (b), and (c) are incorrect because each is a true statement.

23. On July 1, 1990, Ms. K, who is single and owns and operates a specialty shop, paid $15,000 for a new automobile which she uses 60% of the time for business purposes. She purchased no other business assets in 1990. The taxable income of the business before the Sec. 179 deduction is $20,000. What is the maximum allowable Sec. 179 deduction that Ms. K may elect to take in 1990?

a. $1,596.
b. $2,660.
c. $3,000.
d. $9,000.

The correct answer is (a). *(SPE 986 II-65)*
REQUIRED: The Sec. 179 expense deduction in 1990.
DISCUSSION: Sec. 179 allows a taxpayer to treat up to $10,000 of the cost each year of Sec. 179 property acquired after 1986 as an expense. Only the 60% portion of the automobile used for business will qualify, however. Therefore, the Sec. 179 expense would normally be $9,000 (60% x $15,000).
But Sec. 280F limits the first year capital recovery deduction for automobiles to $2,660 for 1990 (Rev. Proc. 90-22). The capital recovery deductions include the amount expensed under Sec. 179 and depreciation. This amount must be reduced by personal use for the automobile during the year. The redetermined amount is the limit times the percentage of business/investment use during the year ($1,596 = $2,660 x .60).
Author's Note: A new Revenue Procedure is published each year with the inflation-adjusted limits for Sec. 280F. At the publication date the inflation-adjusted numbers for 1991 were unavailable.

Module 13.4: Election to Expense

24. Ellwood and Elmo were equal partners in a used guitar store. In 1991, they bought a used amplifier for use in the store to demonstrate guitars. The amplifier cost $25,000. The taxable income of the business before the Sec. 179 deduction is $20,000. How much Sec. 179 expense can Ellwood and Elmo each deduct in 1991 if neither has any other Sec. 179 deductions?

a. $0.
b. $5,000.
c. $10,000.
d. $12,500.

The correct answer is (b). *(Publisher)*
REQUIRED: The cost of used property partners can expense in the year of acquisition.
DISCUSSION: Sec. 179 allows a taxpayer to elect to treat all or part of the cost of Sec. 179 property as an expense. Sec. 179 property is any tangible property, subject to depreciation, which is Sec. 1245 property, and acquired by purchase for use in a trade or business. It does not matter that the property is used. The maximum amount that may be taken into account for this election is $10,000. This limit applies both to the partnership and to each partner [Sec. 179(d)(8)]. Hence, the total amount that the partnership can deduct is $10,000, or $5,000 each for Ellwood and Elmo.

25. In 1991, Walt Sheen purchased and placed in service a packaging machine at a cost of $204,000. He had $3,000 taxable income from his business before considering the deduction allowed under Sec. 179. What is Walt's allowable Sec. 179 deduction for 1991?

a. $10,000.
b. $6,000.
c. $3,000.
d. $0.

The correct answer is (c). *(SPE 990 II-36)*
REQUIRED: The Sec. 179 expense deduction for 1991.
DISCUSSION: Sec. 179 allows a taxpayer to treat up to $10,000 of the cost each year of Sec. 179 property acquired after 1986 as an expense rather than as a capital expenditure. There are certain limitations that can reduce the allowable deduction. One limitation is that the amount deductible under Sec. 179 must be reduced by the amount by which the cost of Sec. 179 property placed in service during the year exceeds $200,000. Walt's deduction is reduced from $10,000 to $6,000 by this limitation. Another limitation is that the total cost that can be deducted is limited to the taxable income from the active conduct of any trade or business during the tax year. Walt had only $3,000 of taxable income. Because this amount is smaller than either the general rule or the limitation based on property placed in service, his deduction is limited to $3,000. The remaining $3,000 ($6,000 – $3,000) may be carried forward to 1992.

26. Kell Corporation's financial accounting income for 1991 includes operating expenses of $4,000 for depreciation of a machine that Kell purchased and placed in service in January 1991 for use in the active conduct of Kell's business. This machine cost $32,000 and has an estimated useful life of 8 years, with no salvage value. No other fixed assets were acquired during 1991. Kell has taxable income and wishes to minimize its 1991 income tax to the fullest possible extent. The proper election was made in connection with the tax treatment of this machine in Kell's 1991 income tax return. Kell's book income before tax for 1991 is $76,000. No other differences between book and tax income exist for 1991. How much can Kell expense under Sec. 179?

a. $0.
b. $5,000.
c. $10,000.
d. $32,000.

The correct answer is (c). *(CPA 1189 Q-46)*
REQUIRED: The Sec. 179 expense deduction for 1991.
DISCUSSION: If a firm wishes to minimize its taxable income for a given year, a Sec. 179 deduction may be made. Sec. 179 allows a taxpayer to elect to treat all or part of the cost of Sec. 179 property as an expense. The maximum amount that may be taken into account under this election is $10,000.

Module 13.5: Depreciation (Assets Acquired 1981 - 1986)

27. Raccoon Tails, Ltd. processes furs for clothing. Raccoon purchased a new hide stripper in 1991 for $20,000. It is 5-year recovery property. Raccoon claimed the maximum expense under Sec. 179. The hide stripper was its only asset acquisition for 1991. Raccoon Tails reports taxable income of $60,000 excluding depreciation for 1991. What is Raccoon's basis for Modified ACRS depreciation?

   a. $10,000.
   b. $12,000.
   c. $15,000.
   d. $20,000.

The correct answer is (a). *(Publisher)*
REQUIRED: The basis for depreciation of property on which an election to use the Sec. 179 expensing has been made.
DISCUSSION: The basis for computing the Modified ACRS depreciation is reduced by the $10,000 election to expense part of the asset's cost under Sec. 179. Thus, the depreciable basis is $10,000 ($20,000 cost − $10,000 Sec. 179 expense).

28. Pat is married and files a joint return. In November 1990, Pat purchased a new car for $10,000 that was used 30% for business. No other assets were purchased in 1990 by Pat for use in his business. Pat's Sec. 179 expense deduction, should he so elect, is $3,000.

The correct answer is (F). *(SPE 1083 I-26)*
DISCUSSION: Sec. 280F(a) limits depreciation on automobiles acquired in 1990 to $2,660 in the first year. Sec. 179 expense is treated as depreciation under Sec. 280F. But Sec. 280F limits the first year deduction for automobiles to $2,660 in 1990 (Rev. Proc. 90-22). This amount must be reduced by personal usage of the automobile during the year. The redetermined limit on depreciation in the first year for Pat is the limit times the percentage of business/investment use during the year ($798 = $2,660 x .30).

13.5 Depreciation (Assets Acquired 1981 - 1986)

29. Which of the following is a correct statement concerning the Accelerated Cost Recovery System (ACRS), for assets placed in service after 1980 but before 1987?

   a. Either ACRS or depreciation under IRC Sec. 167 can be elected.
   b. Depreciation under IRC Sec. 167 is no longer used.
   c. ACRS uses the half-year convention for properties other than 19-year real property.
   d. A taxpayer may change from Sec. 167 depreciation to ACRS.

The correct answer is (c). *(SPE 990 I-40)*
REQUIRED: The correct statement concerning the Accelerated Cost Recovery System (ACRS).
DISCUSSION: ACRS applies to all tangible property subject to depreciation which is placed in service after 1980. For other than real property, ACRS is applied by the use of tables which have the 150%-declining-balance method and the half-year convention built into them. The asset is treated as if placed in service at mid-year. No cost recovery (depreciation) is allowed in the year of disposition.
Answer (a) is incorrect because ACRS is mandatory for depreciable, tangible property placed in service after 1980. Answer (b) is incorrect because depreciation under Sec. 167 still applies to property placed in service prior to 1981 and to intangible property (depreciation of intangibles is sometimes called amortization). Answer (d) is incorrect because a taxpayer may not use ACRS for property placed in service prior to 1981 and no change is allowed.

30. On July 1, 1986, Mr. Fink, a calendar-year taxpayer, purchased and placed in service a new piece of equipment costing $32,000. This equipment is 5-year recovery property and he estimates the salvage value to be $5,000. Fink does not elect to take the Sec. 179 deduction. What is Fink's depreciation deduction for the equipment for 1990?

   a. $4,800.
   b. $5,400.
   c. $6,400.
   d. $6,720.

The correct answer is (d). *(SPE 986 II-63)*
REQUIRED: The cost recovery (depreciation) deduction in 1990 for property acquired in 1986.
DISCUSSION: Under Sec. 168(b) prior to the 1986 TRA, the depreciation on recovery property was computed by applying the applicable percentage in the table to the unadjusted basis of recovery property. The investment tax credit is generally not available for assets purchased after 1985.
As a result, Fink's unadjusted basis for depreciation is $32,000. Salvage value is not taken into account. The applicable percentage for 5-year recovery property in the fifth year is 21%. Accordingly, Fink's depreciation deduction for 1990 is $6,720 (21% x $32,000).

31. Alpha Corporation purchased new office furniture costing $125,000 on January 2, 1986. The assets have a 15-year useful life. Salvage value was estimated at $15,000. Assuming this was the only asset purchase that Alpha made in 1986 and that the maximum Sec. 179 expense deduction was claimed, compute the maximum depreciation for 1990.

  a. $18,000.
  b. $25,200.
  c. $26,250.
  d. $26,400.

The correct answer is (b). *(CMA 1282 3-10)*
REQUIRED: The maximum cost recovery (depreciation) deduction in the fifth year for property placed in service in 1986.
DISCUSSION: Prior to 1987, the maximum Sec. 179 deduction was $5,000. The amount expensed reduces the basis used for depreciation. The investment tax credit is generally not available for assets purchased after 1985.
Alpha's depreciation (cost recovery) deduction was the applicable percentage in the table [former Sec. 168(b)] times the unadjusted basis of the recovery property. Office furniture is 5-year recovery property. In the fifth year, the applicable percentage for 5-year recovery property is 21%. Therefore, Alpha's 1990 depreciation is $25,200 [21% x ($125,000 − $5,000 Sec. 179 expense)].

32. Mike Wright bought a marina in Florida on September 15, 1982. The purchase price was allocated among the land, buildings, and other personal property. The part of the price allocated to the buildings was $225,000. What is Wright's maximum depreciation deduction on the buildings in 1991?

  a. $11,250.
  b. $13,500.
  c. $15,750.
  d. $18,000.

The correct answer is (a). *(Publisher)*
REQUIRED: The maximum amount of 1991 cost recovery (depreciation) under ACRS for real property acquired in 1982.
DISCUSSION: For real property acquired after 1980 and before March 16, 1984, former Sec. 168(c)(2)(D) defined 15-year real property as Sec. 1250 class property which does not have a present class life of 12.5 years or less. Under old Sec. 168(b)(2), 15-year real property is depreciated in accordance with tables which approximate the use of 175%-declining-balance method. Under the tables, the applicable percentage to be applied to the unadjusted basis of the real property is 5% for the tenth year if placed in service in the ninth month of the year of acquisition. Wright's maximum depreciation deduction in 1991 is $11,250 (5% x $225,000).

33. Bearcat, Inc. purchased a building for $750,000 on April 6, 1984. Useful life was estimated to be 40 years and salvage value was estimated at $50,000. If Bearcat elected the optional straight-line method under the Accelerated Cost Recovery System for federal income tax purposes (using the shortest possible life), the 1991 cost recovery deduction would be

  a. $31,250.
  b. $41,667.
  c. $50,000.
  d. $52,500.

The correct answer is (b). *(CMA 682 3-3)*
REQUIRED: The maximum ACRS deduction in 1991 under the optional straight-line method for property acquired in 1984.
DISCUSSION: Former Sec. 168(b)(3) provided that a taxpayer may elect to use the straight-line method over the recovery period. Sec. 168(c) defines real property acquired after March 15, 1984 and before May 9, 1985 as 18-year real property. 18-year real property could be depreciated over 18, 35, or 45 years. Salvage value is ignored under ACRS. The ACRS deduction is

$$\frac{\text{Unadjusted basis}}{\text{Recovery period}} = \frac{\$750,000}{18 \text{ yrs.}}$$
$$= \$41,667$$

Editor's Note: If the published ACRS tables for 18-year property (straight-line method, no mid-month convention) were used, the depreciation would be $45,000 (.06 x $750,000) [Source: Notice 84-16, (I.R.B. 1984-52) Table 18.].

34. For real property (other than low-income housing) with a class life greater than 12.5 years and acquired after May 8, 1985 but before January 1, 1987, what is the statutory recovery period?

   a. 18 years.
   b. 19 years.
   c. 22 years.
   d. 25 years.

The correct answer is (b). *(Publisher)*
REQUIRED: The recovery period for real property acquired between May 8, 1985 and December 31, 1986.
DISCUSSION: Prior to the 1986 TRA, Sec. 168(c)(2)(D) defined the recovery period for real property with a class life greater than 12.5 years and which was not low income housing. For property acquired from January 1, 1981 through March 15, 1984, the recovery period was 15 years. From March 16, 1984 through May 8, 1985, it was 18 years. From May 9, 1985 through December 31, 1986, it was 19 years.

13.6 Depreciation (Assets Acquired after 1986)

35. Which of the following is a correct statement concerning the Modified Accelerated Cost Recovery System (MACRS) for assets acquired after 1986?

   a. The 200%-declining-balance method is used for all property except 27.5-year and 31.5-year property.
   b. An election to use the straight-line method may be made on an annual basis, but only for an entire class of assets.
   c. The alternative depreciation system allows a choice of recovery periods for each class of assets.
   d. For 3-year through 10-year property, only 200%-declining-balance and straight-line methods are available.

The correct answer is (b). *(Publisher)*
REQUIRED: The correct statement about MACRS after the 1986 TRA.
DISCUSSION: ACRS is called Modified Accelerated Cost Recovery System (MACRS) after 1986. Generally for personal property acquired after 1986, MACRS uses the 200%-declining-balance method over a prescribed recovery period. Straight-line depreciation may be elected in any year for one or more classes of property in lieu of the accelerated method. This election is irrevocable once made and must be made for all assets acquired that year in a particular class of property, not on an asset-by-asset basis.
Answer (a) is incorrect because the 200%-declining-balance method is used for 3-year through 10-year property; the 150%-declining-balance method is used for 15-year and 20-year property, and the straight-line method for 27.5-year and 31.5-year property. Answer (c) is incorrect because the alternative depreciation system (used for property predominantly used outside the U.S., tax-exempt use property, etc.) uses different (longer) recovery periods than MACRS, but there is only one for each class of property. Answer (d) is incorrect because a taxpayer may use (for regular tax purposes) the alternative depreciation system used in computing the alternative minimum tax which uses the 150%-declining balance method.

36. All of the following statements regarding the alternative MACRS depreciation system are true except:

   a. The election to use the alternative MACRS system can be revoked.
   b. The election must be made by the due date, including extensions, for the tax return of the year in which the property was placed in service.
   c. The alternative MACRS depreciation system is figured using straight-line method, no salvage value and the class life of the asset or 12 years if no class life is assigned.
   d. Excluding nonresidential real and residential rental property, the election of the alternative MACRS depreciation system for a class of property applies to all property in that class that is placed in service during the tax year of the election.

The correct answer is (a). *(SPE 990 II-38)*
REQUIRED: The incorrect statement regarding the alternative MACRS depreciation system.
DISCUSSION: For personal property acquired after 1986, MACRS uses the 200%-declining-balance method over a prescribed recovery period. The alternative MACRS depreciation system of Sec. 168(g) may be elected in any year for one or more classes of property in lieu of the regular method or the straight-line method of Sec. 168(b)(5). The alternative depreciation system uses the straight-line method over a recovery period established in Sec. 168(g)(2) which is generally longer than that used under regular MACRS. However, this election is irrevocable once made [Sec. 168(g)(7)(B)] and must be made for all assets acquired that year in a particular class of property. Nonresidential real property and residential rental property elections are made on a property-by-property basis.
Answers (b), (c), and (d) are incorrect because each is a true statement regarding the alternative MACRS depreciation system.

37. The changes to ACRS by the 1986 TRA generally apply to property placed in service after 1986. Which of the following is a false statement about exceptions to this general rule?

   a. An election may be made to apply the pre-1986 TRA rules to property placed in service after 1986.
   b. An election may be made to apply the 1986 TRA rules to property placed in service after July 31, 1986.
   c. If a taxpayer leased property in 1985 and 1986 and then purchases it after 1986, MACRS generally may not be used if it allows more depreciation in the first year than ACRS would.
   d. If a taxpayer is not allowed to use MACRS because of the antichurning rules, depreciation must be computed using whatever method was already being used for the property.

The correct answer is (a). *(Publisher)*
REQUIRED: The false statement concerning application of the 1986 TRA changes to ACRS.
DISCUSSION: There is no election available to apply prior law to property placed in service after 1986.
Answer (b) is incorrect because the transition rules did provide an election to apply MACRS to property placed in service after July 31, 1986. Answer (c) is incorrect because the antichurning rules generally prevent taxpayers from using MACRS when it provides more generous depreciation for property the taxpayer owned or used prior to MACRS. Answer (d) is incorrect because if the antichurning rules apply, depreciation is to be determined under whatever depreciation rule was being used before MACRS. This could be ACRS or Sec. 167 depreciation prior to 1981.

38. For depreciation purposes, the half-year convention means that

   a. Depreciation can be claimed in the first tax year of the life of the asset only if the asset is placed in service on or before June 30.
   b. Only one-half of the capital expensing deduction (Sec. 179) can be used.
   c. Only one-half of the full annual depreciation deduction will be allowable in the first tax year of the life of the asset regardless of when the asset is purchased or placed in service during the year.
   d. Depreciation can be claimed in the last tax year of the life of the asset only if the asset is disposed of after June 30.

The correct answer is (c). *(SPE 989 II-38)*
REQUIRED: The correct meaning of the half-year convention.
DISCUSSION: The half-year convention applies to all property placed in service after 1986 except for residential rental and nonresidential real property (to which the mid-month convention applies) and except when the mid-quarter convention applies (see next question). Under the half-year convention, all property to which it applies is treated as placed in service or disposed of at the mid-point of the year.
Answers (a) and (d) are incorrect because they describe the modified half-year convention which is no longer used for tax purposes. Answer (b) is incorrect because the half-year convention only applies to depreciation. The Sec. 179 expensing deduction is available regardless of when the property is purchased or placed in service during the year.

39. In November 1991, Weasleduck, Inc. placed in service 3-year property with a cost of $100,000. The only other property placed in service in 1991 was a piece of machinery with a cost of $50,000. In computing the depreciation deduction for 1991 calendar year, Weasleduck, Inc. must use the

   a. Half-year convention.
   b. Mid-month convention.
   c. Mid-quarter convention.
   d. Full year convention.

The correct answer is (c). *(Publisher)*
REQUIRED: The applicable convention used when a substantial amount of property is placed in service during November.
DISCUSSION: Normally, the half-year convention is required for 3-year property. But Sec. 168(d)(3) provides that when substantial property is placed in service during the last 3 months of the year, the mid-quarter convention must be used for all property placed in service during such year. Substantial property is defined as greater than 40% of the aggregate bases of property placed in service during the year. The $100,000 of 3-year property constitutes 66.66% ($100,000 ÷ $150,000) of all property placed in service that year, so the mid-quarter convention must be used.

Module 13.6: Depreciation (Assets Acquired after 1986)

40. A business auto that is purchased and placed in service in 1991 is classified under the modified accelerated cost recovery system as

a. 3-year property/with annual limitations.
b. 3-year property/without annual limitations.
c. 5-year property/with annual limitations.
d. 5-year property/without annual limitations.

The correct answer is (c). *(SPE 988 II-40)*
REQUIRED: The correct classification of an automobile used in business.
DISCUSSION: Sec. 168(e)(3)(B) specifically provides that an automobile is 5-year property. Sec. 280F(a)(1) provides annual limitations on the amount of depreciation each year for automobiles.
Answer (a) is incorrect because automobiles are 5-year property. Answer (b) is incorrect because automobiles are 5-year property and there are annual limitations on the depreciation. Answer (d) is incorrect because there are annual limitations on the depreciation.

41. Which of the following is a correct statement concerning depreciation of automobiles placed in service in 1990?

a. The amount of depreciation and Sec. 179 expense is limited to $2,660 in the first year.
b. The amount of depreciation is limited to $2,660 per year.
c. If the automobile is used 50% or less for business use, no depreciation is allowed.
d. If the use of an automobile for business decreases to 50% or less after the first year, only the current and subsequent years' depreciation will be affected.

The correct answer is (a). *(Publisher)*
REQUIRED: The correct statement concerning depreciation of automobiles placed in service after 1986.
DISCUSSION: Sec. 280(F) limits the depreciation on automobiles. The maximum amount of depreciation deductible for automobiles acquired in 1990 in the first year is $2,660. The Sec. 179 expense amount is treated as depreciation for this purpose, so the two combined are limited to $2,660 in the first year. This amount is reduced if business use is less than 100%.
Answer (b) is incorrect because depreciation after the first year is limited to $4,200 in the second year, $2,550 in the third year, and $1,475 per year thereafter. Answer (c) is incorrect because depreciation for an automobile used 50% or less in business is computed by the alternative depreciation system. Answer (d) is incorrect because if an automobile's use decreases to 50% or less in subsequent years, any depreciation in prior years in excess of the alternative depreciation system is included in gross income for the years in which the business use decreased to 50% or less.

42. In 1990, Master Corporation provided each one of its salesmen with a new automobile costing $25,000. The automobiles are used 100% of the time in the business. Assuming Master elected a half-year convention in 1990, the maximum 1991 depreciation deduction the corporation may take for any one car is

a. $4,200.
b. $4,100.
c. $2,660.
d. $2,560.

The correct answer is (a). *(CMA 689 3-25)*
REQUIRED: The maximum second-year depreciation deduction for an automobile.
DISCUSSION: Sec. 280F(a) limits the depreciation deduction for an automobile placed in service in 1990 to $2,660 for the first year, $4,200 for the second year, $2,550 for the third year, and $1,475 for each succeeding year (Rev. Proc. 90-22).

Module 13.6: Depreciation (Assets Acquired after 1986)

43. On March 15, 1991, Mr. Driver, a calendar-year taxpayer, purchased and placed in service a fleet of light trucks to be used in his business. Each truck has an ADR mid-point of 8 years. The trucks cost $300,000, and their salvage value is estimated to be 10% of cost. What is the Modified ACRS depreciation deduction for 1991?

a. $37,500.
b. $60,000.
c. $90,000.
d. $120,000.

The correct answer is (b). *(SPE 989 II-65)*
REQUIRED: The 1991 MACRS depreciation deduction for property acquired in 1991.
DISCUSSION: Light duty trucks are now 5-year property subject to the 200%-declining-balance method. Salvage value is treated as zero, the half-year convention applies in the year of acquisition, and the Sec. 179 expensing election is phased out when qualifying property of $210,000 or more is acquired. Driver's depreciation calculation is

Cost	$300,000
200% D.B.	x .4
	$120,000
1/2 yr. convention	x .5
1991 depreciation	$ 60,000

The same amount can be determined using the MACRS tables.

44. Cub Corporation purchased an automated tube bender for $500,000 in 1990. The tube bender, used to manufacture folding chairs, has an estimated life of 10 years and an estimated salvage value of $60,000. It is 5-year property under the MACRS rules. Cub's taxable income for 1991 before the depreciation deduction is $120,000. The maximum depreciation for tax purposes in 1991 is

a. $100,000.
b. $117,600.
c. $120,000.
d. $160,000.

The correct answer is (d). *(CMA 1282 3-9)*
REQUIRED: The maximum depreciation in the second year of use for property acquired in 1990.
DISCUSSION: The depreciation on property under MACRS is computed by applying the applicable method for the class of property to the unadjusted basis of the property ($500,000). There is no Sec. 179 expense deduction because it is phased out when qualifying property of $210,000 or more is acquired.

The applicable depreciation method for 7-year property is the 200%-declining-balance method. As an alternative to computing the depreciation each year on the adjusted basis, then subtracting the depreciation, and the next year recomputing depreciation on the remaining basis, the IRS has developed tables of percentages to apply to the original unadjusted basis. These percentages in effect compute the depreciation at the 200%-declining-balance method. The percentage for 5-year property in the second year is 32%. Therefore, Cub's maximum amount of deductible depreciation for 1991 is $160,000 (32% x $500,000).

45. On April 1, 1989, Mr. C purchased office furniture costing $10,000. The furniture has an ADR midpoint life of 10 years and is 7-year property under the MACRS rules. Mr. C purchased no other assets during 1989 and did not elect a Sec. 179 deduction. What is C's maximum amount of deductible depreciation for 1991?

a. $1,429.
b. $1,440.
c. $1,457.
d. $1,749.

The correct answer is (d). *(SPE 987 II-69)*
REQUIRED: The maximum depreciation in the third year of use for property acquired in 1989.
DISCUSSION: The depreciation on property under MACRS is computed by applying the applicable method for the class of property to the unadjusted basis of the property. The applicable method for 7-year property is the 200%-declining-balance method. Using the IRS table for the 200%-declining-balance method and the half-year convention described in the answer to the preceding question, the percentage in the third year is 17.49%. Therefore, C's maximum amount of deductible depreciation for 1991 is $1,749 (17.49% x $10,000).

Module 13.6: Depreciation (Assets Acquired after 1986)

46. Mainstream Company purchased depreciable equipment in 1990 for $20,000 and claimed the maximum Sec. 179 deduction. The equipment qualified as 5-year property under MACRS. Mainstream sold all of this equipment on June 30, 1991. What is the amount of Mainstream's MACRS deduction for 1991?

a. $0.
b. $1,600.
c. $3,200.
d. $6,400.

The correct answer is (b). *(SPE 990 II-66)*
REQUIRED: The amount of MACRS depreciation in the year of disposition of property acquired after 1986.
DISCUSSION: The deduction for MACRS depreciation is calculated using the 200%-declining-balance method for 5-year property. The basis is reduced by $10,000 (the Sec. 179 deduction). The half-year convention allows one-half year depreciation in the year of acquisition and one-half year depreciation in the year of disposition. Therefore, Mainsteam's 1991 MACRS depreciation is $1,600.

Cost of equipment	$20,000
Less Sec. 179 deduction	(10,000)
Depreciable basis	$10,000
X MACRS percentage (5-year property, Year 2)	x 32%
	$ 3,200
Times one-half (half-year convention)	x .50
1991 depreciation	$ 1,600

The 1991 depreciation amount can also be determined by using the MACRS tables.

47. On January 2, 1991, Mr. Quick, a sole proprietor, purchased a new van to be used in his business. He traded in a used van with an adjusted basis of $2,500 and paid $7,500 cash. He did not elect a Sec. 179 deduction for the van. What is Quick's allowable depreciation deduction for 1991?

a. $2,500.
b. $2,000.
c. $1,500.
d. $1,000.

The correct answer is (b). *(SPE 989 II-64)*
REQUIRED: The allowable depreciation deduction for the year of purchase using the Modified ACRS rules.
DISCUSSION: Under Sec. 168(i), the Modified ACRS percentages are applied to property placed in service after December 31, 1986. Mr. Quick's basis in the new van is determined under the like-kind exchange rules [Sec. 1031(d)]. The basis is $10,000 ($2,500 substituted basis + $7,500 cash). Cars and light trucks (including vans) are specifically included in the 5-year class of property under MACRS. Quick's allowable depreciation deduction can be determined from the MACRS tables as follows for 1991

$$\$10,000 \times 20\% = \$2,000$$

48. On January 1, 1991, Mr. Long purchased and placed in service a passenger automobile that cost $10,000 and qualified as a 100% business vehicle. Long did not elect a Sec. 179 deduction but did make the election to use the alternative MACRS depreciation system. What is Mr. Long's allowable MACRS deduction for 1991?

a. $1,000.
b. $2,000.
c. $3,334.
d. $3,560.

The correct answer is (a). *(SPE 990 II-67)*
REQUIRED: The depreciation deduction for 1991 using the alternative depreciation system.
DISCUSSION: Sec. 168(g)(7) allows a taxpayer to elect the alternative depreciation system. The half-year convention still applies and the election applies for all items in that class of property placed in service during the tax year. The straight-line method is used and the recovery period for automobiles is 5 years [Sec. 168(g)(3)(D)]. Long's depreciation deduction for 1991 is

$$½ \times (\$10,000 \div 5 \text{ years}) = \$1,000$$

49. J acquired a new light-duty truck on January 1 for use in his business. The truck cost $10,000, had an estimated salvage value of $1,500, and a 4-year estimated useful life. If the year were 1980, J would use straight-line depreciation and minimal permitted salvage. If the year were 1991, J would use an accelerated method under MACRS. By how much would J's depreciation deduction in 1991 exceed (fall below) that available in 1980 under these alternatives? Assume that no additional first-year depreciation is taken and that no election to expense (Sec. 179) part of the cost is made under either alternative.

a. $375.
b. $125.
c. $0.
d. ($375).

The correct answer is (d). *(J.G. Burns)*
REQUIRED: The difference between Sec. 167 depreciation and Sec. 168 (MACRS) depreciation.
DISCUSSION: Sec. 167(f) provides that for personal property with a useful life of at least 3 years, salvage value may be reduced by 10% of the basis. Therefore, salvage value is $500 ($1,500 − $1,000), and the basis for straight-line depreciation is $9,500 ($10,000 − $500 salvage value). J's depreciation for 1980 would have been $2,375 ($9,500 ÷ 4 years).
Under Sec. 168, salvage value is not taken into account. The light-duty truck is 5-year property under Sec. 168(e). The applicable method for 5-year property is the 200%-declining-balance method with a half-year convention, so J's 1991 ACRS depreciation would be $2,000 ($10,000 x 40% x 1/2).

1991 ACRS depreciation	$2,000
1980 Sec. 167 depreciation	(2,375)
Difference in methods	$ (375)

50. Ichabod Crane purchased a mechanical horse on January 1, 1990 to use at his riding academy in Sleepy Hollow. He paid $5,000 cash and signed a promissory note for $15,000. The horse was 5-year recovery property and Ichabod elected to use the straight-line method over 5 years to depreciate it. What is Ichabod's basis in the horse at the end of 1991?

a. $3,000.
b. $9,000.
c. $14,000.
d. $16,000.

The correct answer is (c). *(Publisher)*
REQUIRED: The basis of property acquired by becoming personally liable on a debt.
DISCUSSION: The original basis of property is its cost (Sec. 1012), which is reduced by depreciation allowable [Sec. 1016(a)(2)]. The cost of property includes debt on which the purchaser is personally liable since (s)he will be legally obligated to pay this amount. Accordingly, the original basis of the mechanical horse was $20,000 ($5,000 cash + $15,000 debt).
Under Sec. 168, 5-year recovery property may be depreciated on the straight-line method over 5 years. Ichabod's annual depreciation is $4,000 ($20,000 divided by 5 years). Because the property is treated as having been acquired at mid-year in the year of acquisition [Sec. 168(d)(1)], Ichabod's total depreciation at the end of the second year will be $6,000 ($2,000 in the first year + $4,000 in the second year). The basis of the property will be $14,000 ($20,000 cost − $6,000 depreciation).

51. Residential rental property that was placed in service during 1991 using the modified accelerated cost recovery system (MACRS) is depreciated over how many years, using which depreciation method and convention?

a. 15 years, 150%-declining-balance method, half-year convention.
b. 27.5 years, straight-line method, mid-month convention.
c. 31.5 years, straight-line method, mid-month convention.
d. 40 years, 200%-declining-balance method, half-year convention.

The correct answer is (b). *(SPE 989 I-45)*
REQUIRED: The proper recovery period and method for residential real property.
DISCUSSION: Sec. 168(c) provides that the recovery period for residential rental property is 27.5 years. Sec. 168(b)(3) provides that the straight-line method shall be used for residential rental property. Sec. 168(d)(2) provides that mid-month convention shall be used for residential rental property.
Answers (a) and (d) are incorrect because the recovery period is 27.5 years, straight-line method is used, and the mid-month convention applies. Answer (c) is incorrect because the recovery period is 27.5 years.

52. The rock group Redhead bought a studio on July 20, 1991 to record their albums. The purchase price was $900,000 exclusive of land (located in California). The studio has a useful life of 50 years. What is Redhead's maximum cost recovery deduction in 1991?

a. $0.
b. $13,095.
c. $31,500.
d. $36,000.

The correct answer is (b). *(Publisher)*
REQUIRED: The maximum depreciation under MACRS on nonresidential real property acquired in 1991.
DISCUSSION: Under Sec. 168, tangible property is depreciable under the recovery period assigned, regardless of actual useful life. Nonresidential real property is depreciated on the straight-line method over 31.5 years using the assumption that all property is placed in service at mid-month. For nonresidential real property placed in service in July, Redhead's cost recovery deduction is $13,095 [($900,000 ÷ 31.5 years) x (5.5 ÷ 12)]. The same amount can be derived from the MACRS tables (Table 7). The calculation using Table 7 is as follows:

$$13,095 = \$900,000 \times .01455.$$

53. The Bearcat Corporation purchased an apartment building in October 1991. The cost of the building was $4,000,000 and its estimated life was 40 years. Corporate management wants to know the alternative methods of deducting the cost of the building for tax purposes. The company may use the straight-line method over 27.5 years or can elect to use the

a. Straight-line method over a recovery period of 35 or 45 years.
b. Straight-line method over a recovery period of any length between 27.5 and 45 years.
c. Straight-line method over a recovery period of 40 years.
d. Declining-balance method at 125% of the straight-line rate using a recovery period of 27.5 or 40 years.

The correct answer is (c). *(CMA 1283 3-4)*
REQUIRED: The alternative method(s) of depreciating a building acquired in 1991.
DISCUSSION: Apartment buildings acquired after 1986 are classified as residential rental property and are normally depreciated in accordance with the straight-line method over 27.5 years. A taxpayer may elect to use the straight-line method over 40 years for real property under the alternative depreciation system.

Answers (a) and (b) are incorrect because only 27.5 and 40 years are permissible recovery periods. Answer (d) is incorrect because the declining-balance method at 125% of straight-line is not permissible.

54. Mr. Z purchased a single family rental house and placed it in service on April 25, 1991. His basis for the rental house was $80,000 excluding the land. Mr. Z elected to use the alternative MACRS depreciation system on his timely filed return. What is his depreciation deduction for 1991?

a. $2,000.
b. $1,417.
c. $1,336.
d. $1,100.

The correct answer is (b). *(SPE 989 II-63)*
REQUIRED: The depreciation allowable under the alternative MACRS depreciation system.
DISCUSSION: Single family rental homes are classified as residential rental property and are normally depreciated in accordance with the straight-line method over 27.5 years. However, if the taxpayer elects to use the alternative depreciation system, the straight-line method over a period of 40 years for real property will be used. Sec. 168(d)(2) provides that the mid-month convention shall also be used for residential rental property. Thus the depreciation expense for 1991 is calculated as follows:

Cost of home	$80,000
÷ 40 years (alternative depreciation system)	x .025
	$ 2,000
x mid-month calculation (8.5 months ÷ 12)	x .7083
1991 depreciation deduction	$ 1,417

55. When computing the depreciation deduction under the Modified ACRS rules, salvage value should be subtracted from the basis before computing the allowable deduction.

The correct answer is (F). *(SPE 1082 I-17)*
DISCUSSION: Under Sec. 168, no adjustments are made for salvage value.

56. The alternative depreciation system for computing depreciation under the Modified accelerated cost recovery system (MACRS) uses a recovery percentage based on a modified straight-line method that allows the use of any recovery period provided it exceeds the regular recovery period under MACRS.

The correct answer is (F). *(SPE 986 II-12)*
DISCUSSION: The alternative depreciation system uses the straight-line method over a specific recovery period which generally depends on the ADR midpoint for the property. The ADR midpoint is 12 years if the property has no ADR midpoint, and 40 years for residential rental and nonresidential real property.

13.7 Amortization

57. The cost of a building or improvements constructed after 1986 on leased land is recovered

　a. Over a 60-month amortization period.
　b. As an MACRS deduction.
　c. Over the lease term.
　d. Over the lesser of the remaining period of the lease or the MACRS recovery period for the type of improvements.

The correct answer is (b). *(Publisher)*
REQUIRED: The period of time over which a lessee may deduct the cost of improvements constructed on leased land.
DISCUSSION: Sec. 168(i)(8) provides that any building erected or improvements made on leased property after 1986 is recovered as a MACRS deduction. This means the recovery period is determined by the type of property the improvements consist of regardless of the remaining term of the lease. Prior to the 1986 TRA, the recovery period was the lesser of the remaining period of the lease or the recovery period under MACRS rules.

58. Taxpayer A leased an office building on January 1, 1990 for 15 years with no option to renew. On July 1, 1991, A paid $10,000 for a new roof for the building. What is A's allowable amortization deduction for 1991?

　a. $146.
　b. $320.
　c. $417.
　d. $833.

The correct answer is (a). *(SPE 1079 I-69)*
REQUIRED: A taxpayer's allowable amortization deduction for capital improvements on leased property.
DISCUSSION: Sec. 168(i)(8) provides that improvements made on leased property (if the lease is entered into after September 25, 1985) are recovered as a MACRS deduction. A new roof on an office building is considered nonresidential real property and depreciated over a 31.5-year period. The mid-month convention applies. Taxpayer A's allowable deduction in 1991 is $146 [($10,000 ÷ 31.5 years) x (5.5 ÷ 12)].

59. Construction period interest on self-constructed property which is not inventory is generally

　a. Capitalized and recovered as depreciation deductions over the recovery period of the asset.
　b. Capitalized and amortized over a 10-year period.
　c. Expensed in the year incurred.
　d. Accumulated and deducted when the property is sold.

The correct answer is (a). *(Publisher)*
REQUIRED: The proper treatment of construction period interest after 1986.
DISCUSSION: The 1986 TRA added Sec. 263A(f) which provides that interest is capitalized on self-constructed property used in a business and recovered as depreciation deductions over the useful life of the asset. The interest must have been incurred during the production period and the property must have a long useful life, an estimated production period of over 2 years, or an estimated production period over 1 year with a cost of over $1 million.
Answer (b) is incorrect because Sec. 189, which provided for such treatment, has been repealed. Answer (c) is incorrect because Sec. 263A requires production costs (direct and indirect) to be capitalized. Answer (d) is incorrect because such treatment applies to production costs of inventory.

Module 13.7: Amortization

60. In 1990, Mr. D incurred the following expenses in connection with starting a manufacturing business to begin January 1, 1991. All of the expenses are start-up costs that must be capitalized and then amortized except

   a. Salaries and wages for employees who are being trained.
   b. Advertisements for the opening of the manufacturing plant.
   c. Travel expense to secure prospective distributors.
   d. Mr. D's share of real estate taxes on a factory building that he purchased.

The correct answer is (d). *(SPE 1085 II-37)*
REQUIRED: The expense that is not a start-up cost amortizable under Sec. 195.
DISCUSSION: Sec. 195 allows a taxpayer to elect to amortize start-up expenditures over a period of not less than 60 months (beginning with the month in which the business begins). Start-up expenditures are those paid or incurred in connection with investigating the creation or acquisition of an active trade or business, or with creating an active trade or business, and which, if paid or incurred in connection with the expansion of an existing business, would be allowable as a deduction in the year paid or incurred. The kinds of expenditures include those for research of one's product and the market for it. But real estate taxes are deductible under Sec. 164 regardless of whether incurred in a trade or business, so they do not need to be amortized.
Answers (a), (b) and (c) are incorrect because each is a start-up cost amortizable under Sec. 195.

61. Martha, a calendar-year taxpayer, inherited a large sum of money in January 1991 when her wealthy aunt died. Discouraged with the prospect of boring, passive investments, she decided to start an alligator farm after carefully investigating her prospects in the business. She incurred the following expenditures prior to the end of the year:

Market research	$ 800
Trip to Florida alligator farm	1,100
Books on alligator farming and first aid	70
Setting up an accounting system	130
Purchase of land for farm	40,000

If Martha's business is considered to begin on December 1, 1991, how much may she deduct in 1991?

   a. $0.
   b. $35.
   c. $420.
   d. $8,420.

The correct answer is (b). *(Publisher)*
REQUIRED: The amortization in the first year of business for start-up expenditures.
DISCUSSION: Sec. 195 allows a taxpayer to elect to amortize start-up expenditures over a period of not less than 60 months (beginning with the month in which the business begins). Start-up expenditures are those paid or incurred in connection with investigating the creation or acquisition of an active trade or business, or with creating an active trade or business, and which, if paid or incurred in connection with the expansion of an existing business, would be allowable as a deduction in the year paid or incurred. The kinds of expenditures include those for research of one's product and the market for it, and setting up accounting systems. The purchase of real property does not qualify as a start-up expenditure. Martha is entitled to 1 month of amortization (from when she began business) in 1991.

Market research	$ 800
Trip to Florida	1,100
Books	70
Accounting system	130
Total start-up expenditures	$2,100
1991 amortization ($2,100 x 1/60 months)	$ 35

62. The costs of acquiring a lease or leasehold for business purposes may be recovered by amortizing the costs over the term of the lease.

The correct answer is (T). *(SPE 984 II-11)*
DISCUSSION: The cost of acquiring a lease is a capital expenditure that may be amortized over the term of the lease under Sec. 167. A lease is an intangible asset, so Sec. 168 does not apply.

63. On January 2, 1991, Mr. Q, a calendar-year taxpayer, acquired an existing lease on property to be used in his business. Mr. Q paid $25,000 to the previous lessee. In addition, Mr. Q paid a commission of $5,000 to his broker as a finder's fee. The lease had a remaining life of 10 years with an option to renew for 5 years. If the cost of acquiring the lease for the base period is less than 75% of the total cost to acquire the lease, Mr. Q's amortization deduction for 1991 will be $2,000.

The correct answer is (T). *(SPE 1083 II-12)*
DISCUSSION: The $25,000 paid to the previous lessee and the $5,000 commission are costs of acquiring a lease that may be amortized over the term of the lease. Under Sec. 178, the term of the lease includes any period for which the lease may be renewed if less than 75% of the cost of acquiring the lease is attributable to the portion of the lease excluding the option period. The cost is allocated over both periods since it is not specified otherwise. Therefore, two-thirds (which is less than 75%) of the cost applies to the initial term. The $30,000 cost is thus allocated over 15 years, at $2,000 per year.

64. Skypipes, Inc. installed certified pollution control equipment to prevent certain toxic fumes from being discharged into the air. It was certified by the proper state and federal authorities. The equipment neither eliminated the visible exhaust nor increased the company's output or the useful life of the plant. Skypipes, Inc. may amortize the equipment over 60 months.

The correct answer is (T). *(Publisher)*
DISCUSSION: Sec. 169 allows a taxpayer to amortize the cost of a certified pollution control facility over a period of 60 months. A certified pollution control facility is a new, identifiable treatment facility used in connection with a plant or property in operation prior to 1976. The facility must abate or control water or atmospheric pollution or contamination and be certified by both the relevant state and federal authorities. Furthermore, it must not significantly increase the output or capacity, extend the useful life, or reduce the total operating costs of such plant or property, or alter the nature of the manufacturing or production process or facility. It need not eliminate any visible exhaust as long as it does remove pollutants.

65. When a taxpayer enters into a new business as a sole proprietor, costs incurred for advertising the opening of the business and wages paid employees undergoing training must be capitalized if incurred before business operations begin. Such costs can be amortized over a 60-month period.

The correct answer is (T). *(SPE 1083 II-6)*
DISCUSSION: Sec. 195 allows a taxpayer to elect to amortize start-up expenditures over not less than 60 months (beginning with the month in which the business begins). Start-up expenditures are those paid or incurred in connection with creating or investigating the creation or acquisition of an active trade or business. They must, however, be costs that would be deductible in the year paid or incurred if they had been costs of operating an existing trade or business. The costs of advertising the business opening and wages paid to employees undergoing training are all start-up expenditures.

66. A commission paid by the borrower to find and obtain a mortgage for business or income-producing property is a capital expenditure. The commission may not be added to the basis of the property but may be amortized over the life of the mortgage.

The correct answer is (T). *(SPE 989 II-8)*
DISCUSSION: Capitalized expenditures are not deductible in the current year, but must be amortized over the useful life of the asset to which they relate. Since the commission that was paid to obtain the mortgage fits into this category, it must be amortized over the life of the mortgage.
A commission paid by the borrower to locate a mortgage for businesses or income producing property is a capital expenditure. These outlays are amortized over the life of the loan and deducted accordingly (Rev. Rul. 70-360). Those related to a business property are deductible under Sec. 162 and those related to income producing property are deductible under Sec. 212. The commission is not added to the cost of the asset because it would instead be recovered through depreciation.

13.8 Depletion

67. For a taxpayer to claim a deduction for depletion, (s)he must possess an "economic interest" in the natural resource. For an economic interest to be considered present, the taxpayer is only required to

a. Possess an ownership interest in the land containing the mineral in place prior to extraction.
b. Have acquired by investment any interest in the mineral in place.
c. Look solely to the extraction and sale of the mineral for a return of capital.
d. Both (b) and (c).

The correct answer is (d). *(E.D. Fenton)*
REQUIRED: The definition of economic interest for depletion purposes.
DISCUSSION: Reg. 1.611-1(b)(1) states that a taxpayer possesses an economic interest when (s)he has acquired by investment any interest in the mineral in place and secures income derived from the extraction of the mineral to which (s)he must look for a return of capital. The courts have said that an actual cash investment in the property is not necessary. The investment can be in the form of land in a controlling position over the natural resource, or in nonmovable equipment used for the extraction and production of the mineral.
Answer (a) is incorrect because ownership of the land is different from ownership of the mineral rights, and is not required. Answers (b) and (c) are both requirements that must be met.

68. Wendy Flower has an adjusted basis of $20,000 in mineral property. It is estimated there are 40,000 tons of recoverable coal on the property. Wendy produced and sold 10,000 tons during 1991. What is her cost depletion deduction for 1991?

a. $1,000.
b. $5,000.
c. $10,000.
d. $15,000.

The correct answer is (b). *(SPE 1079 I-70)*
REQUIRED: A taxpayer's cost depletion deduction for mineral property.
DISCUSSION: Sec. 611(a) states that a deduction is allowed for reasonable depletion of mines, oil and gas wells, other natural deposits, and timber. Cost depletion for any year is the adjusted basis of the mineral property, divided by the number of units of mineral estimated as of the beginning of the taxable year, times the number of units of mineral sold within the taxable year.

Adjusted basis	$20,000
Divided by units of mineral	÷40,000
Depletion per unit	$ .50
Units sold in 1991	x10,000
Cost depletion deduction	$ 5,000

69. Donny owns and leases a coal mine to Brian. The lease agreement states that Brian will pay Donny $4 per ton royalty on coal mined. What is Brian's percentage depletion deduction for 1991 from the information given below?

Gross income from coal	$250,000
Income from trucking coal	20,000
Royalty paid Donny	30,000
Taxable income on coal (excluding depletion)	40,000
Coal depletion rate	10%

a. $20,000.
b. $22,000.
c. $24,000.
d. $25,000.

The correct answer is (a). *(SPE 1081 II-80)*
REQUIRED: A taxpayer's percentage depletion deduction on a coal mine.
DISCUSSION: Sec. 611(a) authorizes a reasonable allowance for depletion of mines, oil and gas wells, other natural deposits, and timber. Percentage depletion (for other than oil and gas wells) is provided in Sec. 613 as the specified percentage (10% for coal) of the gross income from the property (excluding any rents or royalties paid or incurred by the taxpayer with respect to the property). This depletion allowance may not exceed 50% of the taxpayer's taxable income from the property computed before the allowance for depletion. Percentage depletion is the lesser of

1) 10% of gross income, i.e.,
    10% x ($250,000 − $30,000 royalty) = $22,000; or
2) 50% of taxable income, i.e.,
    50% x $40,000 = $20,000.

Brian's percentage depletion deduction is thus limited to $20,000 (50% of his taxable income).

CHAPTER FOURTEEN
CAPITAL GAINS AND LOSSES

> 14.1 Capital Assets Identified .... (10 questions) 333
> 14.2 Capital Gains from Sale of Stock .... (18 questions) 336
> 14.3 Gains from Sale of Other Capital Assets .... (15 questions) 341
> 14.4 Net Capital Gain Computations .... (8 questions) 345
> 14.5 Nonbusiness Bad Debts .... (8 questions) 348
> 14.6 Section 1244 Stock .... (7 questions) 350
> 14.7 Capital Loss Limitations and Carryovers .... (16 questions) 352
> 14.8 Sales to Related Parties .... (6 questions) 357

14.1 Capital Assets Identified

1. Mr. E, a sole proprietor, is in the process of selling his retail store. Based on the following list of assets used in his business, what is the total amount of E's capital assets?

Accounts receivable	$20,000
Merchandise inventories	30,000
Buildings	40,000
Copyrights	20,000
Goodwill	30,000
Land	40,000
Furniture & fixtures	20,000

   a. $30,000.
   b. $50,000.
   c. $90,000.
   d. $150,000.

The correct answer is (a). *(SPE 1083 II-59)*
REQUIRED: The total amount of a sole proprietor's capital assets.
DISCUSSION: Under Sec. 1221, a capital asset is defined as any property held by the taxpayer (whether or not it is connected with his/her trade or business) that is not specifically excluded by Sec. 1221. Land used in a business, accounts receivable, inventories, and copyrights created by the owner are specifically excluded. Buildings and furniture and fixtures are excluded as depreciable property used in a business. E's only capital asset is the goodwill ($30,000).

2. Joe Hall owns a limousine for use in his personal service business of transporting passengers to airports. The limousine's adjusted basis is $40,000. In addition, Hall owns his personal residence and furnishings, that together cost him $280,000. Hall's capital assets amount to

   a. $320,000.
   b. $280,000.
   c. $40,000.
   d. $0.

The correct answer is (b). *(CPA 1190 Q-28)*
REQUIRED: The amount of capital assets owned by an individual.
DISCUSSION: Capital assets are any property held by the taxpayer (whether or not they are connected with his/her business), but not inventory, depreciable business property, real property used in a trade or business, copyrights and artistic compositions created by the owner, accounts and notes receivable, and certain U.S. government publications acquired at reduced cost (Sec. 1221). Personal use property, such as a residence, is a capital asset.
The limousine is depreciable business property and not a capital asset. The personal residence and furnishings ($280,000) is a capital asset.

3. Which one of the following is a capital asset?

   a. Delivery truck.
   b. Goodwill.
   c. Land used as a parking lot for customers.
   d. Machinery used in business.

The correct answer is (b). *(CPA 587 Q-46)*
REQUIRED: The property which is a capital asset.
DISCUSSION: Capital assets are any property held by the taxpayer not listed in Sec. 1221. Goodwill is not listed in Sec. 1221; therefore, it is a capital asset.
Answers (a) and (d) are incorrect because Sec. 1221 excludes depreciable property used in a trade or business from the definition of a capital asset. Answer (c) is incorrect because Sec. 1221 excludes real property used in a trade or business from the definition of a capital asset.

4. Helen Chambers owns and manages an apartment building. She also paints seascapes which she exhibits and sells, and she published several volumes of art criticism for which she owns the copyrights. With the profits from the books, she acquired stock in a local art supply company. If Helen sold any of the foregoing property, which would give rise to capital gains or losses?

   a. The apartment building.
   b. The paintings.
   c. The copyrights.
   d. The stock in the art supply company.

The correct answer is (d). *(Publisher)*
REQUIRED: The property which is a capital asset.
DISCUSSION: Capital gains and losses result from the sale or exchange of capital assets. Capital assets are defined as all property held by a taxpayer which are not excluded by Sec. 1221. Shares of stock are not specified in Sec. 1221, so stock is a capital asset as long as it is not held by a dealer for sale to customers in his/her trade or business.
   Answer (a) is incorrect because an apartment building is depreciable real property used in a trade or business and is excluded from being a capital asset by Sec. 1221(2). Answers (b) and (c) are incorrect because artistic compositions and copyrights held by the taxpayer who created them are excluded from the definition of a capital asset by Sec. 1221(3).

5. Halbert Zweistein is a renowned physicist and Nobel Prize winner who holds numerous patents. Halbert owns the copyrights to the 75 books he wrote in a long career. He has also collected his voluminous correspondence, notes, journals, and other papers which he plans to sell to a library in a major eastern city. Which of the following will result in capital gain or capital loss?

   a. The sale of the patents.
   b. The lease of the patents.
   c. The sale of the copyrights.
   d. The sale of the papers.

The correct answer is (a). *(Publisher)*
REQUIRED: The asset and transaction which will result in a capital gain or loss.
DISCUSSION: A capital gain or loss results from a sale or exchange of a capital asset. Patents are capital assets since they are not listed as not being capital assets in Sec. 1221.
   Answer (b) is incorrect because, although patents are capital assets, the lease of a patent will result in royalty income rather than capital gain or loss since a lease is not a sale or exchange. If the lease had transferred all substantial rights to a patent, then the income therefrom might produce a capital gain or loss under Sec. 1235. Answers (c) and (d) are incorrect because copyrights and letters held by the taxpayer whose personal efforts created them are not capital assets under Sec. 1221(3).

6. "Bear" Wall is a dealer in stocks. She sells them to customers in the ordinary course of business. "Bull" Street is in the business of trading stocks for his own benefit. He buys and sells stocks as his sole means of support and business activity. Which of the following statements is true?

   a. Stocks held by "Bear" are capital assets but stocks held by "Bull" are not capital assets.
   b. Stocks held by "Bear" are not capital assets but stocks held by "Bull" are capital assets.
   c. Stocks held by both "Bull" and "Bear" are capital assets.
   d. Stocks held by neither "Bull" nor "Bear" are capital assets.

The correct answer is (b). *(Publisher)*
REQUIRED: Whether stocks held by a trader and/or dealer are capital assets.
DISCUSSION: Capital assets are defined as all property held by a taxpayer which is not excluded by Sec. 1221. One exclusion is the stock in trade of a taxpayer properly included in inventory, or property held primarily for sale to customers in the ordinary course of a trade or business. A dealer in stock does hold the stock primarily for sale to customers in the ordinary course of business (unless the dealer "identifies" the stock as an investment by the close of the business day of acquisition). Accordingly, the stocks held by "Bear" are not capital assets.
   Cases have held that a person who trades stocks for his/her own account is entitled to capital gain or loss on the transactions. The stocks of a trader are not considered held for sale to customers, so stocks held by "Bull" are capital assets.
   Answers (a) and (c) are incorrect because the stocks held by "Bear" are not capital assets. Answers (a) and (d) are incorrect because the stocks held by "Bull" are capital assets.

7. Estie Tate is in the real estate business. She purchased a vacant office building for the purpose of reselling it. Estie's sister, not a real estate dealer, owns a large tract of residential land she purchased 7 years ago as an investment. Winfield Nestar is a tax lawyer. He converted an apartment building into condominiums and is trying to sell them. He also owns a tract of land that is zoned for business use and was received in payment for his fees last year. Nestar subdivided this land and is selling it as an office park. Which of the following will produce capital gain or loss?

a. Estie's sister's subdivision of the residential land into five lots and sale to five purchasers.
b. Estie's sale of the office building.
c. Nestar's sale of the condominiums to residents.
d. Nestar's sale of the office park lots.

The correct answer is (a). *(Publisher)*
REQUIRED: The land transaction which will produce capital gain or loss.
DISCUSSION: Generally, the subdivision of land into parcels converts the parcels into property held primarily for sale to customers, so the property is not a capital asset and the gain therefrom is ordinary income. Nevertheless, Sec. 1237 provides that land held by a taxpayer other than a corporation is not deemed to be held primarily for sale to customers solely because the taxpayer subdivided the land for purposes of sale. The land will be considered a capital asset only if the following requirements are met: the taxpayer must not have previously held the land for sale to customers; in the same year in which the sale occurs, the taxpayer must not hold any other real property for sale to customers; no substantial improvements may have been made on the land while held by the taxpayer; and the land must have been held by the taxpayer for at least 5 years. Since Estie's sister meets all of the requirements, her subdivision and sale will produce capital gain or loss.
Answer (b) is incorrect because Estie purchased the office building with the purpose of reselling it to customers in the ordinary course of her trade or business. Therefore, it is not a capital asset under Sec. 1221(1). Answers (c) and (d) are incorrect because the subdivision of a building into condominiums and the subdivision of land converts the property to that held primarily for sale to customers, i.e., the equivalent of inventory.

8. Fully depreciated property used in your trade or business is a capital asset.

The correct answer is (F). *(SPE 1081 II-22)*
DISCUSSION: Property used in a trade or business which is subject to the allowance for depreciation is specifically excluded from capital asset characterization under Sec. 1221(2). It does not matter whether the property is partially or fully depreciated.

9. Capital assets may be given preferential tax treatment. Some examples of capital assets are stocks and bonds held in a personal account, a personal residence, and household furnishings.

The correct answer is (T). *(SPE 1080 I-31)*
DISCUSSION: Net capital gains accruing to individual taxpayers are given a 28% maximum tax rate under Sec. 1(j), but net capital losses receive less favorable treatment than ordinary losses. Net capital gains means the excess of net long-term capital gains over net short-term capital losses. Any net short-term capital gains would be taxed at ordinary income rates, including the 31% rate. An individual's investment securities and personal use property are capital assets because they are not excluded under Sec. 1221.

10. On June 1, 1991, Mr. N transferred all substantial rights to a trade secret to an unrelated third party for $25,000. Mr. N must report the entire proceeds as ordinary income.

The correct answer is (F). *(SPE 1081 II-24)*
DISCUSSION: A trade secret qualifies as a capital asset. It is property (intangible) and not excluded in Sec. 1221. If all substantial rights are transferred, the transaction will be treated as a sale and not a licensing agreement (Sec. 1235). The gain will be capital and short- or long-term depending on the holding period.

14.2 Capital Gains from Sale of Stock

11. During 1989, Mr. F acquired 100 shares of stock in ABC Corporation for $500. During 1991 he sold the stock for $1,000. His adjusted basis in the stock at the time of sale was $500 and he had no other capital gains or losses during the year. What is the amount and character of income to be reported on F's income tax return for 1991?

   a. $500 long-term capital gain.
   b. $500 short-term capital gain.
   c. $500 ordinary income.
   d. $200 long-term capital gain.

The correct answer is (a). *(SPE 988 I-51)*
REQUIRED: The amount and character of the gain or loss on the sale of stock.
DISCUSSION: F's gain is the amount realized less the adjusted basis of the stock. The amount realized is the $1,000 selling price. The adjusted basis is the original $500 purchase price. Therefore, his gain is $500 ($1,000 − $500). Stock acquired as an investment or by a trader is a capital asset. The character of the gain is long-term capital gain. Under Sec. 1222(3) long-term capital gain is gain from the sale or exchange of a capital asset held for more than 1 year.

12. Mr. L purchased stock in Corporation O in 1989 for $500. In 1990, Mr. L received a distribution of $200 at a time when Corporation O had no current or accumulated earnings and profits, so it was a nontaxable return of capital. Mr. L sold his Corporation O stock in 1991 for $700. What is the amount of long-term capital gain to be reported by Mr. L?

   a. $0.
   b. $200.
   c. $400.
   d. $700.

The correct answer is (c). *(SPE 988 I-57)*
REQUIRED: The amount and character of the gain or loss on the sale of the stock in 1991.
DISCUSSION: L's gain will be the amount realized ($700) less the adjusted basis of the stock. The adjusted basis is L's original basis of $500 reduced by the return of capital ($200), or $300 [Sec. 1016(a)(4)]. The $400 gain ($700 − $300) is long-term because the stock had been held for more than 1 year.

13. On April 1, 1991, Mr. D purchased stock for investment purposes. In order to qualify for long-term capital gain or loss treatment the property must be held more than

   a. 6 months.
   b. 9 months.
   c. 12 months.
   d. Not applicable since long-term capital gains do not receive any preferential tax treatment.

The correct answer is (c). *(SPE 988 I-49)*
REQUIRED: The holding period for capital gain to be treated as long-term.
DISCUSSION: For property acquired after 1987, long-term capital gain or loss is the gain or loss from the sale or exchange of a capital asset held for more than 1 year (Sec. 1222).
Answer (a) is incorrect because the 6-month holding period for long-term treatment applied to a property acquired after June 22, 1984 and before January 1, 1988. Answer (b) is incorrect because the 9-month holding period for long-term treatment was only in effect for tax years beginning in 1977. Answer (d) is incorrect because long-term capital gains in excess of capital losses for individual taxpayers are eligible for a 28% maximum tax rate and the deduction for capital losses is limited.

14. On June 1, 1991, Ben Rork sold 500 shares of Kul Corp. stock. Rork had received this stock on May 1, 1991 as a bequest from the estate of his uncle, who died on March 1, 1991. Rork's basis was determined by reference to the stock's fair market value on March 1, 1991. Rork's holding period for this stock was

   a. Short-term.
   b. Long-term.
   c. Short-term if sold at a gain; long-term if sold as a loss.
   d. Long-term if sold at a gain; short-term if sold at a loss.

The correct answer is (b). *(CPA 589 Q-52)*
REQUIRED: The holding period for stock received from a decedent.
DISCUSSION: Under Sec. 1223(11), if property acquired from a decedent is sold or otherwise disposed of by the recipient within 1 year of the decedent's death, then the property is considered to have been held for more than 1 year. Therefore, under Sec. 1223(3), it is long-term.

15. Following are Mr. Orange's capital transactions in 1991:

Acquired	Item	Sold	Selling Price	Cost
09/13/90	Stock	01/07/91	$ 3,000	$ 4,500
02/10/90	Stock	02/25/91	4,000	3,000
06/09/90	Stock	07/06/91	45,000	38,000
10/17/89	Stock	11/16/91	2,000	6,000
03/20/91	Stock	12/10/91	5,500	1,500

Mr. Orange's capital gain (loss) for 1991 is

	Long-term	Short-term
a.	$2,500 gain	$4,000 gain
b.	$3,000 loss	$9,500 gain
c.	$4,000 gain	$2,500 gain
d.	$8,000 gain	$1,500 loss

The correct answer is (c). *(SPE 1077 II-13, 14)*
REQUIRED: The amount of net long-term and short-term capital gain or loss for 1991.
DISCUSSION: For property acquired after 1987, long-term capital gain or loss is the gain or loss from the sale or exchange of a capital asset held for more than 1 year (Sec. 1222). If the capital gain or loss is not long-term, it is short-term.

A net long-term capital gain is the excess of long-term capital gains over long-term capital losses. The three long-term transactions (the sales in February, July, and November) resulted in a net long-term capital gain of $4,000.

A net short-term capital gain is the excess of short-term capital gains over short-term capital losses. A net short-term capital loss is the excess of short-term capital losses over short-term capital gains. There were two short-term transactions: the sales in January and December, resulting in a net short-term capital gain for 1991 of $2,500.

Date of Sale	Long-term	Short-term
01/07/91		$(1,500)
02/25/91	$1,000	
07/06/91	7,000	
11/16/91	(4,000)	
12/10/91		4,000
	$4,000	$ 2,500

16. On June 15, 1991, Tim sold 100 shares of Corporation Y stock for $20 per share. Tim's records relating to the sale reflect the following information:

Date Purchased	Number of Shares	Adjusted Basis
June 1, 1990	40	$25
January 2, 1991	60	$10

What is the character and amount of Tim's gain or loss?

   a. $600 short-term capital gain and $200 long-term capital loss.
   b. $600 short-term capital gain and $200 short-term capital loss.
   c. $600 long-term capital gain and $200 long-term capital loss.
   d. $600 long-term capital gain and $200 short-term capital loss.

The correct answer is (a). *(SPE 989 I-79)*
REQUIRED: The gain from the sale of stock purchased at different times.
DISCUSSION: Under Reg. 1.1012-1(c), the basis and holding period of stock which was acquired in several different transactions is determined by specific identification of the stock sold. If the stock sold cannot be identified to any purchase or lot, it is assumed to be the first stock purchased or acquired; i.e., the FIFO (first-in, first-out) rule is applied.

In this transaction the number of shares sold equals the number purchased. So, the issue is determining the amount and character of gain. The first 40 shares were purchased on June 1, 1990 for $25 per share. The sale produces a long-term capital loss of $200 ($800 – $1,000). The remaining 60 shares were purchased on January 2, 1991 for $10 per share. Their sale results in a short-term capital gain of $600 ($1,200 – $600).

17. Sue Trader purchased 100 shares of JCN stock on January 1, 1990 for $100 per share. On September 1, 1990, she acquired an additional 50 shares of JCN stock at $110 per share. On October 1, 1990, she received a distribution of 200 shares of JCN stock from the estate of a deceased relative. It had been purchased at $60 per share in 1988 and was selling at $120 per share on the date of the decedent's death, which was the valuation used for the decedent's estate tax. On February 1, 1991, Trader sold 200 shares of JCN stock for $150 per share. The shares that were sold cannot be specifically identified. How much and what type of gain does Trader have?

   a. $6,500 long-term capital gain, and $2,000 short-term capital gain.
   b. $6,000 short-term capital gain.
   c. $18,000 long-term capital gain.
   d. $2,123 long-term capital gain, and $5,306 short-term capital gain.

The correct answer is (a). *(Publisher)*
REQUIRED: The gain from the sale of stock when it cannot be determined which lot or purchase the stock came from.
DISCUSSION: Under Reg. 1.1012-1(c), the basis and holding period of stock which was acquired in several different transactions is determined by specific identification of the stock sold. If the stock sold cannot be identified to any purchase or lot, it is assumed to be the first stock purchased or acquired; i.e., the FIFO (first-in, first-out) rule is applied.

Since Trader cannot identify the stock sold to its dates of purchase, she is considered to have sold the first 200 shares purchased or acquired. One hundred shares were purchased on January 1, 1990 for $100 per share, which produced a long-term capital gain upon their sale of $5,000 ($15,000 − $10,000). Another 50 shares were purchased on September 1, 1990 for $110 per share, the sale of which produced a short-term capital gain of $2,000 ($7,500 − $5,500). The remaining 50 shares sold came from the October 1, 1990 distribution with a basis of $120 per share (FMV). These produced a long-term capital gain of $1,500 ($7,500 − $6,000). It is long-term because, even though the beneficiary sold the property within 1 year of the decedent's death, it is considered to have been held longer than 1 year [Sec. 1223(11)].

The transaction produced $6,500 long-term capital gain and $2,000 short-term capital gain.

18. Stanley Garret purchased 1,000 shares of Pat Corporation common stock at $5 per share in 1989. On September 19, 1991, he received 1,000 stock rights entitling him to buy 250 additional shares of Pat Corporation common stock at $10 per share. On the day that the rights were issued, the fair market value of the stock was $12 per share ex-rights and that of the rights was $1 each. Garret did not exercise the rights; he let them expire on November 28, 1991. What should be the loss that Garret can report for 1991?

   a. No gain or loss.
   b. A short-term capital loss of $250.
   c. A long-term capital loss of $385.
   d. A short-term capital loss of $1,000.

The correct answer is (a). *(CPA 576 Q-18)*
REQUIRED: The amount of loss that Garret can report for 1991.
DISCUSSION: When a taxpayer receives nontaxable stock rights, the cost basis of the rights under Sec. 307 is determined by allocating part of the basis of the stock on which the distribution was made. If the fair market value of the rights at the time of the distribution is less than 15% of the fair market value of the stock held at that time, the allocation is elective, but no allocation is made unless the stock rights are sold or exercised. If stock rights are allowed to expire, no allocation is made and no loss is recognized [Reg. 1.307-1(a)].

19. On July 1, 1987, Lila Perl paid $90,000 for 450 shares of Janis Corporation common stock. Lila received a nontaxable stock dividend of 50 new common shares in November 1990. On December 20, 1991, Lila sold the 50 new shares for $11,000. How much should Lila report in her 1991 return as long-term capital gain?

   a. $0.
   b. $1,000.
   c. $2,000.
   d. $11,000.

The correct answer is (c). *(CPA 585 Q-37)*
REQUIRED: The amount of gain that should be reported in 1991.
DISCUSSION: When a shareholder receives a nontaxable stock dividend, the basis of the new stock must be determined by allocating to it part of the adjusted basis of the old stock (Sec. 307). The new shares (50) represented 10% of the total shares owned (500) after the stock dividend. Therefore, the basis of the new shares is $9,000 (10% × $90,000). The holding period of the new shares includes the holding period of the old shares, i.e., from July 1, 1987 [Sec. 1223(5)]. This results in a $2,000 long-term capital gain as computed below.

Sale proceeds	$11,000
Less allocated basis	(9,000)
Realized and recognized gain	$ 2,000

Module 14.2: Capital Gains from Sale of Stock

20. Patrick purchased 100 shares of "I" Company stock in December 1990 for $5,775. The following information reflects the activity of "I" Company stock in 1991. The stock dividends are nontaxable.

February 2, 1991 - 10% stock dividend
March 2, 1991 - 2 for 1 split
August 2, 1991 - 5% stock dividend

On November 2, 1991, Patrick sold 100 shares of "I" Company stock for $3,600. What is Patrick's reportable capital gain or loss on this transaction for 1991?

a. $1,100 gain.
b. $1,600 gain.
c. $2,175 loss.
d. $2,500 gain.

The correct answer is (a). *(SPE 1077 II-23)*
REQUIRED: The capital gain or loss after two tax-free stock dividends and a stock split.
DISCUSSION: When a shareholder receives a tax-free stock dividend or stock split, the basis of the new stock is determined by allocating part of the basis of the original stock to the new shares. The cumulative effect of the stock dividends and split was that Patrick owned 231 shares. Allocating the original cost of $5,775 between the 231 shares results in a $25 per share basis. The sale of 100 shares resulted in a gain of $1,100 ($3,600 proceeds − $2,500 basis).

Date	Occurrence	Total # of Shares
12/90	Original shares	100
02/91	Plus 10%	110
03/91	Plus 100%	220
08/91	Plus 5%	231

Allocation: $5,775 ÷ 231 = $25/share

21. Iam Broke frequently traded on the stock market. On November 1, 1990, when stock prices were very high, Broke sold short (sold without owning any stock by borrowing from the broker) 100 shares of Ducko, Inc. at $80 per share. On July 1, 1991, Broke purchased 100 shares of Ducko for $50 per share and delivered them on December 1, 1991. Broke also purchased 100 shares of High Tech, Inc. on February 1, 1990 for $60 per share. He sold 100 shares of High Tech short on December 1, 1990 at $100 per share. Broke delivered these 100 shares on September 1, 1991. What is Broke's gain on the sales?

a. $4,000 short-term capital gain in 1990, and $3,000 long-term capital gain in 1991.
b. $3,000 long-term capital gain in 1990, and $4,000 short-term capital gain in 1991.
c. $7,000 long-term capital gain in 1990.
d. $7,000 short-term capital gain in 1991.

The correct answer is (d). *(Publisher)*
REQUIRED: The time of recognition and character of gain from short sales of stock.
DISCUSSION: Sec. 1233 provides special rules for determining gains and losses from the short sale of stock. The gain is not recognized until the short sale is closed; i.e., when the stock is delivered to the purchaser. For property acquired after 1987, a gain is short-term capital gain if on the date of the short sale substantially identical property to that sold short had been held for 1 year or less, or if substantially identical property to that sold short is acquired after the short sale and before the short sale is closed.
Broke closed both sales in 1991 so that is when the gain is recognized. The shares of Ducko used to close the first short sale were purchased after the short sale and prior to the closing, so the gain is short-term capital gain. Broke purchased shares of High Tech within 1 year before the short sale of High Tech, so that gain is also short-term. The gain on Ducko is $3,000 ($8,000 − $5,000). The gain on High Tech is $4,000 ($10,000 − $6,000). Broke has $7,000 of short-term capital gains in 1991.

22. In January 1989, Kirk Kelly bought 100 shares of a listed stock for $8,000. In March 1990, when the fair market value was $6,000, Kirk gave this stock to his cousin, Clara. No gift tax was paid. Clara sold this stock in June 1991 for $7,000. How much is Clara's reportable gain or loss in 1991 on the sale of this stock?

a. $0.
b. $1,000 loss.
c. $1,000 gain.
d. $7,000 gain.

The correct answer is (a). *(CPA 1185 Q-32)*
REQUIRED: The amount of reportable gain or loss from the sale of stock received as a gift.
DISCUSSION: The basis of property received by gift is the donor's basis (transferred or carryover basis). If the fair market value (FMV) of the property at the time of the gift is lower, however, the basis for purposes of determining loss is the FMV (Sec. 1015). Clara's basis for gain is $8,000, and her basis for loss is $6,000. Therefore, neither gain nor loss is recognized [Reg. 1.1015-1(a)(2)].

	Gain	Loss
Sales price	$7,000	$7,000
Less basis	(8,000)	(6,000)
Gain (loss)	No gain	No loss

Module 14.2: Capital Gains from Sale of Stock

23. On March 10, 1991, James Rogers sold 300 shares of Red Company common stock for $4,200. Rogers acquired the stock in 1987 at a cost of $5,000. On April 4, 1991, he repurchased 300 shares of Red Company common stock for $3,600 and held them until July 18, 1991, when he sold them for $6,000. How should Rogers report the above transactions for 1991?

a. A long-term capital loss of $800.
b. A long-term capital gain of $1,000.
c. A long-term capital gain of $1,600.
d. A long-term capital loss of $800 and a short-term capital gain of $2,400.

The correct answer is (c). *(CPA 576 Q-16)*
REQUIRED: The amount and character of capital gain after identical stocks are sold and repurchased within 30 days.
DISCUSSION: The sale of stock on March 10 was a wash sale under Sec. 1091 because identical stock was repurchased within 30 days (on April 4). No deduction is allowable for any loss that occurs in a wash sale. The $800 realized loss ($4,200 − $5,000) that occurred in March will not be recognized for tax purposes. The disallowed loss is added to the basis of the stock that is subsequently purchased in April. The basis in the stock purchased in April is $4,400 ($3,600 cost + $800 disallowed loss), and a gain of $1,600 is recognized when the stock is sold for $6,000 on July 18. The holding period of stock acquired in a wash sale includes the holding period of the originally purchased stock, so the gain is long-term.

24. Sandy is an investor in a mutual fund. The fund notified her that it realized a long-term capital gain in 1991. The amount allocated to her account was $5,000. The fund also advised her that it paid federal tax of $1,700 on the gain on her behalf and that it will not distribute the net amount. All of the following statements are true except:

a. In 1991, Sandy must report a long-term capital gain of $5,000.
b. Sandy is allowed a $1,700 credit on her return for the tax paid by the mutual fund.
c. Sandy does not report a long-term gain since no distribution was made.
d. Sandy increases her basis in the stock by $3,300.

The correct answer is (c). *(SPE 990 I-38)*
REQUIRED: The incorrect statement concerning treatment of long-term capital gain from a mutual fund.
DISCUSSION: A mutual fund is a regulated investment company, the taxation of which is determined by Sec. 852. Dividends paid by the mutual fund to shareholders are taxed. Undistributed capital gains must be included in income by shareholders, but a credit is allowed for their proportionate share of any tax on the capital gain paid by the mutual fund. Basis would increase by the net amount of $3,300 ($5,000 capital gain − $1,700 taxes paid) [Sec. 852(b)(3)(A) and (D)].

25. On September 30, 1991, Peter sold 100 shares of Solid Corporation stock for $16,000. Peter inherited the stock from his uncle who died on May 15, 1991. It was included in the uncle's Federal estate tax return at its May 15 fair market value of $18,000. Peter has a long-term capital loss of $2,000 from this transaction.

The correct answer is (T). *(SPE 990 I-13)*
DISCUSSION: Peter acquired the stock from a decedent. He takes the stock's fair market value at the date of the decedent's death as his basis. There is a $2,000 loss ($16,000 − $18,000) on the sale. The character is long-term. When property is acquired from a decedent and a sale subsequently occurs within 1 year of the decedent's death, the property is considered to have been held long-term [Sec. 1223(11)].

26. Mrs. D, a calendar-year, cash-basis taxpayer, sold stock through the stock exchange for $25,000 on December 30, 1990. She had purchased the stock on May 28, 1990 for $20,000. The cash was received and the sale closed by delivery of the stock on January 9, 1991 in accordance with the rules of the stock exchange. Mrs. D has a short-term capital gain of $5,000 on her 1991 return.

The correct answer is (F). *(SPE 1078 I-26)*
DISCUSSION: For sales made after December 31, 1986, both cash and accrual taxpayers must report, in the year of sale, gain or loss from sales of stocks or securities which are traded on an established securities market [Sec. 453(k)(2)]. Mrs. D has a $5,000 gain which occurred on December 30, 1990 and is reported as a short-term capital gain on her 1990 return.

27. Mr. W purchased two shares of XYZ common stock. He paid $90 for the first share and $60 for the second share. XYZ declared a stock dividend which gave stockholders two new shares of common stock for each share they held. After the distribution, Mr. W had six shares of stock with an adjusted basis of $25 each.

The correct answer is (F). *(SPE 1081 I-32)*
DISCUSSION: A taxpayer cannot average the basis for shares of stock in a corporation. The basis for each share is its cost, subject to allocation for stock dividends under Sec. 307. Two new shares are attributable to the $90 share, so each is assigned a basis of $30 ($90 ÷ 3 shares). Two new shares are attributable to the $60 share, so each is assigned a basis of $20 ($60 ÷ 3 shares). After the distribution Mr. W has six shares of stock, three shares with a basis of $30, and three shares with a basis of $20.

28. Jim owns five shares of stock in X Corporation. The corporation declared a 5% stock dividend. It also set up a plan wherein fractional shares were sold and the cash proceeds distributed to the stockholders. Jim should treat the amount he received for the fractional share stock dividend as an ordinary taxable dividend.

The correct answer is (F). *(SPE 1081 I-12)*
DISCUSSION: When a corporation declares a stock dividend, it is not uncommon for some shareholders to be entitled to fractional shares. If cash is distributed in lieu of fractional shares to avoid dealing in fractional shares, the cash received by shareholders is treated as though the fractional shares were distributed as part of the stock dividend and then redeemed by the distributing corporation under Sec. 302 [Reg. 1.305-3(c)]. If the corporation issues and sells the fractional shares and then distributes the proceeds as part of a plan, however, the transaction is treated as if the shareholders had received the fractional shares and then sold them. Jim should treat the amount received as part capital gain and part reduction of basis of his other stock (to the extent basis would have been allocated if the fractional shares had been received).

14.3 Gains from Sale of Other Capital Assets

29. Mr. J bought an asset on June 19, 1990. What is the earliest date on which Mr. J could have sold that asset and qualified for long-term capital gain or loss treatment?

a. December 19, 1990.
b. December 20, 1990.
c. June 19, 1991.
d. June 20, 1991.

The correct answer is (d). *(SPE 987 II-52)*
REQUIRED: The date on which a long-term holding period begins.
DISCUSSION: For assets acquired after 1987, long-term capital gain or loss treatment is provided if the asset is held for more than 1 year. The general rule is that the date the property is acquired is excluded and the date that the property is disposed of is included in this computation of the holding period. Since Mr. J bought the asset on June 19, 1990, his holding period is treated as beginning June 20, 1990. Exactly 1 year is considered to have expired on June 19, 1991. Therefore, on June 20, 1991 more than 1 year has passed which would satisfy the long-term holding period requirement.

30. Jack had the following items of income and loss in 1991:

Wages	$22,500
Nonbusiness bad debt	1,400
Gain on stock held since 1989	2,600
Flood loss to his personal residence owned since 1985	4,100
Loss on stock held since 1988	300
Gain on stock held for 4 months	2,050

What is his taxable capital gain or deductible capital loss for 1991?

a. $1,150 loss.
b. $1,570 gain.
c. $2,500 gain.
d. $2,950 gain.

The correct answer is (d). *(SPE 1077 II-20)*
REQUIRED: The taxable capital gain or deductible capital loss from all the transactions.
DISCUSSION: Jack had a net long-term capital gain of $2,300 resulting from the $2,600 gain on the sale of stock and the $300 loss on the sale of some other stock. Jack had a net short-term capital gain of $650 resulting from the sale of stock held for 4 months and the $1,400 nonbusiness bad debt. Nonbusiness bad debts are treated as short-term capital losses under Sec. 166. The flood loss is an itemized deduction, not a capital loss.

Net long-term capital gain ($2,600 − $300)	$2,300
Net short-term capital gain ($2,050 − $1,400)	650
Taxable capital gain	$2,950

Module 14.3: Gains from Sale of Other Capital Assets

31. On July 1, 1991, Mr. A, a cash-method taxpayer, sold a painting for which he received $50,000 in cash and a note with a face value of $50,000 and a fair market value of $35,000. He paid a commission of $5,000 on the sale. Mr. A had acquired the painting in 1981 and his basis was $5,000. What is A's recognized gain for 1991?

a. $95,000.
b. $90,000.
c. $75,000.
d. $50,000.

The correct answer is (c). *(SPE 1079 I-75)*
REQUIRED: The recognized gain on the sale of the painting.
DISCUSSION: The amount realized under Sec. 1001 includes money received plus the fair market value of other property. Mr. A realized $85,000 ($50,000 cash + $35,000 note). Commissions reduce the amount realized under Reg. 1.263(a)-2. Consequently, Mr. A recognized a gain of $75,000.

Amount realized	$85,000
Less commission	(5,000)
Net proceeds	$80,000
Less adjusted basis	(5,000)
Recognized gain	$75,000

32. In 1991, Mr. Phibbs sold land that had an adjusted basis to him of $65,000 for $90,000 cash plus a painting having a fair market value of $25,000. The buyer assumed Phibbs' $10,000 loan on the land. Mr. Phibbs paid $5,000 in selling expenses. What is the amount of Mr. Phibbs' gain on the sale?

a. $30,000.
b. $45,000.
c. $50,000.
d. $55,000.

The correct answer is (d). *(SPE 990 I-74)*
REQUIRED: The gain when property is given, liabilities assumed and selling expenses incurred.
DISCUSSION: The amount realized under Sec. 1001 includes money received, fair market value of other property received, and any liabilities of which the seller is relieved. Mr. Phibbs realized $125,000 ($90,000 cash + $25,000 FMV painting + $10,000 liability relieved). Under Reg. 1.263(a)-2, commissions reduce the amount realized. Sec. 1001(a) provides that the gain from the sale of property is the excess of the amount realized over the adjusted basis. Therefore, Mr. Phibbs recognized a gain of $55,000.

Amount realized	$125,000
Less commissions paid	(5,000)
Net proceeds	$120,000
Less adjusted basis	(65,000)
Realized and recognized gain	$ 55,000

33. On September 1, 1990, Sam purchased for $9,200 cash a $10,000 bond with 10% annual interest that matures in 2000. Sam did not elect to accrue market discount currently as interest income. On September 2, 1991, Sam sold the bond for $9,400. The amount and character of gain Sam must recognize in 1991 from this transaction is

a. $600 long-term capital loss.
b. $200 short-term capital gain.
c. $80 ordinary income; $120 short-term capital gain.
d. $80 ordinary income; $120 long-term capital gain.

The correct answer is (d). *(Publisher)*
REQUIRED: The amount and character of gain that must be recognized on the sale of a bond purchased at a market discount.
DISCUSSION: Sec. 1276 requires that gain on the disposition of any market discount bond be treated as ordinary income to the extent that the market discount could have been accrued as interest. In this case, the market discount was $800 ($10,000 − $9,200). The accrued market discount is the amount bearing the same ratio to the market discount as the number of days the taxpayer held the bond bears to the number of days from acquisition to maturity. One year ÷ 10 years x $800 = $80 accrued market discount. The total gain was $200 ($9,400 − $9,200), so the gain consists of $80 ordinary income and $120 long-term capital gain.

Module 14.3: Gains from Sale of Other Capital Assets

34. On September 1, 1991, Leslie purchased a 10-year, $10,000 bond with 7% annual interest that matures September 1, 1996. Leslie borrowed $8,000 to help finance the $9,100 purchase price of the bond. For 1991, Leslie's interest expense for the borrowed funds is $321 and the interest income from the bonds is $234. What is the total deduction resulting from this transaction in 1991?

a. $321.
b. $261.
c. $234.
d. $27.

The correct answer is (b). *(Publisher)*
REQUIRED: The total deduction allowed for interest paid on funds borrowed to purchase a market discount bond.
DISCUSSION: Sec. 1277 provides that the net direct interest expense with respect to a market discount bond is deductible only to the extent that it exceeds the market discount allocable to the days during the year the bond was held by the taxpayer. The term "net direct interest expense" means the excess of the interest expense on indebtedness over total interest (including original issue discount) includable in gross income for the taxable year with respect to the bond. The market discount allocable to the taxable year is based on the number of days the bond was held during the taxable year. Interest expense, to the extent of the interest income from the bond, is also deductible.

Interest paid or accrued on debt	$321
Interest from the bond includable in gross income	(234)
Net direct interest	$ 87
Market discount allocable to 1991 {[($10,000 − $9,100) ÷ 5 years] x (122 days ÷ 365 days)}	(60)
Net direct interest deduction	$ 27
Interest deductible to extent of income	234
Total interest deduction	$261

35. Kerry Orange owned a 20% interest for 20 years in the T & T Partnership which owns no unrealized receivables or inventory items. In 1991, he sold his interest for $30,000 and was relieved of his share of partnership liabilities of $2,200. At the date of sale, Orange's total basis in his partnership interest was $24,000. What gain or loss should Orange report?

a. $3,800 ordinary income.
b. $6,000 capital gain.
c. $8,200 capital gain.
d. $8,200 ordinary income.

The correct answer is (c). *(SPE 1077 III-21)*
REQUIRED: The amount and character of gain from the sale of the partnership interest.
DISCUSSION: Gain or loss on the sale of a partnership interest is capital gain or loss under Sec. 741. Liabilities assumed by the purchaser are part of the amount realized on the sale. Therefore, Orange is considered to have received $32,200 for his partnership interest ($30,000 + $2,200). His capital gain is $8,200 ($32,200 − $24,000).

36. On March 1, 1991, Harry Beech received a gift of income-producing real estate having a donor's adjusted basis of $50,000 at the date of the gift. Fair market value of the property at the date of the gift was $40,000. Beech sold the property for $46,000 on August 1, 1991. How much gain or loss should Beech report for 1991?

a. No gain or loss.
b. $6,000 short-term capital gain.
c. $4,000 short-term capital loss.
d. $4,000 ordinary loss.

The correct answer is (a). *(CPA 1184 Q-27)*
REQUIRED: The amount of gain or loss on the sale of property acquired by gift.
DISCUSSION: For the purpose of computing gain, a donee's basis is the same as the donor's basis. For computing loss, the donee takes the lower of the donor's basis or the fair market value of the property (Sec. 1015). Beech has no gain or loss, as shown below.

	Gain	Loss
Amount realized	$46,000	$46,000
Less basis	(50,000)	(40,000)
Gain/loss	No gain	No loss

Module 14.3: Gains from Sale of Other Capital Assets

37. Soft Cream sells franchises to independent operators. In 1991 it sold a franchise to Edward Trent, charging an initial fee of $20,000 and a monthly fee of 2% of sales. Soft Cream retains the right to control such matters as employee and management training, quality control and promotion, and the purchase of ingredients. Mr. Trent's 1991 sales amounted to $200,000. From the transactions with Trent, Soft Cream, an accrual-basis taxpayer, would include in its computation of 1991 taxable income

   a. Long-term capital gain of $24,000.
   b. Long-term capital gain of $20,000, ordinary income of $4,000.
   c. Long-term capital gain of $4,000, ordinary income of $20,000.
   d. Ordinary income of $24,000.

The correct answer is (d). *(CPA 573 Q-12)*
REQUIRED: The amount and character of income from the sale of the franchise.
DISCUSSION: The transfer of a franchise is not treated as a sale or exchange of a capital asset if the transferor retains significant power, rights, or continuing interest with respect to the franchise (Sec. 1253). The right to control employee and management training, quality control and promotion, and the purchase of ingredients constitutes significant power, rights, and continuing interest. Therefore, the transfer is not a sale but merely a licensing agreement, and all the income ($20,000 initial fee and $4,000 monthly fee) is ordinary income.

38. On May 5, 1990 Mr. E purchased a rare gem as an investment. On April 25, 1991 he exchanged it for another rare gem in a nontaxable exchange. On August 7, 1991 he sold it for cash. Any gain or loss on the sale is a long-term capital gain or loss.

The correct answer is (T). *(SPE 1082 I-32)*
DISCUSSION: Property held for investment is a capital asset. The holding period for property received in an exchange includes the period of the property exchanged if the property received is a capital or Sec. 1231 asset and it has the same basis in whole or in part as the property exchanged [Sec. 1223(1)]. Under Sec. 1031, the exchange of the gems is a like-kind exchange and the basis of the gem received is the same as the basis of the gem exchanged. Therefore, the gain or loss on the subsequent sale is a long-term capital gain or loss because the holding period exceeded 1 year.

39. On January 3, 1991 Mrs. Y acquired a patent for her invention. On September 30, 1991 she sold all her substantial rights to this patent. Mrs. Y is entitled to long-term capital gain treatment.

The correct answer is (T). *(SPE 1079 II-40)*
DISCUSSION: Under Sec. 1235, the transfer by the inventor of property which consists of all substantial rights to a patent shall be considered the sale or exchange of a capital asset which has been held for the long-term gain (loss) holding period. The gain on sale of this patent will be considered long-term capital gain even though it had been held for less than 1 year.

40. Mr. B, a car dealer, assigns cars from his new inventory to be used as demonstrators. In June 1991, he sold one demonstrator for $12,000. It cost $10,000 and no depreciation had been deducted. Mr. B should report a $2,000 capital gain.

The correct answer is (F). *(SPE 1081 II-23)*
DISCUSSION: Demonstrators are stock in trade (inventory) and are specifically excluded from the capital asset definition of Sec. 1221. The gain on the sale of inventory is ordinary gain to the taxpayer. However, it could be argued that the demonstrators are Sec. 1231 property if held and depreciated for more than 1 year (but the depreciation would be recaptured under Sec. 1245).

41. In 1985 Mr. C, who is not a dealer in real estate, purchased a tract of land and divided it into four lots. Mr. C substantially increased the value of the lots by installing gas, electricity, sewer, and water, and sold the lots at a gain in 1991. Mr. C is entitled to capital gain treatment on the sale of the lots.

The correct answer is (F). *(SPE 1085 I-34)*
DISCUSSION: The subdivision of land is generally considered to convert investment property to property held for sale in a trade or business, i.e., inventory that produces ordinary income. Sec. 1237 does not allow capital gain in this case because Mr. C made substantial improvements. Installing utilities is not considered substantial improvements only if the property is held by the taxpayer for 10 years or more.

Module 14.4: Net Capital Gain Computations

42. Ashby held a tract of land for 3 years during which time he made no substantial improvements. Ashby made a gift of the land to his son Hank, who held the land for 3 additional years. Hank subdivided the tract without improving it and sold four lots at a gain. Neither Mr. Ashby or Hank are real estate dealers. Hank has a long-term capital gain from the sale of the four lots.

The correct answer is (T). *(SPE 990 I-14)*
DISCUSSION: The gift of the land by Ashby to his son, Hank, allows for Hank to include Ashby's 3-year holding period. At the time of the sale, Hank has a holding period of 6 years. This satisfies one of three requirements under Sec. 1237. The other two requirements are: (1) such tract, or any lot or parcel thereof, had not previously been held by such taxpayer primarily for sale to customers in the ordinary course of a trade or business, and (2) no substantial improvement that substantially enhances the value of the lot or parcel sold is made by the taxpayer on such tract while held by the taxpayer. These two requirements are met in this transaction. Sec. 1237(b)(1) further limits the benefit of capital gains status by allowing no more than five lots or parcels contained in the same tract to qualify for capital gain treatment. In this transaction, there are four lots sold. So all lots qualify for long-term capital gain treatment. The portion of Sec. 1237 that requires ordinary income to be recognized equal to 5% of the selling price when more than five lots are sold does not apply here since only four lots have been sold by the end of the current year.

43. Mr. D is a sole proprietor using the cash method of accounting. In May 1991 he retired and sold his trade accounts receivable totaling $30,000 for $20,000. The result of the sale of the accounts receivable is an ordinary gain of $20,000.

The correct answer is (T). *(SPE 1085 II-24)*
DISCUSSION: Capital assets are defined in Sec. 1221. Accounts receivable are explicitly excluded from the definition of a capital asset. Therefore, the sale of accounts receivable results in ordinary income. Since he was a cash method taxpayer, his basis in the receivables was zero and the entire proceeds were ordinary income.

14.4 Net Capital Gain Computations

Also see Chapter 15 for long-term capital gains under Sec. 1231.

44. Harold Crowe had the following capital transactions for the year 1991:

$3,000 long-term capital loss
9,000 long-term capital gain
2,000 net short-term capital gain

What is the amount of Crowe's reportable capital gain net income in the 1991 Schedule D summary?

a. $4,400.
b. $5,200.
c. $8,000.
d. $11,000.

The correct answer is (c). *(CPA 582 P-58)*
REQUIRED: The amount of capital gain net income in the Schedule D summary.
DISCUSSION: Schedule D is used to report capital gains and losses, and the summary combines the long-term gains/losses with the short-term gains/losses. When these capital gains and losses all net to a gain, it is called "capital gain net income" [Sec. 1222(9)]. This has occurred in the question and is computed below

Net long-term capital gain ($9,000 – $3,000)	$6,000
Net short-term capital gain	2,000
Capital gain net income	$8,000

Do not confuse the term "capital gain net income" with the term "net capital gain." A "net capital gain" is the excess of net long-term capital gains over net short-term capital losses. It does not include net short-term capital gains. The difference is important because starting in 1991 the net capital gain term is used in applying the 28% maximum tax rate on capital gains. The 28% maximum tax rate for individuals does not apply to net short-term capital gains.

Module 14.4: Net Capital Gain Computations

45. The maximum tax rate on net capital gains for individuals for 1991 is

    a. 33%.
    b. 31%.
    c. 28%.
    d. 15%.

46. Tom Brown, a single taxpayer, reported adjusted gross income of $110,000 for 1991. Included in the adjusted gross income is $30,000 of long-term capital gains. Brown claims a standard deduction and one personal exemption. What is the amount of Brown's 1991 tax liability?

    a. $29,975.
    b. $28,308.
    c. $28,255.
    d. $27,408.

The correct answer is (c). *(SPE 988 I-52)*
REQUIRED: The maximum tax rate on net capital gains.
DISCUSSION: For 1991 and later tax years the maximum tax rate for ordinary income will be 31%. The maximum tax rate on net capital gains (i.e., excess of net long-term capital gains over net short-term capital losses) recognized by individuals for 1991 and later tax years is 28%. Therefore, answer (c) is correct.

The correct answer is (d). *(Publisher)*
REQUIRED: The 1991 tax liability for a single individual with adjusted gross income of over $100,000 and capital gain income.
DISCUSSION: The taxpayer's adjusted gross income is reduced by his standard deduction ($3,400) and one personal exemption ($2,150). Under the 1990 Act, there is a phaseout of the personal exemption at the rate of 2% for every $2,500, or fraction thereof, of AGI in excess of $100,000. Tom Brown's AGI exceeds $100,000 by $10,000. There are 4 intervals, so the phaseout is 8% (2% x 4). The resulting loss is $172 ($2,150 x .08). Taxable income is computed below.

AGI	$110,000
Standard deduction	(3,400)
Personal exemption	(2,150)
	$104,450
Phaseout	172
Taxable income	$104,622

In 1991, the maximum tax rate for ordinary income is 31% and for capital gains is 28%. For a single individual the first $20,350 of income is taxed at 15%, the next bracket of income up to $49,300 is taxed at 28%, and the excess over $49,300 is taxed at 31%. For capital gain income, if the taxable income as reduced by net capital gain is greater than the amount of taxable income in the 15% bracket, the tax on capital gains is the sum of (1) the regular tax on taxable income minus net capital gain plus (2) 28% of the net capital gain. The 1991 tax liability is calculated below. Here, the taxable income minus net capital gain exceeds the 15% bracket. Therefore, the income will be calculated as stated above.

Taxable income	$104,622
Less net capital gain	(30,000)
Ordinary taxable income	$ 74,622
First $49,300	$ 11,158
Excess over $49,300	
[31% x ($74,622 – $49,300)]	7,850
Capital gain ($30,000 x .28)	8,400
Total tax liability	$ 27,408

Module 14.4: Net Capital Gain Computations

47. During 1991, Mr. G had the following capital transactions:

	Short-term	Long-term
Gains	$2,600	$5,400
Losses	3,790	1,750

What is the amount of Mr. G's net capital gain (or loss)?

a. $(1,750).
b. $(1,190).
c. $2,460.
d. $3,650.

The correct answer is (c). *(SPE 989 I-76)*
REQUIRED: The amount of net capital gain or loss for 1991.
DISCUSSION: Under Sec. 1222(6), Mr. G has a net short-term capital loss of $1,190. Mr. G. also has a net long-term capital gain of $3,650 under Sec. 1222(7). Net capital gain is defined in Sec. 1222(11) as the excess of net long-term capital gain for the taxable year over the net short-term capital loss for such year. Here, the net capital gain is $2,460 ($3,650 − $1,190).

48. Lewis and Clark are partners who share profits and losses in a ratio of 2:1, respectively. For 1991, the partnership tax return showed a net short-term capital loss of $3,000 and a net long-term capital gain of $15,000. Lewis also had a personal net short-term capital loss of $2,000. What is the net capital gain that should be included in Lewis' taxable income on his 1991 individual income tax return?

a. $2,400.
b. $3,600.
c. $6,000.
d. $10,000.

The correct answer is (c). *(CPA 1174 P-12)*
REQUIRED: The amount of capital gain that should be included in a partner's taxable income.
DISCUSSION: In determining the income from a partnership, each partner is required to take into account separately his/her distributive share of the partnership capital gains and losses. Lewis is entitled to two-thirds of the profits and losses of the partnership. $2,000 of the partnership's $3,000 short-term capital loss was passed through to Lewis to be combined with his personal short-term loss of $2,000 (for a total short-term capital loss of $4,000). In addition, two-thirds of the partnership's $15,000 long-term capital gain was passed through to Lewis ($10,000). The net short-term capital loss and the net long-term capital gain are netted, resulting in a net capital gain of $6,000.

Net short-term capital loss $2,000 + (2/3 x $3,000)	$(4,000)
Net long-term capital gain (2/3 x $15,000)	10,000
Net capital gain	$ 6,000

49. Taxpayer G had the following items of income and loss in 1991:

Wages	$28,000
Nonbusiness bad debt	1,000
Gain on commodity futures held 14 months	1,000
Loss on stock purchased in 1984	800
Flood loss on personal residence owned since 1982	4,500
Gain on stock held 13 months	4,500

What is G's net capital gain or net capital loss for 1991?

a. $200 gain.
b. $800 loss.
c. $3,700 gain.
d. $4,700 gain.

The correct answer is (c). *(SPE 1078 I-78)*
REQUIRED: The amount of net capital gain or loss to be included in taxable income.
DISCUSSION: Nonbusiness bad debts are treated as short-term capital losses. The nonbusiness bad debt is the only short-term transaction. The long-term capital transactions are the $800 loss on stock, the $4,500 gain on stock, and the $1,000 gain on commodity futures. The flood loss is an itemized deduction, not a deductible capital loss.

Net short-term:		
Nonbusiness bad debt		$(1,000)
Net long-term:		
1984 stock loss	$ (800)	
13-month stock gain	4,500	
Commodity futures gain	1,000	4,700
Net capital gain		$ 3,700

50. For the year 1991 Diana Clark had salary income of $38,000. In addition, she had the following capital transactions during the year:

Long-term capital gain	$14,000
Short-term capital gain	6,000
Long-term capital loss	(4,000)
Short-term capital loss	(8,000)

There were no other items includable in her gross income. What is her adjusted gross income for 1991?

a. $38,000.
b. $41,200.
c. $42,800.
d. $46,000.

The correct answer is (d). *(CPA 583 P-44)*
REQUIRED: The amount of adjusted gross income given various capital transactions.
DISCUSSION: In determining the amount of income to be included from capital gains and losses, the long-term capital gains and losses are netted and the short-term capital gains and losses are netted. These totals are then netted to determine the net capital gain.

Net short-term capital loss ($6,000 – $8,000)	$ (2,000)
Net long-term capital gain ($14,000 – $4,000)	10,000
Net capital gain	$ 8,000
Wages	38,000
Adjusted gross income	$46,000

51. Alan Kupper had the following transactions during 1991:

Gain of $7,000 on sale of common stock purchased on January 15, 1990 and sold on April 15, 1991.
Gain of $5,000 on sale of common stock purchased on October 15, 1990 and sold on March 25, 1991.
Receipt of a $10,000 installment payment on an installment contract created in 1983 when Kupper sold for $100,000 (exclusive of 6% interest on installments) land acquired in 1975 for $20,000. The contract provides for ten equal annual principal payments of $10,000 beginning on July 1, 1983 and ending on July 1, 1992.

What is the amount of Kupper's net capital gain for 1991?

a. $15,000.
b. $8,000.
c. $7,500.
d. $6,000.

The correct answer is (a). *(CPA 581 P-51)*
REQUIRED: The amount of net capital gain included in taxable income.
DISCUSSION: The sale of stock in April resulted in a long-term capital gain. The sale of stock in March resulted in a short-term capital gain because the stock was held less than 1 year. The sale of land in 1983 resulted in a long-term capital gain because it had been held more than 1 year. Therefore, Kupper's installment receipt in 1991 is considered long-term, and $8,000 of it represents gain under the installment method.

Long-term gains:	
Sale of stock in April 1991	$ 7,000
Installment payment [($10,000 ÷ $100,000) x $80,000]	8,000
Net capital gain	$15,000

Note that a net capital gain is the excess of net long-term capital gains over net short-term capital losses. Kupper's net short-term capital gain is not included in the net capital gain. However, the net short-term capital gain is included in taxable income (but is not given any special treatment).

14.5 Nonbusiness Bad Debts

52. Gilbert Quinn loaned a friend $2,000 in 1989 and it had not been repaid in 1991 when the friend died insolvent. For 1991, Quinn should account for the nonpayment of the loan as a(n)

a. Ordinary loss.
b. Long-term capital loss.
c. Short-term capital loss.
d. Deduction from adjusted gross income.

The correct answer is (c). *(CPA 1179 Q-28)*
REQUIRED: The treatment of the nonpayment of a personal loan.
DISCUSSION: A nonbusiness debt is defined under Sec. 166 as a debt other than one which is created or acquired in connection with a taxpayer's trade or business. A loan to a friend is a nonbusiness debt. When any nonbusiness debt becomes worthless, the loss is treated as a short-term capital loss. Note that a short-term capital loss is a deduction for adjusted gross income (above the line), but is limited to a total deduction of $3,000 per year for all capital losses in excess of capital gains.

Module 14.5: Nonbusiness Bad Debts

53. Earl Cook, who worked as a machinist for Precision Corp., lent Precision $1,000 in 1987. Cook did not own any of Precision's stock and the loan was not a condition of employment. In 1991, Precision declared bankruptcy, and Cook's note receivable from Precision became worthless. What loss can Cook claim on his 1991 income tax return?

   a. $0.
   b. $500 long-term capital loss.
   c. $1,000 short-term capital loss.
   d. $1,000 business bad debt.

54. Mr. G, a cash-basis taxpayer, loaned his neighbor, Mr. B, $5,000 in 1987. B signed a note and promised to pay G $1,000 a year plus 10% interest on the unpaid principal. B paid principal and interest in 1988 and 1989. No payments were made in 1990 or in 1991. In November 1991, B filed for bankruptcy. G has no chance of recovery. How will G report the loss on his 1991 tax return?

   a. $0 (no deduction).
   b. $3,000 short-term capital loss.
   c. $3,000 long-term capital loss.
   d. $3,000 miscellaneous itemized deduction.

55. In 1991, Mr. K had totally worthless nonbusiness bad debts of $10,000 and business bad debts of $5,000. His taxable income (figured without either of these losses) was $50,000. Mr. K had no other gains or losses. What is the maximum amount Mr. K can deduct with respect to his bad debts in 1991?

   a. $5,000.
   b. $8,000.
   c. $10,000.
   d. $12,000.

56. Nonbusiness bad debts are deductible only as short-term capital losses on Schedule D, Form 1040.

57. Mr. B loaned his sister, Mrs. M, $2,000 in 1984 to assist her in completing her education. Mrs. M did not sign a note, no terms for repayment were established, and B made no efforts to collect the $2,000. Mrs. M filed for bankruptcy in 1991. Mr. B may take a nonbusiness bad debt deduction in 1991.

The correct answer is (c). *(CPA 584 Q-21)*
REQUIRED: The treatment of an uncollectible loan made by an employee to the employer.
DISCUSSION: When a nonbusiness bad debt becomes worthless, the loss that results is treated as a short-term capital loss under Sec. 166. A nonbusiness bad debt is one that is created or acquired other than in connection with a trade or business of the taxpayer. Loans made to employers are not considered business loans unless made as a condition of employment or in order to keep employment. Earl's loss is from a nonbusiness bad debt and is treated as a short-term capital loss in the amount of $1,000.

The correct answer is (b). *(SPE 984 I-66)*
REQUIRED: The proper treatment of an uncollectible nonbusiness loan.
DISCUSSION: A taxpayer is entitled to a deduction when a debt becomes worthless during the tax year. The loss by an individual is considered a short-term capital loss if the debt was a nonbusiness debt. A nonbusiness debt is one not created or acquired in connection with the creditor's trade or business. Assuming G was not in the business of lending money, the debt was a nonbusiness bad debt and the loss is treated as a short-term capital loss. The amount of the loss equals the $5,000 originally loaned less the $2,000 principal collected in 1988 and 1989.

The correct answer is (b). *(SPE 984 II-71)*
REQUIRED: The maximum amount deductible given both business and nonbusiness bad debts.
DISCUSSION: Under Sec. 166, a bad debt is deductible as an ordinary loss in the year the debt becomes worthless as long as it is not a nonbusiness bad debt. Mr. K can deduct the full amount of his business bad debt ($5,000). Nonbusiness bad debts are treated as short-term capital losses. Capital losses are deductible up to the lesser of taxable income or $3,000 in any year. Mr. K can deduct $3,000 of his nonbusiness bad debt in 1991 and the balance in subsequent years. His 1991 deduction is thus $8,000 ($5,000 + $3,000).

The correct answer is (T). *(SPE 989 I-28)*
DISCUSSION: Under Sec. 166, a nonbusiness bad debt is treated as a short-term capital loss. Under Sec. 166, when a nonbusiness bad debt becomes worthless, the resulting loss is treated as a short-term capital loss. Individual taxpayers report short-term capital losses on the Schedule D, Form 1040.

The correct answer is (F). *(SPE 984 I-36)*
DISCUSSION: Under Reg. 1.166-1(c), only a bona fide debt qualifies for deduction as a bad debt. A bona fide debt is one that arises from a debtor-creditor relationship based on a valid and enforceable obligation to pay a sum of money. Since there was no note, no terms for repayment, and no effort by B to collect the $2,000, the debt is not considered a bona fide debt and is not deductible.

58. Mr. B contracted with ACE Home Builders to build his personal residence at a cost of $50,000. B advanced ACE $10,000 prior to the start of construction. Due to insolvency, ACE was unable to start construction and B had to hire another contractor. Since B was unable to collect the $10,000 from ACE, he can take a nonbusiness bad debt deduction of $10,000.

The correct answer is (T). *(SPE 987 I-32)*
DISCUSSION: When the contractor could not perform or return the money, the advance became a bad debt for Mr. B. The debt is nonbusiness because it relates to a personal residence. Nonbusiness bad debts are deductible as short-term capital losses under Sec. 166.

59. In order to protect his investment, Mr. C, an officer and stockholder of Corporation Z, guaranteed payment of a bank loan received by the Corporation. Z defaulted on the loan and Mr. C was required to pay off the balance. Mr. C was unable to collect from Z. Mr. C has a deductible nonbusiness bad debt.

The correct answer is (T). *(SPE 987 I-34)*
DISCUSSION: A nonbusiness bad debt is a debt other than one incurred or acquired in connection with the trade or business of the taxpayer. The investment is not considered a trade or business, and a shareholder who makes a loan to a corporation to protect his/her investment is not considered to have made a business loan. Therefore, Mr. C has a nonbusiness bad debt. It is deductible as a short-term capital loss.

14.6 Section 1244 Stock

60. Which of the following is not a requirement for stock to be qualified as "Small Business Stock" (Sec. 1244)?

   a. The corporation was qualified as a Small Business Corporation.
   b. The stock is not convertible into other securities of the corporation.
   c. The stock was issued for money or property other than stock or securities.
   d. The stock must be voting common stock.

The correct answer is (d). *(SPE 1077 I-171)*
REQUIRED: The item which is not required for stock to qualify as Sec. 1244 stock.
DISCUSSION: A loss on Sec. 1244 stock (limited to $50,000, or $100,000 on a joint return) is treated as an ordinary loss instead of a capital loss. Such stock may be common stock or preferred stock, whether voting or nonvoting.
Answer (a) is incorrect because the corporation must be a "small business corporation," which means its capital does not exceed $1,000,000. Answer (b) is incorrect because the stock may be common stock or preferred stock but not convertible into other securities. Answer (c) is incorrect because the stock must be issued for money or other property, not including stock or securities.

61. Mrs. O sold her interest in a small business corporation (Sec. 1244 stock) and incurred a loss of $150,000. Mrs. O is married and files a joint return. What is the amount and character of her loss?

	Ordinary Loss	Capital Loss
a.	$0	$150,000
b.	$50,000	$100,000
c.	$100,000	$50,000
d.	$150,000	$0

The correct answer is (c). *(SPE 987 II-51)*
REQUIRED: The amount and character of loss from the sale of Sec. 1244 stock.
DISCUSSION: The determination of the recognized loss on the sale of Sec. 1244 stock is the same as with any other asset. However, unlike losses on most long-term capital assets, part of this loss is an ordinary loss. The ordinary loss is limited to $100,000 for a husband and wife who file a joint return. Any loss in excess of the limit is given capital loss treatment. Therefore, $100,000 of the loss is ordinary and the other $50,000 is capital loss.

Module 14.6: Section 1244 Stock

62. During 1991, Mrs. Venture sold her interests in two small business corporations (Sec. 1244). Her loss on Corporation X stock was $120,000 and her loss on Corporation Y stock was $20,000. Mrs. Venture files jointly with her husband. What is the amount and character of Mrs. Venture's loss to be reported on their joint return for 1991?

   a. $140,000 ordinary; $0 capital.
   b. $100,000 ordinary; $40,000 capital.
   c. $40,000 ordinary; $100,000 capital.
   d. $0 ordinary; $140,000 capital.

The correct answer is (b). *(SPE 989 II-48)*
REQUIRED: The amount and character of loss to be reported from Sec. 1244 stock.
DISCUSSION: Unlike losses on most capital assets held long-term, part of the loss from the sale or exchange of Sec. 1244 stock is treated as ordinary loss. Under Sec. 1244(b), the aggregate amount treated by the taxpayer by reason of Sec. 1244 as an ordinary loss shall not exceed $100,000 in the case of a husband and wife filing a joint return. The aggregate Sec. 1244 loss, in this case, is $140,000 ($120,000 from Corp. X + $20,000 from Corp. Y). Subject to the Sec. 1244(b) limitation, $100,000 is allowed as ordinary loss, the remaining $40,000 is treated as a capital loss.

63. Mr. F transferred property with an adjusted basis of $1,000 and a fair market value of $250 to a qualifying corporation for its small business stock (Sec. 1244). He later sold the stock for $200. What is the amount and character of F's loss?

   a. $250 ordinary and $750 capital.
   b. $200 ordinary and $750 capital.
   c. $50 ordinary and $750 capital.
   d. $0 ordinary and $750 capital.

The correct answer is (c). *(SPE 989 II-73)*
REQUIRED: The amount and character of loss when property having basis in excess of FMV is exchanged for Sec. 1244 stock and the stock is later sold for a loss.
DISCUSSION: Under Sec. 1244(d)(1)(A), when property having a basis in excess of its value is exchanged for Sec. 1244 stock, the basis taken in the stock is the basis of the property exchanged. When there is a loss on the sale of the Sec. 1244 stock, however, the basis is reduced by the difference between the basis and the fair market value at the time of the original exchange. In this case, the difference was $750 ($1,000 – $250). This $750 is a capital loss. The new basis is $250 [$1,000 basis – ($1,000 – $250)]. So, the ordinary loss is $50 ($200 sales price – $250 basis).

64. Corporation H was incorporated in 1991 and received $750,000 as a contribution to capital and $300,000 as paid-in surplus in exchange for its stock. Corporation H qualifies as a small business corporation under Sec. 1244 of the Internal Revenue Code.

The correct answer is (F). *(SPE 1083 III-17)*
DISCUSSION: To qualify under Sec. 1244, the corporation must be a small business corporation. To be classified as a small business corporation, the aggregate amount of money and other property received by the corporation for stock, as a contribution to capital and as paid-in surplus, cannot exceed $1,000,000. Even though the paid-in capital exceeds $1,000,000, part of the stock (up to $1,000,000) will be designated by the corporation as qualifying for Sec. 1244 ordinary loss treatment.

65. The AB Partnership acquired $500,000 in qualifying Sec. 1244 stock in Corporation X as an investment in 1986. Corporation X went bankrupt in 1991. Partners A and B have been 50/50 owners since the partnership's inception. Partners A and B are entitled to individually claim $250,000 of ordinary loss with respect to the worthless stock of Corporation X in 1991.

The correct answer is (F). *(SPE 1078 III-26)*
DISCUSSION: An individual taxpayer is entitled to recognize the loss on Sec. 1244 stock as an ordinary loss, subject to a maximum amount of $50,000 per year ($100,000 per year for a husband and wife filing a joint return). If a partnership owns the stock, individual partners are entitled to the Sec. 1244 ordinary loss. Each partner may claim only a $50,000 ($100,000 if filing jointly with spouses) ordinary loss with respect to the worthless stock of Corporation X in 1991. Any remaining loss is a capital loss.

14.7 Capital Loss Limitations and Carryovers

66. The ordinary loss provisions on small business stock (Sec. 1244) are available only to the original owner of the stock.

The correct answer is (T). *(SPE 1082 II-30)*
DISCUSSION: Sec. 1244(a) provides that an individual is entitled to an ordinary loss on a sale of Sec. 1244 stock which was issued to such individual. Reg. 1.1244(a)-1(b) provides that to claim the deduction under Sec. 1244, the individual must have continuously held the stock from the date of issuance. For example, the ordinary loss treatment would not apply to an individual who acquires the stock by gift or inheritance.

67. Mr. J sold land that he had purchased for investment purposes to Ms. P for $5,000 cash and her assumption of an existing mortgage of $2,000 and delinquent back taxes of $1,500. Mr. J's adjusted basis in the land was $10,000 and he paid $600 in selling costs. What is Mr. J's recognized loss?

a. $0.
b. $(1,500).
c. $(2,100).
d. $(2,400).

The correct answer is (c). *(SPE 1082 I-84)*
REQUIRED: The recognized loss from the sale of investment property on which the buyer assumes a mortgage and pays back taxes.
DISCUSSION: The gain or loss from the sale of property is the amount realized less the adjusted basis (Sec. 1001). Mr. J realized $5,000 in cash, relief of a mortgage liability of $2,000, and relief of back taxes of $1,500. This gross amount realized totals $8,500. However, selling costs decrease the amount realized, so Mr. J's net amount realized is $7,900 ($8,500 − $600). Mr. J's recognized loss is $2,100 ($7,900 realized − $10,000 basis). This is a capital loss since property held for investment is a capital asset.

68. In 1991 capital losses incurred by a married couple filing a joint return

a. Will be allowed only to the extent of capital gains.
b. Will be allowed to the extent of capital gains, plus up to $3,000 of ordinary income.
c. May be carried forward up to a maximum of 5 years.
d. Is not an allowable loss.

The correct answer is (b). *(CPA 1188 Q-8)*
REQUIRED: The correct statement concerning deductibility of capital losses incurred by a married couple filing jointly.
DISCUSSION: The amount of capital losses that can be deducted is the lesser of the excess of capital losses over capital gains or $3,000 [Sec. 1211(b)]. The maximum amount in excess of capital gains allowed as a deduction is $3,000 ($1,500 for taxpayers filing separately).
Answer (a) is incorrect because capital losses are deductible in excess of capital gains, but this excess is limited to $3,000. Answer (c) is incorrect because capital losses that are not deductible in the current year may be carried forward indefinitely. Answer (d) is incorrect because capital losses are deductible to the extent of capital gains and any excess is deductible to the extent of $3,000.

69. During 1991, Mr. H, who is married filing separately, made the following sales of stock.

100 shares of ABC Co. on 6/1/91	$1,000
Purchased 2/1/91 for $2,000	
100 shares of XYZ Co. on 9/1/91	750
Purchased 4/1/91 for $1,500	
100 shares of EFG Co. on 11/1/91	1,000
Purchased 9/15/89 for $3,000	

What is the amount of H's deductible capital loss for 1991?

a. $0.
b. $1,500.
c. $3,000.
d. $3,500.

The correct answer is (b). *(SPE 988 I-87)*
REQUIRED: The deductible capital loss for a married taxpayer filing separately.
DISCUSSION: Mr. H has a net short-term capital loss of $1,750 ($1,000 from the stock sold in June and $750 from the stock sold in September). He has net long-term capital loss of $2,000 from the stock sold in November. His total capital loss is therefore $3,750 ($1,000 + $750 + $2,000).
Under Sec. 1211(b), a noncorporate taxpayer is allowed a deduction for capital losses in excess of capital gains limited to the lesser of the excess of capital losses over capital gains, or $3,000. But this $3,000 limitation is $1,500 for a taxpayer who is married filing separately. Therefore, H's deductible capital loss is $1,500.

70. For 1991, Mr. G has a short-term capital loss of $4,000, a short-term capital gain of $1,900, a short-term capital loss carryover from 1989 of $700, a long-term capital gain of $800, and a long-term capital loss of $1,500. What is Mr. G's deductible loss in 1991?

a. $2,300.
b. $2,800.
c. $3,000.
d. $3,500.

The correct answer is (c). *(SPE 1081 I-86)*
REQUIRED: The amount of deductible capital loss that may be claimed for 1991.
DISCUSSION: Short-term capital gains and losses, and long-term capital gains and losses are first netted to determine the capital loss deduction. The carryover from 1989 retains its character as a short-term capital loss and is netted with the other short-term transactions.

Short-term: ($1,900 − $4,000 − $700)	$(2,800)
Long-term: ($800 − $1,500)	(700)
Capital loss	$(3,500)

Since the loss computed above exceeds $3,000, the amount deductible is limited to the lesser of $3,000 or taxable income (Sec. 1211). Long-term capital losses of $500 are carried forward.

71. For the year 1991 Michael King reported salary and taxable interest income of $40,000. His capital asset transactions during the year were as follows:

Long-term capital gains	$ 2,000
Long-term capital losses	(8,000)
Short-term capital gains	1,000

For 1991 King should report adjusted gross income of

a. $35,000.
b. $37,000.
c. $37,500.
d. $39,000.

The correct answer is (b). *(CPA 579 Q-37)*
REQUIRED: The taxpayer's adjusted gross income for 1991.
DISCUSSION: Under Sec. 1211, a taxpayer may deduct the excess of the net long-term capital loss over net short-term capital gain, provided that such amount does not exceed $3,000. Net long-term capital loss is $6,000 ($2,000 − $8,000). King's excess of net long-term capital loss over net short-term capital gain is $5,000 ($6,000 − $1,000). Therefore, the $3,000 limit applies.

Salary and interest income	$40,000
Less capital loss deduction	(3,000)
Adjusted gross income	$37,000

72. On February 16, 1990, Fred Samson purchased 100 shares of Oscar Corp. stock at $40 per share. On July 28, 1991 he sold the 100 shares at $25 per share. On August 10, 1991 his wife purchased 50 shares of Oscar Corp. at $30 per share. These are the only capital asset transactions by the Samsons during 1991. In computing his 1991 taxable income, Fred may deduct from his ordinary income of $15,000 a capital loss in the amount of

a. $375.
b. $750.
c. $1,000.
d. $1,500.

The correct answer is (b). *(CPA 573 Q-9)*
REQUIRED: The amount of capital loss that the taxpayer may deduct from ordinary income.
DISCUSSION: Fred sold 100 shares of stock on July 28 and his wife subsequently purchased 50 shares of the same corporation on August 10. Consequently, 50 of the shares Fred sold are not eligible for the capital loss deduction because this would be considered a wash sale (spouses are treated as the same taxpayer for this purpose). Under Sec. 1091, a wash sale occurs when substantially the same securities are purchased within 30 days of being sold for a loss. A capital loss deduction is available for the other 50 shares. The sale of 50 shares resulted in a $750 loss. The full amount of the loss is deductible.

Sales price (50 x $25)	$ 1,250
Less adjusted basis (50 x $40)	(2,000)
Long-term capital loss	$ (750)

Module 14.7: Capital Loss Limitations and Carryovers

73. On March 1, 1990, Rollin Doe bought 200 shares of Gummit stock at $40 per share. On April 1, 1991, Rollin sold short (sold without delivering) 100 shares of Gummit stock for $50 per share. On December 1, 1991, Rollin bought 100 shares of Gummit stock for $60 per share and closed the short sale by delivering this stock. What is the tax result to Rollin Doe?

a. $1,000 short-term capital loss.
b. $1,000 short-term capital gain.
c. $1,000 long-term capital loss.
d. $1,000 long-term capital gain.

The correct answer is (c). *(Publisher)*
REQUIRED: The gain or loss from a short sale when substantially identical stock has been held long-term.
DISCUSSION: The treatment of gains and losses from short sales of stock is determined under Sec. 1233. If property substantially identical to that which is sold short has been held long-term as of the date of the short sale, any loss incurred on the short sale is long-term. Since Rollin Doe owned 200 shares of Gummit stock for more than 1 year prior to the short sale, any loss will be long-term capital loss. The loss was $1,000 since Rollin Doe received $5,000 on the sale and satisfied it with stock which he purchased for $6,000. Rollin Doe has a $1,000 long-term capital loss.

74. In 1991, Mr. K decided to go into a new business. He incurred the following costs:

Travel to look over various business alternatives	$1,000
Travel to look for possible business locations	500
Market surveys for various businesses	1,500
Legal fees to set up the new business	1,000
Advertising to promote the new business	1,500
Expenses to train employees	2,000

Despite K's efforts, circumstances beyond his control prevented him from actually starting business operations and he abandoned the project late in 1991. How should Mr. K handle these costs in his 1991 tax return?

	Ordinary Loss or Schedule C Loss	Capital Loss
a.	$0	$0
b.	$0	$4,500
c.	$4,500	$0
d.	$4,500	$3,000

The correct answer is (b). *(SPE 1083 II-64)*
REQUIRED: The amount of ordinary loss and capital loss for business start-up costs when the business was abandoned.
DISCUSSION: Business start-up expenditures are normally amortizable under Sec. 195 and not otherwise deductible. However, when the business is disposed of prior to full amortization, the unamortized balance is deductible as a loss [Sec. 195(b)(2)]. The legal fees, advertising, and expenses to train employees are start-up expenditures under Sec. 195. These expenditures total $4,500. The travel and market surveys are not Sec. 195 start-up expenditures and are not deductible at all because they do not relate to the organization of a specific business. Rather, they are merely general investigatory expenditures.

The $4,500 loss is a capital loss because the capitalizable start-up expenditures are deemed to be capital assets since they do not fall within an exclusion specified in Sec. 1221.

75. During 1991, Nancy had the following transactions:

Short-term capital loss	($2,400)
Short-term capital gain	2,000
Short-term capital loss carryover for 1989	(1,400)
Long-term capital gain	3,800
Long-term capital loss	(8,000)

What is the amount of her capital loss deduction in 1991, and what is the amount and character of her capital loss carryover?

	Deduction	Carryover
a.	$0	$6,000 long-term
b.	$3,000	$3,000 long-term
c.	$6,000	$0
d.	$3,000	$3,000 short-term

The correct answer is (b). *(SPE 990 I-79)*
REQUIRED: The taxpayer's current capital loss deduction and carryover.
DISCUSSION: The deduction for any capital loss is the excess of capital losses over capital gains (Sec. 1211). The capital loss deduction, however, is limited to $3,000 in any year. Unused capital losses may be carried forward indefinitely. Short-term capital losses are considered first to determine the character of the carryover. In this case, there is an $1,800 short-term capital loss ($400 current year net loss + $1,400 carryover from 1989). The net long-term capital loss for the year is $4,200 ($3,800 − $8,000). Only $1,200 of the long-term capital loss can be deducted during the current year; the remaining $3,000 is a carryover. The total deduction is $3,000 ($1,800 short-term + $1,200 long-term).

Module 14.7: Capital Loss Limitations and Carryovers

76. During 1991, Stacy, who is single and has no dependents, sold the following shares of stock:

Stock	Date Purchased	Adjusted Basis	Date Sold	Sales Proceeds
Alpha Corp.	12/2/89	$3,500	6/29/91	$1,100
Beta Corp.	7/11/89	2,000	4/15/91	100
Delta Corp.	5/27/90	3,000	5/26/91	1,500
Gamma Corp.	1/22/91	1,500	7/28/91	200

Stacy's taxable income for 1991 is $500 before the personal exemption and capital loss deductions. What is the amount of her allowable capital loss deduction?

a. $0.
b. $500.
c. $1,500.
d. $3,000.

77. Based on the information in Q. 76, what is the amount and character of Stacy's capital loss carryover to 1992?

a. $0 short-term; $4,100 long-term.
b. $2,800 short-term; $1,300 long-term.
c. $2,800 short-term; $3,800 long-term.
d. $2,300 short-term; $4,300 long-term.

78. For 1991, Mr. H had taxable income of $120,000, excluding exemptions and capital transactions. In 1991, H's capital transactions were as follows:

	Short-term	Long-term
Gains	$10,000	$20,000
Losses	(13,000)	(24,000)

In addition, Mr. H had a $2,200 short-term capital loss carryover from 1990. What is the amount of H's capital loss deduction in 1991 and capital loss carryover to 1992?

	Deduction	Carryover Short-term	Long-term
a.	$0	$5,200	$4,000
b.	$3,000	$3,000	$200
c.	$3,000	$0	$3,200
d.	$3,000	$2,200	$4,000

The correct answer is (d). *(SPE 989 I-81)*
REQUIRED: The capital loss deduction for a single taxpayer in 1991.
DISCUSSION: The capital losses from the four transactions are categorized as follows:

Stock	Short-term Gain or Loss	Long-term Gain or Loss
Alpha		$(2,400)
Beta		(1,900)
Delta	$(1,500)	
Gamma	(1,300)	
Total	$(2,800)	$(4,300)

The loss on the Delta stock is short-term since the stock has been held for only 1 year. Normally Sec. 1211 limits the capital loss deduction to $3,000 and $4,100 of excess losses would be carried over to 1992.

However, Stacy's taxable income (before the capital loss and personal exemption deductions) of $500 is less than the $3,000 capital loss deduction and she will obtain a tax benefit from only part of the capital loss deduction. The carryover to 1992 is instead computed as if her capital loss deduction was limited to the $500 of taxable income. Thus, Stacy's carryover to 1992 is $6,600.

The correct answer is (d). *(SPE 989 I-82)*
REQUIRED: The amount and character of the capital loss carryover to 1992.
DISCUSSION: In Q. 76, Stacy reported $7,100 ($2,800 + $4,300) of capital losses, of which $500 were deductible in 1991; $6,600 ($7,100 − 500) of these losses can be carried over to 1992. For 1991's deduction, short-term losses were used first. Because only $500 of losses provided a tax benefit, $2,300 ($2,800 − 500) of the short-term losses are carried over to 1992. In addition, all $4,300 of the long-term capital losses are carried over to 1992.

The correct answer is (d). *(SPE 988 I-82)*
REQUIRED: The capital loss deduction in 1991 and the capital loss carryover to 1992.
DISCUSSION: Mr. H has a net short-term capital loss of $3,000 ($10,000 − $13,000) and a net long-term capital loss of $4,000 ($20,000 − $24,000) for 1991. Mr. H also has a $2,200 short-term capital loss carryover from 1990. The total capital loss of $9,200 ($3,000 + $4,000 + $2,200) is deductible only to the extent of the $3,000 limitation on deductions for capital losses in any 1 year.

For the $3,000 deduction, short-term capital losses are used first. Therefore, $3,000 of the short-term capital loss will be used up in 1991, leaving $2,200 ($3,000 + $2,200 − $3,000) to carry over. None of the long-term capital loss will be used in 1991, leaving all $4,000 to carry over.

Module 14.7: Capital Loss Limitations and Carryovers

79. The income tax treatment of individual and corporate taxpayers agrees in which of the following respects?

    a. Excess capital losses may be carried forward 5 years and losses may not be carried back.

    b. Excess capital losses may be offset against income from other sources, but only to a limited extent.

    c. Excess capital losses retain their identity as either long-term or short-term losses in the year to which they are carried.

    d. None of the above.

The correct answer is (d). *(CPA 1173 Q-4)*
REQUIRED: The correct statement regarding similarity of capital loss treatment for corporate and individual taxpayers.
DISCUSSION: None of the statements is correct (Secs. 1211 and 1212). The only similarities between corporate and individual treatment of capital losses are that the capital loss definition and the netting process are the same.
Answer (a) is incorrect because individuals can carry excess losses forward indefinitely, while corporations may carry them forward for only 5 years. Also, excess capital losses are not carried back by individuals, but are carried back 3 years by corporations. Answer (b) is incorrect because excess capital losses may be offset against ordinary income to a limited extent by individual taxpayers, but corporations may only offset capital losses with capital gains. Answer (c) is incorrect because carryovers do retain their identity as long- or short-term for individuals but not for corporations.

80. Mr. D's capital losses for 1991 exceeded the $3,000 capital loss limitation. He may elect to carry the unused capital loss back to an earlier year.

The correct answer is (F). *(SPE 1081 I-39)*
DISCUSSION: An individual taxpayer may only carry an unused capital loss forward (Sec. 1212). Only corporations are entitled to carry back excess capital losses (for 3 years).

81. When carrying over an individual's unused long-term capital loss, 100% of the loss is carried to the next year and is treated as if it had been incurred in that year.

The correct answer is (T). *(SPE 1079 I-38)*
DISCUSSION: For purposes of capital loss carryovers, the taxpayer carries over the entire loss and uses it as an offset against capital gains and income of the succeeding year just as if the loss had occurred in the succeeding year (Sec. 1212).

82. If an individual has capital losses from 2 or more years and they are carried to the same year, the loss from the earliest year is deducted first. When that loss is completely used up, the loss from the next earliest year is deducted, and so on.

The correct answer is (F). *(SPE 990 III-8)*
DISCUSSION: An individual's capital losses are carried forward indefinitely [Sec. 1212(b)(1)]. The net short-term loss or net long-term capital loss carryover that is not offset against capital gains or deducted in the carryover year is treated as a short-term loss or long-term loss, as the case may be, that is incurred in the succeeding year. These carryovers are offset against capital gains in the succeeding year using the regular combining rules for capital gains and losses. Carryovers that are not offset against capital gains can be deducted starting with the short-term losses first and then the long-term losses. Therefore, the earliest incurred loss is not always deducted first.

14.8 Sales to Related Parties

83. In January 1991, Luther Miller sold stock with a cost basis of $26,000 to his brother, Marvin, for $24,000, the fair market value of the stock on the date of sale. Five months later, Marvin sold the same stock through his broker for $27,000. The tax effect for 1991 of these transactions would be a

a. Nondeductible loss to Luther of $2,000; recognized gain to Marvin of $1,000.
b. Nondeductible loss to Luther of $2,000; recognized gain to Marvin of $3,000.
c. Deductible loss to Luther of $2,000; recognized gain to Marvin of $3,000.
d. None of the above.

The correct answer is (a). *(CPA 577 Q-22)*
REQUIRED: The tax effects of the sale of stock between related parties, followed by a subsequent sale of the same stock.
DISCUSSION: Under Sec. 267, losses are not allowed on sales or exchanges of property between related parties. Brothers are related parties for this purpose. Luther realized a $2,000 loss but may not deduct it. When Marvin subsequently sold the stock he realized a $3,000 gain, but he recognizes only $1,000 of it. The previously disallowed loss is used to offset any subsequent gain on the sale of the property.

84. On July 1, 1991, Daniel Wright owned stock (held for investment) purchased 2 years earlier at a cost of $10,000 and having a fair market value of $7,000. On this date he sold the stock to his son, William, for $7,000. William sold the stock for $6,000 to an unrelated person on November 1, 1991. How should William report the stock sale (before any deduction) on his 1991 tax return?

a. As a short-term capital loss of $1,000.
b. As a long-term capital loss of $1,000.
c. As a short-term capital loss of $4,000.
d. As a long-term capital loss of $4,000.

The correct answer is (a). *(CPA 583 P-48)*
REQUIRED: The treatment of a loss on the sale of stock acquired from a related party in a loss transaction.
DISCUSSION: Under Sec. 267, losses are not allowed on sales or exchanges of property between related parties. A father and son are related parties for this purpose. Thus, Daniel's loss of $3,000 on the sale of the stock to William is disallowed. William takes as his basis for the stock the cost of $7,000. Since William's stock basis is determined by his cost (not by reference to Daniel's cost), there is no carryover of Daniel's holding period to William. Therefore, upon the sale of the stock to an unrelated party for $6,000, William realizes a short-term loss of $1,000.

85. Mitch sold stock he had purchased for $20,000 to his sister Carol for $18,000. Later, Carol sold the stock to an unrelated party for $22,000. What is the amount of Carol's recognized gain?

a. $0.
b. $1,000.
c. $2,000.
d. $4,000.

The correct answer is (c). *(SPE 990 I-76)*
REQUIRED: The amount of recognized gain when stock is sold after acquisition from a related party in a loss transaction.
DISCUSSION: Under Sec. 267, losses are not allowed on sales or exchanges of property between related parties. Brothers and sisters are related parties. Mitch realized a $2,000 ($20,000 – $18,000) loss on the sale but may not deduct it. On the subsequent sale, Carol realized a $4,000 gain ($22,000 sales price – $18,000 basis). However, she only recognizes a $2,000 gain. The disallowed loss is used to offset the subsequent gain on the sale of the property ($4,000 realized gain – $2,000 disallowed loss).

Module 14.8: Sales to Related Parties

86. Mr. M sold stock that cost him $10,000 to his brother for $7,600. Later, Mr. M's brother sold the stock to an unrelated party for $6,900. What is the amount of Mr. M's brother's recognized loss?

a. $3,100.
b. $2,400.
c. $700.
d. $0.

The correct answer is (c). *(SPE 987 I-82)*
REQUIRED: The amount of loss recognized on a subsequent sale of related party property.
DISCUSSION: When Mr. M sold the stock to his brother, Mr. M had a realized loss of $2,400. He was not allowed to recognize the loss because his brother was a related party under Sec. 267.

When Mr. M's brother later resold the stock, he realized a $700 loss based on his purchase price of $7,600. This loss is recognized because he sold the stock to an unrelated party. The fact that Mr. M's $2,400 loss was not recognized does not affect the loss recognized by Mr. M's brother. Only if Mr. M's brother sold the stock at a gain would he be able to offset the gain by Mr. M's disallowed loss.

87. S. Lumlord owns and lives in a large, two-story home situated in a neighborhood adjacent to a large university. S. Lumlord purchased the property several years ago for $60,000. The property has recently been rezoned to permit apartment buildings. S. Lumlord owns 60% of the Gainsburg Student Living Co. and the remainder is owned by a local city commissioner. In 1991, S. Lumlord sells the personal residence, subject to a first mortgage of $40,000, to the Gainsburg Student Living Co. for $30,000 cash and a promissory note secured by a second mortgage for $30,000. The Gainsburg Student Living Co. will rent the rooms in the building to students. How is the gain taxed to S. Lumlord?

a. $0.
b. $30,000 long-term capital gain.
c. $40,000 long-term capital gain.
d. $40,000 ordinary income.

The correct answer is (d). *(Publisher)*
REQUIRED: The treatment of the gain on the sale of depreciable property to a more-than-50%-owned entity.
DISCUSSION: S. Lumlord's gain is $40,000. Lumlord realized $30,000 cash, was relieved of a mortgage of $40,000, and received a note for $30,000. These total $100,000 and, after deducting the basis of $60,000, result in a gain of $40,000.

The gain on a personal residence is normally capital gain, but Sec. 1239 provides that the gain on sale of property between related persons will be treated as ordinary income if the property is depreciable in the hands of the transferee. Related persons include a taxpayer and a more-than-50%-owned entity. Since S. Lumlord owns 60% of the Gainsburg Student Living Co., and the property is depreciable in the hands of the Gainsburg Student Living Co. (because it is being rented), the $40,000 gain will be treated as ordinary income.

88. Mr. J owns 100% of the stock of Corporation K (an S corporation). His mother, Mrs. J, owns 100% of the stock of Corporation L. Corporation K sold a piece of property, with a basis to K of $12,000, to Corporation L for $10,000. Since Corporation K and Corporation L are related parties, Corporation K cannot claim the $2,000 loss.

The correct answer is (T). *(SPE 987 III-19)*
DISCUSSION: Under Sec. 267, losses are not allowed on sales or exchanges of property between related parties. Related parties include a C corporation and an S corporation of which more than 50% is owned by the same person. Constructive ownership rules apply so that an individual is treated as owning stock owned by a family member. As a result, Mr. J is treated as owning the stock that his mother owns. His mother is treated as owning the stock that Mr. J owns. Corporation K and Corporation L are therefore treated as related parties.

CHAPTER FIFTEEN
SALE OF BUSINESS PROPERTY

15.1 Section 1231 Property	(8 questions)	359
15.2 Section 1245 Property	(25 questions)	361
15.3 Section 1250 Property	(16 questions)	368
15.4 Sale of a Business	(6 questions)	374
15.5 Sales to Related Parties	(7 questions)	376
15.6 Effect on Taxable Income	(6 questions)	378

15.1 Section 1231 Property

1. The following property is all used in a trade or business and has been held in excess of 1 year. Which property will not qualify for gains or losses from Sec. 1231 property upon its disposition by sale or exchange?

  a. Property held for production of rent and royalties.
  b. Business property condemned for public use.
  c. Depreciable property used in a trade or business.
  d. Property includable in inventory.

The correct answer is (d). *(SPE 1078 II-53)*
REQUIRED: The property which does not meet the definition of Sec. 1231 property.
DISCUSSION: Gains and losses receive special treatment under Sec. 1231. Property which qualifies under Sec. 1231 generally must have been held for more than 1 year and either have been used in a trade or business or be an involuntarily converted nonpersonal capital asset. Inventory is specifically excluded.
Answer (a) is incorrect because the property is used in a trade or business. Answer (b) is incorrect because condemnation of business property is specifically included as a Sec. 1231 transaction. Answer (c) is incorrect because depreciable property used in a trade or business is a primary example of Sec. 1231 property.

2. Which of the following assets will not qualify for gain or loss treatment under Sec. 1231?

  a. Factory machine, acquired March 1, 1990, sold August 1, 1991.
  b. Land used as a parking lot, acquired August 1, 1990, sold September 1, 1991.
  c. Sculpture acquired August 1, 1990 by an investor for the purpose of making a profit on it, which was destroyed in a fire on September 1, 1991.
  d. Personal automobile, acquired August 1, 1990, destroyed in a collision on September 1, 1991.

The correct answer is (d). *(Publisher)*
REQUIRED: The asset that is not Sec. 1231 property.
DISCUSSION: Sec. 1231 property is depreciable or real property used in a trade or business and held for more than 1 year, or an involuntarily converted nonpersonal capital asset (i.e., held in connection with a trade or business or a transaction entered into for profit) held for more than 1 year. The personal automobile is a personal use capital asset and does not qualify for treatment under Sec. 1231.
Answers (a), (b), and (c) are incorrect because each is an example of Sec. 1231 property.

3. Janice owns a gift shop and lives in the back part of the building. A hurricane destroyed much of the property. Gains or losses on which of the following assets are Sec. 1231 assets, assuming all are held long-term?

  a. Personal automobile.
  b. Portion of the building used as a residence.
  c. Portion of the building used for the gift shop.
  d. Inventory in the gift shop.

The correct answer is (c). *(Publisher)*
REQUIRED: The asset that is Sec. 1231 property.
DISCUSSION: Sec. 1231 applies to property involuntarily converted by storm, if held more than 1 year, and is depreciable or real property used in a trade or business, or a capital asset held in connection with a trade or business or a transaction entered into for profit [Sec. 1231(a)(3)(A)]. The portion of the building used for the gift shop qualifies.
Answers (a) and (b) are incorrect because Sec. 1231 does not apply to personal use property. Answer (d) is incorrect because inventory is not a capital asset, nor is it depreciable or real property.

4. Trudy Holiday has been selling greeting cards for several years as a sole proprietor. In May 1991, she purchased land and a building to use in the greeting card business. In October 1991, she sold the entire business, including inventory held since 1989 and the land and building. Trudy's automobile, used exclusively in her business and purchased in 1989, was swallowed by a sinkhole before the sale in 1991. Which of the following is a Sec. 1231 asset?

   a. The inventory acquired in 1989.

   b. The building.

   c. The land.

   d. The automobile.

The correct answer is (d). *(Publisher)*
REQUIRED: The asset that is Sec. 1231 property.
DISCUSSION: Sec. 1231 property is depreciable or real property used in a trade or business and held for more than 1 year, and nonpersonal capital assets, held more than 1 year, which are involuntarily converted. Trudy's business automobile is Sec. 1231 property because it was held long term and was involuntarily converted.

Answer (a) is incorrect because inventory is not real or depreciable property used in a trade or business.
Answers (b) and (c) are incorrect because the building and land were not held for more than 1 year, so they are not Sec. 1231 property even though they were used in a trade or business.

---

5. During 1991 Budd Weiser sold a building used in his business. His records relating to the sale reflect the following information:

Cash received	$100,000
Fair market value of property received	25,000
Real estate taxes assumed by buyer	2,000
Mortgage assumed by buyer	20,000
Budd's adjusted basis in building sold	80,000

What is the amount of Mr. Weiser's recognized gain?

   a. $67,000.

   b. $65,000.

   c. $47,000.

   d. $42,000.

The correct answer is (a). *(SPE 989 I-74)*
REQUIRED: The amount of recognized gain on the sale of a building used in a business.
DISCUSSION: Under Sec. 1001, the gain on the sale or other disposition of property is the excess of the amount realized over the adjusted basis. The amount realized is the sum of any money received plus the fair market value of the nonmoney property received. The amount realized includes relief from liabilities, and in this case includes the assumption of the mortgage and real estate taxes by the buyer. The full amount realized is recognized unless all or some portion thereof is specifically excluded by another Code Section. Budd Weiser's recognized gain is calculated as follows

Cash received	$100,000
Plus: FMV of property received	25,000
Real estate taxes assumed	2,000
Mortgage assumed	20,000
Amount realized	$147,000
Minus adjusted basis of building	(80,000)
Realized and recognized gain	$ 67,000

---

6. Mary Brown purchased an apartment building on January 1, 1985 for $200,000. The building was depreciated using the straight-line method. On December 31, 1991, the building was sold for $210,000 when the asset basis net of accumulated depreciation was $160,000. On her 1991 tax return, Brown should report

   a. Sec. 1231 gain of $10,000 and ordinary income of $40,000.

   b. Sec. 1231 gain of $40,000 and ordinary income of $10,000.

   c. Ordinary income of $50,000.

   d. Sec. 1231 gain of $50,000.

The correct answer is (d). *(CPA 1180 P-44)*
REQUIRED: The amount and character of gain that must be recognized.
DISCUSSION: When depreciable property used in a trade or business is sold at a gain, first Sec. 1245 and Sec. 1250 are applied, then the balance of the gain not recaptured as ordinary income is Sec. 1231 gain. In this case, Sec. 1245 does not apply (the building is residential rental property acquired before 1987), and Sec. 1250 recapture is limited to the excess of accelerated depreciation taken by the taxpayer over straight-line depreciation. Since the building was depreciated on the straight-line method, the entire $50,000 gain ($210,000 − $160,000) is Sec. 1231 gain.

7. Peterson Corporation sold a parcel of land during 1991 realizing a $30,000 gain. Peterson has used this parcel for a parking lot during the 120 months that it has owned the land. The amount and tax classification of the gain recognized on this sale of land is

   a. A $30,000 Sec. 1245 gain.
   b. A $30,000 Sec. 1250 gain.
   c. A $30,000 Sec. 1231 gain.
   d. Ordinary income of $30,000.

The correct answer is (c). *(CMA 1283 3-5)*
REQUIRED: The amount and type of gain recognized on the sale of a parking lot.
DISCUSSION: Sec. 1231 property includes real property used in a trade or business that is held for more than 1 year.
Answer (a) is incorrect because Sec. 1245 generally only applies to depreciable property other than real property. Answer (b) is incorrect because Sec. 1250 only applies to depreciable real property. Answer (d) is incorrect because the gain is Sec. 1231 gain. As long as Sec. 1231 losses do not exceed Sec. 1231 gains, the gain will be treated as a long-term capital gain.

8. If held long-term, all the following are considered to be Sec. 1231 transactions:

- Sale of depreciable personal property
- Sale of leasehold used in a business
- Sale of rental property
- Net casualty gains on business property
- Business or investment property condemned for public use

The correct answer is (T). *(SPE 1080 I-26)*
DISCUSSION: The sale or exchange of property used in a trade or business [as defined in Sec. 1231(b)] is a Sec. 1231 transaction, whether a gain or loss results. Property used in a trade or business includes real property and depreciable property held for more than 1 year. Net casualty gains and gains or losses from condemnation of either business property or capital assets, held for more than 1 year and in connection with a trade or business or a transaction entered into for profit, are also considered Sec. 1231 transactions.

15.2 Section 1245 Property

9. The Quick Torch Insurance Agency owns the land and building in which its offices are located. The property was acquired in 1982 and regular ACRS depreciation has been taken. The agency also owns its office furniture, company cars, and client files. Which of the following is not Sec. 1245 property?

   a. The building.
   b. The office furniture.
   c. The company cars.
   d. The client files.

The correct answer is (d). *(Publisher)*
REQUIRED: The asset that is not Sec. 1245 property.
DISCUSSION: Sec. 1245 property includes property depreciable under Sec. 167 which is either personal property or specified real property, and most recovery property under Sec. 168. Whether buildings are Sec. 1245 property depends on the year placed in service, whether commercial or residential, and the method of depreciation (see Q. 11). Client files are not Sec. 1245 property because they are neither depreciable nor recovery property.
Answer (a) is incorrect because the building is 15-year real property under ACRS, and it is Sec. 1245 property unless the straight-line method of depreciation is elected. Answers (b) and (c) are incorrect because office furniture and company cars used in a trade or business are Sec. 1245 property.

10. During 1991, Mr. Boyette built and occupied a manufacturing plant for use in his business. All of the following assets located in the building are Sec. 1245 property except

   a. Large mainframe computer system used by Boyette's research department.
   b. Elevators and escalators.
   c. Office furniture.
   d. Packaging machine in the shipping department.

The correct answer is (b). *(SPE 990 II-45)*
REQUIRED: The asset which is not Sec. 1245 property.
DISCUSSION: Sec. 1245 property is property depreciable under Sec. 167 or 168 which is either personal property, specified real property, or most recovery property under Sec. 168. Whether a building is Sec. 1245 property depends on the year it is placed in service, whether it is commercial or residential, and the method of its depreciation. Elevators and escalators placed in service after 1986 are not Sec. 1245 property and are treated as part of the building, which is Sec. 1250 property.
Answers (a), (c), and (d) are incorrect because they are all examples of Sec. 1245 property.

11. Which of the following buildings is Sec. 1245 property? An office building acquired and placed in service in

a. 1980 and depreciated using an accelerated method.
b. 1984 and depreciated using regular ACRS percentages.
c. 1985 and depreciated using the straight-line ACRS method.
d. 1987 and depreciated using the regular MACRS method.

The correct answer is (b). *(Publisher)*
REQUIRED: The asset that is Sec. 1245 property.
DISCUSSION: Nonresidential buildings placed in service after 1980 and before 1987 are Sec. 1245 property unless the straight-line method of depreciation is elected. These buildings are 15-year property, 18-year property, or 19-year property under Sec. 168, depending upon the date placed in service.
Answer (a) is incorrect because buildings placed in service prior to 1981 (prior to ACRS) are Sec. 1250 property, regardless of the method of depreciation used, and regardless of whether used for residential or commercial purposes. Answer (c) is incorrect because nonresidential buildings placed in service from 1981 through 1986 are Sec. 1250 property if the straight-line method of depreciation is elected. Answer (d) is incorrect because both residential and commercial buildings placed in service after 1986 are Sec. 1250 property. The straight-line method of depreciation is required.

12. Which of the following items is not Sec. 1245 property? (All have been subject to an allowance for depreciation.)

a. Amortized certified pollution control facility.
b. Storage facility used for the bulk storage of fungible commodities.
c. Storage facility used to store oranges that have been sorted and boxed.
d. Storage facility used in connection with the distribution of petroleum products.

The correct answer is (c). *(SPE 1085 II-50)*
REQUIRED: The asset that is not Sec. 1245 property.
DISCUSSION: Sec. 1245 property generally includes depreciable personal property, but not most buildings. Some real property is included as Sec. 1245 property, especially certain storage facilities. A storage facility used to store oranges that have been sorted and boxed is not Sec. 1245 property. It is Sec. 1250 property because it is not listed in Sec. 1245(a)(3).
Answer (a) is incorrect because real property subject to amortization under Sec. 169 is Sec. 1245 property. Answer (b) is incorrect because storage facilities used for bulk storage of fungible commodities is listed as Sec. 1245 property in Sec. 1245(a)(3)(B)(iii). Answer (d) is incorrect because a storage facility for petroleum products is also Sec. 1245 property under Sec. 1245(a)(3)(E).

13. If the fair market value of Sec. 1245 property is greater than its basis, which of the following transactions will give rise to Sec. 1245 income?

a. Disposition at death.
b. Disposition by gift.
c. A like-kind exchange in which boot is received.
d. A Sec. 351 exchange with a newly formed corporation for all of its stock.

The correct answer is (c). *(Publisher)*
REQUIRED: The transaction to which Sec. 1245 applies.
DISCUSSION: The general rule of Sec. 1245(a) is that it applies notwithstanding any other section of the Code. However, Sec. 1245(b) provides certain exceptions and limitations for its application. In a like-kind exchange, Sec. 1245 applies to the amount of gain recognized plus the fair market value of non-Sec. 1245 property received which is not already taken into account in calculating the recognized gain. Under Sec. 1031, the amount of gain recognized is the smaller of the gain realized or boot received.
Answers (a) and (b) are incorrect because Sec. 1245(b) provides that it will not apply to dispositions by gift or death. Answer (d) is incorrect because Sec. 1245(b) provides that depreciation will only be recaptured on a Sec. 351 exchange to the extent that gain is recognized under Sec. 351. Generally, no gain is recognized upon the transfer of assets to a new corporation solely for stock.

Module 15.2: Section 1245 Property

14. In July of 1991, Tommy Tutone sold a printing press used in his business that originally cost him $10,000 for $10,000. His adjusted basis at the time of the sale was $1,000 and Tommy paid $1,000 in selling expenses. What is the amount of the gain that would be ordinary income under Sec. 1245?

a. $0.
b. $8,000.
c. $9,000.
d. $10,000.

The correct answer is (b). *(SPE 989 II-74)*
REQUIRED: The amount of gain classified as ordinary income under Sec. 1245.
DISCUSSION: Under Sec. 1001, the gain realized and recognized on the sale of property is the excess of the amount realized over its adjusted basis. Selling expenses also reduce the gain recognized. Thus, Tommy recognizes:

Money received	$10,000
Less: Adjusted basis of printing press	(1,000)
Selling expenses	(1,000)
Realized and recognized gain	$ 8,000

Sec. 1245 requires the recapture of ordinary income up to the amount of depreciation taken. Thus, the full $8,000 recognized gain must be recaptured as ordinary income since $9,000 of depreciation expense was incurred ($10,000 original basis – $1,000 ending basis).

15. On January 2, 1991, Ann Sewald received a gift of an electric typewriter with a fair market value of $350 and an original cost (basis) to the donor of $500. There was no applicable gift tax. During 1991 the typewriter was used in Sewald's business and depreciated using the straight-line MACRS rules over its 5-year recovery period. On December 31, 1991, it was sold for $315. The loss that Sewald can deduct in computing her 1991 taxable income is

a. $0.
b. $35.
c. $135.
d. $185.

The correct answer is (a). *(CPA 574 Q-25)*
REQUIRED: The amount of loss that can be recognized from the sale of the typewriter.
DISCUSSION: Ann's original basis in the electric typewriter was $350, since fair market value is used as the basis if less than the donor's adjusted basis (to determine loss on property received as a gift and always when personal use property is converted to business use). Depreciation was $35 ($350 ÷ 5 years x ½ for half-year convention). The adjusted basis was $315 at the time the typewriter was sold, and there would be no recognized gain or loss on the sale.

Original basis	$350
Less depreciation ($350 ÷ 5 years x ½)	(35)
Adjusted basis	$315
Sales proceeds	$315
Less adjusted basis	(315)
Realized and recognized gain/loss	$ 0

16. In 1991, Mr. Adamson changed jobs and sold his car that he had used 60% for business. Mr. Adamson had purchased the car for $12,000 and sold it for $10,000. He had claimed $2,000 depreciation on the car. What is the taxable gain or deductible loss on the sale, assuming no replacement vehicle was acquired?

a. $0.
b. $800 gain.
c. $800 loss.
d. $2,000 gain.

The correct answer is (b). *(SPE 1085 I-83)*
REQUIRED: The gain or loss recognized upon sale of a car used for both business and personal purposes.
DISCUSSION: Since the taxpayer used the car for both business and personal reasons, the business and personal portions must be computed separately. The adjusted basis of the car for personal use was 40% of the original cost of $12,000, or $4,800. The adjusted basis of the business portion of the car was $5,200 [(60% x $12,000 cost) – $2,000 depreciation]. There was a realized loss of $800 on the personal portion of the car and a realized gain of $800 on the business portion of the car. A loss on the sale of personal use property is not deductible (Sec. 165), so there is a recognized gain on the sale of $800.

	Personal (40%)	Business (60%)
Sales proceeds	$4,000	$6,000
Less Adjusted basis	(4,800)	(5,200)
Realized gain/loss	$ (800)	$ 800
Recognized gain/loss	$ 0	$ 800

Module 15.2: Section 1245 Property

17. In June 1988, Tina bought new hair dryers for her beauty shop at a cost of $6,000. During 1991, Tina remodeled her shop and sold the hair dryers for $7,500. Tina had properly claimed depreciation of $4,740 on the dryers, and has had no net Sec. 1231 losses in any of the years she has been in business. What is the amount and character of Tina's gain?

- a. $4,740 ordinary gain and $1,500 capital gain.
- b. $1,500 capital gain.
- c. $6,240 ordinary gain.
- d. $6,240 capital gain.

The correct answer is (a). *(SPE 990 II-77)*
REQUIRED: The amount and character of the gain on the sale of property given depreciation recapture.
DISCUSSION: The realized gain from the sale of the hair dryers is $6,240 [$7,500 − ($6,000 − $4,740)]. Since the hair dryers are Sec. 1245 property, the recognized gain is characterized as ordinary to the extent of any depreciation that has been taken. Thus, $4,740 will be classified as ordinary income due to depreciation recapture, and the remaining gain of $1,500 will be classified as Sec. 1231 gain.

18. Belle Corporation sold King Company some equipment on February 1, 1991 which had been used in Belle's business operations. The selling price was $50,000 to be paid in two equal installments -- the first on January 1, 1992 and the second on December 1, 1992. The adjusted basis of the equipment was $40,000 after considering depreciation taken to the date of sale of $5,000. Belle made no election regarding the sale on its 1991 return. The amount and character of the gain Belle will report on its 1991 federal income tax return is a

- a. No gain or loss.
- b. $10,000 gain, of which $5,000 is ordinary income and $5,000 is Sec. 1231 gain.
- c. $5,000 gain, of which all $5,000 is ordinary income.
- d. $5,000 gain, of which $2,500 is Sec. 1231 gain and $2,500 is ordinary income.

The correct answer is (c). *(CMA 1281 3-11)*
REQUIRED: The amount and character of recognized gain from the sale of equipment on the installment basis given depreciation recapture.
DISCUSSION: The realized gain from the sale of the equipment is $10,000. Since the equipment is Sec. 1245 property, the realized gain is characterized as ordinary income to the extent of any depreciation that has been taken and must be fully recognized in the year of sale without regard to the timing of payments [Sec. 453(i)]. $5,000 of depreciation was taken, so $5,000 of the realized gain must be recognized as ordinary income in 1991. All of the remaining gain is Sec. 1231 gain, and will be recognized when payments are received (the installment method is required absent an election not to use it).

Sales proceeds	$50,000
Less adjusted basis	(40,000)
Realized gain	$10,000

Recognized gain in 1991 is Sec. 1245 recapture of $5,000.

19. On January 2, 1987, Rob, a sole proprietor, purchased a business truck for $10,000. On January 2, 1989, Rob gave the truck to his son, Scott, who also used it in his business. At the time of the gift, the truck had an adjusted basis to Rob of $5,000 and a fair market value of $3,000. The truck had a remaining useful life of 5 years and no salvage value. Scott elected straight-line depreciation. On January 2, 1991, Scott sold the truck for $6,000. What is the amount and character of Scott's gain?

	Capital Gain	Ordinary Income
a.	$0	$3,000
b.	$0	$4,200
c.	$1,000	$2,000
d.	$3,000	$1,200

The correct answer is (a). *(SPE 990 II-78)*
REQUIRED: The amount and character of the gain on the sale of the truck.
DISCUSSION: Since this property is depreciable business property personal in nature, under Sec. 1245 any realized gain must be recognized as ordinary income to the extent of any depreciation previously taken. Since the truck was acquired by gift from his father, Scott must recapture any depreciation previously taken, including that taken by his father. Scott's basis is a carryover from that of his father. The total depreciation ($5,000 by Rob + $2,000 by Scott) exceeds the realized gain, and therefore the entire gain will be ordinary income.

Sales proceeds		$6,000
Less adjusted basis:		
Carryover basis	$5,000	
Minus depreciation*	(2,000)	(3,000)
Realized and recognized gain		$3,000

*½ year in 1989 and 1991 and a full year in 1990.

Module 15.2: Section 1245 Property

20. On August 15, 1991, Long Corporation sold a machine used in its business for $65,000. The machine was purchased in 1988 and depreciated under the Modified ACRS rules as 7-year recovery period property as follows:

Cost		$60,000
Depreciation - 1988	$ 8,574	
Depreciation - 1989	14,694	
Depreciation - 1990	10,494	
Depreciation - 1991	3,747	
Total depreciation to date of sale		37,509
Adjusted basis of machine at date of sale		$22,491

In 1991, Long Corporation should report

a. $42,509 of long-term capital gain.

b. $37,509 of Sec. 1245 ordinary income, and $5,000 of Sec. 1231 gain.

c. $37,509 of Sec. 1250 ordinary income, and $5,000 of Sec. 1231 gain.

d. $42,509 of Sec. 1231 gain.

The correct answer is (b). *(CMA 1289 3-24)*
REQUIRED: The amount and character of the gain on the sale of a machine given Sec. 1245 depreciation recapture.
DISCUSSION: The realized gain from the sale of the equipment is $42,509 ($65,000 – $22,491). Since the equipment is Sec. 1245 property, the realized gain must be recognized as ordinary income up to the amount of depreciation taken, or $37,509. The remaining $5,000 gain ($42,509 – $37,509) is recognized as Sec. 1231 gain which may be used to offset other Sec. 1231 losses and other capital losses.

21. During 1991, Mr. Monopoly sold equipment used in his business for $11,000. The equipment cost $10,000 and Monopoly had properly claimed Modified ACRS deductions totaling $4,000. Straight-line depreciation, if it had been used, would have been $2,500. What is the amount of gain that should be reported under Secs. 1231 and 1245?

	Sec. 1231	Sec. 1245
a.	$5,000	$0
b.	$3,500	$1,500
c.	$1,000	$4,000
d.	$0	$5,000

The correct answer is (c). *(SPE 987 II-76)*
REQUIRED: The amount of the gain recognized under Secs. 1245 and 1231 on the sale of property depreciated using MACRS.
DISCUSSION: The sale resulted in a $5,000 realized gain as computed below. Since the property was Sec. 1245 property, the realized gain must be recognized as ordinary income to the extent of depreciation taken. Therefore, $4,000 must be recognized as Sec. 1245 ordinary income. The remaining $1,000 ($5,000 gain – $4,000 ordinary income) is recognized as Sec. 1231 gain.

Original cost	$10,000
Less depreciation	(4,000)
Adjusted basis	$ 6,000
Sales proceeds	$11,000
Less adjusted basis	(6,000)
Realized and recognized gain	$ 5,000

22. Burtt Corporation sold its small office building for $220,000 in 1991. Burtt acquired the building in 1986 for $200,000 and made improvements costing $15,000 at that time. During the period of its use, cost recovery on the building under ACRS amounted to $76,000. Depreciation would have been $51,000 under the straight-line method. For tax purposes, Burtt should treat the gain as:

a. $81,000 Sec. 1231 gain.

b. $5,000 Sec. 1231 gain; $51,000 ordinary income.

c. $5,000 Sec. 1231 gain; $76,000 ordinary income.

d. $56,000 Sec. 1231 gain; $25,000 ordinary income.

The correct answer is (c). *(CMA 1284 3-11)*
REQUIRED: The amount of gain on the sale of an office building subject to depreciation recapture.
DISCUSSION: The office building is 19-year real property under the pre-1987 ACRS system. It is also Sec. 1245 recovery property since it does not fall within any of the exceptions (such as residential rental property, low-income housing, or property on which an election to use the straight-line method is made). Under Sec. 1245, all the depreciation is recaptured as ordinary income up to the amount of the gain on the sale.
Basis was $139,000 ($200,000 cost + $15,000 improvements – $76,000 depreciation). The gain on the sale was $81,000 ($220,000 sales price – $139,000 basis). The amount of the gain subject to depreciation recapture is $76,000, the total depreciation taken. The Sec. 1231 gain is $5,000 ($81,000 total gain – $76,000 Sec. 1245 gain).

Module 15.2: Section 1245 Property

23. Belle purchased a new freezer case for her grocery store at a cost of $60,000 on July 1, 1990. Belle elected to expense $10,000 of the cost in 1990 and depreciated the remaining $50,000 basis using MACRS. Depreciation taken totaled $18,000 prior to the December 1, 1991 sale of the equipment. Straight-line depreciation would have been $9,000. The sales price on December 1, 1991 was $52,000. Gain on the sale was

a. $28,000 Sec. 1231 gain.

b. $20,000 Sec. 1231 gain.

c. $18,000 ordinary income, $2,000 Sec. 1231 gain.

d. $20,000 ordinary income.

The correct answer is (d). *(Publisher)*
REQUIRED: The amount and character of gain on the sale when Sec. 179 expense was claimed.
DISCUSSION: The realized gain of $20,000 is subject to recapture under Sec. 1245 because the freezer is depreciated under Sec. 168 and is not excepted by Sec. 1245. Thus, any realized gain is recognized as ordinary income to the extent of any depreciation taken. The $10,000 that was expensed under Sec. 179 counts as depreciation expense in determining the character of the gain. Therefore, all the recognized gain is ordinary income.

Original cost	$60,000
Sec. 179 expense	(10,000)
Depreciation	(18,000)
Adjusted basis	$32,000
Sales proceeds	$52,000
Adjusted basis	(32,000)
Realized and recognized gain	$20,000

24. Mike Verdisco owns the Buffalo Pit Bulls of the Universal Football League. The team purchased a weight machine in December 1990 for $11,000. $10,000 of the purchase price was expensed under Sec. 179. MACRS depreciation claimed was $143 in 1990 and $122 in 1991. In December 1991, when the weight machine had a fair market value of $8,000, the team exchanged it for a whirlpool bath that had a fair market value of $7,000. The team also received $1,000 in cash. What is the gain or loss of the Buffalo Pit Bulls?

a. No gain or loss.

b. $265 of Sec. 1245 gain and $735 of Sec. 1231 gain.

c. $1,000 of Sec. 1245 gain.

d. $7,265 of Sec. 1245 gain.

The correct answer is (c). *(Publisher)*
REQUIRED: The amount and character of gain from a like-kind exchange of Sec. 1245 property.
DISCUSSION: Under Sec. 1031, the exchange of the weight machine for the whirlpool bath qualifies as a like-kind exchange, and the gain recognized is limited to the boot received of $1,000. Under Sec. 1245(b)(4), the amount of recapture in a like-kind exchange is limited to the amount of gain recognized plus the fair market value of property acquired which is not Sec. 1245 property not already included in calculating the gain recognized. The whirlpool bath is Sec. 1245 property. Under Sec. 1245(a)(2), the amount of Sec. 1245 recapture includes both depreciation claimed and the expense deducted under Sec. 179. Consequently, the entire $1,000 gain is recaptured as ordinary income.

25. Gary Lary owns the Boston Maulers of the Universal Basketball League as a sole proprietor. The assets include a device for suspending a player from the ceiling to stretch his/her back to increase height. The machine cost $20,000 when purchased several years ago and $10,000 of straight-line depreciation had been claimed when Gary died on December 31, 1991. Gary willed all of the team assets to Hondo Hadacheck. The device had a fair market value of $15,000 on Gary's death, and a short time later, Hondo sold it for $18,000. How much Sec. 1245 recapture is recognized, and when?

a. None.

b. $5,000 on Gary's death.

c. $3,000 when Hondo sells it.

d. $8,000 when Hondo sells it.

The correct answer is (a). *(Publisher)*
REQUIRED: The amount and timing of depreciation recapture on Sec. 1245 property which is transferred at death and later sold.
DISCUSSION: Under Sec. 1245(b)(2), there is no recapture on disposition by death. When Gary died, the basis of the device was stepped up to its fair market value on the date of death [Sec. 1014(a)]. Therefore, when Hondo sold it for $18,000, he recognized a $3,000 gain ($18,000 − $15,000 basis). Reg. 1.1245-2(c)(3) states that depreciation recapture potential exists following a transfer at death to the extent of the depreciation deductions allowed the transferee before the decedent's death that reduce the transferee's basis in the property under Sec. 1014(b)(9). Generally, such a reduction occurs when property is acquired from a decedent prior to death (e.g., creation of a joint interest involving the decedent and the transferee). Since the property was acquired from Gary Lary at death, and no subsequent depreciation was claimed, no basis reduction occurs under Sec. 1014(b)(9). Therefore, none of the $3,000 recognized gain is depreciation recapture under Sec. 1245.

Module 15.2: Section 1245 Property

26. If you dispose of both depreciable personal property and other property in one transaction and realize a gain, in the absence of an agreement between the buyer and seller, an allocation of the amount realized between the two types of property disposed of in proportion to their fair market values must occur to figure the part of the gain to be reported as ordinary income due to depreciation recapture.

The correct answer is (T) *(SPE 987 I-27)*

DISCUSSION: When different types of property are disposed of in one transaction, an allocation must be made between the different properties. This is especially true when part of the property is depreciable, to account for the depreciation recapture under Sec. 1245. The allocation is generally made on the basis of the relative fair market values of each property or portion of a property. Normally, if the allocation is made in an agreement between the buyer and the seller, the agreement will be used (Sec. 1060). Not only must the amount realized be allocated, but if it is property that has several uses (e.g., business and personal), then the basis of the property must also be allocated in order to determine a gain on the disposition of each.

27. If a portion of an investment is expensed under a Sec. 179 election, the expensed amount cannot be recaptured under Sec. 1245 since it was not depreciation.

The correct answer is (F). *(Publisher)*

DISCUSSION: A Sec. 179 expense deduction is treated as a depreciation deduction for purposes of the Sec. 1245 recapture rules. Gain realized on the disposition of Sec. 179 property is treated as ordinary income to the extent of the amount expensed and depreciation claimed.

28. On July 1, 1986, John purchased a commercial building for $210,000. He allocated $20,000 to land. On June 30, 1991, he sold the building for $200,000 cash. At the time of the sale the accumulated depreciation on the building was $75,800. If John had used the straight-line depreciation method over the same period of time, the depreciation would have been $30,000. John recognizes ordinary income of $75,800 and Sec. 1231 gain of $10,000 on the sale.

The correct answer is (T). *(SPE 990 II-17)*

DISCUSSION: The realized gain from the sale of the building is $85,800 [$200,000 selling price − ($190,000 − $75,800) adjusted basis]. Since the building was placed in service before 1987 and regular ACRS depreciation was claimed, it is Sec. 1245 property, and thus ordinary income must be recognized up to the amount of depreciation taken, or $75,800. The remaining $10,000 recognized gain is Sec. 1231 gain.

29. Section 1245 property includes tangible as well as intangible personal property that is or has been subject to an allowance for depreciation.

The correct answer is (T). *(SPE 989 II-14)*

DISCUSSION: Sec. 1245 property means any property which is or has been property of a character subject to the allowance for depreciation or amortization and is either personal (tangible or intangible) property or other property (not including a building or its structural components). Examples of intangible property that is considered Sec. 1245 property includes leaseholds of Sec. 1245 property, baseball and football players' contracts, and patents.

30. Oil and gas storage tanks, grain storage bins, silos, blast furnaces, coke ovens, and coal tipples are special-purpose structures or storage facilities which qualify as Sec. 1245 property.

The correct answer is (T). *(SPE 1080 II-27)*

DISCUSSION: The properties described in this question are specifically deemed to be Sec. 1245 property under Sec. 1245(a)(3).

31. The deduction for the cost of removal of barriers for the handicapped must be considered similar to depreciation when considering the treatment of gain from a sale of the property.

The correct answer is (T). *(SPE 1078 II-20)*

DISCUSSION: Under Sec. 190 the cost of the removal of barriers for the handicapped is deductible. Under Sec. 1245(a)(3)(C), property which has an adjusted basis which reflects adjustments under Sec. 190 is deemed to be Sec. 1245 property. This deduction must be considered as an adjustment to basis similar to depreciation to prevent the taxpayer from receiving a double tax benefit.

32. Mike made a gift of depreciable personal property to Michelle. If Michelle sells the property she must take into account the post-1961 depreciation claimed by Mike in determining the gain to be reported as ordinary income.

The correct answer is (T). *(SPE 1078 II-23)*
DISCUSSION: Under Sec. 1015, property acquired by gift retains the same basis the donor had at the time of the gift. There is no depreciation recapture under Sec. 1245(b) upon a disposition by gift. The Sec. 1245 taint stays with the property, and Michelle will have depreciation recapture on her sale of the property as if she had taken the depreciation.

33. On January 2, 1990, Charles bought office furniture for $3,000. He deducted $600 in depreciation under MACRS. On January 3, 1991, a fire destroyed the furniture for which he was reimbursed $2,800 by his insurance company. Charles replaced the furniture at a cost of $2,600. Charles has ordinary income of $200.

The correct answer is (T). *(SPE 990 II-18)*
DISCUSSION: Under Sec. 1033, if property is involuntarily converted into property similar or related in service or use, no gain shall be recognized, unless the money received exceeds the adjusted basis of the similar property purchased, then the gain shall be recognized to the extent of excess money received. For this example, the adjusted basis at the time of the involuntary conversion was $2,400 ($3,000 − $600 depreciation). The following calculation will be made to determine the gain recognized:

Insurance Reimbursement	$2,800
Less Adjusted Basis	(2,400)
Gain realized	$ 400

Under Sec. 1033, only $200 of this gain needs to be recognized since the $2,800 Insurance reimbursement less the $2,600 cost of replacement furniture equals $200. The entire $200 is ordinary income, because the furniture is Sec. 1245 property, and $600 of depreciation had been claimed.

15.3 Section 1250 Property

34. HICO, Inc. controls various income-producing real properties. Included among its assets are a shopping mall built in 1980 and depreciated by an accelerated method, an apartment building purchased in 1981 and depreciated by the regular ACRS method, and an office building purchased in 1982 which is depreciated under the straight-line method of ACRS. Which of the following is not Sec. 1250 property?

a. The shopping mall.
b. The apartment building.
c. The land on which the apartment building is built.
d. The office building.

The correct answer is (c). *(Publisher)*
REQUIRED: The asset that is not Sec. 1250 property.
DISCUSSION: Sec. 1250 property is depreciable real property that is not Sec. 1245 property. Since land is not depreciable, it is not Sec. 1250 property (nor Sec. 1245 property).
Answer (a) is incorrect because real property put into service prior to 1981 is Sec. 1250 property unless it is an item specified in Sec. 1245. Answer (b) is incorrect because buildings used for residential rental purposes are Sec. 1250 property regardless of when placed in service. Answer (d) is incorrect because nonresidential buildings placed in service from 1981 through 1986 are Sec. 1250 property if the straight-line method of depreciation is used.

Module 15.3: Section 1250 Property 369

35. Which of the following assets placed in service from 1981 through 1986 is Sec. 1250 property?

a. Low-income housing depreciated by the regular method of ACRS.
b. A warehouse depreciated by the regular method of ACRS.
c. An elevator depreciated by the straight-line method of ACRS.
d. A farmer's silo depreciated by the straight-line method of ACRS.

The correct answer is (a). *(Publisher)*
REQUIRED: The asset that is Sec. 1250 property.
DISCUSSION: Sec. 1250 property is depreciable real property that is not Sec. 1245 property. Low-income housing is not Sec. 1245 property regardless of when placed in service; therefore, it is Sec. 1250 property.
Answer (b) is incorrect because commercial (nonresidential) buildings placed in service from 1981 through 1986 are Sec. 1245 property unless the straight-line method of depreciation is elected. Answer (c) is incorrect because elevators were specifically listed in Sec. 1245(a)(3)(C) as Sec. 1245 property prior to 1987. Answer (d) is incorrect because a facility used for the bulk storage of fungible commodities is specifically listed in Sec. 1245(a)(3)(B).

36. In which of the following transactions will Sec. 1250 recapture be recognized if the property is Sec. 1250 property, its fair market value is in excess of basis, and accelerated depreciation has been claimed?

a. Disposition by gift.
b. Disposition on death.
c. Exchange for all of the stock in a newly formed corporation.
d. A like-kind exchange when the potential recapture is greater than the value of the Sec. 1250 property received.

The correct answer is (d). *(Publisher)*
REQUIRED: The transaction which will give rise to Sec. 1250 recapture.
DISCUSSION: The amount of Sec. 1250 recapture is generally the lesser of the gain recognized or the amount of additional depreciation (accelerated depreciation claimed in excess of straight-line depreciation). However, under Sec. 1250(d)(4), the Sec. 1250 recapture is limited in a like-kind exchange to the greater of the gain recognized on a transaction under the general boot rules or the excess of the potential Sec. 1250 recapture over the fair market value of Sec. 1250 property acquired in the transaction. Therefore, if the additional depreciation amount is greater than the value of the Sec. 1250 property received in the exchange, the additional depreciation will be recaptured up to the amount of the realized gain.
Answers (a) and (b) are incorrect because Sec. 1250(d) excludes these dispositions from causing recapture. Answer (c) is incorrect because Sec. 1250(d)(3) limits the recapture on a Sec. 351 transaction to the gain recognized. In an exchange in which all of the stock in a newly formed corporation is received, there is generally no gain recognized under Sec. 351.

37. During 1991, Ramone sold Sec. 1250 nonresidential real property for $6,000. She had purchased the property in 1978 at a cost of $10,000. Ramone had properly claimed depreciation totaling $5,000 of which $2,000 was depreciation in excess of straight-line. What is the amount of Ramone's Sec. 1250 gain?

a. $0.
b. $1,000.
c. $2,000.
d. $5,000.

The correct answer is (b). *(SPE 987 II-77)*
REQUIRED: The amount of Sec. 1250 gain on the sale of an asset.
DISCUSSION: The amount of Sec. 1250 recapture is the lesser of the gain realized or the amount of additional depreciation (accelerated depreciation claimed in excess of straight-line depreciation). The amount of additional depreciation is $2,000 as given in the question. The realized gain on the transaction is only $1,000 ($6,000 selling price − $5,000 basis). Therefore, the amount of Sec. 1250 gain is limited to the realized gain of $1,000.

38. Mr. Miller bought a house in 1980 for $30,000. He used two-thirds of the house as his personal residence and rented the other one-third. Depreciation totaling $3,000 has been allowed on the rented portion of the house. In 1991, Mr. Miller sold the house for $57,000. What is his net gain on the rental portion?

a. $6,000.
b. $12,000.
c. $18,000.
d. $22,800.

The correct answer is (b). *(SPE 1080 I-82)*
REQUIRED: The amount of gain to be recognized on the rental portion of the house.
DISCUSSION: Since the house was used for personal and rental purposes, the gain on the sale must be computed separately for each portion. Sec. 1250 would apply to the rental portion if accelerated depreciation had been taken, and the balance of the gain would be Sec. 1231 gain. The gain on the personal portion is capital gain.

<u>Rental Portion (1/3)</u>

1/3 of original cost	$10,000
Less depreciation	(3,000)
Adjusted basis	$ 7,000
1/3 of sales proceeds	$19,000
Less adjusted basis	(7,000)
Realized gain	$12,000

39. On December 1, 1980, Mr. D began using in his business a building he constructed at a cost of $125,000. On January 2, 1991 he sold the building for $150,000. Accumulated depreciation on the building on January 2, 1991 was $40,000. Had Mr. D used the straight-line method of computing depreciation, the accumulated depreciation would have been $30,000. What is Mr. D's Sec. 1231 gain?

a. $10,000.
b. $30,000.
c. $40,000.
d. $55,000.

The correct answer is (d). *(SPE 1081 II-85)*
REQUIRED: The amount of the gain that is recognized as Sec. 1231 gain.
DISCUSSION: The realized gain on this sale is $65,000 as computed below. Depreciable real property acquired prior to 1981 is Sec. 1250 property. Sec. 1250 requires that the realized gain be recognized as ordinary income to the extent that depreciation taken is in excess of depreciation under the straight-line method. The accelerated depreciation exceeded the straight-line depreciation by $10,000. This amount is recognized as ordinary income. The remaining realized gain is recognized as Sec. 1231 gain.

Sales proceeds	$150,000
Less adjusted basis ($125,000 − $40,000)	(85,000)
Realized and recognized gain	$ 65,000

Sec. 1250 gain: $40,000 − $30,000 = $10,000
Sec. 1231 gain: $65,000 − $10,000 = $55,000

40. Ralph made a gift of Sec. 1250 property to his son. Ralph had properly claimed depreciation totaling $3,000 of which $750 was additional depreciation. For the year in which the gift was made, the son properly claimed $1,000 in depreciation of which $250 was additional depreciation. On January 2 of the following year, the son sold the property for a gain of $2,000. What is the amount of the son's Sec. 1250 gain?

a. $0.
b. $250.
c. $750.
d. $1,000.

The correct answer is (d). *(SPE 988 II-70)*
REQUIRED: The amount of Sec. 1250 gain on the disposition of property which the seller originally received by gift.
DISCUSSION: Sec. 1250(d) excludes dispositions by gift from causing a recapture. However, the recapture potential carries over to the donee. Therefore, when the son sold the property, there was a depreciation recapture potential of $1,000 ($750 additional depreciation deducted by Ralph and $250 additional depreciation deducted by the son). Since the realized gain of $2,000 is in excess of the $1,000 depreciation recapture potential, the entire depreciation recapture potential is treated as Sec. 1250 gain. This is $1,000. The remaining $1,000 gain is Sec. 1231 gain.

Module 15.3: Section 1250 Property

41. General Company purchased a building on January 2, 1980 for $1,200,000, electing to depreciate it over an estimated useful life of 40 years. On December 31, 1991 General sold the building for $1,300,000. At the time the building was sold, it had an adjusted basis of $750,000. General Company must report a gain of

a. $550,000 ordinary income.
b. $550,000 Sec. 1231 income.
c. $460,000 Sec. 1231 income, and $90,000 ordinary income.
d. $388,000 Sec. 1231 income, and $162,000 ordinary income.

The correct answer is (d). *(CMA 688 3-7)*
REQUIRED: The amount and character of income to be recognized by a corporation in 1991.
DISCUSSION: This transaction resulted in a realized gain of $550,000. Depreciable real property acquired prior to 1981 is Sec. 1250 property. Under Sec. 1250, realized gain is recognized as ordinary income to the extent the depreciation taken exceeds depreciation under the straight-line method. This excess was $90,000 because straight-line depreciation over 40 years computes to $360,000 for the 12 years General used the building. In addition, Sec. 291(a) requires a corporation to treat as additional Sec. 1250 gain 20% of the excess of Sec. 1245 gain (as if the property had been Sec. 1245 property) over the regular Sec. 1250 gain. The remainder of General's realized gain is recognized as Sec. 1231 gain.

Sales proceeds	$1,300,000
Less adjusted basis	(750,000)
Realized and recognized gain	$ 550,000

Sec. 1250 gain:
$450,000 − $360,000 = $ 90,000
Sec. 291 gain:
20% x ($450,000 − $90,000) = 72,000
Total Sec. 1250 gain: $162,000

Sec. 1231 gain:
$550,000 − $162,000 = $388,000

42. Cardinal, Inc. located one of its manufacturing plants in Piedmont, Ohio 15 years ago. As an inducement to locate in Piedmont, the town donated the land for the plant site to Cardinal. The town had originally purchased the land for $40,000 and its value at the time of donation to Cardinal was $50,000. In 1991, Cardinal moved the operations to a new location outside the city limits and sold the land for $200,000 and the old plant for $300,000. The plant had been depreciated using the straight-line method and had an adjusted basis of $150,000 at the date of sale after deducting $90,000 of depreciation. The gain on the sale for federal income tax purposes is a

a. $350,000 Sec. 1231 gain.
b. $300,000 Sec. 1231 gain.
c. $310,000 Sec. 1231 gain.
d. $332,000 Sec. 1231 gain; $18,000 ordinary income.

The correct answer is (d). *(CMA 682 3-4)*
REQUIRED: The amount and character of gain recognized on the sale of the donated land and building.
DISCUSSION: The realized gain on the sale of the donated land is equal to the sales price. The corporation had no basis in the property because the land was donated by the city [Sec. 362(c)]. This gain is all Sec. 1231 gain because the land is real property used in a business and it is not Sec. 1250 property since it is not depreciable.

The sale of the building resulted in a realized gain of $150,000. There is no regular Sec. 1250 gain because straight-line depreciation was taken. However, Sec. 291(a) requires a corporation to treat as additional Sec. 1250 gain 20% of the excess of Sec. 1245 gain (as if the property had been Sec. 1245 property) over the regular Sec. 1250 gain. Any Sec. 1250 gain is recognized as ordinary income. The remainder of the realized gain is Sec. 1231 gain.

	Land	Building
Sales proceeds	$200,000	$300,000
Less adjusted basis	0	(150,000)
Realized gain	$200,000	$150,000

Sec. 291 gain:
20% x ($90,000 depreciation − $0) = $18,000
Sec. 1231 gain:
$200,000 + ($150,000 − $18,000) = $332,000

43. In March 1984, TapKeg Corporation purchased an apartment building for a total purchase price of $3,500,000. The property was placed in service on April 1, 1984. TapKeg depreciated the building using the accelerated cost recovery system and claimed a total of $1,890,000 in depreciation before selling the building. Straight-line depreciation would have been $1,085,000. TapKeg sold the building on December 31, 1991 for $4,000,000. Gain on the sale will be reported as a

a. Sec. 1231 gain of $2,390,000.

b. Sec. 1245 gain of $1,890,000 and Sec. 1231 gain of $500,000.

c. Sec. 1250 gain of $1,022,000 and Sec. 1231 gain of $1,368,000.

d. Sec. 1250 gain of $805,000 and Sec. 1231 gain of $1,585,000.

The correct answer is (c). *(Publisher)*
REQUIRED: The amount and character of gain recognized on the sale of the apartment building.
DISCUSSION: The sale of the apartment building resulted in a realized gain of $2,390,000. The building is Sec. 1250 residential real property since it is excluded from Sec. 1245 property by Sec. 1245(a)(3) as in effect prior to the 1986 TRA. The realized gain is recognized as ordinary income to the extent the depreciation taken exceeded depreciation under the straight-line method. In addition, Sec. 291(a) requires a corporation to treat as additional Sec. 1250 gain 20% of the excess of Sec. 1245 gain (as if the property had been Sec. 1245 property) over the regular Sec. 1250 gain. The remaining portion of the realized gain is recognized as Sec. 1231 gain.

Sales proceeds	$4,000,000
Less basis ($3,500,000 – $1,890,000)	(1,610,000)
Realized and recognized gain	$2,390,000

Sec. 1250 gain:
$1,890,000 – $1,085,000 = $805,000
Sec. 291 gain:
20% x ($1,890,000 – $805,000) = 217,000
Total Sec. 1250 gain = $1,022,000

Sec. 1231 gain:
$2,390,000 – $1,022,000 = $1,368,000

44. Cando Corporation purchased low-income housing on September 28, 1986 for $800,000. It claimed $300,000 in depreciation using the accelerated cost recovery system. Straight-line depreciation would have been $175,000. Cando sold the housing on December 28, 1991 for $600,000. What is the character and amount of Cando's gain or loss on the sale?

a. $200,000 capital loss.

b. $125,000 ordinary income.

c. $100,000 Sec. 1231 gain.

d. $100,000 ordinary income.

The correct answer is (d). *(SPE 1085 II-75)*
REQUIRED: The amount and character of gain or loss to be recognized on the sale of low-income housing.
DISCUSSION: The sale of the property resulted in a realized gain of $100,000. Low-income housing is excluded from Sec. 1245 and is therefore Sec. 1250 property. Under Sec. 1250, realized gain must be recognized as ordinary income to the extent of any depreciation taken in excess of depreciation under the straight-line method. This excess is $125,000. The realized gain on the sale of the property was only $100,000, so the lesser of these two amounts is recognized as ordinary income.

Sec. 291(a) will not affect this transaction because it only increases the Sec. 1250 gain by 20% of what missed Sec. 1245 treatment, which is zero in this case because Sec. 1245 is also limited to the realized gain.

Original cost	$800,000
Less depreciation	(300,000)
Adjusted basis	$500,000
Sales proceeds	$600,000
Less adjusted basis	(500,000)
Realized and recognized gain	$100,000

Excess depreciation:
$300,000 – $175,000 = $125,000

Module 15.3: Section 1250 Property

45. A.K. Rabbits bought an office building in January 1987 for $2,000,000. Rabbits spent an additional $1,000,000 to renovate the plumbing and heating systems in the building before renting it on March 10, 1987. Rabbits chose to use straight-line depreciation and claimed a total of $600,000 in depreciation. On December 31, 1991 the office building had a fair market value of $3,300,000. Rabbits exchanged the office building for an apartment house owned by Fox Corporation with a fair market value of $2,800,000 and basis to Fox of $2,000,000. In the exchange, Fox assumed a $500,000 liability on the office building. Gain or loss on the exchange will be reported

a. $500,000 Sec. 1231 gain.
b. $400,000 Sec. 1250 gain.
c. $500,000 Sec. 1231 gain; $600,000 Sec. 1245 gain.
d. $900,000 Sec. 1231 gain.

The correct answer is (a). *(Publisher)*
REQUIRED: The amount and character of gain or loss recognized on the exchange of the office building.
DISCUSSION: The realized gain on this exchange was $900,000. Since both properties are real property held for use in a trade or business or for investment, the transaction is a like-kind exchange under Sec. 1031. Gain is recognized to the extent of boot received (relief from a liability) of $500,000.

Since the office building was depreciated on a straight-line basis, it is considered Sec. 1250 property. Sec. 1250 recapture is limited to depreciation taken in excess of straight-line depreciation. There is no excess depreciation, so Sec. 1250 does not apply and all the recognized gain is Sec. 1231 gain.

Original cost of office building	$2,000,000
Renovation	1,000,000
Depreciation	(600,000)
Adjusted basis of office building	$2,400,000
FMV of property received	$2,800,000
Liability relieved of	500,000
Amount realized	$3,300,000
Adjusted basis of office building	(2,400,000)
Realized gain	$ 900,000
Recognized gain under Sec. 1031	$ 500,000

46. Karey bought a small shopping mall on July 15, 1987 for a total price of $2,000,000. Karey chose to use straight-line depreciation and deducted $283,100 before the mall was sold for $2,500,000 on December 31, 1991. The gain on the sale should be reported as

a. $283,100 ordinary income and $500,000 Sec. 1231 gain.
b. $500,000 capital gain.
c. $783,100 Sec. 1231 gain.
d. $783,100 ordinary income.

The correct answer is (c). *(Publisher)*
REQUIRED: The amount and character of gain recognized on the sale of the shopping mall.
DISCUSSION: All real property purchased after 1986 is classified as Sec. 1250 property. Under Sec. 1250, only depreciation in excess of straight-line is recaptured. Since real property placed in service after 1986 must be depreciated under the straight-line method according to the MACRS rules, no Sec. 1250 recapture is required for post-1986 real property held for more than 1 year.

Original cost	$2,000,000
Less depreciation	(283,100)
Adjusted basis	$1,716,900
Sales proceeds	$2,500,000
Less adjusted basis	(1,716,900)
Realized and recognized gain	$ 783,100

47. If depreciable real property is held for 1 year or less, any depreciation that has been deducted is treated as additional depreciation for purposes of figuring the part of any gain to be reported as ordinary income.

The correct answer is (T). *(SPE 1082 II-28)*
DISCUSSION: In addition to accelerated depreciation in excess of straight-line, all depreciation is subject to recapture if the Sec. 1250 property has not been held more than 1 year [Sec. 1250(b)(1)].

48. In computing Sec. 1250 recapture on qualified low-income housing for periods after 1975, the applicable percentage is 100%, minus 1% for each full month the property was held in excess of 100 full months.

The correct answer is (T). *(SPE 1079 II-38)*
DISCUSSION: Generally, Sec. 1250 requires that excess depreciation be recaptured in full for periods after 1975. However, certain properties such as low-income housing are provided a partial release under Sec. 1250(a)(1)(B).

49. When residential real property which has been depreciated under the accelerated cost recovery system is sold, gain is recaptured as ordinary income to the extent that depreciation has been taken.

The correct answer is (F). *(Publisher)*
DISCUSSION: Residential real property is classified as Sec. 1250 property. Under Sec. 1250, gain is recaptured as ordinary income only to the extent depreciation taken exceeds depreciation calculated under the straight-line method.

15.4 Sale of a Business

50. Sonny Shapiro was the sole proprietor of a high-volume drug store that he owned for 15 years before he sold it to Dale Drug Stores, Inc. in 1991. Besides the $900,000 selling price for the store's tangible assets and goodwill, Mott received a lump sum of $30,000 in 1991 for his agreement not to operate a competing enterprise within 10 miles of the store's location for a period of 6 years. The $30,000 will be taxed to Mott as

a. $30,000 ordinary income in 1991.
b. $30,000 short-term capital gain in 1991.
c. $30,000 long-term capital gain in 1991.
d. Ordinary income of $5,000 a year for 6 years.

The correct answer is (a). *(CPA 1183 Q-21)*
REQUIRED: The proper treatment of a payment received for an agreement not to compete.
DISCUSSION: The sale of a business often includes a covenant not to compete. Cases and rulings have held that income from the covenant is ordinary income because it is similar to payments for services; it is simply a payment for not performing services.
Answers (b) and (c) are incorrect because the covenant is not a capital asset. Answer (d) is incorrect because the income must all be recognized in the year received.

Questions 51 through 53 are based on the following information. Mr. Rabbit sold his retail business consisting of the following assets, all held long term except for the noncompetition agreement.

1 Goodwill
2 Noncompetition agreement that can be severed from goodwill
3 Exclusive franchise
4 Accounting records
5 Trade accounts receivable
6 Business realty
7 Furniture and equipment
8 Inventory

---

51. Which of Rabbit's assets are capital assets?

a. 1, 5, and 8.
b. 1, 3, and 4.
c. 3, 6, and 7.
d. 2, 3, and 4.

The correct answer is (b). *(SPE 1077 I-179)*
REQUIRED: The items listed that are capital assets.
DISCUSSION: Sec. 1221 defines capital assets as property held by the taxpayer and not excluded by its subsections. Goodwill, an exclusive franchise, and accounting records are capital assets because they are not inventory, depreciable, or otherwise excluded.
Answers (a), (c), and (d) are incorrect because a noncompetition agreement represents ordinary income under cases and rulings, and the other items are excluded from being capital assets by Sec. 1221.

52. Which are real or depreciable property used in a trade or business?

a. 2, 3, and 4.
b. 2 and 6.
c. 6 and 7.
d. 6, 7, and 8.

The correct answer is (c). *(SPE 1077 I-180)*
REQUIRED: The items listed that are real or depreciable property used in a trade or business.
DISCUSSION: Business realty is obviously real property used in a trade or business. Furniture and equipment are depreciated under Sec. 167 before 1981 and under Sec. 168 after 1980.
Answers (a), (b), and (d) are incorrect because goodwill, an exclusive franchise, and accounting records do not have a fixed or determinable life so they are not depreciable. Accounts receivable and inventory are not used in a trade or business (accounts receivable are collected and inventory is sold) so they are not depreciable. A noncompetition agreement is generally considered amortizable rather than depreciable.

Module 15.4: Sale of a Business

53. Refer to the data presented in the information block on page 374. Which are other property generating ordinary income?

a. 1, 2, and 8.
b. 3, 6, and 7.
c. 1, 5, and 8.
d. 2, 5, and 8.

The correct answer is (d). *(SPE 1077 I-181)*
REQUIRED: The items listed that generate ordinary income.
DISCUSSION: The noncompetition agreement generates ordinary income because the seller receives payment for not performing services. Courts have held such payments similar to income from services. Accounts receivable and inventory are not capital assets under Sec. 1221 nor are they Sec. 1231 property; therefore, they produce ordinary income.
Answers (a), (b), and (c) are incorrect because goodwill, an exclusive franchise, and accounting records are capital assets. Business realty and furniture and equipment are Sec. 1231 property.

54. Needle Taylor, a sole proprietor, sold his small clothing business for $50,000 in 1991. The sales agreement does not allocate the sales price among the assets which include accounts receivable, inventory, equipment, and goodwill. How should the $50,000 price be allocated among the assets?

a. Based on the relative adjusted bases of the assets.
b. Based on the relative fair market values of the assets except for goodwill.
c. In any manner so long as it is consistent between the purchaser and seller.
d. In accordance with an IRS determination since the buyer and seller did not agree.

The correct answer is (b). *(Publisher)*
REQUIRED: The proper method for allocating the purchase price among assets when the parties did not agree.
DISCUSSION: When a sole proprietorship is sold (or purchased), the price must be allocated among the assets because the transaction is essentially a sale of each individual asset. The difference between the purchase price and the sum of the fair market values of the tangible and identifiable intangible assets is allocated to goodwill (Sec. 1060). The rest of the allocation is based on the relative fair market values of the assets. Following the Revenue Reconciliation Act of 1990, Sec. 1060(a) provides that, if a transferee and a transferor agree in writing as to the allocation of any consideration, or as to the fair market values of any of the assets, in an applicable asset transfer [defined under Sec. 1060(c)], then such agreement is binding on both the transferor or transferee unless the IRS determines that the allocation is not appropriate. Under long-standing case law, the parties could agree in an arm's-length transaction to an allocation since historically what was beneficial for one party was detrimental to the other; e.g., the seller wanted to allocate more to goodwill because it produced capital gain, while the purchaser wanted to allocate less to goodwill (since it is not depreciable) and more to equipment.
Answers (a) and (c) are incorrect because, when the parties have not agreed, the allocation is based on the relative fair market values, not the adjusted bases of the assets. Answer (d) is incorrect because the IRS has no authority to make a determination other than one based on the relative fair market values of the assets.

55. Mr. Macabee, a sole proprietor on the accrual basis, prepared the following balance sheet for his business on December 15, 1991:

Assets

Accounts receivable		$ 8,000
Inventory		14,000
Equipment (purchased in 1982)	$40,000	
Accumulated depreciation	(30,000)	10,000
Goodwill (tax basis)		15,000
		$47,000

Capital

Macabee, Capital	$47,000

On December 15, 1991 Mr. Macabee sold this business. The allocation of the selling price of $63,000 was stipulated in the sales agreement as follows:

Accounts receivable	$ 8,000
Inventory	17,000
Equipment	16,000
Goodwill	22,000
Total selling price	$63,000

How should this sale be reported in Mr. Macabee's 1991 individual tax return?

a. Zero long-term capital gain and $16,000 ordinary income.

b. Zero ordinary income and $16,000 long-term capital gain.

c. $3,000 ordinary income and $13,000 long-term capital gain.

d. $9,000 ordinary income and $7,000 long-term capital gain.

The correct answer is (d). *(CPA 575 Q-25)*
REQUIRED: The amount and character of gain recognized on the sale of the business.
DISCUSSION: The sale of the business resulted in a realized gain of $16,000. The accounts receivable had a tax basis of $8,000 because they were already recognized as income under the accrual method of accounting. The $3,000 gain on inventory is ordinary income because inventory is not a capital asset under Sec. 1221 nor is it Sec. 1231 property. The realized gain of $6,000 on the equipment must be recognized as ordinary income under the recapture provisions of Sec. 1245 because $30,000 in depreciation had previously been taken on the equipment. Goodwill is a capital asset and the $7,000 realized gain is a capital gain.

Asset	Sales Price	Basis	Gain
Accounts receivable	$ 8,000	$ 8,000	$ 0
Inventory	17,000	14,000	3,000
Equipment	16,000	10,000	6,000
Goodwill	22,000	15,000	7,000
Realized gain			$16,000

Ordinary income:	Inventory	$3,000
	Sec. 1245	6,000
	Total	$9,000
Capital gain:	Goodwill	$7,000

15.5 Sales to Related Parties

56. Justin Justice owns 55% of the outstanding stock of Rego Corporation. During 1991 Rego sold a trailer to Justin for $10,000. The trailer had an adjusted tax basis of $12,000 and had been owned by Rego for 3 years. In its 1991 income tax return, what is the allowable loss that Rego can claim on the sale of this trailer?

a. $0.

b. $2,000 ordinary loss.

c. $2,000 Sec. 1231 loss.

d. $2,000 Sec. 1245 loss.

The correct answer is (a). *(CPA 1186 Q-41)*
REQUIRED: The amount and character of loss on the sale of property by a corporation to a 55% shareholder.
DISCUSSION: Rego realized a $2,000 loss ($10,000 realized − $12,000 adjusted basis). Sec. 267(a) provides that a loss from the sale or exchange of property between related parties is not deductible. Related parties include a corporation and an individual who owns more than 50% of the stock. Since Justin owns more than 50% of the Rego stock, the loss is not deductible.

57. Mom and French have a partnership which buys railroad cars and leases them as tax shelters. Mom is a 55% partner and French is a 45% partner. Mom decided to open a diner as a sole proprietor, so she acquired one of the railroad cars from the partnership to use for her diner. This railroad car had cost the partnership $20,000 and $5,000 of depreciation had been claimed. Because the railroad car was badly in need of repair, Mom bought it for only $12,000. What is the partnership's deductible loss?

a. $0.
b. $3,000 Sec. 1245 loss.
c. $3,000 Sec. 1231 loss.
d. $3,000 capital loss.

The correct answer is (a). *(Publisher)*
REQUIRED: The deductible loss when a partner purchases property from a partnership for less than basis.
DISCUSSION: The partnership realized a loss of $3,000 ($12,000 realized − $15,000 adjusted basis). Sec. 267(a)(1) does not apply to partners and partnerships, but Sec. 707(b) does disallow a loss on the sale or exchange of property between a partnership and a person owning more than 50% of the capital or profit interests in the partnership. Since Mom owns 55% of the partnership, the loss realized on the sale is not deductible by the partnership.

58. Christina and Anne are equal partners in the capital and profits of Agee & Nolan, but are otherwise unrelated. The following information pertains to 300 shares of Mast Corporation stock sold by Anne to Agee & Nolan.

Year of purchase	1980
Year of sale	1991
Basis (cost)	$9,000
Sales price (equal to fair market value)	$4,000

The amount of long-term capital loss that Anne recognized in 1991 on the sale of this stock was

a. $5,000.
b. $3,000.
c. $2,500.
d. $0.

The correct answer is (a). *(CPA 1189 Q-56)*
REQUIRED: The long-term capital loss that Anne recognized on the sale of stock to a partnership which she equally shared in the capital and profits with another partner.
DISCUSSION: Under Sec. 1001, Anne would realize and recognize a $5,000 long-term capital loss on the sale of stock to the partnership, since she held the stock for more than a year. If Anne had owned greater than a 50% interest in the capital profits of Agee & Nolan, Anne would not be able to report her loss on the sale [Sec. 707(b)(1)(A)].

59. Dug Outt, a former baseball coach, decided to open a sporting goods store. He formed a corporation and sold a building for $80,000 to the corporation. The building originally cost Dug $75,000 and $25,000 of straight-line depreciation had been claimed prior to the sale during a period when Dug leased it to a tavern. The corporation will use the building as the location of the sporting goods store. What is Dug's gain on the sale of the building?

a. $0.
b. $5,000 capital gain.
c. $30,000 ordinary income.
d. $25,000 ordinary income and $5,000 capital gain.

The correct answer is (c). *(Publisher)*
REQUIRED: The gain recognized on the sale of depreciated property by a shareholder to a 100% owned corporation.
DISCUSSION: Dug realized a gain of $30,000 ($80,000 realized − $50,000 adjusted basis). There is no depreciation recapture since the straight-line method was used (Sec. 1250). The property is Sec. 1231 property, and the gain would normally be long-term capital gain if Dug had no other Sec. 1231 transactions. However, Sec. 1239(a) provides that any gain recognized on the sale of property between related persons is ordinary income if the property is depreciable in the hands of the transferee. Related persons include a taxpayer and a 50% owned entity. Dug's entire $30,000 gain is therefore ordinary income.

60. Senior sold Junior (his son) a rental residence with an adjusted basis of $60,000 for $40,000. Junior rented the house to a nonrelated tenant for 2 years, properly claiming $8,000 in depreciation on the house. He then sold it for $42,000. As a result of the sale, Junior will

a. Report no gain or loss.
b. Report a $10,000 loss.
c. Report a $10,000 gain.
d. Have his father report a $10,000 loss.

The correct answer is (a). *(J.M. Ruble)*
REQUIRED: The gain or loss upon the sale of property acquired from a related party.
DISCUSSION: Under Sec. 267(a), Senior's $20,000 loss incurred on the sale or exchange of property to Junior is not deductible. Sec. 267(d) provides that, if a loss has previously been disallowed because of the related party rules, any subsequent gain on the sale of such property is recognized only to the extent that the gain exceeds the previously disallowed loss. Thus, the $10,000 gain realized by Junior on the sale of the house (see below) is not recognized because it does not exceed the loss disallowed to Senior.

Sales proceeds		$42,000
Less adjusted basis:		
Cost	$40,000	
Depreciation	(8,000)	(32,000)
Realized gain		$10,000

61. Mr. Manryque sold his warehouse at a loss to his brother. The loss is deductible by Mr. Manryque.

The correct answer is (F). *(SPE 1082 I-34)*
DISCUSSION: Under Sec. 267(a), a loss incurred on the sale or exchange of property between related persons is not deductible. Related persons include brothers.

62. If a husband sells depreciable property to a trust in which his wife is the sole beneficiary, the gain on the sale will be treated as ordinary income.

The correct answer is (T). *(SPE 1077 I-138)*
DISCUSSION: Under Sec. 1239, gain recognized on a sale of property between related persons is ordinary income if the property is depreciable in the hands of the transferee. Related persons include a taxpayer and a trust in which the taxpayer or spouse is a beneficiary.

15.6 Effect on Taxable Income

63. Ben Green operates a parking lot that yielded net income of $13,000 during 1991. The only other transactions that Mr. Green had during the year were a gain of $16,000 on the sale of some Westinghouse Corporation stock that he bought 2 years ago, a loss of $10,000 on the sale of 1 acre of the land used in his parking lot business, and a gain of $4,000 on the sale of ½ acre of the land used in his parking lot business. All of the land used in his parking lot operations was purchased 7 years ago. Mr. Green's net capital gain from sale or exchange of capital assets for 1991 is

a. $16,000.
b. $10,000.
c. $6,400.
d. $5,000.

The correct answer is (a). *(CPA 572 P-4)*
REQUIRED: The net capital gain from the sale of capital assets.
DISCUSSION: Sec. 1222(11) defines "net capital gain" as the excess of the net long-term capital gain for the taxable year over the net short-term capital loss for the year.
Mr. Green had two Sec. 1231 transactions: the $10,000 loss and the $4,000 gain. Real property (land) used in a trade or business is a Sec. 1231 asset, and land is neither Sec. 1245 nor Sec. 1250 property. These result in a net Sec. 1231 loss of $6,000, so both are treated as ordinary gains and losses. The remaining sale resulted in a $16,000 long-term capital gain. Green's net capital gain is $16,000.

Module 15.6: Effect on Taxable Income

64. Steve Bullman sold his business in 1991 for $120,000. The sales contract allocated $40,000 to inventory and $80,000 to real property. The adjusted basis of the inventory was $38,000. The real property, held more than 1 year, had a cost of $40,000 and depreciation claimed on a straight-line basis was $20,000. In 1991, Steve received a down payment of $60,000, of which $40,000 was payment for the inventory. Steve had no other Sec. 1231 transactions. What is the amount and nature of the gain that Steve should report using the installment method?

	Ordinary Income	Capital Gain
a.	$2,000	$15,000
b.	$2,000	$20,000
c.	$40,000	$60,000
d.	$40,000	$80,000

65. During the current year, a corporation retired obsolete equipment purchased in 1981 having an adjusted basis of $30,000 and sold it as scrap for $1,000. The corporation also had $50,000 net income from operations. The taxable income of the corporation was

a. $21,000.
b. $35,000.
c. $49,000 with a capital loss carryover of $27,000.
d. $50,000 with a capital loss carryover of $14,500.

66. During 1991, Mr. Trout had the following losses and gains on property that he had held for more than 1 year:

Loss on sale of real property used in business	$ 900
Casualty loss of a stolen personal auto (excess of loss over insurance and $100 limitation)	400
Involuntary conversion (condemnation) loss of land used in business	300
Gain from insurance reimbursement for hurricane damage to residence	700
Gain from sale of machinery used in business (not recapture)	1,300

Calculate ordinary income or loss under Sec. 1231.

a. No ordinary income or loss.
b. $400 ordinary loss.
c. $1,600 ordinary loss.
d. $400 ordinary income.

The correct answer is (a). *(SPE 1083 II-74)*
REQUIRED: The amount and nature of the gain under the installment method.
DISCUSSION: The sale of the business is essentially a sale of each of the separate assets. The inventory was sold at a gain of $2,000, which is ordinary income because inventory is neither a capital asset nor Sec. 1231 property.

The real property was sold at a gain of $60,000 (see below). Since this is a Sec. 1231 gain, and Steve has no other Sec. 1231 transactions, the entire amount will be considered long-term capital gain. Steve's gross profit percentage on the real property is 75% ($60,000 gain ÷ $80,000 contract price). Under the installment sale rules, Mr. B must recognize $15,000 of the Sec. 1231 (capital) gain (75% x $20,000 received in 1991).

	Inventory	Real Property
Sales proceeds	$40,000	$80,000
Less adjusted basis	(38,000)	(20,000)
Realized gain	$ 2,000	$60,000

The correct answer is (a). *(CPA 1172 P-11)*
REQUIRED: The taxable income of the corporation after retiring obsolete equipment.
DISCUSSION: The corporation realized a loss of $29,000 ($1,000 realized − $30,000 adjusted basis) on the sale of the retired equipment for scrap. This is a Sec. 1231 loss. Since there are no other Sec. 1231 gains or losses to net, it is treated as an ordinary loss. Taxable income is

Income from operations	$50,000
Less loss on equipment	(29,000)
Taxable income	$21,000

The correct answer is (a). *(SPE 1077 III-17)*
REQUIRED: The amount of ordinary income or loss under Sec. 1231.
DISCUSSION: First, gains and losses from casualties and thefts are netted (the "subnet"). If losses exceed gains, all are considered ordinary gains and losses and are not included in further Sec. 1231 computations. If gains exceed losses, this net gain is included in the second computation (the "major net"). Net gains from the "subnet" and all other Sec. 1231 gains and losses are then netted. If losses exceed gains, all gains and losses are ordinary. If gains exceed losses, all gains and losses are long-term capital gains and losses. In this case, there is no subnet computation because the casualty and thefts were on personal use property which is not covered by Sec. 1231 after 1983.

	Major Net
Real property sale	$ (900)
Condemnation	(300)
Machinery sale	1,300
Net gain in major net	$ 100

Since the major net resulted in a net gain, all Sec. 1231 transactions are treated as long-term capital gains and losses.

67. Hoss Cartwrong has owned a cattle ranch in Alaska County, Florida, for 10 years. In 1991, he had the following gains and losses:

Gain when 10 acres of his spread were condemned	$3,000
Loss when breeding cattle were stolen which he had owned for 1½ years	2,000
Gain on the sale of 5 acres used for pasturage	5,000
Loss when the bunkhouse burned	7,000
Insurance reimbursement for the bunkhouse	6,000

Hoss has $30,000 of taxable income from the ranch not including the above occurrences. What is Hoss's taxable income?

a. $40,800.
b. $37,000.
c. $35,000.
d. $32,000.

The correct answer is (c). *(Publisher)*
REQUIRED: The taxable income for 1991 of a person who has several Sec. 1231 transactions.
DISCUSSION: All the property qualifies as Sec. 1231 property except the stolen cattle because Sec. 1231(b)(3) requires breeding cattle to be held 24 months or more to constitute Sec. 1231 property. Therefore, the theft loss is an ordinary loss outside of Sec. 1231.

The computation under Sec. 1231 must be made in two steps. First, gains and losses from casualties and thefts are netted (the "subnet"). Since subnet losses exceed gains, all are considered ordinary gains and losses and are not included in further Sec. 1231 computations. Second, net gains from the "subnet" and all other Sec. 1231 gains and losses are netted (the "major net"). Since gains in the major net exceed losses, all these gains and losses are long-term capital gains and losses. Note that the condemnation is in the "major net" because it is similar to an actual sale rather than a casualty.

Subnet
Loss on bunkhouse	$(7,000)
Reduced by insurance	6,000
Net loss in subnet	$(1,000)

Major Net
Gain on condemnation	$3,000
Gain on sale	5,000
Net gain in major net	$8,000

Taxable Income
Tentative taxable income	$30,000
Loss on theft of cattle	(2,000)
Net loss in subnet	(1,000)
Net gain in major net	8,000
Taxable income	$35,000

68. The results of Digimatic Corporation's first 3 years of operations are presented below.

Year	Results of Operations
1989	Sec. 1231 losses of $10,000
1990	Sec. 1231 losses of $15,000
1991	Sec. 1231 gain of $75,000

Digimatic Corporation's 1991 Sec. 1231 gain can best be characterized as

a. A net long-term capital gain of $75,000.
b. A net long-term capital gain of $50,000.
c. A net long-term capital gain of $50,000 and ordinary income of $25,000.
d. A net long-term capital gain of $25,000 and ordinary income of $50,000.

The correct answer is (c). *(CMA 686 3-25)*
REQUIRED: The characterization of Sec. 1231 gain given prior year Sec. 1231 transactions.
DISCUSSION: The net Sec. 1231 gain for any taxable year is treated as ordinary income to the extent that the gain does not exceed the nonrecaptured net Sec. 1231 losses. The nonrecaptured net Sec. 1231 loss is the excess of all Sec. 1231 losses for the 5 most recent taxable years over the portion of such losses already recaptured.

For Digimatic Corporation in 1991, the nonrecaptured net Sec. 1231 loss is $25,000 ($10,000 in 1989 + $15,000 in 1990). Therefore, the $75,000 net Sec. 1231 gain in 1991 must be treated as $25,000 of ordinary income (recapture of the previous Sec. 1231 losses of $25,000) and $50,000 of long-term capital gain.

CHAPTER SIXTEEN
NONTAXABLE PROPERTY TRANSACTIONS

16.1 Introduction	(5 questions)	381
16.2 Like-Kind Exchanges	(21 questions)	382
16.3 Involuntary Conversions	(23 questions)	389
16.4 Sale of a Principal Residence	(15 questions)	396

16.1 Introduction

1. A property transaction (e.g., sale, exchange, casualty) may give rise to a realized gain or loss which is not recognized. Such a transaction is often referred to as a nontaxable or tax-free transaction. Which of the following is a correct generalization concerning gain which is not recognized in such a transaction?

a. The gain is a tax deferral included in taxable income in the year subsequent to the transaction.

b. When gain is not recognized, a permanent tax savings is effected.

c. The effect of not recognizing gain is generally to cause a deferral of taxation for an indefinite time until the property is again sold, exchanged, or disposed of.

d. The tax on the deferred gain is computed at the rates in effect when the gain was realized.

The correct answer is (c). *(Publisher)*
REQUIRED: The correct statement concerning deferral of gain in a nontaxable transaction.
DISCUSSION: In most cases, a nontaxable transaction results only in deferral of gain. The basis of the new or acquired property is either the same as the basis in the old property, or the cost of the new property less any gain not recognized. With a low basis in the new or acquired property, the deferred gain is generally recognized when the property is again disposed of in a taxable transaction. One major exception to deferral is the one-time exclusion of gain on the sale of a personal residence for taxpayers age 55 and older, for whom there is a permanent tax savings.
Answer (a) is incorrect because the gain is deferred until a taxable transaction occurs. Answer (b) is incorrect because generally there is a tax deferral and not a permanent tax savings. Answer (d) is incorrect because tax on the deferred gain is computed at the rates in effect when the subsequent taxable transaction occurs, not when the deferred gain was realized.

2. The deferral of taxation on unrecognized gains from a nontaxable property transaction

a. Is accomplished by adjustments to the basis of the new or acquired property.

b. Becomes a permanent tax saving if the property is held for the statutory period following the transaction.

c. Has no effect on the basis of the property.

d. Results in a reduction of the basis of the acquired property by the amount of tax paid in a subsequent transfer of the property.

The correct answer is (a). *(Publisher)*
REQUIRED: The correct statement concerning deferral of taxation on nontaxable transactions.
DISCUSSION: A nontaxable property transaction generally results in the deferral of gain rather than a permanent tax savings. This is usually accomplished by transferring the basis of the old property to the new, or by determining the basis of the new or acquired property as its cost less the unrecognized gain.
Answer (b) is incorrect because there is no statutory period after which deferred gain becomes a permanent tax savings. Answer (c) is incorrect because the deferred gain is usually reflected in a lower basis for the new or acquired property. Answer (d) is incorrect because when a subsequent taxable transaction takes place and the gain is recognized, the tax does not alter the basis of the property.

3. Which of the following statements are correct?

1. A sale is generally a transfer of property for money only or for a promise to pay money.
2. An exchange is a transfer of property in return for other property or services.
3. Recognized gain is always the excess of the amount realized over the adjusted basis of the property.
4. Realized loss is always the excess of the adjusted basis of the property over the amount realized.
5. The adjusted basis of the property is always the original cost adjusted for such items as casualty losses, improvements, and depreciation.

   a. 1, 2, and 3.
   b. 1, 2, and 4.
   c. 1, 4, and 5.
   d. 2, 3, and 4.

The correct answer is (b). *(SPE 1080 I-61)*
REQUIRED: The correct statements concerning a sale or exchange of property.
DISCUSSION: Statements 1, 2, and 4 are correct. A sale is generally a transfer of property for money or for a promise to pay money, while an exchange is a transfer of property for something other than money. Sec. 1001(a) defines a realized loss as the excess of the adjusted basis over the amount realized.

Answers (a) and (d) are incorrect because statement 3 is incorrect. Sec. 1001(a) defines a realized gain as the excess of the amount realized over the adjusted basis of the property; a realized gain is not always recognized (e.g., gain from a like-kind exchange under Sec. 1031). Answer (c) is incorrect because statement 5 is incorrect. The adjusted basis of property is not always the original cost adjusted by the items listed in Sec. 1016. Sec. 1015 provides that the basis of property acquired by gift is either the donor's basis or the fair market value of the property on the date of the gift.

4. Advance payment to a contractor, within the qualified replacement period, for construction of replacement property does not qualify as being the purchase of replacement property if construction is not completed within the replacement time period.

The correct answer is (T). *(SPE 1079 II-28)*
DISCUSSION: A person who makes an advance payment to a contractor may receive a right to receive the replacement property at a stated time. The purchase of this right is not the same as the purchase of replacement property (for the purpose of nonrecognition of gain), and it would not satisfy the tests to determine whether the replacement property qualifies. The actual replacement property must be acquired within the time limit.

5. A loss is recognized in a nontaxable exchange to the extent you receive property or cash.

The correct answer is (F). *(SPE 1079 II-23)*
DISCUSSION: A loss is fully recognized on an involuntary conversion (Sec. 1033). A loss cannot be recognized in a like-kind exchange (Sec. 1031) even if nonlike-kind property or cash is received.

16.2 Like-Kind Exchanges

6. All of the following statements regarding tax-free like-kind exchanges are true except:

   a. The property must be held for productive use in a trade or business or it must be investment property.
   b. The property must be tangible property.
   c. The exchange of personal property for similar personal property may qualify for a tax-free exchange.
   d. If you pay money in addition to giving up like property in a like-kind exchange, you may have a taxable gain or deductible loss.

The correct answer is (d). *(SPE 990 I-45)*
REQUIRED: The incorrect statement concerning tax-free like-kind exchanges.
DISCUSSION: Sec. 1031(a)(1) requires that property qualifying for tax-free treatment must be held for productive use in a trade or business or investment. Sec. 1031(a)(2) exempts intangible property such as stocks, bonds, and partnership interests from tax-free exchange treatment. Sec. 1031(a) requires that property exchanged tax-free must be of like-kind. Reg. 1.1031(a)-1(b) states that "like-kind" refers to the nature or character of the property, i.e., a class of property such as real or personal property. Hence, personal property exchanged for similar personal property would qualify for tax-free treatment. Based on the above, statements (a), (b), and (c) are correct.

Although Sec. 1031(b) requires that gain be recognized to the extent of boot received, there is no requirement that gain or loss be recognized to the extent of boot given. Thus, statement (d) is incorrect.

7. For purposes of determining like-kind property for nontaxable exchanges, which of the following items held for business or investment purposes are not like-kind property?

   a. Real estate for real estate.
   b. Car for a truck.
   c. Real estate for personal property.
   d. Personal property for personal property.

The correct answer is (c). *(SPE 1079 II-53)*
REQUIRED: The exchange of property that does not qualify as a like-kind exchange.
DISCUSSION: The term "like-kind" refers to the nature or character of the property, i.e., a class of property such as real or personal property [Reg. 1.1031(a)-1]. An exchange of real estate for real estate qualifies as a like-kind exchange even if the properties are as different as a rental office building and a parking lot. An exchange of personal property for personal property also qualifies as a like-kind exchange. But, an exchange of real estate for personal property does not qualify as a like-kind exchange.
Answers (a), (b), and (d) are incorrect because they are all exchanges of property within the same class and qualify for like-kind treatment when held for business or investment purposes.

8. Assuming all items are held for use in a business or for investment, which of the following does not qualify as a nontaxable like-kind exchange?

   a. The trade of an apartment house for a store building that is subsequently rented out.
   b. The exchange of a vacant city lot for unimproved farm land.
   c. The exchange of real estate you own for a real estate lease that runs 30 years or more.
   d. The exchange of stock of one corporation held for investment for stock of another corporation to be held for investment.

The correct answer is (d). *(SPE 988 II-48)*
REQUIRED: The exchange of property that does not qualify for like-kind treatment.
DISCUSSION: Sec. 1031(a) specifically excludes stocks (and other securities and debt instruments) from qualifying for like-kind exchange treatment. Therefore, even though the exchange of stock is for property within the same class, such an exchange does not qualify for like-kind treatment.
Answer (a) is incorrect because an apartment house and a store building are both real property and qualify as like-kind property even though the buildings are used for different purposes. Answer (b) is incorrect because a vacant city lot and unimproved farm land are both real property, even if one of the properties was improved. Answer (c) is incorrect because a real estate lease that runs 30 years is treated as real property and the exchange of it for other real estate qualifies under Sec. 1031 as long as the parties to the exchange are not dealers in real estate.

9. Alex is a general partner in the XYZ Partnership. The basis of his partnership interest is $50,000 and the fair market value is $100,000. Bill is a limited partner in the ABC Partnership. The basis of his partnership interest is $30,000, and the fair market value is $100,000. Alex and Bill exchange their partnership interests. No other consideration is involved in the exchange. Which of the following is the best answer?

   a. Neither party must recognize gain.
   b. Alex must recognize a gain of $50,000. The receipt of a limited partnership interest for a general partnership interest is not a like-kind exchange.
   c. Bill must recognize a gain of $70,000. The receipt of a general partnership interest for a limited partnership interest is not a like-kind exchange.
   d. Both (b) and (c).

The correct answer is (d). *(M.J. Whiteman)*
REQUIRED: The proper treatment of an exchange of partnership interests.
DISCUSSION: For exchanges after 1984, Sec. 1031 excludes the transfer of partnership interests in different partnerships from the tax-free exchange provisions of Sec. 1031. Therefore, each participant in the exchange should recognize gain equal to the excess of the amount realized over his basis. Tax-free exchanges of interests in the same partnership (e.g., a general interest for a limited interest) are permitted.
Note that this also applies to the exchange of a general partnership interest for a general partnership interest. Under prior law, such an exchange fell within Sec. 1031 provided the property held by the partnerships was like-kind. Now partnership interests will not qualify as tax-free exchanges.

Module 16.2: Like-Kind Exchanges

10. Pat Leif owned an apartment house that he bought in 1976. Depreciation was taken on a straight-line basis. In 1991, when Pat's adjusted basis for this property was $200,000, he traded it for an office building having a fair market value of $600,000. The apartment house has 100 dwelling units, while the office building has 40 units rented to business enterprises. The properties are not located in the same city. What is Pat's reportable gain on this exchange?

a. $400,000 Sec. 1250 gain.
b. $400,000 Sec. 1231 gain.
c. $400,000 long-term capital gain.
d. $0.

The correct answer is (d). *(CPA 586 Q-58)*
REQUIRED: The recognized gain on the exchange of an office building for an apartment building.
DISCUSSION: Sec. 1031(a) provides for the nonrecognition of gain or loss on the exchange of like-kind property held for productive use in a trade or business or for investment. Like-kind refers to the nature or character of property (here, real property) and not to its grade or quality [Reg. 1.1031(a)-1(b)]. The parcels of real property are like-kind property regardless of whether they are improved, unimproved, or used for different purposes.
Leif has a realized gain of $400,000 ($600,000 realized − $200,000 adjusted basis). None of this gain is recognized under Sec. 1031.

11. Bolo Corporation exchanged a machine used in its business and $26,000 cash for an updated version of the same machine. Its old machine had an adjusted basis of $27,000 and a fair market value of $32,000 at the date of the exchange. The new machine had a fair market value of $58,000. What is Bolo's recognized taxable gain on the exchange and Bolo's tax basis of the new machine?

	Bolo's Recognized Taxable Gain	Bolo's Tax Basis of the New Machine
a.	$0	$27,000
b.	$0	$53,000
c.	$5,000	$32,000
d.	$31,000	$58,000

The correct answer is (b). *(CMA 686 3-30)*
REQUIRED: The amount of recognized gain or loss and the new basis of property acquired in a like-kind exchange.
DISCUSSION: The transaction would qualify for like-kind treatment under Sec. 1031 since Bolo is exchanging personal property used in its business for personal property to be used in the business. Gain is recognized in a like-kind exchange only to the extent nonlike-kind property is received. The property received was solely like-kind and therefore no gain or loss would be recognized on this transaction. The basis of the new machine is equal to the adjusted basis of the machine surrendered, increased by the amount of cash given [Sec. 1031(d)].

Adjusted basis of old machine	$27,000
Additional cash given	26,000
Basis of new machine	$53,000

12. Python Corporation wants to obtain commercial property located on Mainstreet. Paul, one of its customers, owns the property and uses it in his business. Python offers to give Paul the land it owns next to his business and inventory items worth $70,000 in exchange for his Mainstreet property. Paul's basis in the Mainstreet property is $160,000 and its fair market value is $350,000. The land owned by Python has an adjusted basis to Python of $90,000 and a fair market value of $280,000. Paul will hold the land he receives from Python for investment purposes. What is the amount of Paul's recognized gain if he accepts the offer?

a. $0.
b. $70,000.
c. $120,000.
d. $290,000.

The correct answer is (b). *(SPE 990 II-76)*
REQUIRED: The recognized gain on the exchange of real property for real property and personal property.
DISCUSSION: The transaction would qualify for like-kind treatment under Sec. 1031 since Paul is exchanging real property used in his trade or business for real property held for investment purposes. Sec. 1031(b) requires gain to be recognized in a like-kind exchange only to the extent that nonlike-kind property is received. Since the inventory items received by Paul are personal property, they are considered nonlike-kind (boot) property. Inventory is also excluded from being like-kind property by Sec. 1031(a)(2)(A).
Paul realizes a gain of $190,000 ($280,000 FMV of new property + $70,000 FMV of inventory − $160,000 basis of old property). The gain recognized is the lesser of the boot received ($70,000) or the realized gain ($190,000).

Module 16.2: Like-Kind Exchanges

13. During 1991, Mr. A exchanged stock and real estate that he held for investment for other real estate he intends to hold for investment. The stock at the time of the exchange had a fair market value of $4,000 and an adjusted basis to A of $1,000. A's old real estate had a fair market value of $150,000 and an adjusted basis to him of $90,000. The real estate acquired by Mr. A had a fair market value of $180,000 at the time of the exchange. What is the amount of A's recognized gain (or loss) on the exchange?

a. $(30,000).
b. $(3,000).
c. $3,000.
d. $30,000.

The correct answer is (c). *(SPE 989 I-75)*
REQUIRED: The recognized gain or loss on an exchange of like-kind property when appreciated boot is given.
DISCUSSION: Neither gain nor loss is recognized on an exchange of like-kind property held for productive use in a trade or business or for investment [Sec. 1031(a)]. In addition, recognition of gain or loss is not triggered when boot is given. However, when boot is given, there is no provision preventing recognition of gain or loss on the boot itself.

The stock Mr. A exchanged with the real estate is boot. Hence, Mr. A realizes and recognizes a $3,000 gain on the stock ($4,000 fair market value − $1,000 adjusted basis). There is no other gain or loss on the exchange because the old and new real estate exchange does qualify under Sec. 1031.

One might question why Mr. A would be able to exchange property having a $154,000 market value for other property having a $180,000 market value. He may be receiving a good deal, or the $180,000 amount may be inflated. Alternatively, there may be another aspect of the transaction that is not obvious, such as Mr. A is receiving compensation, a gift, or repayment of a debt. These other alternatives would possibly change the tax consequences.

14. KMH Corporation exchanged a piece of land with NEB Corporation during 1991. The transaction met the requirements of the like-kind exchange provisions of the Internal Revenue Code. Below is the relevant information pertaining to the land prior to this exchange.

At Date of Exchange	KMH Land	NEB Land
Adjusted basis	$20,000	$10,000
Fair market value	40,000	30,000

In addition, NEB paid KMH $7,000 in cash and assumed KMH's $3,000 mortgage on the land. KMH's recognized gain resulting from this transaction is

a. $0.
b. $3,000.
c. $7,000.
d. $10,000.

The correct answer is (d). *(CMA 690 3-22)*
REQUIRED: The recognized gain or loss on an exchange of like-kind property when boot is received and a mortgage is assumed.
DISCUSSION: Since the transaction qualifies as a like-kind exchange, Sec. 1031(b) requires gain to be recognized only to the extent of boot received. Reg. 1.1031(d)-2 provides that liabilities assumed by the other party are to be treated as money received by the taxpayer. Thus, the total boot received by KMH is $10,000 ($7,000 cash + $3,000 of liabilities assumed).

KMH realizes a gain of $20,000 ($30,000 FMV of property received + $3,000 of liabilities assumed + $7,000 cash − $20,000 basis of property given up). The gain recognized is the lesser of total boot received ($10,000) or the realized gain ($20,000).

Module 16.2: Like-Kind Exchanges

15. On October 1, 1991, Donald Anderson exchanged an apartment building, having an adjusted basis of $375,000 and subject to a mortgage of $100,000, for $25,000 cash and another apartment building with a fair market value of $550,000 and subject to a mortgage of $125,000. The property transfers were made subject to the outstanding mortgages. What amount of gain should Anderson recognize in his tax return for 1991?

a. $0.
b. $25,000.
c. $125,000.
d. $175,000.

The correct answer is (b). *(CPA 582 P-56)*
REQUIRED: The recognized gain in a like-kind exchange of properties subject to mortgages.
DISCUSSION: Anderson's realized gain is computed as follows:

Fair market value of building received		$550,000
Mortgage on old building		100,000
Cash received		25,000
Total amount realized		$675,000
Less: Basis of old building	$375,000	
Mortgage on new building	125,000	(500,000)
Realized gain		$175,000

Under Reg. 1.1031(d)-2, the mortgages are netted so that Anderson is considered to have given $25,000 boot by taking the larger mortgage. The cash boot received by Anderson cannot be netted with the mortgages. Accordingly, Anderson recognizes gain to the extent of the $25,000 cash received.

16. Mr. J traded in his truck that had an adjusted basis of $3,500 and was used in his business, for a new one to be used in his business costing $12,000. Mr. J paid $7,000 in cash and was allowed $5,000 trade-in value for his old vehicle. What is Mr. J's basis in his new truck?

a. $7,000.
b. $8,500.
c. $10,500.
d. $12,000.

The correct answer is (c). *(SPE 988 I-76)*
REQUIRED: The basis of property acquired in a like-kind exchange when boot is given.
DISCUSSION: The basis of property acquired in a like-kind exchange is equal to the adjusted basis of the property surrendered, decreased by any boot received, and increased by any gain recognized or boot given [Sec. 1031(d)]. Mr. J received no boot and recognized no gain on the transaction. His basis in the new truck is $10,500 ($3,500 substituted basis + $7,000 boot given). The information about trade-in value is irrelevant.

17. Fred Phillips traded a business car with an adjusted basis of $2,000 for another business car with a fair market value of $1,800 and cash boot of $500. What is Fred's recognized gain or loss, and what is his basis in the new business car?

a. Recognized gain, $0; basis, $2,000.
b. Recognized gain, $500; basis, $2,300.
c. Recognized gain, $300; basis, $1,800.
d. Recognized loss, $200; basis, $2,500.

The correct answer is (c). *(G.L. Waters)*
REQUIRED: The gain or loss and the basis of property received in a like-kind exchange.
DISCUSSION: Under Sec. 1031(a), neither gain nor loss is recognized on the exchange of like-kind property held for productive use in a trade or business. However, Sec. 1031(b) provides that if boot is received in addition to the like-kind property, gain is recognized to the extent of the fair market value of the boot. The $500 received is boot. Fred's realized gain is $300 ($1,800 FMV of car received + $500 cash − $2,000 basis). Since the realized gain of $300 is less than the boot of $500, the entire $300 gain is recognized.

The basis of property received in a like-kind exchange is the basis of the property given up, increased by any gain recognized, and decreased by any boot received. Thus, Fred's basis is $1,800 ($2,000 substituted basis + $300 gain recognized − $500 boot received).

Module 16.2: Like-Kind Exchanges

18. Mr. N exchanged a press used in his business that had an adjusted basis of $10,000, for a lathe that had a fair market value of $6,000, a band saw that had a fair market value of $2,000, and $500 cash. What is the combined basis of the lathe and band saw?

  a. $10,000.
  b. $9,500.
  c. $8,000.
  d. $7,500.

The correct answer is (b). *(SPE 1085 II-61)*
REQUIRED: The basis of property acquired in a like-kind exchange when boot is received.
DISCUSSION: The exchange qualifies for like-kind treatment under Sec. 1031 since personal property used in Mr. N's business is exchanged for other personal property to be used in the business. The realized loss is $1,500 ($6,000 lathe + $2,000 saw + $500 cash – $10,000 basis), which cannot be recognized under Sec. 1031(c). The basis of the property received is $9,500 ($10,000 adjusted basis of the property surrendered – $500 boot received).

19. Ms. M exchanged an auto used in her business that had an adjusted basis to her of $12,000 with an outstanding liability of $2,000, for a new auto, to be used in her business, with a fair market value of $11,000 and $1,000 in cash. Ms. M's liability was assumed by the other party. What is Ms. M's basis in the new auto?

  a. $9,000.
  b. $10,000.
  c. $11,000.
  d. $12,000.

The correct answer is (c). *(SPE 987 II-62)*
REQUIRED: The basis of property acquired in a like-kind exchange when boot is received.
DISCUSSION: Ms. M recognized a $2,000 gain on the exchange. She received $14,000 (auto with a FMV of $11,000 + $2,000 debt relieved of + $1,000 cash) and she gave up an auto with a basis of $12,000. Mrs. M's realized gain is $2,000 ($14,000 – $12,000 adjusted basis). The recognized gain is the lesser of the $3,000 boot received, or the $2,000 realized gain, or $2,000. Her basis in the new automobile is $11,000 ($12,000 basis of the old car – $3,000 boot received + $2,000 gain recognized).

20. Seminole Airways is a small passenger airline operating in Florida. Due to heavy losses, it decided to get out of the airline business and into real estate investment. As part of its disposition of assets, Seminole traded a hangar (with a fair market value of $100,000 and a basis of $50,000) and an airplane (with a fair market value of $300,000 and a basis of $100,000) for an apartment building with a fair market value of $400,000. The difference between the fair market value and basis of Seminole's assets was entirely due to depreciation subject to recapture. What is Seminole's recognized gain on this transaction?

  a. $0.
  b. $200,000 ordinary income.
  c. $250,000 ordinary income.
  d. $200,000 ordinary income and $50,000 Sec. 1231 gain.

The correct answer is (b). *(Publisher)*
REQUIRED: The amount and character of gain recognized on the exchange of real property and personal property solely for real property.
DISCUSSION: Seminole Airways has a realized gain of $250,000 ($400,000 realized – $50,000 basis in hangar – $100,000 basis in airplane). The hangar and the apartment building are like-kind properties because they are both real property. No gain is recognized on this part of the exchange. The airplane is not like-kind property with respect to the apartment building. Therefore, gain of $200,000 ($300,000 FMV received – $100,000 basis) is recognized. This gain is ordinary under Sec. 1245 as depreciation recapture.

21. If the apartment building in the previous question had a basis of $300,000 and Sec. 167 depreciation subject to recapture of $50,000, what is the prior owner's gain?

   a. $0.
   b. $50,000 ordinary income.
   c. $100,000 ordinary income.
   d. $50,000 ordinary income and $50,000 Sec. 1231 gain.

The correct answer is (d). *(Publisher)*
REQUIRED: The amount and character of gain when real property and personal property are received in exchange for real property.
DISCUSSION: The exchange of the apartment building for the hangar qualifies as a like-kind exchange; however, the receipt of the airplane is boot because it is not like-kind property. Under Sec. 1031(b), gain is recognized to the extent of the fair market value of boot received. The prior owner of the apartment building had a realized gain of $100,000 ($400,000 realized − $300,000 adjusted basis). This entire gain is recognized because boot with a value of $300,000 was received.

The apartment building is Sec. 1250 property because it is real property subject to Sec. 167 depreciation. Under Sec. 1250(a), the amount of recapture is the lesser of the gain recognized or the additional depreciation (depreciation subject to recapture). Consequently, $50,000 of the gain will be recaptured as ordinary income and the remaining $50,000 gain will be Sec. 1231 gain. Since the entire realized gain is already recognized, the fact that the non-Sec. 1250 property that was received is worth $300,000 does not increase the amount of the recognized gain [Sec. 1250(d)(3)].

22. Timbertoppers, Inc. is in the forestry business. It wanted to acquire a parcel of property owned by Woodsy, who held the property for investment. Woodsy would not sell but agreed to exchange the property if Timbertoppers could find other suitable property. Timbertoppers could not locate suitable property immediately, so the parties entered into an agreement by which Timbertoppers took title to Woodsy's property (which had a fair market value of $400,000 and a basis of $50,000) on August 1, 1990, and an escrow was set up in which Timbertoppers placed certificates of deposit as security until real property could be found to suit Woodsy. If one parcel valued at $300,000 is identified 30 days after the escrow and transferred to Woodsy on January 10, 1991, and a second parcel valued at $100,000 is identified 60 days after the escrow and transferred to Woodsy on December 20, 1990, what is Woodsy's gain?

   a. $0.
   b. $100,000 in 1990; $0 in 1991.
   c. $300,000 in 1990; $0 in 1991.
   d. $0 in 1990; $100,000 in 1991.

The correct answer is (b). *(Publisher)*
REQUIRED: The amount of gain on a nonsimultaneous exchange of like-kind properties.
DISCUSSION: Woodsy will realize a gain of $350,000 ($400,000 realized − $50,000 basis). Provided the escrow is arranged so that the certificates of deposit in escrow are clearly the property of Timbertoppers pending performance and Woodsy has no right in such escrow except upon the failure of Timbertoppers to perform, a nonsimultaneous exchange will also qualify for nonrecognition of gain under the case of Starker, 602 F.2d 1341, 1979.

However, Sec. 1031(a)(3) requires, for transfers after July 18, 1984, that the property to be received must be identified as such within 45 days after transferring the old property being exchanged, and the new property must actually be received within 180 days or by the due date of the taxpayer's tax return if sooner. If these requirements are not met, the property received will be treated as boot. These requirements were met for the parcel received on January 10, 1991, but not for the parcel received on December 20, 1990, so Woodsy must recognize $100,000 (the amount of boot) in 1990.

23. On May 1, 1991, Mr. Brown traded an old truck, which had been used in his business, for a new personal automobile. Mr. Brown paid an additional $4,000 for the new automobile. This exchange is a nontaxable exchange.

The correct answer is (F). *(SPE 1077 I-125)*
DISCUSSION: The property given and the property received in an exchange must be held for productive use in a trade or business or for investment for the transaction to qualify as a nontaxable like-kind exchange (Sec. 1031). Since Mr. Brown traded a truck used in his business for a personal automobile, the exchange is not a nontaxable like-kind exchange.

24. Mr. O, a real estate broker and dealer in real property, exchanged a 100-acre tract of farm land held for sale (fair market value $100,000, adjusted basis $50,000) for a one-block parking lot located in a large metropolitan area (fair market value $200,000). In the transaction, Mr. O assumed a $100,000 mortgage. Mr. O must report a $50,000 gain on the exchange.

The correct answer is (T). *(SPE 1083 II-27)*
DISCUSSION: The exchange of property held primarily for sale does not qualify as a nontaxable like-kind exchange because the property is not held for productive use in a trade or business or for investment. Mr. O must recognize the entire gain on the transaction. The amount realized is $100,000 ($200,000 FMV received − $100,000 mortgage assumed). The gain is $50,000 ($100,000 realized − $50,000 basis).

25. Mr. E traded in a large lathe used in his business with an adjusted basis of $7,000 for a smaller lathe valued at $8,000. In addition to the smaller lathe, Mr. E received $2,000 cash. Mr. E's recognized gain is $3,000.

The correct answer is (F). *(SPE 1081 II-20)*
DISCUSSION: Under Sec. 1031(b), a gain realized on a like-kind exchange is recognized to the lesser of gain realized or the value of money or nonlike-kind property received. Mr. E received total consideration of $10,000 (lathe worth $8,000 and cash of $2,000) in exchange for property with an adjusted basis of $7,000. He thereby realized a gain of $3,000. This gain is recognized only to the extent of the cash received, or $2,000.

26. Mr. Knot wants to get a new truck for his business. His old truck has an adjusted basis of $2,600 and a fair market trade-in value of $3,100. The new truck has a sales price of $8,000. The dealer will take Mr. Knot's truck plus $4,900 cash. Mr. Knot's basis in the new truck would be $7,500. However, he wants a higher basis for depreciation, so he agrees to pay the dealer $8,000 cash for the new truck and the dealer agrees to pay him $3,100 cash for the old truck. This transaction is treated as a nontaxable exchange and Mr. Knot's basis in the new truck would still be $7,500, which is the same as if he had traded his old truck.

The correct answer is (T). *(SPE 989 II-13)*
DISCUSSION: The basis of property acquired in a like-kind exchange is equal to the adjusted basis of property surrendered, decreased by any boot received, and increased by any gain recognized or boot given [Sec. 1031(d)]. Thus, Mr. Knot's basis in the new truck would be $7,500 ($2,600 basis of old truck + $4,900 of boot given).
However, the taxpayer attempts to increase his depreciable basis to $8,000 by buying the new truck from the dealer for $8,000 in return for the dealer's promise to pay him $3,100 for his old truck. This attempt would fail since Rev. Rul. 61-119 indicates that a nontaxable exchange exists when a taxpayer sells property to a dealer and then purchases like-kind property from the same dealer. Hence, the property's basis shall be determined under the like-kind exchange rules.

16.3 Involuntary Conversions

27. Which of the following does not constitute an involuntary conversion?

   a. Factory building destroyed by fire.
   b. Embezzlement of funds by a teller working in a bank.
   c. Diamond necklace mislaid or lost by the owner.
   d. Condemnation of land held for investment by a state highway department.

The correct answer is (c). *(SPE 1078 I-56)*
REQUIRED: The occurrence that does not constitute an involuntary conversion.
DISCUSSION: An involuntary conversion results from the destruction, theft, seizure, requisition or condemnation, or the disposition under threat or imminence of requisition or condemnation of the taxpayer's property [Sec. 1033(a)]. Losing or mislaying property does not fall under the definition of an involuntary conversion.
Answers (a), (b), and (d) are incorrect because they result from destruction, condemnation, or theft and do constitute involuntary conversions.

28. If the taxpayer owns an office building that (s)he does not personally manage and the office building is involuntarily converted, which of the following will qualify as replacement property with nonrecognition of gain?

a. A hotel which the taxpayer will personally manage.

b. An interest in a gold mine.

c. An apartment building which the taxpayer will not personally manage.

d. A retail sole proprietorship.

The correct answer is (c). *(Publisher)*
REQUIRED: The property that will qualify as replacement property for an involuntary conversion.
DISCUSSION: Sec. 1033(a) provides for the nonrecognition of gain if property is involuntarily converted and replaced with property similar or related in service or use. "Similar or related in service or use" has been interpreted to mean, for an investor, that the property must have a similar service or use with respect to the taxpayer-owner. Since both the office building and the apartment building are operated as passive leasing investments, the latter will qualify as replacement property.
Answer (a) is incorrect because the active management of a hotel is a different use of property from the passive investment in an office building. Answer (b) is incorrect because an interest in a gold mine is a speculative venture quite different from the passive investment in real property. Answer (d) is incorrect because a sole proprietorship requires an active management role which is different from the passive renting of a building.

29. If the warehouse of a taxpayer who is in the business of retailing goods is involuntarily converted, which of the following replacement properties will qualify for nonrecognition of gain?

a. Land on which to build a new warehouse.

b. An additional retail outlet.

c. Cash that the taxpayer uses to build another warehouse.

d. A building with individual storage lockers leased to the public.

The correct answer is (c). *(Publisher)*
REQUIRED: The property that will qualify as replacement property in an involuntary conversion.
DISCUSSION: Sec. 1033(a) provides for the nonrecognition of gain from an involuntary conversion if property similar or related in service or use replaces the property converted. "Similar or related in service or use" has been interpreted to mean, for owner-users of property, that the replacement property must have a close functional similarity to the property converted. A new warehouse does have the same functional use as a prior warehouse. Under Sec. 1033(a)(2), the receipt of money used to acquire qualified replacement property within 2 years qualifies for nonrecognition of gain.
Answer (a) is incorrect because land does not have the same functional use as a warehouse, even if a warehouse can be built on the land. Answer (b) is incorrect because a retail outlet is used to sell goods to the public, while the functional use of a warehouse is to store goods. Answer (d) is incorrect because a building in which storage lockers are leased to the public does not serve the same function as a building used to store goods for one's own business.

30. N's business building was destroyed by a hurricane. The building had an adjusted basis to N of $200,000 and a fair market value immediately before the hurricane of $300,000. N received a reimbursement of $270,000 from his insurance company and immediately spent $268,000 for a new business building. What amount must N include in his gross income?

a. $(32,000) loss.

b. $(30,000) loss.

c. $2,000 gain.

d. $70,000 gain.

The correct answer is (c). *(SPE 986 I-79)*
REQUIRED: The gross income resulting from the involuntary conversion of insured property.
DISCUSSION: N received insurance proceeds of $270,000 on destroyed property with an adjusted basis of $200,000 and thereby realized a gain of $70,000. Since the replacement property was similar, under Sec. 1033(a)(2), N may elect to recognize the gain only to the extent that the amount realized ($270,000) exceeds the cost of the replacement property ($268,000), or $2,000.

Module 16.3: Involuntary Conversions

31. One of Matthew Corporation's warehouses, on which it had taken straight-line depreciation, was completely destroyed by fire during 1990. The warehouse had an adjusted basis of $75,000 and a market value of $120,000 on the day of the fire. The warehouse was insured for $100,000 and settlement in that amount was received on August 1. On February 16, 1991, Matthew purchased all of the outstanding stock of Warehouse, Inc., a corporation which owned a warehouse equal in size to the destroyed warehouse. Purchase price of the stock was $95,000. How would these events have been reported on Matthew's federal income tax returns for 1990 and 1991 in order to minimize its tax liability?

   a. $20,000 loss in 1990; no effect on the 1991 returns.
   b. $25,000 gain in 1990; $20,000 deduction in 1991.
   c. $5,000 gain in 1990; no effect in 1991.
   d. No effect in 1990; $5,000 gain in 1991.

The correct answer is (c). *(CMA 682 3-9)*
REQUIRED: The amount and timing of a gain recognized on the involuntary conversion of a warehouse.
DISCUSSION: Matthew received insurance proceeds of $100,000 on a destroyed warehouse with an adjusted basis of $75,000, thereby realizing a gain of $25,000. Matthew can elect nonrecognition of the gain by purchasing other similar or related property or by purchasing 80% or more of the stock of a corporation owning similar property [Sec. 1033(a)(2)]. The purchase of the stock qualifies as replacement property and the gain will be recognized under Sec. 1033 only to the extent that the amount realized on the involuntary conversion ($100,000) exceeds the cost of the replacement property ($95,000), or $5,000. The $5,000 gain is realized and must be recognized in 1990, the year in which the conversion occurred and not the year in which reinvestment occurred. An amended 1990 income tax return may be required for Matthew.
   Note that if accelerated depreciation had been taken, the purchase of stock would not be replacement property adequate under Sec. 1250(d)(4) to prevent 1250 recapture from occurring regardless of nonrecognition under Sec. 1033.

32. Michael owned a building with an adjusted basis of $80,000 and land with an adjusted basis of $20,000. A tornado leveled the building. Michael used an insurance settlement of $140,000 plus $25,000 from a mortgage to construct a new building on the same land within 1 year. Assuming he elects any possible gain deferral, his recognized gain from the insurance settlement will be

   a. $0.
   b. $40,000.
   c. $60,000.
   d. $85,000.

The correct answer is (a). *(J.M. Ruble)*
REQUIRED: The recognized gain from an insurance settlement when the proceeds are invested in a similar business.
DISCUSSION: This situation qualifies as an involuntary conversion. Sec. 1033(a) provides that, if the property is converted into money or other property not similar or related in service or use to the converted property, as in the case of insurance proceeds, the taxpayer may elect to defer gain by investing an amount equal to or greater than that of the proceeds received in the conversion. Since Michael reinvested an amount greater than the insurance proceeds in similar property, he will not be required to recognize any gain.

33. In the previous question, assume Michael used only $80,000 of the insurance proceeds and incurred a mortgage liability of $85,000 to construct the new building. His recognized gain from the insurance settlement will be

   a. $0.
   b. $40,000.
   c. $60,000.
   d. $85,000.

The correct answer is (a). *(J.M. Ruble)*
REQUIRED: The amount of gain recognized from the receipt of insurance proceeds.
DISCUSSION: As long as a taxpayer reinvests an amount equal to or greater than the proceeds received upon the involuntary conversion, (s)he may elect to defer all of the gain realized. The source of the funds for reinvestment is immaterial. Michael reinvested $165,000, which is greater than the $140,000 of insurance proceeds, so he will not recognize any gain.

Module 16.3: Involuntary Conversions

34. Gotuda Sugarbowl owned a warehouse that he rented to ABC Company. The warehouse was purchased 6 years ago and has an adjusted basis of $200,000. Early this year the warehouse was condemned by the city of Jones Chapel. The condemnation award was $450,000. Sugarbowl used $400,000 of the award to purchase a new warehouse that will be rented. If Sugarbowl elects to apply the provisions for nonrecognition of gain upon involuntary conversion, what is the recognized gain?

a. $0.
b. $50,000.
c. $150,000.
d. $200,000.

The correct answer is (b). *(G.L. Waters)*
REQUIRED: The amount of gain recognized on an involuntary conversion of property.
DISCUSSION: When property is involuntarily converted and cash received, the taxpayer may elect to recognize gain only to the extent the amount realized exceeds the cost of qualified replacement property [Sec. 1033(a)]. The replacement property must be similar in service or use and the new warehouse should qualify.

Sugarbowl received a $450,000 condemnation award for property with an adjusted basis of $200,000, thereby realizing a gain of $250,000. Since he reinvested $400,000 in qualified replacement property, he can elect to recognize only $50,000 of the gain ($450,000 − $400,000).

35. During 1991, Mr. G had property that had an adjusted basis of $78,000, condemned by the state. The state paid G $93,000 for the property. Mr. G immediately purchased similar new property for $87,000. G properly reported a $6,000 gain on his 1991 federal income tax return. What is the amount of Mr. G's basis in the new property?

a. $72,000.
b. $78,000.
c. $87,000.
d. $93,000.

The correct answer is (b). *(SPE 989 I-90)*
REQUIRED: The basis of replacement property received as a result of an involuntary conversion.
DISCUSSION: Sec. 1033(a)(2) provides for a taxpayer to elect nonrecognition of gain as a result of an involuntary conversion when money is received and used to replace the converted property within 2 years of the conversion. Sec. 1033(a)(2), however, requires recognition of gain to the extent the amount realized on conversion exceeds the cost of replacement property.

Mr. G realizes a $15,000 gain ($93,000 condemnation proceeds − $78,000 basis of converted property) but is only required to recognize $6,000 ($93,000 condemnation proceeds − $87,000 cost of replacement property). Under Sec. 1033(b), the basis of replacement property is its purchase price less any gain not recognized. Therefore, Mr. G's basis in the replacement property is $78,000 ($87,000 cost of replacement property − $9,000 realized gain not recognized).

36. Mercury owned a racetrack, including the land and improvements (track, stands, and buildings). The property was condemned when Mercury's basis in the land was $30,000 and his basis in the improvements was $40,000. Mercury received new land worth $100,000 and cash of $200,000 which he immediately used to build a track, stands, and buildings to operate a new racetrack. Mercury elected to defer as much gain as possible. What is Mercury's basis in the new racetrack?

a. $30,000 in the land and $40,000 in the improvements.
b. $30,000 in the land and $200,000 in the improvements.
c. $100,000 in the land and $40,000 in the improvements.
d. $100,000 in the land and $200,000 in the improvements.

The correct answer is (a). *(Publisher)*
REQUIRED: The basis of replacement property received as a result of an involuntary conversion.
DISCUSSION: Under Sec. 1033(a)(1), no gain is recognized on an involuntary conversion when the converted property is replaced with similar property. Under Sec. 1033(b), the basis of the replacement property is the same as the basis in the converted property. Mercury's basis in the land is therefore $30,000.

Sec. 1033(a)(2) also provides for a taxpayer to elect nonrecognition of gain as a result of an involuntary conversion when money is received and used to replace the converted property within 2 years of the conversion. Under Sec. 1033(b), the basis of such replacement property is its purchase price less any gain not recognized. Therefore, Mercury's basis in the improvements is $40,000 ($200,000 − $160,000 gain not recognized).

Module 16.3: Involuntary Conversions

> Questions 37 and 38 are based on the following two transactions for a sole proprietorship during 1991. These were the only sales or exchanges of capital assets or Sec. 1231 assets.
>
> Sold a machine used in the business for $40,000. It cost $33,000 when purchased in 1988, and its adjusted tax basis when sold was $21,000. Depreciation had been recorded on an accelerated basis; straight-line depreciation would have been $9,900.
>
> Received a $50,000 insurance recovery on a small warehouse destroyed by fire. It was used in the business and depreciated using the straight-line method. Its adjusted tax basis at the date of the fire was $52,400. A new warehouse was rebuilt at a cost of $60,000.

37. What is the combined tax effect of these two transactions?

    a. $7,000 long-term capital gain and $9,600 ordinary income.
    b. $4,600 long-term capital gain and $12,000 ordinary income.
    c. $19,000 long-term capital gain and $2,400 ordinary loss.
    d. $7,000 long-term capital gain; $12,000 ordinary income; and $2,400 ordinary loss.

The correct answer is (d). *(CPA 575 Q-22)*
REQUIRED: The combined tax effect of the sale of depreciable business property and the involuntary conversion of business property.
DISCUSSION: The sale of the machine resulted in a realized gain of $19,000 (amount realized of $40,000 less the adjusted basis of $21,000). A portion of the gain equal to the depreciation already taken is recaptured as ordinary income under Sec. 1245. $12,000 of the gain on the sale of the machine is thus ordinary income. The remaining $7,000 of gain is characterized under Sec. 1231. The involuntary conversion results in a $2,400 realized loss ($50,000 amount realized less $52,400 adjusted basis). Realized losses on involuntary conversions are fully recognized.
Under Sec. 1231(a), if losses on business property from involuntary conversions by casualty or theft exceed such gains, they are not netted with other 1231 gains and losses. The $2,400 loss will be treated as ordinary loss, and netted with the $12,000 of Sec. 1245 ordinary income for a total of $9,600. The $7,000 of Sec. 1231 gain will be treated as long-term capital gain.

38. What is the basis of the new warehouse?

    a. $52,400.
    b. $57,600.
    c. $60,000.
    d. $62,400.

The correct answer is (c). *(CPA 575 Q-23)*
REQUIRED: The basis of a warehouse acquired as a result of an involuntary conversion.
DISCUSSION: Sec. 1033 applies only to gains arising from involuntary conversions, and this was a loss. The realized loss was fully recognized, so the basis of the new warehouse is its cost of $60,000 (Sec. 1012).

Module 16.3: Involuntary Conversions

39. Bennet Hanover purchased a tract of land for $20,000 in 1989 when he heard that a new highway was going to be constructed through the property and that the land would soon be worth $200,000. Highway engineers surveyed the property and indicated that he would probably get $175,000. The highway project was abandoned in 1991 and the value of the land fell to $15,000. Hanover can claim a loss in 1991 of

a. $0.
b. $5,000.
c. $160,000.
d. $180,000.

The correct answer is (a). *(CPA 577 Q-28)*
REQUIRED: The amount of loss recognized from the decrease in value of land held for investment.
DISCUSSION: Sec. 1033 does not apply to losses. Sec. 165 allows a deduction for uncompensated losses sustained during the taxable year. Since Hanover has not sold, exchanged, or otherwise disposed of the land, he has not realized a loss. Therefore, he cannot claim any loss in 1991. When the land is sold or exchanged, his realized loss or gain will be equal to the amount realized minus his adjusted basis.

40. Taxpayer C has a personal residence with an adjusted basis of $50,000 and a fair market value of $60,000. Taxpayer C's property was condemned by the state for a highway project. If C receives $35,000 compensation, what is his gain or deductible loss?

a. $0.
b. $15,000 gain.
c. $15,000 loss.
d. $25,000 loss.

The correct answer is (a). *(SPE 1079 I-51)*
REQUIRED: The gain or deductible loss arising from the condemnation of a personal residence.
DISCUSSION: If Mr. C receives $35,000 for the condemnation of a personal residence with an adjusted basis of $50,000, he will have realized a loss of $15,000. Under Sec. 165(c), however, losses incurred by individuals on personal use assets can only be recognized if they arise from fire, storm, shipwreck, other casualty, or theft. Loss from the condemnation of a personal use asset is never recognized. Furthermore, Sec. 1033 does not apply to losses.

41. You are a calendar-year taxpayer. You were notified by the city council on December 1, 1990 of its intention to acquire your real property used in your business by negotiation or by condemnation. On June 1, 1991, when the property had an adjusted basis of $40,000 to you, the city converted the property and paid you $50,000. When does your replacement period end?

a. June 1, 1993.
b. December 1, 1993.
c. June 1, 1994.
d. December 31, 1994.

The correct answer is (d). *(SPE 986 II-49)*
REQUIRED: The last date to acquire qualified replacement property for nonrecognition of gain on an involuntary conversion.
DISCUSSION: Reg. 1.1033(g)-1(c) provides that in the case of the condemnation of real property held for productive use in a trade or business or for investment, the replacement period ends 3 years after the close of the taxable year in which the gain is realized. Since the gain was realized in 1991, the replacement period ends December 31, 1994.

42. Mr. M read in the newspaper that the state highway department had decided to take his property for public use. Mr. M verified the news by phoning an official of the highway department who is involved in the project acquiring this property. This is a threat of condemnation.

The correct answer is (T). *(SPE 1080 I-35)*
DISCUSSION: A threat of condemnation under Sec. 1033 requires the taxpayer to obtain confirmation that there has been a decision to acquire property for public use and to have reasonable grounds to believe the property will be taken (Rev. Rul. 63-221). Mr. M's reading about the condemnation in the newspaper and his confirming it by phone with a public official give him reasonable grounds to believe the property will be taken. A threat of condemnation sufficient to constitute an involuntary conversion therefore exists.

43. Mr. H has been told by the city council that the city is interested in buying some land that he owns to build a convention center. H knows that the council is negotiating with other landowners to get land at the lowest price possible. A member of the council told H that if none of the landowners sells land voluntarily, the city will probably acquire a site by condemnation. H's land is under threat of imminence of condemnation.

The correct answer is (F). *(SPE 986 I-34)*
DISCUSSION: A threat of condemnation under Sec. 1033 requires the taxpayer to obtain confirmation that there has been a decision to acquire property for public use and to have reasonable grounds to believe the property will be taken (Rev. Rul. 63-221). Since Mr. H knows that the city council is negotiating with other landowners, there is a reasonable possibility that Mr. H's land will not be condemned. A threat of condemnation sufficient to constitute an involuntary conversion does not exist.

44. Mr. K is considered to be under threat or imminence of condemnation if he has received a health department notice that a building he owns is unfit and will be condemned if necessary improvements are not made.

The correct answer is (F). *(SPE 987 II-26)*
DISCUSSION: Involuntary conversions under Sec. 1033 include a condemnation for public use. But a notice that a building will be condemned because it is in need of improvements is not a condemnation for public use. A notice is not an actual condemnation, and a taxpayer's failure to repair property cannot be turned into an involuntary conversion. Therefore, the nonrecognition of gain under Sec. 1033 does not apply.

45. A state government authorized to acquire land to widen a road told Mr. J it wishes to acquire his property. Mr. J went to court to keep his property, but the court ruled for the state government. The government took the property and paid Mr. J an amount fixed by the court. An involuntary conversion has occurred.

The correct answer is (T). *(SPE 984 II-23)*
DISCUSSION: Reg. 1.1033(a)-1(a) provides that an involuntary conversion may be the result of the seizure of property, the requisition or condemnation of property, or the threat or imminence of requisition or condemnation of property. The taking of property by the government is an involuntary conversion.

46. Mr. L owns a rental building with an adjusted basis of $75,000 and a fair market value of $70,000. On July 1, 1991, the state condemned the property for a highway project and paid him $70,000, which he immediately reinvested in a similar rental property. Mr. L may recognize a loss.

The correct answer is (T). *(SPE 1080 II-30)*
DISCUSSION: Mr. L received a $70,000 condemnation award for investment property with an adjusted basis of $75,000, thereby realizing a loss of $5,000. Sec. 165 allows a deduction for any loss on business property sustained during the taxable year which is not compensated. Accordingly, Mr. L may recognize this loss. Note that Sec. 1033 applies only to gains.

47. A taxpayer whose property was involuntarily converted can replace the property for tax postponement purposes by acquiring a controlling interest in a corporation owning property that is similar or related in service or use to the property involuntarily converted.

The correct answer is (T). *(SPE 1077 I-6)*
DISCUSSION: Sec. 1033 permits a taxpayer, whose property was involuntarily converted and who received monetary compensation, to purchase a controlling interest in a corporation owning property which qualifies as replacement property in lieu of purchasing the replacement property directly. The controlling interest must be 80% or more of the corporate stock. Such a purchase allows the taxpayer to postpone recognition of any gain arising from the involuntary conversion.

48. In 1991, Mr. P's dairy herd developed a disease that required him to sell the cows for less than the going market rate. This is considered an involuntary exchange.

The correct answer is (T). *(SPE 1085 II-20)*
DISCUSSION: Livestock sold or exchanged because they are diseased or have been exposed to disease, and which would not otherwise have been sold or exchanged at that particular time, are treated as involuntarily converted [Sec. 1033(d)]. Therefore, Mr. P's selling of the cows is an involuntary conversion.

49. Mr. L planned to build a warehouse for use in his business on unimproved property he owned. The property had an adjusted basis to him of $100,000. During March 1991, before he could build the warehouse, the state condemned the property and reimbursed Mr. L $125,000. During October 1991, Mr. L bought improved real property for $150,000 that had buildings on it which he could use as rentals. The improved real estate qualifies as replacement property and Mr. L may postpone the tax on the gain from the condemnation.

The correct answer is (T). *(SPE 986 II-22)*
DISCUSSION: Under Sec. 1033(a)(2), a taxpayer may elect nonrecognition of gain resulting from an involuntary conversion if money is received and used to replace the converted property within 2 years of conversion. Generally, the replacement must be similar or related in service or use to the converted property. The unimproved property is not similar in service or use to property with rental buildings. However, for real property used in a trade or business or held for investment that is condemned, the replacement property need only be like-kind as under Sec. 1031 [Reg. 1.1033(g)-1]. Both the unimproved and improved property are like-kind under Sec. 1031 so the gain may be deferred under Sec. 1033.

16.4 Sale of a Principal Residence

50. Senior gave his son, Junior, his personal residence with an adjusted basis of $60,000 and a fair market value of $40,000. Junior lived in the house for 2 years and then sold it for $35,000. As a result of the sale, Junior will

a. Report no gain or loss.
b. Report a $5,000 loss.
c. Report a $25,000 loss.
d. Have his father report a $25,000 loss.

The correct answer is (a). *(J.M. Ruble)*
REQUIRED: The deductible loss from sale of a personal residence.
DISCUSSION: Under Sec. 1001(a), gain or loss is the excess of the amount realized over the adjusted basis. The amount realized is $35,000. The adjusted basis is determined under Sec. 1015. The basis for gain is the donor's basis, and the basis for loss is the lower of the donor's basis or the fair market value (FMV) on the date of the gift. Junior's basis is the FMV of $40,000. Thus, he has a realized loss of $5,000 on the sale. However, he cannot deduct a loss on the sale of a personal residence.

51. Richard Rich owns a houseboat in Florida, a condominium in Colorado, a house in California, and stock in a housing cooperative in New York City. For the last 3 years, Richard Rich and his family have spent 3 months in the winter in the Florida houseboat, 1 month in the Colorado condominium, and the rest of the year in the New York City apartment. Prior to the last 3 years, Richard Rich and his family lived in the California house year-round. It is now vacant. Richard just put his stock in the New York City cooperative up for sale. Which property qualifies as a principal residence for both Sec. 1034 and Sec. 121?

a. The Florida houseboat.
b. The Colorado condominium.
c. The California house.
d. The stock in the New York City cooperative.

The correct answer is (d). *(Publisher)*
REQUIRED: The property that qualifies as a principal residence under Secs. 1034 and 121.
DISCUSSION: Principal residence for Sec. 121 has the same meaning as for Sec. 1034 [Reg. 1.121-3(a)], except Sec. 121 requires the property to have been used as a principal residence by the taxpayer for 3 or more years out of the 5-year period ending on the date of sale. A principal residence may include houseboats, condominiums, and stock in a cooperative housing corporation [Reg. 1.1034-1(c)(3)]. The stock in the New York City cooperative qualifies as a principal residence.
Answer (a) is incorrect because the Florida houseboat is not a principal residence since it is only used for 3 months out of the year. Answer (b) is incorrect because the Colorado condominium also has not been used for a sufficient amount of time or with the intent to be a personal residence. Answer (c) is incorrect because, although the California house was a personal residence 3 years ago, it has not been used as a personal residence for 3 years of the preceding 5-year period.

Module 16.4: Sale of a Principal Residence

52. On December 20, 1990, Ms. Rich, age 52, signed a contract to sell her main home which had an adjusted basis to her of $62,100. She purchased her home May 10, 1981. During the 90-day period ending December 20, 1990, she paid $1,800 to replace the roof which she capitalized as part of her adjusted basis, and $200 for decorating expenses. On January 10, 1991 she sold the house for $81,200 and paid $4,800 in selling expenses. On February 11, 1991 she purchased a new home for $73,000. What is the amount of Ms. Rich's taxable gain, deferred gain, and the adjusted basis of the new home?

	Taxable Gain	Deferred Gain	Adjusted Basis
a.	$0	$9,300	$76,400
b.	$0	$12,500	$73,000
c.	$3,200	$9,300	$62,100
d.	$3,200	$9,300	$63,700

53. During 1991, Mr. J sold his personal residence and realized a gain. What is his replacement period for purposes of postponing (rolling over) his gain?

a. Within 2 years before or 2 years after he sold the home.
b. Within 1 year before or 2 years after he sold the home.
c. Within 1 year before or 18 months after he sold the home.
d. Within 18 months before or 18 months after he sold the home.

54. On June 15, 1991, Mr. M sold his home (which he had originally purchased for $35,000) for $60,000. In April 1991 he replaced the roof for $3,000. Selling expenses were $5,000. In November 1991 he bought and began living in a new home that cost $65,000. What is the amount of gain on which tax is deferred?

a. $25,000.
b. $20,000.
c. $19,000.
d. $17,000.

The correct answer is (d). *(SPE 990 I-77)*
REQUIRED: The taxable gain, deferred gain, and adjusted basis of the replacement residence from the sale of a taxpayer's principal residence.
DISCUSSION: Ms. Rich realized a $12,500 gain on the sale of her residence ($81,200 sales price – $4,800 selling expenses – $63,900 basis of old residence). The $1,800 roof replacement is a capital improvement, not a fixing-up cost, and increases the basis of the old residence. Fixing-up costs are those incurred within 90 days of the contract date to assist the sale, such as the $200 of decorating costs in this problem. Under Sec. 1034, Ms. Rich need only recognize gain to the extent that the adjusted sales price exceeds the amount reinvested in a replacement residence. The adjusted sales price of $76,200 ($81,200 sales price – $4,800 selling expenses – $200 fixing-up costs) exceeds the $73,000 reinvested in a replacement residence by $3,200. Hence, the recognized gain is $3,200 while the deferred gain is $9,300 ($12,500 realized gain – $3,200 recognized gain).
Under Sec. 1034(e), the basis of the replacement residence is its cost less the unrecognized gain on the sale of the old residence. Therefore, Ms. Rich's basis in the replacement residence is $63,700 ($73,000 cost of replacement residence – $9,300 deferred gain).

The correct answer is (a). *(SPE 990 I-46)*
REQUIRED: The replacement period for a new personal residence to defer gain on the sale of an old personal residence.
DISCUSSION: Under Sec. 1034(a), a taxpayer may defer the gain on the sale of a principal residence if a replacement principal residence is purchased and used by the taxpayer within a period beginning 2 years before the sale of the old residence and extending 2 years after the sale of the old residence.
Answers (b), (c), and (d) are incorrect because they specify replacement periods different than 2 years before and after the sale of the old residence.

The correct answer is (d). *(SPE 1085 I-84)*
REQUIRED: The amount of gain deferred from the sale of a personal residence and purchase of a new personal residence.
DISCUSSION: Mr. M realized a $17,000 gain on the sale of his personal residence ($60,000 sales price – $5,000 selling expenses – $38,000 adjusted basis of the property). The $3,000 roof replacement is a capital improvement, not a fixing-up cost, and increases the basis of the old residence. Fixing-up costs are those incurred within 90 days to assist in the sale. Under Sec. 1034, Mr. M need only recognize gain to the extent that the adjusted sales price of his old residence exceeds the amount reinvested in a new residence within 2 years. The adjusted sales price of the old residence is $55,000 ($60,000 sales price – $5,000 selling expenses). Mr. M reinvested $65,000 in a new residence within 2 years. Therefore, the recognized gain is zero ($55,000 adjusted sales price – $65,000 reinvestment) and the entire realized gain of $17,000 is deferred.

Module 16.4: Sale of a Principal Residence

55. Mr. R lives in a four-unit apartment building. He used one apartment as his principal residence and rented the other three. Mr. R purchased the building in 1980 for $60,000 and has taken depreciation of $20,000 on the rented portion. On June 1, 1991, Mr. R sold the apartment house for $200,000 and purchased a new home for $45,000. What should Mr. R report as his recognized gain on the sale of the personal portion of his residence?

a. $0.
b. $5,000.
c. $35,000.
d. $40,000.

The correct answer is (b). *(SPE 1083 I-86)*
REQUIRED: The recognized gain resulting from the sale of a personal residence that is part of a rental complex.
DISCUSSION: Mr. R sold the apartment building for $200,000. One-fourth of this amount ($50,000) is attributable to his personal residence. His basis in the personal residence is $15,000 (25% x $60,000 original cost). Mr. R has a realized gain of $35,000 ($50,000 − $15,000). This gain can go unrecognized if the cost of the new residence exceeds the adjusted sales price of the old residence. Since the adjusted sales price of his old residence ($50,000) exceeds the cost of his new residence ($45,000), Mr. R must recognize a $5,000 gain [Sec. 1034(a)].

56. Stockman, under age 55, owned a personal residence in Hometown that he purchased in 1980 for $40,000. He obtained a government job and moved to Capitol City, so he sold the Hometown residence for $60,000 in January 1991 and purchased a new residence in Capitol City for $70,000 in February 1991. After making a blundering statement to the press, Stockman lost his job and moved back to Hometown. Stockman sold the Capitol City house for $75,000 in November 1991 and purchased a new house in Hometown for $55,000 in December 1991. What is Stockman's recognized gain on the sale of these residences?

a. $0.
b. $5,000.
c. $10,000.
d. $15,000.

The correct answer is (c). *(Publisher)*
REQUIRED: The recognized gain when the taxpayer acquires more than one replacement residence within 2 years after the initial sale.
DISCUSSION: Sec. 1034(a) provides that gain on the sale of a personal residence is recognized only to the extent that the selling price exceeds the cost of a replacement residence acquired within 2 years of the sale of the old residence. Sec. 1034(c)(4) provides that if during the 2-year period after the sale of a principal residence the taxpayer acquires more than one principal residence, only the last residence constitutes the replacement residence.
Since Stockman purchased two residences within 2 years after the sale of the house in Hometown, only the last one (purchased in Hometown for $55,000) qualifies as the replacement residence. Stockman's gain on the original Hometown residence was $20,000 ($60,000 − $40,000), of which $5,000 is recognized ($60,000 proceeds − $55,000 replacement cost). Stockman's gain of $5,000 on the Capitol City residence will be recognized. Stockman's total gain is $10,000 ($5,000 on the original Hometown residence and $5,000 on the Capitol City residence).

Module 16.4: Sale of a Principal Residence

57. In 1991, Mr. V, who is 49 years old, sold his principal residence where he had lived since 1979 and purchased a new residence. Mr. V's records reflect the following:

Selling price of old house	$650,000
V's basis in old house	400,000
Qualified fixing-up expenses	10,000
Qualified selling expenses	5,000
Cost of new residence	600,000

What is the amount of taxable gain Mr. V will report on his 1991 return and what is his adjusted basis in his new house?

	Taxable Gain	Adjusted Basis
a.	$45,000	$600,000
b.	$45,000	$400,000
c.	$35,000	$400,000
d.	$35,000	$390,000

The correct answer is (d). *(SPE 987 I-87)*
REQUIRED: The taxable gain on the sale of an old personal residence and the adjusted basis in the new personal residence.
DISCUSSION: Under Sec. 1034(a), gain on the sale of a personal residence is recognized only to the extent that the adjusted selling price exceeds the cost of a new residence acquired within 2 years of the sale of the old residence. Mr. V's realized gain is

Selling price	$650,000
Less:	
Selling expenses	(5,000)
Adjusted basis of old residence	(400,000)
Realized gain	$245,000
Adjusted selling price ($650,000 – $5,000 selling expenses – $10,000 fixing-up costs)	$635,000
Less: Cost of new residence	(600,000)
Recognized gain	$ 35,000

The adjusted basis of the new residence is its cost reduced by the gain not recognized:

Cost	$600,000
Unrecognized gain ($245,000 – $35,000)	(210,000)
Adjusted basis	$390,000

58. Eric Kay, age 59, is single and has no dependents. In 1991, Eric sold his personal residence for the net amount of $300,000 after all selling expenses. He bought the house in 1960 and occupied it until sold. The house had a basis of $100,000 on the date of sale. Eric moved into a rental apartment and does not intend to buy another residence. What is the maximum portion of the gain on sale of the residence that Eric may exclude from his 1991 taxable income?

a. $0.
b. $62,500.
c. $125,000.
d. $200,000.

The correct answer is (c). *(CPA 588 Q-16)*
REQUIRED: The amount of realized gain on the sale of a residence that may be excluded from taxable income.
DISCUSSION: Taxpayers who are 55 or older may make a once-in-a-lifetime election to exclude from income up to $125,000 of gain on a sale of a principal residence as long as the taxpayer owned and occupied the residence for at least 3 of the 5 years ending at the date of the sale (Sec. 121).
Eric's realized gain was $200,000 ($300,000 amount realized – $100,000 basis). He may exclude $125,000 of it from 1991 taxable income.

59. Mr. and Mrs. H, both 66 years old, sold their residence in 1991 for $182,000 and moved to an apartment. They elect to exclude as much of the gain as they can. They purchased the house 20 years ago for $13,000 and have made improvements over the years which total $25,000. The selling expenses were $10,000 and qualified fix-up costs were $350. What, if any, is their recognized gain?

a. $0.
b. $8,650.
c. $9,000.
d. $34,000.

The correct answer is (c). *(SPE 986 I-84)*
REQUIRED: The recognized gain resulting from the sale of a principal residence by taxpayers who are over the age of 55.
DISCUSSION: Since Mr. and Mrs. H are over age 55 and they have lived in the house for a period aggregating 3 years or more during the last 5 years, they are eligible to make the one-time exclusion of gain from the sale of a principal residence under Sec. 121. Note that the $350 of fixing-up costs only reduce adjusted sales price for computing the deferral of gain under Sec. 1034 and are never deductible. The recognized gain on the sale of the residence is

Sales price	$182,000
Less: Selling expenses	(10,000)
Adjusted basis ($13,000 cost + $25,000 improvements)	(38,000)
Realized gain	$134,000
Less Sec. 121 exclusion	(125,000)
Recognized gain	$ 9,000

Module 16.4: Sale of a Principal Residence

60. The following information pertains to the sale of Al Oran's principal residence:

Date of sale	May 1991
Date of purchase	May 1979
Net sales price	$260,000
Adjusted basis	$ 70,000

In June 1991, Oran (age 70) bought a smaller residence for $90,000. Oran elected to avail himself of the exclusion of realized gain available to taxpayers age 55 and over. What amount of gain should Oran recognize in 1991 on the sale of his residence?

a. $45,000.
b. $65,000.
c. $70,000.
d. $90,000.

The correct answer is (a). *(CPA 589 Q-42)*
REQUIRED: The recognized gain resulting from the sale of a principal residence by a taxpayer who is over the age of 55.
DISCUSSION: Mr. Oran realizes a $190,000 gain on the sale of his residence ($260,000 − $70,000). Under Sec. 1034(a), gain on the sale of a personal residence is recognized only to the extent that the adjusted sales price exceeds the cost of a new residence acquired within 2 years of the sale of the old residence. Without considering the Sec. 121 exclusion, Mr. Oran would recognize a $170,000 gain since that is the amount by which the adjusted sales price ($260,000) exceeds the cost of the replacement residence ($90,000). However, since Mr. Oran makes the Sec. 121 election, $125,000 of this gain is excluded. Therefore, Mr. Oran only recognizes a $45,000 gain ($170,000 recognized gain without considering the Sec. 121 exclusion − $125,000 Sec. 121 exclusion).

61. If a principal residence is sold for $90,000 and a replacement residence is acquired within 1 year of the sale for $90,000, the nonrecognition of gain on the sale is mandatory.

The correct answer is (T). *(SPE 1078 I-28)*
DISCUSSION: If a taxpayer purchases a new principal residence within a period beginning 2 years before the date of sale of the old residence and ending 2 years after such date, a gain on the sale of the old residence is recognized only to the extent that the adjusted sales price of the old residence exceeds the taxpayer's cost of the new residence (Sec. 1034). This treatment is mandatory.

62. In 1991, Mr. and Mrs. D sold their principal home for $106,000. Both were over 55 years of age on the date of sale. They had purchased the property 5 years prior to the sale and had lived in the home for a full 36 months during that period. They had never before excluded gain on a sale or exchange of a home. Mr. and Mrs. D qualify for the one-time exclusion on the sale of their home.

The correct answer is (T). *(SPE 990 I-16)*
DISCUSSION: Under Sec. 121, a taxpayer who has attained the age of 55 before the date of sale of his/her principal residence and has lived in the residence for a period aggregating 3 or more of the past 5 years may elect once in his/her lifetime to exclude up to $125,000 of the gain on the sale of his/her principal residence. Since Mr. and Mrs. D were over the age of 55, lived in the house for 3 of the last 5 years, and have never elected the Sec. 121 exclusion, they are eligible for the $125,000 exclusion on the sale of their principal residence. Note that, as a married couple filing jointly, they would still be eligible for Sec. 121 treatment if only one spouse satisfies the age, holding, and use requirements discussed above [Sec. 121(d)(1)(C)].

63. During 1991, Mr. W, who is 55 years old and single, sold his principal residence, which he purchased in 1969, for a gain of $80,000. W had lived in his home until December 1988, at which time he became unable to care for himself and moved to a nursing home. W was residing at the nursing home at the time he sold his home. Mr. W can choose to exclude the gain from his income.

The correct answer is (T). *(SPE 990 I-15)*
DISCUSSION: For sales and exchanges after September 30, 1988, the requirement of living in a residence at least 3 out of 5 years prior to sale is satisfied by time a taxpayer resides in a nursing home due to incapability of self-care if the taxpayer owns the home for the entire period and has actually lived in it for at least 1 year during the 5-year period [Sec. 121(d)(9)].

64. Jay and Gee were married and sold their principal residence for $140,000 in 1991. Their basis in their residence was $60,000. If Jay dies after the sale of the residence but before the purchase of a new residence, Gee can still defer the gain by purchasing a new residence for at least $140,000 within the required time period after Jay's death.

The correct answer is (T). *(SPE 990 I-17)*
DISCUSSION: The deferral provision of Sec. 1034 is available when one spouse dies after the sale and the surviving spouse reinvests the proceeds after the other's death. This provision was enacted in 1988 retroactive for sales and exchanges after 1984. Previously, the deferral was not available if both spouses did not reinvest the proceeds [Sec. 1034(g)].

CHAPTER SEVENTEEN
PARTNERSHIPS

17.1	Partnerships Defined	(10 questions)	401
17.2	Formation of a Partnership	(30 questions)	404
17.3	Partnership's Tax Year	(12 questions)	413
17.4	Partnership Ordinary Income	(11 questions)	416
17.5	Partners' Distributive Shares of Income and Gain	(20 questions)	419
17.6	Partnership Losses	(14 questions)	425
17.7	Guaranteed Payments	(12 questions)	430
17.8	Adjustments to Basis in Partnership Interest	(15 questions)	433
17.9	Transactions Between the Partnership and a Partner	(10 questions)	438
17.10	Current Distributions	(11 questions)	440
17.11	Liquidating Distributions and Retirement of Partners	(23 questions)	443
17.12	Sale of a Partnership Interest	(15 questions)	450
17.13	Family Partnerships	(10 questions)	454
17.14	Filing Requirements and Tax Audit Procedures	(9 questions)	457

Treasury Regulations were issued in 1989 to allocate partnership debt to general and limited partners. These Regulations are quite complex and rely on the concept of "economic risk of loss" for the allocation of recourse debt. In this chapter we assume that the economic risk of loss is equal to a general partner's loss interest for recourse debt with a share of recourse debt allocated to a limited partner only to the extent of any future contributions which the limited partner is obligated to make. In reality, all post-1989 recourse debt is allocated to the partners by assuming a hypothetical liquidation in which all assets have a zero value and all debts are due. Under the new Regulations, allocation of the nonrecourse debt requires that the partners must first share the minimum gain amount and then use a profits interest for any excess. For purposes of this chapter, we assume there is no minimum gain allocation so that nonrecourse debt is allocated among the partners according to their profits interest.

17.1 Partnerships Defined

1. For federal income tax purposes, a partnership is:

a. Required to pay a tax upon its profits which in turn must be assumed by its partners.

b. Considered to be a nontaxable entity but which must file an information return.

c. A taxable entity similar to a trust or estate.

d. Treated the same as an association for tax purposes.

The correct answer is (b). *(SPE 990 II-50)*

REQUIRED: The correct statement concerning the nature of a partnership for tax purposes.

DISCUSSION: Sec. 701 states that the partners, not the partnership, are subject to federal income tax. The partnership is required to file an information return (Form 1065) under Sec. 6031. For the purpose of reporting income, a partnership is a conduit which distributes the income to the partners.

Answer (a) is incorrect because only the partners are liable for income taxes on partnership profits. Answer (c) is incorrect because a partnership is not a taxable entity but an aggregation of partners for the purpose of payment of tax. Answer (d) is incorrect because an association is a taxable entity subject to the corporate income tax, while a partnership is not subject to income tax. However, some partnerships classified as publicly-traded partnerships are taxed as corporations.

Module 17.1: Partnerships Defined

2. For federal income tax purposes, all of the following statements regarding partnerships are true except:

a. The term partnership includes a syndicate, group, pool, joint venture, or other unincorporated organization that is carrying on a business and that may not be classified as a trust, estate, or corporation.

b. A partnership is the relationship between two or more persons who join together to carry on a trade or business.

c. Co-ownership of property that is maintained and leased or rented is considered a partnership if the co-owners provide no services to the tenants.

d. The term "person" when used to describe a partner means an individual, a corporation, a trust, an estate, or another partnership.

The correct answer is (c). *(SPE 990 II-49)*
REQUIRED: The item which is not correct regarding partnerships for federal income tax purposes.
DISCUSSION: Under Reg. 1.761-1(a), mere co-ownership, maintenance, repair, and rental of property does not constitute a partnership. The co-owners are partners only if, in addition to renting the property, they provide additional services to the occupants and share the profits.

Answer (a) is incorrect because it is the definition of a partnership under Code Sec. 761. Answer (b) is incorrect because a partnership is characterized by two or more persons carrying on a trade or business. Answer (d) is incorrect because it is the definition of a person under Sec. 7701(a)(1).

3. Which one of the following is least important when reviewing the partnership agreement for income tax purposes?

a. Income and expense allocation.
b. Modifications of the agreement.
c. Economic effect of allocations to partners.
d. The form of the agreement.

The correct answer is (d). *(SPE 1078 II-58)*
REQUIRED: The least important item when reviewing the partnership agreement for income tax purposes.
DISCUSSION: For income tax purposes, there are no formal requirements regarding the partnership agreement. A partnership agreement or modifications thereof may be oral or written [Reg. 1.761-1(c)].

Answer (a) is incorrect because income and expense allocation is important in determining each partner's taxable income. Answer (b) is incorrect because the partnership agreement includes any modifications made prior to the date prescribed for filing the partnership return. Answer (c) is incorrect because the economic effect of allocations to partners is considered in determining whether the allocation will be allowed for tax purposes.

4. Regulations list six characteristics of a corporation. Some of these characteristics are used to determine whether a limited partnership will be taxed as a partnership or as an association (which is taxed as a corporation). Which of the characteristics are useful in distinguishing a partnership from an association?

1. Associates
2. An objective to carry on business for joint profit
3. Continuity of life
4. Centralized management
5. Limited liability
6. Free transferability of interest

a. 1, 2, 3, and 4.
b. 2, 4, 5, and 6.
c. 3, 4, 5, and 6.
d. All of the above.

The correct answer is (c). *(Publisher)*
REQUIRED: The characteristics used to determine whether a partnership will be taxed as a corporation.
DISCUSSION: Reg. 301.7701-2 lists all the characteristics in the question as those found in a corporation which, taken together, distinguish it from other organizations. Since partnerships and corporations both have associates and an objective to carry on business for joint profit, these are not used to distinguish a partnership from an association. The characteristics used to distinguish a partnership from an association are continuity of life, centralized management, limited liability, and free transferability of interest. Each characteristic is given equal weight, and if an organization has more corporate than noncorporate characteristics, it will be taxed as an association. If there is an equal split or if there are fewer corporate than noncorporate characteristics, the organization will be taxed as a partnership (provided it is not publicly traded).

Answers (a), (b), and (d) are incorrect because associates and an objective to carry on business for joint profit are common to both associations and partnerships.

Module 17.1: Partnerships Defined

5. In which of the following situations will a publicly traded partnership be taxed as a corporation in 1991?

   a. It has been publicly traded since January 1987 and has no new line of business. Its income is solely from a merchandising business.
   b. It was newly formed in 1990. Its income is solely from a merchandising business.
   c. It was newly formed in 1990. Its income is 90% real property rents.
   d. It has been publicly traded since December 1986 and has no new line of business. It would qualify as a regulated investment company if it were a domestic corporation.

The correct answer is (b). *(Publisher)*
REQUIRED: When a publicly-traded partnership will be taxed as a corporation.
DISCUSSION: Sec. 7704 generally requires publicly-traded partnerships to be taxed as corporations. A publicly-traded partnership is any partnership that is traded on an established securities market or is regularly traded on a secondary market (or the equivalent thereof). Partnerships that were not publicly traded prior to 1988 are generally subject to these rules.
Answer (a) is incorrect because for existing partnerships that were publicly traded on December 17, 1987 the provision requiring them to be taxed as a corporation does not apply until taxable years beginning after 1997. Answer (c) is incorrect because a publicly-traded partnership will not be taxed as a corporation if 90% or more of its gross income consists of "qualifying income" for the current tax year and each proceeding tax year beginning after 1987, during which the partnership was in existence. Qualifying income includes real property rents. Answer (d) is incorrect because publicly-traded partnerships will not be taxed as corporations until after 1997 if they were publicly traded on December 17, 1987 and have no new line of business. A partnership that would qualify as a regulated investment company if it were a domestic corporation does not qualify for the exemption for partnerships having 90% qualifying income, but the grandfathering provision of being publicly traded on December 17, 1987 still applies.

6. A partnership agreement for income tax purposes may be oral.

The correct answer is (T). *(SPE 1078 II-34)*
DISCUSSION: For income tax purposes, there are no formal requirements regarding the formalities of a partnership agreement. Such agreements may be oral or written [Reg. 1.761-1(c)].

7. Dick and Barry, both enrolled agents, maintain separate practices but share the same office, equally dividing expenses such as rent and utilities. This arrangement is a partnership for federal income tax purposes.

The correct answer is (F). *(SPE 990 II-19)*
DISCUSSION: Partnerships include organizations which carry on a business, financial operation, or venture with a profit motive. A joint undertaking merely to share expenses is not a partnership [Reg. 1.761-1(a)]. Dick and Barry do not have a partnership for federal income tax purposes.

8. Ms. L and Ms. N, in a joint undertaking, co-own a building that they rent to unrelated individuals. They share the expense of maintaining the building, but provide no other services for the tenants. Ms. L and Ms. N are considered to have a partnership for federal income tax purposes.

The correct answer is (F). *(SPE 989 II-17)*
DISCUSSION: Under Reg. 1.761-1(a), mere co-ownership, maintenance, repair, and rental of property does not constitute a partnership. The co-owners are partners only if, in addition to renting the property, they provide additional services to the occupants and share the profits.

9. Certain investing or operating agreement partnerships may be completely excluded from being treated as a partnership for federal income tax purposes. All of the members must choose to be excluded and the partnership has to file a partnership return, Form 1065, by the due date of the return, including extensions, for the first year it wishes to be excluded.

The correct answer is (T). *(SPE 988 II-17)*
DISCUSSION: Sec. 761(a) allows a partnership which is essentially an operating agreement or that exists for investment purposes only and not for the active conduct of a business to be excluded from treatment as a partnership (under Subchapter K only) if all of the members so elect. Each member must separately include his/her share of the income and deductions.

10. Subchapter K rules apply both to general partnerships and to limited partnerships.

The correct answer is (T). *(Publisher)*
DISCUSSION: Subchapter K is the part of the Code containing most of the tax rules that apply to partnerships. A partnership is defined under Sec. 761(a) as including a syndicate, group, pool, joint venture, or other unincorporated organization which carries on a business and is not a corporation, trust, or estate. Both limited and general partnerships fall within this definition.

17.2 Formation of a Partnership

11. During 1991, Norman contributed property held more than one year to the MaryAnn Partnership for a 40% interest. The total capital after his contribution was $50,000. His tax basis in the property was $8,000, and it had a fair market value of $10,000 at the time of the contribution to the partnership. What gain or loss should Norman report on the contribution of his property to the partnership?

  a. No gain or loss.
  b. $2,000 long-term capital gain.
  c. $12,000 long-term capital gain.
  d. $12,000 long-term capital gain of which $10,000 is deferred.

The correct answer is (a). *(CPA 1174 P-16)*
REQUIRED: The gain or loss that should be reported by a partner on the contribution of property to a partnership.
DISCUSSION: When property is contributed to a partnership in exchange for a partnership interest, the general rule is that no gain or loss is recognized by the partner or the partnership [Sec. 721(a)].
This rule applies even though the contributed property is appreciated and the partner receives a disproportionate interest in the partnership. For assets contributed after March 31, 1984, precontribution gain on the asset will be allocated to the contributing partner when the partnership later sells the asset. Property does not include services, however, and if Norman received part of his interest in the partnership for performing services, he must recognize ordinary income to that extent. See Q. 24.

12. On May 1, 1991, Mr. Good contributed 500 shares of stock in Candid Corporation to the partnership of Murphy & Wooster for a 25% interest in the partnership's capital and profits. The stock, which he purchased in 1979 for $20,000, had a fair market value on May 1 of $100,000. On May 1, 1991, the fair market value of the partnership's net assets, after Good's contribution, was $400,000. What is the amount of Good's gain in 1991 on the exchange?

  a. $0.
  b. $80,000 ordinary income.
  c. $80,000 long-term capital gain.
  d. $80,000 Sec. 1231 gain.

The correct answer is (a). *(SPE 990 II-85)*
REQUIRED: The gain to a partner on the exchange of stock for a partnership interest.
DISCUSSION: Under Sec. 721 no gain or loss is recognized by a partnership or its partners when property is contributed to the partnership in exchange for a partnership interest. Good has a realized gain of $80,000 (25% of the $400,000 value of the partnership minus his $20,000 basis in his contribution). This gain is not recognized under Sec. 721. For assets contributed after March 31, 1984, the precontribution gain on the asset is allocated to the contributing partner when the partnership later sells the asset.
Note that stock does constitute property under Sec. 721. But if the partnership would be an investment company if it were incorporated, the gain will be recognized. For this purpose, an investment company is one in which the partner has diversified his/her interest in stocks and securities and in which 80% or more of the partnership's assets are marketable stocks or securities.

Module 17.2: Formation of a Partnership

13. The Neat Partnership was formed on January 1, 1991. Mr. Groom contributed equipment to Neat for a 50% interest. The equipment had an adjusted basis to Groom of $50,000 and a fair market value of $150,000 at the time of the transfer. The equipment was subject to a mortgage of $15,000 which the partnership assumed. What is Groom's basis in his interest in Neat Partnership?

   a. $35,000.
   b. $42,500.
   c. $50,000.
   d. $150,000.

The correct answer is (b). *(SPE 990 II-84)*
REQUIRED: The taxpayer's basis in a partnership interest when mortgaged property is contributed.
DISCUSSION: Under Sec. 722, the basis of a partnership interest acquired by the contribution of property is the adjusted basis of the property to the contributing partner. Under Sec. 752(b), the assumption by a partnership of a partner's individual liabilities is treated as a distribution of money to the partner, which reduces the basis of the partner's interest (Sec. 733).
Groom's basis is the $50,000 adjusted basis of the equipment contributed less the relieved individual liability ($15,000 x 50% = $7,500). The basis is $42,500 ($50,000 – $7,500).
Note that if Groom had contributed property with a liability in excess of his basis, then gain might have been generated, but only to the extent that the deemed monetary distribution exceeds the basis of the contributed property. This differs from the results of a capital contribution to a corporation under Secs. 351 and 351(c).

14. The following information pertains to Carr's admission to the Smith & Jones partnership on July 1, 1991:

Carr's contribution of capital: 800 shares of Ed Corporation stock bought in 1975 for $30,000; fair market value $150,000 on July 1, 1991.
Carr's interest in capital and profits of Smith & Jones: 25%.
Fair market value of net assets of Smith & Jones on July 1, 1991 after Carr's admission: $600,000.

Carr's gain in 1991 on the exchange of the Ed stock for Carr's partnership interest was

   a. $120,000 ordinary income.
   b. $120,000 long-term capital gain.
   c. $120,000 Section 1231 gain.
   d. $0.

The correct answer is (d). *(CPA 1189 Q-55)*
REQUIRED: The gain to a partner on the exchange of stock for a partnership interest.
DISCUSSION: Under Sec. 721 no gain or loss is recognized by a partnership or its partners when property is contributed to the partnership in exchange for a partnership interest. Carr has a realized gain of $120,000 (25% of the $600,000 value of the partnership minus his $30,000 basis in his contribution). This gain is not recognized under Sec. 721. For assets contributed after March 31, 1984, the precontribution gain on the asset is allocated to the contributing partner when the partnership later sells the asset.
Note that stock does constitute property under Sec. 721. But if the partnership would be an investment company if it were incorporated, the gain will be recognized. For this purpose, an investment company is one in which the partner has diversified his/her interest in stocks and securities and in which 80% or more of the partnership's assets are marketable stocks or securities.

15. Mr. Wheeler received a 40% interest in the profits (but no interest in the capital) of the Shakey Sands Hotel Partnership in return for arranging necessary financing for the partnership. Three weeks after receiving his partnership interest, he sold it for $50,000. Mr. Wheeler's income from the receipt of his partnership interest is

   a. $50,000 ordinary income.
   b. $0 ordinary income.
   c. Ordinary income equal to the fair market value of Mr. Wheeler's services.
   d. None of the above.

The correct answer is (a). *(Publisher)*
REQUIRED: A partner's income on receipt of a profit interest in exchange for services.
DISCUSSION: Sec. 721 does not prevent a partner from recognizing income on the receipt of a partnership interest for services. It is clear that the receipt of a capital interest in a partnership for services must be included in the partner's income in the year of receipt under Sec. 83. It is not so clear that receipt of a profit (rather than capital) interest for services requires the partner to recognize income. However, the case of Diamond (492 F.2d 286, 1974) held that the receipt of a profit interest for services did generate ordinary income equal to the FMV of the profit interest. While the FMV may often not be ascertainable, it is ascertainable when there is a sale of the profit interest shortly after receipt. Mr. Wheeler's income from the receipt of the partnership interest is its $50,000 FMV.

Module 17.2: Formation of a Partnership

16. On June 1, 1991, Don Kerr received a 10% interest in the capital of Rev Company, a partnership, for services rendered. Rev's net assets at June 1 had a basis of $35,000 and a fair market value of $50,000. What income must Kerr include in his 1991 tax return for the partnership interest transferred to him by the other partners?

a. $5,000 capital gain.
b. $5,000 ordinary income.
c. $3,500 capital gain.
d. $3,500 ordinary income.

The correct answer is (b). *(CPA 1189 Q-54)*
REQUIRED: The income recognized when a partnership interest is received for services.
DISCUSSION: An individual must recognize compensation income when a partnership interest is received in exchange for services (whether current or past) rendered [Reg. 1.721-1(b)(1)]. The receipt of a capital interest in a partnership for services must be included in the year of receipt under Sec. 83. The income that should be recognized is the $5,000 (10% x $50,000) fair market value of the partnership interest received unless the interest is nontransferable or subject to a substantial risk of forfeiture. The income is ordinary because it is compensation for services.

17. Ben Krug, sole proprietor of Krug Dairy, hired Jan Karl in 1982 for an agreed salary and the promise of a 10% partnership capital interest if Karl continued in Krug's employ until the end of 1990. On January 1, 1991, when the net worth of the business was $300,000, the partnership was formed as agreed. On what amount will Karl have to pay tax in 1991 for the partnership capital interest received by him?

a. $0.
b. $12,000.
c. $18,000.
d. $30,000.

The correct answer is (d). *(CPA 587 Q-53)*
REQUIRED: Effect of receipt of interest in a partnership for services to a sole proprietor.
DISCUSSION: Ordinary income is recognized if services are rendered in return for property. Since Jan did not perform services for a partnership but worked for a sole proprietor in exchange for an interest in a new partnership, the tax treatment differs slightly from that in the preceding question. The transaction is treated as if Jan received an undivided 10% interest in each of the enterprises's assets and then contributed them to the partnership.
The partnership's basis in the assets deemed contributed by Jan will be their FMV. Jan should recognize income of 10% of the $300,000 net worth of the enterprise, or $30,000.

18. Mr. Horn contributes $10,000 cash and machinery with an adjusted basis of $5,000 and a fair market value of $7,000 to a partnership in exchange for a 50% interest. Mr. Horn's basis in his interest in the partnership is

a. $5,000.
b. $7,500.
c. $15,000.
d. $17,000.

The correct answer is (c). *(SPE 1077 III-28)*
REQUIRED: A partner's basis in a partnership interest received in exchange for cash and property.
DISCUSSION: The basis of a partner's interest acquired by contribution of property and money is the amount of money contributed plus the adjusted basis of property contributed (Sec. 722). Mr. Horn's basis in the partnership interest is

Money contributed	$10,000
Adjusted basis of machinery	5,000
Basis	$15,000

19. Ralph Elin contributed land to the partnership of Anduz & Elin. Elin's adjusted basis in this land was $50,000 and its fair market value was $75,000. Under the partnership agreement, Elin's capital account was credited with the full fair market value of the land. Anduz made a $75,000 cash contribution to the partnership. Thus, each partner's capital account was credited for $75,000. Elin and Anduz share profits and losses equally. What is the adjusted basis of Elin's partnership interest?

a. $25,000.
b. $37,500.
c. $50,000.
d. $75,000.

The correct answer is (c). *(CPA 1183 Q-54)*
REQUIRED: The adjusted basis of a partner's interest acquired by contributing property.
DISCUSSION: The adjusted basis of a partner's interest is the amount of money contributed plus the adjusted basis of property contributed (Sec. 722). Elin's adjusted basis in the partnership interest is $50,000 (adjusted basis of the land contributed). Stated capital account values and contributions by other partners (except liabilities) have no effect on a partner's basis for tax purposes.

Module 17.2: Formation of a Partnership

20. The following information pertains to land contributed by Pink for a 50% interest in a new partnership:

Adjusted basis to Pink	$100,000
Fair market value	300,000
Mortgage assumed by partnership	30,000

The basis for Pink's partnership interest is

a. $70,000.
b. $85,000.
c. $100,000.
d. $300,000.

The correct answer is (b). *(CPA 1188 Q-34)*
REQUIRED: A partner's basis in a partnership interest acquired by contributing property subject to a mortgage.
DISCUSSION: Under Sec. 722, the basis of a partner's interest in a partnership is the partner's adjusted basis in the contributed property. When the partnership assumes a mortgage or takes the property subject to a mortgage, the contributing partner is deemed to have received a distribution of cash to the extent of the relieved liability [Sec. 752(b)]. This deemed distribution reduces the partner's basis. Any excess of this "deemed" distribution over the partner's basis is a gain [Sec. 731(a)].

Adjusted basis of land contributed	$100,000
Less share of mortgage assumed by the other partners (.50 x $30,000)	(15,000)
Basis	$ 85,000

21. In 1991 Dave Burr acquired a 20% interest in a partnership by contributing a parcel of land. At the time of Burr's contribution, the land had a fair market value of $35,000, an adjusted basis to Burr of $8,000, and was subject to a mortgage of $12,000. Payment of the mortgage was assumed by the partnership. Burr's basis for his interest in the partnership is

a. $0.
b. $5,600.
c. $8,000.
d. $23,000.

The correct answer is (a). *(CPA 588 Q-33)*
REQUIRED: A partner's basis in a partnership to which he contributed property with a liability in excess of basis.
DISCUSSION: Under Sec. 722, the basis of an interest in a partnership acquired by the contribution of property is the adjusted basis of such property to the contributing partner. Sec. 752(b) treats a decrease in a partner's individual liabilities by reason of the assumption by the partnership of such liabilities as a distribution of money to the partner, which in turn reduces the basis of the partner's interest under Sec. 733 (but not below zero).

When Burr became a 20% partner, he was relieved of 80% of his $12,000 mortgage, or $9,600. Burr's basis in his partnership interest is the $8,000 basis in the property contributed less the $9,600 liability relieved of. However, his basis may not be less than zero. Note that he also has a gain of $1,600.

22. Mr. McRich is a limited partner with a 60% loss interest and a 30% profit interest in the XYZ Partnership. Mr. McRich contributed $10,000 cash for his partnership interest. At the time of his contribution, the partnership had recourse liabilities of $100,000 and nonrecourse liabilities of $70,000. Mr. McRich's basis in his partnership interest is

a. $10,000.
b. $31,000.
c. $61,000.
d. $91,000.

The correct answer is (b). *(Publisher)*
REQUIRED: A limited partner's basis in a partnership that has both recourse and nonrecourse liabilities.
DISCUSSION: A partner receives a basis in a partnership equal to the basis of the property contributed to the partnership (Sec. 722). Under Sec. 752(a), an increase in a partner's share of liabilities is treated as a contribution of money by such partner, which increases the partner's basis. Partners share recourse liabilities based on their ratio for sharing economic losses [Temp. Reg. Sec. 1.752-1T(d)]. But a limited partner does not share in recourse debts in excess of the additional amount (s)he would actually lose if the partnership could not pay its debt. In the absence of guarantees and special arrangements, this is usually limited to the amount of additional contributions the partner must make. All partners, including limited partners, share true nonrecourse debts first as the minimum gain is shared with the excess shared in the same proportion as profits.

Mr. McRich's basis in the partnership includes the $10,000 cash contributed plus his share of nonrecourse liabilities based on his profit-sharing interest. His total basis in the partnership is $31,000 [$10,000 + $21,000 (30% x $70,000) of nonrecourse liabilities].

23. Jeffrey, the sole proprietor of a hardware business, hired Eastwood on January 1, 1988 for an agreed salary and a promise to give him a 25% ownership interest if he were still employed at the end of 3 years, and an additional 25% interest if he continued in the business for a second 3-year period. On January 1, 1991, a partnership was formed and Eastwood received a 25% interest in the capital and profits of the business. On that date the net worth of the partnership was $60,000. What is Eastwood's tax basis of his partnership interest at January 1, 1991, and what amount should be added to his gross income for 1991?

	Partnership Interest	Addition to Gross Income
a.	$0	$0
b.	$15,000	$15,000
c.	$30,000	$15,000
d.	$30,000	$30,000

The correct answer is (b). *(CPA 1181 P-49)*
REQUIRED: The basis of a partnership interest and the amount of gross income when a partner receives the interest in exchange for services.
DISCUSSION: When a partnership interest is received in exchange for services performed, income equal to the fair market value of the partnership interest must be recognized by the partner [Reg. 1.721-1(b)(1)]. A partner's basis in his/her partnership interest received for services rendered is equal to the income recognized (Reg. 1.722-1). Eastwood must recognize gross income of $15,000 (25% of $60,000), which is the value of the partnership interest received for services rendered. Eastwood's basis in the partnership is $15,000, the amount of income recognized.

24. James Elton received a 25% capital interest in Bredbo Associates, a partnership, in return for services rendered plus a contribution of assets with a basis to Elton of $25,000 and a fair market value of $40,000. The fair market value of Elton's 25% interest was $50,000. How much is Elton's basis for his interest in Bredbo?

a. $25,000.
b. $35,000.
c. $40,000.
d. $50,000.

The correct answer is (b). *(CPA 582 Q-58)*
REQUIRED: The basis of a partner's interest when property and services are contributed.
DISCUSSION: A partner's basis in a partnership is his/her adjusted basis in the property contributed (Sec. 722) plus income recognized by the partner for receiving the interest in exchange for services (Reg. 1.722-1). Reg. 1.721-1(b)(1) states that the value of a partnership interest received as compensation for services is income to the partner (FMV of the interest in capital received). The fair market value of Elton's services is $10,000 ($50,000 FMV of the interest − $40,000 FMV of assets contributed).

Adjusted basis of assets contributed	$25,000
Income recognized for services rendered	10,000
Elton's partnership basis	$35,000

25. Three individuals form a partnership sharing in profits and losses equally. Mr. Aardvark contributes $10,000 cash. Mr. Baboon contributes $5,000 in cash and land worth $5,000 with an adjusted basis of $4,000. Mr. Camel contributes machinery with a fair market value of $16,000 subject to a mortgage of $6,000 which the partnership assumed and with an adjusted basis of $16,000. The adjusted basis of Mr. Baboon's interest in the partnership is

a. $5,000.
b. $9,000.
c. $10,000.
d. $11,000.

The correct answer is (d). *(SPE 1077 III-13)*
REQUIRED: The adjusted basis of a partner's interest received in exchange for cash and property.
DISCUSSION: The basis of a partnership interest acquired by a contribution of property and money is the adjusted basis of property contributed plus the amount of money contributed (Sec. 722). An increase in a partner's share of partnership liabilities is treated as an additional cash contribution [Sec. 752(a)] which increases the partner's basis. Mr. Baboon's adjusted basis is

Money contributed	$ 5,000
Adjusted basis of land contributed	4,000
Share of partnership's liabilities (1/3 of $6,000)	2,000
Baboon's adjusted basis	$11,000

Module 17.2: Formation of a Partnership 409

26. ABC Partnership was formed on March 1, 1991 by three individuals. A contributed $20,000 cash for a 25% interest. B contributed property with an adjusted basis of $28,000 and fair market value of $32,000, subject to a $12,000 mortgage. C contributed property with an adjusted basis of $20,000 and fair market value of $64,000, subject to a $24,000 liability. B and C received 25% and 50% partnership interests, respectively. The partnership assumed all liabilities. On March 1, 1991, B's gain recognized on contribution and basis in partnership interest are:

   a. $0 gain, $19,000 basis.
   b. $9,000 gain, $14,000 basis.
   c. $0 gain, $25,000 basis.
   d. $9,000 gain, $19,000 basis.

The correct answer is (c). *(C.K. Craig)*
REQUIRED: Calculation of gain recognized from partnership contributions and basis in partnership interest. Impact of liabilities when more than one partner contributes property subject to debt.
DISCUSSION: In general, under Sec. 721 no gain or loss shall be recognized by a partnership or any of its partners when contributing property to the partnership in exchange for a partnership interest. The general rule applies in this case, even in the presence of the various liabilities assumed by the partnership.

Under Sec. 722, the basis of an interest in a partnership acquired by a contribution of property, including money, to the partnership is the adjusted basis of such property to the contributing partner increased by the amount of any gain recognized under Sec. 721(b). Within this context, Sec. 752 requires that increases in a partner's share of partnership liabilities be treated as contributions of money and decreases in such liabilities be treated as distributions of money.

As of March 1, 1991, B's basis in the partnership interest is as follows:

Basis in property contributed	$28,000
Less liabilities assumed by partnership ($12,000 x .75)	9,000
Plus liabilities assumed by B ($24,000 x .25)	6,000
Basis in partnership interest to B	$25,000

27. A and B formed a partnership by transferring the following assets to the partnership books. A transferred $25,000 in cash and equipment which cost $27,000, had an adjusted basis of $19,800, and had a fair market value of $30,000. B transferred cash of $50,000. The partnership's basis in equipment transferred to the partnership by A is

   a. $19,800.
   b. $27,000.
   c. $30,000.
   d. $44,800.

The correct answer is (a). *(P.J. Markou)*
REQUIRED: The partnership's basis in contributed property.
DISCUSSION: Under Sec. 723, the partnership's basis for contributed property is the adjusted basis of such property to the contributing partner at the time of contribution, provided it is not an investment partnership. A's basis in the equipment was $19,800, so the partnership's basis in the equipment is $19,800.

28. Mr. A, Mr. B, and Mr. C formed a calendar-year partnership. Profits and losses are to be shared equally. Mr. A contributed a building to be used in the business that had an adjusted basis to him of $10,000 and a fair market value of $13,000. The partnership also assumed Mr. A's $6,000 mortgage on the building. Mr. B and Mr. C each contributed $4,000 in cash to the partnership's capital. What is the partnership's basis for determining depreciation on the building?

   a. $0.
   b. $4,000.
   c. $10,000.
   d. $13,000.

The correct answer is (c). *(SPE 1085 II-82)*
REQUIRED: The partnership's basis in contributed property.
DISCUSSION: Under Sec. 723, the partnership's basis in property is the contributing partner's basis at the time of contribution. Therefore, the partnership's basis in the building is Mr. A's adjusted basis of $10,000. No adjustment in basis of the building is made for the mortgage.

Module 17.2: Formation of a Partnership

29. The holding period of property acquired by a partnership as a contribution to the contributing partner's capital account

a. Begins with the date of contribution to the partnership.
b. Includes the period during which the property was held by the contributing partner.
c. Is equal to the contributing partner's holding period prior to contribution to the partnership.
d. Depends on the character of the property transferred.

The correct answer is (b). *(CPA 1188 Q-36)*
REQUIRED: The holding period of contributed property.
DISCUSSION: The partnership's holding period for contributed property includes the period of time the property was held by the contributing partner [Sec. 1223(2)]. The holding period of the partner "tacks on" because the partnership receives a carryover basis in the contributed property. This is true even if the contributing partner recognizes a gain or loss (due to being relieved of debt in excess of basis).

30. Last year, Jim Cash, one of two equal partners, contributed land with a basis to him of $15,000 and a fair market value of $10,000 to the partnership of which he was a member. His capital account was credited for $10,000. The land was later sold for $8,000. As a result of this sale, Cash must report on his personal income tax return

a. $1,000 loss.
b. $3,500 loss.
c. $5,000 loss.
d. $6,000 loss.

The correct answer is (d). *(CPA 1172 P-8)*
REQUIRED: The tax effect to a partner when property contributed is sold subsequent to formation of the partnership.
DISCUSSION: Under Sec. 721, neither the partnership nor any partner generally recognizes gain or loss when property is contributed in exchange for a partnership interest. Under Sec. 723, the partnership's basis in the property is $15,000 (the contributing partner's basis at the time of contribution). The sale of the property by the partnership resulted in a $7,000 loss ($8,000 proceeds less $15,000 adjusted basis). Under Sec. 704(c), gain or loss from the sale of contributed property must be allocated between the partners to take into account the variation between the property's basis to the partnership and its FMV at the time of contribution for all property contributed after March 31, 1984. Accordingly, Cash must recognize all of the pre-contribution loss of $5,000 ($15,000 basis − $10,000 FMV contribution) plus his $1,000 share of post-contribution loss [1/2 x ($10,000 FMV of contribution − $8,000 sales price)].

31. A and B formed a calendar-year partnership on April 1, 1991. Certain costs were incurred before beginning business September 1, 1991:

Legal fees in drawing up agreement	$ 300
Cost of placing notice required by local law in newspapers	200
Commissions paid to sell limited partners' interests	1,800
Costs of filing with the state	100

What is the allowable deduction for organizational costs in 1991?

a. $20.
b. $40.
c. $90.
d. $160.

The correct answer is (b). *(SPE 1078 II-49)*
REQUIRED: A partnership's allowable deduction for organizational costs.
DISCUSSION: Under Sec. 709(a), organizational expenses are not deductible; however, Sec. 709(b) allows a partnership to amortize organizational expenses over a period of not less than 60 months. The 60-month period starts with the month in which the partnership begins business. The organizational expenses which may be amortized are those which are incident to the creation of the partnership and are chargeable to the capital account.

Legal fees	$300
Cost of notices required by law	200
Costs of filing with the state	100
Total deductible costs	$600

The partnership formed by A and B may deduct $40 [($600 ÷ 60 months) x 4 months]. The commissions paid are syndication expenses which must be capitalized and cannot be amortized [Reg. 1.709-2(b)].

32. Sam and Terry formed the ST Partnership as equal partners on July 15, 1991. As part of the formation, Sam contributed land with a basis to him of $70,000 and a fair market value of $200,000, and Terry contributed property with a basis equal to its fair market value of $100,000. On July 16, 1991, the partnership mortgaged the land for $150,000 and distributed $100,000 cash to Sam. How much gain (loss) should Sam recognize from these transactions?

a. $0.
b. $30,000.
c. $65,000.
d. $130,000.

The correct answer is (c). *(Publisher)*
REQUIRED: The gain (loss) a partner should recognize when (s)he contributes property to a partnership and receives an immediate distribution.
DISCUSSION: Prior to 1984 Sam would have no income ($70,000 basis for property contributed + $75,000 basis for his share of the mortgage liability − $100,000 distribution = $45,000 ending basis). However, Sec. 707(a)(2) will treat such a transaction as a sale of the property by Sam (when the transaction is essentially a sale) with respect to the portion of the property given up to the other partner(s).
Therefore, Sam will be treated as having sold one-half of the property for $100,000 and contributed the other half to the partnership. His gain on the "sale" is $65,000 [$100,000 − (.50 × $70,000)]. He has no gain on his contribution of the remaining one-half of the land.

33. In August 1989, Jacob contributed land (held as an investment) to the Fastbuck Real Estate partnership for a 20% interest. Jacob had a $75,000 basis in the land, and its fair market value at the date of the contribution was $35,000. Fastbuck developed the land into building lots at a total cost of $20,000. During 1991 Fastbuck sold all the lots for a total of $60,000. What is the amount and character of the partnership's gain or loss?

a. $35,000 ordinary loss.
b. $35,000 capital loss.
c. $5,000 ordinary loss.
d. $5,000 capital gain.

The correct answer is (b). *(Publisher)*
REQUIRED: The amount and character of a partnership's gain or loss on the sale of contributed capital gain property.
DISCUSSION: Under Sec. 723, the partnership's basis in the land is $75,000 (the contributing partner's basis at the time of contribution). The partnership increased its basis in the property to $95,000 by the $20,000 development costs. The sale of the property by the partnership resulted in a $35,000 loss ($60,000 proceeds − $95,000 basis). For capital assets contributed to a partnership after March 31, 1984, Sec. 724(c) requires any loss to be treated as a capital loss to the extent of the loss inherent in the property at the time of contribution (basis in excess of FMV). This applies even if the property is not a capital asset in the hands of the partnership. Since Jacob had an inherent capital loss of $40,000 in the property when he contributed it ($75,000 basis − $35,000 FMV), the partnership's $35,000 loss is a capital loss.

34. Taxpayers A and B formed a partnership during 1991. A contributed $25,000 in cash and B contributed a building that cost $10,000 but had a fair market value of $25,000. B does not have a reportable gain for 1991 on the building contributed.

The correct answer is (T). *(SPE 1079 II-24)*
DISCUSSION: Under Sec. 721, a partner does not generally recognize gain or loss when (s)he contributes property to a partnership in exchange for a partnership interest. Furthermore, Sec. 1250(d)(3) limits depreciation recapture to the amount of gain otherwise recognized. Therefore, B has no reportable gain.

35. The amount of any gain recognized by a contributing partner at the time of contribution increases the partner's basis in the partnership.

The correct answer is (F). *(SPE 1078 II-42)*
DISCUSSION: When a partnership interest is acquired by a contribution of property, the partner's basis in the interest is increased by the amount (if any) of gain recognized under Sec. 721(b). Gain may be recognized under Sec. 721(b) if the partnership is in effect an investment company in partnership form. A partner may recognize gain (as a deemed distribution under Sec. 752) if property subject to a liability in excess of basis is contributed, but this gain would not increase basis since the money distribution does not reduce the basis of the interest below zero.

36. Mr. D and Mr. E formed a calendar-year partnership. Mr. D contributed land that had a basis to him of $5,000 and a fair market value of $10,000. The land was contributed subject to a mortgage of $3,000. Mr. E is to manage the partnership's business for which he will receive a one-half interest in the profits, losses, and capital of the partnership. Neither of the partners nor the partnership is required to recognize gain or loss on the formation of the partnership.

The correct answer is (F). *(SPE 1085 II-32)*
DISCUSSION: In general, no gain or loss is recognized by the partnership or the partners when property is contributed to the partnership in exchange for a partnership interest [Sec. 721(a)]. However, Sec. 721 does not prevent a partner from recognizing compensation income when a partnership interest is received in exchange for services. Mr. E must recognize the fair market value of the partnership interest he received as ordinary income.

37. A contribution of property by Partner N to her partnership may be treated as a transaction in which gain or loss is recognized, if after a short period of time, either before or after the contribution, the partnership distributes other property to N and the property contributed by N is retained by the partnership.

The correct answer is (T). *(SPE 989 II-27)*
DISCUSSION: Section 721(a) states that no gain or loss shall be recognized to a partnership or to any of its partners in the case of a contribution of property to the partnership in exchange for an interest in the partnership. Sec. 707(a) permits a partner to engage in a transaction with the partnership when (s)he is not acting in his/her capacity as a partner. Sec. 707(a)(2)(B) states that, if there is a direct or indirect transfer of money or other property by a partner to the partnership and there is a related direct or indirect transfer of money or other property by the partnership to such partners, then the two transfers, when viewed together, are to be characterized as a sale of the property. Because the two transfers take place in a short period of time, the transaction described above must be properly characterized as a sale or exchange of property. As a result, gain or loss will be recognized by Partner N.

38. Partner N contributed property with an adjusted basis of $400 and a fair market value of $1,000 to Partnership B. Partner L contributed $1,000 cash. Under the partnership agreement, each partner will have a capital account reflected in the partnership books of $1,000, but the adjusted basis of Partner N's interest is only $400.

The correct answer is (T). *(SPE 984 II-34)*
DISCUSSION: The basis of a partnership interest acquired by a contribution of property is the adjusted basis of the property contributed (Sec. 722). Although the partners will have equal capital account balances, the adjusted bases of their interests will not be equal.

39. Mr. Snow and Ms. White formed a partnership. Snow contributed $20,000 in cash and White contributed equipment having a fair market value of $20,000 and an adjusted basis to her of $16,000. The partnership's basis in the equipment is $20,000.

The correct answer is (F). *(SPE 990 II-24)*
DISCUSSION: Under Sec. 723, the partnership's basis in property is the contributing partner's basis at the time of the contribution. Therefore, the partnership's basis in the equipment is Ms. White's adjusted basis of $16,000.

40. Syndication fees, which are costs connected with the issuing and marketing of interests in a partnership, such as commissions, professional fees, and printing costs, must be capitalized and amortized over a period of 60 months or more.

The correct answer is (F). *(SPE 989 II-5)*
DISCUSSION: Syndication fees must be capitalized and cannot be amortized. However, Sec. 709(b) allows a partnership to amortize organizational expenses over a period of not less than 60 months. Examples of organizational expenses are filing fees with the state and legal fees incurred in drawing up the partnership agreement.

17.3 Partnership's Tax Year

41. When a partner dies, the partnership tax year must close:

a. On a date selected by the remaining partners.
b. At a date determined by the executor/executrix of the estate.
c. At the date of death.
d. At the end of the regular partnership year.

The correct answer is (d). *(SPE 990 II-51)*
REQUIRED: The date the partnership tax year closes when a partner dies.
DISCUSSION: Under Sec. 706(c)(2)(A)(ii), the taxable year of a partnership with respect to a partner who dies does not close prior to the end of the partnership tax year.

42. With respect to a partner who sells or exchanges his entire interest in a partnership, the closing of the partnership year occurs

a. At the end of the partnership year.
b. On a date selected by the above partner.
c. On the date of the sale or exchange.
d. On a date agreed upon by all partners.

The correct answer is (c). *(P.J. Markou)*
REQUIRED: The date a partnership year closes with respect to a partner who sells or exchanges his partnership interest.
DISCUSSION: Under Sec. 706(c)(2)(A), the taxable year closes with respect to a partner on the date he sells or exchanges his entire interest.

43. In 1991, which taxable year may a newly formed partnership not adopt without obtaining prior approval from the IRS?

a. A taxable year which is the same as that of its majority partners.
b. A calendar year if majority partners and principal partners have varied year-ends.
c. A January 31 year-end if it is a retail enterprise with a natural business year ending January 31 and all of its majority and principal partners are on a calendar year.
d. The taxable year of all its principal partners if its majority partners do not have a common tax year-end.

The correct answer is (c). *(CPA 1186 Q-52)*
REQUIRED: The taxable year a new partnership may not adopt in 1991 without IRS approval.
DISCUSSION: For taxable years beginning after December 31, 1986, a partnership's required taxable year is that of the partner(s) owning more than 50% of partnership capital and profits if they have held the same tax year during the shorter of the preceding 3 years or the lifetime of the partnership. If the majority partner(s) do not have the same taxable year or have not kept their same tax year for the required period, the taxable year of all principal (5%) partners must be adopted. If all principal partners do not have the same taxable year, the calendar year must be used.
Although Sec. 444 permits a partnership to elect a fiscal year, a newly formed partnership may not elect a fiscal year with more than a 3-month deferral period (i.e., the number of months between the beginning of the tax year selected, and the end of the required tax year). A January 31 year-end has an 11-month deferral period. Any other fiscal year may be chosen only with the consent of the IRS and only if a business purpose (e.g., natural business year) is established.

44. Which one of the following statements regarding a partnership's tax year is correct?

a. A partnership formed on July 1 is required to adopt a tax year ending on June 30.
b. A partnership may elect to have a tax year other than the generally required tax year if the deferral period for the tax year elected does not exceed 3 months.
c. A "valid business purpose" can no longer be claimed as a reason for adoption of a tax year other than the generally required tax year.
d. Within 30 days after a partnership has established a tax year, a form must be filed with the IRS as notification of the tax year adopted.

The correct answer is (b). *(CPA 590 Q-25)*
REQUIRED: The correct statement regarding a partnership tax year.
DISCUSSION: Sec. 444 permits a partnership to elect a fiscal year with no more than a 3-month deferral period; i.e., the number of months between the beginning of the tax year selected and the end of the required tax year.
Answer (a) is incorrect because a partnership may elect any taxable year as long as it corresponds to that of its majority partner(s), all its principal partners, any taxable year given that its principal partners change to the same tax year, or a calendar year if all of its principal partners do not have the same tax year. Answer (c) is incorrect because any fiscal year may be chosen if a business purpose is established and the IRS gives its consent. Answer (d) is incorrect because the partnership elects its tax year on its first return which must be filed by the 15th day of the fourth month following the end of its tax year.

45. Which of the following is a true statement with respect to a partnership electing a fiscal year which is not normally required and for which a business purpose does not exist?

   a. The election requires the partners to pay an additional tax on their income from the partnership.
   b. The election requires a payment to approximate the tax the partners would have paid if the partnership switched to its required year.
   c. The election requires minimum distributions to be made to the partners.
   d. Any fiscal year may be selected if the required payment is made.

The correct answer is (b). *(SPE 990 II-52)*
REQUIRED: The true statement concerning a partnership's election of a fiscal year.
DISCUSSION: A partnership may elect, under Sec. 444, a fiscal year other than normally required and for which a business purpose does not exist. However, for the election to be effective, Sec. 7519 requires a payment intended to approximate the tax the partners would have paid if the entity had switched to its required year.
Answer (a) is incorrect because the partnership makes the additional payment (similar to a deposit), not the partners. Answer (c) is incorrect because minimum distributions are required of a personal service corporation to elect a fiscal year, not a partnership. Answer (d) is incorrect because the fiscal year may not result in more than a 3-month deferral (i.e., ends no earlier than September 30 when the partnership's required year is the calendar year) unless the partnership existed in 1986 and is retaining the fiscal year it had at that time.

46. A principal partner is one who owns more than half of the partnership's capital interests.

The correct answer is (F). *(Publisher)*
DISCUSSION: A principal partner is defined in Sec. 706(b)(3) as one having an interest of 5% or more in partnership profits or capital. A partnership must generally use the same taxable year as that of all its principal partners if its majority partner(s) do not have the same taxable year.

47. ABCD partnership was formed on January 1, 1991. Mr. A, Mr. B, and Mr. C are all calendar-year taxpayers. D is a corporation and uses the fiscal year ending June 30 for reporting its taxable income. Each partner owns a 25% interest in the partnership. The partnership is required to use the calendar year as its tax year.

The correct answer is (T). *(SPE 989 II-20)*
DISCUSSION: For taxable years beginning after December 31, 1986, a partnership's required taxable year is that of the partners owning more than 50% of partnership capital and profits, if they have held the same tax year during the shorter of the preceding 3 years or the lifetime of the partnership. Here, three partners own 75% of the capital and profits and they are all calendar-year taxpayers. Therefore, the partnership must use the calendar year.

48. A newly formed partnership may not adopt a calendar year without the consent of the Commissioner of Internal Revenue if both partners report their income on a fiscal year basis ending June 30.

The correct answer is (T). *(SPE 1085 II-29)*
DISCUSSION: Under Sec. 706(b)(1), a partnership may not adopt a taxable year other than that of the partners owning more than 50% of partnership profits and capital if the partners have had the same tax year during the shorter of the preceding 3 years or the life of the partnership. If the principal (5%) partners do not have the same tax year, the partnership may adopt the calendar year. In this question, since a calendar year differs from that of the partners, the partnership needs prior approval from the IRS to adopt a calendar year. Only with IRS approval could the partnership use some other taxable year for which it establishes a business purpose. Although Sec. 444 permits the election of a tax year other than that required by Sec. 706, it may not have more than a 3-month deferral period, i.e., the number of months between the beginning of the tax year selected and the end of the required tax year.

49. Under Sec. 444, certain partnerships may elect to use a tax year that is different from their required tax year. A newly formed partnership that begins operations on December 1, 1991 and is owned by calendar year partners may make a Sec. 444 election to adopt a September 30 tax year, assuming they meet the other requirements.

The correct answer is (T). *(SPE 989 II-21)*
DISCUSSION: Sec. 444 permits the election of a tax year other than that required by Sec. 706. However, it may not have more than a 3-month deferral period, i.e., the number of months between the beginning of the tax year selected and the end of the required tax year. Assuming the partners are calendar-year taxpayers, there is a 3-month deferral period here, but not more than 3 months.

50. Each of Partnership MNO's three equal partners has a different tax year. All three concurrently change in 1991 so that they have the same tax year. The partnership must also change to the same year if no business purpose exists for a fiscal year, and prior approval of the IRS is not required.

The correct answer is (F). *(SPE 1081 II-29)*
DISCUSSION: Under Sec. 706(b)(1), after December 31, 1986, a partnership must adopt the taxable year of partners owning more than 50% of partnership profits and capital if the partners have had the same tax year during the shorter of the three preceding years or the lifetime of the partnership. Because the time period requirement of the majority partner rule is not met in this question, MNO escapes the majority rule. Each of the partners is a principal partner, and the partnership would be required to adopt the taxable year of all principal partners. However, a fiscal year election may be made under Sec. 444 provided there is no more than a 3-month deferral period from the otherwise required year-end.

51. WMW, a partnership, began operations on September 11, 1991, and is qualified to make a Sec. 444 election to use an October 31 tax year for its tax year beginning September 11, 1991. WMW must file Form 8716, Election to Have a Tax Year Other Than a Required Tax Year, by February 15, 1992, which is the due date of the partnership's tax return for the period September 11, 1991 to October 31, 1991.

The correct answer is (T). *(SPE 990 II-22)*
DISCUSSION: A Sec. 444 election is made by filing a properly prepared Form 8716, Election to Have a Tax Year Other Than a Required Tax Year. Under Temp. Reg. 1.444-3T(b), the Form 8716 must be filed by the earlier of (1) the 15th day of the fifth month following the month that includes the first day of the taxable year for which the election will first be effective, or (2) the due date (without regard for extension) of the income tax return resulting from the Sec. 444 election. Under (1) the date would be February 15 (15th day of the fifth month beginning after September) and under (2) the date would be February 15 (15th day of the fourth month beginning after October 31). Since both dates are the same, the Form 8716 must be filed by February 15, 1992.

52. As a general rule, a partnership taxable year is closed by the death of a partner even though the partnership is not terminated.

The correct answer is (F). *(SPE 986 II-27)*
DISCUSSION: Sec. 706(c) provides the general rule that the taxable year of a partnership does not close when a partner dies. The exception is that the taxable year of a partnership does close if the death causes the partnership to terminate (discontinuance of all business, or sale or exchange of 50% or more of profits and capital interest within a 12-month period).

17.4 Partnership Ordinary Income

53. In computing the taxable income of a partnership, a deduction is allowed for

a. Fixed salaries paid to partners for services determined without regard to the income of the partnership.
b. The net operating loss deduction.
c. Contributions to charitable organizations.
d. Personal exemptions of the partners.

The correct answer is (a). *(CPA 580 Q-29)*
REQUIRED: The item that is deductible by a partnership.
DISCUSSION: A partnership's taxable income is computed in the same way as that of an individual except that certain items must be separately stated and certain deductions are not allowed [Sec. 703(a)]. Fixed salaries not based on partnership income and paid to partners for services are deductible.
Answers (b) and (c) are incorrect because the net operating loss deduction and the charitable contribution deduction are not allowed to the partnership. Answer (d) is incorrect because a partnership is not allowed personal exemptions.

54. In the computation of the ordinary income of a partnership, a deduction is allowed for

a. Contributions to qualified charities.
b. The net operating loss deduction.
c. Guaranteed payments to partners.
d. Short-term and long-term capital losses.

The correct answer is (c). *(CPA 1188 Q-37)*
REQUIRED: The deduction allowed in computing the ordinary income of a partnership.
DISCUSSION: The ordinary income of a partnership is the balance of the taxable income excluding all items required to be separately stated under Sec. 702(a). Guaranteed payments to partners are deductible under Sec. 707(c), provided they meet the requirements of Sec. 162(a), i.e., if they are ordinary and necessary business expenses.
Answers (a) and (d) are incorrect because neither is deductible but must be separately stated. Answer (b) is incorrect because the partnership does not have a net operating loss deduction.

55. All of the following items are taken into account in figuring the ordinary income or loss of a partnership except

a. Depletion allowance with respect to partnership oil and gas properties.
b. Rent expense for building where partnership conducts business.
c. Business bad debts.
d. Guaranteed payments to partners.

The correct answer is (a). *(SPE 986 II-50)*
REQUIRED: The deduction not allowed in computing the ordinary income of a partnership.
DISCUSSION: A partnership's ordinary income consists of the balance of the taxable income of a partnership that is not required to be separately stated [Sec. 702(a)(8)]. In computing partnership ordinary income, Sec. 703(a)(2)(F) specifically disallows depletion deductions with respect to oil and gas wells.
Answers (b), (c), and (d) are incorrect because these items are deductible in computing partnership ordinary income.

56. The partnership must make elections as to the tax treatment of all the following items except

a. Partnership accounting methods.
b. Inventory method.
c. Reinvestment of proceeds from an involuntary conversion pursuant to Sec. 1033.
d. Deduction or credit of foreign taxes paid.

The correct answer is (d). *(Publisher)*
REQUIRED: The election that is made by individual partners rather than the partnership.
DISCUSSION: Under Sec. 703(b), almost all elections affecting the computation of taxable income derived from a partnership are made by the partnership. However, there are five elections that are made by the individual partners rather than the partnership. One of these is the election under Sec. 901 to claim a credit for foreign taxes rather than a deduction.
Answers (a), (b), and (c) are incorrect because each is an election that falls under the general rule of Sec. 703(b); i.e., each is made by the partnership rather than the partners.

57. Dunn and Shaw are partners who share profits and losses equally. In the computation of the partnership's 1991 book income of $100,000, guaranteed payments to partners totaling $60,000 and charitable contributions totaling $1,000 were treated as expenses. What amount should be reported as ordinary income on the partnership's 1991 return?

- a. $100,000.
- b. $101,000.
- c. $160,000.
- d. $161,000.

The correct answer is (b). *(CPA 588 Q-36)*
REQUIRED: The amount of the partnership's ordinary income.
DISCUSSION: A partnership's ordinary income consists of the balance of the taxable income of a partnership which is not required to be separately stated [Sec. 702(a)(8)].
Deductible guaranteed payments are not separately stated and do enter into the calculation. Charitable contributions are not deductible in computing a partnership's taxable income and could never enter into the determination of ordinary income. The $1,000 of charitable contributions that were deducted must be added back.

Operating income	$100,000
Plus charitable contributions	1,000
Partnership ordinary income	$101,000

58. The partnership of Truman, Inc. and Hanover realized the following items of income during the year ended December 31, 1991:

Net income from sales	$62,000
Dividends from domestic corporations	4,000
Interest on corporate bonds	3,000
Net long-term capital gains	5,000
Net short-term capital gains	1,000
Net rental income	7,000

Both the partnership and the partners are on a calendar-year basis. The partners both work full-time at the partnership. The total income which should be reported as ordinary income of the partnership for 1991 is

- a. $62,000.
- b. $69,000.
- c. $72,000.
- d. $76,000.

The correct answer is (a). *(CPA 580 Q-31)*
REQUIRED: The amount of ordinary income of the partnership.
DISCUSSION: The ordinary income of a partnership consists of the balance of taxable income which does not have to be separately stated [Sec. 702(a)(8)].
Capital gains must be separately stated to allow the appropriate netting at the partner level. Dividends must also be separately stated because of the availability of a dividends-received deduction to corporate partners. Interest on corporate bonds and dividends are portfolio income and must be separated from active or passive income. Rental income is passive income and must be separately stated. Since these items are separately stated, they do not enter into the partnership's ordinary income computation.

59. For the year ended December 31, 1991, the partnership of Bicent and Tennial reported ordinary income of $260,000, which included the following items of expenses and losses:

Salaries paid (other than to partners)	$70,000
Real estate taxes for partnership office	8,000
Charitable contributions	2,000
Repairs	1,000
Foreign income taxes	5,000
Loss on sale of machinery held 7 years	12,000

As a result of the above items, the partnership should increase its ordinary income and report what amount separately on its tax return?

- a. $19,000.
- b. $23,000.
- c. $27,000.
- d. $72,000.

The correct answer is (a). *(CPA 1177 Q-26)*
REQUIRED: The amount that must be reported separately by the partnership.
DISCUSSION: Partnerships compute taxable income in the same way as individuals except that certain items must be separately stated [Sec. 703(a)]. Partnership ordinary income is the balance of taxable income not required to be separately stated. The sum of the items that the partnership included in its ordinary income computation but which should have been separately stated is

Contributions [Sec. 702(a)(4)]	$ 2,000
Foreign income taxes [Sec. 702(a)(6)]	5,000
Loss on sale of machinery (Sec. 1231 loss) [Sec. 702(a)(3)]	12,000
Total	$19,000

Module 17.4: Partnership Ordinary Income

60. Partnership M, a law partnership, had the following items for 1991:

Income from clients	$200,000
Repairs	1,000
Depreciation	2,000
Dividends on capital stock	500
Other operating expenses	125,000
Charitable contributions	1,500
Sec. 1231 gain on sale of office furniture	1,200
Sec. 1245 gain on sale of office furniture	1,000

What is Partnership M's ordinary income?

a. $70,500.
b. $72,700.
c. $73,000.
d. $73,500.

The correct answer is (c). *(SPE 1080 II-85)*
REQUIRED: The amount of ordinary income of the partnership.
DISCUSSION: Partnership ordinary income is that portion of partnership taxable income which is not required to be separately stated under Sec. 702(a). Charitable contributions are not deductible by a partnership but are required to be separately stated. Dividends must be separately stated because they are portfolio income and must be separated from active and passive income. Sec. 1231 gain must be separately stated. Note that Sec. 1245 gain does not have to be separately stated since it is always taxed as ordinary income. Partnership M's ordinary income is

Income from clients	$200,000
Sec. 1245 gain	1,000
Operating expenses	(125,000)
Repairs	(1,000)
Depreciation	(2,000)
Ordinary income	$ 73,000

61. During 1991, the EEE Partnership paid insurance premiums for the following coverage:

Life insurance on the lives of all the partners in order to get or protect a business loan	$ 700
Group term life on the lives of all the partners with the partnership designated as the beneficiary	300
Worker's compensation on behalf of all the partners	600
Use and occupancy and business interruptions due to fire or other causes	900
Public liability that covers the partnership's liability for bodily injury suffered by persons who are not employees of the partnership and for property damage to others	1,000

What is the amount of the partnership's deductible insurance expense for 1991?

a. $3,500.
b. $2,800.
c. $2,200.
d. $1,900.

The correct answer is (d). *(SPE 989 II-69)*
REQUIRED: The premiums paid on insurance policies taken out by a partnership that are deductible.
DISCUSSION: Section 264(a) denies a deduction for premiums paid on any life insurance policy concerning the life of any officer, employee, or person financially interested in any trade or business carried on by taxpayer, when the taxpayer is directly or indirectly a beneficiary under the policy. The premium paid on life insurance on the lives of all the partners in order to get or protect a business loan is nondeductible (Yarnall, 9 T.C. 616). The premium paid on the group term life insurance on the partners with the partnership being the beneficiary is also nondeductible under Sec. 264(a) since the partners can be considered "financially interested" individuals. Premiums paid on worker's compensation for the partners are nondeductible even though payments for the partnership's employees would be deductible (Rev. Rul. 72-596). The premiums on the business interruption insurance and public liability insurance are trade or business expenses deductible under Sec. 162.

62. Section 179 expensing of assets is deducted on Form 1065 in computing partnership ordinary income.

The correct answer is (F). *(SPE 1081 II-26)*
DISCUSSION: Each partner must take into account separately his/her share of any item which could result in a different tax liability if it were separately taken into account [Reg. 1.702-1(a)(8)(ii)]. Since there is a limit on Sec. 179 expensing of assets at the partner level (as well as at the partnership level), it must be taken into account separately by the partners and not deducted in computing partnership ordinary income.

63. Partner A, whose services are essential to the success of the partnership, may take out insurance on his life and name his co-partners as beneficiaries to induce them to retain their investments in the firm. In such a case, since A is not a direct beneficiary, the premiums would be deductible.

The correct answer is (F). *(SPE 1079 II-19)*
DISCUSSION: Premiums for life insurance on a partner's life are not deductible by the partnership if the insured partner is directly or indirectly a beneficiary of the insurance. Under Reg. 1.264-1(b), Partner A is an indirect beneficiary when the policy is purchased for the purpose of inducing partners to retain their interests. The premiums are not deductible.

17.5 Partners' Distributive Shares of Income and Gain

64. For the year ended December 31, 1991, the partnership of Charles and Paul had book income of $75,000 which included the following:

Short-term capital loss	$(3,100)
Long-term capital gain (on sale of securities)	4,300
Sec. 1231 gain	1,500
Ordinary income (Sec. 1245 recapture)	600
Dividends	200

The partners share profits and losses equally. What should be each partner's share of partnership income (excluding all partnership items which must be accounted for separately) to be reported as taxable for 1991?

a. $35,700.
b. $36,050.
c. $36,150.
d. None of the above.

The correct answer is (b). *(CPA 1176 Q-31)*
REQUIRED: The amount of each partner's share of partnership ordinary income.
DISCUSSION: The ordinary income of a partnership is the portion of taxable income which is not required to be separately stated [Sec. 702(a)(8)]. Note that Sec. 1245 recapture income is not required to be separately stated since it will always be ordinary income. Book income must be adjusted to exclude the effects of all separately stated items.

Book income	$75,000
Add back:	
Short-term capital loss	3,100
Subtract:	
Long-term capital gain	(4,300)
Sec. 1231 gain	(1,500)
Dividends	(200)
Partnership ordinary income	$72,100

Since Charles and Paul share profits and losses equally, each partner's share of partnership ordinary income is 50% of $72,100, or $36,050.

65. For the year ended December 31, 1991, the partnership of Murray and Parker had book income of $100,000 which included the following:

Long-term capital gain (on sale of securities)	$ 7,000
Sec. 1231 loss	(3,000)
Dividends	200
Interest paid to partners for use of capital	12,000

The partners share profits and losses equally. What amount of partnership income (excluding all partnership items which must be reported separately) should each partner report in his individual income tax return for 1991?

a. $47,900.
b. $48,000.
c. $50,000.
d. $53,900.

The correct answer is (a). *(CPA 1180 P-58)*
REQUIRED: The amount of partnership ordinary income that should be reported by each partner.
DISCUSSION: A partnership's ordinary income is the portion of taxable income not required to be stated separately [Sec. 702(a)(8)]. The interest paid to partners is a guaranteed payment which results in an ordinary deduction. Book income may be adjusted to ordinary income by excluding all items of income and adding back all deduction and loss items, which must be separately stated. The partnership's ordinary income is

Book income	$100,000
Add back:	
Sec. 1231 loss	3,000
Subtract:	
Long-term capital gain	(7,000)
Dividends	(200)
Partnership ordinary income	$ 95,800

Because the partners share profits and losses equally, each partner's share of partnership income is $47,900 (50% x $95,800).

Module 17.5: Partners' Distributive Shares of Income and Gain

66. Charles Jordan files his income tax return on a calendar-year basis. He is a 3% partner of a partnership reporting on a June 30 fiscal-year basis. Jordan's share of the partnership's ordinary income was $24,000 for the fiscal year ended June 30, 1990, and $72,000 for the fiscal year ended June 30, 1991. How much should Jordan report on his 1990 return as his share of taxable income from the partnership?

a. $24,000.
b. $36,000.
c. $60,000.
d. $72,000.

The correct answer is (a). *(CPA 581 Q-51)*
REQUIRED: The amount of partnership income that a partner should report when the partnership has a different tax year.
DISCUSSION: When computing taxable income, a partner is required to include his/her share of partnership income and separately stated items for any partnership year that ends within his/her taxable year [Sec. 706(a)]. Since the partnership's fiscal year ending June 30, 1990 ended within Jordan's 1990 calendar year, Jordan must report $24,000 (his share of the partnership's income for the fiscal year ending June 30, 1990).

67. Crater Partnership had 1991 ordinary income of $45,000 and a long-term capital gain of $5,000. Mr. Abbott, who has a 20% interest in the profits and losses of the partnership and basis before 1991 operations of $15,000, had 1991 drawings of $12,500 from the partnership. The other partners withdrew $27,500 during 1991. The partnership agreement does not provide for partner salaries or bonuses. Mr. Abbott had no other capital gains or losses during 1991. By how much will Mr. Abbott's 1991 adjusted gross income increase because of his interest in Crater Partnership?

a. $9,000.
b. $10,000.
c. $12,500.
d. $22,500.

The correct answer is (b). *(CPA 575 Q-19)*
REQUIRED: A partner's income from a partnership when he has draws.
DISCUSSION: Draws by partners, when not paid as salary or bonus, are partnership distributions. Under Sec. 731(a), a partner receiving a distribution from a partnership will not recognize gain unless the distribution exceeds that partner's adjusted basis in the partnership. Abbott has a basis of $15,000 before making an adjustment for current year ordinary income + gains; therefore, he will recognize no current income from his drawings of $12,500. However, a partner is required to include in gross income his/her share of partnership ordinary income and separately stated items under Sec. 702(a).

Partnership's ordinary income (20% x $45,000)	$ 9,000
Long-term capital gain (20% x $5,000)	1,000
Increase in adjusted gross income	$10,000

68. In 1991, the Rainy Day Partnership reported a Sec. 1231 gain of $30,000, a long-term capital loss of $33,000, a $400 charitable contribution, and ordinary income of $40,000. Mr. Umbrella, a single taxpayer with no dependents, owned a 40% profit and loss interest in the partnership. In 1991, Umbrella had a $2,000 long-term capital gain and $30,000 ordinary income but no Sec. 1231 transactions, charitable contributions, or short-term capital gains or losses before considering the partnership results. Umbrella had itemized deductions from AGI of $7,000 without considering partnership results. He has no dependents. Umbrella's taxable income for 1991 was

a. $30,320.
b. $37,490.
c. $39,640.
d. $40,640.

The correct answer is (b). *(Publisher)*
REQUIRED: A partner's taxable income including his share of partnership items.
DISCUSSION: Under Sec. 702(a), each partner separately takes into account his/her distributive share of the partnership's long-term capital gains and losses, Sec. 1231 gains and losses, charitable contributions, and ordinary income of the partnership. Mr. Umbrella's share of each of these items is 40%.

His own ordinary income		$30,000
Partnership ordinary income (40% x $40,000)		16,000
Capital gain:		
Partnership 1231 gain (40% x $30,000)	$12,000	
His own LTCG	2,000	
Partnership LTCL (40% x $33,000)	(13,200)	800
Adjusted gross income		$46,800
Itemized deductions:		
His own	$ 7,000	
Partnership charitable contributions (40% x $400)	160	(7,160)
Personal exemption		(2,150)
Taxable income		$37,490

Module 17.5: Partners' Distributive Shares of Income and Gain

69. CDH Company, a fiscal year partnership, is equally owned by C, D, and H. The partnership reported net income of $120,000 for the taxable year ending October 31, 1990. Partner C, a calendar year taxpayer, withdrew $25,000 from his capital account during the fiscal year. The partnership reported net income of $90,000 for the taxable year ending October 31, 1991. What is the amount of partnership income C must report on his 1990 income tax return?

a. $25,000.
b. $30,000.
c. $40,000.
d. $55,000.

70. A partner's taxable income, arising from the partner's interest in a partnership, includes

a. Only the partner's share of partnership income actually distributed to the partner during the year.
b. The partner's share of partnership income, whether or not distributed to the partner during the year.
c. Only the partner's salary actually paid to the partner during the year.
d. Only the partner's salary and interest paid to the partner during the year, and deducted by the partnership during that year.

71. At June 30, 1991, Burns and Cooper were equal partners in a partnership with net assets having a tax basis and fair market value of $100,000. On July 1, 1991, Todd contributed securities with a fair market value of $50,000 (purchased in 1984 at a cost of $35,000) to become an equal partner in the new firm of Burns, Cooper and Todd. The securities were sold on December 15, 1991 for $65,000. How much of the partnership's capital gain from the sale of these securities should be allocated to Todd?

a. $5,000.
b. $10,000.
c. $15,000.
d. $20,000.

The correct answer is (c). *(SPE 990 II-56)*
REQUIRED: The amount of partnership income that a partner should report when the partnership has a different tax year and a partner has draws.
DISCUSSION: When computing taxable income, a partner is required to include his/her share of partnership income and separately stated items for any partnership tax year that ends within his/her taxable year [Sec. 706(a)]. Here CDH Partnership's fiscal year ending October 31, 1990, ended within C's calendar-year 1990 tax year. C must report $40,000 (his 1/3 share of the $120,000 partnership income for the fiscal year ending October 31, 1990). The withdrawal from C's capital account is merely a reduction in his basis.

The correct answer is (b). *(CPA 1185 Q-57)*
REQUIRED: The amount of partnership income to be reported by the partner.
DISCUSSION: Distributive shares of partnership income are reported by partners for their taxable year during which the end of the partnership taxable year occurs. The partner will be taxed on the partnership income whether it is distributed or not.
Answers (a), (c), and (d) are incorrect because a partner must report and pay tax on his/her distributive share of partnership income, whether or not it is distributed to the partner during the year.

The correct answer is (d). *(CPA 1181 P-53)*
REQUIRED: The amount of partnership capital gain on contributed property to be allocated to the contributing partner.
DISCUSSION: The general rule is that a partner's distributive share should be determined according to the partnership agreement [Sec. 704(a)]. For property contributed after March 31, 1984, Sec. 704(c) requires a special allocation for the difference between fair market value at the time of contribution and basis of contributed property. The gain attributable to the pre-contribution appreciation in the securities must be allocated entirely to Todd, and the gain attributable to post-contribution appreciation should be shared equally by Burns, Cooper, and Todd. Todd's share is

Precontribution appreciation ($50,000 FMV − $35,000 basis)	$15,000
Plus 1/3 of postcontribution appreciation ($65,000 proceeds − $50,000 7/1 FMV)	5,000
Todd's share of the capital gain	$20,000

72. On January 1, 1991, Dan and Lee formed a partnership to manufacture furniture. Dan has been a developer and land dealer. He contributed land from the inventory of his other business that had a $25,000 basis and a fair market value at the time of the transfer of $30,000. Lee contributed $25,000 in cash. Both partners and the partnership use the calendar year and cash method. On October 31, 1991, the partnership sold the land contributed by Dan for $35,000. Which of the following statements is true?

a. For 1991, Dan reports ordinary income of $10,000 and the basis of his partnership interest is $35,000.

b. The partnership reports a capital gain of $10,000.

c. The partnership reports ordinary income of $10,000.

d. The partnership reports capital gain of $30,000 and ordinary income of $5,000.

The correct answer is (c). *(SPE 990 II-83)*
REQUIRED: The correct statement concerning the contribution of inventory to a partnership and its subsequent sale.
DISCUSSION: Under Sec. 724(b) the characterization of the gain or loss on contributed inventory property is carried over from the contributing partner. No gain or loss is recognized by the partner or partnership on the contribution of the land held as inventory. The basis of the land to Dan was $25,000. The land is considered inventory by Dan so when it is sold it is considered ordinary income unless held by the partnership for more than 5 years. Here, the land is sold within 1 year so it retains ordinary income character. There is a $10,000 gain recognized by the partnership on the sale of the land ($35,000 sales price − $25,000 basis). The gain is all ordinary income. The first $5,000 of gain ($30,000 contribution − $25,000 basis) is precontribution gain and allocated to Dan. The remaining $5,000 gain is reported by the partnership as ordinary income and allocated to the partners according to their profits interests.

73. In each of the following situations, assume that capital accounts are maintained in accordance with the Sec. 1.704 regulations, the allocation is reflected in the capital account, and liquidation is in accordance with capital accounts with deficit balances to be restored on liquidation. Which of these special allocations has substantial economic effect?

a. Partner A is allocated $10,000 of Sec. 1231 loss and all other partners are allocated $10,000 of depreciation deductions.

b. Partner A is allocated 10% of all foreign source income of the partnership and all other partners receive the same dollar amount of U.S. source income.

c. Partner A is allocated all income (but not gain or loss) from $100,000 face amount 10% municipal bonds and Partner B is allocated all dividends (but not gain or loss) from $100,000 fair market value of G.M. stock. The interest and dividends are likely to be close to the same amount.

d. Partner A receives all depreciation deductions. Gains and losses from the sale of depreciable assets are allocated pro rata among the partners.

The correct answer is (d). *(Publisher)*
REQUIRED: The special allocation that has substantial economic effect.
DISCUSSION: A partner's distributive share of income, gain, loss, deduction, or credit may be determined by special allocation in the partnership agreement provided it has substantial economic effect [Sec. 704(b)]. Otherwise, the distributive share will be determined in accordance with the partner's interest in the partnership. Under case law and Reg. 1.704-1(b)(2), substantial economic effect exists if the allocation may substantially affect the dollar amount of the partners' shares of the total partnership income or loss independent of tax consequences. Answer (d) has substantial economic effect since Partner A's receipt of funds upon liquidation will be reduced according to the depreciation taken and charged to his/her capital account.

Answer (a) is incorrect because an allocation of Sec. 1231 loss to one partner and equivalent depreciation deductions to other partners is just a means of reducing taxes and does not affect their dollar amounts of partnership income. Answers (b) and (c) are incorrect because the partners' dollar amount of income is directly dependent on the allocations, but that effect is not substantial.

74. In 1991, Stan Steamer contributed $50,000 cash and Pierce Arrow contributed a machine with a fair market value of $50,000 and an adjusted basis of $20,000 to a partnership. Each owned a 50% interest in the partnership. All depreciation on the machine is allocated to Steamer in the partnership agreement. Assuming straight-line depreciation over five years, Steamer's annual depreciation allocation will be

a. $10,000.
b. $5,000.
c. $4,000.
d. $2,000.

The correct answer is (c). *(Publisher)*
REQUIRED: A partner's depreciation under a special allocation to take into account the difference between fair market value and basis of contributed property.
DISCUSSION: Sec. 704(c) used to allow a special allocation of depreciation to take into account the variation between the basis of the property to the partnership and its fair market value at the time of contribution. For property contributed after March 31, 1984, such an allocation is required by Sec. 704(c).
By contributing $50,000, Steamer has in effect purchased a one-half interest in the machine and should be entitled to depreciation based on a $25,000 basis (one-half of the machine's FMV), but he will be limited to the amount of actual depreciation allowed to the partnership ($4,000 per year because the partnership's basis is only $20,000).

75. Which one of the following statements is false?

a. Each individual partner's distributive share of partnership income or loss must be reported on his or her 1040.
b. Generally, a partner's distributive share of income or loss is determined by the partnership agreement.
c. Distributions by the partnership are generally not taxable to the partners unless the distributions are treated as a liquidation or sale or exchange of their capital interests.
d. The partnership is required to file a declaration of estimated tax in any year it anticipates a profit.

The correct answer is (d). *(SPE 1081 II-61)*
REQUIRED: The false statement concerning a partnership.
DISCUSSION: A partnership is not required to file an estimated tax declaration because it is not liable for such tax (Sec. 701). The partnership tax return is only an informational return.
Answer (a) is incorrect because each partner is required to report his/her share of partnership income [Sec. 702(a)], although if a partner is not an individual, it would be reported on a different return. Answer (b) is incorrect because under Sec. 704(a) a partner's distributive share is determined by the agreement unless the allocation does not have substantial economic effect. Answer (c) is incorrect because distributions are generally not taxed to partners since they are taxed as the partnership earns the income whether or not it is distributed.

76. Irving Aster, Dennis Brill, and Robert Clark were partners who shared profits and losses equally. On February 28, 1991, Aster sold his interest to Phil Dexter. On March 31, 1991, Brill died, and his estate held his interest for the remainder of the year. The partnership continued to operate and for the fiscal year ending June 30, 1991 had a profit of $45,000. Assuming that partnership income was earned on a pro rata monthly basis and that all partners were calendar-year taxpayers, the distributive shares to be included in 1991 gross income should be

a. Aster $10,000, Brill $0, Estate of Brill $15,000, Clark $15,000, and Dexter $5,000.
b. Aster $10,000, Brill $11,250, Estate of Brill $3,750, Clark $15,000, and Dexter $5,000.
c. Aster $0, Brill $11,250, Estate of Brill $3,750, Clark $15,000, and Dexter $15,000.
d. Aster $0, Brill $0, Estate of Brill $15,000, Clark $15,000, and Dexter $15,000.

The correct answer is (a). *(CPA 574 Q-3)*
REQUIRED: The correct statement concerning the distributive shares of each partner to be included in gross income.
DISCUSSION: Under Sec. 706(a), a partner includes his/her share of partnership income for a partnership taxable year which ends within the partner's tax year. Sec. 706(d) requires each partner to include only his/her share of partnership income for the period of time (s)he owned the partnership interest; i.e., the partnership tax year closes with respect to a partner who sells his/her entire interest [Sec. 706(c)]. Accordingly, Aster and Dexter must prorate their share of partnership income based on the length of time of ownership. Death of a partner does not close the partnership tax year with respect to the decedent, and the entire amount of Brill's share is included in the estate's income [Reg. 1.706-1(c)(3)].

Profit of $45,000 ÷ 3 partners ÷ 12 months = $1,250 monthly income per partner.
Aster: 8 months x $1,250 = $10,000
Brill's estate: 12 months x $1,250 = $15,000
Clark: 12 months x $1,250 = $15,000
Dexter: 4 months x $1,250 = $5,000

77. Ms. M, a cash-basis, calendar-year taxpayer, became a partner in Partnership C on July 1, 1990 by purchasing her partnership interest for $10,000. C files its return for a fiscal year ending June 30. On December 31, 1990, C made a cash distribution to Ms. M of $5,000. Ms. M's share of C's partnership income for the year ending June 30, 1991 was $10,000. Ms. M does not have to report any income from the partnership on her 1990 return.

The correct answer is (T). *(SPE 1083 II-38)*
DISCUSSION: Sec. 706(a) provides that, when a partner computes taxable income, (s)he must include his/her distributive share of partnership income for any partnership year that ends within his/her taxable year. Ms. M will report her $10,000 share of partnership income for the year ending June 30, 1991 on her 1991 return. The $5,000 cash distribution reduces Ms. M's basis, but it is not income to her since it is not in excess of her basis.

78. The character of a partner's distributive share of a partnership item of income, gain, loss, credit, or deduction that the partner must take into account separately, is determined as if the partner had realized it directly from the same source or incurred it in the same manner as it was realized or incurred by the partnership.

The correct answer is (T). *(SPE 990 II-23)*
DISCUSSION: The question restates Sec. 702(b), under which a partner's share of the partnership income (and other tax items) retains the same character to the partner that it had to the partnership.

79. A partnership agreement may be modified for a particular tax year after the close of that tax year but not later than the date (not including any extension of time) for filing the partnership return for that year.

The correct answer is (T). *(SPE 989 II-19)*
DISCUSSION: Under Sec. 761(c), a partnership agreement (which may be written or oral) includes modifications made prior to or at the time required by law for filing the return, but not including extensions of time to file. Note that any special allocations must meet the requirements of Sec. 704(b) with respect to substantial economic effect. The Sec. 706(d) varying interest rule may apply.

80. For federal income tax purposes, the specific allocations of income, credits, and deductions to the partners will be controlled by the partnership agreement even though it cannot be demonstrated that the allocations have substantial economic effect.

The correct answer is (F). *(SPE 986 II-2)*
DISCUSSION: A partner's distributive share of income, gain, loss, deduction, or credit may be determined by special allocation provided it has substantial economic effect [Sec. 704(b)]. Otherwise, the distributive share will be determined in accordance with the partner's interest in the partnership.

81. Mr. Y, a calendar-year taxpayer, died on September 12, 1991. He was a partner in a March 31 fiscal-year partnership. Under applicable state law, the partnership terminated with the death of Mr. Y. Mr. Y's final return will include his share of the partnership items only from the partnership year ending March 31, 1991, but not the period ending with his death.

The correct answer is (T). *(SPE 1085 II-30)*
DISCUSSION: Sec. 706(a) requires a partner to include his/her share of partnership income for a partnership taxable year ending within the partner's taxable year. Typically, a decedent's final return would only include his share of partnership income for the partnership year ended March 31, 1991. The decedent's distributive share of partnership income from the partnership's fiscal year ending in 1992 would be reported by his estate or successor in interest. Termination of a partnership under state law upon the death of a partner is not a termination for tax purposes [Sec. 706(c)], so the partnership's tax year does not end on the date of death.

82. A partnership does not pay a minimum tax. Each partner must separately take into account his/her distributive share of the partnership's tax preference items.

The correct answer is (T). *(SPE 986 II-33)*
DISCUSSION: Partnerships are not tax-paying entities but are merely conduits to "flow through" tax items to the partners. Partners report their share of partnership taxable income or loss and other items on their individual returns. Partners are subject to the alternative minimum tax on their share of partnership tax preference items.

83. Kelly Green's distributive share of income from the Shamrock Partnership was $22,000 in 1991. Kelly Green received a distribution of $15,000 of Shamrock Partnership's 1990 earnings on December 15, 1991. She should report $15,000 as ordinary income from Shamrock Partnership, a calendar-year partnership, on her 1991 individual return, Form 1040.

The correct answer is (F). *(SPE 1077 I-111)*
DISCUSSION: A partner must report his/her distributive share of partnership income [Sec. 702(a)]. This is because the partner is taxed on the partnership income whether it is distributed or not. Green should thus report $22,000 as income from the partnership.

17.6 Partnership Losses

84. J&D Partnership's books and records reflected the following for the current tax year:

Gross receipts	$90,000
Operating expenses	95,000
Sec. 1231 gain	21,000
Charitable contributions	2,000
Guaranteed payments to partners	40,000
Depletion on oil and gas properties	3,000

What is the amount of the partnership's ordinary loss?

a. $5,000.
b. $45,000.
c. $47,000.
d. $50,000.

The correct answer is (b). *(SPE 986 II-75)*
REQUIRED: The amount of a partnership's ordinary loss.
DISCUSSION: A partnership's ordinary income or loss is the balance of the taxable income (loss) excluding all items required to be separately stated under Sec. 702(a) and disallowed deductions under Sec. 703. The partnership's loss equals $45,000 ($90,000 − $95,000 − $40,000). The Sec. 1231 gain and charitable contributions are items to be separately stated and do not enter into the computation. The depletion deduction with respect to oil and gas properties is disallowed to the partnership by Sec. 703.

85. Ms. Murphy has a 50% interest in a partnership in which she materially participates in the partnership's business. Ms. Murphy's adjusted basis in the partnership was $20,000 at the beginning of 1991. During 1991, the partnership borrowed $320,000 to purchase equipment and pay off an existing note with a balance of $200,000. All of the partners are personally liable for all partnership debts and there are no guarantees or similar arrangements. The partnership sustained a $600,000 loss in 1991. What amount can Ms. Murphy claim as a loss from the partnership on her 1991 individual income tax return?

a. $20,000.
b. $80,000.
c. $120,000.
d $320,000.

The correct answer is (b). *(SPE 990 II-81)*
REQUIRED: A partner's deduction for a partnership loss.
DISCUSSION: In determining his/her income tax, a partner must separately take into account his/her distributive share of the partnership's income, gain, loss, deduction, or credit [Sec. 702(a)]. A partner's distributive share of partnership loss is allowed only to the extent of the adjusted basis of such partner's interest in the partnership [Sec. 704(d)]. The partnership's debt increased by $120,000 ($320,000 new debt − $200,000 old debt) during 1991. Ms. Murphy's basis increased by $60,000 (50% x $120,000).

Ms. Murphy should deduct an $80,000 ordinary loss [the adjusted basis of her partnership interest at year-end ($20,000 + $60,000)]. The remainder of her share of partnership loss [(50% x $600,000) − $80,000 = $220,000] may be deducted in a subsequent year when her basis in the partnership is increased.

Module 17.6: Partnership Losses

86. Partnership Y reported a $50,000 ordinary loss for its first year of operation. Partner A, who materially participates, had invested $10,000 cash in exchange for a 60% interest in partnership profits. The partnership agreement stated that Partner A was liable for all of the partnership's debts. The only partnership debt at year-end was a $10,000 loan from a local bank. Partner A and the general partner had a separate agreement that Partner A's liability to the bank would not exceed $5,000. What is the amount of A's deductible loss?

  a. $30,000.
  b. $20,000.
  c. $15,000.
  d. $10,000.

The correct answer is (c). *(SPE 987 II-81)*
REQUIRED: The amount of a partner's deductible loss.
DISCUSSION: The amount of loss which may be deducted is limited to the partner's adjusted basis in the partnership interest [Sec. 704(d)]. Under Sec. 752 temporary regulations issued in December 1989, A's basis includes recourse debt only in the amount which is his potential economic loss after considering all agreements among the partners. A's basis is, accordingly, $15,000 ($10,000 contribution + $5,000 share of liabilities) and this is his deductible loss.

87. The partners of Martin, Cynthia, and Libby share profits and losses in a ratio of 4:3:3, respectively. All three materially participate in the partnership's business. The tax basis of each partner as of December 31, 1991 was as follows:

Martin	$7,200
Cynthia	6,000
Libby	2,500

During 1991 the partnership incurred an operating loss of $15,000. The loss is not reflected in the tax basis figures shown above. As a result of this loss, Martin, Cynthia, and Libby should deduct, respectively, on their 1991 individual returns

  a. $6,000, $4,500, and $2,500.
  b. $6,000, $4,500, and $4,500.
  c. $7,000, $5,500, and $2,500.
  d. $7,100, $5,400, and $2,500.

The correct answer is (a). *(CPA 1177 Q-24)*
REQUIRED: The amount of each partner's deductible share of the partnership loss.
DISCUSSION: A partner may deduct his/her distributive share of loss as provided in the partnership agreement for a partnership in which (s)he actively participates. The amount of loss which may be deducted is limited, however, to the partner's adjusted basis in the partnership interest [Sec. 704(d)]. The deductible loss of each partner is

Martin: 40% x $15,000 = $6,000
Cynthia: 30% x $15,000 = $4,500
Libby: 30% x $15,000 = $4,500, but limited to adjusted basis of $2,500

Libby will be able to deduct her remaining $2,000 loss at the end of a subsequent year in which her adjusted basis in the partnership is increased.

88. In February 1988, C, B, and A started a partnership to purchase and lease a commercial office building. C actively participates in the partnership's business, but B and A are not involved. Income and losses are shared equally. Each partner invested $50,000 cash and the partnership borrowed $350,000 from the bank on a recourse basis, using the building as security in 1988. The debt remains outstanding. For 1988-1990, the partnership had losses totaling $105,000 and for 1991, a loss of $90,000. What is the amount that C may claim as a loss from the partnership on his 1991 income tax return, assuming he had no passive income.

  a. $25,000.
  b. $30,000
  c. $32,000.
  d. $45,000.

The correct answer is (a). *(SPE 990 II-81)*
REQUIRED: The amount of deductible loss to an active partner given adjusted basis and recourse debt.
DISCUSSION: A passive activity is defined as any activity which involves the conduct of a trade or business in which the taxpayer does not materially participate. The term passive activity includes any rental activity [Sec. 469(c)(2)]. Partner C is allocated one-third of 1991's $90,000 loss, or $30,000. The amount of loss is not limited by C's basis in the partnership which is $131,667 [$50,000 + (1/3 x $350,000 partnership debt) − (1/3 x $105,000 pre-1991 losses)] at the beginning of 1991. Since C actively participates in the activity, (s)he can deduct up to $25,000 of rental real estate activity losses [Sec. 469(i)]. The $25,000 amount is reduced by 50 cents for each dollar that his/her modified adjusted gross income (AGI) exceeds $100,000. The $25,000 loss offset is eliminated when AGI equals $150,000. Since we do not know Partner C's AGI, we can only presume that the entire $25,000 loss can be deducted.

Module 17.6: Partnership Losses

89. Ed and Bob each have 50% interest in Partnership Q. Both Ed's and the partnership returns are filed on a calendar year basis. For its 1990 tax year, Partnership Q had a $12,000 loss. Ed's adjusted basis in his partnership interest on 1/1/90 was $4,000. In 1991, Partnership Q had a profit of $8,000. Assuming there were no other adjustments to Ed's basis in the partnership in 1990 and 1991, what amount of partnership income (loss) should Ed show on his 1990 and 1991 individual income tax returns?

   a. $2,000 loss in 1990; $0 income or loss in 1991.
   b. $4,000 loss in 1990; $2,000 income in 1991.
   c. $4,000 loss in 1990; $4,000 income in 1991.
   d. $6,000 loss in 1990; $4,000 income in 1991.

The correct answer is (b). *(SPE 989 II-76)*
REQUIRED: The share of a partnership loss that may be deducted by a partner.
DISCUSSION: A partner's distributive share of partnership loss is allowed only to the extent of the adjusted basis of such partner's interest in the partnership at the end of the partnership's tax year [Sec. 704(d)]. Any remaining loss which cannot be deducted in the current year may be deducted in a subsequent year when the partner's partnership basis is increased.
   In 1990, Ed should report a $4,000 loss. There is a $6,000 (50% x $12,000) loss but his basis limits the loss to $4,000. The remaining $2,000 ($6,000 loss − $4,000 reported loss) loss may be deducted when his partnership basis is increased. In 1991, Ed's partnership basis is increased by $4,000 (50% x $8,000) profit, so he is entitled to report the remaining $2,000 loss from 1990. In 1991, Ed reports $2,000 ($4,000 income − $2,000 loss) of income.

90. The XYZ Partnership was formed on January 1, 1991 and incurred a $48,000 loss for the year ending December 31, 1991. Each of the three partners shares profits and losses equally. Mr. Y is a passive investor in the partnership. On January 1, 1991, Y contributed $6,000. Mr. Y contributed $10,000 more during 1991 and had draws of $2,500. The partnership has no portfolio income. Without regard to any partnership liabilities, what is Y's deductible loss from XYZ for 1991 if he had $9,500 in income from other passive investments?

   a. $9,500.
   b. $13,500.
   c. $16,000.
   d. $23,500.

The correct answer is (a). *(SPE 1078 II-79)*
REQUIRED: A partner's deductible loss from a passive partnership investment.
DISCUSSION: A partner may deduct his/her distributive share of partnership loss only to the extent of his/her adjusted basis in the partnership at the end of the year in which the loss occurs [Sec. 704(d)]. Further, loss from a passive investment can only offset income from passive investments (Sec. 469). Y's adjusted basis at year-end is

Adjusted basis 1/1/91	$ 6,000
Contributions during 1991	10,000
Distributions	(2,500)
Adjusted basis 12/31/91 before loss	**$13,500**

Y's distributable share of the loss is $16,000 (1/3 x $48,000). Y's allowable loss for 1991 is limited to his December 31, 1991 adjusted basis of $13,500. It is further limited to income from other passive investments of $9,500.

91. ABC is a calendar-year partnership with three partners, A, B, and C. Under the partnership agreement, profits and losses were to be shared in proportion to their contributions. As of January 1, this was 50% for A, 25% for B, and 25% for C. On July 1, B and C each contributed additional amounts so that their new profit and loss sharing ratios were 30% for A, 35% for B, and 35% for C. For the tax year ended December 31, the partnership had a loss of $2,000. This loss was sustained in substantially equal amounts over the course of the partnership's tax year. What is A's share of the partnership loss?

   a. $600.
   b. $800.
   c. $1,000.
   d. $1,600.

The correct answer is (b). *(SPE 984 II-66)*
REQUIRED: The share of partnership loss allocable to a partner when the profit/loss ratio changes during the year.
DISCUSSION: Under Sec. 704(a), a partner's distributive share of loss is determined by the partnership agreement. Furthermore, Sec. 706(d)(1) requires the partners' distributive shares to take into account their varying interests when there has been a change during the year.
   A's share of the partnership loss is 50% for 6 months and 30% for 6 months. Given that the $2,000 loss was incurred uniformly over the year, A's share of the loss is

$$(50\% \times \$1,000) + (30\% \times \$1,000) = \$800$$

Module 17.6: Partnership Losses

92. L, M, and N formed an equal general partnership in January 1991, each contributing $1,000 cash and each actively participating in the business. The partnership is engaged in real estate rental activities and uses the cash method of accounting. The partnership purchased real property for $100,000, paying $3,000 in cash and giving a $97,000 non-recourse note for which none of the partners is personally liable and which is not qualified real estate nonrecourse financing. The partnership incurred an operating loss of $15,000 for 1991. Each partner has adjusted gross income from other activities of approximately $75,000 and no other passive losses. What is each partner's deductible share of the loss?

a. $0.
b. $1,000.
c. $4,000.
d. $5,000.

93. In February 1986, A, B, and C started a partnership to purchase and lease a commercial office building. A actively participates in the partnership's business but B and C are not involved. Income and losses are shared equally. Each partner invested $100,000 cash and the partnership borrowed $700,000 from the bank on a recourse basis, using the building as security in 1986. For 1986-1990, the partnership had losses of $210,000 and for 1991, a loss of $180,000. What amount may B claim as a loss from the partnership on his 1991 income tax return, assuming he has no passive income?

a. $0.
b. $12,000.
c. $60,000.
d. $64,000.

The correct answer is (b). *(SPE 1082 II-61)*
REQUIRED: Each partner's share of a loss from a real estate rental activity, the assets for which were purchased with a nonrecourse note.
DISCUSSION: Under Sec. 465, each partner may deduct a loss only to the extent that (s)he is at risk with respect to the activity. Since the $97,000 note is nonrecourse, none of the partners has any risk with respect to it. Each partner is at risk with respect to only $1,000. Note that Sec. 465 applies at the partner level rather than at the partnership level.

Further, rental activity is generally passive. Passive losses must be netted at the partner level with other passive income and losses. Net passive losses from rental real estate activities may offset up to $25,000 of active or portfolio income for partners who actively participate in the rental activity if their AGI is not too large. Each partner can deduct his/her $1,000 passive loss from the rental real estate activity.

The correct answer is (a). *(SPE 986 II-76)*
REQUIRED: The amount of deductible loss from a passive activity given adjusted basis and recourse debt.
DISCUSSION: Each partner's basis in his partnership interest includes his cash investment plus his allocable share of recourse liabilities or $333,333 [$100,000 + (1/3 x $700,000)]. In 1986-1990, each partner's deductible loss was limited only by his basis (which is also his at-risk basis), so each partner could claim $70,000 in losses and had a $263,333 ($333,333 − $70,000) basis at the beginning of 1991. The passive loss rules generally limit deduction of passive losses to the amount of passive income [Sec. 469(a)]. The special phase-in rules of Sec. 469(m) have expired so none of the passive losses from pre-October 22, 1986 investments are deductible except under the general passive loss rules. For rental real estate activities in which a partner actively participates, up to $25,000 in loss may also be allowed under the passive loss rules. However, B does not actively participate in the partnership, so the $25,000 allowance is not available to him. He can deduct none of his allowable share of partnership losses.

Note that B's partnership basis is reduced by the full amount of losses even though only part is deductible because of the passive loss rules. The suspended losses can be deducted in a later year against passive income. Any loss remaining when the partnership terminates its interest in the building or when B terminates his investment in the partnership in a fully taxable transaction may be deducted by B in the year of the termination [Sec. 469(g)].

94. In February 1984, Mary contributed cash of $50,000 and Kay contributed land with an adjusted basis of $70,000 and a fair market value of $50,000 to form a partnership. All loss from precontribution decline in value of the land is allocated to Kay in the partnership agreement, with all other gain, loss, and income to be shared equally. In 1991, the land was sold for $36,000. Kay's share of the loss from the sale of land is

a. $34,000.
b. $27,000.
c. $17,000.
d. $7,000.

The correct answer is (b). *(Publisher)*
REQUIRED: A contributing partner's share of loss from the sale of property under an agreement to specially allocate precontribution loss.
DISCUSSION: For property contributed before March 31, 1984, Sec. 704(c)(2) allowed partners to specially allocate gain or loss with respect to property contributed to the partnership to take into account the variation between the basis of the property to the partnership and its fair market value at the time of contribution. This allocation is required by Sec. 704(c) for property contributed after March 31, 1984. Mary and Kay did this by allocating the $20,000 ($50,000 FMV – $70,000 basis) of precontribution decline in value. Upon the sale for $36,000, Kay's share of the loss is

Precontribution loss	$20,000
Postcontribution loss [50% x ($50,000 – $36,000)]	7,000
Total share of the loss	$27,000

95. The XYZ partnership is a cash-basis, calendar-year entity. During 1991, the partnership incurred $12,000 in interest expense evenly throughout the year, but the total interest expense was not paid until December 31, 1991. Otherwise, revenues equaled expenses, and XYZ reported a $12,000 loss for the 1991 tax year. Zorro became a 40% partner by making a $10,000 cash contribution on December 1, 1991. How much of the partnership loss can be allocated to him for 1991?

a. $0.
b. $400.
c. $4,800.
d. $10,000.

The correct answer is (b). *(Publisher)*
REQUIRED: The partnership loss that can be allocated to a partner who enters the partnership late in the tax year.
DISCUSSION: Under Sec. 706(d)(1), a partner's distributive share of any item of income, loss, deduction, or credit must take into account the varying interests of the partners during the year. Sec. 706(d)(2) requires cash-basis partnerships to allocate items such as interest to the days of the year to which they are applicable and to the partners based on their ownership interest each day. However, the allocation to partners may be done using a monthly convention for administrative ease.
Since Zorro is a 40% partner, he may be allocated 40% of the loss attributed to the period while a partner. Therefore, Zorro's distributive share of the partnership loss is $400 (40% x $12,000 x 1/12).

96. Your distributive share of partnership loss in the tax year in which the loss occurred is limited to the adjusted basis, before reduction by the current year's loss, of your partnership interest at the beginning of the partnership's tax year in which the loss occurred.

The correct answer is (F). *(SPE 986 II-26)*
DISCUSSION: A partner's distributive share of partnership loss is allowed only to the extent of the adjusted basis of such partner's interest in the partnership at the end (not beginning) of the partnership's tax year but before reduction for any losses of the current year [Sec. 704(d)].

97. A partner in a partnership which invests exclusively in real estate is allowed to use his allocable share of qualified nonrecourse financing as part of his basis for purposes of determining his at-risk loss limitation.

The correct answer is (T). *(SPE 1079 II-33)*
DISCUSSION: An increase in a partner's share of partnership liabilities is considered a contribution of money by the partner to the partnership [Sec. 752(a)]. Nonrecourse loans are treated the same under Sec. 752(c). Under Sec. 722, a partner's adjusted basis is increased by the amount of money contributed to the partnership. Therefore, a partner's basis for determining his/her loss limitation is also increased by his/her share of a nonrecourse loan. Sec. 465 "at risk" limitations do apply to real estate activities, but an investor is considered at risk for his share of qualified nonrecourse financing incurred to hold real property and secured by real property [Sec. 465(b)(6)].

17.7 Guaranteed Payments

98. Which of the following is most likely to qualify as a guaranteed payment under Sec. 707(c)?

a. A, B, and C decide to form a partnership to build an apartment building. A, an architect, draws up the plans for the building. The partnership pays him his usual fee.

b. A and B contribute cash to their partnership as a capital contribution and agree that the partnership will pay them an 8% annual payment for the use of their capital. The partnership pays the annual amount.

c. A, a partner in the AB partnership, lends $10,000 to the partnership on a 10% one-year secured note. Regular payments of interest are made.

d. B, a stockholder and a 30% partner, sells stock to the ABC partnership. The stock is sold for its fair market value.

The correct answer is (b). *(Publisher)*
REQUIRED: The transaction that qualifies as a guaranteed payment.
DISCUSSION: Under Sec. 707(c), guaranteed payments are payments to a partner for services or for the use of capital which are determined without regard to the income of the partnership. If the transaction is other than in the partner's capacity as a member of the partnership, however, it will be treated under Sec. 707(a) and not as a guaranteed payment. The payment of 8% for the use of the partners' capital is a guaranteed payment under Sec. 707(c) and does not fall under Sec. 707(a).
Answer (a) is incorrect because the architectural services rendered for an investment partnership would probably be performance by the partner other than in his/her capacity as a member of the partnership and would fall under Sec. 707(a) rather than Sec. 707(c). Answer (c) is incorrect because a bona fide loan is a transaction under Sec. 707(a) and is treated as occurring between a partnership and one who is not a partner. Answer (d) is incorrect because the sale of property between a partnership and a partner also falls under Sec. 707(a).

99. Nash and Ford are partners who share profits and losses equally. For the year ended December 31, 1991, the partnership had book income of $80,000, which included the following deductions:

Guaranteed salaries to partners:
Nash $35,000
Ford 25,000
Charitable contributions 5,000

What amount should be reported as ordinary income on the partnership return for 1991?

a. $75,000.
b. $85,000.
c. $140,000.
d. $145,000.

The correct answer is (b). *(CPA 1181 P-59)*
REQUIRED: The amount of the partnership's ordinary income.
DISCUSSION: If a payment is made to a partner for services rendered other than in his/her capacity as a partner, the payment is deductible by the partnership under Sec. 707(a). If a payment is made to a partner for services rendered in his/her capacity as a partner, the payment is deductible under Sec. 707(c) as a guaranteed payment provided the amount of the payment is not determined with regard to the income of the partnership. The question states that the payments to the partners are guaranteed payments under Sec. 707(c), and they are therefore deductible. Charitable contributions are not deductible by a partnership [Sec. 703(a)]. The partnership's ordinary income is computed by adding back the charitable contribution deduction to book income.

Book income	$80,000
Plus charitable contributions	5,000
Ordinary income	$85,000

100. Partnership K uses a fiscal year ending October 31 as its tax year. J, a calendar-year partner, received guaranteed payments of $5,000 on November 30, 1989, $15,000 on October 28, 1990, and $15,000 on November 30, 1991. J's distributive share of partnership income for the year ended October 31, 1990 was $75,000. How much income from the partnership must be included on J's 1990 income tax return?

a. $75,000.
b. $95,000.
c. $105,000.
d. $110,000.

The correct answer is (b). *(SPE 986 II-77)*
REQUIRED: The amount of a partner's income from a partnership given guaranteed payments.
DISCUSSION: Guaranteed payments are considered as made to a nonpartner, so they are deductible by the partnership [Sec. 707(c)]. The $75,000 of partnership income is therefore net of the guaranteed payments. A partner's share of partnership income is included in his/her tax year in which the partnership tax year ends. Guaranteed payments are included as income in the recipient's tax year which includes the end of the partnership tax year in which they were deducted. Therefore, the amount of partnership income included on J's return equals $95,000 ($5,000 + $15,000 + $75,000).

Module 17.7: Guaranteed Payments

101. Gilroy, a calendar-year taxpayer, is a long-time partner in the firm of Adams and Company which has a fiscal year ending June 30. The partnership agreement provides for Gilroy to receive 25% of the ordinary income of the partnership. Gilroy also receives a guaranteed payment of $1,000 monthly which is deductible by the partnership. The partnership reported ordinary income of $88,000 for the year ended June 30, 1990, and $132,000 for the year ended June 30, 1991. How much should Gilroy report on his 1990 return as total income from the partnership?

- a. $25,000.
- b. $30,500.
- c. $34,000.
- d. $39,500.

The correct answer is (c). *(CPA 1181 P-58)*
REQUIRED: A partner's income from a partnership including guaranteed payments.
DISCUSSION: In determining his/her income, each partner must take into account his/her distributive share of the partnership's income for the tax year of the partnership which ends within the partner's tax year [Sec. 706(a)]. This means Gilroy must include his share of the $88,000 June 30, 1990 income on his 1990 return. Since guaranteed payments are deductible by the partnership, they are separately included in income by the recipient partner. A partner includes guaranteed payments in income in his/her tax year which includes the end of the partnership tax year in which the guaranteed payments were deducted [Reg. 1.707-1(c)]; i.e., Gilroy includes the guaranteed payments made July 1989 through June 1990 in his 1990 income.

Distributive share of ordinary income (25% x $88,000)	$22,000
Guaranteed payments ($1,000 x 12 months)	12,000
Total 1990 income	$34,000

102. G and H each contributed $25,000 to a newly formed partnership. The partnership agreement provides that G is entitled to a fixed annual salary of $10,000 without regard to the income of the partnership for managing the business. Any profit or loss, after the deduction of G's salary, is to be shared equally between the two partners. The first year's operation resulted in a loss of $15,000 after G's salary was deducted. What amount of net income or loss from the partnership should G report on his individual income tax return assuming he is a material participant in the partnership's business?

- a. $10,000 income.
- b. $2,500 income.
- c. $(2,500) loss.
- d. $(7,500) loss.

The correct answer is (b). *(SPE 986 II-74)*
REQUIRED: The net income of a partner from a guaranteed payment and a partnership loss.
DISCUSSION: A fixed salary paid to a partner for managing the business which is determined without regard to the income of the partnership is a guaranteed payment under Sec. 707(c). Managing the business is a normal activity of a partner, so the payment is not treated under Sec. 707(a). It is deductible by the partnership provided it meets the normal requirements of a trade or business expense under Sec. 162(a). The recipient partner includes the guaranteed payment as ordinary income. G's share of the partnership loss is $7,500 (50% x $15,000). The $10,000 guaranteed payment income minus the $7,500 loss produces net income for G of $2,500. Since G is a material participant in the partnership's business, the passive loss rules do not apply. Note that both the guaranteed payment and the partnership loss should be separately reported, not netted.

103. Milo Denver and Buyhi Carrington are partners in the Denver-Carrington partnership. Under the terms of the partnership agreement, Milo is to receive 25% of all partnership income or loss plus a guaranteed payment of $80,000 per year. In the 1991 tax year, Denver-Carrington had $72,000 of ordinary income before any deduction for Milo's payment. What income (loss) will Milo report on his 1991 tax return assuming he materially participates in partnership activities?

- a. $18,000 partnership income; $80,000 guaranteed payment.
- b. $18,000 partnership income; $62,000 guaranteed payment.
- c. $80,000 guaranteed payment.
- d. $80,000 guaranteed payment; $2,000 partnership ordinary loss.

The correct answer is (d). *(Publisher)*
REQUIRED: The income from a partnership to be reported by a partner who receives a guaranteed payment.
DISCUSSION: The guaranteed payment is deductible by the partnership [Sec. 707(c)]. This leaves a partnership loss of $8,000 ($72,000 − $80,000). Since Milo's share is 25% of profits or losses, he will be treated as receiving 25% of the partnership ordinary loss of $8,000, or $2,000. Milo will report an $80,000 guaranteed payment and a $2,000 ordinary loss. Since Milo is a material participant in the partnership, his loss is not limited by the passive loss rules.

104. In the previous question, what will Buyhi Carrington report as his income (loss) from the partnership assuming he materially participates in the partnership business?

a. $0.
b. $54,000 ordinary income.
c. $10,000 ordinary income.
d. $6,000 partnership ordinary loss.

The correct answer is (d). *(Publisher)*
REQUIRED: The partner's income (loss) when a guaranteed payment to another partner causes a partnership loss.
DISCUSSION: The $80,000 payment to Milo is treated as a guaranteed payment, and it will cause an $8,000 loss to the partnership ($72,000 − $80,000). Since Milo is to receive 25% of the partnership income, Buyhi must receive 75% of the income or loss. This results in a $6,000 ordinary loss (75% × $8,000).

105. Steve manages the ABC partnership, a real estate partnership, in which he is also a partner. Steve receives 30% of all partnership income before guaranteed payments, but not less than $80,000. In 1991, the ABC partnership reports $200,000 of ordinary income. What is Steve's guaranteed payment?

a. $0.
b. $20,000.
c. $60,000.
d. $80,000.

The correct answer is (b). *(Publisher)*
REQUIRED: The partner's guaranteed payment.
DISCUSSION: Guaranteed payments are considered to be made to a nonpartner, so they are deductible by the partnership. Most guaranteed payments are in the form of a specific amount (e.g., a stated salary amount). Some guaranteed payments are in the form of a guaranteed minimum; that is, the partner is guaranteed a minimum amount from the partnership each year. In such a situation, the guaranteed payment is the excess of the partner's guaranteed minimum over the partner's distributive share. This is the situation that exists in this problem. Steve's 1991 guaranteed payment is $20,000 [$80,000 guaranteed minimum − ($200,000 × .30)] and is deductible by the partnership. If the guaranteed minimum were $60,000 or less, no guaranteed payment would exist in 1991.

106. Guaranteed payments made to a cash basis partner for organizing the partnership are deductible by the partnership in the year paid.

The correct answer is (F). *(SPE 989 II-26)*
DISCUSSION: If a payment is made to a partner for services rendered in his/her capacity as a partner, it is treated as a guaranteed payment and is deductible under Sec. 707(c) provided the payment is for services which would have been deductible if performed by an outsider. Section 709(a) disallows a deduction for any amounts paid or incurred to organize a partnership. Sec. 709(b) provides for capitalization of the expenses and amortization over a period of not less than 60 months. The guaranteed payment is not deductible by the partnership in the year the payment is made (Rev. Rul. 75-214).

107. Guaranteed payments made by a partnership to a partner for services or for the use of capital, to the extent they are figured without regard to the income of the partnership, are treated by the partnership in the same way as payments made to a person who is not a partner. This treatment only applies for the purposes of determining gross income and deductible business expenses.

The correct answer is (T). *(SPE 988 II-23)*
DISCUSSION: Guaranteed payments under Sec. 707(c) are not treated for all purposes as if they were payments to an outsider under Sec. 707(a). However, for purposes of determining gross income and business expenses, they are treated as if the partner were an outsider. They generate ordinary income to the recipient and represent either a deduction from ordinary income or a capitalized item to the partnership.

108. Helen, a calendar-year taxpayer, is a partner in a partnership that is on a fiscal year that ends January 31. Starting on February 1, 1991, Helen is entitled to a fixed monthly payment of $1,000 without regard to the income of the partnership. Helen should report the guaranteed payments of $11,000 on her 1991 federal tax return.

The correct answer is (F). *(SPE 990 II-27)*
DISCUSSION: Under Sec. 706(a), a partner must include guaranteed payments deducted in a partnership's taxable year ending within his/her taxable year. The $11,000 in guaranteed payments will be deducted by the partnership in its fiscal year ending January 31, 1992. Thus, Helen will include the payments on her 1992 individual income tax return.

109. Under the terms of a partnership agreement, Tom is entitled to a fixed annual payment of $10,000 without regard to the income of the partnership. Tom's distributive share of the partnership is 20%. The partnership has a $40,000 loss after deducting Tom's guaranteed payment. Tom must report the full amount of the guaranteed payment and separately take into account his share of the partnership loss.

The correct answer is (T). *(SPE 990 II-28)*
DISCUSSION: When computing taxable income, a partner must include his/her distributive share of partnership items for any partnership taxable year ending within his/her taxable year [Sec. 706(a)]. A partner must also include guaranteed payments deducted in a partnership's taxable year ending within his/her taxable year. Because guaranteed payments are considered made to a nonpartner, they are deductible by the partnership [Sec. 707(c)].

17.8 Adjustments to Basis in Partnership Interest

110. Mr. G and Mr. H do business as a partnership. They file partnership and individual returns on a calendar-year basis. The partnership had a loss of $12,000 in 1990 and a profit of $10,000 in 1991. Mr. G's distributive share of the loss in 1990 was $6,000 and his share of the profit in 1991 is $5,000. The adjusted basis of his partnership interest before the 1990 loss was $3,000. What is Mr. G's adjusted basis of his partnership interest at the end of 1991?

a. $0.
b. $2,000.
c. $3,000.
d. $5,000.

The correct answer is (b). *(SPE 984 II-84)*
REQUIRED: The adjusted basis in partnership interest given distributive shares of profit and loss.
DISCUSSION: At the end of the year in which a partner's basis is increased, (s)he is allowed a loss previously disallowed by the Sec. 704(d) basis limitation. Under Sec. 705(a), the adjusted basis of a partner's interest in a partnership is increased or decreased by his/her distributive share of partnership income or losses, respectively. In 1990, Mr. G can deduct only $3,000 of his $6,000 share of the partnership loss because of the basis limitation. After deducting this loss, Mr. G's adjusted basis is zero. In 1991 Mr. G's adjusted basis is increased by his $5,000 share of partnership income. He may also deduct the remaining $3,000 share of the 1990 partnership loss, leaving him with an adjusted basis of $2,000 ($0 + $5,000 − $3,000).

Whether the passive loss rules apply has no effect on basis. Basis is decreased by losses even if the losses are not currently deductible under the passive loss rules.

111. Hall and Haig are equal partners in the firm of Arosa Associates. On January 1, 1991 each partner's adjusted basis in Arosa was $40,000. During 1991 Arosa borrowed $60,000, for which Hall and Haig are personally liable. Arosa sustained an operating loss of $10,000 for the year ended December 31, 1991. The basis of each partner's interest in Arosa at December 31, 1991 is

a. $35,000.
b. $40,000.
c. $65,000.
d. $70,000.

The correct answer is (c). *(CPA 585 Q-57)*
REQUIRED: The adjusted basis of a partner's partnership interest.
DISCUSSION: The adjusted basis of a partner's interest is the original basis of such interest, increased by the partner's distributive share of the partnership's income and allocable portion of liabilities, and decreased by the partner's distributive share of the partnership's loss (Secs. 705 and 752). The bases of Hall's and Haig's interests would each be the same:

Basis on 1/1/91	$40,000
Increase in liabilities (50% x $60,000)	30,000
Share of partnership loss (50% x $10,000)	(5,000)
Basis on 12/31/91	$65,000

Module 17.8: Adjustments to Basis in Partnership Interest

112. Clark and Lewis share profits and losses of 60% and 40%, respectively. The tax basis of each partner's interest in the partnership as of December 31, 1990 was as follows:

| Clark | $24,000 |
| Lewis | $18,000 |

During 1991 the partnership had ordinary income of $50,000 and a long-term capital loss of $10,000 from the sale of securities. There were no distributions to the partners during 1991. What is the amount of Lewis's tax basis as of December 31, 1991?

a. $33,000.
b. $34,000.
c. $38,000.
d. $42,000.

The correct answer is (b). *(CPA 1180 P-60)*
REQUIRED: The tax basis of a partner's interest after a year of operation.
DISCUSSION: Sec. 705(a) provides that the adjusted basis of a partner's interest is the original basis, increased by the partner's distributive share of income of the partnership, and decreased by the partner's distributive share of losses and distributions received from the partnership. Lewis's tax basis is

Lewis's tax basis on 1/1/91	$18,000
Share of income (40% x $50,000)	20,000
Share of loss (40% x $10,000)	(4,000)
Lewis's tax basis on 12/31/91	$34,000

113. Arnold Money invested $20,000 for a one-third interest in capital and profits of a partnership. Subsequent to his investment, the partnership had taxable income of $30,000 and nontaxable income of $6,000, and Money withdrew $9,000. After this series of events, the tax basis of Money's interest in the partnership is

a. $11,000.
b. $20,000.
c. $21,000.
d. $23,000.

The correct answer (d). *(CPA 1172 P-7)*
REQUIRED: The tax basis of a partner's partnership interest.
DISCUSSION: Sec. 705(a) provides that a partner's adjusted basis is the original basis of the interest, increased by the partner's distributive share of partnership income (both taxable and nontaxable), and decreased by distributions from the partnership. Money's original basis is his contribution of $20,000 to the partnership (Sec. 722). Money's basis in the partnership is

Original basis	$20,000
Share of:	
Taxable income (1/3 x $30,000)	10,000
Nontaxable income (1/3 x $6,000)	2,000
Distributions	(9,000)
Tax basis after events	$23,000

114. In January 1991 Martin and Louis formed a partnership with each contributing $75,000 cash. The partnership agreement provided that Martin would receive a guaranteed salary of $20,000 and that partnership profits and losses (computed after deducting Martin's salary) would be shared equally. For the year ended December 31, 1991, the partnership's operations resulted in a loss of $18,000 after payment of Martin's salary. The partnership had no outstanding liabilities as of December 31, 1991. What is the amount of Martin's partnership basis as of December 31, 1991?

a. $46,000.
b. $66,000.
c. $76,000.
d. $86,000.

The correct answer is (b). *(CPA 1179 Q-23)*
REQUIRED: The adjusted basis of a partner's partnership interest.
DISCUSSION: Sec. 705(a) provides that the adjusted basis of a partner's interest is the original basis of such interest, increased by the partner's distributive share of partnership income, and decreased by the partner's share of partnership loss. Sec. 707(c) provides that guaranteed payments (determined without regard to partnership income) are considered as if made to a nonpartner for purposes of computing gross income and business expenses. This means the guaranteed salary paid to Martin is not considered a distribution and does not affect Martin's partnership basis. Martin's partnership basis is

Original basis	$75,000
Share of partnership loss (50% x $18,000)	(9,000)
Year-end basis	$66,000

Module 17.8: Adjustments to Basis in Partnership Interest

115. On January 1, 1991 John Pierce acquired a 10% general interest in the Saratoga partnership for a cash investment of $20,000. He does not participate in the partnership business. In 1991, the partnership reported an ordinary loss of $40,000, of which Pierce's distributive share was $4,000. On January 1, 1991 the partnership had no liabilities; however, during 1991 the partnership had the following transactions:

A $50,000 loan from the Second National Bank due June 30, 1992.

A $100,000 nonrecourse loan (secured by inventory) from the Union Finance Company due December 31, 1992.

The partners share the economic risk of loss from recourse liabilities equally. After allocation of the operating loss, what is the tax basis of Pierce's partnership interest at December 31, 1991?

a. $16,000.
b. $20,000.
c. $21,000.
d. $31,000.

The correct answer is (d). *(CPA 1181 P-60)*
REQUIRED: The adjusted basis of a partner's partnership interest.
DISCUSSION: The adjusted basis of a partner's interest is the original basis of such interest, increased by the partner's distributive share of the partnership's income and allocable portion of liabilities, and decreased by the partner's distributive share of the partnership's loss (Secs. 705 and 752). The basis of a partner's original partnership interest is the amount of any money contributed (Sec. 722). The basis of Pierce's interest is

Original basis	$20,000
Share of partnership loss	(4,000)
Increase in liabilities	
(10% x $50,000)	5,000
(10% x $100,000)	10,000
Year-end basis	$31,000

Note that the nonrecourse loan is included in basis (as a constructive contribution) under Sec. 752. For the purpose of the partners deducting their share of losses, it would not be considered an amount at risk under Sec. 465. Pierce has a sufficient amount at risk to deduct the $4,000 loss.

Since Pierce does not materially participate, his income or loss is passive. The $4,000 passive loss is deductible in 1991 only if Pierce has passive income from other sources. Whether the passive loss rules apply has no effect on basis. Basis is decreased by losses even if the losses are not currently deductible under the passive loss rules.

116. On January 1, 1991, the Hack Partnership was formed. Bill acquired a 20% interest in the partnership by contributing a computer system that had an adjusted basis to him of $15,000, and was subject to a $5,000 liability. During the year, the partnership paid off the entire $5,000 liability. The partnership reported ordinary income of $75,000 on its 1991 partnership return. What is the amount of Bill's basis in the partnership on December 31, 1991?

a. $35,000.
b. $30,000.
c. $25,000.
d. $20,000.

The correct answer is (c). *(SPE 989 II-81)*
REQUIRED: The basis of a partner's partnership interest.
DISCUSSION: Under Sec. 722, the basis of an interest in a partnership acquired by a contribution of property, including money, to the partnership is the adjusted basis of such property to the contributing partner. Under Sec. 752, increases in a partner's share of liabilities are treated as contributions and decreases in such liabilities are treated as distributions. Therefore, Bill's basis is

Original basis (adjusted basis)	$15,000
Liabilities assumed by partnership (80% x $5,000)	(4,000)
Decrease in liabilities (20% x $5,000)	(1,000)
Ordinary income (20% x $75,000)	15,000
Year-end basis	$25,000

117. The Salt and Pepper Partnership was formed in January 1991 when Salt and Pepper each contributed $10,000 cash and together began to operate a business as equal partners. Both work full-time in the partnership. The partnership borrowed $40,000 on a nonrecourse basis during 1991. There are no guarantees or loss limitation agreements. Operations in 1991 resulted in a $5,000 ordinary loss, $2,000 tax-exempt income, and an $800 charitable contribution. What is Salt's basis at the end of the 1991 tax year?

a. $8,100.
b. $27,500.
c. $28,100.
d. $28,500.

The correct answer is (c). *(Publisher)*
REQUIRED: A general partner's basis in a partnership after a year of operations.
DISCUSSION: A contributing partner receives an original basis in a partnership equal to the amount of money contributed. This basis is increased by the partner's share of both recourse and nonrecourse partnership debt under Sec. 752 because either debt is treated as a contribution of money by the partner. The basis of a partner's interest is further increased by both taxable and tax-exempt income under Sec. 705(a)(1), and decreased by partnership losses and nondeductible expenditures (such as charitable contributions) under Sec. 705(a)(2).

Original contribution	$10,000
Partnership liability (50% x $40,000)	20,000
Tax-exempt income (50% x $2,000)	1,000
Ordinary loss (50% x $5,000)	(2,500)
Charitable contribution (50% x $800)	(400)
Year-end basis	$28,100

118. A partnership has three general and two limited partners. Each of the limited partners contributed $5,000. The partnership liabilities are

Accounts payable	$20,000
Accrued expenses	25,000
Mortgage payable (nonrecourse - secured only by a partnership building with a basis of $150,000)	75,000
Nonrecourse notes payable incurred March 15, 1991 (personally guaranteed by general partners)	40,000

If all partners have equal shares of partnership income, loss, and minimum gain, what is each limited partner's share of the liabilities?

a. $5,000.
b. $10,000.
c. $12,500.
d. $15,000.

The correct answer is (d). *(SPE 1078 II-80)*
REQUIRED: The amount of each limited partner's share of liabilities.
DISCUSSION: A limited partner's share of liabilities may not exceed his/her obligation for additional contributions to the partnership, unless no partners have personal liability for a partnership liability. Then all partners (including limited) share the liability based first on their share of minimum gain, then their share of any Sec. 704(c) minimum gain, with the remainder shared based on their profit-sharing ratio [Temp. Reg. 1.752-1(a)]. But limited partners cannot share in nonrecourse debt guaranteed by a general partner after February 29, 1984. In this question, there is no minimum gain. Therefore, each limited partner's share of liabilities is limited to 20% of the nonrecourse mortgage (20% x $75,000 = $15,000), and none of the notes incurred March 15.

119. Mr. J had an adjusted basis of $10,000 in a partnership at the beginning of 1991. Both Mr. J and the partnership are calendar-year taxpayers. During 1991, J received $12,000 in guaranteed payments for services he performed. During the same year, Mr. J withdrew $4,000 in cash from the partnership and was relieved of a partnership liability of which his share amounted to $2,000. Partnership income for 1991 was zero. What is Mr. J's basis in the partnership should he sell his interest January 1, 1992?

a. $4,000.
b. $8,000.
c. $16,000.
d. $20,000.

The correct answer is (a). *(SPE 988 II-76)*
REQUIRED: The adjusted basis of a partner's partnership interest.
DISCUSSION: The adjusted basis of a partner's interest is the original basis of such interest, increased by the partner's distributive share of the partnership's income and allocable portion of liabilities, and decreased by the partner's distributive share of partnership loss and distributions (Secs. 705, 731, and 752). A guaranteed payment does not affect basis.

Beginning basis	$10,000
Cash distribution	(4,000)
Decrease in liabilities	(2,000)
Basis on 1/1/92	$4,000

Module 17.8: Adjustments to Basis in Partnership Interest

120. Partnership LIFE's profits and losses are shared equally among the four partners. The adjusted basis of Partner E's interest in the partnership on December 31, 1990 was $25,000. On January 2, 1991, Partner E withdrew $10,000 cash. The partnership reported $200,000 as ordinary income on its 1991 partnership return. In addition, $5,000 for qualified travel, meals, and entertainment was shown on a separate attachment to E's Schedule K-1 of Form 1065. Due to the limitation, $1,000 of the $5,000 is unallowable as a deduction. What is the amount of E's basis in the partnership on December 31, 1991?

a. $60,000.
b. $61,000.
c. $65,000.
d. $71,000.

The correct answer is (a). *(SPE 988 II-77)*
REQUIRED: The adjusted basis of a partner's partnership interest.
DISCUSSION: The adjusted basis of a partner's interest is the original basis of such interest, increased by the partner's distributive share of the partnership's income and allocable portion of liabilities, and decreased by the partner's distributive share of partnership loss and distributions (Secs. 705, 731, and 752). Partnership basis is also reduced by nondeductible expenses.

Beginning basis	$25,000
Ordinary income (25% x $200,000)	50,000
Cash distribution	(10,000)
Travel, meals, entertainment expense	(5,000)
Year-end basis	$60,000

121. A partner's share of partnership liabilities will be determined in accordance with the partner's ratio for sharing profits under the partnership agreement.

The correct answer is (F). *(SPE 1080 II-37)*
DISCUSSION: Partners share recourse liabilities based on their potential for economic loss (usually their ratio for sharing losses). Only nonrecourse liabilities in excess of minimum gain are shared based on the profit-sharing ratio.

122. Your adjusted basis for an interest in a partnership can be less than zero.

The correct answer is (F). *(SPE 1079 II-20)*
DISCUSSION: A partner's basis may not be decreased below zero [Secs. 705(a)(2) and 733]. Distributions in excess of a partner's basis result in gain to the partner.

123. A partner's basis in a partnership interest is increased by the partner's share of tax-exempt receipts of the partnership.

The correct answer is (T). *(SPE 1082 II-42)*
DISCUSSION: Sec. 705(a) provides the adjustments to a partner's basis for partnership operations. A partner's basis in a partnership interest is increased by the partner's share of tax-exempt income and is decreased by the partner's share of nondeductible expenditures.

124. The amount shown in the partnership books as a partner's capital account is the same as the basis of a partner's interest in the partnership.

The correct answer is (F). *(SPE 1077 I-89)*
DISCUSSION: The basis of a partner's interest in a partnership reflects the money and adjusted basis of any property contributed and includes the partner's share of liabilities. A partner's capital account, however, usually reflects the money and fair market value of property contributed and does not include liabilities. There is no requirement that the capital account and basis relate to each other.

17.9 Transactions Between the Partnership and a Partner

125. Sam owns a 55% interest in the capital and profits of the Gemini Partnership. This year he transferred property to the partnership. On the date of the transfer, the property had an adjusted basis to Sam of $26,300 and a fair market value of $25,000. What amount and type of loss, if any, can Sam recognize in his income tax return for the year in which the property was transferred to the partnership?

a. No gain or loss.
b. $650 capital loss.
c. $1,300 ordinary loss.
d. $1,300 capital loss.

The correct answer is (a). *(CPA 575 Q-18)*
REQUIRED: A partner's amount and type of loss on the transfer of property to a partnership.
DISCUSSION: Under Sec. 721(a), neither the partnership nor the partner recognizes any gain or loss on the contribution of property to the partnership. Nonrecognition is mandatory. However, if Sam sold the property to the partnership, he could recognize gain under Sec. 707(a) but could not recognize loss due to Sec. 707(b).

126. Sara Loy is a member of a four-person equal partnership. Sara is unrelated to the other partners. In 1991, Sara sold 100 shares of a listed stock to the partnership for the stock's fair market value of $20,000. Sara's basis for this stock, that was purchased in 1982, was $14,000. Sara's recognized gain on the sale of this stock was

a. $0.
b. $1,500.
c. $4,500.
d. $6,000.

The correct answer is (d). *(CPA 1187 Q-40)*
REQUIRED: A partner's recognized gain on the sale of stock to the partnership.
DISCUSSION: When a partner engages in a transaction with the partnership not in his/her capacity as a partner, the transaction is considered to occur between the partnership and a nonpartner [Sec. 707(a)]. Therefore, Sara may recognize a $6,000 long-term capital gain ($20,000 proceeds less $14,000 adjusted basis). Note that if Sara had owned more than 50% of the capital or profit interest of the partnership, a gain could still have been recognized, but a loss on a sale to the partnership could not be recognized [Sec. 707(b)(1)].

127. Mr. Jones owns an 80% interest in the capital and profits of the J and J partnership. On April 1, 1991, Mr. Jones bought a warehouse which had been used in the business from the partnership at the building's fair market value of $60,000. The partnership's adjusted basis was $85,000. For the year ended December 31, 1991, the partnership's net income was $105,000 after recording the $25,000 loss on the sale of the warehouse. What is Mr. Jones' distributive share of the partnership's ordinary income for 1991?

a. $64,000.
b. $84,000.
c. $96,000.
d. $104,000.

The correct answer is (d). *(SPE 1085 II-84)*
REQUIRED: An 80% partner's distributive share of ordinary income after purchasing partnership property at less than its basis.
DISCUSSION: Sec. 707(b)(1) provides that losses from sales or exchanges of property between a partnership and a partner owning more than 50% of the capital or profits interest may not be deducted. Consequently, the $25,000 loss on the sale of land to Jones must be added back to the partnership's net income of $105,000.

Partnership's net income	$105,000
Add back nondeductible loss	25,000
Partnership's ordinary income	$130,000
x	80%
Jones' distributive share	$104,000

128. On December 1, 1991, Alan Younger, a member of a three-man equal partnership, bought securities from the partnership for $27,000, their market value. The securities had been acquired by the partnership for $15,000 on August 1, 1991. By what amount will this transaction increase Younger's taxable income for 1991?

a. $0.
b. $1,600.
c. $4,000.
d. $12,000.

The correct answer is (c). *(CPA 1181 P-54)*
REQUIRED: The amount by which a sale by a partnership to a partner will increase the partner's taxable income.
DISCUSSION: The general rule under Sec. 707(a) is that when a partner engages in a transaction with the partnership other than in his/her capacity as a partner, the transaction is considered to occur between the partnership and a nonpartner. This means that the partnership would recognize a gain on the sale of securities. The partnership's gain is a short-term gain of $12,000 ($27,000 proceeds − $15,000 basis). The increase in Younger's taxable income as a result of his share of partnership income is $4,000 (1/3 x $12,000).

129. Kay Shea owns a 55% interest in the capital and profits of Admor Antiques, a partnership. In 1991, Kay sold an oriental lamp to Admor for $5,000. Kay bought this lamp in 1978 for her personal use at a cost of $1,000 and used it continuously in her home until she sold it to Admor. Admor purchased the lamp as inventory for sale to customers in the ordinary course of business. What is Kay's reportable gain in 1991 on the sale of the lamp to Admor?

a. $4,000 ordinary income.
b. $4,000 long-term capital gain.
c. $3,400 ordinary income.
d. $3,400 long-term capital gain.

The correct answer is (a). *(CPA 585 Q-59)*
REQUIRED: A partner's reportable gain from a sale of capital gain property to the partnership.
DISCUSSION: Under Sec. 707(b)(2), gains recognized on sales to or from a person who directly or indirectly owns more than a 50% interest in the partnership or between partnerships in which more than 50% is owned by the same persons, are treated as ordinary income if the property is not a capital asset in the hands of the buyer. Since the lamp will be sold as inventory by the partnership, Kay's reportable gain is $4,000 ordinary income ($5,000 proceeds − $1,000 basis).

130. Walter owned a 30% general partnership interest in the ABC partnership and a 60% general partnership interest in the WXY partnership. Under the terms of the partnership agreement, Walter receives 60% of the profits from each partnership. On April 15, 1991, ABC sold a building to WXY for $200,000. ABC's adjusted basis in the building at the time of the sale was $250,000. ABC will not be allowed to recognize any loss on the sale of the building to WXY.

The correct answer is (T). *(SPE 990 II-26)*
DISCUSSION: Sec. 707(b)(1) provides that losses are not deductible on sales or exchanges of property between a partnership and a partner owning more than a 50% interest in the capital or profits, or two partnerships in which the same person or persons own more than 50% of the capital or profits interests. Walter owns more than a 50% profits interest in both partnerships, so the partnership may not deduct the loss on the sale between the two partnerships.

131. A sale by one partnership to another (each having the same partners) at less than the selling partnership's adjusted basis results in no loss being recognized. If the acquiring partnership later sells the property at a gain, the gain will be taxable only to the extent it exceeds the unrecognized loss.

The correct answer is (T). *(SPE 1078 II-41)*
DISCUSSION: Sec. 707(b)(1) provides that losses from sales or exchanges of property between two partnerships in which the same persons own more than 50% of the capital or profit interest are not deductible. When the property is subsequently sold, any realized gain is recognized only to the extent that it exceeds the unrecognized loss.

Module 17.10: Current Distributions

132. A&B is a partnership that rents commercial office buildings. A and B are brothers. A buys one of the partnership buildings at fair market value and continues renting it. If the partnership has a gain on the sale, the gain is treated as ordinary income.

The correct answer is (T). *(SPE 986 II-28)*
DISCUSSION: When sale or exchange of property occurs between a partnership and a partner owning more than 50% of the capital or profit interest, and the property transferred is not a capital asset to the transferee, the gain is ordinary [Sec. 707(b)(2)]. Under the rules of constructive ownership, A owns 100% (A's 50% + B's 50%) of the partnership, and the building is an asset used in business operations. Thus, the gain on the sale is ordinary.

133. Mr. White, a 50% partner in the Red and White Partnership, loaned the partnership $10,000 on a secured basis with a market interest rate. The partnership can deduct only 50% of the interest paid to Mr. White.

The correct answer is (F). *(Publisher)*
DISCUSSION: A bona fide loan from a partner to a partnership is treated as occurring between a partnership and one who is not a partner under Sec. 707(a). All the interest paid to a partner on borrowed funds is deductible.

134. Nilla Wafer, an accountant, was paid $100 each month to prepare the books for the Wafer-Water Partnership in which Nilla held a 30% interest. The partnership will treat Nilla's $100 payment as a deductible expense.

The correct answer is (T). *(Publisher)*
DISCUSSION: Payments to a partner for services rendered to the partnership are generally deductible. The payment is treated as an ordinary expense under Sec. 707(a) and considered to occur between a partnership and a nonpartner if the services are not generally those performed by a partner. If they are customary partner services, the payment will be treated as a guaranteed payment under Sec. 707(c) and will still be deductible as long as the payment is not determined based on the income of the partnership.

17.10 Current Distributions

135. Hart's adjusted basis of his interest in a partnership was $30,000. He received a nonliquidating distribution of $24,000 cash plus a parcel of land with a fair market value and partnership basis of $9,000. Hart's basis for the land is

   a. $9,000.
   b. $6,000.
   c. $3,000.
   d. $0.

The correct answer is (b). *(CPA 590 Q-26)*
REQUIRED: A partner's basis in property distributed by a partnership.
DISCUSSION: Sec. 732(a) provides that the basis of property distributed to a partner (not in liquidation of his/her interest) is the property's adjusted basis to the partnership immediately before such distribution. This basis, however, cannot exceed the adjusted basis of the partner's interest in the partnership less any money received in the same distribution [Sec. 732(a)(2)]. Hart's basis in the land distributed is

Basis of partnership interest	$30,000
Less cash received	(24,000)
Basis in distributed property	$ 6,000

136. Marvel has an adjusted basis in a partnership interest of $25,000 before receiving a current distribution of $4,000 cash, inventory with an adjusted basis of $6,000 and a fair market value of $9,000, and land with a fair market value of $7,000 and an adjusted basis of $8,000. Sec. 751 does not apply. What is Marvel's basis in the partnership interest after the distribution?

   a. $25,000.
   b. $8,000.
   c. $7,000.
   d. $5,000.

The correct answer is (c). *(Publisher)*
REQUIRED: A partner's basis in the partnership after receiving a current distribution.
DISCUSSION: A partner's basis in a partnership is reduced by the amount of money and the basis to the partner of distributed property in a nonliquidating distribution (Sec. 733). The basis of property to the partner is determined under Sec. 732(a) as the adjusted basis to the partnership immediately before the distribution. Marvel's basis in the partnership after the distribution is

Beginning basis	$25,000
Less: Cash	(4,000)
Inventory	(6,000)
Land	(8,000)
Ending basis	$ 7,000

137. Mondy had an adjusted basis in his/her partnership interest of $39,000 before receiving a current distribution. In the current distribution (to which Sec. 751 does not apply) (s)he received the following:

	Basis	Fair Market Value
Cash	$3,000	$3,000
Inventory	15,000	17,000
Land 1	10,000	15,000
Land 2	20,000	25,000

What is his/her basis in each of the items received?

a. $3,000 cash; $15,000 inventory; $10,000 land 1; $20,000 land 2.
b. $3,000 cash; $12,000 inventory; $12,000 land 1; $12,000 land 2.
c. $3,000 cash; $15,000 inventory; $10,500 land 1; $10,500 land 2.
d. $3,000 cash; $15,000 inventory; $7,000 land 1; $14,000 land 2.

The correct answer is (d). *(Publisher)*
REQUIRED: A partner's basis in property received in a current distribution.
DISCUSSION: A partner's basis in a nonliquidating distribution is determined under Sec. 732(a) as the property's adjusted basis to the partnership immediately before the distribution. This transferred basis is not to exceed the adjusted basis of the partner's interest in the partnership reduced by any money distributed in the same transaction. If this limitation applies (i.e., if the partnership's basis in the property distributed is greater than the partner's basis in the partnership), Sec. 732(c) provides that the basis is allocated first to unrealized receivables and inventory items, and then to any other distributed properties in proportion to their adjusted bases to the partnership.

Mondy will have a $3,000 basis in the cash and a $15,000 basis in the inventory. This leaves $21,000 of basis to allocate to the two parcels of land ($39,000 beginning basis – $3,000 cash – $15,000 inventory). This $21,000 will be allocated to Land 1 and Land 2 in proportion to their adjusted bases to the partnership ($7,000 to Land 1 and $14,000 to Land 2).

138. Betty contributed land with a $6,000 basis and a $10,000 FMV to the ABC partnership in 1990. In 1991 the land was distributed to Sally, another partner in the partnership. At the time of the distribution the land had a $12,000 fair market value and Sally had a $30,000 basis for her partnership interest. What gain is recognized by the partnership on the distribution? What is Sally's basis for the distributed land?

	Gain Recognized	Basis for Land
a.	$0	$0
b.	$0	$6,000
c.	$4,000	$10,000
d.	$6,000	$12,000

The correct answer is (c). *(Publisher)*
REQUIRED: The partner's basis in, and the partnership's gain recognized on the distribution of land.
DISCUSSION: For property contributed to a partnership after October 3, 1989 that had a deferred precontribution gain or loss, the contributing partner must recognize the precontribution gain or loss when the property is distributed to any other partner within 5 years of its contribution [Sec. 704(c)(1)(B)]. The precontribution gain or loss that is recognized by the partnership and allocated to the contributing partner equals the remaining precontribution gain or loss which would have been allocated to the contributing partner if the property had instead been sold for its fair market value on the distribution date. The partnership recognizes a $4,000 gain ($10,000 FMV at contribution date – $6,000 adjusted basis). This gain is allocated to Betty. The partnership's $6,000 basis in the land is increased by the $4,000 gain recognized by the partnership. Sally takes a $10,000 basis for the land and reduces the basis of her partnership interest by a corresponding amount.

139. At a time when Nedra's basis in her partnership interest was $5,000, she received a current distribution of $6,000 cash, and land with an adjusted basis of $2,000 and a fair market value of $3,000. The partnership had no unrealized receivables or substantially appreciated inventory. What is the result of this distribution to Nedra?

a. $0 gain or loss, $0 basis in land, $(1,000) basis in partnership interest.
b. $3,000 capital gain, $2,000 basis in land, $0 basis in partnership interest.
c. $1,000 ordinary income, $2,000 basis in land, $0 basis in partnership interest.
d. $1,000 capital gain, $0 basis in land, $0 basis in partnership interest.

The correct answer is (d). *(Publisher)*
REQUIRED: The tax result of a current distribution to a partner.
DISCUSSION: Gain is not recognized to a partner on a distribution except to the extent that money distributed exceeds the partner's adjusted basis in the partnership interest. Since Nedra received $6,000 when she had a $5,000 basis in the partnership interest, she will recognize a $1,000 gain which is a capital gain under Sec. 741. The basis in the land is zero under Sec. 732(a)(2) since the basis of property received in a distribution may not exceed the partner's basis in the partnership interest less any money received in the distribution. Nedra's basis in the partnership interest after the distribution is zero because her basis was reduced by the money distributed to her (Sec. 733).

Module 17.10: Current Distributions

140. Dale's distributive share of income from the calendar-year partnership of Dale & Eck was $50,000 in 1990. On December 15, 1990, Dale, who is a cash-basis taxpayer, received a $27,000 distribution of the partnership's 1990 income, with the $23,000 balance paid to Dale in May 1991. In addition, Dale received a $10,000 interest-free loan from the partnership in 1990. This $10,000 is to be offset against Dale's share of 1991 partnership income. What total amount of partnership income is taxable to Dale in 1990?

 a. $27,000.
 b. $37,000.
 c. $50,000.
 d. $60,000.

The correct answer is (c). *(CPA 590 Q-24)*
REQUIRED: The total amount of partnership income taxable to a partner within his tax year.
DISCUSSION: Section 706(a) provides that the last day of the partnership's taxable year is the date used by the partners to report their distributive shares of the partnership's items of income, gain, loss, deduction, or credit and the guaranteed payment of salary or interest on capital received from the partnership. The $50,000 should be reported by Dale for 1990. The $10,000 interest-free loan is not considered income to the partner. It will be repaid in the next year but will not lower income in that year. The two distributions are tax-free since Dale has sufficient basis to cover the distributions.

141. The adjusted basis of Mr. E's partnership interest was $65,000. In a partial liquidation, Mr. E exchanged one-half of his interest for the following properties:

	Adjusted Basis	Fair Market Value
Cash	$60,000	$60,000
Inventory	15,000	20,000
Land	15,000	5,000
	$90,000	$85,000

The inventory was not substantially appreciated, nor did the partnership have any unrealized receivables. As a result of the partial liquidation, Mr. E's proportionate share of partnership liabilities also declined by one-half, or $10,000. The partnership had no other liabilities. What is Mr. E's total recognized gain or loss on the disposition?

	Capital Gain	Ordinary Income
a.	$30,000	$5,000
b.	$10,000	$0
c.	$5,000	$0
d.	$0	$0

The correct answer is (c). *(SPE 1083 II-86)*
REQUIRED: The recognized gain or loss on a distribution with no Sec. 751 assets.
DISCUSSION: Gain is recognized by a partner on a distribution only to the extent that money distributed exceeds the partner's adjusted basis in the partnership interest immediately before the distribution [Sec. 731(a)(1)]. The decrease of a partner's proportionate share of partnership liabilities is treated as a cash distribution. The result of the distribution is as follows:

Actual cash received	$60,000
Deemed cash (decrease in liability)	10,000
	$70,000
Less adjusted basis of partnership interest before the distribution	(65,000)
Recognized gain	$ 5,000

This gain is capital gain under Sec. 741. Note that all the remaining assets distributed will have a zero basis and Mr. E's remaining basis in the partnership interest is zero.

142. The M and M partnership made a current distribution to Mac, a partner owning 50% of the partnership, of land with a fair market value of $6,000 (adjusted basis of $4,000) and a building with a fair market value of $100,000 (adjusted basis $40,000). This distribution was proportionate with respect to unrealized receivables and substantially appreciated inventory. The building had Sec. 1250 recapture potential of $55,000. What is the tax effect of this distribution on M and M?

 a. No gain or loss.
 b. $7,000 capital; $55,000 ordinary income.
 c. $2,000 capital; $60,000 ordinary income.
 d. $62,000 capital gain.

The correct answer is (a). *(Publisher)*
REQUIRED: The tax effect to the partnership of a distribution of property with potential recapture.
DISCUSSION: A partnership recognizes no gain on a distribution to a partner of property (even if money is distributed [Sec. 731(b)]) when there is not a disproportionate distribution of unrealized receivables or substantially appreciated inventory. The potential recapture is also not recognized under Sec. 1250(d)(3) when no gain is recognized in a Sec. 731 distribution.

143. When various kinds of property are distributed by a partnership to a partner in a nonliquidating distribution, the basis of the partner's interest in the partnership must first be allocated to depreciable property, then to unrealized receivables. Any remaining basis is then allocated to any other property distributed.

The correct answer is (F). *(SPE 1078 II-43)*
DISCUSSION: Sec. 732(c) states that the basis of distributed properties is allocated first to any unrealized receivables (and inventory items), and then, to the extent of any remaining basis, to any other distributed properties in proportion to their adjusted bases to the partnership. There is no special allocation to depreciable property.

144. Ms. A's adjusted basis in AB Partnership on December 31, 1991, just prior to a nonliquidating distribution, is $10,000. If $11,000 in cash is distributed to A on December 31, 1991, in a nonliquidating distribution, A must include $1,000 in income on her 1991 tax return.

The correct answer is (T). *(SPE 1078 II-44)*
DISCUSSION: Sec. 731(a) provides that in a current distribution by a partnership to a partner, gain is recognized only to the extent that any money distributed exceeds the adjusted basis of the partner's interest in the partnership. Because the $11,000 cash distributed to A exceeded A's adjusted basis in the partnership interest by $1,000, A must include this amount in income in 1991.

145. Partnership V made a nonliquidating distribution to Partner A of $4,000 cash and real property with an adjusted basis to the partnership of $8,000. The fair market value of the real property distributed was $15,000. Partner A's adjusted basis in the partnership at the time of the distribution was $10,000. Partner A's adjusted basis in the distributed real property is $6,000.

The correct answer is (T). *(SPE 984 II-35)*
DISCUSSION: Sec. 732(a) provides that the basis of a nonliquidating property distribution to a partner is the adjusted basis to the partnership immediately before the distribution. This basis, however, may not exceed the adjusted basis of the partner's interest reduced by any money received in the same distribution. A's adjusted basis in the distributed real property is $6,000 ($10,000 adjusted basis in partnership interest − $4,000 cash received).

17.11 Liquidating Distributions and Retirement of Partners

146. The basis of property (other than money) distributed by a partnership to a partner, in complete liquidation of the partner's interest, shall be an amount equal to the

   a. Adjusted basis of such partner's interest in the partnership, increased by any money distributed in the same transaction.
   b. Adjusted basis of such partner's interest in the partnership, reduced by any money distributed in the same transaction.
   c. Fair market value of the property.
   d. Book value of the property.

The correct answer is (b). *(CPA 1186 Q-54)*
REQUIRED: The basis of property received in liquidation of a partnership interest.
DISCUSSION: In a liquidating distribution, a partner's basis for his/her partnership interest is reduced by the amount of money received [Sec. 732(b)]. Any remaining basis is then allocated to other property received.
Answer (a) is incorrect because a cash distribution reduces the partnership interest. Answers (c) and (d) are incorrect because the basis of distributed property is the adjusted basis of the partner's interest less any money received in the same transaction.

147. Ted King's adjusted basis for his interest in Troy Partnership was $24,000. In complete liquidation of his interest in Troy, King received cash of $4,000 and realty having a fair market value of $40,000. Troy's adjusted basis for this realty was $15,000. King's basis for the realty is

   a. $9,000.
   b. $15,000.
   c. $16,000.
   d. $20,000.

The correct answer is (d). *(CPA 585 Q-60)*
REQUIRED: The basis of property received in liquidation of a partnership interest.
DISCUSSION: In a liquidating distribution, a partner's basis for his/her partnership interest is reduced by the amount of money received [Sec. 732(b)]. Any remaining basis is then allocated to other property received. King's partnership interest basis of $24,000 is reduced by the $4,000 cash distributed. Accordingly, King's basis in the realty distributed is the remaining $20,000.

148. Ms. A's interest in Partnership D had an adjusted basis of $40,000. In complete liquidation of D, A received $20,000 cash, inventory items with a basis to D of $10,000, and land used in the partnership more than 1 year with an adjusted basis to D of $15,000 and a fair market value of $18,000. What is A's basis in the land received?

 a. $8,000.
 b. $10,000.
 c. $15,000.
 d. $18,000.

The correct answer is (b). *(SPE 986 II-80)*
REQUIRED: A partner's basis in property received in liquidation.
DISCUSSION: Under Sec. 732(b), the basis of property received by a partner in liquidation of his/her interest in the partnership is the adjusted basis of the partner's interest less any money received in the same distribution. The basis of distributed property is allocated first to inventory items and unrealized receivables up to the amount of the partnership's adjusted basis in these items, then to other distributed properties in proportion to their adjusted bases to the partnership [Sec. 732(c)].

A's adjusted basis in partnership interest	$40,000
Less cash received	(20,000)
Basis to be allocated	$20,000
Less basis allocated to inventory	(10,000)
Basis to be allocated to land	$10,000

149. The Choate, Hamm & Sloan partnership's balance sheet on a cash basis at September 30 of the current year was as follows:

Assets	Basis	Fair Market Value
Cash	$12,000	$ 12,000
Accounts receivable	0	48,000
Land	63,000	90,000
	$75,000	$150,000
Equities		
Notes payable	$30,000	$ 30,000
Choate, capital	15,000	40,000
Hamm, capital	15,000	40,000
Sloan, capital	15,000	40,000
	$75,000	$150,000

If Choate withdraws from the partnership under an agreement whereby he takes one-third of each of the three assets and assumes $10,000 of the notes payable, he should report

 a. $9,000 capital gain.
 b. $9,000 ordinary gain.
 c. $16,000 ordinary gain and $9,000 capital gain.
 d. No gain or loss.

The correct answer is (d). *(CPA 1172 P-9)*
REQUIRED: A partner's gain upon receiving a liquidating distribution from a partnership with unrealized receivables.
DISCUSSION: Under Sec. 731(a), a partner does not recognize gain except to the extent that money distributed exceeds the partner's adjusted basis in the partnership interest. Choate's basis in his partnership interest before the distribution was $25,000 ($15,000 in capital and $10,000 share of liabilities). Cash received was $4,000 (1/3 of $12,000), so he recognized no gain under Sec. 731(a). Gain can also be recognized under Sec. 751 when the partnership has unrealized receivables, but not in this case because Choate received a proportionate share of all partnership property.

There was no loss since the basis of property received exceeded his basis in his partnership interest. In any event, losses can only be recognized if no property other than cash, unrealized receivables, and inventory is received in a liquidating distribution [Sec. 731(a)(2)].

Module 17.11: Liquidating Distributions and Retirement of Partners

150. Sandy's interest in Beach Partnership has an adjusted basis of $120,000. In complete liquidation of her interest she received:

Cash	$40,000
Inventory items with an adjusted basis to Beach of	48,000
Automobile with an adjusted basis to Beach of	16,000
Land with an adjusted basis to Beach of	48,000

What is Sandy's basis in the car and land respectively?

- a. $12,000 and $36,000.
- b. $16,000 and $48,000.
- c. $8,000 and $24,000.
- d. $4,000 and $12,000.

The correct answer is (c). *(SPE 990 II-87)*
REQUIRED: The basis in properties received in liquidation of the partnership interest.
DISCUSSION: Sec. 732(b) provides that the basis of properties distributed by a partnership in a liquidating distribution to a partner is the adjusted basis of the partner's interest in the partnership less any money received in the same distribution. The basis of distributed property is allocated first to inventory items and unrealized receivables up to the amount of the partnership's adjusted basis in these items, then to other distributed properties in proportion to their adjusted bases to the partnership [Sec. 732(c)].

Sandy's adjusted basis in partnership interest	$120,000
Less cash received	(40,000)
Basis to be allocated	$ 80,000
Less basis allocated to inventory	(48,000)
Basis to be allocated to automobile and land	$ 32,000

The basis of the automobile is $8,000 [($16,000 ÷ $64,000) x $32,000]. The basis of the land is $24,000 [($48,000 ÷ $64,000) x $32,000].

151. John Albin is a retired partner of Brill & Crum, a personal service partnership. Albin has not rendered services to Brill & Crum since his retirement in 1984. Under the provisions of Albin's retirement agreement, Brill & Crum is obligated to pay Albin 10% of the partnership's net income each year. In compliance with this agreement, Brill & Crum paid Albin $25,000 in 1991. The partnership earned only ordinary income during 1991. How should Albin treat this $25,000?

- a. Not taxable.
- b. Ordinary income.
- c. Short-term capital gain.
- d. Long-term capital gain.

The correct answer is (b). *(CPA 583 Q-60)*
REQUIRED: The treatment of payments received under a partnership retirement agreement.
DISCUSSION: Payments to a retired partner that are determined by partnership income are distributive shares of partnership income regardless of the period over which they are paid [Sec. 736(a)(1)]. Thus, these payments are taxable to Albin as ordinary income since the partnership income was all ordinary income.

152. Mr. K owned a 50% interest in K&L partnership. It reports income on the accrual basis. On April 1, 1991, the partnership was dissolved and it distributed to K one-half of all partnership assets. The partnership had no liabilities. The following assets were distributed to K:

	Basis	Fair Market Value
Cash	$ 5,000	$ 5,000
Accounts receivable	10,000	10,000
Inventory	8,000	10,000
Land	20,000	50,000

K's basis in the partnership interest was $43,000. As of December 31, 1991, K had sold the inventory for $10,000 and collected all accounts receivable. What gain will K report in 1991?

- a. $2,000 capital gain.
- b. $2,000 ordinary income.
- c. $32,000 capital gain.
- d. $32,000 ordinary income.

The correct answer is (b). *(SPE 1079 II-7)*
REQUIRED: The gain recognized by a partner from partnership assets distributed in liquidation and later sold.
DISCUSSION: Under Sec. 731(a), a partner recognizes no gain when property is distributed by the partnership except to the extent that money distributed exceeds the partner's adjusted basis in the partnership. Since the cash received ($5,000) did not exceed K's basis in the partnership ($43,000), K recognizes no gain under Sec. 731(a). Gain can also be recognized under Sec. 751 when the partnership has substantially appreciated inventory, but not in this case since K received a proportionate share of all partnership property.

Under Sec. 732, the basis of property distributed is the partner's adjusted basis in the partnership interest less any money distributed ($43,000 − $5,000 = $38,000). This basis is first allocated to unrealized receivables and inventory items in an amount not to exceed the adjusted basis of such property to the partnership. K's basis in the inventory is $8,000, and he has a $2,000 gain when it is sold. This gain is ordinary under Sec. 735(a)(2) since the inventory was sold within 5 years of the distribution. K recognizes no gain on collection of $10,000 in accounts receivable since his basis in them is also $10,000.

Questions 153 and 154 are based on the following information. Mr. Bones, a one-third partner, had a $12,000 basis in his partnership interest. Mr. Bones withdrew from the ABC partnership on January 1, 1991 when the partnership had the following balance sheet:

Assets	Basis	FMV
Cash	$12,000	$12,000
Accounts receivable	0	30,000
Land	24,000	27,000
	$36,000	$69,000
Equities		
Accounts payable	$ 9,000	$ 9,000
Abbot, capital	9,000	20,000
Bones, capital	9,000	20,000
Costell, capital	9,000	20,000
	$36,000	$69,000

153. If Mr. Bones received $20,000 cash in a liquidating distribution, what will he report as his gain or loss?

    a. No gain or loss.

    b. $8,000 capital gain.

    c. $11,000 capital gain.

    d. $10,000 ordinary income; $1,000 capital gain.

The correct answer is (d). *(Publisher)*
    REQUIRED: A partner's gain or loss from a liquidating distribution.
    DISCUSSION: Payments made in liquidation of a retiring partner are considered a distribution under Sec. 736(b) to the extent the payments are made in exchange for the interest of the partner in the partnership property. The payments are considered made for the partnership property except for the amount paid for the unrealized receivables of $10,000 (1/3 x $30,000). This amount is treated as a guaranteed payment under Sec. 736(a) and is ordinary income to Mr. Bones.
    Mr. Bones is considered to have received a distribution of $10,000 cash plus $3,000 relief of liabilities (share of accounts payable). Under Sec. 731(a), he will have a capital gain of $1,000 ($13,000 proceeds − $12,000 basis).

154. What gain or loss will the ABC partnership recognize if Bones receives $5,000 cash and accounts receivable with a fair market value of $15,000 in a liquidating distribution?

    a. No gain or loss.

    b. $5,000 ordinary income.

    c. $556 capital gain.

    d. $15,000 ordinary income.

The correct answer is (b). *(Publisher)*
    REQUIRED: The gain or loss to the partnership when a partner receives more than his/her share of unrealized receivables in a liquidating distribution.
    DISCUSSION: If the accounts receivable are distributed, there is no Sec. 736(a) payment. Under Sec. 751(b), when more unrealized receivables are distributed to a partner than his/her share, the partnership is treated as having sold the amount of unrealized receivables in excess of the partner's share. The gain or loss on such a constructive sale is ordinary. Mr. Bones' share of accounts receivable was $10,000 (1/3 x $30,000). Therefore, he received $5,000 excess accounts receivable. These are treated as having been sold to Mr. Bones in exchange for other partnership property of which he did not receive his share. Since the accounts receivable had a zero basis, the partnership will have $5,000 ordinary income.

155. K&C, a boat dealership, distributed a cabin cruiser from its inventory (adjusted basis $25,000, fair market value $40,000) to Mr. C in complete liquidation of his partnership interest (adjusted basis $50,000). Mr. C used the cabin cruiser personally for 6 years, then sold it for $55,000. K&C's inventory is not substantially appreciated and it has no unrealized receivables. Which of the following is true?

   a. In the year of liquidation, Mr. C did not recognize a loss but was entitled to a $50,000 adjusted basis in the cabin cruiser.
   b. In the year of liquidation, Mr. C recognized a capital loss of $10,000.
   c. In the year of liquidation, K&C partnership recognized ordinary income of $15,000.
   d. In the year Mr. C sold his cabin cruiser, he recognized a capital gain of $30,000.

The correct answer is (d). *(SPE 1083 II-87)*
REQUIRED: The true statement about a partnership distribution of inventory in complete liquidation of a partner's interest.
DISCUSSION: Under Sec. 731(a)(2), a partner recognizes loss on a liquidation distribution if (s)he receives no assets other than cash, unrealized receivables, and inventory and if the basis of the assets received is less than his/her basis in the partnership. Therefore, C recognizes a loss of $25,000 ($50,000 − $25,000 basis in boat) on the liquidating distribution. Under Sec. 732, the basis of inventory distributed is the partnership's adjusted basis in the property. Therefore, Mr. C has a $25,000 adjusted basis in the cruiser and a gain of $30,000 on the sale ($55,000 − $25,000). Since the cruiser was sold more than 5 years after the distribution, the gain is capital gain [Sec. 735(a)(2)].
   Answers (a) and (b) are incorrect because C recognized a loss of $25,000 in the year of liquidation. Answer (c) is incorrect because the boat is not substantially appreciated inventory so Sec. 751 does not apply.

156. Mr. W, a calendar-year taxpayer, was a 10% partner in Partnership Z. Z uses a fiscal year ending June 30. Mr. W died on October 1, 1990. Z's taxable income for the fiscal years ending June 30, 1990 and June 30, 1991 was $60,000 and $120,000, respectively. What is the amount of partnership income and self-employment income that must be reported on W's final return?

	Partnership Income	Self-Employment Income
a.	$6,000	$9,000
b.	$6,000	$10,000
c.	$9,000	$6,000
d.	$9,000	$9,000

The correct answer is (b). *(SPE 1083 II-81)*
REQUIRED: The amount of partnership and self-employment income that must be reported in the year of a partner's death. This is a difficult question, but SPE candidates should be aware of it.
DISCUSSION: A partner's income includes his/her distributive share of partnership income for any taxable year of the partnership ending within or with the taxable year of the partner [Sec. 706(a)]. Sec. 706(c)(1) provides that the taxable year of a partnership with respect to a partner who dies does not close prior to the end of the partnership's normal tax year. Accordingly, Mr. W's final return will include only his share of income for the tax year ending June 30, 1990, or $6,000 ($60,000 x 10%).
   For purposes of computing self-employment income (for the self-employment FICA tax), the deceased partner's share of the partnership's ordinary income attributable to the period ending on the first day of the month following the partner's death must also be included. For this calculation, the partnership's income is treated as realized ratably over the partnership taxable year [Sec. 1402(f)]. Accordingly, Mr. W's final return must include self-employment income of $10,000 [$6,000 from the year ending June 30, 1990 plus $4,000 (4/12 x 10% x $120,000) from the year ended June 30, 1991].

157. David Beck and Walter Crocker were equal partners in the calendar-year partnership of Beck & Crocker. On July 1, 1990, Beck died. Beck's estate became the successor in interest and continued to share in Beck & Crocker's profits until Beck's entire partnership interest was liquidated on April 30, 1991. At what date was the partnership considered terminated for tax purposes?

   a. April 30, 1991.
   b. December 31, 1990.
   c. July 31, 1990.
   d. July 1, 1990.

The correct answer is (a). *(CPA 583 Q-57)*
REQUIRED: The date the partnership is considered terminated for tax purposes following a partner's death.
DISCUSSION: A partnership generally does not terminate for tax purposes on the death of a partner since the deceased partner's estate or successor in interest continues to share in partnership profits and losses (Sec. 708). The Beck & Crocker partnership terminated on April 30, 1991 because, when Beck's entire partnership interest was liquidated, the business ceased to be operated as a partnership.

Module 17.11: Liquidating Distributions and Retirement of Partners

158. For tax purposes, a retiring partner who receives retirement payments ceases to be regarded as a partner

    a. On the last day of the taxable year in which the partner retires.

    b. On the last day of the particular month in which the partner retires.

    c. The day on which the partner retires.

    d. Only after the partner's entire interest in the partnership is liquidated.

The correct answer is (d). *(CPA 1185 Q-60)*
REQUIRED: The date a retiring partner ceases to be recognized as a partner.
DISCUSSION: Sec. 736(b)(1) states that payments made in liquidation of the interest of a retiring partner are to be considered a distribution by the partnership. Accordingly, Sec. 706(c)(2)(A) provides that the taxable year of a partnership shall close with respect to a partner whose interest is liquidated. Therefore, a retiring partner remains a partner until his interest has been completely liquidated by partnership distributions.

159. A partner's adjusted basis in his partnership is $40,000. In complete liquidation of his interest he receives $15,000 in cash, inventory items having a basis to the partnership of $22,000, and a company automobile having an adjusted basis to the partnership of $6,000. The automobile also has a $6,000 basis in the hands of the partner.

The correct answer is (F). *(SPE 1077 I-78)*
DISCUSSION: The basis of property received in a liquidating distribution is determined under Sec. 732(b). The partner's adjusted basis in the partnership is first reduced by cash received, then allocated to inventory and unrealized receivables. Any remaining basis is allocated to other assets received. The basis of the automobile is

Adjusted basis in partnership	$40,000
Less cash received	(15,000)
Basis to be allocated	$25,000
Less basis allocated to inventory	(22,000)
Basis of automobile	$ 3,000

160. If the basis of a partner's partnership interest is more than the adjusted basis to the partnership of the unrealized receivables and inventory items distributed, and if no other property is distributed to which (s)he can apply his/her remaining basis, (s)he has an ordinary loss to the extent of the remaining basis of his/her partnership interest.

The correct answer is (F). *(SPE 1083 II-43)*
DISCUSSION: A loss is only recognized under Sec. 731(a)(2) in a liquidation of a partner's interest when the money and basis of unrealized receivables and inventory is less than the partner's partnership basis. Assuming this is a liquidating distribution, the loss is treated as coming from the sale of a capital asset and will generally be a capital loss.

161. Mr. W, a partner in a business consulting firm, received $25,000 as his share of accounts receivable in the firm's dissolution. The partnership used the cash method. If the accounts receivable are later collected, or if Mr. W sells them, the amount he receives will be ordinary income to him.

The correct answer is (T). *(SPE 984 II-39)*
DISCUSSION: Any gain on the sale of accounts receivable distributed by a partnership is treated as ordinary income [Sec. 735(a)]. The character of the income is unchanged by their character in the hands of the partner regardless of the length of time he holds them.

162. On June 15, 1991, Mr. Pill received, in complete liquidation of his partnership interest, land with a fair market value of $20,000 and an adjusted basis to the PK partnership of $16,000. PK purchased the land on March 14, 1979. Mr. Pill acquired his partnership interest on October 15, 1986. Mr. Pill's holding period for the land begins on June 15, 1991.

The correct answer is (F). *(Publisher)*
DISCUSSION: Under Sec. 735(b), a partner's holding period for property received in a distribution includes the partnership's holding period for the property. Since PK's holding period began on March 14, 1979, Mr. Pill's holding period is treated as beginning on that date.

163. Payments to a retiring partner in liquidation of an interest that are treated as distributive shares of partnership income or as guaranteed payments are subject to self-employment tax.

The correct answer is (T). *(SPE 989 II-29)*
DISCUSSION: General partners are treated as self-employed taxpayers. Each partner must report his/her share of partnership net earnings from self-employment. Net earnings from self-employment are the sum of the partner's distributive share of partnership income and guaranteed payments received by the partner from the partnership.

Module 17.11: Liquidating Distributions and Retirement of Partners

164. Payments in liquidation of a partner's entire interest, to the extent that they are made in exchange for the interest in partnership property, are treated as distributions to the partner. However, this treatment does not apply to payments made for unrealized receivables or goodwill in excess of its basis to the partnership, unless the partnership agreement provides for the payment of goodwill.

The correct answer is (T). *(SPE 1080 II-40)*
DISCUSSION: Sec. 736(b)(1) provides that to the extent payments made in liquidation of a partner's interest are made in exchange for the interest, they are considered a distribution by the partnership. Sec. 736(b)(2), however, provides that payments made in exchange for an interest in partnership property do not include amounts paid for unrealized receivables or goodwill of the partnership, unless the partnership agreement provides for a payment of goodwill.

165. If a partnership terminates its existence and the partners, as individuals, continue to make guaranteed installment payments to a previously retired partner, they are entitled to a capital loss in the year of payment in the amount of the total payments made by each.

The correct answer is (F). *(SPE 1083 II-42)*
DISCUSSION: Payments made in liquidation of a retiring partner's interest are considered guaranteed payments if determined without regard to the partnership income and are not paid for partnership property. As guaranteed payments, they are generally deductible by the partnership as ordinary business expenses [Sec. 707(c)]. If the partnership terminates and the former remaining partners continue to make guaranteed payments to the retired partner, they may deduct the payments under Sec. 162 (Rev. Rul. 75-154).

166. Mr. A received $35,000 in liquidation of his interest when he retired from Partnership Z. His adjusted basis in the partnership was $20,000 and the valuation placed on his partnership interest in an arm's-length agreement was $30,000. Mr. A should treat the $5,000 received in excess of the valuation as ordinary income.

The correct answer is (T). *(SPE 1085 II-33)*
DISCUSSION: Under Sec. 736(b)(1), payments made in complete liquidation of a partnership interest are considered distributions by the partnership only to the extent such payments are made in exchange for the interest of the partner in partnership property. Under Reg. 1.736-1(b)(1), payments for an interest in the partnership are those attributable to the value of the partner's interest in the partnership property. The $5,000 for unspecified purposes is a guaranteed payment under Sec. 736(a) and is ordinary income.

167. Partnership C&R had the following assets and no liabilities:

	Adjusted Basis	Fair Market Value
Cash	$ 20,000	$ 20,000
Accounts receivable	10,000	12,000
Trade notes receivable	9,000	8,000
Inventory	11,000	17,000
Land (Sec. 1231 property)	300,000	333,000
	$350,000	$390,000

Partnership C&R inventory items are substantially appreciated and would give rise to ordinary income if gain were recognized on a sale or liquidation of a partnership interest.

The correct answer is (F). *(SPE 1083 II-44)*
DISCUSSION: Inventory items of a partnership are considered to be substantially appreciated if their fair market value exceeds 120% of the adjusted basis of the property and 10% of the fair market value of all partnership property, other than money [Sec. 751(d)]. For this purpose, the term "inventory items" includes inventory and unrealized receivables. The fair market value of the receivables and inventory ($37,000) exceeds 120% of their basis of $30,000. However, the inventory items do not meet the 10% test [10% x ($390,000 FMV – $20,000 cash) = $37,000]. Therefore, the inventory is not substantially appreciated.

168. Partner A sells his entire partnership interest to the partnership for cash. The portion of the money that is attributable to A's share of the partnership's unrealized receivables qualifies for capital gain treatment.

The correct answer is (F). *(SPE 1082 II-45)*
DISCUSSION: A sale by a partner to a partnership is a liquidation. Money attributable to A's share of unrealized receivables is a Sec. 736(a) payment which will be taxed as a guaranteed payment or as a distributive share of partnership income.

17.12 Sale of a Partnership Interest

169. On December 31, 1991, the basis of Partner D's interest in BRBQ Partnership was $30,000, which included his $20,000 share of partnership liabilities for which he was liable. There were no unrealized receivables or substantially appreciated inventory items. D sold his interest in BRBQ for $20,000 cash and was relieved of his share of partnership liabilities. D had already been paid his share of BRBQ's income for 1991. What is the amount of D's gain or (loss)?

a. $20,000.
b. $10,000.
c. $(10,000).
d. $(20,000).

The correct answer is (b). *(SPE 990 II-88)*
REQUIRED: The amount of gain or loss on the sale of a partnership interest.
DISCUSSION: Because there were no unrealized receivables or substantially appreciated inventory, the sale of the interest in the partnership results in capital gain or loss (Sec. 741). The relief from partnership liabilities is treated as an amount realized on the sale [Sec. 752(d)]. Partner D's gain is

Proceeds ($20,000 cash + $20,000 liabilities relieved of)	$40,000
Less adjusted basis	(30,000)
Capital gain	$10,000

170. On August 1, 1991, George Hart, Jr. acquired a 25% interest in the Wilson, Hart, and Company partnership by gift from his father. The partnership interest had been acquired by a $50,000 cash investment by Hart, Sr. on July 1, 1967. The tax basis of Hart, Sr.'s partnership interest was $60,000 at the time of the gift. No gift tax was paid. Hart, Jr. sold the 25% partnership interest for $85,000 on December 17, 1991. What type and amount of gain should Hart, Jr. report on his 1991 tax return?

a. A long-term capital gain of $25,000.
b. A short-term capital gain of $25,000.
c. A long-term capital gain of $35,000.
d. A short-term capital gain of $35,000.

The correct answer is (a). *(CPA 1181 P-56)*
REQUIRED: The amount and type of gain on the sale of a partnership interest acquired by gift.
DISCUSSION: Under Sec. 1015, the basis of property acquired by gift is the same as the adjusted basis of the donor plus gift tax paid by the donor on the property's appreciation. Hart, Jr.'s basis was therefore $60,000 (adjusted basis of the donor at the time of the gift). Sec. 741 provides that the gain on the sale of a partnership interest is capital gain. Hart, Jr.'s gain is long-term since Sec. 1223(2) provides that if property has the same basis as it did in the hands of the previous owner, the holding period of the present owner includes the holding period of the previous owner. Note that this problem assumes there is no change in basis between August 1 and December 17, which would be unlikely. Under this assumption, Hart, Jr.'s gain is

Proceeds	$85,000
Less adjusted basis	(60,000)
Long-term capital gain	$25,000

171. On January 2, 1991, Harvey contributed $12,000 cash to Partnership K, a calendar year partnership, for a one-fifth interest. On February 1, 1991, the partnership borrowed $50,000 from a local bank. Neither Harvey, the other partners, nor the partnership has assumed personal liability for the debt. There is no minimum gain and the partners have no loss limitation agreements. The partnership has no other liabilities and has no unrealized receivables or substantially appreciated inventory items. On November 1, 1991, Harvey received a $15,000 cash distribution from the partnership. For 1991, K reported ordinary income of $60,000 and the partners reported their distributive shares on their individual income tax returns. On January 2, 1992, Harvey sold his interest in K for $20,000. What is the amount of Harvey's capital gain or (loss)?

a. $(1,000).
b. $1,000.
c. $11,000.
d. $13,000.

The correct answer is (c). *(SPE 989 II-85)*
REQUIRED: The capital gain or (loss) recognized on the sale of a partnership interest.
DISCUSSION: A partner's adjusted basis is increased by his/her distributive share of partnership income and decreased by cash distributions from the partnership. The nonrecourse liability is shared according to the profit ratio since there is no minimum gain. Harvey's adjusted basis at the time of sale is $19,000.

Adjusted basis at contribution of cash	$12,000
Plus: 20% of the partnership liabilities	10,000
Less cash distribution	(15,000)
Plus distributive income share (20% x $60,000)	12,000
Adjusted basis 1/2/92	$19,000

The capital gain is $11,000 and is calculated as follows:

Cash proceeds	$20,000
Relief from liabilities	10,000
Amount realized	$30,000
Less adjusted basis	(19,000)
Capital gain	$11,000

Module 17.12: Sale of a Partnership Interest

Questions 172 and 173 are based on the following. The personal service partnership of Allen, Baker & Carr had the following cash basis balance sheet at December 31, 1990:

Assets

	Adjusted Basis Per Books	Market Value
Cash	$102,000	$102,000
Unrealized accounts receivable	--	420,000
Totals	$102,000	$522,000

Liability and Capital

Note payable	$ 60,000	$ 60,000
Capital accounts:		
Allen	14,000	154,000
Baker	14,000	154,000
Carr	14,000	154,000
Totals	$102,000	$522,000

Carr, an equal partner, sold his partnership interest to Dole, an outsider, for $154,000 cash on January 1, 1991. In addition, Dole assumed Carr's share of the partnership's liability.

172. What was the total amount realized by Carr on the sale of his partnership interest?

a. $174,000.
b. $154,000.
c. $140,000.
d. $134,000.

The correct answer is (a). *(CPA 590 Q-22)*
REQUIRED: The amount realized on the sale of a partnership interest.
DISCUSSION: Cash received by the selling partner is included in the amount realized. Also, a selling partner's amount realized includes liabilities assumed by the buyer [Sec. 752(d)]. Therefore, Carr's amount realized is

Cash	$154,000
Liabilities assumed by the buyer (1/3 x $60,000)	20,000
Amount realized	$174,000

173. What amount of ordinary income should Carr report in his 1991 income tax return on the sale of his partnership interest?

a. $0.
b. $20,000.
c. $34,000.
d. $140,000.

The correct answer is (d). *(CPA 590 Q-23)*
REQUIRED: The amount of ordinary income to report on the sale of a partnership interest including Sec. 751 items.
DISCUSSION: Sec. 741 provides that a sale or exchange of an interest in a partnership results in capital gain or loss, except as otherwise provided by Sec. 751. Section 751 requires the amount of money attributable to unrealized receivables of the partnership to be treated as an amount realized from other than the sale of a capital asset. Consequently, the portion of the money attributable to Carr's share of the unrealized receivable will produce ordinary income.

Carr's ordinary income is $140,000 ($420,000 FMV of unrealized receivables times his 1/3 interest) for his share of unrealized receivables under Sec. 751. His basis in the unrealized receivables is the carryover basis he would have in the receivables if he had received them as a distribution from the partnership ($0). Accordingly, his ordinary income is $140,000.

174. Which of the following items is not considered a potential unrealized receivable?

a. Franchise.
b. Farm land.
c. Stock in a Domestic International Sales Corporation.
d. Accounts receivable -- accrual basis taxpayer.

The correct answer is (d). (SPE 1080 II-63)
REQUIRED: The item that is not considered a potential unrealized receivable.
DISCUSSION: The term "unrealized receivable" includes any right to payment not previously includable in income under the partnership's accounting method for goods (if noncapital property) or services [Sec. 751(c)]. Since an accrual-basis taxpayer recognizes income on accounts receivable when earned, they are not potential unrealized receivables.
Answers (a), (b), and (c) are incorrect because each is specifically listed in Sec. 751(c) as a potential unrealized receivable to the extent gain from their sale or exchange would be ordinary income.

175. Mr. Y sold his 30% interest in XYZ partnership in 1991. The partnership was formed in 1980 and it reports income on the accrual basis. Mr. Y's adjusted basis in his partnership interest was $32,700 and the partnership had no liabilities at the date of sale. The partnership had the following assets at the time Mr. Y sold his interest:

	Adjusted Basis	Fair Market Value
Cash	$ 20,000	$ 20,000
Accounts receivable of $10,000 less bad debt reserve of $1,000	0	9,000
Inventory	6,000	10,000
Machinery and equipment Less accumulated depreciation	12,000 (9,000)	6,000 0
Land	80,000	100,000
	$109,000	$145,000

Mr. Y sold his interest for $43,500. What is his gain or loss to be reported in 1991?

	Ordinary Income	Capital Gain
a.	$3,000	$7,800
b.	$4,000	$6,800
c.	$0	$10,800
d.	$4,800	$6,000

The correct answer is (d). (SPE 1079 II-72)
REQUIRED: The amount and character of gain on the sale of a partnership interest including Sec. 751 items.
DISCUSSION: Sec. 741 provides that gain or loss on the sale or exchange of a partnership interest is capital gain or loss. Under Sec. 751(a), gain attributable to unrealized receivables or substantially appreciated inventory is ordinary income. Unrealized receivables include any depreciation recapture. Inventory is appreciated if its fair market value exceeds 120% of its adjusted basis. It is substantial if its fair market value exceeds 10% of the fair market value of all partnership property except money [Sec. 751(d)]. There are three Sec. 751 assets whose basis and FMV are as follows:

	Basis	FMV
Receivables	$ 0	$ 9,000
Inventory	6,000	10,000
Recapture	0	3,000
	$6,000	$22,000

The $22,000 FMV exceeds 10% of $125,000 and $22,000 is also greater than 120% of the $6,000 basis. Y's payment for Sec. 751 assets totals 30% of the FMV of $6,600 and his basis for these assets is the basis he would have had if his 30% interest in each asset had been distributed to him or $1,800. He will recognize ordinary income of $4,800 ($6,600 − $1,800). The $36,900 ($43,500 − $6,600) remainder of his amount realized and the $30,900 ($32,700 − $1,800) remainder of his basis determine his $6,600 capital gain amount.

176. Mrs. C is a limited partner in ABC Partnership. The adjusted basis of her partnership interest at the end of the current year is zero. Mrs. C's share of the partnership liabilities is $15,000, and her share of the ordinary income potential in partnership depreciable property is $5,000. Mrs. C sold her partnership interest for $10,000 cash. What is the amount and character of Mrs. C's gain?

a. $20,000 capital gain.
b. $5,000 ordinary income and $15,000 capital gain.
c. $5,000 ordinary income and $20,000 capital gain.
d. $5,000 ordinary income and $25,000 capital gain.

The correct answer is (c). (SPE 988 II-80)
REQUIRED: The amount and character of gain on the sale of a partnership interest including Sec. 751 items.
DISCUSSION: Sec. 741 provides the general rule that capital gain or loss is recognized on the sale or exchange of a partnership interest. However, under Sec. 751(a), gain attributable to unrealized receivables or substantially appreciated inventory is ordinary income. Recapture potential is considered an unrealized receivable.

Total gain ($25,000 amount realized − $0 basis)	$25,000
Sec. 751 gain (ordinary) on receivables	(5,000)
Capital gain	$20,000

Module 17.12: Sale of a Partnership Interest

177. Marwick sold his 30% interest in the PM partnership to Moses for $90,000 when the PM partnership had the following balance sheet:

Assets	Basis	FMV
Cash	$ 50,000	$ 50,000
Inventory	105,000	110,000
Land	70,000	140,000
	$225,000	$300,000
Equities		
Marwick, capital	$ 67,500	$ 90,000
Plum, capital	157,500	210,000
	$225,000	$300,000

PM had a Sec. 754 election in effect at the time of sale. PM's basis in its assets with respect to Moses is

	Cash	Inventory	Land
a.	$15,000	$31,500	$21,000
b.	$15,000	$31,500	$42,000
c.	$15,000	$33,000	$21,000
d.	$15,000	$33,000	$42,000

The correct answer is (d). *(Publisher)*
REQUIRED: The basis of partnership assets with respect to a purchasing partner when a Sec. 754 election is in effect.
DISCUSSION: The basis of partnership property is not adjusted as the result of a transfer of a partnership interest unless the election under Sec. 754 is in effect. When the Sec. 754 election is in effect, a partnership increases the adjusted basis of the partnership property by the excess of the basis to the transferee partner of his/her interest in the partnership over his/her proportionate share of the adjusted basis of the partnership property [Sec. 743(b)].

PM's increase in basis is the difference between $90,000 and $67,500 (30% x $225,000), or $22,500. This is allocated under Sec. 755 to Sec. 1231 assets or other property on the basis of relative appreciation (Sec. 755). As shown below, the adjustment to inventory is $1,500, which increases its basis to $33,000 from $31,500. The increase in the land is $21,000, which increases its basis to $42,000 from $21,000.

New partner's basis in partnership	$90,000
Share of partnership property basis	(67,500)
Sec. 743(b) adjustment	$22,500
Sec. 755 allocation:	
Inventory ($5,000 ÷ $75,000 x $22,500)	$ 1,500
Land ($70,000 ÷ $75,000 x $22,500)	$21,000

178. Partners A, B, and C, were equal partners in the ABC partnership, a calendar-year partnership. On November 15, 1991, Partners A & B sold their interest to C and withdrew from partnership affairs. At what date was the partnership terminated for tax purposes?

 a. November 15, 1991.
 b. November 30, 1991.
 c. December 31, 1991.
 d. The partnership has not been terminated.

The correct answer is (a). *(SPE 990 II-55)*
REQUIRED: The date a partnership terminated for tax purposes.
DISCUSSION: Under Sec. 708(b)(1), a partnership terminates if no part of its business continues to be carried on by any of its partners in a partnership. The partnership terminated on November 15, 1991, the date on which A and B sold their interest to C. On that date, the business ceased to operate as a partnership because the operation of a partnership requires two or more partners.

179. A partnership is terminated for tax purposes

 a. Only when it has terminated under applicable local partnership law.
 b. When at least 50% of the total interest in partnership capital and profits changes hands by sale or exchange within 12 consecutive months.
 c. When the sale of partnership assets is made only to an outsider, and not to an existing partner.
 d. When the partnership return of income (Form 1065) ceases to be filed by the partnership.

The correct answer is (b). *(CPA 1185 Q-59)*
REQUIRED: The condition that terminates a partnership for tax purposes.
DISCUSSION: Under Sec. 708(b)(1), a partnership terminates for tax purposes only if (1) no part of any business, financial operation, or venture of the partnership continues to be carried on by its partners in a partnership, or (2) within a 12-month period there is a sale or exchange of 50% or more of the total interest in partnership capital and profits.

Answer (a) is incorrect because local law terminations result in tax terminations only if one of the two conditions above is met. Answer (c) is incorrect because a sale of 50% or more of the partnership's capital and profits to an existing partner will terminate the partnership. Answer (d) is incorrect because ceasing to file a return does not terminate a partnership.

180. In a sale or exchange of a partner's interest in a partnership, if the selling partner is relieved of any liabilities of the partnership, (s)he will include that amount in determining the amount realized for the interest in computing any gain or loss.

The correct answer is (T). *(SPE 990 II-29)*
DISCUSSION: In a sale or exchange of a partnership interest, liabilities are treated the same as in connection with the sale or exchange of other property [Sec. 752(d)]. Therefore, a selling partner's relief of liabilities is included in the amount realized.

181. Amounts received by a selling partner that are attributable to that partner's interest in unrealized receivables or substantially appreciated inventory items not held for more than 5 years result in ordinary income or loss.

The correct answer is (T). *(SPE 986 II-3)*
DISCUSSION: Sec. 751(a) provides that money or property received by a partner in exchange for his/her partnership interest attributable to unrealized receivables or substantially appreciated inventory is considered an amount realized from the sale or exchange of a non-capital asset, i.e., ordinary income. Note that this result holds true no matter how long the partnership has held property if the property is an unrealized receivable or substantially appreciated inventory.

182. An election under Sec. 754 to adjust the basis of partnership assets requires adjustments both for transfers of partnership interests and for distributions by the partnership.

The correct answer is (T). *(Publisher)*
DISCUSSION: If an election is in effect under Sec. 754, the basis of assets is required to be adjusted for both transfers of partnership interests under Sec. 743(b) and for distributions by the partnership under Sec. 734(b).

183. Once a Sec. 754 election is made, a partnership can revoke the election with the consent of all partners.

The correct answer is (F). *(Publisher)*
DISCUSSION: A Sec. 754 election may only be revoked with the approval of the district director for the Internal Revenue district in which the partnership return is required to be filed. An application setting forth the grounds on which the revocation is desired must be filed no later than 30 days after the close of the partnership taxable year in which the revocation is intended to take effect. It need only be signed by one partner [Reg. 1.754-1(c)].

17.13 Family Partnerships

184. A family partnership is one in which the members are closely related through blood or marriage. For federal income tax purposes, family members include all the following except:

a. Ancestors.
b. Spouses and lineal descendants.
c. Trusts for their benefit.
d. Brothers and sisters.

The correct answer is (d). *(SPE 990 II-53)*
REQUIRED: The relationship in a family partnership which is not considered a family member.
DISCUSSION: Under Sec. 704(e)(3), "the family of any individual shall include only his spouse, ancestors, and lineal descendants, and any trusts for the primary benefit of such persons." Brothers and sisters do not qualify under this definition.

185. Howard Harper has conducted his hardware store business as a sole proprietorship for 25 years. On May 1, 1991, he gave a one-fourth interest in this business to his son, Lanny. After the transfer of this one-fourth interest, under what circumstances would the business be considered a partnership for federal income tax purposes?

a. Under no circumstances.
b. Only if the son is a bona fide owner of the interest which was said to have been transferred to him.
c. Only if the son gives his father a promissory note for the value of the interest transferred to him.
d. Only if the son works in the hardware store.

The correct answer is (b). *(CPA 1174 P-15)*
REQUIRED: When a person who receives an interest in a business is recognized as a partner.
DISCUSSION: Sec. 704(e)(1) provides that a person is recognized as a partner for tax purposes, whether or not his/her interest was a gift from any other person, as long as (s)he owns a capital interest in a partnership in which capital is a material income-producing factor. If the son is a bona fide owner of the interest, he will be recognized as a partner and the business will be considered a partnership.
Answer (a) is incorrect because the recipient of a gift of a business interest will be recognized as a partner as long as (s)he is a bona fide owner. Answer (c) is incorrect because a partnership interest can be created by gift. Answer (d) is incorrect because a recipient of a partnership interest by gift must work in the partnership to be treated as a partner only if the partnership is a service partnership.

186. Rose ran her bookkeeping business as a sole proprietorship. Rose gave her daughter Ruby a 20% interest in the business when Ruby graduated from the Nearby Vocational School. Under what conditions will the business be considered a partnership for tax purposes?

　a.　Under no conditions.

　b.　Only if Ruby contributes 20% of the capital to the business.

　c.　Only if Ruby actively participates as a partner in the business.

　d.　Under all conditions since Rose made a completed gift.

The correct answer is (c). *(Publisher)*
REQUIRED: The conditions under which the gift of an interest will convert a service enterprise into a partnership.
DISCUSSION: There are no statutory provisions as to when a partner will be recognized in a service partnership. Under case law, all relevant factors must be considered, but active participation in a service partnership is a basic requirement.

Answer (a) is incorrect because a partner can acquire an interest in a partnership by gift. Answer (b) is incorrect because there is no requirement that capital be contributed to the business for a partner to be recognized. Answer (d) is incorrect because the partners must intend and act as partners for a partnership to exist; the legal completion of a gift is not sufficient.

187. Andrew gave his children, Tom and Theresa, each a 20% interest in his manufacturing company. Tom, age 17, is still a minor but has worked in the business since he was 12 and has developed significant management skills. Theresa, age 22, attends college in another state and is not interested in the business. Andrew gave her 20% of the interest in the partnership but, under the terms of the gift, Theresa cannot sell or pledge her interest without her father's written approval. Which of the children, if any, is in partnership with Andrew?

　a.　Neither child is a partner.

　b.　Only Theresa is a partner because Tom, as a minor, cannot be a partner.

　c.　Only Tom is a partner because Theresa has a restricted right to dispose of her interest.

　d.　Both Tom and Theresa are partners.

The correct answer is (c). *(Publisher)*
REQUIRED: The child who will be recognized as a partner after receiving the gift of interest in a manufacturing concern.
DISCUSSION: Sec. 704(e)(1) provides that a person will be recognized as a partner if (s)he owns a capital interest in a partnership in which capital is a material income-producing factor, whether or not such interest was derived by purchase or gift from any other person. Reg. 1.704-1(e) discusses factors which are to be considered in determining whether the donee of a gift has actually acquired ownership of a capital interest in a partnership.

A minor child is generally not recognized as a partner if the interest is not held in trust, except when the child is shown to be competent to manage his/her own property and participate in the partnership activities. Tom should therefore be recognized as a partner. Retained control by the donor of the interest which (s)he has purported to transfer causes the donor to be treated as the continuing owner of the interest. Consequently, Andrew is considered as remaining the substantial owner of Theresa's interest.

188. Mr. B sold 75% of his business to his son A. The resulting partnership had a profit of $60,000. Capital is a material income-producing factor. The father performed services worth $30,000, which was reasonable compensation, and the son performed no services. What is the maximum amount of income A can report from the partnership for the year?

　a.　$7,500.

　b.　$15,000.

　c.　$22,500.

　d.　$45,000.

The correct answer is (c). *(SPE 989 II-78)*
REQUIRED: The donee's distributive share of partnership income when the donor performed services.
DISCUSSION: Under Sec. 704(e)(2), the distributive shares of partnership income of the donor and donee must include a reasonable allowance for services rendered. For this purpose, sales between family members are treated as if a gift was made when allocating income. The balance of income considered attributable to partnership capital must be allocated between the partners in accordance with their respective interests in partnership capital.

Partnership income	$60,000
Less value of B's services	(30,000)
Income to be allocated according to capital interests	$30,000
	× 75%
A's distributive share	$22,500

Module 17.13: Family Partnerships

189. On January 2, 1991, Mrs. W sold 50% of her business to her daughter Leigh. The resulting partnership had a profit of $100,000 for the tax year and capital is a material income-producing factor. Mrs. W performed services for which $40,000 was reasonable compensation. Leigh performed no services. What is the maximum amount of income Leigh can report from the partnership in 1991?

a. $20,000.
b. $30,000.
c. $40,000.
d. $50,000.

The correct answer is (b). *(SPE 990 II-82)*
REQUIRED: The distributive share of partnership income of a family member who purchased his interest.
DISCUSSION: Sec. 704(e)(2) requires that the distributive share of partnership income of a donee must take into account a reasonable allowance for services rendered by the donor. For this purpose, an interest purchased by a family member from another is considered a gift from the seller [Sec. 704(e)(3)]. Therefore, the value of the mother's services must be taken into account in computing the distributive shares as if the mother had given the daughter her interest. The balance of partnership income must be allocated according to their capital interests. Leigh's share is

Partnership income	$100,000
Less value of mother's services	(40,000)
Income to be allocated according to capital interests	$ 60,000
	x 50%
Leigh's share of partnership income	$ 30,000

190. Elizabeth Moore owned a 50% interest in a partnership in which capital is a material income-producing factor. Effective January 1, 1991, pursuant to a model custodian act, she gave 10% of her interest to her minor nephew and 20% of her interest to her minor niece. The custodian is Mrs. Moore's brother, who is the father of the children. The nephew's distributive share of income is used to satisfy part of his father's support obligation, while the niece's share is deposited in her own savings account. Assuming the partnership income for 1991 is $10,000, Mrs. Moore's original 50% distributive share should be included in the respective gross incomes of

a. Mrs. Moore as $4,000 and her niece as $1,000.
b. Mrs. Moore as $3,500 and her brother as $1,500.
c. Mrs. Moore as $3,500, her niece as $1,000, and her brother as $500.
d. Mrs. Moore as $3,500, her niece as $1,000, and her nephew as $500.

The correct answer is (c). *(CPA 574 Q-17)*
REQUIRED: The amount of partnership income which should be included in each person's gross income.
DISCUSSION: A person is recognized as a partner for income tax purposes if (s)he owns a capital interest in a partnership in which capital is a material income-producing factor, whether such interest was derived by purchase or gift [Sec. 704(e)(1)]. The niece and nephew are considered partners since a gift to a minor under a model custodian act generally makes the minor a bona fide owner. However, when the income of a trust is used to satisfy the trustee's obligation of support (the custodian is a trustee), the income so used is taxed to the trustee [Sec. 678(c)]. Since the nephew's distributive share was used to satisfy the support obligation of his father (who is the custodian), it is included in his father's gross income. The amounts to be included in each person's gross income are

Mrs. Moore (35% x $10,000)	$3,500
Niece (10% x $10,000)	1,000
Mrs. Moore's brother (5% x $10,000)	500

191. Partnership G is a family partnership, with Mr. and Mrs. G each owning 30% and their four children each owning 10%. Capital is a material income-producing factor in the partnership, and both Mr. and Mrs. G are active in the business. The children, who are full-time students, acquired their interests in a bona fide gift transaction by Mr. and Mrs. G. There are no limits on the amount that may be allocated to the children as their distributive share of partnership income.

The correct answer is (F). *(SPE 984 II-31)*
DISCUSSION: A person is recognized as a partner for tax purposes if (s)he owns a capital interest in a partnership in which capital is a material income-producing factor, whether such interest was derived by purchase or gift [Sec. 704(e)(1)]. Sec. 704(e)(2), however, requires that the distributive share of partnership income of a donee take into account a reasonable allowance for services rendered by the donor.

Module 17.14: Filing Requirements and Tax Audit Procedures

192. For a family member to be recognized as a partner in a partnership where capital is not a material income-producing factor, the family member must contribute substantial or vital services to the partnership.

The correct answer is (T). *(SPE 988 II-22)*
DISCUSSION: To be recognized as a partner in a service partnership (or when capital is not a material income-producing factor), it must be shown that the parties, in good faith and with a business purpose, intended to act together as a partnership. This is readily shown by a family member contributing substantial or vital services, but all facts and circumstances will be considered to ascertain the essential intent to act together as partners.
For the IRS Enrollment Exam, this question is true since the IRS relies on the substantial or vital services test, but case law has held otherwise if other facts show the intent to form a partnership.

193. For a family member to be recognized as a partner in a partnership where capital is a material income-producing factor, they must acquire their capital interest in a bona fide transaction (even if by gift or purchase from another family member), actually own the partnership interest, and actually have control over the interest.

The correct answer is (T). *(SPE 990 II-25)*
DISCUSSION: Under Sec. 704(e)(1), a person shall be recognized as a partner for purposes of this subtitle if he owns a capital interest in a partnership in which capital is a material income-producing factor, whether or not such interest was derived by purchase or gift from any other person.

17.14 Filing Requirements and Tax Audit Procedures

194. The ABC Partnership, consisting of 20 partners, timely filed its 1990 partnership return on April 15, 1991, but failed to include all the necessary information on the return. On October 8, 1991, it provided the required information but was unable to show reasonable cause for the omission. What is the amount of the penalty to be assessed against the partnership?

   a. $50.
   b. $250.
   c. $350.
   d. $5,000.

The correct answer is (d). *(SPE 1085 II-80)*
REQUIRED: The amount of penalty for failure to provide necessary information on a partnership return.
DISCUSSION: Under Sec. 6698, the penalty for failing to file a complete partnership return is $50 per month (or part of a month) that the partnership return is late or incomplete, up to a maximum of 5 months, times the number of persons who were partners at any time during the tax year. The penalty in this case is $5,000 ($50 per month x 5 months x 20 partners).

195. A fiscal year partnership must file its partnership return on or before the 15th day of the fourth month following the close of the fiscal year, except when that day is a Saturday, Sunday, or legal holiday.

The correct answer is (T). *(SPE 1079 II-43)*
DISCUSSION: Sec. 6072 provides that a partnership must file its return on or before the 15th day of the fourth month following the close of the partnership's taxable year. When that day is a Saturday or legal holiday, Sec. 7503 provides that the time for performance is extended to the next succeeding day which is not a Saturday, Sunday, or legal holiday.

196. Form 1065 (Partnership Return) is required to be filed by the same dates as Forms W-2 and W-3 since it is an information form.

The correct answer is (F). *(SPE 1078 II-36)*
DISCUSSION: Forms W-2 and W-3 must be filed on or before the last day of February following the calendar year [Reg. 31.6071(a)-1(a)(3)(ii)]. Partnership returns must be filed by the 15th day of the fourth month following the close of the partnership's taxable year (Sec. 6072).

197. All partners are required to sign a partnership return.

The correct answer is (F). *(SPE 1078 II-37)*
DISCUSSION: Sec. 6063 provides that a partnership return may be signed by any one of the partners. The signature of a partner on the return is considered evidence that such partner is authorized to sign the return.

198. D, N, and S formed a partnership on December 1, 1991. The partnership is on a calendar-year basis. The agreement calls for each of the partners to put up one-third of the capital required to buy a business by January 15, 1992. No other expenses are incurred. No partnership return is required for 1991.

The correct answer is (T). *(SPE 990 II-20)*
DISCUSSION: For purposes of filing a partnership return, an unincorporated organization will not be considered, within the meaning of Sec. 761(a), to carry on a business, financial operation, or venture as a partnership before the first taxable year in which such organization receives income or incurs any expenditures treated as deductions for federal income tax purposes [Reg. 1.6031-1(a)(1)]. A partnership tax return is not required for the new partnership in 1991 since it apparently did not have any income or expense before 1992. If the business is acquired in 1992, the partnership will have to commence filing partnership tax returns.

199. For partnership tax years beginning after September 3, 1982, each partner is required either to treat items on his/her return consistently with the treatment on the partnership return or to file a statement with his/her return identifying the inconsistency.

The correct answer is (T). *(Publisher)*
DISCUSSION: Under Sec. 6222, a partner is required to treat a partnership item on his/her own return in a manner consistent with the partnership return. This requirement does not apply if the partner files a statement identifying the inconsistency. Sec. 6222 does not apply to partnerships with 10 or fewer partners, each of whom is a natural person (other than a nonresident alien) or estate [Sec. 6231(a)(1)(B)].

200. Since a partnership is not a taxpaying entity, determination of partnership income, loss, deductions, and credits is made for each partner in the partnership.

The correct answer is (F). *(Publisher)*
DISCUSSION: Under Sec. 6221 through 6233, the determination of partnership income, loss, deductions, and credits is made at the partnership level for partnership tax years beginning after September 3, 1982. This does not apply to partnerships with 10 or fewer partners, each of whom is a natural person or an estate.

201. A "tax matters partner" (TMP) has the authority to reach a settlement with the IRS on behalf of any partner who has not clearly stated that (s)he will not be bound by the TMP's settlement.

The correct answer is (T). *(Publisher)*
DISCUSSION: Under Sec. 6224 in an administrative proceeding, a partner who has not filed a statement that the "tax matters partner" will not have authority to enter into a settlement agreement on behalf of such partner is bound by a settlement reached by the tax matters partner. This does not apply to partnerships with 10 or fewer partners, each of whom is a natural person or estate.

202. The IRS must offer every partner in a partnership settlement terms consistent with those offered any one partner in the partnership.

The correct answer is (T). *(Publisher)*
DISCUSSION: Sec. 6224(c)(2) requires the IRS, when it has entered into a settlement agreement with any partner with respect to partnership items, to offer consistent settlement terms to every other partner who so requests. This does not apply to partnerships with 10 or fewer partners, each of whom is a natural person or estate.

CHAPTER EIGHTEEN
CORPORATE FORMATIONS AND OPERATIONS

18.1	Entities Taxed as Corporations	(5 questions)	459
18.2	Organizational Expense	(10 questions)	460
18.3	Corporate Formations	(29 questions)	463
18.4	Assets Acquired for Stock	(9 questions)	472
18.5	Gifts to Corporations	(4 questions)	474
18.6	Business Deductions	(15 questions)	475
18.7	Bonds	(11 questions)	479
18.8	Dividends-Received Deduction	(13 questions)	482
18.9	Charitable Contributions Deduction	(16 questions)	486
18.10	C Corporation Net Operating Losses	(22 questions)	492
18.11	Capital Gains and Losses	(21 questions)	498
18.12	Treasury Stock	(3 questions)	503
18.13	Taxable Income and Tax Calculations	(21 questions)	504
18.14	Alternative Minimum Tax	(21 questions)	511
18.15	Return Filing and Payment Requirements	(17 questions)	516
18.16	Estimated Tax Payments	(10 questions)	520
18.17	Earnings and Profits	(10 questions)	522
18.18	Dividend Distributions to Shareholders	(28 questions)	525

18.1 Entities Taxed as Corporations

1. Several individuals form an unincorporated organization to conduct business and divide profits. The organization has provided for its continuing life, centralized management, limited the liability of its members, and allowed the free transfer of members' interests. How will this organization be taxed?

    a. As an unincorporated association.

    b. As a collapsible corporation.

    c. As a corporation.

    d. As a personal holding company.

The correct answer is (c). *(SPE 989 III-36)*
REQUIRED: The way in which the organization described will be taxed.
DISCUSSION: For the purpose of taxation, an organization may be classified as a corporation, partnership, or trust. The rules for determining these classifications are found in Reg. 301.7701-2, which provides that an organization will be classified as a corporation if it has more corporate characteristics than noncorporate characteristics. The significant corporate characteristics are continuity of life, centralized management, limited liability, and free transferability of interests. Since the organization in question exhibits more corporate characteristics than noncorporate, it will be taxed as a corporation.
Answer (a) is incorrect because an organization which is an unincorporated association is taxed as a corporation. Answer (b) is incorrect because a collapsible corporation as defined by Sec. 341 is a special form of corporation that results in the shareholder recognizing ordinary income when its stock is sold or exchanged. Answer (d) is incorrect because a personal holding company is a corporation and taxed as such, but is also subject to an additional penalty tax if income and stock ownership tests are satisfied.

2. Whether an unincorporated organization should be treated as a corporation for federal income tax purposes is determined by considering all of the following characteristics except:

    a. Continuity of life.

    b. Limited liability.

    c. Equity capital.

    d. Centralization of management.

The correct answer is (c). *(SPE 988 III-42)*
REQUIRED: The characteristic which is not considered when determining if an organization should be taxed as a corporation.
DISCUSSION: Reg. 301.7701-2 provides that an organization will be classified as a corporation if it has more corporate than noncorporate characteristics. The significant corporate characteristics are continuity of life, centralization of management, limited liability, and free transferability of interests. The amount of capital contributed is generally not relevant.

3. Which characteristic of a publicly-traded partnership is most likely to cause it to be taxed as a corporation in 1991?

    a. The partnership was formed after 1987.

    b. 90% of the partnership's gross income consists of interest, dividends, and real property rents.

    c. A market for the partnership interests is created by brokers and dealers.

    d. The partnership was in existence and publicly traded since 1986.

The correct answer is (a). *(Publisher)*
REQUIRED: When a publicly-traded partnership is most likely to be taxed as a corporation.
DISCUSSION: Sec. 7704 requires certain publicly-traded partnerships to be taxed as corporations after 1987. For existing partnerships that were publicly traded on December 17, 1987, the provision does not apply until after 1997. Therefore, if a partnership is formed after 1987, it is likely to be required to be taxed as a corporation.
Answer (b) is incorrect because if 90% of the partnership's gross income is qualifying income (e.g., interest, dividends, or property rents, etc.), then it will not be taxed as a corporation. Answer (c) is incorrect because if brokers or dealers create a market for the partnership interests, the partnership will be considered publicly traded. Answer (d) is incorrect because a partnership that was in existence and publicly traded on December 17, 1987 is "grandfathered" and will not be taxed as a corporation until after 1997 unless it adds a substantial new line of business.

4. A corporation, for federal income tax purposes, includes associations, joint stock companies, insurance companies, and trusts and partnerships that actually operate as associations or corporations.

The correct answer is (T). *(SPE 1083 III-1)*
DISCUSSION: The term "corporation" under federal tax law includes associations, joint stock companies, and life insurance companies [Sec. 7701(a)(3)]. Trusts and partnerships that operate as corporations (i.e., have more corporate than noncorporate characteristics) are also treated as corporations (Reg. 301.7701-2).

5. To be classified as a corporation for federal income tax purposes, a professional service organization must be both organized under a State Professional Association Act and operated as a corporation.

The correct answer is (F). *(SPE 986 III-2)*
DISCUSSION: Generally, if a professional service organization is organized under a State Professional Association Act and operated as a corporation, the IRS will recognize the corporate form. In the case of an individual who incorporates to provide his/her professional services, the IRS would require organization under a State Professional Association Act. The IRS's answer to this question was (T).
However, an organization may qualify as a corporation even if it fails to qualify under a recognized state statute if it satisfies the Reg. 301.7701-2 criteria. In fact, partnerships providing professional services have been held to be associations and taxed as corporations.

18.2 Organizational Expense

6. All of the following items can be amortized as a qualified organizational expense except:

    a. Fee paid to a state for incorporation.

    b. Expense of organizational meeting of directors.

    c. Expense for issuance or sale of stock.

    d. Organizational meetings of stockholders.

The correct answer is (c). *(SPE 990 III-35)*
REQUIRED: The item that is not considered an organizational expense.
DISCUSSION: An organizational expense must be capitalized unless an election is made under Sec. 248 to amortize it over 60 months or more. An organizational expenditure is one incurred in the creation of the corporation. Reg. 1.248-1(b)(3) specifically excludes expenditures connected with issuing or selling stock such as commissions, professional fees, and printing costs. These expenditures represent a reduction in the proceeds from the issuance of the stock and are not amortizable.
Answers (a), (b), and (d) are incorrect because each is an expenditure that will qualify for amortization over 60 months under Sec. 248.

Module 18.2: Organizational Expense

7. Corporation R was organized and began active business on January 4, 1991. R incurred the following expenses in connection with creating the business.

Professional fees for issuance of stock	$ 400
State incorporation fees	200
Printing cost for stock certificates	150
Broker's commissions on sale of stock	700
Legal fees for drafting the charter	600
Expense for temporary directors	500
Total	$2,550

The maximum amount of organizational expense which may be deducted by Corporation R on its 1991 income tax return would be:

   a. $260.

   b. $510.

   c. $1,700.

   d. $2,250.

8. During the first half of 1991, Corporation Z incurred $10,000 of qualifying organizational expenses. On July 1, 1991, Z became actively engaged in business. If an election is made, what is the maximum organizational expense deduction for the period ending December 31, 1991?

   a. $0.

   b. $1,000.

   c. $2,000.

   d. $2,500.

9. The Norton Manufacturing Corporation was organized on June 1, 1991. The following expenses were incurred and paid in the period from June to December 1991.

Fee paid to State of Kansas for incorporation	$ 100
Cost of organizational meetings	300
Printing cost of stock certificates	1,200
Legal fees related to drafting the corporate charter	2,000

Assuming the corporation elects to amortize organizational expenses over the shortest period allowed by law and that it is a calendar-year taxpayer, Norton's 1991 deduction for organizational expenditures is

   a. $720.

   b. $480.

   c. $420.

   d. $280.

The correct answer is (a). *(SPE 990 III-62)*
REQUIRED: The maximum amount of organizational expenses a corporation may deduct on its first tax return.
DISCUSSION: Sec. 248 allows a corporation to elect to amortize its organizational expenses over at least 60 months starting with the month in which it begins business. Organizational expenditures are those incurred incidental to the creation of the corporation. Reg. 1.248-1(b)(3) specifically excludes expenditures connected with issuing or selling stock and with transferring assets to the corporation. Corporation R's 1991 amortization deduction (assuming it is a calendar-year corporation) is

State incorporation fees	$ 200
Legal fees for drafting the charter	600
Expense for temporary directors	500
Total allowable expenses	$1,300
1991 amortization ($1,300 x 12/60 months)	$ 260

The correct answer is (b). *(SPE 1085 III-69)*
REQUIRED: The maximum organizational expense deduction for the first tax year.
DISCUSSION: Sec. 248 allows a corporation to elect to amortize its organizational expenditures over at least 60 months, beginning with the month in which the corporation starts business. Therefore, the corporation may deduct $1,000 ($10,000 x 6/60 months) of organizational expense amortization in its first year (assuming it is a calendar-year corporation).

The correct answer is (d). *(CMA 1289 3-21)*
REQUIRED: The maximum amount of organizational expenses which may be deducted in the first year.
DISCUSSION: Under Sec. 248, a corporation may elect to amortize its organizational expenditures over at least 60 months, starting with the month in which the corporation begins business. Organizational expenditures are incurred incidental to the creation of the corporation. Reg. 1.248-1(b)(3) specifically excludes expenditures connected with issuing or selling shares of stock such as printing costs. Norton Manufacturing Corporation's 1991 deductible amortization is

Fee paid to State of Kansas for incorporation	$ 100
Cost of organizational meetings	300
Legal fees related to drafting the corporate charter	2,000
Total organizational expenditures	$2,400
1991 amortization ($2,400 x 7/60 months)	$ 280

10. Holover Corporation started business on July 1, 1990 and has elected to amortize its organizational expenses of $40,000. The maximum deduction that can be claimed for organizational expense on Holover's 1991 federal income tax return is

   a. $1,000.
   b. $4,000.
   c. $8,000.
   d. $40,000.

The correct answer is (c). *(CMA 685 3-11)*
REQUIRED: The maximum deduction for organizational expense on a corporation's second income tax return.
DISCUSSION: Sec. 248 allows a corporation to elect to amortize its organizational expenditures over at least 60 months, beginning with the month in which the corporation starts business. Therefore, Holover Corporation may deduct $8,000 ($40,000 x 12/60 months) of organizational expense in its second year.

11. Western Corporation began business on July 1, 1991 and elected a tax year ending December 31, 1991. The company elected to amortize organizational expenses over the minimum permissible period. The organizational expenses the company incurred during this first year were as follows

July 15	$ 300
July 20	900
August 15	1,160
October 15	1,000
Total	$3,360

Western's maximum allowable deduction for amortization of organizational expenses for the 1991 taxable year is

   a. $672.
   b. $392.
   c. $336.
   d. $280.

The correct answer is (c). *(SPE 1078 III-61)*
REQUIRED: The allowable deduction for amortization of organizational expenses in a corporation's first year.
DISCUSSION: Under Sec. 248, a corporation may elect to amortize its organizational expenditures over at least 60 months. The amortization begins with the month in which the corporation begins business even if the expenditures are paid later in the year. This election only applies to expenditures incurred before the end of the taxable year in which business commences [Reg. 1.248-1(a)(2)]. The deduction for organizational expenses is

July 15, 1991	$ 300
July 20, 1991	900
August 15, 1991	1,160
October 15, 1991	1,000
Total organizational expenses	$3,360
Amortization in 1991 ($3,360 x 6/60 months)	$ 336

12. Dale Corporation's book income before federal income taxes was $520,000 for the year ended December 31, 1991. Dale was organized 3 years earlier. Organization costs of $260,000 are being written off over a 10-year period for financial statement purposes. For tax purposes, these costs are being written off over the minimum allowable period. For the year ended December 31, 1991, taxable income was

   a. $468,000.
   b. $494,000.
   c. $520,000.
   d. $546,000.

The correct answer is (b). *(CPA 584 Q-1)*
REQUIRED: The taxable income of a corporation whose organization costs are treated differently for tax and financial accounting purposes.
DISCUSSION: Under Sec. 248, a corporation may elect to amortize its organizational expenditures over at least 60 months, beginning with the month in which the corporation begins business. Dale's taxable income is computed by adding back the book amortization costs of $26,000 ($260,000 ÷ 10 years) and then deducting the maximum amount of $52,000 ($260,000 x 12/60 months). Taxable income is $494,000 ($520,000 + $26,000 − $52,000).

13. If a corporation does not make an election to amortize qualifying organizational expenditures for the first tax year, the corporation must capitalize these expenses and not deduct them until the year in which the corporation is liquidated.

The correct answer is (T). *(SPE 990 III-3)*
DISCUSSION: Organizational expenditures must be capitalized. If an election is not made under Sec. 248 to amortize them, they may be deducted only on dissolution of the corporation.

14. A corporation incurs additional expense in setting up its accounting system after the close of the tax year but before the due date of its initial return. This is an organizational expense and may be amortized.

The correct answer is (F). *(SPE 1078 III-1)*
DISCUSSION: Under Sec. 248, a corporation may elect to amortize its organizational expenditures over at least 60 months, beginning with the month in which it begins business. Reg. 1.248-1(a)(2) provides that this election only applies to expenses incurred before the end of the taxable year in which the corporation begins business. Even though the expense of setting up an accounting system may be considered an organizational expenditure, it cannot be amortized since it was incurred after the end of the corporation's first taxable year.

15. Corporation X, a calendar year taxpayer, began business on January 1, 1990. X deducted $10,000 in organizational expenses on its 1990 return which was filed on August 15, 1991. X had properly obtained an extension. On September 1, 1991 (ignoring Saturdays, Sundays, and holidays), after realizing its error, Corporation X filed an amended return electing to amortize its organizational expenses over 60 months. X made a proper election by choosing to amortize its organizational expenses.

The correct answer is (T). *(SPE 989 III-4)*
DISCUSSION: Reg. 1.248-1(c) states that the election to deduct an amortized portion of organizational expenditures be made in a statement attached to the taxpayer's return for the taxable year in which it begins business. The return and statement must be filed not later than the date prescribed by law for filing the return (including any extensions of time) for the taxable year in which the taxpayer begins business. The extended due date in this case is September 15, 1991. Since the amended tax return was filed after the August 1st initial filing and before the September 15th extended due date, the election to amortize the organizational expenditures is considered to have been made in a timely manner.

18.3 Corporate Formations

16. To qualify for tax-free incorporation, a sole proprietor must be in control of the transferee corporation immediately after the exchange of the proprietorship's assets for the corporation's stock. "Control" for this purpose means ownership of stock amounting to at least

   a. 80.00%.
   b. 66.67%.
   c. 51.00%.
   d. 50.00%.

The correct answer is (a). *(CPA 587 Q-45)*
REQUIRED: Minimum stock ownership constituting "control" for purposes of a tax-free incorporation.
DISCUSSION: Sec. 351 provides the rules for a tax-free incorporation. It refers to Sec. 368(c) for the definition of "control." Sec. 368(c) defines "control" as the ownership of stock possessing at least 80% of the total combined voting power of all classes of stock entitled to vote and at least 80% of the total number of shares of all other classes of stock of the corporation.

17. On July 1, 1991, Alan Rees, sole proprietor of Kee Nail, transferred all of Kee's assets to Merit, Inc., a new corporation, solely for a certain percentage of Merit's stock. Al Clyde, who is not related to Rees, also bought some of Merit's stock on July 1. Merit's outstanding capital stock consisted of 1,000 shares of common stock with a par value of $100 per share. For the transfer of Kee Nail's assets to be tax-free, what is the minimum number of shares of Merit's stock that must be owned by Rees and Clyde immediately after the exchange?

   a. 500.
   b. 501.
   c. 800.
   d. 801.

The correct answer is (c). *(CPA 582 Q-45)*
REQUIRED: The minimum number of shares of stock which must be owned by two transferors immediately after the exchange for the transfer to be tax-free.
DISCUSSION: A transfer of assets for stock of a corporation is tax-free under Sec. 351(a) if the transferors are in control of the corporation immediately after the exchange. Therefore, the person who transfers appreciated property will receive the benefit of Sec. 351 if another transferor transfers property (including cash) and together they meet the control test. Sec. 368(c) defines control as the ownership of stock possessing at least 80% of the total combined voting power of all classes of stock entitled to vote and at least 80% of the total number of shares of all other classes of stock of the corporation. Rees and Clyde must own 800 shares (80% x 1,000 shares).

18. Which of the following is not taken into account when determining if a gain or loss should be recognized on the transfer of property to a corporation in exchange for a controlling interest in stock of the corporation?

a. Ownership of at least 80% of the total combined voting power of all stock entitled to vote.
b. Ownership of at least 80% of the total number of shares of all other classes of stock.
c. Receipt of money in addition to stock.
d. Fair market value of property transferred.

The correct answer is (d). *(SPE 1078 III-49)*
REQUIRED: The item not taken into account when determining if gain or loss is recognized on the transfer of property to a corporation.
DISCUSSION: Sec. 351(a) provides that no gain or loss is recognized if one or more persons transfer property to a corporation solely in exchange for stock in such corporation, and immediately after the exchange such person(s) are in control of the corporation. Control is defined in Sec. 368(c) as the ownership of stock possessing at least 80% of the total combined voting power of all classes of voting stock and at least 80% of the total number of shares of all other classes of stock. In a Sec. 351 exchange, the FMV of property transferred is not taken into account when determining the amount of the recognized gain or loss.
Answers (a) and (b) are incorrect because each must be considered when determining if the corporation is controlled by the transferors. Answer (c) is incorrect because Sec. 351(b) provides that gain is recognized when other property or money is received in addition to the stock.

19. Mr. A owned 75% of the voting stock and 85% of the nonvoting stock of Corporation Y. Mr. A transferred property with a fair market value of $90,000 and an adjusted basis of $70,000 to Y for an additional 5% of the voting stock and 5% of the nonvoting stock. What is the amount of gain to be recognized by Mr. A?

a. $0.
b. $8,000.
c. $10,000.
d. $20,000.

The correct answer is (a). *(SPE 1085 III-52)*
REQUIRED: The gain recognized on transfer of assets to a corporation by an existing shareholder in exchange for additional stock.
DISCUSSION: If the requirements of Sec. 351(a) are met, no gain or loss is recognized when property is transferred to a corporation. The requirements are that the transfer be made by one or more persons, solely in exchange for stock, and the transferor(s) must be in control of the corporation immediately after the exchange. Sec. 368(c) defines control as the ownership of at least 80% of both the voting and nonvoting stock. After the transaction, Mr. A owns 80% (75% + 5%) of the voting stock and 90% (85% + 5%) of the nonvoting stock. He therefore meets the criteria and qualifies under Sec. 351(a). No gain or loss is recognized.

20. Philip Hall and Andrew Miles formed a corporation during 1991 to which Hall contributed $50,000 cash and Miles contributed a building (current fair market value of $80,000 and an adjusted basis to Miles of $60,000). Hall and Miles each received 300 shares of the corporation's common stock. As a result of this transaction, Miles should report

a. An ordinary gain of $20,000.
b. A Section 1250 gain of $20,000.
c. A capital gain of $20,000.
d. Neither a gain nor a loss.

The correct answer is (d). *(CPA 577 Q-20)*
REQUIRED: The gain or loss recognized on the transfer of assets to a corporation in exchange for its stock.
DISCUSSION: If the requirements of Sec. 351(a) are met, no gain or loss is recognized when property is transferred to a corporation. The requirements are that the transfer be by one or more persons, solely in exchange for stock, and the transferor(s) must be in control of the corporation immediately after the exchange. Sec. 368(c) defines control as the ownership of at least 80% of both the voting and nonvoting stock. Money qualifies as property under Sec. 351. Hall and Miles meet these criteria so the transfer qualifies under Sec. 351(a). No gain or loss is recognized.
The difference in value of property contributed for equal shares may cause other tax consequences depending on the underlying facts; e.g., Miles may have made a gift to Hall, or Hall may have received compensation from Miles or the corporation.

21. Mr. Green transferred land with a fair market value of $25,000 and an adjusted basis to him of $10,000 to Corporation X in exchange for 100% of X's only class of stock and an automobile owned by X with an adjusted basis to X of $13,000. At the time of the transfer, the stock had a fair market value of $29,000 and the automobile had a fair market value of $11,000. What is the amount of gain to be recognized by Mr. Green due to the transfer?

   a. $30,000.
   b. $19,000.
   c. $13,000.
   d. $11,000.

The correct answer is (d). *(SPE 988 III-74)*
REQUIRED: The recognized gain on the transfer of assets to a corporation in exchange for stock and other property.
DISCUSSION: Under Sec. 351(a), no gain or loss is recognized if property is transferred to a corporation by one or more persons solely in exchange for stock in such corporation, and immediately after the exchange such person(s) are in control (i.e., own at least 80% of the voting and nonvoting stock) of the corporation. If other property or money is received in addition to the stock, gain is recognized by the recipient. Mr. Green's realized gain is

Amount realized	
($29,000 stock + $11,000 vehicle)	$40,000
Less basis of land transferred	(10,000)
Realized gain	$30,000

Under Sec. 351(b), gain is recognized only to the extent of the amount of money received plus the fair market value of other property received. Mr. Green's recognized gain is the fair market value of the vehicle ($11,000). The character of Mr. Green's gain depends on the character of the asset (land) transferred (e.g., capital gain if the land were a capital asset).

Note that if the $15,000 ($40,000 FMV received – $25,000 FMV given) excess value received by Mr. Green was deemed a dividend or compensation for prior services, the amount and/or character of his income or gain that is recognized may change.

22. Mr. Bass transferred a building that had an adjusted basis to him of $300,000 and a fair market value of $500,000, to Corporation C solely in exchange for 100% of C's only class of stock. The building was subject to a mortgage of $100,000, which C assumed for bona fide business purposes. The fair market value of the stock on the date of transfer was $550,000. What is the amount of gain to be recognized by Mr. Bass?

   a. $0.
   b. $100,000.
   c. $200,000.
   d. $250,000.

The correct answer is (a). *(SPE 989 III-67)*
REQUIRED: The gain or loss recognized on the transfer of assets and a liability to a corporation in exchange for its stock.
DISCUSSION: If the requirements of Sec. 351(a) are met, no gain or loss is recognized when property is transferred to a corporation. The requirements are that the transfer be by one or more persons, solely in exchange for stock, and the transferor(s) must be in control of the corporation immediately after the exchange. Sec. 368(c) defines control as the ownership of at least 80% of the voting and nonvoting stock. Mr. Bass meets these criteria so the transfer qualifies under Sec. 351(a). No gain or loss is recognized.

Note that Sec. 357(a) provides that the transfer of the mortgage on the building does not prevent the exchange from qualifying under Sec. 351(a), since the purpose of the liability assumption was not tax avoidance, but had a valid business purpose, and because the amount of the mortgage did not exceed the adjusted basis of the property.

Module 18.3: Corporate Formations

23. During 1991, Mr. Ray transferred $10,000 cash and a building with an adjusted basis to him of $50,000 and a fair market value of $90,000 to Corporation Z for 90% of Z's only class of outstanding stock. In addition, for a bona fide business purpose, Z assumed Ray's outstanding mortgage on the building of $65,000. What is the amount of Ray's recognized gain on the exchange?

a. $0.
b. $5,000.
c. $15,000.
d. $25,000

The correct answer is (b). *(SPE 990 III-56)*
REQUIRED: The gain recognized on an exchange of property with a liability in excess of basis.
DISCUSSION: The general rule of Sec. 351 is that no gain is recognized if a shareholder transfers property in exchange for stock of a corporation as long as the shareholder(s) involved in the transaction control the corporation immediately after the exchange. Control is defined in Sec. 368(c) as 80% of the voting power and 80% of all classes of nonvoting stock. Mr. Ray received 90% of Corporation Z's stock and therefore has control immediately after the exchange. But Sec. 357(c) provides that gain must be recognized by the shareholder to the extent that liabilities assumed, or taken subject to, by the corporation exceed the adjusted basis of all property transferred. The mortgage on the building exceeded the adjusted basis of all the property Mr. Ray transferred by $5,000 [$65,000 − ($50,000 + $10,000)]. Mr. Ray must recognize a gain of $5,000.

24. In 1991 Taxpayer C acquired sufficient stock of Corporation Y in an exchange to meet the nonrecognition of gain or loss requirements. Stock was acquired as follows (stock listed at fair market value)

Received $30,000 in stock for cash of $20,000
Received $100,000 in stock for property with adjusted basis of $50,000
Received $15,000 in stock for services rendered
Received $25,000 in stock for bonds of Corporation Y (basis of $18,000) per conversion privilege

What is the total amount includable in Taxpayer C's income?

a. $10,000.
b. $15,000.
c. $25,000.
d. $82,000.

The correct answer is (b). *(SPE 1078 III-62)*
REQUIRED: The amount included in income from an exchange of property and services for stock.
DISCUSSION: The general rule of Sec. 351 is that no gain or loss is recognized if property is transferred to a corporation by one or more persons solely for stock, and immediately after the exchange such person or persons are in control of the corporation (i.e., own at least 80% of the stock). Sec. 351(d) states, however, that stock issued for services are not issued in return for property. Stock issued for services falls outside the general rule and income must be recognized on such a transfer. The fair market value of stock received for services ($15,000) must be included in C's income. All other stock received was in exchange for property and no gain or loss is recognized on its transfer.
Note that the discrepancy in the amount of stock received for cash does not affect the Sec. 351 transaction as long as it was a bona fide exchange; e.g., the stock may have been overvalued. However, if the excess $10,000 of stock were additional compensation for services, it too would be included in C's income.

25. In 1991, Dr. James Pyle, a cash-basis taxpayer, incorporated his dental practice. No liabilities were transferred. The following assets were transferred to the corporation:

Cash (checking account)	$ 1,000
Equipment	
Adjusted basis	60,000
Fair market value	68,000

Immediately after the transfer, Pyle owned 100% of the corporation's stock. The corporation's total basis for the transferred assets is

a. $69,000.
b. $68,000.
c. $61,000.
d. $60,000.

The correct answer is (c). *(CPA 588 Q-34)*
REQUIRED: The corporation's basis in assets received in exchange for stock.
DISCUSSION: Sec. 362(a) provides that the basis of property acquired by a corporation in connection with a Sec. 351 transaction is the same as the basis in the hands of the transferor (shareholder), increased by the amount of gain recognized by the transferor on such transfer. Since Pyle did not receive any boot, he did not recognize gain. Thus, the corporation's total basis in the transferred assets is the same as that in Pyle's hands ($1,000 + $60,000 = $61,000).

Module 18.3: Corporate Formations

26. Mr. Wind transferred property subject to a $35,000 liability to Corporation X in exchange for 90% of X's only class of stock outstanding. Mr. Wind's adjusted basis in the property transferred was $40,000. The fair market value of the stock at the time of the transfer was $60,000. What is Corporation X's basis in the property received and what is Wind's basis in the stock received?

	Corporation X	Mr. Wind
a.	$35,000	$5,000
b.	$40,000	$5,000
c.	$60,000	$40,000
d.	$75,000	$75,000

The correct answer is (b). *(SPE 990 III-60)*
REQUIRED: The basis of the stock and property exchanged in a Sec. 351 transfer.
DISCUSSION: Sec. 358(a)(1) provides that, in a Sec. 351 exchange, the basis of the stock received by the transferors (shareholders) is the basis of the property transferred decreased by the fair market value of other property received, the amount of any money received, and the amount of loss that was recognized by the taxpayer. The basis is increased by the amount of gain recognized by the taxpayer. Sec. 357(a) exempts the taxpayer from recognizing gain on the transfer due to assumption of the liability. Under Sec. 358(d), the assumption of a liability by the transferee corporation is treated as money received by the taxpayer in the exchange. Thus, Mr. Wind's basis in the stock received is $5,000 ($40,000 basis of property transferred – $35,000 liability).

The basis to Corporation X for the assets received is determined by Sec. 362(a) as the same as that of the transferor ($40,000) plus the gain recognized by the transferor ($0), or $40,000.

27. Mrs. Oak transferred property that had an adjusted basis to her of $175,000 and a fair market value of $200,000 to Corporation T in exchange for 100% of T's only class of stock, $10,000 in cash, and an automobile owned by T with an adjusted basis to T of $12,000. At the time of the transfer, the stock had a fair market value of $120,000 and the automobile had a fair market value of $30,000. What is the amount of Mrs. Oak's basis in Corporation T's stock?

a. $175,000.
b. $145,000.
c. $135,000.
d. $120,000.

The correct answer is (c). *(SPE 989 III-72)*
REQUIRED: The basis of stock received by the shareholder when other property is also received.
DISCUSSION: Sec. 358(a)(1) provides that, in a Sec. 351 exchange, the basis of the stock received by the transferors (shareholders) is the basis of the property transferred decreased by the fair market value of other property received, the amount of any money received, and the amount of loss that was recognized by the taxpayer. The basis is increased by the amount of gain recognized by the taxpayer.

Mrs. Oak received cash of $10,000 and an automobile with a $30,000 fair market value in addition to the stock. These two items reduce her basis in the stock. Mrs. Oak realized a $15,000 net loss on the exchange ($160,000 amount realized – $175,000 adjusted basis), but recognizes no loss. Her basis in the stock is $135,000 ($175,000 basis of property transferred – $10,000 cash received – $30,000 value of automobile received).

28. For bona fide business purposes, Mr. D transferred the following property to Corporation X. X assumed the $50,000 mortgage.

	Asset Basis	Mortgage	Fair Market Value
Building and land	$120,000	$50,000	$160,000
Various equipment	60,000	0	40,000

In the exchange, Mr. D received 100% of X's only class of stock. What is Corporation X's basis in the property received in the exchange?

a. $130,000.
b. $150,000.
c. $180,000.
d. $200,000.

The correct answer is (c). *(SPE 1085 III-70)*
REQUIRED: The basis of assets transferred to a corporation subject to a mortgage.
DISCUSSION: Sec. 362(a) provides that the basis to a corporation of property acquired in a Sec. 351 transaction is the same as the basis in the hands of the transferor, increased by the gain recognized by the transferor. Here, the transfer qualifies as a Sec. 351 transaction since greater than 80% of all stock was transferred to the shareholder. Sec. 357(c) would not cause any recognition of gain on the contribution of the mortgage since the liability did not exceed the adjusted basis of all property transferred. The basis of the property received by Corporation X is therefore the adjusted basis of the property in the hands of the shareholder, which was $180,000 ($120,000 + $60,000).

29. Mr. L transferred the following assets and liabilities to Corporation K:

	Adjusted Basis	Fair Market Value
Building	$10,000	$60,000
Mortgage on building	40,000	40,000
Truck	5,000	10,000
Machine	20,000	15,000

In the exchange, Mr. L received 95% of K's only class of outstanding stock. What is K's total basis in the assets received, assuming that Mr. L properly recognized the correct amount of gain on the exchange?

a. $35,000.
b. $40,000.
c. $65,000.
d. $85,000.

The correct answer is (b). *(SPE 1083 III-65)*
REQUIRED: The basis of assets transferred to a corporation in a Sec. 351 transfer.
DISCUSSION: Sec. 362(a) provides that the basis to a corporation of property acquired in a Sec. 351 transaction is the same as the basis in the hands of the transferor, increased by the gain recognized by the transferor. If property is transferred to a corporation by a person solely in exchange for stock and, immediately after the exchange, the person is in control, the shareholder recognizes no gain or loss on the transfer [Sec. 351(a)]. Mr. L by owning 95% of K's stock is in control of Corporation K after the transfer.

However, Sec. 357(c) provides that, if the liabilities transferred to the corporation exceed the adjusted basis of all the property transferred, the excess is treated as a gain resulting from the sale or exchange. Thus, Mr. L was required to recognize a gain of $5,000 ($40,000 mortgage − $35,000 adjusted basis of assets). K's total basis in the assets received is $40,000 ($35,000 transferred property basis + $5,000 gain recognized by Mr. L).

30. Sam owns 100% of M Corporation's single class of stock. Sam transfers land and a building having a $30,000 and $100,000 adjusted basis, respectively, to M Corporation in exchange for additional M Corporation common stock worth $200,000 and IBM stock worth $20,000. The IBM stock had a $5,000 basis on M Corporation's books. Peter transfers $50,000 in cash for 15% of the M Corporation common stock. What amount of gain or loss is recognized by Sam and M Corporation on the exchange?

	Sam	M Corporation
a.	$0	$0
b.	$0	$15,000
c.	$20,000	$0
d.	$20,000	$15,000

The correct answer is (d). *(Publisher)*
REQUIRED: The gain or loss recognized on the exchange.
DISCUSSION: Sec. 351 states that no gain or loss is recognized when property is transferred to a corporation in exchange for the corporation's stock if the person or persons transferring the property are in control of the corporation immediately after the transfer. "Control" is defined by the Code as at least 80% ownership of the corporation's voting and nonvoting stock. Because Sam meets the control test, he recognizes no gain on the receipt of the M Corporation stock. However, he does recognize a $20,000 gain on the receipt of the IBM stock. Sec. 351(b)(1) states that if other property is received by the transferor, the transferor must recognize gain equal to the fair market value of the property. Therefore, Sam must recognize a $20,000 gain.

M Corporation recognizes no gain or loss on the receipt of the land and building in exchange for its own stock (Sec. 1032). However, M Corporation does recognize a gain on the transfer of the IBM stock. Under Sec. 311, if a corporation distributes appreciated property, the corporation will recognize gain to the extent that the property's fair market value exceeds its adjusted basis. Therefore, M Corporation must recognize a $15,000 gain ($20,000 fair market value − $5,000 basis) on the transfer of the IBM stock to Sam.

Module 18.3: Corporate Formations

31. On June 10, 1990, Celeste purchases a computer for $6,000 which she uses in her sole proprietorship. The computer is 5-year property under the MACRS rules. Depreciation in the amount of $1,200 is claimed by Celeste on the computer in 1990. On February 1, 1991 Celeste transfers the computer and the other assets of her proprietorship to C Corporation in exchange for all of C's stock. No gain or loss is recognized on the exchange. What amount of depreciation is claimed by Celeste and C Corporation on the computer in 1991?

	Celeste	C Corporation
a.	$0	$1,920
b.	$0	$1,200
c.	$160	$1,760
d.	$960	$960

The correct answer is (c). *(Publisher)*
REQUIRED: The correct amount of depreciation claimed by the transferor and the corporation on a transfer of an asset for stock.
DISCUSSION: Under Sec. 362, when property is transferred to a corporation in exchange for its stock in a transaction in which no gain or loss is recognized, the corporation's basis in the property will be the same as the property's basis in the hands of the transferor. Therefore, the computer will have a $6,000 basis to the corporation. Under Sec. 168, 5-year property is depreciated at a rate of 32% in its second year. Since the asset was transferred, the 1991 depreciation must be apportioned between Celeste and C Corporation. The depreciation is apportioned based on the number of complete months each taxpayer owned the property. Celeste's deduction is $160 (1/12 x $6,000 x 32%). C Corporation's depreciation deduction is $1,760 (11/12 x $6,000 x 32%).

32. On August 15, 1990, the ABC Partnership purchases telephone equipment for $10,000. The equipment is 5-year property under the MACRS rules. Depreciation in the amount of $2,000 is claimed by ABC on the equipment in 1990. On March 31, 1991 ABC Partnership is incorporated with its assets being exchanged for King Corporation stock and notes. Gain of $1,000 is recognized on the transfer of the equipment that was purchased in 1990. What amount of depreciation is claimed by ABC and King on the equipment in 1991?

	ABC	King
a.	$800	$2,400
b.	$800	$2,600
c.	$1,600	$1,600
d.	$880	$2,640

The correct answer is (b). *(Publisher)*
REQUIRED: The correct amount of depreciation claimed by the transferor of property and the recipient of the property.
DISCUSSION: Under Sec. 1012, the basis of property is generally the cost of the property. ABC's basis in the telephone equipment is therefore $10,000. Sec. 362 provides that, when property is transferred to a corporation in a transaction to which Sec. 351 applies, the corporation's basis in the property is the same as the transferor's basis, increased in the amount of any gain recognized by the transferor on the transfer. Therefore, King's basis in the property is $11,000 ($10,000 transferor's basis + $1,000 gain recognized by ABC on the transfer).

Because the property was transferred during the second year of its life the depreciation must be apportioned between ABC and King. The depreciation is apportioned based on the number of complete months the property was owned. The step-up in basis of $1,000 is treated as a second property whose depreciation commences on April 1, 1991. Under IRS depreciation tables, depreciation rates of 20% and 32% are applied to 5-year property in its first and second years, respectively. ABC's depreciation deduction is $800 ($10,000 basis x 32% x 3/12). King Corporation's depreciation deduction is $2,600 ($10,000 basis x 32% x 9/12) + ($1,000 basis x 20% x 1).

33. On June 30, 1990, Mr. K purchased a truck. On March 31, 1991, he transferred it to Corporation E in exchange for 90% of the outstanding stock of Corporation E plus $2,000 cash. As of December 31, 1991, what is Corporation E's holding period?

a. 6 months.
b. 9 months.
c. 12 months.
d. 18 months.

The correct answer is (d). *(SPE 1081 III-47)*
REQUIRED: The corporation's holding period of an asset received in a Sec. 351 exchange for its stock.
DISCUSSION: Under Sec. 1223(2), a taxpayer's holding period of property should include the period for which such property was held by another person if such property has the same basis in the taxpayer's hands as it had in the hands of such other person (transferred basis). Therefore, Corporation E may add Mr. K's holding period to its own holding period. E's holding period is 18 months (July 1, 1990 through December 31, 1991).

34. Individual R owns 80% of the outstanding voting stock of Corporation K. In the current year, R exchanged equipment for an additional 10% of the voting stock and a truck. Assuming there is a gain, R must recognize the gain to the extent of the fair market value of the truck.

The correct answer is (T). *(SPE 1081 III-10)*
　　DISCUSSION: Sec. 351(a) provides that no gain or loss is recognized if property is transferred to a corporation by a person solely in exchange for stock, and immediately after the exchange such person is in control (i.e., owns at least 80% of the outstanding stock) of the corporation. But if other property or money is received in addition to the stock or securities, any gain realized must be recognized to the extent of money received plus the fair market value of other property received. If R realizes a gain on the transfer, (s)he must recognize the realized gain to the extent of lesser of the realized gain or the FMV of the truck.

35. No gain or loss is recognized by the transferors or the corporation if there is a transfer of money or property by individuals to the corporation solely in exchange for stock of that corporation and immediately after the exchange the transferors, as a group, own at least 80% of the total combined voting power of all classes of voting stock and at least 80% of the total number of shares of all other classes of the corporation's stock.

The correct answer is (T). *(SPE 988 III-10)*
　　DISCUSSION: Under Sec. 351(a), no gain or loss is recognized if property is transferred to a corporation by one or more persons solely in exchange for stock, and immediately after the exchange such person or persons are in control of the corporation. Sec. 368(c) defines control as the ownership of stock possessing at least 80% of the total combined voting power of all voting stock and at least 80% of the total number of shares of all other classes of stock of the corporation. Sec. 1032 prevents the transferee corporation from recognizing gain when property is received in exchange for the corporation's stock.

36. Mr. C and Mr. N are unrelated individual taxpayers. On June 1, 1991, each transferred property to Corporation J and each received 50% of J's only class of outstanding stock. The property Mr. C transferred had an adjusted basis of $10,000 and a fair market value of $30,000. The property Mr. N transferred had an adjusted basis of $40,000, a fair market value of $45,000, and was subject to a mortgage of $15,000 which was assumed by Corporation J upon transfer. Neither Mr. C nor Mr. N need recognize any gain in this transaction.

The correct answer is (T). *(SPE 1083 III-10)*
　　DISCUSSION: The general rule of Sec. 351(a) is that no gain or loss shall be recognized if property is transferred to a corporation by one or more persons solely in exchange for stock in such corporation and, immediately after the exchange, such person or persons are in control of the corporation. Mr. C and Mr. N each transferred property to the corporation solely in exchange for stock and they controlled the corporation after the transfer (owning at least 80% of the stock). Also, Sec. 357(a) exempts the taxpayer from recognizing gain on the transfer from the assumption of the liability because it is not treated as boot received. Neither Mr. C nor Mr. N need recognize any gain.

37. Mr. Z transfers the business assets of his sole proprietorship to Z Corporation in a nontaxable exchange on September 1, 1991. The holding period for all of Mr. Z's stock in Z Corporation commences on September 1, 1991.

The correct answer is (F). *(Publisher)*
　　DISCUSSION: The holding period of stock received in a tax-free exchange under Sec. 351 is determined under Sec. 1223(1). The holding period includes that for transferred property provided it was either a capital asset or Sec. 1231 property, i.e., real or personal property used in a trade or business. When a sole proprietorship is incorporated, each share of stock has a split holding period under Rev. Rul. 85-164 when either capital asset or Sec. 1231 property is transferred along with ordinary income property.

38. On January 1, 1991, Mr. S transferred property he had originally acquired on July 1, 1990 to Corporation X in a nontaxable exchange for X's stock. On August 1, 1991, Corporation X sold the property for a gain. Corporation X's holding period of the property does not include the period it was held by Mr. S.

The correct answer is (F). *(SPE 1085 III-12)*
　　DISCUSSION: Sec. 1223(2) provides that, in determining a taxpayer's holding period, the period for which property was held by any other person will be included if the property has the same basis as it had in the hands of such other person. Under Sec. 362(a), the corporation's basis for property is the same as the property's basis in the hands of the transferor (shareholder), so Sec. 1223(2) will apply. X's holding period will include the time Mr. S owned the assets.

Module 18.3: Corporate Formations

39. Mr. C transfers a warehouse to O Corporation in exchange for all its stock. The warehouse has an adjusted basis to Mr. C of $60,000 and a fair market value of $80,000. The corporation also assumed the outstanding mortgage on the warehouse of $40,000. Mr. C's basis in the stock received is $40,000.

The correct answer is (F). *(SPE 1080 III-40)*
DISCUSSION: Under Sec. 351(a), no gain or loss is recognized if property is transferred to a corporation by a person solely in exchange for stock, and immediately after the exchange, such person is in control of the corporation (i.e., owns at least 80% of the stock). Sec. 358(a) provides that the basis of stock received in a Sec. 351 transaction is the same as the basis of the property exchanged, increased by the amount of gain recognized by the transferor, and decreased by the amount of money received and the fair market value of any other property received. Although Sec. 357(a) does not treat liabilities assumed, or taken subject to, by the corporation as money or other property for purposes of recognizing gain, they are considered the receipt of money by the shareholder and they decrease basis of the stock under Sec. 358(a). C's basis in the stock received is the same as his adjusted basis in the warehouse less the mortgage on the warehouse, or $20,000 ($60,000 − $40,000).

40. No gain or loss is recognized by a corporation on the receipt of property or money in exchange for its own stock.

The correct answer is (T). *(SPE 1078 III-4)*
DISCUSSION: Sec. 1032 provides that a corporation recognizes no gain or loss on the receipt of money or other property in exchange for its stock.

41. Mr. B owns 100% of the stock of Corporation F. In January 1991, Mr. B transferred land to Corporation F as a contribution to capital. Mr. B's original cost for the land was $8,000. The land had an adjusted basis to Mr. B of $10,000 and a fair market value of $12,000 on the date of the transfer. Corporation F's basis in the land is $10,000.

The correct answer is (T). *(SPE 987 III-78)*
DISCUSSION: Sec. 362(a) provides that a corporation takes a transferred basis in property received as a contribution to capital. B's transaction is a contribution to capital since he received nothing in return and already owned 100% of the Corporation F stock. F's basis in the property would therefore be B's adjusted basis of $10,000.

42. Mr. A formed Corporation X on July 1, 1991 by transferring all of his business assets (adjusted basis $10,000, fair market value $15,000) to the corporation in exchange for 100% of its stock. Corporation X's basis in these assets is $15,000.

The correct answer is (F). *(SPE 1078 III-7)*
DISCUSSION: Sec. 362(a) provides that a corporation's basis in assets acquired in a Sec. 351 transaction is the transferor's basis, increased by any gain recognized by the transferor. Sec. 351 applies since Mr. A transferred assets solely for stock of Corporation X and he met the control test after the exchange. Therefore, Mr. A will recognize no gain on the exchange, and X's basis in the assets will be A's adjusted basis of $10,000.

43. A transfer of your services to a corporation in return for stock will not result in taxable compensation to you.

The correct answer is (F). *(SPE 986 III-11)*
DISCUSSION: Sec. 351(d)(1) provides that any stock issued for services are not considered issued for property. Consequently, the requirement of stock being exchanged for property is not fulfilled and Sec. 351(a) will not apply. Under Secs. 61 and 83, the value of stock received in an exchange for services is included in gross income.

44. The transfer of mortgaged property to a controlled corporation results in no gain or loss being recognized even if the liabilities assumed are in excess of the property's adjusted basis.

The correct answer is (F). *(SPE 1078 III-6)*
DISCUSSION: Under Sec. 357(a), liabilities assumed by a corporation, or taken subject to, are not generally considered money or property (i.e., no gain or loss results). Sec. 357(c) states, however, that if the liabilities exceed the adjusted basis of property transferred, such excess is considered a gain to the transferor from the sale or exchange of an asset.

18.4 Assets Acquired for Stock

45. Mr. Brown transferred property that had an adjusted basis to him of $40,000 and a fair market value of $50,000, to Corporation B in exchange for 100% of B's only class of stock and $15,000 cash. At the time of the transfer, the stock had a fair market value of $35,000. What is the amount of gain to be recognized by Mr. Brown?

a. $0.
b. $10,000.
c. $15,000.
d. $25,000.

The correct answer is (b). *(SPE 989 III-65)*
REQUIRED: The taxable gain from the transfer of property to a controlled corporation.
DISCUSSION: This transfer qualifies under Sec. 351 since Mr. Brown transferred property to a corporation for stock and, immediately after the transfer, controlled the corporation. The realized gain on the transfer is $10,000 ($50,000 realized − $40,000 adjusted basis). When property other than stock is received in a Sec. 351 transfer, any gain is recognized to the extent of the lesser of the realized gain or the amount of other property received [Sec. 351(b)]. Hence, Mr. Brown's gain is limited to the $10,000 realized gain.

46. Ms. M transferred a building to Corporation C. The building had a basis to M of $15,000 and a fair market value of $90,000. In addition, an outstanding mortgage of $20,000 on the building was assumed by C upon the transfer. In return, M received 80% of C's only class of outstanding stock (fair market value of $65,000) and a car with a fair market value of $5,000. What is Ms. M's recognized gain on the transaction?

a. $0.
b. $10,000.
c. $25,000.
d. $45,000.

The correct answer is (b). *(SPE 1083 III-64)*
REQUIRED: The gain recognized by a transferor of a building for stock and a car.
DISCUSSION: Sec. 351(a) provides for nonrecognition of gain or loss if property is transferred to a corporation by a person solely in exchange for stock in the corporation and, immediately after the exchange, such person is in control (owns at least 80% of the stock). If other property or money is received in addition to the stock, any gain realized by the recipient is recognized, but not in excess of the sum of the money plus the fair market value of other property received [Sec. 351(b)]. Also, Sec. 357(c) provides that if the liabilities transferred or assumed ($20,000) are greater than the basis of all the property transferred ($15,000), the excess is treated as a gain from the sale or exchange of property. Ms. M's recognized gain is $10,000 [$5,000 other property (car) + $5,000 excess of mortgage over basis].

47. In a bona fide transaction, Jesse Jenkins transferred land worth $50,000 to his controlled corporation for stock of the corporation worth $20,000 and cash of $20,000. The basis of the property to him was $15,000 and was subject to a $10,000 mortgage which the corporation assumed. Jenkins must report a gain of

a. $10,000.
b. $20,000.
c. $30,000.
d. $35,000.

The correct answer is (b). *(CPA 1172 P-12)*
REQUIRED: The gain recognized by a transferor who exchanges land for stock and cash.
DISCUSSION: Sec. 351(a) provides nonrecognition of gain or loss if property is transferred to a corporation by a person solely in exchange for stock in the corporation and, immediately after the exchange, such person is in control of the corporation (i.e., owns at least 80% of the stock). Under Sec. 351(b), if other property or money is received in addition to the stock, any gain realized by the recipient is recognized to the extent of the amount of money plus the fair market value of other property received. Sec. 351 will apply to Jesse's transaction since its conditions are met even though this is not a corporate formation. Jesse's reportable gain is

Proceeds ($20,000 stock + $20,000 cash + $10,000 liabilities assumed by the corporation)	$50,000
Less adjusted basis of land transferred	(15,000)
Realized gain	$35,000
Gain recognized (limited to cash received)	$20,000

Note that under Sec. 357(a) liabilities assumed by the corporation (which are not in excess of basis) are not considered property or money for the purpose of recognizing gain.

Module 18.4: Assets Acquired for Stock

48. Price Corporation has common stock with a par value of $25 per share. During 1991, Price entered into an exchange whereby the company gave up stock worth $350,000 and received land with a fair market value of $350,000 and an adjusted basis of $100,000. At the time of the exchange, Price common stock was selling for $35 per share. The gain that Price must recognize as a result of the exchange is

  a. $0.
  b. $100,000.
  c. $250,000.
  d. $350,000.

The correct answer is (a). *(CMA 688 3-13)*
REQUIRED: The amount and character of gain or loss recognized by a corporation when it issues its own stock for property.
DISCUSSION: No gain or loss is recognized by a corporation on the receipt of money or other property in exchange for its stock, including treasury stock [Sec. 1032(a)].

49. Mr. Slo transferred property, with a fair market value of $10,000 and an adjusted basis to him of $9,000, to Tina Corporation. Mr. Slo did not own any Tina Corporation stock before this transaction. In exchange, Tina issued and transferred 40% of its stock to Mr. Slo. The stock transferred to Mr. Slo had a fair market value of $12,000 at the time of the exchange. The remaining 60% of Tina's stock is owned by 10 unrelated shareholders. What is Tina Corporation's basis in the property received?

  a. $0.
  b. $9,000.
  c. $10,000.
  d. $12,000.

The correct answer is (d). *(SPE 990 III-59)*
REQUIRED: The corporation's basis in property received in exchange for stock.
DISCUSSION: The basis of property acquired by a corporation as a contribution to capital is the transferor's basis increased by the amount of gain recognized by the transferor [Sec. 362(a)]. The described exchange does not qualify under Sec. 351(a) because Mr. Slo does not control the corporation immediately after the exchange, so Mr. Slo must recognize his entire realized gain.

Mr. Slo's recognized gain:
Amount realized (FMV of shares)	$12,000
Less adjusted basis of property	(9,000)
Realized and recognized gain	$ 3,000

Tina Corporation's basis:
Adjusted basis to Mr. Slo	$ 9,000
Gain recognized by Mr. Slo	3,000
Tina Corporation's basis	$12,000

50. Ms. D transferred the following assets to Corporation E:

	Adjusted Basis	Fair Market Value
Cash	$1,000	$1,000
Equipment	2,000	1,500
Land	4,500	6,000

In exchange, Ms. D received 51% of E's only class of outstanding stock. The stock had no established value. What is Corporation E's total basis in all the assets received, assuming that Ms. D recognized the correct amount of gain on the exchange?

  a. $6,000.
  b. $7,000.
  c. $7,500.
  d. $8,500.

The correct answer is (d). *(SPE 1083 III-66)*
REQUIRED: The corporation's basis in assets acquired in exchange for its stock.
DISCUSSION: Under Sec. 362(a), a corporation's basis in assets acquired as a contribution to capital is the transferor's basis, increased by the amount of gain recognized by the transferor on the transfer. Because less than 80% of E's stock was exchanged for the assets, this transfer does not qualify for nonrecognition under Sec. 351. When the fair market value of property received cannot be ascertained, the amount realized is the fair market value of property given up.

D's recognized gain:
Amount realized (FMV of property given up)	$8,500
Less adjusted basis	(7,500)
Realized and recognized gain	$1,000

Corporation E's basis:
Property's adjusted basis to D	$7,500
Gain recognized by D	1,000
E's basis in assets	$8,500

51. Ms. A transferred money and property to Corporation X, solely in exchange for stock of X. Immediately after the exchange, A owned 10% of the total combined voting power of all classes of stock entitled to vote and 100% of all other classes of stock. No gain or loss will be recognized by A or X.

The correct answer is (F). *(SPE 989 III-2)*
DISCUSSION: Sec. 351 provides the rules for a tax-free incorporation. It refers to Sec. 368(c) for the definition of "control." Sec. 368(c) defines "control" as the ownership of stock possessing at least 80% of the total combined voting power of all classes of stock entitled to vote and at least 80% of the total number of shares of all other classes of stock of the corporation. Since Ms. A owns only 10% of the voting stock, she must recognize gain or loss on the transaction.

52. If a shareholder of a closely-held or solely-owned corporation receives no additional shares for a contribution of property to the corporation, the basis of the property received by the corporation is the same as it was to the shareholder.

The correct answer is (T). *(SPE 986 III-16)*
DISCUSSION: The basis of property acquired by a corporation as a contribution to capital is the transferor's basis increased by the amount of gain recognized by the transferor [Sec. 362(a)]. Likewise, no gain will be recognized on the contribution of property to an 80%-or-more-owned corporation.

53. A corporation's holding period for an asset received in a nontaxable exchange of property for stock includes the time the asset was held by the transferor.

The correct answer is (T). *(SPE 990 III-2)*
DISCUSSION: Sec. 1223(2) provides that, in determining a taxpayer's holding period, the period for which property was held by any other person will be included if the property has the same basis as it had in the hands of such other person. Under Sec. 362(a), the corporation's basis in a Sec. 351 transaction where no gain is recognized is the same as the basis in the hands of the transferor (shareholder), so Sec. 1223(2) will apply. The corporation's holding period will include the time the transferor owned the assets.

18.5 Gifts to Corporations

54. On January 2, 1991, City M gave the A Corporation $200,000 to purchase a building within the city limits. The building was purchased on June 1, 1991 for $150,000. What is the correct method of handling the excess money received?

a. Long-term capital gain.
b. Short-term capital gain.
c. Reduction of basis in other assets.
d. Nontaxable contribution to capital.

The correct answer is (c). *(SPE 1080 III-53)*
REQUIRED: The correct tax treatment of the excess money received as a contribution from a nonshareholder.
DISCUSSION: Sec. 362(c) states that, if money is received by a corporation as a contribution from a nonshareholder, the basis of any property acquired with the money must be reduced by the amount of the contribution. Any excess is to be applied to the reduction of the basis of any other property held by the taxpayer. The reduction of basis is applied first to all depreciable property, then to all amortizable property, and finally to all remaining property [Reg. 1.362-2(b)].
Answers (a) and (b) are incorrect because under Sec. 118, contributions to capital are not included in gross income. Answer (d) is incorrect because Sec. 362(c) requires a reduction in basis.

55. The City of Cleveland transferred land worth $250,000 to Monitor Corporation as part of an inducement to locate a new plant in the city. The land had been acquired by the city several years ago at a cost of $100,000. The income that Monitor must recognize as a result of the transfer and the basis of the land to Monitor are

a. $250,000 of income, $250,000 of basis.
b. $100,000 of income, $100,000 of basis.
c. $0 of income, $100,000 of basis.
d. $0 of income, $0 of basis.

The correct answer is (d). *(CMA 1289 3-18)*
REQUIRED: The income and basis recognized on a contribution of property by a nonshareholder.
DISCUSSION: The general rule of Sec. 118(a) is that gross income does not include any contribution to the capital of a corporation. Monitor Corporation should not include any income with respect to the land contributed.
Sec. 362(c) provides that if property other than money is acquired by a corporation through a contribution from a nonshareholder, the tax basis of such property is zero.

56. In 1991, City M gave Corporation D land as an incentive to relocate and build a plant in City M. Corporation D must include the fair market value of the land as income in 1991.

The correct answer is (F). *(SPE 1079 III-18)*
DISCUSSION: The general rule of Sec. 118(a) is that gross income does not include any contribution to the capital of a corporation. Corporation D should not recognize any income with respect to the land contributed. Instead, D will have a zero basis in the land.

57. If a corporation acquires property as a gift from a city as an inducement to locate there, the corporation has a tax basis in the property equal to the fair market value of the property on the date of the gift.

The correct answer is (F). *(SPE 987 III-12)*
DISCUSSION: Sec. 362(c) provides that, if property other than money is acquired by a corporation through a contribution from a nonshareholder, the tax basis of such property is zero.

18.6 Business Deductions

See Chapter 6 for additional questions on business expenses, and Chapter 13 for questions on depreciation, amortization, and depletion.

58. Expenses that may be deducted for federal income tax purposes entirely in the year incurred by the corporation are

a. Research and experimental expenses.
b. Organizational expenditures.
c. Internally developed computer software costs.
d. Research and experimental expenses and internally developed computer software costs.

The correct answer is (d). *(CMA 1281 3-1)*
REQUIRED: The expenses which may be deducted entirely in the year incurred.
DISCUSSION: Research and experimental expenditures may be either deducted in the year they are paid or incurred or may be deferred and amortized (Sec. 174). Reg. 1.174-2(a) defines research and experimental expenditures as generally including all costs incidental to the development of a model, process, or similar property. Therefore, research and experimental expenses and internally developed computer software costs would both be deductible in the year incurred (Rev. Proc. 69-21). Note that there are certain requirements or qualifications for internal development of computer software to qualify as research and experimental expenditures.
Answers (a) and (c) are incorrect because, although each may be deducted in the year incurred, answer (d) is a better answer. Answer (b) is incorrect because Sec. 248 provides that organizational expenditures may be amortized over 60 or more months, but not expensed.

59. Which one of the following items would not be fully deductible by a corporation?

a. Group term life insurance premiums where the average policy had a face value of $80,000.
b. Entertainment of employees at a Christmas party.
c. Depreciation on luxury cars used entirely for business purposes.
d. Parking fines.

The correct answer is (d). *(CMA 688 3-9)*
REQUIRED: The item that is not deductible for federal income tax purposes.
DISCUSSION: Fines and penalties paid to a governmental unit or agency are not deductible [Sec. 162(f)]. If fines were deductible, the effect of the punishment would be reduced and businesses would be less inclined to adhere to the law.
Answer (a) is incorrect because premiums paid for life insurance are generally deductible as long as the corporation is not the beneficiary. Answer (b) is incorrect because entertaining employees is an ordinary and necessary business expense. Answer (c) is incorrect because the automobile is used entirely (100%) for business purposes. The fact that the automobile is a luxury vehicle only spreads out the depreciation deduction over more years.

Module 18.6: Business Deductions

60. Mr. B is the nonstockholder president of Corporation M. He paid $50 a share for 100 shares of M stock which has a par value of $60 and a fair market value of $100. The stock was subject to a substantial risk of forfeiture at the time of purchase on January 28, 1990. Mr. B sold this stock to his wife on February 1, 1990 for $10 a share. On February 28, 1991, the stock was no longer subject to a substantial risk of forfeiture and had a fair market value of $120 a share. Assume that M withholds any necessary amount on the portion of the income considered compensation to Mr. B. How much can Corporation M deduct on this transaction for 1991?

   a. $0.
   b. $1,000.
   c. $5,000.
   d. $6,000.

The correct answer is (d). *(SPE 1079 III-82)*
REQUIRED: A corporation's deduction when a substantial risk of forfeiture lapses on stock sold to an employee below fair market value.
DISCUSSION: Under Sec. 83(a), an employee includes in income the excess of fair market value of property received for services over the amount paid for such property only when the property is no longer subject to a substantial risk of forfeiture. The employer is allowed a deduction for the amount the employee must include in income when the employee includes it in income [Sec. 83(h)]. Reg. 1.83-6(a)(2) permits a deduction for the income only if the employer withholds any federal income taxes on amounts considered compensation to the employee.

Mr. B's stock was no longer subject to a substantial risk of forfeiture on February 28, 1991. At that time, the fair market value was $120 per share, so his income was $120 minus the $50 he paid for each share. Under Reg. 1.83-1(c), however, B was required to recognize as income in 1990 the $10 per share realized from the sale to his wife since it was not an arm's-length sale. This $10 per share is considered an increase in the amount paid for the stock. Consequently, Mr. B must include $6,000 in income and Corporation M can deduct $6,000 in 1991 [($120 − $60) x 100 shares].

61. During 1991, Phantom Corporation, a cash method corporation, paid the following educational expenses for its employees:

Tuition	$15,000
Textbooks	5,000
Travel	3,000
Laboratory fees	1,000

The education was not required of the employees to maintain or improve their skills in their present positions. For 1991, Phantom can claim a deduction for these expenses of:

   a. $0.
   b. $15,000.
   c. $21,000.
   d. $24,000.

The correct answer is (d). *(SPE 989 III-85)*
REQUIRED: The amount that a corporation may deduct for educational expenses paid for employees.
DISCUSSION: Sec. 162(a) states that a deduction is allowed for the ordinary and necessary expenses paid or incurred during the year in any trade or business. Although an individual may not be entitled to deduct educational expenses not required to maintain or improve skills in the employee's present position [Reg. 1.162-5(a)], an employer can deduct such amounts as compensation paid to or for its employees. As long as the expenses are treated as compensation, even the travel need not be documented as travel and entertainment [Sec. 274(e)].

62. Included in Kell Corporation's operating expenses were the following life insurance premiums:

Term life insurance premiums paid on the life of Kell's controller, with Kell as owner and beneficiary of the policy	$ 2,000
Group-term life insurance premiums paid on employees' lives, with the employees' dependents as owners and beneficiaries of the policies	$18,000

In its 1991 income tax return, what amount should Kell deduct for life insurance premiums?

   a. $20,000.
   b. $18,000.
   c. $2,000.
   d. $0.

The correct answer is (b). *(CPA 1189 Q-45)*
REQUIRED: The amount that a corporation may deduct for payment of life insurance premiums.
DISCUSSION: Kell Corporation may deduct the premiums paid for group-term life insurance under Sec. 162. However, according to Sec. 264, no deduction is allowed for premiums paid for life insurance for which the corporation is the beneficiary. Thus, only the $18,000 paid for its employees' group-term life insurance is deductible by Kell.

Module 18.6: Business Deductions   477

63. Daynite Corporation, a domestic corporation, acquired a 90% interest in KDN Corporation in 1981 for $50,000. During 1991, the stock of KDN was declared worthless. KDN's income for all taxable years was from sources other than passive income. What is the character and amount of the deduction Daynite should take in 1991?

a. Long-term capital loss of $50,000.
b. Ordinary loss of $50,000.
c. Long-term capital loss of $25,000.
d. Long-term capital loss of $3,000.

The correct answer is (b). *(SPE 989 III-41)*
REQUIRED: The character and amount of the deduction of worthless securities.
DISCUSSION: Sec. 165(g)(1) states that, if a security becomes worthless during the taxable year, the resulting loss will be treated as a loss from the sale or exchange of the security. However, Sec. 165(g)(3) provides an exception to this rule in the case of affiliated corporations. Under this exception, if a domestic corporation owns at least 80% of the voting and nonvoting stock of a corporation which derives at least 90% of its income from sources other than passive income, the stock is not treated as a capital asset. Therefore, any loss will be treated as an ordinary loss. Daynite will claim an ordinary loss of $50,000 on the KDN stock.

64. Able Corporation is owned entirely by individual A. Able pays A $300,000 in salary for 1991. As a result of an IRS audit, reasonable compensation for A is determined to be $180,000. Which one of the following statements regarding A's compensation is incorrect?

a. The $120,000 of unreasonable compensation is a dividend to A.
b. The $120,000 of unreasonable compensation cannot be deducted by Able.
c. The $120,000, if repaid by A as part of a repayment agreement, can be deducted by A in the year in which the repayment occurs.
d. The $120,000, if not repaid by A, is treated as a capital contribution made by A to Able.

The correct answer is (d). *(Publisher)*
REQUIRED: The incorrect statement regarding unreasonable compensation to a shareholder.
DISCUSSION: Sec. 162(a) provides that a corporation can deduct a reasonable allowance for salaries or compensation. The unreasonable compensation is normally treated as a constructive dividend to the shareholder (not a capital contribution by the shareholder) under Sec. 301, assuming that the corporation has sufficient earnings and profits.
Answer (a) is incorrect because it is a correct statement of the treatment of unreasonable compensation to a shareholder. Answer (b) is incorrect because Sec. 162(a)(1) only allows a deduction for reasonable salaries. Answer (c) is incorrect because a repayment under an agreement is deductible as a trade or business expense by the employee in the year in which it occurs.

65. With respect to corporations that are non-financial institutions, which one of the following methods is currently acceptable for computing a deduction for bad debts for tax purposes?

a. Allowance method.
b. Aging method.
c. Percentage of accounts receivable method.
d. Direct write-off method.

The correct answer is (d). *(CMA 690 3-21)*
REQUIRED: The method for recognizing a corporation's bad debt expense.
DISCUSSION: For tax years beginning after 1986, the reserve method is no longer allowed (except for certain financial institutions). Corporations that are not financial institutions must use the direct charge-off method or the nonaccrual-experience method.
Answers (a), (b), and (c) are incorrect because the reserve method is not allowed (except for certain financial institutions) after 1986.

66. Carey Corporation, a calendar-year taxpayer, employs the allowance method for its bad debts for financial reporting purposes. The credit balance in the allowance account was $100,000 on December 31, 1990. On December 31, 1991, Carey determined that a reasonable allowance would be $87,500. Carey wrote off $75,000 against the allowance account during 1991. Carey's 1991 deduction for bad debt expense on its federal income tax return is

a. $100,000.
b. $87,500.
c. $75,000.
d. $62,500.

The correct answer is (c). *(CMA 685 5-10)*
REQUIRED: A corporation's bad debt expense in 1991.
DISCUSSION: For tax years beginning after 1986, the reserve method of computing the bad debt deduction is no longer allowed (except for certain financial institutions). The direct charge-off method must be used. Therefore, Carey's 1991 bad debt deduction is $75,000, the actual bad debts amount.

478 Module 18.6: Business Deductions

67. Finway Corporation has paid the following ordinary and necessary business expenses with regard to its sales force.

Daily auto rental	$2,000
Meals at restaurants while traveling	2,500
Meals furnished on business premises	500
Cabs and limousines	1,000
Reimbursements for auto expenses of employees at $.275 per mile (IRS standard mileage rate for 1991)	2,250

The total amount that Finway may deduct for tax purposes is

a. $8,250.
b. $7,750.
c. $7,650.
d. $7,200.

The correct answer is (c). *(CMA 689 3-30)*
REQUIRED: The deductible amount of business expenses.
DISCUSSION: Travel expenses are deductible under Reg. 1.162-2(a). However, Sec. 274(a) limits the deduction of meal expenses while traveling to 80% of expenses incurred. Sec. 274(n)(1) limits the general deduction allowed for meal and entertainment expenses. Section 274(n)(2) provides a series of exceptions to this rule for items excepted from Sec. 274(a) by Sec. 274(e). Although Sec. 274(e)(1) specifically excepts meals furnished on business premises from Sec. 274(a), it is not also excepted from the 80% rule of Sec. 274(n)(1). Therefore, 20% of such expenses are disallowed. Finway's allowable deduction is computed as follows:

Auto rental	$2,000
Meals (80% deductible)	2,000
Meals furnished on business premises (80% deductible)	400
Cabs and limousines	1,000
Reimbursements for auto expenses	2,250
Total	$7,650

68. In 1991, Kara Corp. incurred the following expenditures in connection with the repurchase of its stock from shareholders to avert a hostile takeover

Interest on borrowings used to repurchase stock	$100,000
Legal and accounting fees in connection with the repurchase	400,000

The total of the above expenditures deductible in 1991 is

a. $0.
b. $100,000.
c. $400,000.
d. $500,000.

The correct answer is (b). *(CPA 1188 Q-24)*
REQUIRED: The amount that a corporation may deduct for expenses related to the repurchase of its stock.
DISCUSSION: Under Sec. 163, the interest expense incurred on business borrowings is deductible in the period in which it is paid or accrued. However, other expenses related to a stock repurchase or reorganization are generally not deductible. The Technical Amendments and Miscellaneous Revenue Act of 1988 added Sec. 162(k) which specifically prohibits deductions for amounts paid or incurred in connection with a stock redemption.

69. On December 31, 1990, Upbeat Corporation, a calendar-year accrual method taxpayer, accrued a $25,000 bonus payable to its sole shareholder K. K is a cash method taxpayer. The bonus is paid on March 15, 1991. The bonus cannot be deducted by Upbeat in 1990 but can be deducted in 1991.

The correct answer is (T). *(SPE 989 III-9)*
DISCUSSION: Sec. 267(a)(2) defers the deduction for certain losses and expenses occurring between related taxpayers. A corporation and its sole owner are related taxpayers under Sec. 267(b). The deduction for the bonus is deferred until the day that the amount is includable in individual K's income, or March 15, 1991.

70. Corporation R gave a real estate agency 100 shares of its stock for its advice when the corporation purchased a new office building. If the par value and the fair market value are both $10 a share, the corporation can deduct $1,000 as a current expense.

The correct answer is (F). *(SPE 1079 III-30)*
DISCUSSION: Under Reg. 1.162-1(a), no item may be included in business expenses to the extent it is used by the taxpayer in computing the cost of property included in its inventory or used in determining the gain or loss basis of plant, equipment, or other property. The cost of advice of the real estate agency must be capitalized under Reg. 1.263(a)-2(a) and included as part of the building's basis. Accordingly, Corporation R may not deduct the amount as a current expense.

71. If a corporation grants a transferable nonstatutory stock option in return for noncapital services and the option has an ascertainable fair market value, the corporation can take a current deduction.

The correct answer is (T). *(SPE 1079 III-34)*
DISCUSSION: Under Regs. 1.61-15 and 1.83-7, a nonstatutory stock option is included in the income of the employee when granted if the stock option has an ascertainable fair market value. At the same time, the employer is allowed a deduction in a corresponding amount. It must be for noncapital services so that the amount can be expensed rather than capitalized.

72. A corporation may deduct the premiums paid on permanent group life insurance above $50,000 on its officers if the corporation has no ownership in the policy, is not directly or indirectly the beneficiary, and the officers' compensation, including premiums paid, is considered reasonable.

The correct answer is (T). *(SPE 1079 III-28)*
DISCUSSION: Sec. 162 allows a deduction for ordinary and necessary trade or business expenses incurred. Generally, this includes most expenditures by an employer to promote employee health, goodwill, and welfare, as long as the amount is "reasonable." Therefore, the premiums would be deductible on insurance in amounts both above and below $50,000. Under Sec. 264(a), however, premiums paid on life insurance covering the life of an officer or employee are not deductible if the corporation is directly or indirectly a beneficiary.

18.7 Bonds

73. Delve Co., Inc. issued $1,000,000 of 10-year convertible bonds on October 1, 1981 for $880,000. The amount of bond discount deductible on Delve's income tax return for the year ended March 31, 1991 is

a. $0.
b. $6,000.
c. $12,000.
d. $120,000.

The correct answer is (c). *(CPA 581 Q-56)*
REQUIRED: The amount of bond discount which is deductible by a corporation.
DISCUSSION: Reg. 1.163-4 provides for the corporation issuing bonds at a discount before July 2, 1982 to accrue and deduct a ratable portion of the original issue discount each year. Delve's deduction for bond discount is

Par value	$1,000,000
Less proceeds	(880,000)
Original issue discount	$ 120,000
Monthly portion ($120,000 ÷ 120 months)	$ 1,000
Months outstanding in tax year ending 3/31/91	x 12
Bond discount deductible	$ 12,000

74. Shaney Corporation repurchased its own outstanding bonds in the open market for $258,000 on May 31, 1991. The bonds were originally issued on May 5, 1987 at face value of $250,000. For its tax year ending December 31, 1991, Shaney should report

a. Neither income nor a deduction.
b. A capital gain of $8,000.
c. A capital loss of $8,000.
d. A deduction of $8,000.

The correct answer is (d). *(CPA 1177 Q-22)*
REQUIRED: The tax effect a corporation must report as a result of repurchasing its own bonds.
DISCUSSION: Under Reg. 1.163-4(c), if bonds are issued and subsequently repurchased by the corporation at a price in excess of the issue price, the excess of the purchase price over the issue price is deductible as interest expense for that taxable year. Shaney should therefore report a deduction of $8,000 (repurchase price of $258,000 less issue price of $250,000).

Module 18.7: Bonds

75. On August 1, 1991, Corporation A, which is a calendar-year taxpayer, issued original issue bonds with a face value of $500,000 and carrying an 11% coupon rate. The bonds had a 4-year maturity and an issue price of $456,300. What is A's original issue discount deduction for 1991 assuming a current market yield of 14%?

- a. $10,925.
- b. $8,882.
- c. $4,552.
- d. $3,723.

The correct answer is (d). *(SPE 1078 III-66)*
REQUIRED: A corporation's deduction for original issue discount under the effective yield method.
DISCUSSION: For original issue discount bonds issued after July 1, 1982, Sec. 163(e) provides that the deduction for original issue discount is the aggregate of the daily portions of the original issue discount for the number of days in the year. The daily portions are determined under Sec. 1272(a) as the ratable portion of the excess of the product of the bond's yield to maturity and its adjusted issue price over the interest payable for the bond year. The adjusted issue price is the original issue price adjusted for original issue discount previously taken into income.

Yield times adjusted issue price (14% x $456,300)	$63,882
Less interest payable (11% x $500,000)	(55,000)
Annual discount amortization	$ 8,882
Ratable portion [(153 days left in year divided by 365 days) x $8,882]*	$ 3,723

*August 1, 1991 through December 31, 1991.

76. On May 15, 1983, Corporation A issued callable 20-year convertible bonds at a face value of $200,000 bearing interest at 5% per year. Under the terms of the bonds, the call price before May 15, 1992 is $210,000. On July 1, 1991, Corporation A calls the bonds for $210,000. What amount of the premium can Corporation A deduct on its 1991 income tax return?

- a. $0.
- b. $5,000.
- c. $10,000.
- d. $150,000.

The correct answer is (c). *(SPE 1080 III-68)*
REQUIRED: The amount of premium a corporation may deduct as a result of calling its convertible bonds.
DISCUSSION: Reg. 1.163-4(c) provides that, if bonds are issued and subsequently repurchased by the corporation at a price greater than the issue price, the excess of the purchase price over the issue price is deductible as interest expense for the taxable year. Corporation A can deduct $10,000 (redemption price of $210,000 less issue price of $200,000) in 1991.
Sec. 249 limits the deduction to the amount of the normal call premium on convertible debt. Excess amounts can be deducted only if the taxpayer can show that the excess is not attributable to the conversion feature. Since the call premium does not exceed one year's interest, it is considered a normal call premium and can be deducted in full.

77. Sportsworld, Inc. issued $500,000 face amount of bonds in 1978 and established a sinking fund to pay the debt. An independent trustee was appointed by the bondholders to administer the sinking fund. In 1991, the sinking fund earned $30,000 in interest on bank deposits and $2,000 in net short-term capital gains. How much of this income is taxable to Sportsworld?

- a. $0.
- b. $2,000.
- c. $30,000.
- d. $32,000.

The correct answer is (d). *(CPA 582 Q-42)*
REQUIRED: The amount of income from a sinking fund which is taxable to the corporation.
DISCUSSION: Reg. 1.61-13(b) provides that, if a corporation establishes a sinking fund under the control of a trustee for the payment of its debt, any gain arising from the fund must be included in income of the corporation. Therefore, Sportsworld must include both the interest and the net short-term capital gains in its taxable income ($30,000 + $2,000 = $32,000).

Module 18.7: Bonds

78. On December 31, 1971, Homer Corporation issued $2,000,000 of 50-year bonds for $2,600,000. On December 31, 1991, Homer issued new bonds with a face value of $3,000,000 for which it received $3,400,000 and used part of the proceeds to repurchase for $2,320,000 the bonds issued in 1971. No elections were made to adjust the basis of any property. What is the taxable income to Homer on the repurchase of the 1971 bonds?

  a. $0.
  b. $40,000.
  c. $280,000.
  d. $360,000.

The correct answer is (b). *(CPA 581 Q-44)*
REQUIRED: The amount of taxable income to a corporation on the repurchase of its bonds.
DISCUSSION: Under Reg. 1.61-12(c)(3), if bonds are issued by a corporation and are subsequently repurchased at a price less than the issue price minus any amount of premium already recognized as income, the difference is included in income for the taxable year. Prior to 1987, a corporation could elect under Sec. 108 to exclude the income and reduce the basis of property, but this election is available in post-1986 years only in cases of bankruptcy or insolvency. The amount of income taxable to Homer is

Original issue price	$2,600,000
Less face value	(2,000,000)
Total premium	$ 600,000
Issue price	$2,600,000
Less premium already recognized as income [($600,000 ÷ 50 years) x 20 years]	(240,000)
Issue price less premium already included in income	$2,360,000
Less repurchase price	(2,320,000)
Amount included in 1991 income	$ 40,000

79. If a corporation issues its own bonds at a discount, it has in effect paid additional interest which is deductible over the life of the bonds.

The correct answer is (T). *(SPE 989 III-18)*
DISCUSSION: For bonds issued prior to July 2, 1982, Reg. 1.163-4 permits the deduction of the original issue discount (as interest) over the life of the bond on a ratable basis. For bonds issued after July 1, 1982, Sec. 163(e) allows the deduction of original issue discount over the life of the bond based on the "yield" method of amortizing the discount.

80. On January 1, 1984, Corporation X issued a 10-year $1,000 debenture for $800. In 1991, Corporation X can deduct $20 of the bond discount (1/10 of the original discount) as interest expense.

The correct answer is (F). *(SPE 1081 III-18)*
DISCUSSION: Original issue discount is deductible as interest by the issuer. For bonds issued after July 1, 1982, the issuer is allowed a deduction each year based on the yield to maturity on the bond times the bond's adjusted issue price (issue price plus previously amortized discount) minus any interest paid in cash. Corporation X may therefore deduct bond discount as interest expense, but the amount of the discount is not determined by including the same amount of discount in income in each of the 10 years that the bond is outstanding.

81. Corporation L issued 20-year convertible bonds at a face value of $1,000 bearing interest at 16%. L repurchased these bonds before maturity for $1,100 each. The premium paid to repurchase the bonds is deductible since it does not exceed a normal call premium for comparable nonconvertible corporate indebtedness.

The correct answer is (T). *(SPE 1082 III-13)*
DISCUSSION: Under Sec. 249, if a security is retired at a premium (i.e., at a price greater than the original issue price), the debtor corporation may deduct this premium, limited to a normal call premium on nonconvertible debt. Corporation A's premium is

Repurchase price	$1,100
Less issue price	(1,000)
"Premium" on repurchase	$ 100

Since this premium does not exceed 1 year's interest at the rate stated in the bond, it is considered a normal call premium and may be deducted in full.

82. Corporation P repurchased at a premium convertible bonds it had issued. The amount of the premium that P may deduct as interest may not be in excess of a normal call premium for comparable nonconvertible corporate indebtednesses.

The correct answer is (F). *(SPE 1081 III-19)*
DISCUSSION: Sec. 249 provides the general rule that no deduction is allowed to an issuing corporation for any repurchase premium which exceeds a normal call premium. But a repurchase premium which exceeds a normal call premium may be deducted to the extent that the corporation demonstrates to the commissioner that such repurchase price is not attributable to the conversion feature. Consequently, under certain circumstances the premium which P may deduct may exceed a normal call premium.

83. In 1991, Corporation T transferred stock to its creditors in satisfaction of indebtedness (T is not involved in bankruptcy nor is it insolvent). Corporation T is treated as satisfying the indebtedness in full with money equal to the fair market value of the stock. Therefore, the corporation will have income from discharge of indebtedness to the extent the debt exceeds the value of the stock.

The correct answer is (T). *(SPE 990 III-5)*
DISCUSSION: Under Sec. 61, taxpayers, including corporations, must recognize gain from the discharge of indebtedness. If a corporation transfers stock to its creditors in satisfaction of indebtedness, it will have income from the discharge of the indebtedness to the extent that the debt exceeds the value of the distributed stock. The corporation will not have income from the discharge of indebtedness if it is insolvent or is involved in bankruptcy (Sec. 108).

18.8 Dividends-Received Deduction

84. Which of the following qualifies for the dividends-received deduction?

a. Dividends from a DISC paid out of accumulated DISC income.
b. Dividends on deposits in a mutual savings bank.
c. Dividends from a real estate investment trust.
d. Dividends from a taxable domestic corporation.

The correct answer is (d). *(SPE 1080 III-54)*
REQUIRED: The dividends which qualify for the dividends-received deduction.
DISCUSSION: Sec. 243 permits a corporation to deduct 70% of dividends received from a domestic taxable corporation of which it owns less than 20% of the stock, 80% of dividends received if the stock is 20% or more owned, and 100% of dividends received if the stock is 80% or more owned.
Answer (a) is incorrect because Sec. 246(d) provides that no deduction is allowed with respect to dividends from a DISC (domestic international sales corporation) to the extent that the DISC dividend comes out of accumulated DISC income or previously taxed income. Answers (b) and (c) are incorrect because Sec. 243(c) provides that amounts received as dividends from mutual savings banks or from real estate investment trusts are not eligible.

85. During 1991, the dividends-received deduction for a corporation allows a(n)

a. 85% deduction for all dividends received from non-affiliated corporations.
b. 70% deduction for all dividends received from non-affiliated corporations.
c. 70% deduction for dividends received from a corporation when ownership is less than 20%, 80% deduction for dividends received from non-affiliated corporations when ownership is 20% or more, and 100% deduction for dividends received from affiliated corporations when ownership is 80% or more.
d. 70% deduction for dividends received from a corporation when ownership is less than 20% and an 85% deduction for dividends received from non-affiliated corporations when ownership is 20% or more.

The correct answer is (c). *(CMA 1289 3-13)*
REQUIRED: The percentage of dividends received which qualify for the dividends-received deduction.
DISCUSSION: Sec. 243 permits a corporation to deduct 70% of dividends received from a domestic taxable corporation of which it owns less than 20% of the stock, 80% of dividends received if the stock is 20% or more owned, and 100% of dividends received if the stock is 80% or more owned.

Module 18.8: Dividends-Received Deduction

86. For a domestic corporation to deduct a percentage of the dividends it receives after 1986 from a foreign corporation, certain tests must be met. Which of the following conditions need not be present?

a. The domestic corporation owns at least 10% of the foreign corporation.

b. The foreign corporation has income effectively connected with a trade or business in the U.S.

c. The corporation is not a foreign personal holding company.

d. The foreign corporation has derived income effectively connected with its U.S. business amounting to at least 50% of its gross income from all sources for a 36-month period.

The correct answer is (d). *(SPE 1079 III-49)*
REQUIRED: The condition which need not be met for a domestic corporation to deduct a percentage of dividends received from a foreign corporation.
DISCUSSION: Sec. 245 lists requirements which must be met for the dividends of a foreign corporation to qualify for the dividends-received deduction. These requirements include that the foreign corporation (1) not be a foreign personal holding company; (2) be subject to federal income taxation; (3) be 10% or more owned by the domestic corporation; and (4) have income from effectively connected business sources within the United States. For dividends received before 1987, prior law required the foreign corporation to have derived 50% or more of its gross income from effectively connected business sources within the U.S.

Answers (a), (b), and (c) are incorrect because each is a condition that must be met.

87. Andron Corporation owns 30% of the stock of Blackbird Corporation, 10% of the stock of Connie Corporation, and 80% of the stock of Dannin Corporation. Blackbird and Connie are both U.S. corporations, and Dannin is a foreign (non-U.S.) corporation doing 100% of its business in South America. Andron has taxable income before the dividends-received deduction of $200,000, and has received the following dividends.

Blackbird	$ 5,000
Connie	10,000
Dannin	20,000

The dividends-received deduction for Andron Corporation would be

a. $10,500.
b. $11,000.
c. $12,000.
d. $31,500.

The correct answer is (b). *(CMA 689 3-24)*
REQUIRED: The correct dividends-received deduction (DRD).
DISCUSSION: Under Sec. 243, a corporation is entitled to a special deduction from gross income for dividends received from a taxable domestic corporation. The amount of the deduction is based upon the value and the percentage of the voting stock of the distributing corporation owned by the recipient. The deduction is 70% of dividends received from corporations owned less than 20% by the recipient corporation or 80% of dividends received from a corporation owned more than 20%. The DRD is 100% if the recipient owns 80% or more of the distributing corporation and they are members of the same affiliated group. The total DRD is limited to 70% (80% in the case of a 20% owned corporation) of the recipient corporation's taxable income without regard to any NOL deduction, DRD, capital loss carryback, or adjustments for nontaxed portions of extraordinary dividends received.

Under Sec. 245, a dividends-received deduction is available for dividends received from a foreign corporation if owned 10% or more by a domestic corporation. However, it is available only on the portion of the dividend distribution attributable to income that is effectively connected with the conduct of a U.S. trade or business. Since Dannin Corporation has no effectively connected income, Andron Corporation receives no dividends-received deduction for dividends received from Dannin Corporation. The DRD is $11,000 as computed below.

Corporation	Deduction %	Dividend	DRD
Connie	70%	$10,000	$ 7,000
Blackbird	80%	5,000	4,000
Total			$11,000

Andron may be able to claim a deemed paid foreign tax credit (Sec. 902) with respect to the dividend from Dannin. See Module 11.7 for a discussion of the deemed paid credit.

Module 18.8: Dividends-Received Deduction

88. Evans Inc. has gross income for 1991 of $150,000 excluding dividends of $100,000 received from nonaffiliated, domestic, taxpaying corporations in which Evans owns a 5% interest. The dividends were not from debt-financed portfolio stock. The company's operating expenses for the year are $160,000. Evans Inc.'s allowable dividends-received deduction is

a. $63,000.
b. $72,000.
c. $76,500.
d. $80,000.

The correct answer is (a). *(CMA 688 3-11)*
REQUIRED: A corporation's allowable deduction for dividends received in 1991.
DISCUSSION: Sec. 243 allows a corporation to deduct 70% of dividends received from a domestic corporation of which it owns less than 20% of the stock. Sec. 246(b), however, limits the dividends-received deduction to 70% of the corporation's taxable income, computed without regard to the dividends-received deduction, dividends-paid deduction, net operating loss deduction, capital loss carryback, and certain adjustments for extraordinary dividends. Evans' taxable income before the dividends-received deduction is $90,000 ($150,000 gross profit – $160,000 expenses + $100,000 dividends). Evans' allowable deduction for dividends received is limited to $63,000 (70% x $90,000 taxable income).

89. Universal Corporation had the following items of income and expenses in 1991:

Gross income	$1,000,000
Deductible expenses	1,200,000
Dividends received from domestic corporations (20% owned)	20,000

Universal had no debt related to its stock ownership. Universal is entitled to a dividends-received deduction in 1991 of

a. $0.
b. $16,000.
c. $17,000.
d. $20,000.

The correct answer is (b). *(CMA 685 3-9)*
REQUIRED: The dividends-received deduction for a corporation with a net operating loss.
DISCUSSION: Sec. 243(a) allows a corporation to deduct 80% of the dividends received from domestic corporations where the taxpayer owns 20% or more of the distributing corporation. Sec. 246(b) limits this deduction to 80% of the corporation's taxable income computed without the dividends-received deduction and certain other deductions and losses. This limit, however, does not apply for any taxable year for which there is a net operating loss.
Since Universal has a net operating loss of $180,000 ($1,000,000 income + $20,000 dividends – $1,200,000 expenses), the 80% of income limitation does not apply and the dividends-received deduction will be 80% of dividends received from domestic corporations, which is $16,000 ($20,000 x 80%).

90. For the year ended December 31, 1991, Atkinson, Inc., a calendar-year corporation, had gross business income of $160,000 and dividend income of $100,000 from 25% owned unaffiliated domestic corporations. Business deductions for 1991 amounted to $170,000. The dividends were not from debt-financed portfolio stock. What is Atkinson's dividends-received deduction for 1991?

a. $0.
b. $72,000.
c. $80,000.
d. $90,000.

The correct answer is (b). *(CPA 1182 Q-50)*
REQUIRED: The corporation's dividends-received deduction.
DISCUSSION: Under Sec. 243(a), a corporation is allowed a deduction for 80% of dividends received from unaffiliated domestic corporations of which it owns at least 20% of the stock. Sec. 246(b) limits the dividends-received deduction to 80% of taxable income before inclusion of the dividends-received deduction, dividends-paid deduction, net operating loss deduction, capital loss carrybacks, and certain adjustments for extraordinary dividends. (Note this deduction is 70% of taxable income for dividends from less than 20% owned corporations.) Eighty percent of Atkinson's dividend income is $80,000. However, 80% of the taxable income before the dividends-received deduction is $72,000. This limit will be the dividends-received deduction.

Gross business income	$160,000
Dividend income	100,000
Gross income	$260,000
Less business deductions	(170,000)
Taxable income without dividends-received deduction	$ 90,000
Deduction is lesser of:	
80% of dividend income, or	$ 80,000
80% of taxable income without dividend deduction	$ 72,000

Module 18.8: Dividends-Received Deduction

91. Bailey Corporation owns 15% of the stock of Chandler Company, a domestic corporation. Bailey received a $30,000 dividend from Chandler during 1991. In addition, Bailey had a net loss from operations of $15,000 during 1991. Bailey is entitled to a 1991 dividends-received deduction of

a. $0.
b. $21,000.
c. $24,000.
d. $30,000.

The correct answer is (b). *(CMA 690 3-12)*
REQUIRED: The amount of a corporation's dividends-received deduction.
DISCUSSION: Sec. 243(a) allows a corporation to deduct 70% of the dividends received from domestic corporations where the taxpayer owns less than 20% of the corporation paying the dividends. This deduction is limited to 70% of the corporation's taxable income computed without regard to the dividends-received deduction and certain other deductions and losses, unless there is a net operating loss after deducting the dividends-received deduction [Sec. 246(b)].

Net income from operations	$(15,000)
Plus dividends	30,000
Taxable income (before dividends-received deduction)	$ 15,000
Less dividends-received deduction (70% x $30,000)	(21,000)
Net operating loss	$ (6,000)

Since there is a net operating loss after the dividends-received deduction, the deduction of $21,000 is not limited by taxable income.

92. Maris Corporation purchased 20% of Mantle Corporation's common stock in August 1991 and paid for the purchase with $100,000 cash and $100,000 borrowed from its bank. During 1991, Maris received $30,000 in dividends from Mantle and paid $10,000 in interest expense on the bank loan. Maris did not make any principal payments on the loan during 1991. If Maris had taxable income of $50,000 before special deductions, what is its dividends-received deduction for 1991?

a. $0.
b. $12,000.
c. $14,000.
d. $24,000.

The correct answer is (c). *(Publisher)*
REQUIRED: The corporate dividends-received deduction when stock is debt financed.
DISCUSSION: Sec. 246A restricts the dividends-received deduction when portfolio stock is debt financed. Debt-financed portfolio stock is any stock of a corporation if the taxpayer does not own at least 50% of the stock of such corporation and if, at some time during the base period, portfolio indebtedness exists with respect to the stock. The dividends-received deduction (when the recipient owns 20% or more of the payor corporation) is limited to a percentage equal to 80% times 100% minus the average indebtedness percentage. This percentage is the average amount of portfolio indebtedness divided by the average amount of adjusted basis of the stock during the period. However, the reduction in the dividends-received deduction cannot be more than the interest deducted for the portfolio indebtedness.

Maris's average indebtedness percentage is 50% ($100,000 ÷ $200,000), so the allowable deduction is 40% [80% x (100% − 50%)], giving a dividends-received deduction of $12,000 (40% x $30,000). The full deduction would have been $24,000 (80% x $30,000). The total reduction in the dividends-received deduction ($24,000 − $12,000 = $12,000) is greater than the interest-expense deduction for the period ($10,000), so the reduction is limited by Sec. 246A(e) to the $10,000 of interest expense. Maris's dividends-received deduction is thus $14,000 [(80% x $30,000) − $10,000].

93. Alpha is a U.S. corporation which owns 20% of the stock of Omega, a foreign corporation which is not a foreign personal holding company. In 1991, 40% of Omega's income is from effectively connected business sources in the U.S., and Omega distributes all its current earnings to its shareholders. Alpha's dividend from Omega is $20,000 in 1991. Alpha has no debt related to its stockholdings. What is Alpha's dividends-received deduction?

   a. $0.
   b. $1,280.
   c. $6,400.
   d. $16,000.

The correct answer is (c). *(Publisher)*
REQUIRED: The dividends-received deduction for dividends from a foreign corporation.
DISCUSSION: A portion of dividends from a foreign corporation 10% or more of which is owned by a U.S. corporation qualifies for the dividends-received deduction. The portion of the dividends that qualify is the U.S. source portion of the dividends [Sec. 245(a)]. The U.S. source portion is the portion of undistributed earnings after 1986 attributable to income effectively connected with the conduct of a business in the U.S. and subject to U.S. tax. The dividends-received deduction is 80% for dividends received from corporations in which the recipient owns 20% or more of the stock.
Therefore, Alpha's dividends-received deduction is $6,400 (80% x 40% effectively connected income x $20,000 dividend).

94. Dividends on deposits or withdrawable accounts in mutual savings banks qualify for the dividends-received deduction when received by a corporation.

The correct answer is (F). *(SPE 1079 III-44)*
DISCUSSION: Sec. 243(c) provides that dividends paid by mutual savings banks are not considered dividends (they are more like interest) for the purpose of the dividends-received deduction. Therefore, dividends from mutual savings banks do not qualify for the dividends-received deduction.

95. Small business investment companies may deduct 100% of the dividends received from a taxable domestic corporation.

The correct answer is (T). *(SPE 1081 III-14)*
DISCUSSION: Under Sec. 243(a), a small business investment company operating under the Small Business Investment Act of 1958 may deduct 100% of the dividends received from a domestic taxable corporation.

96. Generally, the total deduction for dividends received is limited to 20% of the taxable income of a corporation. In figuring this limitation, taxable income is determined without regard to any capital loss carryback to the tax year.

The correct answer is (F). *(SPE 990 III-6)*
DISCUSSION: Sec. 246(b) limits the dividends-received deduction to 70% of taxable income computed without regard to deductions for net operating losses, capital loss carrybacks, dividends received, or dividends paid, and certain adjustments for extraordinary dividends, when the taxpayer owns less than 20% of the distributing corporation. The limit is 80% of taxable income (as adjusted) where the taxpayer owns 20% or more of the distributing corporation.

18.9 Charitable Contributions Deduction

97. Which of the following contributions made by Natvale Corporation, a domestic corporation, is not deductible for federal income tax purposes in 1991?

   a. 100 shares of Natvale's preferred stock to Soo Valley Community College; the stock has been held in the treasury ($60 per share FMV on the date of gift).
   b. $2,500 to the local humane society.
   c. $7,500 to the American Red Cross.
   d. $2,000 to Mexican Adoptions, a private foundation in Mexico that operates orphanages.

The correct answer is (d). *(CMA 684 3-11)*
REQUIRED: The contribution not deductible for federal income tax purposes in 1991.
DISCUSSION: Sec. 170(c) defines charitable contributions to include any contribution to an organization operated exclusively for religious, charitable, scientific, or educational purposes. However, the organization must have been created or organized in the United States or selected foreign countries with which the U.S. has a tax treaty. Mexican Adoptions does not qualify since the foundation is organized in Mexico.
Answers (a), (b), and (c) are incorrect because each of the organizations listed qualifies under Sec. 170(c).

Module 18.9: Charitable Contributions Deduction

98. Which of the following statements is true for a corporation?

a. Charitable contributions in excess of the 10% limitation may, subject to limitations, be carried back to each of the preceding 3 years.

b. Charitable contributions in excess of the 10% limitation may, subject to limitations, be carried over to each of the following 5 years.

c. Subject to the 10% limitation, a carryover of excess contributions is used before the contributions made in the carryover year.

d. Charitable contributions in excess of the 10% limitation may be carried over to subsequent years indefinitely.

The correct answer is (b). *(SPE 1083 III-53)*
REQUIRED: The true statement regarding charitable contributions made by a corporation.
DISCUSSION: Sec. 170(b) provides that excess charitable contributions may be carried over to each of the succeeding 5 years, subject to certain limitations. Under Sec. 170(b)(2), the total deductions for charitable contributions of a corporation may not exceed 10% of the taxable income computed before special deductions.
Answer (a) is incorrect because charitable contributions may not be carried back. Answer (c) is incorrect because the current year contributions are used before the carryovers. Answer (d) is incorrect because the carryover is only allowed for 5 years.

99. Brave, Inc. made cash donations of $30,000 to various qualified charities during 1991. The following data for 1991 are also available:

Revenue from operations	$800,000
Interest income from various corporate bonds	150,000
Business expenses (not including the charitable contribution deduction)	700,000

Brave had no dividend income or carryovers of any type for 1991. Brave's allowable charitable deduction for 1991 is

a. $5,000.
b. $12,500.
c. $25,000.
d. $30,000.

The correct answer is (c). *(CMA 1282 3-2)*
REQUIRED: The corporation's deduction for charitable contributions for 1991.
DISCUSSION: A corporation may deduct charitable contributions of up to 10% of the corporate taxable income computed without taking into consideration the charitable contributions and other special deductions. Brave's charitable contribution deduction is

Revenue from operations	$800,000
Interest income	150,000
Business expenses	(700,000)
Taxable income before charitable contribution deduction	$250,000
	x 10%
Charitable contribution deduction limit	$ 25,000

The $5,000 of excess 1991 charitable contributions may be carried forward 5 years and deducted.

100. Marvel Corporation's operating income for 1991 was $200,000 after consideration of $60,000 for charitable contributions. What is the maximum allowable deduction for contributions on Marvel's 1991 federal income tax return?

a. $26,000.
b. $20,000.
c. $12,500.
d. $6,000.

The correct answer is (a). *(SPE 990 III-64)*
REQUIRED: The proper charitable contribution deduction for 1991.
DISCUSSION: Sec. 170(b)(2) provides that the charitable contribution deduction for corporations is limited to 10% of the taxable income computed before the charitable contribution deduction, dividends-received deduction, net operating loss carryback, and capital loss carryback. Marvel's charitable contribution deduction should be $26,000 [($200,000 + $60,000) x 10%].

101. Gero Corporation had operating income of $160,000, after deducting $10,000 for contributions to State University, but not including dividends of $2,000 received from nonaffiliated taxable domestic corporations (not from debt-financed portfolio stock). In computing the maximum allowable deduction for contributions, Gero should apply the percentage limitation to a base amount of

a. $172,000.
b. $170,400.
c. $170,000.
d. $162,000.

The correct answer is (a). *(CPA 1188 Q-26)*
REQUIRED: The base amount for the percentage limitation on charitable contributions.
DISCUSSION: Sec. 170(b)(2) limits the charitable contribution deduction to 10% of a corporation's taxable income computed before the charitable contribution deduction, dividends-received deduction, net operating loss carryback, and capital loss carryback. Gero's base amount to which the percentage limitation should be applied in computing the charitable contribution deduction is $172,000 ($160,000 operating income + $10,000 contributions + $2,000 dividends).

102. During 1991, Corporation Y received $20,000 in dividends from a taxable domestic corporation in which Y had more than 20% ownership. Y received no other dividends. Y's charitable contributions for 1991 totaled $10,000. Y's taxable income for 1991 was $60,000 after the dividends-received deduction but before the deduction for charitable contributions. What is the amount of Corporation Y's charitable contribution deduction for 1991?

a. $4,000.
b. $7,600.
c. $8,000.
d. $10,000.

The correct answer is (b). *(SPE 989 III-75)*
REQUIRED: The charitable contribution deduction for a corporation.
DISCUSSION: Sec. 170(b)(2) provides that the charitable contribution deduction for a corporation may not exceed 10% of the corporation's taxable income computed before the charitable contribution deduction, net operating loss carryback, capital loss carryback, and the dividends-received deduction. Y's charitable contribution is limited to $7,600 as computed below. The excess of $2,400 ($10,000 – $7,600) may be carried over for 5 years.

Y's taxable income before deduction for charitable contributions	$60,000
Add back:	
Dividends-received deduction ($20,000 x 80%)	16,000
Adjusted taxable income	$76,000
	x 10%
10% limit on contribution deduction	$ 7,600

103. During 1990, Q, a cash-basis corporation, made the following contributions:

$1,000 to United Fund
$100 to V.F.W.
$200 to Goodwill Industries
$500 to a community college

In December 1990, due to an unusually high taxable income of $100,000, the board of directors authorized an additional $1,000 contribution to the United Fund to be paid January 31, 1991. What is Corporation Q's charitable contribution deduction on its calendar-year 1990 return?

a. $1,300.
b. $1,700.
c. $1,800.
d. $2,300.

The correct answer is (c). *(SPE 1080 III-55)*
REQUIRED: A corporation's charitable contribution deduction.
DISCUSSION: Under Sec. 170, charitable contributions made to qualified organizations and paid within the taxable year may be deducted from taxable income. All of the organizations listed qualify under Sec. 170(c). But the additional $1,000 paid to United Fund in January 1991 is not deductible in 1990 because only accrual basis corporations may authorize and deduct a contribution in one year and pay it within 2½ months after year-end [Sec. 170 (a)(2)]. A corporation's charitable deduction is limited to 10% of taxable income computed before the contributions deduction, and certain special deductions. Corporation Q's charitable contribution deduction for 1990 is not limited because the qualified contributions ($1,800) do not exceed $10,000 (10% of $100,000 taxable income).

United Fund	$1,000
V.F.W.	100
Goodwill Industries	200
Community college	500
Contribution deduction	$1,800

Module 18.9: Charitable Contributions Deduction

104. Norwood Corporation is an accrual basis taxpayer. For the year ended December 31, 1990, it had book income before tax of $450,000 after deducting a charitable contribution of $50,000. The contribution was authorized by the board of directors in December 1990, but was not actually paid until March 1, 1991. How should Norwood treat this charitable contribution for tax purposes to minimize its 1990 taxable income?

a. It cannot claim a deduction in 1990 but must apply the payment against 1991 income.
b. Make an election claiming a deduction for 1990 of $50,000 with no carryover.
c. Make an election claiming a deduction for 1990 of $45,000 with no carryover.
d. Make an election carrying back the deduction 3 years.

The correct answer is (b). *(CPA 581 Q-48)*
REQUIRED: A corporation's maximum charitable contribution deduction.
DISCUSSION: Sec. 170(a)(2) allows an accrual basis corporation to deduct a charitable contribution if authorized during the taxable year and paid within 2½ months after year-end. Since the contribution was paid by March 15, it is deductible in 1990. Sec. 170(b)(2) provides that the charitable contribution deduction may not exceed 10% of a corporation's taxable income computed before certain special deductions and the charitable contribution deduction. Norwood's maximum 1990 deduction is $50,000, which is within the limit as shown below.

Taxable income after contribution	$450,000
Add back contributions made	50,000
Taxable income before contribution	$500,000
	x 10%
1990 contribution deduction limit	$ 50,000

105. In 1991, Green Corporation had a net operating loss and has a net operating loss carryback of $4,400 available to 1990. Green Corporation had the following income and expenses for 1990 when it was originally reported.

Gross profit	$205,000
Other deductions (including $1,700 of contributions)	194,200

What is the Green Corporation's deduction for contributions when the 1990 taxable income is recomputed?

a. $640.
b. $810.
c. $1,080.
d. $1,250.

The correct answer is (d). *(SPE 1077 III-11)*
REQUIRED: A corporation's contribution deduction when there are NOL carrybacks.
DISCUSSION: Sec. 170(b)(2) limits a corporation's charitable deduction to 10% of the corporation's taxable income computed before the charitable contribution deduction, net operating loss carryback, capital loss carryback, and dividends-received deduction. Green's contribution deduction is $1,250 because the 10% limit is less than actual contributions.

Gross profit	$205,000
Less deductions	(194,200)
Add back contributions made	1,700
Taxable income before special deductions	$ 12,500
	x 10%
Contribution deduction limitation	$ 1,250

106. Corporation D (not an S corporation) donated inventory with a cost of $8,500 and a fair market value of $10,000 to a public charity. The conditions regarding the special rule on appreciation have been met (e.g., the charity used the inventory for the care of the needy). Corporation D's taxable income before the contribution deduction is $95,000. What is Corporation D's allowable contribution deduction?

a. $750.
b. $8,500.
c. $9,250.
d. $9,500.

The correct answer is (c). *(SPE 1081 III-76)*
REQUIRED: A corporation's allowable deduction for charitable contributions of inventory.
DISCUSSION: Normally, the deduction for a contribution of inventory is limited to its basis by Sec. 170(e)(1). However, Sec. 170(e)(3) provides that when a corporation contributes inventory to be used by the donee for the care of the needy, the qualified contribution is reduced by only one-half the amount of potential ordinary income if the property had instead been sold at its fair market value. Corporation D's allowable contribution deduction is $9,250 and is not limited since it does not exceed $9,500 (10% x $95,000 adjusted taxable income).

Contributions	$10,000
Potential ordinary income if sold [($10,000 FMV − $8,500 basis) x 50%]	(750)
Contribution deduction	$ 9,250

Module 18.9: Charitable Contributions Deduction

107. April Corporation's book income before income taxes for 1991 was $60,000. During 1991, April paid $3,000 in cash dividends on its outstanding cumulative preferred stock and $7,000 as a contribution to a qualified charitable organization. For 1991, April's taxable income was

a. $60,000.
b. $60,300.
c. $61,000.
d. $63,000.

The correct answer is (b). *(CPA 580 Q-22)*
REQUIRED: A corporation's taxable income when cash dividends were paid and a contribution was made to a qualified charitable organization.
DISCUSSION: Under Sec. 170, a contribution made to a qualified charitable organization may be deducted from gross income. Sec. 170(b)(2) limits the deduction to 10% of the corporation's taxable income computed before the charitable contribution deduction, net operating loss carryback, capital loss carryback, and dividends-received deduction. Dividends paid are not deductible for either book or taxable income (except with respect to certain public utility company dividends under Sec. 247) so it is irrelevant information. April's contribution deduction is limited to $6,700 since the 10% limit is less than actual contributions. April's taxable income is

Book income	$60,000
Add back contributions made	7,000
Income for computing 10% limit	$67,000
	x 10%
Charitable contribution deduction	$ 6,700
Net income before contribution deduction	$67,000
Less contribution deduction	(6,700)
Taxable income	$60,300

108. For 1991, a corporation had taxable income of $70,000 without regard to the contribution deduction. Contributions made in 1991 totaled $5,000 and a $4,000 carryover of excess contributions from 1990 is available to apply to 1991. What is the amount of contribution carryover available for 1992 and what is its source?

a. $0.
b. $2,000 from 1991.
c. $2,000 from 1990.
d. $3,000 from 1990.

The correct answer is (c). *(SPE 990 III-36)*
REQUIRED: A corporation's excess contribution carryover.
DISCUSSION: Sec. 170(b)(2) limits the charitable contribution deduction to 10% of the corporation's taxable income computed before the charitable contribution deduction and certain special deductions. Sec. 170(d)(2) allows a corporation to carry excess contributions forward for 5 years. The total charitable contribution deduction including contribution carryovers, however, may not exceed the 10% limit. The current contributions are deducted first so that the 1992 carryover consists of $2,000 from 1990.

Contributions made in 1991	$5,000
Carryover from 1990	4,000
	$9,000
1991 deduction limited to 10% x $70,000	(7,000)
Carryover to 1992 from 1990	$2,000

> Questions 109 and 110 are based on Kelli Corporation, which had the following income and expense items during 1991.
>
> | | |
> |---|---:|
> | Dividends received | $ 10,000 |
> | Revenue from operating activities | 130,000 |
> | Expenses from operating activities | 100,000 |
> | Charitable contributions paid | 5,000 |
>
> In addition to the above items, Kelli had a $1,000 unused charitable contribution from 1987.

109. The proper treatment of Kelli Corporation's charitable contributions when calculating its 1991 tax liability is to

a. First apply the carryover from 1987 and then use the current contributions.

b. First use the current contributions and then apply the carryover from 1987.

c. Lump both amounts together and treat the total as contributions made in the current year.

d. Use only the current contributions since unused charitable contributions can only be carried forward for 3 succeeding tax years.

The correct answer is (b). *(CMA 690 3-10)*
REQUIRED: The proper treatment of charitable contribution carryovers.
DISCUSSION: Sec. 170(d)(2) requires the current contributions be used first and then applying carryovers in a first-in, first-out (FIFO) manner. Excess contributions may be carried forward for 5 years.

110. Kelli Corporation's maximum charitable contribution deduction for 1991 is

a. $3,000.
b. $3,500.
c. $4,000.
d. $6,000.

The correct answer is (c). *(CMA 690 3-11)*
REQUIRED: A corporation's maximum charitable contribution deduction.
DISCUSSION: Sec. 170(b)(2) limits the charitable contribution deduction to 10% of the corporation's taxable income computed before any charitable contribution deduction, and without regard to the dividends-received deduction, net operating loss carrybacks, and capital loss carrybacks.
Sec. 170(d)(2) allows a corporation to carry unused charitable contributions forward for 5 years. The total charitable contribution deduction, including carryovers, may not exceed the 10% limit. Current contributions are deducted before carryovers. Kelli Corporation's taxable income for 1991 (computed without regard to the dividends-received deduction or the charitable contributions deduction) is $40,000 ($10,000 dividends + $130,000 operating revenues less $100,000 expenses). Therefore, Kelli Corporation's maximum charitable contribution deduction for 1991 is $4,000 (10% x $40,000).

111. At its December 1990 board meeting, Corporation A, an accrual-method taxpayer, authorized a contribution to Charitable Organization Y. Corporation A's 1990 calendar-year tax return was filed on June 13, 1991. The payment to Y was made on May 1, 1991. Corporation A can deduct the charitable contribution made to Y on its 1990 tax return.

The correct answer is (F). *(SPE 1080 III-15)*
DISCUSSION: A corporation which reports income on the accrual basis may elect to treat a contribution as paid (and therefore deductible) during the taxable year if the board of directors authorizes the contribution during such year and the contribution is paid within 2½ months following the close of the taxable year [Sec. 170(a)(2)]. For Corporation A to deduct the contribution on its 1990 tax return, it would have had to pay the contribution by March 15, 1991, and it would have had to obtain an extension of time to file its return so that the election could have been made on a timely filed return.

18.10 C Corporation Net Operating Losses

112. If a corporation's charitable contributions for the year are more than the allowable limit, the corporation may, subject to certain limitations, carry the excess over to each of the following 5 years.

The correct answer is (T). *(SPE 989 III-6)*
DISCUSSION: Sec. 170(d)(2) provides that a corporation's excess charitable contributions may be carried forward and deducted in the 5 succeeding taxable years.

113. Corporation A had $300,000 of income from business operations and $700,000 of allowable business expenses. It also received $20,000 in dividends from a domestic corporation in which it was a 20% owner. What is the amount of Corporation A's net operating loss?

a. $380,000.
b. $396,000.
c. $397,000.
d. $400,000.

The correct answer is (b). *(SPE 990 III-66)*
REQUIRED: Corporation A's net operating loss when there is dividend income.
DISCUSSION: Sec. 172(c) defines a net operating loss as the excess of deductions over gross income, with certain modifications. One modification is that the dividends-received deduction is computed without regard to the 80% of taxable income limitation in Sec. 246(b).

Gross profit on sales	$ 300,000
Dividends received	20,000
Gross income	$ 320,000
Less: Administrative expenses	(700,000)
Dividends-received deduction (80% x $20,000)	(16,000)
Net operating loss	$(396,000)

114. Based on the following information, what is the amount of Corporation X's net operating loss for calendar year 1991?

Gross income from business operations	$500,000
Dividends from 20% owned taxable domestic corporations	150,000
Business expenses	625,000
1990 net operating loss (available for carryover to 1991)	100,000

a. $0.
b. $3,750.
c. $75,000.
d. $95,000.

The correct answer is (d). *(SPE 987 III-82)*
REQUIRED: The corporation's net operating loss when there is dividend income and a NOL carryover.
DISCUSSION: Sec. 172(c) defines a net operating loss as the excess of deductions over gross income, with certain modifications. One modification is that the dividends-received deduction is computed without regard to the Sec. 246(b) limitation of 80% of taxable income. Also, a deduction for a net operating loss carryover is not allowed in computing a current NOL. Consequently, Corporation X's 1991 NOL is computed as follows:

Gross income from business operations	$500,000
Dividends received	150,000
Gross income	$650,000
Less: Business expenses	(625,000)
Dividends received deduction (80% x $150,000)	(120,000)
Net operating loss	$ (95,000)

115. For the tax year ended December 31, 1991, Orange Corporation had gross income of $600,000 and operating expenses of $900,000. Contributions of $5,000 to qualified charities were included in expenses. In addition to the expenses, Orange Corporation had a net operating loss carryover of $8,000. What is Orange Corporation's net operating loss for 1991?

a. $205,000.
b. $295,000.
c. $300,000.
d. $305,000.

The correct answer is (b). *(SPE 990 III-65)*
REQUIRED: The corporation's net operating loss when there is dividend income and charitable contributions.
DISCUSSION: Sec. 172(c) defines a net operating loss as the excess of deductions over gross income, with certain modifications. One of the modifications is that a deduction for a net operating loss carryover is not allowed in computing a current NOL. Furthermore, a deduction for charitable contributions is not allowed because it is limited to 10% of taxable income (and Orange has a loss). Thus, Orange's NOL for 1991 is $295,000 ($600,000 gross income – $895,000 business expenses).

Module 18.10: C Corporation Net Operating Losses

116. How much of Corporation A's 1990 net operating loss of $100,000 may be deducted in 1991 based on the following information pertaining to A's 1991 return?

Taxable income before the net operating loss deduction	$81,000
Charitable contribution deduction	9,000
Total charitable contributions for 1991	12,000

a. $69,000.
b. $81,000.
c. $90,000.
d. $93,000.

The correct answer is (b). *(SPE 988 III-83)*
REQUIRED: The corporation's utilization of a prior year's net operating loss.
DISCUSSION: The amount of 1990 carryover which may be deducted on the 1991 return is the 1991 taxable income as adjusted under Sec. 172. The charitable contribution limitation is computed after reduction for the net operating loss deduction [($81,000 + $9,000 − $100,000) × 10% = $0]. The unused portion of the charitable contributions of $3,000 ($12,000 total contributions − $0 deductible in 1991) must be carried forward, separately stated, in addition to the remaining net operating loss carryover of $10,000 ($100,000 − $90,000). See Reg. Sec. 1.170A-11(c)(2) for a detailed illustration of the NOL and charitable contribution deduction carryover interaction.

117. Items that pertain to Ward Corporation for 1991 are presented below.

Taxable loss before capital transactions	$(15,000)
Short-term capital gains	10,000
Long-term capital losses	(30,000)

For 1991, Ward Corporation has a net operating loss of

a. $35,000.
b. $15,000 and a capital loss deduction of $3,000.
c. $5,000 and a long-term capital loss of $30,000.
d. $15,000 and a long-term capital loss of $20,000.

The correct answer is (d). *(CMA 686 3-23)*
REQUIRED: A corporation's net operating loss and net capital loss.
DISCUSSION: Under Sec. 172, a corporation may carry back or carry forward a net operating loss. However, a net capital loss may only offset capital gains and may not be combined with a net operating loss. Therefore, Ward has a $15,000 net operating loss and a separate $20,000 ($30,000 − $10,000) long-term capital loss. Corporations carry their capital losses back and forward as short-term losses [Sec. 1212(a)].

118. Yuma Corporation had a net operating loss in 1991. The net operating loss

a. Can only be carried back to each of the three years before 1991 and not carried forward.
b. May be carried back to each of the 3 years before 1991 and then carried forward to each of the 5 years after 1991.
c. Must be carried back to each of the 3 years before 1991 and then carried forward to each of the 7 years after 1991.
d. May be carried back to each of the 3 years before 1991 and then carried forward to each of the 15 years after 1991.

The correct answer is (d). *(CMA 685 3-12)*
REQUIRED: The years to which a corporation may carry a net operating loss.
DISCUSSION: A net operating loss may be carried back to each of the 3 preceding taxable years and carried forward to each of the 15 succeeding taxable years [Sec. 172(b)]. However, an election can be made to forgo the 3-year carryback and only carry the loss forward 15 years [Sec. 172(b)(3)(C)]. In either case, the loss must be carried first to the earliest allowed year.

119. Pike Corporation, a calendar year corporation, had a net operating loss of $60,000 for 1991. Pike correctly deducted $50,000 of the 1991 loss as a carryback. Pike will lose the remaining $10,000 if it cannot be deducted by the end of which tax year?

a. 1995.
b. 2004.
c. 2005.
d. 2006.

The correct answer is (d). *(SPE 990 III-39)*
REQUIRED: The maximum carryover period for a net operating loss.
DISCUSSION: The maximum carryover period for a corporation's net operating loss is 15 years [Sec. 172(b)(1)].

Module 18.10: C Corporation Net Operating Losses

120. During 1991, its first year of operations, KAN Corporation had a loss from operations of $30,000 and short-term capital gains of $10,000. Included in the loss from operations was a net fire loss of $5,000. What is the amount of KAN's net operating loss carryover from 1991?

a. $15,000.
b. $20,000.
c. $25,000.
d. $30,000.

The correct answer is (b). *(SPE 989 III-78)*
REQUIRED: KAN Corporation's net operating loss carryover from first year operations.
DISCUSSION: Under Sec. 172, a net operating loss may be carried back 3 years and forward 15 years. The net operating loss must be carried to the earliest taxable year to which such loss may be carried. Since 1991 is KAN's first year of operation, the net operating loss will be carried forward 15 succeeding taxable years or until used up. The amount of the net operating loss carryover is the excess of deductions over gross income. The fire loss (included in the $30,000 loss) may be fully deducted since KAN is a corporation (Sec. 165). KAN's net operating loss carryover is

Short-term capital gains	$ 10,000
Loss from operations	(30,000)
Net operating loss carryover	$(20,000)

121. Geyer, Inc., a calendar-year corporation, had net income per books of $80,000 for the year 1991. For each of the years 1987-1990, Geyer's net income (loss) per books was as follows:

1987	$ 5,000
1988	15,000
1989	10,000
1990	(60,000)

Included in Geyer's gross revenues for 1990 were taxable dividends of $20,000 received from an unrelated 20% owned domestic corporation. When filing its tax return for 1990 on March 10, 1991, Geyer elected to give up the 3-year carryback of the loss for 1990. Geyer should report a net operating loss carryover on its tax return for 1991 of

a. $30,000.
b. $47,000.
c. $60,000.
d. $76,000.

The correct answer is (d). *(CPA 1180 P-42)*
REQUIRED: Geyer's net operating loss carryover to 1991.
DISCUSSION: Under Sec. 172(b)(1), a net operating loss may be carried back to each of the 3 preceding taxable years and forward to the 15 succeeding taxable years. The net operating loss must be carried to the earliest possible year, unless an election is made to give up the 3-year carryback [Sec. 172(b)(3)(C)]. Since Geyer made this election, the 1990 net operating loss is a carryover to 1991. In computing the net operating loss, the dividends-received deduction is computed without regard to the 80% of taxable income limitation. Geyer's net operating loss carryover is

Net loss per books	$(60,000)
Dividends-received deduction (80% x $20,000)	(16,000)
Net operating loss carryover	$(76,000)

122. Corporation R incurred a net operating loss of $96,000 in 1991 and carried it back to 1988. In 1988, Corporation R had gross income of $470,000 and business expenses of $390,000, including charitable contributions of $1,000. A net operating loss of $70,000 from 1990 had also been carried back to 1988. How much of Corporation R's 1991 net operating loss can be deducted against 1988 income?

a. $0.
b. $10,000.
c. $11,000.
d. $80,000.

The correct answer is (b). *(SPE 1083 III-71)*
REQUIRED: The amount of the 1991 NOL that may be carried back to 1988.
DISCUSSION: Under Sec. 172(b)(1), a net operating loss may be carried back to each of the 3 preceding taxable years and forward to the 15 succeeding taxable years. Unless an election to give up the carryback is made, the loss must be carried back to the earliest possible year. The charitable contribution is still deductible in 1988 because the limitation is on taxable income before a net operating loss carryback [Sec. 170(b)(2)(C)]. For 1988, Corporation R had gross income of $470,000 and business expenses of $390,000, producing income of $80,000. Since a $70,000 NOL from 1990 was carried back to 1988, $10,000 of income remains for that year to which the 1991 NOL may be applied.

Module 18.10: C Corporation Net Operating Losses

123. Corporation X sustained a $10,000 net operating loss reflected on its 1991 calendar-year tax return. Corporation X carried this loss back to its 1988 calendar-year tax return. In 1988 Corporation X had $5,000 of gross income and $3,100 in total expenses of which $100 was a charitable contribution. What is the amount of Corporation X's NOL carryback to 1989?

- a. $0.
- b. $8,000.
- c. $8,100.
- d. $10,000.

The correct answer is (c). *(SPE 1078 III-78)*
REQUIRED: Corporation X's net operating loss carryback to 1989.
DISCUSSION: Under Sec. 172(b)(1), a net operating loss may be carried back to each of the 3 preceding taxable years and forward to the 15 succeeding taxable years. Unless an election to give up the carryback is made under Sec. 172(b)(3)(C), the loss must be carried back to the earliest possible year. Note that the charitable contribution is still deductible in 1988 because the limit is 10% of taxable income before a net operating loss carryback. Corporation X's net operating loss carryback to 1989 is

1991 net operating loss	$10,000
Carried to 1988	(1,900)
Carryback to 1989	$ 8,100

124. KAD, Inc., a calendar-year corporation incorporated in January 1983, had a net operating loss of $75,000 in 1990. For each of the years 1986-1989, KAD reported taxable income (loss) before net operating loss deduction as follows:

1986	$ 15,000
1987	(20,000)
1988	10,000
1989	30,000

When filing its tax returns for both 1987 and 1990, KAD did not elect to give up the carryback of its losses. KAD's taxable income before the net operating loss deduction for 1991 was $80,000. What is the amount of net operating loss KAD should report on its tax return for 1991?

- a. $30,000.
- b. $35,000.
- c. $40,000.
- d. $55,000.

The correct answer is (c). *(SPE 989 III-79)*
REQUIRED: KAD's net operating loss deduction for 1991.
DISCUSSION: Sec. 172(b) provides that a net operating loss may be carried back to each of the 3 preceding taxable years and forward to the succeeding 15 taxable years. Unless an election is made under Sec. 172(b)(3)(C) to give up the carryback, the loss must be carried to the earliest possible taxable year. The amount of loss which may be carried to any tax year is equal to the taxable income after any earlier net operating losses. KAD's 1991 net operating loss deduction is

(1) 1987 net operating loss	$20,000
Carried to 1986	(15,000)
Carried to 1988	(5,000)
Remaining net operating loss	$ 0
(2) 1990 net operating loss	$75,000
Carried to 1988 ($10,000 – $5,000 1987 net operating loss used)	(5,000)
Carried to 1989	(30,000)
Carryover to 1991	$40,000

125. Which one of the following statements about a 1991 corporate net operating loss (NOL) is correct?

- a. The carryback period may be forgone and the carryforward period increased to 18 years.
- b. A dividends-received deduction may not create, nor may it add, to an NOL.
- c. A corporation does not make adjustments to its NOL for nonbusiness deductions.
- d. If the corporation elects to carry back the loss, 1990 would be the first year to which the loss would be carried.

The correct answer is (c). *(CMA 1289 3-15)*
REQUIRED: The correct statement about net operating losses.
DISCUSSION: A corporation does not have any nonbusiness deductions, and therefore does not make any adjustments to its NOL for them.
Answers (a) and (d) are incorrect because Sec. 172(b) provides that a net operating loss must be carried back to each of the 3 preceding taxable years, and carried forward to each of the 15 succeeding taxable years. The net operating loss must be carried to the earliest of the taxable years to which such loss may be carried. Sec. 172(b)(3)(C) allows a corporation to elect to forgo the entire carryback period and only carry the loss forward, but it does not extend the carryforward period. Answer (b) is incorrect because Sec. 172(d)(5) provides that the dividends-received deduction may create or increase an NOL.

Module 18.10: C Corporation Net Operating Losses

126. Which of the following is not true concerning net operating losses?

    a. There are no limitations on the use of net operating losses.

    b. Sec. 382 generally limits the "prechange in ownership" NOLs absorbed in any "postchange in ownership" taxable year.

    c. Sec. 382 limits the use of NOLs to the product of the fair market value of the loss corporation's stock times the "long-term tax-exempt rate."

    d. The Sec. 382 limitation is triggered by a 50 percentage point change in ownership.

The correct answer is (a). *(Publisher)*
REQUIRED: The false statement about net operating losses.
DISCUSSION: Sec. 382 provides that where a corporation has a 50 percentage point or greater change in ownership, special rules shall apply to the use of NOL carryovers incurred prior to the change in ownership and used after the change in ownership. The carryovers are limited by formula, but in concept they are limited to the amount that would be realized each year had the firm sold its assets and invested the proceeds in high-grade tax-exempt securities.
Answers (b), (c), and (d) are all true statements concerning NOLs.

127. Corporation P, a calendar-year taxpayer, sustained a net operating loss in 1990. The return was filed on March 1, 1991. Corporation P uses Form 1120X to carry back the net operating loss. What is the latest date Corporation P can file Form 1120X (ignoring holidays and weekends)?

    a. December 31, 1991.

    b. March 1, 1992.

    c. March 15, 1992.

    d. March 15, 1994.

The correct answer is (d). *(SPE 1080 III-58)*
REQUIRED: The latest date a corporation may file to carry back a net operating loss.
DISCUSSION: Form 1120X, an amended corporate return, must be filed within the time set by law for a refund to be allowed [Sec. 6511(b)]. A claim for refund generally must be filed within 3 years of the time the return was filed or 2 years from the time the tax was paid, whichever expires later [Sec. 6511(b)]. However, if the return is filed before the due date, the 3-year period starts to run from the date the return was due [Sec. 6513(a)]. Corporations on the calendar year must file income tax returns by March 15 (ignoring holidays and weekends). The latest date Corporation P may file Form 1120X is March 15, 1994 (3 years from the due date of the return).

128. Corporation L incurred a net operating loss for the year ended June 30, 1991. Corporation L was granted an automatic 6-month extension and filed its tax return on December 15, 1991. If Corporation L wishes to use Form 1139 to carry back the net operating loss, it must do so on or before which of the following dates? (Assume none of the dates falls on a Saturday, Sunday, or legal holiday.)

    a. September 15, 1991.

    b. December 31, 1991.

    c. April 15, 1992.

    d. June 30, 1992.

The correct answer is (d). *(SPE 1083 III-54)*
REQUIRED: The date on or before which the form for obtaining a quick refund must be filed.
DISCUSSION: Sec. 6411 provides a procedure that allows a taxpayer to obtain a quick refund for certain loss and credit carrybacks, including a net operating loss carryback. The corporate application for such a refund is Form 1139. Application for a quick refund may not be filed sooner than the due date of the return for the year of the loss, nor later than 12 months from the end of such tax year. Therefore, Corporation L must file Form 1139 on or before June 30, 1992.

129. In 1988, Corporation XYZ's taxable income was $25,000. For 1991, it had a $25,000 net operating loss. On a timely filed return, it must carry the entire 1991 net operating loss back to the 1988 tax year before the net operating loss can be carried forward.

The correct answer is (F). *(SPE 1081 III-22)*
DISCUSSION: Sec. 172(b) provides that a net operating loss must be carried back to each of the 3 preceding taxable years, and carried forward to each of the 15 succeeding taxable years. The net operating loss must be carried to the earliest of the taxable years to which such loss may be carried. However, under Sec. 172(b)(3)(C), a taxpayer such as Corporation XYZ may elect to forgo the entire carryback period and only carry the loss forward.

Module 18.10: C Corporation Net Operating Losses

130. Stone Corporation, a calendar-year taxpayer, had modified taxable income in 1988 and 1989. In 1990, Stone Corporation incurred a net operating loss and elected to forgo the carryback period. Stone incurred another net operating loss in 1991. Since Stone elected to forgo the carryback period for 1990, it cannot carry the 1991 net operating loss back to 1988.

The correct answer is (F). *(SPE 990 III-9)*
DISCUSSION: Under Sec. 172(b)(3)(C), a taxpayer may elect to relinquish the entire carryback period with respect to a particular net operating loss. This election, however, only applies to the net operating loss of the taxable year for which the election is made. The election made by Stone applies only to the 1990 net operating loss. Stone may carry the 1991 net operating loss back to 1988.

131. In 1990, Corporation K had a net operating loss and timely elected to forgo the carryback period. Prior to filing its 1991 tax return, Corporation K filed Form 1120X for 1990, which revoked the election to forgo the carryback period. Corporation K may now carry back the 1990 loss.

The correct answer is (F). *(SPE 984 III-14)*
DISCUSSION: Sec. 172(b)(3)(C) allows a taxpayer to forgo the carryback option and only use the carryforward period. Once the election is made for any taxable year, however, it is irrevocable for that taxable year.

132. If a corporation has a net operating loss, it can carry back the loss to get a refund of previously paid taxes. The corporation can get a refund more quickly by filing an Amended U.S. Corporate Income Tax Return (Form 1120X) than by filing a Corporate Application for Tentative Refund (Form 1139).

The correct answer is (F). *(SPE 984 III-15)*
DISCUSSION: Form 1139 is used to obtain the quick refund for loss and credit carrybacks provided for in Sec. 6411. Form 1120X is an amended tax return that is not required to be processed as quickly.

133. If a corporation has a net operating loss (NOL), and does not elect to forgo the carryback period, it must first carry the entire NOL to the earliest carryback year, then carry any excess NOL, after subtracting modified taxable income, to the next carryback year, and so on.

The correct answer is (T). *(SPE 989 III-8)*
DISCUSSION: A net operating loss may be carried back to each of the 3 preceding taxable years and carried forward to each of the 15 succeeding taxable years [Sec. 172(b)(1)]. However, an election can be made to give up the 3-year carryback and only carry the loss forward 15 years. In either case, the loss must be carried first to the earliest allowed year.

134. A corporation must deduct as much of its net operating loss as possible. Any of the NOL that is left over after modified taxable income is reduced to zero can be carried over to the next year.

The correct answer is (T). *(SPE 988 III-19)*
DISCUSSION: Sec. 172 provides that net operating losses must be used to their fullest extent in each year to which they are carried. Therefore, the taxpayer cannot pick and choose which years to take the net operating loss, except to elect to forgo the net operating loss carryback under Sec. 172(b)(3)(C).

18.11 Capital Gains and Losses

135. Wonder Inc. had 1991 taxable income of $200,000 exclusive of the following:

Gain on sale of land used in business	$25,000
Loss on sale of machinery used in business	(13,000)
Loss on sale of securities held 3 years	(4,000)
Loss on sale of securities held 3 months	(3,000)

On what amount of taxable income should Wonder compute tax?

 a. $200,000.
 b. $202,500.
 c. $205,000.
 d. $212,000.

The correct answer is (c). (CPA 1176 Q-24)
REQUIRED: A corporation's taxable income with both capital and Sec. 1231 gains and losses.
DISCUSSION: The sale of the land and machinery used in the business are Sec. 1231 transactions, assuming the assets were held more than 1 year. Since the gain and loss net to a gain, they are considered a long-term capital gain and loss. The securities are capital assets so the losses are capital losses. Under Sec. 1211, a corporation may only deduct capital losses to the extent of capital gains. In this case, the capital losses are fully deductible because they do not exceed the $12,000 net Sec. 1231 gain.

Taxable income before capital gains/losses		$200,000
Capital gains/losses:		
Gain on sale of land	$25,000	
Loss on sale of machinery	(13,000)	
Loss on sale of securities (held 3 years)	(4,000)	
Loss on sale of securities (held 3 months)	(3,000)	
Net capital gain		5,000
Taxable income		$205,000

136. In 1991, its first year of operations, Rowley Corporation, not a dealer in securities, realized taxable income of $128,000 from the operation of its business. In addition to its regular business operations, it realized the following gains and losses from the sale of marketable securities:

Short-term capital gain	$10,000
Short-term capital loss	(4,000)
Long-term capital gain	12,000
Long-term capital loss	(32,000)

What is Rowley's total taxable income for 1991?

 a. $114,000.
 b. $124,000.
 c. $128,000.
 d. $134,000.

The correct answer is (c). (CPA 1181 P-51)
REQUIRED: A corporation's total taxable income including capital gains and losses.
DISCUSSION: Sec. 1211 provides that a corporation may only deduct capital losses to the extent of capital gains (without regard to whether they are short- or long-term). Therefore, Rowley may only deduct $22,000 of its capital losses since capital gains are $22,000 ($10,000 short-term and $12,000 long-term). The balance of the capital losses may be carried forward 5 years. Rowley's total taxable income is

Income from operations	$128,000
Capital gains	22,000
Capital losses	(22,000)
Taxable income	$128,000

137. In 1991, Little Company sold land, that had been held strictly for investment purposes, for $70,000. The original cost of the land when purchased 2 years ago was $80,000. During 1991, Little also had a capital gain of $6,000 and received dividends from investments of $3,000. The amount of the loss that is deductible by Little in 1991 from the sale of the land is

 a. $0.
 b. $3,000.
 c. $6,000.
 d. $9,000.

The correct answer is (c). (CMA 690 3-14)
REQUIRED: The amount of capital losses allowed as an offset against other taxable income.
DISCUSSION: Sec. 1211 provides that a corporation may only deduct capital losses to the extent of capital gains (without regard to whether they are short- or long-term). Therefore, Little can only deduct $6,000 of its net long-term capital loss in 1991. The remaining $4,000 long-term capital loss will be carried over to 1992.

Module 18.11: Capital Gains and Losses

138. General Corporation, a calendar-year taxpayer, reported taxable income of $100,000, all ordinary, on its 1991 corporate income tax return. The company has discovered that it inadvertently omitted a long-term capital gain of $15,000 from the return. General Corporation's 1991 income tax liability should have been larger by

a. $4,200.
b. $5,100.
c. $5,550.
d. $5,850.

The correct answer is (d). *(CMA 1283 3-3)*
REQUIRED: The effect of a long-term capital gain on a corporation's tax liability.
DISCUSSION: Long-term capital gain is included in a corporation's taxable income. The tax rate is 39%, which is the top corporate rate of 34% plus the 5% surtax for income in excess of $100,000. The 34% corporate alternative tax rate for long-term capital gains under Sec. 1201 is not applicable at current tax rates. Thus, General Corporation's tax liability will be increased by $5,850 (39% x $15,000).

139. Ross Corporation, a calendar-year taxpayer, had taxable income of $90,000 for 1991, which included a net capital gain of $10,000. What is Ross Corporation's income tax for 1991?

a. $18,850.
b. $19,850.
c. $20,300.
d. $21,150.

The correct answer is (a). *(Publisher)*
REQUIRED: The amount of a calendar-year corporation's tax for 1991.
DISCUSSION: The alternative tax under Sec. 1201 is not applicable at current tax rates. All income is taxed at the same rate under Sec. 11. Therefore, Ross's 1991 income tax is

15% x $50,000	$ 7,500
25% x $25,000	6,250
34% x $15,000	5,100
Income tax	$18,850

140. In 1989, Corporation E had a net short-term capital gain of $15,000, a net long-term capital gain of $8,000, and an $11,000 short-term capital loss carryback from 1991. In 1989, what is Corporation E's net long-term capital gain after the carryback?

a. $0.
b. $4,000.
c. $6,000.
d. $8,000.

The correct answer is (d). *(SPE 1081 III-50)*
REQUIRED: A corporation's net long-term capital gain after a capital loss carryback.
DISCUSSION: Sec. 1212(a)(1) provides that if a corporation has a net capital loss, the capital loss may be carried back to each of the 3 preceding taxable years, and forward to each of the 5 succeeding taxable years. The carryback or carryforward is treated as a short-term capital loss in each such taxable year. Corporation E's net long-term capital gain is $8,000 since the capital loss carryback is treated as a short-term capital loss. In addition, Corporation E has a net short-term capital gain of $4,000 ($15,000 − $11,000).

141. Which one of the following statements is applicable to corporate capital gains for a tax year ending December 31, 1991?

a. Long-term capital gains are eligible for an alternative tax rate of 28%.
b. If 1991 capital losses exceed capital gains, only $3,000 of the excess is currently deductible.
c. Capital gains are excluded in computing the 10% of income limitation for charitable contribution purposes.
d. Whether carried forward or backward, excess long-term capital losses are treated as short-term capital losses for the year to which they are carried.

The correct answer is (d). *(CMA 1289 3-14)*
REQUIRED: The correct statement about corporate capital gains.
DISCUSSION: Sec. 1212(a)(1) provides that if a corporation has a net capital loss, the capital loss may be carried back to each of the 3 preceding taxable years, and forward to each of the 5 succeeding taxable years. The carryback or carryforward is treated as a short-term capital loss in each such taxable year.
Answers (a) and (b) are incorrect because they apply to individuals, not corporations. Answer (c) is incorrect because Sec. 170(b)(2) defines taxable income for charitable contribution purposes to include corporate capital gains.

Module 18.11: Capital Gains and Losses

142. Smyth Corp. has both a capital loss and a net operating loss for 1991. The capital loss

a. Cannot be deducted currently, but can be carried forward for 5 years.
b. Is included in the net operating loss.
c. Cannot be deducted currently, but can be carried back 3 years, and then carried forward 5 years.
d. Is treated as an ordinary loss under the Tax Reform Act of 1986.

The correct answer is (c). *(CMA 688 3-10)*
REQUIRED: The proper treatment of a net capital loss.
DISCUSSION: A corporation's losses from the sale or exchange of capital assets are allowed only to the extent of the net gain from such sales or exchanges [Sec. 1211(a)]. The net capital loss (excess of capital losses over capital gains) may be carried back to each of the 3 preceding years and forward to each of the 5 succeeding taxable years (Sec. 1212).
Answer (a) is incorrect because there is also a 3-year carryback. Answer (b) is incorrect because a net operating loss is defined as not including capital losses. Answer (d) is incorrect because there is no provision showing capital losses to be treated as ordinary losses.

143. Corporation Z's net long-term capital loss exceeded its net short-term capital gain by $5,000 in calendar year 1991. To what taxable year is the net capital loss first carried?

a. 1986.
b. 1988.
c. 1990.
d. 1992.

The correct answer is (b). *(SPE 1078 III-54)*
REQUIRED: The taxable year to which a net capital loss is first carried.
DISCUSSION: A corporation's net capital loss is the excess of short- and long-term capital losses over short- and long-term capital gains. Under Sec. 1212(a)(1), a corporation which has a net capital loss may carry the capital loss back to each of the 3 preceding taxable years, and forward to each of the 5 succeeding taxable years. The entire amount of the net capital loss must be carried to the earliest of the allowable taxable years. Corporation Z's net capital loss must first be carried back 3 years to 1988. Unlike the net operating loss provisions, there is not an election to forgo the carryback.

144. Corporation B had a net capital loss of $18,000 in 1990 and a net capital loss of $14,000 in 1991. B's net capital gains in 1987, 1988, and 1989 were $13,000, $14,000, and $6,000, respectively. What amount of the 1991 net capital loss will be absorbed by the 1988 net capital gain?

a. $2,000.
b. $8,000.
c. $9,000.
d. $14,000.

The correct answer is (c). *(SPE 986 III-70)*
REQUIRED: The amount of capital loss carryback to 1988 that originated in 1991.
DISCUSSION: Under Sec. 1212, a net capital loss is carried back to the preceding 3 taxable years and then carried forward to the succeeding 5 taxable years. The losses are used on a first-in, first-out basis. The 1990 net capital loss will be carried back first to 1987, where it will offset $13,000 in net capital gain, and then to 1988 where it will offset $5,000 of capital gain. This leaves $9,000 of net capital gain in 1988 which is then offset by $9,000 of 1991 capital loss. The remaining net capital loss from 1991 will be carried to 1989.

145. Ryan Corporation had the following gains and losses during 1991:

Long-term capital gain	$5,000
Long-term capital loss	8,000
Short-term capital gain	3,000
Short-term capital loss	7,000
Sec. 1245 gain from depreciation recapture	6,000

The nature and amount of Ryan's 1991 capital loss carryback/carryforward is a

a. $1,000 short-term capital loss.
b. $1,000 long-term capital loss.
c. $7,000 short-term capital loss.
d. $3,000 long-term capital loss and a $4,000 short-term capital loss.

The correct answer is (c). *(CMA 684 3-8)*
REQUIRED: The nature and amount of the capital loss carryback/carryforward.
DISCUSSION: The Sec. 1245 gain from depreciation recapture is treated as ordinary income and does not enter into the capital loss computation. The capital losses for each year are allowed only to the extent of capital gains (Sec. 1211). Thus, only the excess of the capital losses over the capital gains may be carried back or forward. The carryback/carryforward must be treated as a short-term capital loss in each year to which it is carried.

	Short-term	Long-term
Capital gains	$ 3,000	$ 5,000
Capital losses	(7,000)	(8,000)
Net capital loss	$(4,000)	$(3,000)

Module 18.11: Capital Gains and Losses

146. Corporation X is a calendar-year taxpayer which began operations in 1986. It incurred the following during the years indicated:

	Net Long-term Capital Gain (Loss)	Net Short-term Capital Gain (Loss)
1986	($1,000)	-0-
1987	-0-	($2,000)
1988	$2,000	-0-
1989	-0-	($3,000)
1990	$1,000	-0-
1991	-0-	($1,000)

What is the carryover to 1992 identified as to year and amount?

  a. ($1,000); 1988 - $2,000, 1989 - ($3,000).
  b. ($2,000); 1989 - ($3,000), 1990 - $1,000.
  c. ($4,000); 1986 - ($1,000), 1989 - ($3,000).
  d. ($4,000); 1989 - ($3,000), 1991 - ($1,000).

147. In 1991, Bell Corporation (its first year of operations) had net short-term capital gains of $3,000 and net long-term capital losses of $8,000. How will the capital loss carryover be treated in Bell's 1992 income tax return?

  a. Ordinary loss.
  b. Sec. 1231 loss.
  c. Long-term capital loss.
  d. Short-term capital loss.

148. The following information was taken from Wolverine Corporation's 1991 federal income tax return:

Gross income	$700,000
Dividends-received deduction	60,000
Other business deductions	750,000
Net short-term capital loss	5,000
Net long-term capital loss	10,000

Which one of the following most accurately reflects Wolverine Corporation's federal income tax position for 1991?

  a. Net operating loss of $50,000; the dividends-received deduction and the capital losses are separate carryback and carryover items.
  b. Net operating loss of $50,000; only the capital losses are separate carryback and carryover items.
  c. Net operating loss of $65,000; the dividends-received deduction is not allowed and cannot be carried over.
  d. Net operating loss of $110,000; the capital losses are separate carryback and carryover items.

The correct answer is (d). *(SPE 1078 III-75)*
REQUIRED: The amount and year of origination of a capital loss carryover.
DISCUSSION: Sec. 1211 provides that corporations may only deduct capital losses to the extent of capital gains. Under Sec. 1212, if a corporation has a net capital loss, it may be carried back to each of the 3 preceding taxable years, and carried forward to each of the 5 succeeding taxable years. Oldest net capital losses are used first against capital gains. The year and the amount of Corporation X's capital loss carryover to 1992 are

Year	Net Capital Gain (Loss)	Year Used and Amount	Remaining
1986	($1,000)	1988 - $1,000	-0-
1987	($2,000)	1988 - $1,000 1990 - $1,000	-0-
1989	($3,000)	-0-	$3,000
1991	($1,000)	-0-	$1,000
Capital loss carryover			$4,000

The correct answer is (d). *(CPA 1174 P-2)*
REQUIRED: The character of a capital loss carryover.
DISCUSSION: Under Sec. 1212, a corporation may carry capital losses back to each of the 3 preceding taxable years, and forward to each of the 5 succeeding taxable years. The capital loss which is carried back or forward is treated as a short-term capital loss in each such taxable year. Consequently, the capital loss carryover in Bell's 1992 tax return will be treated as a short-term capital loss and is deductible only against capital gains.

The correct answer is (d). *(CMA 681 3-9)*
REQUIRED: The most accurate reflection of a corporation's federal income tax position.
DISCUSSION: Sec. 1211(a) provides that a corporation may only deduct capital losses to the extent of capital gains. Any net capital loss may be carried back 3 years and forward 5 years. Therefore, the capital losses are separate carryback and carryover items (not included in Wolverine's net operating loss).

The dividends-received deduction limitation based on taxable income does not apply when the taxpayer has a net operating loss. Since Wolverine has a net operating loss, it may take the full deduction. Wolverine's net operating loss is

Gross income	$ 700,000
Less:	
Business deductions	(750,000)
Dividends-received deduction	(60,000)
Net operating loss	$(110,000)

149. Laser Corporation, during its first year of operations in 1990, incurred an operating loss of $50,000 and a long-term capital loss of $8,000. In 1991 the corporation had ordinary taxable income totaling $125,000, a net short-term capital gain of $10,000, and a net long-term capital gain of $15,000. Laser Corporation's taxable income classified by type of tax treatment for 1991 is

    a. $67,000 ordinary income and $25,000 long-term capital gain.

    b. $75,000 ordinary income and $17,000 long-term capital gain.

    c. $77,000 ordinary income and $15,000 long-term capital gain.

    d. $85,000 ordinary income and $7,000 long-term capital gain.

The correct answer is (c). *(CMA 1281 3-10)*
REQUIRED: The amount and classification of a corporation's taxable income.
DISCUSSION: Sec. 172 allows a net operating loss to be carried back 3 years and forward 5 years. Since Laser incurred a $50,000 operating loss during its first year of operations, it may only carry this loss forward. Under Sec. 1211(a), a corporation may only deduct capital losses to the extent of capital gains. A net capital loss may be carried back 3 years and forward 5 years and is treated as a short-term capital loss in each such year. Since the net capital loss of $8,000 occurred during Laser's first year of operations, it must be carried forward 5 years. A net short-term capital gain is treated the same as ordinary income when there are no net long-term losses to offset it. Laser's ordinary income is

1991 ordinary income	$125,000
1990 NOL carryover	(50,000)
1991 net short-term capital gain ($10,000 – $8,000 carryover)	2,000
1991 income receiving ordinary tax treatment	$ 77,000

150. A corporation may deduct capital losses only to the extent of

    a. $3,000.

    b. Taxable income before any capital loss deduction.

    c. Total net capital loss.

    d. Its capital gains.

The correct answer is (d). *(SPE 989 III-40)*
REQUIRED: The amount of capital losses deductible in a tax year.
DISCUSSION: Sec. 1211 provides that a corporation may only deduct capital losses to the extent of capital gains. Any excess capital losses are carried back 3 years and carried forward 5 years.

151. Corporation P's net long-term capital gain exceeds its net short-term capital loss by $20,000 for 1991. P's taxable income is $60,000. P will benefit from using the alternative tax rate on capital gains.

The correct answer is (F). *(SPE 986 III-6)*
DISCUSSION: The 1986 TRA amended the corporate alternative tax rate. Long-term capital gains of a corporation are now taxed at an alternative rate of 34%. Since this rate is the same as the 1991 ordinary rates, the alternative tax for capital gains is not applicable until a later change occurs.

152. Corporation A, which was organized in 1989, sustained net capital losses of $40,000 and $30,000 for 1990 and 1991, respectively. In 1989, A had taxable income of $45,000 including short-term capital gains of $20,000 and long-term capital gains of $30,000. After applying the capital loss carrybacks, A has $20,000 available for carryover from 1991.

The correct answer is (F). *(SPE 1083 III-16)*
DISCUSSION: A corporation may carry back its net capital losses 3 years as long as the carryback does not increase or produce a net operating loss [Sec. 1212(a)(1)]. Corporation A may carry back only $45,000, thereby reducing its 1989 taxable income to zero. Therefore, A has $25,000 ($70,000 net capital losses – $45,000) of capital losses available for carryover to 1992.

153. In 1991, Corporation A had a net short-term capital gain of $3,000 and a net long-term capital loss of $9,000. Corporation A should treat the net capital loss of $6,000 as a long-term capital loss when carried back or forward.

The correct answer is (F). *(SPE 986 III-19)*
DISCUSSION: The net capital loss for the corporation may be carried back 3 years and forward 5 years. Sec. 1212(a) provides that a capital loss carried back or forward to other taxable years is treated as a short-term capital loss in each such taxable year.

154. Capital losses that cannot be used by a corporation in its current year may be carried back to the 3 years preceding the year of the losses and, if not completely used up, carried forward to future tax years, for up to 5 years.

The correct answer is (T). *(SPE 989 III-7)*
DISCUSSION: If a corporation has a net capital loss, the amount of such loss may be carried back 3 years and forward 5 years [Sec. 1212(a)]. The net capital loss must be carried to the earliest of the taxable years to which such loss may be carried. A corporation may not elect to forgo the carryback.

155. If a corporation has two or more capital loss carrybacks to the same taxable year, the loss from the latest year is deducted first.

The correct answer is (F). *(SPE 987 III-14)*
DISCUSSION: If a corporation has two or more capital loss carrybacks to the same year, the earliest such loss must be applied first [Sec. 1212(a)]. This rule is to the corporation's advantage since the loss from the latest year can be carried forward longer.

18.12 Treasury Stock

156. During 1991, Webster Corporation repurchased 2,000 shares of its $1 par common stock in the open market for $5,000. Webster later resold 1,000 of these treasury shares to new shareholders when the stock was selling for $4 per share. Webster will report a gain (loss) on its 1991 tax return of

a. $0.
b. $(1,000).
c. $1,500.
d. $3,000.

The correct answer is (a). *(CMA 690 3-15)*
REQUIRED: The amount of gain which a corporation recognizes on the purchase and sale of its treasury stock.
DISCUSSION: Under Sec. 1032(a), a corporation recognizes no gain or loss on the receipt of money or other property in exchange for its own stock, including treasury stock. Webster, therefore, should not report any gain.

157. When Kile Corporation was organized in 1975, it received $100,000 from the sale of 10,000 shares of its $10 par value common stock. In 1989, Kile reacquired 300 of these shares as treasury stock at a cost of $6,000. In 1991, Kile sold the 300 shares of treasury stock to an unrelated party for $7,500. How much capital gain should Kile report in its 1991 tax return in connection with the sale of these 300 shares?

a. $4,500.
b. $3,000.
c. $1,500.
d. $0.

The correct answer is (d). *(CPA 1183 Q-50)*
REQUIRED: The amount of gain that a corporation should recognize on the purchase and sale of its treasury stock.
DISCUSSION: A corporation does not recognize any gain or loss on the sale or exchange of its own stock, including treasury stock [Sec. 1032(a)]. Kile Corporation should report no gain.

158. The following information pertains to treasury stock sold by Lee Corporation to an unrelated broker in 1991:

Proceeds received	$50,000
Cost	30,000
Par value	9,000

What amount of capital gain should Lee recognize in 1991 on the sale of this treasury stock?

a. $0.
b. $8,000.
c. $20,000.
d. $30,500.

The correct answer is (a). *(CPA 1188 Q-22)*
REQUIRED: The gain a corporation should report as a result of the purchase and sale of treasury stock.
DISCUSSION: Under Sec. 1032(a), a corporation does not recognize gain or loss on the receipt of money or other property in exchange for its stock, including treasury stock. Therefore, no gain or loss is recognized by Lee as a result of the treasury stock transactions.

18.13 Taxable Income and Tax Calculations

159. All of the following statements about the corporate tax rates for tax years beginning on or after July 1, 1987 are true except:

a. Corporate taxable income is subject to tax under a three-bracket graduated rate system.
b. The tax rate is 15% of the first $50,000 of taxable income.
c. The tax rate is 30% if taxable income is over $50,000 but not over $75,000.
d. A 5% surtax is charged on taxable income between $100,000 and $335,000.

The correct answer is (c). *(SPE 990 III-40)*
REQUIRED: The statement which does not describe the current corporate tax system.
DISCUSSION: The current corporate tax system under Sec. 11 is based on a three-bracket graduated rate system as follows:

$0 - $50,000	15%	
$50,000 - $75,000	25%	
Over $75,000	34%	

A surtax of 5% is charged on income between $100,000 and $335,000, which eliminates the benefit of the lower brackets.

160. Catz, Inc. is a calendar-year corporation with taxable income of $95,000 for 1991 and no capital gains. Catz, Inc.'s income tax liability is

a. $23,750.
b. $22,150.
c. $21,250.
d. $20,550.

The correct answer is (d). *(Publisher)*
REQUIRED: The 1991 income tax liability of a calendar-year corporation.
DISCUSSION: Sec. 11 imposes a tax on the taxable income of every corporation. The 1991 tax liability of Catz, Inc. is

$50,000 x 15%	$ 7,500
$25,000 x 25%	6,250
$20,000 x 34%	6,800
Tax liability	$20,550

161. Tina, Inc., a calendar-year corporation, has taxable income of $150,000 for 1991 with no capital gains. Tina's tax liability before credits for 1991 is

a. $39,250.
b. $41,750.
c. $48,000.
d. $50,250.

The correct answer is (b). *(E.D. Fenton)*
REQUIRED: A corporation's tax liability before credits when income exceeds $100,000.
DISCUSSION: Corporations with taxable income in excess of $100,000 must increase the tax liability computed under the graduated rates by the lesser of (1) 5% of such excess or (2) $11,250. Corporations with taxable income of $335,000 or more will realize no benefits from the graduated rates of Sec. 11.

15% of $50,000	$ 7,500
25% of $25,000	6,250
34% of $75,000	25,500
Tax per graduated rates	$39,250
Add: 5% x $50,000 excess	2,500
Tax liability	$41,750

162. For the calendar year 1991, Sun Corporation had operating income of $80,000, exclusive of the following capital gains and losses:

Long-term capital gain	$14,000
Short-term capital gain	6,000
Long-term capital loss	(2,000)
Short-term capital loss	(8,000)

What is Sun Corporation's income tax liability for 1991?

a. $18,850.
b. $19,850.
c. $20,300.
d. $21,150.

The correct answer is (a). *(SPE 990 III-67)*
REQUIRED: The 1991 income tax liability of a calendar-year corporation.
DISCUSSION: Sec. 11 imposes a tax on the taxable income of every corporation. Sun Corporation's taxable income includes $80,000 of operating income and a net long-term capital gain of $10,000 [($14,000 − $2,000) + ($6,000 − $8,000)], or $90,000. The 1991 tax liability of Sun Corporation is

$50,000 x 15%	$ 7,500
$25,000 x 25%	6,250
$15,000 x 34%	5,100
	$18,850

163. The following information is available for Briner Corporation for the tax year ended December 31, 1991:

Revenues from sales	$8,000,000
Cost of goods sold	(4,000,000)
Operating expenses	(2,000,000)
Taxable income	$2,000,000

The tax liability for Briner's tax year ended December 31, 1991 is

a. $668,250.
b. $680,000.
c. $681,250.
d. $682,250.

The correct answer is (b). *(W. Wallace)*
REQUIRED: A corporation's income tax liability when income exceeds $335,000.
DISCUSSION: Sec. 11 imposes a tax on the increments that make up the first $100,000 of taxable income of 15%, 25%, and 34%, respectively. Thereafter, the rate is 34%. However, an additional 5% surtax is added to the $100,000 to $335,000 range to cause taxpayers with income in excess of $335,000 to pay a flat 34%. Briner's tax is therefore $680,000 ($2,000,000 x 34%).

164. The Tinkers, Evers, and Chance Corporations have taxable income, all resulting from regular operations, of $100,000, $300,000 and $450,000, respectively. None is a member of a controlled group. The tax liabilities before credits in 1991 are

	Tinkers	Evers	Chance
a.	$22,250	$ 90,250	$141,250
b.	$22,250	$100,250	$153,000
c.	$25,750	$117,750	$186,750
d.	$34,000	$102,000	$153,000

The correct answer is (b). *(C.J. Skender)*
REQUIRED: The 1991 income tax liabilities of three corporations.
DISCUSSION: Sec. 11 imposes a tax on the taxable income of every corporation. The amounts are determined by using the graduated rates below. Graduated tax rates are phased out by imposing an additional 5% tax on income between $100,000 and $335,000, which effectively offsets the graduated rates on the initial $75,000.

	Tinkers	Evers	Chance
15% x $50,000	$ 7,500	$ 7,500	$ 7,500
25% x $25,000	6,250	6,250	6,250
34% x taxable income in excess of $75,000	8,500	76,500	127,500
5% x taxable income (limited to $335,000) minus $100,000)	0	10,000	11,750
Tax liability	$22,250	$100,250	$153,000

Corporations with taxable income in excess of $335,000 are taxed at an effective 34% rate (34% x $450,000 income of Chance = $153,000).

165. Cato Corporation is owned by three engineers all of whom are employed by the corporation. It primarily performs civil engineering activities with respect to construction projects. During 1991 Cato Corporation earns $150,000 of taxable income. Cato has not elected to be taxed under Subchapter S. What is Cato's 1991 regular tax liability?

a. $39,250.
b. $41,750.
c. $45,000.
d. $51,000.

The correct answer is (d). *(Publisher)*
REQUIRED: The correct corporate tax liability for 1991.
DISCUSSION: Cato Corporation is a personal service corporation. Sec. 448(d)(2) defines a personal service corporation as a corporation substantially all of the activities of which involve the performance of services in the field of health, law, engineering, architecture, accounting, actuarial science, performing arts, or consulting, and whose stock is owned by employees who perform the services. Under Sec. 11(b)(2), the taxable income of a personal service corporation is taxed at a flat rate of 34%. Therefore, Cato Corporation's 1991 tax liability is $51,000 (34% x $150,000).

166. Which one of the following statements about the taxation of personal service corporations is incorrect?

a. Personal service corporations are subject to the "flat" 34% tax rate only if more than 75% of their gross income is earned income.

b. Taxable income of a qualified personal service corporation is taxed at a 34% rate without benefit of the 15% and 25% reduced rates.

c. Substantially all of the stock of the corporation must be owned by current or retired employees (or their estates or heirs) that are employed performing services for the corporation in connection with activities in certain professional fields.

d. The fields covered by the personal service corporation rules are health, law, engineering, architecture, accounting, actuarial science, performing arts, or consulting.

The correct answer is (a). *(Publisher)*
REQUIRED: The incorrect statement about the taxation of personal service corporations.
DISCUSSION: Under Sec. 448(d)(2), a personal service corporation has two main characteristics: (1) substantially all of its activities must involve the performance of services in the field of health, law, engineering, architecture, accounting, actuarial science, performing arts, or consulting, and (2) substantially all of its stock must be owned by employees who perform the services. Sec. 11(b)(2) provides that the taxable income of a personal service corporation is taxed at a flat rate of 34%. There is no requirement that more than 75% of the gross income be earned income for the flat 34% tax rate.

167. For the year 1991, Corporation Z had $60,000 of taxable income from operations. It also sold depreciable assets to its 100% shareholder as follows

Sale Date	Property	Sales Price	Cost	Total Depreciation Claimed
1/30/91	A	$ 4,000	$ 8,000	$3,000
6/10/91	B	7,000	8,000	4,000
12/10/91	C	15,000	15,000	3,000

What is Z's corporate income tax for 1991?

a. $9,750.
b. $11,250.
c. $11,500.
d. $14,000.

The correct answer is (c). *(SPE 1078 III-67)*
REQUIRED: A corporation's income tax liability given sales of assets to its sole shareholder.
DISCUSSION: Under Sec. 267, losses on sales or exchanges between certain related parties are not recognized. A corporation and its 100% shareholder are related, so the loss on property A is not recognized. The gains of $3,000 each on property B and property C are treated as ordinary income (if not already taxed as ordinary income under one of the recapture provisions) because gains on the sale of depreciable property between certain related parties are ordinary under Sec. 1239. For this purpose also, the corporation and its 100% shareholder are related parties. Accordingly, total income is $66,000 ($60,000 + $3,000 + $3,000), which is taxed under rates below for 1991.

15% x $50,000	$ 7,500
25% x $16,000	4,000
Tax liability	$11,500

Module 18.13: Taxable Income and Tax Calculations

168. The Sunra Corporation had the following data available for 1991

- Gross profit on sales — $40,000
- Dividend income from nonaffiliated domestic corporations (not debt financed – 20% owned) — 2,000
- Operating expenses (exclusive of charitable contributions) — 28,000
- Charitable contributions — 1,500

Sunra's taxable income was

a. $10,600.
b. $10,900.
c. $11,000.
d. $12,400.

The correct answer is (c). *(CPA 1172 P-2)*
REQUIRED: The corporation's taxable income given deductions and expenses.
DISCUSSION: Sec. 63(a) defines taxable income as gross income less deductions allowed. Sec. 162 allows a deduction for ordinary and necessary business expenses. Sec. 170 allows a deduction for contributions made to qualified charitable organizations, limited to 10% of taxable income computed before the charitable contribution deduction and the dividends-received deduction. In this case, the limit applies because taxable income before special deductions is $14,000 ($40,000 + $2,000 – $28,000), and the $1,400 limit is less than actual contributions. Sec. 243 allows a deduction for dividends received from 20% or more owned domestic corporations of 80% of the dividends received, which is $1,600 (80% x $2,000). Sunra's taxable income is

Gross profit	$40,000
Dividend income	2,000
Gross income	$42,000
Less:	
Operating expenses	(28,000)
Charitable contributions	(1,400)
Dividends received deduction	(1,600)
Taxable income	$11,000

169. Which of the following determinations made in corporate financial accounting may need adjustment to conform with tax accounting requirements?

a. Dividend revenue from other domestic corporations.
b. Charitable contribution expense.
c. Insurance expense.
d. (a), (b), and (c).

The correct answer is (d). *(S. Byrd)*
REQUIRED: The difference(s) between financial and tax accounting for corporations.
DISCUSSION: For tax purposes, dividend revenue from domestic corporations may be eligible for the dividends-received deduction; charitable contributions are limited to 10% of the taxable income after adjustments; and insurance expense may be reduced by the amount paid for life insurance (when the corporation is a beneficiary). These deductions and limitations do not apply for financial accounting purposes.

170. In the reconciliation of income per books with income per return,

a. Only temporary differences are considered.
b. Only permanent differences are considered.
c. Both temporary and permanent differences are considered.
d. Neither temporary nor permanent differences is considered.

The correct answer is (c). *(CPA 1185 Q-49)*
REQUIRED: Differences included in the reconciliation of income per books with income per return.
DISCUSSION: Reconciling income per books with income per return considers both temporary differences (i.e., differences expected to be eliminated in the future such as an accelerated method of depreciation for tax purposes and a straight-line method for financial reporting purposes) and permanent differences (i.e., differences not expected to be eliminated in the future such as that caused by the deduction of federal income tax for financial reporting purposes).

171. Wright Corporation reported $100,000 of book income before income taxes for the year ended December 31, 1991. The income statement disclosed the following information:

Christmas gifts to 40 customers at $100 each.

Dividends of $20,000 received from Morley, Ltd., a 20% owned corporation not subject to United States income tax.

Insurance premiums of $15,000 on a policy insuring the life of the president of the corporation, under which Wright Corporation is the beneficiary.

What should Wright report as its taxable income for 1991?

   a. $98,000.
   b. $103,000.
   c. $115,000.
   d. $118,000.

The correct answer is (d). *(CPA 1180 P-52)*
REQUIRED: The amount of a corporation's taxable income.
DISCUSSION: Under Sec. 274(b), business gifts are limited to $25 for each gift. Under Sec. 245, dividends received from foreign corporations are eligible for the dividends-received deduction only if the corporation is subject to U.S. income tax. Under Sec. 264, no deduction is allowed for life insurance premiums on a policy covering the life of an officer if the corporation is directly or indirectly a beneficiary. Wright's taxable income is

Pre-tax income per books	$100,000
Add back:	
Christmas gifts (40 x $75)	3,000
Insurance premiums	15,000
Taxable income	$118,000

Note that the portion of Christmas gifts added back is the excess deduction taken in computing book income. Also, the dividends were included in book income, but no dividends-received deduction is allowed.

172. For the year ended December 31, 1991, Maple Corporation's book income, before federal income tax, was $100,000. Included in this $100,000 were the following

Provision for state income tax	$1,000
Interest earned on U.S. Treasury Bonds	6,000
Interest expense on bank loan to purchase U.S. Treasury Bonds	2,000

Maple's taxable income for 1991 was

   a. $96,000.
   b. $97,000.
   c. $100,000.
   d. $101,000.

The correct answer is (c). *(CPA 590 Q-35)*
REQUIRED: A corporation's taxable income given book income and some of its components.
DISCUSSION: State income taxes are deductible, unlike federal income taxes. There is no exclusion for interest income on U.S. obligations. Relatedly, the interest on debt to carry the U.S. obligations is deductible. Therefore, book income and taxable income are the same, $100,000.

173. For the year ended December 31, 1991, Murray Corporation, a calendar-year corporation, reported book income before income taxes of $120,000. Included in the determination of this amount were the following items

Loss on sale of building depreciated on the straight-line method	$(12,000)
Gain on sale of land used in business	7,000
Loss on sale of investments in marketable securities (long-term)	(8,000)

For the year ended December 31, 1991, Murray's taxable income was

   a. $113,000.
   b. $120,000.
   c. $125,000.
   d. $128,000.

The correct answer is (d). *(CPA 580 Q-32)*
REQUIRED: The amount of a corporation's taxable income.
DISCUSSION: The building and the land are Sec. 1231 assets assuming they have been held more than 1 year. Since these two sales net to a loss, they are treated as an ordinary gain and an ordinary loss under Sec. 1231 and no adjustment is needed for them between book and taxable income. The loss on the sale of investments in marketable securities is a capital loss which may only be deducted to the extent of capital gains. Since Murray has no capital gains, the loss on the sale of investments may not be deducted in 1991. Murray's taxable income is

Book income	$120,000
Add back capital loss on investments	8,000
Taxable income	$128,000

Module 18.13: Taxable Income and Tax Calculations

174. Grady Corporation's book income before income taxes was $300,000 for 1991 after recording amortization of organization costs. Organization costs of $140,000 incurred at the organization date 2 years earlier are being written off over a 10-year period for financial reporting purposes and over the minimum period for income tax purposes. Assuming there were no other reconciling items, what is Grady's taxable income for 1991?

a. $272,000.
b. $286,000.
c. $300,000.
d. $314,000.

The correct answer is (b). *(CPA 1180 P-55)*
REQUIRED: The amount of a corporation's taxable income.
DISCUSSION: Sec. 248 provides that a corporation may elect to amortize organizational expenditures over a period of at least 60 months. The amortization per books is $14,000 ($140,000 divided by 10 years). The amortization for tax purposes is $28,000 ($140,000 divided by 5 years). Consequently, an additional $14,000 ($28,000 − $14,000) is deductible in 1991. Grady's taxable income for 1991 is

Book income	$300,000
Less: Additional amortization	(14,000)
Taxable income	$286,000

175. For 1991, accrual basis Corporation A's books and records reflected the following

Net income per books	$104,000
Accrued federal income tax	50,000
Net capital loss	4,000
Tax-exempt interest	5,000
Book depreciation in excess of allowable tax depreciation	2,000

Based on the above facts, what is the amount of Corporation A's taxable income?

a. $84,000.
b. $85,000.
c. $155,000.
d. $165,000.

The correct answer is (c). *(SPE 987 III-81)*
REQUIRED: A corporation's taxable income for 1991.
DISCUSSION: Federal income tax, excess capital losses, and book depreciation in excess of tax depreciation are not deductible. These amounts must be added back to book income. Tax-exempt interest is not taxable and must be subtracted from book income. These adjustments are done on Schedule M-1 of the corporation tax return.

Net income per books	$104,000
Add back:	
Federal income tax	50,000
Net capital loss	4,000
Excess book depreciation	2,000
	$160,000
Subtract:	
Tax-exempt interest	(5,000)
Taxable income	$155,000

176. In 1991, Conrad Inc. has the following results

Taxable income	$62,500
Federal income taxes	12,000
Tax-exempt interest income	8,000
Capital loss in excess of capital gain	6,000
Modified ACRS depreciation in excess of book depreciation	3,000

The corporation's net book income for 1991 is

a. $33,500.
b. $55,500.
c. $67,500.
d. $69,500.

The correct answer is (b). *(CMA 1289 3-20)*
REQUIRED: Net book income in 1991 of Conrad Inc.
DISCUSSION: On Schedule M-1 of a corporate tax return (Form 1120), adjustments must be made to taxable income to arrive at book income. Federal income taxes are subtracted, tax-exempt interest income is added, a net capital loss is subtracted, and tax depreciation in excess of book depreciation is added.

Taxable income	$62,500
Add back:	
Tax-exempt interest income	8,000
Excess tax depreciation	3,000
	$73,500
Subtract:	
Federal income taxes	(12,000)
Net capital loss	(6,000)
Net book income	$55,500

177. Dantor Corporation, a domestic corporation, has $250,000 of taxable income from business conducted solely in the U.S. Dantor also operates two foreign branch offices. The Hamburg branch has $50,000 of taxable income related to business conducted solely in Germany. The Rome branch has $150,000 of taxable income, of which 50% is related to business conducted solely in Italy and 50% is related to business conducted solely in the U.S. Dantor's income subject to taxation in the U.S. is

a. $250,000.
b. $325,000.
c. $400,000.
d. $450,000.

The correct answer is (d). *(CMA 689 3-26)*
REQUIRED: The amount of income subject to taxation in the U.S.
DISCUSSION: Reg. 1.11-1 states that as a general rule, a domestic corporation will be taxed on its worldwide income with no distinction between income from sources inside or outside the U.S. Therefore, the entire $450,000 of income earned by Dantor is subject to taxation in the U.S.

178. Barbaro Corporation's retained earnings balance at January 1, 1991 was $600,000. During 1991, Barbaro paid cash dividends of $150,000 and received a federal income tax refund of $26,000 (which was not included in book income) as a result of an IRS audit of Barbaro's 1989 tax return. Barbaro's net income per books for the year ended December 31, 1991 was $274,900 after deducting federal income tax of $133,300. How much should be shown in the reconciliation Schedule M-2 of Form 1120 as Barbaro's retained earnings at December 31, 1991?

a. $493,600.
b. $600,900.
c. $626,900.
d. $750,900.

The correct answer is (d). *(CPA 583 Q-49)*
REQUIRED: The amount of unappropriated retained earnings on Schedule M-2 of Form 1120.
DISCUSSION: Schedule M-2 in the corporation's tax return is used to compute unappropriated retained earnings, which equals the balance at the beginning of the year plus book net income less distributions of cash, stock, or property. Other adjustments may be made as necessary. The federal income tax refund requires a positive adjustment. The balance of retained earnings at year-end is

Balance, 1/1/91	$600,000
Plus:	
Net income for year	274,900
Federal income tax refund	26,000
Less cash dividends	(150,000)
Balance, 12/31/91	$750,900

179. Corporation T's records reflect the following information:

Net income per books	$50,000
Federal income tax	8,500
Refund of prior year's income tax	1,000
Contributions carryover from prior year	300
Increase in reserve for contingencies	1,200
Unappropriated retained earnings at beginning of year	40,000
Cash dividends paid	2,000
Stock dividends paid	1,500
Tax-exempt interest	3,500

Based on this information and using generally accepted accounting principles, what is T's unappropriated retained earnings balance at the end of the year?

a. $74,000.
b. $77,800.
c. $85,300.
d. $86,300.

The correct answer is (c). *(SPE 1081 III-77)*
REQUIRED: A corporation's unappropriated retained earnings balance.
DISCUSSION: A corporation's unappropriated retained earnings balance is computed on Schedule M-2 of Form 1120. The balance at the end of the year is the beginning balance, plus net income per books, less distributions of cash, property, or stock. Other adjustments may be made as necessary. T's unappropriated retained earnings balance is

Beginning balance	$40,000
Add:	
Net income per books	50,000
Less:	
Reserve for contingencies	(1,200)
Cash dividends paid	(2,000)
Stock dividends paid	(1,500)
Unappropriated retained earnings	$85,300

The refund of prior year's income tax is not added back because it was included in this year's book income (FASB 16 and APB 30). The reserve for contingencies is subtracted because it represents an amount which is appropriated. The other items in the facts not used in the answer only represent differences between book and taxable income which do not affect retained earnings.

18.14 Alternative Minimum Tax

Author's Note: The Tax Extension Act of 1991 (P.L. 100-227) extended the exemption for untaxed appreciation of charitable contributions of tangible personal property from the list of tax preference items for the alternative minimum tax [Sec. 57(a)(6)]. For tax years beginning in 1992, the exclusion is generally available only for contributions made before July 1, 1992.

180. The alternative minimum tax for corporations after 1986 is

a. The excess of (1) a tentative minimum tax of 20% of alternative minimum taxable income reduced by an exemption amount over (2) the regular tax.

b. 20% of alternative minimum taxable income reduced by an exemption amount.

c. 20% of taxable income adjusted for tax preferences.

d. 15% of the excess of (1) the sum of tax preferences over (2) the greater of $10,000 or the regular tax.

The correct answer is (a). *(Publisher)*
REQUIRED: The calculation for alternative minimum tax for corporations after 1986.
DISCUSSION: The alternative minimum tax for tax years after 1986 is imposed by Sec. 55 for both individuals and corporations. The term "alternative" is a misnomer because the tax as defined by Sec. 55 is imposed only to the extent that it exceeds the regular tax. It is really an add-on tax. The tax is (1) a tentative tax of 20% of the excess of alternative minimum taxable income over an exemption amount, (2) reduced by the regular tax.
Answer (b) is incorrect because the amount computed is only added to tax to the extent it exceeds the regular tax. Answer (c) is incorrect because it does not take into account (1) adjustments to taxable income other than tax preferences, and (2) the exemption amount. Answer (d) is incorrect because it describes the corporate minimum tax before 1987.

181. If a corporation's tentative minimum tax exceeds the regular tax, the excess amount is

a. Subtracted from the regular tax.
b. Payable in addition to the regular tax.
c. Carried back to the third preceding taxable year.
d. Carried back to the first preceding taxable year.

The correct answer is (b). *(CPA 590 Q-37)*
REQUIRED: The correct application of the alternative minimum tax.
DISCUSSION: Sec. 55 provides that the excess of the tentative minimum tax over the regular tax is payable in addition to the regular tax. This excess is called the alternative minimum tax and is due on the same date as the regular tax.

182. Alternative minimum taxable income after 1986 is

a. The sum of all tax preferences.
b. Taxable income increased by tax preferences and adjusted by various other statutory modifications.
c. Taxable income adjusted by tax preferences and reduced by an exemption amount.
d. Computed the same for corporations and individuals.

The correct answer is (b). *(Publisher)*
REQUIRED: The correct statement about alternative minimum taxable income.
DISCUSSION: Taxable income is adjusted by various statutory items to arrive at alternative minimum taxable income. Adjustments are made to numerous items taken into account in determining taxable income as well as some additional adjustments. Tax preference items are also added to taxable income to arrive at alternative minimum taxable income.
Answer (a) is incorrect because the sum of all tax preferences is only one adjustment to taxable income to arrive at alternative minimum taxable income. Answer (c) is incorrect because the exemption amount is not taken into account in calculating alternative minimum taxable income. The exemption amount is subtracted from alternative minimum taxable income before the tax rate of 20% is applied. Answer (d) is incorrect because many of the adjustments differ for individuals and corporations; many are also the same.

183. Beta Corporation has alternative minimum taxable income in 1991 of $220,000. What is its exemption amount?

a. $10,000.
b. $17,500.
c. $22,500.
d. $40,000.

The correct answer is (c). *(Publisher)*
REQUIRED: A corporation's exemption amount for the alternative minimum tax.
DISCUSSION: The basic exemption amount is $40,000. However, this is reduced by 25% of the excess of alternative minimum taxable income over $150,000. Therefore, Beta's exemption amount is reduced by $17,500 [($220,000 − $150,000) x 25%] to $22,500.

184. For property placed in service after 1986, which of the following is a correct statement of the depreciation adjustment required to compute alternative minimum taxable income?

  a. The alternative depreciation system of Sec. 168(g) is used in its entirety.
  b. The alternative depreciation system of Sec. 168(g) is used with the 150%-declining-balance method (switching to straight-line when larger) for personal property.
  c. There is no adjustment for depreciation on real property.
  d. It is the same as for property placed in service prior to 1987.

The correct answer is (b). *(Publisher)*
REQUIRED: The correct statement concerning the adjustment for depreciation on property placed in service after 1986.
DISCUSSION: The deduction allowed for depreciation of any tangible property (personal and real) placed in service after 1986 is generally determined under the alternative depreciation system of Sec. 168(g). However, for personal property the 150%-declining-balance method is used and switches to a straight-line method in the first year the straight-line method yields a larger deduction. For nonresidential real and residential rental property, the straight-line method is used over a 40-year recovery period [Sec. 56(a)(1)].
Answer (a) is incorrect because the 150%-declining-balance method is used for personal property. Answer (c) is incorrect because real property must generally be depreciated over 40 years instead of 27.5 years or 31.5 years, depending on the type of property. Answer (d) is incorrect because, for property placed in service prior to 1987, accelerated depreciation over straight-line is a tax preference item. This generally only applies to real property.

185. Which of the following is not an adjustment to taxable income in order to compute alternative minimum taxable income?

  a. The percentage-of-completion method must be used for long-term contracts entered into after March 1, 1986.
  b. The alternative tax net operating loss is only allowed up to 90% of alternative minimum taxable income.
  c. The installment method is not allowed for sales of inventory and items held for sale to customers by dealers.
  d. The bad debt deduction is reduced by the excess of the reserve method over actual write-offs.

The correct answer is (d). *(Publisher)*
REQUIRED: The item which is not an adjustment in computing alternative minimum taxable income.
DISCUSSION: After 1986, the reserve method is no longer allowed for bad debts. There is no adjustment related to bad debts in computing alternative minimum taxable income.
Answers (a), (b), and (c) are incorrect because each is a required adjustment in computing alternative minimum taxable income as provided by Secs. 56(a)(3), 56(a)(4), 56(d)(1), and 56(a)(6), respectively.

186. Which of the following is a correct statement of the adjusted current earnings adjustment to alternative minimum taxable income?

  a. It is an increase by the excess of adjusted current earnings over alternative minimum taxable income.
  b. It is a decrease by the excess of alternative minimum taxable income over adjusted current earnings.
  c. It only applies to personal holding companies.
  d. It only applies after 1989.

The correct answer is (d). *(Publisher)*
REQUIRED: The correct statement concerning the adjusted current earnings adjustment to alternative minimum taxable income.
DISCUSSION: The adjusted current earnings adjustment only applies for taxable years beginning after 1989.
Answers (a) and (b) are incorrect because the adjusted current earnings calculation requires alternative minimum taxable income to be increased by 75% of the excess of adjusted current earnings of the corporation over the alternative minimum taxable income, or reduced by 75% of the excess of alternative minimum taxable income over the adjusted current earnings of the corporation. The reduction is limited to the excess of the aggregate increases in alternative minimum taxable income from prior years (due to this adjustment) over the aggregate reductions for the prior years. Answer (c) is incorrect because the adjusted current earnings adjustment applies to regular corporations but not to S corporations, regulated investment companies, or real estate investment trusts.

Module 18.14: Alternative Minimum Tax

187. All of the following represent tax preference items in figuring a corporation's alternative minimum taxable income except

a. Intangible drilling costs.
b. Percentage depletion.
c. Net operating losses.
d. Certain tax-exempt interest.

The correct answer is (c). *(SPE 990 III-41)*
REQUIRED: The item that is not a tax preference item for purposes of calculating the alternative minimum tax.
DISCUSSION: Net operating losses are not tax preference items under Sec. 57.
Answers (a), (b), and (d) are incorrect because they are items of tax preference under Sec. 57.

188. Tiger Corporation reports adjusted current earnings (ACE) of $600,000 for 1991. Its alternative minimum taxable income (excluding the alternative tax NOL deduction and the ACE adjustment) is $250,000. Its alternative minimum taxable income is

a. $250,000.
b. $375,000.
c. $512,500.
d. $600,000.

The correct answer is (c). *(Publisher)*
REQUIRED: The correct alternative minimum taxable income for 1991.
DISCUSSION: After 1989, the adjusted current earnings of corporations are treated as a tax preference. Sec. 56(g) states that the alternative minimum taxable income of a corporation must be increased by 75% of the amount by which the adjusted current earnings exceed the alternative minimum taxable income (determined without regard to the adjusted current earnings and the alternative tax net operating loss deduction). Therefore, Tiger Corporation's alternative minimum taxable income for 1991 is $512,500 [$250,000 + 75% x ($600,000 − $250,000)].

189. Bear Corporation reports the following adjusted current earnings (ACE) and alternative minimum taxable income (AMTI) amounts (excluding the ACE adjustment and alternative tax NOL deduction) for the period 1990 through 1992.

	1990	1991	1992
ACE	$200	$200	$200
AMTI	100	200	400

What is Bear Corporation's ACE adjustment for 1992?

a. $0.
b. $75.
c. $150.
d. $200.

The correct answer is (b). *(Publisher)*
REQUIRED: Calculate the ACE adjustment for 1992.
DISCUSSION: Sec. 56(g) provides that the ACE adjustment shall be 75% of the difference between ACE and AMTI (excluding the ACE adjustment and the alternative tax NOL deduction). However, in a tax year where AMTI exceeds ACE, the negative adjustment is limited to the aggregate positive adjustments for prior years over the aggregate negative adjustments for prior years. Bear's AMTI exceeds its ACE by $200 in 1992, 75% of which equals $150. However, this amount is limited to the $75 positive adjustment made in 1990 [($200 ACE − $100 AMTI) x 75% = $75].

190. Which one of the following items properly reported by the corporation in determining alternative minimum taxable income is not adjusted in order to determine adjusted current earnings?

a. Life insurance policy proceeds received by the corporation on the death of a corporate officer.
b. Organizational expenditures that were amortized under Sec. 248.
c. Sales reported by a nondealer using the installment method of accounting.
d. Long-term capital gains.

The correct answer is (d). *(Publisher)*
REQUIRED: The item not adjusted in order to determine adjusted current earnings.
DISCUSSION: Sec. 56(g) lists adjustments that apply in determining adjusted current earnings. These adjustments include life insurance proceeds received by the corporation on the death of a corporate officer, organizational expenditures that were amortized under Sec. 248, and sales reported by a nondealer using the installment method of accounting. Long-term capital gains are not included as an adjustment in determining adjusted current earnings.

Module 18.14: Alternative Minimum Tax

191. Which of the following statements is incorrect concerning the calculation of adjusted current earnings (ACE) for tax years beginning after 1989?

a. The starting point for the ACE calculation is the taxpayer corporation's alternative minimum taxable income.

b. Build-ups in life insurance contracts are included in ACE.

c. Amortization of organizational expenditures are not included in ACE.

d. The book underreported profits (BURP) adjustment is included in ACE.

The correct answer is (d). (Publisher)
REQUIRED: The statement which is incorrect concerning the calculation of adjusted current earnings.
DISCUSSION: The adjusted current earnings (ACE) adjustment replaced the book underreported profits (BURP) adjustment for tax years beginning after 1989 [Sec. 56(g)].
Answers (a), (b), and (c) are correct statements concerning the calculation of the adjusted current earnings.

192. What would be the alternative minimum tax for a corporation whose tax return reflects the following?

Alternative minimum taxable income	$107,500
Foreign tax credits	1,375
Regular tax	6,890

a. $5,235.

b. $12,125.

c. $13,235.

d. $13,500.

The correct answer is (a). (SPE 988 III-73)
REQUIRED: The corporation's alternative minimum tax.
DISCUSSION: Sec. 55 imposes a minimum tax on corporations. First, a tentative tax of 20% is computed on the excess of the alternative minimum taxable income over an exemption amount. The exemption amount is $40,000 provided the alternative minimum taxable income does not exceed $150,000. The minimum tax is the excess of this tentative tax over the regular tax.
The corporation's alternative minimum taxable income of $107,500 is reduced by the exemption amount of $40,000. The tentative tax is $13,500 ($67,500 x 20%). The minimum tax is $5,235.

Tentative tax	$13,500
Less regular tax	(6,890)
Tentative minimum tax	$ 6,610
Less foreign tax credits	(1,375)
Alternative minimum tax	$ 5,235

The alternative minimum tax can be reduced by a foreign tax credit which is limited to 90% of the tentative minimum tax. This limit does not restrict the ability to claim the foreign tax credit here.

193. In 1991, Perrot Corporation had alternative minimum taxable income of $200,000 and a regular tax liability of $30,000. What is Perrot's alternative minimum tax?

a. $0.

b. $2,000.

c. $4,500.

d. $7,500.

The correct answer is (c). (Publisher)
REQUIRED: The corporation's alternative minimum tax.
DISCUSSION: Sec. 55 imposes a minimum tax on corporations. First, a tentative tax is computed at 20% of the excess of the alternative minimum taxable income over an exemption amount. The basic exemption amount is reduced by 25% of the excess of alternative minimum taxable income over $150,000. The minimum tax is then the excess of the tentative tax over the regular tax.
Since Perrot Corporation has alternative minimum taxable income of $200,000, its exemption amount is $27,500 {$40,000 − [25% x ($200,000 − $150,000)]}. Perrot's tentative tax is $34,500 [20% x ($200,000 alternative minimum taxable income − $27,500 exemption amount)]. The alternative minimum tax is $4,500 ($34,500 − $30,000).

194. Corporation X had $100,000 of taxable income in 1991 on which its regular tax is $22,250. Depreciation on machinery placed in service after 1986 amounted to $100,000 (it would be $70,000 using the 150%-declining-balance method). Depreciation on real estate placed in service in 1986 amounted to $15,000 (it would be $10,000 using the straight-line method). Charitable contributions for 1991 were $10,000, consisting of T Corporation stock with a basis of $3,000. The full $10,000 was deducted in determining taxable income. Adjusted current earnings amounted to $182,000. The 1991 alternative minimum tax (AMT) for Corporation X is

a. $0.
b. $2,400.
c. $5,250.
d. $12,400.

The correct answer is (c). *(Publisher)*
REQUIRED: The alternative minimum tax for a corporation.
DISCUSSION: Sec. 55 imposes an alternative minimum tax on corporations. First, a tentative tax of 20% is computed on the excess of the alternative minimum taxable income (AMTI) over an exemption amount. The alternative minimum tax is the excess of the tentative minimum tax over the regular tax. Depreciation on personal property placed in service after 1986 is computed using 150%-declining-balance method. Depreciation on real property placed in service prior to 1987 is generally depreciated using the straight-line method. The untaxed appreciation allowed as a regular tax deduction for charitable contributions must be added back as a tax preference item since the stock is not tangible personal property. Alternative minimum taxable income must also be increased by 75% of the amount by which the adjusted current earnings exceeds the alternative minimum taxable income.

Regular taxable income		$100,000
Adjustments for AMTI:		
Depreciation on equipment ($100,000 – $70,000)		30,000
Tax preference items:		
Excess depreciation on real estate		5,000
Untaxed appreciation of property contributed to charity		7,000
Tentative AMTI		$142,000
Adjusted Current Earnings	$182,000	
Tentative AMTI	(142,000)	
ACE/AMTI tax difference	$ 40,000	
Times: Percentage	x .75	
ACE/AMTI adjustment		$ 30,000
AMTI		$172,000
Less exemption*		(34,500)
AMT tax base		$137,500
AMT rate		x 20%
Total tentative tax		$ 27,500
Less regular tax		(22,250)
AMT		$ 5,250

*The exemption amount is reduced as follows:

Initial exemption		$ 40,000
Less: Excess of AMTI over $150,000	$172,000 (150,000) $ 22,000	
Times: Percentage	x .25	$ 5,500
Exemption		$34,500

195. The adjusted current earnings adjustment equals 50% of the positive or negative difference between adjusted current earnings and alternative minimum taxable income.

The correct answer is (F). *(Publisher)*
DISCUSSION: Sec. 56(g) provides that the adjusted current earnings adjustment equal 75% of the positive or negative difference between adjusted current earnings and alternative minimum taxable income. Sec. 56(g)(2)(B) limits a negative adjustment to excess of the aggregate positive adjustments in prior years over the aggregate negative adjustments in prior years.

18.15 Return Filing and Payment Requirements

196. Dividends-received deductions are not allowed in determining adjusted current earnings.

The correct answer is (F). *(Publisher)*
DISCUSSION: The 100% and 80% dividends-received deductions are permitted in determining the adjusted current earnings adjustment. However, the 70% dividends-received deduction is not permitted.

197. A corporation may have to pay the alternative minimum tax if taxable income for regular income tax purposes, when combined with certain adjustments and preference items that apply in computing the alternative minimum tax, total more than $40,000.

The correct answer is (T). *(SPE 990 III-10)*
DISCUSSION: Under Sec. 55, the alternative minimum tax must be considered if taxable income plus tax preferences and adjustments exceeds the $40,000 exemption. The corporation must pay the alternative minimum tax if the tentative minimum tax exceeds its regular tax.

198. Corporation X carries its net operating loss for 1991 back to 1988 for which X incurred an alternative minimum tax liability. Corporation X must recompute its alternative minimum tax liability for 1988.

The correct answer is (T). *(SPE 987 III-17)*
DISCUSSION: When the taxable income of a corporation is adjusted in any tax year, the alternative minimum tax must be recomputed as well as the regular tax.

199. For tax year 1990 and later years, a corporation is permitted to claim the entire amount of the excess of its alternative minimum tax liability over its regular tax liability as a minimum tax credit.

The correct answer is (T). *(Publisher)*
DISCUSSION: For tax years beginning after December 31, 1989, a corporation that pays an alternative minimum tax liability in one year may use the tax as a credit in later years to offset the regular tax liability in the carryover year. The maximum minimum tax credit that can be used in the carryover year equals the regular tax liability minus all available tax credits against such tax over the tentative minimum tax for the year.
The credit is now available for deferral and exclusion adjustments and preferences. Previously, the credit was only available for deferral items. The corporation minimum tax credit rules are different from those applying to individual taxpayers [Sec. 53(d)(1)(B)(iv)].

200. If a corporation did not use all of its alternative minimum tax credit in 1991, it may carry the balance forward up to a maximum of 15 years.

The correct answer is (F). *(SPE 990 III-12)*
DISCUSSION: Sec. 53 allows for an unlimited carryover of alternative minimum tax credit.

18.15 Return Filing and Payment Requirements

201. Under which of the following circumstances would a corporation be required to file a federal income tax return?

a. The corporation has disposed of all of its assets except for a small sum of cash retained to pay state taxes to preserve its corporate charter.
b. A corporation with no assets, stops doing business and dissolves, and is treated as a corporation under state law for limited purposes connected with winding up its affairs.
c. The corporation has dissolved and is in bankruptcy.
d. In 1990, Corporation M ceased doing business and disposed of all of its assets. However, during all of 1991, M was in the process of suing Corporation B.

The correct answer is (a). *(SPE 990 III-33)*
REQUIRED: The corporation that is required to file a federal income tax return.
DISCUSSION: Sec. 6012(a)(2) requires every corporation subject to taxation under subtitle A of the Code to file a federal income tax return.
Answers (b), (c), and (d) are incorrect because the corporation in each of these situations has ceased business and dissolved. Reg. 1.6012-2(a)(2) states that for federal income tax purposes a corporation is not in existence if it has ceased business and dissolved.

Module 18.15: Return Filing and Payment Requirements

202. P Corporation filed a federal tax return and appropriately paid $1,150,000 for its federal tax liability incurred for the full calendar year 1990. In early 1991, P estimated its 1991 tax liability and paid a total of $1,200,000 in equal installments on appropriate due dates. On February 12, 1992, the corporation's 1991 return was completed. The return indicated an actual liability of $1,300,000. The corporation desires to defer the payment of the balance of tax due as long as possible. What is the amount and due date(s) of the corporation's minimum obligation (not considering weekends and holidays)?

a. $50,000 on March 15 and September 15.
b. $50,000 on March 15 and June 15.
c. $100,000 on March 15.
d. $100,000 on September 15.

The correct answer is (c). *(SPE 1079 III-50)*
REQUIRED: The amount and due date(s) of a corporation's smallest tax payment(s).
DISCUSSION: A corporation's entire tax liability is due on the same date as the return. Under Sec. 6072(b), a calendar-year corporation must file its income tax return on or before the 15th day of March following the close of the calendar year. P Corporation must therefore pay $100,000 of tax on March 15. An extension of time to file the tax return does not provide an extension of time to pay the tax liability without incurring interest and/or penalty.

203. Excluding extensions, which one of the following 1120 returns is filed late ignoring the possibility that a date may be a Saturday, Sunday, or holiday?

	Tax Year Ended	Date Filed
a.	January 31, 1991	April 15, 1991
b.	August 31, 1991	November 2, 1991
c.	July 31, 1991	October 30, 1991
d.	December 31, 1991	March 15, 1992

The correct answer is (c). *(SPE 990 III-34)*
REQUIRED: The 1120 return that is filed later than required by the Code.
DISCUSSION: Sec. 6072(b) requires calendar year corporate taxpayers to file a return by March 15 of the following year. Fiscal year corporate taxpayers must file by the 15th day of the third month following the close of the fiscal year. Answer (c) reflects a late tax return since the due date is October 15, 1991.
Answers (a), (b), and (d) are incorrect because they reflect timely filed tax returns.

204. A calendar-year corporation receives an automatic extension of time for filing its 1991 return by submitting an application for extension on Form 7004. What is the due date for filing the corporation's return (not considering weekends and holidays)?

a. March 15, 1992.
b. August 15, 1992.
c. September 15, 1992.
d. September 30, 1992.

The correct answer is (c). *(SPE 987 III-49)*
REQUIRED: The due date for a corporation filing for an automatic extension.
DISCUSSION: Sec. 6072(b) provides that a corporation must file its return on or before the 15th day of the third month following the close of the tax year. For a calendar-year-end corporation, the due date for a 1991 tax return is March 15, 1992. By filing Form 7004, the corporation will receive an automatic extension for filing the tax return, which moves the due date to September 15, 1992.

205. Which of the following is not a requirement a corporation must meet in order to report its taxable income on Form 1120-A?

a. Its gross receipts, total income, and total assets must each be under $100,000.
b. It does not have foreign shareholders who own, directly or indirectly, 50% or more of its stock.
c. It is not a personal holding company.
d. It is not undergoing a dissolution.

The correct answer is (a). *(SPE 989 III-38)*
REQUIRED: The item that is not a requirement in order to file its taxable income on Form 1120-A.
DISCUSSION: To file form 1120-A, corporate gross receipts, total income, and total assets must each be less than $250,000.
Answers (b), (c), and (d) are incorrect because each is a requirement to file Form 1120-A.

Module 18.15: Return Filing and Payment Requirements

206. A calendar-year corporation filed its 1990 return on April 30, 1991 without securing an extension of time to file. It could not show reasonable cause. If the tax due was $5,000 and no payments had been made prior to filing, the failure to file and failure to pay penalties would equal:

a. $250.
b. $500.
c. $750.
d. $1,000.

The correct answer is (b). *(SPE 987 III-72)*
REQUIRED: The delinquency penalty for failure to file a return and pay taxes by the due date.
DISCUSSION: A delinquency penalty is imposed by Sec. 6651(a) for failure to file a tax return or to pay tax. The penalty for failure to file is 5% of the amount of tax for each month or fraction of a month that the failure to file a return continues. The penalty for failure to pay is 0.5% of the amount of tax for each month or fraction of a month that the failure to pay continues. If the taxpayer fails to file the tax return and to pay the tax, the 5% failure to file penalty is reduced by the 0.5% failure to pay penalty. The corporation's delinquency penalty for failure to file its return and pay its taxes is

Tax due	$5,000
Total penalty percentage	x 5%
Monthly penalty	$ 250
Months outstanding	x 2
Failure to file and failure to pay penalty	$ 500

207. The results of an examination of PKP Corporation's 1990 tax return reflected an additional tax liability of $10,000 which was caused by the negligent actions of the corporate officers. PKP owes the IRS

a. $10,000.
b. $10,500.
c. $11,000.
d. $12,000.

The correct answer is (d). *(M. Yates)*
REQUIRED: The penalty for underpayment of tax due to negligence.
DISCUSSION: Sec. 6662(b)(1) provides that an accuracy-related penalty shall be assessed against any underpayment of tax liability that is attributable to negligence or intentional disregard of rules and regulations. The amount of the penalty is 20% of the underpayment which is attributable to the negligent item(s).

Additional tax liability	$10,000
Times: Penalty rate	x 20%
Negligence penalty	$ 2,000
Additional tax liability	$10,000
Negligence penalty	2,000
Total owed the IRS	$12,000

208. A corporation with no assets is not required to file a federal income tax return after it stops doing business and dissolves, even if it is treated as a corporation under state law for limited purposes connected with winding up its affairs.

The correct answer is (T). *(SPE 987 III-3)*
DISCUSSION: Under Reg. 1.6012-2(a)(2), a corporation that has ceased doing business, dissolved, and retained no assets is not in existence even if, under state law, it is treated as continuing to wind up its affairs. Accordingly, no tax return is required.

209. In 1990, Corporation M ceased doing business and disposed of its assets. However, during all of 1991, Corporation M was in the process of suing Corporation B. Corporation M is required to file a tax return for 1991.

The correct answer is (F). *(SPE 1081 III-1)*
DISCUSSION: Under Reg. 1.6012-2(a)(2), a corporation that has ceased doing business, dissolved, and retained no assets is not in existence even if, under state law, it is treated as continuing to wind up its affairs such as suing and being sued. Accordingly, no tax return is required.

210. A corporation on a fiscal year is required to file its tax return on or before the 15th day of the 4th month following the close of its fiscal year.

The correct answer is (F). *(SPE 987 III-4)*
DISCUSSION: Sec. 6072(b) provides that corporate income tax returns made on the basis of a fiscal year must be filed on or before the 15th day of the third month following the close of the fiscal year.

Module 18.15: Return Filing and Payment Requirements

211. If a due date for filing a corporate tax return falls on a Saturday, Sunday, or a holiday, the return must be filed by the last business day before that Saturday, Sunday, or holiday.

The correct answer is (F). *(SPE 1078 III-15)*
DISCUSSION: Sec. 7503 provides that when the last day prescribed by the Internal Revenue laws for performing any act falls on a Saturday, Sunday, or legal holiday, the performance of such act is considered timely if performed on the next succeeding day which is not a Saturday, Sunday, or legal holiday.

212. A corporation will receive an automatic extension of time for filing a return by submitting an application for extension on Form 7004 and paying any tax due by the original due date of the corporation's income tax return.

The correct answer is (T). *(SPE 984 III-5)*
DISCUSSION: Reg. 1.6081-3(a) allows a corporation an automatic extension of 6 months for filing its income tax return if the corporation files the appropriate form (7004) and pays its estimated unpaid tax liability on or before the due date of the return.

213. Corporation Z, a calendar year taxpayer, submitted a timely application for automatic extension of time for filing its 1990 federal income tax return. At the time of filing the application, Z determined its tax liability to be $20,000. During 1990, Z had made estimated tax payments totaling $10,000. On August 15, 1991, Z filed its return and paid the balance due of $10,000. Z is not subject to the failure to pay penalty.

The correct answer is (F). *(SPE 989 III-1)*
DISCUSSION: Sec. 6151(a) requires the tax to be paid when the return is due. Sec. 6651 imposes a penalty of 0.5% per month (or part of a month) for failure to pay tax when due.

214. Interest is charged by the IRS at the applicable annual rate on the difference between the tentative tax reported on a request for extension of time for filing and the actual tax a corporation must pay when it files its Form 1120.

The correct answer is (T). *(SPE 1078 III-17)*
DISCUSSION: Under Sec. 6601(a), interest is imposed on the underpayment of tax. Interest is charged on the difference between the tentative tax and the actual tax a corporation must pay when filing its Form 1120. The tentative tax must be timely paid to obtain the extension. The underpayment is the additional actual tax.

215. Corporation Y filed its income tax return for 1991, showing a balance of $5,000 due after taking into account estimated tax payments. Upon filing, Corporation Y deposited $3,000 to an authorized commercial bank depository. The remaining $2,000 was deposited 3 weeks later. The corporation's penalty for failure to pay will be $20.

The correct answer is (F). *(SPE 1083 III-4)*
DISCUSSION: Sec. 6151(a) requires the tax to be paid when the return is due. Sec. 6651 imposes a penalty of 0.5% per month (or part of a month) for failure to pay tax when due. The unpaid amount is $2,000, so the penalty is $10 (.005 x $2,000).

216. A corporation that does not file its income tax returns by the due date (including extensions) is subject to a delinquency penalty of 5% of the tax due if the delinquency is not more than 1 month. An additional 5% is imposed for each additional month or fraction thereof during which the delinquency continues, not exceeding a total of 50%.

The correct answer is (F). *(SPE 1078 IV-50)*
DISCUSSION: Sec. 6651(a) imposes a penalty upon a taxpayer who fails to file a required return by the prescribed due date. This penalty is equal to 5% of the amount of tax if the failure is not for more than 1 month, and an additional 5% for each month or fraction of a month the failure continues, but not to exceed 25%.

217. During 1991, Corporation D, a U.S. corporation, made payments to a nonresident alien individual. Corporation D is required to file Form 1042, U.S. Annual Return of Income Tax to be Paid at Source, even though no income tax was withheld and deducted because of a specific exemption.

The correct answer is (T). *(SPE 1081 III-44)*
DISCUSSION: Every withholding agent is required to file an annual return, Form 1042, of the tax required to be withheld on payments made to nonresident aliens and foreign corporations. This form, which is due on or before March 15, must be filed even though no tax was withheld [Reg. 1.1461-2(b)].

18.16 Estimated Tax Payments

Author's Note: The Tax Extension Act of 1991 increased the minimum estimated tax payments for all corporations for tax years 1992 through 1996. The 90% of current tax year liability minimum to avoid an underpayment penalty became: 93% for 1992, 94% for 1993 and 1994, 95% for 1995 and 1996. The minimum amount is slated to return to 90% for 1997. P.L. 100-244 (enacted 2/7/92) changed the portion of the current tax liability that must be paid in to avoid the estimated tax underpayment penalty to the following: 1992, 93%; 1993-1996, 95%.

218. Finbury Corporation's taxable income for the year ended December 31, 1991 was $2,000,000. For Finbury to escape the estimated tax underpayment penalty for the year ending December 31, 1992, its 1992 estimated tax payments must equal at least

   a. 80% of the 1992 tax liability.
   b. 90% of the 1992 tax liability.
   c. 93% of the 1992 tax liability.
   d. 100% of its 1991 tax liability.

The correct answer is (c). *(CPA 583 Q-45)*
   REQUIRED: The minimum amount of estimated tax payments to avoid the underpayment penalty for 1992.
   DISCUSSION: Sec. 6655(b) provides that a corporation will not be considered to have underpaid its income tax if it pays an amount equal to 93% of the tax shown on the return for taxable year 1992.
   Answers (a) and (b) are incorrect because the applicable percentage is 93%. Answer (d) is incorrect because a large corporation (one with taxable income of $1,000,000 or more during any of the 3 prior years) may not use last year's tax as an exception to the penalty.

219. On March 31, G, a calendar-year corporation, determined its estimated tax liability to be $12,000. It should have made estimated tax payments of

   a. $4,000 no later than the 15th day of the 3rd, 6th, and 10th months.
   b. $4,000 no later than the 15th day of the 4th, 7th, and 9th months.
   c. $3,000 no later than the 15th day of the 3rd, 6th, 9th, and 12th months.
   d. $3,000 no later than the 15th day of the 4th, 6th, 9th, and 12th months.

The correct answer is (d). *(SPE 986 III-44)*
   REQUIRED: When a calendar-year corporation's estimated tax payments are due.
   DISCUSSION: A corporation is required to pay ¼ of its estimated taxes each quarter. However, the first payment is not due until April 15. Therefore, G must pay $3,000 (25% x $12,000) on the 15th day of the 4th, 6th, 9th, and 12th months of the year.

220. For 1992, Corporation N, a calendar year taxpayer, had a tax liability of $100,000, consisting of $45,000 in regular taxes, and $55,000 in alternative minimum taxes. N's 1991 tax liability was $200,000. What is the amount N must have paid for each quarter for 1992 to avoid any penalty or interest for underpayment of estimated tax?

   a. $22,500.
   b. $23,250.
   c. $25,000.
   d. $50,000.

The correct answer is (b). *(SPE 990 III-68)*
   REQUIRED: A corporation's estimated tax payments given a liability for both the regular tax and the alternative minimum tax.
   DISCUSSION: Sec. 6655(b) provides that a corporation will not be considered to have underpaid its income tax if it pays an amount equal to 93% of the tax shown on the return for taxable year 1992. The definition of tax for this purpose is found in Sec. 6655(f). For tax years beginning after 1986, this definition of tax includes the alternative minimum tax.
   Corporation N has a total tax liability of $100,000 for 1992. It must pay 93% of this amount in estimated taxes in order to avoid any penalties or interest. The quarterly payment is $23,250 (¼ x $93,000).

221. In order for Corporation X, a calendar year taxpayer, to be required to make estimated tax payments in 1992, its expected tax liability would have to be

   a. $500 or more.
   b. $600 or more.
   c. $1,000 or more.
   d. $2,000 or more.

The correct answer is (a). *(SPE 989 III-43)*
   REQUIRED: The amount of estimated tax liability that requires a corporation to make estimated tax payments.
   DISCUSSION: All corporations must make estimated tax payments, except those which have an estimated tax liability of less than $500 [Sec. 6655(f)].

Module 18.16: Estimated Tax Payments

222. Corporation T had a credit of $1,400 from its 1991 calendar-year return to be applied to its 1992 estimated tax. Its 1991 tax was $1,800. Corporation T accurately estimates its tax for 1992 to be $1,600. Corporation T will be assessed a penalty if it makes no additional estimated tax payments.

The correct answer is (T). *(SPE 1081 III-7)*
DISCUSSION: Under Sec. 6655, a corporation is subject to a penalty for underpayment of its estimated tax. Although a penalty will not be assessed if the tax is less than $500, Corporation T's 1992 tax is $1,600. Corporation T must make total estimated payments equal to $1,488 (93% x $1,600) to avoid the penalty. The $1,400 credit from its 1991 return reduces the remaining estimated payments to $88.

223. A corporation's estimated tax payments must be deposited with an authorized commercial bank, trust company, domestic building and loan association, credit union, or Federal Reserve bank. Each deposit must be accompanied by Form 8109.

The correct answer is (T). *(SPE 1080 III-5)*
DISCUSSION: Reg. 31.6302-1 states that a corporation must deposit estimated tax payments with a Federal Reserve bank, or with an authorized commercial bank. Form 8109 must accompany each remittance of tax.

224. A corporation has the option of annualizing income and paying its estimated taxes accordingly. If later during 1992, a corporation's income increased so that an earlier estimated tax payment was inadequate, the corporation has to pay enough in the subsequent quarter's installment to have paid 93% of the tax due on the new annualized income.

The correct answer is (F). *(Publisher)*
DISCUSSION: Sec. 6655(e) requires that the estimated payment in the subsequent quarter be large enough so that 100% of the shortfall has been paid in. A corporate taxpayer who continues to use the annualization exception for making its estimated tax payments will in later quarters have paid in 93% of the tax due on the new annualized income. If this amount is paid in when income is increasing, 100% of the shortfall will be paid in as is required by Sec. 6655(e).

225. There will be no failure to pay estimated tax penalty for a calendar-year corporation who has determined by April 1st of the tax year that it will owe $10,000 tax, if the corporation makes one estimated tax payment of $10,000 on December 15 of that tax year.

The correct answer is (F). *(SPE 987 III-8)*
DISCUSSION: Sec. 6655 imposes a penalty upon a corporation for the underpayment or late payment of estimated tax. The penalty is assessed for the period of the underpayment, which is from the due date of the estimated payment until the earlier of the date it is paid or the due date of the income tax return. To avoid a penalty, the corporation should make quarterly estimated tax payments in 1992 of $2,325 ($10,000 x 93% x 25%).

226. Corporation L underpays its 1992 estimated tax. Penalty for underpayment is figured on the amount by which any installment is less than the amount that would be required to be paid if the estimated tax were equal to 80% of the tax shown on the return for that year.

The correct answer is (F). *(Publisher)*
DISCUSSION: At least 93% of a corporation's final tax must be paid in installments on a quarterly basis for 1992. If this 93% requirement is not met, the corporation will be subject to a penalty on the amount by which the installment payments are less than 93% of the tax due. The penalty will not apply if a corporation (other than a large corporation) timely pays either an installment based on 100% of its tax liability for the prior year, or 93% of the tax which would be due on its income computed on an annualized or seasonal basis.

227. A calendar-year corporation made 4 quarterly estimated tax payments for 1992 totaling $20,000. On February 1, 1993, the corporation determined that its income tax liability is $17,000. Although the corporation has not filed its 1992 income tax return at this time, it may file for a quick refund of estimated tax payments.

The correct answer is (T). *(SPE 990 III-14)*
DISCUSSION: Sec. 6425 provides that a corporation that makes an overpayment of estimated income tax may file an application (Form 4466) after the close of the tax year and before the 15th day of the third month after year-end for an adjustment. The adjustment will only be allowed if it is (1) at least 10% of the amount that the corporation estimates as its income tax liability for the taxable year, and (2) at least $500. Since the adjustment of $3,000 ($20,000 − $17,000) meets both of the requirements, the corporation is eligible for a quick refund.

18.17 Earnings and Profits

228. Which of the following items is not included in determining a corporation's current earnings and profits amount?

   a. Life insurance proceeds.
   b. Municipal bond interest income.
   c. Charitable contributions made in excess of the 10% of adjusted taxable income limitation.
   d. Dividends-received deduction.

The correct answer is (d). *(Publisher)*
REQUIRED: The item not included in determining current earnings and profits.
DISCUSSION: Sec. 312 provides a partial definition of earnings and profits. The dividends-received deduction is not a deduction for computing earnings and profits because it is not an economic reduction or outlay of the corporation's assets.
Answers (a), (b), and (c) are all items that must be included in calculating current earnings and profits under Sec. 312 and the related regulations. Each represents an increase or decrease in the corporation's assets.

229. Francis Corporation had taxable income of $260,000 for its initial taxable year. A review of company records revealed the following information.

1. The 1991 tax depreciation expense on Furniture and Fixtures, the only asset owned by Francis Corporation, was $10,000. If Francis had used the alternative depreciation system (straight-line method), depreciation expense deducted would have been $5,000.
2. Francis had tax-exempt interest income of $22,000 that has not been included in taxable income.
3. Francis paid dividends of $16,000 that were not deducted.
4. Francis had $20,000 of returns and allowances that were deducted on the return.
5. Francis reported a $20,000 gain on an installment sale of a noninventory item. The total gain on the sale was $100,000.

Earnings and profits for Francis Corporation in 1991 were

   a. $351,000.
   b. $346,000.
   c. $271,000.
   d. $266,000.

The correct answer is (a). *(CMA 689 3-27)*
REQUIRED: The earnings and profits in 1991.
DISCUSSION: In computing earnings and profits of a corporation, all income that is nontaxable or exempt from tax is added to taxable income. The earnings and profits are reduced by any expenditures or expenses of the corporation that are not deductible for tax purposes. Depreciation is usually determined under the alternative depreciation system (straight-line method). If depreciation reported for tax purposes exceeds straight-line depreciation, the difference is added back to taxable income. A corporation that sells property on the installment basis is treated for earnings and profits purposes as if it had not used the installment method. No adjustment is required for returns and allowances since deducting returns and allowances is an acceptable tax accounting procedure for computing taxable income and earnings and profits. The computation of earnings and profits for Francis Corporation in 1991 is as follows

Taxable income	$260,000
Depreciation ($10,000 – $5,000)	5,000
Tax-exempt interest income	22,000
Installment sale gain not reported for tax purposes ($100,000 – $20,000)	80,000
Dividends paid	(16,000)
Earnings and profits	$351,000

Module 18.17: Earnings and Profits

230. Corporation W, which uses the accrual method of accounting, had earnings and profits of $95,000 on December 31, 1990. Based on the following information, compute earnings and profits as of December 31, 1991.

Taxable income per return	$185,000
Contributions in excess of limitation	1,500
Interest paid for tax-exempt bonds	1,000
Tax-exempt interest received	3,000
Federal income taxes	55,400
MACRS depreciation from post-1986 property acquisitions on return in excess of alternative depreciation system straight-line depreciation	1,500

- a. $214,600.
- b. $220,600.
- c. $226,600.
- d. $228,600.

The correct answer is (c). *(SPE 1083 III-73)*
REQUIRED: The earnings and profits balance as of December 31, 1991.
DISCUSSION: Calculation of earnings and profits begins with taxable income according to the tax return. Tax-exempt income is added to the taxable income and nondeductible expenditures are subtracted, e.g., federal income taxes, charitable contributions in excess of the limitation, and interest paid for tax-exempt bonds. Also, earnings and profits are calculated based upon straight-line depreciation using the alternative depreciation system, so excess MACRS depreciation must be added back for property acquired after 1986.

E&P at 12/31/90	$ 95,000
Taxable income for 1991	185,000
Add: Tax-exempt interest	3,000
Excess depreciation	1,500
Deduct: Excess contributions	(1,500)
Interest paid on tax-exempt bonds	(1,000)
Federal income taxes	(55,400)
E&P at 12/31/91	$226,600

231. T, a calendar-year corporation that began doing business January 1, 1984, had $35,000 in accumulated earnings and profits on January 1, 1991. T had an operating loss of $60,000 for the first 6 months of 1991, but had $10,000 in earnings for the entire year. T made a distribution of $25,000 cash to its stockholders on April 1, 1991. What is the amount of T's accumulated earnings and profits on January 1, 1992?

- a. $0.
- b. $10,000.
- c. $20,000.
- d. $45,000.

The correct answer is (c). *(SPE 989 III-82)*
REQUIRED: The effect of a cash distribution to stockholders upon the corporations earnings and profits (E&P).
DISCUSSION: Determination must first be made as to whether or not the cash distribution is a dividend. Sec. 316 defines a dividend as a distribution of earnings and profits. Reg. 1.316-1(a)(1)(ii) states that current E&P is to be computed at the end of the tax year without regard to distributions during the year. At December 31, 1991, T has a current E&P of $10,000 and accumulated E&P of $35,000. The cash distribution comes first from current E&P ($10,000 − $10,000 = $0), with the balance from accumulated E&P, thereby leaving a $20,000 balance ($35,000 − $15,000 = $20,000).

232. Orville Company had earnings and profits of $82,000 for the year ended December 31, 1991, before distribution of dividends. On December 31, 1991, the company distributed inventory with a fair market value of $16,000 and an adjusted basis of $12,000 as a dividend to its sole individual stockholder, Orville. The company values its inventory by the first-in, first-out method. Assume the corporate tax rate is 34%. What should be the earnings and profits after distribution of the dividend for the year ended December 31, 1991?

- a. $66,000.
- b. $68,640.
- c. $70,000.
- d. $82,000.

The correct answer is (b). *(Publisher)*
REQUIRED: The earnings and profits of a corporation after distributing a dividend of inventory.
DISCUSSION: The general rule under Sec. 311(a) is that a corporation recognizes no gain or loss on the distribution of property with respect to its stock. An exception to this nonrecognition principle is the distribution of property with an FMV in excess of its basis. A gain is recognized to the extent of such excess. Thus, Orville Company must recognize a $4,000 gain ($16,000 − $12,000) and pay $1,360 ($4,000 × .34) in taxes on the gain [Sec. 311(b)].

Sec. 312(b) provides that when appreciated assets are distributed, earnings and profits are increased by the excess of fair market value over the adjusted basis of the assets, and decreased by the fair market value.

E&P before distribution	$82,000
Increase by gain recognized ($16,000 − $12,000)	4,000
Decrease by FMV	(16,000)
Decrease by taxes paid	(1,360)
E&P after distribution	$68,640

Module 18.17: Earnings and Profits

233. During 1991, Fiddle Corporation made the following distribution to an individual shareholder who owns 40% of Fiddle's only class of stock.

Cash	$20,000
Real estate:	
Adjusted basis to Fiddle	75,000
Fair market value	85,000
Subject to a mortgage of	15,000

The shareholder assumed the $15,000 mortgage on the property. Fiddle had earnings and profits of $70,000 prior to the distribution. The real estate is Sec. 1245 property to Fiddle. Assume a 34% corporate tax rate. What is the "net" adjustment to be made to the earnings and profits account due to this distribution?

a. $10,000 increase.
b. $60,000 decrease.
c. $70,000 decrease.
d. $76,600 decrease.

The correct answer is (c). *(SPE 990 III-71)*
REQUIRED: The reduction in a corporation's earnings and profits (E&P) due to a distribution.
DISCUSSION: Upon the distribution, Fiddle Corporation recognizes a $10,000 increase in earnings and profits for the gain recognized under Sec. 311(b) ($85,000 fair market value − $75,000 adjusted basis) and a $3,400 decrease in earnings and profits for federal income taxes on the gain ($10,000 gain x .34). This provides an earnings and profits balance of $76,600 ($70,000 + $10,000 − $3,400). The real estate distribution produces a $70,000 reduction in earnings and profits ($85,000 fair market value of real estate − $15,000 liability attaching to real estate). In addition, a cash distribution of $20,000 is made which results in a total reduction of $90,000 ($70,000 + $20,000). This total exceeds the available E&P of $76,600. Because a distribution cannot create an E&P deficit, the E&P balance is reduced to zero. The "net" adjustment is thus $70,000.

234. Corporation R, a calendar-year corporation, began business in 1984. It had accumulated earnings and profits of $40,000 as of January 1, 1991. R had a deficit in earnings and profits of $30,000 for 1991. A distribution of $10,000 was made to the stockholders on July 1, 1991. What is the amount of R's accumulated earnings and profits on January 1, 1992?

a. $0.
b. $5,000.
c. $10,000.
d. $20,000.

The correct answer is (a). *(SPE 990 III-70)*
REQUIRED: The earnings and profits of a corporation after distributing a dividend, with a current year E&P deficit.
DISCUSSION: Sec. 312(a) provides that earnings and profits of a corporation shall be decreased by the amount of money distributed. This decrease is limited to the amount of earnings and profits of the corporation. The current year E&P deficit is assumed to occur ratably during the year.

E&P 1/1/91	$40,000
E&P deficit through 6/30/91 ($30,000 x 50%)	(15,000)
	$25,000
Dividend	(10,000)
	$15,000
E&P deficit 7/1/91-12/31/91	(15,000)
E&P balance 12/31/91	$ 0

235. Under the Tax Reform Act of 1986, in determining the amount of corporate earnings and profits, depreciation for tangible property placed in service after 1986 must be calculated using the "Alternative Depreciation System" rather than the "Modified Accelerated Cost Recovery System."

The correct answer is (T). *(SPE 987 III-21)*
DISCUSSION: Earnings and profits must be computed using the alternative depreciation system of Sec. 165(g)(3) [Sec. 312(k)(3)]. The alternative depreciation system uses the straight-line depreciation method over longer recovery periods, rather than accelerated methods over shorter recovery periods, as is used under MACRS.

236. Corporation C makes a cash distribution to its shareholders. C's earnings and profits should be reduced by this cash distribution, but not below zero.

The correct answer is (T). *(SPE 984 III-18)*
DISCUSSION: Sec. 312(a) provides that earnings and profits of a corporation shall be decreased by the amount of money distributed. This decrease is limited to the amount of earnings and profits of the corporation.

237. Corporation X elected to expense the cost of certain property under Sec. 179. In computing earnings and profits, the Sec. 179 deduction is deducted ratably over a 5-year period that begins in the year the cost is expensed.

The correct answer is (T). *(SPE 1083 III-24)*
DISCUSSION: Sec. 312(k)(3)(B) provides that any amount deductible under Sec. 179 shall be allowed as a deduction ratably over 5 years in computing the earnings and profits of a corporation.

18.18 Dividend Distributions to Shareholders

See Chapter 12 for additional questions on stock dividends and stock rights. See Chapter 14 for additional questions on sales of corporate stock.

238. A distribution of stock or stock rights is generally considered a dividend unless it is which of the following?

   a. Distribution in lieu of money.
   b. Proportionate distribution.
   c. Distribution with respect to preferred stock.
   d. Distribution of convertible preferred stock.

The correct answer is (b). *(SPE 990 I-39)*
REQUIRED: The distribution of stock or stock rights which would not be considered a dividend.
DISCUSSION: A proportionate distribution of stock or stock rights would not be considered a dividend under Sec. 305(a) and would not be included in the gross income of the distributee. Answers (a), (c), and (d) are incorrect because as a distribution in lieu of money, a distribution with respect to preferred stock and a distribution of convertible preferred stock are all exceptions under Sec. 305(b) to the general rule, and such distributions would receive dividend treatment.

239. XYZ, a calendar-year corporation, had accumulated earnings and profits of $5,000 as of January 1, 1991. XYZ's earnings and profits for 1991 were $8,000. During 1991, XYZ distributed one stock right for each of the 10,000 outstanding shares of its only class of stock. The fair market value of each stock right was $15. The corporation gave shareholders the option of receiving the stock rights or cash. No other dividends were paid in 1991. Ms. Y is a 10% shareholder and elects to receive the stock rights. What is the amount of the distribution that is includable in Ms. Y's 1991 gross income?

   a. $0.
   b. $500.
   c. $1,300.
   d. $1,500.

The correct answer is (c). *(SPE 990 I-63)*
REQUIRED: The amount includable in gross income from a distribution of stock rights.
DISCUSSION: When a shareholder has the option of receiving either stock rights or cash, the entire amount of the distribution received by the shareholder will be treated as a taxable dividend under Sec. 305(b)(1). Sec. 316(a) defines a dividend as a distribution made from current and accumulated earnings and profits. The amount by which the distribution exceeds current and accumulated earnings and profits shall be treated as a return of capital and will reduce the shareholder's basis in the stock. XYZ's total distribution is $150,000 (10,000 x $15). The amount considered a dividend would be $13,000 ($8,000 + $5,000), and the remaining $137,000 would be a return of capital. The total amount taxable to Ms. Y would be $1,300 ($13,000 x 10%). Accordingly, Ms. Y would reduce the basis in her 1,000 shares of stock by $13,700 ($137,000 x 10%).

Module 18.18: Dividend Distributions to Shareholders

> Questions 240 and 241 are based on the following information. In January 1991, Joan Hill bought one share of Orban Corporation stock for $300. On March 1, 1991, Orban distributed one share of preferred stock for each share of common stock held. This distribution was nontaxable. On March 1, 1991, Joan's one share of common stock had a fair market value of $450, while the preferred stock had a fair market value of $150.

240. After the distribution of the preferred stock, Joan's bases for her Orban stocks are

	Common	Preferred
a.	$300	$0
b.	$225	$75
c.	$200	$100
d.	$150	$150

The correct answer is (b). *(CPA 586 Q-54)*
REQUIRED: The allocation of basis after stock is received as a stock dividend.
DISCUSSION: Sec. 307(a) provides that if a shareholder receives a nontaxable stock dividend, the basis of the old stock must be allocated between the old and the new stock based on their relative fair market values. The basis allocation is computed as follows:

Common basis: $\dfrac{\$450}{\$450 + \$150} \times \$300 = \$225$

Preferred basis: $\dfrac{\$150}{\$450 + \$150} \times \$300 = \$75$

241. The holding period for the preferred stock starts in

a. January 1991.
b. March 1991.
c. September 1991.
d. December 1991.

The correct answer is (a). *(CPA 586 Q-55)*
REQUIRED: The holding period for preferred stock distributed in a nontaxable transaction.
DISCUSSION: Sec. 1223(5) requires that stock with a basis determined by reference to the basis of other stock (Sec. 307) shall include in its holding period the holding period of the referenced stock.

242. Mr. P owned 100 shares of Corporation C common stock. During 1991, Mr. P received $300 in cash dividends, 50 additional shares of C's common stock and the right to purchase 50 more shares. The fair market values of the stock and stock rights were $200 and $100, respectively. The distributions were not disproportionate and the shareholders were not given an option to receive cash instead of the stock or stock rights. What amount of the distributions is includable in Mr. P's income for 1991?

a. $300.
b. $400.
c. $500.
d. $600.

The correct answer is (a). *(SPE 989 I-63)*
REQUIRED: The amount of income a shareholder must report from dividends of cash, stock and stock rights.
DISCUSSION: The $300 in cash dividends are included in taxable income under the general rule of Sec. 61(a)(7). Cash dividends from taxable domestic corporations are included in income provided they are paid out of earnings and profits (which is assumed unless information is given otherwise in the question). However, under Sec. 305(a), gross income generally does not include a proportionate stock dividend when the shareholder did not have the right to receive cash. Rights to purchase stock are also treated as a stock dividend for this purpose. There are exceptions under Sec. 305(b), but the usual stock dividend paid on common stock falls within the general rule and is not included in the shareholder's income. Therefore, Mr. P will not include any gross income from the stock dividend or distribution of stock rights.

Mr. P's total taxable income from these distributions is the $300 of cash dividends. Note that under Sec. 307(a), Mr. P will be required to allocate some of the basis of his original shares of common stock to the stock and stock rights received as distributions.

243. The following information relates to the Stout Company for 1991.

Accumulated earnings and profits at 1/1/91	$ 6,000
Earnings and profits for the year ended 12/31/91	20,000
Dividends distributed to individual shareholders during 1991	30,000

The amount of dividends that is taxable to the individual shareholders as dividend income in 1991 is

a. $6,000.
b. $20,000.
c. $26,000.
d. $30,000.

The correct answer is (c). *(CMA 690 3-13)*
REQUIRED: The amount of the dividend distribution taxable to the shareholders.
DISCUSSION: A corporate distribution is a dividend that must be included in the recipient's gross income under Sec. 301(c)(1) to the extent it comes from accumulated or current earnings and profits of a corporation. To the extent the distribution exceeds current and accumulated earnings and profits, it is treated as a return of capital to the shareholder. Since Stout Corporation had only $26,000 ($6,000 + $20,000) of earnings and profits, the distribution will be taxed as a dividend only to the extent of the $26,000.

244. Davies Corporation had an E&P deficit of $160,000 at December 31, 1990. Its net income per books was $80,000 for 1991. Cash dividends on common stock totaling $40,000 were paid in December 1991. Davies should report the distribution to its shareholders as

a. Return of capital 100%.
b. Ordinary dividends 25%; return of capital 75%.
c. Ordinary dividends 50%; return of capital 50%.
d. Ordinary dividends 100%.

The correct answer is (d). *(CPA 1180 P-57)*
REQUIRED: The character of a corporate distribution to the shareholders.
DISCUSSION: A corporate distribution is considered a dividend and must be included in the recipient's income under Sec. 301(c)(1) to the extent it comes from accumulated or current earnings and profits. A distribution is considered made from the most recently accumulated earnings and profits [Sec. 316(a)]. Davies' distribution is considered to come entirely from the $80,000 current E&P even though there is a deficit in accumulated E&P. Note that earnings and profits are not the same as net income; however, if there is $80,000 of net income, there likely will be sufficient earnings and profits for the dividend. The distribution is, therefore, entirely ordinary dividend income to the shareholders.

245. Corporation Z, a calendar-year corporation, had accumulated earnings and profits of $20,000 as of January 1, 1991. For the first 6 months of 1991, Z had operating income of $15,000. On July 1, 1991, Z distributed a dividend of $16,000 to its shareholders. The company had a deficit in earnings and profits for the year of $30,000. What portion of the distribution is taxable to the shareholders as ordinary income?

a. $0.
b. $5,000.
c. $15,000.
d. $16,000.

The correct answer is (b). *(SPE 1083 III-72)*
REQUIRED: The portion of the distribution taxable as ordinary income given a current deficit in E&P.
DISCUSSION: A corporate distribution is taxable to the recipient to the extent it comes from accumulated or current earnings and profits [Sec. 301(c)(1)]. When there is a deficit in current E&P, the distribution is regarded as coming out of accumulated E&P on the date of distribution after taking into account the deficit up to that date [Reg. 1.316-2(b)]. The deficit is prorated over the year if actual amounts are not known. In this case, actual amounts are not known because the operating income for the first 6 months is not equal to E&P.

Accumulated E&P	$20,000
Current deficit in E&P on July 1, 1991 (½ x $30,000)	(15,000)
Accumulated E&P, July 1, 1991	$ 5,000

Since Z has accumulated E&P of $5,000, the distribution is a taxable dividend to this extent. The balance of $11,000 is a return of capital.

Module 18.18: Dividend Distributions to Shareholders

246. Core Corporation reported current year earnings and profits of $250,000. It distributed a building with an adjusted basis to Core of $170,000 and a fair market value of $230,000, to its sole shareholder. The building had a mortgage of $90,000 which the shareholder will assume. What is the amount of the dividend received by the shareholder?

a. $80,000.
b. $140,000.
c. $230,000.
d. $250,000.

The correct answer is (b). *(SPE 990 III-69)*
REQUIRED: The amount of a dividend received by a shareholder.
DISCUSSION: Sec. 301(b)(1) provides that the distribution to a shareholder is equal to the fair market value of the property distributed. Under Sec. 301(b)(2)(A), this amount must be decreased by any liabilities assumed by the shareholder or to which the property is subject. The distribution to the shareholder is $140,000 ($230,000 FMV − $90,000 liability).

Under Sec. 316, a distribution is a dividend to the extent that it comes from earnings and profits. The earnings and profits would be increased by the gain (net of tax) on the distribution. Gain is recognized to the extent the FMV of the building exceeds the adjusted basis [Sec. 311(b)], or $60,000. In any event, the corporation has at least $250,000 of earnings and profits. Therefore, the entire $140,000 is a dividend.

247. In 1986, Mr. P purchased stock for $1,000. In 1990 he received a return of capital of $800 and reduced the basis of his stock by that amount. In 1991, he received another return of capital which amounted to $300, which reduced the basis of his stock to zero. At no time did the corporation have earnings and profits. He would report the $100 that was in excess of his basis as

a. Interest.
b. Long-term capital gain.
c. Dividend.
d. Short-term capital gain.

The correct answer is (b). *(SPE 988 III-54)*
REQUIRED: The portion of a distribution to be treated as a gain from a sale or exchange of property by an individual shareholder.
DISCUSSION: A corporate distribution is a "dividend" that must be included in the recipient's gross income under Sec. 301(c)(1) to the extent it comes from accumulated or current earnings and profits of a corporation. To the extent the distribution exceeds current and accumulated earnings and profits, it is treated as a return of capital to the shareholder. Once the basis of the stock has been reduced to zero, any distributions received are treated as a gain from the sale of the stock. Mr. P's capital gain is long-term because he held the stock for more than 1 year.

248. Dahl Corporation was organized and commenced operations in 1930. At December 31, 1991, Dahl had accumulated earnings and profits of $9,000 before a dividend declaration and distribution. On December 31, 1991, Dahl distributed cash of $9,000 and a vacant parcel of land to Mr. Green, Dahl's only stockholder. At the date of distribution, the land had a basis of $5,000 and a fair market value of $40,000. What was Mr. Green's taxable dividend income in 1991 from these distributions assuming a 34% corporate tax rate?

a. $9,000.
b. $32,100.
c. $44,000.
d. $49,000.

The correct answer is (b). *(CPA 1190 Q-26)*
REQUIRED: The amount of a corporation's dividend distribution made to a sole shareholder.
DISCUSSION: Under Sec. 301(b)(1), the amount of a distribution to a distributee equals the amount of money received plus the fair market value of nonmoney property received. Sec. 311(b) requires Dahl Corporation to recognize gain on the distribution of appreciated property of $35,000 ($40,000 FMV − $5,000 adjusted basis). The total amount of Dahl's distribution is

Cash	$ 9,000
Basis of property plus gain (equal to FMV)	40,000
Total distribution	$49,000

Sec. 316 provides that a distribution is a dividend to the extent it comes from earnings and profits. Dahl's $9,000 E&P must be increased by the gain on the distribution and decreased by taxes on the gain. This calculation is as follows:

E&P - 12/31/91	$ 9,000
Gain on land distribution	35,000
Taxes on gain (34% x $35,000)	(11,900)
E&P after Sec. 311(b) adjustment	$32,100

Thus, only $32,100 of the total $49,000 paid is considered a dividend distribution. The remaining $16,900 is either a return of capital or a capital gain depending on Mr. Green's stock basis [Sec. 301(c)(2) and (3)].

Module 18.18: Dividend Distributions to Shareholders

249. Corporation T, with earnings and profits of $60,000, distributed cash of $20,000 and property with a fair market value of $25,000 and an adjusted basis of $30,000 to its corporate shareholders. What is the amount of the distribution received by the shareholders?

a. $20,000.
b. $30,000.
c. $45,000.
d. $50,000.

The correct answer is (c). *(SPE 984 III-73)*
REQUIRED: The amount of a distribution received by corporate shareholders.
DISCUSSION: Sec. 301(b) provides that the amount distributed to a shareholder (corporate or noncorporate) is equal to the amount of money received, plus the fair market value of other property received. Corporation T distributed cash of $20,000 plus property with a fair market value of $25,000. Hence, the corporate shareholders will recognize a distribution of $45,000.

250. Corporation P distributed depreciable personal property having a fair market value of $7,500 to its shareholders. The property had an adjusted basis of $4,000 to the corporation. P had properly deducted $2,000 in depreciation on the property. What amount must Corporation P include in ordinary income as a result of the distribution?

a. $0.
b. $2,000.
c. $3,500.
d. $7,500.

The correct answer is (b). *(SPE 987 III-84)*
REQUIRED: Corporation's ordinary income upon the distribution of depreciable property.
DISCUSSION: Sec. 311(b) requires that gain on the distribution of appreciated property be recognized as if the property had been sold. Therefore, Corporation P will recognize $3,500 ($7,500 fair market value − $4,000 basis) of total gain. $2,000 of this gain will be ordinary income as a result of Sec. 1245 depreciation recapture.

251. Corporation K distributed a parcel of real estate in 1991 to a stockholder which had an adjusted basis to the corporation of $50,000 and an estimated fair market value of $75,000. The property was subject to a mortgage of $80,000, which was assumed by the stockholder. What is Corporation K's recognized gain (or loss) on the distribution to the stockholder?

a. $(5,000).
b. $0.
c. $30,000.
d. $50,000.

The correct answer is (c). *(SPE 1080 III-59)*
REQUIRED: A corporation's recognized gain (or loss) on the distribution of property with a mortgage in excess of basis.
DISCUSSION: Sec. 311(b) requires a corporation to recognize gain to the extent the FMV of property distributed exceeds the adjusted basis of such property. If liabilities exceed basis, FMV is treated as not less than the liabilities assumed or acquired by the shareholder [Sec. 311(b)(2)]. Therefore, the FMV is treated as $80,000.

FMV of property distributed	$80,000
Less adjusted basis	(50,000)
Gain recognized under Sec. 311(b)	$30,000

252. Corporation Q, a calendar-year corporation that began doing business on January 1, 1982, had accumulated earnings and profits of $20,000 as of January 1, 1991. On April 1, 1991, Q distributed $15,000 cash to its shareholder. Q had a $40,000 deficit in earnings and profits for 1991. Mrs. D, Q's sole shareholder, had an adjusted basis of $12,000 in her Q stock before the distribution. What is the amount of Mrs. D's basis in the stock after the distribution?

a. $12,000.
b. $7,000.
c. $2,000.
d. $0.

The correct answer is (b). *(SPE 989 III-81)*
REQUIRED: The calculation of a shareholder's remaining basis when a distribution represents both dividend and return of capital.
DISCUSSION: A corporate distribution is taxable to the recipient to the extent it comes from accumulated or current earnings and profits [Sec. 301(c)(1)]. When there is a deficit in current E&P, the distribution is regarded as coming out of accumulated E&P on the date of distribution after taking into account the deficit up to that date [Reg. 1.316-2(b)]. The deficit is prorated over the year if actual amounts are not known. Q's prorated current E&P as of April 1, 1991, is a $10,000 deficit. Of the $15,000 distribution, $10,000 represents dividend ($20,000 accumulated E&P − $10,000 deficit in current E&P as of April 1, 1991). The $5,000 balance represents a return of capital. Mrs. D's basis in the stock after the distribution is $7,000 ($12,000 adjusted basis − $5,000 return of capital).

253. On April 1, 1991, Stan Corporation bought 1,000 shares (30%) of Lee Corporation common stock for $40,000. On August 1, 1991, Stan received a $7,000 cash distribution that was a dividend on these shares. The fair market value of the shares on the ex-dividend date was $30,000. Stan claimed the full 80% dividends received deduction. On November 1, 1991, Stan sold the Lee stock to an unrelated third party for $50,000. What is Stan's gain on the sale?

a. $10,000.
b. $15,600.
c. $17,000.
d. $50,000.

The correct answer is (b). *(Publisher)*
REQUIRED: A corporate shareholder's gain on sale of stock after an extraordinary dividend.
DISCUSSION: A corporation's basis in stock is reduced by the nontaxed portion of an extraordinary dividend if the stock has been held for 2 years or less (Sec. 1059). An extraordinary dividend is a dividend paid after March 1, 1984 which exceeds 10% of the shareholder's basis in the stock (or if the taxpayer can establish it, the taxpayer may use the fair market value for dividends declared after July 18, 1986 in taxable years ending after such date). The nontaxable portion is the amount of the dividends-received deduction.

Stan Corporation held the Lee stock for less than 2 years and the dividend was greater than 10% of its basis or ex-dividend fair market value, so Stan Corporation must reduce its basis in the Lee stock by the nontaxable portion of the dividend (80% x $7,000 = $5,600). Stan's gain is $15,600 [$50,000 − ($40,000 − $5,600)].

254. Corporation Z sold equipment used in its business to its sole shareholder Mr. Y for $10,000. On the date of the sale, the fair market value of the equipment was $15,000 and Z's adjusted basis was $12,000. Corporation Z has $30,000 of earnings and profits. What amount of the transfer is considered to be a dividend to Mr. Y?

a. $20,000.
b. $5,000.
c. $2,000.
d. $0.

The correct answer is (b). *(SPE 989 III-80)*
REQUIRED: The amount of dividend income to a stockholder from a bargain purchase.
DISCUSSION: A transaction that is a constructive distribution will be treated as a dividend for tax purposes if sufficient E&P is available. A bargain purchase of corporate property by shareholders is such a transaction [Reg. 1.301-1(j)]. Under Sec. 301(b)(1), the amount of a distribution to a distributee is the fair market value of the property distributed. The difference between the fair market value and the amount paid by the shareholder is treated as a constructive distribution.

FMV of equipment	$15,000
Less amount paid	(10,000)
Distribution	$ 5,000

To the extent the distribution comes from earnings and profits, it is treated as a dividend [Sec. 316(a)]. Since Corporation Z had earnings and profits of $30,000 (plus the gain recognized on the part sale - part distribution involving Mr. Y), the entire $5,000 distribution should be considered a dividend.

255. Corporation T, a domestic corporation, distributes the following dividends to its shareholders in 1991

$1,000 to Shareholder A, an unrelated foreign corporation
$1,200 to Shareholder B, a foreign partnership
$1,300 to Shareholder C, a resident alien
$1,400 to Shareholder D, a nonresident alien, with an address in care of another person in the United States

All income of Corporation T was from sources within the United States. On what amount of dividends must T withhold tax?

a. $0.
b. $1,000.
c. $2,200.
d. $3,600.

The correct answer is (d). *(SPE 1083 III-62)*
REQUIRED: The amount of dividends on which the distributor must withhold tax.
DISCUSSION: Sec. 1441 requires the corporation paying dividends to a foreign partnership and a nonresident alien to withhold tax on such amounts. Sec. 1442 requires the same withholding on dividends paid to foreign corporations. There is no special withholding requirement for resident aliens.

Therefore, the withholding by Corporation T is required for shareholders A, B, and D. Their dividends total $3,600.

Module 18.18: Dividend Distributions to Shareholders

256. In 1989, Mr. P bought 100 shares of stock in Corporation X for $20 per share. In 1990, Mr. P bought 100 shares of Corporation X stock for $28 per share. In 1991, X declared a 2-for-1 stock split. The fair market value of the stock at the time of the split was $50 per share. What is Mr. P's basis in Corporation X stock?

   a. 200 shares @ $10 per share,
      200 shares @ $14 per share.
   b. 400 shares @ $12 per share.
   c. 400 shares @ $50 per share.
   d. 100 shares @ $20 per share,
      100 shares @ $28 per share,
      200 shares @ $50 per share.

The correct answer is (a). *(SPE 988 I-79)*
REQUIRED: The basis of stock to the shareholder after a stock split.
DISCUSSION: Sec. 307 requires a shareholder to allocate the basis of the old shares to the new shares. Mr. P's total basis is apportioned among the new shares as follows

1st purchase: $\dfrac{\$20 \times 100 \text{ shares}}{200 \text{ shares}} = \$10 \times 200 \text{ shares}$

2nd purchase: $\dfrac{\$28 \times 100 \text{ shares}}{200 \text{ shares}} = \$14 \times 200 \text{ shares}$

257. A corporation must file a Form 1099-DIV, Statement for Recipients of Dividends and Distributions, with the IRS for each stockholder to whom the corporation paid gross dividends of $10 or more during the calendar year. For 1991 dividends, Form 1099-DIV must be filed with the IRS on or before

   a. December 31, 1991.
   b. January 31, 1992.
   c. February 28, 1992.
   d. March 15, 1992.

The correct answer is (c). *(SPE 990 III-42)*
REQUIRED: The due date of Form 1099-DIV.
DISCUSSION: Reg. 1.6041-6 requires that Form 1099-DIV be filed on or before February 28 of the year following the year in which gross dividends of $10 or more are paid to shareholders.

258. If the common stockholders of a corporation receive a pro rata distribution of preferred stock and have the option to immediately redeem the preferred stock for money, the distribution is considered to be in lieu of money and is included in the gross income of the stockholders.

The correct answer is (T). *(SPE 986 III-22)*
DISCUSSION: Under Sec. 305, a stock dividend is not generally taxable. However, Sec. 305(b) provides exceptions to this general rule. One is for distributions payable in either stock or property. The option of immediate redemption of preferred stock for money effectively makes the distribution payable in either stock or property (money), so it is taxable.

259. A distribution by a corporation to a shareholder that exceeds the corporation's earnings and profits is not a dividend.

The correct answer is (T). *(SPE 1079 III-43)*
DISCUSSION: Sec. 316(a) defines a dividend as a distribution of property by a corporation with respect to its stock which comes from accumulated and current earnings and profits. Any distribution that does not come from the corporation's earnings and profits is not considered a dividend.

260. A distribution from a corporation that is deemed to be a return of capital on stock reduces the basis of the stock and is not taxed until the basis in the stock is fully recovered.

The correct answer is (T). *(SPE 1083 I-15)*
DISCUSSION: A distribution in excess of the corporation's earnings and profits is deemed to be a return of capital on the stock. The amount of such distribution reduces the basis of the stock, and any amounts received in excess of the basis are treated by the recipient as a gain from the sale or exchange of property [Sec. 301(c)(3)].

Module 18.18: Dividend Distributions to Shareholders

261. T Corporation, with earnings and profits of $10,000, distributed $15,000 cash to Mr. A, an individual stockholder. The adjusted basis of Mr. A's stock is $12,000. Mr. A should include $10,000 as dividend income and $5,000 as gain from the sale of property on his income tax return.

The correct answer is (F). *(SPE 1080 III-24)*
DISCUSSION: Sec. 316(a) defines a dividend as a distribution of property by a corporation with respect to its stock which comes from accumulated and current earnings and profits. Sec. 301(c) provides that the amount of the distribution that is a dividend is income to the recipient. The portion of the distribution that is not a dividend reduces the adjusted basis of the recipient's stock. Therefore, Mr. A should include $10,000 as dividend income and treat the remaining $5,000 as a reduction of the adjusted basis of his stock.

262. If common stockholders of a corporation receive a distribution of common and preferred stock resulting in a receipt of preferred by some and common by others, the distribution is taxable as a dividend provided there are sufficient earnings and profits.

The correct answer is (T). *(SPE 1085 III-20)*
DISCUSSION: Sec. 305(b)(3) states that if a distribution results in the receipt of common stock by some shareholders and preferred stock by other shareholders, the general rule of Sec. 305(a) shall not apply and the distribution will be taxed as a dividend under Sec. 301.

263. A corporation distributes property with a fair market value of $18,000 and an adjusted basis of $21,000 to a shareholder. The property's basis in the shareholder's hands is $21,000.

The correct answer is (F). *(Publisher)*
DISCUSSION: Under Sec. 301(d), the basis of property received by a distributee in a dividend distribution is the fair market value of such property. The distributee will have a basis in the property of $18,000, even though the corporation's basis was greater.

264. A corporation distributes property on June 1, 1991 with a fair market value of $30,000 and an adjusted basis of $24,000 to a shareholder. The distributee's holding period includes the holding period of the distributing corporation.

The correct answer is (F). *(Publisher)*
DISCUSSION: Under Sec. 301(d), the basis of property received by a distributee in a dividend distribution is the fair market value of the property. Since the basis for the property does not carry over from the distributing corporation, the carryover holding period provided in Sec. 1223 will not apply. The holding period will commence on the distribution date.

265. For tax years beginning after 1986, the amount of a corporate distribution to both corporate and noncorporate shareholders is determined by the amount of money received and the fair market value of all other property received.

The correct answer is (T). *(SPE 989 III-15)*
DISCUSSION: Sec. 301(b)(1) provides that the amount of any distribution of property made by a corporation to a shareholder shall be the amount of money received plus the fair market value of the other property received. Prior to 1987, different rules existed for determining the amount of income recognized by corporate and noncorporate shareholders when a dividend of nonmonetary property was received.

CHAPTER NINETEEN
ADVANCED CORPORATE TOPICS

19.1	Stock Redemptions	(22 questions)	533
	Liquidations		
19.2	Partial Liquidations	(6 questions)	540
19.3	Complete Liquidations	(15 questions)	542
19.4	Liquidations of Subsidiary Corporations	(5 questions)	546
19.5	Corporate Divisions and Reorganizations	(11 questions)	547
19.6	Consolidated Tax Returns	(9 questions)	551
19.7	Multiple Corporations	(13 questions)	554
19.8	Accumulated Earnings Tax	(13 questions)	557
19.9	Personal Holding Company Tax	(8 questions)	561
	S Corporations		
19.10	S Corporation Election	(15 questions)	563
19.11	S Corporation Income	(7 questions)	567
19.12	S Corporation Losses	(6 questions)	569
19.13	Distributions from S Corporations	(7 questions)	571
19.14	Taxes Levied on the S Corporation	(12 questions)	573
19.15	S Corporation Filing and Estimated Tax Requirements	(7 questions)	577
19.16	Termination of S Corporation Status	(6 questions)	578

19.1 Stock Redemptions

1. All of the following statements regarding stock redemptions are correct except

- a. A redemption occurs when a corporation reacquires its stock in exchange for property.
- b. The term property includes money, securities, and any other property except stock in the distributing corporation.
- c. The stock that is redeemed by a corporation may not be held as treasury stock.
- d. Redemptions that are not complete or partial liquidations can be distributions in part or full payment for the stock surrendered.

The correct answer is (c). *(SPE 990 III-45)*

REQUIRED: The statement regarding stock redemptions that is not correct.

DISCUSSION: Sec. 317(b) states that stock is treated as redeemed by a corporation if the corporation acquires its stock from a shareholder in exchange for property, whether or not the acquired stock is canceled, retired, or held as treasury stock.

Answer (a) is true because Sec. 317(b) provides that stock is treated as redeemed when a corporation acquires its own stock from a shareholder in exchange for property. Answer (b) is true because property, as defined by Sec. 317(a), includes almost anything distributed by a corporation except its own stock or rights to acquire its own stock. Answer (d) is true because under Sec. 302 several types of redemptions are treated as part or full payment for the stock even though there is no partial or complete liquidation of the corporation.

Module 19.1: Stock Redemptions

2. Corporation Y distributed $70,000 cash to shareholder Z in redemption of all his stock. Z's basis in the stock is $20,000 and his pro rata share of Y's earnings and profits is $30,000. Assuming all the requirements for a redemption are met, how should Z treat the distribution for federal income tax purposes?

a. $0.
b. $20,000 dividend.
c. $30,000 dividend; $20,000 capital gain.
d. $50,000 capital gain.

The correct answer is (d). *(SPE 990 III-78)*
REQUIRED: The treatment of a distribution in redemption of stock for federal income tax purposes.
DISCUSSION: Under Sec. 302(b)(3), if a corporation redeems all of its stock owned by a shareholder, the redemption is treated as a distribution in part or full payment in exchange for the stock. Since Corporation Y redeemed all of shareholder Z's stock, the $70,000 distribution is treated as payment for the stock, and any gain is treated as capital gain. The amount of the gain is computed under Sec. 1001, and is the amount by which the distribution exceeds the shareholder's basis in the stock. In this case, the gain is $50,000 ($70,000 distribution less $20,000 basis). Since the stock is a capital asset, the recognized gain is a capital gain.

Because the distribution is treated as being in exchange for the stock and not as a dividend, the amount of the corporation's earnings and profits is irrelevant. Earnings and profits affect distributions only when those distributions have the character of dividends.

3. Mr. X owned 40% of Corporation B's only class of stock outstanding. The remaining 60% of B's stock was owned by Mr. Y (not related to Mr. X). B redeemed all of X's stock for $75,000 and one-half of Y's stock for $50,000. Mr. X's and Mr. Y's basis in their stock of Corporation B was $30,000 and $25,000, respectively. B's earnings and profits were $200,000. Assuming that no partial liquidation occurred, what is the amount and character of X's and Y's recognized gains?

	Mr. X	Mr. Y
a.	$45,000 capital gain	$25,000 dividend
b.	$75,000 dividend	$50,000 dividend
c.	$45,000 capital gain	$25,000 capital gain
d.	$45,000 capital gain	$50,000 dividend

The correct answer is (d). *(SPE 990 III-76)*
REQUIRED: The amount and character of gain resulting from a corporate distribution.
DISCUSSION: Under Sec. 302(b)(3), if a corporation redeems all of its stock owned by a shareholder, the shareholder is treated as having sold his stock to the corporation and will report a capital gain if the amount of the distribution exceeds his basis in the stock. Therefore, Mr. X has a capital gain of $45,000 ($75,000 distribution − $30,000 basis).

If the distribution is not a redemption of all the shareholder's stock, Sec. 302(b)(2) must be applied to determine whether the distribution will be treated as a payment in exchange for the stock or as a dividend. One of the requirements of Sec. 302(b)(2) is that the shareholder must own less than 50% of the total combined voting power of all classes of stock immediately after the redemption. Alternatively, the distribution must be not essentially equivalent to a dividend under Sec. 302(b)(1). This alternative requires a meaningful reduction in the shareholder's interest in the distributing corporation.

Since all of Mr. X's stock was redeemed, Mr. Y owns 100% of the voting stock. Therefore, the requirements of Secs. 302(b)(2) or 302(b)(1) are not met, and the $50,000 distribution is treated as a dividend since it is less than B Corporation's earnings and profits.

4. The Z Corporation's common stock is owned by the following individuals and corporations:

	Number of shares
Mr. B	20
Mrs. B	20
T Corporation	30
X Corporation	30
	100

The B family does not own any of the T or the X Corporation stocks. Mr. B would like to redeem some of his shares and have the redemption treated as an exchange. The minimum number of Mr. B's shares that Z Corporation must redeem in order for the redemption to qualify for exchange treatment under the substantially disproportionate rules of Sec. 302(b)(2) is (rounded to the nearest share):

a. 5.
b. 8.
c. 9.
d. 12.

The correct answer is (d). *(C.K. Craig)*
REQUIRED: The substantially disproportionate rules of Sec. 302(b)(2).
DISCUSSION: Under Sec. 302(b)(2), a stock redemption will be considered substantially disproportionate and will receive exchange treatment if two requirements are met: (1) the shareholder's stock ownership percentage is less than 50% after the redemption; and (2) the shareholder's stock ownership percentage after the redemption is less than 80% of the stock ownership percentage before the redemption.

When computing the ownership percentages, the stock attribution rules of Sec. 318 must be applied. Mr. B is deemed to own not only his stock but also the stock of his wife, or a total of 40 shares of Z stock.

The minimum number of shares that must be redeemed may be determined algebraically.

$$\frac{40 - x}{100 - x} \leq .32,$$ where x is the minimum number of shares needed to be redeemed.

Note that when calculating the ownership percentage after the redemption, both the numerator and denominator must be reduced by the shares redeemed. Solving the equation produces an X value of 12, or 12 shares of Z stock that must be redeemed. Immediately after the redemption Mr. and Mrs. B will each own 28 (8 for Mr. B + 20 for Mrs. B) of the 88 (or 31.81818%) outstanding shares.

5. Rambo Corporation owns, as an investment, 10% of the stock of Duntulum Corporation with a basis of $8,000 and a market value of $50,000. Rambo uses the Duntulum stock to redeem approximately 1%, or $10,000 par value, of its own outstanding stock from unrelated, noncorporate shareholders. As a result of this transaction, Rambo must report

a. $42,000 gain.
b. No gain or loss.
c. $2,000 gain.
d. $50,000 gain.

The correct answer is (a). *(CPA 1172 P-3)*
REQUIRED: The amount of gain recognized by the distributing corporation on a redemption using appreciated property.
DISCUSSION: The general rule under Sec. 311(a) is that a corporation does not recognize gain or loss on the distribution of property with respect to its stock. However, Sec. 311(b) requires a corporation that distributes appreciated property to recognize gain equal to the excess of the fair market value of the property over its adjusted basis, as if the stock were sold to the distributee immediately before the exchange. Rambo's gain is determined as follows:

FMV of stock distributed	$50,000
Less adjusted basis	(8,000)
Recognized gain	$42,000

6. Corporation H has 1,000 shares of stock issued and outstanding. Mr. K, the founder, owns 40% of the stock, his wife owns 10%, his son owns 20%, and the balance is owned by unrelated parties. Under the constructive ownership rules of the stock redemption provisions, what percentage of stock is Mr. K considered to own?

a. 50%.
b. 60%.
c. 70%.
d. 100%.

The correct answer is (c). *(SPE 1082 III-57)*
REQUIRED: The percentage of stock a taxpayer is considered to own under the constructive ownership rules for a stock redemption.
DISCUSSION: The stock redemption provisions found in Sec. 302 use the constructive ownership rules of Sec. 318. Under the Sec. 318(a)(1) rules, an individual is considered to own the stock owned by members of his/her family including his/her spouse, children, grandchildren, and parents. Therefore, Mr. K owns 40% of the stock directly, and he indirectly owns the stock owned by his wife and son. Mr. K has direct and indirect ownership of 70% of Corporation H. For that matter, so do his wife and son.

Module 19.1: Stock Redemptions

7. Corporation Z has 100 shares of stock issued and outstanding owned by the following:

Shares	Shareholder
10	Mr. R
10	Mrs. R (Mr. R's wife)
10	R's son
10	R's mother
10	R's brother
10	R's uncle
10	Partnership X (R is a 10% partner)
10	Corporation A (R is a 40% shareholder)
10	Corporation B (R is a 50% shareholder)
10	Corporation C (R is an 80% shareholder)
100	

Neither R's relatives nor the partnership or corporations are partners in X or shareholders in A, B, or C. Under constructive ownership rules for Sec. 302 stock redemptions, what percentage of stock is R considered to own?

a. 54%.
b. 58%.
c. 64%.
d. 67%.

The correct answer is (a). *(SPE 986 III-51)*
REQUIRED: The percentage of stock a taxpayer is considered to own under the constructive ownership rules.
DISCUSSION: Sec. 318 contains the constructive ownership rules for stock redemptions. An individual is considered to own the stock owned by his/her spouse, children, grandchildren, and parents, but not by brothers, sisters, aunts, or uncles. If a stockholder owns 50% or more in value of the stock of a corporation, (s)he is considered to own the stock the corporation owns in proportion to the value of the stock that (s)he owns in the corporation. Stock owned directly or indirectly by a partnership is considered to be owned proportionately by the partners.

	Shares Owned
R owns personally	10
From R's wife	10
From R's son	10
From R's mother	10
From Partnership X (10% x 10 shares)	1
From Corporation B (50% x 10 shares)	5
From Corporation C (80% x 10 shares)	8
Shares actually and constructively owned under Sec. 318	54

8. Wind Corporation has 100 shares of its only class of stock outstanding. Mr. C owns 15 shares, his wife 20 shares, his son 50 shares and his son's daughter 15 shares. Under the constructive ownership rules for stock redemptions, how many shares of Wind's stock is the son's daughter considered to own?

a. 15.
b. 50.
c. 65.
d. 100.

The correct answer is (c). *(SPE 990 III-46)*
REQUIRED: The number of shares of stock constructively owned by a shareholder in a family corporation.
DISCUSSION: Under Sec. 318, a shareholder is considered to constructively own stock that is in fact owned by another shareholder. Sec. 318(a)(1)(A) states that a shareholder is considered to own the stock owned by the shareholder's spouse, children, grandchildren, and parents. The son's daughter is considered to own the 15 shares owned by herself and the 50 shares owned by her father. She is not considered to constructively own her grandparents' shares because the statute does not attribute a grandparent's stock ownership to a grandchild (although a grandchild's stock ownership is attributed to a grandparent).

Note that Sec. 318(a)(5)(B) prevents double attribution so that the daughter is not considered to constructively own stock that her father would be considered to constructively (and not actually) own.

9. T, an individual shareholder, owned 25% of the Towne Corporation stock. Pursuant to a series of stock redemptions, Towne redeemed 10% of the shares of stock T owned in exchange for land having a fair market value of $30,000 and an adjusted basis of $10,000. T's basis for all of his Towne stock was $200,000. T reported the redemption transaction as if it were a dividend. T's basis in the land and his Towne stock (immediately after the redemption) is

a. Land, $30,000; stock, $200,000.
b. Land, $10,000; stock, $180,000.
c. Land, $30,000; stock, $180,000.
d. Land, $10,000; stock, $200,000.

The correct answer is (a). *(Publisher)*
REQUIRED: The basis in land received in a redemption of stock treated as a dividend, and the basis in the stock after the redemption.
DISCUSSION: Under Sec. 302, if a redemption of shares does not qualify as a sale or exchange, it is treated as a dividend under Sec. 301. Sec. 301(b)(1) provides that the amount of a dividend distribution is the amount of money received plus the fair market value of the property received, so T has a $30,000 dividend. Sec. 301(d) provides that the basis of property received in a distribution will be the fair market value of such property. Therefore, T's basis in the land is $30,000. A dividend distribution does not affect the basis in a shareholder's stock, so T's stock basis remains $200,000 [Reg. 1.302-2(c)].

Module 19.1: Stock Redemptions

10. Mr. Mendez owned all 1,000 shares (100%) of Ore Corporation's only class of stock outstanding. Mr. Mendez's basis in the stock was $20,000 ($20 per share). Ore redeemed 500 shares of Mendez's stock for $15,000. What is Mr. Mendez's basis in his remaining 500 shares of Ore's stock?

　a. $0.
　b. $10,000.
　c. $15,000.
　d. $20,000.

The correct answer is (d). *(SPE 990 III-77)*
REQUIRED: The shareholder's basis in his remaining stock following a partial redemption.
DISCUSSION: The shareholder's basis in his remaining stock will depend upon the treatment of the distribution. If the distribution is essentially equivalent to a dividend, the shareholder's basis in the remaining stock will be increased by the basis of the stock that is redeemed [Reg. 1.302-2(c)]. If the distribution is treated as payment for the shareholder's redeemed stock, the basis of the redeemed stock offsets the amount received by the shareholder and the basis of the remaining shares is unchanged. Sec. 302 governs the determination of the distribution's character. The applicable requirements, when a complete termination of interest does not occur, are that immediately after the redemption the shareholder must own less than 50% of the total combined voting power of all classes of voting stock and the percentage of stock ownership after the redemption must be less than 80% of the percentage ownership immediately before the redemption. Alternatively, the distribution must be not essentially equivalent to a dividend under Sec. 302(b)(1). This alternative requires a meaningful reduction in the shareholder's interest in the distributing corporation.

Since Mr. Mendez is the only shareholder, he still owns 100% of Ore Corporation's stock after the redemption. Therefore, the requirements of Secs. 302(b)(2) or 302(b)(1) are not met and the distribution is considered to be a dividend. The $10,000 (.50 x $20,000) basis of the shares redeemed is added to the $10,000 basis for the remaining shares so that the total basis remains at $20,000.

11. Corporation Z has 500 shares of its only class of stock outstanding. A and B each own 200 shares and C owns 100 shares. None of the parties is related. During 1991, Z redeemed 100 shares from both A and B, and 50 shares from C. This redemption is considered to be a distribution equivalent to a dividend.

The correct answer is (T). *(SPE 989 III-17)*
DISCUSSION: Sec. 302 determines whether a redemption is considered to be a distribution equivalent to a dividend or as payment for the stock eligible for capital gain or loss treatment. Under Sec. 302(b)(2), a substantially disproportionate redemption qualifies for capital gain or loss treatment. For a redemption to be substantially disproportionate, the shareholder must own less than 50% of all outstanding voting stock immediately after the redemption, and his/her total percentage of ownership must be less than 80% of his/her ownership percentage immediately before the redemption.

Each of the three shareholders owns less than 50% of all outstanding voting stock immediately after the redemption, so the first test is met. However, the percentage of stock owned by each shareholder has not changed as a result of the redemption. Therefore, the second test is not met and the redemption is not substantially disproportionate. The redemption is considered to be a distribution equivalent to a dividend since a meaningful reduction in the shareholders' ownership interests did not occur [Sec. 302(b)(1)].

12. Corporation K distributed land used in its business to its shareholders in redemption of some of its outstanding stock. At the time of the distribution, the land had an adjusted basis to K of $200,000, and a fair market value of $500,000. Corporation K does not recognize any gain on this distribution.

The correct answer is (F). *(SPE 990 III-20)*
DISCUSSION: Sec. 311(b) states that if a corporation distributes property to a shareholder with a fair market value in excess of its basis, the corporation shall recognize gain as if the property had been sold to the distributee at its fair market value. Corporation K would recognize a gain of $300,000 on the distribution ($500,000 selling price − $200,000 basis) whether stock is redeemed or not.

13. Mr. G actually and constructively owned 90% of the only stock issued and outstanding of Corporation V as of March 1, 1991. On March 2, 1991, V redeemed some of Mr. G's stock for property. After the redemption, Mr. G actually and constructively owned 60% of V's stock. This exchange is considered a substantially disproportionate redemption.

The correct answer is (F). *(SPE 1083 III-32)*
DISCUSSION: For the redemption to be considered substantially disproportionate, Mr. G's ownership after the redemption would have to be less than 50% of the voting power of all classes of outstanding stock entitled to vote (he does not meet this requirement). Also, his percentage of the total of outstanding voting stock after the redemption would have to be less than 80% of his percentage ownership of the stock immediately before the redemption (he meets this requirement). Since Mr. G's ownership after the redemption is not less than 50%, however, this exchange is not considered substantially disproportionate.

14. Corporation Y has 1,000 shares of one class of stock outstanding which are owned by Mrs. H (500 shares) and her son (500 shares). Y distributed cash to Mrs. H in full payment for her 500 shares. Mrs. H remained in the employ of Y as an officer and director. This redemption is considered to be a dividend distribution to Mrs. H.

The correct answer is (T). *(SPE 986 III-28)*
DISCUSSION: Since Mrs. H maintained an interest in the corporation, that of an officer and director, the waiver of the family attribution rules under Sec. 302(c)(2)(A) is not possible. Therefore, the Sec. 318 attribution rules continue to apply and the distribution to her is not a termination of her interest. Under Sec. 318(a)(1), Mrs. H is deemed to own her son's 100% interest in Corporation Y and she does not have a substantial reduction in her interest. Therefore, the distribution is treated as a dividend under Sec. 301.

15. Some redemptions of stock by a corporation that are not in complete or partial liquidation are treated as distributions in part or full payment in exchange for the stock. The gain or loss to the stockholder may be a capital gain or loss if the distribution is in complete redemption of all the stock of the corporation actually owned by the stockholder, even if some family members still own stock in the corporation.

The correct answer is (T). *(SPE 984 III-21)*
DISCUSSION: Under Sec. 302(b)(3), a complete termination of a shareholder's interest will be treated as a distribution in part or full payment in exchange for his/her stock. Under Sec. 302(c)(2), for purposes of determining whether a complete termination has occurred, the family stock attribution rules of Sec. 318 do not apply if, immediately after the distribution, the former stockholder has no interest in the corporation other than an interest as a creditor, does not acquire any such interest within 10 years from the date of the distribution, and files an agreement to notify the IRS of any acquisition of stock in the corporation within 10 years from the date of the redemption.

16. Corporation W has 2,000 shares of its only class of stock outstanding. Mr. D owns 1,500 shares and his son, Randy, owns 500 shares. W redeemed all 1,500 shares from Mr. D for $45,000. Mr. D kept his position in W as an officer and director. This redemption qualifies for capital gain treatment by Mr. D since all of his ownership in W has been terminated.

The correct answer is (F). *(SPE 990 III-19)*
DISCUSSION: Under Sec. 302(b)(3), a redemption qualifies for capital gain treatment if it is a complete redemption of all the shareholder's stock. The redemption must completely terminate the shareholder's interest in the corporation. The distributee cannot retain an interest in the corporation as an officer, director, or employee, but can retain a creditor interest [Sec. 302(c)(2)(A)(i)]. If the distributee retains such an interest, the attribution rules of Sec. 318(a)(1) will apply. Since Mr. D retains an interest in the corporation other than a creditor interest, Sec. 318(a)(1) will attribute his son's stock ownership to him and he will be considered to own 100% of the corporation's stock after the redemption. The distribution will not qualify for capital gain treatment and will be treated as a dividend.

Module 19.1: Stock Redemptions

17. Corporation Z has only one class of stock outstanding, composed of 300 shares which are owned by three unrelated parties. Mr. K and Mrs. Y each own 125 shares and Mrs. P 50 shares. If Z makes a cash redemption of 75 shares from both Mr. K and Mrs. Y, and 25 shares from Mrs. P the proceeds will qualify for capital gain or loss treatment by the shareholders as a disproportionate distribution.

The correct answer is (F). *(SPE 988 III-25)*
DISCUSSION: For the redemption to be considered substantially disproportionate under Sec. 302(b)(2), each shareholder's ownership percentage before and after the redemption is tested. The shareholder must own less than 50% of the voting power of all classes of outstanding voting stock after the redemption and his/her total percentage ownership after the redemption must be less than 80% of his/her percentage ownership immediately before the redemption.

	Percentage Ownership Before	After
Mr. K	41.67%	40%
Mrs. Y	41.67%	40%
Mrs. P	16.66%	20%
	100.00%	100%

None of the shareholders meets the 80% test. Therefore, the redemption distribution will be taxed as a dividend to all three shareholders to the extent of Corporation Z's earnings and profits.

18. Stone Corporation is owned entirely by individual shareholder S. One-half of S's shares are redeemed by the corporation for $75,000. S's basis in these shares is $5,000. S can report a capital gain on the redemption transaction since it is not essentially equivalent to a dividend distribution.

The correct answer is (F). *(Publisher)*
DISCUSSION: Under Sec. 302(b)(1), a redemption which is not essentially equivalent to a dividend is treated as a sale or exchange. However, when any part of the stock of a sole shareholder is redeemed, it is unlikely to qualify for sale or exchange treatment (Davis, 397 U.S. 301, 1970). Since S's redemption also fails the substantially disproportionate test of Sec. 302(b)(2), it will most likely be treated as a dividend to shareholder S.

19. Mr. A owns all of the stock of J and K Corporations. The adjusted basis for the 1,000 shares of each corporation's stock that he holds is $20,000 and $50,000, respectively. A sells 200 shares of the J Corporation stock to K Corporation for $50,000. At the time of the sale J and K Corporations have earnings and profits balances of $40,000 and $70,000, respectively. The sale results in Mr. A reporting a $46,000 capital gain.

The correct answer is (F). *(Publisher)*
DISCUSSION: The situation described is treated as a related party stock redemption under Sec. 304. Redemption of a shareholder's stock in one controlled corporation by a corporation also controlled by that shareholder will be tested under Sec. 302 to determine if it is a dividend or a sale or exchange of stock. The redemption transaction will be treated as if A made a contribution to K's capital and then A's stock in Corporation K received for the capital contribution had been redeemed. However, the Sec. 302 test will be applied to A's holdings in Corporation J. Since A owns all of the stock of Corporation J (both before and after the redemption), the redemption will be treated as a dividend distribution. The earnings and profits to be considered in determining the result to shareholder A are the earnings and profits of K Corporation ($70,000) and then J Corporation ($40,000). Therefore, all $50,000 that A receives will be considered a dividend.

20. Mr. X holds 30% of the common stock of X-Ray Corporation and 250 shares of X-Ray's preferred stock. The common stock and preferred stock have adjusted bases of $100,000 and $15,000, respectively. The preferred stock is Sec. 306 stock. X-Ray redeems all of Mr. X's preferred stock for $25,000 when X-Ray has earnings and profits of $40,000. Mr. X should report a $10,000 long-term capital gain as a result of the redemption, and the basis of his common stock remains $100,000.

The correct answer is (F). *(Publisher)*
DISCUSSION: When Sec. 306 stock is redeemed, the full amount received by the shareholder is treated as a Sec. 301 distribution. Mr. X has a $25,000 dividend since there are sufficient earnings and profits. The basis of his common stock is increased (to $115,000) by the $15,000 basis in the redeemed preferred shares [Reg. 1.302-2(c)].

Module 19.2: Partial Liquidations

21. Mr. Y also holds 30% of the common stock of X-Ray Corporation (in Q. 20) and 250 shares of X-Ray's preferred stock (Sec. 306 stock). Mr. Y also has a basis of $100,000 in his common stock and $15,000 in his preferred stock. However, X-Ray redeemed all of Mr. Y's preferred stock for $25,000 at a date when X-Ray has only $15,000 of earnings and profits. X-Ray had $100,000 of earnings and profits when Mr. Y originally received the preferred stock. Mr. Y has dividend income of $15,000, and the basis in his common stock is increased to $105,000.

The correct answer is (T). *(Publisher)*
DISCUSSION: When Sec. 306 stock is redeemed, the full amount received by the shareholder is treated as a Sec. 301 distribution. Mr. Y has a $15,000 dividend since there are only $15,000 of earnings and profits at the time of the redemption. Unlike a sale of Sec. 306 stock, it is the earnings and profits at the time of redemption which are important rather than the earnings and profits at the time the preferred stock was distributed. Mr. Y's basis in the preferred stock is reduced by the additional $10,000 received in the redemption which is not a dividend. The remaining $5,000 basis of the preferred stock is assigned to the common stock, which increases its basis to $105,000.

22. Tiger Corporation has 1,000 shares of stock outstanding. Three hundred of the shares are owned by individual K who dies on March 12, 1990. K's cost basis for his Tiger stock is $100,000. The stock was valued at $600,000 for estate tax purposes. K's gross estate was $1,000,000. Debts of his estate were $100,000. Funeral expenses and death taxes incurred by the estate were $150,000. $100,000 of the Tiger stock was redeemed by the estate on April 5, 1991 in order to provide liquidity to the estate. The $100,000 proceeds are taxed as a dividend to the estate.

The correct answer is (F). *(Publisher)*
DISCUSSION: Under Sec. 303, an estate may treat a stock redemption as a sale or exchange of property. In order to obtain this favorable treatment, the value of the stock that is being redeemed must be greater than 35% of the value of the gross estate after taking the deductions allowed under Sec. 2053 (funeral expenses, administration expenses, claims against the estate, and unpaid mortgages) and Sec. 2054 (casualty and theft losses). The stock being redeemed is valued at its value for estate tax purposes. Death taxes are categorized as a claim against the estate.
After deducting the allowable expenses, K's estate is valued at $750,000 ($1,000,000 gross estate − $100,000 debts and $150,000 funeral expenses and death taxes). The value of the redeemed stock is 80% of the value of the gross estate after taking the allowable deductions ($600,000 ÷ $750,000). The requirement of Sec. 303 is met, and the redemption is treated as a sale or exchange of the stock, and not as a dividend.

19.2 Partial Liquidations

23. How does a noncorporate shareholder treat the gain on a redemption of stock that qualifies as a partial liquidation of the distributing corporation?

a. Entirely as capital gain.
b. Entirely as a dividend.
c. Partly as capital gain and partly as a dividend.
d. As a tax-free transaction.

The correct answer is (a). *(CPA 1189 Q-52)*
REQUIRED: The proper treatment accorded a partially liquidating distribution received by a noncorporate shareholder.
DISCUSSION: Sec. 302(b)(4) states that a noncorporate shareholder who receives a distribution in redemption of stock in a partial liquidation treats the distribution as payment in exchange for the stock. Any gain on the exchange will be treated entirely as a capital gain.

24. During 1991, Corporation T distributed machinery having a fair market value of $300,000 and an adjusted basis to T of $150,000, to Mr. K in exchange for 85% of K's interest in T. This distribution was under a plan of partial liquidation that resulted in a contraction of the business. K's adjusted basis in the stock exchanged with T was $180,000. T had an earnings and profit balance of $500,000 prior to the partial liquidation. What is the character and amount of K's recognized gain on the distribution?

a. $120,000 capital gain.
b. $150,000 capital gain.
c. $150,000 capital loss.
d. $300,000 dividend income.

The correct answer is (a). *(SPE 990 III-74)*
REQUIRED: The amount and character of gain recognized by a noncorporate shareholder in a partial liquidation.
DISCUSSION: Under Sec. 302(b)(4), a redemption made in partial liquidation of an interest held by a noncorporate shareholder is treated as a distribution in exchange for the stock. The shareholder will treat any gain on the redemption as a capital gain. The amount of the gain is computed under Sec. 1001. Under Sec. 301(b)(1), the amount of the distribution is the fair market value of the property. Mr. K will recognize a gain of $120,000 on the distribution ($300,000 fair market value of the distributed property − $180,000 basis in the stock). The entire gain will receive capital gain treatment.

Module 19.2: Partial Liquidations

25. On January 1, 1991, Can Corporation distributed Sec. 1231 land with a market value of $300,000 and an adjusted basis of $205,000 under a plan of partial liquidation under the Sec. 302(b)(4) rules. The distribution was made to individual shareholder C who had owned 40% of Can since it was founded. C's stock interest redeemed in the partial liquidation had a basis of $140,000. What is the amount and character of gain (loss) that Can should recognize on the distribution?

   a. $160,000 Sec. 1231 gain.
   b. $95,000 Sec. 1231 gain.
   c. $95,000 capital gain.
   d. $65,000 Sec. 1231 loss.

The correct answer is (b). *(Publisher)*
REQUIRED: The amount and character of gain or loss recognized by a corporation on distributing property in a partial liquidation.
DISCUSSION: The distribution of appreciated property in a partial liquidation falls under Sec. 311(b), which requires the distributing corporation to recognize gain on the distribution as if the property had been sold to the distributee immediately before the distribution. Therefore, Can will recognize a Sec. 1231 gain of $95,000 ($300,000 − $205,000).

26. A corporation making any distribution in liquidation must file a Form 1099-DIV in each calendar year of the liquidation for each shareholder to whom it makes distributions that are equal to or exceed $600. These forms must be filed with the Internal Revenue Service on or before

   a. December 31 of the calendar year.
   b. January 31 of the year after the close of the calendar year.
   c. March 15 of the year after the close of the calendar year.
   d. The last day of February of the year after the close of the calendar year in which the distribution is made.

The correct answer is (d). *(SPE 989 III-45)*
REQUIRED: When Form 1099-DIV must be filed.
DISCUSSION: A corporation making any distribution in complete or partial liquidation must file a Form 1099-DIV in each calendar year of the liquidation for each shareholder to whom it makes a distribution of $600 or more. These forms must be sent to the shareholders by January 31 of the year following the calendar year in which the liquidating distribution is made and filed with the IRS by February 28 [Reg. 1.6043-2(a)].

27. A proportionate distribution to a corporate shareholder by a corporation in partial redemption of stock, pursuant to a plan of partial liquidation, is treated as a dividend to the extent of the earnings and profits of the distributing corporation.

The correct answer is (T). *(SPE 990 III-18)*
DISCUSSION: Sec. 302(b)(4) allows shareholders who receive redemptions in partial liquidation to treat the distribution as payment for their stock. Any gain on the redemption is eligible for capital gain treatment. The provisions of Sec. 302(b)(4) apply only to noncorporate shareholders. Therefore, a corporation that receives a redemption in partial liquidation must treat the distribution as a dividend to the extent of earnings and profits of the distributing corporation. The distribution is not eligible for capital gain treatment unless one of the three other exchange exceptions of Sec. 302(b) apply (i.e., a complete termination, substantially disproportionate, or not essentially equivalent to a dividend). None of these exceptions applies here.

28. Corporation B has been in business since 1975. On January 1, 1991, a fire destroyed some of the assets of the corporation, causing a cessation of part of its activities. As a result, B's president decided on a permanent contraction of the business. On May 31, 1991, the corporation distributed unused insurance proceeds, recovered as a result of the fire, in exchange for some of its outstanding stock. The distribution consisted of $25,000 in cash. B had earnings and profits of $50,000 prior to the distribution. This distribution will qualify as a partial liquidation.

The correct answer is (T). *(SPE 1083 III-30)*
DISCUSSION: Sec. 302(e) provides that a distribution qualifies as a partial liquidation if it is not essentially equivalent to a dividend. A distribution meets this requirement if it is attributable to the termination of one of the corporation's businesses, i.e., a bona fide contraction of the corporate business. The distribution of unused insurance proceeds recovered as a result of a fire that destroyed part of a business qualifies as a partial liquidation (Reg. 1.346-1). Note that only noncorporate shareholders are eligible to treat the redemption as a sale or exchange under Sec. 302(b)(4). Corporate shareholders must apply one of the other exceptions of Sec. 302(b).

19.3 Complete Liquidations

29. Lori owned two blocks of Sting Corporation stock which had the following characteristics:

Block	Shares	Acquired	Basis
1	100	5/01/90	$10,000
2	25	7/02/91	6,250

Lori's two blocks of stock combined represented 10% of Sting's outstanding stock. Pursuant to Sting's complete liquidation, Lori received a $25,000 cash distribution on December 1, 1991 in exchange for her 125 shares of stock. Sting's earnings and profits balance immediately before any liquidating distributions was $25,000. What is the amount and character of gain or loss that Lori should report as a result of the liquidation?

a. No gain or loss.
b. $25,000 dividend income.
c. $8,750 long-term capital gain.
d. $10,000 long-term capital gain, $1,250 short-term capital loss.

The correct answer is (d). *(SPE 990 III-73)*
REQUIRED: The amount and character of gain or loss to be reported as a result of a complete liquidation.
DISCUSSION: Sec. 331 provides capital gain or loss treatment for distributions received by a shareholder in complete liquidation of a corporation. The gain or loss will be long-term or short-term depending on the length of time the stock has been held (Sec. 1222).
The shareholder's gain or loss is the difference between the amount realized and the basis in the stock. The amount realized by Lori is $200 per share ($25,000 distribution ÷ 125 shares owned). The sale of Block 1 produces a gain of $10,000 [100 shares x ($200 selling price less $100 per share basis)]. The gain is long-term because the stock was held for more than 1 year. The sale of Block 2 produces a loss of $1,250 [25 shares x ($250 per share basis – $200 per share selling price)]. The loss is short-term because the stock was held less than 1 year.

30. Mr. L owned 100 shares of stock in Willow Corporation. During 1991, Willow completely liquidated and distributed the following to L.

Cash	$25,000
Land:	
Fair market value	450,000
Subject to a mortgage of	200,000

Mr. L's adjusted basis in Willow's stock was $50,000 and he will assume the mortgage on the land. What is L's basis in the land received?

a. $50,000.
b. $75,000.
c. $250,000.
d. $450,000.

The correct answer is (d). *(SPE 990 III-75)*
REQUIRED: The basis of land received in a complete liquidation.
DISCUSSION: Sec. 334(a) states that if property is received in complete liquidation, and if gain or loss is recognized on receipt of such property, the basis of the property in the distributee's hands will be the fair market value of the property at the time of the distribution.
Mr. L will recognize a gain of $225,000 on the receipt of the cash and land [($450,000 fair market value of land + $25,000 cash – $200,000 liability) – his $50,000 basis in the stock]. Since he recognizes a gain, the provisions of Sec. 334(a) apply and his basis in the land received is its fair market value at the time of distribution.

Module 19.3: Complete Liquidations

31. Krol Corporation distributed marketable securities in redemption of its stock in a complete liquidation. On the date of distribution, these securities had a basis of $100,000 and a fair market value of $150,000. What gain does Krol have as a result of the distribution?

a. $0.
b. $50,000 capital gain.
c. $50,000 Sec. 1231 gain.
d. $50,000 ordinary gain.

The correct answer is (b). *(CPA 590 Q-28)*
REQUIRED: The gain to a corporation on the distribution of property in redemption of its stock in a complete liquidation.
DISCUSSION: Sec. 336 provides that gain or loss is recognized when a corporation distributes property as part of a complete liquidation. Therefore, Krol Corporation will recognize a $50,000 ($150,000 − $100,000) gain. It is a capital gain because the marketable securities are a capital asset.

32. Edgewood Corporation was liquidated in 1991 by Roberts, its sole shareholder. Pursuant to the liquidation, Roberts' stock in Edgewood was canceled and he received the following assets on July 15, 1991:

	Basis to Edgewood	Fair Market Value
Cash	$ 40,000	$ 40,000
Accounts receivable	20,000	20,000
Inventory (FIFO)	30,000	45,000
Land	50,000	75,000
	$140,000	$180,000

How much gain should be recognized by Edgewood Corporation on the liquidation?

a. $0.
b. $15,000.
c. $25,000.
d. $40,000.

The correct answer is (d). *(CPA 1182 Q-59)*
REQUIRED: The amount of gain recognized by a corporation on a liquidating distribution of property.
DISCUSSION: Under Sec. 336(a), a corporation recognizes gain or loss upon making a liquidating distribution of its assets as if the property had been sold for its fair market value immediately before the distribution. Edgewood would therefore have a gain of $40,000 ($180,000 fair market value of property distributed − $140,000 basis of property distributed). The character of this gain would depend upon the nature of the assets (in the hands of the distributing corporation) distributed.

33. In 1991, Individual Z contributed property with an adjusted basis of $1,000 and a fair market value of $100 to Alpha Corporation. Z owned 10% of Alpha. The purpose of the contribution was to recognize a loss by Alpha on its liquidation. The following year Alpha adopted a plan of complete liquidation in order to recognize the loss on the contributed property of Z. In computing the loss, Alpha's basis will be

a. $0.
b. $100.
c. $900.
d. $1,000.

The correct answer is (b). *(Publisher)*
REQUIRED: A corporation's basis for computing loss in a liquidation when the property was acquired in order to recognize a loss.
DISCUSSION: Normally gain or loss is recognized by a corporation on a liquidating distribution of its assets [Sec. 336(a)]. But if a principal purpose of the contribution of property to a corporation in advance of a liquidation is to recognize loss upon sale or distribution of the property, then the basis for determining loss on such property acquired by the corporation in a Sec. 351 transaction, or as a contribution to capital, will be reduced (but not below zero) by the excess of the basis of the property on the date of contribution over its fair market value on such date.

These requirements are met by Individual Z and Alpha Corporation with respect to the property contributed. Therefore, Alpha's basis for determining loss will be $100 ($1,000 − $900 excess of basis over fair market value at the time of contribution). If the fair market value is less than $100 at the time of liquidation, Alpha will still be able to recognize a loss with respect to that difference. On the other hand, if the fair market value has increased to greater than $1,000, then Alpha could recognize a gain using $1,000 as the basis for determining gain.

34. Individual Y owns 55% of Beta Corporation. In 1990, Y contributed property with an adjusted basis of $20,000 and a fair market value of $8,000 to Beta in a transaction qualifying under Sec. 351. In 1991, Beta adopted a plan of complete liquidation and distributed this same property to Y. At this time the property had a basis of $18,000 and a fair market value of $5,000. How much loss will Beta recognize on the distribution?

   a. $0.
   b. $1,000.
   c. $12,000.
   d. $13,000.

The correct answer is (a). *(Publisher)*
REQUIRED: The loss recognized in a liquidation on the distribution of recently contributed property to a related shareholder.
DISCUSSION: Normally gain or loss is recognized on a liquidating distribution of assets [Sec. 336(a)]. However, under Sec. 336(d)(1), a loss is not recognized in a liquidation on the distribution of property to a related person (which includes a greater than 50% shareholder) unless the property is distributed to all shareholders on a pro rata basis and the property was not acquired in a Sec. 351 transaction or contribution to capital during the 5 preceding years (also known as disqualified property). Since the distribution was of property acquired in a Sec. 351 transaction within the 5 preceding years, no loss is recognized on the distribution of the disqualified property to the related person. The fact that the distribution was not pro rata does not affect the ability to recognize the loss.

35. The effect of Sec. 336 (by requiring the distributing corporation to recognize gain) is that the shareholders will realize more from the liquidation since the shareholders' gain will be less.

The correct answer is (F). *(Publisher)*
DISCUSSION: Sec. 336 requires a corporation to recognize gain and loss when it distributes property as part of a complete liquidation. Since the corporation will owe taxes on the gain, there will be less net assets to actually distribute to the shareholders. Therefore, the shareholders will realize less from the liquidation even though their taxes will also be less. The only reason their taxes are less is because there will be less gain to tax.

36. Corporation Z is a cash basis taxpayer. In 1991, Z distributed $50,000 of its accounts receivable to individual shareholder Able pursuant to its complete liquidation. Z does not need to recognize income as a result of the distribution and Able takes a zero basis for the accounts receivable.

The correct answer is (F). *(Publisher)*
DISCUSSION: Sec. 336 provides that gain or loss is recognized when a corporation distributes property as part of a complete liquidation. Therefore, Corporation Z will recognize $50,000 ($50,000 − $0 basis) of income. It will be ordinary income because collection of the accounts receivable would have resulted in ordinary income being reported. Able's basis in the accounts receivable will be their $50,000 fair market value [Sec. 334(a)].

37. A distribution received by a shareholder as a result of a complete liquidation when the shareholder receives less than her basis in the stock results in ordinary income being reported.

The correct answer is (F). *(SPE 1079 III-23)*
DISCUSSION: Sec. 331 provides that when amounts are distributed in complete liquidation of a corporation, the distribution is treated as part or full payment in exchange for the stock. Thus, if the stock is a capital asset in the hands of the shareholder, any amount realized which is less than the shareholder's basis will result in a capital loss or a Sec. 1244 ordinary loss being recognized.

38. A corporation will recognize a gain or loss on the distribution of its property to its noncorporate shareholders in complete liquidation of the corporation, the same as if the corporation had sold the property to its shareholders at fair market value.

The correct answer is (T). *(SPE 990 III-17)*
DISCUSSION: Sec. 336(a) provides that, if a corporation distributes property in complete liquidation, the corporation will be treated as having sold the property to the distributee(s) at its fair market value. The liquidating corporation will recognize a gain to the extent that the fair market value of the distributed property exceeds its adjusted basis. Note that Sec. 336(d) prohibits the recognition of loss on certain types of distributions including distributions to related persons.

Module 19.3: Complete Liquidations

39. The basis of property received in a distribution in complete liquidation (when gain or loss is recognized by the shareholders on receipt of the property) is its adjusted basis at the time of distribution.

The correct answer is (F). *(SPE 1077 I-94)*
DISCUSSION: Under Sec. 334(a), if property is received in a distribution in a complete liquidation and gain or loss is recognized on the receipt of such property, the basis of the property in the hands of the shareholder is the fair market value of the property at the time of the distribution.

40. Corporation G, in complete liquidation, distributed to Shareholder Y cash of $5,000 and $8,000 in 1990 and 1991, respectively. The corporation is not required to file Form 1099-DIV until 1991, the year of the final distribution.

The correct answer is (F). *(SPE 1079 III-13)*
DISCUSSION: In a complete liquidation which is to be accomplished by a series of partial distributions, a corporation is required to file Form 1099-DIV each calendar year in which it distributes a partial payment of $600 or more [Reg. 1.6043-2(a)].

41. A corporation may request an advance ruling from the Internal Revenue Service before entering into transactions such as liquidations and stock redemptions.

The correct answer is (T). *(SPE 984 III-19)*
DISCUSSION: Corporations may request advance rulings from the IRS before entering into transactions such as liquidations and stock redemptions. However, there are limitations, e.g., the IRS will not ordinarily issue an advance ruling for a partial liquidation unless it results in at least a 20% reduction in (1) gross revenue, (2) net fair market value of assets, and (3) employees (Rev. Proc. 91-3).

42. Within 30 days after the adoption of a resolution or plan (including any amendment or supplements to it) for the dissolution of a corporation or its complete or partial liquidation, the corporation must file an information return (Form 966, Corporate Dissolution or Liquidation) with the Internal Revenue Service Center with which the corporation is required to file its income tax returns.

The correct answer is (T). *(SPE 988 III-52)*
DISCUSSION: A corporation must report the adoption of a plan of liquidation to the IRS within 30 days by filing Form 966, an information return [Sec. 6043(a)].

43. Corporation T is deemed to be a collapsible corporation under the provisions of Sec. 341. Individual A owned 15 of T's 100 outstanding shares of common stock since its formation. A's basis for these shares is $15,000. T Corporation is liquidated on December 7, 1991 after being in business for 2 years. Pursuant to the liquidation, A receives cash and property worth $22,500. As a result of the liquidation, A reports a $7,500 long-term capital gain.

The correct answer is (T). *(Publisher)*
DISCUSSION: Under the general rules of Sec. 331(a), amounts received in a distribution in complete liquidation of a corporation are normally treated as payments in exchange for the stock which will result in recognition of a capital gain. Since Sec. 336(a) requires the recognition of gain by T when making a liquidating distribution, the Sec. 341(b)(1)(A) substantial realization of income test has likely been met and the corporation will not be deemed to have been formed with an intent towards collapsing the corporation. If this requirement has been met, the shareholder will have capital gain instead of ordinary income.

19.4 Liquidations of Subsidiary Corporations

44. At January 1, 1991, Pearl Corporation owned 90% of the outstanding stock of Seso Corporation. Both companies were domestic corporations. Pursuant to a plan of liquidation adopted by Seso in March 1991, Seso distributed all of its property in September 1991 in complete redemption of all its stock, when Seso's accumulated earnings equaled $18,000. Seso had never been insolvent. Pursuant to the liquidation, Seso transferred to Pearl a parcel of land with a basis of $10,000 and a fair market value of $40,000. How much gain must Seso recognize in 1991 on the transfer of this land to Pearl?

a. $0.
b. $18,000.
c. $27,000.
d. $30,000.

The correct answer is (a). *(CPA 1183 Q-51)*
REQUIRED: The amount of gain that must be recognized by a subsidiary on the distribution of appreciated property to its parent in a complete liquidation.
DISCUSSION: Generally Sec. 337 requires that a controlled corporation recognize no gain or loss upon making a liquidating distribution of property to its parent corporation. This exception to the general rule of Sec. 336 applies only if the control requirement is met. The control requirement is that the parent corporation must own at least 80% of the voting power and 80% of the total value of the stock of the corporation being liquidated.
Under this rule, Seso will recognize no gain on the transfer of the land to Pearl.

45. Lark Corporation and its wholly owned subsidiary, Day Corporation, both operated on a calendar year. In January 1991, Day adopted a plan of complete liquidation. Two months later, Day paid all of its liabilities and distributed its remaining assets to Lark. These assets consisted of the following:

Cash $50,000
Land (at cost) 10,000

Fair market value of the land was $30,000. Upon distribution of Day's assets to Lark, all of Day's capital stock was canceled. Lark's basis for the Day stock was $7,000. Lark's recognized gain in 1991 on receipt of Day's assets in liquidation was

a. $0.
b. $50,000.
c. $53,000.
d. $73,000.

The correct answer is (a). *(CPA 585 Q-42)*
REQUIRED: A corporation's gain upon the complete liquidation of a subsidiary corporation.
DISCUSSION: Sec. 332 requires that a parent corporation recognize no gain or loss upon the receipt of a liquidating distribution from a controlled corporation. Control for purposes of Sec. 332 means ownership of at least 80% of the subsidiary's voting power and 80% of the total value of the stock.

46. Stone Corporation purchased all of the stock of Rock Corporation in 1979 for $120,000. In November 1991, Rock is liquidated. Stone receives all of Rock's assets, which have a basis to Rock of $150,000 and a fair market value of $250,000. At the time of liquidation, Rock had earnings and profits of $100,000. What gain does Stone recognize as a result of the liquidation, and what is the basis of the properties received in the liquidation?

	Gain	Basis
a.	$130,000	$250,000
b.	$100,000	$250,000
c.	$0	$150,000
d.	$0	$120,000

The correct answer is (c). *(Publisher)*
REQUIRED: The gain recognized upon the liquidation of a subsidiary and the basis of property received in the liquidation.
DISCUSSION: Under Sec. 332, a subsidiary in which the parent corporation owns at least 80% of the voting power and 80% of the total value of the stock can be liquidated without recognition of gain or loss. The parent corporation takes a carryover basis in the property received in the liquidation [Sec. 334(b)(1)]. Accordingly, Stone takes Rock's basis in the assets of $150,000.
Note that Stone Corporation's basis in its Rock Corporation stock has disappeared. It is neither assigned to the assets nor used by Stone to calculate any recognized gain or loss.

47. When a parent corporation completely liquidates its 80%-owned subsidiary, the parent (as stockholder) will ordinarily

    a. Be subject to capital gains tax on 80% of the long-term gain.

    b. Be subject to capital gains tax on 100% of the long-term gain.

    c. Have to report any gain on liquidation as ordinary income.

    d. Not recognize gain or loss on the liquidating distribution(s).

The correct answer is (d). *(CPA 1185 Q-54)*
REQUIRED: The correct statement about a complete liquidation of a subsidiary under Sec. 332.
DISCUSSION: When a subsidiary corporation is liquidated into the parent corporation in a Sec. 332 transaction, no gain or loss is recognized on the liquidation.
Answers (a), (b), and (c) are incorrect because the parent corporation recognizes no gain under Sec. 332.

48. Which one of the following statements is correct regarding the complete liquidation of a subsidiary corporation under Sec. 332?

    a. Gain is recognized on the liquidation only to the extent of the parent corporation's ratable share of the subsidiary's earnings and profits.

    b. The tax attributes of the subsidiary corporation carry over to the parent.

    c. The liquidated corporation recognizes no gain or loss on the liquidation except for depreciation recapture under Sec. 1245 and Sec. 1250.

    d. The minority shareholders must, like the parent corporation, recognize no gain or loss on the liquidation.

The correct answer is (b). *(Publisher)*
REQUIRED: The correct statement of a complete liquidation of a subsidiary under Sec. 332.
DISCUSSION: When a subsidiary corporation is liquidated into the parent corporation in a Sec. 332 transaction, no gain or loss is recognized by either corporation on the liquidation. The tax attributes of the subsidiary corporation do carry over to the parent corporation under Sec. 381.
Answer (a) is incorrect because no gain is recognized on the liquidation of a subsidiary corporation under Sec. 332. Answer (c) is incorrect because Sec. 1245 and 1250 recapture is not recognized; it carries over to the new owner of the property [Secs. 1245(b)(3) and 1250(d)(3)]. Answer (d) is incorrect because Sec. 332 applies only to the parent corporation. Minority shareholders treat the liquidating distribution under Sec. 331.

19.5 Corporate Divisions and Reorganizations

49. Which one of the following is not a corporate reorganization as defined in the Internal Revenue Code?

    a. Stock redemption.

    b. Recapitalization.

    c. Mere change in identity.

    d. Statutory merger.

The correct answer is (a). *(CPA 1186 Q-45)*
REQUIRED: The transaction that does not constitute a corporate reorganization.
DISCUSSION: A stock redemption is normally a taxable transaction to the shareholder(s). It is not a taxable transaction to the corporation unless appreciated property is used to make the redemption. However, stock redemptions do not fall under the corporate reorganization rules defined in Sec. 368(a)(1).
Answer (b) is incorrect because a recapitalization is a Type E reorganization [Sec. 368(a)(1)(E)]. Answer (c) is incorrect because a mere change in identity is a Type F reorganization [Sec. 368(a)(1)(F)]. Answer (d) is incorrect because a statutory merger is a Type A reorganization [Sec. 368(a)(1)(A)].

Module 19.5: Corporate Divisions and Reorganizations

50. Pursuant to a plan of corporate reorganization adopted in June 1991, Lois Pell exchanged 100 shares of Ral Corporation common stock that she had purchased in March 1991 at a cost of $10,000 for 150 shares of Lars Corporation common stock having a fair market value of $12,000. Pell's recognized gain on this exchange was

  a. $0.
  b. $2,000 ordinary income.
  c. $2,000 short-term capital gain.
  d. $2,000 long-term capital gain.

The correct answer is (a). *(CPA 1187 Q-36)*
REQUIRED: The amount of gain recognized in a corporate reorganization.
DISCUSSION: An exchange of stock for stock in obtaining control of a corporation is a Type B reorganization [Sec. 368(a)(1)(B)]. Sec. 354(a)(1) provides that no gain or loss is recognized in a reorganization if stock or securities are exchanged solely for stock or securities in the same corporation or in another corporation that was a party to the reorganization. For Pell, since no boot was received, there would be no gain recognized on the transaction, long-term capital gain or otherwise.

51. On July 1, 1991, in connection with a recapitalization of Yorktown Corporation, Robert Moore exchanged 1,000 shares of stock which cost him $95,000 for 1,000 shares of new stock worth $108,000 and bonds in the principal amount of $10,000 with a fair market value of $10,500. What is the amount of Moore's recognized gain during 1991?

  a. $0.
  b. $10,500.
  c. $23,000.
  d. $23,500.

The correct answer is (b). *(CPA 1181 P-41)*
REQUIRED: The amount of gain recognized by a shareholder receiving stock and bonds for stock in a recapitalization.
DISCUSSION: A recapitalization is a Type E reorganization under Sec. 368(a)(1)(E). Sec. 354(a)(1) provides that no gain or loss is recognized if stock or securities in a corporation are exchanged solely for stock or securities in the same or another corporation pursuant to a plan of reorganization. Therefore, the exchange of the stock for stock qualifies as a tax-free exchange. The bonds are generally considered securities and would qualify except that Sec. 354(a)(2) denies tax-free treatment when securities (bonds) are received but none are surrendered. Under Sec. 356, the gain recognized is the lesser of the realized gain or the fair market value of the nonqualifying property received (in this case, the bonds).
The realized gain is the total amount realized of $118,500 ($108,000 stock + $10,500 bonds) less basis of $95,000 in the stock given up, or $23,500. The recognized gain is limited to $10,500 (the FMV of the bonds received).

52. With regard to corporate reorganizations, which one of the following statements is correct?

  a. A mere change in identity, form, or place of organization of one corporation does not qualify as a reorganization.
  b. The reorganization provisions cannot be used to provide tax-free treatment for corporate transactions.
  c. Securities in corporations not parties to a reorganization are always "boot."
  d. A "party to the reorganization" does not include the consolidated company.

The correct answer is (c). *(CPA 587 Q-58)*
REQUIRED: The correct statement regarding reorganizations.
DISCUSSION: Under Sec. 368(b), a corporation must be a party to a reorganization in order for its property, stock, or securities, to be exchanged tax free. Securities in corporations not parties to a reorganization are boot.
Answer (a) is incorrect because this is a Type F reorganization under Sec. 368(a)(1)(F). Answer (b) is incorrect because Sec. 368 provides for tax-free treatment of corporate reorganizations. Answer (d) is incorrect because Sec. 368(b) includes the new corporation, the consolidated corporation in a Type A reorganization which is a consolidation, as a party to the reorganization under Sec. 368(b).

Module 19.5: Corporate Divisions and Reorganizations

53. Pursuant to a plan of corporate reorganization adopted in 1991, Myra Eber exchanged 1,000 shares of Faro Corporation common stock that she had purchased for $75,000, for 1,800 shares of Judd Corporation common stock having a fair market value of $86,000. As a result of this exchange, Eber's recognized gain and her basis in the Judd stock should be

	Recognized Gain	Basis
a.	$11,000	$86,000
b.	$11,000	$75,000
c.	$0	$86,000
d.	$0	$75,000

The correct answer is (d). *(CPA 585 Q-54)*
REQUIRED: The gain recognized on an exchange of stock in a Type B reorganization and the basis in the new stock.
DISCUSSION: Under Sec. 354(a)(1), a stockholder does not recognize any gain or loss in a reorganization on an exchange of stock or securities in a corporation solely for stock or securities in the same or another corporation that is a party to the reorganization. Since, pursuant to a reorganization, Eber exchanged shares of Faro stock solely for shares of Judd stock, Eber will recognize no gain.
Under Sec. 358, when a Sec. 354 exchange takes place with no recognition of gain or loss, the property received in the transaction has the same basis as the property exchanged. Thus, Eber's basis in the new stock will be the same as her $75,000 basis in the stock exchanged.

54. Pursuant to a plan of reorganization adopted in 1991, Eagle Corporation exchanged property with an adjusted basis of $100,000 for 10,000 of the shares of the Hawkeye Corporation. The shares of Hawkeye had a fair market value of $120,000 on the date of the exchange. Eagle Corporation was liquidated shortly after the exchange with its sole shareholder A receiving the Hawkeye shares. The sole shareholder A had a $110,000 basis in the Eagle shares surrendered. As a result of this exchange, A's recognized gain and her basis in the Hawkeye stock are as follows:

	Recognized Gain	Stock Basis
a.	$0	$100,000
b.	$0	$110,000
c.	$0	$120,000
d.	$20,000	$120,000

The correct answer is (b). *(Publisher)*
REQUIRED: The gain recognized on receipt of stock for property under a plan of reorganization and the basis in the acquired stock.
DISCUSSION: Sec. 354(a) provides that no gain or loss is recognized on a Type C reorganization if a shareholder exchanges property pursuant to a plan of reorganization solely for stock or securities in another corporation. A will recognize no gain.
The basis of the stock received by the shareholder is determined under Sec. 358(a) and is the same as the basis of the stock exchanged. The shareholder's basis in the Eagle stock exchanged was $110,000, so his basis in the Hawkeye stock received will also be $110,000.

55. Pursuant to a plan of reorganization adopted in 1991, Summit Corporation exchanged 1,000 shares of its common stock and paid $40,000 cash for Hansen Corporation's assets with an adjusted basis of $200,000 (fair market value of $300,000). Hansen Corporation was liquidated shortly after the exchange with its shareholders receiving the Summit stock and cash. The 1,000 shares of Summit common stock had a fair market value of $260,000 on the date of the exchange. What is the basis to Summit of the assets acquired in the exchange?

a. $200,000.
b. $240,000.
c. $260,000.
d. $300,000.

The correct answer is (a). *(CPA 1182 Q-55)*
REQUIRED: The basis to the acquiring corporation of assets received in a Type C reorganization.
DISCUSSION: Summit Corporation's exchange of 1,000 shares of common stock and $40,000 cash for the assets of Hansen Corporation will qualify as a Type C reorganization assuming that all or substantially all of Hansen's assets are acquired and that Hansen distributes the stock, securities, and other property it receives, as well as its other property it has retained, as part of the reorganization [Sec. 368(a)]. As a result of a Type C reorganization, Hansen, the transferor corporation, will have a realized gain of $100,000 ($300,000 received − $200,000 adjusted basis). Sec. 361, however, provides that in a qualifying reorganization, the transferor corporation recognizes no gain, if the assets other than stock or securities received are distributed immediately to its shareholders or creditors.
The basis of the assets to Summit, determined under Sec. 362(b) equal the transferor's adjusted basis in the assets ($200,000) increased by any gain recognized by the transferor ($0) or $200,000.

Module 19.5: Corporate Divisions and Reorganizations

56. Pursuant to a tax-free reorganization in 1991, Sandra Peel exchanged 100 shares of Lorna Corporation stock for 100 shares of Wood Corporation stock and in addition received $1,000 cash, which was not in excess of Peel's ratable share of Lorna's undistributed earnings and profits. Peel paid $20,000 in 1980 for the Lorna stock. The Wood stock had a fair market value of $24,000 on the date of the exchange and represented a 5% interest in the outstanding Wood stock. What is the recognized gain to be reported by Peel in 1991?

   a. $0.
   b. $1,000 dividend.
   c. $1,000 long-term capital gain.
   d. $5,000 long-term capital gain.

The correct answer is (c). *(CPA 582 Q-46)*
REQUIRED: The amount and character of gain recognized upon the tax-free reorganization.
DISCUSSION: Sec. 354 provides that no gain or loss is recognized in a reorganization if stock or securities are exchanged solely for stock or securities in the same or another corporation. When property other than stock or securities is received, Sec. 356(a)(1) requires gain to be recognized to the extent of the lesser of the realized gain or the other property (boot) received. Realized gain is $5,000 (stock of $24,000 + cash of $1,000 − basis of $20,000), but the gain recognized is limited to the $1,000 of cash received.

Under Sec. 356(a)(2), this gain is treated as a dividend if the exchange has the effect of a dividend distribution and there are earnings and profits. Because Peel received equivalent stock and her ratable share of earnings and profits exceeds the recognized gain, the $1,000 gain would ordinarily be a dividend.

Note that in determining dividend equivalency, the Sec. 302(b) redemption rules are applied to the stock of the acquiring company. In applying the Sec. 302 rules, Peel is considered to have received all stock in the transaction and then redeemed a portion of the stock for cash [Clark, 109 U.S. 1455 (1989)]. Sec. 302 is tested against Peel's stock ownership in the acquiring corporation. Peel's receipt of cash likely will qualify under Sec. 302(b)(1) as being not essentially equivalent to a dividend since she owns a minority position in Wood before the hypothetical redemption and has had a meaningful reduction in her interest in Wood as a result of the hypothetical redemption. This permits a capital gain to be recognized.

57. Single Corporation, which is owned equally by four individual shareholders, owns all of the stock of Double Corporation. The Double Corporation stock was acquired 8 years ago. It has a fair market value of $80,000 and an adjusted basis of $20,000. Single distributes the Double stock equally to the four shareholders as part of a spinoff transaction at the time that it has $120,000 of earnings and profits. What amount and type of income do each of Single's shareholders report as a result of the distribution?

   a. $20,000 dividend income.
   b. $20,000 capital gain.
   c. $15,000 capital gain.
   d. $0.

The correct answer is (d). *(Publisher)*
REQUIRED: The income recognized by shareholders in a spinoff distribution.
DISCUSSION: Sec. 355 provides that a corporation may transfer to its shareholders tax-free the stock of a controlled corporation, provided certain conditions are met. The distributing corporation must have at least 80% control of the distributed corporation before the spinoff occurs. After the distribution, both the distributing corporation and the controlled corporation must be engaged in the active conduct of a trade or business. In addition, the trade or business must have been conducted throughout the 5-year period ending on the date of distribution, must not have been acquired in a taxable transaction within the preceding 5-year period, and may not have been conducted by another corporation whose control was acquired in a taxable transaction during this 5-year period. The distributing corporation must transfer control to the shareholders in the spinoff. Single Corporation meets all of these requirements, so the distribution of the Double stock to Single's shareholders results in the recognition of no income or gain.

58. Changing the state in which a corporation is incorporated represents a Type F reorganization.

The correct answer is (T). *(Publisher)*
DISCUSSION: A Type F reorganization is defined by Sec. 368(a)(1)(F) as a mere change in identity, form, or place of organization of a single corporation. Under Rev. Rul. 57-276, reincorporation in another state qualifies as a Type F reorganization.

Module 19.6: Consolidated Tax Returns

59. A transfer of an operating division of an existing corporation to a newly created subsidiary corporation, followed by the distribution of all of the subsidiary corporation's stock by the transferor corporation, can be accomplished tax-free under the Type D reorganization rules.

The correct answer is (T). *(Publisher)*
DISCUSSION: A Type D reorganization is defined by Sec. 368(a)(1)(D) as a transfer by a corporation of all or part of its assets to another corporation which is controlled immediately after the transfer by the transferor corporation or its shareholders. The stock or securities of the controlled corporation must also be distributed by the transferor corporation in a transaction which qualifies under Sec. 354, 355, or 356. The distribution in the question would be covered by Sec. 355, and the entire transaction can be accomplished tax-free as a Type D reorganization.

19.6 Consolidated Tax Returns

60. Which of the following corporations is considered to be an "includable corporation" in an affiliated group of corporations?

a. Holding company.
b. Foreign Sales Corporation (FSC).
c. Real estate investment trust.
d. Regulated investment company.

The correct answer is (a). *(CPA 1175 Q-30)*
REQUIRED: The organization that is considered an "includable corporation."
DISCUSSION: An "includable corporation" means any corporation except those corporations listed in Sec. 1504(b). A holding company is not listed as an exception. A holding company is generally one which conducts little or no active business and only holds stock in other corporations. The significance of includable corporations is that they may be part of an affiliated group which may file a consolidated tax return.
Answers (b), (c), and (d) are incorrect because FSCs (foreign sales corporations), real estate investment trusts, and regulated investment companies are specifically excluded under the definition of includable corporations in Sec. 1504(b).

61. Dana Corporation owns stock in Seco Corporation. For Dana and Seco to qualify for the filing of consolidated returns, at least what percentage of Seco's total voting power and total value of stock must be directly owned by Dana?

	Total Voting Power	Total Value of Stock
a.	51%	51%
b.	51%	80%
c.	80%	51%
d.	80%	80%

The correct answer is (d). *(CPA 1188 Q-28)*
REQUIRED: The percentage of total voting power and total value of stock that must be owned in order to file a consolidated tax return.
DISCUSSION: Sec. 1504(a)(2) requires a corporation to own 80% of the total voting power and 80% of the total value of the stock (excluding certain preferred stock issues) in order to file a consolidated return.

62. All of the following are true with respect to the filing of consolidated tax returns except that

a. Each corporation that has been a member of a parent-subsidiary affiliated group during any part of the taxable year for which the consolidated return is to be filed must consent to the filing.
b. Once a consolidated return is filed, the controlled group must continue to file consolidated returns unless it obtains permission from the IRS to do otherwise.
c. The filing of consolidated returns is available to brother-sister corporations.
d. By filing a consolidated return, the corporations in the group can eliminate intercompany profits and losses.

The correct answer is (c). *(CMA 690 3-18)*
REQUIRED: The incorrect statement concerning the filing of consolidated tax returns.
DISCUSSION: Corporations must be members of an affiliated group to file a consolidated tax return. An affiliated group consists of one or more chains of includable corporations that are connected through stock ownership with a common parent corporation. There is an 80% of voting power and 80% of value ownership requirement. Only parent-subsidiary affiliated groups will meet this requirement of having a common parent corporation. Brother-sister corporations do not have a common parent and therefore cannot file a consolidated tax return.
Answers (a), (b), and (d) are incorrect because they are correct statements concerning the filing of consolidated tax returns.

Module 19.6: Consolidated Tax Returns

63. Consolidated returns may be filed

a. Either by parent-subsidiary corporations or by brother-sister corporations.
b. Only by corporations that formally request advance permission from the IRS.
c. Only by parent-subsidiary affiliated groups.
d. Only by corporations that issue their financial statements on a consolidated basis.

The correct answer is (c). *(CPA 588 Q-28)*
REQUIRED: The requirement for corporations to file consolidated tax returns.
DISCUSSION: Corporations must be members of an affiliated group to file a consolidated tax return (Sec. 1501). An affiliated group consists of one or more chains of includable corporations that are connected through stock ownership with a common parent corporation. There is an 80% ownership requirement. Only parent-subsidiary affiliated groups will meet this requirement of having a common parent corporation.
Answer (a) is incorrect because brother-sister corporations exist if two corporations are owned by five or fewer persons with certain stock ownership requirements [Sec. 1563(a)]. They do not have a common parent corporation; it may be one or more individuals who own the stock. Answer (b) is incorrect because there is no requirement that formal advance permission be obtained from the IRS. Answer (d) is incorrect because corporations are not required to issue financial statements on a consolidated basis in order to file tax returns on a consolidated basis.

64. A group of corporations (A, B, C, D, and E) all having only one class of stock have the following ownership and classification:

Corp. A - Domestic corporation which owns 85% of B, 20% of C, and 100% of E's outstanding stock.
Corp. B - Domestic corporation which owns 70% of C and 100% of D's outstanding stock.
Corp. C - Domestic corporation which owns 10% of A's stock.
Corp. D - B's Foreign Sales Corporation (FSC).
Corp. E - Foreign corporation which owns 10% of C and 5% of B's stock.

Which are members of an affiliated group?

a. A and B.
b. B, C, and D.
c. A, B, C, D, and E.
d. A, B, and C.

The correct answer is (d). *(SPE 1078 III-51)*
REQUIRED: The corporations that are members of an affiliated group.
DISCUSSION: Under Sec. 1504(a), an affiliated group means one or more chains of includable corporations connected through stock ownership with a common parent corporation if at least 80% of the total voting power and value is owned directly by one or more of the other corporations, and if the common parent corporation owns directly at least 80% of the total voting power and value of at least one of the other corporations. Although Corporations D and E are wholly owned, they are not members of the affiliated group because foreign corporations (which include FSCs) are excluded from the definition of includable corporations by Sec. 1504(b).
Corporation A is the common parent because it owns 85% of Corporation B directly, and Corporation A combined with Corporation B owns 90% of Corporation C. Thus, Corporations A, B, and C are members of an affiliated group.

65. Parent Corporation and Subsidiary Corporation file consolidated returns on a calendar-year basis. In January 1990, Subsidiary sold land, which it had used in its operations, to Parent for $75,000. Immediately before this sale, Subsidiary's basis for the land was $45,000. Parent held the land primarily for sale to customers in the ordinary course of business. In July 1991, Parent sold the land to Dubin, an unrelated individual, for $90,000. In determining the consolidated Sec. 1231 net gain for 1991, how much should Subsidiary take into account as a result of the 1990 sale of the land from Subsidiary to Parent?

a. $45,000.
b. $30,000.
c. $22,500.
d. $15,000.

The correct answer is (b). *(CPA 1186 Q-48)*
REQUIRED: The amount and character of gain to be reported in the consolidated return for 1991.
DISCUSSION: The regulations under Sec. 1502 provide most of the rules for reporting income in a consolidated return. Under Reg. 1.1502-13, a sale or exchange of property between members of the consolidated group is a "deferred intercompany transaction." In the case of non-depreciable property (e.g., land) not sold on the installment basis, the gain is not reported until the property is sold outside the group, i.e., in 1991. Therefore, Subsidiary should report no income in the consolidated return for 1990 as a result of the sale.
For 1991, however, Subsidiary should recognize the full amount of the deferred intercompany gain of $30,000 ($75,000 − $45,000). Parent should also recognize gain of $15,000 ($90,000 − $75,000).

Module 19.6: Consolidated Tax Returns

66. In the consolidated income tax return of a corporation and its wholly-owned subsidiary, what percentage of cash dividends paid by the subsidiary to the parent is tax-free?

a. 0%.
b. 70%.
c. 80%.
d. 100%.

The correct answer is (d). *(CPA 590 Q-36)*
REQUIRED: The percentage of cash dividends paid by a subsidiary corporation that is tax-free to its parent corporation.
DISCUSSION: Reg. 1.1502-14(a) states that a dividend distributed by one member of a group filing a consolidated tax return to another member of that group is eliminated. The recipient of the dividend makes an adjustment to its separate taxable income that eliminates the dividend from the affiliated group's consolidated taxable income. This elimination process is to be distinguished from the dividends-received deduction allowed by Sec. 243. Under that section, a domestic corporation is allowed to deduct a percentage of the dividends received from another domestic corporation. The dividends-received deduction does not apply to dividends received from other group members for affiliated groups that file a consolidated tax return.

67. Able Corporation and Baker Corporation file a consolidated return on a calendar-year basis. In 1990, Able sold land to Baker for its fair market value of $50,000. At the date of sale, Able had an adjusted basis in the land of $35,000 and had held the land for several years as an investment. Baker held the land primarily for sale to its customers in the ordinary course of its business and sold it to a customer in early 1991 for $60,000.

As a result of the sale of the land in 1991, the corporations should report on their consolidated return

a. $10,000 ordinary gain.
b. $25,000 ordinary gain.
c. $25,000 long-term capital gain.
d. $15,000 long-term capital gain and $10,000 ordinary gain.

The correct answer is (d). *(CPA 1172 P-5)*
REQUIRED: The amount and character of gain to be reported on the consolidated return.
DISCUSSION: Under Reg. 1.1502-13, a sale or exchange of property between members of an affiliated group is a "deferred intercompany transaction." In the case of nondepreciable property (e.g., land) not sold on the installment basis, the gain is not reported until the property is sold outside the group, i.e., in 1991. The character of the deferred gain on an intercompany transaction is determined at the time of the deferred intercompany transaction as if it had not been incurred by a consolidated member; i.e., Able's gain is long-term capital gain. Baker's gain is ordinary since it held the land primarily for sale to its customers.

	Able	Baker
Sales price	$50,000	$60,000
Adjusted basis	(35,000)	(50,000)
Gain	$15,000	$10,000

68. Consolidated tax returns must be filed by all members of an affiliated group once they have made the appropriate election.

The correct answer is (T). *(Publisher)*
DISCUSSION: The election to file a consolidated tax return must be made with the consent of every includable corporation in an affiliated group (Sec. 1501). Once the election is filed, all members must continue to file the consolidated return unless permission is obtained from the IRS to file separately [Reg. 1.1502-75(a)(2)].

19.7 Multiple Corporations

69. Which one of the following statements about a controlled group of corporations is not correct?

a. Any controlled group may elect to file consolidated federal income tax returns.
b. A parent corporation and its 80%-owned subsidiary make up a controlled group.
c. All members of a controlled group need not use the parent's tax year.
d. Members of a controlled group are entitled to only one accumulated earnings tax credit.

The correct answer is (a). *(CMA 686 3-22)*
REQUIRED: The false statement concerning a controlled group of corporations.
DISCUSSION: Under Sec. 1563(a), a controlled group of corporations may be a parent-subsidiary controlled group, a brother-sister controlled group, or a combined group. Either a parent-subsidiary controlled group or the parent-subsidiary portion of a combined group may file a consolidated tax return because there is a common parent corporation and the includable corporations are all 80% owned. However, a brother-sister controlled group exists when two or more corporations are owned by five or fewer persons who own at least 80% of the voting stock or 80% of the value of the outstanding stock. There is no common parent corporation, so a consolidated tax return could not be filed. The affiliated group definition requires ownership of 80% of the voting stock and 80% of the value of the controlled corporation. The controlled group definition is an "or" test, and some controlled groups may meet one of the tests, but not both of the tests and not be able to file a consolidated return.

Answer (b) is incorrect because it describes a parent-subsidiary controlled group. Answer (c) is incorrect because there is no requirement that members of a controlled group use the parent's tax year. Answer (d) is incorrect because one of the purposes of ascertaining whether a controlled group exists is to allocate to the group the accumulated earnings tax credit, the $40,000 alternative minimum tax exemption, the graduated rates, etc.

70. The only class of outstanding stock of Corporations L, M, N, O, and P is owned by the following unrelated individuals:

Individual	L	M	N	O	P
G	30%	40%	50%	50%	5%
H	10%	5%	10%	20%	5%
I	30%	40%	30%	10%	5%
J	30%	15%	10%	20%	5%
K	-0-	-0-	-0-	-0-	5%

Which of the following corporations are members of a brother-sister controlled group?

a. Only L, M, N, and O.
b. Only M, N, O, and P.
c. Only L, M, O, and P.
d. Only L, M, and N.

The correct answer is (a). *(SPE 1080 III-80)*
REQUIRED: The corporations that are members of a brother-sister controlled group.
DISCUSSION: The significance of a controlled group is that members are not allowed many of the benefits of separate corporations; e.g., all members must share the graduated tax rates, accumulated earnings credit, 100% general business tax credit offset, etc., as one corporation. Under Sec. 1563(a), a brother-sister controlled group means two or more corporations of which five or fewer persons who are individuals, estates, or trusts own at least 80% of the voting power or value of each corporation, and more than 50% of the voting power or value of the stock of each corporation counting only identical ownership interests (i.e., the smallest amount owned by each person in any of the corporations is all that is counted in the other corporations for the 50% test).

Individual K's ownership is not counted because (s)he does not own stock in each corporation. Corporation P does not pass the 80% test (see below) and so is not included in the 50% test. The 50% test is met for L, M, N, and O.

Total Percent of Each Corporation Owned		Identical Percent Owned in Each of L, M, N, O	
Corporation L	100%	Individual G	30%
Corporation M	100%	Individual H	5%
Corporation N	100%	Individual I	10%
Corporation O	100%	Individual J	10%
Corporation P	20%	Total	55%

Module 19.7: Multiple Corporations

71. The only class of outstanding stock of Corporations N, O, P, Q, and R is owned by the following unrelated individuals:

Individuals	Corporations/Percent of Stock Owned				
	N	O	P	Q	R
V	40%	40%	40%	40%	40%
W	20%	-0-	10%	20%	30%
X	10%	10%	20%	20%	10%
Y	30%	-0-	30%	10%	-0-
Z	-0-	50%	-0-	10%	-0-

Which corporations are members of a brother-sister controlled group?

a. N and O.
b. N, P, and Q.
c. N, O, P, and Q.
d. N, O, P, Q, and R.

The correct answer is (b). *(SPE 1081 III-49)*
REQUIRED: The corporations that are members of a brother-sister controlled group.
DISCUSSION: Under Sec. 1563(a), a brother-sister controlled group exists when two or more corporations are owned by five or fewer persons who own at least 80% of the voting power or value of each corporation, and more than 50% of the voting power or value of all stock is owned by the group taking into account only the stock ownership of each person that is identical with respect to each corporation.

Each person whose ownership is counted in the 80% test must own stock in each corporation in the controlled group. Only Corporations N, P, and Q meet both tests using shareholders V, W, X, and Y.

Total Percent of Each Corporation Owned		Identical Percent Owned in Each of N,P,Q	
Corporation N	100%	Individual V	40%
Corporation P	100%	Individual W	10%
Corporation Q	90%	Individual X	10%
		Individual Y	10%
		Total	70%

72. A controlled group of corporations that has filed an apportionment plan to divide the taxable income brackets

a. Must divide them equally.
b. Must divide them in accordance with the taxable income of each corporation.
c. May have more than one apportionable $50,000 amount in their lowest taxable income bracket.
d. May adopt an unequal apportionment plan.

The correct answer is (d). *(SPE 986 III-43)*
REQUIRED: The correct statement about the apportionment of the taxable income brackets.
DISCUSSION: Under Sec. 1561(a), component members of a controlled group of corporations are entitled to the taxable income brackets of Sec. 11 as if they were one corporation. The tax brackets are allocated equally unless the members agree otherwise. The members may adopt an unequal apportionment plan.

73. Corporations X, Y, and Z are component members of a controlled group of corporations on December 31, 1991. For the taxable year ending December 31, 1991, they allocate the taxable income brackets under an apportionment plan as follows:

Corporation X	1/4 of each tax bracket
Corporation Y	1/2 of each tax bracket
Corporation Z	1/4 of each tax bracket

Corporation Y has taxable income of $80,000 for 1991. What is Corporation Y's income tax liability?

a. $8,575.
b. $15,450.
c. $17,075.
d. $21,325.

The correct answer is (d). *(SPE 1079 III-73)*
REQUIRED: The 1991 income tax liability of a member of a controlled group.
DISCUSSION: Under Sec. 1561(a)(1), component members of a controlled group of corporations are limited to using the taxable income brackets in Sec. 11 as if they were one corporation. Unless the members agree otherwise, the tax brackets are allocated equally. Under the apportionment plan, Y is entitled to 50% of each tax bracket. Y's income tax is

Tax Brackets	50%	Tax
1st $50,000	$25,000 x 15%	$ 3,750
Next $25,000	12,500 x 25%	3,125
Remainder	42,500 x 34%	14,450
		$21,325

Note that, although each tax bracket is allocated in the same manner here, different allocations would be permitted. Note that we do not know the total taxable income of the controlled group. Some of the income that is taxed at the 34% marginal tax rate may be taxed at a 39% rate because of the additional 5% tax imposed by Sec. 11(b). The additional 5% tax will not apply unless the total taxable income of the controlled group exceeds $100,000.

556   Module 19.7: Multiple Corporations

74. A calendar-year corporation that is a member of a controlled group has taxable income for the 1991 return of $45,000. Its apportionment of each of the taxable income brackets is $15,000. Compute its tax using the tax table below:

Taxable Income Over	But Not Over	The tax is	Of the Amount Over
$ 0	$50,000	15%	$ 0
50,000	75,000	$ 7,500 + 25%	50,000
75,000		$13,750 + 34%	75,000

a. $8,250.
b. $11,100.
c. $12,000.
d. $13,000.

The correct answer is (b). *(SPE 987 III-73)*
REQUIRED: The 1991 income tax of a member of a controlled group.
DISCUSSION: Sec. 1561(a)(1) requires the income tax brackets to be apportioned among the members of a controlled group. The members can elect an apportionment schedule of their choice or in default the brackets will be prorated equally among the members.
The corporation's 1991 tax will be

$15,000 x 15% = $ 2,250
15,000 x 25% = 3,750
15,000 x 34% = 5,100
                $11,100

Note that we do not know the total taxable income of the controlled group. Some of the income that is taxed at the 34% marginal tax rate may be taxed at a 39% rate because of the additional 5% tax imposed by Sec. 11(b). The additional 5% tax will not apply unless the total taxable income of the controlled group exceeds $100,000.

75. For a domestic corporation in 1991, the general business tax credit is limited to the lesser of its net income tax, with certain adjustments for other credits, over the greater of its tentative minimum tax for the year or 25% of its net regular tax liability for the year that exceeds $25,000. How does a controlled group of corporations treat the $25,000?

a. Each corporation is allowed $25,000.
b. The $25,000 is divided equally among the corporations.
c. The $25,000 is divided among the corporations in any manner they choose.
d. The $25,000 is divided according to each corporation's tax liability.

The correct answer is (c). *(SPE 984 III-62)*
REQUIRED: The correct method of apportionment of the $25,000 amount in determining the general business tax credit with respect to a controlled group.
DISCUSSION: Sec. 38(c)(2)(B) provides that, for members of a controlled group, the $25,000 amount must be apportioned among the members as the regulations provide. The regulations allow the members to do so in any manner they choose. They need to agree on an apportionment plan.
Answer (a) is incorrect because the controlled group is limited to the $25,000 in total. Answers (b) and (d) are incorrect because the members may divide the $25,000 as they choose, but if they do not agree, it is divided equally among them.

76. Which one of the following methods is acceptable to determine an arm's length price on the sale of tangible property among a group of controlled entities (Sec. 482)?

a. Relative sales-value method.
b. Resale price method.
c. Direct costing method.
d. Standard cost method.

The correct answer is (b). *(CMA 1289 3-16)*
REQUIRED: The acceptable method to determine an arm's length price on the sale of tangible property among a group of controlled entities.
DISCUSSION: Where one member of a group of controlled entities sells tangible property to another member of the group at other than an arm's length price, an allocation must be made between the buyer and the seller to reflect an arm's length price for such sale. An arm's length price is the price that an unrelated party would have paid for the property under the same circumstances. Reg. 1.482-2(e) lists three methods of determining an arm's length price and the standards for applying each method. These methods are the comparable uncontrolled price method, the resale price method, and the cost plus method.
Answers (a), (c), and (d) are incorrect because they are not listed as allowable methods for determining an arm's length price.

77. Mr. T owns 100% of the single classes of outstanding stock of Corporations A and B. Corporation A owns 90% of the single class of outstanding voting stock of Corporation Z. Corporations A, B, and Z are members of a controlled group of corporations.

The correct answer is (T). *(SPE 1080 III-17)*
DISCUSSION: Under Sec. 1563(a), Corporations A, B, and Z are a combined group because A and B are a brother-sister controlled group and A and Z are a parent-subsidiary controlled group. Mr. T's 100% ownership of A and B satisfies the 80% and 50% common ownership tests for a brother-sister controlled group. A's 90% ownership satisfies the 80% required ownership for a parent-subsidiary controlled group.

78. Corporation D owns 80% of Corporation H's single class of stock. Corporations D and H are brother-sister corporations.

The correct answer is (F). *(SPE 1081 III-16)*
DISCUSSION: Under Sec. 1563(a)(1), Corporations D and H are members of a parent-subsidiary controlled group, not a brother-sister controlled group.

79. Corporations A, B, and C are taxable domestic corporations that each have a single class of stock outstanding. Corporation A owns 90% of the stock of Corporation B. Corporation B owns 80% of the stock of Corporation C. Corporations A, B, and C form a controlled group of corporations.

The correct answer is (T). *(SPE 984 III-13)*
DISCUSSION: A parent-subsidiary controlled group consists of at least two corporations. One corporation (the parent) must directly own 80% or more of the voting power or 80% or more of the value of a second corporation (a subsidiary) [Sec. 1563(a)(1)]. Other corporations are also included in the group if the parent, subsidiary, and other group members together directly own sufficient stock (80%) in the corporations. Corporation A owns 90% of Corporation B, thus making A and B a parent-subsidiary group. Since Corporation B owns 80% of Corporation C, C is also a member of the controlled group.

80. In 1991 tax rate for corporations with taxable income of $0 to $50,000 is 15%. Two calendar year corporations, which are members of the same controlled group, each have $50,000 of taxable income in 1991. The tax that each of the corporations would report would be $7,500.

The correct answer is (F). *(SPE 987 III-7)*
DISCUSSION: The members of a controlled group may divide the tax brackets as they choose under 1561(a). Only in the absence of an apportionment schedule or if a specific equal apportionment election is made for the first bracket are the brackets divided equally among the group members. In either case, each corporation would be limited to $25,000 taxed at a 15% rate if the first tax bracket was divided equally.

81. Members of a controlled group of corporations must divide the $40,000 exemption allowed for the alternative minimum tax among themselves in proportion to their respective regular tax amounts.

The correct answer is (F). *(SPE 984 III-7)*
DISCUSSION: Under Sec. 1561(a), the members of a controlled group may divide the $40,000 alternative minimum tax exemption among themselves in any manner they choose. If they do not so agree, it is divided equally.

19.8 Accumulated Earnings Tax

82. The accumulated earnings tax does not apply to

   a. Corporations that have more than 100 stockholders.
   b. Personal holding companies.
   c. Corporations filing consolidated returns.
   d. Corporations that have more than one class of stock.

The correct answer is (b). *(CPA 588 Q-32)*
REQUIRED: The type of corporation to which the accumulated earnings tax is not applicable.
DISCUSSION: The accumulated earnings tax is imposed by Sec. 531 on unreasonably large accumulations of earnings in a corporation. The purpose of the tax is to require the shareholders to include the earnings in their income, usually as dividends. Under Sec. 532, the accumulated earnings tax does not apply to personal holding companies since they are already subject to a penalty tax on undistributed income.
Answers (a), (c), and (d) are incorrect because the tax applies to each.

Module 19.8: Accumulated Earnings Tax

83. The accumulated earnings tax

a. Can be avoided by sufficient dividend distributions.
b. Is 50% of accumulated taxable income.
c. Applies to both corporations and partnerships.
d. Only applies to controlled and affiliated corporate groups.

The correct answer is (a). *(Publisher)*
REQUIRED: The correct statement concerning the accumulated earnings tax.
DISCUSSION: The accumulated earnings tax is imposed by Sec. 531 on unreasonably large accumulations of earnings in a corporation. If the corporation pays out sufficient dividends, it will not have unreasonably large accumulations of earnings and will not be subject to the tax.
Answer (b) is incorrect because the tax is 28% of the accumulated taxable income. Answer (c) is incorrect because the accumulated earnings tax applies only to corporations, not to partnerships. Answer (d) is incorrect because the accumulated earnings tax can apply to any corporation (not subject to the personal holding company tax) which has unreasonably large accumulated earnings.

84. In determining whether a corporation is subject to the accumulated earnings tax, which of the following items is not a subtraction in arriving at accumulated taxable income?

a. Federal income tax.
b. Capital loss carryback.
c. Dividends-paid deduction.
d. Accumulated earnings credit.

The correct answer is (b). *(CPA 580 Q-35)*
REQUIRED: The item that does not reduce accumulated taxable income.
DISCUSSION: The accumulated earnings tax is applied to accumulated taxable income, defined in Sec. 535(a) as taxable income, subject to certain adjustments. Capital loss carrybacks and carryovers are not allowed. Instead, capital losses are deductible in full in the year incurred (but must be reduced by prior net capital gain deductions).
Answer (a) is incorrect because federal income taxes are deducted as an adjustment to taxable income. Answers (c) and (d) are incorrect because the dividends-paid deduction and the accumulated earnings credit are subtracted from adjusted taxable income.

85. An item not subtracted in determining accumulated taxable income for the accumulated earnings tax is

a. Dividends paid within 2½ months after the end of the corporate tax year.
b. Net capital losses.
c. Net long-term capital gains reduced by the attributable taxes.
d. A net operating loss deduction from a prior year.

The correct answer is (d). *(CMA 1284 3-2)*
REQUIRED: The item that does not reduce accumulated taxable income.
DISCUSSION: The accumulated earnings tax is applied to the accumulated taxable income, defined in Sec. 535(a) as taxable income, subject to certain adjustments. Net operating losses are not allowed.
Answer (a) is incorrect because dividends paid (including those declared and then paid within 2½ months of year-end) reduce adjusted taxable income to compute accumulated taxable income. Answer (b) is incorrect because net capital losses are deductible in full for the accumulated earnings tax. Answer (c) is incorrect because there is allowed as a deduction the net long-term capital gain reduced by taxes attributable to such net capital gain.

86. The minimum accumulated earnings credit in 1991 is

a. $150,000 for all corporations.
b. $150,000 for nonservice corporations only.
c. $250,000 for all corporations.
d. $250,000 for nonservice corporations only.

The correct answer is (d). *(CPA 583 Q-42)*
REQUIRED: The amount of the minimum accumulated earnings credit.
DISCUSSION: The accumulated earnings credit is defined as the increase in the reasonable needs of a business during the tax year. Without showing a reason for the accumulation, the minimum accumulated earnings credit is $250,000 for nonservice corporations [Sec. 535(c)(2)]. The credit is $150,000 for certain service corporations such as those in the fields of health, law, engineering, architecture, accounting, actuarial science, performing arts, or consulting.

Module 19.8: Accumulated Earnings Tax

87. Which of the following would not be considered reasonable needs of a business in determining the accumulated earnings tax?

a. Specific plans to update factory machinery.
b. Definite long-range commitment to purchase raw materials.
c. A feasible long-range plan to expand factory production.
d. Specific and feasible plan to declare a stock dividend to all shareholders.

The correct answer is (d). *(SPE 1080 III-49)*
REQUIRED: The item not considered as meeting the reasonable needs of a business with regard to the accumulated earnings tax.
DISCUSSION: For a corporation to justify its accumulation of earnings, there must be evidence that the future needs of the business will require such an accumulation and that the corporation has specific and feasible plans for the use of the accumulation. A specific plan to declare a stock dividend to all shareholders will not qualify as the reasonable needs of a business since such dividends usually do not involve a use of funds. The accumulated earnings tax was imposed to prevent corporations from accumulating excess earnings and not distributing them as taxable dividends.
Answers (a), (b), and (c) are incorrect because they are specifically listed as reasonable grounds for accumulating earnings in Reg. 1.537-2.

88. To avoid a tax on unreasonably accumulated earnings, a corporation may show that earnings and profits are being retained for

a. Loans to shareholders.
b. Protection against unrealistic business hazards.
c. Retirement of bona fide business indebtedness.
d. Investments in properties unrelated to the business activities of the corporation.

The correct answer is (c). *(CMA 685 3-15)*
REQUIRED: The item considered as meeting the reasonable needs of a business with regard to the accumulated earnings tax.
DISCUSSION: For a corporation to justify its accumulation of earnings, there must be evidence that the future needs of the business will require such an accumulation and that the corporation has specific and feasible plans for the use of the accumulation. The retirement of bona fide business indebtedness is considered to be a future need of the business.
Answers (a), (b), and (d) are incorrect because they are not considered to be future needs of the business but represent actions taken by the corporation which are likely to trigger imposition of the accumulated earnings tax.

89. Which of the following might create a potential liability for the accumulated earnings tax?

a. Manufacturing corporation has retained earnings of $200,000.
b. Corporation is in the process of expanding its facilities.
c. Corporation makes regular and substantial distributions to its shareholders.
d. Corporation is planning to redeem all the shares of one of its current shareholders.

The correct answer is (d). *(SPE 987 III-52)*
REQUIRED: The item most likely to cause a corporation to be subject to the accumulated earnings tax.
DISCUSSION: For a corporation to justify its accumulation of earnings, there must be evidence that the future needs of the business will require such an accumulation and that the corporation has specific and feasible plans for the use of the accumulation. A plan to redeem the shares of a shareholder will not qualify as the reasonable needs of a business, because the tax was created to prevent earnings accumulation.
Answer (a) is incorrect because a manufacturing corporation has a minimum accumulated earnings credit of $250,000. Answer (b) is incorrect because expansion of facilities is reasonable grounds to accumulate earnings. Answer (c) is incorrect because a corporation that makes regular and substantial distributions to its shareholders is not likely to unreasonably accumulate earnings. Answer (d) is correct only if the plan involves a deceased shareholder whose stock is included in his gross estate [Sec. 537(a)(2)].

90. Daystar Corp., which is not a mere holding or investment company, derives its income from retail sales. Daystar had accumulated earnings and profits of $145,000 at December 31, 1990. For the year ended December 31, 1991, it had earnings and profits of $115,000 and a dividends-paid deduction of $15,000. No throwback distributions have been made. It has been determined that $20,000 of the current and accumulated earnings and profits for 1991 is required for the reasonable needs of the business. How much is the allowable accumulated earnings credit at December 31, 1991?

- a. $105,000.
- b. $125,000.
- c. $150,000.
- d. $250,000.

The correct answer is (a). *(CPA 582 Q-44)*
REQUIRED: The allowable accumulated earnings credit.
DISCUSSION: The accumulated earnings credit of Sec. 535(c) is the greater of (1) the difference between $250,000 and the accumulated earnings and profits at the end of the prior year, or (2) the current earnings and profits retained for the reasonable needs of the business minus the long-term capital gain adjustments of the current year. The dividends-paid deduction is used to compute the accumulated taxable income, but not the accumulated earnings credit.

The difference between $250,000 and Daystar's accumulated earnings and profits at the end of the prior year ($145,000) is $105,000. Since this is greater than the $20,000 of reasonable needs of the business, the available accumulated earnings credit is $105,000. $100,000 ($115,000 current E&P – $15,000 dividends-paid deduction) will be used in 1991 and $5,000 will be available in following years.

91. An amount necessary to redeem the corporation's stock included in a deceased stockholder's gross estate may be used in determining the reasonable needs of a business.

The correct answer is (T). *(SPE 1081 III-6)*
DISCUSSION: Under Sec. 537(a)(2), the reasonable needs of the business include the amount needed to redeem stock included in the gross estate of a decedent stockholder.

92. In determining if a corporation has accumulated earnings and profits beyond its reasonable needs, the listed and readily marketable securities owned by the corporation and purchased out of its earnings and profits are to be valued at net liquidation value, not at cost.

The correct answer is (T). *(SPE 1079 III-37)*
DISCUSSION: The Supreme Court in Ivan Allen Co. (422 U.S. 617, 1975) held that for accumulated earnings tax purposes, the value of appreciated securities should be measured by their net liquidation value, or their fair market value less the cost of conversion into cash.

93. Corporation A is a law firm with accumulated retained earnings of $240,000. A has determined that it has no plans for expansion or other business needs for the earnings. A may be subject to the accumulated earnings tax.

The correct answer is (T). *(SPE 986 III-7)*
DISCUSSION: Under Sec. 535(c)(2)(B), certain service corporations are limited to a $150,000 minimum accumulated earnings credit. Law is one of the functions specifically listed in this provision. Since the law firm has accumulated earnings in excess of its minimum credit with no business plans for the funds, it may be subject to the tax.

94. The Bardahl formula determines the amount of earnings that satisfies working capital needs by estimating a corporation's future expenses using estimated future data.

The correct answer is (F). *(Publisher)*
DISCUSSION: The Bardahl formula is used to determine the reasonable accumulation of earnings to satisfy working capital needs based on historical data. The formula uses the average operating cycle from historical data to estimate how much is necessary to operate on the average in the future.

Module 19.9: Personal Holding Company Tax   561

19.9 Personal Holding Company Tax

95. The personal holding company tax

a. Qualifies as a tax credit that may be used by partners or stockholders to reduce their individual income taxes.
b. May be imposed on both corporations and partnerships.
c. Should be self-assessed by filing a separate schedule with the regular tax return.
d. May be imposed regardless of the number of equal stockholders in a corporation.

The correct answer is (c). *(CPA 588 Q-31)*
REQUIRED: The true statement regarding the personal holding company tax.
DISCUSSION: The personal holding company tax should be self-assessed by a corporation by filing Schedule PH along with its regular Form 1120 tax return.
Answers (a) and (b) are incorrect because the personal holding company tax does not apply to partnerships. Answer (a) is also incorrect because no credit is available for personal holding company taxes paid. Answer (d) is incorrect because the personal holding company tax may be imposed only if more than 50% of the value of a corporation's stock is owned by five or fewer individuals.

96. When passive investment income is involved, the personal holding company tax may be imposed

a. On both partnerships and corporations.
b. On companies whose gross income arises solely from rentals, if the lessors render no services to the lessees.
c. If more than 50% of the company is owned by five or fewer individuals.
d. On small business investment companies licensed by the Small Business Administration.

The correct answer is (c). *(CPA 585 Q-44)*
REQUIRED: The correct statement about the personal holding company tax.
DISCUSSION: The personal holding company tax is imposed by Sec. 541 on undistributed income of a personal holding company. A personal holding company is a corporation which is owned 50% or more by five or fewer shareholders any time during the last half of the year, and which has 60% of its income as personal holding company income (generally passive income).
Answer (a) is incorrect because the personal holding company tax applies only to corporations. Answer (b) is incorrect because rents are excluded from personal holding company income if they constitute more than 50% of the corporation's adjusted ordinary gross income and there is only a limited amount of other personal holding company income. Answer (d) is incorrect because small business investment companies are specifically excluded by Sec. 542(c) from being personal holding companies.

97. Which of the following types of income is not considered personal holding company income?

a. Dividends.
b. Interest.
c. Royalties.
d. Personal services income.

The correct answer is (d). *(SPE 1080 III-52)*
REQUIRED: The type of income that is not personal holding company income.
DISCUSSION: The personal holding company tax is imposed by Sec. 541 on undistributed income of a personal holding company. A personal holding company is a corporation which is owned 50% or more by five or fewer shareholders any time during the last half of the year, and which has 60% of its income as personal holding company income. Under Sec. 543(a), personal holding company income is generally passive income such as dividends, interest, and royalties. Personal services income is generally not included in the definition of personal holding company income.
Note that personal services income is included in the personal holding company income definition only if earned by a 25% or more stockholder from a personal service contract and either some person other than the corporation has the right to designate the individual who is to perform the services or the individual who is to perform the services is designated by name or description in the contract.

Module 19.9: Personal Holding Company Tax

98. Benson, a singer, owns 100% of the outstanding capital stock of Lund Corporation. Lund contracted with Benson, specifying that Benson was to perform personal services for Magda Productions, Inc., in consideration of which Benson was to receive $50,000 a year from Lund. Lund contracted with Magda, specifying that Benson was to perform personal services for Magda, in consideration of which Magda was to pay Lund $1,000,000 a year. Personal holding company income will be attributable to

   a. Benson only.
   b. Lund only.
   c. Magda only.
   d. All three contracting parties.

The correct answer is (b). *(CPA 1188 Q-29)*
REQUIRED: The corporation the personal holding company income will be attributed to.
DISCUSSION: Sec. 543(a)(7) includes amounts received by corporations under personal service contracts involving a 25% or more shareholder as personal service company income provided the contract designates specifically that only the shareholder will provide the services. As such, Lund has personal service income of $1,000,000 a year.
Answer (a) is incorrect because Benson is an individual, and personal holding company income only applies to corporations. Answer (c) is incorrect because Magda is paying the income, not receiving it. Answer (d) is incorrect because answers (a) and (c) are incorrect.

99. Ati Corporation has two stockholders. Ati derives all of its income from investments in stocks and securities, and it regularly distributes 51% of its taxable income as dividends to its stockholders. Ati is a

   a. Personal holding company.
   b. Regulated investment company.
   c. Corporation subject to the accumulated earnings tax.
   d. Corporation subject to tax only on income not distributed to stockholders.

The correct answer is (a). *(CPA 1189 Q-49)*
REQUIRED: The correct term for a corporation having only two shareholders and deriving its income solely from investments in stock and securities.
DISCUSSION: Under Sec. 542, a corporation is a personal holding company if at least 60% of its adjusted gross income for the year is "personal holding company income" and at any time during the last half of the taxable year more than 50% of the value of its outstanding stock is owned by not more than five individuals. "Personal holding company income," under Sec. 543, includes income received from stocks and securities.
Answer (b) is incorrect because a regulated investment company must be registered under the Investment Company Act of 1940 or file an election to be a regulated investment company. Answer (c) is incorrect because personal holding companies are not subject to the accumulated earnings tax. Answer (d) is incorrect because a personal holding company is subject to the regular tax on corporate income as well as a 28% tax on its undistributed personal holding company income.

100. Which of the following rates is used to compute the personal holding company tax for tax years beginning in 1991?

   a. 28%.
   b. 38.5%.
   c. 46%.
   d. 50%.

The correct answer is (a). *(SPE 1080 III-51)*
REQUIRED: The personal holding company tax rate in 1991.
DISCUSSION: Under Sec. 541 for 1991, the personal holding company tax is equal to 28% of the undistributed personal holding company income. The application of the tax is straightforward. The difficulties arise in determining whether a corporation is a personal holding company and the amount of undistributed personal holding company income.

101. Alpha Properties is owned by three shareholders. During 1991, Alpha reported the following:

Rental income	$200,000
Dividend income	20,000
Depreciation expense	40,000
Property taxes	10,000
Interest expense on mortgage on rental property	50,000

Alpha's adjusted ordinary gross income (AOGI) and personal holding company income (PHCI) are

a. AOGI, $120,000; PHCI, $20,000.
b. AOGI, $220,000; PHCI, $120,000.
c. AOGI, $120,000; PHCI, $120,000.
d. AOGI, $220,000; PHCI, $220,000.

The correct answer is (a). *(Publisher)*
REQUIRED: The adjusted ordinary gross income and personal holding company income.
DISCUSSION: Sec. 543(b) defines ordinary gross income as gross income less capital gains and Sec. 1231 gains. Ordinary gross income is further reduced by a number of items, including depreciation, property taxes, and interest allocable to rental property, to arrive at adjusted ordinary gross income. Alpha has gross income of $220,000. Adjusted ordinary gross income is $120,000 ($220,000 gross income – $100,000 rental expenses).

Personal holding company income (PHCI) includes dividends, interest, annuities, royalties, rents, and similar passive income [Sec. 543(a)]. Rents are excluded, however, if they constitute more than 50% of the corporation's adjusted ordinary gross income and if PHCI other than rents (reduced by dividend distributions) is not in excess of 10% of ordinary gross income. For this purpose, rents are rental income minus depreciation, property taxes, and allocable interest. Alpha's PHC rent is $100,000 ($200,000 rental income – $100,000 depreciation, property taxes, and interest). Since the rent is more than 50% of adjusted ordinary gross income ($220,000) and the other PHCI ($20,000) is less than 10% of ordinary gross income (10% x $220,000 = $22,000), the rent will not be included as PHCI. Therefore, only dividend income of $20,000 is PHCI, and Alpha is not a personal holding company.

102. Kee Holding Corp. has 80 unrelated equal stockholders. For the year ended December 31, 1991, Kee's income comprised the following:

Net rental income	$ 1,000
Commissions earned on sales of franchises	3,000
Dividends from taxable domestic corporations	90,000

Deductible expenses for 1991 totaled $10,000. Kee paid no dividends for the past 3 years. Kee's liability for personal holding company tax for 1991 will be based on

a. $12,000.
b. $11,000.
c. $9,000.
d. $0.

The correct answer is (d). *(CPA 587 Q-44)*
REQUIRED: The amount of undistributed personal holding company income.
DISCUSSION: To be defined as a personal holding company under Sec. 542, more than 50% in value of the outstanding stock must be owned during the last half of the taxable year, either directly or indirectly, by not more than five individuals. Since Kee Holding Corporation is owned by 80 unrelated stockholders, each of whom owns an equal amount of shares, any five shareholders own only 6.25% of the corporation. Since five or fewer stockholders do not own more than 50% of the corporation, it is not a personal holding company, there is no undistributed personal holding company income, and there is no personal holding company tax.

19.10 S Corporation Election

103. What is the maximum number of stockholders allowable for eligibility as an S corporation?

a. 5.
b. 15.
c. 25.
d. 35.

The correct answer is (d). *(CPA 1185 Q-41)*
REQUIRED: The maximum number of shareholders allowable for eligibility as an S corporation.
DISCUSSION: Under Sec. 1361(b), one of the requirements of an S corporation is that it have no more than 35 shareholders. Note: Husbands and wives are counted as a single shareholder for purposes of Sec. 1361(b), so in effect 70 individuals, who were married, would constitute only 35 shareholders.

Module 19.10: S Corporation Election

104. Which one of the following conditions would prevent a corporation from qualifying as an S corporation?

 a. A corporation that has an estate as a shareholder.
 b. A corporation that is not a member of an affiliated group.
 c. A corporation that has only one class of stock.
 d. A corporation that has nonresident aliens as shareholders.

The correct answer is (d). *(SPE 990 III-47)*
REQUIRED: The condition that would prevent a corporation from qualifying as an S corporation.
DISCUSSION: A small business corporation (S corporation) is defined in Sec. 1361. Sec. 1361(b)(1)(C) specifically prohibits an S corporation from having a nonresident alien as a shareholder. Thus, a corporation having a nonresident alien as a shareholder would be ineligible for S corporation status.
Answer (a) is incorrect because an estate can be a shareholder in an S corporation. Answer (b) is incorrect because a corporation that is not a member of an affiliated group can be an S corporation. Answer (c) is incorrect because an S corporation can have only one class of stock.

105. Which one of the following is not a requirement to make an S corporation election?

 a. Corporate net assets must be valued at less than $10,000.
 b. Shareholder election must be unanimous.
 c. Only one class of stock can be outstanding.
 d. The corporation must be a domestic corporation.

The correct answer is (a). *(CMA 1287 3-9)*
REQUIRED: The item not required to make an S corporation election.
DISCUSSION: No valuation requirements exist for an S corporation. Net assets may be valued at any amount.
Answer (b) is incorrect because all shareholders must elect S corporation status. Answer (c) is incorrect because an S corporation may have only one class of stock. Answer (d) is incorrect because an S corporation must be a domestic corporation.

106. Which of the following will prevent a corporation from qualifying as an S corporation?

 a. Deriving more than 40% of its gross receipts from passive income sources.
 b. Having a partnership as a shareholder.
 c. Owning more than 50% of the stock of a domestic corporation.
 d. Having 35 shareholders.

The correct answer is (b). *(SPE 989 III-46)*
REQUIRED: The action that will prevent an S corporation election.
DISCUSSION: An S corporation may not have more than 35 shareholders; shareholders who are not individuals, estates, or certain kinds of trusts; a nonresident alien as a shareholder; or more than one class of stock [Sec. 1361(b)]. Having a partnership as a shareholder will prevent a corporation from making an S corporation election.
Answer (a) is incorrect because earning passive income will not prevent a corporation from electing S corporation treatment if it has no Subchapter C earnings and profits. Further, the termination of S corporation status will not occur unless the S corporation had Subchapter C earnings and profits at the end of each of 3 consecutive years, and for each of those years has passive income in excess of 25% of gross receipts. Answer (c) is incorrect because only if 80% of the stock of a domestic corporation is owned do corporations become affiliated and ineligible to be S corporations. Answer (d) is incorrect because having 35 shareholders is permissible for an S corporation.

107. Which of the following tax years may an S corporation use for its taxable year beginning after 1986 (assuming no business purpose exists for another year and assuming an election is not made under Sec. 444)?

 a. A calendar year.
 b. A year ending in the last quarter of the calendar year.
 c. The same year as the majority of its shareholders.
 d. Any year it already used before 1987.

The correct answer is (a). *(SPE 990 III-48)*
REQUIRED: The correct taxable year for an S corporation after 1986.
DISCUSSION: For taxable years beginning after 1986, an S corporation is required to use a calendar year unless it establishes a business purpose for using another year and the IRS consents [Sec. 1378(a)]. Otherwise, a fiscal year can be elected under Sec. 444 if a required payment is made.
Answers (b), (c), and (d) are incorrect because none of them is permitted unless a business purpose is established or an election is made under Sec. 444.

Module 19.10: S Corporation Election

108. Lindal Corporation, organized in 1991, immediately filed an election for S corporation status under the rules of Subchapter S. What is the maximum amount of passive investment income that Lindal will be allowed to earn and still qualify as an S corporation?

a. 80% of gross receipts.
b. 50% of gross receipts.
c. 20% of gross receipts.
d. No limit on passive investment income.

The correct answer is (d). *(CPA 584 Q-16)*
REQUIRED: The maximum amount of passive investment income allowable to an S corporation.
DISCUSSION: There is no limit on the amount of passive investment income that a corporation can earn and still qualify as an S corporation. S corporation status can be terminated if the corporation has had passive investment income in excess of 25% of gross receipts for 3 consecutive taxable years and has had Subchapter C earnings and profits at the end of each of these taxable years. Subchapter C earnings and profits are those accumulated during a taxable year for which a Subchapter S election was not in effect [Sec. 1362(d)(3)].

109. Which of the following statements is false about making an election to be taxed under Subchapter S?

a. The S corporation election can be filed only in the first 2½ months of the tax year.
b. The S corporation election that is filed too late to be effective for the current tax year takes effect the next tax year.
c. All persons owning stock on the date the election is filed or during any time in the pre-election period of the election year must consent to the election if it is to be effective in the tax year in which it is filed.
d. Each new shareholder of the S corporation who owns more than 50% of the S corporation stock may revoke the election within 60 days after the stock acquisition.

The correct answer is (a). *(Publisher)*
REQUIRED: The false statement regarding making an S corporation election.
DISCUSSION: Sec. 1362(b) provides that an election to be taxed as an S corporation may be made any time during the preceding taxable year or on or before the 15th day of the third month of the current taxable year.
Answer (b) is incorrect because an election filed after the first 2½ months of a tax year will be effective for the next tax year. Answer (c) is incorrect because the election of S corporation status must be with the consent of all shareholders who own stock on the date the election is filed and all shareholders who owned stock in the pre-election period of the election year if the election is to be effective in the tax year in which it is filed. Answer (d) is incorrect because a new shareholder who owns more than 50% of the S corporation stock may revoke the election within 60 days after his/her stock acquisition and also at any time thereafter [Sec. 1362(d)(1)].

110. Tau Corporation, which has been operating since 1982, has an October 31 year-end, which coincides with its natural business year. On May 15, 1991, Tau filed the required form to elect S corporation status. All of Tau's stockholders consented to the election, and all other requirements were met. The earliest date that Tau can be recognized as an S corporation is

a. November 1, 1990.
b. May 15, 1991.
c. November 1, 1991.
d. November 1, 1992.

The correct answer is (c). *(CPA 1187 Q-27)*
REQUIRED: The earliest date an S corporation election will be effective.
DISCUSSION: Sec. 1362(b) allows a corporation to make a proper election within the first 2½ months of the year and be effective the first day of that tax year. An election made after the first 2½ months of the year is effective as of the next year. Since Tau Corporation filed its election outside the 2½-month period, the election will be effective for the first day of the next tax year beginning November 1, 1991.
Note that an S corporation may have a fiscal year that coincides with its natural business year (with IRS consent).

111. A corporation may elect S corporation status for its 1991 calendar year by making a proper election on its

   a. 1990 corporation income tax return, Form 1120, filed by its original due date.
   b. 1991 S corporation return, Form 1120-S, filed on or before March 15, 1992.
   c. S corporation election, Form 2553, filed any time during 1990, or on or before March 15, 1991.
   d. Short year corporation income tax return with its year beginning on January 1, 1991, and filed by April 15, 1991.

The correct answer is (c). *(SPE 986 III-53)*
REQUIRED: The correct method of electing S corporation status.
DISCUSSION: The election to be taxed under Subchapter S is made on Form 2553 (Election by small business corporation to tax corporate income directly to shareholders). This form may be filed during the previous tax year or within 2½ months of the beginning of the current tax year [Sec. 1362(b)]. In the case of a calendar-year corporation, this would mean filing before March 15, 1991.

112. R Corporation, a domestic corporation, has eleven shareholders. Ten shareholders are individuals and the eleventh is a partnership composed of twenty-four individuals. R Corporation can qualify for S corporation status.

The correct answer is (F). *(SPE 984 III-22)*
DISCUSSION: An S corporation may only have shareholders who are individuals, estates, and certain kinds of trusts [Sec. 1361(b)]. Having a partnership as a shareholder will prevent a corporation from making an S corporation election regardless of the number of partners or other shareholders.

113. For purposes of qualifying for an S corporation election, a husband and wife who own stock in the corporation as joint tenants are treated as one individual in counting the number of shareholders.

The correct answer is (T). *(SPE 1078 III-37)*
DISCUSSION: To qualify for the S corporation election, a corporation may not have more than 35 shareholders. Under Sec. 1361(c), a husband and wife are treated as one shareholder for this purpose.

114. Corporation V is a newly organized corporation. If at least 80% of the stockholders sign a consent, Corporation V's choice of S corporation status is valid.

The correct answer is (F). *(SPE 1085 III-32)*
DISCUSSION: The election of S corporation status by a corporation is valid only if all shareholders on the date of the election consent to the election [Sec. 1362(a)(2)].

115. Mr. P, Mr. W, and Mrs. S are the only shareholders in a domestic corporation. At a board of directors meeting on February 15, 1991, W and S voted to elect S corporation status for 1991. Mr. P was available but would not sign the consent. W and S filed the election form, Form 2553, the next day. This constitutes a valid election for S corporation status.

The correct answer is (F). *(SPE 990 III-22)*
DISCUSSION: Sec. 1362(a)(2) states that an election for S corporation status is valid only if all persons who are shareholders consent to the election. Thus, if Mr. P does not consent to the election, it will not be valid.

116. Corporation T wishes to elect S corporation status for calendar year 1991. T has 26 shareholders including a qualified Subchapter S trust with seven beneficiaries, only one of which is an income beneficiary. In addition, T has common stock outstanding with differences in voting rights although the dividend rights and liquidation preferences for each share are equal. Corporation T can elect S corporation status.

The correct answer is (T). *(SPE 989 III-19)*
DISCUSSION: An S corporation can have no more than 35 shareholders and can have only one class of stock. Only individuals, estates, and certain trusts may be shareholders. Under Sec. 1361(c)(2)(A)(i), a Qualified Subchapter S Trust may be a shareholder in an S corporation. The deemed owner of the trust is treated as the shareholder. Under Sec. 1361(c)(4), differences in common stock voting rights are disregarded. A corporation will not be treated as having more than one class of stock solely because there are differences in voting rights among the shares of common stock.

Module 19.11: S Corporation Income

117. A new corporation electing to be an S corporation for a tax year beginning in 1991 may make a Sec. 444 election to adopt a fiscal tax year only if the months between the beginning of the tax year elected and the close of the first required tax year is 3 months or less.

The correct answer is (T). *(SPE 989 III-20)*
DISCUSSION: Sec. 444 allows an S corporation to elect a taxable year other than the calendar year. Sec. 444(b)(1) states that the election may be made only if the period between the beginning of the tax year elected and the close of the first required tax year (known as the deferral period) is 3 months or less.

19.11 S Corporation Income

118. In computing the nonseparately stated income or loss of an S corporation, which of the following items can be deducted by the corporation?

a. Charitable contributions.
b. Intangible drilling and development costs the corporation elects to expense.
c. Interest expense on investments.
d. Corporate organizational costs.

The correct answer is (d). *(SPE 989 III-48)*
REQUIRED: The item that can be deducted by an S corporation in computing nonseparately stated (ordinary) income or loss.
DISCUSSION: The computation of an S corporation's nonseparately stated (ordinary) income or loss is governed by Sec. 1363(b). That section states that Sec. 248 applies to S corporations. Sec. 248 allows corporate organizational costs to be amortized over a period of not less than 60 months.
Answer (a) is incorrect because Sec. 1363(b)(2), with reference to Sec. 703(a)(2), does not allow an S corporation to deduct charitable contributions. Answers (b) and (c) are incorrect because items that are separately stated are not allowed as deductions to the S corporation. Intangible drilling and development costs the corporation elects to expense and investment interest expense are not included in nonseparately stated (ordinary) income or loss, but are separately stated and pass through directly to the shareholders.

119. An S corporation may deduct

a. Charitable contributions within the percentage of income limitation applicable to corporations.
b. Net operating loss carryovers.
c. Foreign income taxes.
d. Compensation of officers.

The correct answer is (d). *(CPA 1189 Q-51)*
REQUIRED: The item an S corporation may deduct.
DISCUSSION: Sec. 1363(b) provides that the taxable income of an S corporation shall be computed in the same manner as that of an individual, except as otherwise provided. Compensation of officers will be treated as an ordinary and necessary business expense and will result in a reduction of nonseparate income.
Answers (a), (b), and (c) are incorrect because Sec. 1363(b)(2) states that the deductions referred to in Sec. 703(a)(2) are not allowed to an S corporation. Charitable contributions, net operating loss carryovers, and foreign income taxes are all referred to in Sec. 703(a)(2).

120. At the beginning of 1991, W, an S corporation, is owned equally by two individual shareholders, D and K. During 1991, W had ordinary income of $183,000, a net long-term capital gain of $91,500 and charitable contributions of $27,450. What is the amount of ordinary income, capital gain, and charitable contribution from W's activities that D and K must report in 1991?

	Ordinary Income	Capital Gain	Charitable Contribution
a.	$54,500	$0	$0
b.	$84,500	$45,750	$13,725
c.	$89,500	$45,750	$13,725
d.	$91,500	$45,750	$13,725

The correct answer is (d). *(SPE 990 III-80)*
REQUIRED: The amount of ordinary income, capital gains, and charitable contributions that must be reported by equal shareholders of an S corporation.
DISCUSSION: Each shareholder of an S corporation must report his/her share of the corporation's ordinary income. Accordingly, D and K will each report $91,500 of ordinary income from W. The capital gains are also passed through to D and K. Under Sec. 1366(b), the capital gains will retain their character in the shareholders' hands. The charitable contributions cannot be deducted by the S corporation. They will be passed through to D and K and will retain their character. Because D and K are equal shareholders, they will each report one-half of the capital gains ($45,750 = .50 x $91,500) and charitable contributions ($13,725 = .50 x $27,450) resulting from W's activities.

Module 19.11: S Corporation Income

121. Towne Corporation was owned entirely by individual T from January 1, 1991 until October 1, 1991, at which time she sold her entire stockholdings to individual A. During 1991, Towne reported ordinary income of $146,000. It made a $30,000 cash distribution to T on July 1, 1991. How much income should be reported by individuals T and A in 1991 as a result of Towne Corporation's activities, assuming a valid S corporation election has been in effect at all times since its inception?

a. T, $30,000; A, $116,000.
b. T, $0; A, $146,000.
c. T, $139,200; A, $6,800.
d. T, $109,200; A, $36,800.

122. Mr. Star has a $100,000 basis in the stock of an S corporation. Which of the following items would not decrease his basis in the stock?

a. The amount of the deduction for depletion that is more than the basis of the property being depleted.
b. Distributions by the S corporation that are a return of capital.
c. Any expense of the S corporation that is not deductible in figuring its income and not properly chargeable to the capital account.
d. All loss and deduction items of the S corporation that are separately stated and passed through to the shareholder.

123. Fun Corporation, an S corporation since its organization, is owned entirely by Ms. F. The corporation uses a calendar year as its taxable year. Ms. F paid $250,000 for her Fun stock when the corporation was formed on January 1, 1991. For 1991 Fun reported the following results:

Ordinary income	$50,000
Tax-exempt bond interest income	12,000
Long-term capital gains	17,000
Short-term capital loss	(4,000)

No distributions were made during 1991. Ms. F's addition to her gross income because of her Fun stock ownership and her basis for the Fun stock on December 31, 1991 are

a. Income, $63,000; basis, $325,000.
b. Income, $50,000; basis, $250,000.
c. Income, $63,000; basis, $250,000.
d. Income, $75,000; basis, $325,000.

The correct answer is (d). *(Publisher)*
REQUIRED: The shareholders' income from an S corporation when the shares are transferred during the year.
DISCUSSION: Sec. 1366(a) provides that each shareholder shall include his/her pro rata share of the corporation's income. Sec. 1377(a) defines pro rata share as the taxpayer's share of the corporation's income determined on a per day basis. Individual T owned the shares for 273 days, while individual A owned the shares for 92 days. Towne Corporation reported ordinary income of $146,000 for the full year, which is $400 per day ($146,000 ÷ 365 days). Therefore, T must report income of $109,200 (273 days x $400), and A must report income of $36,800 (92 days x $400). The cash distribution to T is not in excess of her basis for the stock and does not result in any further taxation to T (Sec. 1368), except that it reduced her basis so that she incurred a larger gain on the sale of the stock.

The correct answer is (a). *(SPE 989 III-51)*
REQUIRED: The item that would not decrease an S corporation shareholder's stock basis.
DISCUSSION: Sec. 1367(a)(2) provides guidelines covering decreases in the basis of S corporation stock. Decreases in basis are caused by distributions, losses and deductions not included in nonseparately computed (ordinary) income, any nonseparately computed (ordinary) loss, and any expense of the corporation that is not deductible in computing its taxable income and not properly chargeable to the capital account. Basis is also decreased by the amount of the deduction for depletion that does not exceed the basis of the property being depleted. The amount of any deduction for depletion that exceeds the property's basis does not decrease the shareholder's basis in the S corporation stock.
Answers (b), (c), and (d) are incorrect because they are items that decrease a shareholder's basis in the S corporation stock.

The correct answer is (a). *(Publisher)*
REQUIRED: The amount to be included in an S corporation shareholder's gross income and the shareholder's basis in the S corporation stock.
DISCUSSION: As the sole shareholder of Fun Corporation, Ms. F will report all ordinary income from Fun during 1991 as part of her gross income [Sec. 1366(a)]. She will report ordinary income of $50,000, long-term capital gain of $17,000, and short-term capital loss of $4,000, for a net increase in gross income of $63,000.
Ms. F's basis in her S corporation stock is increased by all items of income which must be separately stated plus the nonseparately stated (ordinary) income [Sec. 1367(a)]. Her increase in basis includes the three items included in her gross income and the tax-exempt interest which must be separately reported to her. Her basis is

Beginning basis	$250,000
Ordinary income	50,000
Tax-exempt interest	12,000
Long-term capital gain	17,000
Short-term capital loss	(4,000)
Basis on 12/31/91	$325,000

124. Milam, Inc. is an S corporation with ordinary income of $60,000. Milam owns all of the stock in the corporation. The following data are also available for the tax year ended December 31, 1991:

Milam's 1/1/91 stock basis	$ 3,000
Cash distribution to Milam	27,000
Tax-exempt interest	2,000
Sec. 1250 gain	28,000
Long-term capital loss	4,000
Short-term capital loss	6,000

Milam's stock basis at the end of 1991 is

a. $38,000.
b. $35,000.
c. $28,000.
d. $26,000.

The correct answer is (c). *(W. Wallace)*
REQUIRED: The basis of the shareholder's stock in an S corporation after adjustments.
DISCUSSION: Sec. 1367 provides guidelines for adjustments to the basis of a shareholder's S corporation stock. The increases include items of income (including tax-exempt income) that are passed through to the shareholder, non-separately stated income, and the excess of deductions for depletion over the basis of the property subject to depletion. The basis of Milam's stock is decreased for any distributions made by the corporation not includable in income, non-separately stated loss, and separately stated loss and deduction items, expenses of the corporation not deductible in computing its taxable income, and the amount of the shareholder's deduction for depletion for any oil and gas property held by the S corporation. The Sec. 1250 gain is not added to basis because it is already included in Milam's ordinary income.

Milam's basis at 1/1/91	$ 3,000
Ordinary income of S corporation	60,000
Tax-exempt interest	2,000
Distribution to Milam	(27,000)
Long-term capital loss	(4,000)
Short-term capital loss	(6,000)
Milam's basis at 12/31/91	$28,000

19.12 S Corporation Losses

125. Shareholder A owned one-half of the stock of an electing S corporation on December 31, 1991. The corporation reported a $36,500 ordinary loss for the calendar year 1991. Shareholder A acquired his stock on July 1, 1991. There were no other ownership changes. What is Shareholder A's pro rata share of the 1991 loss?

a. $18,250.
b. $9,200.
c. $9,125.
d. $0.

The correct answer is (b). *(SPE 987 III-87)*
REQUIRED: The ordinary loss allocable to a shareholder of an S corporation who bought his/her stock during the year.
DISCUSSION: An S corporation shareholder includes his/her pro rata share of loss from the S corporation [Sec. 1366(a)]. Sec. 1377(a) defines pro rata share as the taxpayer's share of loss determined on a per-day basis. A owned the stock for 184 days.
The loss for the whole year was $36,500, which is $100 per day ($36,500 ÷ 365 days). Therefore, A's share is $9,200 [184 days x ($100 ÷ 2)] because A owned only 50% of the stock for those days.

126. Corporation D, a calendar year S corporation, was formed January 1, 1990. Mr. Jones owns 50% of D's stock which had a basis to him of $125,000 on January 1, 1990. On February 1, 1990, Corporation D borrowed $20,000 from its bank and $25,000 from Mr. Jones for use in its business. Jones materially participates in the company. D had losses from operations of $120,000 in 1990 and $210,000 in 1991. D has not repaid any of the loan from Mr. Jones. What amount of Mr. Jones' share of D's 1991 loss is deductible on his 1991 individual return?

a. $90,000.
b. $100,000.
c. $105,000.
d. $210,000.

The correct answer is (a). *(SPE 988 III-88)*
REQUIRED: The amount of loss deductible by an S corporation shareholder in the current year.
DISCUSSION: Under Sec. 1366(d)(1), a taxpayer may deduct losses in the amount of the sum of (1) his/her adjusted basis in the stock, plus (2) the adjusted basis of any corporate indebtedness to him/her. For 1990, Jones may deduct his entire 50% share of losses since his limit ($125,000 basis + $25,000 debt) is greater than his share of losses (50% x $120,000 = $60,000). The limit for 1991 is $90,000 ($125,000 basis − $60,000 1990 loss + $25,000 debt). Since the allocable share of the loss of $105,000 (50% x $210,000) is greater than the limit, Jones may only deduct $90,000 in 1991. The remaining $15,000 in losses may be carried over indefinitely. Since Jones materially participates, the passive loss limitation rules do not apply. The corporation's debt to the bank does not affect Jones' basis or loss limitation.

Module 19.12: S Corporation Losses

127. With regard to S corporations and their stockholders, the "at-risk" rules applicable to losses

    a. Depend on the type of income reported by the S corporation.

    b. Are subject to the elections made by the S corporation's stockholders.

    c. Take into consideration the S corporation's ratio of debt to equity.

    d. Apply at the shareholder level rather than at the corporate level.

The correct answer is (d). *(CPA 1189 Q-50)*
REQUIRED: The correct application of the at-risk rules to S corporations and shareholders.
DISCUSSION: The at-risk rules of Sec. 465 do not apply directly to S corporations. They do apply to individuals as shareholders of S corporations. The at-risk rules are incorporated into Sec. 1366(d) to limit a shareholder's deduction for losses and other deductions from an S corporation to the total of (1) the adjusted basis of the shareholder's stock in the S corporation and (2) the shareholder's adjusted basis of any debt owed by the S corporation to the shareholder.
Answers (a), (b), and (c) are incorrect because none of them has any effect on the at-risk rules.

Questions 128 and 129 are based on Day Corporation, an S corporation, which reported a $73,000 ordinary loss for 1991. Day uses the calendar year as its taxable year as do all of its shareholders. Individual B owns 25% of the Day stock at all times during 1991. B's basis in his Day Corporation stock at the beginning of 1991 was $10,000. B materially participates in Day's business. At the end of 1991 Day is liable for the following:

Third-party creditors	$15,000
Individual B	3,000
Other shareholders	9,000

---

128. What amount of Day's losses may be deducted by B in 1991 and what amount of Day's losses can be carried over by B to 1992?

    a. Deducted, $18,250; carryover, $0.

    b. Deducted, $13,000; carryover, $0.

    c. Deducted, $13,000; carryover, $5,250.

    d. Deducted, $18,000; carryover, $250.

The correct answer is (c). *(Publisher)*
REQUIRED: The amount of loss deductible by an S corporation shareholder in the current year and the amount carried over to future years.
DISCUSSION: A shareholder in an S corporation includes his/her pro rata share of all items of income, loss, deduction, and credit from the S corporation [Sec. 1366(a)]. B is a 25% shareholder and is allocated 25% of the $73,000 ordinary loss for 1991, or $18,250. However, Sec. 1366(d) limits the losses taken into account by a shareholder to the sum of the shareholder's basis in the stock and his/her basis in any debt of the S corporation to that shareholder. Individual B's limit for deduction of losses is $13,000 ($10,000 basis in stock + $3,000 basis in loan to Day). The remaining loss of $5,250 which cannot be deducted in the current year can be carried forward indefinitely until B has sufficient basis. Since B materially participates, the passive loss rules do not apply.

---

129. What is B's basis in his Day Corporation stock and his basis in the indebtedness he is owed by Day Corporation at the end of 1991?

    a. Stock, $0; indebtedness, $3,000.

    b. Stock, $0; indebtedness, $0.

    c. Stock, $15,000; indebtedness, $3,000.

    d. None of the above.

The correct answer is (b). *(Publisher)*
REQUIRED: A shareholder's basis in S corporation stock and in the debt owed to the shareholder after deducting losses.
DISCUSSION: When a shareholder deducts losses of an S corporation, his/her basis in the stock is decreased (but not below zero) by the amount of the deduction [Sec. 1367(a)]. When a loss is deducted in excess of the S corporation shareholder's basis in the stock, the basis in debt owed to the shareholder is reduced (but not below zero). Accordingly, B has a zero basis in both the stock and the debt. Future earnings of the corporation will be used first to restore the basis in the debt, and then to increase the basis in the stock [Sec. 1367(b)(2)].

130. Only those S corporation shareholders holding stock on the last day of the tax year may claim their distributive shares of corporate losses and deductions on their individual tax returns.

The correct answer is (F). *(SPE 988 III-29)*
DISCUSSION: Sec. 1366(a) says that a shareholder must include his pro rata share of the loss and deductions, which is determined on a per-day basis under Sec. 1377(a). The shareholder is not required to own the stock at the end of the year.

19.13 Distributions from S Corporations

131. Mr. Sharp received a distribution from an S corporation that was in excess of the basis of his stock in the corporation. The S corporation had no accumulated earnings and profits. Mr. Sharp should treat the distribution in excess of his basis as:

a. A return of capital.
b. A capital gain.
c. Previously taxed income.
d. A reduction in the basis of his stock.

The correct answer is (b). *(SPE 989 III-50)*
REQUIRED: The treatment of a distribution in excess of a shareholder's basis when the corporation has no earnings and profits.
DISCUSSION: Sec. 1368(b) provides that distributions made by an S corporation having no accumulated earnings and profits reduce the stock's basis. Any distribution in excess of the adjusted basis of the stock shall be treated as gain from the sale or exchange of property. Since Mr. Sharp's S corporation stock is considered a capital asset, the gain is capital gain.

132. Wiggins was the sole shareholder of the Tamale Corporation, a calendar-year S corporation. Tamale was indebted to Wiggins in the amount of $5,000. For the year 1991, Tamale earned $25,000 of ordinary income and distributed $10,000 as a dividend to Wiggins. How much income should Wiggins report from Tamale Corporation for the year 1991?

a. $0.
b. $10,000.
c. $25,000.
d. $35,000.

The correct answer is (c). *(Publisher)*
REQUIRED: The amount of income a shareholder should recognize from an S corporation.
DISCUSSION: Although shareholders of regular corporations report income only as it is distributed to them (usually as dividends), shareholders of S corporations are treated differently. All of an S corporation's income is taxed to the shareholders each year whether distributed or not (Sec. 1366). This increases the shareholder's basis. Distributions in general then reduce the shareholder's basis. Wiggins must report the entire $25,000 of ordinary income of the S corporation in his/her own return. The debt of Tamale to Wiggins does not affect this income computation.

133. The books and records of F, a calendar year S corporation since 1983, reflect the following information for 1991.

Accumulated adjustments account - 1/1/91 $ 30,000
Accumulated earnings and profits - 1/1/91   75,000
Ordinary income for 1991   102,000

F has only one shareholder, T, whose basis in F's stock was $50,000 on January 1, 1991. During 1991, F distributed $150,000 to T. What is the amount of this distribution that should be treated as a capital gain by T?

a. $0.
b. $20,000.
c. $130,000.
d. $150,000.

The correct answer is (a). *(SPE 990 III-81)*
REQUIRED: The capital gain recognized by a shareholder on a distribution by an S corporation.
DISCUSSION: Distributions by S corporations with accumulated earnings and profits are governed by Sec. 1368(c). The portion of the distribution that does not exceed the accumulated adjustments account balance reduces the shareholder's basis. The remaining distribution is treated as a dividend to the extent of accumulated earnings and profits. Any remaining distribution is treated as a recovery of the shareholder's remaining basis in the S corporation stock and a capital gain to the extent it exceeds such basis.
At the end of 1991, F's accumulated adjustments account will be $132,000 ($30,000 + $102,000) because of F's 1991 income. T's basis in the stock will be $152,000 ($50,000 beginning basis and $102,000 ordinary income from 1991). The first $132,000 of the distribution will reduce T's stock basis to $20,000. The remaining $18,000 of the distribution will be treated as a dividend. Because the distribution did not exceed T's basis in the stock, no capital gain results.

134. An S corporation's accumulated adjustments account measures the amount of earnings that may be distributed tax-free. Which one of the following statements is true?

a. Must be adjusted downward for the full amount of federal income taxes attributable to any taxable year in which the corporation was a C corporation.

b. Must be adjusted upward for the full amount of federal income taxes attributable to any taxable year in which the corporation was a C corporation.

c. Must be adjusted upward or downward for only the federal income taxes affected by capital gains or losses, respectively, for any taxable year in which the corporation was a C corporation.

d. Is not adjusted for federal income taxes attributable to a taxable year in which the corporation was a C corporation.

The correct answer is (d). *(CPA 1188 Q-25)*
REQUIRED: The correct statement regarding items which affect the accumulated adjustments account.
DISCUSSION: Sec. 1368(e)(1)(A) states that the accumulated adjustments account is not adjusted for federal income tax attributable to a C corporation tax year.
Answers (a), (b), and (c) are incorrect because no adjustment is made to the accumulated adjustments account for federal income taxes for a year when the corporation was a C corporation. Such taxes reduce the S corporation's other adjustments account.

135. JLK Corporation was formed in 1981 and elected a calendar tax year. It elected S corporation status in 1982. On December 31, 1991, JLK made a $50,000 distribution to its founder and sole shareholder, John. JLK had a previously taxed income account of $9,000 and $1,000 of accumulated earnings and profits at the time of the distribution. The accumulated adjustments account balance on January 1, 1991 was zero. During 1991, JLK earned $12,000 of ordinary income. John's basis in his JLK stock on January 1, 1991 was $10,000. How much income will John report from this S corporation investment in 1991 and what is its character?

	Ordinary Income	Capital Gain
a.	$12,000	$0
b.	$13,000	$0
c.	$50,000	$10,000
d.	$13,000	$27,000

The correct answer is (d). *(Publisher)*
REQUIRED: The amount and character of income reported by a shareholder of an S corporation.
DISCUSSION: Distributions by S corporations with accumulated earnings and profits (E&P) are governed by Sec. 1368(c). The portion of the distribution not in excess of the accumulated adjustments account reduces the shareholder's basis. Money distributions next come from previously taxed income after the accumulated adjustments account has been exhausted. These distributions reduce the shareholder's basis. Distributions next come out of accumulated E&P and are taxable as dividends. Any remaining distribution is treated as a capital gain to the extent it exceeds the shareholder's remaining stock basis.
At the end of 1991, JLK's accumulated adjustments account balance is $12,000. John's basis in the stock will be $22,000. The first $12,000 of the distribution comes out of the accumulated adjustments account and reduces the stock basis to $10,000. The next $9,000 comes out of previously taxed income and reduces the stock basis to $1,000. The next $1,000 comes out of accumulated E&P and is taxable as a dividend (thereby resulting in $13,000 of ordinary income). The next $1,000 reduces the stock basis to zero and causes the last $27,000 of the distribution to be a capital gain.

136. Distributions made by an S corporation result in the recognition of gross income only when made out of accumulated earnings and profits, or when the sum of the amount of cash and the fair market value of the property distributed to a shareholder exceeds the basis of his/her stock investment in the corporation.

The correct answer is (T). *(Publisher)*
DISCUSSION: Distributions made by an S corporation are generally considered to be the return of income which has already been taxed to the shareholder and, accordingly, are made without recognition of additional income (Sec. 1368). If the corporation has no accumulated earnings and profits, all distributions will reduce the basis of the stock until the basis reaches zero, and further distributions will be treated as gain from the sale or exchange of the stock. If the corporation has accumulated earnings and profits, distributions are first made from the accumulated adjustments account, then from accumulated earnings and profits (dividends), and lastly are treated as gain from the sale or exchange of property to the extent they are in excess of the shareholder's remaining basis for the stock.

137. In 1991, an S corporation distributed property to a shareholder that had a fair market value in excess of its adjusted basis to the S corporation. The shareholder must use the fair market value of the property in determining the amount of the distribution as opposed to the basis of the property in the hands of the S corporation.

The correct answer is (T). *(SPE 984 III-25)*
DISCUSSION: When an S corporation distributes property (not in liquidation) which has a FMV in excess of basis, then the S corporation must recognize gain as if it sold the property at its FMV [Sec. 311(b)]. The FMV of the property then reduces the shareholder's basis for the stock.

19.14 Taxes Levied on the S Corporation

138. In which of the following instances will the corporation, all S corporations, be subject to tax?

a. ABL had passive investment income in 1991 equal to 10% of its gross receipts.

b. XYZ sold an asset in 1991 at a gain which had a value in excess of its basis when contributed to XYZ. XYZ elected S corporation status for its first year of existence, which was 1987.

c. PQR sold an asset at a gain in 1991 which had a value in excess of basis when PQR elected S corporation status in 1988. PQR began operations in 1987.

d. XYZ had a capital gain in 1991 on an asset acquired in December 1988. XYZ elected S corporation status in January 1988 after 2 years of operations.

The correct answer is (c). *(Publisher)*
REQUIRED: The instance in which an S corporation will be subject to tax.
DISCUSSION: If a C corporation makes an S corporation election after 1986, a corporate level tax is imposed on any gain that arose prior to the conversion if the gain is recognized by the S corporation through sale, collection, exchange, or distribution within 10 years after the date on which the S election took effect. Since PQR had a built-in gain when it elected S corporation status in answer (c), this portion of the gain will be recognized by PQR and taxed under Sec. 1374 when it sells the asset.

Answer (a) is incorrect because an S corporation is only taxed on excess net passive income when passive investment income exceeds 25% of gross receipts and there are Subchapter C earnings and profits (i.e., earnings and profits accumulated while a C corporation). Answer (b) is incorrect because the taxation on built-in gains of an S corporation does not apply when a corporation has always been an S corporation. Answer (d) is incorrect because an S corporation does not have built-in gains if the asset was acquired after S corporation status was in effect, and built-in gains are the only way in which an S corporation which elects S corporation status after 1986 is taxed on capital gains.

139. If an S corporation recognizes a built-in gain and pays tax on it, the shareholders

a. Report only gain from the transaction that is in excess of the built-in gain, i.e., on appreciation accruing after the first day of the first taxable year for which the corporation was an S corporation.
b. Report no gain from the transaction.
c. Report their share of the entire gain in their own taxable income and obtain a credit for their share of taxes paid by the S corporation.
d. Report their share of the entire gain reduced by the taxes paid by the S corporation.

The correct answer is (d). *(Publisher)*
REQUIRED: The effect on shareholders when an S corporation recognizes a built-in gain.
DISCUSSION: The built-in gain of an S corporation is only the excess of the fair market value over the basis that existed on the first day of the first taxable year for which the corporation was an S corporation. Any additional appreciation after the effective date of the S election is not a built-in gain but is treated as ordinary or capital gains of the S corporation. Shareholders must include in their own gross income their share of these gains of the corporation. In addition, a shareholder must include his/her share of the built-in gain, but the amount of built-in gain is reduced by any taxes paid by the S corporation [Sec. 1366(f)(2)].

140. Prail Corporation is a C corporation that on February 1, 1991 elected to be taxed as a calendar-year S corporation. On June 15, 1991, Prail sold land with a basis of $100,000 for $200,000 cash. The fair market value of the land on January 1, 1991 was $150,000. Prail had no other income or loss for the year and no carryovers from prior years. What is Prail's tax?

a. $7,500.
b. $17,000.
c. $22,250.
d. $34,000.

The correct answer is (b). *(Publisher)*
REQUIRED: An S corporation's tax when it sells property with a built-in gain.
DISCUSSION: The corporate level tax is imposed on an S corporation on any gain that arose prior to the conversion (S election) if the gain is recognized by the S corporation through sale, collection, exchange, or distribution within 10 years after the first day of the first taxable year for which the corporation is an S corporation. Prail's built-in gain is $50,000 ($150,000 fair market value − $100,000 basis). The tax is imposed by the highest rate of tax in Sec. 11(b) on the lesser of the net recognized built-in gain or the amount which would be the taxable income if the corporation was not an S corporation. These two amounts are equal for Prail in 1991, so the tax is $17,000 (34% x $50,000).

Prail's shareholders will report their share of the $83,000 gain ($100,000 gain − $17,000 tax paid) and will pay tax on that gain at their individual tax rates.

141. Bligh, Inc. is a calendar-year C corporation that on December 15, 1988 elected to be taxed as an S corporation commencing with 1989. On January 1, 1989, it had land with a basis of $50,000 and a fair market value of $125,000. Bligh sold the land on September 20, 1991 for $150,000 (its basis was still $50,000). Bligh had a net loss from other operations for 1991 of $15,000 and a net operating loss carryover from 1988 of $10,000. What is Bligh's tax?

a. $17,000.
b. $20,400.
c. $22,100.
d. $25,500.

The correct answer is (c). *(Publisher)*
REQUIRED: An S corporation's tax on a built-in gain when it also has current ordinary losses and an NOL carryover.
DISCUSSION: The built-in gain of an S corporation is the excess of fair market value over basis of an asset that existed on the first day of the first taxable year for which the corporation was an S corporation. This built-in gain is recognized when the asset is sold within 10 years thereafter. Bligh's recognized built-in gain is $75,000 ($125,000 − $50,000). The tax on the built-in gain is 34% [the highest rate specified in Sec. 11(b)] on the lesser of the net recognized built-in gain or the amount which would be the taxable income if the corporation was not an S corporation. Net operating loss carryovers from C corporation taxable years are allowed to reduce the recognized built-in gain. Therefore, Bligh's tax is computed on the lesser of $65,000 ($75,000 built-in gain − $10,000 NOL carryover) or taxable income of $85,000 ($100,000 gain − $15,000 loss from other operations). Bligh's tax is $22,100 (34% x $65,000).

142. T, an S corporation, is liable for the tax on its excess net passive income for 1991 of $10,000. What is the amount of the tax?

   a. $1,000.
   b. $3,400.
   c. $4,800.
   d. $5,000.

The correct answer is (b). *(SPE 986 III-85)*
REQUIRED: The amount of the tax on excess net passive income of an S corporation.
DISCUSSION: Sec. 1375(a) provides that the tax on the excess net passive income of an S corporation is the excess net passive income times the highest corporate tax rate (34%). Thus, the tax is $3,400 ($10,000 x 34%).

143. For 1991, Real Corporation, an S corporation, had gross receipts of $100,000, including passive investment income of $75,000. Real also had Subchapter C earnings and profits at the end of the year. Real incurred $50,000 in expenses directly related to the earning of the passive investment income. Taxable income for the S corporation is $40,000. The tax on the excess net passive income is

   a. $2,835.
   b. $5,670.
   c. $11,340.
   d. $22,860.

The correct answer is (b). *(SPE 990 III-79)*
REQUIRED: The tax on the excess net passive income of an S corporation.
DISCUSSION: The excess net passive income is an amount bearing the same ratio to net passive income (passive investment income less directly connected expenses) as the excess of passive investment income over 25% of gross receipts bears to the passive investment income. The tax is imposed at the highest rate in Sec. 11(b), which is 34% in 1991.

x = excess net passive income

$$x = (\$75,000 - \$50,000) \times \frac{[\$75,000 - (25\% \times \$100,000)]}{\$75,000}$$

$x = \$16,667$

Tax = $16,667 x 34% = $5,670 (*rounded*)

144. All of the following factors serve to determine whether an S corporation may be subject to the tax on excess net passive income except

   a. The S corporation has Subchapter C earnings and profits at the end of the tax year.
   b. Passive investment income is more than 25% of its gross receipts.
   c. More than 50% of loans payable are not at-risk.
   d. The S corporation has been an S corporation from the date of its incorporation.

The correct answer is (c). *(SPE 988 III-61)*
REQUIRED: The factor not considered when determining if the excess net passive income tax applies.
DISCUSSION: Under Sec. 1375, the excess net passive income tax applies when the S corporation was previously a C corporation, has accumulated earnings and profits (also known as Subchapter C earnings and profits), and has gross receipts of which more than 25% is passive investment income. Therefore (c) is not part of the criteria for applying this tax.

Answers (a), (b), and (d) are all considerations in determining applicability of the excess net passive income tax.

145. Tango Corporation, a calendar-year corporation, elects to be taxed as an S Corporation on December 1, 1990. The election is effective for tax year 1991. During 1991 Tango sold land and marketable securities that resulted in the recognition of a $60,000 gain and a $40,000 loss, respectively. The land was used as a parking lot in its business and had a $90,000 fair market value and a $30,000 basis on January 1, 1991. The marketable securities had a $50,000 fair market value and a $90,000 adjusted basis on January 1, 1991. The $40,000 built-in loss can be used to offset the $60,000 built-in gain recognized in 1991 in calculating the built-in gains tax.

The correct answer is (T). *(Publisher)*
DISCUSSION: Sec. 1374 imposes a tax on the built-in gains of a corporation that elects S corporation status after 1986. Built-in gain is defined as the gain accruing on an asset during the period prior to the S corporation election and recognized by the S corporation during a 10-year period beginning with the first day of the S corporation's first taxable year. The tax is applied to the S corporation's net recognized built-in gain, which is defined by Sec. 1374(d)(2) as the lesser of (1) the net of the S corporation's built-in gains and losses or (2) the corporation's taxable income if it were taxed as a C corporation without regard to the dividends-received or dividends-paid deduction or the NOL deduction. The net of the built-in gains and losses is obtained by offsetting built-in losses against built-in gains. Therefore, the $40,000 loss from the sale of the marketable securities can be used to offset the $60,000 gain from the sale of the parking lot in calculating the built-in gains tax.

146. Giant Corporation, a cash basis calendar-year corporation, elects to be taxed as an S corporation on February 1, 1991. The election is effective for tax year 1991. On January 1, 1991 Giant had uncollected accounts receivable of $175,000 and unpaid accounts payable (all of which are deductible) of $115,000. During 1991, all receivables were collected and all payables were paid. Assuming no other transactions or events, Giant Corporation's built-in gains tax base is $175,000.

The correct answer is (F). *(Publisher)*
DISCUSSION: Sec. 1374(d)(5)(A) states that an item of income attributable to the period before the S corporation election took effect is treated as a recognized built-in gain if it is taken into account during the 10-year recognition period (the 10-year period beginning with the first day of the S corporation's first taxable year). Sec. 1374(d)(5)(B) states that any amount allowed as a deduction during the recognition period that was attributable to the period before the S corporation election took effect is treated as a recognized built-in loss. Therefore, Giant Corporation has a recognized built-in gain of $175,000 and a recognized built-in loss of $115,000.

The built-in gains tax base is the net recognized built-in gain, which is defined by Sec. 1374(d)(2) as the lesser of (1) the net of the S corporation's built-in gains and losses or (2) taxable income if it were taxed as a C corporation without regard to the dividends-received or dividends-paid deduction or NOL deduction. Since there were no other transactions or events, the built-in gains tax base is the same under either formula. Giant Corporation's built-in gains tax base is $60,000 ($175,000 − $115,000).

147. P, an S corporation since the date of its incorporation, has passive income for 1991 in excess of 25% of its gross receipts. It is subject to a tax at the rate of 34% on excess net passive income.

The correct answer is (F). *(SPE 986 III-31)*
DISCUSSION: An S corporation which has passive income in excess of 25% of its gross receipts is subject to a tax at the rate of 34% in 1991 on its excess net passive income, but only if it has Subchapter C earnings and profits at the close of such taxable year. A corporation which has been an S corporation since the date of its incorporation would not have any Subchapter C earnings and profits and therefore would not be subject to the tax.

148. The tax on built-in gains generally does not apply to any corporation if an election to be an S corporation was in effect for each of its tax years.

The correct answer is (T). *(SPE 990 III-24)*
DISCUSSION: For a former C corporation electing S corporation status after 1986, Sec. 1374 imposes a tax on any gain accruing prior to the conversion which is recognized by the S corporation within a 10-year period beginning with the first day of the first taxable year for which the corporation was an S corporation. Sec. 1374(c) states that this tax is not imposed on a corporation that has always been an S corporation.

149. King Corporation is a C corporation that elects on December 15, 1990 to be taxed as an S corporation commencing with the 1991 tax year. King Corporation has used the LIFO inventory method for the last 5 of the 8 years it has been in existence. King Corporation must include the excess of the inventory's December 31, 1990 value using a FIFO cost flow assumption over its value using a LIFO cost flow assumption in its 1990 gross income. The tax payable as a result of the income that is recognized is payable in four installments.

The correct answer is (T). *(Publisher)*
DISCUSSION: Sec. 1363(d)(1) states that a C corporation that inventories its goods under the LIFO method for its last taxable year before an S corporation election becomes effective must include in its gross income a LIFO recapture amount. Sec. 1363(d)(3)(C) defines LIFO recapture amount as the amount by which the value of the inventory assets under the FIFO method exceeds the value of the inventory assets under the LIFO method. The tax payable as a result of the income that is recognized is payable in four installments [Sec. 1363(d)(2)(A)].

19.15 S Corporation Filing and Estimated Tax Requirements

Author's Note: The increase in the minimum estimated tax payments for C corporations described in Chapter 18 (page 520) also applies to S corporations. In 1992, an S corporation has to pay in the lesser of: (1) 93% of its current year tax liability, or (2) the sum of 93% of its built-in gains tax, capital gains tax, and recaptured investment tax credits plus 100% of its preceding year excess passive investment income tax to avoid an underpayment penalty.

150. Which of the following is not information required to be included in an S corporation income tax return?

a. Items of gross income and allowable deductions.
b. Names and addresses of all persons owning stock in the corporation at any time during the tax year.
c. Each shareholder's adjusted basis in the corporation's stock.
d. Number of shares owned by each shareholder at all times during the tax year.

The correct answer is (c). *(SPE 1081 III-59)*
REQUIRED: The item not required as information on an S corporation income tax return.
DISCUSSION: Sec. 6037 prescribes the requirements for information to be included in an S corporation tax return. There is no requirement that each shareholder's adjusted basis in the corporation's stock be included.
Answers (a), (b), and (d) are incorrect because each is specifically required in Sec. 6037 to be included in an S corporation tax return.

151. For 1991 an S corporation does not have to make estimated tax payments with respect to which one of the following taxes?

a. Built-in gains tax.
b. Alternative minimum tax.
c. Excess passive investment income tax.
d. Investment tax credits that are recaptured.

The correct answer is (b). *(Publisher)*
REQUIRED: The tax for which an S corporation does not have to make estimated tax payments.
DISCUSSION: Sec. 6655(g)(4) states that S corporations must make estimated tax payments with respect to the built-in gains tax, the excess passive investment income tax, and the investment credits that are recaptured. There is no requirement that an S corporation make estimated tax payments with respect to the alternative minimum tax.

152. The Form 1120S return must be filed by the 15th day of the third month following the end of the corporate year and must include the names and addresses of all shareholders during the year.

The correct answer is (T). *(SPE 1078 III-43)*
DISCUSSION: Form 1120S is the form used by an S corporation. It, like a regular corporate return, must be filed by the 15th day of the third month following the end of the corporate year [Sec. 6072(b)]. The names and addresses of all shareholders must be included on the return under Sec. 6037.

153. R, a calendar-year S corporation, has until April 15, 1991 to file its 1990 Form 1120S.

The correct answer is (F). *(SPE 1081 III-36)*
DISCUSSION: An S corporation has until the 15th day of the third month following the end of its taxable year to file its return [Sec. 6072(b)]. Thus, a calendar-year S corporation has until March 15 to file its return.

154. For 1991 an S corporation does not have to make estimated tax payments unless the tax amount owed is at least $500.

The correct answer is (T). *(Publisher)*
DISCUSSION: Sec. 6655(f) states that a corporation, including an S corporation, does not have to make estimated tax payments if the tax owed is less than $500.

155. For 1992 S corporations owing $500 or more in estimated taxes can avoid an underpayment penalty by paying in the lesser of 93% of the tax shown on the current year's tax return or 93% of the tax shown on the prior year's tax return provided both returns are for a 12-month period.

The correct answer is (F). *(Publisher)*
DISCUSSION: Under Sec. 6655(g)(4)(C), an S corporation owing $500 or more in estimated taxes can avoid an underpayment penalty in 1992 by paying in the lesser of (1) 93% of the tax shown on the current year's tax return or (2) the sum of 93% of the built-in gains tax, capital gains tax, and recaptured investment tax credit for the current year and 100% of the excess passive investment income tax reported for the preceding taxable year. These requirements are applicable only if both returns are for a 12-month period.

156. Abe Snake owns 50% of the stock of Delta Corporation, an electing calendar-year S corporation. During 1991 Delta made estimated tax payments on its $30,000 built-in gains tax liability. Abe's ratable share of Delta's ordinary income for 1991 is $80,000. In addition, long-term capital gains of $30,000 are separately passed through to Abe. Because Delta made $30,000 in estimated tax payments, Abe does not have to include his share of Delta's income in calculating his quarterly estimated tax payments.

The correct answer is (F). *(Publisher)*
DISCUSSION: Sec. 1366(f)(2) states that the built-in gains tax imposed on an S corporation is treated as a loss sustained by the S corporation. The character of the loss is determined by allocating it proportionately among the recognized built-in gains that gave rise to the tax. Sec. 1366(a)(1) states that a shareholder must take into account his/her share of the S corporation's items of income, loss, deduction, or credit that are passed through directly to the shareholder, and the S corporation's nonseparately computed income or loss. The estimated tax Delta paid on its built-in gains will affect the amount that passes through to Abe. It does not relieve him of the requirement that he include his share of Delta's income in calculating his quarterly estimated tax payments.

19.16 Termination of S Corporation Status

157. All of the following will result in the termination of a corporation's status as an S corporation except

   a. Transfer of stock to a partnership.
   b. Acquiring 80% of an operating subsidiary.
   c. Having passive investment income of more than 25% of gross receipts in its initial year.
   d. Creating a second class of voting common stock in its initial year.

The correct answer is (c). *(SPE 986 III-57)*
REQUIRED: The event that will not terminate a corporation's S corporation status.
DISCUSSION: Failing the passive income test will only terminate S corporation status if the corporation has Subchapter C corporation earnings and profits and if the test is failed for 3 consecutive years. A corporation in its initial year could meet neither of these requirements.
Answer (a) is incorrect because an S corporation may not have a partnership as a shareholder. Answer (b) is incorrect because an S corporation may not be a member of an affiliated group. Answer (d) is incorrect because an S corporation may only have one class of stock.

Module 19.16: Termination of S Corporation Status

158. Which of the following events could cause an S corporation to cease to qualify as an S corporation?

a. Transferring its stock to a corporation or partnership.
b. A shareholder has zero basis in his stock.
c. A 25% shareholder sells his shares to an individual who wants to revoke the corporation's S status.
d. The corporation is liable for tax on excess net passive investment income for 2 consecutive years.

The correct answer is (a). *(SPE 989 III-52)*
REQUIRED: The event that could cause an S corporation to cease to qualify as an S corporation.
DISCUSSION: An S corporation is a small business corporation whose shareholders have made an election under Sec. 1362(a). S corporation status may be terminated by the action of a majority of the shareholders. It may also be terminated if the corporation ceases to meet the requirements of a small business corporation. One of those requirements is that the corporation have as shareholders only individuals, estates, and certain trusts. Therefore, transferring its stock to a corporation or partnership may cause an S corporation to cease to qualify as an S corporation.

Answer (b) is incorrect because a shareholder's stock basis has no effect on an S corporation's status. Answer (c) is incorrect because an election may be revoked only if shareholders holding more than one-half of the shares of stock consent to the revocation. Answer (d) is incorrect because the corporation must have passive investment income that exceeds 25% of gross receipts for 3 consecutive years (and must also have Subchapter C earnings and profits at the end of each of the 3 years) for the election to be terminated.

159. Which of the following statements about the termination or revocation of an election to be taxed as an S corporation is correct?

a. Once an election is revoked, a new election cannot be made for 3 years.
b. The occurrence of an event that terminates an S corporation election causes the election to be revoked as of the first day of the taxable year.
c. The termination of an S corporation election causes all prior year losses that have not been deducted by the shareholders to be lost.
d. Having passive investment income of more than 25% of gross receipts in its initial year will not result in the termination of a corporation's status as an S corporation.

The correct answer is (d). *(SPE 989 III-53)*
REQUIRED: The correct statement concerning the termination or revocation of an S corporation election.
DISCUSSION: An S corporation election may be revoked by shareholders holding more than one-half of the shares of stock. It may also be terminated if the corporation ceases to be a small business corporation as defined by Sec. 1361(b)(1) or if the corporation's passive investment income exceeds 25% of gross receipts for 3 consecutive taxable years (and the corporation has Subchapter C earnings and profits at the end of each year). Having passive investment income of more than 25% of gross receipts in its initial year will not result in the termination of a corporation's status as an S corporation because of the requirement that the passive investment income must exceed 25% of gross receipts for 3 consecutive years, and the corporation must have Subchapter C earnings and profits.

Answer (a) is incorrect because under Sec. 1362(g) a new election cannot be made for 5 years. Answer (b) is incorrect because the occurrence of an event that terminates an S corporation election causes the election to be terminated on the day preceding the date the event occurs. Answer (c) is incorrect because shareholders may continue to deduct losses that were not deducted in prior years during the post-termination period which is usually 1 year [Sec. 1366(d)(3)].

Module 19.16: Termination of S Corporation Status

160. The S corporation status can only be revoked if the shareholders who collectively own more than what percentage of the outstanding shares in the S corporation's stock consent to its revocation?

a. 50%.
b. 66 2/3%.
c. 75%.
d. 80%.

The correct answer is (a). *(SPE 984 III-53)*
REQUIRED: The percentage of shares required to revoke S corporation status.
DISCUSSION: Sec. 1362(d)(1) provides that an S corporation's status may be revoked by an election of the shareholders holding more than half of the shares of a corporation.

161. Corporation B, an S corporation, terminated its status as an S corporation on December 31, 1991. Generally, how many tax years must it wait before it can become an S corporation again?

a. 1.
b. 3.
c. 5.
d. 10.

The correct answer is (c). *(SPE 984 III-54)*
REQUIRED: The number of tax years a corporation must wait to become an S corporation again after terminating such status.
DISCUSSION: According to Sec. 1362(g), a corporation that was an S corporation and terminated such status must wait 5 years before electing S corporation status again unless early IRS approval is given.

162. The S corporation status would terminate at the end of 1991 for which of the following?

a. Incorporated in 1983. First year of S status was 1987. Passive investment income equaled 29% of gross receipts in 1989, 27% in 1990, and 25% in 1991. Subchapter C earnings and profits were $10,000 at the end of each year.

b. Incorporated in 1983. First year of S status was 1987. Earnings and profits from C corporation tax years of $10,000. In 1989, passive investment income equaled 35% of gross receipts. The corporation had no passive investment income in prior or later years.

c. Incorporated in 1985. First year of S status was 1988. Passive investment income equaled 27% of gross receipts in 1989, 26% in 1990, and 44% in 1991. Subchapter C earnings and profits were $10,000 at the end of each year.

d. Incorporated in 1985. First year of S status was 1986. Passive investment income equaled 19% of gross receipts in 1989, 34% in 1990, and 35% in 1991.

The correct answer is (c). *(SPE 990 III-50)*
REQUIRED: The condition that would terminate S corporation status.
DISCUSSION: Sec. 1362(d)(3) provides that S corporation status will be terminated when passive investment income exceeds 25% of gross receipts for 3 consecutive taxable years and the corporation has Subchapter C earnings and profits. Answer (c) is the only one that meets both requirements.

Answer (a) is incorrect because in 1991 passive investment income equaled but did not exceed 25% of gross receipts. Passive investment income must exceed 25% of gross receipts for 3 consecutive taxable years. Answer (b) is incorrect because the corporation had passive investment income in only 1 year. Therefore, the condition that passive investment income exceed 25% of gross receipts for 3 consecutive taxable years is not met. Answer (d) is incorrect because in 1989 passive investment income was only 19% of gross receipts.

CHAPTER TWENTY
INCOME TAXATION OF ESTATES AND TRUSTS

20.1 Income and Deductions of Estates and Trusts	(21 questions)	581
20.2 Distributable Net Income (DNI)	(4 questions)	586
20.3 Distributions from Estates and Trusts	(24 questions)	588
20.4 Grantor Trusts	(4 questions)	595
20.5 Tax Years, Return Filing, and Estimated Taxes	(14 questions)	597
20.6 Income in Respect of a Decedent	(7 questions)	600

20.1 Income and Deductions of Estates and Trusts

See Chapter 4, Gross Income, for income and deductions included on a decedent's final return.

1. The taxable income of estates and trusts is generally computed in the same manner as that of which type of taxpayer?

    a. Association.

    b. Corporation.

    c. Individual.

    d. Partnership.

The correct answer is (c). *(Publisher)*
    REQUIRED: The taxpayer whose computation of taxable income is most similar to that of estates and trusts.
    DISCUSSION: Except as otherwise provided, the taxable income of an estate or trust is computed in the same manner as that of individuals [Sec. 641(b)]. Most of the variations from the computation of an individual are contained in Sec. 642. Another difference is that an estate or trust is entitled to a deduction for distributions of income to beneficiaries.
    Answer (a) is incorrect because an association is taxed as a corporation. Answer (b) is incorrect because the taxation of a corporation is very different than an estate or trust. Answer (d) is incorrect because a partnership has a unique method of taxation which does not apply to an estate or trust.

2. In 1991, the estate of Mr. B received the income listed below. No income was distributed to Mr. B's beneficiaries in 1991. All of the following items are considered taxable income of the estate except

    a. Dividends received.

    b. Partnership income.

    c. Interest on life insurance.

    d. Life insurance proceeds.

The correct answer is (d). *(SPE 984 III-57)*
    REQUIRED: The item that is not included in the gross income of an estate.
    DISCUSSION: An estate (or trust) is taxed very similarly to an individual. Items included in the gross income of an individual are generally included in the gross income of an estate. Life insurance proceeds are excluded from gross income by Sec. 101(a), unless the policy was transferred for valuable consideration.
    Answers (a), (b), and (c) are incorrect because each is an item of gross income for an estate or trust under Sec. 61.

3. Ross, a calendar-year, cash-basis taxpayer who died in June 1991, was entitled to receive a $10,000 accounting fee that had not been collected before the date of death. The executor of Ross's estate collected the full $10,000 in July 1991. This $10,000 should appear in

   a. Only the decedent's final individual income tax return.
   b. Only the estate's fiduciary income tax return.
   c. Only the estate tax return.
   d. Both the fiduciary income tax return and the estate tax return.

The correct answer is (d). *(CPA 1188 Q-19)*
REQUIRED: The correct treatment of income earned before death but not received until after death.
DISCUSSION: Income that a decedent had a right to receive prior to death but which was not includable on his/her final income tax return is income in respect of a decedent (see Module 20.6). The $10,000 is properly includable in the estate's (fiduciary) income tax return because Ross was a cash-basis taxpayer and would not properly include income not yet received at the time of death in his final return. Since the money was owed to Ross (he has a right to receive it), it is an asset of the estate and must be included on the estate tax return also.
Answer (a) is incorrect because Ross was a cash-basis taxpayer and would not properly include income not received at the time of death. Answer (b) is incorrect because the $10,000 is an asset of the estate and must also be included on the estate tax return. Answer (c) is incorrect because the $10,000 is income to the estate and must also be included on the income tax return.

4. Charmaine, who was single, died on September 15, 1991. She had purchased land in February 1991 for $10,000. When she died, the land had a fair market value of $10,500. The alternative valuation date was not elected. Her estate, the legal owner, sold the land in December 1991 for $12,000. Her estate also received the following:

Salary owed Charmaine	$3,000
Interest from banks	1,000
Dividends	800

What is the taxable income of Charmaine's estate before the personal exemption if no distributions were made to beneficiaries during 1991?

   a. $3,800.
   b. $4,800.
   c. $6,300.
   d. $6,800.

The correct answer is (c). *(SPE 990 III-84)*
REQUIRED: The taxable income of an estate before deducting the personal exemption.
DISCUSSION: Except as otherwise provided, the taxable income of an estate is computed in the same manner as that of individuals. The salary, interest, and dividends are income to the estate if earned, but not collected, by the decedent before death. The income earned by the decedent but taxable to the estate is $4,800 ($3,000 + $1,000 + $800).
The estate's basis in the land is its fair market value at the date of death [Sec. 1014(a)]. The sale of the land produces a capital gain of $1,500 ($12,000 selling price − $10,500 basis). Therefore, the total taxable income of the estate before deducting the personal exemption is $6,300.

Module 20.1: Income and Deductions of Estates and Trusts

5. The estate of Mr. N paid or incurred the expenses listed below. Which one of these items is not an allowable deduction of an estate on Form 1041, U.S. Fiduciary Income Tax Return?

a. Administrative expenses.
b. Losses on sale of property.
c. Medical and dental expenses.
d. Net operating losses of the estate.

The correct answer is (c). *(SPE 1081 III-61)*
REQUIRED: The item that is not an allowable tax deduction for an estate.
DISCUSSION: Sec. 641(b) provides that the taxable income of an estate (or trust) is computed the same as for an individual except as otherwise provided. Medical and dental expenses that are paid by the estate within 1 year after death may be deducted on the decedent's final return [Sec. 213(c)]. Otherwise, they are deductible for estate tax purposes under Sec. 2053, but they are not deductible on the estate income tax return. If they are deducted on the decedent's final income tax return, a waiver must be filed that they will not be deducted on the estate tax return.
    Answer (a) is incorrect because administrative expenses are deductible on the estate's income tax return if not claimed for estate tax purposes and a waiver of the right to deduct such items for estate tax purposes is filed [Sec. 642(g)]. Answer (b) is incorrect because a loss on the sale of property is deductible on the estate income tax return (the same as if by the decedent). Answer (d) is incorrect because net operating losses are deductible by an estate [Sec. 642(d)].

6. Which of the following expenses may be deducted in computing the taxable income of an estate (Form 1041)?

1. Funeral expenses of decedent
2. Medical and dental expenses of decedent paid by estate
3. Alimony payments paid out of estate income
4. Decedent's prior year net operating loss carryover
5. Estate net income distributed to beneficiaries

a. 1 and 3.
b. 2.
c. 3 and 5.
d. 4 and 5.

The correct answer is (c). *(SPE 1078 III-60)*
REQUIRED: The expense that may be deducted on the income tax return of an estate.
DISCUSSION: Since the taxable income of an estate is generally computed in the same manner as that of an individual, the alimony is deductible by the estate. Secs. 651 and 661 provide a deduction for estate income which is distributed to beneficiaries.
    Answer (a) is incorrect because funeral expenses may only be deducted for estate tax purposes. Answer (b) is incorrect because medical and dental expenses of the decedent must be deducted on either the decedent's final income tax return or on the estate tax return [Sec. 213(c)]. Answer (d) is incorrect because net operating losses of an individual do not carry over to his/her estate, but end upon death.

7. Which of the following statements relating to the charitable contribution deduction on an income tax return of an estate is true?

a. The AGI limitation applies the same as for individuals.
b. To be deductible by an estate, a specific provision for the contribution must be in the will of the decedent.
c. If there is no will, a contribution deduction will be allowed if all beneficiaries agree to the contribution.
d. A credit for political contributions is allowable.

The correct answer is (b). *(SPE 988 III-63)*
REQUIRED: The correct statement concerning deduction for a charitable contribution on an income tax return of an estate.
DISCUSSION: Although the taxable income of an estate is generally computed in the same manner as in the case of an individual, Sec. 642(c) provides that a deduction for a charitable contribution is only available if paid pursuant to the terms of the will of the decedent.
    Answer (a) is incorrect because Sec. 642(c) allows an unlimited deduction for charitable contributions paid if pursuant to a provision in the will of a decedent. Answer (c) is incorrect because Sec. 642(c) does not provide for beneficiaries to agree to the contribution. Answer (d) is incorrect because the political contribution credit no longer exists for either individuals, estates, or trusts.

Module 20.1: Income and Deductions of Estates and Trusts

8. The amount of the personal exemption allowed to an estate and a simple trust is

	Estate	Simple Trust
a.	$1,000	$1,000
b.	$600	$300
c.	$600	$100
d.	$300	$100

The correct answer is (b). *(Publisher)*
REQUIRED: The personal exemption deductible by an estate and a simple trust.
DISCUSSION: Sec. 642(b) provides a $600 personal exemption for an estate. A simple trust is one that is required to distribute all of its income currently and is entitled to an exemption of $300. A complex trust is one that is not required to distribute all of its income currently and is only entitled to a personal exemption of $100.

9. The trust agreement creating Trust X provides for all income of the trust to be distributed to the beneficiaries and requires a reserve equal to tax depreciation to be charged to income. If the trust has gross income of $30,000, expenses charged to income of $28,000, and depreciation of $3,000, how much depreciation can Trust X deduct?

a. $0.
b. $300.
c. $2,000.
d. $3,000.

The correct answer is (d). *(Publisher)*
REQUIRED: The amount of depreciation the trust can deduct.
DISCUSSION: Sec. 642(e) allows an estate or trust a deduction for depreciation to the extent it is not allowable to beneficiaries. Under Sec. 167(d) and Reg. 1.167(h)-1(b), in the absence of provisions in the trust instrument apportioning the deduction, the deduction is apportioned between the trust and its beneficiaries based on the income allocable to each. Since a reserve is required under the trust instrument, the depreciation deduction is allocated to the trust to the extent income is set aside for a depreciation reserve and actually remains in the trust. The entire $3,000 of depreciation is allocated to and deductible by the trust.

If no reserve were required under the trust instrument or local law, the beneficiaries would be entitled to the depreciation deduction, since the trust must distribute all of its income currently.

10. For 1991, Estate D has gross income of $80,000 of which $20,000 is allocated to corpus and $60,000 to the beneficiaries after expenses. Depreciation for the year is $8,000. The decedent's will does not provide a reserve for depreciation. What is the amount of depreciation that Estate D can deduct?

a. $0.
b. $2,000.
c. $6,000.
d. $8,000.

The correct answer is (b). *(SPE 989 III-88)*
REQUIRED: The amount of depreciation deductible by the estate.
DISCUSSION: Sec. 642(e) allows an estate to deduct depreciation only to the extent not allowable to beneficiaries. Under Sec. 167(d), in the absence of provisions in the estate instrument apportioning the deduction, the deduction is apportioned between the estate and the beneficiaries on the basis of the income allocable to each. Therefore, the depreciation deduction allowed to the estate is $2,000.

$$\left(\frac{\$20,000}{\$80,000} \times \$8,000 \right)$$

11. Which of the following is a correct statement concerning net operating losses (NOLs) of trusts and estates?

a. NOLs are not deductible by either trusts or estates.
b. NOLs are deductible by trusts, but not by estates.
c. NOLs of trusts and estates are deductible each year by the beneficiaries.
d. NOL carryovers of trusts and estates are passed through to the beneficiaries in the last year of the estate or trust.

The correct answer is (d). *(SPE 989 III-62)*
REQUIRED: The correct statement concerning net operating losses of trusts and estates.
DISCUSSION: Under Sec. 642(h), if on termination, an estate or trust has a net operating loss carryover, such carryover is allowed as a deduction to the beneficiaries. In effect, the net operating loss carryover is passed through to the beneficiaries in the last year of the estate or trust.

Answers (a) and (b) are incorrect because net operating losses are deductible by both estates and trusts under Sec. 642(d). Answer (c) is incorrect because beneficiaries are entitled to net operating losses of trusts or estates only if there are carryover net operating losses in the year of termination.

12. Estate Z paid the following expenses (which did not relate to the income tax return) in its final taxable year.

Attorney fees	$6,000
Accountant fees	3,000
Executor fees	10,000
Miscellaneous administration expenses	4,000

How much can Estate Z deduct on its income tax return without waiving the deduction of these expenses for estate tax purposes?

a. $0.
b. $4,000.
c. $19,000.
d. $23,000.

The correct answer is (a). *(Publisher)*
REQUIRED: The deduction for administration expenses without waiving the deduction for estate taxes.
DISCUSSION: Attorney fees, accountant fees, and executor fees are all administration expenses deductible for estate tax purposes under Sec. 2053. They may be deducted on the income tax return only if there is a statement filed that such amounts have not been allowed as deductions under Sec. 2053 and the right to deduct such amounts under Sec. 2053 is waived. Therefore, Estate Z can deduct none of these items without filing a waiver.

13. Trust X invests solely in stocks and bonds. During the year it received

Interest from corporate bonds	$6,000
Interest from tax-exempt municipal bonds	2,000
Taxable dividends	2,000

Trust X also paid its trustee $1,000 for earning all of the above investment income. What is Trust X's taxable income before the exemption?

a. $7,000.
b. $7,200.
c. $9,000.
d. $9,800.

The correct answer is (b). *(Publisher)*
REQUIRED: The taxable income of a trust, before its exemption, given both taxable and tax-exempt income and a trustee fee.
DISCUSSION: Taxable income of a trust (or estate) is computed similarly to that of an individual [Sec. 641(b)]. Interest from the corporate bonds and the taxable dividends must be included in income. Interest from municipal bonds is not included in income (Sec. 103).
The trustee fee is generally deductible, except for the portion relating to the municipal bonds (Sec. 265). The fee must be allocated between the taxable and the tax-exempt income. Since the interest from municipal bonds is 20% of the total accounting income ($2,000/$10,000), 20% of the fee will not be deductible. Any expenses directly connected with the tax-exempt interest also would have been entirely nondeductible.

Interest from corporate bonds	$6,000
Dividends	2,000
Trustee fee ($1,000 − $200)	(800)
Taxable income before exemption	$7,200

14. An executor or administrator of a decedent's estate must report estate income using the same method of accounting used by the decedent.

The correct answer is (F). *(SPE 986 III-33)*
DISCUSSION: An estate is a new taxable entity. Under Reg. 1.446-1(e)(1), a taxpayer filing its first return may adopt any permissible method of accounting. Therefore, the estate may use the accrual method regardless of the method used by the decedent.

15. Only items of income accrued or received before the decedent's death are accounted for in computing gross income to be included in Form 1041, U.S. Fiduciary Income Tax Return.

The correct answer is (F). *(SPE 1080 III-33)*
DISCUSSION: Items of income that are accrued (if the decedent is an accrual-method taxpayer) or received (if the decedent is a cash-method taxpayer) before the decedent's death must be included in the decedent's final income tax return. All other items of income received or accrued by the estate are included in Form 1041.

16. If a decedent was using the cash method of accounting, all income earned, even though not received before death, is included in the decedent's final income tax return.

The correct answer is (F). *(SPE 987 III-35)*
DISCUSSION: For a cash-method taxpayer, income is generally only included when received. Therefore, if a cash-method decedent does not receive income prior to death, it is not included in his/her final income tax return. Instead it will be included in the income tax return of the decedent's estate.

17. An estate, or other recipient, that acquires property from a decedent and sells or otherwise disposes of the property within 12 months of the decedent's death is considered to have held the property for the required long-term holding period of more than 12 months.

The correct answer is (T). *(SPE 988 III-32)*
DISCUSSION: Sec. 1223(11) provides that a person who acquires property from a decedent will be treated as having held the property for more than 12 months if disposed by such person within 12 months. In other words, the recipient of property from a decedent is treated as holding the property for the long-term holding period.

18. Carryover losses resulting from net operating losses or capital losses sustained by the decedent prior to death may be taken as a deduction on the estate's income tax return (Form 1041).

The correct answer is (F). *(SPE 989 III-26)*
DISCUSSION: An estate is a new taxable entity. There is no provision allowing either operating losses or capital losses of an individual to be carried over to an estate after death. Carryover losses of an individual end with the decedent's final return.

19. In 1990, the estate of Ms. Wills was entitled to claim a net operating loss deduction of $8,000. The estate will file another return for 1991. Paul is the sole beneficiary of the estate. The net operating loss deduction will flow through to his individual 1990 income tax return.

The correct answer is (F). *(SPE 990 III-29)*
DISCUSSION: As a separate taxable entity, net operating loss deductions of an estate or trust are not allowed to be passed through to the beneficiaries. However, under Sec. 642(h), any unused net operating loss carryovers are passed through to the beneficiaries in the year the estate or trust terminates.

20. Funeral expenses of the decedent can be deducted on the Form 1041, U.S. Fiduciary Income Tax Return, in the year that the decedent's death occurs.

The correct answer is (F). *(SPE 1080 III-34)*
DISCUSSION: Funeral expenses of a decedent are deductible for estate tax purposes under Sec. 2053. They may not be deducted on Form 1041. Furthermore, the estate has a new tax year which begins on the date of death and is not necessarily a calendar year.

21. An estate income tax return may claim only one $600 personal exemption.

The correct answer is (T). *(SPE 989 III-29)*
DISCUSSION: An estate is allowed one personal exemption of $600 each year [Sec. 642(b)], but it is not allowed a standard deduction or personal exemption deduction for dependents.

20.2 Distributable Net Income (DNI)

22. Which of the following is not a modification of taxable income used to determine distributable net income?

a. The personal exemption is added back.
b. Capital gains are subtracted to the extent allocated to corpus and not distributed or set aside for a beneficiary.
c. Tax-exempt interest is added.
d. The net operating loss deduction is added back.

The correct answer is (d). *(Publisher)*
REQUIRED: The item that is not a modification of taxable income to determine DNI.
DISCUSSION: Distributable net income (DNI) is an important concept because it is essentially the limit on both the deduction for distributions to beneficiaries and the amount of income the beneficiaries must recognize from distributions. DNI is defined in Sec. 643(a) as taxable income with certain modifications. These modifications do not include adding back the net operating loss deduction.
Answers (a), (b), and (c) are incorrect because each is a modification listed in Sec. 643(a) in computing DNI.

Module 20.2: Distributable Net Income (DNI)

23. An estate has $8,000 of dividends from domestic corporations and $6,000 of tax-exempt interest. Its only expense is $1,000 of interest incurred to carry the tax-exempt bonds. What is the estate's distributable net income?

- a. $7,400.
- b. $8,000.
- c. $12,400.
- d. $13,000.

The correct answer is (d). *(Publisher)*
REQUIRED: The estate's distributable net income.
DISCUSSION: Under Sec. 643(a), distributable net income includes dividends and tax-exempt interest less expenses allocable to it. The personal exemption is not allowed. Here, the estate's taxable income is $7,400 ($8,000 dividends − $600 personal exemption). The estate's distributable net income is

Taxable income	$ 7,400
Add back personal exemption	600
Add tax-exempt interest (net $1,000 of nondeductible interest)	5,000
Distributable net income	$13,000

24. A simple trust has long-term capital gains allocable to corpus of $20,000, taxable interest income of $3,000, and dividends from domestic corporations of $7,000. What is the trust's distributable net income?

- a. $9,900.
- b. $10,000.
- c. $18,000.
- d. $29,900.

The correct answer is (b). *(Publisher)*
REQUIRED: The simple trust's distributable net income.
DISCUSSION: Under Sec. 643(a), distributable net income (DNI) of a trust is taxable income with the personal exemption added back and capital gains excluded provided the capital gains are allocated to corpus. In most cases, capital gains are allocated to corpus, not to the income interest of the beneficiaries. Rather than compute taxable income and adjust it to DNI, a short-cut is to simply include the items that belong in DNI.

Interest income	$ 3,000
Dividends	7,000
Distributable net income	$10,000

25. A simple trust has tax-exempt interest income of $10,000 and rental income of $15,000. There are fiduciary fees of $5,000 entirely allocable to the rental income. There is $2,000 of depreciation, but the trust is not required to set up a reserve. All the income is distributable to the beneficiaries. What is the trust's distributable net income?

- a. $8,000.
- b. $10,000.
- c. $18,000.
- d. $20,000.

The correct answer is (d). *(Publisher)*
REQUIRED: The simple trust's distributable net income.
DISCUSSION: Under Sec. 643(a), distributable net income is taxable income with tax-exempt interest added and no personal exemption allowed. This trust is not allowed a depreciation deduction because there is no reserve and all the income is distributable to the beneficiaries [Reg. 1.167(h)-1(b)]. The income beneficiaries will be entitled to the depreciation deduction in addition to their income from the trust. The trust's taxable income is $9,700 (rental income $15,000 − fiduciary fees $5,000 − personal exemption $300). The trust's distributable net income is

Taxable income	$ 9,700
Add back personal exemption	300
Add tax-exempt interest	10,000
Distributable net income	$20,000

20.3 Distributions from Estates and Trusts

26. Which of the following should be allocated entirely to corpus of an estate or trust if the will or trust agreement does not provide otherwise?

a. Royalties for the extraction of natural resources.
b. Gain on the sale of estate or trust property.
c. Tax-exempt interest income.
d. Insurance proceeds for lost profits under strike insurance for a baseball team.

The correct answer is (b). *(Publisher)*
REQUIRED: The receipt allocated to corpus rather than fiduciary income.
DISCUSSION: The allocation between corpus (principal) and fiduciary income is generally provided under local law. Most states follow the Revised Uniform Principal and Income Act, which allows the allocation to be modified by the will or trust agreement. However, the general treatment is that gain on the sale of estate or trust property, and any replacement of estate or trust property, is allocated to corpus.
Answer (a) is incorrect because royalties are an income receipt. The Uniform Principal and Income Act does allocate royalties between income (72½%) and corpus (27½%). Answer (c) is incorrect because most interest receipts are allocated to income whether taxable or tax-exempt. Answer (d) is incorrect because insurance proceeds for lost profits is the replacement of income.

27. Which of the following receipts should be allocated by a trustee exclusively to income?

a. A stock dividend.
b. A very large year-end cash dividend.
c. A liquidating dividend whether in complete or partial liquidation.
d. A stock split.

The correct answer is (b). *(CPA 1178 L-37)*
REQUIRED: The receipts that should be allocated exclusively to income.
DISCUSSION: Cash dividends are exclusively allocable to income. Cash dividends are not a change in the form of the principal, rather they represent earnings from the principal (corpus). For simple trusts (i.e., trusts that must distribute all of their income currently), extraordinary dividends (whether paid in cash or property) or taxable stock dividends can be excluded from "income" if they are not distributed or credited to a beneficiary because the fiduciary in good faith determines that the governing instrument and local law allocate such amounts to corpus [Sec. 643(a)(4)].
Answers (a), (c), and (d) are incorrect because stock dividends, liquidating dividends, and stock splits are allocated exclusively to principal.

28. Shepard created an inter vivos trust for the benefit of his children with the remainder to his grandchildren upon the death of his last surviving child. The trust consists of both real and personal property. One of the assets is an apartment building. In administering the trust and allocating the receipts and disbursements, which of the following would be improper?

a. The allocation of forfeited rental security deposits to income.
b. The allocation to principal of the annual service fee of the rental collection agency.
c. The allocation to income of the interest on the mortgage on the apartment building.
d. The allocation to income of the payment of the insurance premiums on the apartment building.

The correct answer is (b). *(CPA 581 L-51)*
REQUIRED: The improper allocation of receipts and disbursements between principal and income.
DISCUSSION: The annual service fee of a rent collection agency represents an ordinary operating expense of the trust. Since it is an expense incurred in the production of income, it is properly chargeable to income.
Answer (a) is incorrect because the allocation is proper. A rent security deposit secures the payment of rent, and provides coverage for minor damages requiring repairs. Since the rent is allocated to income and the repairs are chargeable to income, it follows that the deposits should also be allocated to income. Answer (c) is incorrect because interest expense is properly charged to income. Answer (d) is incorrect because insurance premiums represent an ordinary operating expense properly chargeable to income.

Module 20.3: Distributions from Estates and Trusts

29. Which of the following receipts or disbursements by a trustee should be credited to or charged against income?

   a. Principal payment on real property subject to a mortgage.
   b. Capital gain distributions received from a mutual fund.
   c. Stock rights received from the distributing corporation.
   d. The discount portion received on redemption of treasury bills.

The correct answer is (d). *(CPA 1178 L-40)*
REQUIRED: The receipts or disbursements credited to or charged against income.
DISCUSSION: The discount portion received on redemption of treasury bills is credited to income. The discount represents a return on investment (earnings) of trust assets, and therefore is the equivalent of interest, which is allocable to income.
Answer (a) is incorrect because the payment of the principal of a mortgage is allocable to principal of the trust. The payment or receipt of the noninterest portion of a mortgage is a mere change in the form of trust assets. Answer (b) is incorrect because a capital gain is credited to principal. Capital gains (and capital losses) represent mere changes in the form of trust assets. Answer (c) is incorrect because stock rights from the distributing corporations are allocated to principal in the same manner as stock dividends.

30. A trust which is required to distribute all of its income currently, does not make a distribution other than of current income, and does not make charitable contributions is called a

   a. Complex trust.
   b. Estate.
   c. Simple trust.
   d. Totten trust.

The correct answer is (c). *(Publisher)*
REQUIRED: The type of trust that is defined in the question.
DISCUSSION: A simple trust is one whose governing instrument requires that the trust distribute all of its income currently, does not provide for any charitable contributions, and does not make any distributions other than of current income [Reg. 1.651(a)-1]. The distinction between a simple and a complex trust is important because Secs. 651 and 652 apply to distributions from simple trusts, while Secs. 661 and 662 apply to distributions from complex trusts and estates.
Answer (a) is incorrect because a complex trust is a trust other than a simple trust, i.e., one which distributes other than current income. Answer (b) is incorrect because an estate is the entity which holds a decedent's property until distribution to beneficiaries. Answer (d) is incorrect because a Totten trust is a revocable account at a financial institution in which the donor places funds in his/her name as trustee for some other person.

31. Trust M, a simple trust, has dividends of $4,000 and rent receipts of $8,000. It paid fiduciary fees of $1,000. There is depreciation of $2,000, but no reserve for depreciation is required. What is Trust M's distribution deduction?

   a. $9,000.
   b. $10,000.
   c. $11,000.
   d. $12,000.

The correct answer is (c). *(Publisher)*
REQUIRED: The amount of a simple trust's distribution deduction.
DISCUSSION: Sec. 651 provides the deduction for the distribution of fiduciary income from a simple trust. Fiduciary income is the accounting income determined under the trust agreement or will, and local law. The deduction is the amount of fiduciary income required to be distributed, but limited to the amount of distributable net income (DNI). For this purpose, DNI does not include items of fiduciary income which are not included in gross income.
The fiduciary income of Trust M is $11,000 (dividends $4,000 + rent $8,000 − fiduciary fees $1,000). Since there is no reserve, depreciation is not charged to income. DNI is also $11,000, as is the distribution deduction.

Module 20.3: Distributions from Estates and Trusts

32. Trust M, a simple trust, has dividends of $4,000 and rent receipts of $8,000. It paid fiduciary fees of $1,000. There is depreciation of $2,000, but no reserve for depreciation is required. There is only one beneficiary, who is single. What is the beneficiary's increase in taxable income from the trust?

   a. $0.
   b. $9,000.
   c. $10,000.
   d. $11,000.

The correct answer is (b). *(Publisher)*
REQUIRED: The increase in a beneficiary's taxable income from a simple trust.
DISCUSSION: Sec. 652 provides that the fiduciary income of a simple trust is included in the gross income of the beneficiaries (whether or not distributed), but limited to DNI of the trust. Under Sec. 652(b), the income retains the same character in the hands of the beneficiary as in the hands of the trust.

Trust M had $11,000 of fiduciary income, so this amount, limited to DNI (which is also $11,000), is included in the beneficiary's gross income. Also, the depreciation is deductible by the beneficiary since it was not deductible by the trust. Therefore, the beneficiary's increase in taxable income is $9,000 ($11,000 fiduciary income − $2,000 depreciation pass through).

33. Trust N, a simple trust, has taxable interest of $5,000, tax-exempt interest of $10,000, and short-term capital gain of $20,000. What is Trust N's distribution deduction?

   a. $5,000.
   b. $15,000.
   c. $25,000.
   d. $35,000.

The correct answer is (a). *(Publisher)*
REQUIRED: A simple trust's distribution deduction.
DISCUSSION: Sec. 651 allows a distribution deduction for a simple trust equal to the fiduciary income of the trust, but limited to the distributable net income (DNI). For this purpose, DNI does not include any items of fiduciary income which are not included in gross income.

Trust N's fiduciary income is $15,000 ($5,000 taxable interest + $10,000 tax-exempt interest). Capital gains are allocated to corpus, not income. Trust N's DNI is also $15,000, but for the purpose of the distribution deduction, it does not include tax-exempt interest and is limited to $5,000. Therefore, the distribution deduction is also limited to $5,000.

The reason the distribution deduction is so limited is that the tax-exempt interest was not included in the trust's gross income, so no deduction should be allowed for it.

34. Trust N, a simple trust, has taxable interest of $5,000, tax-exempt interest of $10,000, and short-term capital gain of $20,000. There are two equal beneficiaries. How much gross income does each beneficiary have from Trust N?

   a. $2,500.
   b. $5,000.
   c. $7,500.
   d. $15,000.

The correct answer is (a). *(Publisher)*
REQUIRED: The amount of gross income each beneficiary has from a simple trust.
DISCUSSION: Sec. 652(a) requires a beneficiary of a simple trust to include in gross income the amount of fiduciary income (whether or not distributed) but not to exceed the amount of distributable net income. The character of the income in the hands of the beneficiary is the same as in the hands of the trust [Sec. 652(b)].

The beneficiaries of Trust N are to receive $15,000 of fiduciary income. Since distributable net income is also $15,000, that amount must be included by the beneficiaries. However, $10,000 is tax-exempt interest which is excluded from the beneficiaries' gross incomes since it retains its character in the hands of the beneficiaries. The beneficiaries must include $5,000 in total in their gross incomes, and each beneficiary must include $2,500 as his/her share.

Module 20.3: Distributions from Estates and Trusts

35. Bob Jones is sole beneficiary of a trust which requires that all income, but no corpus, be distributed currently. The trust's distributable net income for 1991 was $20,000, of which $4,000 is a long-term capital gain allocated to income and $2,500 is interest on tax-exempt municipal bonds. Jones received a $15,000 distribution on December 20, 1991, and the remaining $5,000 on January 10, 1992. Assuming Jones has no other income for 1991, his adjusted gross income should be

 a. $20,000.
 b. $17,500.
 c. $15,000.
 d. $12,500.

36. A complex trust is a trust that

 a. Must distribute income currently, but is prohibited from distributing principal during the taxable year.
 b. Invests only in corporate securities and is prohibited from engaging in short-term transactions.
 c. Permits accumulation of current income, provides for charitable contributions, or distributes principal during the taxable year.
 d. Is exempt from payment of income tax since the tax is paid by the beneficiaries.

37. Phillip died in 1990 leaving all his property to his three children. In 1991, Phillip's estate had $25,000 in distributable net income. The executor of Phillip's estate, who has full discretion as to when income is to be distributed, made a cash payment of $10,000 to each of the children. What is the amount of the estate's distribution deduction?

 a. $30,000.
 b. $25,000.
 c. $20,000.
 d. $10,000.

The correct answer is (b). *(CPA 574 Q-20)*
REQUIRED: The adjusted gross income of the sole beneficiary of a simple trust.
DISCUSSION: Sec. 652 requires the beneficiary of a simple trust (one which is required to distribute all income currently) to include in gross income the amount of fiduciary income of the trust (whether distributed or not), but limited to the amount of distributable net income. The amount included in a beneficiary's gross income retains the same character as in the hands of the trust.
Although Jones only received $15,000 in 1991, all of the distributable net income (which is the same as fiduciary income in this case) must be included in his gross income in 1991. Since the income retains the same character in the hands of the beneficiary as in the hands of the trust, Bob is entitled to exclude the $2,500 of interest on municipal bonds. Therefore, Bob's adjusted gross income is $17,500 ($20,000 distributable net income – $2,500 tax-exempt interest).

The correct answer is (c). *(CPA 588 Q-20)*
REQUIRED: The characteristics of a complex trust.
DISCUSSION: A complex trust is one that can accumulate income, provide for charitable contributions, or distribute amounts other than income [Reg. 1.661(a)-1]. These characteristics distinguish a complex trust from a simple trust.
Answer (a) is incorrect because a complex trust may distribute principal. Answer (b) is incorrect because a complex trust is not required to invest only in corporate securities and is not prohibited from engaging in short-term transactions. Answer (d) is incorrect because a complex trust, like a simple trust, is taxed on income not distributed to beneficiaries.

The correct answer is (b). *(SPE 989 III-57)*
REQUIRED: The amount of a complex trust's distribution deduction.
DISCUSSION: The distribution deduction for complex trusts and estates is determined under Sec. 661. Phillip's estate is complex because there is no required income distribution. The deduction is the sum of the fiduciary income required to be distributed and any other amounts properly distributed, but limited to distributable net income (DNI).
Since $30,000 was distributed ($10,000 x three children), the deduction is $30,000 limited to the amount of DNI. The DNI is $25,000, which is less than the amount distributed. Therefore, the estate's distribution deduction is limited to $25,000.

38. Trust A, a complex trust, is not required to distribute any income currently. It has $10,000 of taxable interest. Trust A distributes $5,000 of income and $2,000 of corpus to its beneficiaries. What is Trust A's distribution deduction?

a. $5,000.
b. $7,000.
c. $10,000.
d. $20,000.

The correct answer is (b). *(Publisher)*
REQUIRED: The amount of a complex trust's distribution deduction.
DISCUSSION: The distribution deduction for complex trusts and estates is determined under Sec. 661. The deduction is the sum of the fiduciary income required to be distributed and any other amounts properly distributed, but limited to distributable net income (DNI).
Trust A has fiduciary income of $10,000 and DNI is also $10,000. Since $7,000 was distributed, the deduction is also $7,000. The deduction is allowed for the distribution of any amount (whether current income, accumulated income, or corpus), limited to the amount of the distributable net income. In effect, the distributable net income flows out of the trust with any distribution including that of corpus.

39. Trust A, a complex trust, is not required to distribute any income currently. It has $10,000 of taxable interest. Trust A distributes $5,000 of income and $2,000 of corpus to its beneficiaries. How much must the beneficiaries include in their taxable income from the trust?

a. $3,500.
b. $5,000.
c. $7,000.
d. $10,000.

The correct answer is (c). *(Publisher)*
REQUIRED: The amount of income from a complex trust that beneficiaries must include in their taxable income.
DISCUSSION: Under Sec. 662, beneficiaries of a complex trust are required to include in gross income the amounts of fiduciary income required to be distributed and all other amounts which are distributed, but limited to DNI. The amounts included in the beneficiaries' gross income retain the same character as in the hands of the estate or trust and are treated as consisting of the same proportion of each class of item entering into the computation of DNI.
Since $7,000 was distributed to the beneficiaries (and DNI is not less), the beneficiaries must include $7,000 in gross income.

40. Estate B has $8,000 of dividends, $10,000 of taxable interest, and $6,000 of tax-exempt interest. If it distributes $30,000 to its sole beneficiary, what is Estate B's distribution deduction?

a. $10,000.
b. $18,000.
c. $24,000.
d. $30,000.

The correct answer is (b). *(Publisher)*
REQUIRED: The distribution deduction for an estate.
DISCUSSION: An estate (and a complex trust) is allowed a deduction under Sec. 661 for amounts which are distributed, but not to exceed DNI. No deduction is allowed for any item of DNI which is not also included in gross income of the estate or trust.
Estate B has $24,000 of fiduciary income and DNI. Although it distributed $30,000 to its beneficiary, the deduction is limited to DNI. Furthermore, no deduction is allowed for the $6,000 of tax-exempt interest since it is not included in the estate's gross income. Therefore, Estate B's distribution deduction is $18,000 ($8,000 of dividends + $10,000 of taxable interest).

41. Using the same facts as in the previous question, how much must the beneficiary include in his/her taxable income from the estate?

a. $10,000.
b. $18,000.
c. $24,000.
d. $30,000.

The correct answer is (b). *(Publisher)*
REQUIRED: The amount the beneficiary must include in taxable income from an estate.
DISCUSSION: Under Sec. 662, beneficiaries of an estate (and a complex trust) must include in gross income the amounts distributed from the trust, but limited to DNI. The amounts included in the beneficiaries' gross incomes retain the same character as in the hands of the estate, and are treated as having the same proportion of each class of item entering into the DNI computation. The beneficiary of Estate B will include $24,000 from the trust as DNI, but will exclude $6,000 of tax-exempt interest, so the net amount included in the beneficiary's taxable income is $18,000.

42. Trust C, a complex trust, is not required to distribute any income currently to its two beneficiaries. It has $10,000 of taxable interest and $10,000 of tax-exempt interest for the year. Trust C distributes $8,000 of income to Beneficiary A and $2,000 of corpus to Beneficiary B. What is Trust C's distribution deduction?

   a. $2,000.
   b. $2,500.
   c. $5,000.
   d. $10,000.

The correct answer is (c). *(Publisher)*
REQUIRED: The amount of a complex trust's distribution deduction when it has tax-exempt income.
DISCUSSION: The distribution deduction for complex trusts and estates is determined under Sec. 661. The deduction is the sum of the fiduciary income required to be distributed and any other amounts properly distributed, but limited to distributable net income (DNI). This amount eligible for the deduction is treated as consisting of the same proportion of each type of income included in the DNI. Furthermore, no deduction is allowed for any portion treated as distributed which is not included in gross income of the trust or estate.
   Trust C has both fiduciary income and DNI of $20,000. The amount of each portion of DNI that is treated as distributed will be 50% (since half of the DNI is tax-exempt). $10,000 of DNI in total is distributed, of which $5,000 is treated as tax-exempt income. Thus, the distribution deduction is $5,000. This portion of distributable income flows out of the trust with any distribution including that of corpus.

43. Trust C, a complex trust, is not required to distribute any income currently to its two beneficiaries. It has $10,000 of taxable interest and $10,000 of tax-exempt interest for the year. Trust C distributes $8,000 of income to Beneficiary A and $2,000 of corpus to Beneficiary B. How much must the beneficiaries include in their taxable income from the trust?

	Beneficiary A	Beneficiary B
a.	$8,000	$2,000
b.	$4,000	$1,000
c.	$2,500	$2,500
d.	$4,000	$0

The correct answer is (b). *(Publisher)*
REQUIRED: The amount of income from a complex trust with tax-exempt income that beneficiaries must include in taxable income.
DISCUSSION: Under Sec. 662, beneficiaries of complex trusts are required to include in gross income the amounts of fiduciary income required to be distributed and all other amounts which are distributed, but limited to DNI. The amounts included in the beneficiaries' gross income retain the same character as in the hands of the estate or trust and are treated as consisting of the same proportion of each classified item entering into the computation of DNI.
   Since Beneficiary A received a distribution of $8,000, half of which is treated as tax-exempt income, A must include $4,000 in gross income. Since Beneficiary B received a distribution of $2,000, half of which is treated as tax-exempt income, B must include $1,000 in gross income.

44. If you are the beneficiary of an estate that must distribute all its income currently (and none is tax-exempt), you must report your share of

   a. The distributable net income plus all other amounts actually paid to you.
   b. The distributable net income that you have actually received.
   c. The distributable net income whether or not you have actually received it.
   d. None of the above.

The correct answer is (c). *(SPE 986 III-59)*
REQUIRED: The amount of income to be reported by a beneficiary of an estate.
DISCUSSION: Under Sec. 662, a beneficiary of an estate (or complex trust) must include in gross income the amounts required to be distributed currently and any additional amounts actually distributed, but both amounts limited to distributable net income (DNI). Therefore, if all income is taxable and required to be distributed currently, the beneficiary must include all DNI in income even if not actually received.
   Answer (a) is incorrect because DNI is the limit on a beneficiaries' taxable income from an estate (or complex trust). Answer (b) is incorrect because DNI is included when required to be distributed even if not actually received.

45. Under the terms of Mr. B's will, $5,000 a year is to be paid to his widow and $2,500 to each of his two children out of the estate income during the period of administration. There are no charitable contributions. For 1991, the distributable net income of the estate was $8,000. What amount is the widow required to include in gross income?

a. $5,000.
b. $4,000.
c. $2,500.
d. $2,000.

The correct answer is (b). *(SPE 984 III-79)*
REQUIRED: The amount a beneficiary should include in gross income from an estate.
DISCUSSION: Under Sec. 662, a beneficiary of an estate includes in gross income the amount distributed from an estate, but limited to the distributable net income (DNI) of the estate. If the amount distributed exceeds DNI, each beneficiary includes a proportionate amount of the DNI based on the total amount distributed to all beneficiaries [Sec. 662(a)(1)]. The widow received 50% of total distributions to beneficiaries ($5,000/$10,000), so she will include $4,000 in her gross income (50% x $8,000 DNI).

46. A will provided for $25,000 to be distributed to beneficiary A, property valued at $30,000 with a basis of $20,000 to be distributed to beneficiary B, and the residue (valued at $40,000) to be distributed to beneficiary C. If the estate has $50,000 of distributable net income, how much is included in the gross income of all three beneficiaries of the estate?

a. $40,000.
b. $45,000.
c. $50,000.
d. $95,000.

The correct answer is (a). *(Publisher)*
REQUIRED: The amount of distributions from an estate that beneficiaries must include in gross income when there are specific bequests.
DISCUSSION: Generally, a beneficiary of an estate must include in gross income the amount distributed from an estate, limited to the DNI of the estate (Sec. 662). Sec. 663(a)(1), however, provides that a gift or bequest of a specific sum of money or specific property which is paid or credited at one time or in no more than three installments is not included in amounts distributed under Sec. 662. The bequest is excluded from the beneficiaries' gross income by Sec. 102(a).
The $25,000 distributed to beneficiary A and the property valued at $30,000 distributed to beneficiary B are specific bequests and are not included in the beneficiaries' gross incomes. The $40,000 residue is not a specific bequest because it is not a specific sum of money until the taxable estate is computed. $40,000 is considered a distribution under Sec. 662 and is included in gross income, limited to DNI. Since the $40,000 distributed is less than DNI, the entire $40,000 is included in the gross income of beneficiary C.

47. Estate X has DNI of $10,000. Its sole distribution during the year is property with a basis of $8,000 and a fair market value of $12,000. This property is not a specific bequest. What is the beneficiary's basis in the property and how much must (s)he include in income?

	Income	Basis
a.	$8,000	$8,000
b.	$10,000	$10,000
c.	$10,000	$12,000
d.	$12,000	$12,000

The correct answer is (a). *(Publisher)*
REQUIRED: A beneficiary's income and basis in property distributed from an estate.
DISCUSSION: Under Sec. 662, beneficiaries of an estate must include in gross income the amounts distributed from the estate, but limited to DNI. Sec. 643(e) provides that the basis of property received by a beneficiary is the adjusted basis of the property in the hands of the estate, adjusted for any gain or loss recognized by the estate on the distribution. The amount of the distribution under Sec. 662 is the lesser of the basis of the property in the hands of the beneficiary, or the fair market value of the property.
No gain is recognized on the distribution of the property unless the executor elected to treat it as a sale. Hence, the beneficiary's basis in the property is $8,000 (the adjusted basis in the hands of the estate). The amount of the distribution and the amount of the income to the beneficiary are both $8,000 (the lesser of the basis of the property in the hands of the beneficiary or its fair market value).

48. Estate X has DNI of $10,000. Its sole distribution during the year is property with a basis of $8,000 and a fair market value of $12,000. This property is not a specific bequest. Assume that the executor elects to recognize gain on the distribution. What is the beneficiary's basis in the property and how much must (s)he include in income?

	Income	Basis
a.	$8,000	$8,000
b.	$10,000	$10,000
c.	$10,000	$12,000
d.	$12,000	$12,000

The correct answer is (c). *(Publisher)*
REQUIRED: The beneficiary's income and basis in property given an election by the estate to recognize gain.
DISCUSSION: An estate may elect to recognize gain under Sec. 643(e) equal to the fair market value of the property in excess of its basis. In such case, the distribution under Sec. 662 is the fair market value of the property. A capital gain generally does not increase DNI since it is allocable to corpus, so the beneficiary must include $10,000 in gross income (the lesser of the amount of the distribution or the DNI).
The beneficiary's basis in the property is the adjusted basis of the property in the hands of the estate adjusted for any gain or loss recognized by the estate on the distribution. The estate's basis in the property was $8,000, and it had a $4,000 gain. Therefore, the beneficiary's basis is $12,000.

49. Trust X has $10,000 of distributable net income each year. The trustee accumulates the income for 3 years and does not distribute any to the sole beneficiary, Letty, age 30. In year four, the trustee distributes $30,000 when Trust X's DNI is only $5,000. Which of the following is correct?

a. Letty will include only $5,000 of income from the trust in year four.
b. Letty will include $30,000 of income from the trust in year four.
c. Letty will be taxed in year four on the $25,000 in excess of current DNI as if it had been distributed in the prior years.
d. The trustee has saved taxes equal to the difference between Letty's and Trust X's tax rates by planning distributions in years when DNI is low.

The correct answer is (c). *(Publisher)*
REQUIRED: The correct statement about an accumulation distribution from a trust.
DISCUSSION: Under Sec. 662, a beneficiary of an estate or complex trust includes in gross income the amount distributed, but limited to DNI. However, Sec. 666 requires an accumulation distribution to be taxed to the beneficiary of a trust (but not an estate) as if the distribution had been made in the preceding years. The accumulated distribution is the amount of the current distribution in excess of current DNI.
Answer (a) is incorrect because Letty will not only include $5,000 of trust income in year four, but she will also be taxed on the remainder of the distribution as if it had been made in the previous years. Answer (b) is incorrect because $25,000 of income will be taxed as if distributed in the prior years, and only $5,000 will actually be included in her year four income. Answer (d) is incorrect because the accumulation distribution rules of Sec. 666 prevent the saving of taxes by accumulating income.

20.4 Grantor Trusts

50. If approval or consent of an adverse party is not required for the exercise of the power, which of the following powers held by the grantor of a trust will not cause the income of the trust to be taxable to the grantor?

a. The power to allocate income of a trust among two noncharitable beneficiaries.
b. The power to borrow trust funds interest free.
c. The power to revoke the trust.
d. The power to use income of the trust for the support of a dependent (other than the grantor's spouse) if it is not so used.

The correct answer is (d). *(Publisher)*
REQUIRED: The power held by a grantor that will not cause the trust income to be taxable to the grantor.
DISCUSSION: Under Sec. 671, the income attributable to that portion of a trust of which a grantor is treated as an owner is taxed to the grantor. Under Sec. 677(b), income of a trust is not considered taxable to the grantor merely because the income may be applied or distributed for the support of a beneficiary (other than the grantor's spouse) whom the grantor is legally obligated to support, unless such income is actually so applied or distributed.
Answer (a) is incorrect because the grantor is treated as the owner of a trust in which (s)he has the power to control the beneficial enjoyment of the corpus or the income [Sec. 674(a)]. Answer (b) is incorrect because the grantor is treated as the owner of a trust in which (s)he has the power to borrow funds without interest or without adequate security [Sec. 675(2)]. Answer (c) is incorrect because the grantor is treated as the owner of a trust in which (s)he has the power to revoke the trust [Sec. 676(a)].

51. Grantor set up two irrevocable trusts: Trust Y and Trust Z. The income of Trust Y is to be accumulated for distribution to Grantor's spouse after Grantor's death. The income of Trust Z is to be accumulated for the children of Grantor, and the trustee has the discretion to use any part of the income for the children's support. Half of the income is so used in the current year. Which statement is correct?

a. All the income from both trusts is taxed to Grantor.
b. None of the income from either trust is taxed to Grantor.
c. No income from Trust Y is taxed to Grantor and half of the income from Trust Z is taxed to Grantor.
d. All the income from Trust Y and half from Trust Z is taxed to Grantor.

The correct answer is (d). *(Publisher)*
REQUIRED: The correct statement concerning the taxation of trust income to the grantor.
DISCUSSION: Under Sec. 677(a), a grantor is treated as the owner of a trust the income of which may be distributed or accumulated for the grantor's spouse (without the approval or consent of an adverse party). Therefore, all of the income from Trust Y is taxed to Grantor.

The grantor is also taxed on income from a trust in which the income may be applied for the benefit of the grantor [Sec. 677(a)]. Use of income for the support of a dependent is considered the application of income for the benefit of the grantor. Under Sec. 677(b), however, the income of a trust that may be applied for the support of a dependent is not taxable to the grantor if it is not actually used. Therefore, only half of the income of Trust Z (used for the children's support) is taxed to Grantor.

52. Martins created and funded an irrevocable 15-year trust in 1985 for the benefit of his minor children. At the end of the 15 years, the principal reverts to Martins. Martins named the Bloom Trust Company as trustee and provided that Bloom would serve without the necessity of posting a bond. In understanding the trust and the rules applicable to it, which of the following is correct?

a. If Martins dies 10 years after creation of the trust, it is automatically revoked and the property is distributed to the beneficiaries of his trust upon their attaining age 21.
b. Martins may revoke the trust after 11 years, since he created it, and the principal reverts to him at the expiration of the 15 years.
c. The facts indicate that the trust is a separate legal entity for both tax and nontax purposes.
d. The trust is not a separate legal entity for federal tax purposes.

The correct answer is (c). *(CPA 582 L-57)*
REQUIRED: The correct statement concerning an irrevocable trust for the benefit of minors.
DISCUSSION: Any trust that is validly created is a separate legal entity for nontax purposes. A trust funded before March 2, 1986 and that is to last longer than 10 years is generally treated as a separate entity for tax purposes provided the grantor holds no disqualifying power(s) under Secs. 671-677. The major requirements are that for at least 10 years the trust must be irrevocable, and the income of the trust must not be used for the benefit of the grantor.

Answer (a) is incorrect because a trust which is irrevocable for a 15-year term is not terminated by the death of the grantor. At the end of the 15-year period, the assets of the trust would revert to the heirs of the deceased grantor (absent a provision otherwise in the trust agreement). Answer (b) is incorrect because a grantor who creates an irrevocable trust may not revoke it during the term of its existence. Answer (d) is incorrect because the trust is generally a separate legal entity for tax purposes as discussed above.

53. Zekes created and funded a trust in December 1986 for his children's education. They were ages 13 and 15 when the trust was created. The trust is irrevocable for 10 years, and at the end of that time all corpus will revert to Zekes. In 1991, the trust has distributable net income of $10,000 and taxable income of $9,000, and the trustee spent $5,000 for the children's education. Who is taxed on the income?

a. $5,000 to the children, $4,000 to the trust.
b. $5,000 to the children, $4,000 to Zekes.
c. $9,000 to Zekes.
d. $10,000 to Zekes.

The correct answer is (c). *(Publisher)*
REQUIRED: The person(s) taxed on the income from a trust irrevocable for 10 years.
DISCUSSION: Under Sec. 673(a), the grantor is treated as the owner of a trust or any portion of a trust with respect to transfers to the trust after March 1, 1986 in which (s)he has a reversionary interest which exceeds 5% of the value of such portion. The remainder interest in a 10-year trust with income only being paid out is over 50%. Since Zekes' interest exceeds 5%, all the income is taxed to Zekes during the existence of the trust. The amounts expended on behalf of the children are treated as gifts to the children (although to the extent expended for education, the amount is excluded from taxable gifts under Sec. 2503(e).

20.5 Tax Years, Return Filing, and Estimated Taxes

54. For income tax purposes, all estates

a. Must adopt a calendar year, except for existing estates with fiscal years that ended in 1987.
b. May adopt a calendar year or any fiscal year.
c. Must adopt a calendar year regardless of the year the estate was established.
d. Must use the same taxable year as that of its principal beneficiary.

The correct answer is (b). *(CPA 588 Q-18)*
REQUIRED: The taxable year required of estates.
DISCUSSION: An estate is a new taxable entity and may choose a taxable year ending within 12 months after the date of the decedent's death [Reg. 1.441-1(b)].
Answer (a) is incorrect because there is no requirement for an estate to adopt the calendar year. Answer (c) is incorrect because an estate is not required to use a calendar year, but this rule would apply to most trusts. Answer (d) is incorrect because there is no provision for an estate to use the taxable year of its principal beneficiary.

55. All trusts, except tax-exempt trusts,

a. Must adopt a calendar year, except for existing trusts with fiscal years that ended in 1987.
b. May adopt a calendar year or any fiscal year.
c. Must adopt a calendar year regardless of the year the trust was established.
d. Must use the same taxable year as that of its principal beneficiary.

The correct answer is (c). *(CPA 588 Q-17)*
REQUIRED: The required tax year of a trust.
DISCUSSION: Sec. 645 requires all trusts, both new and existing (for the first taxable year beginning after December 31, 1986), to adopt the calendar year as their taxable year. Only tax-exempt trusts and wholly charitable trusts are exceptions from this rule.
Answer (a) is incorrect because there is no provision to grandfather existing trusts to a fiscal year. Answer (b) is incorrect because trusts must adopt a calendar year. Answer (d) is incorrect because there is no provision for a trust to adopt the same tax year as its principal beneficiary.

56. Trust X is a simple trust that was created on August 1, 1985 and elected a taxable year ending July 31. Trust X is neither tax-exempt nor wholly charitable. Annual trust income totals $120,000 (none is tax-exempt) and is earned evenly throughout the year. Barbara Jones is the sole beneficiary. How much gross income should she include in her 1990 tax return from the trust if she minimized her 1987 income?

a. $62,500.
b. $120,000.
c. $132,500.
d. $170,000.

The correct answer is (c). *(Publisher)*
REQUIRED: A beneficiary's gross income from a trust that had to change from a fiscal year to a calendar year.
DISCUSSION: Trust income is included in the beneficiary's tax year in which the trust year ends regardless when the income is distributed to the beneficiary. Therefore, for the tax year ending December 31, 1990, Jones must include the entire $120,000 of annual trust income in her gross income.
In addition, Sec. 645 requires trusts to adopt a calendar year for tax years beginning after 1986. That means Trust X must also have a short taxable year beginning August 1, 1987 and ending December 31, 1987. The amount of income included in Jones' gross income for the short taxable year is $50,000 (5/12 year x $120,000 annual income). This is the trust's income for the months August 1987 through December 1987. However, a transition rule allows this $50,000 to be included in her income ratably over a 4-year period unless she elects to include it all in 1987. Therefore, she need only include $12,500 (1/4 x $50,000) of this $50,000 in her gross income for each of the calendar years 1987 through 1990. Jones' total taxable income from the trust for 1990 will be $132,500 ($120,000 + $12,500).

57. A domestic estate that has only U.S. citizens as beneficiaries must file a Form 1041 if the gross income of the estate in 1991 is at least

a. $1.
b. $500.
c. $600.
d. $2,000.

The correct answer is (c). *(SPE 988 III-62)*
REQUIRED: When an estate must file an income tax return.
DISCUSSION: Under Sec. 6012(a)(3), every estate which has gross income of $600 or more must file a tax return.

58. Estate J, a calendar-year domestic estate, had gross income of $9,850 for 1991. Without considering any extensions of time and ignoring Saturdays, Sundays, and holidays, what income tax return must the estate file and by what date?

	Income Tax Return	Date
a.	Form 1040	March 15, 1991
b.	Form 1040	April 15, 1991
c.	Form 1041	April 15, 1991
d.	Form 1041	June 15, 1991

The correct answer is (c). *(SPE 1082 III-55)*
REQUIRED: The income tax return required by an estate and the date by which it must be filed.
DISCUSSION: Under Sec. 6012(a)(3), every estate which has gross income of $600 or more must file an income tax return. Under Reg. 1.6012-3, the return to be filed by a fiduciary for an estate or a trust is Form 1041. Sec. 6072 requires the return for a calendar-year estate to be filed on or before April 15 following the close of the calendar year.

59. A trust must file an income tax return (Form 1041) if it has

a. Any gross income.
b. $100 of gross income.
c. $300 of gross income.
d. Any taxable income.

The correct answer is (d). *(Publisher)*
REQUIRED: When a trust must file an income tax return.
DISCUSSION: Under Sec. 6012(a)(4), every trust which has any taxable income must file a tax return, or any trust which has gross income of $600 or more regardless of the amount of taxable income must file a tax return.
Answers (a), (b), and (c) are incorrect because, if there is no taxable income, a trust may not file a tax return until it has $600 of gross income.

60. With regard to estimated income tax, estates

a. Must make quarterly estimated tax payments starting no later than the second quarter following the one in which the estate was established.
b. Are exempt from paying estimated tax during the estate's first 2 taxable years.
c. Must make quarterly estimated tax payments only if the estate's income is required to be distributed currently.
d. Are not required to make payments of estimated tax.

The correct answer is (b). *(CPA 588 Q-19)*
REQUIRED: The correct statement concerning estimated tax payments for estates.
DISCUSSION: Sec. 6654(l) requires estates to make estimated payments of income tax except during the first 2 taxable years of existence. No estimated payments are required during the estate's first 2 taxable years.
Answer (a) is incorrect because estates need not make estimated tax payments for the first 2 years of existence. Answer (c) is incorrect because estimated tax payments are required after the first 2 years regardless of the required distribution of income. Answer (d) is incorrect because estates are required to make payments of estimated tax after the first 2 years of existence.

61. With respect to estimated tax payments for tax years beginning after 1987,

a. A trust must pay them, but not an estate.
b. A trust must pay 80% of its tax in quarterly payments, or 100% of the prior year tax if less.
c. A trust or estate (unless otherwise exempt) must pay 90% of its tax in quarterly payments, or 100% of the prior year tax if less.
d. Neither an estate nor a trust is required to pay them.

The correct answer is (c). *(Publisher)*
REQUIRED: The correct statement regarding estimated tax payments for estates and trusts.
DISCUSSION: Sec. 6654(l) requires both trusts and estates to make estimated payments of income tax. Four installments of estimated tax for each taxable year are due on April 15, June 15, September 15, and January 15 of the following taxable year. The total of these four installments of estimated tax must be the lesser of (1) 90% of the final tax due on the trust or estate tax return, or (2) 100% of its tax for the prior year.
The one exception is that an estate is not required to pay estimated taxes for its first 2 taxable years of its existence. After that, filing is required the same as for a trust.

62. On the first U.S. Fiduciary Income Tax Return, Form 1041, the executor or administrator selects the accounting method to be used to report the income of the estate.

The correct answer is (T). *(SPE 1085 III-38)*
DISCUSSION: Under Sec. 6012(b), returns of an estate or trust are made by the fiduciary (the executor or administrator of the estate). An estate is a new taxable entity, and under Reg. 1.446-1(e)(1) a taxpayer filing its first return may adopt any permissible method of accounting to compute taxable income. Accordingly, the executor or administrator of an estate must choose the accounting method.

63. The first income tax return of an estate, Form 1041, is due on the 15th day of the fourth month following the death of a taxpayer.

The correct answer is (F). *(SPE 1077 I-4)*
DISCUSSION: An estate is a new taxable entity and may choose a taxable year ending within 12 months after the date of the decedent's death [Reg. 1.441-1(b)]. Form 1041 is due on the 15th day of the fourth month following the close of whatever year is chosen (Sec. 6072).

64. Trust W uses a calendar year-end. For the year ended December 31, 1991, Trust W has $500 of gross income and $100 of taxable income. Trust W must file Form 1041 on or before April 15, 1992 unless an extension of time is obtained.

The correct answer is (T). *(Publisher)*
DISCUSSION: Sec. 6012 requires every trust which has any taxable income or which has gross income of $600 or more (regardless of the amount of taxable income) to file an income tax return. Although Trust W did not have $600 of gross income, it did have $100 of taxable income, so it must file an income tax return. A trust is required to use Form 1041 under Reg. 1.6012-3. The return is due on or before the 15th day of the fourth month after year-end (Sec. 6072).

65. For tax years beginning after 1986, estates with tax years ending 2 or more years after the date of the decedent's death must pay estimated tax in the same manner as individuals.

The correct answer is (T). *(SPE 989 III-25)*
DISCUSSION: Sec. 6654(l)(1) requires estates and trusts to make estimated tax payments in the same manner as individuals. Sec. 6654(1)(2) creates an exception to this general rule. Under this exception, estates and grantor trusts that receive the residue of a probate estate under the grantor's will are not required to pay estimated taxes for the first 2 taxable years of their existence. After this 2-year period expires, the estate must make estimated tax payments.

66. Ms. Penny died October 15, 1990. During 1991, her estate received $5,000 in interest income. In September 1991, all of her estate's assets were distributed and the estate terminated. The executor of her estate is required to make estimated tax payments.

The correct answer is (F). *(SPE 990 III-25)*
DISCUSSION: Sec. 6654(l) requires that estates and trusts make estimated tax payments. However, Sec. 6654(l)(2) exempts an estate from making estimated tax payments with respect to any taxable year ending before the date 2 years after the date of the decedent's death. Since the estate terminates before this 2-year period ends, the executor of the estate is not required to make estimated tax payments.

67. A trustee may elect to treat a payment of estimated tax made by the trust as a payment made by a beneficiary of the trust.

The correct answer is (T). *(Publisher)*
DISCUSSION: Sec. 643(g) allows a trustee to elect to treat any portion of a payment of estimated tax made by the trust as a payment made by the beneficiary of the trust. For any amount the trustee so elects, it shall be treated as paid or credited to the beneficiary on the last day of such taxable year, the same as a distribution.

20.6 Income in Respect of a Decedent

68. Which one of the following statements concerning the consequences of income being classified as "income in respect of a decedent" is correct?

a. It receives no step-up in basis upon the decedent's death.
b. It is all treated as ordinary income to recipient.
c. It is all taxable to the decedent's estate.
d. It must be included in the decedent's final return.

The correct answer is (a). *(SPE 990 III-52)*
REQUIRED: The correct statement of the consequences of income in respect of a decedent.
DISCUSSION: Sec. 1014(a) provides that the basis of property acquired from a decedent is generally the fair market value of the property on the date of the decedent's death. Sec. 1014(c) provides that property which constitutes a right to receive income in respect of a decedent does not receive a step-up in basis. Therefore, it has a carryover basis.
Answer (b) is incorrect because income in respect of a decedent is treated as having the same character it would have had in the hands of the decedent [Sec. 691(a)(3)]. Answer (c) is incorrect because income in respect of a decedent is included when received (as if on a cash basis) by the person who receives it [Sec. 691(a)(1)]. Answer (d) is incorrect because income in respect of a decedent is that which is earned by the taxpayer but not received prior to his/her death, nor accrued prior to his/her death if on the accrual method, so it is not included in the decedent's final return.

Module 20.6: Income in Respect of a Decedent

69. Income in respect of a cash basis decedent

a. Covers income earned before the taxpayer's death but not collected until after death.
b. Receives a stepped-up basis in the decedent's estate.
c. Must be included in the decedent's final income tax return.
d. Cannot receive capital gain treatment.

The correct answer is (a). *(CPA 1190 Q-39)*
REQUIRED: The correct statement regarding income in respect of a decedent.
DISCUSSION: Reg. 1.691(a)-1(b) defines income in respect of a decedent as those amounts to which a decedent was entitled as gross income but which were not includable in computing taxable income on his final return. For cash basis taxpayers, income in respect of a decedent is income earned by the decedent before death, but not paid until after death. A common example of income in respect of a decedent is salary earned by an employee prior to death, but not paid by the employer until after death.
Answer (b) is incorrect because Sec. 1014(c) prevents the decedent's estate from receiving a stepped-up basis for the income in respect of a decedent. Answer (c) is incorrect because income in respect of a decedent is included in the fiduciary tax return (not the decedent's). Answer (d) is incorrect because income in respect of a decedent is treated as having the same character it would have had in the hands of the decedent [Sec. 691(a)(3)].

70. Which of the following received after a decedent's death is not income in respect of a decedent?

a. Salary earned by the decedent, but not received prior to death.
b. Installment gain in payments from a contract entered into prior to death.
c. Rent for the month after the decedent's death but pursuant to a lease entered into prior to death.
d. Collection on a cash-basis taxpayer's accounts receivable which existed at the date of death.

The correct answer is (c). *(Publisher)*
REQUIRED: The receipt that is not income in respect of a decedent.
DISCUSSION: Income in respect of a decedent is provided for under Sec. 691, but there is no statutory definition. It is generally considered to be all amounts of gross income that the decedent had a right to receive prior to death but which were not properly includable on his/her final income tax return. Rent which accrues after death is not something the decedent had a right to receive prior to death, so it is not income in respect of a decedent.
Answer (a) is incorrect because salary earned but not received prior to death is not properly includable in the final return of the decedent, so it is income in respect of a decedent. Answer (b) is incorrect because a decedent would be required to include in gross income payments on a contract entered into prior to death if received prior to death, so after death the gain or income portion of these payments is income in respect of a decedent. Answer (d) is incorrect because collections on accounts receivable for a cash-basis taxpayer represent income already earned by the decedent, so they are income in respect of a decedent.

71. Mr. A sold a tract of land and reported the sale using the installment method of accounting. The net sale price was $80,000 and the cost basis was $40,000. After A's death, the final $10,000 installment (plus interest) was collected by his personal representative. What amount (other than interest) must be reported as profit on a Form 1041, U.S. Fiduciary Income Tax Return, for the year in which the $10,000 was received?

a. $10,000.
b. $5,000.
c. $2,500.
d. $0.

The correct answer is (b). *(SPE 987 III-89)*
REQUIRED: The amount of the payments received after death that are income in respect of a decedent.
DISCUSSION: Income in respect of a decedent is that which the decedent had a right to receive prior to death but which was not properly includable on his/her final income tax return. It retains its same character to the recipient as it would have been in the hands of the decedent. There is no step-up in basis under Sec. 1014(c), so the same gross profit margin is used on an installment receipt. The gross profit margin was 50% ($40,000 ÷ $80,000), so $5,000 (50% x $10,000) is income in respect of a decedent. The remaining $5,000 is merely a return of capital.
The interest on the installment debt is not income in respect of a decedent except for the portion accrued before death. All the interest received must also be reported on Form 1041.

72. Income that a decedent would have reported had death not occurred that is received by the administrator or executor of the decedent's estate is exempt from federal income tax.

The correct answer is (F). *(SPE 986 III-32)*
DISCUSSION: Income in respect of a decedent is that which is earned by the taxpayer but not received prior to his/her death, nor accrued prior to his/her death if on the accrual method, so it is not included in the decedent's final return. Income in respect of a decedent is included in the recipient's (e.g., the estate's) income in the year received or accrued.

73. On March 20, 1991, Mr. L, a cash-method taxpayer, sold his truck for $10,000 payable September 20, 1991. His adjusted basis for the truck was $8,000. Mr. L died June 15, 1991, before receiving payment. The gain realized on the sale is not income in respect of a decedent.

The correct answer is (F). *(SPE 1085 III-37)*
DISCUSSION: Since Mr. L sold the truck prior to death, he was entitled to receive the gross income prior to death. Since payment was not received until after death and is not properly includable on his final income tax return, the profit is income in respect of a decedent. Under Sec. 691(a)(1), it is included in the recipient's income in the year received.

74. Mr. A, a single, cash-basis taxpayer, died on October 31, 1991. A salary check that was received on October 31, 1991 but not cashed is not income in respect of a decedent.

The correct answer is (T). *(SPE 984 III-33)*
DISCUSSION: Income in respect of a decedent is all gross income the decedent was entitled to prior to death, but was not properly includable in his/her final income tax return. A salary check received on October 31 by someone who died on that date should be included in the final income tax return of the decedent. The check is considered the equivalent of cash and need not be cashed to recognize the income.

CHAPTER TWENTY-ONE
ACCOUNTING METHODS

21.1	Cash Method	(24 questions)	603
21.2	Accrual Method	(18 questions)	611
21.3	Hybrid Method	(5 questions)	616
21.4	Long-Term Contracts	(13 questions)	617
21.5	Installment Sales	(24 questions)	622
21.6	Inventories	(24 questions)	629
21.7	Change of Accounting Methods	(5 questions)	636
21.8	Tax Year	(12 questions)	638
21.9	Recordkeeping Requirements	(12 questions)	641

21.1 Cash Method

Also see Chapter 9, "Deductions from AGI," for additional questions covering prepaid interest and discounted notes.

1. For taxable years beginning after 1986, which of the following is prohibited from using the cash receipts and disbursements method?

   a. Individual taxpayers.
   b. Small farming businesses.
   c. Personal service corporations.
   d. Tax shelters.

The correct answer is (d). *(Publisher)*
REQUIRED: The type of taxpayer prohibited from using the cash method in taxable years beginning after 1986.
DISCUSSION: Sec. 448 limits the use of the cash method by certain business entities; i.e., they are required to use the accrual method. Many C corporations, partnerships with a C corporation as a partner, and tax shelters are not permitted to use the cash receipts and disbursements method. Tax shelters are defined broadly to include syndicates, enterprises whose interests must be registered as a security, and any arrangement the principal purpose of which is the avoidance of federal income tax.
    Answer (a) is incorrect because individuals may use the cash method of accounting. Answer (b) is incorrect because farming businesses are only required to use the accrual method if they are tax shelters or operated by a corporation or a partnership with a corporation as a partner [Sec. 447(a)]. This rule does not apply to S corporations, corporations owned 50% or more by the same family with annual gross receipts of $25 million or less, and other corporations with annual gross receipts of $1 million or less [Sec. 447(c)]. Answer (c) is incorrect because personal service corporations engaged in rendering professional services and owned primarily by the employees who provide the services are not required to use the accrual method.

2. Which of the following entities may not use the cash method for taxable years beginning after 1986?

    a. A partnership with average annual gross receipts in excess of $5 million.

    b. A C corporation whose average annual gross receipts for the preceding three taxable years do not exceed $5 million.

    c. A C corporation substantially owned by its employees and whose business is selling goods with average annual gross receipts in excess of $5 million since its inception.

    d. An S corporation.

The correct answer is (c). *(Publisher)*
REQUIRED: The business not allowed to use the cash method for taxable years beginning after 1986.
DISCUSSION: Certain entities are required by Sec. 448 to use the accrual method of accounting after 1986. A C corporation is one such entity unless it is a qualified personal service corporation or its annual gross receipts are small enough. To qualify as a personal service corporation, substantially all of the corporation's activities must involve the performance of services in health, law, engineering, architecture, accounting, actuarial science, performing arts, or consulting. A C corporation's average gross receipts must be $5 million or less for the prior three years to qualify for the cash method based on gross receipts.
Answer (a) is incorrect because a partnership may use the cash method unless it has a C corporation as a partner. Answer (b) is incorrect because Sec. 448(b) allows entities which meet this gross receipts test to use the cash method of accounting. Answer (d) is incorrect because S corporations may also use the cash method (if not a tax shelter).

3. Dowd, a cash-basis engineering consultant, wanted to defer income to 1992. A client who was in Dowd's office on December 31, 1991, offered to pay his $2,000 bill immediately, but Dowd told him to pay in January. A check for $5,000 from another client arrived in the mail on December 29 and Dowd told his office manager not to deposit it until January. Dowd also told his office manager not to send a client a bill for $3,000 for services performed in 1991 until January. How much income from these transactions should Dowd report in 1991?

    a. $8,000.
    b. $7,000.
    c. $5,000.
    d. $0.

The correct answer is (b). *(SPE 990 II-58)*
REQUIRED: The income of a cash-basis taxpayer that must be recognized before year-end.
DISCUSSION: Although a cash-basis taxpayer generally recognizes income only when cash or the equivalent of cash is received, income is also recognized upon its constructive receipt. Under Reg. 1.451-2, income is constructively received when it is credited to a taxpayer's account, set apart for him/her, or otherwise made available so that (s)he may draw upon it at any time. Dowd must recognize the $2,000 of income from the client who offered to pay the bill. The $5,000 check received on December 29 must also be reported as income in 1991 because a check is the equivalent of cash. However, income is not recognized merely upon failure to send out a bill. A taxpayer is not required to aggressively seek payment, but (s)he may not turn his/her back upon it when it is available. Dowd must report $7,000 in 1991.

4. Mat West, a cash-basis taxpayer, owned interests in several corporations. The Wireless Corporation made a practice of sending dividend checks out to all shareholders on the last day of December so the shareholders would not receive them until January. West received a $50 dividend check from Wireless on January 3, 1992. The Palace Hotel, Inc., in which West was an officer, mailed its dividend checks in the same manner as Wireless. However, West's $400 check was placed on his office desk on December 31, 1991. West owned a controlling interest in Gambling Saloon, Inc. and told the bookkeeper not to write his check, which was to be for $6,000, even though all other shareholders' checks were written and delivered in December 1991. How much dividend income does West have in 1991?

    a. $0.
    b. $450.
    c. $6,400.
    d. $6,450.

The correct answer is (c). *(Publisher)*
REQUIRED: The amount of dividend income to be recognized by a cash-basis taxpayer.
DISCUSSION: Although dividends can be constructively received like any other income, a special rule has developed with respect to dividends. If a dividend is declared payable in December and the corporation follows its usual practice of paying the dividends by checks mailed so that the shareholders do not receive them until January of the following year, such dividends are not considered to have been constructively received in December [Reg. 1.451-2(b)]. However, dividends are constructively received when unqualifiedly made subject to the demand of the shareholder.
Therefore, West has constructively received the $400 from Palace Hotel, Inc. which was placed on his desk in 1991, and the $6,000 from Gambling Saloon, Inc. which he declined to receive. West has $6,400 of dividend income in 1991.

Module 21.1: Cash Method

5. What is the amount of income to be reported by Mr. X in 1991 under the cash method of accounting for the following items?

- Check for $1,200 received January 4, 1991 for services rendered in December 1990.
- Check for $900 received December 26, 1991 for services rendered in October 1991; did not cash until January 5, 1992.
- Dividend check for $500. Check was dated December 31, 1991, but it is the practice of the issuing corporation to mail checks so they will not be received until January of the following year.
- Check for $600 received on April 1, 1991 for interest on corporate bonds held for the period October 1, 1990 through March 31, 1991. Interest is paid semi-annually on April 1 and October 1.
- Rental income of $800 for December 1991 received January 3, 1992.

   a. $1,800.
   b. $2,700.
   c. $3,500.
   d. $4,000.

The correct answer is (b). *(SPE 1085 II-59)*
REQUIRED: The amount of income recognized under the cash method of accounting.
DISCUSSION: A cash-basis taxpayer recognizes income when cash or its equivalent is received and when income is constructively received. Under Reg. 1.451-2, income is constructively received when it is credited to a taxpayer's account, set apart for him/her, or otherwise made available so that (s)he may draw upon it at any time. The $1,200 check for 1990 services, the $900 check for 1991 services, and the $600 check for bond interest are cash equivalents received during 1991. Mr. X's income under the cash method totals $2,700. It does not matter that the $900 check was not cashed until January 5, 1992, since the money had been set aside for Mr. X and was available for his use.

The dividends of $500 are not treated as received since it was the usual practice of the corporation to delay them. Since the rent was not received until 1992, there is no reason to include it in 1991.

6. Mr. Goodman, a calendar-year sole proprietor, uses the cash method of accounting. Mr. Goodman had the following items of income in December 1991.

Payments received on account December 28; deposited in operating account January 2, 1992	$6,000
December client billings for services performed during 1991	5,000
Payment received in December for services to be performed during 1992; deposited in operating account December 31	9,000

What is the amount Mr. Goodman must include in his income for 1991?

   a. $6,000.
   b. $9,000.
   c. $11,000.
   d. $15,000.

The correct answer is (d). *(SPE 989 II-56)*
REQUIRED: The amount of income recognized under the cash method of accounting.
DISCUSSION: A cash-basis taxpayer recognizes income when cash or its equivalent is received and when income is constructively received. Reg. 1.451-2 provides that constructive receipt of income occurs when it is credited to a taxpayer's account, set apart for him/her, or otherwise made available so that (s)he may draw upon it at any time. In this instance, Mr. Goodman must include in income $15,000. The payments received ($6,000) in December have been made available to the taxpayer. The other payment ($9,000) for services to be rendered in 1992 has been deposited in December and must be included in income in 1991. The mere billing for services performed does not constitute income to a cash-basis taxpayer. The $5,000 in client billings will be included in income when received.

Module 21.1: Cash Method

7. In July 1991, Mr. Brown, a cash-basis, calendar-year farmer, had his bean crop damaged by a flood. He normally would have reported the income from the crop in 1992. On November 1, 1991, he received a $40,000 payment under the Disaster Assistance Act of 1988 due to the damage to his beans. Regarding Mr. Smith's reporting of the $40,000 for federal income tax purposes, which of the following statements is correct?

   a. $40,000 must be included in his gross income for 1991.
   b. The $40,000 is nontaxable income.
   c. He may elect to postpone reporting the $40,000 to 1992 by attaching a statement to his 1991 income tax return. The statement must include information required by a specific section of the Income Tax Regulations.
   d. He may note on his Schedule F, Form 1040 that $40,000 from the Disaster Assistance Act will be reported in 1992.

The correct answer is (c). *(SPE 990 II-47)*
REQUIRED: The amount to be reported by a cash-basis farmer when his crop is destroyed by a flood and he receives payments under the Disaster Assistance Act of 1988.
DISCUSSION: Sec. 451(d) provides that payments from the Disaster Assistance Act of 1988 for crop loss from drought, flood, or any other natural disaster shall be treated as insurance proceeds. These payments (in the form of insurance proceeds) may be included in income in the year of receipt, or the taxpayer may elect to include the proceeds in income in the year following the year of destruction as damage, if it can be established that under current practice income from such crops would have been reported in the following taxable year. A statement verifying that these requirements have been met must be attached to the 1991 tax return [Reg. 1.451-6(b)].

8. M, a cash-basis taxpayer, leased property on June 1, 1991 to P at $325 a month. P paid M $325 as a security deposit which will be returned at the end of the lease. In addition, P paid $650 in advance rent which is to be applied as rent to the last 2 months in the lease term. The lease is to run for a 2-year period. What is M's rental income for 1991?

   a. $2,275.
   b. $2,600.
   c. $2,925.
   d. $3,250.

The correct answer is (c). *(SPE 1081 I-70)*
REQUIRED: A cash-basis taxpayer's income from prepaid rent and a security deposit.
DISCUSSION: Sec. 451(a) provides that any item of gross income is included in income in the year of receipt, unless properly accounted for otherwise. Reg. 1.451-1(a) states that under the cash method of accounting, an amount is includable in gross income when actually or constructively received. Reg. 1.61-8(b) requires advance rent payments to be included in gross income in the year of receipt regardless of the accounting method used. The security deposit is not income since M is obligated to return it and does not have an unrestricted right to it. M's rental income for 1991 is

Advance rental payments	$ 650
Current rent (7 months x $325)	2,275
Rental income for 1991	$2,925

9. Dave operates a home improvement business as a sole proprietor. On December 31, 1991, he received a delivery of plasterboard and gave the deliveryman a check for $300. Later that day he bought paint, brushes and some power tools for use in his business. He bought the paint and brushes for $125 from the Bright Paint Store and charged them on a bank credit card. He bought the tools for $150 from Power Hardware Company and charged them on his Power Hardware credit card. What is the amount of these expenditures that Dave can deduct as business expense in 1991?

   a. $575.
   b. $425.
   c. $300.
   d. $275.

The correct answer is (b). *(SPE 990 II-57)*
REQUIRED: A cash-basis taxpayer's deduction for payments made by check and charge card.
DISCUSSION: Reg. 1.461-1(a)(1) provides that deductions are allowed under the cash method of accounting in the taxable year when paid. A mere promise to pay is generally not considered payment under the cash method of accounting.
A check is considered the equivalent of cash, and payment is considered made when the check is delivered or sent. A charge on a hardware store credit card is merely a promise to that hardware store to pay and is not considered payment until the charge card bill is paid. On the other hand, use of a bank credit card involves a third party. It is equivalent to obtaining a loan from the bank and paying the hardware store. Therefore, the charge with a bank credit card is payment at the time of the charge. Dave's business expense deductions for 1991 are $425 ($300 by check + $125 on the bank credit card).

Module 21.1: Cash Method

10. Mr. J, a cash-method taxpayer, operates a business and files his return on a calendar-year basis. In 1990, Mr. J took out a 3-year fire insurance policy on his building effective November 1, 1990. On January 1, 1991, Mr. J paid a premium of $1,800 for the 3 years. What amount may Mr. J deduct as an insurance expense in 1991?

   a. $100.
   b. $600.
   c. $700.
   d. $1,800.

The correct answer is (c). *(SPE 1081 II-79)*
REQUIRED: The amount a cash-basis taxpayer may deduct as insurance expense.
DISCUSSION: Sec. 461(a) provides that a deduction must be taken in the taxable year which is proper under the method of accounting used by the taxpayer. Reg. 1.461-1(a)(1) states that a taxpayer who uses the cash method of accounting generally should deduct allowable deductions in the taxable year in which they are paid. An exception to this rule occurs if an expenditure results in the creation of an asset having a useful life which extends substantially beyond the close of the taxable year. In such a case, the asset should be capitalized and the basis should be amortized ratably over its life. Mr. J may deduct the premiums applicable to 1990 (November and December) and 1991.

Monthly insurance expense ($1,800 divided by 36 months)	$ 50
Months deductible in 1991 (November and December of 1990 + 1991 calendar year)	x 14
Insurance expense	$700

11. On April 1, 1991, Ms. G, a calendar-year, cash-basis taxpayer, entered into a 3-year lease for a building to be used in her business. The lease is for the period July 1, 1991 through June 30, 1994, and provides for annual payments of $6,000. On April 1, 1991, G paid $18,000 in advance. What is the amount of G's deductible rental expense for 1991?

   a. $3,000.
   b. $4,500.
   c. $6,000.
   d. $18,000.

The correct answer is (a). *(SPE 987 II-40)*
REQUIRED: A cash-basis taxpayer's deductible rent expense.
DISCUSSION: The prepaid rent must be amortized over the period to which it applies. Although an expense is generally deductible if only prepaid for the next year, the Special Enrollment Exam consistently requires amortization of any prepaid expense. Ms. G's rent expense is $3,000 [($18,000 ÷ 36 months) x 6 months].

12. Dr. Berger reports on the cash basis. The following items pertain to Dr. Berger's medical practice in 1991:

Cash received from patients in 1991	$200,000
Cash received in 1991 from third-party reimbursers for services provided by Dr. Berger in 1990	30,000
Salaries paid to employees in 1991	20,000
Year-end 1991 bonuses paid to employees in 1992	1,000
Other expenses paid in 1991	24,000

What is Dr. Berger's net business income for 1991 from his medical practice?

   a. $155,000.
   b. $156,000.
   c. $185,000.
   d. $186,000.

The correct answer is (d). *(CPA 1183 Q-36)*
REQUIRED: The net business income of cash-basis taxpayers.
DISCUSSION: Under Sec. 451(a) and Reg. 1.451-1(a), a cash-basis taxpayer generally includes an item in income when it is actually or constructively received. Under Sec. 461(a) and Reg. 1.461-1, a cash-basis taxpayer may generally deduct an expense only in the year of actual payment. Dr. Berger's net income from his business is

Income:	
Cash from customers	$200,000
Cash from third parties	30,000
Expenses:	
Salaries	(20,000)
Other business expenses	(24,000)
Net business income	$186,000

The 1991 year-end bonuses paid in 1992 will be deductible in 1992.

13. Paul Charles, a cash-basis taxpayer, owns an apartment house. In computing net rental income for 1991, the following data are obtained:

An analysis of the 1991 bank deposit slips shows rents received in the amount of $15,000.

In December 1991, Mr. Charles received a $600 negotiable non-interest-bearing promissory note dated December 1, 1991 as rent for the months of December 1991 and January 1992 (fair market value $550).

Pursuant to instructions from Mr. Charles, a past-due rent check of $175 was given to the building superintendent on December 29, 1991. He mailed it to the rental office on the 30th; it was received on January 2 and deposited on January 3, 1992.

The lease of the tenant in Apt. 4A expired on December 31, 1991 and the tenant left improvements valued at $500. The improvements were not in lieu of any rent required to have been paid.

In computing his 1991 taxable income, Mr. Charles will report gross rents of

a. $16,275.
b. $16,225.
c. $15,725.
d. $15,500.

The correct answer is (c). *(CPA 573 Q-4)*

REQUIRED: The amount of rental income includable by a cash-basis taxpayer.

DISCUSSION: Under the general rule of Sec. 451(a) and Reg. 1.451-1(a), a taxpayer who uses the cash method of accounting includes an item in gross income when it is actually or constructively received. Reg. 1.451-2(a) provides that an item is constructively received if it is set apart for the taxpayer or could be collected by the taxpayer during that taxable year.

The bank deposits and the promissory note were income actually received. Only the fair market value of the note is included in income in 1991, however, since that is all Charles could realize on it (cash equivalency). Prepaid rent (January) is included in income when received. Upon collection of the note in 1992, an additional $50 will be recognized. The rent check of $175 was constructively received since Charles's agent received it. Improvements left by a tenant (not in lieu of rent) are excluded from gross income (Sec. 109).

Actually received:	
Bank deposits	$15,000
FMV of note	550
Constructively received:	
Rent check given to building supervisor	175
Gross rents	$15,725

14. L.E. operates an accounting service as a sole proprietorship. For income tax purposes, L.E. reports on the cash and calendar-year bases. During 1991, L.E. made the following expenditures in connection with his business

Utility bills for services received in 1991		$4,000
Property taxes applicable to:		
1991	$2,000	
1992	2,400	4,400
Business loan interest applicable to:		
1990	$1,500	
1991	1,500	
1992	1,500	4,500
Computer rental applicable to:		
1991	$12,000	
1992	3,000	15,000

If L.E. makes no tax elections applicable to 1991, what is the allowable amount of his business deductions for 1991?

a. $27,900.
b. $26,400.
c. $24,900.
d. $23,400.

The correct answer is (d). *(E. Grams)*

REQUIRED: The amount of a cash-basis taxpayer's business deductions.

DISCUSSION: Under Sec. 461(a) and Reg. 1.461-1, expenses may be deducted by a cash-basis taxpayer when actually paid. Exceptions to this rule are that a cash-basis taxpayer is required to capitalize (1) payments that create assets having a useful life extending substantially beyond the end of the taxable year and (2) payments for prepaid interest [Sec. 461(g)]. The utility bills and property taxes are fully deductible in the year paid. The business loan interest is deductible except for that applicable to 1992, which must be capitalized and deducted in 1992. The prepayment of computer rental arguably creates an asset that will extend beyond the end of the taxable year. On this basis the payment applicable to 1992 must be capitalized and deducted in 1992, but there is case law to the contrary which would allow the deduction in 1991 for payments that relate to the next year.

Utility bills	$ 4,000
Property taxes	4,400
Business loan interest (excluding	
$1,500 applicable to 1992)	3,000
Computer rentals (excluding	
$3,000 applicable to 1992)	12,000
Total allowable deduction	$23,400

Module 21.1: Cash Method

15. Which of the following is not considered "constructive receipt" of income?

  a. Ms. K was informed her check for services rendered was available on December 15, 1991, but she waited until January 15, 1992 to pick up the check.

  b. Earned income of Mr. D was received by his agent on December 29, 1991, but not received by D until January 5, 1992.

  c. Mr. W received a check on December 30, 1991 for services rendered, but was unable to make a deposit until January 4, 1992.

  d. A payment on a sale of real property was placed in escrow on December 15, 1991, but not received by Ms. B until January 10, 1992 when the transaction was closed.

The correct answer is (d). *(SPE 990 I-42)*
REQUIRED: The payment not considered constructive receipt of income.
DISCUSSION: The general rule under Sec. 451(a) and Reg. 1.451-1(a) is that an item is included in gross income by a cash-basis taxpayer when it is actually or constructively received. Income is constructively received in the taxable year during which it is credited to the taxpayer's account, set apart for him/her, or otherwise made available so that (s)he could have drawn upon it during the taxable year if notice of intention to withdraw had been given. However, income is not constructively received if its receipt is subject to substantial limitations or restrictions. The payment in escrow is subject to substantial limitations or restrictions on receipt and thus not constructively received.
Answer (a) is incorrect because the check was available to Ms. K. Answer (b) is incorrect because a payment in the hands of an agent is available to the taxpayer-principal. Answer (c) is incorrect because the receipt of a check is equivalent to the receipt of cash.

16. Pierre, a headwaiter, received tips totaling $2,000 in December 1990. On January 5, 1991 Pierre reported this tip income to his employer in the required written statement. At what amount, and in which year, should this tip income be included in Pierre's gross income?

  a. $2,000 in 1990.
  b. $2,000 in 1991.
  c. $1,000 in 1990, and $1,000 in 1991.
  d. $167 in 1990, and $1,833 in 1991.

The correct answer is (b). *(CPA 1188 Q-3)*
REQUIRED: When tips should be included in income.
DISCUSSION: Normally, a cash-basis taxpayer includes income when received. However, tips are specially treated. An employee who receives $20 or more in tips in a month (as a result of working for one employer, and not combined from several jobs) must report the total tips to the employer by the 10th day of the next month [Sec. 6053(a)]. These tips are treated as paid when the report is made to the employer [Sec. 451(c)]. Since Pierre properly reported his December 1990 tips to his employer in January 1991, the tips are not included in gross income until 1991.

17. Farmer John, a cash-basis taxpayer, bought $3,000 of cattle feed in 1991 for use in 1992. John's other farming expenses for 1991 amounted to $2,000. In prior years he also had prepaid expenses in excess of nonprepaid expenses. How much and when is the cattle feed deductible?

	1991	1992
a.	$0	$1,000
b.	$0	$3,000
c.	$1,000	$2,000
d.	$3,000	$0

The correct answer is (c). *(Publisher)*
REQUIRED: The amount of prepaid feed a farmer may deduct.
DISCUSSION: Reg. 1.162-12 provides that farmers (but not farming syndicates) may deduct prepaid feed when the expenditure is incurred even if it is to be consumed by the livestock in a subsequent year. After 1986, even individual farmers' deduction of prepaid farm supplies is limited by Sec. 464(f) to 50% of other farming expenses incurred during the taxable year. Farmer John's deduction of prepaid cattle feed for 1991 is thus limited to $1,000 (50% x $2,000 other expenses).
If the farmer has a principal residence on a farm or his/her principal occupation is farming and if the aggregate of prepaid farm supplies for the prior 3 taxable years is less than 50% of the aggregate of other deductible farming expenses, then the 50% limitation does not apply for the current year.

18. All of the following items are deductible on a cash basis decedent's final return except:

a. Decedent's net operating loss from business operations.
b. Medical expenses paid after the date of death by the surviving spouse for the care of the decedent.
c. Personal exemption for the decedent.
d. Moving expenses incurred, but not paid before date of death.

The correct answer is (d). *(SPE 989 III-54)*
REQUIRED: The expenses that are deductible on a cash basis decedent's final tax return.
DISCUSSION: When a taxpayer dies, his income tax liability must be determined using his/her regular accounting method for the period of time from the beginning of his/her tax year to the date of death. Under Reg. 1.461-1, a cash method of accounting taxpayer deducts expenses when they are paid. Deductions of a decedent are not accrued on his/her final return unless his/her established accounting method requires it, but are deductible by the estate or other person who is liable for their payment. In the case of the moving expenses they would be deducted by the estate in the year that they were paid.
The decedent's net operating loss can be deducted in his/her final tax return. Medical expenses paid by a surviving spouse after the date of death are deductible on a joint return filed with the decedent for the year of death or on his/her separate return. A decedent is allowed a personal exemption in his/her final tax return.

19. Y separately operates a small grocery store and a pick-up and delivery messenger service. Y may use the same accounting method and keep one complete set of books for both businesses.

The correct answer is (F). *(SPE 1081 IV-43)*
DISCUSSION: Under Reg. 1.446-1(a)(4), a taxpayer is required to maintain accounting records to enable him/her to file a correct tax return. Each business is required to keep a separate set of books, so Y may not keep one set of books for both the grocery store and the messenger service. However, Y may use the same accounting method for both businesses or may use a different method of accounting for each business [Reg. 1.446-1(d)]. The grocery store will be required to use the accrual method of accounting for its inventory purchases and sales since inventories are a material income-producing factor [Reg. 1.446-1(c)(2)].

20. A lawyer using the cash method of accounting may deduct uncollectible fees as a bad debt.

The correct answer is (F). *(SPE 1077 I-100)*
DISCUSSION: Under Sec. 165, the deduction for a loss is limited to the adjusted basis of the property. Under the cash method of accounting, fees which have not been collected have not been included in income and, therefore, have no basis. Without any basis, there is no loss to deduct.

21. Mr. X signed a note for $1,500 on May 31, 1991 at a 12% interest rate, agreeing to repay it in 12 equal installments beginning on April 1, 1992. Interest of $180 was subtracted from the face value of the note and Mr. X received $1,320. Mr. X uses the cash method. He may deduct the $180 interest in 1991.

The correct answer is (F). *(SPE 1081 I-26)*
DISCUSSION: Under Reg. 1.461-1(a)(1), a taxpayer using the cash method of accounting generally deducts expenses when they are paid. However, a taxpayer who receives a loan at a discount has not paid the discount (interest) until the loan is repaid. A cash-basis taxpayer deducts the discount ratably as the loan is repaid.

22. Mr. Grey owns a cattle ranch in Texas. This area suffered a severe drought in 1991 and was designated as eligible for federal assistance. Mr. Grey normally buys cattle, raises them for 2 years, then sells them. As a result of the drought, his cattle had to be sold after holding them only 1 year. Under these conditions, Mr. Grey may elect to postpone reporting the income from the sale in 1991 to 1992.

The correct answer is (T). *(SPE 989 II-16)*
DISCUSSION: Sec. 451(e)(1) provides an exception to the general rule of cash basis accounting by allowing taxpayers to defer recognition of income from sale or exchange of livestock until the tax year following the year in which the sale or exchange occurred. This exception applies only if the sale or exchange would not have occurred were it not for drought conditions and the drought conditions resulted in the area being designated as eligible for federal government assistance.

23. Mr. Sharp is a 50% shareholder in Corporation W. On November 30, 1991 the corporation declared a cash dividend payable on December 15, 1991. On December 10, Sharp notified W not to issue him his dividend check until January 15, 1992, since this would enable W to delay drawing on its line of credit from State Bank. Mr. Sharp should include the dividend income from W in his income for 1992.

The correct answer is (F). *(SPE 990 I-7)*
DISCUSSION: Under Reg. 1.451 income is constructively received when it is set apart for the taxpayer or otherwise made available so that (s)he may draw upon it at any time. In this case, the dividend is available to Mr. Sharp on December 15, 1991. Mr. Sharp must report the dividend income in 1991.

24. Mr. C is a cash-basis, calendar-year taxpayer. He owns several shares of stock in a mutual fund. On December 29, 1991 the fund credits to his account a capital gain distribution of $600. C received the $600 on January 15, 1992. C must report the $600 capital gain distribution as a capital gain on his 1991 return.

The correct answer is (T). *(SPE 1083 I-14)*
DISCUSSION: The general rule under Sec. 451(a) and Reg. 1.451-1(a) is that income is included by a cash-basis taxpayer when it is actually or constructively received. Income is deemed to be constructively received if it is credited to the taxpayer's account. Hence, C must report the $600 distribution in 1991. Sec. 852(b)(3)(B) holds that a capital gain dividend of a mutual fund is reported as a long-term capital gain.

21.2 Accrual Method

25. M, an accrual-method taxpayer using the calendar year, had the following transactions during 1991

Recovery of an account receivable written off and deducted in a prior year which did not reduce income subject to tax	$ 5,000
Sales to a customer who is directed to transmit the payment to M's brother	3,500
Amounts received in settlement of a breach of contract suit	22,500
Goods shipped on consignment December 15, 1991 and sold by M's agent on January 10, 1992	13,000

What amount must M include in gross income?

a. $8,500.
b. $26,000.
c. $27,500.
d. $31,000.

The correct answer is (b). *(SPE 1081 II-73)*
REQUIRED: The amount that an accrual-method taxpayer must include in gross income.
DISCUSSION: Reg. 1.446-1(c)(1) provides the general principles to be used in the accrual method. Income is included in the taxable year in which all the events have occurred which fix the right to receive such income and the amount can be determined with reasonable accuracy. The sales to a customer are included in income since the direction to pay M's brother is merely an assignment of income. Proceeds from settlement of a lawsuit are included in income when received because that is when the amount can be determined with reasonable accuracy.
The recovery of a bad debt is excluded from income if the prior deduction did not reduce taxes (Sec. 111). Goods shipped on consignment do not produce income until sold since the all events test has not been satisfied [Reg. 1.446-1(c)].

Sales to customer who is directed to pay M's brother	$ 3,500
Amounts received in settlement of breach of contract suit	22,500
Includable in gross income	$26,000

26. Mr. J, a calendar-year taxpayer using the accrual method, had the following transactions during 1991:

Recovery of an account receivable that had been written off and deducted in 1989 (did not reduce income subject to tax)	$15,000
Rental income (tenant made payments to J's son)	6,000
Performed legal services for RJB Corporation in return for 100 shares of stock in RJB which had a	
Par value	1,000
Fair market value	24,000

What amount must Mr. J include in his gross income for 1991?

  a. $21,000.
  b. $22,000.
  c. $30,000.
  d. $45,000.

The correct answer is (c). *(SPE 990 II-61)*
REQUIRED: The amount includable in gross income for an accrual-method taxpayer.
DISCUSSION: Income is included in the taxable year in which all the events have occurred which fix the right to receive such income and the amount can be determined with reasonable accuracy. The rental income is included in gross income. The direction to pay Mr. J's son is merely an assignment of income. The payment for legal services performed is also included in gross income. The fair market value of the stock is the amount included [Sec. 83(a)].

Under Sec. 111, the recovery of a bad debt is excluded from income if the previous deduction did not reduce taxes.

Rental income (tenants directed to pay J's son)	$ 6,000
Legal services performed (FMV of stock)	24,000
Includable in gross income	$30,000

27. In 1991 Mr. A started a business that rents, sells, and repairs video recorders. Mr. A uses the accrual method of accounting and the calendar year as his tax year. The 1991 business receipts included payments for 1-year service contracts and payments for prepaid rent on video recorders. The video recorders are offered for sale without service contracts in the normal course of business. Which of the following statements regarding Mr. A's reporting of gross income is correct?

  a. He must include the payments for prepaid rent in gross income for 1991, but may include the payments for 1-year service contracts as he earns them over the periods of the contracts.

  b. He may include the payments for prepaid rent and 1-year service contracts in gross income as he earns them over the periods of the contracts.

  c. He must include the payments for 1-year service contracts in gross income for 1991, but may include the payments for prepaid rent over the periods of the rental contracts.

  d. He must include the payments for prepaid rent and for 1-year service contracts in gross income for 1991.

The correct answer is (a). *(SPE 1085 II-38)*
REQUIRED: The income an accrual basis taxpayer reports from prepaid services and rent.
DISCUSSION: An accrual-method taxpayer must report income when all events have occurred which fix the right to receive such income and the amount thereof can be determined with reasonable accuracy [Reg. 1.451-1(a)]. As a general rule, an accrual-method taxpayer must recognize prepaid income when received. This is true for rent, but prepaid income for services may be accrued over the period for which the services are to be performed provided that the period is not to extend past the end of the next tax year (Rev. Proc. 71-21).

All of Mr. A's prepaid rent must be recognized when received. The prepaid income for services may be accrued over the period of the service contract, since the service period is for 1 year only.

Module 21.2: Accrual Method

28. Perry Refrigerators, an accrual-basis, calendar-year company for both tax and financial reporting, received a $600 payment from the September 1990 sale of a $1,000 refrigerator. The cost of the refrigerator to Perry was $550, and the refrigerator was in stock on December 31, 1990. The refrigerator was shipped to the customer in March 1991 after the remaining $400 was paid. When is Perry required to report income from the sale of the refrigerator?

   a. $600 in 1990 and $400 in 1991.
   b. $550 in 1990 and $450 in 1991.
   c. $1,000 in 1990.
   d. $1,000 in 1991.

The correct answer is (d). *(R. Fernandez)*
REQUIRED: The period in which to report payments for goods sold.
DISCUSSION: As a general rule, an accrual-basis taxpayer reports advance payments for the sale of merchandise when they are earned (e.g., when the goods are shipped). This rule applies only if such payments are reported for tax purposes no later than they are reported for accounting purposes. Even when this is true, Reg. 1.451-5(c)(1) limits the time of deferral if the taxpayer has received substantial advance payments (defined as greater than the seller's cost of goods sold) and the goods are on hand or available from normal channels. When these two conditions are met, as in this problem, the advance payments must be reported in the earlier of the year reported for financial purposes (1991) or the second taxable year after the tax year in which the advance payments become substantial (1990 + 2 = 1992).

29. Which of the following statements is not correct?

   a. A cash-method taxpayer must report the increase in redemption value each year on U.S. savings bonds issued on a discount basis.
   b. An accrual-method taxpayer must report the increase in redemption value each year on U.S. savings bonds issued on a discount basis.
   c. A cash-method taxpayer may defer the reporting of interest on Series E or EE U.S. savings bonds until the bonds are cashed or the year the extended maturity period ends, whichever is earlier.
   d. A cash-method taxpayer must report interest when received on U.S. savings bonds issued at face value.

The correct answer is (a). *(SPE 1081 I-48)*
REQUIRED: The incorrect statement concerning U.S. savings bonds issued at a discount.
DISCUSSION: A cash-method taxpayer is required to report interest only when actually or constructively received. On a discount bond, interest is received when the bond is surrendered. Sec. 454(a) provides that a cash-basis taxpayer may elect to treat the annual increase in redemption value of Series E or EE bonds as income each year.
Answer (b) is true because a taxpayer must report interest as it accrues under the accrual method of accounting. Answer (c) is true because Series E and EE bonds are noninterest-bearing bonds issued at a discount. The interest is not received until they are cashed or they mature. Answer (d) is true because U.S. savings bonds issued at face value pay interest twice a year and this interest must be included by a cash-method taxpayer when received.

30. Mr. S owns and operates an art studio. On December 1, 1990 he received an advance payment of $12,000 from Ms. A to give her 12 painting lessons. The agreement stated that one lesson would be given in 1990 and 11 lessons in 1991. However, due to Ms. A's health, one lesson scheduled for July 1991 was not given until January 1992. S uses the calendar year and the accrual method of accounting. Assuming S elects to defer the advance payments, when must S report the income from painting lessons?

   a. $12,000 in 1990.
   b. $1,000 in 1990 and $11,000 in 1991.
   c. $1,000 in 1990, $10,000 in 1991, and $1,000 in 1992.
   d. $12,000 in 1991.

The correct answer is (b). *(SPE 990 II-35)*
REQUIRED: The amount an accrual basis taxpayer includes in income from prepaid services.
DISCUSSION: Generally, an accrual basis taxpayer must recognize prepaid income when received. Prepaid income for services may be accrued over the period for which the services are to be performed provided that the period does not extend past the end of the next tax year (Rev. Proc. 71-21).
Here, the services are to be performed during a 1-year period. Therefore, the income is recognized in that 1-year period. The first lesson of 12 to be performed is given in December 1990, so $1,000 is includable in 1990. The income must be reported by December 1991, even though one lesson is rescheduled until January 1992. Therefore, $11,000 is included in 1991.

31. Mr. D, a calendar-year taxpayer, uses the accrual method of accounting in his manufacturing business. In 1989, D's brother, Mr. E, a calendar-year, cash-basis taxpayer, was selected to be the foreman of a project in which E would receive a $10,000 bonus upon completion of the project. Work on the project began in 1989 and was completed in December 1990. The bonus was paid to E in January 1991. When may Mr. D deduct the bonus paid to his brother?

  a. 1989.
  b. A portion in both 1989 and 1990.
  c. 1990.
  d. 1991.

The correct answer is (d). *(SPE 990 II-32)*
REQUIRED: The taxable year in which an accrual basis taxpayer may deduct a bonus paid to a related party cash-basis taxpayer.
DISCUSSION: Mr. D and Mr. E are related parties under Secs. 267(b)(1) and 267(c)(4). When related parties are involved, Sec. 267(a)(2) requires the matching of the deduction claimed by a payor and the income reported by a payee in the case of expense or interest transaction. In this instance, the payee is a cash-basis taxpayer and he will include the payment in income in the taxable year received (1991). The payor (Mr. D) can then deduct the payment in 1991.

32. LeDoran Sports Cars purchased supplies from a new supplier in 1990. The total invoice was for $12,000, but LeDoran claimed that only one-half of the order was received and paid only $6,000 in 1990. Both parties honestly disputed the bill and LeDoran refused to pay the contested amount. They went to court and a judgment requiring LeDoran to pay an additional $3,000 was issued in 1991. How should LeDoran report the expense?

  a. $6,000 in 1990 and $3,000 in 1991.
  b. $9,000 in 1990.
  c. $9,000 in 1991.
  d. $12,000 in 1990 and $3,000 of income in 1991.

The correct answer is (a). *(Publisher)*
REQUIRED: The correct method for deducting a disputed liability.
DISCUSSION: Under the accrual method of accounting, an expense is deductible for the taxable year in which all events (including economic performance) have occurred which determine the fact of the liability and the amount thereof can be determined with reasonable accuracy [Reg. 1.461-1(a)(2)]. When there is a dispute and the amount of a liability is contested, it cannot be said that all events have occurred to determine the entire amount of the liability or that the amount can be determined with reasonable accuracy. Therefore, any part of a liability that remains unpaid and is honestly disputed may not be deducted.

Since $6,000 of the liability was not disputed, it should be deducted in 1990 when LeDoran became liable. The remaining $3,000 should be deducted in 1991. Note that Sec. 461(f) allows the deduction of a contested amount that is paid but remains contested.

33. All the following statements regarding accounting methods are true except:

  a. If inventory is a material, income-producing item for your business, you must use the accrual method for your sales and purchases.
  b. If you use the cash method for reporting expenses, you can use the accrual method for figuring income.
  c. If you use the accrual method for reporting expenses, you can use the cash method for figuring income.
  d. If you operate more than one business, you may use a different accounting method for each separate and distinct business if the method clearly reflects income.

The correct answer is (c). *(SPE 989 II-32)*
REQUIRED: The incorrect statement regarding accounting methods.
DISCUSSION: Under Reg. 1.446-1(c)(1)(iv), if a taxpayer uses the accrual method of accounting to report expenses, then (s)he must use the accrual method in reporting income items.

Answer (a) is incorrect because Reg. 1.446-1(c)(2) states that where an inventory is used, the accrual method of accounting must be used for purchases and sales. Answer (b) is incorrect because it is not specifically excepted and as long as a combination of two different accounting methods clearly reflects income and is consistently used, then it is allowed. Answer (d) is incorrect because Reg. 1.446-1(d)(1) states a taxpayer with two or more separate businesses may use a different method of accounting for each trade or business provided that the income from each is clearly reflected.

34. Shady Deal Corporation agreed to purchase the services of an expert appraiser as a consultant over the next 2 years. Every 6 months, the appraiser will value art works owned by Shady Deal for purposes of determining their resale value. Shady Deal paid the cash-basis appraiser $20,000 on December 31, 1990 for work to be performed in June and December of both 1991 and 1992. Shady, an accrual-basis, calendar-year corporation, may deduct

   a. $20,000 in 1990.
   b. $10,000 in 1991; $10,000 in 1992.
   c. $15,000 in 1991; $5,000 in 1992.
   d. $20,000 in 1992.

The correct answer is (b). *(Publisher)*
REQUIRED: The correct amount and timing of deductions for an accrual-basis taxpayer.
DISCUSSION: An accrual-basis taxpayer can deduct an expense when (1) all events have occurred that established the existence of the liability, and (2) the amount of the liability can be determined with reasonable accuracy (the "all events" test). In addition, Sec. 461(h) provides that the "all events" test will not be satisfied for an accrual-basis taxpayer until economic performance has occurred. Economic performance occurs in the case of payments made to another person for services when such other person actually renders the services. Shady will be allowed to deduct the payment to the appraiser ratably as the appraiser performs the appraisals. Shady may therefore deduct $10,000 in 1991 and $10,000 in 1992.

35. An accrual-method taxpayer must recognize income from providing services during 1991 even if before year-end it appears that the purchaser will not be able to pay.

The correct answer is (F). *(Publisher)*
DISCUSSION: Under the accrual method of accounting, income is recognized if all the events have occurred which fix the right to receive the income and the amount thereof can be determined with reasonable accuracy [Reg. 1.451-1(a)]. But amounts to be received for services need not be accrued if on the basis of experience they will not be collected [Sec. 448(d)(5)]. This exception to the accrual method is not available if the taxpayer charges interest or a penalty for late payment.

36. Under the accrual method of accounting, all items of income are included in gross income when they are earned even though the right to receive the income is contingent upon a future year's event.

The correct answer is (F). *(SPE 990 II-1)*
DISCUSSION: Under the accrual method of accounting, an item is includable in gross income when all the events have occurred which fix the right to receive the income and the amount thereof can be determined with reasonable accuracy [Reg. 1.451-1(a)]. If the right to receive the income is contingent upon a future year's event occurring, then it is not includable in gross income until the future point in time that all the events have occurred which fix the right to receive the income.

37. When inventories are necessary to clearly show income, you must use the accrual method of accounting for sales, purchases, and all other items of income and expense.

The correct answer is (F). *(SPE 988 II-3)*
DISCUSSION: Sec. 446(a) provides that taxable income shall be computed under the method of accounting on the basis of which a taxpayer regularly computes income and keeps books. Each taxpayer must choose a method that, in the opinion of the Commissioner, clearly reflects income. However, a taxpayer who maintains inventory must use the accrual method of accounting with regard to purchases and sales [Reg. 1.446-1(c)(2)] but is not required to use the accrual method for other items of income or expense. A combination of the accrual and cash methods of accounting is known as the hybrid method.

38. A farmer who uses the accrual method of accounting may not make the election to postpone reporting the proceeds from a sale of livestock owing to drought conditions.

The correct answer is (T). *(SPE 1083 II-32)*
DISCUSSION: Under Sec. 451(e), the special rule that allows taxpayers to postpone reporting the proceeds of a sale of livestock owing to drought conditions is not available to accrual-method taxpayers or to anyone whose principal trade or business is not farming.

39. In 1990, Ms. P, an accrual-basis, calendar-year taxpayer, under a contract, received an advance payment covering services to be performed ratably through the end of 1991. If for some reason, Ms. P cannot perform all the services by the end of 1991, she may postpone including the advance payments in income until she earns them.

The correct answer is (F). *(SPE 989 II-2)*
DISCUSSION: As a general rule, an accrual-method taxpayer must recognize prepaid income when received, if the right to receive such income is fixed and the amount thereof can be determined with reasonable accuracy. However, prepaid income for services may be accrued over the period for which the services are to be performed, provided the period does not extend past the end of the next tax year (Rev. Proc. 71-21). Even if for some reason Ms. P cannot perform all the services by the end of 1991, she must include the remaining income in 1991.

40. K and N are sisters operating separate businesses. K uses the accrual method of accounting and N uses the cash method. In December 1991, K purchased non-inventory materials on account from N. K paid for those materials in April 1992. K may not deduct the expense on her 1991 return.

The correct answer is (T). *(SPE 990 II-2)*
DISCUSSION: Sec. 267(a)(2) provides that the deduction for an amount payable to a related party is allowed only when it is includable in the gross income of the person to whom the payment is made. Under Sec. 267(c)(4) siblings are family members and K and N are therefore considered related parties under Sec. 267(b)(1). Accordingly, K will be allowed a deduction in 1992.

41. For accrual basis taxpayers, vacation pay earned and vested by their employees can be deducted in the year earned only if it is paid within 2½ months after the close of the taxable year.

The correct answer is (T). *(SPE 990 II-5)*
DISCUSSION: The employer's deduction for accrued vacation pay is restricted by the Sec. 461(h) economic performance rules. Under these rules, the deduction is allowed in the year economic performance occurs; that is, for employee benefits in the year when the employer makes the payment. Under the Sec. 461(h)(3) recurring item exception, however, a deduction is allowed for an accrual-method taxpayer who pays vacation pay on a regular basis in the year the recurring item requirements are met even though the economic performance test is not yet satisfied. To use this exception, the vacation pay must be paid within 2½ months of the end of the tax year. If the 2½-month requirement is not met, the Sec. 404 deferred compensation rules generally will delay the claiming of the deduction until it is paid.

42. Mr. Oak, an accrual-basis, calendar-year taxpayer, sells refrigerators at the retail level. For 1991, his sales totaled $550,000, which included $50,000 from the sale of 1-year service contracts for the refrigerators. From past experience, Mr. Brown knows that for 1992 he will have expenses of $20,000 relating to those contracts. Since he is on the accrual basis, Mr. Brown can deduct the $20,000 in 1991, as a contingent liability.

The correct answer is (F). *(SPE 989 II-9)*
DISCUSSION: Under the accrual method of accounting, an expense is deductible for the taxable year in which all events (including economic performance) have occurred which determine the fact of the liability and the amount thereof can be determined with reasonable accuracy. Here, the events that determine the fact of the liability have not occurred.

21.3 Hybrid Method

43. Mr. G opened a small grocery store. The sale of inventory is an income-producing factor. Mr. G may select either the cash or accrual method of accounting for his grocery business.

The correct answer is (F). *(SPE 1078 II-3)*
DISCUSSION: Reg. 1.446-1(c)(2) states that where an inventory is used, the accrual method of accounting must be used for purchases and sales. Mr. G must use the accrual method of accounting for his purchases and sales, but he may use the cash method of accounting for noninventory transactions. This combination of methods is commonly referred to as a hybrid method.

44. Mrs. J owns a boutique. She may use the accrual method of accounting for purchases and sales and the cash method for figuring all other items of income and expense.

The correct answer is (T). *(SPE 984 II-3)*
DISCUSSION: Reg. 1.446-1(c)(1)(iv) provides that any combination of permissible methods will be allowed if such combination clearly reflects income and is consistently used. It specifically states that a taxpayer using the accrual method for purchases and sales may use the cash method for all other items of income and expense.

45. A manufacturing business in which inventories are necessary to show income correctly must use the accrual accounting method for purchases and sales.

The correct answer is (T). *(SPE 987 II-5)*
DISCUSSION: Under Reg. 1.446-1(c)(2), where an inventory is necessary to the taxpayer's business, the accrual method of accounting must be used with regard to purchases and sales. The cash method of accounting may be used for other receipts and expenses provided it clearly reflects income [Sec. 446(b)].

46. A sole proprietorship that is required to report sales and purchases using the accrual method may use the cash method for reporting expenses if it clearly reflects income.

The correct answer is (T). *(SPE 986 II-5)*
DISCUSSION: Reg. 1.446-1(c)(2) provides that when an inventory is used, the accrual method of accounting must be used for purchases and sales. Reg. 1.446-1(c)(1)(iv) specifically states that a taxpayer using an accrual method of accounting with respect to purchases and sales may use the cash method in computing all other items of income and expense.

47. A sole proprietorship may use the cash method for reporting gross income and the accrual method for reporting expenses.

The correct answer is (F). *(SPE 987 II-6)*
DISCUSSION: Although hybrid methods of accounting are allowed, a taxpayer who uses the cash method to report gross income must also use the cash method to report expenses. Relatedly, a taxpayer who uses the accrual method to report expenses must also use the accrual method to report income. This is necessary to clearly reflect the income of the business.

21.4 Long-Term Contracts

48. For long-term contracts entered into after July 11, 1989, Sec. 460 requires, with limited exceptions, use of the percentage-of-completion method. For this purpose, which of the following is not a characteristic of a long-term contract?

   a. A contract for the manufacture, building, installation, or construction of property not completed within the taxable year in which it was entered.
   b. A contract for the manufacture of an item that normally takes more than 12 months to complete, regardless of the contract period.
   c. A contract for the manufacture of a unique item not normally carried in finished goods inventory.
   d. A contract estimated to be completed within 2 years of commencement of construction, and the taxpayer's average annual gross receipts for the prior 3 taxable years are $10 million or less.

The correct answer is (d). *(Publisher)*
REQUIRED: The item not characteristic of a long-term contract.
DISCUSSION: Sec. 460(e) provides that a construction contract (other than a home construction contract) is not long-term if it is estimated (when entered into) that it will be completed within 2 years of commencement (when construction costs are first incurred), and the taxpayer's average annual gross receipts for the prior 3 taxable years are $10 million or less. If a contract is not long-term because of these criteria, the taxpayer may use the completed-contract method.
Answer (a) is incorrect because it is the general definition of a long-term contract [Sec. 460(f)(1)]. Answers (b) and (c) are incorrect because they are alternative requirements for manufacturing contracts to be considered long-term.

49. Which one of the following statements is not correct about using the percentage-of-completion method to account for long-term contracts?

  a. The percentage-of-completion capitalized-cost method of accounting is generally available for long-term contracts if the taxpayer makes the appropriate election.
  b. The percentage-of-completion is determined by comparing costs allocated to the contract and incurred before the end of the taxable year with the estimated total contract costs.
  c. In determining the taxable income from the long-term contract under the percentage-of-completion method, a taxpayer may elect not to recognize income or account for costs from the contract for a taxable year if less than 10% of the estimated total contract costs have been incurred by the end of the taxable year.
  d. All income from the long-term contract must be included in gross income no later than the taxable year after the taxable year in which the contract was completed.

The correct answer is (a). *(Publisher)*
REQUIRED: The item not characteristic of the percentage-of-completion method to account for long-term contracts.
DISCUSSION: After July 11, 1989 the percentage-of-completion capitalized-cost method of accounting is no longer acceptable.
Answer (b) is incorrect because it describes the application of the percentage-of-completion method under Sec. 460(b)(1)(A). Answer (c) is incorrect because a taxpayer may elect to use the 10% method under Sec. 460(b)(5). Answer (d) is incorrect because it is required under Sec. 460(b)(1)(B).

50. On January 5, 1991, Mr. D, a calendar-year taxpayer with average annual gross receipts of $4 million, contracted to build a road for X County for $1 million. The road will be completed by December 31, 1992. Mr. D has elected the completed-contract method to report his income. On December 31, 1991 the county engineer on the project certified that 65% of the road had been completed. Costs in the amount of $500,000 were incurred during 1991 with respect to the contract. How much net profit should Mr. D report on this contract in 1991?

  a. $0.
  b. $50,000.
  c. $75,000.
  d. $150,000.

The correct answer is (a). *(SPE 1079 II-65)*
REQUIRED: The net profit on a long-term contract under the completed-contract method of accounting.
DISCUSSION: For long-term contracts entered into after July 11, 1989, Sec. 460 requires with limited exceptions use of the percentage-of-completion method. However, since the contract in the question is estimated to be able to be completed in less than 2 years and the taxpayer's average annual gross receipts are $10 million or less, this is not treated as a long-term contract for purposes of Sec. 460. Therefore, the completed-contract method may be used. Reg. 1.451-3(d) states that, under the completed-contract method, gross income and expenses allocable to the long-term contract are accounted for in the taxable year in which such contract is completed. Since Mr. D's contract is not completed until 1992, no income or expenses allocated to the contract should be included in income for 1991. However, business expenses such as interest paid and depreciation on idle equipment that are not related to the contract can be deducted in 1991.

51. Costs which may be allocated to long-term contracts include all of the following except

  a. Production period interest.
  b. Direct costs of the contract.
  c. Marketing, selling, and advertising expenses.
  d. All costs incurred by reason of the taxpayer's long-term contract activities.

The correct answer is (c). *(Publisher)*
REQUIRED: The costs not allocable to long-term contracts.
DISCUSSION: Marketing, selling, and advertising expenses are not included in the costs of long-term contracts, as well as independent research and development costs and expenses of unsuccessful bids and proposals [Sec. 460(c)(4)].
Answer (a) is incorrect because Sec. 460(c)(3) provides that interest costs shall be allocated to a long-term contract in the same manner as to property produced by the taxpayer under Sec. 263A(f). The production period is amended slightly for long-term contracts. Answers (b) and (d) are incorrect because direct costs and all other costs incurred by reason of the taxpayer's long-term contract activities are allocated to long-term contracts.

Module 21.4: Long-Term Contracts

52. Granite Construction Co. contracted to build a dam for $5.4 million. The construction is to last 1.5 years. Granite elects the completed-contract method. Granite's annual gross receipts are less than $10 million. During 1991, Granite incurred the following costs

Depreciation on idle equipment	$ 45,000
Salaries for construction workers	390,000
Rent on construction equipment	250,000
Materials on dam	800,000
Interest on corporate debt (not related to this project)	12,000

How much can Granite deduct in 1991?

a. $0.
b. $57,000.
c. $307,000.
d. $1,440,000.

The correct answer is (b). *(Publisher)*
REQUIRED: Deductible business expenses under the completed-contract method of accounting.
DISCUSSION: Under the completed-contract method of accounting, gross income and expenses allocable to the long-term contract are accounted for in the taxable year in which such contract is completed [Reg. 1.451-3(d)(1)]. All costs that are not incidental to and necessary for the performance of the long-term contract may be deducted in the year paid or accrued. In determining what costs are properly allocable to a long-term contract, a form of the full absorption method of accounting is provided in Reg. 1.451-3(d)(5). Those costs that are directly or indirectly related to the contract are allocated to it and accumulated in an inventory account. Depreciation on idle equipment and interest on general corporate debt can be deducted in the current year ($57,000).

Note that complex cost allocation rules apply for indirect expenses incurred on contracts not completed within 3 years. But small contractors (less than $25 million average annual gross receipts) are exempt from these cost allocations (Reg. 1.451-3).

53. Corporation V, a calendar-year corporation, is in the construction business and uses the percentage-of-completion method of accounting for long-term contracts. On March 1, 1991, V signed a long-term contract to construct a building. It began construction on the same date. The contract provides for a payment of $300,000 and completion by November 1, 1992. In 1991, V incurred costs totaling $180,000. On December 31, 1991, V estimated the total contract costs would be $270,000. Using the cost-comparison method, how much gross income from the contract must V report in 1991?

a. $180,000.
b. $200,000.
c. $270,000.
d. $300,000.

The correct answer is (b). *(SPE 984 III-72)*
REQUIRED: The long-term contract income under the percentage-of-completion method.
DISCUSSION: According to Reg. 1.451-3(c), under the percentage-of-completion method, the portion of the gross contract price corresponding to the percentage of the entire contract completed during the taxable year is included in gross income for such taxable year.

Using the cost comparison technique, the percentage of completion (66 2/3%) is determined by comparing the costs incurred ($180,000) with the estimated total costs ($270,000). The gross income includable in 1991 is $200,000 ($300,000 total contract price x 66 2/3% percentage of completion).

54. Mr. Smart contracted for the construction of a building on July 1, 1991. The contract provided for a payment of $240,000 for the building to be completed on April 1, 1992. Smart is a calendar-year taxpayer and has elected the percentage-of-completion method to report his income. On December 31, 1991, the architect of the project certified that 40% of the project had been completed. $98,000 of costs were incurred during 1991 with respect to the contract. How much profit or loss should Smart report on his 1991 income tax return in connection with the construction project?

a. None.
b. ($2,000).
c. $56,800.
d. $96,000.

The correct answer is (b). *(SPE 1077 III-12)*
REQUIRED: The profit or loss on a long-term contract under the percentage-of-completion method of accounting.
DISCUSSION: Reg. 1.451-3(c) states that under the percentage-of-completion method, the portion of the gross contract price that corresponds to the percentage of the entire contract that has been completed during the taxable year must be included in gross income for such taxable year. Instead of comparing costs, the percentage of completion may be determined by a qualified professional such as an architect. All costs (taking into account beginning and ending inventories of materials) incurred during the taxable year are deducted in that taxable year. Smart's loss is

Includable income (40% of $240,000)	$96,000
Less costs incurred in 1991	(98,000)
Loss for 1991	$(2,000)

Module 21.4: Long-Term Contracts

55. Which one of the following statements is not correct about using the percentage-of-completion method to account for long-term contracts?

   a. The completed-contract method of accounting can be used for any home construction contract.

   b. The percentage-of-completion capitalized-cost method of accounting can be used for residential construction contracts.

   c. Under the percentage-of-completion capitalized-cost method, 70% of the items with respect to the contract are taken into account under the percentage-of-completion method and the remaining 30% of the items are taken into account under the taxpayer's normal method of accounting for residential construction contracts.

   d. Taxpayers entering into residential or home construction contracts can elect to use either the percentage-of-completion capitalized-cost or completed-contract methods.

The correct answer is (d). *(Publisher)*
REQUIRED: The incorrect statement about the percentage-of-completion capitalized-cost method and long-term contracts.
DISCUSSION: Under Sec. 460(e)(1), home construction contracts are excepted from the long-term contract rules, and therefore can use their regular method of accounting or the completed-contract method. Residential construction contracts (that are not also home construction contracts) fall under the percentage-of-completion capitalized-cost method. This method is required under Sec. 460(e)(5) except that 70% of the items under the contract are taken into account under the percentage-of-completion method and 30% under the taxpayer's regular accounting method instead of the 90% and 10% proportions used under the general percentage-of-completion capitalized-cost method rule. Taxpayers under the residential or home construction contract rules cannot make an election to use either percentage-of-completion, capitalized cost, or completed-contract methods.

56. X Corporation entered into a long-term contract in January 1991 to build an apartment building for $10 million. X Corporation normally uses the completed-contract method to account for long-term contracts. At the end of the first year, X Corporation had incurred $3.6 million of the total estimated $8 million in costs for the contract. The contract was completed in 3 years. Using the percentage-of-completion capitalized-cost method to account for the long-term contract, X Corporation would include in gross income for the first year

   a. $1.35 million.
   b. $3.15 million.
   c. $4.05 million.
   d. $4.5 million.

The correct answer is (b). *(Publisher)*
REQUIRED: The gross income from a long-term contract under the percentage-of-completion capitalized-cost method.
DISCUSSION: The contract entered into by X Corporation is a residential construction contract, but not a home construction contract. The percentage-of-completion capitalized-cost method must be used to account for the contract. Under the residential construction contract rules for the percentage-of-completion capitalized-cost method, 70% of the items with respect to the contract are taken into account under the percentage-of-completion method and the remaining 30% of the items are taken into account under the taxpayer's normal method of accounting for contracts entered into on or after July 11, 1989 [Sec. 460(e)(5)]. Based on the cost-comparison method, X Corporation is 45% complete with its contract ($3.6 million divided by $8 million). Under the percentage-of-completion method, X Corporation would include $4.5 million of the contract price in gross income (45% x $10 million). Therefore, under the percentage-of-completion capitalized-cost method, X Corporation would include $3.15 million in gross income (70% x $4.5 million).

In addition, 70% of the $3.6 million of costs would be deducted. The remaining 30% of the contract can be reported under the completed-contract method; i.e., the rest of the income will be reported when the contract is completed.

57. Under the look-back method related to long-term contracts, interest is computed

a. On tax with respect to only 100% of a contract entered into after July 11, 1989 if the percentage-of-completion method is used.
b. On the difference in tax if income is calculated under the percentage-of-completion method or completed-contract method.
c. On tax with respect to the portion of income determined under the completed-contract method if the percentage-of-completion capitalized-cost method is used.
d. Using the federal short-term rate for original issue discount bonds.

The correct answer is (a). *(Publisher)*
REQUIRED: The correct statement concerning the look-back method of computing interest.
DISCUSSION: The look-back method is used to compute interest on the underpayment or overpayment of tax caused by actual costs varying from estimated costs for each of the contract years [Sec. 460(b)(2)]. Interest must be computed under the look-back method for the entire amount when the percentage-of-completion method is used. The look-back method can be applied to 70% of the amount when the percentage-of-completion capitalized-cost method is used for residential construction contracts.

Answers (b) and (c) are incorrect because the look-back method refers to the difference between the actual and estimated costs on the percentage-of-completion portion of the contract, not the completed-contract portion. Answer (d) is incorrect because the general overpayment rate established by Sec. 6621 is used, compounded daily.

58. Upon completion of a long-term contract, interest is computed under the look-back method by applying the Sec. 6621 general overpayment rate to the over- or underpayment of tax for each year. The over- or underpayment is determined by allocating contract income among taxable years prior to the year of contract completion on the basis of

a. The estimated price and estimated costs.
b. The estimated price and actual contract price.
c. The estimated costs and actual costs of construction.
d. The actual contract price and actual costs.

The correct answer is (d). *(Publisher)*
REQUIRED: The calculation of over- or underpayment of tax under the look-back method.
DISCUSSION: Interest is computed under the look-back method by (1) allocating income under the contract among taxable years before the year in which the contract is completed, on the basis of the actual contract price and actual costs, (2) determining the over- or underpayment of tax for each year (solely for purposes of computing such interest), and (3) applying the Sec. 6621 general overpayment rate to the over- or underpayment [Sec. 460(b)(2)].

59. Corporation A uses the calendar-year and the percentage-of-completion method to report its income. Corporation A's average annual gross receipts exceed $20 million. On June 1, 1991, Corporation A contracted to build a condominium complex for $15,000,000. The completion date was scheduled for June 1, 1993. On December 31, 1991 the complex was 20% completed. Corporation A received payments of $3,750,000 and incurred expenses of $2,000,000 during 1991 on this contract. The amount to be reported as gross receipts for 1991 is $3,750,000.

The correct answer is (F). *(SPE 1083 III-19)*
DISCUSSION: Reg. 1.451-3(c) provides that, under the percentage-of-completion method, the portion of the gross contract price corresponding to the percentage of the entire contract completed during the taxable year must be included in gross income for such taxable year. Consequently, Corporation A will report gross receipts of $3,000,000 ($15,000,000 contract price x 20%).

Note: It is not known if the contract in question satisfies the residential construction contract definition of Sec. 460(e)(6)(B). If 80% of the estimated total contract costs are attributable to dwelling units, then the percentage-of-completion capitalized-cost method of accounting must be used. If this is the case, the answer will still be false.

60. On September 15, 1991, Corporation R entered into a contract to build a shopping center at a total estimated contract price of $20,000,000. The project is scheduled for completion in September 1996. Corporation R, whose average annual gross receipts for the 3 prior years was $15,000,000, may elect to defer reporting any income or loss from the contract until the project is completed.

The correct answer is (F). *(SPE 987 III-18)*
DISCUSSION: A construction contract that is estimated to be completed within 2 years of commencement, when the taxpayer's average annual gross receipts are $10 million or less, may use the completed-contract method rather than the methods prescribed by Sec. 460. Corporation R may not use the completed-contract method of accounting.

21.5 Installment Sales

61. For tax years beginning after 1987, the installment method may not be used for

a. Sales of personal property (except farm property) by dealers who regularly sell this type of personal property on an installment plan.
b. Sales of real property (except farm property and certain sales of residential lots or timeshares) held by a dealer for sale in the ordinary course of business.
c. Both (a) and (b) above are correct.
d. Neither (a) nor (b) above is correct.

The correct answer is (c). *(Publisher)*
REQUIRED: Transactions for which the installment method of accounting is disallowed.
DISCUSSION: For taxable years beginning after 1987, use of the installment method is usually disallowed for dispositions of property by dealers [Sec. 453(b)(2)]. This includes any disposition of (1) personal property, if the person regularly sells such personal property on the installment plan, and (2) real property held by the taxpayer for sale to customers in the ordinary course of his/her trade or business. Exceptions are made for property used or produced in the trade or business of farming, and, if so elected, sales of residential lots or timeshares, subject to interest payments on the deferred tax [Sec. 453(l)].

62. On January 1, 1991, Corporation M sold farmland held for investment with an adjusted basis of $2,000 for $10,000. The sales contract provided for a down payment on January 1, 1991 of $4,000, with the remaining $6,000 due on June 15, 1992. The interest rate stated in the contract is 12%. M received the $4,000. How much gain from the installment sale should be reported in 1991?

a. $0.
b. $3,200.
c. $4,000.
d. $8,000.

The correct answer is (b). *(SPE 984 III-85)*
REQUIRED: The amount of gain in the year of an installment sale.
DISCUSSION: The amount of gain under Sec. 453 is the proportion of the payments received in the year that the gross profit bears to the total contract price. M's gross profit is $8,000 ($10,000 sales price − $2,000 adjusted basis). Since $4,000 was received in the year of sale, the gain is $3,200.

$$\frac{\$8,000 \text{ gross profit}}{\$10,000 \text{ contract price}} \times \$4,000 = \$3,200$$

63. Mr. P purchased property from Mr. A by assuming an existing mortgage of $12,000 and agreeing to pay an additional $6,000, plus interest, over the next 3 years. Mr. A had an adjusted basis of $8,800 in the building and paid selling expenses totaling $1,200. What was the sales price and the contract price in this transaction?

	Sales Price	Contract Price
a.	$6,000	$12,000
b.	$18,000	$10,000
c.	$18,000	$8,000
d.	$18,000	$6,000

The correct answer is (c). *(SPE 989 I-95)*
REQUIRED: The sales price and contract price in an installment sale transaction.
DISCUSSION: The sales price includes any cash paid, relief of seller's liability by buyer, and any installment note given by the buyer. Here, the sales price is $18,000 ($12,000 relief of liability + $6,000 installment note). The contract price is the total amount the seller will ultimately collect from the buyer. However, if an existing mortgage assumed by the buyer exceeds the adjusted basis of the property, such excess (reduced by selling expenses) is treated as a payment and must be included both in the contract price and in the first year's payment received. The contract price is $8,000 ($6,000 note + $3,200 mortgage in excess of basis − $1,200 selling expenses).

64. During 1991, Mr. C sold property that had an adjusted basis to him of $19,000. The buyer assumed C's existing mortgage of $15,000 and agreed to pay an additional $10,000 consisting of a cash down payment of $5,000, and payments of $1,000, plus interest, per year for the next 5 years. Mr. C paid selling expenses totaling $1,000. What is C's gross profit percentage?

a. 20%.
b. 40%.
c. 50%.
d. 80%.

The correct answer is (c). *(SPE 989 I-94)*
REQUIRED: The gross profit percentage for an installment sale.
DISCUSSION: The gross profit percentage is the proportion of gross profit in relation to total contact price. The gross profit is the selling price reduced by the adjusted basis of the property and any selling expenses. The contract price is the total amount the seller will ultimately collect from the buyer. C's gross profit is $5,000 ($25,000 sales price − $19,000 basis − $1,000 selling expenses). The contract price totals $10,000. Thus, the gross profit percentage is 50% ($5,000 gross profit ÷ $10,000 contract price).

Module 21.5: Installment Sales

65. During 1991, Z sold property that had an adjusted basis to him of $5,000. The buyer assumed Z's existing loan on the property of $3,000 and agreed to pay an additional $10,000 cash consisting of a down payment of $2,000 and payments of $2,000, plus interest, per year for the next 4 years. Z received $2,000 in 1991. Using the installment method of accounting, what is the amount of gain Z should report in 1991?

a. $1,000.
b. $1,230.
c. $1,600.
d. $2,000.

The correct answer is (c). *(SPE 990 I-94)*
REQUIRED: The amount of gain to report in the year of an installment sale.
DISCUSSION: An installment sale is a disposition of property in which at least one payment is to be received after the close of the taxable year in which the disposition occurs (Sec. 453). Under the installment method (applicable unless the taxpayer elects otherwise), income recognized for any taxable year is the proportion of the payments received in that year which the gross profit bears to the total contract price. The gross profit is the selling price (less selling expenses) minus the adjusted basis of the property ($13,000 − $5,000 = $8,000). The contract price is the total amount the seller will ultimately collect from the purchaser ($10,000). This means the contract price does not include any existing mortgage assumed by the buyer. Z's gain is

$$\frac{\$8,000 \text{ gross profit}}{\$10,000 \text{ contract price}} \times \$2,000 = \$1,600$$

66. All of the following statements concerning "unstated interest" are true except:

a. If you use the installment method for reporting your gain on a sale, both the selling price and the contract price must be reduced by any unstated interest.
b. If an installment sale with some or all of the payments due more than 1 year after the date of the sale does not provide for interest, a part of each payment due more than 6 months after the date of the sale will be treated as interest.
c. If the unstated interest rules apply, both the buyer and the seller must treat a part of the installment sale price as interest.
d. Unstated interest does not affect the amount of the gain.

The correct answer is (d). *(SPE 989 I-57)*
REQUIRED: The statement concerning "unstated interest" that is incorrect.
DISCUSSION: Sec. 483 indicates how unstated interest is accounted for by a purchaser and a seller. Total unstated interest equals the excess of the sum of the payments due under a contract to which Sec. 483 applies over the sum of the present values of the contract and interest payments due under the contract [Sec. 483(b)]. Reg. Sec. 1.483-2(a) requires unstated interest to be excluded from the selling price for the property. Therefore, the amount of the gain realized on the sale is affected by the unstated interest and answer (d) is false. All of the other answers are true. Unstated interest affects the contract price and selling price when using the installment method. The Sec. 483 imputed interest rules apply only to payments on account of a sale or exchange of property due more than 6 months after the date of the sale provided some or all of the payments are due more than 1 year after the sale or exchange. The Sec. 483 imputed interest rules apply to buyer and seller alike.

67. Mr. D sold his home for $250,000 using the installment method. His adjusted basis in his home at the date of sale was $175,000. He also incurred selling expenses of $25,000. Mr. D postponed $25,000 of his gain because of a purchase of a new home. What is D's gross profit percentage under the installment method?

a. 10%.
b. 20%.
c. 30%.
d. 40%.

The correct answer is (a). *(SPE 990 I-93)*
REQUIRED: The gross profit percentage for an installment sale of a home.
DISCUSSION: Under Sec. 453, income recognized on an installment sale is the proportion of payments received in the year that the gross profit bears to the total contract price. The gross profit is generally the selling price less the basis in the property and less selling expenses. For a sale of a personal residence, it is also reduced by gain postponed owing to the purchase of a new home. The contract price is the selling price reduced by any indebtedness the buyer assumed or took subject to.

Mr. D's gross profit is $25,000 ($250,000 selling price − $175,000 adjusted basis − $25,000 selling expenses − $25,000 postponed gain). His contract price is $250,000 (selling price). Mr. D's gross profit percentage is 10% ($25,000 ÷ $250,000).

68. Mr. A sold his business in 1991 for $120,000. The contract allocated $40,000 to inventory and $80,000 to real property. The book value of the inventory was $38,000. The real property had a cost of $40,000 and depreciation claimed on a straight-line basis was $20,000. In 1991, Mr. A received a downpayment of $60,000 of which $40,000 was payment for the inventory. Mr. A had no other Sec. 1231 transactions. What is the amount and nature of the gain that Mr. A should report in 1991 using the installment method?

 a. $40,000 ordinary income, $60,000 capital gain.
 b. $68,000 ordinary income, $10,000 capital gain.
 c. $2,000 ordinary income, $20,000 capital gain.
 d. $2,000 ordinary income, $15,000 capital gain.

69. In 1991, Mr. U sold property with an adjusted basis to him of $1,000 for $10,000. The sales agreement called for a down payment of $1,000 and payments of $1,500 in each of the next 6 years to be made from an irrevocable escrow account, established by the buyer, that contains the balance of the purchase price plus interest. What is the amount of gain Mr. U should report on his 1991 return?

 a. $9,000.
 b. $1,350.
 c. $1,000.
 d. $900.

70. On August 1, 1991, Roger Company sold machinery used in its business for a total price of $20,000, payable in four equal annual installments of principal plus interest at 14%. The first payment was due and paid on December 31, 1991. At the time of the sale, Roger had a $4,000 basis in the machinery and $8,000 Sec. 1245 depreciation recapture potential. There were no other Sec. 1231 transactions. Ignoring the interest income, what amount must Roger recognize in 1991?

 a. $4,000 ordinary income.
 b. $8,000 ordinary income and $4,000 capital gain.
 c. $8,000 ordinary income and $2,000 capital gain.
 d. $8,000 ordinary income and $8,000 capital gain.

The correct answer is (d). *(SPE 1080 II-79)*
REQUIRED: The amount and nature of the gain under the installment method.
DISCUSSION: An installment sale is a disposition of property in which at least one payment is to be received after the close of the taxable year in which the disposition occurs. However, sales of inventory consisting of personal property are not installment sales as a general rule [Sec. 453(b)(2)]. A's sale of inventory produces $2,000 of ordinary income ($40,000 − $38,000).

The sale of the real property was an installment sale. Under the installment method, income recognized for any year from a disposition is that proportion of the payments received in that year which the gross profit bears to the total contract price. A's gross profit is $60,000 ($80,000 selling price − $20,000 adjusted basis). The contract price is the total amount the seller will ultimately collect from the purchaser ($80,000). The gain is Sec. 1231 gain since straight-line depreciation was used. In 1991, Mr. A should report Sec. 1231 gain of $15,000.

$$\frac{\$60{,}000 \text{ gross profit}}{\$80{,}000 \text{ contract price}} \times \$20{,}000 = \$15{,}000$$

Assuming no other transactions involving Sec. 1231 occurred in 1991, the gain is capital gain.

The correct answer is (a). *(SPE 987 I-64)*
REQUIRED: The amount of gain to be reported in the year of an installment sale when the remaining payments are escrowed.
DISCUSSION: An installment sale is a disposition of property in which at least one payment has to be received after the close of the tax of the year in which the disposition occurs. Funds can be escrowed provided they are still the property of the purchaser and can revert to the purchaser. But if the escrow is irrevocable, then the seller really has the right to the funds. Therefore, Mr. U will be treated as having received all $10,000 in the year of sale and must report a gain of $9,000 ($10,000 sales price − $1,000 basis) in 1991.

The correct answer is (c). *(Publisher)*
REQUIRED: The amount and character of gain that must be recognized under the installment method on the sale of depreciable property.
DISCUSSION: Sec. 453(i) requires full recognition of depreciation recapture in the year of sale regardless of payments. Any amounts treated as ordinary income by reason of the recapture provisions are added to the basis of the property for determining gain or loss. The total gain is $16,000 ($20,000 selling price − $4,000 basis). Therefore, Roger must recognize the full $8,000 of Sec. 1245 depreciation recapture as ordinary income in 1991.

This amount is added to the basis for determining the remaining installment gain or loss. The revised gain is thus $8,000 ($20,000 selling price − $12,000 adjusted basis). The gross profit percentage is 40% ($8,000 gross profit ÷ $20,000 contract price). This percentage will be applied to each of the four equal annual payments to determine the amount of Sec. 1231/capital gain for each year. For 1991, the capital gain is $2,000 [40% x ($20,000 ÷ 4)].

Module 21.5: Installment Sales

71. Jake sold an office building in 1990 on the installment method for $5.5 million. At the end of 1991 he is still owed $4.9 million on the debt from the sale. In which situation will Jake have to pay interest on the deferred tax of his 1991 sales if they are all installment sales with no payments in 1991?

   a. In 1991 he sells a rental duplex for $160,000.

   b. In 1991 he sells a rental duplex for $150,000 and an apartment complex for $4.9 million.

   c. In 1991 he sells a rental duplex for $160,000 and an apartment complex for $4.9 million.

   d. More than one of the above.

The correct answer is (c). *(Publisher)*
REQUIRED: When interest is required to be paid on the deferred tax on installment sales.
DISCUSSION: Interest is charged under Sec. 453A on the deferred tax of non-dealer installment sales of over $150,000 involving any type property. Excluded is personal use property, property produced or used in the trade or business of farming, time shares and residential lots. The interest is only charged if the obligation is outstanding at the end of the year and the taxpayer has non-dealer installment receivables totaling over $5 million at the end of the year from sales of property described above that occur during the year. If in 1991 Jake sells a rental duplex for $160,000 and an apartment complex for $4.9 million, his 1991 installment sales (in receivables at year-end) will exceed $5 million. Therefore, the interest will be charged on the deferred tax.

Answer (a) is incorrect because Jake would not have installment receivables at year-end from 1991 sales in excess of $5 million. The receivable from the property sold in 1990 does not count towards the $5 million minimum. Answer (b) is incorrect because sales of property for $150,000 or less are not counted towards the $5 million minimum; therefore, Jake would have receivables from appropriate 1991 sales of only $4.9 million. Answer (d) is incorrect because only answer (c) is correct.

72. Robert, a calendar-year taxpayer, sells an office building in 1991 for $9 million, receiving $1 million cash in 1991 and a note for $8 million. Assume Robert's gross profit percentage is 30% and the Sec. 6621 rate for underpayments is 10% in December 1991. The highest tax rate for individuals in 1991 is 31%. What is the interest on the deferred tax for 1991?

   a. $0.

   b. $27,900.

   c. $28,350.

   d. $74,400.

The correct answer is (b). *(Publisher)*
REQUIRED: The interest on the deferred tax for 1991.
DISCUSSION: Interest is computed each year at the underpayment rate of Sec. 6621 that is in effect for the month in which the tax year ends. The interest is computed on "applicable percentage" of the deferred tax. The applicable percentage is equal to the total face amount (not the balance) of receivables from the current year outstanding at year-end in excess of $5 million divided by the total face amount of receivables outstanding at year-end from current year sales. The deferred tax is the amount of gain not recognized as of the end of the year multiplied by the highest tax rate applicable to the taxpayer.

At the end of 1991, Robert's deferred taxes are $744,000 ($8 million x 30% gross profit x 31% tax rate). The applicable percentage is 37.5% ($3 million ÷ $8 million). The interest for 1991 is $27,900 ($744,000 x 37.5% x 10% interest rate).

73. When property (other than marketable securities) is sold to a related person on the installment method, which of the following will cause the seller to recognize the remainder of the gain on the installment obligation before all payments are received?

a. The seller dies.
b. The buyer dies.
c. The buyer resells the property more than 2 years later.
d. The buyer gives the property away within 2 years of the installment sale.

The correct answer is (d). *(Publisher)*
REQUIRED: When income recognition from an installment obligation will be accelerated.
DISCUSSION: To prevent intermediary sales on an installment basis to related parties followed by other dispositions, Sec. 453(e) requires the amount realized on a second disposition of property to be treated as received by the person who made the first installment sale to a related party. This rule also applies to a disposition by gift. When the buyer gives the property away, the FMV of the property is deemed realized by the original seller to accelerate the installment obligation.
Answers (a) and (b) are incorrect because the death of either the buyer or seller generally does not accelerate the installment obligation. Answer (c) is incorrect because the second disposition rule does not apply to dispositions more than 2 years after the first installment sale, except for marketable securities.

74. In 1990 Corporation W sold real property and elected to report the realized gain on the installment method of accounting. W distributed the installment receivable to a shareholder as a dividend in 1991. W's basis in the receivable was $25,000, the remaining balance to be received was $40,000, and the fair market value of the receivable was $40,000. What amount of income, if any, should Corporation W report on the transfer?

a. $0.
b. $15,000.
c. $25,000.
d. $40,000.

The correct answer is (b). *(SPE 1082 III-75)*
REQUIRED: The income recognized on the disposition of an installment obligation.
DISCUSSION: Sec. 453B provides that, when an installment obligation is disposed of, gain or loss is recognized to the extent of the difference between the basis of the obligation and the amount realized (or the fair market value of the obligation if disposed of other than by sale or exchange).
Since Corporation W disposed of the installment obligation other than by sale or exchange, the excess of the fair market value of the obligation over W's basis in the obligation is recognized as income on the transfer. This amount of income is $15,000 ($40,000 fair market value – $25,000 basis). The gain is treated as resulting from the sale or exchange of the property in respect of which the installment obligation was originally held.

75. In 1990 Neptune sold his lakefront lot in which he had a basis of $14,000 on the installment method for $28,000. Neptune received $8,000 in the year of sale and $1,000 in 1991 before having to repossess the land after payments stopped. What is Neptune's gain on the repossession?

a. $0.
b. $5,000.
c. $6,000.
d. $10,000.

The correct answer is (b). *(Publisher)*
REQUIRED: The gain on repossession of real property which was sold under the installment method.
DISCUSSION: Sec. 1038(b) provides that on the repossession of real property which was sold on the installment method, gain is recognized to the extent the payments received prior to the repossession exceed the gain on the property reported in periods prior to the repossession. This gain is limited to the total gain realized on the sale of the property, less the gain recognized in prior periods.
Neptune's gain on the repossession is $5,000 ($9,000 received prior to repossession – $4,000 recognized gain in 1990). The limitation is $10,000 ($14,000 gain realized in 1990 – $4,000 recognized in 1990), which does not apply because it is greater than the gain computed.

Module 21.5: Installment Sales

76. L.E. operates an accounting service as a sole proprietorship. For income tax purposes, he reports on the cash and calendar-year bases. During 1991, L.E. received the following receipts in connection with his business, which was his only source of income

Cash collected for services:
Rendered in 1990	$ 2,000	
Rendered in 1991	90,000	
To be rendered in 1992	5,000	$97,000

Cash collection on land contract:
Principal	$40,000	
Interest (14%)	2,000	$42,000

L.E. acquired the land at a cost of $30,000 in 1989 for future use as a building site. However, the land was never developed and L.E. sold it on March 18, 1991 for $60,000, with $20,000 of principal payments deferred until 1992. The $20,000 deferred payment is evidenced by a negotiable note with a fair market value of $20,000. If L.E. makes no tax elections applicable to 1991, what amount of gross income must he report for 1991?

a. $107,000.
b. $119,000.
c. $134,000.
d. $139,000.

The correct answer is (b). *(E. Grams)*
REQUIRED: The amount of gross income for 1991.
DISCUSSION: A cash-basis taxpayer generally reports income attributable to services in the taxable year cash is received. The installment method applies to this sale of land because L.E. did not elect otherwise. Income recognized under the installment method is determined by applying the gross profit percentage ($30,000 gross profit ÷ $60,000 contract price = 50%) to the amount of payments received during the taxable year. L.E.'s gross income for 1991 is

Income from services	$ 97,000
Interest income	2,000
Installment sale income (50% x $40,000)	20,000
Gross income	$119,000

77. Given the same facts as in the preceding question, assume that on December 31, 1991, uncollected billings for 1991 services amounted to $9,000. At that date, no accrued interest was uncollected. What amount of gross income must L.E. report for 1991 if he is an accrual rather than a cash-basis taxpayer?

a. $107,000.
b. $121,000.
c. $134,000.
d. $139,000.

The correct answer is (b). *(E. Grams)*
REQUIRED: The gross income of an accrual-basis taxpayer.
DISCUSSION: An accrual-basis taxpayer generally reports income in the taxable year the right to receive the income becomes fixed. An accrual-basis taxpayer must generally report advance payments of income in the year received under the "claim of right" doctrine. However, Rev. Proc. 71-21 allows the income from services to be reported when earned if all of the services are required to be performed by the end of the tax year following the year of receipt. Accordingly, the $5,000 for services to be rendered in 1992 can be reported in 1992.

L.E. already reported the $2,000 of income for services rendered in 1990. The installment method also applies to an accrual-basis taxpayer unless he elects otherwise (which he did not). L.E.'s adjusted gross income is

Income accrued for 1991 services	$ 9,000
Income received for 1991 services	90,000
Interest income	2,000
Installment sale income (50% x $40,000)	20,000
Gross income	$121,000

Module 21.5: Installment Sales

78. In 1987, Mr. B sold his personal property on contract for $200,000 which resulted in a capital gain of $100,000. Mr. B properly elected to use the installment method of reporting and through 1990 had collected $40,000 on the contract. At the start of 1991, the buyer defaulted on the contract and Mr. B repossessed the property. At the time of repossession the property had a fair market value of $160,000. What is the gain or loss to be reported on the repossession?

   a. $20,000 capital gain.
   b. $60,000 ordinary income.
   c. $80,000 capital gain.
   d. $100,000 capital gain.

The correct answer is (c). *(SPE 1080 I-85)*
REQUIRED: The amount and character of gain (loss) on the repossession of personal property by a taxpayer who uses the installment method.
DISCUSSION: Under Sec. 453B(f)(1), a vendor recognizes a gain or loss (capital if the asset was capital) on the repossession of property sold on the installment method. The gain or loss is the difference between the fair market value of the repossessed property and basis of the obligations of the purchaser so satisfied.

Fair market value of property		$160,000
Less: Balance of contract due	$160,000	
Unrealized profit (50%)	(80,000)	
Basis of contract		(80,000)
Capital gain on repossession		$ 80,000

79. Mrs. L sold a business asset with an adjusted basis of $50,000 encumbered with a $25,000 mortgage. The buyer agreed to pay Mrs. L $100,000 over the next 5 years and in addition assumes the mortgage on the property. The contract price is $100,000.

The correct answer is (T). *(SPE 1081 II-21)*
DISCUSSION: Under Sec. 453, the contract price is generally the total amount the seller will ultimately collect from the purchaser. Reg. 15A.453-1(b)(2)(iii) provides that an existing mortgage assumed by the buyer is only included in the contract price to the extent that it exceeds the basis of the property. Since the mortgage assumed by the buyer does not exceed the adjusted basis of the property, the contract price is $100,000.

80. In 1991, Mr. L, a calendar-year taxpayer, sold his motorcycle with an adjusted basis of $500 for $700. He agreed to accept a lump sum payment in 1992. The gain on this sale qualifies for the installment method of reporting.

The correct answer is (T). *(SPE 1081 I-37)*
DISCUSSION: Under Sec. 453(b), an installment sale is a disposition of property where at least one payment is to be received after the close of the taxable year in which the disposition occurs. Since Mr. L will receive one payment after 1991, this sale qualifies for the installment method. Mr. L must elect to have the installment method not apply.

81. Y, a dealer regularly engaged in the sale of personal property on a revolving credit plan, may report his income from such sales in 1991 on the installment method, regardless of the selling price of the products sold or the amount collected in the year of sale.

The correct answer is (F). *(SPE 1080 II-5)*
DISCUSSION: Sec. 453(k) provides that any disposition of personal property under a revolving credit plan may not be reported under the installment method for tax years beginning after 1986. Sec. 453(b) excludes dealer dispositions of personal property from using the installment method.

82. Upon disposition of an installment obligation, any gain or loss recognized will always be ordinary income.

The correct answer is (F). *(SPE 990 I-28)*
DISCUSSION: Sec. 453B(a) provides that any gain or loss on the disposition of an installment obligation is considered as resulting from the sale or exchange of the property for which the installment obligation was received. The character of the gain (loss) will be determined by the kind of property for which the installment obligation was issued.

Module 21.6: Inventories 629

83. The cancellation of an installment obligation is treated as a disposition other than by sale or exchange. The gain or loss is the difference between the basis of the obligation and the fair market value of the repossessed property resulting in the cancellation of the indebtedness at the time of the cancellation.

The correct answer is (T). *(SPE 988 I-23)*
DISCUSSION: Under Sec. 453B(f)(1), a vendor recognizes a gain or loss on the repossession of property sold on the installment method. The gain or loss is the difference between the fair market value of the repossessed property and the basis of the obligation of the purchaser so satisfied.

84. Mr. B sells an automobile on which a Sec. 1245 gain is recognized to Mrs. B. The property will be used in Mrs. B's sole proprietorship. The installment method of accounting does not apply to the sale.

The correct answer is (F). *(Publisher)*
DISCUSSION: The installment method of accounting applies to the sale in question. The controlled entity sale rules of Sec. 453(g)(1) do not apply since a husband and wife are not related parties under the Sec. 1239(b) related party definition. However, even though the installment method of accounting applies to the sale, the realized gain able to be reported using the installment method is reduced by all recapture income (e.g., Sec. 1245 income) that must be recognized in the year of sale [Sec. 453(i)(1)]. Only gain realized in excess of the recapture income, if any, is reported using the installment method.

21.6 Inventories

85. Which of the following is the most important principle in valuing inventories?

   a. Generally accepted accounting principles.
   b. Clear reflection of income.
   c. Lower of cost or market.
   d. Full absorption costing.

The correct answer is (b). *(Publisher)*
REQUIRED: The overriding principle in valuing inventories.
DISCUSSION: Reg. 1.471-2(a) provides that the method of valuing inventory must conform as nearly as possible to the best accounting practice in the trade or business, and it must clearly reflect income. Courts have held that the overriding concern is the clear reflection of income. Conformity to the best accounting practice is considered only a method of achieving a clear reflection of income. The inventory practice should also be consistent from year to year to clearly reflect income.
Answer (a) is incorrect because generally accepted accounting principles are an important factor in valuing inventories, but the clear reflection of income overrides it. Answers (c) and (d) are incorrect because lower of cost or market and full absorption costing are merely methods of valuing inventory, not overriding principles.

86. The uniform capitalization rules apply to which one of the following properties?

   a. Property you produce under a long-term contract.
   b. Personal property you purchase for resale if your average annual gross receipts are $10,000,000 or less.
   c. Costs paid or incurred by an individual (other than as an employee), or a qualified employee-owner of a personal service corporation in the business of being a writer, photographer, or artist.
   d. Real property or tangible personal property which you produce for sale to customers.

The correct answer is (d). *(SPE 989 II-34)*
REQUIRED: The item to which the uniform capitalization rules apply.
DISCUSSION: Under Sec. 263A(b)(1), the uniform capitalization rules apply to real or tangible personal property produced by the taxpayer.
Answer (a) is incorrect because it is specifically excepted under Sec. 263A(c)(4). Answer (b) is incorrect because it is an exception under Sec. 263A(b)(2)(B). Answer (c) is incorrect because it is specifically excepted under Sec. 263A(h).

630 Module 21.6: Inventories

87. The uniform capitalization rules apply to all of the following business related costs except:

a. Direct materials costs.

b. Indirect costs.

c. Interest on debt to finance the production of real or tangible personal property with a class life of 20 years or more.

d. Marketing, selling, advertising, and distribution costs.

The correct answer is (d). *(SPE 988 II-36)*
REQUIRED: The business related costs to which the uniform capitalization rules do not apply.
DISCUSSION: For costs incurred after 1986, Sec. 263A establishes a uniform set of rules requiring the capitalization of certain previously deductible production costs. Marketing, selling, advertising, and distribution costs are period costs and are not capitalized.
Answers (a) and (b) are incorrect because both the direct costs and a proper share of indirect costs (including taxes) allocable to property must be capitalized. Answer (c) is incorrect because interest is capitalized if it is paid or incurred during the production period and is allocable to property produced by the taxpayer.

88. Mr. Jones built a machine at a total cost of $4,000,000 to be used in his business. The machine has an estimated production period of 3 years. Mr. Jones incurred interest on a $3,000,000 loan, the proceeds of which were used to build the machine. He also incurred interest on $6,000,000 of other debt in his business. The interest incurred on how much debt must be capitalized?

a. $0.

b. $3,000,000.

c. $4,000,000.

d. $6,000,000.

The correct answer is (c). *(Publisher)*
REQUIRED: The amount of debt on which interest must be capitalized for the construction of property to be used by the taxpayer.
DISCUSSION: When assets are built for a taxpayer's own use, the taxpayer must capitalize production costs and recover them as depreciation deductions over the useful life of the asset. Interest is capitalized only if it is paid or incurred during the production period and is allocable to property produced by the taxpayer. Such property must have a long useful life, an estimated production period over 2 years, or an estimated production period over 1 year and a cost of over $1,000,000 [Sec. 263A(f)]. This applies to interest directly attributable to production expenditures plus interest on any other indebtedness that could have been avoided if the production expenditure had not been incurred.
The interest on Mr. Jones' $3,000,000 loan plus $1,000,000 of other debt, which could have been paid off, for a total of $4,000,000, must be capitalized.

89. All of the following inventory practices are acceptable for tax purposes except

a. LIFO method of identifying inventory.

b. Specific cost identification method of inventory valuation.

c. Deducting a reserve for price changes in the value of the inventory.

d. Perpetual inventory systems.

The correct answer is (c). *(SPE 988 II-34)*
REQUIRED: The method that is not acceptable for valuing inventory.
DISCUSSION: Reg. 1.471-2(f) gives examples of unacceptable methods of valuing inventory. One is deducting a reserve for price changes from inventory or estimating depreciation on the value of inventory.
Answer (a) is incorrect because the LIFO method of identifying inventory means "last in, first out" and is acceptable. Answer (b) is incorrect because the specific cost identification method is acceptable. It refers to actually identifying each item of inventory and the item's cost. Answer (d) is incorrect because a perpetual inventory system is also acceptable. The inventory account is charged with cost of goods purchased and credited with value of goods sold.

Module 21.6: Inventories

90. All of the following are acceptable in valuing inventory for federal income tax purposes except:

a. Allocating indirect production costs to inventory by means of the manufacturing burden rate method.

b. Identifying direct material costs with particular units or groups of the product.

c. Allocating variable indirect production costs to cost of goods produced while treating fixed indirect production costs as currently deductible period costs.

d. Figuring cost of goods on hand by use of perpetual inventories when the account is charged with cost of goods purchased and credited with value of goods sold.

The correct answer is (c). *(SPE 984 II-48)*
REQUIRED: The method that is not acceptable for valuing inventory.
DISCUSSION: Reg. 1.471-2(f) gives examples of unacceptable methods for valuing inventory. One is the allocation of only variable costs to cost of goods produced while treating fixed costs as period costs. This approach is commonly referred to as the "direct cost" method.
Answers (a), (b), and (d) are incorrect because each is an acceptable method of valuing inventory.

91. Which of the following occupations or businesses would generally not be required to use inventories in determining gross profit?

1. Manufacturer of toys
2. Doctors
3. Grocery store
4. Painters
5. Clothing store

a. 1 and 3.
b. 1, 2, and 5.
c. 2 and 4.
d. 4 and 5.

The correct answer is (c). *(SPE 1078 II-50)*
REQUIRED: The businesses generally not required to use inventories in determining gross profit.
DISCUSSION: Reg. 1.471-1 provides that inventories at the beginning and end of each taxable year are necessary in every case in which the production, purchase, or sale of merchandise is an income-producing factor. The production, purchase, or sale of merchandise is not an income-producing factor for doctors or painters.
Answers (a), (b), and (d) are incorrect because the production, purchase, or sale of merchandise would be an income-producing factor for a manufacturer of toys, a grocery store, and a clothing store.

92. Which of the following items is not included in inventory?

a. Raw material.
b. Goods you received on consignment.
c. Work in process.
d. Finished goods.

The correct answer is (b). *(SPE 1080 II-50)*
REQUIRED: The item that is not included in inventory.
DISCUSSION: Reg. 1.471-1 provides that inventory should include all finished goods, work in process, and raw materials and supplies which will physically become a part of merchandise intended for sale. Merchandise should be included in inventory only if title thereto is vested in the taxpayer. In the case of goods received by the taxpayer on consignment, the title remains with the consignor and the goods are not included in inventory.

93. All of the following costs must be included in valuing inventory using the full absorption method except

a. Materials that become an integral part of the finished product.
b. Shift differential pay to production workers.
c. Payroll taxes related to production workers.
d. Research and experimentation costs.

The correct answer is (d). *(SPE 986 II-41)*
REQUIRED: The item that is not included in inventory under the full absorption method.
DISCUSSION: Under the full absorption method of inventory costing, both direct and indirect production costs must be taken into account. Research and experimentation costs are not considered production costs [Reg. 1.263A-1T(b)(2)(v)(D)].
Answers (a), (b), and (c) are incorrect because each is a direct production cost under Reg. 1.263A-1T(b)(2).

Module 21.6: Inventories

94. Mr. Cheta owns a retail hardware store. Which of the following should be included in his ending inventory?

a. Envelopes and stationery not for sale.
b. Lawnmower sold but not yet delivered.
c. Shipment of nails purchased f.o.b. supplier but still in transit.
d. Small power tools rented to customers.

The correct answer is (c). *(SPE 1077 I-167)*
REQUIRED: The item(s) included in a retail hardware store owner's ending inventory.
DISCUSSION: Reg. 1.471-1 provides that inventory should include all merchandise if title thereto is vested in the taxpayer. The title to items shipped f.o.b. supplier transfers to the purchaser as soon as the items leave the supplier. Therefore, Mr. Cheta has title to the shipment of nails.
Answer (a) is incorrect because the envelopes and stationery were not acquired for sale. Answer (b) is incorrect because the title has been transferred to the purchaser. Answer (d) is incorrect because the small power tools are not intended for sale.

95. For federal tax purposes, all of the following affect the cost of goods sold except

a. Cash discounts taken that are credited to a separate discount account.
b. Trade discounts taken.
c. Purchase returns and allowances.
d. Freight-in on raw materials.

The correct answer is (a). *(SPE 984 II-49)*
REQUIRED: The item that does not affect the cost of goods sold for federal tax purposes.
DISCUSSION: Under Reg. 1.471-3(b), the cost of merchandise purchased during the taxable year includes the invoice price less trade or other discounts, except for strictly cash discounts that are deducted at the option of the taxpayer.
Answer (b) is incorrect because trade discounts do affect the cost of goods sold [Reg. 1.471-3(b)]. Answer (c) is incorrect because purchase returns decrease the cost of goods on hand (inventory). Answer (d) is incorrect because the cost of raw materials includes transportation or other necessary charges incurred in acquiring possession of goods.

96. Mr. B properly uses the lower of cost or market method of valuing his inventory. B's closing inventory for 1991 consisted of the following:

Items	Cost	Market
L	$300	$500
M	200	100
N	650	250

What is the value of B's closing inventory?

a. $350.
b. $650.
c. $850.
d. $1,150.

The correct answer is (b). *(SPE 987 II-68)*
REQUIRED: The value of inventory using the lower of cost or market method.
DISCUSSION: The two basic methods of valuing inventory are to use cost and lower of cost or market. When using the lower of cost or market, the cost and market value of each item on hand at the inventory date must be compared. It is not acceptable to value the entire inventory at cost and also at market and then use the lower of these two. The computation is below:

Items	Cost	Market	Lower of Cost or Market
L	$300	$500	$300
M	200	100	100
N	650	250	250
Total			$650

Module 21.6: Inventories

97. For 1991, Mr. P, who uses the FIFO method of identifying inventory, had a beginning inventory of 3,500 units consisting of the following:

1,000 purchased 4/20/90 @ $1.00 per unit
2,000 purchased 6/24/90 @ $2.00 per unit
500 purchased 7/24/90 @ $3.00 per unit

During 1991, Mr. P purchased the following units:

3,000 purchased 9/25/91 @ $4.00 per unit
1,000 purchased 12/1/91 @ $5.00 per unit

During 1991, P sold 2,300 units. What is the value of P's ending inventory on December 31, 1991.

    a. $13,300.
    b. $15,300.
    c. $19,900.
    d. $22,900.

The correct answer is (c). *(SPE 990 II-63)*
REQUIRED: The cost of ending inventory using the FIFO method.
DISCUSSION: The FIFO ("first in, first out") method is based on a flow of goods assumption. The cost of goods sold under the FIFO method contains the costs of the earlier acquired units. The cost of the ending inventory contains the costs of the more recently acquired items. The ending inventory is $19,900 with a total of 5,200 units on hand (3,500 beginning inventory + 4,000 purchased − 2,300 sold).

Date Purchased	Units	Price	Total
6/24/90	700	$2.00	$ 1,400
7/24/90	500	3.00	1,500
9/25/91	3,000	4.00	12,000
12/1/91	1,000	5.00	5,000
Ending inventory	5,200		$19,900

98. Mr. Y, who uses the LIFO method in computing his inventory, had 1,000 units left at the end of 1991. Based on the following information, what is the value of Y's inventory on December 31, 1991?

	Units	Cost Per Unit	Market Value Per Unit
Opening inventory	500	$2.00	$3.00
Purchases: 9/25/91	1,500	3.00	3.00
11/15/91	1,000	4.00	4.00

    a. $2,500.
    b. $3,000.
    c. $4,000.
    d. $5,000.

The correct answer is (a). *(SPE 990 II-62)*
REQUIRED: The value of ending inventory using the LIFO method.
DISCUSSION: The LIFO ("last in, first out") method is a flow of goods assumption. The cost of goods sold under the LIFO method contains the costs of the most recently purchased units. The cost of the ending inventory contains the costs of the earlier acquired units. The ending inventory for 1991 is $2,500 given 1,000 units on hand at December 31.

Date Purchased	Units	Price	Total
Opening inventory	500	$2.00	$1,000
9/25/91	500	3.00	1,500
Ending inventory	1,000		$2,500

Note that a taxpayer who uses the LIFO method must value inventory at cost, rather than at lower of cost or market.

99. For calendar-year 1991, Ms. K's books and records reflect the following information regarding item X.

Opening inventory
  500 units purchased in July 1990 at $1.00 per unit
  300 units purchased in December 1990 at $3.00 per unit.
Purchased during 1991
  500 units in April at $2.00 per unit
  400 units in August at $3.00 per unit
Sold in 1991
  1,400 units

What is the cost of goods sold under both the FIFO and LIFO methods of identifying inventory?

	FIFO	LIFO
a.	$2,450	$3,000
b.	$2,700	$3,300
c.	$2,850	$3,075
d.	$1,400	$4,200

The correct answer is (b). *(SPE 988 II-57)*
REQUIRED: The value of cost of goods sold determined under the FIFO and the LIFO methods.
DISCUSSION: FIFO ("first in, first out") is a flow of goods assumption. The cost of goods sold under the FIFO method consists of the earliest purchased units. LIFO ("last in, first out") is another flow of goods assumption in which cost of goods sold consists of the most recently purchased units. The value of X's cost of goods sold is

Date Purchased	FIFO	
July 1990	500 @ $1.00	$ 500
December 1990	300 @ $3.00	900
April 1991	500 @ $2.00	1,000
August 1991	100 @ $3.00	300
Cost of goods sold	1,400 units	$2,700

Date Purchased	LIFO	
July 1990	200 @ $1.00	$ 200
December 1990	300 @ $3.00	900
April 1991	500 @ $2.00	1,000
August 1991	400 @ $3.00	1,200
Cost of goods sold	1,400 units	$3,300

Module 21.6: Inventories

100. M is a manufacturing company. It uses the same accounting method for financial reports as for tax purposes. In M's financial reports, inventory costs include depreciation of production machinery. Its records reflect the following

Interest expense on loans to finance production machinery	$10,000
Repairs and maintenance expense on production machinery	20,000
Depreciation expense on production machinery	40,000
Tools and equipment exhausted within 1 year	35,000
Research and experimental expenses	55,000
Quality control costs	25,000
Vacation and holiday pay (factory labor)	30,000

What amount must M include in indirect costs in valuing inventory for tax purposes?

a. $80,000.
b. $110,000.
c. $120,000.
d. $150,000.

The correct answer is (c). *(SPE 1081 II-75)*
REQUIRED: The amount which a manufacturer must include in indirect costs in valuing inventory for tax purposes.
DISCUSSION: Under the uniform capitalization rules of Sec. 263A, a manufacturer must use the full absorption method of inventory costing and include indirect production costs. Temp. Reg. Sec. 1.263A-1T(b) prescribes the basic rules about the direct and indirect costs included in inventory by a manufacturer under the uniform capitalization rules. These rules provide that maintenance and repair expenses, utilities, rent, indirect labor and production wages, indirect materials and supplies, tools and equipment not capitalized, and costs of quality control and inspection must be included in inventory costs regardless of their treatment in a manufacturer's financial reports. Depreciation allowable for tax purposes is included in inventory irrespective of what is done on the financial statements.

Costs not included in inventory include interest, research and experimental expenses, and marketing expenses. The interest is capitalized as part of the machinery's cost. Vacation and holiday pay for factory labor is a direct production cost, not an indirect cost. The amount which M must include in indirect costs is

Repairs and maintenance	$ 20,000
Depreciation expense	40,000
Tools and equipment used	35,000
Quality control costs	25,000
Indirect costs includable	$120,000

101. Inventory data for ABC Retailing Co. at December 31, 1991 are as follows:

	Cost	Retail
Sales		$95,000
Inventory, 1/1/91	$10,000	24,000
Purchases	40,000	84,000
Additional markups		18,000
Markup cancellations		6,000
Markdowns		9,000
Markdown cancellations		4,000

What is the ending inventory at approximate lower of cost or market under the retail method?

a. $8,334.
b. $8,696.
c. $20,000.
d. None of the above.

The correct answer is (a). *(K. McMullen)*
REQUIRED: Ending inventory under the retail method to approximate lower of cost or market method.
DISCUSSION: Calculated as follows:

	Cost	Retail
Inventory, 1/1/91	$10,000	$ 24,000
Purchases	40,000	84,000
Markups (net)		12,000
	$50,000	$120,000

$50,000 ÷ $120,000 = 41.67%

Markdowns	(5,000)
Sales	(95,000)
Ending inventory at retail	$ 20,000
	x 41.67%
Ending inventory at LCM	$ 8,334

Under lower of cost or market, it is assumed that goods marked down are either sold at year-end or that any decline in profitability of these goods must be recognized if they are still in inventory. With that in mind, net markdowns are treated like sales in calculating percentage of cost versus retail. The lower of cost or market percentage will always be lower than the cost percentage when markdowns occur.

Module 21.6: Inventories 635

102. XYZ Company adopted dollar-value LIFO for inventory valuation on January 1, 1991 when the price index for its type of goods was 120. Its inventory on that date at average cost was $150,000. At December 31, 1991, inventory costed at year-end prices was $210,000, when the price index was 144. What is the cost of its December 31, 1991 inventory under dollar-value LIFO?

   a. $30,000.
   b. $150,000.
   c. $180,000.
   d. $210,000.

The correct answer is (c). *(K. McMullen)*
REQUIRED: The value of ending inventory using dollar-value LIFO.
DISCUSSION: Costing of inventory under dollar-value LIFO entails first determining if a new layer of LIFO inventory has been created during the year. To discover this, the ending inventory taken at current replacement cost must be restated at beginning costs, and then compared to beginning inventory.

Ending inventory at current costs	$210,000
Price index change	x 120/144
Ending inventory at beginning costs	$175,000
Beginning inventory	(150,000)
New layer at beginning costs	$ 25,000

The new layer at beginning costs is then restated by applying the price index change to create the new layer at current costs. Then it is added to the base layer to arrive at ending inventory under dollar-value LIFO.

New layer at beginning costs	$ 25,000
Price index change	x 144/120
New layer at ending costs	$ 30,000
Original layer	150,000
Ending inventory at dollar-value LIFO	$180,000

Note that Sec. 474 provides an option for eligible small businesses (those with average annual gross receipts for the 3 preceding taxable years of $5 million or less) whereby such small businesses may elect to use a simplified dollar-value LIFO method of pricing inventories.

103. The cost of inventory must be reduced by cash discounts.

The correct answer is (F). *(Publisher)*
DISCUSSION: Under Reg. 1.471-3, cash discounts (those received for paying early) may reduce the cost of inventory or be treated as income, as long as a consistent method is followed. On the other hand, trade discounts (discounts for volume) must be reflected in a lower cost of inventory.

104. All taxpayers who are engaged in manufacturing or production must use the full absorption method to value their inventory.

The correct answer is (T). *(SPE 1083 II-9)*
DISCUSSION: Sec. 263A(a) provides that the cost of goods purchased or manufactured by a taxpayer must be determined by the full absorption method of inventory costing. The costs that are capitalized are described in the uniform capitalization rules of Temp. Reg. Sec. 1.263A-1T(b).

105. Taxpayers who change to LIFO inventory valuations have 3 years (beginning with the year of change) to take back into income inventory write-downs from use of lower of cost or market valuations.

The correct answer is (T). *(Publisher)*
DISCUSSION: Under Sec. 472(d), the beginning inventory for the first taxable year that LIFO is used must be valued at cost. Any change in the inventory amount resulting from changing the beginning inventory to cost (e.g., from lower of cost or market) must be taken into account ratably for the first 3 years beginning with the adoption of LIFO.

106. Under the LIFO method of identifying inventory, a taxpayer has the option of using the cost method or the lower of cost or market method in valuing your inventory.

The correct answer is (F). *(SPE 987 II-11)*
DISCUSSION: A taxpayer who uses the LIFO method must value inventory at cost, rather than at the lower of cost or market.

107. For tax purposes, if using the lower of cost or market method for inventory valuation, the taxpayer has the option of comparing the total cost of inventory to total market value or comparing each inventory item to its market value.

The correct answer is (F). *(SPE 984 II-8)*
DISCUSSION: Reg. 1.471-4(c) states that when inventory is valued on the basis of lower of cost or market, each item included in the inventory must be valued at the lower of its cost or market value. There is no option of comparing total cost to total market value.

108. A deduction for a reserve for price changes or an estimated amount for depreciation in the value of inventory is allowable assuming this method is used consistently from year to year for all inventory items.

The correct answer is (F). *(SPE 1083 II-8)*
DISCUSSION: Under Reg. 1.471-2(f), unacceptable methods for valuing inventories include deducting from inventory an estimated amount for depreciation in its value or a reserve for price changes.

21.7 Change of Accounting Methods

109. Which of the following items is not a change in the method of accounting requiring the consent of the IRS?

a. Change from the cash method to accrual method or vice versa.
b. Change in the method or basis used to value inventories.
c. Change in method of figuring depreciation (except certain changes to the straight-line method).
d. An adjustment in the useful life of a depreciable asset.

The correct answer is (d). *(SPE 988 II-32)*
REQUIRED: The change that does not require the permission of the IRS.
DISCUSSION: To change an accounting method, the taxpayer must generally obtain the permission of the IRS [Sec. 446(e)]. However, the taxpayer is only required to notify the Commissioner of a change in the useful life of a depreciable asset if the taxpayer and the Commissioner had entered into a written agreement specifying the useful life. Note that most assets have fixed periods over which to compute depreciation under ACRS and MACRS. This does not apply to intangible property where the useful life is relevant or to property placed in service prior to 1981.
Answers (a), (b), and (c) are incorrect because each is a change in the overall plan of accounting for gross income or deductions or a change in the treatment of any material item used in such overall plan and thus qualifies as a change in accounting method [Reg. 1.446-1(e)(2)].

110. A taxpayer is not required to obtain the permission of the Commissioner of Internal Revenue to change from the

a. LIFO method to the FIFO method of valuing inventories.
b. Units-of-production method to the straight-line method of computing depreciation.
c. Cash basis to the accrual basis of reporting income.
d. Accrual method to the installment method of reporting income.

The correct answer is (d). *(CPA 572 P-8)*
REQUIRED: The change that does not require the permission of the IRS.
DISCUSSION: The general rule of Sec. 446(e) is that to change an accounting method, the taxpayer must obtain the permission of the IRS. The installment method of reporting income may be used by a taxpayer under the conditions of Secs. 453 or 453A, but does not require the permission of the IRS. However, the installment method of accounting is generally no longer available for sales made by dealers [Sec. 453(l)]. It can still be used by dealers for certain properties and by nondealers.
Answers (a), (b), and (c) are incorrect because each requires the permission of the IRS. Reg. 1.446-1(e)(2) provides that a change in the method of accounting includes a change in overall plan of accounting for gross income or deductions, or a change in the treatment of any material item used in such overall plan.

111. Which one of the following changes requires permission from the Internal Revenue Service?

a. A change from the FIFO method to the LIFO method for valuing inventories.
b. A correction of an error in calculating the tax liability of a previous year.
c. A change from the declining-balance method to the straight-line method for depreciating an asset.
d. A change from the cash method to the accrual method.

The correct answer is (d). *(CMA 681 3-12)*
REQUIRED: The change that requires permission from the IRS.
DISCUSSION: Sec. 446(e) requires the taxpayer to obtain permission from the IRS to change a method of accounting. A change from the cash method to the accrual method is a change in the method of accounting which requires permission from the IRS [Reg. 1.446-1(e)(2)(ii)(a)].
Answers (a) is incorrect because the LIFO method may be elected by a taxpayer, although the IRS may impose conditions of adjustments to be made in making such election. Answer (b) is incorrect because a correction of an error in calculating tax is not a change in accounting method [Reg. 1.446-1(e)(2)(ii)(b)]. Answer (c) is incorrect because Sec. 167(e)(1) permits a change from a declining-balance method to the straight-line method without consent of the IRS. Note that most assets have specified methods for being depreciated under ACRS and MACRS. A taxpayer can elect the straight-line method of depreciation under ACRS or MACRS for certain classes of property or certain properties (depending on the type of asset) without obtaining IRS permission.

112. All of the following changes in method of accounting require the consent of the Commissioner of Internal Revenue except

a. From the cash or accrual method to a long-term contract method.
b. From the cash method to the accrual method.
c. Change in the method or basis used to value inventories.
d. From the declining-balance method to the straight-line method of figuring depreciation.

The correct answer is (d). *(SPE 986 II-39)*
REQUIRED: The change in method of accounting not requiring the consent of the IRS.
DISCUSSION: Sec. 167(e)(1) provides an exception to the general rule of Sec. 446(e) and permits a change from the declining-balance method of depreciation to the straight-line method without consent of the IRS. Note that most assets have specified methods for being depreciated under ACRS and MACRS. A taxpayer can elect the straight-line method of depreciation under ACRS or MACRS for certain classes of property or certain properties (depending on the type of asset) without obtaining IRS permission.
Answers (a), (b), and (c) are incorrect because each requires the permission of the IRS.

113. When you file your first tax return, you may, without the consent of the IRS, choose any appropriate accounting method. The method you choose must clearly show your income and must be used from year to year, unless you get a consent from the IRS to change your accounting method.

The correct answer is (T). *(SPE 989 II-1)*
DISCUSSION: A taxpayer may choose any appropriate accounting method without the consent of the IRS as long as it clearly reflects income. Under Sec. 446(e), a taxpayer must obtain permission from the IRS in order to change a method of accounting.

21.8 Tax Year

114. All of the following tax years are acceptable tax years except:

a. 52- to 53-week tax year.

b. A short tax year which occurred because a business was not in existence for an entire year.

c. A short tax year which occurred because a business had a change in accounting period.

d. A fiscal tax year (other than a 52- to 53-week tax year) that ends on any day of the month other than the last day.

The correct answer is (d). *(SPE 989 II-31)*
REQUIRED: The incorrect statement regarding tax years.
DISCUSSION: Under Sec. 441(e), a fiscal year is a period of 12 months ending on the last day of any month other than December.
Answer (a) is incorrect because a 52- to 53-week tax year is allowed under Sec. 441(f). Answer (b) is incorrect because a short tax year is allowed for a business not in existence for an entire year under Sec. 443(a)(2). Answer (c) is incorrect because a short tax year is permitted when an accounting period is changed under Sec. 443(a)(1).

115. For the first 6 months of 1991, Mr. S, who files jointly with his wife, had an adjusted gross income of $30,000 and itemized deductions of $6,000. He is entitled to a total of four exemptions. Mr. S changed his accounting period and is required to file a short period return for the six-month period. What is Mr. S's annualized income?

a. $48,000.
b. $39,400.
c. $19,700.
d. $15,400.

The correct answer is (b). *(SPE 1080 II-66)*
REQUIRED: The annualized income of a taxpayer who changes accounting periods.
DISCUSSION: Sec. 443(a)(1) requires a taxpayer who changes accounting periods to file a short period return, in which income must be annualized [Sec. 443(b)]. Income is annualized by multiplying the short period modified taxable income (gross income minus deductions allowed and using a proportionate amount of personal exemptions) by 12, dividing the result by the number of months in the short period. S's annualized income is

Adjusted gross income	$30,000
Less itemized deductions	(6,000)
Less personal exemptions (4 x $2,150 x 6/12 months)	(4,300)
Taxable income for short period	$19,700
	x 12/6
Annualized income	$39,400

Note that Mr. S would compute tax on $39,400 and then pay one-half the tax (6/12 months).

116. A calendar-year accounting period covers a 12-month period and may end on the last day of any month of the year.

The correct answer is (F). *(SPE 984 II-2)*
DISCUSSION: A calendar-year accounting period covers a 12-month period ending on December 31. The taxpayer may choose a fiscal year covering a 12-month period ending on the last day of any month except December.

117. Mr. P established a calendar tax year when he filed his first individual income tax return. Mr. P in a later year began business as a sole proprietorship and wished to change his tax year to a fiscal year ending in January. P may change his tax year without securing permission from the Commissioner of Internal Revenue.

The correct answer is (F). *(SPE 990 II-3)*
DISCUSSION: Sec. 442 provides that a taxpayer must obtain consent from the IRS before changing his/her annual accounting period. An application to change tax years is made on Form 1128.

118. An application to change a tax year (Form 1128), to be timely, must be filed with the Internal Revenue Service on or before the 15th day of the second month following the close of the short period.

The correct answer is (T). *(SPE 1080 II-2)*
DISCUSSION: Reg. 1.442-1(b) provides that a taxpayer must file an application on Form 1128 to change the tax year on or before the 15th day of the second calendar month following the close of the short period.

119. Because this is the first year for Mr. Pluto to file a federal income tax return, the 12-month period ending February 15, 1991 can be adopted if the election is timely.

The correct answer is (F). *(SPE 1077 I-87)*
DISCUSSION: In a taxpayer's first year, any taxable year which meets the requirement in Sec. 441 may be adopted without obtaining prior approval. Sec. 441, however, allows only the adoption of a calendar or fiscal year as a taxable year. A calendar year is the period of 12 months ending on December 31. A fiscal year is a period of 12 months ending on the last day of any month other than December, or a 52- to 53-week annual accounting period. Because the 12-month period ending February 15 is not a fiscal or calendar year, it is not an allowable tax year.

120. A calendar-year C corporation that has been inactive for a number of years can change to a June 30 fiscal year when business is resumed.

The correct answer is (T). *(SPE 1079 III-8)*
DISCUSSION: Under Reg. 1.442-1(c)(2), a corporation may change its accounting period without prior approval if the following conditions are met: (1) the corporation has not changed its accounting period within the preceding 10 calendar years, (2) the short tax year has no net operating loss, (3) the taxable income for the short tax year when annualized is at least 80% of the taxable income from the preceding full tax year, and (4) if the corporation has a special status, it must retain this status. If a corporation has been inactive, these requirements would probably be met. Also, Rev. Rul. 60-51 allows a corporation that has been inactive (in effect not in existence) for several years to adopt a new accounting year without consent.

121. In order to adopt a 52- to 53-week year a corporation must file a statement showing:

1. The day of the week upon which the tax year will always end;
2. Whether it will end on the last such day of the week occurring in the calendar month or on the date such day of the week occurs nearest the end of the month; and
3. The month in which (or with reference to which) the tax year will end.

The correct answer is (T). *(SPE 1080 III-41)*
DISCUSSION: Reg. 1.441-2(c) requires a statement to be filed for a taxpayer to adopt a 52- to 53-week year. This statement must include the following information: (1) the calendar month with reference to which the tax year will end, (2) the day of the week on which the tax year will always end, and (3) whether the tax year will end on the last such day of the week occurring in the calendar month or on the date such day of the week occurs nearest the end of the month.

122. Under the Tax Reform Act of 1986, a corporation that is newly formed must always use the calendar year as its tax year.

The correct answer is (F). *(SPE 987 III-6)*
DISCUSSION: In general, in a corporation's first year, it may choose any taxable year which meets the requirement in Sec. 441 without obtaining prior approval. This is true for a C corporation. But an S corporation is generally only allowed a calendar year or a fiscal year for which a business purpose is established. A personal service corporation is generally only allowed a calendar year. But both the S corporation and the personal service corporation may elect, under Sec. 444, some other fiscal year. But to make this election, an S corporation must make a required payment and a personal service corporation must make minimum distributions to its shareholders.

123. A partnership may elect a fiscal year after 1986 when the deferral of income to the partners is for not more than a 3-month period.

The correct answer is (T). *(Publisher)*
DISCUSSION: Under Sec. 706, a business purpose must be established to permit after 1986 the use of a taxable year other than one determined under the normal rules, e.g.; that of the majority partner(s). A 3-month deferral of income is not a business purpose. But Sec. 444 allows a partnership to elect a fiscal tax year if a required payment is made. The fiscal year may be the fiscal year the partnership had at the end of 1986 or a fiscal year with no more than a 3-month deferral period. But if the fiscal year at the end of 1986 had less than a 3-month deferral, then a new fiscal year may not have a greater deferral.

124. An S corporation's taxable year beginning after 1986 is restricted to a calendar year or a fiscal year for which a business purpose can be established.

The correct answer is (F). *(Publisher)*
DISCUSSION: After 1986, Sec. 1378(a) specifies that an S corporation's taxable year is restricted to a permitted year. A permitted year is a calendar year or a fiscal year for which a business purpose is established. But Sec. 444 allows an S corporation to elect a fiscal tax year if a required payment is made. The fiscal year may be the fiscal year the S corporation had at the end of 1986 or a fiscal year with no more than a 3-month deferral period. But if the fiscal year at the end of 1986 had less than a 3-month deferral, then a new fiscal year may not have a greater deferral.

125. Personal service corporations must use a calendar year after 1986 unless the IRS consents otherwise.

The correct answer is (F). *(Publisher)*
DISCUSSION: Sec. 441(i) requires that personal service corporations must use a calendar year after 1986 unless the IRS consents to some other year based on a business purpose. But Sec. 444 allows a personal service corporation to elect a fiscal tax year if it makes "minimum distributions to its shareholders." The fiscal year may either be the fiscal year the personal service corporation had at the end of 1986 or a fiscal year with no more than a 3-month deferral period. But if the fiscal year at the end of 1986 had less than a 3-month deferral, than a new fiscal year may not have a greater deferral.

21.9 Recordkeeping Requirements

126. Which of the following items represents sufficient documentary evidence to substantiate expenditures for travel, entertainment, or gift expenses?

    a. A canceled check written to pay a motel bill on a business trip.

    b. A statement from the taxpayer's employer.

    c. An account book maintained daily by the taxpayer for her business meals (no meal was over $10).

    d. Memos on a desk calendar.

The correct answer is (c). *(SPE 1080 I-54)*
REQUIRED: The item providing sufficient documentary evidence to substantiate expenditures for travel, entertainment, or gift expenses.
DISCUSSION: Temp. Reg. 1.274-5T outlines the rules for substantiation. Substantiation of who, when, where, why, and the amount is generally required. A taxpayer must maintain adequate records or sufficient evidence corroborating the taxpayer's statement. An account book maintained daily by the taxpayer would meet the rules for substantiation. Documentary evidence such as a receipt is not required for meals costing less than $25.
Answer (a) is incorrect because the business purpose is not evident from a canceled check. Answer (b) is incorrect because a statement from the taxpayer's employer is not an adequate record. Answer (d) is incorrect because memos on a desk calendar are usually not made at or near the time of expenditure. The record should be made at or near the time of the expenditure.

127. A business operated as a sole proprietorship must use the double-entry accounting method to reflect both income and expenses for computing taxable income.

The correct answer is (F). *(SPE 1082 II-2)*
DISCUSSION: Under Sec. 446(a), a taxpayer is required to compute taxable income using the method of accounting regularly used in keeping his/her books. There are no specified methods as long as the method used clearly reflects income.

128. Federal law does not require a taxpayer to maintain any special form of records but the records must be such that the taxpayer can prepare a complete and accurate income tax return.

The correct answer is (T). *(SPE 988 IV-35)*
DISCUSSION: Sec. 6001 requires every person liable for any tax imposed by the Internal Revenue Code to keep records sufficient to establish the amount of items required to be shown by such a person in any return of tax or information. Reg. 31.6001-1(a), however, states that no particular form is required for keeping records.

129. Adequate records must include sufficient documents (sales slips, invoices, canceled checks, etc.) that clearly establish the income, deductions, and credits shown on the return.

The correct answer is (T). *(SPE 1078 IV-70)*
DISCUSSION: Reg. 1.6001-1(a) provides that books of accounts or records should be sufficient to establish the amount of gross income, deductions, credits, or other matters required to be shown by such persons in any tax or information return.

130. For federal tax purposes, an automatic data processing recordkeeping system must provide an audit trail so that details (invoices and vouchers) may be identified and made available upon request.

The correct answer is (T). *(SPE 1081 IV-40)*
DISCUSSION: Rev. Proc. 86-19 sets forth the guidelines for record requirements in an ADP system. One of the requirements is that an audit trail must be designed so that details underlying the summary accounting data, such as invoices and vouchers, may be identified and made available to the IRS upon request.

131. Microfilm and microfiche reproductions of general books of accounts, such as cash books, journals, voucher registers, and ledgers, are accepted by the Internal Revenue Service for recordkeeping if they comply with applicable revenue procedures.

The correct answer is (T). *(SPE 984 IV-47)*
DISCUSSION: Rev. Proc. 81-46 sets forth the conditions under which microfilm reproductions will be considered books and records under Sec. 6001. As long as the microfilm and microfiche reproductions satisfy the requirements, they will be accepted by the IRS for recordkeeping.

132. If you receive a cash gift from a relative, you should maintain a record to substantiate its receipt in order to prevent it from later being characterized as taxable income.

The correct answer is (T). *(SPE 1077 IV-31)*
DISCUSSION: If the IRS challenges the treatment of an item, the taxpayer must produce sufficient records to support his/her claim. Therefore, it would be a good idea to record the receipt of a cash gift from a relative.

133. An accountant should furnish records or information to the Internal Revenue Service on first request, even if (s)he feels the information is privileged.

The correct answer is (F). *(SPE 1080 IV-22)*
DISCUSSION: If an accountant feels information is privileged, (s)he should not furnish the records or information to the IRS since unauthorized disclosure of information by preparers of returns can constitute a misdemeanor, punishable by fines up to $1,000 and/or imprisonment of up to 1 year [Sec. 7216(a)].

134. You must keep records on employment taxes (income tax withholding, social security, and federal unemployment tax) for at least 4 years after the due date of the return or after the date the tax is paid, whichever is later.

The correct answer is (T). *(SPE 990 IV-27)*
DISCUSSION: The general rule of Reg. 31.6001-1(e)(2) is that persons required to keep records concerning a tax must maintain them for at least 4 years after the due date of the return or after the date the tax is paid, whichever is later.

135. Employers are not required to retain withholding exemption certificates (Form W-4) filed by employees after the date of the current year's returns.

The correct answer is (F). *(SPE 1081 IV-42)*
DISCUSSION: Under Reg. 31.6001-5(a)(13), employers are required to retain in their records Form W-4 for each employee. These records must be retained for at least 4 years [Reg. 31.6001-1(e)(2)].

136. Purchasing property with a long life, adopting the LIFO method of inventory, and changing a method of accounting are all examples of business decisions which may require a person to maintain records longer than the general requirement of 3 years after the return was due or filed or 2 years after the date the tax was paid, whichever is later.

The correct answer is (T). *(SPE 989 IV-35)*
DISCUSSION: Reg. 1.6001-1(e) provides that a taxpayer's records must be kept as long as the contents may be material in the administration of any Internal Revenue law. Since the IRS generally has 3 years from the date a return was due or filed, or 2 years from the date the tax was paid, whichever is later, to assess tax [Sec. 6501(a)], a taxpayer must retain his/her records at least until the later time.

137. You should keep records that verify your basis in property for as long as they are needed to figure the basis of the original or replacement property.

The correct answer is (T). *(SPE 987 IV-33)*
DISCUSSION: Records relating to the basis of property should be retained as long as they may be material [Reg. 1.6001-1(e)]. The basis of property is material until the statute of limitations expires for the year sold.

643

CHAPTER TWENTY-TWO
EMPLOYMENT TAXES AND WITHHOLDING

22.1 Social Security Tax Overview	(6 questions)	643
22.2 Employee versus Independent Contractor	(6 questions)	644
22.3 FICA for Employees	(20 questions)	645
22.4 FICA for the Self-Employed	(21 questions)	650
22.5 Filing a Social Security Tax Return	(4 questions)	656
22.6 Federal Unemployment Tax	(5 questions)	657
22.7 Withholding	(16 questions)	659

22.1 Social Security Tax Overview

1. During the examination of the financial statements of Viscount Manufacturing Corporation the CPAs noted that although Viscount had 860 full-time and part-time employees, it had completely overlooked its responsibilities under the Federal Insurance Contributions Act (FICA). Under these circumstances, which of the following is true?

a. No liability under the Act will attach if the employees voluntarily relinquish their rights under the Act in exchange for a cash equivalent paid directly to them.

b. If the union which represents the employees has a vested pension plan covering the employees which is equal to or exceeds the benefits available under the Act, Viscount has no liability.

c. Since employers and employees owe FICA taxes at the same rate and since the employer must withhold the employees' tax from their wages as paid, Viscount must remit to the government a tax double the amount assessed directly against the employer.

d. The Act does not apply to the part-time employees.

The correct answer is (c). *(CPA 1177 L-13)*
REQUIRED: The correct statement concerning an employer's responsibility under FICA.
DISCUSSION: Both employers and employees owe FICA taxes at the same rate. Under Sec. 3102, an employer is liable for collecting (withholding) the employees' tax from wages. Employers who fail to collect these taxes are responsible for the employees' tax, in addition to their own. Furthermore, Viscount could be subject to a 100% penalty under Sec. 6672 in addition to the taxes, if the failure to withhold or pay is willful.
Answer (a) is incorrect because coverage under the Social Security Act is mandatory and employees may not give up Social Security rights in exchange for money paid directly or indirectly to them. Answer (b) is incorrect because coverage under Social Security is mandatory and not replaceable by union benefits or pension plans. Answer (d) is incorrect because the Social Security Act applies to all employees, including part-time employees.

2. All of the following items of information are required to be maintained for Social Security tax purposes except

a. The amount and date of each wage, annuity, or pension payment.

b. The dates and amounts of tax deposits made.

c. The names, addresses, and Social Security numbers of employees and recipients of payments.

d. Any agreement between the employee and employer for the voluntary withholding of additional amounts of FICA tax.

The correct answer is (d). *(SPE 986 IV-69)*
REQUIRED: The information not required to be maintained by an employer for Social Security tax purposes.
DISCUSSION: Circular E provides a list of records which should be kept for at least 4 years for employment tax purposes. An employee may have additional amounts of income tax withheld, but it makes no sense to have additional amounts of FICA tax withheld because there is a cap on the amount of FICA tax; i.e., there would be no agreement between an employee and an employer for such voluntary withholding.
Answers (a), (b), and (c) are incorrect because these are records of an employer which should be maintained for 4 years.

3. The Social Security Act provides for the imposition of taxes and the disbursement of benefits. Which of the following is a correct statement regarding these taxes and disbursements in 1991?

    a. Only those who have contributed to Social Security are eligible for benefits.

    b. As between an employer and its employee, the tax rates are the same.

    c. A deduction for federal income tax purposes is allowed the employee for Social Security taxes paid.

    d. Social Security benefits are fully includable in gross income for federal income tax purposes unless they are paid for disability.

The correct answer is (b). *(CPA 581 L-59)*
REQUIRED: The correct statement concerning the Social Security tax and benefits.
DISCUSSION: Under the Federal Insurance Contributions Act (FICA), the tax rate for employers and employees is the same (7.65% in 1991). This requirement of shared responsibility has been followed since the Social Security Act was enacted in 1935.
Answer (a) is incorrect because benefits under Social Security benefits are paid to more than those who have contributed to it. Many of the recipients of Social Security benefits are surviving spouses or children of retired, deceased, or disabled workers. Answer (c) is incorrect because employment taxes are not deductible by an employee (Sec. 3502), although they are deductible by an employer carrying on a trade or business. Answer (d) is incorrect because Social Security benefits are included in gross income only to the extent that a recipient's income is in excess of certain statutory amounts.

4. Bank Z makes annuity payments as an agent for an employees' trust and the trust is the payor. If the trust has withholding taxes due, but no employees with wages subject to FICA taxes, it should file Form 941E.

The correct answer is (T). *(SPE 1080 II-10)*
DISCUSSION: Form 941 is used to report withholding and Social Security taxes collected by an employer. If an employer collects withholding taxes, but has no employees with wages subject to Social Security taxes, the proper form for reporting withholding taxes collected is Form 941E. The E refers to the exempt status with regard to the Social Security taxes.

5. Every employer required to report employment taxes or give tax statements to employees must obtain an employer identification number.

The correct answer is (T). *(SPE 1079 II-35)*
DISCUSSION: Any employer who is required to report employment taxes or give tax statements to employees must obtain an identification number in order to facilitate the filing of the information (Sec. 6109).

6. Although an organization is recognized as tax exempt, it is responsible for withholding, depositing, and reporting federal income tax, FICA tax, and FUTA tax on wages paid to its employees.

The correct answer is (T). *(SPE 986 IV-53)*
DISCUSSION: Employers are required to perform these functions. The term employer includes exempt organizations.

22.2 Employee versus Independent Contractor

7. Certain sales agents are classified as independent contractors for purposes of the employment taxes. To which of the following does this safe harbor not apply?

    a. Licensed real estate agent.

    b. Seller of consumer goods in the home to a buyer for resale.

    c. Seller of consumer goods in the home, not for resale.

    d. Seller whose remuneration is based on hours worked.

The correct answer is (d). *(Publisher)*
REQUIRED: The seller who is not within the safe harbor provisions as an independent contractor.
DISCUSSION: A safe harbor is provided for certain real estate agents and direct sellers to be classified as independent contractors, but the seller's remuneration must be directly related to the sales or output and not based on hours worked (Sec. 3508).
Answers (a), (b), and (c) are incorrect because a licensed real estate agent and a seller of consumer goods in the home rather than in a permanent retail establishment (whether or not for resale) will not be classified as employees if substantially all of their remuneration is directly related to sales or output rather than to the number of hours worked, and if the services are pursuant to a written contract which provides that the individual will not be treated as an employee with respect to such service for federal tax purposes.

8. If A has the legal right to control both the method and the result of B's services, B is an employee under common law.

The correct answer is (T). *(SPE 1078 II-29)*
DISCUSSION: The status of a taxpayer as an employee under common law is important because an employee under common law is an employee for federal employment tax purposes, although this is not the exclusive test [Sec. 3121(d)]. Under common law principles, an employee is a person whose performance is subject to the control of the employer. This control extends not only to the result but to the details and means by which the result is accomplished by the employee.

9. A homeworker, working according to specifications of the person for whom the services are performed, on materials or goods furnished by and required to be returned to that person, is not an employee for Social Security tax purposes.

The correct answer is (F). *(SPE 1077 I-105)*
DISCUSSION: Under Sec. 3121(d)(3)(C), an employee is defined as including a homeworker performing work according to the specifications of and with materials or goods furnished by the "employer" which are required to be returned to him/her.

10. A commission-driver who distributes soft drinks for a principal is an employee for Social Security tax purposes.

The correct answer is (T). *(SPE 1077 I-129)*
DISCUSSION: Under Sec. 3121(d)(3)(A), an employee is defined as including any person who performs services for remuneration as an agent-driver or commission-driver engaged in distributing meats, vegetables, fruits, beverages, etc., for his/her principal.

11. Drivers for M Trucking Co. often engage laborers to unload their trucks. This is done with the implied consent of M, and the drivers pay the unloaders from funds provided by M. The unloaders are employees of M Trucking Co.

The correct answer is (T). *(SPE 1085 II-15)*
DISCUSSION: Under common law principles, an employee is defined as a person whose performance (both method and result) is subject to the control of the employer. Since the drivers (employees of M) presumably control the performance of the unloaders, these persons are effectively controlled by M, who also consented to their hiring and provides funds for their compensation.

12. Sue and Bob Johnson have a babysitter who was sent to them by a babysitting agency. The agency sets the babysitter's fee, requires regular reports from the sitter, and exercises control over the sitter relative to dress and rules of conduct. The Johnsons are required to pay employment taxes and file Forms 940 and 942 for wages paid to the sitter.

The correct answer is (F). *(SPE 988 I-26)*
DISCUSSION: When an agency provides a worker, sets the fee, and exercises control over the worker, the agency is the employer of that worker. Therefore, the agency, not the Johnsons, is liable for Social Security taxes and needs to file Forms 940 and 942. Furthermore, the agency is an independent contractor with respect to the Johnsons.

22.3 FICA for Employees

13. The federal Social Security Act
    a. Does not apply to self-employed persons.
    b. Excludes professionals such as accountants, lawyers, and doctors.
    c. Provides for a deduction by the employee which is available against his/her federal income tax.
    d. Provides that bonuses and commissions paid as compensation are included as wages in the calculation of employer-employee contributions.

The correct answer is (d). *(CPA 1175 L-44)*
REQUIRED: The correct statement concerning the federal Social Security Act.
DISCUSSION: The definition of wages on which contributions are based includes all remuneration for employment [Sec. 3121(a)]. Bonuses and commissions are wages and are used in the calculation of the employer-employee contributions.
Answer (a) is incorrect because the Social Security Act does apply to self-employed persons and coverage is mandatory. Answer (b) is incorrect because the Social Security Act does not exclude professionals such as accountants, lawyers, and doctors. Answer (c) is incorrect because an employee may not deduct his/her Social Security tax (Sec. 3502).

Module 22.3: FICA for Employees

14. The Social Security tax does not apply to which of the following?

a. Medical and hospital reimbursements by the employer which are excluded from gross income.
b. Compensation paid in forms other than cash.
c. Self-employment income of $1,000.
d. Bonuses and vacation time pay.

The correct answer is (a). *(CPA 1181 L-30)*
REQUIRED: The payment to which the Social Security tax does not apply.
DISCUSSION: The Social Security tax imposed by the Federal Insurance Contribution Act (FICA) applies to virtually all compensation received for employment, including money or other forms of wages, bonuses, commissions, vacation pay, severance allowances, and tips. Reimbursements by one's employers for medical and hospital expenses which are not included in gross income are not subject to FICA [Sec. 3121(a)(2)]. However, sick pay, which is a wage payment paid when unable to work, is subject to FICA.

Answers (b) and (d) are incorrect because they are subject to FICA. Answer (c) is incorrect because self-employment income is taxed for the same Social Security benefits although the tax is imposed by Sec. 1401 rather than Secs. 3101 and 3111.

15. For 1991, Mr. K, a farmer-employer, would have to pay Social Security taxes on which of the following?

a. $400 cash wages paid to Mr. K's 17-year-old son.
b. $800 cash wages paid to Mr. K's father.
c. $100 cash wages paid to Mr. K's wife. Total cash wages paid to all employees is $1,300.
d. 100 bushels of soybeans with a fair market value of $600 given to an unrelated person by Mr. K in lieu of wages.

The correct answer is (b). *(SPE 1085 II-51)*
REQUIRED: The item on which a farmer-employer must pay Social Security tax in 1991.
DISCUSSION: The Social Security taxes are imposed by Secs. 3101 and 3111 on wages paid by an employer. Wages are defined in Sec. 3121(a) as all remuneration for employment, not including that paid for agricultural labor unless the cash remuneration in such year is $150 or more to the employee, or the employer pays at least $2,500 during the year for all agricultural labor [Sec. 3121(a)(8)]. Mr. K's father earned more than $150, and his wages therefore qualify under the definition of wages. Employment for FICA purposes includes that of a parent by a child.

Answer (a) is incorrect because employment for FICA purposes excludes services performed by a child under 18 in the employ of his/her parent. Answer (c) is incorrect because after 1987, an individual in the employ of his/her spouse is no longer automatically exempt from the FICA tax. However, Mrs. K earned less than $150 and total wages paid to agricultural labor is less than $2,500, her wages are exempt from the FICA tax. Answer (d) is incorrect because wages subject to FICA tax do not include compensation paid in forms other than cash for agricultural labor.

16. Ernesto is an employee of Med-Tech Corporation for all of 1991. He earned $80,000 in salary. What is the amount of Social Security taxes paid by Med-Tech Corporation with respect to Ernesto?

a. $3,924.
b. $4,085.
c. $4,471.
d. $6,120.

The correct answer is (c). *(Publisher)*
REQUIRED: The Social Security taxes required to be paid by an employer in 1991.
DISCUSSION: Beginning in 1991, the two components of the FICA tax [old-age, survivors, and disability insurance (OASDI)] and Medicare have different wage ceilings. The OASDI rate is 6.20% each for employers and employees up to a maximum of $53,400. The Medicare rate is 1.45% for employers and employees up to a maximum of $125,000. The employment taxes paid by Med-Tech with respect to Ernesto in 1991 are as follows:

OASDI	$53,400 x .0620 =	$3,311
Medicare	$80,000 x .0145 =	1,160
Total		$4,471

Module 22.3: FICA for Employees

17. You are the accountant for Company R and you are requested to file Form 941, Employer's Quarterly Federal Tax Return for Federal Income Tax withheld from wages and for Federal Insurance Contributions Act Taxes, for the second quarter of 1991. Given the following information, what is the total FICA tax due for the second quarter (rounded to the nearest dollar)?

Employee	Wages Paid Second Quarter	Wages Paid First Quarter
X	$ 5,000	$ 5,000
Y	12,000	29,000
Z	5,000	0

a. $2,884.
b. $2,946.
c. $3,304.
d. $3,366.

The correct answer is (d). *(SPE 1079 II-84)*
REQUIRED: The amount of Social Security tax due during the second quarter of 1991.
DISCUSSION: Beginning in 1991, the two components of the FICA tax (Social Security and Medicare) must be reported separately on Form 941. The rate for Social Security is 6.20% each for employers and employees up to a maximum of $53,400. The rate for Medicare is 1.45% each for employers and employees up to a maximum of $125,000. The tax is paid until the maximum wage is reached, then no FICA tax is paid for the rest of the year; i.e., it is not paid ratably over the year. The total wages subject to FICA taxes in the second quarter of 1991 amount to $22,000. All wages are subject to taxes since none of the employees' total wages paid through the second quarter exceeds either of the maximum amounts for withholding. The total FICA tax for both components is 7.65% in 1991. However, the employee and the employer are each required to pay the 7.65%, and the combined percentage of 15.30% is reported on Form 941, divided into its two components.

Employee	Wages Subject to Tax
X	$ 5,000
Y	12,000
Z	5,000

$22,000 x 15.30% = $3,366

18. Mrs. C is employed part-time as a waitress with restaurants A and B. During the month of June she received tips totaling $15 from her employment at A, and tips totaling $85 from her employment at B. For employment tax purposes, what amount of June tips must Mrs. C report to her employers?

a. $0.
b. $65.
c. $85.
d. $100.

The correct answer is (c). *(SPE 984 I-54)*
REQUIRED: The amount of income from tips which the employee must report to her employers.
DISCUSSION: Under Sec. 3121(a)(12), an employee is only required to report tips if they exceed $20 in one month. This $20 applies to each place of employment. Therefore, Mrs. C must report her tips to her employer at restaurant B, but she is not required to report her tips to her employer at restaurant A.

19. An employee who has had Social Security tax withheld in an amount greater than the maximum for a particular year may claim

a. The excess as a credit against income tax, if that excess was withheld by one employer.
b. The excess as a credit against income tax, if that excess resulted from correct withholding by two or more employers.
c. Reimbursement of such excess from his employers if that excess resulted from correct withholding by two or more employers.
d. Such excess as either a credit or an itemized deduction, at the election of the employee, if that excess resulted from correct withholding by two or more employers.

The correct answer is (b). *(CPA 588 Q-10)*
REQUIRED: The correct statement about the result of Social Security tax withheld in excess of the maximum amount.
DISCUSSION: When an employee overpays the Social Security tax, Sec. 6413(a) provides that proper adjustments shall be made, without interest, pursuant to regulations. If the overpayment cannot be adjusted, the amount shall be refunded pursuant to regulations [Sec. 6413(b)]. If the overpayment resulted from correct withholding by two or more employers, the extra Social Security tax may be used to reduce income taxes.
Answer (a) is incorrect because only when an employee has worked for two or more employers can the extra Social Security tax be used to reduce income taxes. Answer (c) is incorrect because it is not the employer's responsibility to refund the tax (the employer turned it over to the government). Answer (d) is incorrect because the overpayment is not available as a deduction.

20. A waiter works in a restaurant and earns more than $1,000 in tips monthly. His tips are subject to income tax withholding and the employer's portion of Social Security taxes.

The correct answer is (T). *(SPE 987 II-35)*
DISCUSSION: The Social Security employer tax and income tax withholding applies to wages that are paid by the employer to the employee. Under Sec. 3401(f), tips are considered to be wages. The employer is required to collect employee Social Security tax and income tax on tips reported by an employee. The employer must also pay the employer portion of the Social Security tax on tips reported by an employee. Sec. 6053(a) requires an employee receiving tips in a calendar month to report the amount of such tips on or before the 10th day of the following month. The employer may stop collecting employee Social Security tax and paying employer Social Security tax when the employee's wages and reported tips total $53,400 ($125,000 for Medicare payments) for 1991.

21. The mandatory gratuity charges assessed on members by a country club are not tips, but wages subject to withholding for income and Social Security taxes and are also subject to FUTA.

The correct answer is (T). *(SPE 1078 II-30)*
DISCUSSION: Mandatory gratuity charges assessed by the employer are not considered tips since they are under the control and possession of the employer. When the employer distributes part or all of these charges to the employee, this is considered to be a wage paid by the employer and thus is subject to income tax withholding, FICA, and FUTA (Rev. Rul. 66-74). FUTA is the Federal Unemployment Tax.

22. Mr. C works as a waiter at a restaurant. The restaurant requires customers who use its banquet room to pay a service charge, which is given to the waiters and waitresses. C's share of this service charge is not a tip reportable to his employer.

The correct answer is (T). *(SPE 1083 I-12)*
DISCUSSION: Service charges collected by an employer from customers and given to the waiters and waitresses are not considered tips since they are under the control of the employer. When the employer distributes these charges to the employees, they are considered wages paid by the employer subject to income tax withholding, FICA, and FUTA.

23. Mr. X worked at Zee Restaurant and received $25 in tips for 1 month. That same month he also worked at Cheap Restaurant and received $15 in tips. Mr. X must report his tips to both of his employers.

The correct answer is (F). *(SPE 988 I-5)*
DISCUSSION: Every employee who receives tips that are wages (i.e., tips in any calendar month of at least $20) must file a written report on or before the 10th day following such month [Sec. 6053(a)]. Mr. X must report his tips to Zee Restaurant but is not required to report them to Cheap Restaurant because tips of less than $20 in a month are not considered to be wages [Sec. 3121(a)(12)].

24. Mr. A works part-time as a waiter for a restaurant. Mr. A splits all of his tips with the busboy, giving him one-fourth. In January 1991, Mr. A received tips totaling $100 and gave the busboy $25 for his share. Mr. A is required to report $75 in tips to the employer, but the busboy does not have to report his $25 share.

The correct answer is (F). *(SPE 1085 II-16)*
DISCUSSION: Under Sec. 3121(a)(12), an employee is required to report tips if they exceed $20 in any one month. Therefore, both Mr. A and the busboy must report tips earned in January 1991.

25. If you do not report tips to your employer as required, you may be subject to a penalty equal to 50% of the employee Social Security tax, in addition to the tax that you owe.

The correct answer is (T). *(SPE 986 I-16)*
DISCUSSION: If the failure is the result of willful neglect rather than reasonable cause, the employee must pay the FICA tax on the unreported tips plus 50% of such tax [Sec. 6652(b)].

Module 22.3: FICA for Employees 649

26. Ms. C is a waitress at a restaurant employing over 100 employees where tipping is customary. The restaurant's food and beverage sales totaled $2,000,000 for the year. Employees reported tips of $80,000 or 4% of total sales. The restaurant will allocate among the employees who receive tips directly from customers the excess of 8% of total sales over the 4% reported. The allocated amount will be reported by the restaurant on C's W-2 separate from wages and reported tips. However, no allocation will be made to C if she reported tips at least equal to her share of 8% of total sales.

The correct answer is (T). (SPE 986 I-14)

DISCUSSION: A large food or beverage establishment (one providing food or beverage for consumption on the premises, where tipping is customary, and having more than 10 employees on a typical day in all food or beverage operations) must allocate tips if employees report tips of less than 8% of gross receipts (less carryout sales and sales with a 10% service charge added) [Sec. 6053(c)(3)]. The 8% threshold may be reduced (but not below 2%) by petition of the employer or a majority of the employees.

27. All of the following employees are subject to the withholding of Social Security taxes.

1. Resident alien, services performed in United States.
2. Son under 18 employed by parent.
3. Parent employed by son in course of his business.
4. Full-time life insurance salesman.
5. Federal employees.

The correct answer is (F). (SPE 1080 II-11)

DISCUSSION: Under Sec. 3121(b)(3), a child under the age of 18 in the employ of his/her father or mother is not subject to the withholding of Social Security taxes. Federal employees are no longer exempt as they are no longer covered under a separate retirement plan. Aliens who perform services in the U.S., parents of employer children, and insurance sales people are all subject to FICA.

28. Since noncash items are difficult to value, only wages paid in cash are subject to federal employment taxes.

The correct answer is (F). (SPE 1080 II-9)

DISCUSSION: Under Sec. 3121(a), wages are all forms of compensation paid for employment including the cash value of compensation paid in any medium other than cash. Wages are equal to cash plus the fair market value of any property received for services performed.

29. Ms. B pays $100 per month to Ms. W, a household employee, to take care of her disabled dependent. Ms. B does not have to pay Social Security tax on Ms. W's wages.

The correct answer is (F). (SPE 1081 I-42)

DISCUSSION: An employer must pay FICA tax on the wages of an employee providing domestic service in a private home if the employee is paid $50 or more in a quarter.

30. Mr. G was employed by B from January to September 1991 and was paid $60,000 in earned wages. On October 15, 1991, he started a new job with S. If G informs his new employer that he has already met the wage limitation for FICA tax, and provides verification, S is not required to withhold FICA tax from G's wages for 1991.

The correct answer is (F). (SPE 1083 II-22)

DISCUSSION: Each employer must withhold a deduction for Social Security taxes from its employee's wages. No provision allows an employer to take into account that an employee has already reached the annual limit while working for another employer. Only when both corporations have a common paymaster can wages be accumulated from different employers to reach the wage limitation. Note: For 1991 and later years G has met the OASDI limit for FICA taxes, but not the Medicare limit.

31. If you worked for only one employer and more than the maximum Social Security tax was withheld, you may claim the extra amount as a credit to reduce your income tax when you file your return.

The correct answer is (F). (SPE 986 I-15)

DISCUSSION: Sec. 6413(a) provides that proper adjustments, with respect to both the tax and the amount to be deducted, shall be made, without interest, pursuant to regulations. If the overpayment cannot be adjusted, the amount shall be refunded pursuant to regulations [Sec. 6413(b)]. Only when you worked for two or more employers can the extra Social Security tax be used to reduce income taxes.

32. In June 1991, Corporation Y purchased all of the assets of Corporation Z. Ms. B, who had worked for Z, continued to work for Y. Ms. B had received $20,000 in wages in 1991 before the date of the purchase. Corporation Y is subject to the Social Security tax (OASDI portion) on only the first $33,400 of wages paid to Ms. B during the rest of 1991.

The correct answer is (T). *(SPE 1085 III-44)*
DISCUSSION: The employee and the employer pay the full FICA taxes on the first $53,400 of an employee's wages for calendar year 1991. Wages paid in excess of $53,400 are still subject to the Medicare tax up to $125,000 in wages. The successor employer (one acquiring all or substantially all of the property used in the business of the predecessor) may use the wages paid by the predecessor employer to the employee in calculating the $53,400 or $125,000 tax limits.

22.4 FICA for the Self-Employed

33. The federal Social Security Act

a. Applies to self-employed persons.
b. Excludes professionals such as accountants, lawyers, and doctors.
c. Provides for a deduction by the employee against his/her federal income tax.
d. Applies to professionals at their option.

The correct answer is (a). *(CPA 1176 L-47)*
REQUIRED: The correct statement concerning the federal Social Security Act.
DISCUSSION: The Social Security Act applies to self-employed persons who must pay a tax on self-employment income (15.3% on the first $53,400 and 2.90% on wages between $53,400 and $125,000 in 1991).
Answers (b) and (d) are incorrect because the Social Security Act does not exclude professionals from mandatory coverage. Answer (c) is incorrect because an employee's contribution to Social Security is not deductible for federal income tax purposes. After 1989, one-half of a self-employed person's self employment tax is deductible for federal income tax purposes [Sec. 164(f)].

34. All of the following individuals are generally subject to the self-employment tax except

a. Grocery store sole proprietor.
b. Bricklayer - independent contractor.
c. Minister - member of the clergy.
d. Factory worker - paid on piecemeal basis.

The correct answer is (d). *(SPE 984 II-63)*
REQUIRED: The individual not subject to the self-employment tax.
DISCUSSION: The self-employment tax applies to those individuals who have self-employment income. A factory worker paid on a piecemeal basis is an employee of a factory regardless of the method of payment. Therefore, the factory worker is subject to the FICA tax for employees rather than self-employed persons.
Answers (a) and (b) are incorrect because each is a self-employed individual with self-employment income. Answer (c) is incorrect because a minister is generally subject to the self-employment tax, although (s)he may make an irrevocable election to be exempt from it.

35. For self-employment tax purposes, which of the following is not considered earnings from self-employment?

a. Net profit of a delicatessen operated by a sole proprietor.
b. Salary received by a corporate officer who is also the sole shareholder.
c. Distributive share of income from an operating partnership received by a general partner.
d. Guaranteed payment received from a partnership by a limited partner for services (s)he has performed.

The correct answer is (b). *(SPE 1081 II-68)*
REQUIRED: The earnings not subject to self-employment taxes.
DISCUSSION: Self-employment income is defined in Sec. 1402 generally as the net income derived by an individual from a trade or business. Wages and salary from a corporation are not self-employment income; they are earnings of an employee regardless of his/her stock ownership.
Answers (a), (c), and (d) are incorrect because each constitutes income derived from a trade or business and therefore would be considered net earnings from self-employment.

Module 22.4: FICA for the Self-Employed

36. Which of the following are includable in net earnings from self-employment for a farmer?

1. Taxable patronage dividends
2. Taxable commodity credit loans
3. Prizes on farm livestock
4. Gain on sale of breeding stock
5. Crop damage insurance payments

   a. 1, 2, 3, and 4.
   b. 1, 2, 3, and 5.
   c. 1, 2, 4, and 5.
   d. 1, 3, 4, and 5.

The correct answer is (b). *(SPE 1077 I-183)*
REQUIRED: Receipts includable in the net earnings from self-employment for a farmer.
DISCUSSION: The patronage dividend is a distribution from a cooperative out of its earnings from business done with the recipient. To a farmer, it represents increased earnings or a reduction of expenses from the business of farming. Commodity credit loans are secured by the commodity the farmer produces, and this commodity is usually sold to satisfy the loan. Therefore, when the loan is taxable (Sec. 77 election), it represents the sale of the farmer's product. Prizes on farm livestock are self-employment income because they are income produced as a result of the farmer's business. Crop damage insurance payments are a replacement for lost profits on crops, which would have been self-employment income of the farmer.

Answers (a), (c), and (d) are incorrect because gain on the sale of breeding stock is not income earned in the ordinary course of a farmer's business. It is a gain on a Sec. 1231 asset, not self-employment income.

37. Gilda Bach is a cash-basis self-employed consultant. For the year 1991 she determined that her net income from self-employment was $80,000. In reviewing her books you determine that the following items were deducted in arriving at the net income of $80,000:

Salary drawn by Gilda Bach	$20,000
Estimated federal income taxes paid	6,000
Malpractice insurance premiums	4,000
Cost of attending professional seminar	1,000

Based upon the above information, what should Gilda Bach report as her net earnings from self-employment for 1991?

   a. $91,000.
   b. $101,152.
   c. $106,000.
   d. $110,000.

The correct answer is (b). *(CPA 579 Q-38)*
REQUIRED: The amount of income to be reported as net earnings from self-employment.
DISCUSSION: The net income per books amounted to $80,000. It is necessary to add back the salary that was drawn ($20,000) since an individual may not claim a deduction for salary which is paid to him/herself. In addition, the estimated federal income taxes paid of $6,000 are not deductible. The malpractice insurance premium and the cost of attending the seminar are deductible business expenses. Bach's tentative net self-employment income is $106,000.

Net income per books	$ 80,000
Items added back	
Salary	20,000
Federal income taxes	6,000
Tentative net earnings from self-employment	$106,000

The tentative net earnings from self-employment are reduced by the product of one-half of the OASDI tax rate (6.20%) times the lesser of net earnings from self-employment or the $53,400 ceiling (in 1991) plus the product of one-half of the Medicare tax rate (1.45%) times the lesser of net earnings from self-employment or the $125,000 ceiling [Sec. 1402(a)(12)]. This reduction is calculated as follows

$$\$4,848 = (.0620 \times \$53,400) + (.0145 \times \$106,000)$$

Net earnings from self-employment for Gilda Bach equals $101,152 ($106,000 − $4,848).

Author's Note: Some tax commentators have raised a question about whether the self-employment tax deduction is calculated as shown above or is 7.65% times all self-employment income. A literal reading of the statute would imply the latter, although theoretically a deduction would not be permitted for the OASDI tax on self-employment income in excess of $53,400 which is not paid by the taxpayer.

Module 22.4: FICA for the Self-Employed

38. Which one of the following statements about the self-employment tax is false?

    a. The maximum self-employment tax that can be owed by a self-employed individual is 15.30% times $53,400 or $8,170.20.

    b. Self-employed individuals may deduct as a business expense one-half of their self-employment taxes for income tax purposes.

    c. In addition to deducting one-half of the self-employment taxes for income tax purposes, self-employment net earnings can be reduced by the product of the net earnings from self-employment times one-half of the self-employment tax rate.

    d. The old-age, survivors, and disability insurance (OASDI) portion of the self-employment tax has a $53,400 net earnings ceiling while the hospital insurance (Medicare) portion of the self-employment tax has a $125,000 net earnings ceiling.

The correct answer is (a). *(Publisher)*
REQUIRED: The false statement about the self-employment tax for 1991.
DISCUSSION: The maximum self-employment tax that can be owed by a self-employed individual is 15.30% on the first $53,400 of self-employment income, or $8,170.20. However, in addition, a 2.90% hospital insurance (Medicare) tax can be levied on self-employment income from $53,400 to $125,000. This additional tax levy is $2,076.40. Total FICA taxes of $10,246.60 can be collected from a self-employed individual.

Answers (b), (c), and (d) are incorrect because they are true statements about the self-employment tax.

39. Mr. and Mrs. B file a joint income tax return. Mr. B owns and operates a grocery store that had a net income of $15,000 in 1991. Mrs. B is a self-employed physical therapist and her net income was $42,900. What is the total amount of self-employment tax Mr. and Mrs. B must report on their joint return for 1991?

    a. $2,295.

    b. $6,564.

    c. $8,182.

    d. $8,859.

The correct answer is (c). *(SPE 1082 II-90)*
REQUIRED: A couple's self-employment tax for 1991.
DISCUSSION: The tax on self-employment income is imposed by Sec. 1401 on all taxpayers whose net earnings from self-employment exceeds $400. For 1991, the tax is divided into two components, the Social Security and Medicare taxes, which are based on the net earnings from self-employment. The Social Security tax is imposed at a 12.40% rate up to a $53,400 maximum. The Medicare tax is imposed at a 2.90% rate up to a $125,000 maximum. Taxpayers may reduce their net earnings from self-employment by the product of one-half of the Social Security tax rate (6.20%) times the lesser of net earnings from self-employment or the $53,400 ceiling (in 1991) plus the product of one-half of the Medicare tax rate (1.45%) times the lesser of net earnings from self-employment or the $125,000 ceiling [Sec. 1402(a)(12)]. The self-employment tax is then computed separately for each spouse. Their taxes are

	Mr. B	Mrs. B
Net income	$15,000	$42,900
Less: one-half of self-employment tax rate times net income	(1,147)	(3,282)
Net earnings from self-employment	$13,853	$39,618
Times: tax rate	x 0.153	x 0.153
Self-employment tax	$ 2,120	$ 6,062

The total self employment tax for Mr. and Mrs. B is $8,182 ($2,120 + $6,062).

Module 22.4: FICA for the Self-Employed

40. Sabrina is a cash basis self-employed accountant. During 1991, she had the following income and expense items

Gross receipts	$90,000
Operating expenses	45,000
Guaranteed payments from partnership for service to partnership	5,500
Share of income from partnership that operates bakery	10,200
Net operating loss carryover	(6,000)
Share of S Corporation's taxable income	7,000
Gain on sale of a computer used in the business	500

What is the amount of earnings Sabrina will have to pay the OASDI portion of the self-employment tax on for 1991?

a. $53,400.
b. $56,056.
c. $56,509.
d. $60,700.

The correct answer is (a). *(SPE 990 II-90)*

REQUIRED: The amount of earnings on which the Social Security portion of the self-employment tax must be paid in 1991.

DISCUSSION: Sec. 1401 imposes a tax on an individual's self-employment income. Under Reg. 1.1402, net earnings from self-employment includes the net income from a trade or business, guaranteed payments for services from a partnership, and a partner's distributive share of income from a partnership. Gains from the disposition of property, NOL carryovers, and income from S corporations are not included in the computation of net earnings from self-employment.

For 1991, the self-employment tax is divided into two components: Social Security and hospital insurance. The maximum net earnings subject to the Social Security portion are $53,400 for 1991. Sabrina's net earnings from self-employment total $60,700 ($90,000 gross receipts less $45,000 operating expenses) plus $5,500 guaranteed payments and $10,200 partnership income). Sec. 1402(a)(12) allows a further reduction in net earnings from self-employment equal to one-half of the 12.40% Social Security tax rate times net earnings from self-employment (but not in excess of the $53,400 ceiling on the Social Security portion of the tax) plus one-half of the 2.90% hospital insurance tax rate times the amount of net earnings from self-employment (but not in excess of the $125,000 ceiling on the hospital insurance portion of the tax). This reduces the net earnings to $56,509 [$60,700 − ($53,400 x .0620) − ($60,700 x .0145)]. Since Sabrina's net earnings from self-employment ($56,509) exceed the Social Security (OASDI) ceiling ($53,400), Sabrina will have to pay the Social Security portion of the tax on $53,400.

41. Assume the same facts as in the preceding problem. What is the amount of earnings Sabrina will have to pay the hospital insurance (Medicare) portion of the self-employment tax on for 1991?

a. $53,400.
b. $56,509.
c. $60,700.
d. $125,000.

The correct answer is (b). *(Publisher)*

REQUIRED: The amount of earnings on which the hospital insurance portion of the self-employment tax must be paid in 1991.

DISCUSSION: The hospital insurance portion of the self-employment tax has a $125,000 ceiling. Since Sabrina's net earnings from self-employment $56,509 do not exceed the hospital insurance ceiling ($125,000), Sabrina will pay the hospital insurance portion of the tax on $56,509.

Module 22.4: FICA for the Self-Employed

42. Mr. Y operates his own tax practice. For 1991, his books and records reflect the following

Fees received	$65,000
Operating expenses	24,300
Loss on office equipment destroyed by fire	(400)
Gain on sale of computer used in the business	350

Mr. Y also had a part-time job for which he received $6,500 in wages that were subject to Social Security tax. What is the amount of earnings Mr. Y will have to pay self-employment tax on?

a. $40,700.
b. $40,650.
c. $40,300.
d. $37,586.

The correct answer is (d). *(SPE 987 II-88)*

REQUIRED: The amount of earnings subject to self-employment tax.

DISCUSSION: The self-employment tax is imposed at a 15.30% tax rate on the first $53,400 of net earnings from self-employment in 1991 reduced by any wages that were already subject to the Social Security tax. The ceiling for Mr. Y in 1991 is $46,900 ($53,400 − $6,500). (Since net earnings do not exceed $53,400 a separate ceiling on the Medicare tax is not calculated.)

Mr. Y's tentative net earnings from self-employment for 1991 is $40,700 ($65,000 − $24,300 operating expenses). The casualty loss of business property and the gain on the sale of business property are not included in the calculation of net earnings from self-employment. The tentative amount is reduced by the product of one-half of the self-employment tax rate (7.65%) times the net earnings from self-employment ($40,700) [Sec. 1402(a)(12)]. Net earnings from self-employment for Mr. Y equals $37,586 ($40,700 − $3,114).

43. In 1991, Mr. K had $30,600 from wages subject to Social Security tax and net earnings from self-employment of $30,000. What is the amount of K's self-employment tax for 1991?

a. $3,488.
b. $3,697.
c. $4,239.
d. $4,590.

The correct answer is (b). *(SPE 986 II-54)*

REQUIRED: The self-employment tax of a person who earned wages as an employee in 1991.

DISCUSSION: For 1991, the self-employment tax is separated into two components, Social Security and hospital insurance. The Social Security tax is 12.40% of the first $53,400 of self-employment income. The hospital insurance tax is 2.9% of the first $125,000 of self-employment income. In computing the self-employment tax taxpayers may reduce the net earnings from self-employment by one-half of the self-employment tax rate times the net earnings from self-employment income (before this adjustment). Assume such an adjustment has been made in arriving at the $30,000 amount. Mr. K's employment taxes on wages of $30,600 has already been paid through withholding by his employer. Therefore, he must pay the combined tax on $22,800 ($53,400 − $30,600). He must pay the hospital insurance tax on the remaining $7,200 ($30,000 − $22,800). Mr. K's self-employment tax is thus $3,697 [(15.3% x $22,800) + (2.9% x $7,200)].

44. A partner must include his/her distributive share of partnership income or loss in computing net earnings from self-employment.

The correct answer is (T). *(SPE 1077 I-55)*

DISCUSSION: Under Sec. 1402(a), net earnings from self-employment include the distributive share (whether or not distributed) of ordinary income or loss from any trade or business carried on by a partnership of which the taxpayer is a member. Special rules apply to limited partners in a limited partnership in determining their self-employment income [Sec. 1402(a)(13)].

45. An inactive partner's distributive share of his partnership income is not considered to be net earnings from self-employment to the partner for self-employment tax purposes.

The correct answer is (F). *(SPE 988 II-29)*

DISCUSSION: Under Sec. 1402(a), net earnings from self-employment include the partner's distributive share of ordinary income or loss whether distributed or not. There is no requirement that the partner be active in the partnership. Also, an inactive partner's distributive share is considered net earnings from self-employment.

Module 22.4: FICA for the Self-Employed

46. Mr. Q owns and operates a hotel that provides housekeeping and maid services for the occupants. The rents received are considered earnings from self-employment.

The correct answer is (T). *(SPE 1081 II-44)*
DISCUSSION: Rents received from operating a hotel are considered net earnings from self-employment derived by an individual from conducting a trade or business under Sec. 1402(a).

47. The rentals that an individual receives from real estate and from personal property leased with the real estate are earnings from self-employment even though the individual is not engaged in a trade or business as a real estate dealer.

The correct answer is (F). *(SPE 1078 I-21)*
DISCUSSION: Rentals an individual receives from real estate and from personal property leased with the real estate are earnings from self-employment under Sec. 1402 when the individual is engaged in the trade or business of dealing in real estate. When such rentals are not received in the conduct of a trade or business, they are not net earnings from self-employment [Sec. 1402(a)(1)].

48. Mr. T operates an appliance repair shop with a fiscal year ending June 30. On January 1, 1991, the maximum earnings subject to the self-employment tax increased. T must compute the maximum earnings subject to the self-employment tax for the fiscal year ending June 30, 1991 based upon a weighted average of the maximums for 1990 and 1991.

The correct answer is (F). *(SPE 1083 II-48)*
DISCUSSION: Since Mr. T's business uses a tax year other than a calendar year, he must use the tax rate and the maximum income limit in effect at the beginning of the fiscal year (July 1, 1990) throughout the year. Hence, the change in the income limit on January 1, 1991 does not affect his self-employment tax for the fiscal year.

49. The net operating loss deduction should not be used to reduce net earnings from self-employment when figuring the self-employment tax.

The correct answer is (T). *(SPE 984 II-43)*
DISCUSSION: The net operating loss deduction is not allowed under Sec. 1402(a)(4) in computing the net earnings from self-employment.

50. H and his spouse W file a joint return. H has net earnings from a sole proprietorship of $35,000. H and W may split the $35,000 and file separate Forms 1040 (Schedules SE) in order to provide Social Security coverage for W.

The correct answer is (F). *(SPE 1078 II-28)*
DISCUSSION: If one spouse has net earnings from self-employment and the couple elects to file separate tax returns, the spouse who had the net earnings from self-employment will report the entire amount. The spouse who did not have the net earnings from self-employment would report none of the income. Even spouses in community property states are required to report net earnings from self-employment for FICA tax purposes in this manner.

51. Mr. Y is a bricklayer working full time at an aluminum plant repairing furnaces. On some evenings and weekends, he works for himself doing odd jobs such as building fireplaces, repairing chimneys and laying patios for individual homeowners. For 1991, Y's earnings from the plant, which were subject to withholding, totaled $39,200. His net earnings from doing odd jobs totaled $20,000. Mr. Y is liable for the self-employment tax on $14,200.

The correct answer is (F). *(SPE 986 II-31)*
DISCUSSION: Sec. 1402(b) defines self-employment income as the net earnings from self-employment derived by an individual, but not in excess of the taxable limit for the year less wages received during the year. The limit for combined Social Security and hospital insurance taxes is $53,400 in 1991. Above the $53,400 limit, only the hospital insurance tax is imposed. Assuming the Sec. 1402(a)(12) adjustment for one-half of self-employment taxes has been made to arrive at the $20,000 net earnings, Mr. Y's self-employment income subject to the social security portion of the tax is $14,200. However, all $20,000 of his self-employment income is subject to the hospital insurance portion of the tax.

52. You are exempt from Social Security self-employment tax if you are a United States citizen employed in the United States by an international organization or a foreign government.

The correct answer is (F). *(SPE 986 I-12)*
DISCUSSION: Wages received by a U.S. citizen employed in the U.S. by an international organization or a foreign government are excluded from the employment taxes of Sec. 3121. Under Sec. 1402, however, these earnings are picked up as net earnings from self-employment (any trade or business) to the extent they are not covered by the employment taxes of Sec. 3121. There is no similar exemption under Sec. 1402.

53. An ordained, licensed, or commissioned minister must include the rental value of a home provided him as part of his pay for duties performed, as earnings from self-employment for purposes of Social Security self-employment tax.

The correct answer is (T). *(SPE 989 I-8)*
DISCUSSION: Under Sec. 1402(a)(8), an ordained, licensed, or commissioned minister must include the rental value of a home provided him as part of his pay for duties performed as earnings from self-employment for purposes of the self-employment tax. This is true even though the rental value of such a home is not included in gross income for income tax purposes.

22.5 Filing a Social Security Tax Return

54. During 1991, M paid $20 a week to a 17-year-old girl to babysit and perform domestic services in M's home after school and on weekends while M was working. Which of the following applies?

a. Form 941 must be filed.
b. Form 942 must be filed.
c. Form 943 must be filed.
d. No returns need be filed.

The correct answer is (b). *(SPE 1078 II-56)*
REQUIRED: The appropriate form to file when reporting wages paid to a domestic servant.
DISCUSSION: A domestic worker in a private home is subject to tax if his/her wages are at least $50 in any calendar quarter. When the domestic worker is subject to taxation, the employer must withhold FICA taxes and file the appropriate forms. Form 942 is a simplified form which may be used by employers of domestic workers in private homes.
Answer (a) is incorrect because Form 941 is the standard employer's quarterly federal tax return which need not be filed when Form 942 is used. Answer (c) is incorrect because Form 943 is used by employers of agricultural workers.

55. Mr. J, a farmer, has seven farm employees. Which one of the following returns is Mr. J required to file for taxes withheld from wages?

a. Form 941.
b. Form 941E.
c. Form 942.
d. Form 943.

The correct answer is (d). *(SPE 1082 II-54)*
REQUIRED: The appropriate form to file with respect to Social Security taxes withheld from agricultural employees.
DISCUSSION: An employer of agricultural employees is required to withhold both Social Security taxes and income taxes from wages. Form 943 is used by employers of agricultural workers to report the withholding of Social Security taxes.
Answer (a) is incorrect because Form 941 is the standard employer's quarterly federal tax return which need not be filed when Form 943 is filed. Answer (b) is incorrect because Form 941E is used to report wages exempt from the Social Security tax. Answer (c) is incorrect because Form 942 is used by employers of domestic workers in private homes.

56. Mr. C, a calendar-year taxpayer, uses the accrual method of accounting. He pays his employees on the 3rd day of each month. As of December 31, 1991, accrued wages for the month of December were $30,000. Wages paid October 3 totaled $20,000; November 3, $25,000; and December 3, $22,000. Mr. C's 4th quarter return, Form 941, should show total wages of

   a. $45,000.
   b. $67,000.
   c. $75,000.
   d. $97,000.

The correct answer is (b). *(SPE 1082 II-74)*
REQUIRED: The amount of wages which should be reported on an employer's 4th quarter return of Form 941.
DISCUSSION: Taxable wages and employment taxes are reported only when wages are actually paid. Employment taxes are imposed by a separate part of the Internal Revenue Code and have no relationship to the employer's method of accounting for income tax purposes. Therefore, accrued wages are not included on Form 941; only wages actually paid are included. Mr. C's 4th quarter return should show total wages of

Paid October 3	$20,000
Paid November 3	25,000
Paid December 3	22,000
Total wages in 4th quarter	$67,000

57. If you withhold income tax from wages or are liable for Social Security taxes, you must file a quarterly return on Form 941 unless the wages you paid were for domestic service or agricultural labor.

The correct answer is (T). *(SPE 1077 I-17)*
DISCUSSION: If you, as an employer, pay wages and withhold taxes on those wages, you are required to file Form 941 as a collecting agent. If the wages that you paid were for domestic services, then you would be required to file Form 942 instead. If the wages that you paid were for agricultural labor, you would be required to file Form 943.

22.6 Federal Unemployment Tax

58. All of the following individuals who perform services for a business are subject to taxes under the Federal Insurance Contributions Act (FICA) and the Federal Unemployment Tax Act (FUTA) except

   a. Part-time employee.
   b. Officer of a corporation.
   c. Office manager.
   d. Director of a corporation.

The correct answer is (d). *(SPE 984 II-56)*
REQUIRED: The individual who is not subject to FICA and FUTA.
DISCUSSION: Employees are subject to both FICA and FUTA. Self-employed persons are subject to self-employment taxes but not unemployment taxes. The director of a corporation is a self-employed individual, not an employee, so (s)he is not subject to FUTA.
Answers (a), (b), and (c) are incorrect because each is an employee subject to FICA and FUTA.

59. Given the following wage information, what are the total gross wages subject to Federal Unemployment Tax for 1991?

Employee	Wages Paid During 1991
T	$ 4,200
E	5,800
M	22,900

   a. $7,000.
   b. $12,000.
   c. $16,000.
   d. $17,000.

The correct answer is (d). *(SPE 1079 II-85)*
REQUIRED: The amount of gross wages subject to Federal Unemployment Tax for 1991.
DISCUSSION: Under Sec. 3306(b)(1), wages are taxed for federal unemployment taxes up to $7,000 for each employee. Wages earned in excess of $7,000 are not subject to federal unemployment taxes. The full amount of wages paid during 1991 to employee T and employee E is taxable. Only $7,000 of the wages paid to M is subject to federal unemployment taxes. Thus, the total amount of wages paid in 1991 that is subject to federal unemployment taxes is $17,000.

Employee	Wages Subject to Unemployment Tax
T	$ 4,200
E	5,800
M	7,000
Total	$17,000

Module 22.6: Federal Unemployment Tax

60. The theatrical agency of Power & Tyrone employs two people full-time. Which of the following is true with regard to federal unemployment insurance?

a. In terms of industry and number of employees, Power & Tyrone is within the class of employers covered by the Federal Unemployment Tax Act.

b. Service agencies are exempt.

c. Since the number of employees is small, an exemption can be obtained from coverage if a request is filed with the appropriate federal agency.

d. If the employees all reside in one state and do not travel interstate on company business, Power & Tyrone is exempt from compliance with the act.

The correct answer is (a). *(CPA 1177 L-15)*
REQUIRED: The correct statement regarding federal unemployment insurance.
DISCUSSION: An employer that (1) employs one or more persons covered by the Social Security Act for at least part of a day in each of 20 different calendar weeks in a year or the preceding year or (2) pays wages of $1,500 or more during any calendar quarter in a year or the preceding year must pay a federal unemployment tax on the first $7,000 of each employee's wages [Sec. 3306(a)]. Thus, a theatrical agency employing two persons full-time would fall within the class of employers covered by the federal unemployment tax.

Answer (b) is incorrect because businesses classified as service agencies are not exempt. Answer (c) is incorrect because no exemption can be obtained by filing a request with any federal agency. Answer (d) is incorrect because, for purposes of Social Security and its various benefits, employment is considered to affect interstate commerce and falls within federal jurisdiction regardless of residence and travel.

61. C, a sole proprietor, has three employees. His FUTA tax liability for each quarter of 1991 was as follows

1st Quarter	$50
2nd Quarter	45
3rd Quarter	65
4th Quarter	50

Assuming the due date does not fall on a Saturday, Sunday, or legal holiday, C was required to make his first deposit of FUTA tax by which date?

a. April 30, 1991.

b. July 31, 1991.

c. October 31, 1991.

d. January 31, 1992.

The correct answer is (c). *(SPE 1083 II-55)*
REQUIRED: The date the employer is required to deposit FUTA taxes.
DISCUSSION: Form 940 is required to be filed by January 31 each year with respect to FUTA taxes for the prior calendar year. However, quarterly payments must be made as soon as the liability for unpaid taxes exceeds $100. These quarterly payments are due on April 30, July 31, October 31, and January 31.

Since C's FUTA tax liability did not reach $100 until the third quarter, the first deposit of FUTA tax is due by October 31, 1991.

62. After 1987, the services of an individual who works for his/her spouse in a trade or business are covered by Social Security taxes, but not by federal unemployment taxes.

The correct answer is (T). *(SPE 989 II-28)*
DISCUSSION: Sec. 3101 imposes Social Security taxes on the income of every individual. No exemptions are provided after 1987 for an individual who works for his/her spouse in a trade or business. Sec. 3301 imposes federal unemployment taxes on employers. However, under Sec. 3306(c)(5), the employer does not have to pay federal unemployment taxes on services performed by the employer's son or daughter if they are under age 21 and the employer's spouse.

22.7 Withholding

63. Which of the following employee benefits is not subject to income tax withholding by an employer?

a. Bonuses only paid at year-end.
b. Sick pay.
c. Medical expense reimbursements under a self-insured plan.
d. Employee's personal use of company car.

The correct answer is (c). *(Publisher)*
REQUIRED: The employee benefit which is not subject to withholding for income taxes.
DISCUSSION: Sec. 3402(a) requires every employer who pays wages to withhold from the wages a tax determined in accordance with tables prescribed by the Secretary of the Treasury. These wages are defined in Sec. 3401(a) as all remuneration for services performed by an employee including the cash value of all noncash payments. However, wages do not include medical care reimbursements under a self-insured medical reimbursement plan since such reimbursements are excluded from the employee's income under Sec. 105.
Answer (a) is incorrect because bonuses are wages subject to withholding whenever they are paid. Answer (b) is incorrect because sick pay is also subject to withholding since there is no exclusion for it from gross income. Answer (d) is incorrect because an employee's personal use of a company car is noncash remuneration and is subject to withholding.

64. The penalty for willful failure to collect or pay over to the government the amounts required to be withheld from employees is what percentage of the tax?

a. .5%.
b. 5%.
c. 50%.
d. 100%.

The correct answer is (d). *(Publisher)*
REQUIRED: The percentage of the tax which may be imposed as a penalty against an employer for willful failure to withhold income tax.
DISCUSSION: Under Sec. 6672, any person required to collect, account for, and pay over any Internal Revenue tax and who willfully fails to do so may be liable for a penalty equal to the total amount of the tax not collected and paid over. For not withholding income tax, the employer may, therefore, suffer a 100% penalty. In addition, the employer is liable for the payment of the tax required to be deducted and withheld from employees' wages (Sec. 3403). As a result, the employer who fails to withhold can be required to pay, not just withhold, the tax and still be subject to a 100% penalty.

65. Corporation X, a foreign corporation engaged in the conduct of a U.S. trade or business, received interest income from the following U.S. sources in 1991. All of the income is effectively connected with the conduct of a U.S. trade or business. What amount is subject to withholding tax?

Passbook savings	$2,500
Certificates of deposit	3,000
Deposits with an insurance company	1,500

a. $0.
b. $2,500.
c. $3,000.
d. $7,000.

The correct answer is (a). *(SPE 1081 III-68)*
REQUIRED: The amount of income of a foreign corporation that is subject to withholding tax.
DISCUSSION: Under Reg. 1.1441-4(a), no withholding is required for income received by a foreign corporation if the income is effectively connected with the conduct of a trade or business within the U.S. Under Sec. 864(c)(2), interest income from passbook savings, certificates of deposit, and deposits with an insurance company are all considered income effectively connected with the conduct of a trade or business within the U.S. if the income items satisfy an "asset-use" test or if the trade or business activities were a material factor in the production of the income.

66. Corporation R, a domestic corporation, distributed the following dividends to its shareholders in 1991

$5,000 to Shareholder A, a foreign partnership
$4,000 to Shareholder B, an unrelated foreign corporation
$3,000 to Shareholder C, a resident alien
$2,000 to Shareholder D, a nonresident alien

All of the income of Corporation R was from sources within the United States. On what amount of dividends must R withhold tax?

a. $0.
b. $7,000.
c. $9,000.
d. $11,000.

The correct answer is (d). *(SPE 990 III-43)*
REQUIRED: The amount of dividends subject to withholding.
DISCUSSION: Under Sec. 1441(a), a corporation paying a dividend from income from sources within the United States to any nonresident alien individual or any foreign partnership is required to deduct and withhold a tax equal to 30% (or a lower rate specified in a tax treaty) of the dividend. Sec. 1442(a) requires that a tax of 30% (or a lower rate specified in a tax treaty) be withheld on dividends paid to a foreign corporation that are derived from gross income from sources within the United States. The total amount of dividends on which R must withhold tax is $11,000 ($5,000 + $4,000 + $2,000).

67. All of the following items of gross income earned by a foreign corporation in the United States are subject to 30% withholding except

a. Rents.
b. Sale of real property.
c. Interest.
d. Dividends.

The correct answer is (b). *(SPE 990 III-55)*
REQUIRED: The item of gross income earned by a foreign corporation in the United States that is not subject to 30% withholding.
DISCUSSION: Sec. 1442(a) states that in the case of foreign corporations, a tax of 30% is to be withheld on items of income provided in Sec. 1441. Sec. 1441(b) states that items of income subject to withholding are interest, dividends, rent, salaries, wages, premiums, annuities, compensations, remunerations, emoluments, or other fixed or determinable annual or periodical gains. A sale of real property is not subject to withholding unless it is a U.S. real property interest [as defined by Secs. 897(c) and 1445(a) and Reg. 1.1445-2(a)]. If the real property is a U.S. real property interest, then withholding is required at a 10% rate on the amount realized from the sale [Sec. 1445(a)].

68. On which of the following is withholding not required?

a. Payments of dividends or interest of $10 or more when the payee has furnished his/her taxpayer identification number.
b. Payments to an independent contractor of $600 or more for services if the taxpayer identification number of the independent contractor is not provided.
c. Payments of deferred compensation if the recipient has not elected otherwise.
d. Payments to foreign persons for the purchase in 1991 of U.S. real property used in a business.

The correct answer is (a). *(Publisher)*
REQUIRED: The payments on which the payor is not required to withhold income taxes.
DISCUSSION: The Sec. 3406 back-up withholding rules requires the payor to withhold 20% of dividend or interest payments of $10 or more. Withholding is not required, however, if the payee furnishes his/her taxpayer identification number to the payor. The payor is then required to report the payment to the IRS.
Answer (b) is incorrect because the payor must withhold 20% of such payments unless the independent contractor gives the taxpayer identification number to the payor. Answer (c) is incorrect because Sec. 3405 requires the payor of periodic payments (such as deferred compensation) to withhold an amount as if it were paid as wages. However, an individual may elect against this withholding. Answer (d) is incorrect because Sec. 1445 requires anyone who purchases real property from a foreign person to withhold 10% of the amount the foreign person has realized on the sale. The purchase of a personal residence for $300,000 or less is one of several exceptions.

Module 22.7: Withholding

69. Corporation N declared a dividend. Mr. Snead, a shareholder of N, should receive $500 when the dividend is paid. Mr. Snead refuses to provide Corporation N with his Social Security number for N's information returns. How much should Corporation N withhold from Mr. Snead's dividend for backup withholding?

   a. $0.
   b. $50.
   c. $100.
   d. $125.

The correct answer is (c). *(SPE 989 III-44)*
REQUIRED: The amount of backup withholding.
DISCUSSION: Dividends paid to a domestic shareholder are generally not subject to withholding. However, under Sec. 3406(a)(1)(A), if a payee refuses to furnish his taxpayer identification number to a payor, the payor is required to deduct and withhold from the payment a tax of 20%. Therefore, Corporation N must withhold $100 (20% x $500) from the dividend paid to Mr. Snead.

70. All of the following statements regarding employer withholding requirements on moving expense allowances or reimbursements are true except

   a. The employer is not required to withhold income tax and Social Security tax on deductible moving expense allowances.
   b. The employer is required to withhold income tax on both deductible and nondeductible moving expense reimbursements.
   c. The employer is required to withhold income tax and Social Security tax if the employee probably will not meet the time test.
   d. The employer must first apply a reimbursement to deductible moving expenses where there is no specific allocation to either deductible or nondeductible moving expenses.

The correct answer is (b). *(SPE 987 I-54)*
REQUIRED: The false statement about withholding requirements on moving expense allowances.
DISCUSSION: Generally, an employer is required to withhold from all remuneration paid to an employee, but Sec. 3401(a)(15) exempts payments to an employee if it is reasonable to believe that a corresponding deduction is allowable for moving expenses.
Answers (a), (c), and (d) are correct statements about withholding requirements on moving expenses.

71. On January 3, 1991, an employee of Corporation T filed a Form W-4, Employee's Withholding Allowance Certificate, claiming 25 withholding allowances. T must notify the employee that this number of withholding allowances is excessive, and disregard the Form W-4 for withholding purposes.

The correct answer is (F). *(SPE 1082 III-47)*
DISCUSSION: When an employee files a W-4 claiming 10 or more withholding allowances, the employer is required to send the IRS a copy of the W-4 if the employee is still employed at the end of the quarter. The employer is not required to disregard the Form W-4 for withholding purposes. The IRS will notify the employer as to what action to take. An employee can be liable for penalties and criminal prosecution for fraudulent filings of Form W-4.

72. Mr. A moved and his employer reimbursed him for his expenses. At the time the reimbursement was paid, A's employer reasonably believed A would meet the distance and time tests, and that the expenses would be deductible. The employer is required to withhold a reasonable amount of income tax in connection with the reimbursement for these expenses.

The correct answer is (F). *(SPE 984 I-18)*
DISCUSSION: Generally, an employer is required to withhold from all remuneration paid to an employee, but Sec. 3401(a)(15) exempts payments to an employee if it is reasonable to believe that a corresponding deduction is allowable for moving expenses.

73. If no income tax is withheld, an employer must keep a record of the fair market value and date of each payment of noncash compensation made to a retail commission salesperson.

The correct answer is (T). *(SPE 1083 IV-48)*
DISCUSSION: Reg. 31.3402(j)-1 allows an employer to disregard wages paid in a medium other than cash for services by a retail commission salesperson if the employer ordinarily pays in cash. In that case, however, the employer must keep a record of the fair market value and date of each payment of noncash compensation.

74. Corporation F, a foreign corporation, has a store located in the United States that sells cosmetics. Generally, the income derived from selling the cosmetics is effectively connected with the conduct of a business within the United States and not subject to the withholding tax on foreign corporations.

The correct answer is (T). *(SPE 984 III-39)*
DISCUSSION: Income derived from selling cosmetics through a store located in the United States is treated as income effectively connected with the conduct of a trade or business within the United States. Under Secs. 1441 and 1442, no withholding is required for any income (other than compensation for personal services) that is effectively connected with the conduct of a trade or business within the United States.

75. Corporation N, a foreign corporation, received a dividend payment from Corporation O, a U.S. corporation. Corporation O will compute the withholding on the total amount of the dividend payment less the dividend-received deduction.

The correct answer is (F). *(SPE 990 III-31)*
DISCUSSION: A dividends-received deduction is only available to a foreign corporation on its dividend income received from a domestic corporation that is effectively connected with the conduct of a U.S. trade or business. Sec. 1441(c) provides an exemption from the 30% withholding requirement of Sec. 1441(a) for income effectively connected with the conduct of a U.S. trade or business. The U.S. taxes due on such income are paid by the foreign corporation by making estimated tax payments.

76. If, as a withholding agent, you are not able to easily determine the relationship between yourself and a foreign payee or the relationship between a foreign payee and a foreign corporation, you should withhold at a rate of 30% from the amount paid for the services rendered.

The correct answer is (T). *(SPE 989 III-34)*
DISCUSSION: Under Regs. 1.1441-3(b)(3) and 1.1441-4(b)(2)(iii), if a withholding agent is not able to readily determine the relationship between the agent and a foreign payee or the relationship between a foreign payee and a foreign corporation, the agent is required to withhold 30% of the amount paid.

77. Form 1042, Annual Withholding Tax Return for U.S. Source Income of Foreign Persons, is due by March 15 of the year following the tax year even if there was no withholding because of a specific withholding exemption.

The correct answer is (T). *(SPE 989 III-35)*
DISCUSSION: A U.S. corporation that makes payments to a nonresident alien is required to file Form 1042 each year even if no income tax is withheld because of exemptions to which the nonresident alien was entitled.

78. Form 1042S, Foreign Person's U.S. Source Income Subject to Withholding, is required for each payee (recipient) of income to whom payments were made during the calendar year, regardless of the amount of tax withheld.

The correct answer is (T). *(SPE 990 III-32)*
DISCUSSION: Reg. 1.1461-2(c) states that every withholding agent is required to file Form 1042S for each payee of income to whom payments were made during the calendar year. The form is required regardless of the amount of tax withheld.

CHAPTER TWENTY-THREE
WEALTH TRANSFER TAXES

Gift Tax
23.1	Gifts Defined	(8 questions)	663
23.2	Valuation of Gifts	(6 questions)	666
23.3	Exclusions and Deductions from Gifts	(14 questions)	667
23.4	Gift-Splitting	(11 questions)	671
23.5	Calculation of Gift Tax	(8 questions)	673
23.6	Reporting Gifts	(5 questions)	675

Estate Tax
23.7	Inclusions in the Gross Estate	(16 questions)	676
23.8	Valuation of Estate Property	(9 questions)	681
23.9	Deductions from the Gross Estate	(7 questions)	683
23.10	Calculation of Estate Tax	(6 questions)	685
23.11	Estate Tax Payment and Returns	(8 questions)	686

Generation-Skipping Transfer Tax
23.12	Generation-Skipping Transfers	(9 questions)	688
23.13	Taxable Amount and Taxpayer Identification	(4 questions)	691
23.14	Calculation of Generation-Skipping Transfer Tax	(4 questions)	693

23.1 Gifts Defined

1. Which of the following situations would not constitute a transfer that comes within the gift tax statutes?

a. An individual creates a trust under the terms of which a child is to get income for life and a grandchild the remainder at the child's death.

b. An individual, with personal funds, purchases real property and has title conveyed to the individual and the individual's brother as joint tenants.

c. An individual creates a trust giving income for life to his wife and providing that, at her death, the corpus is to be distributed to his son. The individual reserves the right to revoke the transfer at any time without the consent of the other parties.

d. An individual, with his own funds, purchases a U.S. Savings Bond made payable to himself and his wife. His wife surrenders the bond for cash to be used for her benefit.

The correct answer is (c). *(SPE 1080 III-65)*

REQUIRED: The transfer that would not come within the gift tax statutes.

DISCUSSION: The gift tax applies to most gratuitous shifting of property or property rights during one's lifetime. The concept of a gift for gift tax purposes is generally broader than (and not well integrated with) the narrow concept of a gift for income tax exclusion purposes. Sec. 2511(a) provides that the gift tax applies to transfers made in trust, to indirect gifts, and to intangible property in addition to outright and direct transfers of tangible property. However, the gift tax only applies to completed gifts, and Reg. 25.2511-2(c) provides that a gift is incomplete if the donor retains the power to revest the beneficial title to the property in him/herself. If the transfer is revocable without the consent of the other parties, it is not complete and not taxable.

Answer (a) is incorrect because the gift tax applies to gifts made in trust, to income interests, and to remainder interests. Answer (b) is incorrect because the brother received an ownership interest in the land so the part interest is taxable. Answer (d) is incorrect because the individual has conferred a benefit upon his wife in the amount of the bond surrendered.

2. Raff created a joint bank account for himself and his friend's son, Dave. There is a gift to Dave when

   a. Raff creates the account.
   b. Raff dies.
   c. Dave draws on the account for his own benefit.
   d. Dave is notified by Raff that the account has been created.

The correct answer is (c). *(CPA 1188 Q-17)*
   REQUIRED: The time when a completed gift is made.
   DISCUSSION: A gift is complete when the donor has so parted with dominion and control as to leave him/her no power to change its disposition [Reg. 25.2511-2(b)]. Raff made an indirect transfer of the money to Dave by opening the bank account. Only when Dave withdraws the money will Raff lose all dominion and control over the property so that the action will complete the gift [Reg. 25.2511-1(h)(4)].
   Answer (a) is incorrect because when Raff creates the account, he can still withdraw the money so that it is not a completed gift. Answer (b) is incorrect because when Raff dies, there may be no transfer to Dave or there may be a devise, but not a gift because a gift only occurs during lifetime. Answer (d) is incorrect because notice has no effect here since Dave must draw on the account for a completed gift.

3. Which of the following represents taxable gifts?

   I. Transfer of wealth to a dependent family member that represents support.
   II. Payment of son's tuition for law school.
   III. Payment of $10,000 of medical bills for a friend.

   a. None of the above is a taxable gift.
   b. Only I is a taxable gift.
   c. Only II is a taxable gift.
   d. Both II and III are taxable gifts.

The correct answer is (a). *(Publisher)*
   REQUIRED: The taxable gift(s) among the items listed.
   DISCUSSION: Sec. 2503, which defines taxable gifts, specifically excludes bona fide transfers made on behalf of any individual as tuition to an educational organization or as payment to someone who provides medical care for such individual. Accordingly, neither payment of a son's tuition for law school (II) nor payment of $10,000 of medical bills for a friend (III) is a taxable gift.
   Item I is not a taxable gift because transfers that represent support are not considered gifts at all.

4. All of the following statements relating to qualified transfers for gift tax purposes are true except

   a. The exclusion for a qualified transfer is in addition to the annual exclusion.
   b. A qualified transfer is allowed without regard to the relationship between the donor and donee.
   c. Only that part of a payment to a qualified educational institution that applies to direct tuition costs is a qualified transfer.
   d. A payment made directly to an individual to reimburse him for his medical expenses is a qualified transfer.

The correct answer is (d). *(SPE 986 III-61)*
   REQUIRED: The false statement about qualified transfers for gift tax purposes.
   DISCUSSION: Sec. 2503(e) provides an exclusion from the gift tax for transfers made to pay tuition at an educational institution or to pay medical bills. Answer (d) is a false statement because the qualified transfer must be made directly to the provider of medical care.
   Answers (a), (b), and (c) are incorrect because each is a true statement with respect to Sec. 2503(e) which permits the exclusion of qualified transfers.

Module 23.1: Gifts Defined 665

5. During 1991, Mr. & Mrs. X made joint gifts to their son of the following items:

A painting with an adjusted basis of $15,000 and a fair market value of $45,000.
Stock with an adjusted basis of $27,000 and a fair market value of $30,000.
An auto with an adjusted basis of $15,000 and a fair market value of $17,000.
An interest free loan of $8,000 for a boat (for the son's personal use) on January 1, 1991, which was repaid by their son on December 31, 1991. Assume the applicable federal rate was 11% per annum.

What is the gross amount of gifts includable in Mr. & Mrs. X's gift tax return?

a. $92,880.
b. $92,000.
c. $57,880.
d. $57,000.

The correct answer is (b). *(SPE 988 III-90)*
REQUIRED: The gross amount of gifts including an interest-free loan.
DISCUSSION: The amount of a gift made in property is the fair market value of the property on the date of the gift [Sec. 2512(a)]. The auto, painting, and stock have a combined fair market value of $92,000.
In general, an interest-free loan results in deemed transfers of interest between the borrower and lender. When the two parties are related, the lender is deemed to have made a gift of the interest amount to the borrower [Sec. 7872(a)(1)]. However, Sec. 7872(c)(2) excludes gift loans between individuals from this provision if the aggregate outstanding principal does not exceed $10,000. Accordingly, the $8,000 interest-free loan does not result in a gift.

6. A gift is complete if a donor has parted with dominion and control over the transferred property or property interest and if the donor is left without the power to change its disposition whether for the benefit of the donor or for the benefit of others.

The correct answer is (T). *(SPE 1079 III-40)*
DISCUSSION: Reg. 25.2511-2 discusses the effect of the donor's dominion and control over transferred property. If the donor has so parted with dominion and control over the property as to leave him/her no power to change its disposition, whether for his/her own benefit or for the benefit of another, the gift is complete.

7. A sale is completed in the ordinary course of Mr. Jones' business and the sales price is less than the fair market value of the property. The difference between the fair market value and the sales price is not a gift.

The correct answer is (T). *(Publisher)*
DISCUSSION: Sec. 2512(b) provides that, when property is transferred for less than an adequate and full consideration in money or money's worth, the amount by which the value of the property exceeds the value of the consideration is deemed a gift. However, a sale, exchange, or other transfer of property made in the ordinary course of business (in a transaction that is bona fide, at arm's length, and free from any donative intent) is made for adequate and full consideration in money or money's worth (Reg. 25.2512-8).

8. Donative intent must be present before a gift tax can be levied.

The correct answer is (F). *(Publisher)*
DISCUSSION: Donative intent on the part of the transferor is not an essential element in application of the gift tax to the transfer. Application of tax is based on objective facts of the transfer and circumstances under which it is made, rather than on subjective motives of the donor [Reg. 25.2511-1(g)(1)].

23.2 Valuation of Gifts

9. On December 1, 1990, Sam gave his son, Stan, land with a fair market value of $14,000 on the date of the gift. Sam paid gift tax of $4,200. Sam had purchased the land in 1985 for $10,000 which was his adjusted basis on the date of the gift. On January 1, 1991, Stan sold the land for $13,000. What was the value of the land for gift tax purposes and what was Stan's basis?

	Gift Tax Value	Stan's Basis
a.	$13,000	$14,200
b.	$10,000	$11,200
c.	$14,000	$10,000
d.	$14,000	$11,200

The correct answer is (d). *(Publisher)*
REQUIRED: The value of land for gift tax purposes and the donee's basis in the land.
DISCUSSION: The amount of a gift made in property is the fair market value of the property on the date of the gift [Sec. 2512(a)]. The fair market value of Sam's property on the date of the gift was $14,000.

The basis of property acquired by gift generally is the same as it was in the hands of the donor [Sec. 1015(a)], increased by the portion of the gift tax attributable to the appreciation in value of the property [Sec. 1015(d)(6)].

$$\frac{\$4,000 \text{ appreciation}}{\$14,000 \text{ total gift}} \times \$4,200 \text{ tax} = \$1,200$$

Stan's basis in the land is $11,200 ($10,000 basis of the donor + $1,200 of gift tax attributable to the appreciation of the property).

10. When her father died on March 1, 1991, Mary, age 25, inherited an income interest for life in a $100,000 trust. When she dies, Steve, age 18, will receive the remainder interest. Under the regulations in effect at her father's death, what are the values of Mary's and Steve's interests (assuming a 9.60% interest rate is specified by the IRS for March 1991)?

	Mary's Interest	Steve's Interest
a.	$0	$100,000
b.	$96,971	$3,029
c.	$97,216	$2,784
d.	$100,000	$0

The correct answer is (b). *(Publisher)*
REQUIRED: The values of the life and remainder interests in a trust.
DISCUSSION: Annuity interests are valued from actuarial tables that were promulgated in IRS Notice 89-20. The actuarial tables must be used regardless of the actual earnings rate of the annuity. Code Sec. 7520 added in 1988 calls for the actuarial tables to be revised every month. These tables incorporate an interest rate, rounded to the nearest 0.2% that is 120% of the Federal midterm rate applicable for the month of the transfer. These tables were revised to take into account the most recent mortality experience.

Based on the annuity table R(1), Mary's age, and a 9.6% interest rate, the income interest is calculated by multiplying the total trust assets by a factor of .96971. The value of Steve's interest is determined by multiplying the total trust assets by the remainder interest factor for Mary's age (.03029). Thus, the values of the two interests are $96,971 for Mary and $3,029 for Steve.

11. On May 4, 1991, David gave his brother Larry one share of ABC stock, which was traded on an exchange. May 4 was a Saturday, and these were the quoted prices on Friday and Monday:

	Sales Price		
Date	High	Low	Closing
5/3/91	100	93	97.5
5/6/91	100.5	95.5	97

What is the fair market value of David's gift?

a. $96.50.
b. $97.25.
c. $97.50.
d. $98.00.

The correct answer is (b). *(Publisher)*
REQUIRED: The fair market value of the donor's gift of stock.
DISCUSSION: If there is a market for stocks on a stock exchange, the mean between the highest and lowest quoted selling prices on the date of the gift is the fair market value per share. If there were no sales on the date of the gift, the fair market value is determined by taking a weighted average of the means between the highest and lowest sales on the nearest date before and the nearest date after the date of the gift. The average is to be weighted inversely by the respective number of trading days between the selling dates and the date of the gift [Reg. 25.2512-2(b)].

The mean sales price on May 3, one trading day before the date of David's gift, was 96.5, and the mean sales price on May 6, one trading day after the date of the gift, was 98. The fair market value of David's gift is determined as follows:

$$\frac{(1 \text{ day} \times 96.5) + (1 \text{ day} \times 98)}{2 \text{ days}} = \$97.25 \text{ per share}$$

Module 23.3: Exclusions and Deductions from Gifts

12. The amount of a gift for gift tax purposes is its fair market value on the date it is given.

The correct answer is (T). *(SPE 1082 III-42)*
DISCUSSION: The amount of a gift made in property is the fair market value of the property at the date of the gift (Reg. 25.2512-1). The fair market value is that which would occur in an arm's-length transaction between a willing buyer and a willing seller in the normal market.

13. During 1991, Ms. T gave her brother rental property with a fair market value of $80,000 and an adjusted basis to Ms. T of $60,000. The value of this gift for gift tax purposes is $80,000.

The correct answer is (T). *(SPE 984 III-37)*
DISCUSSION: The amount of a gift made in property is its fair market value at the date of the gift [Sec. 2512(a)]. Ms. T's gift to her brother is $80,000.

14. In valuing closely held stock, the nature and history of the business are two factors that are usually considered.

The correct answer is (T). *(Publisher)*
DISCUSSION: Factors taken into consideration in valuing stock when selling prices or bid and asked prices are unavailable include the company's net worth, prospective earning power and dividend paying capacity, and other relevant factors. Rev. Rul. 59-60 adds the nature and history of the business from its inception as important factors in valuing closely held stock.

23.3 Exclusions and Deductions from Gifts

15. During 1991, Mr. C, a U.S. citizen, made the following gifts:

- $15,000 cash to his son; $50,000 to his wife, also a U.S. citizen
- Equipment to his brother (fair market value $12,000, adjusted basis $8,000)
- $100,000 in cash to city W for construction of a new city park

Without considering gift-splitting, what is the total of Mr. C's exclusions and deductions for his 1991 gift tax return?

   a. $160,000.
   b. $168,000.
   c. $170,000.
   d. $177,000.

The correct answer is (c). *(SPE 984 III-80)*
REQUIRED: The amount of exclusions and deductions for gifts.
DISCUSSION: The first $10,000 of a gift of a present interest in property made to any person during the calendar year may be excluded [Sec. 2503(b)]. This provision allows Mr. C a total of $40,000 in exclusions ($10,000 x 4 gifts). In addition, Sec. 2522(a)(1) provides that a gift to a city may be deducted as a charitable gift. The gift to the spouse of the taxpayer is eligible for a deduction under Sec. 2523. Both of these deductions are available for the balance of the gifts not excluded (Sec. 2524). The total of C's deductions and exclusions is, therefore, $170,000 ($40,000 in exclusions + $90,000 deduction for the gift to the city + $40,000 deduction for the gift to his wife).

16. In 1991, Blum, who is single, gave an outright gift of $50,000 to a friend, Gould, who needed the money to pay medical expenses. In filing the 1991 gift tax return, Blum was entitled to a maximum exclusion of

   a. $20,000.
   b. $10,000.
   c. $3,000.
   d. $0.

The correct answer is (b). *(CPA 1188 Q-20)*
REQUIRED: The maximum exclusion for a gift used to pay medical expenses.
DISCUSSION: The first $10,000 of gifts of present interest to each donee is excluded [Sec. 2503(b)]. In addition, an unlimited exclusion is available for amounts paid on behalf of the donee as medical care [Sec. 2503(e)]. However, the transfer for medical care must be made directly to the person who provides it (not the donee). Therefore, this exclusion is not available for Blum. Blum's maximum exclusion is the $10,000 per donee per year.

17. In 1991, Jean Camp contributed to the National Wildlife Foundation a remainder interest in 100 acres of land with a fair market value of $100,000 and a basis of $20,000. The remainder interest has a .20994 actuarial factor. Jean only specified the property was to be used for "conservation purposes" in general. Her taxable gift in 1991 is

  a. $0.
  b. $4,199.
  c. $20,994.
  d. $100,000.

The correct answer is (a). *(Publisher)*
REQUIRED: The taxable gift which results from a gift of a remainder interest in real estate to a qualified organization in 1991.
DISCUSSION: Gifts of a remainder interest are valued at the actuarial factor times the fair market value, so Camp's gift amount is $20,994 ($100,000 x .20994). The actuarial factor is based on tables published by the IRS in Notice 89-60, the age of the donor, and the applicable interest rate for the month of the transfer. Gifts to a charity of less than an entire interest in property generally do not result in a charitable contribution deduction. A charitable contribution deduction is allowed for a gift of a remainder interest in real property made to a qualified organization after 1986 for any "conservation purposes" (Sec. 2522). Camp's taxable gift is $0 ($20,944 gift amount – $20,944 charitable contribution deduction).

18. Mary made the following gifts in 1991:

Gift	Donee	Value
Cash	Son	$14,000
6-month certificate of deposit	Daughter	6,000
Antique furniture	Sister	24,000
Stocks in trust		
Life estate	Brother	78,000
Remainder	Daughter	22,000

Mary's taxable gifts for 1991 total

  a. $128,000.
  b. $114,000.
  c. $108,000.
  d. $86,000.

The correct answer is (c). *(Publisher)*
REQUIRED: The donor's taxable gifts for 1991.
DISCUSSION: Taxable gifts means the total amount of gifts made during the calendar year reduced by the charitable and marital deductions [Sec. 2503(a)]. The first $10,000 of gifts of present interests made to each donee during the year is excluded [Sec. 2503(b)].
Mary transferred $144,000 of property by gift during the year. The only gift not subject to the exclusion is the gift of the trust remainder, since it is a future interest. The exclusion for the gift to Daughter is limited to the $6,000 certificate of deposit.

Total amount of gifts	$144,000
Less exclusions:	
Son	(10,000)
Daughter	(6,000)
Sister	(10,000)
Brother	(10,000)
Taxable gifts	$108,000

19. During 1991, Nancy, who is single, made the following gifts:

Paid $12,000 in medical bills for her friend. The payments were paid directly to her friend's doctor
$15,000 to her mother to help her with rent and groceries
$20,000 to her nephew Tom to get him started in business
Nancy also had made a $50,000 interest free demand loan to her nephew James in 1990. The loan is still outstanding at the end of 1991. The applicable federal interest rate during 1991 remained constant at 10%.

What is the amount of Nancy's taxable gifts in 1991?

  a. $39,000.
  b. $15,000.
  c. $12,000.
  d. $10,000.

The correct answer is (b). *(SPE 990 III-87)*
REQUIRED: The correct amount of taxable gifts.
DISCUSSION: Under Sec. 2503, gifts are taxable to the extent that they exceed $10,000 unless they are made on behalf of any individual as tuition to an educational organization or as payment to someone who provides medical care to such individual. The payment must be made directly to the educational organization or person providing medical care.
The $12,000 Nancy paid directly to her friend's doctor is not a taxable gift. The gifts to her mother and to her nephew Tom are each taxable to the extent that they exceed the $10,000 exclusion of Sec. 2503(b). An interest-free loan generally results in a deemed transfer of interest between the borrower and the lender [Sec. 7872(a)]. The lender is deemed to have made a gift of the foregone interest to the borrower. The amount of Nancy's gift to her nephew James is deemed to be $5,000. Because the amount of deemed interest is less than the $10,000 exclusion, it is not a taxable gift.

20. During 1991, Rosemary made the following gifts:

$25,000 to her son for his personal use
$30,000 to her husband for a car
$20,000 to her church as a donation
Jewelry with an adjusted basis of $12,000 and a fair market value of $37,000 to her daughter

Rosemary does not live in a community property state and does not elect gift-splitting. What is the amount of Rosemary's taxable gifts?

a. $17,000.
b. $27,000.
c. $42,000.
d. $52,000.

The correct answer is (c). *(SPE 989 III-90)*
REQUIRED: The correct amount of taxable gifts.
DISCUSSION: The first $10,000 of gifts of present interest to each donee is excluded under Sec. 2503(b). Rosemary's gift to her son is taxable to the extent that it exceeds this exclusion. The $30,000 gift to her husband is not taxable because Sec. 2523 allows a deduction for a gift to a spouse equal to the value of the gift. The $20,000 donation to the church does not result in a taxable gift because Rosemary is allowed a deduction for the amount of the gift under Sec. 2522. The amount of a gift made in property is the fair market value of the property at the date of the gift. The gift is taxable to the extent that the fair market value of the property exceeds the $10,000 exclusion. Rosemary's taxable gifts total $42,000 ($15,000 taxable gift to her son and $27,000 taxable gift of jewelry to her daughter).

21. When Jim and Nina became engaged in April 1991, Jim gave Nina a ring that had a fair market value of $50,000. After their wedding in July 1991, Jim gave Nina $75,000 in cash so that Nina could have her own bank account. Both Jim and Nina are U.S. citizens. What was the amount of Jim's 1991 gift tax marital deduction?

a. $0.
b. $75,000.
c. $115,000.
d. $125,000.

The correct answer is (b). *(CPA 1190 Q-36)*
REQUIRED: The correct marital deduction for 1991.
DISCUSSION: Sec. 2503(b) allows an individual a $10,000 annual exclusion for gifts of present interests made to each donee during the calendar year. Sec. 2523 permits a marital deduction when a donor transfers property during the calendar year by gift to a donee who at the time of the gift is the donee's spouse. Sec. 2524 states that the deductible marital deduction amount may not exceed the includable gift; that is, the amount of the gift in excess of the annual exclusion. The fair market value of the ring would not qualify for the marital deduction because Nina was not Jim's spouse at the time she received the ring. $10,000 of the value of the ring would, however, qualify for the annual exclusion. The $75,000 Jim gave Nina to open her own bank account would qualify for the deduction because Jim and Nina were married when the gift was made and the annual exclusion had been exhausted with the gift of the ring.

22. Mr. C made the following gifts during 1991:

- $1,000 each month to a university to pay tuition costs for his niece.
- An undeveloped tract of land to his sister that had an adjusted basis to Mr. C of $4,000 and a fair market value of $25,000.
- Various shares of stock to his wife that had an adjusted basis to Mr. C of $15,000 and a fair market value of $40,000.

Mr. C did not consent to gift-splitting. What is the total amount of taxable gifts for 1991?

a. $0.
b. $15,000.
c. $27,000.
d. $77,000.

The correct answer is (b). *(SPE 1085 III-85)*
REQUIRED: The amount of the donor's taxable gifts.
DISCUSSION: Taxable gifts means the total amount of gifts made during the calendar year, less the charitable and marital deductions [Sec. 2503(a)]. The first $10,000 of gifts of present interests to each donee is excluded [Sec. 2503(b)]. In addition, an unlimited educational exclusion is available for amounts paid on behalf of a donee as tuition to an educational organization [Sec. 2503(e)]. The gift to the donor's spouse is eligible for a marital deduction equal to the value of the property transferred after any applicable exclusions (Sec. 2523).

Donee	Amount	Exclusion/Deduction	Taxable
Niece	$12,000	$12,000	$ 0
Sister	25,000	10,000	15,000
Wife	40,000	40,000	0
Total taxable gifts			$15,000

23. If an individual donor makes a gift of future interest whereby the donee is to receive possession of the gift at some future time, the annual exclusion for gift tax purposes is

a. $0.
b. $3,000.
c. $5,000.
d. $10,000.

The correct answer is (a). *(CPA 589 Q-58)*
REQUIRED: The annual exclusion for a gift of a future interest.
DISCUSSION: Sec. 2503(b) allows an annual exclusion of $10,000 to each donee. The exclusion is specifically limited to gifts of present interest. A gift of a future interest does not qualify for the exclusion.

24. In March 1991, Ted Thrifty created a trust for his son, Doug. Under the terms of the trust, Doug is to get for life the entire income from the property with the remainder going to Ted's grandson at the death of Doug. The annual exclusion for gifts would apply to Ted's gift in trust to his son, Doug.

The correct answer is (T). *(SPE 989 III-31)*
DISCUSSION: Sec. 2503(b) allows a donor to exclude the first $10,000 of each gift made in a calendar year. The exclusion applies only to gifts of present interests. Ted's gift in trust to his son qualifies for the exclusion because it is a present interest in the income of the trust. Under Reg. 25.2503-3, an unrestricted right to the immediate use, possession, or enjoyment of property or the income from property (such as a life estate) is a present interest in property and qualifies for the exclusion.

25. The annual exclusion of $10,000 per donee can be used for no more than 15 donees in any one calendar year.

The correct answer is (F). *(Publisher)*
DISCUSSION: Sec. 2503(b) places no limitation on the number of donees for which the $10,000 exclusion may be taken. The exclusion is limited only to gifts of present interests in property, not future interests.

26. Gifts between spouses never generate taxable gifts.

The correct answer is (F). *(Publisher)*
DISCUSSION: The marital deduction provided in Sec. 2523 is not available to a donor who is not a citizen or resident. Furthermore, Sec. 2523(b) disallows the deduction in most cases if the interest passing to the spouse by gift is a terminable interest. A terminable interest is generally one that could terminate or fail and pass to someone else in such a way that the interest would not be included in the spouse's estate.

27. If a special election is made, a marital deduction can be taken for a transfer of a terminable interest in 1991.

The correct answer is (T). *(Publisher)*
DISCUSSION: A donor is allowed a deduction for qualified terminable interest property (QTIP) if the donee spouse makes an election to treat it as such [Sec. 2523(f)]. The donee spouse must be entitled to all the income from the property, payable annually or at more frequent intervals, and no person may have a power to appoint any part of the property to any person other than the spouse [Sec. 2056(b)(7)(B)]. The result is that the donor is entitled to the marital deduction, but the donee spouse must include the entire value of the property in his/her estate (Sec. 2044). For transfers made after December 31, 1985, an election for this treatment must be made by the due date of the gift tax return, including extensions.

28. A charitable deduction is available equal to the fair market value of property donated to a qualified charitable organization reduced by the $10,000 exclusion.

The correct answer is (T). *(Publisher)*
DISCUSSION: Sec. 2522 allows a deduction for the fair market value of property donated to a qualified charitable organization. Sec. 2524 limits the charitable deduction to the portion of the gift not excluded, i.e., in excess of $10,000.

23.4 Gift-Splitting

29. All of the following statements concerning gift-splitting are true except:

a. The annual gift tax exclusion allows spouses who consent to split their gifts to transfer up to $20,000 to any one person during any calendar year without gift tax liability, if the gift qualifies as a present interest.

b. To qualify for gift-splitting, a couple must be married at the time the gift is made to a third party.

c. For gift tax purposes, a husband and wife must file a joint income tax return to qualify for the gift-splitting benefits.

d. Both spouses must consent to the use of gift-splitting.

The correct answer is (c). *(SPE 990 III-54)*
REQUIRED: The statement that is not true for gift-splitting.
DISCUSSION: Sec. 2513 allows a gift to be treated as made one-half by the donor and one-half by the donor's spouse. There is no requirement that the spouses file a joint income tax return.
Answer (a) is incorrect because gift-splitting allows spouses who consent to split their gifts to exclude the first $20,000 of each gift of a present interest. Answer (b) is incorrect because the donor must be married at the time of the gift to qualify for gift-splitting. Answer (d) is incorrect because both spouses must consent to the use of gift-splitting.

30. In March 1991, H transferred $200,000 to daughter and $200,000 to son. In July 1991, H's wife transferred $5,000 to son. No other gifts were made. H and his wife elected to split the gifts on their gift tax returns. What is the amount of 1991 taxable gifts made by H and H's wife?

	H	W
a.	$182,500	$182,500
b.	$192,500	$192,500
c.	$360,000	$5,000
d.	$380,000	$0

The correct answer is (a). *(SPE 990 III-88)*
REQUIRED: The correct amount of taxable gifts by spouses who elect to use gift-splitting.
DISCUSSION: Sec. 2513 allows a gift to be treated as made one-half by the donor and one-half by the donor's spouse. Because H and W elect to split their gifts, they can each take advantage of the $10,000 annual exclusion per donee.

Donee	Amount	Exclusion	Taxable
Son	$205,000	$20,000	$185,000
Daughter	200,000	20,000	180,000
Total taxable gifts			$365,000

Because the spouses elected to split their gifts, each spouse is treated as having made one-half of each gift. Thus, H and W are each treated as having made $182,500 of taxable gifts in 1991.

31. During 1991, Warren made the following gifts:

Cash to son Ronald	$ 40,000
Land to wife Laura	100,000
Cash to First Church	30,000
Painting to niece Suzie	18,000

Warren and Laura elect gift-splitting. Laura's only gift in 1991 is a $50,000 cash gift to her mother. What is the amount of the taxable gifts to be reported by Warren in 1991?

a. $188,000.
b. $44,000.
c. $25,000.
d. $10,000.

The correct answer is (c). *(Publisher)*
REQUIRED: Warren's total taxable gifts after gift-splitting.
DISCUSSION: If both spouses consent, a gift made by one spouse to any person other than the other spouse is considered as made one-half by each spouse [Sec. 2513(a)]. In addition to his own gifts, Warren is treated as having made one-half of Laura's gift to her mother. By splitting the gifts, each spouse can take advantage of the $10,000 per donee exclusion.

Donee	Amount	Exclusion/ Deduction	Taxable
Ronald	$ 20,000	$ 10,000	$10,000
Laura	100,000	100,000	0
Church	15,000	15,000	0
Suzie	9,000	9,000	0
Laura's mother	25,000	10,000	15,000
Total taxable gifts			$25,000

Module 23.4: Gift-Splitting

32. During 1991, Mr. Jones made gifts to his son of the following items:

A minivan with an adjusted basis of $12,000 and fair market value of $14,000

Bonds with an adjusted basis of $5,000 and fair market value of $17,000

Antique furniture with an adjusted basis of $12,000 and a fair market value of $35,000

An interest-free $10,000 loan on January 1, to buy a boat for his personal pleasure. His son repaid the loan in full on December 31, 1991. The applicable federal interest rate was 10%.

Mr. and Mrs. Jones elect gift-splitting. What is the total amount of their taxable gifts to their son in 1991?

a. $9,000.
b. $30,000.
c. $46,000.
d. $66,000.

The correct answer is (c). *(SPE 989 III-89)*
REQUIRED: The total amount of taxable gifts by spouses who elect gift-splitting.
DISCUSSION: Gift-splitting allows spouses to treat each gift as made one-half by each. This allows each spouse to exclude the first $10,000 of each gift of a present interest to a third person in a calendar year, for a total exclusion of $20,000 per donee. Thus, Mr. and Mrs. Jones may exclude $20,000 of the total gifts made to their son in 1991.
The amount of a gift made in property is the fair market value of the property on the date of the gift. The taxable gifts made to the son total $66,000 in 1991 ($14,000 minivan + $17,000 bonds + $35,000 furniture). Applying the available exclusion to these gifts reduces the taxable gifts to $46,000. The interest-free loan does not qualify as a gift.
Sec. 7872(c)(2) creates an exception for loans between individuals when the amount of the loan does not exceed $10,000. Accordingly, the $10,000 interest-free loan does not result in a gift.

33. Mr. and Mrs. John Hance jointly gave a $100,000 outright gift in 1991 to an unrelated friend, Fred Green, who needed the money to pay some legal expenses. In filing their gift tax returns for 1991, Mr. and Mrs. Hance elected gift-splitting and were entitled to exclusions aggregating

a. $0.
b. $6,000.
c. $10,000.
d. $20,000.

The correct answer is (d). *(CPA 1183 Q-25)*
REQUIRED: The amount of exclusions available to a couple who elect gift-splitting.
DISCUSSION: If Mr. and Mrs. Hance elect gift-splitting, each will be treated as if (s)he had made a $50,000 cash gift to the donee. Since the gift was of a present interest, a $10,000 exclusion is available for each donor of the split gift. Therefore, Mr. and Mrs. Hance have total exclusions aggregating $20,000 (2 x $10,000).

34. A gift made by a person to someone other than a spouse may be considered as made one-half by each spouse.

The correct answer is (T). *(SPE 989 III-33)*
DISCUSSION: Sec. 2513 allows spouses to treat a gift made to a third person as made one-half by the donor and one-half by the donor's spouse. The spouses must make a proper election to split their gifts and must signify their consent on the gift tax return.

35. The annual gift exclusion allows spouses who consent to split their gifts to transfer up to $20,000 to any one person during any calendar year without any gift tax liability, if the gift qualifies as a present interest.

The correct answer is (T). *(SPE 1085 III-41)*
DISCUSSION: Sec. 2513 allows a gift made by either spouse to a third party to be treated as made one-half by each spouse, if both spouses consent to the gift-splitting election. In addition, Sec. 2503(b) allows each spouse to exclude from his/her taxable gifts the first $10,000 of gifts (of present interests) made to each donee. Thus, a gift of a $20,000 present interest, split between spouses, will not result in any gift tax liability.

36. In order for a husband and wife to qualify for gift-splitting they must have been married the entire year.

The correct answer is (F). *(SPE 989 III-32)*
DISCUSSION: Sec. 2513(a) provides that to qualify for gift-splitting, the individual must be married at the time of the gift. There is no requirement that the donor and his/her spouse be married the entire year.

37. For gift tax purposes, a husband and wife must file a joint gift tax return to qualify for the gift-splitting benefits.

The correct answer is (F). *(SPE 1082 III-43)*
DISCUSSION: There is no such thing as a joint gift tax return. Each spouse must file his/her own gift return. The gift-splitting provision under Sec. 2513 applies when the spouses have each signified consent to gift-splitting for all gifts made during the calendar year by signing the consent on the other spouse's return.

38. Gift-splitting provisions are advantageous only if one spouse made no gifts during the tax year.

The correct answer is (F). *(Publisher)*
DISCUSSION: When both spouses have made gifts but the gifts made by one spouse are much larger than those made by the other spouse, the progressive structure of the gift tax rates makes the election of gift-splitting advantageous. Furthermore, gift-splitting allows the $10,000 exclusion to be used by each spouse for each donee who receives a present interest.

39. Gifts made to qualified charitable organizations do not qualify for gift-splitting.

The correct answer is (F). *(Publisher)*
DISCUSSION: Neither Sec. 2513 nor Sec. 2522 disallows the deduction for gifts made to qualified charitable organizations if gift-splitting is elected.

23.5 Calculation of Gift Tax

40. In 1991, Rose made her first taxable gift when she gave her sister, Lily, stock with a fair market value of $900,000. What is Rose's gift tax due for 1991?

a. [$248,300 + 39%($140,000)].
b. [$248,300 + 39%($150,000)].
c. [$248,300 + 39%($140,000)] − $155,800.
d. [$248,300 + 39%($140,000)] − $192,800.

The correct answer is (d). *(Publisher)*
REQUIRED: The donor's gift tax payable for 1991.
DISCUSSION: The donor's taxable gift is the $900,000 of stock transferred by gift reduced by the $10,000 exclusion under Sec. 2503(b), or $890,000. Since the donor has never made any other taxable gifts, the tax imposed is computed on the $890,000 of taxable gifts [Sec. 2502(a)]. The tax rates in Sec. 2001(c) are used. For taxable gifts in excess of $750,000 but not over $1,000,000, the tax is $248,300 plus 39% of the excess over $750,000. Furthermore, Sec. 2505(b) allows a credit equal to $192,800. Rose's gift tax due is $248,300, plus 39% of $140,000, minus the $192,800 unified credit.

41. In 1991 Mr. X made a gift to his brother of land which had an adjusted basis to X of $10,000 and a fair market value of $20,000. Mr. X did not consent to gift-splitting with his spouse. Mr. X made no other gifts in 1991 and had made no taxable gifts in prior years. What amount of gift tax should Mr. X pay for 1991?

a. $0.
b. $2,000.
c. $3,400.
d. $4,400.

The correct answer is (a). *(SPE 1085 III-86)*
REQUIRED: The donor's gift tax payable for 1991.
DISCUSSION: The amount of a gift made in property is the fair market value of the property on the date of the gift [Sec. 2512(a)]. Without a gift-splitting election, the donor's taxable gift is the $20,000 of land transferred by gift reduced by the $10,000 exclusion under Sec. 2503(b), or $10,000. Since the donor has never made any other taxable gifts, the tax imposed is computed on the $10,000 of taxable gifts [Sec. 2502(a)]. The tax rates in Sec. 2001(c) are used. For taxable gifts not over $10,000, the tax is 18% of the amount of taxable gifts, or $1,800. Furthermore, Sec. 2505(a) allows a credit equal to $192,800. Mr. X's gift tax due is zero.

Module 23.5: Calculation of Gift Tax

42. Mr. C, who is single and a U.S. citizen, made the following gifts in 1991:

Cash to nephew	$200,000
Cash to sister	200,000
Property to brother (FMV)	400,000
Cash to the local university building fund	200,000

C had not made any gifts in prior years. What is C's net gift tax liability?

a. $63,300.
b. $100,300.
c. $159,800.
d. $256,100.

The correct answer is (a). *(SPE 984 III-82)*
REQUIRED: The gift tax payable on gifts made to relatives and a university in 1991.
DISCUSSION: The total of the taxable gifts is the total gift amount of $1,000,000 minus exclusions for each gift and a deduction for the gift to the university.

	Total Gifts	Exclusions and Deductions	Taxable Gifts
Nephew	$ 200,000	$ (10,000)	$190,000
Sister	200,000	(10,000)	190,000
Brother	400,000	(10,000)	390,000
University	200,000	(200,000)	0
Total	$1,000,000	$(230,000)	$770,000

The tax is calculated only on the $770,000 of taxable gifts for 1991 since this is the first year in which taxable gifts have been made [Sec. 2502(a)]. The tax rates in Sec. 2001(c) are used. The tentative tax is $256,100 [$248,300 + .39 x ($770,000 − $750,000)]. This tax is reduced by the $192,800 unified credit for 1991 [Sec. 2505(a)], leaving a gift tax liability of $63,300.

43. Sharon made a gift of land in 1991 with a fair market value of $1,010,000 to her daughter. She made no gifts in 1986-1990. In 1985, she used $121,800 of her unified credit to offset gift tax otherwise due. What amount of unified credit can Sharon use to offset gift tax due on the 1991 gift?

a. $192,800.
b. $79,300.
c. $71,000.
d. $17,000.

The correct answer is (c). *(Publisher)*
REQUIRED: The amount of unified credit the donor may use to offset the gift tax in 1991.
DISCUSSION: For gifts made in 1991, the unified credit is $192,800 reduced by the amount allowable as a unified credit for all preceding calendar years [Sec. 2505(a)]. Since Sharon used $121,800 of unified credit in previous years, the amount of unified credit she may use in 1991 is $71,000 ($192,800 − $121,800).

44. In 1991, Spencer, a single taxpayer, made a $1,000,000 taxable gift to his brother Tracy. The only other taxable gifts Spencer has made were a $2,000,000 taxable gift to Tracy in 1979, and a $500,000 taxable gift to his sister Katharine in 1981. Spencer paid a total gift tax on the 1979 and 1981 gifts of $987,800. What is the gift tax due from Spencer for his 1991 gifts?

a. $345,800.
b. $385,200.
c. $1,373,000.
d. $1,565,800.

The correct answer is (b). *(Publisher)*
REQUIRED: The donor's gift tax payable for 1991.
DISCUSSION: The gift tax imposed is equal to the excess of a tentative tax on the sum of taxable gifts for the current year and for each preceding year, over a tentative tax computed on the sum of the taxable gifts for each preceding year [Sec. 2502(a)]. Sec. 2505 allows a unified credit in 1991 equal to $192,800 reduced by the amounts allowable as credits to the individual for all preceding years. The taxpayer's last gift was in 1981 and the allowable unified credit in that year was $38,000.

Tentative tax on $3,500,000	$1,565,800
Tentative tax on $2,500,000	(1,025,800)
	$ 540,000
Unified credit ($192,800 − $38,000)	(154,800)
Gift tax payable	$ 385,200

45. To calculate the tax due on the current year's taxable gifts, the tax paid on all prior years' taxable gifts is subtracted from the tax calculated using the current year's tax rates and cumulative lifetime taxable gifts.

The correct answer is (F). *(Publisher)*
DISCUSSION: To calculate the tax due on the current year's taxable gifts, the tentative tax (computed using current tax rates) on all taxable gifts in the preceding years is subtracted from the tentative tax (computed using current tax rates) on the sum of the current year's taxable gifts and the taxable gifts of all preceding years [Sec. 2502(a)].

Module 23.6: Reporting Gifts

46. The marginal tax rate on cumulative gifts in excess of $3,000,000 is 55% for 1991.

The correct answer is (F). *(Publisher)*
DISCUSSION: The top rate in 1987 was 55% on taxable gifts over $3,000,000 (53% on taxable gifts between $2,500,000 and $3,000,000). The 1987 Revenue Act retained the maximum rate of 55% through 1992 on cumulative gifts in excess of $2,500,000. A 5% surtax also applies to cumulative transfers (gifts and bequests) of between $10,000,000 and $21,040,000 to phase out the benefits of the graduated rates and unified credit.

47. The unified credit available to offset tax due on the current year's gifts is equal to the statutory credit for the current year. For 1991, that credit is $192,800.

The correct answer is (F). *(Publisher)*
DISCUSSION: The unified credit available to offset tax due on the current year's gifts is equal to the statutory credit for the current year reduced by the sum of the amounts allowed as a credit to the individual for all preceding calendar years [Sec. 2505(a)]. For 1991, the statutory credit is $192,800.

23.6 Reporting Gifts

48. On February 4, 1991, Mr. Smith made a gift in an amount sufficient to require the filing of a federal gift tax return. On October 5, 1991, Mr. Smith died. Assuming extensions have not been obtained, the gift tax return, Form 709, must be filed by (assuming none of the dates are Saturdays, Sundays, or holidays):

 a. March 15, 1991.
 b. April 15, 1991.
 c. March 15, 1992.
 d. April 15, 1992.

The correct answer is (d). *(SPE 989 III-63)*
REQUIRED: The date Form 709, United States Gift Tax Return, is due.
DISCUSSION: Under Sec. 6075, gift tax returns are due on or before the 15th day of April following the close of the calendar year in which a gift was made. Since Mr. Smith made a gift in 1991, Form 709 is due by April 15, 1992.
If the date falls on a weekend or holiday, then the return is due the next business day.
An estate tax return may be required of Mr. Smith's estate. This return is due no later than 9 months after the date of death unless an extension is obtained [Sec. 6075(a)]. The due date for the gift tax return for the year of death is no later than the estate tax return due date [Sec. 6075(b)(3)]. This does not change the answer here.

49. For transfers by gift during 1991, one must file a gift tax return for which of the following?

 a. A transfer of a present interest in property that is not more than the annual exclusion.
 b. A qualified transfer for educational or medical expenses.
 c. A transfer to one's spouse that qualified for the unlimited marital deduction.
 d. A transfer of $18,000 to a son for which one's spouse has agreed to gift-splitting.

The correct answer is (d). *(SPE 984 III-35)*
REQUIRED: The transfer for which a gift tax return must be filed.
DISCUSSION: Sec. 6019 provides that a gift tax return must be filed for almost all taxable gifts. Specifically excluded from the requirement for filing are transfers that qualify for and do not exceed the $10,000 annual exclusion of Sec. 2503(b) or the Sec. 2503(e) exclusion for educational or medical expenses. In addition, transfers to a spouse that qualify for the unlimited marital deduction also do not require the filing of a gift tax return. However, a gift tax return must be filed for a transfer that exceeds the annual exclusions even if no tax will be paid because the donor's spouse agrees to gift-splitting.

50. A U.S. citizen does not have to file a gift tax return for any year unless taxable gifts exceed $25,000.

The correct answer is (F). *(SPE 1078 III-48)*
DISCUSSION: Sec. 6019 provides that a gift tax return must be filed unless all gifts made may be excluded under the $10,000 exclusion of Sec. 2503(b), the Sec. 2503(e) exclusion for transfers in payment of medical or tuition expenses, or may be deducted under the marital deduction of Sec. 2523(a).

51. Mr. J made a $21,000 payment directly to an educational organization for the tuition of another individual. This is considered a qualified transfer and does not require the donor to file a gift tax return.

The correct answer is (T). *(SPE 988 III-37)*
DISCUSSION: Qualified transfers under the Sec. 2503(e) exclusion for medical or tuition expenses do not require the donor to file a gift tax return.

52. Mr. C, a U.S. citizen, made the following gifts during 1991:

Cash to brother - $5,000
Automobile to son with a fair market value of $18,000; adjusted basis to C of $8,000
Rental property to spouse with a fair market value of $50,000; adjusted basis to C of $32,000

Mr. C is not required to file a gift tax return for 1991.

The correct answer is (F). *(SPE 984 III-36)*
DISCUSSION: Sec. 6019 provides that a gift tax return must be filed unless all gifts may be excluded under Sec. 2503(b) or Sec. 2503(e), or may be deducted under the marital deduction of Sec. 2523(a). The gift of the automobile to the son with a fair market value of $18,000 exceeds the $10,000 that can be excluded under Sec. 2503(b). Hence, a gift tax return must be filed for 1991.

23.7 Inclusions in the Gross Estate

53. A decedent's gross estate includes the value of all property to the extent of the decedent's interest in the property at the time of death. Which one of the following items is not included in the gross estate?

a. Medical insurance reimbursements that were due the individual at death.
b. The value of the part of a deceased husband's real property allowed to his widow for her lifetime (dower interest).
c. Proceeds of life insurance on the decedent's life if the decedent possessed incidents of ownership in the policy.
d. Outstanding dividends declared to decedent after the date of death.

The correct answer is (d). *(SPE 1081 III-64)*
REQUIRED: The item not included in a decedent's gross estate.
DISCUSSION: Under Sec. 2033, the value of a gross estate includes the value at the time of death of all property in which the decedent had an interest at the time of death. A shareholder only has a right to or interest in dividends which have been declared by the directors. Since the dividends were declared after death, the decedent had no interest in them at the time of his/her death and they are not included in the gross estate. Note that, if the dividends had been declared (and the record date had passed) before the decedent's death, but not paid, they would be includable in the gross estate.
Answer (a) is incorrect because medical insurance reimbursements due the individual at death are considered property in which the decedent had an interest. Answer (b) is incorrect because Sec. 2034 provides that dower interests will not prevent the inclusion of such property in the decedent's gross estate. Answer (c) is incorrect because Sec. 2042 provides that the value of the gross estate includes proceeds of life insurance when the decedent possessed incidents of ownership in the policy.

54. Which of the following items of property would be included in the gross estate of a decedent who died in 1991?

1. Clothes and jewelry of the decedent.
2. Cash of $400,000 given to decedent's friend in 1989. No gift tax was paid on the transfer.
3. Land purchased by decedent and held as joint tenants with rights of survivorship with decedent's brother.

a. 1, 2, and 3.
b. 1 and 3.
c. 1 and 2.
d. 2 and 3.

The correct answer is (b). *(Publisher)*
REQUIRED: The items of property included in the decedent's gross estate.
DISCUSSION: Under Secs. 2031 and 2033, a decedent's gross estate includes the value of all property, real or personal, tangible or intangible, wherever situated, to the extent the decedent owned a beneficial interest at the time of death. Clothes and jewelry of the decedent are included in the gross estate. Sec. 2040(a) provides for the inclusion of all property held as joint tenants with right of survivorship by the decedent and any other person, except the part of the property shown to have originally belonged to the other person and for which adequate and full consideration was not provided by the decedent. Therefore, the full value of the land is also included in the decedent's gross estate.
Answers (a), (c), and (d) are incorrect because gifts made prior to death are not included in the estate of a decedent who dies after 1981, except for certain transfers such as those in which a life estate is retained or the transfer is of life insurance [Sec. 2035(d)].

55. Mr. X died on September 24, 1991. His will required the transfer of all possessions to his sister. At the date of death, the assets transferred were

	Adj. Basis	FMV
Apartment house	$275,000	$420,000
Stock	25,000	40,000
Dividends on above stock (declared 9/30/91)	3,000	3,000
Medical insurance reimbursement (check received 9/20/91 but not cashed)	5,000	5,000
Cash	50,000	50,000

The executrix did not elect the alternate valuation date. What is Mr. X's gross estate for purposes of an estate tax return, Form 706?

a. $358,000.
b. $503,000.
c. $515,000.
d. $518,000.

56. Following are the fair market values of Wald's assets at the date of death

Personal effects and jewelry	$150,000
Land bought by Wald with Wald's funds 5 years prior to death and held with Wald's sister as joint tenants with right of survivorship	800,000

The executor of Wald's estate did not elect the alternate valuation date. The amount includable as Wald's gross estate in the federal estate tax return is

a. $150,000.
b. $550,000.
c. $800,000.
d. $950,000.

The correct answer is (c). *(SPE 1085 III-83)*
REQUIRED: The value of the decedent's gross estate for purposes of an estate tax return.
DISCUSSION: Under Sec. 2033, the value of a gross estate includes the value at the time of death of all property in which the decedent had an interest at the time of death. A shareholder only has a right to or interest in dividends which have been declared by the directors. Since the dividends were declared after death, the decedent had no interest in them at the time of his death and they are not included in the gross estate. Note that if the dividends had been declared (and the record date had passed) before the decedent's death but not paid, they would be includable in the gross estate. Medical insurance reimbursements due the individual at death are considered property in which the decedent had an interest. Here the reimbursements were actually received. Thus, the decedent's gross estate includes

Apartment house	$420,000
Stock	40,000
Medical insurance reimbursement	5,000
Cash	50,000
Gross estate	$515,000

The correct answer is (d). *(CPA 1190 Q-37)*
REQUIRED: The amount includable on the estate tax return.
DISCUSSION: Under Sec. 2033, the value of the gross estate includes the value of all property in which the decedent had an interest at the time of death. Therefore, the value of the personal effects and jewelry is included in the gross estate.
Sec. 2040 states that a decedent's gross estate includes the value of property held jointly at the time of the decedent's death by the decedent and another person with right of survivorship. The amount of the value to be included depends upon how much of the purchase price or other consideration was supplied by the decedent. If the decedent furnished only a part of the purchase price, only a corresponding portion of the property is so included. If, as in this case, the decedent furnished the entire purchase price of the jointly held property, the value of the entire property is included in the gross estate. Therefore, Wald must include the entire value of the jointly held property in his gross estate.

57. Mr. Good died on April 15, 1991. His assets and their fair market value at the time of his death were

Cash	$ 10,000
Home	140,000
Life insurance payable to Mr. Good's estate	200,000
Series EE bonds	90,000
Municipal bonds	180,000

Mr. Good had borrowed $10,000 against the cash value of his life insurance policy. Mr. Good's estate is liable for the loan. What is the total amount of Mr. Good's gross estate for federal estate tax purposes?

 a. $240,000.
 b. $420,000.
 c. $610,000.
 d. $620,000.

The correct answer is (d). *(SPE 990 III-85)*
REQUIRED: The value of the decedent's gross estate for federal estate tax purposes.
DISCUSSION: Under Sec. 2033, the value of a gross estate includes the value at the time of death of all property in which the decedent had an interest at the time of death. Sec. 2042 requires the inclusion of proceeds from life insurance policies where the proceeds are receivable by or for the benefit of the estate. U.S. savings bonds purchased by a decedent with his own funds are includable in his gross estate if registered in his own name or with another person as co-owner. The value of the municipal bonds is includable in the gross estate. The fact that the income generated by municipal bonds is tax exempt does not prevent them from being included in the gross estate. The federal estate tax is a tax upon the value of the property and not upon the income the property generates. The cash and the value of the home are also included in the gross estate. The estate's liability for the loan does not affect the amount of the gross estate unless the estate actually pays the loan.

58. Mr. C died on June 30, 1991. Based on the following facts, compute Mr. C's gross estate.

In 1990, C gave cash of $50,000 to his friend. No gift tax was paid on the gift.

C held property jointly with his brother. Each paid $30,000 of the total purchase price of $60,000. Fair market value of the property at date of death was $100,000.

In 1989, C purchased a life insurance policy on his life and gave it as a gift to his sister. C retained the right to change the beneficiary. Upon C's death, his sister received $150,000 under the policy.

In 1982, C gave his son a summer home (fair market value in 1982 - $125,000). C continued to use it until his death pursuant to an understanding with his son. Fair market value at date of death was $175,000.

 a. $200,000.
 b. $250,000.
 c. $375,000.
 d. $425,000.

The correct answer is (c). *(SPE 1083 III-83)*
REQUIRED: The gross estate of a decedent who died in 1991.
DISCUSSION: For decedents dying after 1981, gifts made prior to death are not included in the estate except for certain transfers such as those in which a life estate is retained or those involving life insurance [Sec. 2035(d)]. Therefore, the cash gift to a friend is not included in Mr. C's estate but the life insurance is. The life insurance is also included because the right to change the beneficiary is an incident of ownership under Sec. 2042.

The value of property owned jointly is included [Sec. 2040(a)]. To the extent it can be shown that consideration for the acquisition of the jointly held property was provided by the other joint tenant, a proportionate part is excluded (1/2). Thus, $50,000 of the fair market value of the property held with the brother must be included in the estate.

Sec. 2036 requires inclusion in the gross estate of all property that the decedent transferred without full consideration while retaining for life its possession or enjoyment. Accordingly, the $175,000 fair market value of the summer home is included in C's gross estate. The gross estate therefore totals $375,000 ($50,000 + $150,000 + $175,000).

Module 23.7: Inclusions in the Gross Estate

59. Proceeds of a life insurance policy payable to the estate's executor, as the estate's representative, are

   a. Includable in the decedent's gross estate only if the premiums had been paid by the insured.
   b. Includable in the decedent's gross estate only if the policy was taken out within 3 years of the insured's death under the "contemplation of death" rule.
   c. Always includable in the decedent's gross estate.
   d. Never includable in the decedent's gross estate.

The correct answer is (c). *(CPA 1188 Q-18)*
REQUIRED: The correct treatment of life insurance proceeds payable to the executor of an estate.
DISCUSSION: Sec. 2042 requires inclusion in the gross estate of the amounts receivable by all beneficiaries from insurance under policies on the life of the decedent with respect to which the decedent possessed at his/her death any incidents of ownership or where the proceeds are receivable by or for the benefit of the estate. If they are payable to the executor, they are receivable for the benefit of the estate and are always included in the decedent's gross estate.
Answer (a) is incorrect because payment of premiums is not a determinative factor, rather possessing incidents of ownership is determinative. Answer (b) is incorrect because life insurance is always included in a decedent's estate if payable to or for the benefit of the estate or if the decedent has any incidents of ownership. There is no need for contemplation of death rule. Answer (d) is incorrect because life insurance generally is included in a decedent's gross estate unless (s)he had no incidents of ownership and it is not received by and for the benefit of the estate.

60. Dr. Kildare, a dentist, used the cash method of accounting. At the time of his death, April 5, 1990, he had $5,000 of unpaid accounts. His estate collected the entire $5,000 by the end of October 1990. Dr. Kildare's estate was settled May 5, 1991. Which return should the $5,000 be included on?

   a. Dr. Kildare's final income tax return.
   b. Dr. Kildare's beneficiary's tax return.
   c. Dr. Kildare's estate tax return, Form 706.
   d. Both (a) and (c).

The correct answer is (c). *(SPE 989 III-55)*
REQUIRED: The return on which income earned prior to death but received after death should be reported.
DISCUSSION: The gross estate of a decedent includes under Sec. 2033 the value of all property, whether real or personal, tangible or intangible, and wherever situated, beneficially owned by the decedent at the time of his death. Notes or other claims held by the decedent are included. Thus, the accounts would be included in Dr. Kildare's gross estate. The $5,000 would be included in the estate tax return, Form 706.
Answer (a) is incorrect because only amounts that are both earned and collected by the decedent prior to death are included in the decedent's final income tax return. Answer (b) is incorrect because amounts collected by a decedent's estate are not reported by beneficiaries.

61. In December 1988, Ms. J assigned all rights under a life insurance policy in her name to another person. She did not receive any money or something of equal value in return. Ms. J was required to file a gift tax return. Ms. J died in February 1991. The proceeds of the life insurance policy are included in Ms. J's gross estate.

The correct answer is (T). *(SPE 988 III-33)*
DISCUSSION: Although Ms. J no longer had an ownership interest in the life insurance policy at the time of her death, the value of the proceeds of the policy are included in her estate because she made a gift of the policy within 3 years of death [Sec. 2035(c)].

62. The gross estate, for purposes of the Federal Estate Tax, includes one-half of the value of property owned by the decedent and spouse as tenants with right of survivorship if the decedent and spouse are the only joint tenants. This is true regardless of which spouse furnished the consideration for the property.

The correct answer is (T). *(SPE 987 III-38)*
DISCUSSION: Under Sec. 2040(a), the decedent's estate normally includes the value of all property held as joint tenants with right of survivorship except to the extent it can be shown that any other joint tenants provided consideration for the property originally. But in the case of spouses owning property as joint tenants with right of survivorship, when one of the spouses dies, only one-half of the property is included in the decedent's estate regardless of who furnished consideration for the property [Sec. 2040(b)].

63. The gross estate will include the value of an annuity that a beneficiary is due to receive if the decedent possessed the right to receive such annuity either alone or with another person or persons during his/her lifetime.

The correct answer is (T). *(SPE 1083 III-42)*
DISCUSSION: Under Sec. 2039, the gross estate includes the value of any annuity receivable by a beneficiary by reason of surviving the decedent if (1) the annuity was payable to the decedent, or (2) the decedent possessed the right to receive such annuity or payment, either alone or in conjunction with another for his/her life or for any period not ascertainable without reference to his/her death, or for any period that does not end before his/her death.

64. Employer B carries a group life insurance policy on its employees. The employees own the right to change the beneficiaries and the right to terminate the policy. If an employee dies, the proceeds from the policy must be included in the decedent's gross estate.

The correct answer is (T). *(SPE 1081 III-40)*
DISCUSSION: Sec. 2042 provides that proceeds from a life insurance policy under which the decedent possessed incidents of ownership must be included in the value of his/her gross estate. The right to change beneficiaries or to terminate the policy is each a sufficient incident of ownership to require the property to be included in the decedent's gross estate.

65. Rob is trustee of a trust established by Martha which gave the income interest to Bert for life. As trustee, Rob has the right to choose between Bert and Nan for the remainder interest. If Rob has that right to choose between Bert and Nan on the date of his death, the fair market value of the trust assets must be included in Rob's estate.

The correct answer is (F). *(Publisher)*
DISCUSSION: Sec. 2041 requires inclusion in the decedent's gross estate of the value of any property with respect to which the decedent had at the time of his/her death a general power of appointment created after October 21, 1942. A general power of appointment is a power exercisable in favor of the decedent, his/her estate, his/her creditors, or the creditors of his/her estate [Sec. 2041(b)]. Since Rob could only choose to give the trust remainder to Bert or Nan, he only had a limited power of appointment and the value of the trust assets is not included in his gross estate.

66. For estate tax purposes, U.S. Government bonds and other U.S. Government indebtednesses are included in the gross estate even if, by law, they are generally exempt from all federal taxes.

The correct answer is (T). *(SPE 989 III-27)*
DISCUSSION: Reg. 20.2033-1 states that statutory provisions which exempt bonds, notes, bills, and certificates of indebtedness of the Federal Government and the interest thereon from taxation are generally not applicable to the estate tax, since the estate tax is an excise tax on the transfer of property at death and is not a tax on the property transferred.

67. Ike Hogg paid $4,000 of the $12,000 purchase price when he purchased property as joint tenants with his sister Ima. The property had a fair market value of $21,000 on the date of Ike's death and his gross estate must include $7,000 of that value.

The correct answer is (T). *(Publisher)*
DISCUSSION: The decedent's gross estate includes the full value of property held as joint tenants with right of survivorship, except to the extent it can be shown the other joint tenant provided consideration [Sec. 2040(a)]. Since the decedent's sister provided two-thirds of the consideration to purchase the property, only one-third of the value of the property at the date of the decedent's death ($7,000) is included in his gross estate.

68. The gross estate includes the value of the surviving spouse's lifetime interest in the deceased spouse's real property.

The correct answer is (T). *(SPE 989 III-28)*
DISCUSSION: Under Sec. 2034, a decedent's gross estate includes any interest in property of the decedent's surviving spouse existing at the time of the decedent's death as dower or courtesy. Thus, the full value of property is included in the decedent's gross estate, without deducting the surviving spouse's interest.

23.8 Valuation of Estate Property

69. If the executor of a decedent's estate elects the alternate valuation date and none of the property included in the gross estate has been sold or distributed, the estate assets must be valued as of how many months after the decedent's death?

- a. 3.
- b. 6.
- c. 9.
- d. 12.

The correct answer is (b). *(CPA 1190 Q-38)*
REQUIRED: The number of months after the decedent's death at which estate assets are valued under the alternate valuation date.
DISCUSSION: Under Sec. 2032, if the executor of an estate elects the alternate valuation date, and the property in the gross estate has not been sold or distributed, the estate assets are valued as of the date 6 months after the decedent's death. If property is sold or distributed within the 6-month period, it is valued as of the date of sale or distribution.

70. All of the following statements about the alternate valuation method for property included in the decedent's gross estate are correct except

- a. The election applies to all of the property in the estate other than property for which the special use valuation applies.
- b. Property affected by mere lapse of time is valued at date of death and includes those properties affected by the time value of money.
- c. If the alternate valuation method is elected, property disposed of within 6 months after the decedent's death is valued as of the date of disposition.
- d. Property not disposed of within 6 months after the decedent's death is valued as of 6 months after the decedent's death.

The correct answer is (b). *(SPE 984 III-59)*
REQUIRED: The false statement concerning the alternate valuation method.
DISCUSSION: The alternate valuation method is to value the estate property as of 6 months after death, or when disposed of if earlier (Sec. 2032). However, property affected by mere lapse of time is valued as of the date of death with adjustments for differences in value 6 months after death which are not due to mere lapse of time. Properties affected by mere lapse of time do not include those due to time value of money such as obligations of payment. They refer to property interests the value of which is based on years such as life estates, remainder interests, patents, etc.
Answers (a), (c), and (d) are incorrect because each is a true statement about the alternate valuation method for property included in an estate.

71. With regard to the federal estate tax, the alternate valuation date

- a. Is required to be used if the fair market value of the estate's assets has increased since the decedent's date of death.
- b. If elected on the first return filed for the estate, may be revoked in an amended return provided that the first return was filed on time.
- c. Must be used for valuation of the estate's liabilities if such date is used for valuation of the estate's assets.
- d. Can be elected only if its use decreases both the value of the gross estate and the estate tax liability.

The correct answer is (d). *(CPA 589 Q-60)*
REQUIRED: The correct statement about the alternate valuation date.
DISCUSSION: Sec. 2032 states the requirements for electing the alternate valuation date for property included in the decedent's gross estate. The effect of the election is to value all estate property on the date 6 months after death or when disposed of, if earlier. This election can only be made for estates of decedents dying after July 18, 1984, if the result is a reduction in both the value of the gross estate and the federal estate tax liability.
Answer (a) is incorrect because there is no requirement that the alternate valuation date be used if the fair market value of the estate's assets has increased since the decedent's date of death. Answer (b) is incorrect because the alternate valuation date election is irrevocable. Answer (c) is incorrect because there is no requirement that the alternate valuation date be used for valuation of the estate's liabilities.

Module 23.8: Valuation of Estate Property

72. Mr. Ash died on June 15, 1991. The assets in his estate were valued on his date of death and alternate valuation date respectively as follows:

Asset	Date of Death Valuation	Alternate Valuation
Home	$250,000	$300,000
Stock	425,000	450,000
Bonds	200,000	125,000
Patent	100,000	95,000

The patent had 10 years of its life remaining at the time of Mr. Ash's death. The executor sold the home on August 1, 1991, for $275,000. If Mr. Ash's executor elects the alternate valuation date method, what is the value of Mr. Ash's estate?

a. $895,000.
b. $945,000.
c. $950,000.
d. $970,000.

The correct answer is (c). *(SPE 990 III-86)*
REQUIRED: The correct value of the decedent's estate if the alternate valuation date is elected.
DISCUSSION: Under Sec. 2032, if the executor elects to use the alternate valuation date, the estate's assets are valued as of the date 6 months after the decedent's death. Assets that are sold or distributed within that 6-month period are valued as of the date of sale or distribution. Any asset which is affected by mere lapse of time is valued as of the date of the decedent's death, but adjusted for any difference in its value not due to mere lapse of time as of the date 6 months after the decedent's death. Assets which are affected by mere lapse of time include patents, life estates, remainders, reversions, and other like properties.
Because the home was sold within the 6-month period after the decedent's death, it is valued as of the date of sale. Its value for estate tax purposes is therefore $275,000. The stock and the bonds are included in the estate at their alternate valuation date value. The patent is an asset which is affected by mere lapse of time and is included in the estate at its date of death value. The value of Mr. Ash's estate is $950,000 ($275,000 + $450,000 + $125,000 + $100,000).

73. Alyssa, a widow, died on August 1, 1990. At her death, she had the following assets:

Asset	Alyssa's Basis	Fair Market Value 8/1/90	2/1/91
Car	$18,000	$14,000	$12,000
IBM stock	20,000	30,000	28,000
Jewelry	180,000	235,000	236,000
Residence	305,000	400,000	405,000

The IBM stock was distributed to Alyssa's daughter on October 5, 1990 when its fair market value was $24,000. All other assets remained in the estate on February 1, 1991. Alyssa's lowest permissible gross estate valuation is

a. $523,000.
b. $675,000.
c. $677,000.
d. $679,000.

The correct answer is (c). *(Publisher)*
REQUIRED: The lowest gross estate valuation for a decedent.
DISCUSSION: The executor of Alyssa's estate may choose to value the estate at either the date of her death or the alternate valuation date (Sec. 2032). The alternate valuation date may only be elected if both the value of the gross estate and the estate tax liability are decreased [Sec. 2032(c)]. Using the alternate valuation date, the IBM stock must be valued as of its distribution on 10/5/90. The chart below compares the alternate valuation with the date of death value of the estate and the estate tax under each method, assuming the gross estate and taxable estate are equal. Since the alternate valuation yields both a lower total estate and a lower estate tax, it gives the lowest permissible gross estate value.

Assets	Date of Death Value	Alternate Valuation
Car	$14,000	$12,000
IBM stock	30,000	24,000
Jewelry	235,000	236,000
Residence	400,000	405,000
Estate value	$679,000	$677,000
Estate tax after unified credit	$29,230	$28,490

74. The election of the alternate valuation method changes the rule that the gross estate includes property that the decedent owned or had an interest in on the date of death.

The correct answer is (F). *(SPE 989 III-30)*
DISCUSSION: The alternate valuation method is only a method of placing a value on the property in an estate. It does not affect the property that must be included in the estate.

Module 23.9: Deductions from the Gross Estate

75. If an executor of an estate elects to use the alternate valuation method, any property that is sold, exchanged, or otherwise disposed of within 6 months after the decedent's death is valued as of the date of the decedent's death.

The correct answer is (F). *(SPE 1083 III-44)*
DISCUSSION: If the alternate valuation election is made, property held in the estate 6 months after the decedent's death is valued on that date. However, Sec. 2032 provides that, in the case of property distributed, sold, exchanged, or otherwise disposed of within 6 months after the decedent's death, such property shall be valued as of the date of disposition.

76. The gross estate for federal estate tax purposes includes the value of all property to the extent of the decedent's interest in the property at time of death. "Value" is the lesser of the decedent's adjusted basis or the fair market value of the property.

The correct answer is (F). *(SPE 1080 III-38)*
DISCUSSION: Under Sec. 2033, the gross estate includes the value of all property to the extent of the decedent's interest in the property at time of death. Under Sec. 2031 and the regulations, value is the fair market value of the property unless a special valuation rule is used (Sec. 2032A). Adjusted basis is irrelevant.

77. If certain conditions are met, the executor of an estate may elect to value real property devoted to farming or used in a closely held business on the basis of its current use as a farm or its use in the business, rather than its fair market value determined on the basis of its highest and best use.

The correct answer is (T). *(SPE 1080 III-36)*
DISCUSSION: Real property is generally valued at its highest and best use. Sec. 2032A provides that, if certain conditions are met, qualified real property used in farming or in a closely held trade or business other than farming may be valued on the basis of its actual use. However, this only applies to qualified real property and is available only if current use valuation is elected on the first estate tax return filed.

23.9 Deductions from the Gross Estate

78. Which of the following is not an allowable deduction against a decedent's gross estate?

a. Administration and funeral expenses.
b. Claims against the estate.
c. Penalty incurred as the result of a late payment of the federal estate tax.
d. Casualty and theft losses.

The correct answer is (c). *(SPE 989 III-60)*
REQUIRED: The item which is not an allowable deduction from the decedent's gross estate.
DISCUSSION: Secs. 2053, 2054, and 2055 provide the allowable deductions from the gross estate. There is no provision allowing the deduction of a penalty incurred as the result of a late payment of the federal estate tax.
Answers (a), (b), and (d) are incorrect because each is an allowable deduction against a decedent's gross estate.

79. Which one of the following is a valid deduction from a decedent's gross estate?

a. Expenses of administering and settling the estate.
b. State inheritance tax.
c. Income tax paid on income earned and received after the decedent's death.
d. Federal estate tax.

The correct answer is (a). *(CPA 1190 Q-40)*
REQUIRED: The item which is a valid deduction from a decedent's gross estate.
DISCUSSION: Sec. 2053 allows deductions for funeral expenses, administration expenses, claims against the estate, and unpaid mortgages or other indebtedness related to property included in the gross estate. Thus, expenses of administering and settling the estate are a valid deduction from a decedent's gross estate.
Answer (b) is incorrect because there is no deduction for state inheritance taxes. Instead, there is a credit under Sec. 2011 for all state death taxes. Answers (c) and (d) are incorrect because there is no deduction for income tax paid on income earned and received after the decedent's death or for federal estate taxes.

Module 23.9: Deductions from the Gross Estate

80. B died in 1991. The state of residence was not a community property state. From the items listed below, what are the allowable deductions from the gross estate?

Funeral expenses	$ 3,500
Executor and administrative fees	5,000
Mortgage on jointly held property, one-half purchase price paid by B	70,000
Transfers of cash to B's spouse	60,000
Expense of filing estate's income tax return	500

a. $68,500.
b. $73,500.
c. $103,500.
d. $135,000.

The correct answer is (c). *(SPE 1078 III-85)*
REQUIRED: The amount of allowable deductions from the gross estate.
DISCUSSION: Under Sec. 2053, deductions from the gross estate are allowed for funeral expenses, administration expenses, and claims against the estate for unpaid mortgages on property in which the value of the decedent's interest is included in the value of the gross estate. Only one-half of the mortgage may be deducted because only one-half the value of the property is included in B's estate. Sec. 2056 allows a marital deduction from the gross estate for most transfers to a surviving spouse. There are no provisions allowing the expense of filing the estate's income tax return to be deducted against the gross estate. Such amount can be deducted on the estate's income tax return. The allowable deductions are computed as follows:

Funeral expenses	$ 3,500
Executor and administrative fees	5,000
Mortgage (1/2 of $70,000)	35,000
Cash to spouse	60,000
Allowable deductions	$103,500

81. Alan Curtis, a U.S. citizen, died on March 1, 1991 leaving an adjusted gross estate with a fair market value of $1,400,000 at the date of death. Under the terms of Alan's will, $375,000 was bequeathed outright to his widow. The remainder of Alan's estate was left to his mother. Alan made no taxable gifts during his lifetime. In computing the taxable estate, the executor of Alan's estate should claim a marital deduction of

a. $250,000.
b. $375,000.
c. $700,000.
d. $1,025,000.

The correct answer is (b). *(CPA 1187 Q-12)*
REQUIRED: The amount of the marital deduction.
DISCUSSION: A deduction from the gross estate is allowed for all property transferred in a qualified manner to the surviving spouse (Sec. 2056). Leaving it to the surviving spouse outright will qualify. Therefore, Alan's estate should claim a marital deduction of the entire $375,000 bequeathed to Alan's widow.

82. Medical expenses, if deducted only on the estate tax return, are fully deductible as administration expenses.

The correct answer is (T). *(SPE 1080 III-39)*
DISCUSSION: Sec. 2053 allows a deduction from the gross estate for claims against the estate. Medical expenses are deductible. Sec. 213(c) provides that medical expenses paid within 1 year of death may be deducted on either the estate tax return or the final income tax return of the decedent, but not on both returns.

83. Administration expenses and debts of the decedent are deductible in arriving at a taxable estate on Form 706 and on the estate's income tax return, Form 1041.

The correct answer is (F). *(SPE 1077 I-38)*
DISCUSSION: Administration expenses and debts of a decedent are deductible on the estate tax return under Sec. 2053 and some may also qualify as deductions for income tax purposes on the estate's income tax return. Sec. 642(g), however, disallows a double deduction and requires a waiver of the right to deduct them on Form 706 in order to claim them on Form 1041.

84. Mr. C died on December 25, 1991. According to Mr. C's will, all his property was transferred to his wife whom he had married on July 22, 1991. The property does not qualify for the estate tax marital deduction because Mr. C and his wife had not been married for one calendar year.

The correct answer is (F). *(SPE 986 III-36)*
DISCUSSION: Sec. 2056(a) allows a marital deduction for the value of any interest in property which passes from the decedent to the surviving spouse (which is not a terminable interest), but only to the extent that the interest is included in the gross estate. There is no requirement that the decedent be married for any set length of time.

23.10 Calculation of Estate Tax

85. All of the following credits are deducted from the gross estate tax to determine the net estate tax payable except

a. Credit for foreign death taxes.
b. Credit for state death taxes.
c. Credit for gift taxes.
d. Credit for the marital deduction.

The correct answer is (d). *(SPE 988 III-67)*
REQUIRED: The credit which is not deductible in the determination of the estate tax payable.
DISCUSSION: There is no credit for a marital deduction. Instead the marital deduction is deductible in arriving at the taxable estate. The estate tax is then computed on the taxable estate.
Answer (a) is incorrect because there is a credit for death taxes paid to foreign governments. Answer (b) is incorrect because there is a credit for death taxes paid to states. Answer (c) is incorrect because indirectly there is a credit for gift taxes. This is because the gross estate tax is computed on the taxable estate and all prior transfers. Subtracted from that is the amount of tax paid on prior transfers (gifts) based on current rates to arrive at the net estate tax.

86. Dinah Mite died in 1991 with a taxable estate of $2,000,000 and had made no taxable gifts during her lifetime. Her estate will pay a state death tax of $100,000. Her federal estate tax due is

a. $488,400.
b. $588,000.
c. $680,800.
d. $681,200.

The correct answer is (a). *(Publisher)*
REQUIRED: The federal estate tax payable after credits in 1991.
DISCUSSION: The estate tax is imposed in Sec. 2001. Sec. 2011(a) allows a credit for state death taxes paid; however, Sec. 2011(b) limits the amount of this credit in the case of a taxable estate of $2,000,000 to $99,600. For decedents dying in 1991, Sec. 2010 allows a unified credit of $192,800.

Tax on $2,000,000	$780,800
State death tax credit	(99,600)
Unified credit	(192,800)
Estate tax payable	$488,400

87. John died in 1991 with a taxable estate of $2,000,000 and adjusted taxable gifts of $1,000,000. During his life he used unified credits of $79,300. The unified credit that his estate will subtract from tentative estate tax due is

a. $17,000.
b. $79,300.
c. $113,500.
d. $192,800.

The correct answer is (d). *(Publisher)*
REQUIRED: The amount of unified credit available for the estate tax.
DISCUSSION: In the case of decedents dying in 1991, the unified credit allowed under Sec. 2010 is $192,800 [Sec. 2010(a)]. The unified credit against the estate tax is not reduced by the amount of unified credit used against the gift tax during life. There is not a double benefit; instead, the unified credit used for lifetime gifts is taken into account in the initial computation of the estate tax; i.e., tax on the sum of the taxable estate plus prior gifts, less gift taxes imposed at current rates.

88. Using the same facts as in the previous question, John paid gift taxes during his lifetime of $266,500. What is his estate tax due?

a. $831,500.
b. $1,024,300.
c. $1,098,000.
d. $1,290,800.

The correct answer is (a). *(Publisher)*
REQUIRED: The amount of estate tax payable after credits.
DISCUSSION: Sec. 2001 imposes a tax equal to the excess of a tentative tax (computed on the sum of the taxable estate and the adjusted taxable gifts) over the tax which would have been payable on gifts if the current rate schedule had been in effect at the time of the gifts [Sec. 2001(b)]. The tax rate schedules are in Sec. 2001(c).

Estate tax on $3,000,000		$1,290,800
Gift tax on $1,000,000	$345,800	
Unified gift credit	(79,300)	
		(266,500)
Tentative estate tax		$1,024,300
Unified credit		(192,800)
Estate tax payable		$831,500

89. Kary died in 1991 with a taxable estate of $3,500,000 and adjusted taxable gifts of $1,000,000. She used a unified credit of $62,800 during her life and paid gift taxes of $283,000. Kary lived in a state that assesses a state death tax of $342,400 on this estate. The tax due on Kary's estate is

a. $1,410,800.
b. $1,540,800.
c. $1,832,800.
d. $2,115,800.

The correct answer is (a). *(Publisher)*
REQUIRED: The tax due on the decedent's estate.
DISCUSSION: The tax due is equal to the tax imposed under Sec. 2001 reduced by allowable credits. The tax imposed under Sec. 2001(b) is equal to the excess of a tentative tax (computed on the sum of the taxable estate and the adjusted taxable gifts), over tax that would have been payable on gifts if the current rate schedule had been in effect at the time of the gifts [Sec. 2001(b)]. Sec. 2011(a) allows a credit for state death taxes paid; however, Sec. 2011(b) limits the amount of this credit in the case of a taxable estate of $3,500,000 to $229,200. For decedents dying in 1991, the unified credit against the estate tax is $192,800 (Sec. 2010).

Estate tax on $4,500,000	$2,115,800
Gift tax on $1,000,000	$345,800
Unified gift credit	(62,800)
	(283,000)
Tentative estate tax	$1,832,800
State death tax credit	(229,200)
Unified credit	(192,800)
Estate tax payable	$1,410,800

90. Alvin died in March 1989. Under the terms of his will, Alvin left $1,000,000 in assets to his brother Bill. Bill died in December 1991. The assets inherited from Alvin were included in Bill's taxable estate. The amount of federal estate tax paid by Alvin's estate that is attributable to these assets was $100,000. The amount of tax paid by Bill's estate attributable to these assets is $75,000. Bill's estate can claim a credit of $100,000 for tax on the prior transfer.

The correct answer is (F). *(SPE 990 III-27)*
DISCUSSION: Sec. 2013 allows a credit for taxes paid on prior transfers. The credit applies to a transfer of property by or from a person who died within 10 years before, or within 2 years after, the decedent's death. The credit serves to prevent an estate from being diminished by successive taxes on the same property within a brief period. The credit is subject to the limitations of Sec. 2013(c) and must be adjusted if the transferor predeceased the decedent by more than 2 years.
Under Sec. 2013(c), the credit is the lesser of (1) the estate tax paid by the transferor on the assets, or (2) the amount by which the transferred assets increase the decedent's estate tax. Since the amount by which the transferred assets increased Bill's estate tax ($75,000) is less than the amount of estate tax paid by Alvin attributable to the assets ($100,000), the credit is $75,000.
Because Alvin predeceased Bill by more than 2 years, this credit must be adjusted. Sec. 2013(a)(1) allows the decedent to claim 80% of the credit if the transferor died within the third or fourth years before the decedent's death. Therefore, the credit allowable to Bill's estate for tax on the prior transfer is $60,000 (80% x $75,000).

23.11 Estate Tax Payment and Returns

91. Which of the following rules does not apply to the filing of an estate tax return of a U.S. citizen?

a. Form 706 is the form that is used to file an estate tax return.
b. The return is due 9 months after the date of death unless an extension of time for filing has been granted.
c. The return is filed with the Internal Revenue Service Center for the state in which the decedent was domiciled.
d. For 1991, the value of the gross estate must be over $500,000.

The correct answer is (d). *(SPE 1085 III-62)*
REQUIRED: The rule not applicable for filing an estate tax return.
DISCUSSION: Sec. 6018 provides that an estate tax return must be filed when the gross estate of a decedent exceeds $600,000.
Answers (a), (b), and (c) are incorrect because each is a rule applicable to the filing of an estate tax return.

Module 23.11: Estate Tax Payment and Returns

92. If a citizen or resident of the United States dies during 1991, an estate tax return must be filed if the gross estate at the date of death was valued at more than:

   a. $500,000.
   b. $600,000.
   c. $750,000.
   d. $1,000,000.

The correct answer is (b). *(SPE 989 III-58)*
REQUIRED: The amount of the gross estate that requires filing an estate tax return.
DISCUSSION: Sec. 6018 provides that when the gross estate of a decedent exceeds $600,000, the personal representative must file an estate tax return.

93. Unless an extension of time to file is granted, an estate tax return, Form 706 is due:

   a. 3 months after the date of the decedent's death.
   b. 6 months after the date of the decedent's death.
   c. 9 months after the date of the decedent's death.
   d. 12 months after the date of the decedent's death.

The correct answer is (c). *(SPE 989 III-59)*
REQUIRED: The date on which the estate tax return is due.
DISCUSSION: Sec. 6075(a) provides that estate tax returns must be filed within 9 months after the date of the decedent's death.

94. Sec. 6166 contains provisions for extending the time for paying estate taxes when the estate consists largely of an interest in a closely held business. An interest in a closely held business does not include

   a. An interest in a sole proprietorship.
   b. An interest in a partnership carrying on a trade or business if 20% or more of the capital interest in such partnership is included in the gross estate or there are 15 or fewer partners.
   c. Stock in a corporation carrying on a trade or business if 20% or more in value of the voting stock of such corporation is included in the gross estate or there are 15 or fewer shareholders.
   d. Stock in an S corporation carrying on a trade or business if 15% or more in value of the voting stock of such corporation is included in the gross estate or there are 35 or fewer shareholders.

The correct answer is (d). *(E. Fenton)*
REQUIRED: The interest that is not an interest in a closely held business for extensions of time to pay estate taxes.
DISCUSSION: Under Sec. 6166, estates that include a substantial interest in a closely held business may be allowed to delay payments of a portion of the estate tax due if the interest exceeds 35% of the adjusted gross estate. Sec. 6166(b) defines an interest in a closely held business to include a corporation carrying on a trade or business if 20% or more in value of the voting stock of such corporation is included in the gross estate or there are 15 or fewer shareholders. There are no separate requirements for S corporations.
Answer (a) is incorrect because a sole proprietorship is included as a closely held business. Answer (b) is incorrect because an interest in a partnership is included as a closely held business if the partnership is carrying on a trade or business and if 20% or more of the capital interest in the partnership is included in the gross estate or there are 15 or fewer partners. Answer (c) is incorrect because a closely held business does include stock in a corporation carrying on a trade or business if 20% or more in value of the voting stock is included in the gross estate or there are 15 or fewer shareholders.

95. Extensions of time for filing the estate tax return and for paying the estate tax are permitted by law. Both extensions are requested by filing Form 4768 and, if granted, will be for no more than 6 months from the original due date for each.

The correct answer is (F). *(SPE 986 III-34)*
DISCUSSION: Under Sec. 6161(a)(1), the time for paying the estate tax may be extended by a reasonable period not to exceed 12 months. However, a satisfactory showing of undue hardship is required [Reg. 20.6161-1(b)]. The extension for filing the return is 6 months [Sec. 6081(a)].

96. An executor or administrator may be granted up to 6 months' additional time to file a United States Estate Tax Return.

The correct answer is (T). *(SPE 1082 III-38)*
DISCUSSION: An extension up to 6 months for filing any return may be granted under Sec. 6081(a).

97. In 1980, Mr. Grant, a United States citizen, made adjusted taxable gifts of $310,000. He died on March 15, 1991. At the time of his death, the fair market value of his assets were his home $200,000, car $10,000 and investments $250,000. None of Mr. Grant's gifts are included in his estate. Mr. Grant's executor is required to file Form 706, United States Estate Tax Return.

The correct answer is (T). *(SPE 990 III-26)*
DISCUSSION: The executor of an estate is required to file Form 706, United States Estate Tax Return, if the gross estate at the decedent's death exceeds $600,000. Adjusted taxable gifts made by the decedent during his/her lifetime are added to the estate. Therefore, the adjusted taxable gifts of $310,000 are added to the value of the assets (which total $460,000). The value of the estate exceeds the $600,000 threshold and the executor will be required to file an estate tax return.

98. The executor of James Bank's estate distributed the entire net estate to the beneficiaries before paying the estate's tax liability of $400. John Bank received $600 as a general bequest as his share of the estate. John could be assessed the entire $400 tax due.

The correct answer is (T). *(SPE 990 III-28)*
DISCUSSION: The executor of an estate is ultimately liable for the payment of estate taxes (Sec. 2002). However, the taxes are actually paid out of the estate property. Sec. 2205 provides that, if a part of the estate is distributed and the tax on that portion of the estate is paid out of other property, an equitable contribution of taxes is recoverable from the beneficiary to whom the property was distributed.

23.12 Generation-Skipping Transfers

99. Which of the following is subject to the generation-skipping transfer tax?

   a. Margaret wrote her will in 1985 establishing a generation-skipping trust. Her will was unchanged when she died in November 1986.
   b. Sam wrote his will in 1960 but amended it in 1985 to add a generation-skipping trust. Sam was mentally incompetent from January 1986 to his death in February 1989.
   c. Carol wrote a will in May 1986 which established a generation-skipping trust. She made no changes in her will before her June 1989 death.
   d. Carlisle established in 1983 a generation-skipping trust by gift for the benefit of her descendants. The irrevocable trust was unchanged and no corpus was added prior to her death in 1989.

The correct answer is (c). *(Publisher)*
REQUIRED: The trust subject to the generation-skipping transfer tax (GSTT).
DISCUSSION: Generally, the GSTT imposed by Sec. 2601 applies only to a generation-skipping transfer made after October 22, 1986. There are three exceptions: (1) The tax is not imposed on a generation-skipping transfer under a trust which was irrevocable on September 25, 1985, to the extent that the transfer is not made out of corpus added to the trust after September 25, 1985. (2) The tax is also not imposed on a transfer under a will executed before October 22, 1986 if the decedent dies before 1987. (3) The tax is not imposed on the generation-skipping transfer of a decedent who was mentally incompetent on October 22, 1986 and remains such so as not to be able to change the disposition before death. Since Carol died in 1989 and the corpus was placed in the trust at that time, none of the exceptions applies and her testamentary generation-skipping trust is subject to the GSTT.
Answer (a) is incorrect because the will was in existence on October 22, 1986, not amended after that date with respect to the generation-skipping transfer, and the decedent died before 1987. Answer (b) is incorrect because Sam was mentally incompetent on October 22, 1986 and remained so until his death. Answer (d) is incorrect because the irrevocable generation-skipping trust was in existence on September 25, 1985, it was not amended after that date, and no corpus was added after September 25, 1985.

Module 23.12: Generation-Skipping Transfers

100. Which of the following is a correct statement of the events which may trigger a generation-skipping transfer tax?

    a. A taxable termination only.
    b. A taxable distribution only.
    c. A taxable termination or a taxable distribution but not a direct skip.
    d. A taxable termination, a taxable distribution, or a direct skip.

The correct answer is (d). *(Publisher)*
REQUIRED: Identification of the event which may trigger a generation-skipping transfer tax.
DISCUSSION: A generation-skipping transfer is defined as a taxable termination, a taxable distribution, or a direct skip [Sec. 2611(a)]. A taxable termination is a termination (by death, lapse of time, release of power, or otherwise) of an interest in property held in trust unless immediately after the termination a non-skip person has an interest in the property or if at no time after the termination may a distribution be made to a skip person [Sec. 2612(a)]. A taxable distribution means any distribution from a trust to a skip person if it is not a taxable termination or a direct skip [Sec. 2612(b)]. A direct skip is a transfer subject to the estate tax or the gift tax of an interest in property to a skip person. A skip person is a natural person assigned to a generation which is two or more generations below the generation assignment of the transferor or a trust where all interests are held by skip persons [Sec. 2613(a)].

101. Thomas (age 63) established a trust and named his second wife Theresa (age 50) as income beneficiary for 20 years. After 20 years, Thomas's son Trevor (age 40) and nephew Bob (age 25) are to receive lifetime income interests. After the death of both Trevor and Bob, the remainder passes equally to Thomas's granddaughter Sara (age 20) and great-granddaughter Hope (age 1). How many younger generations are there in this trust arrangement?

    a. 4.
    b. 3.
    c. 2.
    d. 1.

The correct answer is (b). *(Publisher)*
REQUIRED: The number of younger generations in the trust arrangement.
DISCUSSION: Younger generations refer to generations younger than the transferor's generation. An individual who is a lineal descendant of a grandparent of the grantor is assigned to that generation which results from comparing the number of generations between the grandparent and such individual with the number of generations between the grandparent and the transferor [Sec. 2651(b)(1)]. An individual who has been married to the transferor is assigned to the transferor's generation [Sec. 2651(c)(1)].
Since Theresa is married to the transferor, she is assigned to the same generation as Thomas. Trevor and Bob are assigned to one generation below the transferor's generation. Sara is assigned to two generations below the transferor's generation. Hope is assigned to three generations below the transferor's generation.

102. In the previous question, assume Trevor died 22 years after the trust was established and Bob died 34 years after the trust was established. Assuming both Sara and Hope were alive when Bob died, how many times is the generation-skipping transfer tax levied?

    a. Never.
    b. Once.
    c. Twice.
    d. Three times.

The correct answer is (b). *(Publisher)*
REQUIRED: The number of times the generation-skipping transfer tax is levied.
DISCUSSION: The generation-skipping transfer tax (GSTT) is imposed on generation-skipping transfers which are any taxable distributions or terminations with respect to a generation-skipping trust or direct skips [Sec. 2611(a)]. A taxable termination means the termination of an interest held in trust unless (1) immediately after the termination a non-skip person has an interest in the trust, or (2) at no time after the termination may a distribution be made to a skip person [Sec. 2612(a)(1)]. A skip person is a natural person assigned to a generation which is two or more generations below the transferor or a trust all interests of which are held by skip persons. A non-skip person is any person who is not a skip person [Sec. 2613(b)].
Trevor and Bob are one generation below the transferor and are non-skip persons. There is no taxable termination on Trevor's death since Bob, a non-skip person, has an interest in the trust. Both Sara and Hope are skip persons, so there is a taxable termination on Bob's death.

103. Which of the following statements about the generation-skipping transfer tax (GSTT) is false?

a. Distributions to a beneficiary from a generation-skipping trust trigger the GSTT even if they are made out of current income.

b. A termination of an interest held in trust by a non-skip person does not trigger application of the GSTT if someone who is not a skip person continues to have an interest in the property.

c. The grantor's own child and his sister's child will be considered to be the same generation no matter what their relative ages are.

d. Congress exempted transfers of up to $2,000,000 for the grandchild of the grantor from application of the GSTT for direct transfers after December 31, 1989.

The correct answer is (d). *(Publisher)*
REQUIRED: The false statement concerning the generation-skipping transfer tax.
DISCUSSION: Answer (d) is false because a transfer to a grandchild after December 31, 1989 is considered to be a direct skip and subject to the GSTT. The special exemption from the GSTT for direct skips was applicable only for direct transfers to a grandchild on or before December 31, 1989 if the aggregate transfers to the grandchild did not exceed $2,000,000.
Answer (a) is incorrect because generation-skipping distributions from a trust are subject to tax whether the distributions are from trust income or corpus [Sec. 2612(b)]. However, an income tax deduction is available for the GSTT on the distribution of income [Sec. 164(a)]. Answer (b) is incorrect because a taxable termination does not occur if immediately after the termination, a non-skip person has an interest in the property. A skip person is a natural person assigned to a generation two or more generations below the transferor; a non-skip person is anyone who is not a skip person. Answer (c) is incorrect because a lineal descendant of a grandparent of the transferor is assigned to that generation which results from comparing the number of generations between the grandparent and such individual with the number of generations between the grandparent and the transferor, regardless of age.

104. N.Y. Life, age 55 years exactly, wants to provide for the financial security of her secretary, Sue, and other unrelated friends. She establishes a trust. Sue, age 65, will receive income from the trust for her life. On Sue's death, Sam, another friend who is currently 51, will receive income for his lifetime. Upon his death, the remainder interest will be divided equally between Kevin (age 39) and Stan (age 43). How many times will this trust be subject to a GSTT?

a. None. No GSTT will be assessed.

b. One.

c. Two.

d. Three.

The correct answer is (a). *(Publisher)*
REQUIRED: The number of times a GSTT will be assessed under the trust arrangement.
DISCUSSION: A taxable termination is a termination of an interest in property held in trust unless immediately after the termination a non-skip person has an interest in the property, or at no time after the termination may a distribution be made to a skip person. An individual is a skip person if (s)he is assigned to a generation which is two or more generations below the generation assignment of the transferor. An individual who is not a lineal descendant (or married to a lineal descendant) of a grandparent of the transferor is assigned to a generation based on the date of such individual's birth. An individual born not more than 12½ years after the transferor is assigned to the transferor's generation; an individual born 12½ to 37½ years after the transferor is assigned to the first generation younger than the transferor [Sec. 2651(d)].
Since Sue is older than the transferor, she is not a younger generation beneficiary. Since Sam and Stan were both born within 12½ years of the transferor's birth, they are assigned to the same generation as the transferor and are not younger generation beneficiaries. Since Kevin was born more than 12½ years but not more than 37½ years after the date of the birth of the transferor, he is assigned to the first generation younger than the transferor and is the only younger generation beneficiary under this trust.
No one with an interest at any time in the trust is two or more generations younger than Sue, so no one is a skip person. With no skip person, there is no taxable termination, and no generation-skipping transfer tax is due.

105. The transferor's child and the transferor's nephew are in different younger generations if their ages are more than 25½ years apart.

The correct answer is (F). *(Publisher)*
DISCUSSION: Since the transferor's child and nephew are both lineal descendants of a grandparent of the transferor, they are assigned to that generation which results from comparing the number of generations between the transferor's grandparent and themselves with the number of generations between the grandparent of the transferor and the transferor [Sec. 2651(b)(1)]. Since the number of generations between the transferor's child and the transferor's grandparent, and the transferor's nephew and the transferor's grandparent, is always the same, the transferor's child and nephew will always be assigned to the same generation.

106. Kay has an interest in a generation-skipping trust if she has only a future right to receive income or corpus from the trust.

The correct answer is (F). *(Publisher)*
DISCUSSION: An interest in a trust exists if a person has a present (not future) right to receive income or corpus from the trust, or is a permissible recipient of such income or corpus [Sec. 2652(c)].

107. Interests in a generation-skipping trust can pass between beneficiaries of the same generation without triggering the generation-skipping transfer tax.

The correct answer is (T). *(Publisher)*
DISCUSSION: There must be a taxable distribution, termination, or direct skip for the tax to apply. A transfer is not a generation-skipping transfer if (1) the property transferred has already been taxed under the GSTT, (2) the transferee of that prior transfer was the same (or lower) generation as the transferee for the current event, and (3) the transfers do not have the effect of avoiding tax. While interpretation of the third requirement is uncertain, requirements (1) and (2) could apply to the transfer from one skip person (Individual A) to another skip person (Individual B) of the same generation.

23.13 Taxable Amount and Taxpayer Identification

108. Which of the following is a true statement about the taxable amount of a generation-skipping transfer?

a. The taxable amount for a direct skip and a taxable termination are the same.
b. The taxable amount for a taxable termination is the value of the property received by the transferee reduced by expenses incurred by the transferee in connection with the determination, collection, or refund of the GSTT.
c. The taxable amount for a taxable distribution is the value of all property distributed less allowable expenses, debt, and taxes.
d. If a generation-skipping transfer tax on a taxable distribution is paid by the generation-skipping trust, an amount equal to the taxes paid by the trust will be treated as a taxable distribution.

The correct answer is (d). *(Publisher)*
REQUIRED: The correct statement about the taxable amount of a generation-skipping transfer.
DISCUSSION: Under Sec. 2603, the transferee is liable for the GSTT on a taxable distribution. Therefore, if the GSTT on a taxable distribution is paid by the trust, the transferee is deemed to have received an additional taxable distribution equal to the amount of taxes paid by the trust [Sec. 2621(b)].
Answer (a) is incorrect because the taxable amount of a direct skip is the amount received by the transferee before taxes (Sec. 2623) but the taxable amount of a taxable termination (Sec. 2622) is the value of all property with respect to which the termination occurred reduced by deductions similar to those deductible against a gross estate under Sec. 2053 (taxes, debt, certain expenses). Answer (b) is incorrect because it describes the taxable amount of a taxable distribution (Sec. 2621) but not a taxable termination. Answer (c) is incorrect because the taxable amount of a taxable distribution is the value of property received by the transferee less any expense incurred by the transferee in connection with the determination, collection, or refund of the GSTT.

109. When Sam died, his property was placed in trust with his son David and David's daughter Carole eligible to receive principal and income in the trustee's discretion. When the property was placed in trust its value was $5,000,000 and the GST exemption was not allocated to this trust. Carole received a distribution of $8,000,000 when the trust's value totaled $10,000,000. The appraisal to value trust assets cost $40,000 and was paid by the trust. What is the taxable amount of the generation-skipping transfer and who is responsible for the tax payment?

	Taxable Amount	Taxpayer
a.	$7,960,000	Trust
b.	$5,040,000	David
c.	$7,960,000	Carole
d.	$8,000,000	David

The correct answer is (c). *(Publisher)*
REQUIRED: The taxable amount and identification of the taxpayer of a taxable distribution.
DISCUSSION: This is a taxable distribution because it is a distribution to a skip person (Carole) and a nonskip person (David) still has an interest in the trust. The amount of a taxable distribution is the value of property received by the transferee minus costs of determination, collection, and refund of the GSTT paid by the transferee (Sec. 2621). Since the trust paid the cost of appraisal, only $7,960,000 in assets remained to pass to Carole. The value of assets received by Carole is not further reduced since she incurred no additional costs associated with payment of the GSTT.
Carole is responsible for the tax payment as the transferee of a taxable distribution [Sec. 2603(a)(1)].

110. A generation-skipping transfer does not include a termination of a trust created by Sheila with income to her son and a remainder interest to her granddaughter if her son has power over the trust which will cause the trust assets to be taxed in the son's estate.

The correct answer is (T). *(Publisher)*
DISCUSSION: The transfer of property from the trust created by Sheila to her son and granddaughter is not a generation-skipping transfer. Whenever trust property is subject to the gift tax or the estate tax, the donor or decedent that is taxed becomes the new transferor of the property for purposes of the GSTT [Sec. 2652(a)(1)]. Because Sheila's son must include the trust assets in his estate upon his death as a result of the power which he holds over the trust, Sheila's son is considered the transferor for the income and remainder interests which are transferred. Any property that is transferred from the trust to the granddaughter is only transferred to the first generation below Sheila's son and is therefore not a generation-skipping transfer.

111. Tracy's will established a trust for his grandchildren solely to pay college tuition for the grandchildren. The distributions to pay the college tuition are generation-skipping transfers.

The correct answer is (F). *(Publisher)*
DISCUSSION: A transfer which would not be a taxable gift if made inter vivos because of the exclusion for payment of medical expenses or tuition is not a generation-skipping transfer [Sec. 2611(b)(1)]. Tracy's payment of a grandchild's tuition would not be a taxable gift so the trust distribution to pay the tuition is not subject to the GSTT.

23.14 Calculation of Generation-Skipping Transfer Tax

112. Which of the following statements about the generation-skipping transfer exemption is false?

a. An individual (or his/her executor) can allocate a $1,000,000 exemption to property with respect to which (s)he is the transferor.

b. All appreciation which occurs to property covered by the allocation of the $1,000,000 exemption is also covered by the exemption up to a limit of $5,000,000.

c. If a married couple elect gift-splitting for a transfer, the transferred property may be allocated a GSTT exemption of up to $2,000,000.

d. The GST exemption may be allocated to an inter vivos transfer on a timely filed gift tax return or later statement of allocation filed with the IRS.

The correct answer is (b). *(Publisher)*
REQUIRED: The false statement about the generation-skipping transfer exemption of $1,000,000.
DISCUSSION: If all or part of the $1,000,000 exemption is allocated to trust property, all appreciation which occurs after the allocation to the property covered by the exemption is also exempt from the GSTT. There is no $5,000,000 limit.
Answers (a), (c), and (d) are incorrect because each is a true statement about the GST $1,000,000 exemption [Secs. 2631(a), 2632(a), and 2642].

113. In 1990, Jim's will established a trust for his son, Kevin, and grandsons. In 1991, a taxable termination occurred when Kevin died and trust assets were distributed to grandsons, Mark and John. Jim's executor allocated his $1,000,000 exemption to the trust which had a value of $4,500,000 at that time. When the taxable termination occurred in 1991, trust assets had a value of $8,500,000. State death taxes attributable to trust property were $500,000. What is the inclusion ratio used to calculate the GSTT?

a. 1/8.
b. 1/4.
c. 3/4.
d. 7/8.

The correct answer is (c). *(Publisher)*
REQUIRED: The inclusion ratio for a generation-skipping transfer with an exemption and death taxes.
DISCUSSION: The inclusion ratio multiplied by the maximum federal estate tax rate determines the tax rate for a generation-skipping transfer. The inclusion ratio is 1 minus a fraction whose numerator is the GST exemption allocated to the trust and whose denominator is generally the value of the property transferred into the trust reduced by the sum of (1) federal estate taxes or state death taxes attributable to the property and paid by the trust and (2) charitable deductions with respect to the trust property [Sec. 2642(a)]. The inclusion ratio in this case is

$$1 - \frac{\$1,000,000}{\$4,500,000 - \$500,000} = 3/4$$

114. What is the generation-skipping transfer tax due on the taxable termination described in the question above?

a. $1,650,000.
b. $1,856,250.
c. $3,300,000.
d. $3,506,250.

The correct answer is (d). *(Publisher)*
REQUIRED: The calculation of the generation-skipping transfer tax on a taxable termination.
DISCUSSION: The generation-skipping transfer tax is the product of the taxable amount times the applicable rate (Sec. 2602). The applicable rate is the maximum federal estate tax rate for the date of the taxable termination, taxable distribution, or direct skip (55% for 1991) times the inclusion ratio (3/4 from Q. 113) (Sec. 2641). The taxable amount of a taxable termination is the value of all property with respect to which the taxable termination has occurred ($8,500,000) reduced by expenses, deductions, and taxes which would be allowable under Sec. 2053 if this were an estate. State death taxes are not allowable deductions under Sec. 2053(c)(1)(B), so the taxable amount is $8,500,000. The generation-skipping transfer tax is $3,506,250 ($8,500,000 x 55% x 3/4), and the tax will be paid by the trustee from trust assets.

115. Pearl gave $5,000,000 in securities to her granddaughter Ruby in 1991. Pearl, a widow, had never made any gift to Ruby prior to the 1991 transfer. Pearl allocated $500,000 of her GST exemption to this direct skip. What is the generation-skipping transfer tax amount and who must pay it?

	Tax	Payor
a.	$2,475,000	Pearl
b.	$2,475,000	Ruby
c.	$2,750,000	Pearl
d.	$2,750,000	Ruby

The correct answer is (a). *(Publisher)*
REQUIRED: The calculation of the generation-skipping transfer tax on a direct skip in 1991.
DISCUSSION: The GSTT is the product of the taxable amount of the transfer times the applicable rate (Sec. 2602). The applicable rate is the maximum federal estate tax rate for the date of the direct skip (55% for 1991) times the inclusion ratio (Sec. 2641). The taxable amount of the transfer is $5,000,000. The inclusion ratio is one minus the fraction whose numerator is the GST exemption allocated to the property transferred, and whose denominator is the value of the transfer involved in the direct skip reduced by federal estate tax, state death taxes, and charitable deductions related to the property. The inclusion ratio in this case is:

$$1 - \frac{\$500,000}{\$5,000,000} = .90$$

The generation-skipping transfer tax is the product of the taxable amount (i.e., amount transferred times the inclusion ratio) times the applicable rate (Sec. 2602). The applicable rate is the maximum federal estate tax rate for decedents dying on the date of the direct skip (55% for 1991). The tax on this transfer is $2,475,000 ($5,000,000 x 55% x .90). The transferor, Pearl, is liable for the tax on the direct skip (Sec. 2603).

CHAPTER TWENTY-FOUR
PREPARER RULES AND PRACTICE BEFORE THE IRS

	Tax Return Preparer Rules		
24.1	Coverage of Tax Return Preparer Rules	(4 questions)	695
24.2	Identification of Tax Return Preparers	(14 questions)	696
24.3	Activities of Tax Return Preparers	(5 questions)	699
24.4	Required Copies of Returns	(5 questions)	699
24.5	Signature, Identification, and Reporting Requirements	(12 questions)	700
24.6	Penalties on Tax Return Preparers	(23 questions)	702
	Practice Before the IRS		
24.7	Eligibility for Enrollment	(6 questions)	707
24.8	Enrollment Process	(7 questions)	708
24.9	Renewal of Enrollment - CPE	(7 questions)	709
24.10	Conduct of an Enrolled Agent	(22 questions)	711
24.11	Suspension and Disbarment	(24 questions)	715
24.12	Practice Before the IRS by Persons Without Enrollment	(13 questions)	719

24.1 Coverage of Tax Return Preparer Rules

1. Preparers of which of the following returns are not covered by the preparer rules?

  a. Individual income tax.
  b. Corporate income tax.
  c. Fiduciary income tax.
  d. Estate tax.

The correct answer is (d). *(SPE 1078 IV-79)*
REQUIRED: The type of return for which preparers are not covered by the rules instituted by the Tax Reform Act of 1976.
DISCUSSION: Sec. 7701(a)(36) defines an income tax return preparer as any person who prepares or employs persons to prepare for compensation any return of tax or claim for refund under Subtitle A. Subtitle A of the Internal Revenue Code includes income taxes on all entities. The estate tax falls within Subtitle B, and preparers of such returns are not covered by the tax return preparer rules.
  Answers (a), (b), and (c) are incorrect because each is a tax covered by Subtitle A of the Internal Revenue Code, and preparers of returns for these taxes are subject to the preparer rules.

2. Which one of the following types of returns is not covered by the preparer rules?

  a. Gift tax returns.
  b. Partnership returns.
  c. DISC returns.
  d. S corporation returns.

The correct answer is (a). *(SPE 1081 IV-82)*
REQUIRED: The type of return which is not covered by preparer rules.
DISCUSSION: Sec. 7701(a)(36) defines a tax return preparer as any person who prepares or employs persons to prepare for compensation any tax return or claim for refund under Subtitle A. Gift taxes are imposed by Subtitle B, and preparers of gift tax returns are not covered by preparer rules.
  Answers (b), (c), and (d) are incorrect because each is a return for a tax imposed by Subtitle A, and preparers of each are covered by the preparer rules.

3. All of the following tax returns are covered by the preparer penalty provisions of the Internal Revenue Code except

a. An individual income tax return (Form 1040).
b. A partnership return (Form 1065).
c. A corporation tax return (Form 1120).
d. An excise tax return (Form 720).

The correct answer is (d). *(SPE 987 IV-71)*
REQUIRED: The type of return which is not covered by preparer rules.
DISCUSSION: Sec. 7701(a)(36) defines a tax return preparer as any person who prepares or employs persons to prepare for compensation any tax return or claim for refund under Subtitle A. The rules governing excise taxes are found within Subtitles D and E, and the preparers of excise tax returns are not covered by the preparer rules.
Answers (a), (b), and (c) are incorrect because each is a return for a tax imposed by Subtitle A, and the preparers of such returns are subject to the preparer rules.

4. Preparers of information returns, Forms 1099, are not covered by the preparer rules.

The correct answer is (T). *(SPE 1078 IV-23)*
DISCUSSION: Return preparers are those who prepare or employ others to prepare for compensation returns for tax imposed by Subtitle A [Sec. 7701(a)(36)]. Since information returns are required by Subtitle F, they are not covered by the preparer rules.

24.2 Identification of Tax Return Preparers

5. Which of the following is an income tax return preparer as defined in the regulations relating to return preparers?

a. Mr. A engages a number of persons to prepare income tax returns on a commission basis, but does not himself prepare returns.
b. Mr. B, controller of Corporation X, prepares and files X's corporate tax return.
c. Mr. C owns and operates a payroll service. Service provided clients includes the preparation of all employment tax returns.
d. Mr. D, an attorney, regularly advises clients in arranging future business transactions to minimize income tax.

The correct answer is (a). *(SPE 1085 IV-67)*
REQUIRED: The income tax return preparer as defined in the regulations.
DISCUSSION: Under Sec. 7701(a)(36), an income tax return preparer is any person who prepares for compensation or employs others to prepare for compensation any income tax return or claim for refund under Subtitle A.
Answer (b) is incorrect because Sec. 7701(a)(36)(B)(ii) provides that a person who prepares a return for the employer by whom (s)he is regularly and continuously employed is not considered an income tax return preparer. Answer (c) is incorrect because employment tax returns are not considered income tax returns. Answer (d) is incorrect because advising clients on specific issues of law with respect to the consequences of contemplated actions (rather than events that have already occurred) does not constitute income tax return preparation.

6. All of the following are income tax return preparers except

a. A person who prepares a substantial portion of the return for a fee.
b. A person who prepares a claim for a refund for a fee.
c. A person who gives an opinion about theoretical events that haven't occurred.
d. A person who prepares a United States return for a fee outside the United States.

The correct answer is (c). *(SPE 987 IV-67)*
REQUIRED: The person who is not an income tax return preparer.
DISCUSSION: Under Sec. 7701(a)(36), an income tax return preparer is any person who prepares for compensation or employs others to prepare for compensation any income tax return or claim for refund under Subtitle A. A person who gives an opinion about events that have not happened is not a tax return preparer.
Answers (a), (b), and (d) all represent tax return preparers under the regulations.

7. The duties in the preparation of Corporation XYZ's income tax return were assigned and completed as follows:

Joe — obtained the necessary information, applied the tax law to the information, and performed the necessary calculations.

Sue — Joe's supervisor, reviews Joe's work. In her review, Sue reviews the information provided and the application of the tax laws.

Company A — A computer tax service which takes the information provided by Sue, verifies the mathematical accuracy and prints the return form.

Pat — A partner in the firm where Joe and Sue work. Pat reviews the return, the information provided, and applies this information to XYZ's affairs. Pat also verifies that the partnership's policies have been followed and makes the final determination.

Who is the preparer of XYZ's return and therefore required to sign it?

a. Joe.
b. Sue.
c. Company A.
d. Pat.

The correct answer is (d). *(SPE 989 IV-68)*
REQUIRED: The preparer of the tax return.
DISCUSSION: Sec. 7701(a)(36)(A) defines an income tax return preparer as any person who prepares for compensation, or who employs one or more persons to prepare for compensation, any income tax return or claim for refund of income tax under Subtitle A. Reg. 1.6695-7(b)(2) states that if more than one income tax return preparer is involved in the preparation of a return or a claim for refund, the individual preparer who has the primary responsibility as between or among the preparers for the overall substantive accuracy of the preparation of the return or claim is considered to be the income tax return preparer for purposes of determining who is required to sign the return. Because Pat makes the final determination regarding the return, she is considered to be the preparer and is required to sign the return.

Answers (a) and (b) are incorrect because neither Joe nor Sue has primary responsibility for the overall substantive accuracy of the return. Answer (c) is incorrect because a person or company furnishing typing, reproducing, or other mechanical assistance is not an income tax return preparer [Sec. 7701(a)(36)(B)(i)].

8. An income tax return preparer is any person who prepares all or a substantial portion of any return of tax or of any claim for refund of tax, under Subtitle A of the Internal Revenue Code.

The correct answer is (F). *(SPE 1083 IV-30)*
DISCUSSION: Sec. 7701(a)(36) specifically provides that income tax return preparers are those who prepare income tax returns or claims for refund of income taxes for compensation under Subtitle A. If not compensated, a person is not an income tax return preparer. Also, a person who prepares returns for his/her regular employer or a fiduciary who prepares a return or claim for refund for his/her trust is not considered an income tax return preparer.

9. Completion of a single schedule of a tax return will be considered a "substantial portion" if that schedule is the dominant portion of the entire tax return.

The correct answer is (T). *(SPE 1079 IV-5)*
DISCUSSION: Under Reg. 301.7701-15(b)(1), whether a schedule of a return is a substantial portion is determined by comparing the length and complexity of that portion to the return as a whole. A schedule which is the dominant portion of an entire tax return will usually be considered a substantial portion of the tax return.

10. A person who prepares only a portion of a return will not be considered a preparer if that portion involves gross income, deductions, or the basis for determining tax credits of

1. Under $2,000 or
2. Under $100,000 and less than 20% of gross income (or 20% of adjusted gross income on an individual return) of the return as a whole.

The correct answer is (T). *(SPE 1078 IV-24)*
DISCUSSION: Reg. 301.7701-15(b)(2) provides that a schedule or portion of a return is not considered a substantial portion if it involves gross income, deductions, or amounts on the basis of which credits are determined which are (1) less than $2,000, or (2) less than $100,000 and also less than 20% of the gross income (or adjusted gross income if an individual) as shown on the return.

11. The preparer of a Form 1065, U.S. Partnership Return of Income, can be considered the preparer of a partner's individual income tax return if the entries on the partnership return that are reportable on the partner's return constitute a substantial portion of the partner's return.

The correct answer is (T). *(SPE 1082 IV-28)*
DISCUSSION: Under Reg. 301.7701-15(b)(3), a preparer of one return is not considered a preparer of another return just because entries affect the other return, unless the entries (e.g., on a partnership return) are directly reflected on the other return (e.g., a partner's return) and constitute a substantial portion of the other return.

12. Mr. C, a certified public accountant, prepared a claim for refund which resulted from an examination by the Internal Revenue Service. Mr. C is considered a tax return preparer.

The correct answer is (F). *(SPE 1080 IV-44)*
DISCUSSION: Under Sec. 7701(a)(36)(B)(iv), a person is not considered an income tax return preparer if the preparation of a claim for refund is in response to a notice of deficiency issued by the IRS.

13. Mr. P, employed in the accounting department of Partnership T, prepares the partnership's income tax return. Mr. P is not considered a return preparer.

The correct answer is (T). *(SPE 1080 IV-47)*
DISCUSSION: Under Sec. 7701(a)(36)(B)(ii), a person who prepares a return or claim for refund of the employer by whom (s)he is regularly and continuously employed is not considered an income tax return preparer. Since P is an employee of the partnership, he is not considered a return preparer.

14. Anyone who prepares a return or claim for a refund as a fiduciary is not covered by the preparer rules.

The correct answer (T). *(SPE 1081 IV-26)*
DISCUSSION: Sec. 7701(a)(36)(B)(iii) provides that a person is not considered a tax return preparer merely because (s)he prepares a return or claim for refund as a fiduciary.

15. A person who is compensated for preparing a relative's claim for refund is not covered by the preparer rules.

The correct answer is (F). *(SPE 1079 IV-2)*
DISCUSSION: The preparer rules apply to any person who prepares for compensation any return of tax or claim for refund of tax imposed by Subtitle A. If this definition is met, the person is considered a return preparer regardless of his/her relationship with the taxpayer.

16. B is a college student working his way through school. During the tax season, he is paid to prepare his friends' tax returns. B was paid $250. B is not an income tax preparer.

The correct answer is (F). *(SPE 1083 IV-31)*
DISCUSSION: Sec. 7701(a)(36) defines an income tax return preparer as any person who prepares for compensation any return of tax or any claim for refund of tax imposed by Subtitle A.

17. A person who prepares a return or claim for refund for a taxpayer with no explicit or implicit agreement for compensation is not a preparer, even though the person receives a gift, return service, or favor.

The correct answer is (T). *(SPE 984 IV-30)*
DISCUSSION: Reg. 301.7701-15(a)(4) provides that a person must prepare a return or claim for refund for compensation to be an income tax return preparer. A person who prepares a return with no explicit or implicit agreement for compensation is not a preparer, even if (s)he receives a gift, return service, or favor.

18. A person shall not be an income tax return preparer merely because a person furnishes typing, reproducing, or other mechanical assistance.

The correct answer is (T). *(SPE 1077 IV-55)*
DISCUSSION: Sec. 7701(a)(36)(B)(i) provides that a person is not considered an income tax return preparer merely because (s)he furnishes typing, reproducing, or mechanical assistance.

24.3 Activities of Tax Return Preparers

19. When preparing a return involving a deduction for travel and entertainment expenses, the return preparer must make reasonable inquiries to determine that the taxpayer's records are adequate to substantiate the deduction.

The correct answer is (T). *(SPE 1082 IV-34)*
DISCUSSION: Reg. 1.6694-1(b)(2)(ii) provides that a return preparer should make appropriate inquiries of the taxpayer to determine the existence of facts and circumstances required by a Code section or regulations incidental to claiming a deduction. This applies to adequate documentation for travel and entertainment expenses and other deductions, even if the amount is minimal.

20. Generally, in preparing a return, the preparer may in good faith rely without verification upon information furnished by the taxpayer and need not make reasonable inquiries if the information as furnished appears to be incorrect or incomplete.

The correct answer is (F). *(SPE 986 IV-20)*
DISCUSSION: Reg. 1.6694-1(b)(2)(ii) requires a return preparer to make reasonable inquiries if the information as furnished appears incorrect or incomplete. The preparer may not ignore the implications of information furnished.

21. Mr. A, a partner in an accounting firm, discovers that one of his clients omitted a substantial amount of gross income. Mr. A should immediately notify his partners and the Internal Revenue Service.

The correct answer is (F). *(SPE 1080 IV-21)*
DISCUSSION: Unless the understatement of gross income was done willfully or recklessly or was the result of a position that did not have a realistic possibility of being sustained on its merits, Mr. A will not be liable for a penalty (Sec. 6694). When a taxpayer's liability has been understated, there is no requirement that the tax return preparer notify the IRS.

22. Ms. A, an enrolled agent, prepared and signed as the preparer Mr. B's 1990 income tax return. Mr. B's refund check was properly mailed to Ms. A. Ms. A may endorse and cash Mr. B's refund check.

The correct answer is (F). *(SPE 984 IV-40)*
DISCUSSION: Sec. 6695(f) provides that any tax return preparer who endorses or otherwise negotiates a check issued to a taxpayer (other than the preparer) will be penalized $500 with respect to each such check.

23. If, in good faith, a preparer reasonably takes the position that a revenue ruling does not accurately reflect the Internal Revenue Code, the preparation of a return by the preparer in conflict with the revenue ruling does not result in an understatement that is due to the taking of an unrealistic position.

The correct answer is (T). *(SPE 986 IV-16)*
DISCUSSION: Under Sec. 6694(a), a preparer who takes a position contrary to a rule or regulation is not guilty of taking an unrealistic position if there was a realistic possibility of the position being sustained on its merits.

24.4 Required Copies of Returns

24. An income tax return preparer must furnish a completed copy of the original return to the taxpayer not later than the time the original return is presented for the signature of the taxpayer.

The correct answer is (T). *(SPE 984 IV-36)*
DISCUSSION: Sec. 6107(a) requires all income tax return preparers to furnish a completed copy of the return to the taxpayer not later than the time such return or claim for refund is presented for the taxpayer's signature.

25. An income tax return preparer does not have to furnish a completed copy of the original return to the taxpayer provided a copy of the return is retained by the preparer.

The correct answer is (F). *(SPE 990 IV-17)*
DISCUSSION: Under Sec. 6107(a), any income tax return preparer with respect to any return or claim for refund must furnish a completed copy of the return or claim to the taxpayer no later than the time such return or claim is presented for the taxpayer's signature.

26. An income tax return preparer who fails to furnish a copy of the return or claim for refund to the taxpayer shall be subject to a $50 penalty for the failure unless it is shown that the failure is due to reasonable cause and not due to willful neglect.

The correct answer is (T). *(SPE 988 IV-21)*
DISCUSSION: For documents prepared in 1990 and later years, Sec. 6695(a) provides that an income tax return preparer with respect to any return or claim for refund who fails to furnish a copy of the return to the taxpayer when the return is presented for the taxpayer's signature must pay a penalty of $50, unless the failure is due to reasonable cause and not willful neglect.

27. A tax return preparer is required to retain and keep available for a 3-year period a copy of any return prepared or retain a record of the name, taxpayer identification number, and taxable year of the taxpayer (or nontaxable entity) for whom the return was prepared, and the type of return prepared.

The correct answer is (T). *(SPE 990 IV-19)*
DISCUSSION: Sec. 6107(b) requires an income tax return preparer to retain a completed copy of each return or claim prepared, or a list of the names and taxpayer identification numbers of the taxpayers for whom such returns or claims were prepared. Under Reg. 1.6107-1(b)(1)(ii), the list must include the taxable year of the taxpayer and the type of return or claim for refund prepared. This copy or list must be retained by the income tax return preparer for 3 years after the close of the return period.

28. An income tax return preparer can satisfy the regulation requiring the preparer to retain a copy or record of each return prepared by retaining a photocopy of only the completed first page of each return prepared.

The correct answer is (T). *(SPE 987 IV-21)*
DISCUSSION: The tax return preparer is required to keep either a copy of the return or some record with includes the name, taxpayer identification number, taxable year, and type of return or claim for refund filed [Reg. Sec. 1.6107-1(b)(1)]. The first page of the return includes the required information.

24.5 Signature, Identification, and Reporting Requirements

29. Mr. K employs X, Y, and Z to prepare income tax returns for taxpayers. X and Y collect the information from taxpayers and apply the tax laws. The return forms are completed by a computer service. One day, when certain returns prepared by X and Y were ready for their signatures, X was out of town for 2 weeks and Y was out of the office for the day. Which one of the following statements is correct?

   a. Z may sign the returns prepared by X and Y, if Z reviews the information obtained by X and Y from the taxpayers and reviews the preparation of the returns.

   b. Z may sign the returns prepared by X, if Z reviews the information obtained by X from the taxpayers and reviews the preparation of the returns.

   c. Z may sign the returns prepared by Y if he reviews the information obtained by Y from the taxpayers and reviews the preparation of the returns.

   d. X and Y must sign the returns that each one prepared.

The correct answer is (b). *(SPE 990 IV-62)*
REQUIRED: The correct statement about who may sign an income tax return.
DISCUSSION: Reg. 1.6695-1(b)(1) requires an individual who is an income tax return preparer to manually sign the return after it has been completed and before it is presented to the taxpayer. If the preparer is unavailable for signature, another preparer must review the entire preparation of the return and then must manually sign the return. Z may sign the returns prepared by X, provided that Z reviews the information obtained by X relative to the taxpayer and Z reviews the preparation of each return prepared by X. Z may not sign the returns prepared by Y because Y is considered to be available.

Module 24.5: Signature, Identification, and Reporting Requirements

30. Preparers are required to sign all the returns they prepare and show their identification numbers.

The correct answer is (T). *(SPE 1079 IV-6)*
DISCUSSION: Reg. 1.6695-1(b) requires each individual income tax preparer to manually sign each return or claim for refund after it is completed and before it is presented to the taxpayer for signature. Under Sec. 6109(a)(4), any return or claim for refund filed with the IRS prepared by an income tax return preparer must include his/her identifying number.

31. The requirement that a preparer manually sign a return after it is completed and before it is presented to the taxpayer may be satisfied by a photocopy of the copy of the return which the preparer manually signed. However, the preparer is required to retain the manually signed copy of the return.

The correct answer is (T). *(SPE 988 IV-22)*
DISCUSSION: Reg. 1.6695-1(b)(4)(i) provides that the manual signature requirement may be satisfied by a photocopy of the copy of the return or claim for refund which was manually signed by the preparer. The manually signed copy of the return must be retained by the preparer.

32. A preparer is required to enter an identification number on the taxpayer's copy of the return.

The correct answer is (F). *(SPE 1080 IV-54)*
DISCUSSION: An income tax return preparer is not required to sign or affix an identification number to the taxpayer's copy of a federal income tax return (Rev. Rul. 78-317).

33. An enrolled agent will not meet the requirement of the regulations relating to tax return preparers for furnishing the preparer's identifying number on tax returns they are required to sign by entering his or her enrolled agents identifying number.

The correct answer is (T). *(SPE 988 IV-23)*
DISCUSSION: An income tax return preparer required by Reg. 1.6695-1(b) to sign the return or claim for refund must also include his/her identifying number. Reg. 301.6109-1 provides that the identifying number of an individual is his/her Social Security number.

34. Mr. V is a partner in DAV Tax Service, and is responsible for the overall substantive accuracy of all income tax returns prepared by subordinates. Mr. V neither gathers the necessary information nor prepares the income tax forms. Mr. V is considered to be the preparer and should sign the returns as the preparer.

The correct answer is (T). *(SPE 990 IV-18)*
DISCUSSION: Reg. 1.6695-1(b)(2) states that, if more than one income tax return preparer is involved in the preparation of a return or claim for refund, the preparer who has primary responsibility for the overall accuracy of the preparation of such return or claim is required to manually sign the return.

35. L, an accounting firm, employs R and S to prepare income tax returns for taxpayers. R collected the information from the taxpayers and applied the tax laws to the information. The return forms are completed by a computer service company. On the day the returns prepared by R are ready for his signature, which is several days prior to their due date, R is visiting another office in the city for the day. If S reviews the information obtained by R from the taxpayers and reviews the preparation of the returns, she may sign the returns prepared by R.

The correct answer is (F). *(SPE 1083 IV-37)*
DISCUSSION: Reg. 1.6695-1(b)(1) provides that if the preparer is unavailable for signature, another preparer shall review the entire preparation of the return or claim for refund, and then shall manually sign the return or claim for refund. But since R is only out of the office for the day and several days remain before the due date of the returns, R is not considered unavailable. Therefore, S may not sign the returns.

36. N, a taxpayer, employs A, a law firm, to prepare his income tax return. A assigns T, an employee, to prepare N's tax return. T obtains the necessary information to complete the return and makes determinations with respect to the proper application of the tax laws. The information is then forwarded to E, a computer tax service which performs the mathematical computations and prints out the tax return. The completed tax return is then returned to T, who reviews the accuracy of the return. T must sign the return as preparer.

The correct answer is (T). *(SPE 986 IV-19)*
DISCUSSION: Reg. 1.6695-1(b)(1) provides that an income tax return preparer shall manually sign the return after it is completed and before it is presented to the taxpayer for signature. If more than one income tax preparer (e.g., the law firm) is involved in preparing the return, the individual preparer (e.g., T) who has primary responsibility for the overall accuracy of the return is considered the preparer for this purpose. The computer service is not a preparer because it only provides mechanical assistance.

37. Preparers employed by others or partners in partnerships must enter their Social Security numbers on tax returns. Furnishing the identification number of the employer or partnership is optional.

The correct answer is (F). *(SPE 989 IV-24)*
DISCUSSION: Under Reg. 1.6109-2(a), an income tax return preparer must include his/her identifying number. If there is a partnership or employment arrangement between two or more preparers, the identifying number of the partnership or employer must also be included.

38. If the preparer is an employee of a firm, corporation, or another individual, then that preparer must sign the return and enter his/her name, identification number, and home address.

The correct answer is (F). *(SPE 1077 IV-48)*
DISCUSSION: Regs. 1.6109-2 and 1.6695-1(b) provide that a return must be signed by the preparer and must bear the identifying number of the preparer required to sign. If there is a partnership or employment arrangement, the identifying number of the partnership or the employer must also appear on the return or claim. But the address which must be included is that of the preparer's place of business where the return or claim was prepared, not the preparer's personal address.

39. Returns mechanically completed by a computer facility that the preparer does not control may be filed with an attestation manually signed by the preparer when the return information is submitted to the computer facility. The attestation must be attached to the return when filed.

The correct answer is (T). *(SPE 1080 IV-55)*
DISCUSSION: Reg. 1.6695-1(b)(4)(ii) provides that if a return is mechanically completed by computer not under the control of the individual preparer, the manual signature requirement may be satisfied by a manually signed attestation by the preparer attached to the return.

40. Each person who employs or engages one or more income tax return preparers to prepare returns other than for that person must retain a record of the name, taxpayer identification number, and principal place of work of each preparer employed. That record must be available for inspection upon request by the district director of the Internal Revenue Service.

The correct answer is (T). *(SPE 990 IV-20)*
DISCUSSION: A person who employs one or more income tax return preparers to prepare a return or claim for refund must make a return setting forth the name, identifying number, and place of work of each income tax return preparer employed by him/her. Sec. 6060(b) allows the IRS to approve an alternative method of reporting.
Reg. 1.6060-1 states that the requirements of Sec. 6060 are satisfied by retaining a record of the name, identifying number, and principal place of work of each income tax return preparer employed, and making that record available for inspection upon request by the district director for the 3-year period following the close of the return period to which that record relates.

24.6 Penalties on Tax Return Preparers

41. John is an income tax return preparer. He prepares a tax return for a client and takes a position that he knows does not have a realistic possibility of being sustained on its merits. He does not disclose this position on the tax return. The position John takes causes the client's tax liability to be substantially understated. John is subject to a penalty of

   a. $50.
   b. $100.
   c. $250.
   d. $1,000.

The correct answer is (c). *(Publisher)*
REQUIRED: The penalty for understatements due to unrealistic positions.
DISCUSSION: Sec. 6694(a) provides for a penalty of $250 to be assessed against a tax return preparer who takes an unrealistic position with regard to a tax matter that produces an understatement of tax liability. The penalty is applicable if the return preparer knew, or reasonably should have known, that there was not a realistic possibility of the position being sustained on its merits and the position was not disclosed or was frivolous. The preparer may be relieved of the penalty if it can be shown that there is reasonable cause for the understatement and that the preparer acted in good faith.

Module 24.6: Penalties on Tax Return Preparers

42. A penalty may be assessed against an income tax return preparer who takes an unrealistic position that causes an understatement of liability on a return. For purposes of assessing the penalty, "understatement of liability" means

a. Any understatement of tax liability greater than $100.

b. Any understatement of the tax liability or overstatement of the amount to be refunded or credited.

c. Any understatement that exceeds 10% of the tax liability shown on the return.

d. Any overstatement of the amount refundable that exceeds 10% of the amount refundable shown on the claim for refund.

The correct answer is (b). *(Publisher)*
REQUIRED: The correct meaning of "understatement of liability."
DISCUSSION: Sec. 6694(e) defines "understatement of liability" for purposes of assessing penalties against return preparers as any understatement of the net amount of tax payable under Subtitle A or any overstatement of the net amount creditable or refundable under Subtitle A. Under Sec. 6694(d), penalties will not be assessed against tax return preparers unless there has been an understatement of liability.

43. Ralph is an income tax return preparer. He obtains an important new client by implying that the returns he prepares always generate refunds. While preparing the client's return, Ralph learns that the client owes a substantial amount of tax. In order to produce a refund for the client, Ralph intentionally disregards rules and regulations. Ralph is subject to a penalty of

a. $100.
b. $250.
c. $500.
d. $1,000.

The correct answer is (d). *(Publisher)*
REQUIRED: The penalty for willful or reckless conduct by a return preparer.
DISCUSSION: Sec. 6694(b) provides for a penalty of $1,000 to be assessed against a return preparer whose willful or reckless conduct in preparing a tax return causes an understatement of liability. The penalty is applied if the understatement is due to either a willful attempt to understate the tax liability or to any reckless or intentional disregard of rules or regulations by the return preparer. The penalty is assessed against each return containing an understatement of liability caused by the return preparer's willful or reckless conduct.

44. Which of the following statements about a tax return preparer's willful understatement of a tax liability is not correct?

a. A tax return preparer is considered to have willfully attempted to understate liability if the preparer disregards information furnished by the taxpayer and it results in an understatement of the taxpayer's tax liability.

b. Willful understatement of a taxpayer's tax liability by a tax return preparer will always result in a $1,000 penalty being imposed.

c. A tax return preparer may rely in good faith upon information provided by a tax return preparer without obtaining verification.

d. The willful understatement penalty is imposed upon a tax return preparer only when an understatement of the taxpayer's liability occurs.

The correct answer is (b). *(Publisher)*
REQUIRED: The false statement relating to the willful understatement penalty.
DISCUSSION: The $1,000 willful understatement penalty is not imposed in all situations involving a willful attempt to understate a taxpayer's tax liability. For example, Sec. 6694(d) permits abatement of the return preparer's penalty when it is established in final administrative determination or final judicial decision that the taxpayer's liability was not understated on his return or refund claim even though willful understatement on the part of the tax return preparer may have occurred (e.g., a willful overstatement of deductions that results in an underpayment is more than offset by a failure to exclude income that results in a larger overpayment).
Answer (a) is incorrect because a preparer is considered to have willfully attempted to understate the liability if (s)he disregards information furnished by the taxpayer or other persons and it results in an understatement of the taxpayer's tax liability [Reg. 1.6694-1(b)(2)(i)]. Answer (c) is incorrect because a tax return preparer can in good faith rely upon information furnished by the taxpayer without having to obtain third-party verification [Reg. 1.6694-1(b)(2)]. The tax return preparer, however, may not ignore the implications of information furnished by the taxpayer. Answer (d) is incorrect because the willful understatement is only imposed when an understatement of a tax liability occurs [Reg. 1.6694-1(b)(1)].

Module 24.6: Penalties on Tax Return Preparers

45. Scott is an income tax return preparer. While preparing a return for a client, he knowingly takes an unrealistic position that he does not disclose. He also intentionally disregards rules and regulations. The position Scott takes causes an understatement of the client's liability. With regard to the penalties that may be assessed against Scott, which of the following statements is true?

   a. Only the penalty for understatement of liability due to unrealistic positions may be assessed against Scott.
   b. Only the penalty for willful or reckless conduct may be assessed against Scott.
   c. Scott must pay both the penalty for understatement of liability due to an unrealistic position and the penalty for willful or reckless conduct.
   d. Scott is liable for both penalties, but the penalty for willful or reckless conduct will be reduced by the amount of the penalty for understatement due to unrealistic positions.

The correct answer is (d). *(Publisher)*
REQUIRED: The correct statement regarding penalties that may be assessed against a return preparer who takes an unrealistic position and who also engages in willful or reckless conduct.
DISCUSSION: Sec. 6694(a) provides a penalty of $250 to be assessed against a return preparer who takes an unrealistic position that causes an understatement of liability. The penalty is applicable if the preparer knew, or reasonably should have known, that the position was unrealistic and the preparer did not disclose the position, or if the position was frivolous. Sec. 6694(b) assesses a $1,000 penalty against a return preparer whose willful or reckless conduct causes an understatement of liability. The penalty is applicable if the understatement of liability is due to the preparer's willful attempt to understate the tax liability or his/her reckless or intentional disregard of rules or regulations. Sec. 6694(b) also states that the $1,000 penalty is to be reduced by the $250 penalty assessed under Sec. 6694(a) if the preparer is subject to both. Thus, a preparer who is subject to both the penalty for understatement due to unrealistic positions and the penalty for willful or reckless conduct will pay a total penalty of $1,000.

46. After a statement of notice and demand is made for an assessed preparer penalty, a return preparer must either pay the entire assessment or pay 15% or more of the assessment and file a claim for refund. If the preparer chooses the latter, then the claim for refund must be filed within how many days?

   a. 30.
   b. 60.
   c. 90.
   d. 120.

The correct answer is (a). *(SPE 990 IV-61)*
REQUIRED: The number of days within which a claim for refund must be filed.
DISCUSSION: A tax return preparer who has received a statement of notice and demand for an assessed preparer penalty may either pay the entire assessment or pay at least 15% of the assessment and file a claim for refund. Under Sec. 6694(c), a tax return preparer who chooses to pay at least 15% of the assessment and file a claim for refund must file the claim within 30 days after the day on which the notice and demand for payment of the penalty is made.

47. Robert, a tax return preparer, intentionally disregards regulations in preparing a return for a client. As a consequence, the tax liability shown on the return is understated. The client is subsequently audited by the Internal Revenue Service and the penalty for willful or reckless conduct is assessed against Robert. Robert's client appeals the IRS's audit determination. An appeals officer determines that the client did not take several allowable deductions. These deductions eliminate the understatement produced by Robert's intentional disregard of regulations. Which of the following statements concerning the penalty assessed against Robert is true?

   a. Robert is still liable for the penalty.
   b. The penalty will be reduced in proportion to the reduction in the tax liability.
   c. The penalty will be abated and any amount Robert may have paid will be refunded.
   d. Robert may pay 15% of the penalty and bring an action in the United States District Court for determination of his liability for the penalty.

The correct answer is (c). *(Publisher)*
REQUIRED: The correct statement concerning the penalty assessed against a tax return preparer.
DISCUSSION: Sec. 6694(d) states that the penalty for understatements due to unrealistic positions or the penalty for willful or reckless conduct will be abated if a final administrative determination or a final judicial decision is made that there was no understatement of liability. If the return preparer has paid any part of the penalty, the payment will be refunded. "Understatement of liability" means any understatement of the net amount of tax payable under Subtitle A.

Module 24.6: Penalties on Tax Return Preparers

48. In which of the following situations will the preparer be liable for the $50 penalty for failure to provide a copy of the return to the taxpayer?

   a. Failure was due to reasonable cause.
   b. Failed to provide copy of claim for refund that he or she prepared.
   c. Failed to provide copy of return that he or she is preparer of solely by giving advice on specific issues of law.
   d. Failed to provide copy of return that he or she is preparer of solely because of having prepared another return which affects amounts reported on the return.

The correct answer is (b). *(SPE 989 IV-67)*
REQUIRED: The situation in which a return preparer will be liable for the penalty for failure to provide a copy of the return to the taxpayer.
DISCUSSION: Sec. 6107(a) requires an income tax return preparer to furnish a completed copy of the return or the claim for refund to the taxpayer. Under Sec. 6695(a), any income tax return preparer who fails to provide a copy of the return or the claim for refund is subject to a $50 penalty unless the failure is due to reasonable cause and not due to willful neglect. Sec. 7701(a)(36)(A) defines an income tax return preparer as any person who prepares for compensation, or who employs one or more persons to prepare for compensation, any income tax return or claim for refund of income taxes. Reg. 301.7701-15(a)(2) states that a person who only gives advice on specific issues is generally not considered to be an income tax return preparer. Reg. 301.7701-15(b)(3) states that a preparer of one return is not considered to be a preparer of another return merely because an entry or entries reported on the return may affect any entry reported on the other return.

49. An income tax return preparer shall pay a penalty of $50 for each return or claim for refund that (s)he prepares that lacks his/her signature unless it is shown that such failure is due to reasonable cause.

The correct answer is (T). *(SPE 1077 IV-50)*
DISCUSSION: Sec. 6695(b) provides that, unless the failure of an income tax return preparer to sign a return is due to reasonable cause, (s)he will be penalized $50 for each such failure.

50. Preparers who fail to properly sign the returns they prepared, or who do not furnish the required tax preparer identification numbers, may be fined $50 for each improper signature and an additional $50 for each identification number omitted.

The correct answer is (T). *(SPE 1078 IV-30)*
DISCUSSION: Sec. 6695(b) provides a penalty of $50 for the failure of an income tax return preparer to sign the returns prepared. Sec. 6695(c) also provides a penalty of $50 for each failure of an income tax return preparer to provide his/her identifying number.

51. The penalty for a preparer who fails to retain a copy or record of income tax returns and claims for refunds under Internal Revenue Code Sec. 6695(d), is $25 for each failure up to a maximum of $25,000 for a single return period.

The correct answer is (F). *(SPE 989 IV-25)*
DISCUSSION: Sec. 6107(b) requires an income tax return preparer to retain a completed copy of the return or claim for refund for 3 years after the close of the return period. Sec. 6695(d) imposes a penalty of $50 for each failure to retain a completed copy of the return or claim for refund for the required period, unless it is shown that the failure is due to reasonable cause and not due to willful neglect. The maximum penalty imposed on any preparer is limited to a maximum of $25,000 for a single return period.

52. The penalty for understatements due to unrealistic positions cannot be asserted unless there is an understatement of tax liability.

The correct answer is (T). *(Publisher)*
DISCUSSION: Sec. 6694(a) provides for a penalty of $250 when an understatement of liability is due to an unrealistic position by the income tax return preparer. Sec. 6694(d) provides for the penalty to be abated if a final determination shows no understatement.

53. An income tax return preparer who causes the tax liability on a return to be understated by intentionally disregarding rules or regulations is subject to a penalty of $500 for each such return, up to a maximum of $25,000 for a return period.

The correct answer is (F). *(Publisher)*
DISCUSSION: Under Sec. 6694(b), if any part of any understatement of liability is due to the reckless or intentional disregard of rules and regulations by a person who is an income tax return preparer, the preparer is liable for a penalty of $1,000 with respect to the return. There is no maximum penalty.

54. A return preparer who is subject to both the penalty for understatement due to unrealistic positions and the penalty for willful or reckless conduct must pay a total penalty of $1,000.

The correct answer is (T). *(Publisher)*
DISCUSSION: Under Sec. 6694(a), the penalty for understatements due to unrealistic positions is $250. Sec. 6694(b) provides a penalty of $1,000 for willful or reckless conduct that results in an understatement of liability. Sec. 6694(b) further states that, if a person is subject to both penalties, the $1,000 penalty for willful or reckless conduct must be reduced by the $250 penalty imposed for understatements due to unrealistic positions. Thus, an income tax return preparer subject to both penalties will pay a total penalty of $1,000.

55. An income tax return preparer who knowingly takes an unrealistic position that causes an understatement of liability is liable for the penalty for understatements due to unrealistic positions whether or not there was a reasonable cause for the understatement and the preparer acted in good faith.

The correct answer is (F). *(Publisher)*
DISCUSSION: Under Sec. 6694(a), an income tax return preparer who knowingly takes an unrealistic position that causes an understatement of liability is subject to a penalty of $250 unless it is shown that there is reasonable cause for the understatement and the preparer acted in good faith.

56. There is no limitation period for assessing the penalty against an income tax return preparer for willful or reckless conduct that results in an understatement of liability.

The correct answer is (T). *(Publisher)*
DISCUSSION: There is no limitation period for assessing the penalty against an income tax return preparer for willful or reckless conduct that results in an understatement of liability [Sec. 6696(d)]. There is a 3-year limitation period to assess the penalty for understatements due to unrealistic positions under Sec. 6694(b), or any of the procedural penalties under Sec. 6695.

57. A preparer's employer may also be liable for the penalty for willful or reckless conduct if the employer participated in the violation.

The correct answer is (T). *(Publisher)*
DISCUSSION: Reg. 1.6694-1(b)(1) states that an employer or partnership of a preparer subject to the penalty for willful understatement of liability is not also liable for the penalty unless the employer or partnership (or one of its officers or general partners) participated in the willful attempt to understate the liability. Sec. 6694(b) provides a penalty for willful or reckless conduct. Willful attempt to understate liability is one aspect of willful or reckless conduct [Sec. 6694(b)(1)].

58. No more than one preparer may be subject to the penalty for willful or reckless conduct on the same tax return.

The correct answer is (F). *(Publisher)*
DISCUSSION: Reg. 1.6694-1(b)(1) provides that if an understatement of tax liability is due to a willful attempt by one or more income tax return preparers, each such preparer will be subject to a separate penalty. Proposed Reg. 1.6694-1(b)(1) holds for documents prepared and advice given after December 31, 1991 that no more than one individual associated with a firm (e.g., as a partner or employee) is treated as a preparer with respect to a return or refund claim.

59. When the Internal Revenue Service assesses the return preparer a negligence penalty under Internal Revenue Code Sec. 6694, the preparer may, within 30 days, pay 15% of the penalty and file a claim for refund for the amount paid. If the claim is then denied, the preparer has 60 days to bring suit in the district court to determine the liability for the penalty.

The correct answer is (F). *(SPE 989 IV-23)*
DISCUSSION: If a claim for refund filed by an income tax return preparer who has paid 15% of the assessed penalty is denied, the preparer has 30 days to bring suit in the district court to determine the liability for the penalty [Sec. 6694(c)(2)].

60. If a District Court finds that an income tax return preparer has continually or repeatedly engaged in guaranteeing the payment of tax refunds to his/her client-taxpayers, the court may enjoin such person from acting as an income tax return preparer.

The correct answer is (T). *(SPE 1077 IV-53)*
DISCUSSION: Sec. 7407(b) states that if a court finds that an income tax return preparer has (1) negligently or intentionally disregarded rules or regulations, or willfully understated tax liability, (2) misrepresented his/her eligibility to practice before the IRS, (3) guaranteed a tax refund or the allowance of a tax credit, or (4) engaged in other fraudulent or deceptive conduct which substantially interferes with the administration of the Internal Revenue Laws, the court may enjoin such person from further engaging in such conduct. If the court finds that the preparer has continually or repeatedly engaged in such action, the court may enjoin the person from acting as an income tax return preparer.

61. The $250 penalty for understatement of the taxpayer's tax liability due to an unrealistic position being taken can be abated if the tax return preparer adequately discloses the relevant facts concerning the position in the return or in a statement attached to the return.

The correct answer is (T). *(Publisher)*
DISCUSSION: Three requirements must be satisfied for the Sec. 6694 understatement penalty to be imposed. They are: (1) part of the understatement is due to a position for which there was not a realistic possibility of being sustained on its merits, (2) any person who is an income tax preparer with respect to such return or claim knew (or reasonably should have known) of such position, and (3) such position was not disclosed as provided in Sec. 6662(d)(2)(B)(ii) or was frivolous. Sec. 6662(d)(2)(B)(ii) requires that the relevant facts affecting the item's tax treatment be adequately disclosed in the return or in a statement attached to the return. Making the required disclosure, therefore, should eliminate the penalty.

62. Mr. Q, a tax return preparer, was assessed a negligence penalty relating to his preparation of Mr. P's 1989 tax return. Mr. Q paid the penalty immediately. Mr. P's examination was resolved 4 years later at the appeals level of the Internal Revenue Service with the tax liability being accepted as originally filed. Mr. Q's assessed negligence penalty will be abated without consideration of any period of limitations.

The correct answer is (T). *(SPE 984 IV-34)*
DISCUSSION: Sec. 6694(d) provides that, if at any time there is a final administrative determination or final judicial decision that there was no understatement of liability after a penalty for negligence has been assessed, such assessment shall be abated. If any portion of such penalty was paid, the amount paid shall be refunded without regard to any period of limitations.

63. An income tax return preparer, other than a preparer-bank, that collects return preparation fees by endorsing and cashing income tax refund checks for clients and withholding the amount of the fee will be subject to a $500 penalty for each check negotiated in this manner.

The correct answer is (T). *(SPE 988 IV-26)*
DISCUSSION: Sec. 6695(f) provides that any income tax return preparer who endorses or otherwise negotiates any check made in respect of income taxes that is issued to a taxpayer will be subject to a penalty of $500 with respect to each such check. This does not apply to the deposit by a bank in the taxpayer's account.

24.7 Eligibility for Enrollment

64. Enrollment to practice may be granted only to natural persons who are citizens of the United States.

The correct answer is (F). *(SPE 1078 IV-8)*
DISCUSSION: The rules relating to practice before the Internal Revenue Service are set forth in Treasury Department Circular No. 230 (31 CFR Subtitle A Part 10). Under Sec. 10.4(c), enrollment to practice may be granted only to natural persons, but there is no requirement of citizenship.

65. The enrollment of any agent is terminated if the enrolled agent becomes eligible to practice before the Internal Revenue Service as an attorney or certified public accountant under the regulations set forth in Treasury Department Circular No. 230.

The correct answer is (T). *(SPE 1085 IV-5)*
DISCUSSION: Circular No. 230, Sec. 10.4(d), provides that enrollment is not available for persons who qualify to practice as attorneys or CPAs. They are automatically entitled to practice before the IRS.

66. The word attorney, as it relates to practice before the Internal Revenue Service, means any individual who has completed law school and received his or her degree.

The correct answer is (F). *(SPE 1079 IV-33)*
DISCUSSION: As it relates to practice before the Internal Revenue Service, "attorney" means any person who is a member in good standing of the bar of the highest court of any state, possession, territory, commonwealth, or the District of Columbia [Sec. 10.2(b) of Circular No. 230].

67. The two conditions which must be met before CPAs or attorneys may practice before the IRS are that they must not be under disbarment or suspension and they must have prepared the tax return which is being examined.

The correct answer is (F). *(SPE 1078 IV-2)*
DISCUSSION: Sec. 10.3 of Circular No. 230 provides that attorneys and CPAs may practice before the IRS if they are not currently under suspension or disbarment and if they file a written declaration that they are currently qualified and have been authorized to represent the party on whose behalf they are acting. Attorneys and CPAs need not have prepared the tax return which is being examined.

68. Certified public accountants must file written declarations that they are currently qualified and have been authorized to represent the party on whose behalf they are acting each time they represent a different client.

The correct answer is (T). *(SPE 1079 IV-32)*
DISCUSSION: Sec. 10.3 of Circular No. 230 requires attorneys and CPAs to file a written declaration that they are currently qualified and are authorized to represent the particular party on whose behalf they are acting each time they represent a different client.

69. An employee of a state whose duties require him/her to investigate state tax matters may not practice before the Internal Revenue Service if his/her employment might disclose information applicable to federal tax matters.

The correct answer is (T). *(SPE 1083 IV-2)*
DISCUSSION: Sec. 10.3(g) of Circular No. 230 provides that no state employee whose duties require him/her to pass upon, investigate, or deal with tax matters of such state may practice before the IRS if such employment may disclose information applicable to federal tax matters.

24.8 Enrollment Process

70. Mr. A has been a self-employed tax practitioner all his working life. Which one of the following conditions must be met for Mr. A to be eligible for enrollment?

a. Over 21 years of age and a U.S. citizen.
b. Pass a written examination and have creditable conduct.
c. Pass a written examination and be a U.S. citizen.
d. Pass a written examination and be over 21 years of age.

The correct answer is (b). *(SPE 1078 IV-78)*
REQUIRED: The conditions that must be met for a self-employed tax practitioner to be eligible for enrollment.
DISCUSSION: Sec. 10.4(a) of Circular No. 230 provides that enrollment may be granted to an applicant who passes a written examination and who has not engaged in any conduct which would justify the suspension or disbarment of an enrolled agent.
Answers (a), (c), and (d) are incorrect because there is no longer a requirement of age or citizenship to be eligible for enrollment.

71. Enrollment may be granted to a former Internal Revenue Service employee who, by virtue of his or her past service and technical experience in the Internal Revenue Service, qualifies for such enrollment without taking a written test.

The correct answer is (T). *(SPE 1079 IV-38)*
DISCUSSION: Sec. 10.4(b) of Circular No. 230 provides that the Commissioner may grant enrollment to an applicant who by virtue of his/her past service and technical experience in the Internal Revenue Service has qualified for such enrollment. To determine whether an applicant qualifies, the scope and extent of employment, length of employment, and recommendation of the superior officer in the division that such employment took place are all considered.

72. An enrolled agent meets the conference and practice requirements for filing a written declaration that he or she is currently qualified to represent taxpayers before the Service by annually filing a written statement to that effect in the Service's district headquarters office for the geographical area in which the enrolled agent practices.

The correct answer is (F). *(SPE 987 IV-28)*
DISCUSSION: Sec. 10.3(c) of Circular No. 230 provides that any person enrolled as an agent may practice before the Internal Revenue Service. There is no requirement that an enrolled agent file a written declaration.

73. An applicant for enrollment could have to submit to an oral examination under oath if so determined by the Commissioner.

The correct answer is (T). *(SPE 1080 IV-12)*
DISCUSSION: Sec. 10.5(b) of Circular No. 230 provides that, as a condition to consideration of an application for enrollment, the Commissioner may require the applicant to file additional information and to submit to any written or oral examination under oath or otherwise.

74. Upon receipt of a properly executed application for enrollment to practice before the Internal Revenue Service, the Director of Practice may grant an applicant temporary recognition to practice pending a determination as to whether enrollment to practice should be granted.

The correct answer is (T). *(SPE 989 IV-3)*
DISCUSSION: Sec. 10.5(c) of Circular No. 230 allows the Commissioner to grant an applicant temporary recognition to practice pending a determination as to whether enrollment to practice should be granted. Such temporary recognition is only granted if the application is properly executed and is regular on its face.

75. Issuance of temporary recognition allows an applicant for enrollment to practice before the Internal Revenue Service but it does not constitute enrollment to practice or a finding of eligibility for enrollment.

The correct answer is (T). *(SPE 984 IV-5)*
DISCUSSION: Although an applicant for enrollment may be granted temporary recognition to practice before the IRS, Sec. 10.5(c) of Circular No. 230 specifically provides that this shall not constitute enrollment to practice or a finding of eligibility. The temporary recognition may be withdrawn at any time.

76. An individual whose application for enrollment has been denied by the Director of Practice has 90 days after receipt of the decision in which to appeal to the Secretary of the Treasury.

The correct answer is (F). *(SPE 989 IV-4)*
DISCUSSION: The Director of Practice approves or denies enrollment applications. If denied an application for enrollment, the applicant may file a written appeal to the Secretary of the Treasury within 30 days after receipt of the notice of denial. A decision on the appeal will be rendered by the Secretary of the Treasury as soon as practicable [Sec. 10.5(d) of Circular No. 230].

24.9 Renewal of Enrollment - CPE

77. When would an enrollment card issued on May 15, 1991 terminate?

- a. June 1, 1992.
- b. February 1, 1993.
- c. April 1, 1993.
- d. May 16, 1994.

The correct answer is (c). *(SPE 990 IV-89)*
REQUIRED: The date of termination of an enrollment card issued on May 15, 1991.
DISCUSSION: Sec. 10.6(b) of Treasury Department Circular No. 230 states that the Director of Practice will issue an enrollment card to each individual whose application for enrollment to practice before the Internal Revenue Service is approved. Sec. 10.6(d)(2) states that for enrollment cards issued after April 1, 1990, the effective date of renewed enrollment is April 1, 1993. Thus, an enrollment card issued on May 15, 1991, will terminate on April 1, 1993.

78. All of the following statements concerning continuing professional education (CPE) requirements for enrolled agents are true except:

   a. (S)he must complete a minimum of 48 hours of CPE credit if enrolled for the entire enrollment cycle.
   b. (S)he must complete a minimum of 16 hours of CPE credit in each year of an enrollment cycle if enrolled for the entire cycle.
   c. An individual who receives initial enrollment during an enrollment cycle must complete 2 hours of CPE credit for each month enrolled.
   d. The Director of Practice may grant a waiver from the CPE requirements for a given period if there is a compelling reason and the request for waiver is appropriately documented.

The correct answer is (a). *(SPE 990 IV-90)*
REQUIRED: The false statement about continuing professional education requirements for enrolled agents.
DISCUSSION: The requirements for continuing professional education for enrolled agents are found in Sec. 10.6 of Treasury Department Circular No. 230. For renewed enrollment effective April 1, 1990 and every third year thereafter, Sec. 10.6(e)(2)(ii) states that a minimum of 16 hours of continuing education credit must be completed in each year of an enrollment cycle. Sec. 10.6(e)(2)(i) states that a minimum of 72 hours of continuing education credit must be completed during each 3-year enrollment cycle.
Answers (b), (c), and (d) are true statements concerning continuing professional education requirements for enrolled agents.

79. An individual who becomes enrolled to practice before the Internal Revenue Service in 1991 must meet certain continuing professional education requirements and apply for renewal of enrollment by January 31, 1993 in order to maintain active enrollment status.

The correct answer is (T). *(SPE 990 IV-54)*
DISCUSSION: Applications for renewal are required between November 1, 1992 and January 31, 1993 to maintain active enrollment status [Circular 230, Sec. 10.6(d)]. In order to qualify for renewal, 72 hours of CPE are normally required during the 3-year enrollment cycle. If initial enrollment is during an enrollment cycle (such as during 1991 or 1992), then 2 hours of CPE is required for each month enrolled during the enrollment cycle [Circular No. 230, Sec. 10.6(e)].

80. For an enrolled agent to maintain active status, (s)he is required to have his/her enrollment renewed in accordance with Treasury Department Circular No. 230. However, if an enrolled agent does not receive notification of the renewal requirement from the Director of Practice, such agent will be relieved of the requirement.

The correct answer is (F). *(SPE 989 IV-62)*
DISCUSSION: Sec. 10.6(d) of Circular No. 230 states that an individual enrolled to practice before the IRS is required to have his/her enrollment renewed as set forth in Circular 230 in order to maintain active enrollment. Failure by such individual to receive notification from the Director of Practice of the renewal requirement is not justification for circumvention of such requirement.

81. An enrolled agent meets the conference and practice and Circular 230 requirements for filing a written declaration that (s)he is currently qualified to represent taxpayers before the Service by annually filing a written statement to that effect in the Service's district headquarters office for the geographical area in which the enrolled agent practices.

The correct answer is (F). *(SPE 989 IV-30)*
DISCUSSION: Sec. 601.502(b) CFR states that an enrolled agent may not appear in a representative capacity on behalf of any taxpayer unless the enrolled agent presents satisfactory identification and is recognized to practice before the Internal Revenue Service. A person will be recognized to practice before the Service if (s)he meets the requirements set forth in Circular 230. Sec. 10.3 of Circular 230 states that an enrolled agent may represent a taxpayer upon the filing of a written declaration that (s)he is currently qualified as an enrolled agent and is authorized to represent the particular party on whose behalf (s)he acts. The evidence of recognition must be submitted when the enrolled agent appears for the initial meeting in the first office of the Internal Revenue Service in which (s)he represents the taxpayer (Sec. 601.503 CFR).

82. To qualify for continuing education credit, a course of learning taken by an enrolled agent must be a qualifying program consisting of current subject matter in federal taxation or federal tax related matters and be conducted by a qualifying sponsor.

The correct answer is (T). *(Publisher)*
DISCUSSION: Sec. 10.6(f)(1) of Circular 230 states that for a course of learning to qualify for continuing education credit for an enrolled agent, the course must be a qualifying program designed to enhance the professional knowledge of an individual in federal taxation or federal tax related matters and be conducted by a qualifying sponsor. The program may include accounting, financial management, and business computer science as well as taxation.

83. Participation of an enrolled agent as an instructor at an educational program meeting the continuing education requirements of Circular 230 will earn the agent continuing education credit.

The correct answer is (T). *(Publisher)*
DISCUSSION: Sec. 10.6(f)(2)(iii) of Circular 230 provides that 1 hour of continuing education credit will be awarded for each contact hour completed as an instructor, discussion leader, or speaker by an enrolled agent at an education program that meets the continuing education requirements of Circular 230. Moreover, 2 hours of credit will be awarded for actual subject preparation time for each contact hour, subject to recordkeeping requirements.

24.10 Conduct of an Enrolled Agent

84. If an enrolled agent knows that a client has not complied with the revenue laws of the United States with respect to a matter administered by the IRS, the enrolled agent is required to:

a. Advise the client of the noncompliance.
b. Immediately notify the IRS.
c. Advise his client and notify the IRS.
d. Do nothing until the client advises him to take corrective action.

The correct answer is (a). *(SPE 990 IV-56)*
REQUIRED: The action required by an enrolled agent who knows that a client has not complied with the revenue laws.
DISCUSSION: Sec. 10.21 of Treasury Department Circular No. 230 requires an attorney, certified public accountant, or enrolled agent who knows that a client has not complied with the revenue laws of the United States to promptly advise the client of the noncompliance.
Answers (b), (c), and (d) are incorrect because they are not actions that an enrolled agent is required to take.

85. Which of the following statements may not be used when an enrolled agent advertises?

a. Name, address, and office hours.
b. Names of associates of the firm.
c. Claims of quality of service which cannot be verified.
d. Membership in professional organizations.

The correct answer is (c). *(SPE 1080 IV-89)*
REQUIRED: The statement which may not be used when an enrolled agent advertises.
DISCUSSION: An enrolled agent may not use or participate in the use of any form of public communication containing a false, fraudulent, misleading, deceptive, or unfair statement or claim. This prohibition specifically includes statements pertaining to the quality of services rendered unless subject to factual verification [Sec. 10.30(a)(1) of Circular No. 230].
Answers (a), (b), and (d) are incorrect because each is specifically allowed to be disclosed in advertising by Sec. 10.30(b) of Circular No. 230.

86. An enrolled agent may be suspended from practice for advertising that (s)he is an expert in certain areas of taxation when such a statement is not authorized by state or federal agencies having jurisdiction over the practitioners.

The correct answer is (T). *(SPE 1080 IV-25)*
DISCUSSION: Circular No. 230 allows advertising and solicitation as long as it does not contain a false, fraudulent, misleading, deceptive, or unfair statement or claim. This prohibition specifically includes claims of specialized expertise not authorized by state or federal agencies having jurisdiction over the practitioner. Under Sec. 10.52 of Circular No. 230, an enrolled agent may be suspended from practice before the Internal Revenue Service for willful violations of any of the regulations contained in Circular 230.

87. An enrolled agent may publish a statement that his or her practice is limited to certain areas.

The correct answer is (T). *(SPE 989 IV-9)*
DISCUSSION: Under Sec. 10.30(b)(1) of Circular No. 230, it is permissible for attorneys, CPAs, and enrolled agents to advertise that the individual's or firm's practice is limited to certain areas.

88. Enrolled agents may publish the following information when communicating their services to the public: "enrolled to practice before the Internal Revenue Service."

The correct answer is (T). *(SPE 984 IV-14)*
DISCUSSION: Sec. 10.30(b)(1) of Circular No. 230 specifically permits an enrolled agent to use the phrase "enrolled to practice before the Internal Revenue Service" when advertising.

89. If a practitioner who is eligible to practice before the Internal Revenue Service uses radio or television to advertise fee information, the broadcast must be prerecorded and the practitioner must retain a recording of the actual transmission.

The correct answer is (T). *(SPE 989 IV-8)*
DISCUSSION: Sec. 10.30(d) of Circular No. 230 provides that if radio or television broadcasting is used, the broadcast must be prerecorded and the practitioner must retain a recording of the actual audio transmission.

90. An enrolled agent may solicit new business in matters related to the Internal Revenue Service by mailings provided the contents of the mailing are designed for the general public.

The correct answer is (T). *(SPE 987 IV-7)*
DISCUSSION: Solicitation by mailings directed to specific circumstances unique to the recipient is not allowed. This does not apply to mailings the contents of which are designed for the general public [Sec. 10.30(a)(2) of Circular No. 230].

91. Tina, an enrolled agent, wanted to have Bethany as a new client. Without invitation, Tina approached Bethany at the local fitness center and explained how she could assist Bethany with her federal tax matters and would like to have her as a client. Tina is in violation of the solicitation regulations set forth in Treasury Department Circular No. 230.

The correct answer is (T). *(SPE 990 IV-6)*
DISCUSSION: Sec. 10.30(a) of Circular No. 230 provides that an enrolled agent shall not directly or indirectly make any uninvited solicitation of employment in matters relating to the Internal Revenue Service. For this purpose, solicitation includes in-person contact. Tina's in-person contact with Bethany would be in violation of this regulation.

92. An individual who has been granted temporary recognition to practice before the Internal Revenue Service by the Director of Practice, is entitled to publicly advertise that (s)he is "enrolled to represent taxpayers before the Internal Revenue Service."

The correct answer is (F). *(SPE 989 IV-7)*
DISCUSSION: Although Sec. 10.30(b) of Circular No. 230 provides that an enrolled agent may advertise the fact that (s)he is enrolled to practice before the Internal Revenue Service, Sec. 10.5(c) provides that temporary recognition to practice does not constitute enrollment practice. Therefore, someone who has been granted temporary recognition is not enrolled to practice and may not advertise as such.

93. Ms. K is an enrolled agent and a notary public. She is representing Mr. D before the Internal Revenue Service. The revenue agent involved in the case requests certified copies of various contracts relating to the sale of a building. K may secure copies of the contracts and then certify them using her notary public stamp.

The correct answer is (F). *(SPE 989 IV-10)*
DISCUSSION: Sec. 10.27 of Circular No. 230 provides that an enrolled agent may not administer oaths or certify papers as a notary public in connection with matters in which (s)he is employed as agent or in which (s)he may be in any way interested before the IRS.

94. Enrolled agents shall exercise due diligence in preparing or assisting in the preparation of documents or other papers relating to Internal Revenue Service matters.

The correct answer is (T). *(SPE 984 IV-11)*
   DISCUSSION: Sec. 10.22(a) of Circular No. 230 requires attorneys, CPAs, and enrolled agents to exercise due diligence in preparing or assisting in the preparation of, approving, and filing returns, documents, and other papers relating to IRS matters.

95. An enrolled agent, attorney, or CPA must file a written declaration that (s)he is currently qualified as an enrolled agent, attorney, or CPA and is authorized to represent the particular party on whose behalf (s)he is acting when appearing for the initial meeting in the first office of the Internal Revenue Service in which (s)he represents the party.

The correct answer is (T). *(SPE 990 IV-23)*
   DISCUSSION: No person may appear in a representative capacity on behalf of any taxpayer before the IRS unless a written declaration is filed that the representative is qualified to practice before the IRS and authorized to represent the party [26 CFR 601.502 and 601.503(a)].

96. Doug, who is not recognized to practice before the Internal Revenue Service, is employed by Sandy, an enrolled agent. One of Sandy's clients has been notified that his 1987 income tax return has been selected for audit by the IRS. Sandy had prepared the return and signed it as the preparer. Doug cannot represent the client as his advocate at the audit even if he has Sandy's written authority to do so and has the client's power of attorney.

The correct answer is (T). *(SPE 990 IV-2)*
   DISCUSSION: Each person must be eligible to practice before the IRS before (s)he can represent a taxpayer. This eligibility cannot be delegated to employees.

97. No enrolled agent shall charge an unconscionable fee for representation of a client in any matter before the Internal Revenue Service.

The correct answer is (T). *(SPE 1079 IV-46)*
   DISCUSSION: Sec. 10.28 of Circular No. 230 provides that no attorney, CPA, or enrolled agent may charge an unconscionable fee for representation of a client before the IRS.

98. On December 17, 1990, Stan, an enrolled agent, placed an ad in a local newspaper and a trade magazine that he would prepare a complex Form 1040 for $200. On January 2, 1991, the owner of Stan's office building unexpectedly increased his rent by a large amount. Stan determined he would have to charge $230 to make a profit. Stan is bound to the $200 rate for at least 30 days from the last publication of the $200 rate.

The correct answer is (T). *(SPE 990 IV-5)*
   DISCUSSION: Attorneys, CPAs, and enrolled agents are bound to charge in accordance with published fee information for a reasonable period of time, but not less than 30 days from the last publication of such information [Sec. 10.30(c)(3) of Circular No. 230].

99. Ms. E is an enrolled agent who prepared the tax returns of Mr. A and Mr. B (buyer and seller, respectively). Ms. E may not, under any circumstances, represent A and B before the IRS with regard to the buy and sell transaction.

The correct answer is (F). *(SPE 1078 IV-19)*
   DISCUSSION: Under Sec. 10.29 of Circular No. 230, an attorney, CPA, or enrolled agent may represent conflicting interests before the IRS if all directly interested parties expressly consent after full disclosure has been made. Therefore, if A and B consent to E's representing them both, she may do so.

100. An enrolled agent may be suspended from practice before the IRS for negotiating federal income tax refund checks of his/her clients.

The correct answer is (T). *(SPE 1078 IV-15)*
   DISCUSSION: Sec. 10.31 of Circular No. 230 provides that attorneys, CPAs, and enrolled agents may not endorse or otherwise negotiate any income tax refund check issued to a client. Sec. 10.52 provides that any attorney, CPA, or enrolled agent may be disbarred or suspended from practice before the IRS for willful violations of any of the regulations contained in Circular No. 230.

101. An enrolled agent can knowingly accept assistance in a specific matter from a person who substantially participated personally in such matter as an Internal Revenue Service employee.

The correct answer is (F). *(SPE 1077 IV-36)*
DISCUSSION: Under Sec. 10.24 of Circular No. 230, no attorney, CPA, or enrolled agent may knowingly and directly or indirectly accept assistance from any former government employee, in violation of Sec. 10.26. Sec. 10.26(b)(2) prohibits a former government employee who participated in a transaction from representing or knowingly assisting, in that transaction, any person who is or was a specific party to that transaction.

102. When practicing before the Service, an enrolled agent may accept assistance from a person currently suspended from practice before the Service if no compensation is paid for the assistance.

The correct answer is (F). *(SPE 984 IV-12)*
DISCUSSION: Sec. 10.24 of Circular No. 230 provides that in practice before the IRS, no attorney, CPA, or enrolled agent shall knowingly accept assistance from any person who is under disbarment or suspension from practice before the IRS.

103. Enrolled agents are required to promptly submit records or information upon a proper and lawful request by a revenue agent in connection with an examination of a taxpayer, unless the enrolled agent believes in good faith and on reasonable grounds that such record or information is privileged or that the request is of doubtful legality.

The correct answer is (T). *(SPE 988 IV-7)*
DISCUSSION: Sec. 10.20(a) of Circular No. 230 provides that no attorney, CPA, or enrolled agent shall neglect or refuse promptly to submit records or information in any matter before the IRS, upon proper and lawful request by a duly authorized officer or employee of the IRS, unless (s)he believes in good faith and on reasonable grounds that such information is privileged or that the request is of doubtful legality.

104. Pursuant to the regulations set forth in Treasury Department Circular No. 230 with respect to practice before the IRS, attorneys, certified public accountants, and enrolled agents may not advertise fixed fees for specific services or hourly rates.

The correct answer is (F). *(SPE 1085 IV-10)*
DISCUSSION: Under Sec. 10.30(c) of Circular No. 230, fixed fees for specific routine services, hourly rates, the range of fees for particular services, and the fee charged for an initial consultation may be advertised. The availability of a written fee schedule may also be published.

105. Mr. B, a former Internal Revenue Service employee, is currently a partner in partnership K. Ten months before ending his government employment, Mr. B was involved in rendering technical advice on a particular situation. Eight months after Mr. B's government employment ended, another partner of partnership K, Mr. Y, wants to represent a person who was a party to the above situation. Mr. Y may represent the person if partnership K isolates the former Internal Revenue Service employee, Mr. B, in such a way that he does not assist in the representation.

The correct answer is (T). *(SPE 1081 IV-9)*
DISCUSSION: Former IRS employees may not represent or assist anyone in a matter administered by the IRS if (s)he participated in the transaction. Members of a firm of which a former IRS employee is a member may represent or assist a person who was a specific party in a transaction in which the former IRS employee participated if certain conditions are met. These conditions include (1) the employee not discussing employment in the firm with a firm member who had knowledge of his participation in the transaction until his/her IRS employment is ended or until 6 months after the termination of his/her participation in the transaction, whichever is earlier, and (2) the firm's isolating the former IRS employee so that (s)he does not assist in the representation [Sec. 10.26(c) of Circular No. 230].

24.11 Suspension and Disbarment

106. Which of the following is not an example of disreputable conduct for which an enrolled agent may be disbarred or suspended from practice before the Internal Revenue Service?

- a. Maintaining a partnership for the practice of tax law and accounting with a person who is under disbarment from practice before the Internal Revenue Service.
- b. Conviction of any offense involving dishonesty, or breach of trust.
- c. Soliciting new business in matters relating to the Internal Revenue Service through the publishing of a range of fees for particular services.
- d. Circulating or publishing malicious or libelous matter in connection with practice before the Internal Revenue Service.

The correct answer is (c). *(SPE 987 IV-61)*
REQUIRED: The action which would not require the disbarment of an enrolled agent.
DISCUSSION: The Secretary of the Treasury may suspend or disbar from practice before the IRS any attorney, CPA, or enrolled agent who is shown to be incompetent, disreputable, or who refuses to comply with the rules and regulations relating to practice before the IRS, or who, with intent to defraud, willfully and knowingly deceives, misleads, or threatens any claimant or potential claimant (Sec. 10.50 of Circular No. 230). Soliciting new business by publishing a range of fees for particular services is an acceptable practice for an enrolled agent.
Answers (a), (b), and (d) are incorrect because each is listed as disreputable conduct for which an enrolled agent may be disbarred or suspended in Sec. 10.51 of Circular No. 230.

107. All of the following are examples of disreputable conduct for which an enrolled agent may be disbarred or suspended from practice before the Internal Revenue Service except

- a. Solicitation by mailings, the contents of which are designed for the general public.
- b. Endorsing or otherwise negotiating a refund check made in respect of income taxes which is issued to a taxpayer other than the enrolled agent.
- c. Maintaining a partnership for the practice of tax law and accounting with a person who is under disbarment from practice before the Internal Revenue Service.
- d. Failure to properly and promptly remit funds received from a client for the purpose of payment of taxes.

The correct answer is (a). *(SPE 986 IV-62)*
REQUIRED: The action for which an enrolled agent may not be disbarred or suspended from practice.
DISCUSSION: Sec. 10.51 of Circular No. 230 lists several examples of disreputable conduct for which an enrolled agent may be disbarred or suspended from practice before the Internal Revenue Service. The actions listed in answers (b), (c), and (d) are prohibited.
Solicitation by mailings, the contents of which are designed for the general public, is not considered disreputable conduct under Sec. 10.30(a)(2) of Circular No. 230.

108. The Director of Practice may take into consideration a petition for reinstatement from any person disbarred from practice before the Internal Revenue Service after a period of how many years?

- a. Never.
- b. 2 years.
- c. 3 years.
- d. 5 years.

The correct answer is (d). *(SPE 987 IV-63)*
REQUIRED: The number of years after disbarment when reinstatement may be considered.
DISCUSSION: Under Sec. 10.75 of Circular No. 230, the Director of Practice may entertain a petition for reinstatement from any person disbarred from practice before the IRS after 5 years following such disbarment. Reinstatement is only granted if the Director of Practice is satisfied that the petitioner will conduct him/herself according to the regulations relating to practice before the IRS.

109. A proceeding for disbarment or suspension from practice before the Internal Revenue Service against an attorney, certified public accountant, or enrolled agent can only be instituted by which of the following?

  a. The District Director of Internal Revenue where the alleged misconduct occurred.
  b. The Director of Practice.
  c. An Administrative Law Judge.
  d. Any officer or employee of the Internal Revenue Service.

The correct answer is (b). *(SPE 988 IV-57)*
REQUIRED: The person who must institute a disbarment or suspension proceeding.
DISCUSSION: Sec. 10.54 of Circular No. 230 provides that whenever the Director of Practice has reason to believe any enrolled agent has violated any of the laws or regulations governing practice before the Internal Revenue Service, (s)he may reprimand such person or institute a proceeding for disbarment or suspension. The proceeding is instituted by a complaint naming the respondent and signed by the Director of Practice.

110. All of the following statements regarding proceedings for disbarment or suspension of an attorney, certified public accountant, or enrolled agent from practice before the Internal Revenue Service are true except

  a. A complaint shall contain a clear and concise description of the allegations which constitute the basis for the proceedings.
  b. Failure to answer the complaint as required will render a decision by default against the respondent.
  c. Every allegation in the complaint which is not denied will be deemed to be admitted by the respondent and may be considered as proved.
  d. The respondent to the complaint must file his answer with the Director of Practice within 15 days from the date the complaint is served.

The correct answer is (d). *(SPE 988 IV-56)*
REQUIRED: The false statement about disbarment or suspension proceedings.
DISCUSSION: Sec. 10.58 of Circular No. 230 provides that the respondent's answer shall be filed in writing within the time specified in the complaint, unless an application is made and the time is extended by the Director of Practice or the Administrative Law Judge.
Answer (a) is incorrect because a complaint is sufficient if it fairly informs the respondent of the charges so that (s)he can prepare a defense (Sec. 10.56). Answer (b) is incorrect because failure to answer constitutes an admission of allegations and a waiver of a hearing (Sec. 10.58). Answer (c) is incorrect because no further evidence in respect of such an allegation need be proved at a hearing if the respondent does not deny it (Sec. 10.58).

111. An enrolled agent may be disbarred or suspended for giving false or misleading information to the Internal Revenue Service.

The correct answer is (T). *(SPE 1077 IV-22)*
DISCUSSION: Sec. 10.51(b) of Circular No. 230 provides that giving false or misleading information to the Department of the Treasury (of which the IRS is a part) is considered disreputable conduct for which an attorney, CPA, or enrolled agent may be disbarred or suspended.

112. The use of abusive language or publishing malicious or libelous matter in connection with practice before the Service is disreputable conduct for which an enrolled agent may be suspended from practice before the Internal Revenue Service.

The correct answer is (T). *(SPE 984 IV-15)*
DISCUSSION: Sec. 10.51(i) of Circular No. 230 provides that disreputable conduct includes contemptuous conduct in connection with practice before the IRS, including the use of abusive language and publishing malicious or libelous matter.

113. The Director of Practice may confer with an attorney, certified public accountant, or enrolled agent concerning allegations of misconduct irrespective of whether a proceeding for disbarment or suspension has been instituted against him.

The correct answer is (T). *(SPE 987 IV-10)*
DISCUSSION: Sec. 10.55 of Circular No. 230 provides that the Director of Practice may confer with an attorney, CPA, or enrolled agent concerning allegations of misconduct regardless of whether a proceeding for disbarment or suspension has been instituted.

114. Except in cases of willfulness, or when time, the nature of the proceeding, or the public interest does not permit, the Director of Practice may not institute a proceeding of disbarment or suspension against any attorney, certified public accountant, or enrolled agent without giving notice in writing to the proposed respondent and allowing the respondent the opportunity to demonstrate or achieve compliance with all lawful requirements.

The correct answer is (T). *(SPE 1085 IV-12)*
DISCUSSION: Unless one of the stated exceptions applies, a proceeding under Sec. 10.54 of Circular 230 is not instituted until facts or conduct warranting such action are called to the respondent's attention in writing and (s)he is given an opportunity to comply with the requirements.

115. A complaint instituted by the Director of Practice against an enrolled agent is considered sufficient if it fairly informs the respondent of the charges against him/her so that (s)he is able to prepare a defense.

The correct answer is (T). *(SPE 984 IV-17)*
DISCUSSION: Sec. 10.56(a) of Circular No. 230 provides that a complaint shall be deemed sufficient if it fairly informs the respondent of the charges against him/her so that (s)he is able to prepare a defense.

116. A complaint filed by the Director of Practice against an enrolled agent must be served upon the agent by certified mail or first-class mail allowing a minimum of 7 days from the date of service of the complaint for the agent to file a reply.

The correct answer is (F). *(SPE 1083 IV-14)*
DISCUSSION: A complaint may be served on the enrolled agent by certified mail, by delivery in person, or by first-class mail if the certified matter is not claimed or accepted by the respondent [Sec. 10.57(a) of Circular No. 230]. The enrolled agent must have at least 15 days from the date of service or complaint to file his/her answer [Sec. 10.56(b) of Circular No. 230].

117. An enrolled agent's answer to a complaint filed against the enrolled agent by the Director of Practice shall contain a statement of facts which constitute the grounds of defense, and it shall specifically admit or deny each allegation set forth in the complaint.

The correct answer is (T). *(SPE 986 IV-8)*
DISCUSSION: However, the respondent may not deny a material allegation that (s)he knows to be true or state that (s)he lacks sufficient information to form a belief when (s)he in fact possesses such information. Special matters of defense may also be affirmatively stated. An allegation that is not denied is deemed to be admitted and proved (Sec. 10.58 of Circular No. 230).

118. If an enrolled agent has been requested by the Director of Practice to provide the Director with any information (s)he may have concerning the violation of the regulations governing practice before the Internal Revenue Service by any person and/or to testify at a proceeding for disbarment or suspension of an enrolled agent, CPA, or attorney, the enrolled agent must do so unless (s)he believes in good faith and on reasonable grounds that such information is privileged or that the request by the Director is of doubtful legality.

The correct answer is (T). *(SPE 989 IV-5)*
DISCUSSION: Sec. 10.20(a) of Circular No. 230 provides that no attorney, CPA, or enrolled agent shall neglect or refuse promptly to submit records or information in any matter before the IRS, upon proper and lawful request by a duly authorized officer or employee of the IRS, unless (s)he believes in good faith and on reasonable grounds that such information is privileged or that the request is of doubtful legality.

119. An Administrative Law Judge presides at the hearing on a complaint for the disbarment or suspension of an enrolled agent, attorney, or CPA. The enrolled agent, attorney, or CPA may appear at this hearing in person or be represented by another who does not have to be an enrolled agent, attorney, or CPA.

The correct answer is (T). *(SPE 989 IV-12)*
DISCUSSION: Sec. 10.63 of Circular No. 230 provides that a respondent may appear in person or may be represented by counsel or other representative who need not be enrolled to practice before the IRS.

120. Hearings presided over by an Administrative Law Judge on a complaint for disbarment or suspension shall be stenographically recorded and transcribed and the testimony of witnesses shall be taken under oath or affirmation.

The correct answer is (T). *(SPE 984 IV-20)*
DISCUSSION: Sec. 10.65(a) of Circular No. 230 provides that hearings shall be stenographically recorded and transcribed, and the testimony of witnesses shall be taken under oath or affirmation.

121. Before the decision is made in a disbarment hearing on a complaint against an enrolled agent, the enrolled agent will be given a reasonable opportunity to submit proposed findings and conclusions and the supporting reasons.

The correct answer is (T). *(SPE 1082 IV-12)*
DISCUSSION: Sec. 10.69 of Circular No. 230 provides that the Administrative Law Judge shall afford the parties a reasonable opportunity to submit proposed findings and conclusions and supporting reasons therefor. This does not apply if the respondent has failed to answer the complaint or a party has failed to appear at the hearing.

122. Mr. B, an enrolled agent, has been properly notified to appear at a hearing on a complaint for his disbarment or suspension from practice before the IRS. If Mr. B fails to appear, he shall be deemed to have waived his right to a hearing, and the Administrative Law Judge may make his/her decision against Mr. B by default.

The correct answer is (T). *(SPE 984 IV-21)*
DISCUSSION: Sec. 10.65(b) of Circular No. 230 provides that if either party to the proceeding fails to appear at the hearing after due notice has been sent to him/her, (s)he is deemed to have waived the right to a hearing, and the Administrative Law Judge may decide against the absent party by default.

123. The same rules of evidence that prevail in courts of law prevail in disbarment hearings on complaints against enrolled agents.

The correct answer is (F). *(SPE 1080 IV-27)*
DISCUSSION: Sec. 10.66(a) of Circular No. 230 provides that the rules of evidence which prevail in courts of law and equity are not controlling in hearings on complaints for the disbarment or suspension of attorneys, CPAs, and enrolled agents. The Administrative Law Judge may exclude irrelevant, immaterial, or unduly repetitious evidence.

124. An enrolled agent may offer his/her consent to suspension of practice before the Internal Revenue Service in order to avoid the institution of a suspension proceeding.

The correct answer is (T). *(SPE 1083 IV-15)*
DISCUSSION: Sec. 10.55(b) of Circular No. 230 provides that an attorney, CPA, or enrolled agent may offer his/her consent to suspension from practice before the IRS to avoid the institution or conclusion of a disbarment or suspension proceeding.

125. The decision of the Administrative Law Judge on a complaint for disbarment or suspension of an enrolled agent may be appealed to the Secretary of the Treasury by either party.

The correct answer is (T). *(SPE 1082 IV-79)*
DISCUSSION: Sec. 10.71 of Circular No. 230 provides that either party may appeal the decision of the Administrative Law Judge to the Secretary of the Treasury. The appeal must be made within 30 days of the date of the decision.

126. Any individual who prepares a return and signs as a preparer may appear before the Internal Revenue Service as the taxpayer's representative even if (s)he is under suspension from practice.

The correct answer is (F). *(SPE 1079 IV-41)*
DISCUSSION: Sec. 10.73 of Circular No. 230 provides that a suspended agent shall not be permitted to practice before the IRS during the period of suspension. This prohibition is not waived for return preparers.

127. An individual who is eligible to practice before the IRS may be disbarred or suspended from practice before the IRS for maintaining a partnership for the practice of tax law or accounting with a person who is under disbarment or suspension from practice before the IRS.

The correct answer is (T). *(SPE 990 IV-7)*
DISCUSSION: Sec. 10.51(h) of Circular No. 230 provides that disreputable conduct for which an attorney, CPA, or enrolled agent may be disbarred or suspended from practice before the IRS includes maintaining a partnership to practice law or accounting with a person who is under disbarment or suspension from practice before the IRS.

128. Godfrey, an enrolled agent, was suspended from practice before the Internal Revenue Service in February, 1991. Prior to his suspension, Godfrey had been representing Sal whose 1989 return was being audited by the IRS. Because of Godfrey's suspension, which was not related to his work on Sal's audit, Sal hired Tiffany, an enrolled agent to represent him. Tiffany may employ Godfrey to assist her on Sal's audit.

The correct answer is (F). *(SPE 990 IV-4)*
DISCUSSION: Sec. 10.24 of Circular No. 230 provides that no attorney, CPA, or enrolled agent may, in practice before the IRS, knowingly and directly or indirectly employ or accept assistance from any person who is under disbarment or suspension from practice before the IRS.

129. An enrolled agent, in practice before the Internal Revenue Service, may share fees with a person who is under disbarment from practice before the Internal Revenue Service if it is done indirectly.

The correct answer is (F). *(SPE 1085 IV-9)*
DISCUSSION: No attorney, CPA, or enrolled agent knowingly and directly or indirectly may share fees with disbarred or suspended persons (Sec. 10.24 of Circular No. 230).

24.12 Practice Before the IRS by Persons Without Enrollment

130. The Commissioner may authorize any person to represent another without enrollment on a specific matter.

The correct answer is (T). *(SPE 1081 IV-6)*
DISCUSSION: Sec. 10.7(b) of Circular No. 230 provides that the Commissioner may authorize any person to represent another without enrollment for the purpose of a particular matter.

131. An individual who is a regular full-time employee of a partnership may represent the partnership before the Internal Revenue Service.

The correct answer is (T). *(SPE 1081 IV-4)*
DISCUSSION: Sec. 10.7(a)(1) of Circular No. 230 provides that an individual may represent a partnership of which (s)he is a regular full-time employee or member without enrollment.

132. Trusts, receiverships, guardianships, or estates may be represented by their trustees, receivers, guardians, administrators, or executors, even if they are not enrolled agents, attorneys, or CPAs.

The correct answer is (T). *(SPE 988 IV-5)*
DISCUSSION: Sec. 10.7(a)(3) of Circular No. 230 provides that trusts, receiverships, guardianships, and estates may be represented by their trustees, receivers, guardians, administrators, or executors without enrollment.

133. An individual who is not an attorney, CPA, or enrolled agent, who is a regular full-time employee of Corporation X, may represent X before the Internal Revenue Service provided that individual presents satisfactory identification.

The correct answer is (T). *(SPE 988 IV-3)*
DISCUSSION: Sec. 10.7(a)(2) of Circular No. 230 provides that corporations may be represented by bona fide officers or regular full-time employees without enrollment if satisfactory identification is presented.

134. A full-time employee of a sole proprietorship may represent his/her employer in an examination with an IRS agent without being an enrolled agent.

The correct answer is (T). *(SPE 1078 IV-3)*
DISCUSSION: An unenrolled individual may represent another individual who is his/her regular full-time employer before the IRS [Sec. 10.7(a)(1) of Circular No. 230].

135. Enrollment is not required for representation outside of the United States before personnel of the Internal Revenue Service.

The correct answer is (T). *(SPE 1077 IV-32)*
DISCUSSION: Sec. 10.7(a)(6) of Circular No. 230 provides that enrollment is not required for representation outside the United States before personnel of the IRS.

136. An elected member of Congress may represent someone before the Internal Revenue Service for compensation.

The correct answer is (F). *(SPE 1079 IV-35)*
DISCUSSION: Sec. 10.3(f) of Circular No. 230 provides that no member of Congress may practice before the IRS in connection with any matter for which (s)he directly or indirectly receives, agrees to receive, or seeks any compensation.

137. An officer or employee of the U.S. Government may practice before the IRS to represent a member of his/her immediate family or any other person or estate for which (s)he serves as a guardian, executor, administrator, trustee, or other personal fiduciary.

The correct answer is (T). *(SPE 1085 IV-2)*
DISCUSSION: Sec. 10.3(f) of Circular No. 230 provides that no officer or employee of the United States in the executive, legislative, or judicial branch of the government, or in any agency of the United States may practice before the Service. However, such officer or employee may represent a member of his/her immediate family or any other person or estate for which (s)he serves as guardian, executor, administrator, trustee, or other personal fiduciary.

138. An individual may, without enrollment, represent without compensation a member of his/her immediate family.

The correct answer is (T). *(SPE 1077 IV-21)*
DISCUSSION: Sec. 10.7(a)(1) of Circular No. 230 provides that an unenrolled individual may represent without compensation a member of his/her immediate family.

139. Practice before the Internal Revenue Service includes the representation of a client at conferences, hearings, and meetings.

The correct answer is (T). *(SPE 984 IV-1)*
DISCUSSION: Sec. 10.2(a) of Circular No. 230 provides that practice before the Internal Revenue Service includes presenting to the IRS or any of its officers or employees all matters relating to a client's rights, privileges, or liabilities. This includes representing a client at conferences, hearings, and meetings.

140. The appearance of an individual as a witness for the taxpayer is considered practice before the Internal Revenue Service.

The correct answer is (F). *(SPE 1085 IV-1)*
DISCUSSION: Under Sec. 10.2(a) of Circular No. 230, "practice before the IRS" does not include the preparation of a tax return, the appearance of an individual as a witness for the taxpayer, or the furnishing of information at the request of the IRS.

141. An unenrolled agent who has not prepared the tax return of taxpayer A may represent A before a revenue agent in the conduct of an examination, providing the unenrolled agent has A's written authorization.

The correct answer is (F). *(SPE 1078 IV-4)*
DISCUSSION: "Practice before the IRS" includes representing a client at conferences, hearings, and meetings. To practice before the IRS, an individual must be an attorney, CPA, or an enrolled agent (Sec. 10.2 and 10.3 of Circular No. 230). Therefore, an unenrolled agent may not represent a client in an examination even with the client's written authorization.

142. A practitioner who is not an attorney, CPA, or enrolled agent, who signs a return as having prepared it for the taxpayer may, with proper authorization from the taxpayer, appear as the taxpayer's advocate, with or without the taxpayer, before revenue agents and examining officers of the Examination Division of the Internal Revenue Service with respect to the taxpayer's tax liability for the period covered by that return.

The correct answer is (T). *(SPE 988 IV-6)*
DISCUSSION: Sec. 10.7(a)(7) of Circular No. 230 provides that any individual, who is not under disbarment or suspension from practice and who prepares a return for a taxpayer and signs it as the preparer, may appear without enrollment as the taxpayer's representative, with or without the taxpayer, before revenue agents and examining officers with respect to the tax liability of the taxpayer for the taxable year or period covered by that return. Proper authorization from the taxpayer is required. This exception does not apply to appearances before the Collection Division.

CHAPTER TWENTY-FIVE
FEDERAL TAX PROCESS AND PROCEDURE

25.1	Sources of Tax Law	(20 questions)	721
25.2	Legislative Process	(6 questions)	726
	Administrative Process		
25.3	Return Examination	(14 questions)	728
25.4	Power of Attorney and Tax Information Authorization	(26 questions)	731
25.5	Appeals Within the IRS	(8 questions)	736
25.6	Deficiencies and Assessments	(7 questions)	737
25.7	IRS Collection Procedures	(23 questions)	739
25.8	Claims for Refund	(11 questions)	744
	Judicial Review		
25.9	Tax Court	(15 questions)	747
25.10	District Court and Claims Court	(7 questions)	749
25.11	Appeals	(6 questions)	750

25.1 Sources of Tax Law

1. Which of the following is the most authoritative source of tax law?

- a. U.S. Constitution.
- b. Internal Revenue Code.
- c. Code of Federal Regulations.
- d. Treasury Regulations.

The correct answer is (b). *(Publisher)*
REQUIRED: The most authoritative source of tax law.
DISCUSSION: The Internal Revenue Code is the body of tax statutes created by Congress as the law of federal taxation. It is not the sole source of tax law because it cannot possibly apply directly to every situation. The rest of the sources of tax law are generally interpretations and applications of the Internal Revenue Code.

Answer (a) is incorrect because the U.S. Constitution's 16th Amendment merely allows the government to collect taxes on incomes without apportionment among the states. This is the authority for the Internal Revenue Code. Answer (c) is incorrect because the Code of Federal Regulations is a compendium of federal administrative regulations classified into a numerical system of categorization. It encompasses much more than taxes. Answer (d) is incorrect because the Treasury Regulations (part of the Code of Federal Regulations) are merely interpretations and applications of the Internal Revenue Code by the Treasury Department, which has the responsibility of carrying out the Internal Revenue Code. The IRS is an agency of the Treasury Department.

2. Which of the following is a false statement regarding court cases, revenue rulings, and revenue procedures?

   a. Supreme Court decisions on federal tax matters are published in Internal Revenue Bulletins.
   b. Announcements concerning the Internal Revenue Service's acquiescence or non-acquiescence in Tax Court decisions that are adverse to the government's position (other than memorandum decisions) are published in Internal Revenue Bulletins.
   c. The Internal Revenue Service does not publish decisions by United States District Courts or the United States Claims Court. To find these decisions one must look to publications issued by commercial printing houses.
   d. The denial of a writ of certiorari by the Supreme Court is the equivalent of a reversal or disagreement.

The correct answer is (d). *(SPE 984 IV-85)*
REQUIRED: The false statement regarding court cases, revenue rulings, and revenue procedures.
DISCUSSION: The denial of a writ of certiorari by the Supreme Court is simply the Court's decision not to hear the case. The Supreme Court selects only those cases that it thinks are of sufficient public interest to warrant a Supreme Court hearing. The denial is neither a reversal nor a disagreement. Moreover, while the effect of the denial is to let stand the result in the court below, the denial does not signify agreement with the decision.
Answers (a), (b), and (c) are true statements regarding cases, revenue rulings, and revenue procedures.

3. Which of the following statements is false?

   a. The Bulletin Index-Digest System is designed primarily to help you find the Service's position on any tax issue pertaining to the Internal Revenue Code that is covered in materials published in the Internal Revenue Bulletin.
   b. All Supreme Court decisions on Federal tax matters are published in the Internal Revenue Bulletin (IRB) and Cumulative Bulletin (CB).
   c. Tax Court decisions are published in the Internal Revenue Bulletin.
   d. Cumulative supplements for the Bulletin Index-Digest System are issued quarterly for the income tax service.

The correct answer is (c). *(SPE 1085 IV-75)*
REQUIRED: The false statement regarding court cases and the Bulletin Index-Digest System.
DISCUSSION: Supreme Court decisions on federal tax matters, IRS acquiescence or nonacquiescence in Tax Court decisions, revenue rulings, and revenue procedures are published in the Internal Revenue Bulletin. Tax Court decisions themselves are not published in the Bulletin.
Answers (a), (b), and (d) are true statements regarding court cases and the Bulletin Index-Digest System.

4. Which of the following statements regarding Treasury Regulations is false?

   a. Regulations are binding on all courts except the Supreme Court.
   b. Interpretative regulations are issued under the general mandate of Code Sec. 7805(a).
   c. Some Code sections specifically authorize regulations to provide the details of the meaning and rules for that particular section. These are called legislative regulations.
   d. Temporary regulations are issued to provide guidance for the public and IRS employees until final regulations are issued.

The correct answer is (a). *(SPE 987 IV-80)*
REQUIRED: The false statement regarding Treasury Regulations.
DISCUSSION: Treasury Regulations explain the language of the Internal Revenue Code (IRC) by giving explanations, definitions, examples, and rules that clarify the intent of Congress. They are not binding on any court if they conflict with the IRC.
Answers (b), (c), and (d) are true statements regarding regulations.

Module 25.1: Sources of Tax Law

5. All of the following statements relating to Treasury Regulations are true except:

a. Temporary regulations are issued to provide guidance for the public and IRS employees until final regulations are issued.

b. Public hearings are always held on temporary regulations.

c. Final regulations supersede temporary regulations.

d. Proposed regulations are issued to solicit public written comments.

The correct answer is (b). *(SPE 989 IV-76)*
REQUIRED: The false statement about Treasury Regulations.
DISCUSSION: The Treasury Department issues regulations as interpretations of the Internal Revenue Code. The regulations explain the language of the Code and give definitions, examples, and rules that provide assistance in understanding the intent of the revenue statutes. Regulations are generally first issued to the public in proposed form. Practitioners and the public are invited to comment on the regulation and suggest changes before the regulation becomes final. The Treasury Department sometimes issues temporary regulations. These regulations give the public, practitioners, and IRS personnel guidance until appropriate final regulations are issued. Any temporary regulation issued after November 20, 1988 will expire within 3 years after the date of issuance and must be issued as a proposed regulation [Sec. 7805(e)]. Because temporary regulations are also issued in proposed form, public hearings are not held on the temporary regulations. The public is always given the opportunity to comment on the proposed regulations. These comments may be in written form (e.g., written data, views, arguments, etc.) without public hearings being held. While in effect, temporary regulations have the same authority as final regulations.

Answers (a), (c), and (d) are true statements regarding regulations.

6. All of the following statements regarding revenue rulings and revenue procedures are true except:

a. Revenue rulings are the published conclusions of the Internal Revenue Service concerning the application of tax law to an entire set of facts.

b. Revenue Procedures are official statements of procedures that either affect the rights or duties of taxpayers or other members of the public.

c. The purpose of these rulings and procedures is to promote a uniform application of the tax laws.

d. Taxpayers cannot appeal adverse return examination results that are based on revenue rulings to the Tax Court or other federal courts.

The correct answer is (d). *(SPE 990 IV-76)*
REQUIRED: The false statement regarding revenue rulings and revenue procedures.
DISCUSSION: A revenue ruling sets forth the IRS's interpretation of the tax law. It is binding on IRS employees but not on courts. Taxpayers may appeal adverse examination decisions whether or not based on a revenue ruling.

Answers (a), (b), and (c) are true statements regarding revenue rulings and procedures.

7. Which of the following statements is false?

   a. If the Commissioner of Internal Revenue has filed nonacquiescence to a decision of the Tax Court he cannot revise it and must appeal to a higher court.

   b. Decisions of the courts other than the Supreme Court do not require the Internal Revenue Service to alter its position for all other taxpayers.

   c. A petition to the Supreme Court to have a case that it is not obliged to review is by writ of certiorari which is initially requested by the appealing party.

   d. The writ of certiorari is issued by the Supreme Court to the lower appellate court requesting the record of a case for review.

The correct answer is (a). *(SPE 988 IV-75)*
REQUIRED: The false statement about court decisions and tax law.
DISCUSSION: The Commissioner may at any time revise a nonacquiescence to a Tax Court decision. A nonacquiescence means the Commissioner does not endorse the principles in an adverse, regular, reported decision of the Tax Court.
Answers (b), (c), and (d) are all true statements.

8. The courts give great importance to the literal language of the Internal Revenue Code but they also consider the history of a particular section of the Code, its relationship to other Code sections, and reports of congressional committees.

The correct answer is (T). *(SPE 989 IV-53)*
DISCUSSION: In applying the Internal Revenue Code to the facts of a case, the courts attempt to carry out the intent of Congress as expressed in the language of the Code. Therefore, they give great importance to the Code's literal language. The courts may also consider other sources that help explain or clarify the intent of a particular section. The reports of the congressional committees, the history of the section, and the relationship to other Code sections may be considered by the courts in determining the intent of Congress.

9. Interpretive regulations are Treasury Regulations issued under the general mandate of a specific section of the Internal Revenue Code.

The correct answer is (T). *(SPE 989 IV-60)*
DISCUSSION: Interpretive regulations are authorized by Sec. 7805(a), which empowers the Secretary of the Treasury to prescribe all needful rules and regulations for enforcement of the Internal Revenue Code. Interpretive regulations serve to make the language of the Code easier to understand and apply. Regulations which are specifically authorized to provide the details of the meaning and rules for a particular code section are called statutory or legislative regulations.

10. There are two types of income tax regulations, interpretive and legislative. These regulations provide explanations, definitions, examples, and rules which explain the language of the Code. Accordingly, your research of a particular Code section cannot be considered complete until you have read the regulations which interpret it.

The correct answer is (T). *(SPE 990 IV-38)*
DISCUSSION: Treasury regulations explain the language of the Internal Revenue Code by giving explanations, definitions, examples, and rules that clarify the intent of Congress. Interpretive regulations make the language of the statutes easier to understand and apply. Legislative regulations are those that are specifically authorized by Congress to provide the details of the meaning and rules for a particular Code section. Courts place great importance on the regulations and will follow them in rendering a decision unless they are plainly inconsistent with the Code. Regulations are also important because they state the position of the Internal Revenue Service. Proper research of a particular Code section requires that the applicable provision in the regulations also be researched.

Module 25.1: Sources of Tax Law

11. All regulations are written by the Office of Chief Counsel. Internal Revenue Service employees and all courts, except the Supreme Court, are bound by these regulations.

The correct answer is (F). *(SPE 990 IV-39)*
DISCUSSION: Regulations are written either by the Legislation and Regulations Division or the Employee Plans, Exempt Organizations Division of the Office of the Chief Counsel, IRS, and are approved by the Chief Counsel and the IRS Commissioners. Courts generally give great importance to the regulations, but are not bound by them. Courts may declare a regulation to be invalid if the regulation conflicts with, or is inconsistent with, the Internal Revenue Code.

12. Temporary regulations explain and define by examples and rules the Commissioner's interpretation of the Code. They are issued only after public hearings are held that allow oral or written comments.

The correct answer is (F). *(SPE 986 IV-60)*
DISCUSSION: Treasury regulations explain the language of the Code by giving explanations, definitions, examples, and rules that clarify the intent of Congress. Temporary regulations give the public, practitioners, and IRS personnel guidance until final regulations are issued. Any temporary regulation issued after November 20, 1988 will expire within 3 years after the date of issuance and must be issued as a proposed regulation. Public hearings are held for some proposed regulations. Alternatively, the IRS may only permit written comments to be filed with respect to other proposed regulations.

13. The courts are bound by legislative regulations but not by interpretive regulations.

The correct answer is (F). *(SPE 988 IV-52)*
DISCUSSION: The two types of income tax regulations are interpretive and legislative (statutory). The Secretary of the Treasury is given the power to issue regulations by specific Code sections. These are called legislative or statutory regulations. Legislative regulations promulgated by the Treasury have the full force and effect of law unless they conflict with the IRC, so they are not always binding.
Interpretive regulations are authorized by Sec. 7805(a), which empowers the Secretary to prescribe all needful rules and regulations for enforcement of the Code. Interpretive regulations also are not binding on a court. The weight given to an interpretive regulation by a court depends upon all the circumstances of a case.

14. Revenue Rulings represent the conclusions of the Service on the application of the law to the pivotal facts stated in the revenue ruling.

The correct answer is (T). *(SPE 987 II-52)*
DISCUSSION: A revenue ruling (abbreviated Rev. Rul.) is substantive, pertains to a specific set of facts, and sets forth the IRS's interpretation of the tax law and its application to those facts. IRS employees must follow published rulings.

15. The purpose of revenue rulings is to promote a uniform application of the tax law to an entire set of facts. Therefore, IRS employees must follow the rulings while taxpayers can appeal adverse return examination decisions based on these rulings.

The correct answer is (T). *(SPE 989 IV-56)*
DISCUSSION: Revenue rulings are published in the Internal Revenue Bulletin (published weekly) and the Cumulative Bulletin (published semiannually). Each issue of the Internal Revenue Bulletin states that, in applying published rulings, the effect of subsequent legislation, regulations, court decisions, rulings, and procedures must be considered, and concerned persons are cautioned against reaching the same conclusions in other cases unless the facts and circumstances are substantially the same. Revenue rulings are interpretations by the IRS and therefore need not be followed if another interpretation is justified.

16. A revenue procedure is a published official statement by the Internal Revenue Service regarding procedures affecting the rights or duties of taxpayers.

The correct answer is (T). *(SPE 1082 IV-69)*
DISCUSSION: Revenue procedures are procedural in nature. They are official statements published by the IRS which affect the rights and duties of taxpayers and are important in dealing with the IRS.

17. Revenue rulings, revenue procedures, and all Supreme Court decisions on federal tax matters are published in the Internal Revenue Bulletin (I.R.B.).

The correct answer is (T). *(SPE 1082 IV-70)*
DISCUSSION: The Internal Revenue Bulletin is published weekly, and includes Treasury decisions, statutes, committee reports, Supreme Court decisions affecting internal revenue, lists of the acquiescences and nonacquiescences of the IRS to decisions of the Tax Court, and administrative rulings.

18. In interpreting and applying the Internal Revenue Code to specific cases, courts are required to apply it in accordance with the law of the state in which the taxpayer and court are located.

The correct answer is (F). *(Publisher)*
DISCUSSION: The Internal Revenue Code is federal law. The only courts in which a federal tax case may be brought are the U.S. Tax Court, U.S. District Court, and U.S. Claims Court. Each of these courts is a federal court and is not bound by state laws, except as the state law may affect or determine the underlying transactions which are the subject of taxation. Even then, generally only the decision of the highest court in the state will be followed with respect to the application of a state law.

19. The commissioner of Internal Revenue is obliged to follow a Supreme Court decision but not the decisions of the other courts. Thus, decisions of the lower courts are binding on the Service only for the particular taxpayer and for the years litigated.

The correct answer is (T). *(SPE 987 IV-57)*
DISCUSSION: Decisions of courts other than the Supreme Court are binding on the Commissioner only for the particular taxpayer in question and only for the years litigated. Decisions of the Supreme Court are binding on the Commissioner for all taxpayers and also for future years.

20. A decision is the court's statement of opinion on a legal point other than the principal issue in the case. The decision has legal sanction and is enforceable.

The correct answer is (F). *(SPE 984 IV-76)*
DISCUSSION: The decision is the court's final determination of the application of the relevant law to the facts in a given case. The decision has legal sanction and is enforceable. Dictum is a court's statement of opinion on a legal point other than the principal issue in the case. Dictum does not have legal sanction and is not enforceable.

25.2 Legislative Process

21. Prior to becoming law, a proposed statute is called a bill. A revenue bill is one which concerns taxation (the raising of revenue). Where must a revenue bill originate?

a. The House of Representatives.
b. The President.
c. The Joint Committee on Taxation.
d. The Senate.

The correct answer is (a). *(Publisher)*
REQUIRED: Where a revenue bill is required to originate.
DISCUSSION: Under the U.S. Constitution, a revenue bill must originate in the House of Representatives. This is a formality because a bill drafted by someone else, e.g., the administration, may be introduced onto the floor of the House by any Representative.
Answer (b) is incorrect because the President can only introduce a revenue bill indirectly by persuading a Congressman to introduce it on the floor of the House. Answer (c) is incorrect because the Joint Committee on Taxation is a permanent committee whose function is to continually review the operation and administration of the tax system and propose improvements. It too can introduce a revenue bill only indirectly. Answer (d) is incorrect because a revenue bill does not reach the Senate until it has been approved by the House of Representatives.

22. When does a revenue bill go to the Senate Finance Committee?

a. After approval by the House Ways and Means Committee.
b. After approval by the Senate.
c. After the President vetoes it.
d. After it is referred to the Senate.

The correct answer is (d). *(Publisher)*
REQUIRED: When a revenue bill goes to the Senate Finance Committee.
DISCUSSION: The Senate Finance Committee operates similarly to the House Ways and Means Committee. Each studies a revenue bill after it has been introduced onto the floor of the House or Senate, holds hearings, and prepares a report for consideration by the entire legislative body. A revenue bill begins with its introduction onto the floor of the House, referral to the Ways and Means Committee, and return to the floor of the House for a vote. If the bill is approved by the House, it is referred to the Senate, which forwards it to the Senate Finance Committee. After the Senate Finance Committee, it goes back to the floor of the Senate for a vote.
Answer (a) is incorrect because a revenue bill must be approved by the House of Representatives after its review in the Ways and Means Committee. Answer (b) is incorrect because a revenue bill is not approved by the Senate until it goes through the Senate Finance Committee. Answer (c) is incorrect because if the President vetoes a revenue bill, it goes back to the Senate and House and becomes law if passed by two-thirds majority of each.

23. When or where are public hearings held on a revenue bill?

a. On the floor of the House and the Senate.
b. In the House Ways and Means Committee and the Senate Finance Committee.
c. In the Joint Conference Committee.
d. Upon first introduction to the House of Representatives.

The correct answer is (b). *(Publisher)*
REQUIRED: The time or place of public hearings held on a revenue bill.
DISCUSSION: In both the House Ways and Means Committee and the Senate Finance Committee, public hearings are usually held on a revenue bill to allow the administration, taxpayers, and other groups to express their views.
Answer (a) is incorrect because the members of Congress may debate a bill on the floor of the House and Senate, but that is not the place for public hearings. Answer (c) is incorrect because the Joint Conference Committee privately reconciles different versions of a bill passed by the House and Senate but does not usually hold public hearings. Answer (d) is incorrect because the first introduction to the House of Representatives is a mere formality before the bill is seriously considered.

24. As revenue bills go through Congress, they are usually approved in different versions since amendments are frequently made. Which committee is responsible for reconciling the House and Senate versions?

a. Joint Conference Committee.
b. Joint Committee on Taxation.
c. House Ways and Means Committee.
d. Senate Finance Committee.

The correct answer is (a). *(Publisher)*
REQUIRED: The committee which is responsible for reconciling House and Senate versions of a revenue bill.
DISCUSSION: As revenue bills go through Congress, amendments are made. Thus, the Senate usually passes a different version of a bill from that approved in the House. The Joint Conference Committee includes members of both the Ways and Means Committee and the Finance Committee, who attempt to reconcile the differences. The new version goes to the House and Senate to be voted upon.
Answer (b) is incorrect because the Joint Committee on Taxation provides only advisory assistance. Answer (c) is incorrect because the Ways and Means Committee merely reports to the House prior to initial approval. Answer (d) is incorrect because the Finance Committee performs the same function in the Senate as the Ways and Means Committee in the House.

25. A useful by-product of the legislative process is legislative history, which is used to help interpret the new law. Which of the following is the most useful part of the legislative history of a revenue bill?

a. Committee hearings.
b. Committee reports.
c. Senate debates.
d. Explanation accompanying the introduction of a bill.

The correct answer is (b). *(Publisher)*
REQUIRED: The most useful part of the legislative history of a revenue bill.
DISCUSSION: The committee reports usually contain a general explanation of the proposed legislation for the entire legislative body to consider. This explanation may contain reasons for the legislation, its potential impact, and its background. These reports come from the House Ways and Means Committee, Senate Finance Committee, and the Joint Conference Committee. They are frequently used to interpret new laws and are even cited by courts.

Answer (a) is incorrect because committee hearings only contain long testimony from various groups about what they think is important. Answer (c) is incorrect because Senate debates may provide the background of a new law but add little to its interpretation. Answer (d) is incorrect because bills are dramatically changed by the time they are approved by the legislative body, so an original explanation is not extremely useful.

26. As tax legislation proceeds from introduction to enactment, it is usually accompanied by reports of the House Ways and Means Committee, Senate Finance Committee, and frequently a Conference Committee report. These reports do not constitute "law," but they are a good source of information in interpreting Congressional intent.

The correct answer is (T). *(SPE 987 IV-59)*
DISCUSSION: The committee reports usually contain a general explanation of the proposed legislation for the entire legislative body to consider. This explanation may contain reasons for the legislation, its potential impact, and its background. The reports are frequently used to interpret new laws and are even cited by courts.

25.3 Return Examination

27. Before the initial in-person interview between the IRS and the taxpayer to determine or collect any taxes, a taxpayer should receive which one of the following publications from the IRS?

a. Publication 586A, The Collection Process (Income Tax Accounts), or Publication 594, The Collection Process (Employment Tax Accounts).
b. Publication 1, Your Rights as a Taxpayer.
c. Publication 5, Appeal Rights and Preparation of Protests for Unagreed Cases.
d. Form 2848, Power of Attorney and Declaration of Representative.

The correct answer is (b). *(SPE 990 IV-84)*
REQUIRED: The correct publication a taxpayer should receive from the IRS before the initial in-person interview.
DISCUSSION: Sec. 7521(b) provides that prior to the initial in-person interview, an officer or employee of the IRS must provide to the taxpayer an explanation of the audit process and the taxpayer's rights under such process, or if the interview is related to the collection of any tax, an explanation of the collection process and the taxpayer's rights under such process. This explanation is provided in Publication 1 (Your Rights as a Taxpayer).

Module 25.3: Return Examination

28. All of the following reasons are acceptable for transferring an examination from one IRS district to another except:

   a. Books and records are located in another district.
   b. The taxpayer's residence has changed since the return was filed.
   c. The place of examination is for the convenience of the Internal Revenue Service.
   d. The place of examination is solely for the convenience of the taxpayer's representative (books and records are located at his client's office which is located within the current IRS district).

The correct answer is (d). *(SPE 990 IV-57)*
REQUIRED: The reason which is not acceptable for transferring an examination from one IRS district office to another.
DISCUSSION: When a request is received to transfer a return to another district for examination, the district director having jurisdiction may transfer the case to the district director of such other district. The IRS will determine the time and place of the examination. In determining whether a transfer should be made, circumstances considered include the change of the taxpayer's domicile, discovery that the taxpayer's books and records are kept in another district, change of domicile of an executor or administrator to another district, and the effective administration of the tax laws [26 CFR 601.105(k)]. The convenience of the taxpayer's representative is not an acceptable reason to transfer an examination.
Answers (a), (b), and (c) are incorrect because each contains reasons considered acceptable by the IRS in deciding whether to transfer an examination.

29. Harold Thompson, a self-employed individual, had income transactions for 1987 (duly reported on his return filed in April 1988) as follows:

Gross receipts	$400,000
Less cost of goods sold and deductions	(320,000)
Net business income	$ 80,000
Capital gains	36,000
Gross income	$116,000

In March 1991, Thompson discovers that he had inadvertently omitted some income on his 1987 return. He retains Mann, CPA, to determine his position under the statute of limitations. Mann should advise Thompson that the 6-year statute of limitations would apply to his 1987 return only if he omitted from gross income an amount in excess of

   a. $20,000.
   b. $29,000.
   c. $100,000.
   d. $109,000.

The correct answer is (d). *(CPA 583 P-55)*
REQUIRED: The amount of gross income omission that would trigger the 6-year statute of limitations.
DISCUSSION: The normal statute of limitations is 3 years after the later of the due date of the return or when the return was filed. A 6-year statute of limitations applies if gross income omitted from the return exceeds 25% of gross income reported on the return [Sec. 6501(e)(1)]. For a trade or business, gross income means the total of the amounts received from the sale of goods before deductions and cost of goods sold. The 6-year statute of limitations will apply if Thompson omitted from gross income an amount in excess of $109,000 [25% x ($400,000 + $36,000)].

30. In the case of an examination of a return in which the same items are being questioned that were questioned in either of the 2 previous years, and the earlier examination resulted in no change to the tax liability, a taxpayer should

   a. Ignore the appointment letter.
   b. Notify the person whose name and phone number appear in the appointment letter.
   c. File a claim Form 1040X.
   d. Appear for the appointment, but decline to furnish requested information.

The correct answer is (b). *(SPE 1085 IV-65)*
REQUIRED: The proper action when an examination is based on a previously resolved issue.
DISCUSSION: If the same items were examined in either of the previous 2 years and the examination resulted in no change to the tax liability, the taxpayer should notify the person whose name and phone number appear in the appointment letter. The IRS will suspend but not cancel an audit (while reviewing its files to determine whether to proceed) so as to avoid repetitive examinations of the same items (IRS Publication No. 556).

31. Mr. B lives in Ohio. Because of his extensive real estate holdings and other business interests, his books and records are located with his accountant in Arizona. If Mr. B's return is selected for examination by the Internal Revenue Service, he may request a transfer of the examination to the appropriate Arizona office of the Internal Revenue Service.

The correct answer is (T). *(SPE 986 IV-9)*
DISCUSSION: In most cases, an income tax examination is conducted in the Internal Revenue District office nearest the taxpayer's place of residence. The examination may be transferred to another IRS district office if the taxpayer's books and records are kept in another district, the taxpayer has changed domicile, or if an executor or administrator has moved to another district. The IRS has authority to determine the time and place of the examination.

32. F's individual returns for 1988 and 1989 were examined by the Internal Revenue Service for alimony payments and exemptions claimed. No change was made to F's tax liability for 1988 or 1989. F's 1990 return was selected for examination under the Taxpayer Compliance Measurement Program (TCMP). F will be able to have the examination of the 1990 return suspended pending a review by the Internal Revenue Service to determine if it should proceed.

The correct answer is (F). *(SPE 986 IV-11)*
DISCUSSION: When a return is selected as part of a random sample for the Taxpayer Compliance Measurement Program (TCMP), the audit will not be suspended even if an examination of the taxpayer's return in either of the 2 prior years resulted in no change (IRS Publication No. 556). The TCMP audit is a review of the entire return for noncompliance, not an audit of specific items that are error-prone.

33. Taxpayers or their authorized representatives may request a conference with the examining agent's supervisor if they are not in agreement with changes proposed by the examining agent.

The correct answer is (T). *(SPE 1078 IV-13)*
DISCUSSION: If the taxpayer does not agree with the adjustments proposed, the examiner will fully explain the alternatives available. These alternatives include an interview with a supervisor, immediately if practicable [26 CFR 601.105(c)]. If a taxpayer wishes to take advantage of this alternative, (s)he should request such a conference.

34. If a taxpayer's return is changed as a result of an examination, the results may not be revealed to anyone who is not employed by the Internal Revenue Service.

The correct answer is (F). *(SPE 1080 IV-43)*
DISCUSSION: The general rule of Sec. 6103 is that tax returns and return information are confidential and are not subject to disclosure. There are exceptions to this rule, including a designee of the taxpayer, state tax officials, persons having a material interest, and Congressional committees. A change in a taxpayer's return would be considered "return information" and would be subject to the disclosure rules [Sec. 6103(b)(2)].

35. Mr. B owed an additional $5,000 tax as a result of the examination of his 1990 federal income tax return. The Internal Revenue Service gave this information, under an exchange agreement, to the state in which Mr. B lives. The Internal Revenue Service has violated Mr. B's right to privacy and may be sued for damages.

The correct answer is (F). *(SPE 1082 IV-25)*
DISCUSSION: Sec. 6103(d) allows returns and return information to be disclosed upon written request of the principal state tax official for the purpose of administering state tax laws. "Return information" includes data received or prepared by the IRS regarding a return, deficiency, or penalty. The IRS may disclose this information to the state in which B lives.

36. The filing of a Notice of Federal Tax Lien puts the public on notice that the IRS has a lien on all property, real or personal, belonging to the taxpayer.

The correct answer is (T). *(SPE 990 IV-43)*
DISCUSSION: Sec. 6323(a) states that a lien for taxes is not valid as against any purchaser, holder of a security interest, mechanic's lienor, or judgment lien creditor until proper notice has been filed. Filing a Notice of Federal Tax Lien puts the public on notice that the IRS has a lien on the taxpayer's property and establishes the IRS's priority in proceedings by creditors against the taxpayer's property.

37. When an audit is initiated by the IRS, the taxpayer must be provided with a comprehensive notice of his/her rights during the audit, as well as the procedures for appeal, claiming repetitive examinations, and making complaints.

The correct answer is (T). *(Publisher)*
DISCUSSION: Much of this has been done by the IRS in the past, but often piecemeal. In 1988, Sec. 7521 was added to the tax law requiring this comprehensive notice at the beginning of the process. This information is generally provided in IRS Publication No. 1 (Your Rights as a Taxpayer).

38. Audio recordings of an interview process between the IRS and the taxpayer are not allowed.

The correct answer is (F). *(Publisher)*
DISCUSSION: Sec. 7521(a) allows taxpayers to make audio recordings of the interview but with advance request and at the taxpayer's expense. IRS officers and employees are also permitted to make audio recordings of the interview. Advance permission of the taxpayer is required and a copy of the transcript or recording must be provided the taxpayer.

39. An interview with the IRS must be suspended immediately if the taxpayer indicates a desire to consult with a representative.

The correct answer is (T). *(Publisher)*
DISCUSSION: Sec. 7521(b) requires the interview to be suspended in such a situation.

40. The taxpayer can be required to accompany a representative (attorney, CPA, enrolled agent, or person permitted to practice before the IRS) to an interview without issuing a summons.

The correct answer is (F). *(Publisher)*
DISCUSSION: The taxpayer need not accompany such representative to any interview unless the IRS issues a summons. Such a summons is subject to judicial review.

25.4 Power of Attorney and Tax Information Authorization

41. All of the following statements concerning the Service's Centralized Authorization File (CAF) number are true except:

a. The CAF number entitles the person to whom it is assigned to practice before any office of the Internal Revenue Service except a regional Appeals Office.

b. The CAF allows Service personnel to identify representatives and the scope of their authority and will automatically direct copies of notices and correspondence to the person authorized by the taxpayer.

c. A CAF number is a unique number that will be assigned to any person who files with the Service a power of attorney and a written declaration that he or she is currently qualified to practice before the IRS and is authorized to represent the particular party on whose behalf he or she acts.

d. A CAF number is a unique number that will be assigned to any person who files with the Service a tax information authorization.

The correct answer is (a). *(SPE 989 IV-69)*
REQUIRED: The false statement concerning the CAF number.
DISCUSSION: The CAF number is the unique number that the Internal Revenue Service will assign to a representative after he or she has filed a Power of Attorney or Tax Information Authorization with an IRS office that is using the CAF system. It entitles the person to whom it is assigned to practice before any office of the Internal Revenue Service except the Regional Appeals Office.
Answers (b), (c), and (d) are correct statements concerning the IRS's centralized authorization file.

42. Which of the following would not be a proper execution of a power of attorney or tax information authorization?

   a. For a corporation, by an officer having authority to bind the corporation.
   b. For a deceased taxpayer, by the executor or administrator.
   c. For a taxpayer with a court-appointed guardian, by the one appointed.
   d. For a partnership, by any partner.

The correct answer is (d). *(SPE 1078 IV-80)*
REQUIRED: The improper execution of a power of attorney or tax information authorization.
DISCUSSION: The rules for execution of a power of attorney and a tax information authorization are contained in 26 CFR 601.504(b). If the power of attorney is for a partnership, all partners must sign or a duly authorized member may sign, but not just any partner.
Answers (a), (b), and (c) are incorrect because each individual listed has the authority to properly execute a power of attorney.

43. A power of attorney or tax information authorization should contain all of the following information except

   a. The taxpayer's intent as to the scope of authority of the representative.
   b. The divisions of the IRS which are involved in the matter covered by the power of attorney.
   c. Type of tax involved.
   d. The year(s) or period(s).

The correct answer is (b). *(SPE 1085 IV-68)*
REQUIRED: Information not required in a power of attorney or tax information authorization.
DISCUSSION: A power of attorney or tax information authorization need not list the divisions of the IRS which are involved in the matter. Required information includes the taxpayer's intention as to the scope of the authority of the representative, the tax matter(s) to which the authority relates, and the year(s) or period(s) involved.
Answers (a), (c), and (d) are incorrect because each item is required in a power of attorney or tax information authorization.

44. Form 2848, Power of Attorney and Declaration of Representative, properly executed by the taxpayer, permits the taxpayer's representative to make substitution of representatives without the taxpayer's specific grant of authority to do so.

The correct answer is (T). *(SPE 990 IV-25)*
DISCUSSION: A properly executed Power of Attorney and Declaration of Representative permits the taxpayer's representative to make substitution of representatives without the taxpayer's specific grant of authority to do so. However, if the taxpayer wishes to authorize the taxpayer's representative to make substitution of representatives or delegate authority to other representatives, the power of attorney must state this intention [26 CFR 601.504(a)].

45. A properly executed power of attorney can be used in connection with more than one particular type of tax.

The correct answer is (T). *(SPE 990 IV-26)*
DISCUSSION: The formal requirements for execution of a power of attorney are found in 26 CFR 601.504. A power of attorney may relate to more than one matter, as, for example, a power of attorney that relates to more than one particular type of tax. The specific type of types of tax should be stated on the power of attorney. A general reference to "all taxes" is not acceptable.

46. If a court having jurisdiction over a debtor appoints a trustee, receiver, or an attorney (designated to represent a trustee, receiver, or debtor in possession), then documents from the court attesting to this appointment preclude the necessity of a power of attorney or a tax information authorization.

The correct answer is (T). *(SPE 1078 IV-42)*
DISCUSSION: Proof of appointment by a court having jurisdiction over the debtor (of a trustee, receiver, or attorney) is generally sufficient to authorize disclosure without a power of attorney or tax information authorization [26 CFR 601.502(c)(3)].

47. A power of attorney or a tax information authorization is not required by the Internal Revenue Service in cases docketed in the Tax Court.

The correct answer is (T). *(SPE 988 IV-34)*
DISCUSSION: A power of attorney or a tax information authorization is not required in cases docketed in the Tax Court. The Tax Court rules provide that counsel for a taxpayer must be admitted to practice before the Tax Court. When the taxpayer's petition to Tax Court is signed by counsel admitted to practice before the Tax Court, that counsel will be recognized as representing that party.

Module 25.4: Power of Attorney and Tax Information Authorization

48. A tax information authorization is not required of a taxpayer's representative at a conference with IRS officials which is also attended by the taxpayer.

The correct answer is (T). *(SPE 988 IV-30)*
DISCUSSION: 26 CFR 601.502(c)(3) provides that a tax information authorization is not required of a taxpayer's representative at a conference which is also attended by the taxpayer.

49. A taxpayer's representative who is recognized to practice before the Internal Revenue Service attends an estate tax case conference without the executor or administrator. No tax information authorization is necessary if the representative is the preparer of the estate tax return and the attorney of record for the executor or administrator before the court where the will is probated or the estate administered.

The correct answer is (T). *(SPE 1078 IV-7)*
DISCUSSION: 26 CFR 601.502(c)(3) provides that a tax information authorization or power of attorney is not required at a conference concerning an estate tax case (even though the executor or administrator is not present at the conference) if the representative presents evidence that (s)he is recognized to practice before the IRS, prepared the estate tax return on behalf of the executor or administrator, and is the attorney of record for the executor or administrator before the court where the will is probated or the estate is administered.

50. Either a tax information authorization or a power of attorney is required for a practitioner to receive a notice of deficiency under Sec. 6212.

The correct answer is (T). *(SPE 1080 IV-2)*
DISCUSSION: 26 CFR 601.502(c)(2) requires a tax information authorization for a taxpayer's representative to receive a notice of deficiency under Sec. 6212. A tax information authorization is not required if the representative has filed a power of attorney for the same matters. Therefore, either a tax information authorization or a power of attorney will fulfill the requirements.

51. A taxpayer's representative is not required to file a tax information authorization in order to receive or inspect confidential information on behalf of the taxpayer if the representative has filed a properly executed power of attorney in connection with the same year and same type of tax, and the power of attorney has not been revoked.

The correct answer is (T). *(SPE 986 IV-22)*
DISCUSSION: 26 CFR 601.502(c)(2) requires a tax information authorization for a taxpayer's representative to receive or inspect confidential tax information on behalf of the taxpayer unless the representative has filed a power of attorney to perform the specific acts.

52. A power of attorney is not required for a practitioner to sign a waiver of notice of disallowance of a claim or credit for a refund.

The correct answer is (F). *(SPE 1079 IV-22)*
DISCUSSION: 26 CFR 601.502(c)(1) specifically provides that a power of attorney is required for a taxpayer's representative to execute a waiver of notice of disallowance of a claim for credit or refund.

53. A taxpayer's representative is not required to submit to the Internal Revenue Service a power of attorney executed by the taxpayer, if the representative wishes to execute a closing agreement under Sec. 7121 of the Internal Revenue Code.

The correct answer is (F). *(SPE 986 IV-21)*
DISCUSSION: 26 CFR 601.502(c)(1) specifically provides that a power of attorney is required for a taxpayer's representative to execute a closing agreement under Sec. 7121.

54. A taxpayer's representative is required to submit to the Internal Revenue Service a power of attorney properly executed by the taxpayer if the representative wishes to extend the statutory period for assessment or collection of a tax on behalf of the taxpayer.

The correct answer is (T). *(SPE 988 IV-28)*
DISCUSSION: Under 26 CFR 601.502(c)(1), a power of attorney is required for a taxpayer's representative to execute a consent to extend the statutory period for assessment or collection of a tax. The power of attorney must be in proper form and must be executed by the taxpayer.

55. A power of attorney is required for the execution of a waiver of restriction on assessment or collection of a deficiency in tax by the practitioner.

The correct answer is (T). *(SPE 1079 IV-21)*
DISCUSSION: 26 CFR 601.502(c)(1) provides that a power of attorney is required for a taxpayer's representative to execute a waiver of restriction on assessment or collection of a deficiency in tax.

56. The right for a taxpayer's representative to receive refund checks must be specifically granted by the taxpayer in IRS Form 2848 or a general power of attorney.

The correct answer is (T). *(SPE 987 IV-30)*
DISCUSSION: 26 CFR 601.502(c)(1) provides that for a taxpayer's representative to receive a refund check the taxpayer must specifically authorize this in IRS Form 2848 (Power of Attorney and Declaration of Representative). But the representative is not authorized to endorse and collect the refund check.

57. If a joint return is involved and the husband and wife are to be represented by the same representative, the power of attorney requires the signature of both husband and wife unless one spouse is duly authorized in writing to sign for the other spouse.

The correct answer is (T). *(SPE 990 IV-24)*
DISCUSSION: 26 CFR 601.504(b)(ii) states that if a joint return is involved and the husband and wife are to be represented by the same representative, the power of attorney must be signed by both spouses unless one spouse is duly authorized in writing to sign for the other spouse.

58. A power of attorney is given for representation in tax matters. For acts to be performed, it lists, "in all tax matters." This is not a valid authorization.

The correct answer is (T). *(SPE 1078 IV-36)*
DISCUSSION: Use of technical language in the preparation of a power of attorney is not necessary, but the instrument should clearly express the taxpayer's intentions. It must clearly specify which acts the representative is authorized to perform [26 CFR 601.504(a)]. "In all tax matters" is not sufficient.

59. If a taxpayer has more than one representative in a matter, and does not designate on the power of attorney which representative is to receive copies of notices and other written communication, it is the practice of the Service to give such copies to the representative first named on the power of attorney with the latest date.

The correct answer is (T). *(SPE 989 IV-32)*
DISCUSSION: 26 CFR 601.506(a) states that if a taxpayer designates more than one representative to receive copies of notices and other written communications, the IRS will give copies of such communications to no more than two representatives so designated. It is the Service's practice to give such copies to the representative first named on the power of attorney with the latest date unless the taxpayer lists the names of not more than two representatives to receive copies of written communications.

60. An attorney, certified public accountant, or a person enrolled to practice before the Internal Revenue Service is not required to file a power of attorney in any form to receive or inspect confidential information about his/her clients' tax matters.

The correct answer is (F). *(SPE 984 IV-27)*
DISCUSSION: Any taxpayer representative must file either a power of attorney or a tax information authorization to receive or inspect confidential tax information. A representative who is recognized to practice before the IRS, such as an attorney, CPA, or enrolled agent, need only execute a declaration on the power of attorney that (s)he is so recognized. The declaration is in lieu of the general procedure of having two disinterested individuals witness the power of attorney [26 CFR 601.504(d)(2)].

61. A corporate power of attorney must be signed by a witness attesting to its validity or have the corporate seal affixed in order for it to be valid.

The correct answer is (F). *(SPE 990 IV-22)*
DISCUSSION: It is not necessary that a power of attorney or a tax information authorization granted by a corporation be attested or that the corporate seal be affixed. Spaces provided on these authorization forms for affixing the corporate seal are for the convenience of the corporations required by charter or law to affix their corporate seals in the execution of instruments [26 CFR 601.504(c)].

62. A single Form 2848, Power of Attorney and Declaration of Representative, may not cover more than one tax matter or more than one taxable year.

The correct answer is (F). *(SPE 1082 IV-37)*
DISCUSSION: 26 CFR 601.504(a) states that a power of attorney or tax information authorization may relate to more than one matter (e.g., a taxpayer's income taxes for several different taxable years). The power of attorney must clearly express the taxpayer's intention as to the scope of the authority of the representative, and must also clearly specify the tax matter(s) to which the authority relates.

63. If a power of attorney has been filed, a new power of attorney must be filed if the taxpayer changes the authority granted to a representative.

The correct answer is (T). *(SPE 1080 IV-7)*
DISCUSSION: 26 CFR 601.505(c)(1) provides that a new power of attorney must be filed if a power of attorney has been filed and if, with respect to the same matter, the taxpayer desires to change the authority granted to a representative.

64. A new power of attorney or tax information authorization is required if the taxpayer desires to add to or reduce the number of persons authorized to represent the taxpayer before the Internal Revenue Service in a tax matter.

The correct answer is (T). *(SPE 984 IV-45)*
DISCUSSION: 26 CFR 601.505(c)(1) provides that a new power of attorney must be filed if a power of attorney was previously filed and the taxpayer desires to change the authority granted to a representative, including changing the number of authorized representatives.

65. A new tax information authorization will revoke a prior power of attorney if the taxpayer signs a statement listing the names and addresses of those individuals listed under the prior power of attorney whose authority is revoked.

The correct answer is (T). *(SPE 989 IV-28)*
DISCUSSION: 26 CFR 601.505(c)(2) provides that a new power of attorney will be deemed to revoke a prior power of attorney unless the new power of attorney contains a clause specifically stating that it does not revoke a prior power of attorney. A similar rule applies to new tax information authorizations. A new tax information notice will revoke a prior power of attorney if the taxpayer signs a statement listing the names and addresses of the individuals listed under the prior power of attorney whose authority is revoked.

66. An Internal Revenue Service examiner cannot, under any circumstances, bypass a taxpayer's representative and contact the taxpayer directly if the representative holds a valid power of attorney from the taxpayer.

The correct answer is (F). *(SPE 986 IV-24)*
DISCUSSION: Generally, an IRS examiner cannot bypass a taxpayer's representative and contact the taxpayer directly if the representative holds a valid power of attorney. However, if the representative has unreasonably delayed or hindered the examination by failing to furnish necessary nonprivileged information, an examiner who receives permission from the chief of examination for the district may contact the taxpayer directly [26 CFR 601.505(b)].

25.5 Appeals Within the IRS

67. All of the following should be contained in a written protest letter except

a. A statement that the taxpayer wants to appeal the findings of the examiner to the Appeals Office.

b. The date and symbols from the letter showing the proposed adjustments and findings being protested.

c. Tax periods or years involved.

d. A statement indicating whether the examination was originally handled through correspondence, by a tax auditor, or by an IRS agent.

The correct answer is (d). *(SPE 984 IV-80)*
REQUIRED: The item that is not required in a written protest.
DISCUSSION: IRS Publication No. 5 (Appeal Rights and Preparation of Protests for Unagreed Cases) provides that a written protest should contain a statement that the taxpayer wants to appeal the findings of the examining officer, the date and symbols from the letter transmitting the proposed adjustments and findings protested, the taxpayer's name and address, the tax periods or years involved, an itemized schedule of the adjustments with which the taxpayer does not agree, a statement of facts supporting the taxpayer's position on any contested factual issue, and a statement outlining the law or authority relied upon. A statement indicating whether the examination was originally handled through correspondence, by a tax auditor, or by an IRS agent is not required.
Answers (a), (b), and (c) are incorrect because each should be included in a written protest.

68. Mr. K, who lives in Dallas, Texas, received a letter from the IRS stating that the result of a recent field examination is a tax deficiency of $15,000. The examination was handled by a revenue agent at Mr. K's place of business. The letter also states that Mr. K has a right to file a protest if he does not agree with the proposal. Generally, how many days does K have to file a written protest?

a. 15 days.

b. 30 days.

c. 60 days.

d. 90 days.

The correct answer is (b). *(SPE 990 IV-59)*
REQUIRED: The number of days granted to file a written protest.
DISCUSSION: If a written protest is required, it must be filed within the 30-day period granted in the letter transmitting the report of examination. A written protest is required unless the change does not exceed $2,500 or the examination was conducted through correspondence or in an IRS office by a tax auditor [26 CFR 601.105(d)(1) and (2)].

69. In response to a preliminary (30-day) letter, a written protest discussing the facts and legal arguments must accompany a written request for an Appeals Conference in which of the following cases?

a. A proposed $2,000 tax increase.

b. The tax return examination was made in an IRS office by a tax auditor.

c. The tax return examination was made by correspondence.

d. A proposed disallowance of a $3,000 refund claim.

The correct answer is (d). *(SPE 987 IV-65)*
REQUIRED: The situation which requires a written protest in a request for an Appeals Conference.
DISCUSSION: A written protest is required if the change exceeds $2,500 [26 CFR 601.105(e)]. The protest must be filed within the 30-day period granted in the letter transmitting the report of examination.
Answer (a) is incorrect because a written protest is not required for changes which do not exceed $2,500. Answer (b) is incorrect because a written protest is not required for examinations conducted in an IRS office by a tax auditor. Answer (c) is incorrect because a written protest is not required for examinations made by correspondence.

70. Mr. K's income tax return was audited by the Internal Revenue Service. The Service determined that K's income tax liability was greater than that shown on his return. If K disagrees, he must participate in a conference with an IRS Appeals Office before he can appeal to the courts.

The correct answer is (F). *(SPE 988 IV-16)*
DISCUSSION: 26 CFR 601.105 gives taxpayers the right to appeal within the Service. However, appeal is at the option of the taxpayer, and (s)he may take the case to court instead [26 CFR 601.106(b)].

Module 25.6: Deficiencies and Assessments

71. Only one level of appeal exists within the Internal Revenue Service. All appeals are made to the Appeals Office.

The correct answer is (T). *(SPE 1080 IV-42)*
DISCUSSION: Other than a conference with the examining agent's supervisor, there is only one level of appeal within the IRS. All appeals are made to the Appeals Office in the taxpayer's region [26 CFR 601.105(c) and (d) and 601.106].

72. Conferences with the Internal Revenue Service Appeals Office are available to taxpayers if their reasons for disagreement are based solely on constitutional grounds.

The correct answer is (F). *(SPE 1082 IV-23)*
DISCUSSION: 26 CFR 601.106(b) provides that the appeals process does not extend to cases based solely on moral, religious, political, or constitutional grounds.

73. Mr. V's income tax return was examined by an IRS tax auditor in an IRS office. The tax auditor proposed an additional tax liability of $12,000. Mr. V does not agree with the auditor's findings and wishes to schedule a conference with an IRS Regional Appeals Office. V must file a written protest of the auditor's findings to obtain an appeals conference.

The correct answer is (F). *(SPE 990 IV-11)*
DISCUSSION: Under 26 CFR 601.105(d) and 601.106(a)(1)(ii), a written protest is required in a field examination case when the total amount of proposed adjustment exceeds $2,500. If the examination was conducted by an IRS tax auditor in an IRS office, a written protest is not required regardless of the amount of proposed adjustment.

74. In any case in which the taxpayer's representative is unable or unwilling to declare of his or her own knowledge that the facts in a claim, written argument, brief, or recitation of facts are true and correct, the Internal Revenue Service may request the taxpayer to make such a declaration under penalty of perjury.

The correct answer is (T). *(SPE 1081 IV-39)*
DISCUSSION: If a taxpayer's representative sends in the protest, (s)he must declare that (s)he prepared it and personally knows the statements of fact are true and correct (IRS Publication No. 556). Alternatively, the taxpayer must make such a declaration under penalty of perjury (IRS Publication No. 556 and Rev. Proc. 61-36).

25.6 Deficiencies and Assessments

75. Which of the following is usually required before taxes may be assessed?

a. A deficiency must be assessed.
b. The taxpayer must file a return.
c. A waiver of restrictions on assessment must be filed.
d. It must be 3 years after the return was filed.

The correct answer is (a). *(Publisher)*
REQUIRED: The action which is usually required before taxes may be assessed.
DISCUSSION: The assessment of taxes is made by recording the liability of the taxpayer in the office of the Secretary of the Treasury (Sec. 6203). Taxes shown on a return filed by a taxpayer, overstatements of credits, and mathematical errors may be assessed immediately (Sec. 6201). However, in the case of a deficiency (the tax imposed in excess of the sum of the amount shown on the return plus amounts previously assessed), a notice of deficiency must be sent to the taxpayer prior to assessment [Sec. 6213(a)]. The taxpayer has 90 days after the notice of deficiency is mailed to file a petition in Tax Court (which prevents the assessment of taxes until the decision of the Tax Court is final). If a petition is not filed, taxes may be assessed 90 days after the notice of deficiency is mailed.
Answer (b) is incorrect because if the taxpayer does not file a return, the IRS may file a return for him/her and an assessment may be made for any deficiency after the required procedures are followed. Answer (c) is incorrect because although a waiver of restrictions on assessment will allow the taxes to be assessed immediately, they may also be assessed 90 days after a deficiency notice is mailed. Answer (d) is incorrect because an assessment of tax must generally be made within (not after) 3 years after the return was filed [Sec. 6501(a)]. The IRS has longer to assess if there is a substantial omission of gross income (in excess of 25%) or a willful attempt to evade tax.

76. Which of the following is not a situation in which taxes may be assessed without the issuance of a statutory notice of deficiency?

   a. Overstatement of a credit on a return.
   b. Mathematical error on a return.
   c. There is a waiver of restrictions on assessment.
   d. The taxpayer has not filed a return.

The correct answer is (d). *(Publisher)*
REQUIRED: The situation which does not allow taxes to be assessed without issuance of a notice of deficiency.
DISCUSSION: There are several exceptions to the requirement that a notice of deficiency be mailed to the taxpayer (and 90 days elapse) before taxes may be assessed. However, the failure of a taxpayer to file a return does not allow the immediate assessment of taxes. A deficiency must be determined and a statutory notice of deficiency must be mailed.
Answer (a) is incorrect because Sec. 6201(a)(3) provides that an overstatement of credits may be assessed without restriction. Answer (b) is incorrect because Sec. 6213(b) allows the assessment without restriction of additional amounts of tax owing because of mathematical or clerical errors in a return. Answer (c) is incorrect because a waiver of restrictions on assessment is formal permission by the taxpayer to the IRS to assess taxes without mailing a notice of deficiency [Sec. 6213(d)].

77. Ronald Raff filed his 1990 individual income tax return on January 15, 1991. There was no understatement of income on the return, and the return was properly signed and filed. The statute of limitations for Raff's 1990 return expires on (assuming no relevant day is a Saturday, Sunday, or holiday)

   a. January 15, 1994.
   b. April 15, 1994.
   c. January 15, 1997.
   d. April 15, 1997.

The correct answer is (b). *(CPA 1184 Q-38)*
REQUIRED: The statute of limitations for a properly filed return.
DISCUSSION: Under Sec. 6501(a), the general statute of limitations for assessment of a deficiency is 3 years from the date the return was filed or due. Under Sec. 6501(b), an income tax return filed before the due date for the return is considered to be filed on the due date for statute of limitations purposes. Since Raff's return was due April 15, 1991, the statute of limitations will expire 3 years from that date.

78. On April 15, 1991, a married couple filed their joint 1990 calendar-year return showing gross income of $80,000. Their return had been prepared by a professional tax preparer who mistakenly omitted $30,000 of income which, in good faith, the preparer considered to be nontaxable. No information with regard to this omitted income was disclosed on the return or attached statements. By what date must the Internal Revenue Service assert a notice of deficiency before the statute of limitations expires?

   a. December 31, 1993.
   b. April 15, 1994.
   c. December 31, 1996.
   d. April 15, 1997.

The correct answer is (d). *(CPA 589 Q-56)*
REQUIRED: The date by which the IRS must assert a notice of deficiency.
DISCUSSION: Sec. 6501(e) provides that if an omission in excess of 25% of gross income stated in the return occurs, the statute of limitations for assessment is 6 years from the date the return was filed (or the due date, if later). This applies even if the omission is made in good faith.

79. What is the statute of limitations on a return which was required to be filed but was never filed?

   a. It never ends.
   b. 3 years.
   c. 6 years.
   d. 7 years.

The correct answer is (a). *(M. Yates)*
REQUIRED: The statute of limitations on a return that was never filed.
DISCUSSION: When a return is not filed, the statute of limitations time period never begins and therefore never ends [Sec. 6501(c)(3)].

80. All of the following statements relating to the statutory notice of deficiency are true except:

    a. If a taxpayer pays the tax after the statutory notice of deficiency has been issued, the taxpayer can no longer petition the Tax Court for review.

    b. The notice of deficiency provides the taxpayer 90 days (150 days if the taxpayer lives outside the United States) to either agree to the deficiency or file a petition with the Tax Court for a redetermination of the deficiency.

    c. The notice of deficiency is not an assessment.

    d. The Service may, with the taxpayer's consent, rescind a notice of deficiency issued after 1985 and once rescinded it is treated as if it never existed.

The correct answer is (a). *(SPE 989 IV-65)*
REQUIRED: The false statement about the notice of deficiency.
DISCUSSION: Normally, once a taxpayer pays the tax, the Tax Court does not have jurisdiction and the taxpayer must file a claim for a refund in U.S. District Court or the Claims Court. However, Sec. 6213(b)(4) provides that payment of additional tax due after the mailing of a notice of deficiency does not deprive the Tax Court of jurisdiction over the deficiency.

Answers (b), (c), and (d) are incorrect because each statement is true. Sec. 6213(a) provides that a taxpayer may file a petition with the Tax Court for a redetermination of the deficiency within 90 days (or 150 if the taxpayer lives outside the U.S.) after the notice of deficiency is mailed. If 90 days (or 150) pass and a petition is not filed, taxes may be assessed and the taxpayer must pay the tax and file a claim for refund.

81. Ms. A was audited for 1989 and agreed to the findings of the Internal Revenue Service examiner that she owed an additional $500. Ms. A will be charged interest on the additional tax from the due date of the return to the billing date if she does not pay the tax when she signs the agreement form. However, Ms. A will not be billed for more than 30 days interest from the date she signs the agreements.

The correct answer is (T). *(SPE 988 IV-17)*
REQUIRED: The date to which interest will be charged on a deficiency.
DISCUSSION: Sec. 6601(c) provides that if a taxpayer files an agreement waiving the restrictions on assessment of deficiency, and notice and demand for payment are not made within 30 days after filing such waiver, interest will be suspended 30 days after signing of the waiver.

Once the demand for payment is made, interest does not accrue after the date of demand if the tax is paid within 10 days after the date of such demand [Sec. 6601(e)(3)].

Thus, Ms. A will not be billed for more than 30 days of interest from the date she signs the agreement. The interest rate charged for underpayments of tax by individuals for returns due after 1986 is the short-term federal rate plus three percentage points (Sec. 6621).

25.7 IRS Collection Procedures

82. The collection process begins:

    a. At the IRS service center where notices are generated requesting payment.

    b. In an IRS Automated Collection Branch when a telephone contact is made with the taxpayer.

    c. Only after the Problem Resolution Officer has acted upon the taxpayer's claim.

    d. When a notice of federal tax lien is filed.

The correct answer is (a). *(SPE 990 IV-85)*
REQUIRED: The correct statement concerning the IRS collection process.
DISCUSSION: Sec. 6301 authorizes the Internal Revenue Service, on behalf of the Secretary of the Treasury, to collect taxes imposed by the internal revenue laws. The collection process begins at the IRS service center where notices are generated requesting payment. Reg. 301.6303-1 states that the district director or the director of the regional service center shall, after the making of a tax assessment, give notice to the person liable for the unpaid tax, stating the amount of the tax and demanding payment.

Answers (b), (c), and (d) are incorrect because they are steps in the collection process that occur subsequent to the taxpayer receiving notice and demand for payment from the service center.

83. The initial action required in the collection process is:

a. The filing of a Notice of Levy.
b. An assessment.
c. The receipt of the fourth notice by certified mail.
d. A notification of a pending examination audit.

The correct answer is (b). *(SPE 990 IV-79)*
REQUIRED: The initial action required in the collection process.
DISCUSSION: Sec. 6201(a) authorizes the Internal Revenue Service to make a determination of all taxes. If the IRS makes a determination that a tax liability exists, the IRS has the authority under Sec. 6201(a) to assess the tax. The assessment of the taxes is the initial action required in the collection process.
Answers (a) and (c) are incorrect because they are steps in the collection process that occur subsequent to the assessment. Answer (d) is incorrect because a notification of a pending examination is part of the examination process, not the collection process.

84. If a taxpayer believes IRS collection personnel have not administered the tax laws properly, (s)he may apply for which of the following from the IRS Problem Resolution Program office?

a. An offer in compromise.
b. An installment agreement.
c. A taxpayer assistance order.
d. A case review.

The correct answer is (c). *(SPE 990 IV-83)*
REQUIRED: The form of relief a taxpayer may request from the Problem Resolution Program.
DISCUSSION: The Problem Resolution Program is designed to aid taxpayers who have been unable to resolve their tax problems after repeated attempts to do so using normal procedures. If a taxpayer suffers or is about to suffer a significant hardship because of the collection of a tax liability, (s)he may apply for a taxpayer assistance order from the Problem Resolution Program. A Problem Resolution Officer reviews the application and may issue a taxpayer assistance order, which may direct the collection function to take actions to relieve the hardship (Sec. 7811).
Answers (a), (b), and (d) are not forms of relief which may be obtained from the Problem Resolution Program.

85. Taxpayers have a right by law to submit an offer in compromise on their unpaid tax liability. An offer in compromise is:

a. An installment agreement.
b. A request for abatement of tax.
c. Based upon doubt as to liability or doubt as to collectability.
d. The payment of tax liability if the penalties and interest are waived.

The correct answer is (c). *(SPE 990 IV-82)*
REQUIRED: The correct definition of an offer in compromise.
DISCUSSION: Under Sec. 7122, the Commissioner of the Internal Revenue Service has the authority to compromise all taxes, interest, and penalties arising under the internal revenue laws, except those relating to alcohol, tobacco, and firearms. A compromise may be made on one or both of two grounds: (1) doubt as to the liability for the amount owed or (2) doubt as to the taxpayer's ability to make full payment. The doubt as to the liability for the amount owed must be supported by the evidence. In the case of inability to pay, the amount offered must exceed the total value of the taxpayer's equity in all his/her assets, and must give sufficient consideration to present and future earning capacity. A compromise may be entered into by the IRS whether a suit has been instituted or not, and may be entered into after a judgment has been rendered.
Answers (a), (c), and (d) are not correct definitions of an offer in compromise.

Module 25.7: IRS Collection Procedures

86. During the period of an installment agreement:
   a. All payments must be made timely and interest and penalties continue to accrue.
   b. Timely payments suspend the accrual of interest and penalties.
   c. Payments can only be made by certified check.
   d. A release of Notice of Federal Tax Lien is filed.

The correct answer is (a). *(SPE 990 IV-87)*
REQUIRED: The correct statement concerning an installment agreement.
DISCUSSION: Under Sec. 6159, the IRS is authorized to enter into written agreements with a taxpayer for the payment of a tax liability in installments. Once an installment agreement is made, the taxpayer must make each payment on time. Interest and penalties will continue to accrue. Failure to pay an installment can result in the termination of the agreement.
Answers (b), (c), and (d) are not correct statements concerning an installment agreement.

87. Assessments, except for jeopardy situations, can be collected by levy after the "Notice of Intent to Levy" is provided and the taxpayer "neglects or refuses" to pay within what period of time?
   a. 10 days.
   b. 30 days.
   c. 45 days.
   d. Immediately.

The correct answer is (b). *(SPE 990 IV-86)*
REQUIRED: The period of time within which an assessment can be collected by levy after the "Notice of Intent to Levy" is provided.
DISCUSSION: Sec. 6331(a) states that if any person liable for tax neglects or refuses to pay the tax within 10 days after notice and demand, the assessment can be collected by levy. Before the levy can be made, a Final Notice (Notice of Intent to Levy) must be given to the taxpayer. This notice must be given in person, left at the taxpayer's dwelling or usual place of business, or sent by certified or registered mail to the taxpayer's last known address. The Final Notice (Notice of Intent to Levy) must be given to the taxpayer at least 30 days in advance [Sec. 6331(d)(2)].

88. Which of the following is not a legal requirement that must be met before levy action can be taken?
   a. The taxpayer must have been audited by the IRS.
   b. An unpaid tax liability must exist.
   c. A notice and demand for payment must have been sent to the taxpayer's last known address.
   d. A Final Notice (Notice of Intent to Levy) must be given to the taxpayer at least 30 days in advance.

The correct answer is (a). *(Publisher)*
REQUIRED: The event that is not a legal requirement that must be met before levy action can be taken.
DISCUSSION: Sec. 6331 authorizes the Internal Revenue Service to collect unpaid taxes by levying upon the taxpayer's property. Before levy action can be taken, it must first be determined that a tax liability exists. Within 60 days after making the assessment, the IRS is required to give a notice and demand for payment to the taxpayer. This notice must be left at the taxpayer's dwelling or usual place of business, or sent by mail to the taxpayer's last known address [Sec. 6303(a)]. If the taxpayer neglects or refuses to pay the tax within 10 days after notice and demand, a Final Notice (Notice of Intent to Levy) must be given to the taxpayer at least 30 days in advance [Sec. 6331(b)]. There is no requirement that a taxpayer first be audited.

89. Jeopardy levies may occur when the IRS waives the 10-day notice and demand period and/or Final Notice (Notice of Intent to Levy) 30-day period because:
   a. A delay would endanger the collection of tax.
   b. The seized property is perishable in nature.
   c. The taxpayer has filed for bankruptcy protection.
   d. The IRS is working in conjunction with the Drug Enforcement Administration.

The correct answer is (a). *(SPE 990 IV-80)*
REQUIRED: The reason jeopardy levies may occur.
DISCUSSION: Under Sec. 6331(a), a taxpayer has 10 days to pay the tax after receiving a Notice and Demand for Tax. If the taxpayer neglects or refuses to pay the tax within that time, the IRS may issue a Final Notice (Notice of Intent to Levy) giving the taxpayer 30 days to pay the tax. If the tax is not paid within that period, the IRS may proceed to collect the tax by levy upon the taxpayer's property. If the IRS makes a finding that the assessment or collection of the tax deficiency is in jeopardy, the IRS may waive the 10-day Notice and Demand period and/or the Final Notice (Notice of Intent to Levy) 30-day period. Jeopardy levies may occur when delay would endanger collection of the tax, interest, penalties, etc. (Sec. 6861).
Answers (b), (c), and (d) are not reasons for jeopardy levies.

90. Unless seized property is perishable, the IRS will:

   a. Advertise the sale for 90 days before the sale.
   b. Conduct the sale after the 60th day.
   c. Request sealed bids for the property.
   d. Wait at least 10 days before conducting the sale.

The correct answer is (d). *(SPE 990 IV-88)*
REQUIRED: The time period for the sale of nonperishable seized property.
DISCUSSION: After seizure of property, the IRS gives notice of sale to the public and to the taxpayer from whom the property was seized. Under Sec. 6335(d), the time of sale must be not less than 10 days nor more than 40 days from the time of giving public notice. Sec. 6336 provides an exception to this rule in the case of perishable goods, which must be returned to the taxpayer if he pays the appraised value of the goods or posts a bond. If the taxpayer does not pay such amount or post a bond, the goods must be sold immediately.

Answer (a) is incorrect because the IRS may sell the property after 10 days of giving public notice. Answer (b) is incorrect because the sale must be conducted not more than 40 days from the time of giving public notice. Answer (c) is incorrect because the property may be sold by public auction as well as by public sale under sealed bids.

91. A levy is the taking of property to satisfy a tax liability.

The correct answer is (T). *(SPE 990 IV-46)*
DISCUSSION: Sec. 7701(a)(21) defines a levy as the power of distraint and seizure by any means. Sec. 6331(a) authorizes the Internal Revenue Service to take (seize) property if a taxpayer neglects or refuses to pay a tax liability. The seized property can be sold to satisfy the unpaid liability.

92. Unemployment benefits are the only property exempt from levy by federal law.

The correct answer is (F). *(SPE 990 IV-48)*
DISCUSSION: Sec. 6334 lists various types of property that are exempt from levy. Unemployment benefits are one type of exempt property [Sec. 6334(a)(4)]. Among the other types of exempt property are wearing apparel, school books, workers' compensation, and undelivered mail.

93. A taxpayer's principal residence is exempt from levy by the IRS by federal law unless jeopardy exists or prior written approval of the IRS district director or assistant district director has been secured.

The correct answer is (T). *(SPE 990 IV-53)*
DISCUSSION: Under Sec. 6334(a)(13), a taxpayer's principal residence is generally exempt from levy by the IRS. However, under Sec. 6334(e), levy is allowed on a taxpayer's principal residence if the district director or assistant district director approves such a levy in writing or if the collection of the tax is in jeopardy.

94. Mr. P's 1990 individual income tax return was examined which resulted in a deficiency of $5,000. P signed an agreement form and paid the additional tax. The interest due from P will be figured from the due date of the return to the date of payment.

The correct answer is (T). *(SPE 990 IV-14)*
DISCUSSION: Under Sec. 6601(a), interest on any underpayment of tax begins to accrue on the date the tax liability arises, which is generally the due date of the return computed without regard to extensions. The interest continues to accrue until the date the tax is paid, except in those cases where the taxpayer signs an agreement form without paying the tax and then pays the tax within 10 days of the date of the Notice and Demand for Tax. Since Mr. P paid the additional tax when he signed the agreement form, the interest will be figured from the due date of the return to the date of payment.

Module 25.7: IRS Collection Procedures

95. Once served, a levy on salary or wages continues for 90 days, or until the tax liability is satisfied.

The correct answer is (F). *(SPE 990 IV-47)*
DISCUSSION: Under Sec. 6331(e), a levy on salary or wages continues from the date the levy is first made until the tax liability is satisfied, the levy is released, or the levy becomes unenforceable due to lapse of time.

96. Mr. M was audited for 1989 and agreed to the findings of the Internal Revenue Service examiner that he owned an additional $5,000. Mr. M did not pay the deficiency when he signed the agreement form. If Mr. M does not pay the amount due within 10 days of the billing date, he could be assessed more interest and/or penalties.

The correct answer is (T). *(SPE 989 IV-18)*
DISCUSSION: Under Sec. 6601(a), interest on an underpayment of tax is figured from the date the tax was due (generally, the due date of the return computed without regard to extensions) to the date the tax is paid. In cases where a taxpayer agrees that additional tax is owed, but does not pay the tax when the agreement form is signed, the taxpayer receives a Notice and Demand for Tax. Sec. 6601(e)(3) states that if the additional tax is paid within 10 days of such notice, interest will cease to accrue as of the date of the notice rather than on the date of payment. However, if the additional tax is not paid within the 10-day period, Sec. 6601(e)(2) states that the general rule of Sec. 6601(a) takes effect and the interest will continue to accrue until the tax is paid.

97. A Chapter 7 bankruptcy discharges all of the unpaid tax liability of a sole proprietor.

The correct answer is (F). *(SPE 990 IV-45)*
DISCUSSION: Under Sec. 6871, upon the adjudication of bankruptcy, the IRS may immediately asses any tax deficiency (including interest, penalties, etc.) that has not previously been assessed. Bankruptcy does not discharge a sole proprietor's unpaid tax liability. The IRS will file a proof of claim in the bankruptcy court and will attempt to satisfy the deficiency from the assets in the bankruptcy estate.

98. If at any step of the collection process a taxpayer does not agree with the recommendations of an IRS collection employee, the taxpayer has the right to discuss the matter with the employee's manager.

The correct answer is (T). *(SPE 990 IV-51)*
DISCUSSION: When the Internal Revenue Service sends a Notice and Demand for Tax to a taxpayer, the notice is accompanied by a publication outlining the taxpayer's rights. One of these rights is the right to discuss the collection matter with the IRS collection employee's manager. If at any step of the collection process a taxpayer does not agree with the recommendations of the IRS employee, the taxpayer has the right to discuss the matter with the employee's manager.

99. Submission of an Offer in Compromise by a taxpayer automatically suspends collection of an account.

The correct answer is (F). *(SPE 990 IV-52)*
DISCUSSION: A taxpayer has the right to submit an offer in compromise. Sec. 7122 authorizes the Commissioner of the Internal Revenue Service to compromise taxes (including interest, penalties, additional amounts or additions to the tax) arising under the internal revenue laws. Reg. Sec. 301.7122-1(d)(2) states that the submission of an offer in compromise does not automatically operate to suspend collection of an account. If there is any indication that the filing of the offer is solely for the purpose of delaying collection of the tax or that delay would negatively affect collection of the tax, the IRS will continue collection efforts. However, enforcement of collection may be deferred if such a deferral will not jeopardize the government's interests.

100. A Taxpayer Assistance Order (Form 911) can be secured to resolve any disagreement between the taxpayer and the IRS.

The correct answer is (F). *(SPE 990 IV-42)*
DISCUSSION: Under Sec. 7811(a), a Taxpayer Assistance Order may be issued by the Office of the Ombudsman. The order will be issued only if the Ombudsman determines that the taxpayer is suffering or is about to suffer a significant hardship as a result of the manner in which the internal revenue laws are being administered.

101. The effect of a request for prompt assessment by a corporation in the process of dissolution is to limit the time in which an assessment of tax may be made or a proceeding in court without assessment for collection of tax may be begun. The assessment must be made or the proceeding started within 12 months from the date the request is filed.

The correct answer is (F). *(SPE 989 III-16)*
DISCUSSION: Under Sec. 6501(d), when a request for prompt assessment is made, the tax for which a corporation contemplating dissolution, a corporation in the process of dissolution, or a corporation that has undergone dissolution may be liable must be assessed (or the proceeding started) within 18 months from the date the request is filed.

102. If a person liable for tax neglects or refuses to pay the tax after demand has been made, a lien in favor of the government attaches to the taxpayer's property. The lien is automatically valid against all the taxpayer's creditors.

The correct answer is (F). *(Publisher)*
DISCUSSION: Sec. 6321 states that if a taxpayer neglects or refuses to pay a deficiency after demand, a lien attaches to all the taxpayer's property. Sec. 6323(a) states that this lien is not valid against any purchaser, holder of a security interest, mechanic's lienor, or judgment lien creditor until the IRS files a Notice of Federal Tax Lien.

103. The recording of a Notice of Federal Tax Lien will not restrict the taxpayer's ability to sell or transfer property during the existence of the lien.

The correct answer is (F). *(SPE 990 IV-44)*
DISCUSSION: The recording of a Notice of Federal Tax Lien serves to put potential purchasers of the taxpayer's property on notice that the government has a claim against the property. Such a recording may restrict the taxpayer's ability to sell or transfer the property during the existence of the lien.

104. A statutory notice of deficiency provides the taxpayer 90 days (150 if the taxpayer resides outside the U.S.), to either agree to the deficiency or to file a petition with the United States Tax Court.

The correct answer is (T). *(SPE 990 IV-15)*
DISCUSSION: Sec. 6212 authorizes the Internal Revenue Service to issue a statutory notice of deficiency if a determination is made that a tax deficiency exists. Under Sec. 6213(a), a taxpayer has 90 days, or 150 days if the notice is addressed to a person outside the United States, after the notice of deficiency is mailed to either agree to the deficiency or file a petition with the United States Tax Court.

25.8 Claims for Refund

105. Mr. Smith filed his 1990 individual income tax return on March 30, 1991 and attached a check for the tax due as shown on the return. On January 15, 1992, Mr. Smith discovered that he understated his itemized deductions on his 1990 tax return. What is the last day on which he can file a claim for refund (assuming no relevant days are a Saturday, Sunday, or holiday)?

   a. March 30, 1993.
   b. April 15, 1993.
   c. March 30, 1994.
   d. April 15, 1994.

The correct answer is (d). *(SPE 990 IV-58)*
REQUIRED: The date for filing an amended return to claim a refund.
DISCUSSION: Sec. 6511(b) states that a claim for refund must be made within the time limits specified in the statute of limitations on refunds. Sec. 6511(a) states that a refund may be paid 3 years from the time the return was filed or 2 years from the time the tax was paid, whichever is later. Under Sec. 6513(a), a return filed early is deemed filed on its due date. Therefore, Mr. Smith must file a claim for refund no later than April 15, 1994.

Module 25.8: Claims for Refund

106. Richard Baker filed his 1990 individual income tax return on April 15, 1991. On December 31, 1991, he learned that 100 shares of stock that he owned had become worthless in 1990. Since he did not deduct this loss on his 1990 return, Baker intends to file a claim for refund. This refund claim must be filed no later than April 15 of which year (assuming no relevant days are Saturdays, Sundays, or holidays)?

a. 1992.
b. 1994.
c. 1997.
d. 1998.

The correct answer is (d). *(CPA 1184 Q-39)*
REQUIRED: The date for filing a refund claim for losses on worthless securities.
DISCUSSION: Sec. 6511(d) allows a 7-year period of limitation for filing a refund claim if the overpayment of tax is due to losses from worthless securities. The period of limitation is 7 years from the date prescribed for filing the return for the year with respect to which the claim is made.

107. Ms. B filed her 1990 Form 1040 on April 15, 1991, but did not pay her tax liability of $3,000. On June 15, 1992, she paid the tax in full. In 1993, Ms. B discovered additional deductions for 1990 that will result in a refund of $1,000. To receive her refund, Ms. B must file an amended income tax return by (assuming no relevant days are Saturdays, Sundays, or holidays)

a. June 15, 1994.
b. April 15, 1994.
c. June 15, 1995.
d. April 15, 1995.

The correct answer is (a). *(SPE 988 IV-58)*
REQUIRED: The date for filing a refund claim for taxes paid after the related return was filed.
DISCUSSION: Sec. 6511(b) states that a claim for a refund must be filed within the time limits established in the statute of limitations on refunds. Sec. 6511(a) provides that refunds may be made 3 years from the time the return was filed or 2 years from the time the tax was paid, whichever is later. Here, 2 years from the time the tax was paid is the later date, so B must file a claim before June 15, 1994.

108. If an individual paid income tax in 1990 but did not file a 1990 return because his income was insufficient to require the filing of a return, the deadline for filing a refund claim is

a. Two years from the date the tax was paid.
b. Two years from the date a return would have been due.
c. Three years from the date the tax was paid.
d. Three years from the date a return would have been due.

The correct answer is (a). *(CPA 1190 Q-22)*
REQUIRED: The deadline for filing a refund claim when no return is filed.
DISCUSSION: Sec. 6511(a) and (b) state that a claim for refund must be filed within 3 years from the time the return was filed or 2 years from the time the tax was paid, whichever is later. Sec. 6511(a) further states that if no return was filed, the claim for refund is due within 2 years from the time the tax was paid.

109. Mr. D's 1988 individual tax return was examined by the Internal Revenue Service in 1989. Mr. D paid $6,000 in additional tax as proposed on September 15, 1989. On September 15, 1991, Mr. D obtained additional information on the 1988 return that would eliminate the additional tax he paid. Mr. D can file a claim for a $6,000 refund on Form 1040X.

The correct answer is (T). *(SPE 1079 IV-81)*
DISCUSSION: A claim for a credit or refund of an overpayment of tax, in respect of which tax the taxpayer is required to file a return, must be filed within 3 years from the time the return was filed or 2 years from the time the tax was paid, whichever is later [Sec. 6511(a)]. Mr. D can file a claim for a refund on Form 1040X.

110. Ms. Smith, a calendar-year taxpayer, made estimated tax payments of $1,000 and got an extension of time to August 15, 1988 to file her 1987 income tax return. She filed her return on November 1, 1988, 2½ months after the extension period ended, and paid an additional $400 tax due on that date. On September 26, 1991, Ms. Smith filed an amended return and claimed a refund of $800. The maximum refund she could receive is $400.

The correct answer is (T). *(SPE 990 I-1)*
DISCUSSION: Sec. 6511(a) and (b) state that a claim for refund must be filed within 3 years from the time the return was filed or 2 years from the time the tax was paid, whichever is later. The limitation on the amount of refund that may be received if the claim was filed within the 3-year period is the portion of the tax paid within the 3 years prior to filing the claim plus any extension period for filing the return.

Ms. Smith filed the claim more than 2 years after paying the tax but less than 3 years from the time of filing the return. She may only receive a refund for the amount paid within 3 years plus 4 months (the extension was from April 15 to August 15) prior to September 26, 1991. Since Ms. Smith paid only $400 during this period, her refund is limited to $400.

111. Taxpayers may file a claim for refund of income taxes that they believe are erroneous by filing Form 843.

The correct answer is (F). *(SPE 1078 IV-66)*
DISCUSSION: A claim for refund of previously paid income taxes is made by filing Form 1040X. Form 843 is used to file a claim for refund of other than income taxes.

112. XYZ, Inc., a calendar-year corporation, reported a net operating loss on its 1990 tax return. The NOL was carried back to the 1987 tax return for a tax refund. The claim for refund was filed on July 15, 1991. The refund was paid by the Internal Revenue Service on August 20, 1991. XYZ will receive interest on the refund for the period March 15, 1991 to July 15, 1991.

The correct answer is (F). *(M. Yates)*
DISCUSSION: Normally, interest on a refund is paid from the date of the overpayment (here, the date prescribed for filing the return) to a date preceding the date of the refund check by not more than 30 days [Sec. 6611(b)(2)]. However, Sec. 6611(e) provides that no interest will be paid on a refund of tax made within 45 days after the due date of the return or the date the return is filed, whichever is later. A claim for refund is a return. Since only 39 days passed between the date the refund claim was filed and the date of the refund, there will be no interest paid on the refund.

113. Once a notice of refund claim disallowance is issued by the IRS, the taxpayer has 2 years from the date of mailing of the notice to file a refund suit in the U.S. District Court having jurisdiction or in the U.S. Claims Court.

The correct answer is (T). *(SPE 1083 IV-20)*
DISCUSSION: A suit for refund may be filed in District Court or Claims Court within 2 years from when the notice of disallowance of a claim for refund was mailed unless the taxpayer and the Internal Revenue Service agree on an extension [Sec. 6532(a)].

114. In a civil proceeding against the U.S. in tax matters, a taxpayer as the prevailing party must prove his/her position is substantially justified in order to receive an award for litigation costs.

The correct answer is (F). *(Publisher)*
DISCUSSION: Sec. 7430 allows an award for litigation costs if the taxpayer is the prevailing party and establishes that the position of the U.S. was not substantially justified.

115. A prevailing party who otherwise qualifies and does not unreasonably lengthen civil proceedings may receive an award for attorneys' fees limited to $75 per hour.

The correct answer is (T). *(Publisher)*
DISCUSSION: Litigation costs will be denied entirely to a prevailing party who unreasonably lengthens any portion of the civil proceedings. Sec. 7430 limits the amount of reasonable litigation costs to be paid for attorneys' services to $75 per hour, unless the court justifies a higher rate. The maximum rate for expert witnesses is the highest compensation rate for expert witnesses paid by the U.S.

25.9 Tax Court

116. The maximum amount of deficiency per tax year or tax period that may be heard by the Small Tax Case Division of the U.S. Tax Court is:

   a. $2,500.
   b. $5,000.
   c. $10,000.
   d. $15,000.

The correct answer is (c). *(SPE 990 IV-60)*
REQUIRED: The maximum deficiency that may be handled by the Small Tax Case Division of the U.S. Tax Court.
DISCUSSION: The Tax Reform Act of 1984 increased the deficiency or overpayment limit for cases that may be heard by the Small Tax Case Division of the Tax Court. The limit is now $10,000 [Sec. 7463(a)]. It is the taxpayer's option (subject to agreement by the Tax Court) for the case to be heard by the Small Tax Case Division.

117. The Tax Court has jurisdiction over all of the following taxes except:

   a. Income.
   b. Employment.
   c. Estate.
   d. Gift.

The correct answer is (b). *(SPE 989 IV-77)*
REQUIRED: The type of tax over which the Tax Court has no jurisdiction.
DISCUSSION: The tax court is a court of limited jurisdiction. Sec. 7442 states that the Tax Court has such jurisdiction as is conferred on it by this title, by Chapters 1, 2, 3, and 4 of the Internal Revenue Code of 1939, by Title II and Title III of the Revenue Act of 1926, or by laws enacted subsequent to February 26, 1926. The Tax Court's jurisdiction covers income, estate, gift, excise, and private foundation taxes. The Tax Court has no jurisdiction over employment taxes. Note: Sec. 7442 remains unchanged from the time of enactment of the Internal Revenue Code of 1954. Presumably the term "this title" refers to both the Internal Revenue Codes of 1954 and 1986 (Title 26).

118. The United States Tax Court is an independent judicial body that has no connection with the Internal Revenue Service.

The correct answer is (T). *(SPE 1081 IV-74)*
DISCUSSION: Congress established the Tax Court to adjudicate tax disputes between taxpayers and the government when a deficiency notice has been issued.

119. If the examination of a taxpayer's return by the Internal Revenue Service results in a disagreement over whether the taxpayer owes additional income tax, the Service must issue a formal letter called a notice of deficiency before the taxpayer can appeal his/her case to the Tax Court.

The correct answer is (T). *(SPE 1085 IV-14)*
DISCUSSION: To be able to take a case to the Tax Court, the taxpayer must have received a notice of deficiency from the IRS and have petitioned the Tax Court within 90 days after the notice was sent. If (s)he pays the tax, (s)he must file a claim for refund with the IRS, then file a suit in District Court or Claims Court if the claim is denied.

120. Before taking an income tax case to the Tax Court, a taxpayer must first have a conference at the IRS Appeals Office in his/her region.

The correct answer is (F). *(SPE 1083 IV-23)*
DISCUSSION: To file suit in the Tax Court, a taxpayer must receive a notice of deficiency from the IRS. The taxpayer is not required to have a conference at the IRS Appeals Office.

121. Mr. W does not agree with the proposed tax deficiency of $20,000 resulting from an IRS examination of his 1990 income tax return. He has been unable to resolve his case within the administrative processes of the Internal Revenue Service. The United States Tax Court is the only court that he may petition without first making payment on the contested deficiency.

The correct answer is (T). *(SPE 990 IV-12)*
DISCUSSION: Under Sec. 6213(a), if a taxpayer files a petition with the Tax Court within 90 days of receiving a notice of deficiency, a tax may not be assessed until the final decision of the Tax Court is rendered. If the taxpayer pays the tax and a claim for refund is disallowed by the IRS, the taxpayer may file a suit for refund in the U.S. District Court or in the U.S. Claims Court.

122. Correspondence in connection with cases docketed in the Tax Court will be addressed to counsel of record before the Court in lieu of a power of attorney or tax information authorization.

The correct answer is (T). *(SPE 989 IV-33)*
DISCUSSION: Tax Court Rule 21(b)(2) states than in lieu of notice to the court that some other counsel is to receive correspondence, correspondence will be addressed to the counsel whose appearance was first entered of record.

123. Both the taxpayer and the Government may appeal "small tax case procedure" decisions of the Tax Court to the Court of Appeals.

The correct answer is (F). *(SPE 988 IV-53)*
DISCUSSION: Sec. 7463(b) provides that a decision entered in any case in the Small Tax Case Division of the Tax Court shall not be reviewed by any other court.

124. "Practice before the Internal Revenue Service" includes the representation of clients in the United States Tax Court for cases being handled under the "small tax case procedure."

The correct answer is (F). *(SPE 990 IV-1)*
DISCUSSION: "Practice before the Internal Revenue Service" comprehends all matters connected with presentation to the Internal Revenue Service or any of its officers or employees relating to a client's rights, privileges, or liabilities under laws or regulations administered by the IRS. Such presentations include the preparation and filing of necessary documents, correspondence with and communication to the IRS, and the representation of a client at conferences, hearings, and meetings. It does not include the representation of clients in the United States Tax Court for cases being handled under the "small tax case procedure." The Tax Court of the United States has its own rules concerning who is allowed to practice before it in regular case and small tax case matters (Sec. 7452).

125. Whether or not the Commissioner of Internal Revenue decides to appeal an adverse Tax Court decision, he may nonacquiesce in the case which means that the Service does not accept the adverse decision and will not follow it in cases on the same issue.

The correct answer is (T). *(SPE 987 IV-54)*
DISCUSSION: The Commissioner may announce his/her acquiescence or nonacquiescence with regard to the regular, reported decisions of the Tax Court. Acquiescence is the Commissioner's public endorsement of a Tax Court decision. In some cases, only specific issues are acquiesced, or the agreement may be in result only.

126. The Commissioner of Internal Revenue will announce acquiescence or nonacquiescence only when the Tax Court's decision is adverse to the Service's position.

The correct answer is (T). *(SPE 988 IV-55)*
DISCUSSION: The Commissioner is not required to endorse the general principles embodied in the decisions of the courts. (S)he may announce an acquiescence or nonacquiescence with regard to the regular, reported decisions of the Tax Court. The announcement relates only to the issue(s) decided adversely to the government.

127. The Commissioner of Internal Revenue may subsequently revise a nonacquiescence but not an acquiescence.

The correct answer is (F). *(SPE 1083 IV-77)*
DISCUSSION: The Commissioner may at any time revise a nonacquiescence to a decision in a prior case. Likewise, an acquiescence may be withdrawn at any time with retroactive effect if the purpose is to correct a mistake in the application of tax law.

128. A Tax Court memorandum decision is a report of a Tax Court decision thought to be of little value as a precedent because the issue has been decided many times.

The correct answer is (T). *(SPE 987 IV-58)*
DISCUSSION: Tax Court memorandum decisions have very little value as precedents. These decisions generally concern routine matters where the law has previously been determined.

129. The Tax Court exclusively hears tax cases nationwide. It decides cases consistently throughout the United States.

The correct answer is (F). *(Publisher)*
DISCUSSION: While the Tax Court is the only forum that exclusively hears tax cases, it does not always decide similar cases in the same way. Under the decision in <u>Golsen</u>, 54 T.C. 742 (1970), the Tax Court will follow the rule adopted by the Court of Appeals to which the taxpayer would appeal an adverse decision. Thus, if the Circuits are in conflict on a particular issue, the Tax Court may decide the issue differently depending upon the origin of the case.

130. Although the Tax Court can decide a case in favor of the taxpayer, it has no authority to order the refund of overpayments made by the taxpayer.

The correct answer is (F). *(Publisher)*
DISCUSSION: The 1988 Tax Act expanded the jurisdiction of the Tax Court. It now allows the Tax Court to order the refund of overpayments determined in Tax Court [Sec. 6512(b)] as well as restrain assessments or collection of tax at issue before the Tax Court [Sec. 6213(a)].

25.10 District Court and Claims Court

131. One difference between the Tax Court and the District Court is that

a. The tax must be paid first to go to Tax Court but not District Court.
b. A trial by jury can be obtained in Tax Court but not in District Court.
c. One can appeal an adverse decision of the Tax Court to the appropriate Circuit Court of Appeals, while an appeal from District Court can be filed only with the Supreme Court.
d. A trial by jury can be had in District Court but not in Tax Court.

The correct answer is (d). *(M.J. Whiteman)*
REQUIRED: The correct statement about the differences between the Tax Court and the District Court.
DISCUSSION: Taxpayers who choose to have their cases heard before the District Court may request a trial by jury. Cases heard before the Tax Court are decided by judges.
Answer (a) is incorrect because the taxpayer must pay the deficiency and then sue for refund in the District Court. The taxpayer need only receive a Notice of Deficiency to file a petition in the Tax Court. Answer (b) is incorrect because a trial by jury is available in District Courts but not in the Tax Court. Answer (c) is incorrect because decisions of both the Tax Court and the District Courts may be appealed to the Circuit Courts of Appeal. Note that "small tax case procedure" decisions of the Tax Court may not be appealed.

132. Within 6 months from the date he filed it, Y received a formal notice from the IRS by certified mail disallowing his $10,000 tax refund claim. What is Y's appeal?

a. File a protest and request that the matter be referred to the IRS Appeals Office.
b. File suit in his United States District Court or the United States Claims Court no later than 2 years after the date of the notice.
c. File a petition with the United States Tax Court.
d. File a petition with the United States Tax Court and ask that it be handled under the "small tax case procedure."

The correct answer is (b). *(SPE 987 IV-66)*
REQUIRED: The appeal for a taxpayer whose refund is disallowed.
DISCUSSION: Sec. 6532(a)(1) provides the general rule that a suit must be brought within 2 years of the date of the notice. Appeal may be made to the United States District Court or the United States Claims Court.
Answer (a) is incorrect because the IRS Appeals Office deals with appeals before refunds are paid. Answers (c) and (d) are incorrect because the Tax Court generally handles cases when the tax in dispute has not been paid. Its jurisdiction to handle overpayments does not extend to the issue described here [Sec. 6512(b)].

133. A taxpayer has 3 years from the date of mailing by the IRS of the notice of claim disallowance to file a refund suit in either United States District Court or United States Claims Court.

The correct answer is (F). *(SPE 990 IV-9)*
DISCUSSION: Under Sec. 6532(a)(1), a taxpayer has 2 years from the date of mailing by the IRS of the notice of claim disallowance to bring a suit for refund in either the district court or the U.S. Claims Court. Sec. 6532(a)(2) does permit an extension of time to file if the taxpayer and the Internal Revenue Service so agree.

134. If a taxpayer wants to file a refund suit in the United States District Court having jurisdiction or in the United States Claims Court, for contested income tax or on estate tax or gift tax issues considered in previously examined returns, he or she should file a claim for refund and request in writing that the claim be immediately rejected by the IRS.

The correct answer is (T). *(SPE 989 IV-14)*
DISCUSSION: Before a taxpayer may file a refund suit in the United States District Court or the United States Claims Court, (s)he must first have paid the tax and filed a claim for refund with the Internal Revenue Service. Only after the IRS rejects the claim for refund may a taxpayer file a refund suit in the District Court or Claims Court. If a taxpayer wishes to file such a suit, (s)he should file a claim for refund with the Internal Revenue Service and request in writing that the claim be immediately rejected.

135. If the Internal Revenue Service has not acted upon your claim for refund within 6 months from the date you filed it, you can file suit for refund in your United States District Court or the United States Claims Court.

The correct answer is (T). *(SPE 1077 IV-10)*
DISCUSSION: Sec. 6532(a)(1) states that a taxpayer cannot file a suit for refund before the IRS has acted on the claim or until 6 months have elapsed.

136. The difference between District Courts and the Claims Court is that District Courts may hear any tax case and the Claims Court may only hear refund cases.

The correct answer is (F). *(Publisher)*
DISCUSSION: Both District Courts and the Claims Court hear only refund cases in tax matters. A taxpayer must pay a tax, file a claim for refund with the IRS, and have the claim for refund denied before the taxpayer may file a tax case in the District Courts or the Claims Court (to obtain a refund of the tax paid). The District Courts hear any type of case which may be heard in federal court. The Claims Court hears only limited types of cases, including tax, government contracts, patents, and customs cases.

137. The Commissioner of Internal Revenue does not file either acquiescence or nonacquiescence to adverse court decisions other than those of the Tax Court.

The correct answer is (T). *(SPE 987 IV-55)*
DISCUSSION: The IRS only files acquiescence or nonacquiescence with respect to Tax Court decisions, not any other decisions.

25.11 Appeals

138. All of the following statements concerning court appeals and court petitions are true except:

a. Both the taxpayer and the Government may appeal decisions of the Tax Court or District Court to the Court of Appeals.

b. The decisions of Courts of Appeal and some decisions of other federal courts may be reviewed by the United States Supreme Court.

c. For federal tax purposes, the most common type of case that the Supreme Court hears is one in which a federal tax statute is ruled to be invalid.

d. If a taxpayer's claim for refund is denied by the Internal Revenue Service or if no decision is made in 6 months, the taxpayer may petition either the United States Claims Court or the United States Circuit Court of Appeals.

The correct answer is (d). *(SPE 990 IV-77)*
REQUIRED: The false statement concerning court appeals and court petitions.
DISCUSSION: If a taxpayer's claim refund is denied by the Internal Revenue Service or if no decision is made in 6 months, the taxpayer may petition either the United States Claims Court or the District Court. The United States Court of Appeals hears appeals from decisions of the Tax Court, the District Court, and the Claims Court. Cases appealed from the Tax Court and District Court are heard in the Circuit Court of Appeals for the taxpayer's jurisdiction. Appeals from the Claims Court are heard by the Court of Appeals for the Federal Circuit. It is not a court of original jurisdiction.
Answers (a), (b), and (c) are correct statements concerning court appeals and court petitions.

Module 25.11: Appeals 751

139. Appeal from the Claims Court is to the
  a. U.S. Circuit Court of Appeals.
  b. U.S. Court of Appeals for the Federal Circuit.
  c. U.S. Tax Court.
  d. U.S. Supreme Court.

The correct answer is (b). *(J.P. Trebby)*
REQUIRED: The appellate court to which appeals from the Claims Court are taken.
DISCUSSION: The U.S. Court of Appeals for the Federal Circuit is the appellate court to which appeals from the Claims Court are taken.
Answer (a) is incorrect because the U.S. Circuit Court of Appeals is the appellate court that hears appeals from the U.S. District Court and the U.S. Tax Court. Answer (c) is incorrect because it is a court of original jurisdiction, not an appellate court. Answer (d) is incorrect because, in tax cases, there is no direct appeal to the Supreme Court from the Claims Court or from any other court of original jurisdiction.

140. If a taxpayer's case is handled in the Tax Court under the "small tax case procedures," the decision of the Tax Court is final and cannot be appealed.

The correct answer is (T). *(SPE 989 IV-17)*
DISCUSSION: Under Sec. 7463(b), all decisions made by the Tax Court under the Small Tax Case procedures are final and may not be appealed.

141. If one District Court has rejected the Commissioner of Internal Revenue's position, then the Commission cannot take that position before any other District Court in the Court of Appeals Circuit.

The correct answer is (F). *(SPE 990 IV-37)*
DISCUSSION: The Internal Revenue Service is not bound by the decisions of District Courts. Therefore, if one District Court has rejected the Commissioner of Internal Revenue's position, the Commissioner may take the same position before any other District Court in the Court of Appeals Circuit. However, if the Court of Appeals for the Circuit has rendered a decision against the Commission of Internal Revenue's position, then the other district courts in the circuit are bound by that decision.

142. All of the following statements are true.

A petition to the Supreme Court to have a case that it is not obliged to review is by writ of certiorari.
The writ of certiorari is initially requested by the appealing party.
The writ of certiorari is issued by the Supreme Court to the lower appellate court requesting the record of a case for review.

The correct answer is (T). *(SPE 987 IV-56)*
DISCUSSION: A petition to the Supreme Court to hear a case is by writ of certiorari requested by the appealing party. If the Court decides to hear the case, the writ is presented to the lower appellate court ordering the record of the case to be sent for review.

143. Decisions of the Courts of Appeal and some decisions of other Federal courts may be reviewed by the United States Supreme Court. The Supreme Court is obligated to hear all cases that it has been requested to review.

The correct answer is (F). *(SPE 989 IV-59)*
DISCUSSION: Generally, the Supreme Court hears cases only at its discretion and if the issue is of sufficient importance. It is not obligated to hear all cases that it has been requested to review.

SUCCESSFUL CAREERS IN ACCOUNTING BEGIN WITH THE GLEIM SERIES OF OBJECTIVE QUESTIONS AND EXPLANATIONS . . .

... AND CONTINUE THROUGH
MULTIPLE CERTIFICATION PROGRAMS

BOOKS AVAILABLE FROM GLEIM PUBLICATIONS, INC.

THE GLEIM SERIES

OBJECTIVE QUESTIONS AND EXPLANATIONS STUDY BOOKS

To help accounting and business law students and professional accountants, we have developed a series of five objective question study manuals. The books in the series cover

**AUDITING & EDP • FINANCIAL ACCOUNTING • FEDERAL TAX
MANAGERIAL ACCOUNTING • BUSINESS LAW/LEGAL STUDIES**

Each manual is a comprehensive, carefully organized compendium of 1,800 to 2,500 objective questions taken from past CPA, CIA, CMA, and other professional certification exams. Where appropriate, questions have been modified to reflect changes in the law, authoritative pronouncements, etc. Hundreds of author-developed questions have been added to each book to assure complete coverage of the topics, not just what has been tested on previous professional exams.

Our exclusive answer explanations (why the right answer is correct; why the wrong answers are incorrect) appear to the immediate right of the questions to eliminate the wasted effort of turning pages back and forth. Because the questions are so comprehensive, each book provides "programmed learning." In addition to helping you learn faster and more easily, these books help you improve your college examination scores and look ahead to professional examinations.

The questions in each book are organized by topic in "modules" within each chapter. The tables of contents of most related textbooks are presented and cross-referenced to the modules in each respective *OBJECTIVE QUESTION AND EXPLANATION* book. As you study a particular chapter in your own text, you know exactly where relevant questions appear in your *OBJECTIVE QUESTION AND EXPLANATION* book. Additionally, each book has a detailed index to assist you in locating questions relevant to the particular topic you are studying.

OTHER BOOKS

CIA EXAMINATION REVIEW, *CMA EXAMINATION REVIEW,* and *CPA EXAMINATION REVIEW*[1] are each two-volume, comprehensive study programs designed to prepare you to pass the CIA (Certified Internal Auditor), CMA (Certified Management Accounting), and CPA (Certified Public Accountant) examinations.

Each set of books contains structured, point-by-point coverage of all material tested, and clear and concise phraseology to help you understand and remember the concepts. They also explain the respective certification programs, introduce you to examination preparation and grading procedures, and help you organize your examination strategy. In addition, these books contain past exam questions (the multiple-choice questions are, of course, accompanied by our exclusive answer explanations).

HOW TO ORDER THESE BOOKS

Any of the books described above can be obtained by completing the order form on page 755 and mailing it to us. All orders are shipped within one day of receipt.

---

[1] Published by John Wiley & Sons, Inc.

GLEIM PUBLICATIONS, INC. • P.O. Box 12848 • Gainesville, FL 32604 • (800) 87-GLEIM

"THE GLEIM SERIES" OBJECTIVE QUESTION AND EXPLANATION BOOKS
- AUDITING & EDP .... (720 pages • 1,819 questions) ...... $16.95 $_____
- BUSINESS LAW/LEGAL STUDIES ..... (800 pages • 1,928 questions) ...... $16.95 $_____
- FEDERAL TAX .... (784 pages • 2,523 questions) ...... $16.95 $_____
- FINANCIAL ACCOUNTING .... (736 pages • 1,837 questions) ...... $16.95 $_____
- MANAGERIAL ACCOUNTING .... (672 pages • 1,967 questions) ...... $16.95 $_____

CIA EXAMINATION REVIEW *(4th Edition, published January 1991)*
- VOLUME I: Outlines & Study Guides .... (800 pages) .... $23.95 $_____
- VOLUME II: Problems & Solutions .... (728 pages) .... $23.95 $_____
- CIA 1992 Updating Edition .... $15.95 $_____
- Save $8.85! Order all three .... $55.00 $_____

CMA EXAMINATION REVIEW *(5th Edition, published February 1992)*
- VOLUME I: Outlines & Study Guides .... (792 pages) .... $24.95 $_____
- VOLUME II: Problems & Solutions .... (816 pages) .... $24.95 $_____

CPA EXAMINATION REVIEW *(published by John Wiley & Sons, Inc.)*
- TWO-VOLUME SET *(19th Edition, published June 1992)*
  - Volume I: Outlines & Study Guides ..... (1,408 pages) .... $41.00 $_____
  - Volume II: Problems & Solutions .... (1,168 pages) .... $41.00 $_____
- THREE-VOLUME SET *(published January 1992)*
  - Auditing .... (622 pages) .... $26.95 $_____
  - Business Law .... (570 pages) .... $26.95 $_____
  - Theory and Practice .... (1,472 pages) .... $36.95 $_____

Shipping .... $____3.00
Add applicable sales tax for shipments within Florida .... $_____
Foreign Surcharge (call or write for charges) .... $_____
Payment must be in U.S. dollars and payable on a U.S. bank .... TOTAL $_____

---

1. We process and ship orders daily, generally 1 day after receipt of your order.
2. Please PHOTOCOPY this order form as necessary.
3. No CODs. All mail orders from individuals must be prepaid and are protected by our unequivocal refund policy.
   Library and company orders may be purchased on account. Shipping and handling charges will be added to the invoice and to all telephone orders.
4. Gleim Publications, Inc. guarantees the immediate refund of all resalable texts if returned within 30 days. Our shipping charge is nonrefundable.

NAME (please print) _____

ADDRESS _____

_____

CITY _____ STATE _____ ZIP _____

__ MasterCard   __ VISA   __ Check/Money Order

MC/VISA ____-____-____-____   Exp. __/__
                                      Mo. / Yr.

Signature _____

122B

Printed 05/92.
Prices subject to change without notice.

Our telephone operators are available to take your calls from 8:00 a.m. to 7:00 p.m., Monday through Friday, and 9:00 a.m. to 2:00 p.m. Saturday, Eastern time.

NOTES

TO: Professional Accountants
FROM: Irvin N. Gleim

For over a decade, I have been recommending multiple certification, not only to earn professional credentials, but also for professional development.

- **CIA** Certified Internal Auditor
- **CMA** Certified Management Accountant
- **CPA** Certified Public Accountant
- **CISA** Certified Information Systems Auditor

The exams are, for the most part, synergistic. Once you have trained yourself to take a two- to three-day accounting examination, you should take advantage of your preparation effort and sit for other certification exams as well. Most are administered at similar times during the year.

Currently, I author review books for the CIA, CMA, and CPA exams and a review supplement for the CISA exam. Each set of books is a comprehensive study program designed to prepare you to pass that particular exam. They contain structured, point-by-point coverage of all material tested, and clear and concise phraseology to help you understand and remember the concepts. They also explain the respective certification programs, introduce you to examination preparation and grading procedures, and help you organize your examination strategy. In addition, these books contain past exam questions (the multiple-choice questions are, of course, accompanied by our exclusive answer explanations).

If you are interested in pursuing the CIA, CISA, CMA, and/or CPA designation, I urge you to consider my books. An order form is provided for your convenience. Or you may call (800) 87-GLEIM from 8 am - 7 pm, Monday - Friday, or 9 am - 2 pm Saturdays, Eastern Time.

AUDITING & EDP OBJECTIVE QUESTIONS AND EXPLANATIONS *(CISA Supplement)* .... $16.95 $_____

CIA EXAMINATION REVIEW *(4th Edition, published January 1991)*
- VOLUME I: Outlines & Study Guides .... (800 pages) ...... $23.95 $_____
- VOLUME II: Problems & Solutions .... (728 pages) ...... $23.95 $_____
- CIA 1992 Updating Edition .... $15.95 $_____
- Save $8.85! Order all three .... $55.00 $_____

CMA EXAMINATION REVIEW *(5th Edition, published February 1992)*
- VOLUME I: Outlines & Study Guides .... (792 pages) ...... $24.95 $_____
- VOLUME II: Problems & Solutions .... (816 pages) ...... $24.95 $_____

CPA EXAMINATION REVIEW *(published by John Wiley & Sons, Inc.)*
TWO-VOLUME SET *(19th Edition, published June 1992)*
- Volume I: Outlines & Study Guides .... (1,408 pages) ...... $41.00 $_____
- Volume II: Problems & Solutions .... (1,168 pages) ...... $41.00 $_____

THREE-VOLUME SET *(published January 1991)*
- Auditing .... (622 pages) ...... $26.95 $_____
- Business Law .... (570 pages) ...... $26.95 $_____
- Theory and Practice .... (1,472 pages) ...... $36.95 $_____

Shipping .... $___3.00
Add applicable sales tax for shipments within Florida .... $_____
Foreign surcharge (call or write for charges) .... $_____
Payment must be in U.S. dollars and payable on a U.S. bank .... TOTAL $_____

Printed 05/92. Prices subject to change without notice.

---

1. We process and ship orders daily, generally 1 day after receipt of your order.
2. Please PHOTOCOPY this order form as necessary.
3. No CODs. All mail orders from individuals must be prepaid and are protected by our unequivocal refund policy.
   Library and company orders may be purchased on account. Shipping and handling charges will be added to the invoice.
4. Gleim Publications, Inc. guarantees the immediate refund of all resalable texts if returned within 30 days. Our shipping charge is nonrefundable.

NAME (please print) _____

ADDRESS _____

_____

CITY _____ STATE _____ ZIP _____

__ MasterCard   __ VISA   __ Check/Money Order

MC/VISA __ __ __ __ - __ __ __ __ - __ __ __ __ - __ __ __ __   Exp. ____ / ____
                                                                    Mo. / Yr.

Signature _____

122B

Gleim Publications, Inc

Continuing Professional Education
SELF-STUDY COURSE CATALOG

WHY SELF-STUDY: To provide an alternative to conventional CPE delivery:
- Interactive
- Programmed learning
- Effective
- Challenging
- Easy-to-use *(see next page)*
- Broad coverage

WHERE: Wherever you can carry two books weighing less than 4 lbs. - home, office, train, plane, etc. No inconvenient out-of-town travel and expense.

WHEN: Whenever you have available time. Study may be completed at your own pace in any time segments, long or short.

PRESENTATION METHODS: *Objective Question "Quizzer" Format* -- for review and reinforcement of basic-intermediate knowledge, completely updated to reflect the most recent authoritative pronouncements, tax law, etc.--see next page.
PREREQUISITE: Previous study of or prior experience with the topic.

Outline - Illustration - Study Question Format -- for new topics--see page 760.
PREREQUISITE: An undergraduate major in business or equivalent.

APPROVED CPE: Our certificate of completion has been accepted by all boards of accountancy, the Accreditation Council for Accountancy and Taxation, the U.S. Department of Treasury, California and Oregon Tax Preparer Programs, Institute of Internal Auditors, Institute of Certified Management Accountants, and many others. We currently interact with 65 accounting related agencies in the U.S. that require CPE.

VARIOUS CPE RULES: Most of the 65 agencies have their own rules regarding what types of subject categories are acceptable for CPE credit. Since the individual courses in our programs cover a wide variety of topics some courses may not be acceptable in your jurisdiction.
Call us for assistance: **(800) 87-GLEIM.**

CREDIT FOR SELF-STUDY CPE: The AICPA standard for measuring CPE credit for formal, non-interactive self-study CPE programs states that CPE credit should equal one-half of the average completion time, as determined by the program developer through pretesting. For example, a course that takes an average of 800 minutes to complete is recommended for 8 contact hours of CPE credit. The recommended credit we indicate is based on this AICPA standard. Note, however, that many jurisdictions that require reporting of CPE credit will allow "full credit" for our programs, i.e., a course that takes an average of 800 minutes to complete is recommended for 16 contact hours of CPE credit.
Call us for assistance: **(800) 87-GLEIM.**

AUTHORS: Irvin N. Gleim, Terry L. Campbell, William A. Collins, Dale Flesher, William A. Hillison, John L. Kramer, Jordan B. Ray. All are professional educators.

EXPIRATION DATE: One year or 30 days after you are notified of program retirement by first class mail, whichever occurs later.

Gleim Publications, Inc. is registered with the National Association of State Boards of Accountancy as a sponsor of continuing professional education on the National Registry of CPE Sponsors. State boards of accountancy have final authority on the acceptance of individual courses. Complaints regarding registered sponsors may be addressed to NASBA, 545 Fifth Avenue, New York, NY 10017-3698, 1-800-CPA-CPE1.

FIVE CPE PROGRAMS
USING OBJECTIVE QUESTION FORMAT

These CPE programs constitute a totally different approach to CPE. Each program contains multiple individual courses based on self-diagnosing objective questions. They are designed to meet the needs of practitioners by providing low-cost, easy-to-use, effective CPE.

All of these programs provide you with an opportunity to review and study a wide range of topics.

- First, they provide a self-diagnosis of your knowledge.

- Second, they constitute a review and study of the professional and technical standards that have come to be the basic proficiency package expected of professional accountants. As such, each individual course is a formal program of learning that contributes directly to your professional competence.

- Third, they are interactive in the sense that you must continually respond to multiple-choice or true-false questions. Thus, you challenge yourself to do well. When you have difficulty, a thorough, easy-to-understand explanation is provided.

- Fourth, these courses are organized in a programmed learning format through a careful ordering of questions, i.e., from general to specific, easy to difficult, etc.

EASY TO USE

You are formally registered when we receive your order, which gets shipped within 24 hours. With each program, you receive:

1. Objective Question and Explanation Study Book.

2. CPE final exam book with complete easy-to-follow instructions.

3. One machine-readable final exam answer sheet (see note below), course evaluation questionnaire, and a special protective return envelope.

- You study the questions and explanations in the Objective Question and Explanation Study Book when and where you want.

- Then you take a final exam (open book) and record your answers on our machine-readable answer sheet.

- Lastly, you return the answer sheet and evaluation form in the protective return envelope to us for grading. If you score 70% or above, we will send you a certificate of completion. In the event of a failure, your answer sheet will be returned to you for correction after your additional study. Our charge for regrading is $15.

NOTE: In each program, you have the option of taking all of the courses, just one course, or any combination of individual courses. All of the courses in a single program can be completed at no additional charge by using the one answer sheet provided with each program. If you prefer to obtain CPE credit for a few courses at a time, there is a $15 grading fee (additional answer sheet) for each subsequent submission.

SAME-DAY grading service, available Mon.-Fri.: Send your materials and $50 prepayment (check, VISA, MC) via Federal Express (priority, so we receive it by noon) to 4201 N.W. 95th Blvd., Gainesville, FL 32606. We will hand grade your answer sheet and send the results back to you via Federal Express the same day.

AUDITING & EDP CPE
8 separate courses with up to 45* CPE hours -- **all for $75**

		Credit Hours
1.	Audit Environment, Standards, and Ethics	7
2.	Internal Control	6
3.	Audit Evidence and Procedures	8
4.	Electronic Data Processing	8
5.	Statistical Sampling	3
6.	Audit Reports	6
7.	Special Reports and Other Reporting Issues	3
8.	Internal Auditing	4

BUSINESS LAW CPE
11 separate courses with up to 48* CPE hours -- **all for $60**

1.	Our Legal System and Environment	5
2.	Torts, Consumer Law, and Accountants' Liability	4
3.	Contracts	5
4.	Sales, International Law, and Ethics	4
5.	Commercial Paper and Antitrust	4
6.	Property and Computer Law	5
7.	Assurance of Creditors' Interests	4
8.	Corporations and Securities Regulation	5
9.	Insurance and Bankruptcy	4
10.	Estate Planning, Employment Regulation, and Environmental Law	4
11.	Agency and Partnerships	4

FEDERAL TAX CPE
14 separate courses with up to 56* CPE hours -- **all for $95**

1.	Gross Income and Exclusions	4
2.	Business Expenses and Losses	3
3.	Investment and Personal Deductions	5
4.	Individual Loss Limits, Tax Calculations, and Credits	4
5.	Property I	5
6.	Property II	5
7.	Partnerships	4
8.	Corporate Formations and Operations	5
9.	Advanced Corporate Topics	3
10.	Accounting Methods and Employment Taxes	4
11.	Estates, Trusts, and Wealth Transfer Taxes	4
12.	Tax Preparer Rules, Process, and Procedures	4

1990 Tax Law Changes

13.	1990 Act: Individuals	2
14.	1990 Act: Business Provisions	4

FINANCIAL ACCOUNTING CPE
13 separate courses with up to 46* CPE hours -- **all for $95**

1.	Basic Concepts and the Accounting Process	4
2.	Current Assets	4
3.	Noncurrent Assets	4
4.	Current and Noncurrent Liabilities	3
5.	Present Value, Pensions, and Leases	4
6.	Shareholders' Equity and EPS	4
7.	Income Tax Allocation, Accounting Changes, Error Corrections	2
8.	Financial Statements and Disclosures	3
9.	Statement Analysis, Interim Statements, and Segment Reporting	4
10.	Equity Method and Business Combinations	5
11.	Price-Level Changes and Foreign Exchange	2
12.	Government and Nonprofit Accounting	4
13.	Specialized Industry and Partnership Accounting	3

MANAGERIAL ACCOUNTING CPE
11 separate courses with up to 43* CPE hours -- **all for $60**

1.	Cost Accounting Overview and Job Order Costing	4
2.	Process Costing; Spoilage, Waste, & Scrap	4
3.	Joint Products and By-Products	2
4.	Service Cost Allocations and Direct Costing	3
5.	Cost-Volume-Profit Analysis	5
6.	Budgeting and Responsibility Accounting	4
7.	Standard Costs	6
8.	Nonroutine Decisions and Inventory Models	4
9.	Capital Budgeting	4
10.	Probability and Statistics; Regression Analysis	4
11.	Linear Programming and Other Quantitative Approaches	3

* See the discussion of determining self-study CPE credit on page 758.

EARN CONTINUING EDUCATION CREDIT WHILE PREPARING FOR THE CMA EXAM!

- **BECOME A CMA:** CMA stands for Certified Management Accountant. Our CMA CPE program is based on the study of outlines, examples, and study questions from Gleim's two-volume *CMA Examination Review*, and will thoroughly prepare you to pass the CMA exam.

- **BROADEN YOUR BACKGROUND:** Comparable to a mini-MBA program, this will assist you both in your own business endeavors and with your clients. It is more user-oriented with respect to financial statements instead of preparer-oriented.

OUTLINE • ILLUSTRATION • STUDY QUESTION FORMAT

CMA CPE 31 separate courses with up to 94 CPE hours -- all for $125

	Credit Hours*
PART 1: ECONOMICS, FINANCE, AND MANAGEMENT	
1. Microeconomics	4
2. Macroeconomics	2
3. International Economics	2
4. Institutional Environment of Business	3
5. Working Capital Finance	4
6. Capital Structure Finance	4
7. Organization Theory	3
8. Motivation and the Directing Process	3
9. Planning and Budgeting	1
10. Communication	1
11. Ethics and the Management Accountant	1
PART 2: FINANCIAL ACCOUNTING AND REPORTING	
12. Financial Accounting: Development of Theory and Practice	2
13. Financial Statement Presentation	10
14. Special Financial Reporting Problems	3
15. SEC Reporting Requirements	1
16. Ratio and Accounts Analysis	3
17. Internal Control	2
18. External Auditing	4
19. Income Taxes	3
PART 3: MANAGEMENT REPORTING, ANALYSIS, AND BEHAVIORAL ISSUES	
20. Process and Job Order Costing	5
21. Direct (Variable) Costing and The Controlling Process	3
22. Budgeting and Responsibility Accounting	3
23. Standard Costs and Variance Analysis	2
PART 4: DECISION ANALYSIS AND INFORMATION SYSTEMS	
24. Incremental Costing	2
25. Cost-Volume-Profit Analysis	1
26. Capital Budgeting	2
27. Decision Making Under Uncertainty	4
28. Inventory Models	2
29. Quantitative Methods	5
30. Information Systems	6
31. Internal and Operational Auditing	3

*See page 758.

ALL REPORTING AGENCIES ACCEPT GLEIM CPE. HERE ARE 27 THAT GRANT 1 CONTACT HOUR FOR EACH 50 MINUTES OF COMPLETION TIME IN A GLEIM CPE PROGRAM

As of February 1992 the following CPE accreditation agencies grant 1 contact hour for each 50 minutes of completion time in a Gleim CPE Program. Thus, the credit indicated on this brochure can be doubled (see discussion on page 758). We encourage you to verify the self-study measurement standard (as it relates to Gleim's CPE) with your CPE reporting agencies.

State Boards of Accountancy

Alabama	Idaho	Mississippi
Alaska	Iowa	Ohio
Arkansas	Maine	South Dakota
Colorado	Massachusetts	Tennessee
Delaware	Michigan	Utah
Hawaii	Minnesota	West Virginia
		Wyoming

Other Organizations

Accreditation Council for Accountancy (ACA)
California Department of Consumer Affairs, Tax Preparer Program (CATP)
EDP Auditors Association (CISA)
General Accounting Office (GAO)
Institute of Internal Auditors (CIA)
National Association of Enrolled Agents (NAEA)
Oregon Board of Tax Service Examiners (ORTP)
U.S. Treasury Department (IRS)

NEW COMPUTER SOFTWARE
(Mark the box on the next page to receive more information.)

CPE Report Generator (Fall 1992) $30

- Keeps track of your individual CPE reporting requirements for up to 12 different CPE reporting agencies.
- Provides status reports on your progress.
- Prints out agency-specific facsimile reports of your continuing education credits earned that you can attach to or copy on your official reporting forms.

Interactive Diagnostic Testing CPE

- Complete your continuing education requirements on your PC. Later this year we will have all of our objective question CPE courses (see page 759) available on computer diskette.
- Obtain immediate feedback and evaluation as you interact with our databases of questions, answers, and explanations.

AVAILABLE NOW:

    Auditing Standards and Ethics $35.00
    (Recommended for 10 hours of CPE credit)

WHY SELF STUDY?

COST/BENEFIT: Formal correspondence courses have the greatest potential to help participants learn more (and with better results) at a lower cost. Travel is expensive. So are rooms and good lecturers.

MORE EFFICIENT

1. The cost of formal correspondence course preparation and delivery is largely fixed. Once a course is developed into textual, audio-video, CBI, etc., the cost of incremental courses is negligible. We produce interactive correspondence courses for most "general" CPE courses so as to cost participants $6 or less per credit hour.

2. Travel costs (including travel time) are eliminated by formal correspondence courses.

3. Formal correspondence courses are convenient -- they can be undertaken when and where the participant desires. This flexibility can save practitioners many billable hours and also results in better (and more timely) service to clients.

4. Textual self-study CPE materials should constitute excellent reference books (ours do!) at no additional cost.

5. Most CPAs relied heavily on self-study to prepare for the CPA exam (even if they took a review course) and thus are experienced at using self-study textual material.

MORE EFFECTIVE

1. Formal correspondence courses require individual study and effort in contrast to merely being "in attendance."

2. When formal correspondence courses are interactive, they provide more opportunity for individual participation than most seminars and professional conferences. We use true/false study questions to ask participants questions that they need to be asked. We also include questions that participants should be asking and then answer them.

3. The AICPA Standards for CPE Reporting require self-study programs to provide evidence of completion (e.g., completed workbook or examination) and a certificate of completion supplied by the sponsor. Our programs comply with these standards.

The existence of a "final examination," whether in workbook or exam mode, is excellent motivation for participants to study and learn versus simply becoming familiar with the subject matter, as occurs at many CPE seminars and professional conference CPE programs.

Detach and order today -or- Call (800) 87-GLEIM -or- FAX (904) 375-6940

Gleim Publications Inc.

Post Office Box 12848
University Station
Gainesville, Florida 32604
(800) 87-GLEIM

CPE Programs Available

AUDITING & EDP	@ $75.00	$ _____
BUSINESS LAW	@ $60.00	_____
FEDERAL TAX	@ $95.00	_____
FINANCIAL ACCOUNTING	@ $95.00	_____
MANAGERIAL ACCOUNTING	@ $60.00	_____
CERTIFIED MANAGEMENT ACCOUNTANT	@ $125.00	_____

IDT Course Available:

Auditing Standards and Ethics .... @ $35.00 _____

☐ 3½ diskette   ☐ 5¼ diskette

Shipping for prepaid orders (nonrefundable) 3.00

Add applicable sales tax for shipments within Florida ..... $ _____

TOTAL $ _____

☐ Please send me more information about CPE Report Generator and Interactive Diagnostic Testing

Printed 05/92. Prices subject to change without notice.

Please type or print legibly. This information is used to establish a permanent record for maintaining your progress and mailing certificates of completion.

NAME (please print) _____

Social Security No. ___ ___ ___ - ___ ___ - ___ ___ ___ ___
(for CPE record keeping purposes only)

Address _____

_____

City _____ State _____ Zip _____

Check enclosed _____ Credit Card _____ Bill Me _____

MasterCard/VISA # _____ Exp. Date ___/___ (Month/Year)

___ ___ ___ ___ - ___ ___ ___ ___ - ___ ___ ___ ___ - ___ ___ ___ ___

Signature _____

Gleim Publications guarantees an immediate refund for all resalable materials if returned within 30 days.

NOTES

INDEX

Abandoned spouse 231
Abandonment of property 101
Accelerated
    Cost recovery system (1981-1986) 319
    Income recognition 626
Accident
    Or health insurance 75
    Payments 76
Accounting certification programs 29
Accounts receivable 345, 448
Accrual
    Basis taxpayer 627
    Method 611, 615
Accumulated
    Adjustments account 572
    Earnings tax 557, 559, 560
    Income tax 557, 558
Acquiescence 748
ACRS 320
Active participation 145
Activities of preparers 699
Adjusted
    Basis in partnership interest 433, 434
    Basis of partners' interest 437
    Current earnings 513, 514
    Gross income 148
Adjustments to basis 305, 306
    In partnership interest 433
Administration expenses 684
Advance rental payments 62, 63
Affiliated group 552
Alimony 66, 67, 157-161
Allocation between principal and income 588
Alternate valuation
    Date 681, 682
    Election 683
    Method 681, 682
Alternative
    MACRS 327
    Minimum tax 245-249, 511, 513-516, 520, 557
Amended return 176
American Institute of CPAs 38
Amortization 328
    Of bond premiums 199
    Of lease 330
Annual exclusion 670
Annualized income 638
Annuity income 63
Answer sheets, IRS SPE 25
Answers beside questions 4
Appeals 718, 736, 737, 750
Appeals within the IRS 736
Application for special enrollment examination 20
Applying for the SPE, Form 2587 19
Apportionment plan 555
Appraisal fees 191
Appreciated property 300
Appreciation 469
Assessment of taxes 737

Assets
    Acquired for stock 472
    Subject to mortgage 467
Assignment
    Income 68
    Of income 68
    Of rental income 70
    Of salary 70
Assumption of
    Liabilities 342
    Mortgage 385, 386
At-risk
    Limitations 138-140
    Rules 137
Authoritative tax citations 6
Automatic extension 519
    Of time to file 236
Automobiles 113
    Depreciation 319, 323
    Expense 209
Awards from employer 84

Back property taxes 175
Backup withholding 660, 661
Bad debts 108, 610
    Deductions 107
    Expense 106, 477
    Recovery 53, 106
Bankrupt financial institution 199
Bankruptcy 743
Bardahl formula 560
Bargain purchase 530
Bartering 47
Basis
    Contributed property 475
    Converted personal residence 314
    Distributed properties 443
    Exchanged property 289
    Exchanged stock and property 467
    Partners' interest 408
    Personal residence 301, 399
    Property 386, 387
        Received by distributee 532
    Replacement property 392
    Shares of stock 290
Beneficiary's taxable income 592
Bequests from decedents 89
Bonds 479
    Discount 479
    Interest income 61
    Repurchase premium 481, 482
Bonuses 607
    Paid to related party 614
Book under-reported profits 514
Boot 386, 387
Bribes 104
Brokerage expenses 206, 213
Brother-sister controlled group 554, 555, 557

Built-in gains 574
Business
   Deductions 475
   Energy credit 271, 273
   Expense 478
      Reimbursement 148
   Gifts 118, 119
   Periodicals 206
   Travel 110
   Use of home 123

Corporation net operating losses 492
CAF number 731
Cafeteria benefit plan 83, 85
Calculation of
   Generation-skipping tax 693
   Gift tax 673
Calculators on the IRS exam 25
Cancellation of installment obligation 629
Capital
   Assets 333-335
   Gain 571
      Computations 345-348
   Gains and losses 498
   Losses 352, 353
      Carryback 499
      Carryover 352, 354, 356
      Deduction 355, 478
      Limitations 352
Capitalization of
   Expenditures 101, 102
   Interest 630
Carryback
   Net operating loss 136
   Of passive losses 141
Carryover
   Net operating loss 136
   Of passive losses 141
   Of unused loss 140
Cash
   Method 603-605
   Rebates 290
Cash-basis taxpayer 627
Casualty and theft losses 130, 193
Casualty loss 130, 132, 193, 194
   Deduction 197
   Definition 198
   Inventory 188, 190
   On residence 195
Certified
   Historic structure 274, 275
   Pollution control facility 330
Change in
   Accounting period 639
   Accounting method 636, 637
   Tax year 638, 639
   Taxable year 597
Chapter cross-references to SPE 29

Charitable
   Contribution 184-186, 490
      Carryforward 191
      Carryovers 189
      Deduction 486-489, 583
      Limitations 187, 188
      Of inventory 192
      Of land 192
   Organizations 185
Child
   As partner 455
   Employed by parents 649
   Support 160
Childcare
   Credit 258-262, 282
   Expenses 192
CIA
   Exam 30
   Examination Review 32
Citations 6
Civic achievement award 94
Claim for refund 704, 744-746, 749, 750
Claims
   Court 749, 750
   For refund 744
Closely held
   Business 687
   Corporation 143
CMA
   Exam 30
   Examination Review 33
Co-owners of bonds 69
Code of Federal Regulations 6
Combined group 557
Community property 295
Company car 121
Compensation for
   Injuries or sickness 75
   Services 53
Complete liquidation 542-545
Completed copy of return 700
Completed-contract method 618, 619, 621
Complex trust 591
   Beneficiary income 593
   Distribution deduction 591, 592
Computational problems 6
Condemnation 394, 395
   Award 395
Conditional sales contract 127
Conservation expenditures 128
Consolidated tax return 551-553
Constructed building 287
Construction
   Period
      Interest 288
      Tax 288
   Wages 105

Index

Constructive
   Ownership rules 535, 536, 538
   Receipt 611
      Of income 609
Continuing professional education 710, 711
Contract
   Price paid 628
   Research 269
Contributed capital gain property 411
Contribution
   Carryover 490-492
   Of inventory 422, 472
   Of property 189, 190, 412
      By nonshareholder 474
Controlled
   Corporation 472
   Group 554-556
Conventions 111, 117
Conversion of nonbusiness property 291
Convertible bond premium 480
Corporate
   Alternative minimum tax 511, 512
   Bond income 57
   Capital gain 499
   Capital loss 500
      Carryback 500
      Carryover 501-503
   Dissolution 744
   Distributions 534
   Divisions and reorganizations 547
   Formations 463, 464
   Recapitalization 548
   Reorganization 547-549
   Tax year 640
   Taxable income 507-510
Corporation
   Defined 460
   NOL 492, 493, 495, 496
Corporation's basis in
   Assets 466
   Contributed property 471
   Property received 473
Cosmetic surgery 172
Cost of
   Goods sold 101
   Purchasing property 290
Country club dues 114-116, 208
Court decisions 724
Covenant not to compete 52, 105
CPA
   Exam 30
   Examination Review 34
   Requirements by state 37
Credit
   For the elderly 262-264
   Limitations and carryovers 280
Cumulative bulletin 722
Current distributions 440

Death
   Benefits 88
   Of partner 415
   Payments 87
Debts of decedent 684
Decedent's final return 424
Declining-balance method 315, 316
Deductions from gifts 667
Deferral of gain 381
Deficiencies and assessments 737
Delinquency penalty 518
Delinquent filing penalty 234
Demolition
   Costs 286
   Expenses 106
Demonstrator automobiles 344
Dependents 219, 220
   Care assistance 85
Depletion 331
Depreciable
   Basis 313
   Property 624
      Acquired by gift 368
Depreciation
   Of pre-1981 assets 315
   On home 125
   Recapture 364, 366, 373
Destroyed property, replacement 299
Different tax years 421
Direct skips 694
Directly related expenses 116
Disability
   Benefits 103
   Payments 77
Disabled access credit 284
Disallowed interest deduction 180
Disaster Assistance Act of 1988 606
Disbarment or suspension proceeding 716
Disclosure 730
Discount on treasury obligations 56
Discriminatory plans 83
Disposition of installment obligation 626
Disputed liability 177, 614
Disreputable conduct 716, 718
Distributable net income 586, 587
Distribution of
   Appreciated property 535, 537
   Inventory 447
   Property 529
   Recapture property 442
Distributions from
   Estates 588
   Estates and trusts 588
   Trusts 588
Distributive share of partnership income 654
District Court 749-751

Index

Dividends 532
   And interest 73
   Distributions 527, 528
      To shareholders 525
   From REIT 59
   From stock 56
   Income 73, 604, 611
   Withholding 530, 660
Dividends-received deduction 482, 484, 486, 516
Divorce income 65, 66
Divorced parents 223, 224
Dollar value LIFO 635
Donated
   Building 371
   Intent 665
   Land 371
Donee's basis in land 666
Draught 611
   Conditions 615
Draws by partners 420
Due
   Date of return 519
   Diligence 713

Early payment penalty 106
Earned income credit 253-256, 281
Earnings and profits 522-525
Education expenses 207
Educational
   Assistance
      Benefits 85
      Program 215
   Expenses 214
   Grants 49
Effect on taxable income 378
Effective yield method 480
Election
   Of fiscal year 414
   To expense 317
Employee
   Benefits 77, 659
   Compensation 120
   Definition 645
   Discounts 78
   Educational expenses 476
   FICA 645
   Health plans 48
   Trade and business expenses 147
Employment
   Agency fees 214
   Income 48
   Taxes 642
Encumbered property 297
Energy
   Property 272
   Tax credit recapture 276, 277
Enrolled agent
   Advertisement 711, 712
   Conduct 711
   Disbarment 715

Enrollment
   Before the IRS 18
   Eligibility 707
   Process 708
   Renewal 709, 710
Entertainment 110
   Expenses 114, 116, 117, 215
Entities taxed as corporations 459
Equivalent of cash 47
Escrowed payments 624
Essay questions 6
Estate
   Accounting methods 599
   Administrative expenses 585
   Beneficiary
      Basis 594
      Income 593, 594
   Deductions 583
   Depreciation deduction 584
   Distribution deduction 592
   Election to recognize gain 595
   Estimated taxes 597, 599, 600
      Payments 598, 599
   Income and deductions 581
   Income tax return 598
   Net operating losses 584, 586
   Personal exemption 584, 586
   Property valuation 681
   Return filing 597
   Tax
      Calculation 685, 686
      Payment 687
      Payment and returns 686
      Return, due date 687
      Return, extension 688
      Return, filing 686, 687
      Year 597
   Taxable
      Income 581, 582
      Year 597
Estimated tax 249, 252, 423, 521
   Farmers and fishermen 252
   Payments 219, 520
   Penalty 250
   Requirements for S corporation 577
Examination
   Repetitive 729
   Transfer 729, 730
Excess
   Alimony 160
      Payments 68
   Contributions to IRA 164
   Net passive income 575, 576
Exchange
   Between partnership and partner 440
   Of partnership interests 383
   Of services 51
Excise tax return 696
Exclusions
   And deductions from gifts 667
   From gifts 667
   Of interest 74
Extension for filing 517
Extraordinary dividend 530

Index

Failure to
- File 236
    - Corporate 518
    - Penalty 233
- Pay
    - Penalty 233
    - Taxes, corporate 518
- Provide a copy of return 705
- Retain copy 705

Family
- Corporations 536
- Partnerships 454-456
- Separation allowances 41

Farm
- Expense 128
- Interest 183
- Residence rental value 129

Federal
- Disaster area 198
- Tax textbooks 7
    - Commerce Clearing House, Inc. 7, 8
    - Everett, Boley, Duncan, and Jamison 8
    - Hoffman and Raabe 9
    - Hoffman and Willis 9
    - Hoffman, Willis, and Smith 10
    - Kramer and Phillips 10, 11
    - Phillips and Kramer 11
    - Pratt, Burns, and Kulsrud 11, 12
    - Prentice Hall, Inc. 13
    - Raby, Tidwell, and White 13
    - Sommerfeld and Jones 13
    - Sommerfeld, Madeo, and Milliron ... 14
- Unemployment tax 657, 658

FICA
- For employees 645
- Tax 95, 643

FIFO valuation method 633
52- to 53-week year 639

Filing
- Requirements 232, 457, 458, 517
- Status 226

Final Return 236, 610
- Income 71, 72

Fines 105
First-tier deductions 199
Flood damage 130

Foreign
- Compensation 92
- Corporations 483, 486, 659, 660
- Income exclusion 91
- Tax credit 266, 267, 283

Forgiveness of indebtedness 46

Form
- 1040A 235
- 1040EZ 235
- 1041, due date 599
- 1099-DIV 531
- 1120S due date 577, 578
- 23, IRS enrollment 18
- 2587 19
- 4190A 19
- 941 657
- 941E 644
- 942 656
- 943 656

Former IRS employees 714
Fringe benefits 48, 77, 78
Full absorption method 632, 635
Funeral expenses 586

Gain
- On sale of partnership interest 452
- Or loss on distribution 442
- To partner 404

Gambling losses 205, 207
Gasoline tax credit 257

General
- Business credit 282, 556
    - Carryback and carryover 283
    - Limitations and carryovers 280
- Sales taxes 103
- Tax credit limitation 281

Generation-skipping transfer 688, 692
- Exemption 693
- Tax 688-691
- Taxable amount 692

Gifts 93
- And prizes 93
- Defined 663, 664
- From employer 84
- In property 667
- Of future interest 670
- Of stock 666
- Property 309
- Reporting 675, 676
- Splitting 671-673
- Tax
    - Calculation 673-675
    - Returns 695
    - To corporations 474

Goodwill 104, 286
Grading of IRS exam 21
Grant or trust 595

Gross
- Estate
    - Deductions 683, 684
    - Inclusions 676-680
- Income 41
- Profit percentage 623

Guaranteed payment 430-433
Guide dog 171

Half-year convention 322
Handicapped barriers 367
Head of household 227
Health insurance
- Credit 256
- Premiums 103

Hedging 129
High income tax payers 217, 218
Highly compensated individual 81, 82
Hobby loss 129, 209
Holding period 307, 308, 336, 337
- For property 448
- Of asset 469
- Of contributed property 410
- Of stock 470

Index

Home
    Improvements 169, 172
    Mortgage interest credit 264, 265
    Office deductions 126
    Worker 645
Hospital insurance 653
Housing allowance 91
Hybrid method 616, 617

Identification requirements 700, 701
Immediate distribution 411
Improvements on
    Leased property 127
    Rental property 126
Inactive director 53
Includable corporation 551
Inclusion ratio 693
Income
    In respect of a decedent 600-602
    Prior to death 679
    Tax refund check 713
Independent contractor 644
Indirect costs 634
Inheritance
    Income 45
    Taxes 173
Inherited
    Installment note 294
    Property 293, 295
Innocent spouse 230
Installment
    Agreement 741
    Basis 364
    Method 379
    Sales 622
Institute of
    Certified Management Accountants 38
    Internal Auditors 38
Insurance
    Claims 195, 199
    Expense 168, 607
    Policy premiums 103, 418
    Premiums 96-98
    Recovery 198
    Reimbursement 300
        For medical expenses 75
    Settlement 391
Interest
    Expense 177, 182
    Income 53, 54, 73
    On deferred tax 625
    On underpayment 519
    Received on state obligations 56
Interest-free loans 665
Internal Revenue
    Bulletin 722, 725, 726
    Code 6, 721, 724, 726
Interpretive regulations 724

Inventory 615, 616, 629
    And insurance reimbursement 130-132
    Cash discounts 635
    Valuation 631
Investment
    Counseling 207
    Interest
        Deduction 179, 180
        Expense 181
Involuntary conversions 299, 310, 368, 389-396
IRA
    Contribution 161-164
    Income 65
Irrevocable trust 596
IRS
    Collection
        Procedures 739, 740
        Process 739
    Enrollment, dates of exam 19
    SPE study material 21
    Special Enrollment
        Exam 17
        Qualifications 19
ITC recapture 275
    On final return 277
Itemized deductions 238, 239
Items included, gross income 41

Jeopardy levy 741
Joint
    Return 231, 232
    Tenancy 680
    Tenant property 296
Judicial decisions, tax citations 6

Keogh plan 166
    Contributions 165
Kickbacks 104, 105

Land clearing expenses 128
Legal expenses 206
Legislative
    Process 726
    Regulations 724
Levy 742, 743
Liabilities transferred to corporation ... 471
Liability in excess of basis 407, 466
Libel lawsuit payments 76
Life insurance 79, 80
    Payments 123
    Policy 679
        Interest 55
    Premiums 476
    Proceed income 42
    Proceeds 679

LIFO
- Recapture ... 577
- Valuation method ... 633, 635, 636

Like-kind exchange ... 298, 302, 366, 368, 373, 382-389
- With boot ... 361, 385

Limitation for high income taxpayers ... 217
Limitations and carryovers ... 352
Liquidating distribution ... 443, 446, 448
- Partnership ... 444

Liquidation of
- Partner's interest ... 449
- Partnership interest ... 443, 445
- Subsidiary ... 546, 547

Litigation costs ... 746
Livestock ... 395
Living quarters ... 84

Loan
- Commitment fees ... 106
- Discounts ... 610
- From partner to partnership ... 440

Lodging expense ... 168

Long-term
- Capital gain property ... 189
- Contracts ... 617, 618
- Lease ... 126

Look-back method ... 621
Loss on liquidation ... 448

Low-income
- Housing ... 368
  - Credit ... 278, 279
- Rental housing credit ... 278

Lower of cost or market ... 632, 636

Lump sum
- Death benefit ... 87
- Purchase price ... 286, 287

MACRS ... 324, 325

Marital
- Deduction ... 669, 670, 684
- Status ... 230

Market discount bonds ... 342, 343
Married child ... 226
Meals furnished by employer ... 84

Medical
- Expenses ... 167, 168, 667, 684
  - Deduction ... 169, 170
    - Of child ... 171
    - Reimbursements ... 50
- Reimbursement plan ... 104
- Reimbursements ... 81

Microfilm and microfiche ... 642
Mid-quarter convention ... 322
Minimum tax ... 245, 424
- Credit ... 248

Ministers ... 50
- Rental value of home ... 656

Minor child ... 242

Miscellaneous
- Expenses ... 98
- Itemized deduction ... 199

Modified accelerated cost recovery system ... 312, 321
Modules ... 2

Mortgage
- Commissions ... 330
- Interest ... 183
- To property ... 405

Moving expenses ... 200-204
- Allowances ... 661
- Reimbursements ... 42

Multiple
- Choice answering technique ... 15
- Corporations ... 554
- Support agreement ... 223

Mutual
- Funds ... 340
  - Income ... 57
- Savings banks ... 486

Negligence penalty ... 518

Net
- Earnings from self-employment ... 650, 651, 654, 655
- Operating loss ... 133-135, 484
  - Carryback ... 136
  - Deduction ... 655
- Rental income ... 150

New business ... 99

NOL
- Carryback ... 494-497
- Carryover ... 493, 494

Nonacquiescence ... 748
Nonbusiness bad debts ... 342, 348-350
Noncash charitable contribution ... 190
Noncustodial parent ... 225
Nondiscrimination requirements ... 82
Nonperishable seized property ... 742

Nonrecourse
- Debt ... 280
- Liabilities ... 407, 437

Nonrefundable personal credits ... 265
Nonresident aliens ... 92
Nonsimultaneous like-kind exchange ... 388

Nontaxable
- Distributions ... 74
- Transactions ... 298

Not-for-profit activity ... 130, 156

Notice of
- Federal Tax Lien ... 730, 744
- Intent to Levy ... 741

Objective question
- Study ... 5
- Uniqueness ... 4

Offer in compromise ... 740, 743
Office in the home ... 124
Order of questions ... 3

Ordinary
- And necessary expenses ... 95
- Income ... 375, 418, 430

Organizational expenses ... 460-463
Original issue discount ... 58, 61, 480, 481

Parent subsidiary controlled group 557
Partial
   Liquidations 540, 541
   Redemptions 537
Partially
   Reimbursed expenses 212
   Worthless debts 109
Partners'
   Basis in property 440, 441
   Current distributions 440
   Deductible loss 426, 427
   Deduction for loss 425
   Depreciation deduction 423
   Distributive
      Income and gain 419
      Share 419, 423
   Interest 406
   Passive loss 143
   Taxable income 420
Partnerships 377
   Agreement 402, 403, 424
   Basis 412
      In contributed property 409
   Capital gain 421
   Definition 401
   Formation 404
   Interest 297
      For services 405, 406, 408
   Liabilities 429, 436
   Liquidation 445
   Losses 425
   Ordinary income 416, 417
   Organizational costs 410
   Penalties 457
   Retirement agreement 445
   Tax year 413, 415, 457, 640
   Taxed as corporation 402
Pass statistics, IRS SPE 22
Passive
   Activities 141
      Losses 141, 428
   Income 142
   Loss 144
   Partnership investment loss 427
Patents 344
Payment
   By charge card 606
   By check 606
   In property 53, 120
   Of another's debt 98
   Requirement 517, 519
   To former spouses 68
   To partner for services 440
Penalties 105
   Early withdrawal 55
   Failure to collect tax 659
   Underpayment of estimated tax 521
Pension income 64
Per diem expenses 117
Percentage-of-completion
   Capitalized cost method 620
   Method 618, 619, 621

Performance of services 50
Performing artist 149
Permanent group life insurance 479
Personal exemptions 219-222
Personal
   Holding company
      Income 561-563
      Tax 561
      Tax rate 562
   Injury
      Damages 47
      Income 41
   Interest 105
      Expense 177, 178
   Property used in business 288
   Service corporations 506
      Tax year 640
Plan of liquidation 545
Points 102
Power of attorney 731-735
Practice before the IRS 720
Precontribution loss 429
Premiums for life insurance 419
Prepaid
   Feed 609
      And seed 129
   Income 616
   Rent 126, 606, 612
   Services 612, 613
Preparer
   Identification number 702
   Penalties 702
Preparing for exam success 23
Present interest 670
Principal
   Partner 414
   Residence 742
Prizes 93
Problem resolution program 740
Production of income 154
Professional
   Accounting examination 17
   Journals 204
   Service organization 460
Profit-loss ratio change 427
Property
   Acquired from decedent 310
   Assessments 150
   Received
      By gift 291, 292
      For services 296
   Sale income 45
   Subject to
      Debt 409
      Mortgage 407
   Taxes 175
Proposed Treasury Regulation 6
Protests 736, 737
Public utility dividend 75
Publicly-traded partnership 403, 460
Purchased property 285

Index

Q
Qualified
- Charitable organization ... 192
- Resident interest ... 179
- Terminal interest property ... 670
- Transfers ... 664, 676
- Tuition reduction ... 85

Qualifying widower ... 228

R
Real
- Estate
  - Rental activity ... 428
  - Tax deduction ... 175
  - Property taxes ... 103, 151, 177

Recapture of alimony ... 159
Recordkeeping requirements ... 115, 116, 610, 641
Recourse liabilities ... 407, 437

Recovery
- Of prior deduction ... 47
- Period ... 326
- Property ... 311-313

Rehabilitation
- Credit ... 273
  - Recapture ... 276
- Expenditure credit ... 277

Reimbursement
- Automobile expenses ... 112
- Medical expenses ... 172

Reinstatement after disbarment ... 715

Related
- Party ... 616
  - Redemption ... 539
  - Sales ... 357
  - Transactions ... 290, 357, 358, 378
- Shareholders ... 544

Remainder interest ... 668

Rental
- Expense ... 126, 150, 607
- Income ... 61, 62, 608
- Losses ... 145
- Of personal residence ... 153, 370
- Property expenses ... 150
- Real estate activities ... 143

Repair and maintenance ... 100
Replacement property ... 390, 394

Reporting
- Gifts ... 675
- Requirements ... 700

Repossession of
- Personal property ... 628
- Real property ... 626

Repurchase of
- Bonds ... 479, 481
- Stock ... 478

Required
- Copies of return ... 699
- Tax year ... 414

Resale price method ... 556

Research
- And development credit ... 268
- And experimentation credit ... 268
- Credit ... 269

Residential real property ... 374

Restricted stock ... 298
Retail valuation method ... 634
Retired partner ... 448

Retirement
- Of partners ... 443
- Payments ... 164

Return
- Examination ... 728
- Filing and payment requirements ... 516
- Preparer
  - Activities ... 699
  - Definition ... 696-698

Revenue
- Bill ... 726-728
- Procedures ... 723, 726
  - By IRS ... 6
- Rulings ... 723, 725
  - By IRS ... 6

Revolving credit plan ... 628
Royalty expenses ... 154

S
S corporation
- At-risk rules ... 570
- Built-in gains ... 576, 577
- Distributions ... 571, 573
- Election ... 563-566
- Estimated tax payments ... 577, 578
- Filing requirements ... 577, 578
- Income ... 567
- Losses ... 569
  - Carryovers ... 570
- NOL carryovers ... 574
- Passive investment income ... 565
- Shareholder income ... 572
- Tax year ... 567, 640
- Taxable year ... 564
- Taxes ... 573
- Termination ... 578-580

Safety achievements awards ... 83
Salary ... 97, 121, 122

Sale of
- Apartment building ... 372
- Automobile ... 363
- Business ... 374, 376
  - Building ... 360
- Capital assets ... 341, 378
- Contributed property ... 410
- Franchise ... 344
- Gifted
  - Property ... 292, 343
  - Stock ... 339
- Low-income housing ... 372
- Obsolete equipment ... 379
- Office building ... 365
- Parking lot ... 361
- Partnership interest ... 343, 450, 451
- Passive activity ... 146
- Personal residence ... 301
- Principal residence ... 396-400
  - Taxpayers over 55 ... 400
- Real property ... 344
- Stock ... 289, 336-338
- Truck ... 364

Sale to partnership by partner 449
Sales
   Between partnership 439
   Of capital gain property to partnership 439
   Of stock to partnership 438
   Taxes 177, 290
   To related parties 376
Salesperson's automobile expense 210
Salvage value 328
Savings
   Account interest 55
   Bonds 613
Scholarships 47, 89, 90
   And fellowships 89
Section
   179 .... 317-319, 366, 367, 419
      Deduction 314
   306 stock 540
   336 544
   351 transfer 465, 466, 468, 470, 471
   444 415
      Election 415
   754 election 453, 454
   1231 498
      Property 359
   1244 stock 350-352
   1245 property 361-363
   1250 property 368
Second-tier deductions 204
Security deposit 606
Seizure of property 395
Self-employed
   FICA 650
   Health insurance 156
   Retirement plan 165
Self-employment
   Income 51, 447
   Tax 448, 650, 652
      Couple 652
Separately reported amounts 417
Series EE
   Bonds 60, 71
   Interest 59
Series HH bond 60
Service partnership 457
Settlement agreement 458
Shareholder
   Meetings 212
   Stock basis 568, 569
Shopping mall 373
Short sales of stock 339, 354
Signature requirements 700, 701
Simple trust 589
   Beneficiary income 590, 591
   Distribution deduction 589, 590
   Personal exemption 584
Sinking fund 480
Small
   Business investment companies 486
   Tax case division 747

Social Security
   Benefits 86, 87
   Tax 234, 643-647
      Return 656
Sources of
   Objective questions 2
   Tax law 721
Special
   Allocation 422, 424
   Enrollment Exam 6, 17
      Questions 21
      Sites 20
Specific bequests 594
Spin-off distribution 550
Sporting events 117
Spouse's medical expenses 171
Standard
   Deduction 237
   Mileage rate 113, 209
Start-up
   Costs of abandoned business 354
   Expenses 104, 329, 330
State
   Bond income 42
   CPA requirements 35
   Income taxes 173
      Refund 176
   Lottery income 43
   Tax 95
      Refund income 44
Statute of limitations 738
   6-year 729
Statutory Notice of Deficiency 738, 739, 744
Stock 310
   And bond income 56
   Dividends 303, 304, 338, 339, 341, 526, 531
      And stock rights 303
   For partnership interest 405
   For services 49, 471
   From decedent 340
   Options 60, 479
   Received for services 297
   Redemptions 533, 536
   Rights 303, 304, 525, 526
   Split 339, 531
Straight-line method 315
Student's maintenance 186
Studying for the special enrollment exam 22
Subchapter K 404
Subsidiary corporations 546
Substantial risk of forfeiture 476
Substantially disproportionate distributions .. 535, 538
Substantiation of business expense 115
Sum-of-the-year's-digits method 316
Support
   For dependents 224, 225
   Of parents 226
Supreme Court 726, 751
Surviving spouse 229, 231
Suspension
   And disbarment 715, 717-719
   From practice 715
Syndication fees 412

Index

TAMRA 6
Targeted jobs credit 270, 271, 282, 284
Tax
   Audit procedures 457
   Calculations 236, 504, 505
   Citations 6
   Court 747-749
      Memorandum decisions 748
   Exempt income 593
   Forms, SPE 6
   Home 117
   Information authorization 731-735
   Itemized deduction 174
   Liability 240, 241
   Matters partner (TMP) 458
   Preference 246, 247, 513
   Reform Act of 1984 6
   Reform Act of 1986 6
   Return
      Preparation fees 205
      Preparer rules 695
      Preparers 696
   Textbooks 7
   Year 638
Tax-exempt bonds 74
Tax-free reorganization 550
Taxable
   Amount of distribution 442
   Gifts 668, 669
   Income 504
      And tax calculations 504
   Termination 693
   Year 414
Taxes 173
Taxpayer Assistance Order 744
Taxpayer's rights 731
Taxpayers over 65 232
Temporary
   Recognition to practice 712
   Treasury Regulation 6
Termination of
   Partnership 447, 453
   Shareholder's interest 538
Textbooks, federal tax 7
Theft loss 132
Time budgeting on SPE exam 28
Tips 609, 647-649
Transactions between partnership and partner . . . 438
Transfer of
   Assets 465
   Liabilities 465
Transferred property 665
Transportation expense 210-212, 216
Travel
   As education 214
   By spouse 112
   Expenses 110, 111, 118, 211, 212, 216
Treasury
   Regulations 6, 722, 723, 725
   Stock 503

Trust
   Accumulation distribution 595
   Depreciation deduction 584
   Estimated taxes 597
      Payments 599
   Income 46
      And deductions 581
      Tax return 598
   Life interests 666
   Net operating losses 584
   Remainder interests 666
   Return filing 597
   Tax years 597
   Taxable income 581, 585
Tuition and books 208
Type
   B reorganization 549
   C reorganization 549
   D reorganization 551
   F reorganization 550

U.S. Court of Appeals 751
Uncollectible fees 610
Understatement of liability 703
Unearned income, minor child 242-244
Unemployment
   Benefits 742
   Compensation income 42
Unenrolled persons 719, 720
Uniform capitalization rules 291, 629, 630
Union dues 206
Unrealistic positions 702, 704-707
Unrealized receivable 452
Unreasonable compensation 477
Unreimbursed employee business expenses 208
Unstated interest 183, 623
Unused passive losses 141
Used property 318

Vacant land 106
Vacation
   Home 151
   Pay 616
Valuation
   Of gifts 666
   Real property 683

Wash sales 340
Widows 229
Willful
   Or reckless conduct 703, 704, 706
   Understatement penalty 703
Withholding 659
   Allowances 661
   Exemption certificates 642
   Foreign corporation 659, 660, 662
   Requirements 519

Work clothing 205
Worthless securities 477, 745
Writ of Certiorari 751

Zero coupon bond 61

Please forward your suggestions, corrections, and comments concerning typographical errors, etc., to Irvin N. Gleim • c/o Gleim Publications, Inc. • P.O. Box 12848 • University Station • Gainesville, Florida • 32604. Please include your name and address so we can properly thank you for your interest.

1. _____

2. _____

3. _____

4. _____

5. _____

6. _____

7. _____

8. _____

9. _____

10. _____

11. _____

12. _____

13. _____

14. _____

15. _____

16. _____

17. _____

18. _____

19. _____

20. _____

21. _____

22. _____

23. _____

24. _____

Name: _____

Company: _____

Address: _____

City/State/Zip: _____